THE WAITE GROUP®

# Visual Basic SuperBible

## TAYLOR MAXWELL
## BRYON SCOTT

WAITE GROUP
PRESS™

Corte Madera, California

**Editorial Director:** *Scott Calamar*
**Development Editor:** *Mitchell Waite*
**Content Editor:** *Heidi Brumbaugh*
**Technical Editor:** *Daniel Derrick*
**Project Manager:** *Harry Henderson*
**Design and Production:** *Barbara Gelfand*
**Illustrations:** *Frances Hasegawa*
**Cover Design:** *Kathy Locke; Locke & Veach*
**Production Manager:** *Julianne Ososke*

© 1992 by The Waite Group, Inc.
Published by Waite Group Press, 200 Tamal Plaza, Corte Madera, CA 94925.

Waite Group Press is distributed to bookstores and book wholesalers by Publishers Group West, Box 8843, Emeryville, CA 94662, 1-800-788-3123 (in California 1-510-658-3453).

Printed in the United States of America
92 93 94 95 • 10 9 8 7 6 5 4 3 2 1


Maxwell, Taylor.
  Visual BASIC superbible / Taylor Maxwell, Bryon Scott.
      p.  cm.
  At head of title: The Waite Group.
  Includes bibliographical references.
  ISBN 1-878739-12-3 : $39.95
  1. Windows (Computer programs) 2. Microsoft Visual BASIC. I. Scott, Byron. II. Waite Group. III. Title.
  QA76.76W56M515  1992
  005.4'3--dc20                                                    92-14459
                                                                        CIP

# DEDICATION

For my wife Marcia.

—*Taylor Maxwell*

For my wife JoAnn.

— *Bryon Scott*

# ACKNOWLEDGMENTS

The authors gratefully acknowledge Mitchell Waite for the opportunity to write this book. We would like to thank Harry Henderson for his helpful editing, suggestions, comments, and for wrapping up this project.

Thanks to Heidi Brumbaugh for her grammatical expertise, and to Scott Calamar for his encouragement and all of his help in getting this book published. Thanks also to Dan Derrick for his technical review.

Taylor Maxwell would like to thank his father Taylor H. Maxwell Sr. for all of his help and encouragement. Thanks to all of the people on the MSBasic forum on Compuserve for the wealth of information about Visual Basic that exists there. This book would not have been possible without the support of family and friends including most especially my very loving wife Marcia.

Bryon Scott would like to give special thanks to Bob Traxler, for putting up with a tired and grouchy employee during the course of this project. Finally, thanks to my lovely wife, JoAnn. Without her dedication and support, I would have never been able to accomplish what I have. I love you.

# PREFACE

In a way, the story of Visual Basic begins more than 25 years ago at Dartmouth College, more than a decade before the first personal computers came on the market. Professors John G. Kemeny and Thomas E. Kurtz had a problem. At a time when "computers" meant huge mainframes and batches of punched cards, Dartmouth had decided that all of its students would become "computer literate." After all, computers were already making an impact in just about every field of study from physics to linguistics. Students were likely to be using computers throughout their careers in unforeseen ways.

Kemeny and Kurtz believed that to make computers accessible, there had to be a simpler way to program them. The most popular languages of the time, FORTRAN and COBOL, were awkward and tedious to use. Equally important, programming had to become interactive. Instead of submitting hundreds of punched cards and waiting a day or more for results, students should be able to type in a command or simple program and see the results immediately. If students could get immediate feedback, they would feel free to experiment with new commands and features. They could tinker with programs and easily try out new ideas.

To meet these needs, the two Dartmouth professors simplified the FORTRAN language, added some new features, and in 1965 came up with BASIC (the acronym stood for "Beginner's All-purpose Symbolic Instruction Code"). Instead of using punch cards, students sat at teletype terminals that looked something like a typewriter on steroids. They typed in their programs, typed "run," and the results were banged out immediately on the teletype. Thousands of people began to think of computers differently.

The next chapter in our story took place in the mid to late 1970s, when the first true personal computers became available. Machines such as the Apple II, TRS-80, Commodore Pet, Atari 800, and their more obscure brethren proliferated. So too did a tiny company called Microsoft. Before there was an MS-DOS or an IBM PC, Microsoft was known for its BASIC interpreters. Just about every PC had its own version of Microsoft BASIC, usually stored in a ROM chip so that it would be available as soon as you booted up. And while a select group of wizards used assembly language to hand-craft the movement of bytes through the early 8-bit microprocessors, the rest of us turned to BASIC. Very little commercial software was available in the early years of personal computing. We spent many hours typing in BASIC listings from magazines and books, sometimes translating them from one machine's BASIC to another's. And when the IBM PC came out in 1982, Microsoft not only provided its DOS, it also provided the on-board BASIC interpreter, called BASICA. As personal computers continued to penetrate the business world, the demand for software grew. The trickle of explorers on the programming frontier soon became a torrent.

Every frontier needs its maps. One of the first sources of reliable and accessible books on personal computing was Mitchell Waite and The Waite Group. Mitch gave himself and his fellow authors a mandate to show readers how to really put BASIC through its paces. Authors were required to make their books thorough, accurate, and useful. Just as important, they were encouraged to make them *fun*. An example was The Waite Group's *BASIC Programming Primer*, first published in 1982. This book offered practical programs for such things as loan amortization and metric conversion, but it also offered a "Micro Space Invaders" game, Tic-Tac-Toe, and (in a later edition) a program that solved Rubik's cubes. With this and other Waite Group books, readers learned to write programs that drew colorful graphics, formatted text, dialed modems, and even played tunes.

But all was not well in the world of BASIC. Early BASICs, such as BASICA, suffered from serious structural problems. First of all, BASICA was interpreted, not compiled. This meant that each program instruction had to be decoded each time it was run, resulting in sluggish performance. And as programs became longer and more complex, programmers began to turn increasingly to the techniques of "structured programming." Unfortunately early BASIC was not well-suited to structured programming. All BASIC variables were "global," meaning that they could be changed willy-nilly from anywhere in the program. And while BASICA had simple subroutines, it did not have the self-contained procedures and modules needed for structured programming.

Microsoft met these concerns in the mid-1980s by coming out with QuickBASIC. This new BASIC was compiled rather than interpreted. It supported procedures and modules, as well as long user-defined functions. Line numbers were no longer needed, and the troublesome GOTO statement could be dispensed with in nearly all cases. Finally, QuickBASIC offered an integrated programming environment (pioneered by Borland's Turbo Pascal). Programmers could now edit, compile, run, debug, and revise programs from the same screen.

The Waite Group provided this second generation of BASIC programmers with such popular guides as the *Microsoft QuickBASIC Bible* and the *Microsoft QuickBASIC Primer Plus*. These books served the new, more sophisticated BASIC by integrating principles of structured programming with an even more thorough exploration of the BASIC language. Now readers could write programs to control the new laser printers, and to draw graphics using the more detailed and complex EGA and VGA graphics modes.

The new BASICs, such as QuickBASIC, were powerful and easy to use. Unfortunately, however, programs in the MS-DOS world were often *hard* to use. Many programs (and DOS itself) required the typing in of precise commands, and text was displayed line by line in a way not unlike teletypes back in the 1960s. Programmers responded to user complaints by designing menus, and eventually dialog boxes and screen windows. The mouse, with its ability to point to, select, and manipulate objects, became increasingly prevalent. But all these improvements in the user interface required tedious coding in each program. Furthermore, there was no standard as to how menus, dialog boxes, and other objects would behave. As a result, users had to relearn the interface each time they used a new program. No wonder they looked enviously at their colleagues' Macintoshes.

Microsoft had decided early on that the character-based PC was reaching a dead end. The result was a massive development project through most of the 1980s. Finally, with Windows 3.0 in 1990, the GUI ("Graphical User Interface") for PCs came of age.

Now PC users had a consistent, easy-to-use interface for their applications. Windows has redefined what it means to use a PC.

At first Windows' friendliness did not extend to the programmer. Until very recently, learning to write Windows programs was like a Westerner learning Japanese. The language needed for programming Windows was not merely different, it was different in different ways. Old PC programs were structured hierarchically, with the main program calling subroutines in a predictable order. Graphics, when used at all, were essentially an afterthought.

Windows programs, on the other hand, consisted of a kind of "ecology" of coexisting objects that send and receive "messages" describing their status. These objects, such as menus, windows, buttons, and lists, can be activated at almost any time by the user. While an old DOS program tended to control the user, a Windows program is controlled *by* the user, usually with the mouse. And in Windows everything you see on the screen, including text, is really a graphical object. Even experienced programmers had to learn to think in a radically different way.

Fortunately Windows provides a tremendous amount of built-in functionality to support the objects that make up a Windows application. But programming in Windows "the old way" required the use of C, a concise but rather cryptic language. It required an expensive, often cumbersome C compiler, plus something called the "Software Development Kit" (SDK). While the SDK offered some tools for creating screen objects, the tools were limited and not well-integrated. Furthermore, programming Windows required mastery of hundreds of C functions, many requiring numerous arguments. When it cost at least $1000 and several months of study to learn Windows programming, it seemed like the good old days of free and easy experimentation were gone for good.

Finally programming tools began to catch up with Windows. Products such as Borland's Turbo C++ for Windows, Turbo Pascal for Windows, and Microsoft's QuickC for Windows offer a Windows-based programming environment and libraries of predefined objects that considerably simplify Windows programming. But for many of us the best news of all came in 1991 with the release of Microsoft Visual Basic.

Visual Basic marries two powerful ideas. The first is: Use Windows to design Windows programs. Select and customize your menus, windows, dialog boxes, buttons, and other features right on the screen where you can see how they'll look. The user interface, traditionally one of the hardest parts of program to write, becomes a snap. The second idea is: Use the simple but powerful Basic language to specify what will happen when the user selects an object, and get the instant feedback for which BASIC is famous.

And so we've come full circle. BASIC is back, and programming is exciting and fun again. At last, Windows is as friendly for the programmer as it is for the user. We at Waite Group Press are proud to provide new maps for the third generation of BASIC programmers. Just as BASIC has evolved, so also have we refined our Bibles as reference tools. We have made sure that you can both explore the features and capabilities of Visual Basic and zero in on the answers to your programming questions.

The frontier is wide open again. We believe that for Windows programmers, the best is yet to come!

# INTRODUCTION

The *Visual Basic SuperBible* is designed to be both a ready reference and a study aid. Chapter 1, *Using the Visual Basic SuperBible,* explains in detail how the book is organized and gives suggestions on how to use it effectively. This brief introduction will simply give a few tips to help you get started.

The *Visual Basic SuperBible* has no additional hardware or system requirements. If you can run Windows, you can run Visual Basic. If you can run Visual Basic, you can run any of the program projects described in this book and provided on the accompanying disk. To get started with the example projects, turn to Appendix F, *How to Use the Project Disk.*

While the *Visual Basic SuperBible* isn't designed to be a tutorial, you don't have to know much about Visual Basic to use this book effectively. Reading Chapter 2, *Introducing Visual Basic,* and Chapter 3, *Programming with Objects,* will give you an overview of how Visual Basic works and of what it offers. If you haven't run Microsoft's online Visual Basic tutorial (by choosing Tutorial from the Help menu in Visual Basic), we suggest that you do so, and that you look over the *Microsoft Visual Basic Programmer's Guide* that comes in your Visual Basic package. After you've learned the fundamentals and created a few applications of your own, we recommend that you look at our companion book, *The Waite Group's Visual Basic How-To.* This book provides a wealth of programming techniques for just about any situation you might encounter. See Appendix E, *Further Reading,* for other book suggestions.

If you're currently working on a programming project, you can quickly look up any object, method, statement, or function in the alphabetical "jump table" on the inside cover of this book. To find out what language features are related to a task you want your program to perform, turn toward the Task Jump Table on the inside back cover.

Do you want to learn more about a particular aspect of Visual Basic? Just turn to the table of contents, find the chapter or appendix that deals with your topic, and jump in. Other than the first three chapters, which lay the groundwork for the rest of the book, each chapter is self-contained.

We hope you will enjoy using this book in your work with Visual Basic. While we were writing this book, hardly a day went past without our being reminded of just how much fun Visual Basic is. Happy programming!

# TABLE OF CONTENTS

# CONTENTS

## PART 2     USING FORMS AND CONTROLS

# PART 3   DRAWING GRAPHICS

## Chapter 10    Drawing Shapes                                                   283

# PART 4    DISPLAYING FONTS AND TEXT

## Chapter 11    Displaying Text with Objects                                     321

## PART 6    DESIGNING DIALOG, LIST, AND COMBO BOXES

# PART 7   MANAGING DATA FLOW

# APPENDICES

## Appendix B     Visual Basic Language Reference     709

Note: see the *Alphabetical Jump Table for individual reference entries*

## Appendix C     Debugging Techniques     803

# PART ONE
# GETTING STARTED

# Using the *Visual Basic SuperBible*

**V**isual Basic's object-oriented nature requires a variety of programming perspectives—more so than with its procedural predecessors, such as QuickBASIC. For instance, you may be designing a new application from scratch. You might begin by visualizing the application in your mind's eye as the user will see it. You start work on the screen layouts, selecting the appropriate forms, objects, and controls needed to communicate with the user. You then code the BASIC statements that make up the "engine" of the program, the code that performs calculations, formats text, or draws images.

Another time, you might have an existing BASIC program and desire to create a user-friendly "front end" for it using Visual Basic. Here you may work from the inside out. First you look at the kind of input the application needs, and then you design your screens to provide the most efficient and comfortable way for the user to interact with your program. You may also want to use Visual Basic's powerful form and printer facilities to improve the appearance of the program's output.

Designing a Visual Basic program is an interactive process, and your perspective may well change between "outside in" and "inside out" even during the same project. This means that the kind of information you need from a reference book will also change. You may need to review the characteristics and properties of Visual Basic's 20 built-in objects, explore a particular property, event, or statement in more detail, or match up a desired program function with appropriate Visual Basic techniques.

*Visual Basic SuperBible* is designed with these shifts of perspective in mind. We combine a detailed, systematic reference with a variety of access methods for getting at the information you need. Wherever you're coming from, we'll make sure you get where you need to go.

## How the *Visual Basic SuperBible* is Organized

The *Visual Basic SuperBible* is designed to be a complete, versatile tool for expanding and honing your knowledge of Visual Basic. The *Visual Basic SuperBible* combines topical organization by part and chapter with direct access to the elements of Visual Basic alphabetically by entry name and by programming task.

### Overall Organization: Parts and Chapters

The *Visual Basic SuperBible* is organized into 25 chapters arranged in seven topical parts, plus six important appendices.

Part 1, *Getting Started,* is your overview of the book and of the Visual Basic language. In this chapter you will become acquainted with the book's features and different ways to use them. In Chapter 2, *Introducing Visual Basic,* you will look at the main features of the Visual Basic language and the topics to be covered in the rest of the book. In Chapter 3, *Programming with Objects,* you will see how to create each of the 20 objects that make up the "core" of the Visual Basic programming environment and that provide so much built-in functionality.

Part 2, *Using Forms and Controls,* is devoted to these key building blocks of Visual Basic applications. In Chapter 4, *Setting Up Forms,* you will learn how to place forms on the screen; and in Chapter 5, *Designing the Application's Appearance,* you will learn how to customize the way forms look and behave on the screen. In Chapter 6, *Using Forms and Controls in Program Code,* and Chapter 7, *Responding to Changes in Properties,* you will work with code statements that refer to and manipulate forms as the program runs, and learn to manage the events that allow you to respond to changes the user makes.

Part 3, *Drawing Graphics,* looks at the creation of graphics, which are especially important in the graphics-based Windows environment. In Chapter 8, *Setting Up Graphical Objects,* you will explore the use of the picture box for drawn and bitmapped graphics, while Chapter 9, *Designing with the Coordinate System,* shows you the meaning of the coordinates and measurements employed for placing graphics. In Chapter 10, *Drawing Shapes,* you will explore the techniques for drawing, coloring, and filling in shapes.

Part 4, *Displaying Fonts and Text,* covers the use of text in Visual Basic. In Chapter 11, *Displaying Text with Objects,* you will learn how to add text to the objects on the screen. In Chapter 12, *Defining and Using Fonts,* you will find out how to enhance the appearance of text output by selecting from the many fonts and typestyles available in Windows. In Chapter 13, *Getting User Input with Text Boxes,* you will learn how to set up and use the text box, Visual Basic's answer to the traditional programmer's headache of data entry and editing.

Part 5, *Mousing, Dragging, and Key Processing,* begins with the interaction between Visual Basic applications and the mouse. In Chapter 14, *Responding to Mouse Events,* you will study the events that allow you to track what the user is doing with the mouse and to respond to single and double clicks. In Chapter 15, *Managing the Dragging Event,* you will see how you can enable the user to manipulate objects in your application by dragging with the mouse. Finally, in Chapter 16, *Handling Keyboard Input,* you will learn how to provide a complete keyboard interface for your application through direct handling of the keyboard, including special keys and key combinations.

Part 6, *Designing Dialog, List, and Combo Boxes,* looks in detail at the various kinds of boxes that Visual Basic provides for displaying choices to the user and getting selections or text input. In Chapter 17, *Creating and Using Dialog Boxes,* you will survey the features you can use in dialog boxes to present information and options. In Chapter 18, *Using List and Combo Boxes,* and Chapter 19, *Managing Files in Drive, Dir, and File List*

*Boxes,* you will learn how to present selections to the user with general purpose list boxes, combo boxes (which allow the user to either select a listed item or type in an alternate selection), and the special boxes that provide for selection of drives, directories, and files. In Chapter 20, *Operating Scroll Bars,* you will learn how to add the handy feature of scroll bars, allowing for the display of large amounts of text (or large pictures) regardless of the size of the window.

Part 7, *Managing Data Flow,* deals with ways in which a Visual Basic application can transfer or exchange data with the outside world. In Chapter 21, *Establishing and Controlling the Application Focus,* you will see how you can control which application (or part of an application) will receive user input. Your Visual Basic application can also find out the date and time from the system clock; and in Chapter 22, *Timing and Time Information,* you will learn how to format date and time information and how to set timers that will execute code at specified intervals. In Chapter 23, *Using the Windows Clipboard,* you will begin to explore the question of transferring data between applications, showing how your application can use the standard Windows clipboard for the purpose. In Chapter 24, *Sending Data to the Printer,* you will learn how Visual Basic treats the printer much like a screen form, giving you complete control over the printed page, and you will learn how to place and format text. Finally, in Chapter 25, *Transferring Data with Dynamic Data Exchange (DDE),* you will explore the powerful but rather esoteric Windows feature called Dynamic Data Exchange (DDE). When working with applications that support DDE, your Visual Basic application can interactively update both applications with the latest results from processing.

Finally, the appendices in the *Visual Basic SuperBible* present additional useful information. In Appendix A, *Visual Basic Language Tutorial,* you can review the statements and functions you use in the Visual Basic code, which provide additional control over the behavior of objects as well as the ability to peform math and process textual data. In Appendix B, *Visual Basic Language Reference,* you can look up each Visual Basic function or statement in an alphabetical reference. In Appendix C, *Debbuging Techniques,* you will find techniques you can use to test and debug your Visual Basic applications. Appendix D introduces you to another esoteric but powerful topic: how to use the Windows API from Visual Basic. The Windows API (Application Program Interface) provides hundreds of functions that can supplement Visual Basic's many built-in capabilities. If you would like to learn more about the BASIC language in Visual Basic, or general concepts of Windows programming, Appendix E, *Further Reading,* provides a selection of books for your further study. Finally, Appendix F explains how to use the accompanying disk of example programming projects.

### The Example Project Disk

The *Visual Basic SuperBible* is accompanied by a disk containing the end-of-chapter projects in ready-to-run program files. Appendix F explains the simple steps needed for running these programs. Since you won't have to undertake the tedious and mistake-prone process of typing in all these projects by hand, you will be able to see right away how each project works. Because Visual Basic is so interactive, you'll be able to easily tinker with the projects and perhaps add your own features—an excellent way to master the techniques you've been reading about!

**Figure 1.1  The detailed Table of Contents shows the book's organization and contents**

## The Detailed Outline

The *Visual Basic SuperBible* also includes a detailed outline (see Figure 1.1). This outline shows each major topic heading within the chapter, and the name of each reference entry included in the chapter. Use this outline to become more familiar with the contents of each chapter as well as the name of the properties, events, and methods discussed.

## What's in a Chapter?

Each chapter of the Visual Basic SuperBible (except for Chapters 1 and 2, which are organized as overviews) begins with a brief introductory narrative that describes the significance of the chapter's topic and gives an overview of the contents. The introductory material often includes tables that concisely summarize the use of the elements of Visual Basic discussed in the chapter.

## What's in a Reference Entry?

The bulk of each chapter consists of alphabetical reference entries covering each Visual Basic element related to the chapter topic. For example, Chapter 4, *Setting Up Forms,* has a reference entry for each property that a form can have as well as each statement that manipulates forms and each event that can affect a form. What's in a Reference Entry?

The reference entries are designed to put the most concise information first: what this feature does and the rules (syntax) for using it. With the exception of those in Chapter 3, the reference entries in the *Visual Basic Super Bible* follow the format shown in Figure 1.2.

The elements of a reference entry include the following:

- The *entry name* is the name of the object, property, event, or statement being described. This is the name by which the entry is listed in the detailed Table of Contents and in the Alphabetical Jump Table.

- *Objects affected* is a list of the 20 Visual Basic objects with bullets next to those objects that can be used with this feature. Properties are often implemented for more than 1 object. In some cases statements don't affect any objects directly; in such cases this section is omitted. Events (such as mouse or keyboard events) are usually defined for many different objects.

- The *purpose* of the item is given in a short statement. The purpose is the answer to the question, "What is this used for?" Some considerations involved in the use of the item are summarized, but details are given later in the entry.

- The *general syntax* shows the order in which the item name and any arguments must be given when you use the item in program code. The arguments are described in generic terms, such as "file," rather than the name of a specific file. Where appropriate, the BASIC data declarations are given to show what type of data (integer, double, string, and so on) is required for each argument. Arguments in square brackets ([ ]) are optional. Where needed, the description of each argument is elaborated in a table.

- The *example syntax* provides an actual illustration of how the item might be used in a program, using real arguments.

- The bulk of the reference entry is made up of the *description* section, which gives the details of the item's usage and behavior, and relationship to other elements of Visual Basic. For complex items the description is broken down into individual topics.

- Sometimes a *comment* concludes the reference entry, pointing out some special circumstance or "quirk" of which the programmer should be aware.

## Reference Entries for Objects (Chapter 3)

The reference entries in Chapter 3, *Programming with Objects,* are organized somewhat differently from those in the rest of the book. Since the focus in Chapter 3 is on objects, the entry for each object brings together the properties and events used with that object, which are summarized in tables. Note that each property or event has its own entry elsewhere in the book (to find the entry, use the Alphabetical Jump Table, described later.) Each object reference entry consists of the following parts:

- The *purpose* is a brief statement of what the object does in a Visual Basic application.

- The *appearance* of the object is shown in a screen dump figure illustrating a typical example of the object as seen by the user.

**DrawWidth Property**

**Objects Affected**

| | | | | |
|---|---|---|---|---|
| Check | Clipboard | Combo | Command | Dbug |
| Dir | Drive | File | ▶ Form | Frame |
| Label | List | Menu | Option | ▶ Picture |
| ▶ Printer | Screen | Scroll | Text | Timer |

**Purpose**

The DrawWidth property sets the width of lines drawn on a form, picture box, or Printer object. A value given to the DrawWidth property represents the thickness of the line in pixels. When this property's value increases, the border around a drawn shape such as a circle or square thickens. On an object with a larger DrawWidth property, a line drawn with the Line method produces a thick line. With a DrawWidth property set larger than 1, the PSet method produces brushlike effects that are the width set by the DrawWidth property. Table 10.9 summarizes the arguments of the DrawWidth property.

**General Syntax**

```
form.DrawWidth[=size%]
picturebox.DrawWidth[=size%]
Printer.DrawWidth[=size%]
```

| Argument | Description |
|---|---|
| form | FormName property of form |
| control | CtlName property of picture box |
| Printer | Printer object |
| size% | Value representing the width of lines around shapes in pixels |

Table 10.9 Arguments of the DrawWidth property

**Example Syntax**

```
'Shows the widths of the different settings
'of the DrawWidth property by drawing lines
'with successively higher settings.
Sub Form_Click ()
    Static X As Integer       'Defines the static variable X
    Static Y As Integer       'Defines the static variable Y
    CX = ScaleWidth / 500     'Defines CX as 1/500 of form's width
    CY = ScaleHeight / 10     'Defines CY as 1/10 of form's height
    DrawWidth = DrawWidth + 1 'Increments the DrawWidth by 1
    X = CX                    'Defines X as CX
    Y = Y + CY                'Increments Y by CY
    For L = 1 To 499          'Run this statement 499 times
        X = X + CX            'Increments X by CX
        PSet (X, Y)           'Draws a point on a form
    Next L                    'Run the For statement again
    X = 0                     'Sets X to zero
End Sub
```

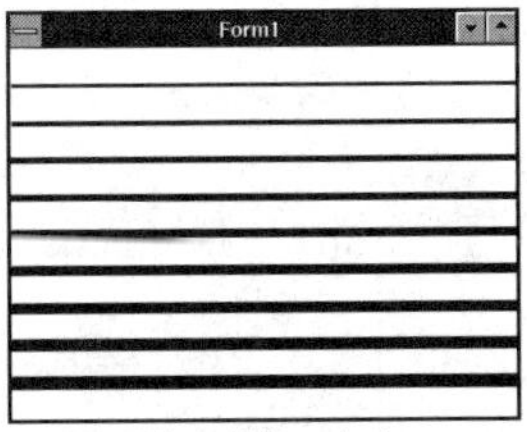

Figure 10.7 DrawWidth property in the example syntax

**Description**

The DrawWidth property sets the thickness of a line drawn on a form, picture box, or Printer object. Every DrawWidth property expression begins with the name of the affected object (the FormName of the form, the CtlName of the Picture box, or printer for Printer object). When a DrawWidth property expression has no name, the form's DrawWidth property changes. This property includes a variable labeled size% in the general syntax. The size% variable refers to the value given to the DrawWidth property. Each object begins with a default DrawWidth property set to 1. With this value, any lines drawn are 1 pixel thick. Additionally, every increase in this value represents that number of pixels for any lines drawn.

In the example syntax, the DrawWidth property of the form increases by 1 with each click of the form. Notice that the line created by the PSet method is successively thicker. Figure 10.7 shows what this example might look like on your screen.

**The Circle, Line, and PSet Methods**

When the DrawWidth property of a form, picture box, or Printer object changes from the default value of 1, it affects the output of the Circle, Line, and PSet methods. With a larger DrawWidth property setting, any circles displayed have enlarged borders. The Line method produces a line with a thickness set by the DrawWidth property. Using the PSet method, a point appears in the size indicated by the DrawWidth property. In the example syntax, the PSet method acts in conjunction with the DrawWidth property to draw a series of spots that make up a line on the screen.

**The DrawStyle Property**

If the DrawWidth property changes to greater than 1, a DrawStyle property less than or equal to 4 does not affect the appearance of a drawn line, which will be solid. With the DrawWidth property set to 1, the DrawStyle property changes the line or lines in a drawn shape from a solid line to dashes, dots, or a combination of the two depending on that property's value. When the DrawWidth property is larger than 4, a line drawn by either the Circle or Line method is solid. This does not affect the actual setting of the DrawStyle property.

**Example**

In the Shape Project at the end of this section, the DrawWidth property of the Draw picture box determines the thickness of the lines and border around a shape. When the Width menu is selected on the Shape form, the user sees a list of the numbers 1 through 10. At program start up, the checked number is the number 1 representing the thickness in pixels of lines drawn on the Draw picture box. Selecting another number on the Width menu causes the next shapes to have lines with that thickness. The DrawWidth property sets the thickness of lines. Each new number selected from the Width menu, changes the DrawWidth property of the Draw picture box. The possible settings of the DrawWidth property are not limited to between 1 and 10.

**Comments**

The DrawWidth property does not affect the setting of the DrawStyle property.

**Figure 1.2 Parts of a Reference Entry**

- The *properties, events, and methods* section uses tables to summarize the properties (characteristics) that the object can have, the events to which the object can respond, and the methods that your program can use to manipulate the object.

- Finally, there is a *description* consisting of several paragraphs that summarize the use of object and the considerations involved in programming.

### Chapter Projects

Following the reference entries, each chapter (starting with Chapter 4) concludes with a Visual Basic project that illustrates many of the features discussed in the chapter, as shown in Figure 1.3.

Each chapter project is a complete, runnable Visual Basic program. In the interest of space and with the need to focus on particular aspects of Visual Basic, however, these projects are not full-fledged applications. Each project includes the following elements:

- A project overview discussing what the project does and what Visual Basic features it illustrates.

- Instructions for assembling the project, including tables showing what objects to create, which properties to set, and the value to be set for each property. A screen dump is provided so you can check the appearance of your forms against the specifications given. Where needed, another figure shows what the program looks like when running.

- The code to be entered into Visual Basic for each event, including all necessary global values and subroutines.

- Where needed, additional notes are provided on how to run the finished project.

### How to Use the Visual Basic SuperBible

Now that you know how the *Visual Basic SuperBible* is organized, let us look at the many ways that you can access its information. Chances are you will use one or more of the following tools to find the information you need while developing your Visual Basic programs.

**Assembling the Project: Setup Form**

1. Begin a new project by selecting the File menu and the New project option. Make a new form (the Setup form) with the objects and properties shown in Table 4.13.

| Object | Property | Setting |
|--------|----------|---------|
| Form | Caption | Setup |
| | ControlBox | True |
| | Icon | \VB\ICONS\COMPUTER\KEY06.ICO |
| | FormName | Setup |
| | MaxButton | True |
| | MinButton | True |
| Command button | Caption | Show Modeless Form |
| | CtlName | SetMode |

**Table 4.13 Elements of the Setup form**

2. Size the objects on the screen, as shown in Figure 4.12.

3. Enter the following code in the General Declarations section. This code declares the variables that define the dimensions of the form's command button.

```
Dim ConvertHeight As Integer
Dim ConvertWidth As Integer
Dim OldFormHeight As Integer
Dim OldFormWidth As Integer
Dim OldHeight As Integer
Dim NewHeight As Integer
Dim OldWidth As Integer
Dim NewWidth As Integer
Dim OldLeft As Integer
Dim NewLeft As Integer
Dim OldTop As Integer
Dim NewTop As Integer
```

4. Enter the following code in the Form_Load event. This routine saves the form's current dimensions and loads the Display form.

```
Sub Form_Load ()
    OldFormHeight = Setup.Height
    OldFormWidth = Setup.Width
    OldHeight = SetMode.Height
```

**Figure 1.3 A chapter project**

## Looking Up Reference Entries

Suppose you are designing your program's user interface and you decide that you need to get a short bit of text from the user (perhaps the user's name). If you know that the InputBox$ function can do the job of asking the user for some text, you can turn to the Alphabetical Jump Table shown in Figure1.4 and skim until you find the entry for InputBox$.

The Alphabetical Jump Table, found on the inside front cover of this book, is simply a list of all the reference entries in the *Visual Basic SuperBible*, with the page number on which each entry begins. When you know what object, property, event, method, statement, or function you want, and simply desire more information about it, the Alphabetical Jump Table is the fastet way to get to the desired information.

## Looking Up Topics

While you can find reference entries in the index, the Alphabetical Jump Table is faster for that purpose because it has *only* reference entries. The index, on the other hand, gives the page numbers throughout the book where a topic (such as "forms") or a particular item (such as "Change event") is discussed.

## Finding Out How to Do Something in Visual Basic

When you're in the midst of developing a program, you often think "functionally." That is, you know what you need your program to do, but you may not know exactly how to accomplish it. For example, you may know that you need to get some text from the user, but you're not sure what methods Visual Basic provides for the purpose. This is where the Task Jump Table (on the inside back cover of the book) comes in. This table, shown in Figure 1.5, is organized by programming task. In our example you skim along the table until you find "Text box" and discover the pages where methods for doing so are discussed.

## Reviewing Visual Basic in Depth

Finally, you may decide that you want to review an area of Visual Basic programming in depth. To do so, simply look at the outline and browse the topic headings there. You

LOF (function), 765
Log (function), 765
LostFocus (event), 530
LSet (statement), 766
LTrim$ (function), 767
Max (property), 509
MaxButton (property), 100
Menu (control), 69
Mid$ (function), 767
Mid$ (statement), 768
Min (property), 510
MinButton (property), 102
Minute (function), 556
MkDir (statement), 768
Month (function), 573
MouseDown (event), 382
MouseMove (event), 385
MousePointer (property), 144
MouseUp (event), 387
MsgBox (function), 440

**Figure 1.4 The alphabetical jump table**

Determine color of a point: **Point**, 223
Get handle to manipulate a graphics image: **Image**, 214
Control redrawing of graphics: **AutoRedraw, Paint**, 208, 218
Save graphics to a file: **SavePicture**, 232

**Graphics (Setup)**
Create a graphic object: **Picture** (control), 73
Set measure to use for graphics coordinates: **ScaleMode**, 265
Establish graphics coordinates: **Scale, ScaleHeight, ScaleLeft, ScaleTop, ScaleWidth**, 258, 260, 263, 267, 269
Determine current position for drawing: **CurrentX, CurrentY**, 248
Position a graphic object: **Left, Top**, 142, 149

**Figure 1.5 The task jump table**

can then proceed to read individual reference entries or entire chapters, using the introductory discussion, reference entries, and chapter project to sharpen and complete your understanding of the topic presented.

As you have seen, there are many ways you can use and benefit from the *Visual Basic SuperBible*. We recommend that you read Chapters 2 and 3 to review your understanding of Visual Basic. If you find that you aren't sure of your undersanding of a particular topic, you may want to study its chapter in depth and perhaps take advantage of the tutorials and advanced programming tips offered in the books discussed in Appendix E.

# Introducing Visual Basic

## Why Visual Basic?

I t has been said that the third time's a charm. This cliche applies very neatly to the Microsoft Windows graphical operating environment. After trying twice, somewhat unsuccessfully, to introduce a graphical environment to the IBM PC and compatible market, Microsoft finally seems to have hit the target with Windows 3.0 and 3.1. The sudden popularity of this environment has created a large need for programs that run under it. Unfortunately, the development of Windows applications has traditionally been an excruciating process with a steep learning curve—nothing like the popular and accessible programming environments such as Microsoft's Quick BASIC, which made it easy to develop a variety of applications in the old world of character-based DOS.

Originally, the only tool available for creating Windows programs was Microsoft's Windows Software Development Kit (SDK). However, this approach had several drawbacks. First, not only did you have to purchase the kit, but you had to either own the Microsoft C compiler, or purchase that as well. Second, the SDK is a large, unwieldy, and often difficult to learn library of hundreds of routines, many with complicated syntax. You could find yourself spending more time mastering the SDK than programming. Also, this method of development required that you write the program under the DOS environment, compile it, and then run the program in Windows. An error in the program's logic meant you had to exit Windows, edit the program, recompile, get back into Windows, and then retest. As you may guess, this could quickly get very tiring.

Microsoft found a solution to this problem by going back to its oldest roots, which were not in the C language but in BASIC. Just about every personal computer that came on the market in the late 1970s and early 1980s had a version of Microsoft BASIC. The key idea of BASIC has always been its interactive nature. Unlike the tedious compile /link/run/debug process used in C, BASIC let you write some code, test it right away, and make changes "on the fly." Over the years, Microsoft considerably enhanced its original BASIC, developing QuickBASIC, which added a compiler for speed and efficiency while retaining fast interaction, and also added powerful new control structures, flexible data types, and new commands for interacting with DOS and creating graphics. It's not surprising, therefore, that when Microsoft looked for a way to make Windows programming easier and more interactive, it turned to a marriage of BASIC and an interactive, highly visual way to design programs by designing forms, controls, and other objects (see Figure 2.1). The result, Visual Basic, is for anyone who wishes to develop Windows applications but does not have the time or resources to use the SDK or Microsoft C. The Visual Basic environment runs under Windows, and requires no extra libraries to produce Windows applications. Development, testing, editing, and retesting can all be done within Windows.

The remainder of this chapter surveys the Visual Basic topics covered in this book. If you have just started using Visual Basic, reading this overview will help you grasp the concepts and procedures needed for successful programming. Even if you are an experienced Visual Basic programmer, the overview can help orient you to the organization of the *Visual Basic SuperBible*.

## Programming with Objects *(Chapter 3)*

Most DOS programs are executed in a linear manner. When a program begins, execution starts at the top and works its way down, one instruction at a time, with branches to subroutines here and there. This works fine for DOS because it is a single-task system, and it does not need to make provisions for several programs running at the same time.

Windows, however, is a multitasking system, in which more than one program may be running concurrently. Because of this programs must be designed to be "event driven"—programs don't control the computer, they react to events that happen in

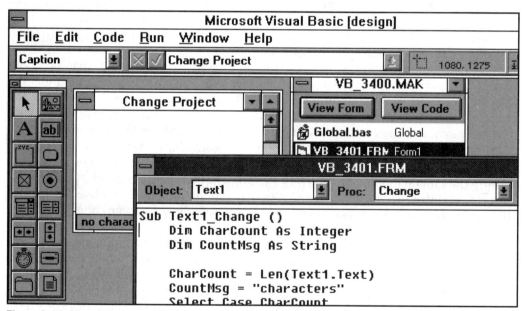

Figure 2.1 In Visual Basic, you design forms and controls, and then write the necessary code

the computer. Event-driven programs have a set of objects that wait for a specific event to occur, and then execute program code to react to the event. This enables programs to run in the background while other programs are waiting for an event to occur.

Visual Basic comes with 20 predefined objects. Each of these objects reacts to a specific event or set of events. There are three types of objects: forms, controls, and special objects. Each object has assigned to it a set of properties, methods, and events. Reviewing the objects discussed in this chapter will give you a broad picture of Visual Basic's capabilities.

## Forms

Forms are used to define a window on the screen. You design an application by placing controls on forms. An application can have more than one form. This allows you to design a main screen area for your program, as well as one or more custom message or dialog boxes.

## Controls and Control Arrays

Controls are objects that are placed on a Visual Basic form. Each control is used to perform a specific function. For instance, command buttons, check boxes, and list boxes are some of the controls provided with Visual Basic. Each control has an icon in the Visual Basic Toolbox window (see Figure 2.2). You create a control by clicking on its icon, and then drawing the control on a form.

You may also create "control arrays." A control array is a group of the same type of controls that all share the same name and events. Although the elements of a control array share the same name, each is a separate control and is referenced by a unique index number. Two properties, CtlName and Index, are used to define a control array. The CtlName property is the same for all elements of the array. The Index property is used to reference a particular element in the control array.

A control array can be created at design time merely by assigning the same name to two controls' CtlName property. This causes Visual Basic to display a dialog box that asks if you wish to create a control array. If you answer "Yes," Visual Basic automatically assigns unique values to the Index properties of each control in the array.

Elements of a control array can also be created dynamically. In other words, a control array may have only one control in its group when created at design time, but more controls may be added to the group while the program is running. You create a

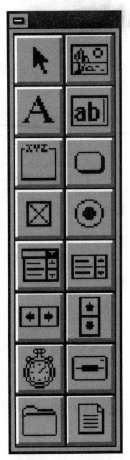

**Figure 2.2 Use the Visual Basic Toolbox to select objects to work with**

control array element dynamically with the Load statement. You may also remove an element from a control array by using the UnLoad statement. Control arrays thus allow you to manage controls flexibly and dynamically, and to select the appropriate control in response to events.

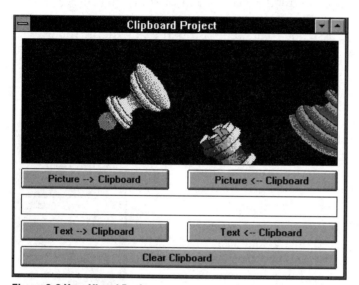

Figure 2.3 Your Visual Basic program can use the Windows Clipboard to transfer text or graphics

## Special Objects

Visual Basic also provides four special objects that are neither forms nor controls. These are the Screen, Clipboard, Printer, and Debug objects.

The Screen object gives your program the ability to reference other objects globally. Your program can use the Screen object to determine which is the active form or control, and how many and what types of fonts are available to the system on which the application is being run.

The Clipboard object gives your program the ability to interact with the Windows clipboard area. Using this object, Visual Basic programs can copy text or graphics to and from the clipboard (see Figure 2.3). Detailed information on how to use this object can be found in Chapter 23, *Using the Windows Clipboard.*

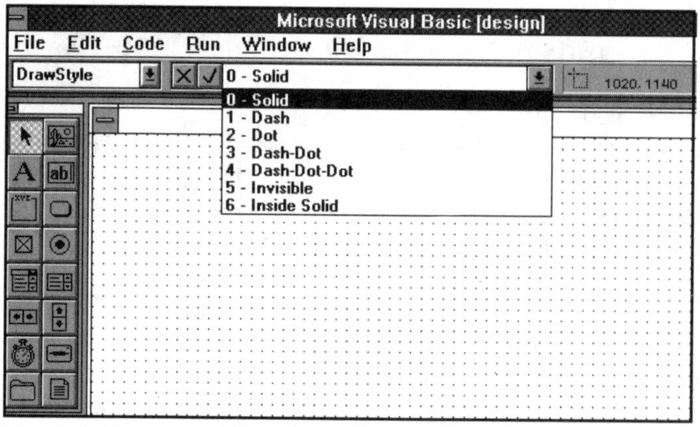

Figure 2.4 You can set the values of object properties at design time

The Printer object is used to generate output to the printer. Since the Windows environment handles the actual printing duties, your Visual Basic program doesn't really send output to the printer. Instead, the Printer object sends that output to the Windows printing routines, which in turn send the data to the printer. The Printer object is covered in Chapter 24, *Sending Data to the Printer.*

The Debug object, which is used only within the Visual Basic environment, can help with the testing and debugging of a program. This object is covered in detail in Appendix B, *Debugging Techniques*.

## Properties

Properties are used to define the appearance of an object and how it will react to a user's actions. You can set the properties for an object when you design an application. In most cases, properties can also be changed by the application while it is running.

Use the properties bar, just under the Visual Basic menus, to set a property during the design phase of a program. This bar consists of two drop-down list boxes (see Figure 2.4). The first lists all the properties that are available at design time for the currently selected object. The second lists the available settings for the selected property. If there is not a fixed set of values for the current property, you may change the setting by editing the text within the text box portion of the drop-down list.

The value of most properties can also be read or changed within the program's code, while a program is running. Use the following syntax in your program to refer to a property:

```
ObjectName.PropertyName
```

Or, if the object is part of a control array, indicate the specific element of the array as follows:

```
ObjectName(Index).PropertyName
```

For instance, if a project has a picture control that has been named Pict1, we could place the value of its Height property in a variable with the following statement:

```
A% = Pict1.Height
```

## Methods

Methods are used within an application's code to cause an action to occur to a Visual Basic object. Methods are very much like regular language statements, but their actions are performed directly on an object. Each method may have one or more arguments that detail specifically how the method will operate. The syntax for executing a method is as follows:

```
ObjectName.MethodName [arguments]
```

Or, if the object is part of a control array, indicate the specific element of the array as follows:

```
ObjectName(Index).MethodName [arguments]
```

The ObjectName specifies on which object the method is to take place. The MethodName is the method to be executed. If the method has any arguments, they are specified after the method name. For instance:

```
Pict1.Line (100, 100)-(200, 200)
```

In the above example, the Line method would be executed upon the object named Pict1. This method would draw a line on the object starting at horizontal position 100 and vertical position 100, and ending at horizontal position 200 and vertical position 200.

## Events

Events are predefined Visual Basic procedures that occur when an object has been activated. This is usually caused by the user performing some sort of action on the object. Each object has it own unique set of events. Each event reacts to a different action. Initially, an event will have no instructions associated with it. An event starts out as an empty template in which you may place Visual Basic statements, functions, or methods that will be executed when the event occurs. While you are in the design phase of a program, you may double-click on any object that you have drawn on a form, or double-click on the form itself. Doing so will display a "Code" window in which you may edit the object's events. The code window has two drop-down list boxes. The first, on the right, lists all the objects that reside on the current form. The second lists all the events associated with the current object. Each event begins with a Sub statement and an event name, and ends with an End Sub statement. When an event is first chosen, it will have the following format:

```
Sub ObjectName_EventName([arguments])

End Sub
```

Or, if the object is part of a control array, an argument is added to the event to specify the particular element of the array on which the event occurred:

```
Sub ObjectName_EventName([Index As Integer, ][arguments])

End Sub
```

As you can see, events are in the same format as a Visual Basic Sub procedure definition. All you have to do is plug in the instructions you wish to execute when the event occurs. (The BASIC language statements and functions supported by Visual Basic are described in Appendix A, *Visual Basic Language Summary*.) To illustrate, let's again use the example of the picture control Pict1. One of the events associated with a picture control is the Click event, which occurs when the user clicks on the picture. In the following event, we instruct the program to draw a line on the Pict1 picture control when the user clicks on it.

```
Sub Pict1_Click()
    Pict1.Line (100, 100)-(200, 200)
End Sub
```

## Setting Up Forms *(Chapter 4)*

To begin designing a Visual Basic program, you must first set up the forms on which your application will be based. Some forms will be used as the main screen area for your program, some for dialog boxes, and others to display miscellaneous messages. You have considerable control over the apperance and behavior of forms.

You may have noticed that in most Windows programs, the main window has a grey control box in the upper left-hand corner, and minimize and maximize buttons in the right-hand corner. You can specify whether the form you are designing has these items by setting the ControlBox, MinButton, and MaxButton properties for the form. You may also specify a title for your form by setting the Caption property.

## Managing Forms

You can designate one form to be the "startup" form for your application. This causes the form to be automatically loaded and displayed when your program begins. Any other forms in your project must be loaded into memory by your program's code. This is done with either the Load statement or the Show method. The Load statement merely loads a form into memory; it does not display it. To display a form, use the Show method. If a form is not currently loaded in memory when the Show method is executed, it will automatically be loaded.

Any time a form is loaded into memory, any code within its Load event is executed. This event can be used to initialize the form's variables and controls.

Forms can also be hidden. This is done by using the Hide method on a form. Hiding a form causes it to become invisible. However, this does not unload it from memory. Your program can still perform methods on the form and on its controls.

You can use the Unload statement to unload a form from memory. Executing the Unload statement on a form that is currently displayed causes the form to disappear from the screen before being erased from memory. If an application only has one form currently loaded, and the Unload statement is used on it, this causes the program to end.

Unloading a form initiates the form's Unload event. You can add code for this event to take care of any house cleaning that may need to be done before a form is exited.

## Forms and the Desktop

When a form is displayed with the Show method, you may specify its modal state. The modal state of a form refers to what type of control a form has over the rest of the desktop. A form can be modal or modeless.

When a modal form is displayed, it retains control of the desktop until it is closed. The user cannot switch to any other window from the same application while a modal form is displayed. This type of form is used primarily for dialog boxes. For instance, when you choose to open a Visual Basic project, an Open Project dialog box appears on the screen. As long as this box is open, you are not permitted to change to any other Visual Basic window. Therefore the Open Project window is a modal window.

A modeless form places no restrictions on which window is active. When a modeless form is displayed, the user can switch to any other window on the desktop. Visual Basic's Project window is a modeless window.

# Designing the Application's Appearance *(Chapter 5)*

The appearance of the screen elements of your application can be distinctive and tailored to the kind of information involved. You determine the appearance of the forms

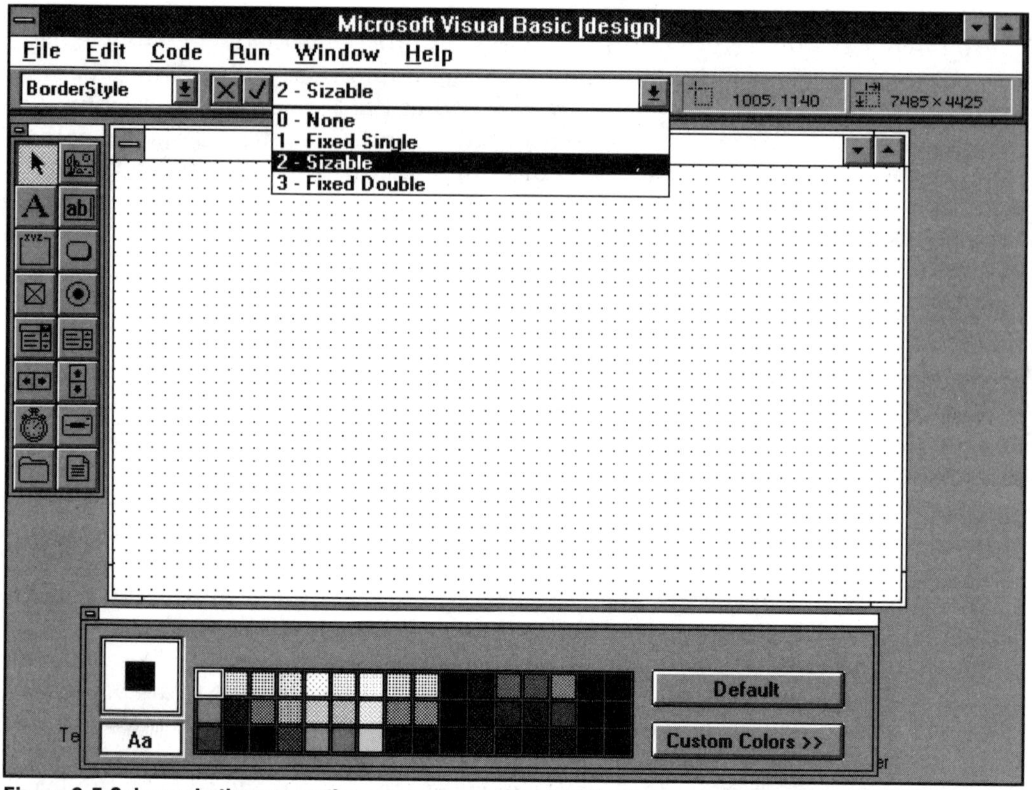

**Figure 2.5 Color and other properties can make your application's screen distinctive**

and controls in your application by setting the appropriate properties. You can specify the label (caption) for a form or control, its dimensions, its foreground and background color, and the kind of border it will have (see Figure 2.5). You can also specify an icon to represent a form when it is minimized, and a pointer to be used when the mouse is moved over the form.

## Using Forms and Controls in Program Code *(Chapter 6)*

Every form and control has a name that you can use to refer to it in your BASIC code. (As you have seen, controls in a control array are further differentiated by an index number.) The syntax section of the reference entries for items that reference a form or control shows precisely how to specify the name in your code. For example, the Height property of MyForm can be changed to 100 as follows:

```
MyForm.Height = 100
```

Objects are often scaled to other objects. For example, you can make MyForm the same size as the screen with this code:

```
MyForm.Height = Screen.Height
MyForm.Width = Screen.Width
```

Here you reference both MyForm and the Screen object, which (among other properties) tracks the height and width of the display.

## Code Modules

Sometimes you will want to write code procedures that affect more than one form. You do this by creating a module and writing code in its code window. This is particularly useful if the same procedure is to be used with several different forms: Any changes to the procedure will only have to be made in one place, and your code is also less bulky.

# Responding to Changes in Properties *(Chapter 7)*

Almost every control in Visual Basic has one property that can be directly changed by the user. For instance, the Text box control is used to display and edit text. When text is entered or edited by the user, the Text property of the text box is changed.

In most cases, you will want your program to be informed when such a change is made. After all, when the user types or selects some text, he or she probably wants your program to do something with it! For this reason, almost every control has a Change event assigned to it. This event is activated any time the control's primary property is changed.

One notable exception to the "one primary property per control" idea is the File List Box control. This control has not one but two change events. These are the PathChange and PatternChange events, which occur when the control's directory path or file pattern change, respectively.

# Setting Up Graphical Objects *(Chapter 8)*

Visual Basic has a powerful array of graphics methods. Many of the instructions that were statements in the classic BASIC languages have been changed into Visual Basic methods, and are now executed directly on a Visual Basic form or picture control.

The most basic of graphics operations is to display a picture or icon on a form or in a picture box. If a picture is contained inside a BMP (Windows bitmap), ICO (Windows icon), or WMF (Windows metafile) file, it can be displayed on a form or picture box by setting that object's Picture property to the file's name at design time. This causes the picture contained in the specified file to be loaded into and displayed on the form or picture box. A picture can also be loaded into a form or picture box at run time with the LoadPicture function.

### Graphics Permanence

In the Windows environment, graphics that are generated by your program can easily be covered up by other windows on the workspace. When this happens there must be some sort of system set up to ensure that your graphics are re-drawn when finally uncovered. Performing this task can be done automatically, using the AutoRedraw property, or manually, using the Paint event.

If you set the AutoRedraw property of a form or picture box to True, a copy of the screen image of that object is kept in memory. Any graphics methods that are performed on the object while AutoRedraw is True are also drawn on the memory image copy of the object. If the object gets covered by another window, it uses its memory copy to restore its image when it is uncovered. Using this technique is very convenient, but it takes more memory and graphics methods are performed at a slower rate.

The Paint event occurs any time a previously covered form or a picture box becomes uncovered, or when one of these objects is resized. This event does not occur when the AutoRedraw property is set to True. If the graphics you have placed on this object are fairly simple and easily redrawn, you may wish to leave the object's AutoRedraw property set to False, and place code in the Paint event to redraw the graphics when needed.

### Specifying Color

In Visual Basic, colors are represented by a 4-byte integer that indicates a mixture of the three electronic primary colors: blue, green, and red. The first byte of this number is ignored. The second, third, and fourth bytes represent how much blue, red and green, respectively, will be used in the color mixture. Each color can be assigned a value between 0 and 255 (or 0 to FF in hexadecimal notation), which indicates that color's intensity in the mixture.

You may represent a color by three means. The first method involves using a hexadecimal numeric literal. In this method, two hexadecimal digits are used for each byte in the color number. Therefore, the first two digits will always be zero, because the first byte of a color number is not used. The second two digits will represent the intensity of blue in the color, from hexadecimal 0 to hexadecimal FF. The third and fourth two-digit groups would also be hexadecimal values in the range from 0 to FF, representing the intensity of green and red, respectively. In this manner, you can represent a color of blue with the number &HFF0000, green with &H00FF00, and red with &H0000FF (&H is the prefix used in Visual Basic to indicate that a number is represented in hexadecimal notation).

The second method for specifying a color is the RGB function. This function lets you supply a decimal number for each electronic primary color, and returns a color number based on these values. Each primary color is represented by a number between 0 and 255.

In the QuickBASIC languages, you could set the current color by using the COLOR statement. This statement determined the foreground and background color of any successive screen operations. Using this statement, a program was allowed to choose from one of 16 colors on a palette. This brings us to the third method for setting a color number in Visual Basic, which involves the use of the QBColor function. QBColor is used to translate an old QuickBASIC color number (from 0 to 15) to the 4-byte format used by Visual Basic.

The final color-related element in Visual Basic is the Point method. This method determines the current color setting at a specific position on a form or picture box. This is useful when you wish to change one color to another. The code fragment below uses the Point and PSet methods to change all points on a form that are blue to red.

```
For x! = 0 To ScaleWidth
    For y! = 0 to ScaleHeight
        PointColor& = Point(x!, y!)
        If PointColor! = &HFF0000 Then PSet (x!, y!), &H0000FF
    Next
Next
```

# Designing with the Coordinate System *(Chapter 9)*

All the Visual Basic graphics methods use a coordinate system to specify where on the object to perform an action. A coordinate consists of two numbers, separated by a comma, that represent the horizontal (generally called X) and vertical (generally called Y) positioning for the method. By default, the upper left-hand corner of a form or picture box is referenced as coordinate 0, 0. You can specify a point by using coordinates that are relative to the upper left-hand corner. When this type of coordinate is supplied, it is called an absolute coordinate.

Each form or picture box has two properties, CurrentX and CurrentY, which indicate where the last graphics method ended its operation on that object. Coordinates in Visual Basic can also be specified relative to the point specified by these properties. When this type of coordinate is supplied, it is called a relative coordinate.

## Video Displays and Object Coordinates

Now that we know how to reference a point on a form or picture, let's discuss what we're referencing. In the QuickBASIC language, graphics statements specified a position by referring to a pixel on the screen. A pixel is the smallest point on a screen that may be set to a color. Every pixel on a screen consists of three very small lights called "guns." Each pixel has one red, one green, and one blue gun. Turning on one or more of a pixel's guns causes a color to be displayed at that point on a screen.

Unfortunately, when Visual Basic was created, it needed to support no less than six standards for video displays. Each of these standards supported a different number of pixels per screen. For instance, the Hercules Graphics Card (HGC) displayed 720 horizontal pixels by 348 vertical pixels, while the Enhanced Graphics Adapter (EGA) displayed 640 by 350 pixels. This meant you had to be able to specify a screen position in your program without having to know what type of video display your program was running on.

To solve this problem, Visual Basic allows you to set the type of coordinates you are using with the ScaleMode, ScaleHeight, and ScaleWidth properties. These properties are used to determine whether the forms and controls in your programs will be measured in twips (see Figure 2.6), points, pixels, characters, inches, millimeters, or centimeters, or if you're going to use a user-defined system.

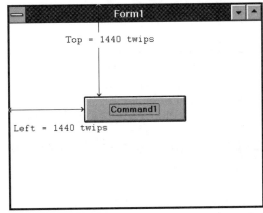

# Drawing Shapes *(Chapter 10)*

You can use two kinds of graphics with Visual Basic. One kind is the bitmap designed pixel by pixel with a paint program

**Figure 2.6 Twips are an absolute unit of measure that you can use to lay out the position of a control, such as this command button**

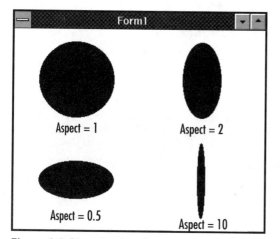

**Figure 2.7 Changing the Aspect argument to the Circle method results in different circular shapes**

such as Windows Paintbrush and stored in bitmap (.BMP) files. The other kind of graphics are lines and curves that can be generated with program statements in traditional BASIC. With Visual Basic, you use the Circle and Line methods to draw simple shapes on a form or picture box (see Figure 2.7). Other methods make it easy to control the general appearance of a shape and its boundaries. The FillColor and FillStyle properties determine the color and "texture" of the interior of a shape. By setting the DrawMode property to an appropriate value, you can control the interaction between new drawings and existing ones.

## Displaying Text with Objects
### (Chapter 11)

With traditional DOS programs, text is flung out onto the screen and is then no longer the concern of the programmer. Visual Basic, however, deals with Windows, where text is part of an object that can be resized by the user. In fact, text drawn on an object such as a form or picture box is really graphics, and is subject to the usual Windows procedures for repainting. Since the font and point size chosen for the form, picture box, or Printer object can vary, you first need to use the TextHeight and TextWidth methods to obtain the dimensions needed by the string you wish to print. You can then use the Print method to position the string in the output area (see Figure 2.8).

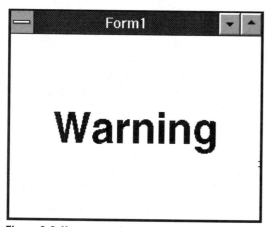

**Figure 2.8 You can scale and print text on a form**

## Defining and Using Fonts (Chapter 12)

Windows allows the programs that run under it to work with more than one font. Windows comes with several standard fonts, and many third-party fonts are available (see Figure 2.9). Your program can find out how many and what types of fonts are available to it by using the FontCount and Fonts properties with the Screen and Printer objects. The Fonts property is an array of font names available for the specified object, and the FontCount property indicates the number of entries in the Fonts property array.

You may change an object's font type by setting its FontName property to the name of the desired font. The size of the chosen font is controlled with the FontSize property.

You can display special effects on the chosen font by setting the FontBold, FontItalic, FontStrikeThru, FontTransparent, or Font-Underline properties.

## Getting User Input with Text Boxes
### (Chapter 13)

Most applications involve four primary tasks: collecting information, processing it, storing it, and making it easily retrievable. A program may work with many types of information, but the most common is text, or alphanumeric, information. Text consists of letters, numbers, and punctuation that have been typed in from the keyboard by the user. Instead of making you write extensive routines to capture and process the user's keystrokes, Visual Basic has provided the text box control. Your programs can use this control to collect alphanumeric information from the user. The text box provides the user with convenient cursor-positioning and editing capabilities (see Figure 2.10).

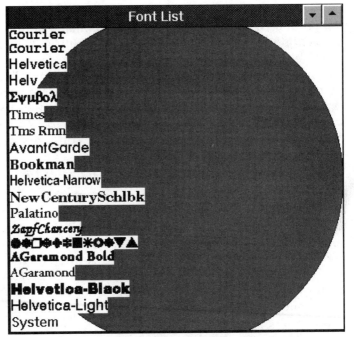

Figure 2.9 A variety of fonts are available to your Visual Basic application

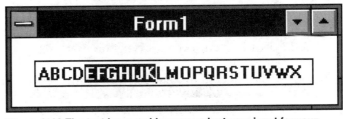

Figure 2.10 The text box provides convenient user input for your Visual Basic application

## Responding to Mouse Events (Chapter 14)

A distinctive feature of Windows is that users come to rely on the mouse for much of their interaction with your application. The mouse (or an equivalent pointing device) is used to select items, initiate actions, and to drag items to different areas of the screen. In a Windows program, therefore, mouse support cannot be an afterthought: Each of your application's controls must be integrated with the operation of the mouse. Visual Basic makes handling the mouse easy. In Visual Basic, your programs define mouse-oriented events that specify how a particular mouse action will be handled. These events tell your program when the user has pressed or released any of the buttons on the mouse, or when the user moves the mouse. You can plug code into these events to handle the user's mouse actions.

Several mouse operations have a standard meaning when used on specific objects. For instance, a single mouse click on a command button is most often used to initiate the action that is related to the command button. When working with list or combo boxes, a single click signifies that an item is selected, and a double-click usually means the user wishes to perform an action on the double-clicked item. It is suggested that you code your programs with these standard mouse operations in mind. If you don't know how an object should react to a mouse action, find another Windows program with a similar object, and set up your object's events to emulate that. This ensures that your Windows applications will have an interface consistent with other Windows programs.

## Managing the Dragging Event *(Chapter 15)*

One of the unique tasks that can be performed by the mouse is dragging. Dragging involves grabbing an item with the mouse and moving it to another position on the screen. This is usually accomplished by placing the mouse's pointer on top of the item, and pressing and holding down the left mouse button. You can then drag the item by moving the mouse pointer to the desired position on the screen. You can place code in the mouse events to perform this task, or you can set an object up so that Visual Basic automatically handles any dragging operations on it. Visual Basic has a full set of events and properties that occur when the user begins dragging an object, or when an object is being dragged over another object.

## Handling Keyboard Input *(Chapter 16)*

Keyboard input is handled much like the mouse. Visual Basic has attached events to the keyboard that occur any time a key is pressed, held down, or released.

The KeyDown event occurs when the user presses or holds down any key on the keyboard (see Figure 2.11). This includes keys that send unprintable characters, such as the Insert and Delete keys. If the user holds a key down, this event will be called repeatedly for that key.

The KeyPress event occurs when the user presses and then releases any key on the keyboard that generates a printable ASCII character. Simply put, the printable ASCII characters consist of the upper- or lower-case letters A through Z, the numbers 0 through 9, and the following punctuation characters: ',./<>?;:'[]{}~!@#$%^&*()_+|\'.

The KeyUp event is the inverse of the KeyDown event.

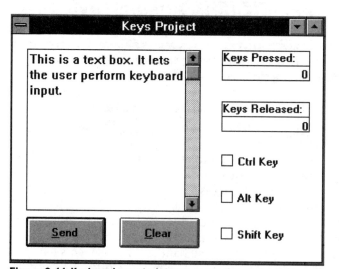

**Figure 2.11 Keyboard events let you recognize and handle any form of keyboard input**

It occurs when a user releases any key on the keyboard. Like KeyDown, this event responds to unprintable character codes.

You may also assign special actions to the Enter and Escape keys. This is done by creating command buttons on a form and setting their Default and Cancel properties. Setting a command button's Default property to True causes its Click event to occur when the user presses the Enter key. In other words, when the user presses Enter, the default action for the command button is executed. A similar relationship is held by a button's Cancel property and the Escape key.

Finally, Visual Basic has the SendKeys statement, which simulates keyboard input. This statement can be used to send keystrokes to your applications or to other Windows programs. This is useful when you wish to send data to a program that does not support Dynamic Data Exchange (DDE).

## Creating and Using Dialog Boxes *(Chapter 17)*

Dialog boxes are another distinctive feature of Windows programs. You can use them to alert the user to important information, to allow the user to tailor the operation of the

program, or to get information needed to complete an operation. While elaborate operations are best done with forms designed for the purpose, Visual Basic provides a set of three predefined dialog boxes in the form of language functions and statements. These dialog boxes allow your programs to perform simple, no-frills interaction with the user without having to design a new form

**Figure 2.12 This simple dialog box can be used to con** **irrevocable action**

for each instance. Two of these dialog boxes, provided by the Input$ and MsgBox tions, return a value based on the user's actions when that dialog box is displayed. third, provided by the MsgBox statement, merely displays a message in a box and ret no value.

You can also include a predefined icon in a message box to heighten visual impact Figure 2.12).

## Using List and Combo Boxes *(Chapter 18)*

In many of the programs you write, you will want to present the user with a list items and let the user choose one item from the list. Generally, you would want th user to choose from a list in order to reduce typing errors by the user, and to hel ensure valid data entry. For this purpose, Visual Basic has the list box control. A list bo appears on a form as a box that contains one or more text items. The user can choos an item by clicking on it with the mouse, or by using the up and down direction key on the keyboard. When an item in a list box has been selected, that item will automati-

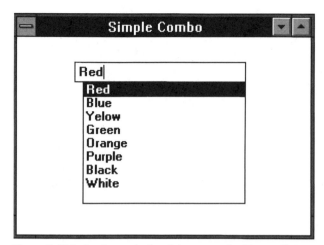

**Figure 2.13 A simple combo box lets users select from a list or type in their own selection**

cally be highlighted by having its color set to white on black. If the area needed to display the list of items exceeds the area defined on the form for the list box, scroll bars are automatically added to the right edge of the box. This allows the user to scroll up and down the list with the mouse.

## Combo Boxes

Sometimes you may wish to get text input from a user, but at the same time you want your program to suggest a predefined list of items as possible values. Visual Basic provides a solution to this situation with the combo box control. Using this control, you can draw a "simple combo" box on your form. A simple combo box is one control that has the features of both a text box and a list box. With this control, a list box appears directly below an edit area that looks and acts just like a text box control. The user can either type or edit text in this edit area, or select an item from the attached list.

## Drop-Down Lists and Combos

List and simple combo boxes are very useful, but they often require a large amount of screen area in order to display enough items in the list to make the box meaningful. To remedy this, the Combo box control has been set up so it can be used in one of three formats, each looking and working a little differently. One of the formats, the simple combo, was discussed in the previous paragraph. The other two formats are called "drop-down" boxes, because the list portion of these boxes is not displayed until the user wishes. At that time, the list will drop-down from the edit portion of the box, and the user can then select an item from the list. One of these two formats is called the drop-down list box. This form of the combo box control restricts the user to those items that are in its list. The other format, called the drop-down combo box, lets the user type and edit text in its edit area as well as select an item from its list. The format used for a combo box is determined by the setting of that box's Style property.

## Specifying Selections for Lists and Combos

When a program begins, the lists provided by these controls are empty. If your program has any of these controls, the list portion of the control needs to be loaded with items from which the user can choose. This process is performed with the AddItem method, which assigns entries to a list. By default, the AddItem method will automatically position the new entry in the list. Alternatively, your program can specify a particular position in the list in which to place the new entry.

The inverse of the AddItem method is the RemoveItem method, which deletes entries from a list or a combo box's list. Unlike the AddItem method, your program must specify which particular item in the list is to be removed.

At design time, when you create a list or combo box, you can set it up so that it automatically sorts its list as items are added to it. This is done by setting the box's Sort property to True. A list or combo box's Sort property can only be set at design time. Once the program is running, this property cannot be changed.

# Managing Files in Drive, Directory, and File List Boxes *(Chapter 19)*

As mentioned previously, most programs have four main tasks: collecting, processing, storing, and retrieving information. The second of these tasks, storage, is mostly done on floppy or hard disk drives in the form of files. For this purpose, Visual Basic has included three controls: the drive, directory, and file list boxes. These controls are used in conjunction with each other to provide a visual interface for navigating the DOS file system.

## Types of Storage Devices

Virtually every system that runs your programs will have access to at least one disk drive. In the DOS file system, each drive available to the computer is assigned a drive letter that uniquely identifies that drive. A drive can further be identified by its label, an 11-character name that can optionally be assigned to it by the user. There are generally three types of disk drives. First is the removable floppy disk drive. Users can insert and remove the disk media from a removable floppy disk drive at will. This allows the user to save files to a floppy disk, and then use that disk on another computer. Second, your program can access a fixed hard drive. Fixed drives have the advantage of having a large capacity, but usually cannot be removed from the computer. Finally, if the computer your program is running on is attached to a network, it may have access to a shared network drive. A network drive is physically located in a separate computer, but the network interface means that information can be stored or retrieved on that drive by remote computers. All network drives have a unique name by which the network software can identify them. When a remote computer wishes to use a network drive, it specifies that drive's network name, and assigns it a logical drive letter. Once this has been done, programs can access the network drive by the assigned drive letter.

Your programs can let the user choose a source or destination drive for file operations with the drive list box. This control is a drop-down list box whose entries list all the available drive letters on the system upon which your program is run. If a listed drive is a fixed hard disk drive, its label, if any, is also listed. If a listed drive is connected through a network, its network name is displayed along with its logical drive letter.

## Navigating the Directory Structure

Way back in the dark ages, when DOS was first written for the IBM PC, it was a flat file system. This means that all the files on a disk drive were contained in the same directory, regardless of whether or not the files were related to each other. Version 2 of DOS borrowed the hierarchial directory scheme from the UNIX operating system. This scheme involves a root directory, which can hold a limited number of files. The root directory can have underneath it one or more optional child directories, which can hold an unlimited number of files. The child directories are called subdirectories, and can in turn have any number of levels of subdirectories.

As you can imagine, navigating through all the possible directories on a disk could be a daunting task. However, Visual Basic's Directory list box provides you with a way to allow the user to perform this task visually. The directories of a disk are displayed in a directory list box in a tree-like structure. The user can then select a directory entry by clicking on it, or change to a directory by double-clicking on it.

One or more files can be contained in each directory. You can use the file list box control to allow the user to choose a particular file within a directory. By manipulating this control's properties, you can limit the displayed files to match a particular file pattern, or to list only those files whose archive bits match a particular setting (see Figure 2.14).

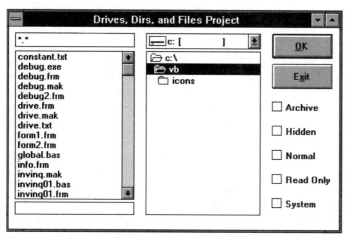

Figure 2.14 You can combine drive, directory, and file lists to give complete control over file selection

When working in a networked environment, the drives, directories, and files available to a program can change at any time without notice to the program. For that reason, it's not a bad idea to use the Refresh method on a regular basis with these controls. When this method is executed, the specified control is refreshed with the most current information. Strategically, there are optimum areas in which to place the Refresh method. One technique involves creating a Timer control (discussed later) on your form, and using its Timer event to refresh all the file related list boxes at a regular timed interval. The other technique is to execute the Refresh method in the list box's GotFocus event (also discussed later).

## Operating Scroll Bars *(Chapter 20)*

When the number of items in a list or combo box exceeds the display area for that control, Visual Basic automatically adds scroll bars to the box so the user can quickly scroll through the list with the mouse. You can also instruct Visual Basic to add a horizontal or vertical scroll bar to the edges of a mulitple-line text box. In some instances, however, you may need to attach a scroll bar to an object that does not automatically have this capability. For this purpose, Visual Basic provides the vertical and horizontal scroll bar controls.

The scroll bar controls consist of grey bars with arrows at each end. Between the arrows is a small scroll button. The position of this button represents a value relative to the length of the bar. Each scroll bar has a minimum and a maximum possible value, set by the scroll bar's Min and Max properties. In order to determine the setting of the scroll bar's button, your program can examine the bar's Value property. This property is a numeric representation of the button's position on the bar in relation to the values of the Min and Max properties.

### Scroll Bars as Positioning Tools

There are two primary purposes for using the scroll bars controls. The first and most obvious purpose is to scroll the contents of a box up or down, or left or right. This is sometimes needed when a box or window is not large enough to display the entire item that it contains. For instance, if you load a large graphic image from a file into a smaller picture box control, the entire graphic will not be displayed. If you want to allow the user to view the undisplayed areas of the image, you can attach scroll bars with which the user can specify which portion of the image to display (see Figure 2.15).

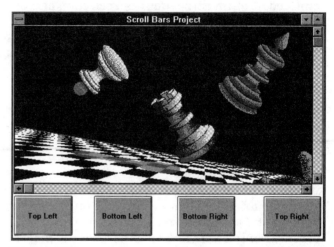

**Figure 2.15 You can use scroll bars to allow the user to examine different parts of a large graphic image**

### Scroll Bars as Slider Controls

Another use for scroll bars is to provide a visual technique for setting the value of a number. This is analogous to a slider control, like the volume and tone controls on some radios. Because the position of the scroll bar's button indicates a numeric value relative to the bar's possible minimum and maximum values, the user can set a numeric value by manipulating a scroll bar's button. For instance, imagine you're developing a program that can shrink and grow a graphic image. You wish to let the user set the size of the image from 50 to 200 percent of its original size. Instead of making the user type in a percentage in a text box, and then auditing the box to see if the value is in the desired range, you could set up a scroll bar with its Min and Max properties set to 50 and 200, respectively. The user could then set the desired image size by manipulating the scroll bar button.

## Establishing and Controlling the Application Focus *(Chapter 21)*

The control that is actively set up to receive any input from the keyboard is said to "have the focus." More often than not, the forms you design for your Visual Basic applications will contain more than just one control. Chances are, many of the controls on the same form will be able to react to keyboard input in one way or another. However, we don't want to have all of the controls battling each other over which one receives any keystrokes entered by the user, so there must be a system for determining which of the controls will react to the keyboard. In Visual Basic, only one control at a time can own the focus. Because Windows can have more than one application running at a time, focus can also refer to the form or program that is the parent of the control with the focus. In other words, your Visual Basic program as a whole may have (or not have) the focus in relation to other programs on the desktop.

### Forms that Seize the Focus

Not all forms and controls can receive the focus at all times. When a modal form is displayed, it restricts the user from selecting any other forms from the same application until the modal form is closed. In essence, a modal form prevents any other forms from the same program from receiving the focus. By the same token, no control on any of these other forms can receive the focus as long as the modal form is displayed.

### Disabling the Focus

In some cases, you might not want a control to receive the focus even though Visual Basic allows it. For example, because the focus refers to the control that will receive keyboard input, you should prevent controls that cannot process input from the keyboard from receiving the focus. The scroll bars control, which we'll discuss in more detail later, can only be controlled by the user via the mouse. Therefore, because it cannot process keyboard input, it would be foolish to allow it to receive the focus. If such a control does receive the focus, it will not affect your program in a harmful manner; but because the user won't be able to see which is the active control, it might cause confusion. In order to prevent a control from receiving the focus, set that control's TabStop property to False.

Finally, any control that has its Enabled property set to False cannot receive the focus.

### Changing the Focus

The focus can be moved from one running application to another in two ways. First, the user can point to an application's window or icon with the mouse, and click the left mouse button. Second, you can move the focus to another running program by using the AppActivate statement within your program's code.

The focus can be moved to another control in one of three ways. First, the user can point to a control with the mouse and click the left mouse button. If the selected control is eligible to receive the focus, it becomes the active control. Second, the user can cycle through all the eligible controls on a form by pressing the Tab key. This moves the focus from one control to another in the order determined by the TabIndex property of all of the controls on the form. Finally the focus can be changed by using the SetFocus method within your program's code. This method allows your program to directly set the focus to a particular control. A control keeps the focus until the focus is moved to another control. The exception to this rule is the Menu control. Just prior to executing any of its events, the Menu control returns the focus to the control that owned it before the menu was opened.

When a control in your program receives the focus, its GotFocus event is initiated. You can use this event to prepare the control for the user's actions. For instance, as mentioned previously, you might use the GotFocus event to update the entries in a file list box when it receives the focus.

## Timing and Time Information *(Chapter 22)*

Sometimes the world inside the computer must be synchronized with the passage of real time. For example, a particular operation may need to be scheduled to be performed at a certain time each day. Much like QuickBASIC, Visual Basic has a Timer function, which uses the system clock to return the number of seconds that have elapsed since midnight. This function can be used to time specific operations (see Figure 2.16). For instance, you can determine how long it takes a fragment of code to execute by assigning the returned value from the Timer function to a variable just prior to the beginning of the code fragment. At the end of the code fragment, you assign the Timer function to another variable. You can then subtract the starting variable from the ending variable to determine the number of seconds that elapsed while the code was running.

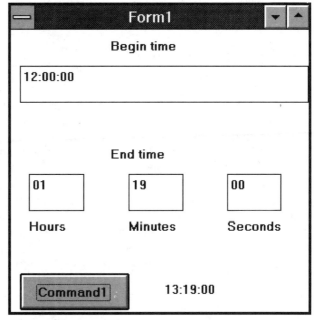

QuickBASIC also has an ON TIMER GOSUB statement, which allows a program to repeatedly execute a set of commands at a predefined interval. However, Visual Basic has no such statement. Instead, it provides a control called the Timer. By setting the Interval property of the Timer, you can cause the Timer control's Timer event to occur on a regular timed

**Figure 2.16 You can easily time intervals with reference to the system clock**

schedule. This control is useful when you need to insert a clock or regularly update a displayed value in a program.

Visual Basic automatically provides time information through a variety of functions, statements, and events. You can obtain the current date and time through a serial number that can be broken down into month, day, hour, minute, and second.

## Using the Windows Clipboard *(Chapter 23)*

The Windows clipboard is an area in memory that has been set aside for programs to use for copying and pasting information. It can be used to store several types of information. First, and most common, is text. Text information consists of any characters that can be represented by an ASCII code. Generally, these are the upper- and lower-case letters A through Z, the numerals 0 through 9, and punctuation characters, such as commas, periods, and exclamation points. The clipboard can also store graphic images that are in one of three formats: Windows bitmap, Windows metafile, and device independent bitmap (DIB). Finally, Windows uses the clipboard area to store information during Dynamic Data Exchange (DDE) conversations (selected topics on DDE are covered later in this chapter, and again in Chapter 25, *Transferring Data with Dynamic Data Exchange*). The clipboard can hold one entry each of all of these types of information. When a piece of information is copied to the clipboard, it replaces any information of the same type that was previously stored there.

Your Visual Basic programs can access this area by manipulating the Clipboard object. This object has five associated methods with which you can determine what type of data is on the clipboard, and copy text or graphics to or from the clipboard. These are GetFormat, GetText, GetData, SetText, and SetData.

### Retrieving Information from the Clipboard

Before your program retrieves information from the clipboard, it needs to determine if the clipboard contains the desired type of information. This is done by using the GetFormat method with the Clipboard object. With this method, your program specifies a data type. If the clipboard contains that information, the method will return a True (-1) value; if not, it returns False (0).

Once you've determined that the desired information is available, you can use either the GetText or GetData methods with the Clipboard object to retrieve it. The GetText method retrieves text information, and it can also be used to retrieve DDE information by specifying that format. You can assign the results of this method to any Visual Basic string, or any control property that is in string format. (A string is a variable type in the Visual Basic language. Variables and their types are covered later in this chapter.)

The GetData method retrieves graphics. By default, this method returns a Windows bitmap. Optionally, your program can specify which type of graphic information it is requesting, bitmap, metafile, or DIB. You can use this method to assign an image from the clipboard to the Picture property of a form or picture control.

### Sending Information to the Clipboard

The converse of the GetText and GetData methods are the SetText and SetData methods. SetText is used to copy text information to the clipboard. Like GetText, it can also be used to copy DDE information by specifying that format. SetData is used to copy the image of a Form object or picture control to the clipboard. With this method, your program supplies the Picture or Image property of the object, and optionally specifies the image format (bitmap, metafile, or DIB).

## Sending Data to the Printer *(Chapter 24)*

One of the advantages of programming for the Windows environment is that your programs do not have to know specific information about the brands and styles of peripheral hardware connected to the system upon which they are run. Windows handles the low-level input and output to devices such as screens and printers. This makes it very simple for you to create programs that output complex forms and graphics to the printer.

In most languages, the printer is treated as a sequential output device. Programs are allowed to write data to a printer one character at a time, and once this is done there can be no going back. Visual Basic, however, takes a very different approach. It provides a special object, appropriately called the Printer object, to handle printed output.

Instead of outputting data in a character-by-character manner, the Printer object is a page-oriented device. The Printer object sets up in memory the image of a blank printer page. Any methods executed on the Printer object occur on this page in memory and are held there until your program tells the printer object to start a new page.

Any of the methods used for drawing graphics or printing characters on a form or picture can be used on the Printer object. When you execute methods such as Pset, Line, and Circle on the Printer object, their output goes to the current printer page in memory. The only difference between using these methods on the screen and using them with a printer is that most printers can only perform their operations in black and white. With such printers, specifying the color in a graphics method has no effect.

## Coordinate Systems on the Printer Object

As mentioned previously, output to the Printer object is directed to a printer page in memory. The size of this page will depend on the particular brand and model of printer. The absolute size of each page is measured in twips. A twip is defined as 1/20 point, which is 1440 twips per printed inch. Therefore, if the default printer has its page size defined as 8-1/2 x 11 inches, the size of the Printer object's print page will be 12240 x 15840 twips. Your program can determine the absolute height and width of the printer page by using the Height and Width properties with the Printer object. However, the values returned by these properties do not necessarily reflect the usable page area. This is because every printer has a unique border area around the page in which it cannot print. The actual size of the usable print area can be obtained with the ScaleHeight and ScaleWidth properties of the Printer object.

## Controlling the Printer Page

Your program needs to inform the Printer object when it is done printing a page of output. This is done with the NewPage method. This method ends the output to the current print page in memory and creates a new blank page on which any new output to the Printer object will occur. The NewPage method also updates the Page property of the Printer object.

The Page property is a counter, that reflects the number of pages that have been printed to the Printer object. Each time your program executes the NewPage method, this property is incremented. The Page property is a read-only property. The only way it can be reset is to execute the EndDoc method.

The EndDoc method tells the Printer object that your program has completed printing the current document. When it is executed, all of the printer pages that have been stored in memory by the Printer object are then sent to the Windows printing routines. Windows then handles the task of outputting those pages to the printer. If your

program has sent output to the Printer object since the last NewPage method was
executed, EndDoc will automatically send a NewPage.

### Printing Forms

Visual Basic also provides a very useful method for printing forms. The PrintForm
method is used with a form object, and sends a copy of that form to the printer. Any
graphics, text, or controls (with the exception of the menu controls) on that form are
printed on the printer.

## Transferring Data with Dynamic Data Exchange (DDE) *(Chapter 25)*

Dynamic Data Exchange (DDE) is a protocol developed by Microsoft for the Windows
environment. It allows you to establish real-time communication between two Windows applications. In other words, DDE allows programs to "talk" to each other. What
makes DDE useful is that it allows the user to set up data links between documents that
have been created by the same or two different applications. Depending on how this
link is set up, the data in one document will automatically be updated when the data
in the other changes. Whenever two applications talk with each other using Dynamic
Data Exchange, it is called a DDE conversation. All DDE conversations consist of four
elements: the client, the server, the topic, and the item.

Every DDE conversation involves two applications exchanging information. The
conversation is started when one of the two applications requests data from the other.
The program that requests the data is called the client application, and the program
that supplies the data is called the server application. In order for a DDE conversation
to occur, both the client and the server must be running. If the client requests data
from an application that is not currently running, a dialog box appears informing the
user of this, and the user is asked if the server application should be executed. When
the conversation is initiated, the client application can set up the link between the two
programs in two ways. First, it can instruct the server application to update the link
every time the requested data changes. This is called a "hot link." Second, the link can
be set up so that information is exchanged only when the client requests it. This is
called a "cold link."

When a conversation is started, the client application must inform the server application of what particular piece of data it is requesting. This is done by specifying a
topic and an item. The topic of a DDE conversation refers to the general form or document on which the requested data resides. The item of a DDE conversation refers to
the specific piece of data requested. The server application defines which of its objects
are available as DDE topics and DDE items. For instance, in a DDE conversation with a
spreadsheet application as the server, the spreadsheet document could be a DDE topic,
and the data in a particular cell in that spreadsheet could be a DDE item. If you wish to
use another application as a DDE server, you will need to refer to its documentation in
order to find out what it defines as a DDE topic and a DDE item.

Your Visual Basic programs can be set up as DDE clients as well as DDE servers. You
can even set up an application to be both server and client. Keep in mind, however,
that not all Windows programs can perform DDE operations. Before you attempt to
create a DDE link between your application and another, make sure the other application has the capabilities needed to participate in a DDE conversation.

In order to define the parameters of a DDE conversation, Visual Basic has associated with the text box, picture box, and label controls a group of four properties: LinkTopic, LinkItem, LinkMode, and LinkTimeOut. You can use these properties to define the server application and DDE topic, the DDE item, whether the DDE link will be hot or cold, and how long to wait for the DDE conversation to begin before issuing an error. See Chapter 25, *Transferring Data with Dynamic Data Exchange,* for details.

# Visual Basic Language Summary *(Appendix A)*

Visual Basic's objects and controls deal mostly with providing you, the programmer, with visual tools for building an intuitive user interface. In most cases, however, these tools cannot perform the actual processing of data, which is the heart of any application. This task is handled by Visual Basic's programming language. This language is based on Microsoft's very popular QuickBASIC language. As a matter of fact, most of the commands in Visual Basic have the same syntax and effects as their QuickBASIC counterparts. (The "compatibility boxes" in the reference entries in Appendix A indicate whether a given Visual Basic statement or function has a counterpart in QuickBASIC 4.5 or Microsoft BASIC Professional Development System 7.0.) Therefore, if you're already a QuickBASIC programmer, the Visual Basic language will be old hat. If not, don't fret. Visual Basic is a straightforward, easy-to-understand language.

## Variables

Any programming language needs a technique for storing and accessing data in the computer's memory. In more primitive times, this was done by having the program refer to the actual address of the physical memory location. Using this technique required the programmer to have an intimate knowledge of how the computer's memory was set up. It also meant that the programmer had to handle all the chores related to allocating memory to data. Fortunately, this is no longer the case. Most modern programming languages, including Visual Basic, allow the programmer to allocate memory by declaring variables.

A variable is a symbolic name for a location in memory. In your programs, you can read and write to memory by assigning a value from or to a variable. Smart programmers will assign a name to a variable that describes the purpose of the data that it represents. This practice is helpful in making your programs more readable. For instance, if you were to set up a variable that will hold the total dollar amount of an invoice, you could name it something ambiguous, such as X. As you are writing the program, that variable name would be fresh in your mind, and you'd have no problem deciphering what it represents. However, suppose you have to come back many months later to make changes to the program. At that time, the meaning of X will not be so fresh in your mind, and you could waste a lot of time just trying to figure out what it means. A better solution would be to give the variable a name that will give you a hint as to what it represents, such as InvoiceTotal. This variable name is descriptive enough so that when you come back to the program to make modifications, you don't need to trace through the whole program to find out what it represents.

Visual Basic has some rules regarding how you may set up a variable name. These rules help Visual Basic to tell the difference between variables that you set up and other elements of the language. These rules are:

1. A variable name may be no longer than 40 characters.

2. The first character of a variable name must be a letter (A through Z). This letter can be upper- or lower-case.

3. The remaining characters can be letters (A through Z or a through z), numbers (0 through 9), or underscores (_).

4. The last character can be one of these type declaration characters (explained later): %, &, !, #, @, $.

5. The variable name cannot be a Visual Basic reserved word. Reserved words include Visual Basic properties, events, methods, operators, statements, and functions.

## Operators

Operators are used to perform an operation with one or more elements in a Visual Basic line of code. For instance, the plus sign (+) is an arithmetic operator. It adds two or more numeric values. Visual Basic has three types of operators: arithmetic, relational, and logical. Arithmetic operators perform math functions on numeric values. Relational operators are used to compare the values of two items. You can use relational operators to determine if one value is equal to, greater than, or less than another value. Logical operators perform bitwise operations on numeric variables. Each logical operator will change the bit values of a numeric variable in a different way.

## Statements and Functions

The core of the Visual Basic language is based on commands, which come in two types: statements and functions. A statement is a command that performs a prescribed task. A function is similar to a statement in that it also performs a task. Additionally, a function returns a value of some sort based on the results of the task. You can modify the behavior of a statement or function by supplying arguments to the command. Statements and functions use the information supplied in these arguments to direct them in their task.

# Debugging Techniques *(Appendix C)*

Once you've written a Visual Basic program, your job is only half done. Although it can catch your syntax errors, Visual Basic is not intelligent enough to know when you've made an error in your programming logic. Logic errors can only be found by rigorously testing and retesting your completed program. Once you find a logic error, you need to determine the cause of the error and fix it. When this happens, it's always nice if the environment in which you are programming provides you with some tools to aid you in your quest for an error-free program. Unlike its DOS cousin QuickBASIC, Visual Basic does not support Watch variables, which let you watch the contents of a variable as the program is running. Fortunately, Visual Basic does provide some tools designed to help you debug programs.

## The Immediate Window

When you start a program while in the Visual Basic environment, your form becomes the window on the desktop with the focus. Another window, called the Immediate window, is displayed underneath your form. At any time while your program is in run mode, you may break out of your program and bring the Immediate window to the forefront. Once you've done so, you can type real-time Visual Basic commands into this window, and they will be executed immediately. This window is very useful for examining the contents of variables and properties at certain points during a program's execution.

## The Debug Object

Hand in hand with the Immediate window is the Debug object. This object can only be accessed in your program while it is running under the Visual Basic environment. It is used with the Print method; when executed, its arguments are printed in the Immediate Window. This allows you to place Print methods at strategic areas in your program that can print the value of certain variables or properties. You can use this in place of the omitted Watch variable feature.

## Breakpoints

Most times while you are trying to debug a program, you will have a fairly good idea as to where in your program an error is occurring. You may want the program to execute normally until just prior to reaching the area of the suspected error. For this reason, Visual Basic lets you set "breakpoints" in your program. Setting a breakpoint makes your program stop at the indicated line, as if the user had pressed Ctrl and Break keys simultaneously. You set a breakpoint by placing the insertion point on the line where you wish to halt program execution and choosing the Toggle Breakpoint option from the Run menu. You can also toggle a breakpoint by pressing the F9 function key.

## Stepping Through a Program

Any time your program halts while running under the Visual Basic environment, it goes into what is called "break" mode. This can happen when you press the Ctrl and Break keys simultaneously, or when the program reaches a breakpoint, or when the program encounters an error. Once in break mode, you can cause your program to execute one line of code at a time. This is called stepping through a program. Visual Basic provides two ways to step through a program. The single step executes one Visual Basic command at a time. If the command includes executing a user-defined subprocedure, that subprocedure is loaded into the Code window, and its commands are then stepped through as well. A single step is executed by choosing the Single Step option from the Run menu, or by pressing the F8 function key. The second way to step through code is called a procedure step. A procedure step executes a subprocedure in one fell swoop. You are not shown the commands inside the subprocedure. A procedure step is executed by choosing the Procedure Step option from the Run menu, or by pressing the Shift key and the F8 function key.

### Set Next Statement

Visual Basic actually lets you change your program's code while in break mode and then continue executing after the changes have been made. Sometimes you will want to see how these changes are going to work as soon as you make them. In order to do this, you can use the Set Next Statement command. This command lets you specify at which statement to continue execution after it has been halted.

# Using the Windows API *(Appendix D)*

Long ago, a wise programmer figured out that writing programs in a structured manner, and relegating specific tasks to routines that could be called from anywhere in a program, meant that these routines could also be used in other programs to perform the same tasks. Then one day another programmer took this idea one step further, and invented a way to compile all of these reusable routines into an object file that could be linked to the compiled version of the program being developed. Thus was born the linkable programming library.

Windows programs take this concept one step further. When the Windows operating environment was created, it included the ability for Windows programs to utilize Dynamic Link Libraries (DLLs). Dynamic Link Libraries are collections of working routines that can be linked to a Windows program. In this respect, DLLs are very much like the classic type of linkable library. The difference between the two is that in order to use routines in a classic library, the programmer needs to link the library to the program during the compilation process. A program that uses routines in a DLL, however, is fully compiled without the library. When the program begins, it searches for the appropriate DLL library file, and links to it at run time. All that is required is for the program to know the name of the DLL file and the syntax needed to execute the routines in the library. Several programs can share the same DLL in memory, considerably reducing the amount of memory needed by the sum of the running applications.

One nice thing about Windows is that most of its Application Program Interface (API) is accessible through dynamic link libraries. An API defines the manner in which a program can be written in order to interact with a particular environment. In Windows, programs can access the API by calling routines from certain dynamic link libraries that come with the environment.

Fortunately, Visual Basic provides your programs with the ability to execute routines that are contained in these DLLs. Before you try to call a DLL, you need to tell Visual Basic about the DLL by placing a Declare statement in the global module of your program (see Appendix A for the syntax of the Declare statement). Once this is done, you can call the DLL routine in the same manner as for any other Visual Basic Sub procedure or function.

# Further Reading *(Appendix E)*

There is no limit to exploration and no end to learning. We conclude the *Visual Basic SuperBible* with a description of books from Waite Group Press and others that can help you master various aspects of Visual Basic. You will also find books on QuickBASIC and related languages, since much of the functionality of QuickBASIC is included in Visual Basic. We also include some titles about Windows programming.

# Programming with Objects 3

## Visual Basic Objects

As you have no doubt noticed while working in the Windows environment, every Windows program shares several features. Pull-down menus, list boxes, and buttons seem to be in almost every Windows program you use. Because of this, Visual Basic provides several predefined "objects" that inherently perform these tasks.

A Visual Basic object is a logical item that performs a specific purpose. Most objects have certain properties that define in detail how they will appear and react to the user. Most objects also have a set of events assigned to them that define what actions are to be taken when they are manipulated by the user. You then add Visual Basic code to specify the appropriate behavior.

These objects are what make Visual Basic a programming "environment" instead of just a programming language. If you were working with a programming language, you would have to write code that would define each object and specify its behavior and how it acts once the user uses it—or obtain a library of such objects written by another programmer. In Visual Basic, each control is already predefined. The properties and behavior of an object are easily set up without doing any programming. The only coding that you need to do is to define how an object will react to the user's actions.

Each object in Visual Basic has a set of properties associated with it. The appearance and behavior of an object are defined by the settings of these properties. Initially, an object's properties are set at design time. In most cases, these settings can also be read or changed by the program while it is running. However, some properties are read only at run time, meaning their value can only be set when the program is in its design phase. Other properties cannot be set during the design phase; you must make any changes to the properties in the program's code.

Visual Basic also assigns a set of events to each object. These events are Visual Basic Sub procedures that occur when the user performs an action with an object. If you double-click on an object in design phase, Visual Basic's Code window is displayed. From here, you may define the actions to be taken when a particular event occurs. (See Appendix A, *Visual Basic Language Summary*, for an explanation of Sub procedures and a description of the statements and functions you can use in Visual Basic code.)

The final element that is related to an object are its methods. Methods are commands that perform an action with or on an object. They are used in a similar manner to Visual Basic's statements or functions, but their operations are performed directly on a form control or object when invoked by code.

Visual Basic has 20 predefined objects. These objects are summarized in Table 3.1. Note that the word "object" is used in two senses in Visual Basic. Each of the items in the table is an "object" as described above, but some objects are also "controls." A control, as the name implies, is an object that the user can use to communicate with or control the application. Objects that are not controls are not directly manipulated by the user.

| Use This... | | To Do This... |
| --- | --- | --- |
| Check box | Control | Display a choice that the user can turn on or off. |
| Clipboard | Object | Copy and paste text or graphics to and from the Windows clipboard |
| Combo box | Control | Display a list box with a text input area |
| Command button | Control | Display a button that performs a function when the user clicks on it |
| Debug | Object | Get help in the development/debugging process of a program |
| Directory list box | Control | Allow the user to choose a disk directory from a list box |
| Drive list box | Control | Allow the user to choose a disk drive from a drop-down list box |
| File list box | Control | Allow the user to choose a file in a specific directory from a list box |
| Form | Object | Define a window on the screen on which   objects may be placed |
| Frame | Control | Define an area on a form that can contain several related controls |
| Label | Control | Place a text label on a Form, picture, or frame |
| List box | Control | Display a list of items in a box from which the user can choose |
| Menu | Control | Define pull-down menus that appear at the top of a form |
| Option button | Control | Define a group of choices where only one choice may be selected |
| Picture box | Control | Define an area on a Form for displaying graphics |
| Printer | Object | Generate output to the printer |
| Screen | Object | Activate a specific form or control at run time |
| Scroll bars | Control | Provide a visual method for setting a value |
| Text box | Object | Define an area on a form for text editing |
| Timer | Object | Provide a program with timing capabilities |

**Table 3.1 Visual Basic objects**

In this chapter, we will explore the purposes and uses of each of these objects. In each entry, the object's related properties, events, and methods are discussed. An accompanying figure shows each object's appearance on the screen, unless the object is not visible. Also, if the object is covered in a later chapter of this book, you will be directed there for an example of how it is used.

# Check Box Control

## Purpose

The check box control presents the user with an on/off choice. The user can either select or deselect this control by clicking on it. Your program can determine whether the user has selected this control by examining its properties.

## Properties, Events, and Methods

Tables 3.2, 3.3, and 3.4 list the properties, events, and methods that relate to the check box control.

| Use This Property... | To Do This... |
| --- | --- |
| BackColor, ForeColor | Read or set the background and foreground colors of this object |
| Caption | Assign text to this object |
| CtlName | Set the name by which this control will be referenced |
| DragIcon | Read or set what is displayed when this control is dragged |
| DragMode | Determine if drag operations are to occur manually or automatically |
| Enabled | Read or set whether this object can react to events |
| FontBold, FontItalic, FontStrikeThru, FontTransparent, & FontUnderline | Read or set special effects for this object's font |
| FontName | Read or set the name of this object's font |
| FontSize | Read or set the size of this object's font |
| Height | Read or set the height of this object |
| Index | Uniquely identify an element of a control array |
| Left | Read or set the left edge position of this control on a picture or form |
| MousePointer | Read or set the shape of the mouse pointer when it's over this object |
| Parent | Read the name of the form to which the control belongs |
| TabIndex | Read or set the placement of this control within the form's tab order |
| TabStop | Read or set whether control is included in the form's tab order |
| Tag | Read or set text information that is particular to this object |
| Top | Read or set the coordinate of this control's top edge |
| Value | Read or set the current setting of this control |
| Visible | Read or set whether this object is visible |
| Width | Read or set the width of this object |

Table 3.2 Properties of the check box control

| Use This Event... | To Do This... |
|---|---|
| Click | React to the user clicking on this object |
| DragOver | React to the user dragging another object over this object |
| GotFocus | Initiate an action when this object receives the focus |
| KeyDown | Initiate an action when the user presses or holds a key down |
| KeyPress | React to the user typing an ASCII character |
| KeyUp | Initiate an action when the user releases a key on the keyboard |
| LostFocus | Initiate an action when this object loses the focus |

Table 3.3 Events of the check box control

| Use This Method... | To Do This... |
|---|---|
| Drag | Control manual dragging of a check box |
| Move | Change the position of a check box |
| Refresh | Cause a check box to be updated immediately |
| SetFocus | Move the focus to the specified check box |

Table 3.4 Methods of the check box control

## Description

The check box control is used to present the user with a choice that has only two possible settings. It consists of a small box, which may be checked or empty, and some accompanying text (see Figure 3.1). When the user clicks on this control, the status of the box is reversed: If it was checked before the user clicked it, the box will now be empty; if it was empty, it will now be checked. Unlike the option button, the operation of each check box on a form, label, or picture is independent of all other check boxes. In other words, changing the status of one check box does not affect other check boxes.

The program can set or read the current status by manipulating the Value property. This property has three possible settings. A setting of 0 indicates the box is currently empty. A setting of 1 means the box is currently checked. A setting of 2 indicates the control is greyed. The Value property can only be set to 2 by your program's code. This allows your programs to have an alternate method for indicating that a check box has been selected. When a check box is greyed, the box is filled in with a greyish color. However, this does not disable the control. It can still receive the focus, and will still react to the user's activity. If clicked on while in this state, the check box's Value property will be set to 0, and the box will be cleared.

The Caption property is used to define the text that will accompany the check box. The size and style of this text is defined by the settings of the Font... properties. If an ampersand (&) is included in the Caption property, the letter following the ampersand will be underlined, and the check box may be selected by holding down the Alt key and pressing that letter. For instance, if a check box's Caption property is set to &Cash, the displayed text will be "<u>C</u>ash" and the user can select the box by pressing Alt+C.

When the user clicks on this control, its Click event is activated. This event is used so the program can react immediately to any changes in the setting of the check box. This event is also initiated if the user presses the space bar while this control has the focus, or any time the check box's Value property is changed within the program's code.

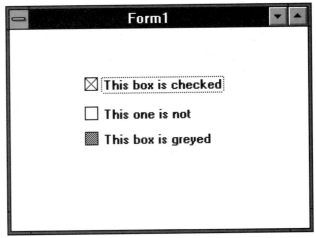

Figure 3.1 How a check box control looks on a form

# Clipboard Object

## Purpose

The Clipboard object is used to copy and paste data to and from the clipboard area of the Windows environment. This enables you to transfer data between most Windows applications as well as between forms or other objects in the same application.

## Properties, Events, and Methods

Table 3.5 lists the methods that relate to the Clipboard object. This object has no associated properties or events.

| Use This Method... | To Do This... |
| --- | --- |
| Clear | Clear the contents of the clipboard |
| GetData | Return graphics information from the Clipboard |
| GetFormat | Return whether or not the clipboard holds a desired type of data |
| GetText | Return text information from the clipboard |
| SetData | Send graphics information to the clipboard |
| SetText | Send text information to the clipboard |

Table 3.5 Methods of the Clipboard object

## Description

One of the advantages to using the Windows operating environment is that all Windows programs can copy and retrieve text and graphics to and from an area in the environment called the clipboard. The clipboard is a temporary holding area for data that has been cut or copied from the current or other program.

This clipboard area is an element of the operating environment, and as such can be used by any program running in the environment. This means you can cut or copy information from one program and paste it into another. All Windows programs can use the clipboard area.

Generally, the clipboard can hold three types of items. First, it can hold text. Text is any letters, numbers or characters that can be represented by an ASCII code. Second, it can hold graphics. Windows lets the user cut and paste pictures as well as text. Finally, the clipboard can hold DDE messages being sent from one program to another. For more information on working with DDE messages, see Chapter 25, *Transferring Data with Dynamic Data Exchange*.

The clipboard may hold only one of each of type of these data items at a time. When a program copies an item to the clipboard, it replaces any item of the same type that previously resided there.

Visual Basic's Clipboard object is used to access the Windows clipboard area. The GetText and SetText methods retrieve and send text from and to the clipboard. GetData and SetData are used to retreive and send graphics from and to the clipboard. The GetFormat method tests whether a specific type of data is currently being held by the clipboard.

The Clipboard object is discussed in detail in Chapter 23, *Using the Windows Clipboard*.

# Combo Box

## Purpose

The combo box control provides three techniques for presenting a list of choices to the user.

## Properties, Events, and Methods

Tables 3.6, 3.7, and 3.8 list the properties, events, and methods that relate to the combo box.

| Use This Property... | To Do This... |
| --- | --- |
| BackColor, ForeColor | Read or set the background and foreground colors of this object |
| CtlName | Set the name by which this control will be referenced |
| DragIcon | Read or set what is displayed when this control is dragged |
| DragMode | Determine if drag operations are to occur manually or automatically |
| Enabled | Read or set whether this object can react to events |
| FontBold, FontItalic, FontStrikeThru, FontTransparent, & FontUnderline | Read or set special effects for this object's font |

| | |
|---|---|
| FontName | Read or set the name of this object's font |
| FontSize | Read or set the size of this object's font |
| Height | Read or set the height of this object |
| Index | Uniquely identify an element of a control array |
| Left | Read or set the left edge placement of this control on a picture or form |
| List | Read or set the value of a listed item |
| ListCount | Read the number of items in a list |
| ListIndex | Read or set the index of the currently selected item in a list |
| MousePointer | Read or set the shape of the mouse pointer when it's over this object |
| Parent | Read the name of the form to which this control belongs |
| SelLength | Read or set the number of characters selected in a text box |
| SelStart | Read or set the starting position of selected text in a text box |
| SelText | Read or replace the selected text in a text box |
| Sorted | Read or set whether Visual Basic will automatically sort the list |
| Style | Read or set the style of a combo box |
| TabIndex | Read or set the placement of this control within the form's tab order |
| TabStop | Read or set whether this control is part of the form's tab order |
| Tag | Read or set text information that is particular to this object |
| Text | Read or set the text contained in a text or combo box |
| Top | Read or set the coordinate of this control's top edge |
| Visible | Read or set whether this object is visible |
| Width | Read or set the width of this object |

**Table 3.6 Properties of the combo box control**

| Use This Event... | To Do This... |
|---|---|
| Change | React to a change in a combo box's text property (Style = 0 or 1) |
| Click | React to the user clicking on this object |
| DblClick | React to the user double-clicking on this object |
| DragDrop | React to the user dragging and dropping an object onto this object |
| DragOver | React to the user dragging another object over this object |
| DropDown | React to the user clicking on the down scroll arrow of a combo box |
| GotFocus | Initiate an action when this object receives the focus |
| KeyDown | Initiate an action when the user presses or holds a key down |
| KeyPress | React to the user typing an ASCII character |
| KeyUp | Initiate an action when the user releases a key |
| LostFocus | Initiate an action when this object loses the focus |

**Table 3.7 Events of the combo box control**

| Use This Method... | To Do This... |
|---|---|
| AddItem | Add an item to a list or combo box's list |
| Drag | Control manual dragging of this control |
| Move | Change the position of this control |
| Refresh | Cause this object to be updated immediately |
| RemoveItem | Delete items from a list |
| SetFocus | Move the focus to this control |

**Table 3.8 Methods of the combo box control**

## Description

Combo boxes provide a combination of the list box and the text Box objects. All combo boxes have an edit area and a list area. The currently selected item is always displayed in the edit area of a combo box. The list area, when visible, appears below the edit area. The user may choose an item from the list portion of a combo box by clicking on it or by using the up and down arrow keys to move the reverse highlight to the desired item. If there are more items in the list than can be displayed in the list portion of the combo box, Visual Basic will automatically add a vertical scroll bar on the right edge of the list. The user can then use this scroll bar to move up or down in the list.

There are three types of combo boxes: the drop-down combo, the simple combo, and the drop-down list box. Setting the Style property determines which type will be used. The Style property can only be set at design time. It is a read-only property at run time.

Setting the Style property to 0 causes a combo box to become a drop-down combo. The drop-down combo box displays the currently selected item in an edit area similar to a text box (see Figure 3.2). A down scroll arrow is displayed to the right of the edit area. The list portion of this combo box stays hidden until the user clicks the down scroll arrow. This causes the list of items to "drop-down." The user may either choose an item from the list, or type an entry in the edit area.

Setting the Style property to 1 causes a combo box to become a simple combo. The simple combo box also has an edit area in which the currently selected item is displayed (see Figure 3.3). The list portion of this combo box is always visible under the edit area. As with the drop-down combo, the user may either choose an item from the list or type an entry in the edit area.

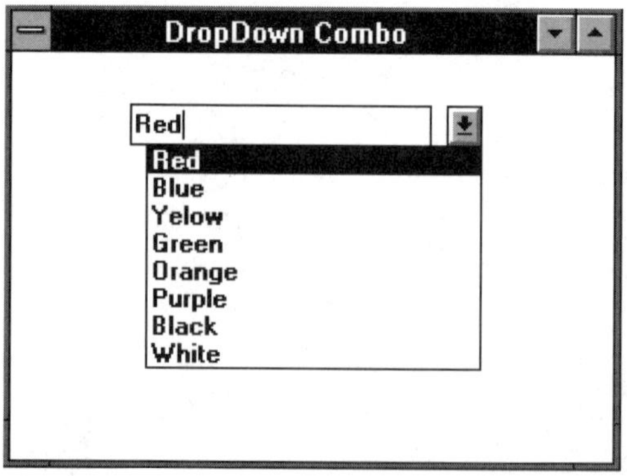

**Figure 3.2 How the drop-down combo box looks on a form**

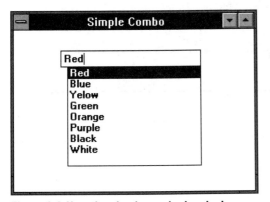

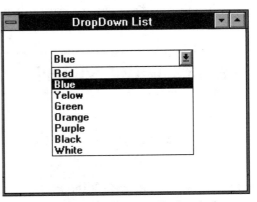

**Figure 3.3 How the simple combo box looks on a form**

**Figure 3.4 How the drop-down list box looks on a form**

Setting the Style property to 2 causes a combo box to become a drop-down list. The drop-down list box is similar in structure to the drop-down combo box. As with the drop-down combo, the list area stays hidden until the user clicks on the down scroll arrow. However, the user cannot edit the text in the edit area, but can only choose an item from the list portion of the drop-down list (see Figure 3.4).

The Text property can be used to read the text associated with the currently selected list item. If no item is currently selected, this property will return a null string. The Text property can also be set during run time for the drop-down and simple combo boxes, but is a read-only property with the drop-down list box.

The List property provides a method for reading and setting a list's contents in a manner similar to accessing and assigning values in an array. The List property is followed by an index number in parentheses that identifies which list entry is being referenced. The index numbering of the list is 0-based. Therefore, if a list contains five items, the first item is index number 0, and the highest index number is 4. The number of items in a list can be determined by using the ListCount property.

The ListCount property is used to determine the number of items that have been added to a combo box. Each time the AddItem method is used on a combo box control, this property is incremented. Using the RemoveItem method decrements it.

The ListIndex property returns the index number of the currently selected item in a list. If no item is currently selected, a -1 is returned. If the user enters text in the edit area of the simple or drop-down combo box, and that text does not match a listed item, this property will also return a ListIndex value of -1.

The program may also set the currently selected item of a list by setting this property. When using the ListIndex property to set the currently selected list entry, the program must use an index number that references a currently existing item in the list. For instance, if a list has five items in it, an index number of 0 to 4 must be specified, or an "Invalid property array index" error will occur.

The AddItem and RemoveItem methods add and delete items from a combo box's list. This object is discussed in detail in Chapter 18, *Using List and Combo Boxes*.

# Command Button Control

## Purpose

The command button control displays a button that performs a function when the user clicks on it.

## Properties, Events, and Methods

Tables 3.9, 3.10, and 3.11 list the properties, events, and methods that relate to the command button control.

| Use This Property... | To Do This... |
|---|---|
| BackColor, ForeColor | Read or set the background and foreground colors of this object |
| Cancel | Assign a command button's Click event to the Escape key |
| Caption | Assign text to this object |
| CtlName | Set the name by which this control will be referenced |
| Default | Assign a command button's Click event to the Enter key |
| DragIcon | Read or set what is displayed when this control is dragged |
| DragMode | Determine if drag operations are to occur manually or automatically |
| Enabled | Read or set whether this object can react to events |
| FontBold, FontItalic, FontStrikeThru, FontTransparent, & FontUnderline | Read or set special effects for this object's font |
| FontName | Read or set the name of this object's font |
| FontSize | Read or set the size of this object's font |
| Height | Read or set the height of this object |
| Index | Uniquely identify an element of a control array |
| Left | Read or set the left edge placement of this control on a picture or form |
| MousePointer | Read or set the shape of the mouse pointer when it's over this object |
| Parent | Read the name of the form to which this control belongs |
| TabIndex | Read or set the placement of this control within the form's tab order |
| TabStop | Read or set whether this control is part of the form's tab order |
| Tag | Read or set text information that is particular to this object |
| Top | Read or set the coordinate of this control's top edge |
| Visible | Read or set whether this object is visible |
| Width | Read or set the width of this object |

Table 3.9 Properties of the command button control

| Use This Event... | To Do This... |
|---|---|
| Click | React to the user clicking on this object |
| DragDrop | React to the user dragging and dropping an object onto this object |
| DragOver | React to the user dragging another object over this object |
| GotFocus | Initiate an action when this object receives the focus |
| KeyDown | Initiate an action when the user presses or holds a key down |
| KeyPress | React to the user typing an ASCII character |
| KeyUp | Initiate an action when the user releases a key |
| LostFocus | Initiate an action when this object loses the focus |

**Table 3.10 Events of the command button control**

| Use This Method... | To Do This... |
|---|---|
| Drag | Control manual dragging of this control |
| Move | Change the position of this control |
| Refresh | Cause this object to be updated immediately |
| SetFocus | Move the focus to this control |

**Table 3.11 Methods of the command button control**

## Description

A command button is a graphic object that represents a task to be performed. When the button is pressed, its related task is activated.

The user can press a button by clicking on it or by pressing the Enter key or the space bar while the button has the focus. Doing so causes the command button's Click event to be initiated. This event defines the actions to be taken when the button is pressed.

The Caption property defines the text that is to be displayed on the button (see Figure 3.5). If an ampersand (&) is included in the Caption property, the letter following the ampersand will be underlined, and the button may be selected by holding down the Alt key and pressing that letter. For instance, if a button's Caption property is set to &Cash, the displayed text will be "Cash," and the user can select the button by pressing Alt+C.

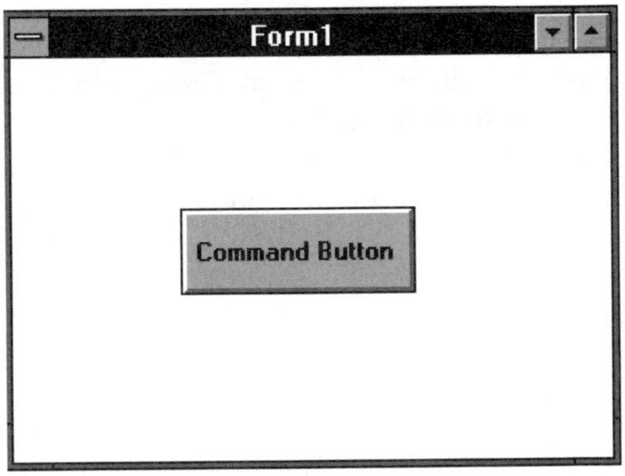

In most cases, a form has one command button that is used to perform the default action for that form. The Default property allows the programmer to assign that default action to the Enter key so that pressing Enter has the same effect as clicking on the command button. This property can either be set to True (-1) or

**Figure 3.5 How a command button looks on a form**

False (0) by the programmer at design time, or by the application during run time. Because only one button on a form may be the default, setting this property to True for one button automatically sets it to False for all the other buttons on the same form.

Sometimes it is necessary to give the user a way to back out of, or cancel, an operation. The Cancel property allows the programmer to assign that cancel action to the Escape key. This property can either be set to True (-1) or False (0) by the programmer at design time, or by the application during run time. Because only one button on a form may be the cancel button, setting this property to True for one button automatically sets it to False for all the other buttons on the same form.

The Default and Cancel properties are covered in greater detail in Chapter 16, *Handling Keyboard Input.*

# Debug Object

## Purpose

The Debug object uses the Print method to send output to the Immediate window when a program is run under the Visual Basic environment.

## Properties, Events, and Methods

Table 3.12 lists the method that relates to the Debug object. This object has no associated properties or events.

| Use This Method... | To Do This... |
| --- | --- |
| Print | Print text on a form or picture box |

Table 3.12 The one Debug method

## Description

The Immediate window automatically opens when a program is run under the Visual Basic environment. While in run mode, the program can send text to this window by executing the Print method with the Debug object. This is generally used to check the value of a variable at a specific point in a program. For instance, the following code will send the value of the variable A% to the Immediate window:

```
Debug.Print A%
```

This object is covered in greater detail in Appendix B, *Debugging Techniques.*

# Directory List Box Control

## Purpose

The directory list box control displays a list box from which the user can navigate through all the directories on the selected disk drive.

## Properties, Events, and Methods

Tables 3.13, 3.14, and 3.15 list the properties, events, and methods that relate to the directory list box control.

| Use This Property... | To Do This... |
| --- | --- |
| BackColor, ForeColor | Read or set the background and foreground colors of this object |
| CtlName | Set the name by which this control will be referenced |
| DragIcon | Read or set what is displayed when this control is dragged |
| DragMode | Determine if drag operations are to occur manually or automatically |
| Enabled | Read or set whether this object can react to events |
| FontBold, FontItalic, FontStrikeThru, FontTransparent, & FontUnderline | Read or set special effects for this object's font |
| FontName | Read or set the name of this object's font |
| FontSize | Read or set the size of this object's font |
| Height | Read or set the height of this object |
| Index | Uniquely identify an element of a control array |
| Left | Read or set the left edge placement of this control on a picture or form |
| List | Read the value of a listed item |
| ListCount | Read the number of items in a list |
| ListIndex | Read or set the index of the currently selected item in a list |
| MousePointer | Read or set the shape of the mouse pointer when it's over this object |
| Parent | Read the name of the form to which this control belongs |
| Path | Read or set the currently selected directory path |
| TabIndex | Read or set the placement of this control within the form's tab order |
| TabStop | Read or set whether this control is part of the form's tab order |
| Tag | Read or set text information that is particular to this object |
| Top | Read or set the coordinate of this control's top edge |
| Visible | Read or set whether this object is visible |
| Width | Read or set the width of this object |

Table 3.13 Properties of the directory list box control

| Use This Event... | To Do This... |
| --- | --- |
| Change | React to a change in the control's Drive property |
| Click | React to the user clicking on this object |
| DragDrop | React to the user dragging and dropping an object onto this object |
| DragOver | React to the user dragging another object over this object |
| DropDown | React to the user clicking on the down scroll arrow of a combo box |
| GotFocus | Initiate an action when this object receives the focus |
| KeyDown | Initiate an action when the user presses or holds a key down |
| KeyPress | React to the user typing an ASCII character |
| KeyUp | Initiate an action when the user releases a key |
| LostFocus | Initiate an action when this object loses the focus |
| MouseDown | React to the user pressing any mouse button |
| MouseMove | React to the user moving the mouse over this object |
| MouseUp | React to the user releasing any mouse button |

Table 3.14 Events of the directory list box control

| Use This Method... | To Do This... |
| --- | --- |
| Drag | Control manual dragging of this control |
| Move | Change the position of this control or form |
| Refresh | Cause this object to be updated immediately |
| RemoveItem | Delete items from a list |
| SetFocus | Move the focus to this control |

Table 3.15 Methods of the directory list box control

## Description

The directory list box displays a hierarchical directory tree in a box. Each directory entry displays a small folder icon next to the name of the directory (see Figure 3.6). This object is used in conjunction with the Drive and File list box objects, to give the user a method for navigating the DOS file system.

The top of the displayed directory tree represents the root directory of the drive currently selected for that directory box. Displayed under the root directory will be each subdirectory that is part of the path to the current directory. The folder icons for these directories will be displayed as open. Also displayed are all subdirectories that are one level below the current directory. The folder icons for these directories are displayed as closed.

The user may select a different directory by clicking on its entry in the box. This sets the ListIndex property to the selected directory. This does not, however, change the current directory for the list box. To change the current directory, the user must double-click on an entry. This not only changes the ListIndex property for the box, but it also changes the Path property to the new directory. You can also set these properties directly in your code. In that case, the directory list box will visually reflect these changes.

The Path property is used to set or read the current drive and path for the directory list box. Whenever the Path property is changed, the directory list box's Change event is activated. This event is used so the program can react to the user changing the current directory.

Please see Chapter 19, *Managing Files in Drive, Directory, and File List Boxes,* for more information on the use of the directory list box control.

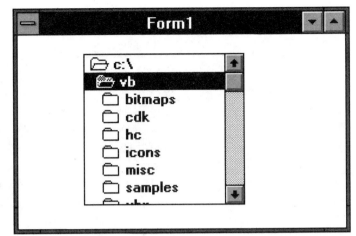

Figure 3.6 How the directory list box control looks on a form

# Drive List Box Control

### Purpose

The drive list box control displays a drop-down list box that allows the user to choose an available disk drive.

### Properties, Events, and Methods

Tables 3.16, 3.17, and 3.18 list the properties, events, and methods that relate to the drive list box control.

| Use This Property... | To Do This... |
| --- | --- |
| BackColor, ForeColor | Read or set the background and foreground colors of this object |
| CtlName | Set the name by which this control will be referenced |
| DragIcon | Read or set what is displayed when this control is dragged |
| DragMode | Determine if drag operations are to occur manually or automatically |
| Drive | Read or set the current selected drive |
| Enabled | Read or set whether this object can react to events |
| FontBold, FontItalic, FontStrikeThru, FontTransparent, & FontUnderline | Read or set special effects for this object's font |
| FontName | Read or set the name of this object's font |
| FontSize | Read or set the size of this object's font |
| Height | Read or set the height of this object |

*Table 3.16 (continued)*

| Use This Property... | To Do This... |
| --- | --- |
| Index | Uniquely identify an element of a control array |
| Left | Read or set the left edge placement of this control on a picture or form |
| List | Read the value of a listed item |
| ListCount | Read the number of items in a list |
| ListIndex | Read or set the index of the currently selected item in a list |
| MousePointer | Read or set the shape of the mouse pointer when it's over this object |
| Parent | Read the name of the form to which this control belongs |
| TabIndex | Read or set the placement of this control within the form's tab order |
| TabStop | Read or set whether this control is part of the form's tab order |
| Tag | Read or set text information that is particular to this object |
| Top | Read or set the coordinate of this control's top edge |
| Visible | Read or set whether this object is visible |
| Width | Read or set the width of this object |

**Table 3.16 Properties of the drive list box control**

| Use This Event... | To Do This... |
| --- | --- |
| Change | React to a change in the control's Path property |
| DragDrop | React to the user dragging and dropping an object onto this object |
| DragOver | React to the user dragging another object over this object |
| GotFocus | Initiate an action when this object receives the focus |
| KeyDown | Initiate an action when the user presses or holds a key down |
| KeyPress | React to the user typing an ASCII character |
| KeyUp | Initiate an action when the user releases a key |
| LostFocus | Initiate an action when this object loses the focus |

**Table 3.17 Events of the drive list box control**

| Use This Method... | To Do This... |
| --- | --- |
| Drag | Control manual dragging of this control |
| Move | Change the position of this control or form |
| Refresh | Cause this object to be updated immediately |
| SetFocus | Move the focus to this control |

**Table 3.18 Methods of the drive list box control**

## Description

The drive list box, used in conjunction with the directory and file list boxes, gives the user a way to navigate the DOS file system. It is a drop-down list box in which the current drive is displayed in the text area (see Figure 3.7). When the user clicks on the down scroll arrow of the box, a list of drives available to the user's system drops down. The user may change the current drive by clicking on one of the listed entries.

When the program starts running, Visual Basic automatically explores the user's system and adds all of the floppy, fixed, and network drives to the list. Drive list items that reflect local fixed disks will also display that disk's label with the drive letter. For network drives, the network name of the drive is also displayed.

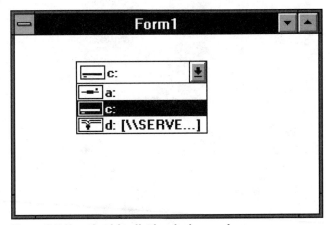

**Figure 3.7 How the drive list box looks on a form**

This control's Drive property may be used to set or read the current drive. When this property has been changed, either by user input or by instructions in the program, the Change event is activated.

If the program is being run on a network, the Refresh method can by used to update the entries for this control. This will cause any changes in shared drives to be reflected in the list entries.

Please see Chapter 18, *Managing Files in Drive, Directory, and File List Boxes,* for more information on the drive list box control.

# File List Box Control

## Purpose

The file list box control displays a list box that lists the files in a specific directory.

## Properties, Events, and Methods

Tables 3.19, 3.20, and 3.21 list the properties, events, and methods that relate to the file list box control.

| Use This Property... | To Do This... |
|---|---|
| Archive | Read or set  whether files with their archive bit set will be displayed |
| BackColor, ForeColor | Read or set the background and foreground colors of this object |
| CtlName | Set the name by which this control will be referenced |
| DragIcon | Read or set what is displayed when this control is dragged |
| DragMode | Determine if drag operations are to occur manually or automatically |
| Enabled | Read or set whether this object can react to events |
| FileName | Read or set the current selected file |
| FontBold, FontItalic, FontStrikeThru, FontTransparent, & FontUnderline | Read or set special effects for the font used with this object |
| FontName | Read or set the name of this object's font |
| FontSize | Read or set the size of this object's font |
| Height | Read or set the height of this object |
| Hidden | Read or set  whether files with their hidden bit set will be displayed |
| Index | Uniquely identify an element of a control array |
| Left | Read or set the left edge placement of this control on a picture or form |
| List | Read the value of a listed item |
| ListCount | Read the number of items in a list |
| ListIndex | Read or set the index of the currently selected item in a list |
| MousePointer | Read or set the shape of the mouse pointer when it's over this object |
| Normal | Read or set whether to display files with system and hidden bits off |
| Parent | Read the name of the form to which this control belongs |
| Path | Read or set the currently selected path |
| Pattern | Read or set the file name pattern |
| ReadOnly | Read or set whether files with their read only bits set will be displayed |
| System | Read or set whether files with their system bits set will be displayed |
| TabIndex | Read or set the placement of this control within the form's tab order |
| TabStop | Read or set whether this control is part of the form's tab order |
| Tag | Read or set text information that is particular to this object |
| Top | Read or set the coordinate of this control's top edge |
| Visible | Read or set whether this object is visible |
| Width | Read or set the width of this object |

**Table 3.19 Properties of the file list box control**

| Use This Event... | To Do This... |
| --- | --- |
| Click | React to the user clicking on this object |
| DblClick | React to the user double-clicking on this object |
| DragDrop | React to the user dragging and dropping an object onto this object |
| DragOver | React to the user dragging another object over this object |
| GotFocus | Initiate an action when this object receives the focus |
| KeyDown | Initiate an action when the user presses or holds a key down |
| KeyPress | React to the user typing an ASCII character |
| KeyUp | Initiate an action when the user releases a key |
| LostFocus | Initiate an action when this object loses the focus |
| MouseDown | React to the user pressing any mouse button |
| MouseMove | React to the user moving the mouse over this object |
| MouseUp | React to the user releasing any mouse button |
| PathChange | Initiate an action when the current path of a file list box has changed |
| PatternChange | Initiate an action when the file pattern of a file list box has changed |

Table 3.20 Events of the file list box control

| Use This Method... | To Do This... |
| --- | --- |
| Drag | Control manual dragging of this control |
| Move | Change the position of this control or form |
| Refresh | Cause this object to be updated immediately |
| SetFocus | Move the focus to this control |

Table 3.21 Methods of the file list box control

## Description

The file list box, used in conjunction with the drive and directory list boxes, gives the user a way to navigate the DOS file system. This control lists all the files in the directory specified by the control's Path property (see Figure 3.8). The files that are displayed are also limited to those whose file names match the control's Pattern property.

The Path property is used to set or read the directory path for the files to be displayed. It is not available during design time. At the start of the program, it defaults to the current default directory. If the Path property is changed, the PathChange event will be activated.

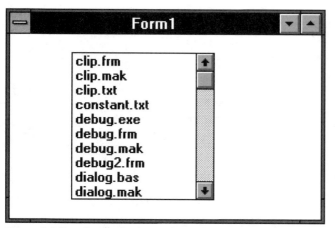

**Figure 3.8 How the file list box control looks on a form**

The Pattern property is used to define a subset of files within the directory specified by the Path property. This property consists of any full or partial file name, and can contain the wild card characters * and ? which match file names according to the standard rules for DOS.

The currently selected file in a list box may be read or set by using the FileName property. This property is changed any time the user clicks on a new file name within the File list box.

The file list box control and its related properties, methods, and events are covered in Chapter 19, *Managing Files in Drive, Directory, and File List Boxes*.

# Form Object

## Purpose

The Form object defines a visual work area on the Windows desktop in which controls can be arranged. Forms can be used to set up any windows, dialogs, or message boxes that are required for a program.

## Properties, Events, and Methods

Tables 3.22, 3.23, and 3.24 list the properties, events, and methods that relate to the Form object.

| Use This Property... | To Do This... |
|---|---|
| AutoReDraw | Read or set whether graphic pictures will be redrawn automatically |
| BackColor, ForeColor | Read or set the background and foreground colors of this object |
| BorderStyle | Determine whether this object has a border, and if it does, set its style |
| ControlBox | Determine if this control box is displayed on a form |
| CurrentX, CurrentY | Read or set the current graphics position on this object |

| | |
|---|---|
| DrawMode | Read or set the appearance of drawings by graphics methods |
| DrawStyle | Read or set the style of lines drawn by graphics methods |
| DrawWidth | Read or set the size of lines drawn by graphics methods |
| Enabled | Read or set whether this object can react to events |
| FillColor | Read or set the color used by graphics methods for fill-in effects |
| FillStyle | Read or set the pattern used by graphics methods for fill-in effects |
| FontBold, FontItalic, FontStrikeThru, FontTransparent, & FontUnderline | Read or set special effects for this object's font |
| FontName | Read or set the name of this object's font |
| FontSize | Read or set the size of this object's font |
| FormName | Set the name by which a form is referenced |
| hDC | Read the Windows device handle for this object |
| Height | Read or set the height of this object |
| hWnd | Read the Windows handle for a form |
| Icon | Read or set the icon used when a form is minimized |
| Image | Read the Windows device handle for this object's persistant bitmap |
| Left | Read or set the left edge placement of this control on a picture or form |
| LinkMode | Read or set a DDE conversation to hot, cold, or none |
| LinkTopic | Read or set the topic of a DDE conversation |
| MaxButton | Read or set whether a maximize button will appear on a form |
| MinButton | Read or set whether a minimize button will appear on a form |
| MousePointer | Read or set the shape of the mouse pointer when it's over this object |
| Picture | Read or assign a graphic image to a picture or form |
| ScaleHeight | Read or set the number of units that define the height of this object |
| ScaleLeft | Read or set the coordinates for the left edge of this object |
| ScaleMode | Read or set the unit of measurement used to place and size objects |
| ScaleTop | Read or set the coordinates for the top edge of this object |
| ScaleWidth | Read or set the number of units that define the width of this object |
| ScrollBars | Determine whether scroll bars appear in a multiple-line text box |
| Tag | Read or set text information that is particular to this object |
| Top | Read or set the coordinate of this control's top edge |
| Visible | Read or set whether this object is visible |
| WindowState | Read or set whether a form is maximized, minimized, or normal |

**Table 3.22 Properties of the Form object**

| Use This Event... | To Do This... |
|---|---|
| Click | React to the user clicking on this object |
| DblClick | React to the user double-clicking on this object |
| DragDrop | React to the user dragging and dropping an object onto this object |
| DragOver | React to the user dragging another object over this object |
| GotFocus | Initiate an action when this object receives the focus |
| KeyDown | Initiate an action when the user presses or holds a key down |
| KeyPress | React to the user typing an ASCII character |
| KeyUp | Initiate an action when the user releases a key |
| LinkClose | React to the termination of a DDE conversation |
| LinkError | React to an error in a DDE conversation |
| LinkExecute | React to a DDE Execute command from a DDE client application |
| LinkOpen | React to the initiation of a DDE conversation |
| Load | Initiate an action when a form is first loaded into memory |
| LostFocus | Initiate an action when this object loses the focus |
| MouseDown | React to the user pressing any mouse button |
| MouseMove | React to the user moving the mouse over this object |
| MouseUp | React to the user releasing any mouse button |
| Paint | Initiate an action when a form or picture needs to be re-drawn |
| Resize | Initiate an action when a form is first displayed or its size is changed |
| UnLoad | Initiate an action when a form is removed from memory |

Table 3.23 Events of the Form object

| Use This Method... | To Do This... |
|---|---|
| Circle | Create a circle or ellipse on a form or picture box |
| Cls | Clear graphics and text that have been drawn on the form at run time |
| Hide | Make a form invisible |
| Line | Draw a line on a form or picture |
| Move | Change the position of this control or form |
| Point | Return the color setting of a specified point on a form or picture box |
| Print | Print text on a form or picture box |
| PrintForm | Send a copy of a form to the printer |
| Pset | Set the color of a specified point on a form or picture box |
| Refresh | Cause this object to be updated immediately |
| Scale | Define the coordinate system used for the form |
| SetFocus | Move the focus to this form |
| Show | Display a previously hidden form |
| TextHeight | Return the height of text in this object's font |
| TextWidth | Return the width of text in this object's font |

Table 3.24 Methods of the Form object

## Description

A form is a window that you create to use as the screen area for an operation in your program. A program can have one or more forms. Each form represents a window in your program (see Figure 3.9). You can then use Visual Basic's Toolbox to draw controls, such as command buttons, text, and check boxes on the form (see Figure 3.10). You can create a variety of effects by choosing appropriate controls and manipulating their properties (see Figure 3.11).

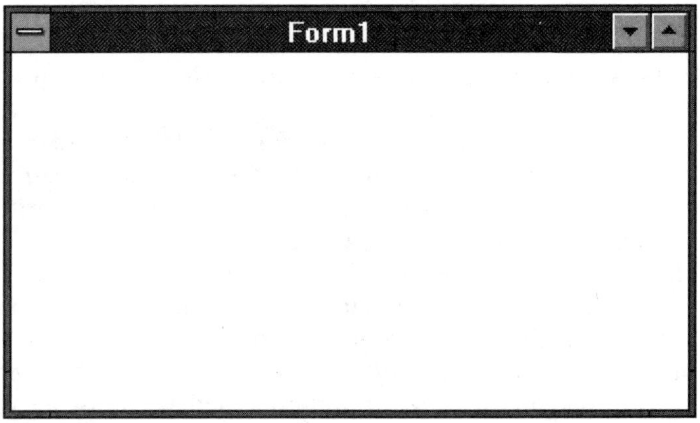

Forms define a logical, as well as visual, portion of your program. Each form has its own separate code area. Any procedures entered into a form's code area are local to that form, and cannot be accessed by rou-

Figure 3.9 A blank form

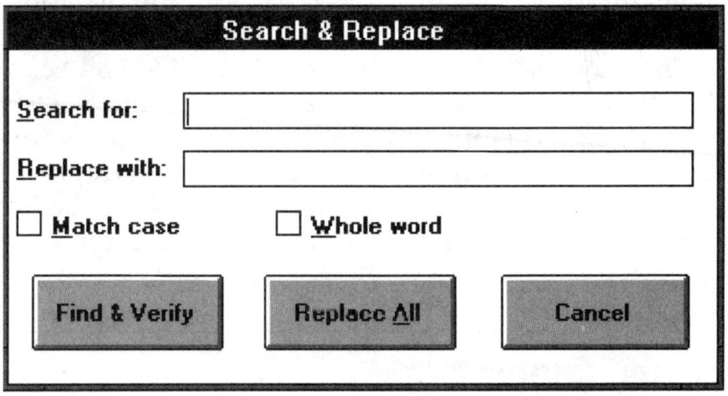

Figure 3.10 A search and replace dialog box created from a form

tines in other forms or code modules. The code portion of a form can contain three types of program code: the General Declarations area, programmer-defined procedures, and object-related events.

A form's general declarations area is used to declare variables, arrays, and constants. Items declared in this area will be accessible to any program code that also resides in the code area of the same form. Procedures that are contained in other forms will not be able to use these variables or constants.

This is a simple message box that was created on a form. The form's ControlBox, MinButton and MaxButton properties are set to False. Along with setting the form's Caption property to a null value, this causes the box to appear without a title bar. Also, the form's BorderStyle property was set to 1 (fixed single), which accounts for the thin border.

Figure 3.11 A simple message box created with a form

Programmer-defined Sub procedures and functions are self-contained procedures that you write to handle specific tasks or return certain values. Please refer to Appendix A, *The Visual Basic Language,* for more on the use of language elements and the definition and use of Sub procedures.

The program code for each of a form's related events is placed in the form's code area. This also holds true for any controls that have been drawn on a form. The event procedures for those controls are also placed in the form's code area.

Each form has a name by which it may be referenced. This name is set at design time, and is specified by the FormName property. This property is not available at run time; however, the name you assign to it at design time is the same name you use to reference the form within your program's code. For more information on referencing forms, please see Chapter 6, *Using Forms and Controls in Program Code.*

The Load and UnLoad statements load and erase a form from memory at run time. Loading a form does not automatically display it. This is done with the Show method. If the UnLoad statement is used on a form, and that form is the only form remaining in memory for that project, the program is ended.

The Show method will display a form that had been previously hidden or not yet displayed. This method is also used to determine if a form is to be modal or modeless. A modal form is a form that does not allow any other window on the desktop to receive the focus until it is closed. A modeless form places no restrictions on where the focus goes. A form may be again hidden with the Hide method.

Please refer to Chapter 4, *Setting Up Forms,* for more information on this object.

# Frame Control

## Purpose

The frame control is used to visually group together controls that are functionally related, based on how they are used in a program.

## Properties, Events, and Methods

Tables 3.25, 3.26, and 3.27 list the properties, events, and methods that relate to the frame control.

| Use This Property... | To Do This... |
| --- | --- |
| BackColor, ForeColor | Read or set the background and foreground colors of this object |
| Caption | Assign text to this object |
| CtlName | Set the name by which this control will be referenced |
| DragIcon | Read or set what is displayed when this control is dragged |

| | |
|---|---|
| DragMode | Determine if drag operations are to occur manually or automatically |
| Enabled | Read or set whether this object can react to events |
| FontBold, FontItalic, FontStrikeThru, FontTransparent, & FontUnderline | Read or set special effects for this object's font |
| FontName | Read or set the name of this object's font |
| FontSize | Read or set the size of this object's font |
| Height | Read or set the height of this object |
| Index | Uniquely identify an element of a control array |
| Left | Read or set the left edge placement of this control on a picture or form |
| MousePointer | Read or set the shape of the mouse pointer when it's over this object |
| Parent | Read the name of the form to which this control belongs |
| TabIndex | Read or set the placement of this control within the form's tab order |
| TabStop | Read or set whether this control is part of the form's tab order |
| Tag | Read or set text information that is particular to this object |
| Top | Read or set the coordinate of this control's top edge |
| Visible | Read or set whether this object is visible |
| Width | Read or set the width of this object |

Table 3.25 Properties of the frame control

| Use This Event | To Do This... |
|---|---|
| DragDrop | React to the user dragging and dropping an object onto this object |
| DragOver | React to the user dragging another object over this object |

Table 3.26 Events of the frame control

| Use This Method... | To Do This... |
|---|---|
| Drag | Control manual dragging of this control |
| Move | Change the position of this control or form |
| Refresh | Cause this object to be updated immediately |

Table 3.27 Methods of the frame control

## Description

You may draw a frame on a form, and then in turn draw other controls upon the frame. This causes the controls to be visually grouped together. If the frame is moved to a new location on the form, its controls are moved with it.

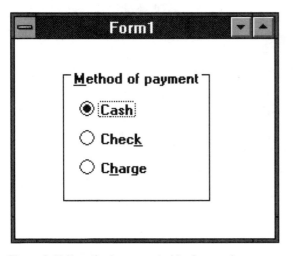

**Figure 3.12 How the frame control looks on a form**

When option button controls are placed upon a frame (see Figure 3.12), not only are they visually grouped together, but they become logically grouped as well. When several option buttons share a frame, they become mutually exclusive. That is to say, when one button is selected, all the other buttons in the same frame get unselected. This is how you can create "radio buttons."

If you wish to place controls on a frame, the frame must be drawn first. Then any controls that are to be within the frame must be drawn on it. You cannot move an already drawn control onto a frame.

A title may be displayed at the upper left-hand corner of the frame by setting its Caption property.

# Label Control

### Purpose
The label control labels an area of a frame, form, or picture.

### Properties, Events, and Methods
Tables 3.28, 3.29, and 3.30 list the properties, events, and methods that relate to the label control.

| Use This Property... | To Do This... |
| --- | --- |
| Alignment | Align text to the right, left, or center within the control |
| BackColor, ForeColor | Read or set the background and foreground colors of this object |
| BorderStyle | Determine whether this object has a border, and if it does, set its style |
| Caption | Assign text to this object |
| CtlName | Set the name by which this control will be referenced |
| DragIcon | Read or set what is displayed when this control is dragged |

| | |
|---|---|
| DragMode | Determine if drag operations are to occur manually or automatically |
| Enabled | Read or set whether this object can react to events |
| FontBold, FontItalic, FontStrikeThru, FontTransparent, & FontUnderline | Read or set special effects for this object's font |
| FontName | Read or set the name of this object's font |
| FontSize | Read or set the size of this object's font |
| Height | Read or set the height of this object |
| Index | Uniquely identify an element of a control array |
| Left | Read or set the left edge placement of this control on a picture or form |
| LinkItem | Read or set the item in a DDE conversation |
| LinkMode | Read or set a DDE conversation to hot, cold, or none |
| LinkTimeout | Read or set the amount of time before a DDE conversation times out |
| LinkTopic | Read or set the topic of a DDE conversation |
| MousePointer | Read or set the shape of the mouse pointer when it's over this object |
| Parent | Read the name of the form to which this control belongs |
| TabIndex | Read or set the placement of this control within the form's tab order |
| TabStop | Read or set whether this control is part of the form's tab order |
| Tag | Read or set text information that is particular to this object |
| Top | Read or set the coordinate of this control's top edge |
| Visible | Read or set whether this object is visible |
| Width | Read or set the width of this object |

**Table 3.28 Properties of the label control**

| Use This Event... | To Do This... |
|---|---|
| Change | React to a change in the control's Caption property |
| Click | React to the user clicking on this object |
| DblClick | React to the user double-clicking on this object |
| DragDrop | React to the user dragging and dropping an object onto this object |
| DragOver | React to the user dragging another object over this object |
| LinkClose | React to the termination of a DDE conversation |
| LinkError | React to an error in a DDE conversation |
| LinkOpen | React to the initiation of a DDE conversation |
| MouseDown | React to the user pressing any mouse button |
| MouseMove | React to the user moving the mouse over this object |
| MouseUp | React to the user releasing any mouse button |

**Table 3.29 Events of the label control**

| Use This Method... | To Do This... |
| --- | --- |
| Drag | Control manual dragging of this control |
| LinkExecute | Send a DDE Execute command to a DDE server application |
| LinkPoke | Send data from a DDE client to a DDE server |
| LinkRequest | Ask for data from a DDE server |
| LinkSend | Send graphic data to a DDE client |
| Move | Change the position of this control or form |
| Refresh | Cause this object to be updated immediately |

Table 3.30 Methods of the label control

### Description

The label control is used to place non-editable text on a form, frame or picture. Most often this control is used to display a meaningful name that describes the purpose of a text, list, or combo box control. (In Figure 3.13, "Search for:" and "Replace with:" are such descriptive labels.)

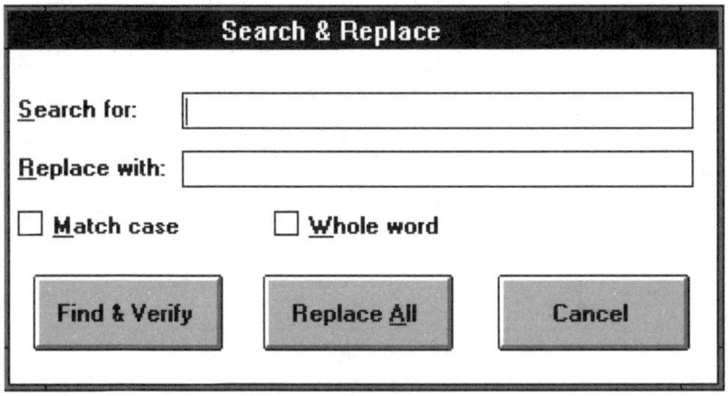

Figure 3.13 How a label control looks on a form

The text displayed by a label control is defined by its Caption property. At design time, this property can be assigned a one-line text string. If needed, at run time the program's code may assign this property a string that contains carriage return/linefeed pairs to create a multiple-line label.

# List Box Control

### Purpose

The list box control displays a box with a list of items from which the user may make a selection.

### Properties, Events, and Methods

Tables 3.31, 3.32, and 3.33 list the properties, events, and methods that relate to the list box control.

| Use This Property... | To Do This... |
| --- | --- |
| BackColor, ForeColor | Read or set the background and foreground colors of this object |
| CtlName | Set the name by which this control will be referenced |
| DragIcon | Read or set what is displayed when this control is dragged |
| DragMode | Determine if drag operations are to occur manually or automatically |
| Enabled | Read or set whether this object can react to events |
| FontBold, FontItalic, FontStrikeThru, FontTransparent, & FontUnderline | Read or set special effects for this object's font |
| FontName | Read or set the name of this object's font |
| FontSize | Read or set the size of this object's font |
| Height | Read or set the height of this object |
| Index | Uniquely identify an element of a control array |
| Left | Read or set the left edge placement of this control on a picture or form |
| List | Read or set the value of a listed item |
| ListCount | Read the number of items in a list |
| ListIndex | Read or set the index of the currently selected item in a list |
| MousePointer | Read or set the shape of the mouse pointer when it's over this object |
| Parent | Read the name of the form to which this control belongs |
| Sorted | Read or set whether Visual Basic will automatically sort the list |
| TabIndex | Read or set the placement of this control within the form's tab order |
| TabStop | Read or set whether this control is part of the form's tab order |
| Tag | Read or set text information that is particular to this object |
| Text | Read the currently selected item |
| Top | Read or set the coordinate of this control's top edge |
| Value | Read or set the current setting of this control |
| Visible | Read or set whether this object is visible |
| Width | Read or set the width of this object |

**Table 3.31 Properties of the list box control**

| Use This Event... | To Do This... |
| --- | --- |
| Click | React to the user clicking on this object |
| DblClick | React to the user double-clicking on this object |
| DragDrop | React to the user dragging and dropping an object onto this object |
| DragOver | React to the user dragging another object over this object |
| GotFocus | Initiate an action when this object receives the focus |
| KeyDown | Initiate an action when the user presses or holds a key down |

*Table 3.32 (continued)*

| Use This Event... | To Do This... |
| --- | --- |
| KeyPress | React to the user typing an ASCII character |
| KeyUp | Initiate an action when the user releases a key |
| LostFocus | Initiate an action when this object loses the focus |
| MouseDown | React to the user pressing any mouse button |
| MouseMove | React to the user moving the mouse over this object |
| MouseUp | React to the user releasing any mouse button |

**Table 3.32 Events of the list box control**

| Use This Method... | To Do This... |
| --- | --- |
| AddItem | Add an item to a list box |
| Drag | Control manual dragging of this control |
| Mouse | Change the position of this control or form |
| Refresh | Cause this object to be updated immediately |
| SetFocus | Move the focus to this control |

**Table 3.33 Methods of the list box control**

## Description

The user may choose an item from a list box by clicking on it or by using the up and down arrow keys to move the reverse highlight to the desired item (see Figure 3.14). If there are more items in the list than can be displayed in the area defined for the box, Visual Basic will automatically add a vertical scroll bar on the right edge of the list. The user can then use this scroll bar to move up or down in the list.

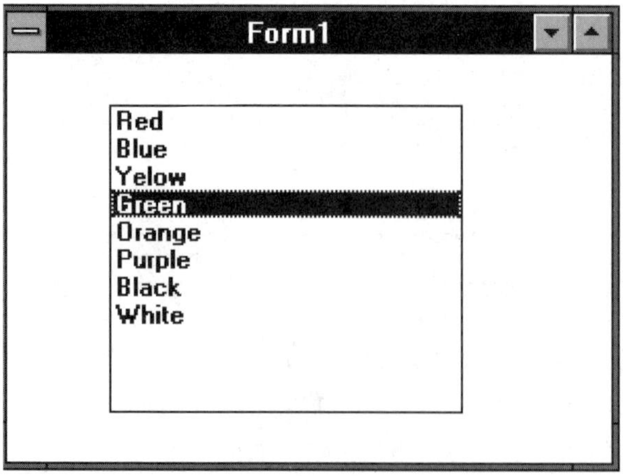

The List property provides a way to read and set a list's contents in a manner similar to accessing and assigning values in an array. The List property is followed by an index number in parentheses, which identifies which list entry is being referenced. The index numbering of the list is 0-based. Therefore, if a list contains five items, the first item is index number 0 and the highest index number is 4. The

**Figure 3.14 How a list box control looks on a form**

number of items in a list can be determined by using the ListCount property.

The ListIndex property returns the index number of the currently selected item in a list. If no item is currently selected, a -1 is returned.

The program may also set the ListIndex property directly. When using the ListIndex property to set the currently selected list entry, you must use an index number that references a currently added item in the list. For instance, if a list has five items in it, an index number from 0 to 4 must be specified, or an "Invalid property array index" error will occur.

The AddItem and RemoveItem methods add and delete list entries to and from a list box control.

This object is discussed in detail in Chapter 18, *Using List and Combo Boxes*.

# Menu Control

## Purpose

The menu control defines a pull-down menu system for a form.

## Properties, Events, and Methods

Tables 3.34 and 3.35 list the properties and events that relate to this object. There are no methods associated with the menu control.

| Use This Property... | To Do This... |
| --- | --- |
| Caption | Assign text to this object |
| Checked | Place or remove a check mark from a menu item |
| CtlName | Set the name by which this control will be referenced |
| Enabled | Read or set whether this object can react to events |
| Index | Uniquely identify an element of a control array |
| Parent | Read the name of the form to which this control belongs |
| Visible | Read or set whether this object is visible |

Table 3.34 Properties of the menu control

| Use This Event... | To Do This... |
| --- | --- |
| Click | React to the user clicking on this object |

Table 3.35 The one menu control event

## Description

The major functions performed by most Windows programs are accessible with a pull-dow menuing system (see Figures 3.15 and 3.16). Visual Basic provides you with the Menu Design window, which lets you define a such a system with up to five levels of sub-menus. Each menu, and each option on each menu, is assigned a CtlName by which that menu or option is referenced.

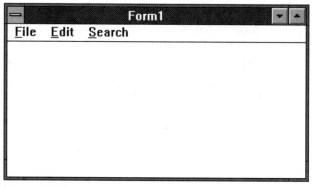

**Figure 3.15 A form with File, Edit and Search menus**

When a user chooses a menu or option, that menu's or option's Click event occurs. Code can be placed in this event to perform the task related to the menu or option chosen by the user.

The Enabled property may be set to 0 to disable a particular menu or menu option. Doing so prevents the user from being able to choose that item. Disabling a menu effectively disables all options under that menu. A disabled item is displayed in grey.

The Checked property may have a value of True (-1), meaning checked, or False (0), meaning not checked. When a menu item's Checked property is True, a small check mark will be displayed next to that menu item to show its current setting. For instance, if a menu option turns a particular function on or off, the Checked property may be used to indicate the current status of the function.

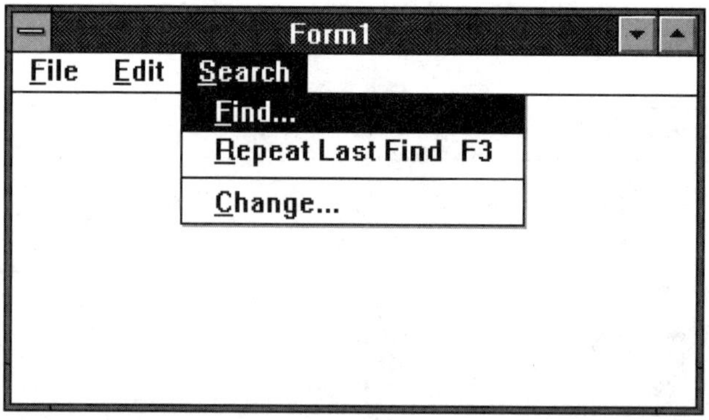

In the Menu Design window, if a value is assigned to the Index property for a menu item, that menu item becomes part of a control array. This gives the program the opportunity to dynamically add and delete menu options at run time, by using the Load and UnLoad statements (see Chapter 4, *Setting Up Forms,* for more on these statements).

**Figure 3.16 The same form with its Search menu open**

# Option Button Control

## Purpose

The option button control provides a technique for presenting a group of choices where only one choice may be selected. In other words, the option button control is used when the selection of one choice excludes the selection of any other related choices.

## Properties, Events, and Methods

Tables 3.36, 3.37, and 3.38 list the properties, events, and methods that relate to the option button control.

| Use This Property... | To Do This... |
|---|---|
| BackColor, ForeColor | Read or set the background and foreground colors of this object |
| Caption | Assign text to this object |
| CtlName | Set the name by which this control will be referenced |
| DragIcon | Read or set what is displayed when this control is dragged |
| DragMode | Determine if drag operations are to occur manually or automatically |
| Enabled | Read or set whether this object can react to events |
| FontBold, FontItalic, FontStrikeThru, FontTransparent, & FontUnderline | Read or set special effects for this object's font |
| FontName | Read or set the name of this object's font |
| FontSize | Read or set the size of this object's font |
| Height | Read or set the height of this object |
| Index | Uniquely identify an element of a control array |
| Left | Read or set the left edge placement of this control on a picture or form |
| MousePointer | Read or set the shape of the mouse pointer when it's over this object |
| Parent | Read the name of the form to which this control belongs |
| TabIndex | Read or set the placement of this control within the form's tab order |
| TabStop | Read or set whether this control is part of the form's tab order |
| Tag | Read or set text information that is particular to this object |
| Top | Read or set the coordinate of this control's top edge |
| Value | Read or set whether the Option button is selected |
| Visible | Read or set whether this object is visible |
| Width | Read or set the width of this object |

Table 3.36 Properties of the option button control

| Use This Event... | To Do This... |
|---|---|
| Click | React to the user clicking on this object |
| DblClick | React to the user double-clicking on this object |
| DragDrop | React to the user dragging and dropping an object onto this object |
| DragOver | React to the user dragging another object over this object |
| GotFocus | Initiate an action when this object receives the focus |
| KeyDown | Initiate an action when the user presses or holds a key down |
| KeyPress | React to the user typing an ASCII character |
| KeyUp | Initiate an action when the user releases a key |
| LostFocus | Initiate an action when this object loses the focus |

**Table 3.37 Events of the option button control**

| Use This Method... | To Do This... |
|---|---|
| Drag | Control manual dragging of this control |
| Move | Change the position of this control or form |
| Refresh | Cause this object to be updated immediately |
| SetFocus | Move the focus to this control |

**Table 3.38 Methods of the option button control**

## Description

The option button control consists of a small circle accompanied by text. Generally, the text defines the purpose of the button. Clicking on a button causes the circle to be filled in with a solid dot. This happens regardless of whether or not the circle had already been filled in.

Option buttons generally work in groups (see Figure 3.17). A group of option buttons is created when two or more option buttons are drawn on the same form, frame, or picture. When this is the case, all the option buttons in the same group become mutually exclusive. That is to say, when one button is clicked, it gets selected and all other buttons in the same group become unselected.

To create a group of option buttons, first draw the frame or picture on which they will be placed. Then draw the buttons on the frame or picture. To have more than one group of option buttons on the same form, create a frame for each group and then place the buttons in the appropriate frame.

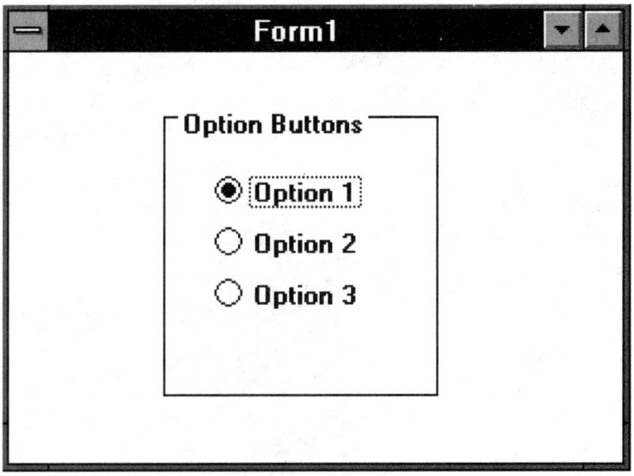

The Caption property defines the text that is to be displayed to the right of the button. If an ampersand (&) is included in the Caption property, the letter following the ampersand will be underlined, and the option button may be selected by holding down the Alt key and pressing that letter. For instance, if an option button's Caption property is set to &Cash, the displayed text will be "Cash" and the user can select the button by pressing Alt+C.

The status of an option button control may be set or read by the program's code by using the Value property. This property will be True (-1) if the button is selected and False (0) if not.

When an option button is selected, its Click event is initiated. This allows the program to react immediately to the setting of the button.

**Figure 3.17 How a group of option buttons looks on a form**

# Picture Control

## Purpose

The picture control defines an area on a form, frame or another picture in which graphics may be displayed. Alternately, the picture control can be used much like the frame control to group together controls that are functionally related based on how they are used in a program.

## Properties, Events, and Methods

Tables 3.39, 3.40, and 3.41 list the properties, events, and methods that relate to the picture control.

| Use This Property... | To Do This... |
| --- | --- |
| AutoReDraw | Read or set whether graphic pictures will be redrawn automatically |
| AutoSize | Read or set whether the size of a picture is controlled by its source file |
| BackColor, ForeColor | Read or set the background and foreground colors of this object |
| BorderStyle | Determine whether this object has a border, and if it does, set its style |
| CtlName | Set the name by which this control will be referenced |
| CurrentX, CurrentY | Read or set the current graphics position on this object |
| DragIcon | Read or set what is displayed when this control is dragged |
| DragMode | Determine if drag operations are to occur manually or automatically |
| DrawMode | Read or set the appearance of drawings by graphics methods |
| DrawStyle | Read or set the style of lines drawn by graphics methods |
| DrawWidth | Read or set the size of linesdrawn by graphics methods |
| Enabled | Read or set whether this object can react to events |
| FillColor | Read or set the color used by graphics methods for fill-in effects |
| FillStyle | Read or set the pattern used by graphics methods for fill-in effects |
| FontBold, FontItalic, FontStrikeThru, FontTransparent, & FontUnderline | Read or set special effects for this object's font |
| FontName | Read or set the name of this object's font |
| FontSize | Read or set the size of this object's font |
| hDC | Read the Windows device handle for this object |
| Height | Read or set the height of this object |
| Image | Read the Windows device handle for an picture's persistant bitmap |
| Index | Uniquely identify an element of a control array |
| Left | Read or set the left edge placement of this control on a picture or form |
| LinkItem | Read or set the item in a DDE conversation |
| LinkMode | Read or set a DDE conversation to hot, cold, or none |
| LinkTimeout | Read or set the amount of time before a DDE conversation times out |
| LinkTopic | Read or set the topic of a DDE conversation |
| MousePointer | Read or set the shape of the mouse pointer when it's over this object |
| Parent | Read the name of the form to which this control belongs |
| Picture | Read or assign a graphic image to a picture or form |
| ScaleHeight | Read or set the number of units that define the height of this object |
| ScaleLeft | Read or set the coordinates for the left edge of this object |
| ScaleMode | Read or set the unit of measurement used to place and size objects |
| ScaleTop | Read or set the coordinates for the top edge of this object |
| ScaleWidth | Read or set the number of units that define the width of this object |
| TabIndex | Read or set the placement of this control within the form's tab order |
| TabStop | Read or set whether this control is part of the form's tab order |
| Tag | Read or set text information that is particular to this object |
| Top | Read or set the coordinate of this control's top edge |
| Visible | Read or set whether an object is visible |
| Width | Read or set the width of this object |

**Table 3.39 Properties of the picture control**

| Use This Event... | To Do This... |
| --- | --- |
| Change | React to a change to the image pointed to by the Picture property |
| Click | React to the user clicking on this object |
| DblClick | React to the user double clicking on this object |
| DragDrop | React to the user dragging and dropping an object onto this object |
| DragOver | React to the user dragging another object over this object |
| GotFocus | Initiate an action when this object receives the focus |
| KeyDown | Initiate an action when the user presses or holds a key down |
| KeyPress | React to the user typing an ASCII character |
| KeyUp | Initiate an action when the user releases a key |
| LinkClose | React to the termination of a DDE conversation |
| LinkError | React to an error in a DDE conversation |
| LinkOpen | React to the initiation of a DDE conversation |
| LostFocus | Initiate an action when this object loses the focus |
| MouseDown | React to the user pressing any mouse button |
| MouseMove | React to the user moving the mouse over this object |
| MouseUp | React to the user releasing any mouse button |
| Paint | Initiate an action when a form or picture needs to be redrawn |

Table 3.40 Events of the picture control

| Use This Method... | To Do This... |
| --- | --- |
| Circle | Create a circle or ellipse on a form or picture box |
| Cls | Clear graphics and text that have been created at run time |
| Drag | Control manual dragging of this control |
| Line | Draw a line on a form or picture |
| LinkExecute | Send a DDE Execute command to a DDE server application |
| LinkPoke | Send data from a DDE client to a DDE server |
| LinkRequest | Ask for data from a DDE server |
| LinkSend | Send graphic data to a DDE client |
| Move | Change the position of this control or form |
| Point | Return the color setting of a specified point on a form or picture box |
| Print | Print text on a form or picture box |
| PrintForm | Send a copy of a form to the printer |
| Pset | Set the color of a specified point on a form or picture box |
| Refresh | Cause this object to be updated immediately |
| Scale | Define the coordinate system used with the picture control |
| SetFocus | Move the focus to this control |
| TextHeight | Return the height of text in this object's font |
| TextWidth | Return the width of text in this object's font |

Table 3.41 Methods of the picture control

## Description

The picture control is used for two different purposes. Primarily, it is used to display a graphic image on a form (see Figure 3.18). However, you can also place controls on a picture in the same manner as placing them on a form or frame. This gives you an alternative to the frame control for grouping together other controls.

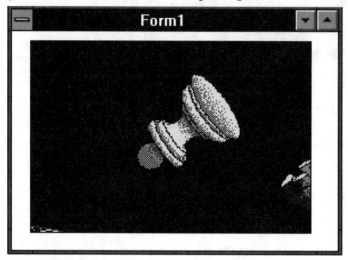

**Figure 3.18 How the picture control looks on a form**

The picture property defines the graphic image to be displayed by this control. The picture control can display icons, Windows bitmaps, and Windows metafiles.

The size of the picture control defines how much of a graphic image is displayed. If a graphic image is too large to be displayed within the boundries of a picture control, you can use two picture controls, placing one on top of the other, to simulate scrolling of the image. This technique is demonstrated in Chapter 20, *Operating Scroll Bars*.

If other controls are drawn on a picture control, they work in the same manner as if they'd been drawn on a frame control. Because the border can be turned off by using the picture control's BorderStyle property, this provides a technique for grouping several controls together without displaying a frame around them.

Please refer to Chapter 8, *Setting Up Graphical Objects*, for more information on this control and its related properties, events, and methods.

# Printer Object

## Purpose

The Printer object is used to generated printed hard copy output by assembling pages to be sent to the printer.

## Properties, Events, and Methods

Tables 3.42 and 3.43 list the properties and methods that relate to the Printer object. This object has no associated events.

| Use This Property... | To Do This... |
|---|---|
| CurrentX, CurrentY | Read or set the current graphics position on this object |
| DrawMode | Read or set the appearance of graphics methods |
| DrawStyle | Read or set the style of lines drawn by graphics methods |
| DrawWidth | Read or set the size of lines drawn by graphics methods |
| FillColor | Read or set the color used by graphics methods for fill-in effects |
| FillStyle | Read or set the pattern used by graphics methods for fill-in effects |
| FontBold, FontItalic, FontStrikeThru, FontTransparent, & FontUnderline | Read or set special effects for this object's font |
| FontCount | Read the number of fonts available to the system |
| FontName | Read or set the name of this object's font |
| Fonts | Read the names of the fonts available to the system |
| FontSize | Read or set the size of this object's font |
| hDC | Read the Windows device handle for this object |
| Height | Read or set the height of this object |
| Page | Read the current output page of the Printer object |
| ScaleHeight | Read or set the number of units that define the height of this object |
| ScaleLeft | Read or set the coordinates for the left edge of this object |
| ScaleMode | Read or set the unit of measurement used to place and size objects |
| ScaleTop | Read or set the coordinates for the top edge of this object |
| ScaleWidth | Read or set the number of units that define the width of this object |
| Width | Read or set the width of this object |

Table 3.42 Properties of the Printer object

| Use This Method... | To Do This... |
|---|---|
| Circle | Create a circle or ellipse on a form or picture box |
| EndDoc | End output to the Printer object, and send data to the printer |
| Line | Draw a line on a form or picture |
| NewPage | End output to the current printer page and begin a new one |
| Print | Print text on a form or picture box |
| Pset | Set the color of a specified point on a form or picture box |
| Scale | Define the coordinate system used with the Picture control |
| TextHeight | Return the height of text in this object's font |
| TextWidth | Return the width of text in this object's font |

Table 3.43 Methods of the Printer object

## Description

Many programs need to create some sort of printed hard copy output. Because the Windows environment handles all printer output, Visual Basic has included the pre-defined Printer object. This object sends printer output commands from your programs to the Windows routines that in turn send the output to the printer.

When working in other languages (such as QuickBASIC), the printer is treated as a sequential output device. Once an item is written to the printer, the print position advances and there can be no going back. With Visual Basic, however, this is not true.

You can think of the Printer object as a form that cannot be viewed until the Visual Basic program tells Windows to print it. This "form" represents one page of printed output. In most cases, until your program instructs Windows to print it, anything can be done to a page of printer output. This is very advantageous, as it allows the program to move the print position anywhere on a page, regardless of where it currently resides. This makes outputting graphics and special printing effects to the printer very easy.

When creating a printed document, the program works one page at a time. All the output for a specific page is first set up by using many of the same methods that work on a form. These include the Circle, Line, Print, PSet, TextHeight, and TextWidth methods. The program determines where these methods are to write to a page by specifying coordinates on the page as arguments to the method or by setting the page's CurrentX, and CurrentY properties. Each of the properties works in the same manner as when they're used on a form. The exception occurs when the printer is not a color printer. In that case, if a color parameter is used for a method, it is ignored and the output is always black.

When the program is finished creating the current page, it can use the NewPage method. This ends the current page, saves it in memory, and clears the Printer object's work area for the next page.

As each page is generated, Visual Basic keeps track of the current page number with the Page property, which is specific to the Printer object. This property can never be set (either at design or run time), but it can be read and thereby printed on each page.

When all printing is finished, the EndDoc method is used to send all the printer output to the Windows printing routines. Windows then takes care of the chores associated with sending the output to the printer.

Please refer to Chapter 24, *Sending Data to the Printer,* for more information on this object and its uses.

# Screen Object

## Purpose

The Screen object has four basic purposes. First, it defines the physical height and width of the display. Next, it provides access to screen fonts that are available to the system. Third, it is used to reference the currently active form or control. Finally, it is used to set or read the current shape of the mouse cursor.

## Properties, Events, and Methods

Table 3.44 lists the properties that relate to the Screen object. This object has no associated events or methods.

| Use This Property... | To Do This... |
| --- | --- |
| ActiveControl | Reference the current control with the focus |
| ActiveForm | Reference the current form with the focus |
| FontCount | Read the number of fonts available to the system for screen display |
| Fonts | Read the names of the fonts available to the system for screen display |
| Height | Read the height of the screen |
| MousePointer | Read or set the shape of the mouse pointer for all objects |
| Width | Read the width of the screen |

**Table 3.44 Properties of the Screen object**

## Description

The Height and Width properties of the Screen object define the dimensions of the screen in twips. A twip is defined as 1/20 point, which equates to 1440 twips per printed inch. This gives the Visual Basic program a method for displaying forms and controls in the proper absolute proportions, regardless of the type of display being used. These properties are discussed in Chapter 5, *Designing the Application's Appearance.*

The FontCount and Fonts properties are used to determine the number and types of fonts available for display on a form or control on the screen. The use of fonts is covered in Chapter 12, *Defining and Using Fonts.*

When used with its ActiveControl and ActiveForm properties, the Screen object will reference the control or form that currently has the focus. For more information on referencing forms and controls, please see Chapter 6, *Using Forms and Controls in Program Code.*

Setting the Screen object's MousePointer property overrides the MousePointer property setting for all forms and controls in the program. Setting this property to 0 for the Screen object returns control of this property setting to the individual forms and controls. More discussion on the MousePointer property can be found in Chapter 5, *Designing the Application's Appearance.*

# Scroll Bars Control

## Purpose

Scroll bars give the user the ability to position text or graphics or set a value by manipulating a visual object. Scroll bars are most commonly used to control the up and down and left to right movement of a graphic view port or list.

## Properties, Events, and Methods

Tables 3.45, 3.46, and 3.47 list the properties, events, and methods that relate to this object.

| Use This Property... | To Do This... |
|---|---|
| CtlName | Set the name by which this control will be referenced |
| DragIcon | Read or set what is displayed when this control is dragged |
| DragMode | Determine if drag operations are to occur manually or automatically |
| Enabled | Read or set whether this object can react to events |
| Height | Read or set the height of this object |
| Index | Uniquely identify an element of a control array |
| LargeChange | Read or set the amount of change when a user clicks on the bar |
| Left | Read or set the left edge placement of this control on a picture or form |
| Max | Read or set the maximum value possible in a scroll bar |
| Min | Read or set the minimum value possible in a scroll bar |
| MousePointer | Read or set the shape of the mouse pointer when it's over this object |
| Parent | Read the name of the form to which this control belongs |
| SmallChange | Read or set the amount of change when a user clicks on an arrow |
| TabIndex | Read or set the placement of this control within the form's tab order |
| TabStop | Read or set whether this control is part of the form's tab order |
| Tag | Read or set text information that is particular to this object |
| Top | Read or set the coordinate of this control's top edge |
| Value | Read or set the current setting of this control |
| Visible | Read or set whether an object is visible |
| Width | Read or set the width of this object |

Table 3.45 Properties of the scroll bars control

| Use This Event... | To Do This... |
|---|---|
| Change | React to a change in the control's Value property |
| DragDrop | React to the user dragging and dropping an object onto this object |
| DragOver | React to the user dragging another object over this object |
| GotFocus | Initiate an action when this object receives the focus |
| KeyDown | Initiate an action when the user presses or holds a key down |
| KeyPress | React to the user typing an ASCII character |
| KeyUp | Initiate an action when the user releases a key |
| LostFocus | Initiate an action when this object loses the focus |

Table 3.46 Events of the scroll bars control

| Use This Method... | To Do This... |
|---|---|
| Drag | Control manual dragging of this control |
| Move | Change the position of this control or form |
| Refresh | Cause this object to be updated immediately |
| SetFocus | Move the focus to this control |

**Table 3.47 Methods of the scroll bars control**

## Description

Scroll bars are primarily used to control scrolling of a picture or a list of items. They can also be used as a graphic technique for setting a particular value. For instance, in the Mouse settings of the Windows Control Panel, the user can set the speed of the mouse by manipulating a horizontal scroll bar.

Scroll bars are graphic objects that consist of a bar with arrows at each end and a button between the arrows (see Figure 3.19). There are two types of scroll bars: vertical and horizontal.

The button's position within the scroll bar is directly related to the value represented by the scroll bar. For horizontal scroll bars, the button is in the leftmost position when the value of the scroll bar is at its minimum setting,

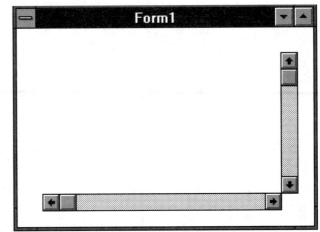

**Figure 3.19 How the scroll bar controls look on a form**

and at the rightmost when the value is at its maximum. A minimum value on a vertical scroll bar places the button at the top, while the maximum value places the button at the bottom. Any value in between places the button on the bar in a position proportional to the value represented by the bar.

The value represented by the scroll bar can be changed in four ways. First, the user can click on either arrow. This causes the value represented by the scroll bar to be incremented or decremented by a small amount in the direction of the selected arrow. Second, the user may click the scroll bar on one side of the button or the other. This causes the scroll bar's value to be affected in a similar manner as with clicking an arrow, but the amount of change is greater. The user can also click and drag the button to a specific position on the bar. This causes the value of the Scroll bar to be set according to the position of the button. Finally, the value of a scroll bar can be set in the program's code.

The events, methods, and properties that relate to scroll bars are discussed in Chapter 20, *Operating Scroll Bars*.

# Text Box Control

## Purpose

The text box control is used for displaying and editing text.

## Properties, Events, and Methods

Tables 3.48, 3.49, and 3.50 list the properties, events, and methods that relate to the text box control.

| Use This Property... | To Do This... |
|---|---|
| BackColor, ForeColor | Read or set the background and foreground colors of this object |
| BorderStyle | Determine whether this object has a border, and if it does, set its style |
| CtlName | Set the name by which this control will be referenced |
| DragIcon | Read or set what is displayed when this control is dragged |
| DragMode | Determine if drag operations are to occur manually or automatically |
| Enabled | Read or set whether this object can react to events |
| FontBold, FontItalic, FontStrikeThru, FontTransparent, & FontUnderline | Read or set special effects for this object's font |
| FontName | Read or set the name of this object's font |
| FontSize | Read or set the size of this object's font |
| Height | Read or set the height of this object |
| Index | Uniquely identify an element of a control array |
| Left | Read or set the left edge placement of this control on a picture or form |
| LinkItem | Read or set the item in a DDE conversation |
| LinkMode | Read or set a DDE conversation to hot, cold, or none |
| LinkTimeout | Read or set the amount of time before a DDE conversation times out |
| LinkTopic | Read or set the topic of a DDE conversation |
| MousePointer | Read or set the shape of the mouse pointer when it's over this object |
| Multiline | Read or set whether a text box can edit multiple-lines |
| Parent | Read the name of the form to which this control belongs |
| ScrollBars | Determine whether scroll bars appear in a multiple-line text box |
| SelLength, SelStart, &, SelText | Read, set, or replace selected text in a text box |
| TabIndex | Read or set the placement of this control within the form's tab order |
| TabStop | Read or set whether this control is part of the form's tab order |
| Tag | Read or set text information that is particular to this object |
| Text | Read or set the text contained in a text box |

| Top | Read or set the coordinate of this control's top edge |
| Visible | Read or set whether an object is visible |
| Width | Read or set the width of this object |

**Table 3.48 Properties of the text box control**

| Use This Event... | To Do This... |
| --- | --- |
| Change | React to a change in the text box control's Text property |
| DragDrop | React to the user dragging and dropping an object onto this object |
| DragOver | React to the user dragging another object over this object |
| GotFocus | Initiate an action when this object receives the focus |
| KeyDown | Initiate an action when the user presses or holds a key down |
| KeyPress | React to the user typing an ASCII character |
| KeyUp | Initiate an action when the user releases a key |
| LinkClose | React to the termination of a DDE conversation |
| LinkError | React to an error in a DDE conversation |
| LinkOpen | React to the initiation of a DDE conversation |
| LostFocus | Initiate an action when this object loses the focus |

**Table 3.49 Events of the text box control**

| Use This Method... | To Do This... |
| --- | --- |
| Drag | Control manual dragging of this control |
| LinkExecute | Send a DDE Execute command to a DDE server application |
| LinkPoke | Send data from a DDE client to a DDE server |
| LinkRequest | Ask for data from a DDE server |
| Move | Change the position of this control or form |
| Refresh | Cause this object to be updated immediately |
| SetFocus | Move the focus to this control |

**Table 3.50 Methods of the text box control**

## Description

The text box control is a rectangle in which the user may enter or edit text. When a text box control receives the focus, an insertion point appears in the box. The insertion point is a slim flashing vertical line that indicates where any new text will be entered within the box. This line can be moved by using the direction keys or by clicking on the desired position in the text box with the mouse. A Visual Basic text box automatically inherits all the conventions of a standard Windows text box, including the ability to cut, copy, and paste to and from the Windows clipboard area.

The Text property is used to set or read the text that is currently in a text box. The style and size of the text are determined by the control's font properties.

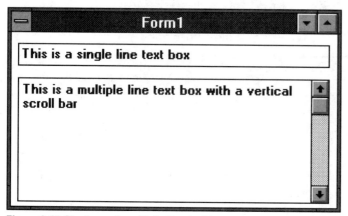

**Figure 3.20 Single- and multiple-line text boxes**

By default, a text box consists of only one line of text. Setting the MultiLine property to True (-1) will allow the user to enter more than one line of text (see Figure 3.20). If you set the MultiLine property to True, you may wish to also set the ScrollBars property to True. This causes a vertical scroll bar to automatically appear at the right of the text box if the entered text exceeds the screen area defined for the box. Please see Chapter 13, *Getting User Input With Text Boxes,* for more information on these properties.

When a text box control has the focus, each keystroke can be intercepted by the program with the KeyDown, KeyPress, and KeyUp events. This allows a program to create validity checking on edit fields. For instance, if you wish to limit the number of characters entered in a text box, you could use the KeyPress event to determine the current length of the text in a text box before allowing the next keystroke to be added to the text. More information on these events can be found in Chapter 16, *Handling Keyboard Input.*

A text box control can be used as a client in a Dynamic Data Exchange.

# Timer Control

## Purpose

The timer control is used to run code at regular intervals.

## Properties, Events, and Methods

Tables 3.51 and 3.52 list the properties and event that relate to the timer control. This control has no associated methods.

| Use This Property... | To Do This... |
| --- | --- |
| CtlName | Set the name by which this control will be referenced |
| Enabled | Read or set whether this object can react to events |
| Index | Uniquely identify an element of a control array |
| Interval | Read or set the length of time between each call to a Timer event |
| Parent | Read the name of this control's parent form |
| Tag | Read or set text information that is particular to this object |

Table 3.51 Properties of the timer control

| Use This Event... | To Do This... |
| --- | --- |
| Timer | Initiate an action at a regular timed interval |

Table 3.52 Events of the timer control

## Description

The timer control is invisible on a form and cannot be manipulated directly by the user (see Figure 3.21). The main purpose for a timer is to define an activity that is to take place at a regular interval. This is useful for writing routines that are to run in the background of an application with no need for user interaction.

The activity to be performed by the timer is defined by placing code in the control's timer event. The timer control's Interval property specifies how often this event is to be executed. This control, and its properties and events, are covered in Chapter 22, *Timing and Time Information*.

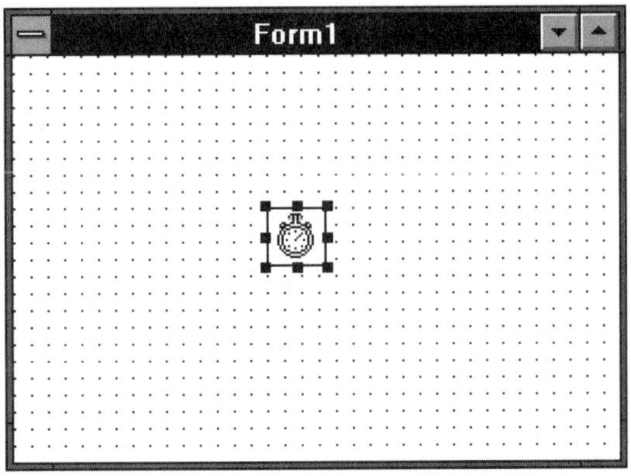

Figure 3.21 How the timer control looks on a form
*Note:* This control is invisible at run time

# PART TWO
# USING FORMS
# AND CONTROLS

# Setting up Forms

Forms, or organized display formats for displaying and soliciting information, are at the heart of most applications. Prior to the release of Microsoft Visual Basic in May of 1991, form setup frequently required several pages of code. This made the process of setting up the forms to be used by Windows applications a tedious chore involving hundreds of lines of code statements invoking functions with complex syntax. Even the familiar "Hello World" window required at least three pages of code to get the window onto the screen. Unfortunately, this complexity effectively placed Windows programming out of the reach of most users. Visual Basic simplifies the process of setting up forms. In fact, designing forms visually and interactively is the heart of Visual Basic programming.

## Forms and Form Setup

Each form in a program has a purpose. For example, there are data entry forms for data bases. Some forms display warning messages when a problem occurs. A communications program might have a form with a list of phone numbers. The user interacts with each of these forms in specified ways.

In Visual Basic, setting up a form requires decisions about four elements: the maximize button, the minimize button, the control box, and the border. These elements directly affect the ways the user will be able to manipulate this form.

Like a standard window, a Visual Basic form can be minimized to an icon, restored to its previous size,

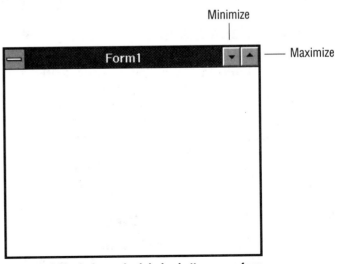

**Figure 4.1 Maximize and minimize buttons on a form**

or maximized to the full screen. To maximize a form, press the maximize button in the upper right corner of the form. To minimize a form, press the minimize button in the upper right corner of the form. Figure 4.1 shows a window's minimize button (on the left) and maximize button (on the right).

## The Control Box

The control box contains the commands that manipulate the basic appearance and position of the form. The control box is a drop-down menu that Windows activates when the user presses the Alt and - keys simultaneously, or clicks on the control box on the upper left corner of the form. The control box can have a combination of the following commands: Restore, Move, Size, Maximize, Minimize, Close, and Switch To. The Maximize and Minimize options appear here when their buttons are in the right corner of the form. Choosing one of these command options from the control box has the same effect as pressing the buttons. The Size option lets the user manually change the form's size. The Move option lets the user change the position of the form on the screen without using the mouse. The Close option removes the form from the screen and memory. The Switch To option brings the task switch box up on the screen.

## Types of Borders

Forms have four possible border styles: none, sizeable, fixed single, and fixed double. A form with no border has no maximize button, minimize button, or control box. This border style is a popular choice for warning boxes, which do not need these options. Users can change the size of sizeable forms, just as the name suggests. Both the fixed single and fixed double borders disable the user's ability to change the form's size with the mouse; however, the user can still maximize or minimize the form.

## Managing Form Display

Forms can be "loaded" and "unloaded" from the memory of the computer. Once a form is loaded into memory, you must explicitly show the form to make it visible. Similarly, you can hide a form from view without removing it from memory. The concepts of "hide" and "show" involve the visibility of forms on the screen. Shown forms display visibly on the screen. A hidden form is invisible to the user. Forms appear and disappear on the screen with the Show and Hide methods. The Show method reveals a form on the screen. If the form is not in memory, then it loads first. Hide takes a displayed form and hides it from sight. A hidden form remains in the current operating memory of the computer.

## Appearance of Forms in Visual Basic

Developing a Visual Basic application usually begins with designing a form's basic appearance. The MaxButton property controls whether the maximize button appears on the form. The ControlBox property determines whether a control box appears on the form. The BorderStyle property determines which type of border appears around the form. The Load and Unload statements take forms in and out of memory. The Show and Hide methods make forms appear and disappear on the screen. Any time the form's size is changed, Visual Basic generates a Resize event. The form's WindowState property reflects whether a form is maximized, minimized, or normal.

Table 4.1 displays the methods, statements, events, and properties that decide the basic setup of a form.

| Use or Set This... | | To Do This... |
|---|---|---|
| ControlBox | Property | Determine if the ControlBox can appear on the top left corner of a form |
| Hide | Method | Make a form invisible on the screen |
| Load | Event | Initiate an action when a form loads into memory |
| Load | Statement | Load a form into memory but do not make it visible |
| MaxButton | Property | Determine if the maximize button can appear on the top right corner of a form |
| MinButton | Property | Determine if the minimize button can appear on the top right corner of a form |
| Resize | Event | Initiate an action when a form's size changes |
| Show | Method | Load a form into memory and make it visible |
| Unload | Event | Initiate an action when a form is removed from memory |
| Unload | Statement | Remove a form from memory |
| WindowState | Property | Set or return whether the form is minimized, maximized, or normal |

Table 4.1 Methods, statements, properties, and events dealing with setting up a form

The methods, statements, properties, and events in Table 4.1 are investigated in detail in the following pages. Step-by-step directions describe how to assemble the sample Setup project at the end of this chapter. This project will give you hands-on experience with each Visual Basic feature described in this chapter.

# ControlBox Property

## Objects Affected

| Check | Clipboard | Combo | Command | Dbug |
|---|---|---|---|---|
| Dir | Drive | File | ▶ Form | Frame |
| Label | List | Menu | Option | Picture |
| Printer | Screen | Scroll | Text | Timer |

## Purpose

The ControlBox property governs whether a control box will appear in the top left corner of a form. There are two possible settings for the ControlBox property, True (-1)

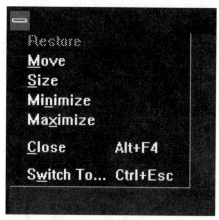

**Figure 4.2 The control box of a form**

and False (0). True is the default setting. A control box contains commands that let the user change the appearance of, or even close, a form. In some situations, you might want to block these commands from the user. For example, a warning box in an application might work best with the control box disabled. Only the OK command button could be used to remove the alert box from the screen. Letting the user use the Close command instead would bypass any events linked to the OK button. Figure 4.2 displays what a control box looks like when opened. Tables 4.2 and 4.3 summarize the meaning of the arguments of the Control Box property.

## General Syntax

```
[form.]ControlBox[= True|False]
```

| Argument | Description |
|----------|-------------|
| form | Identifies the FormName property of the referenced form |
| | If no name precedes, then the code references the current form's ControlBox property |

**Table 4.2 Argument of the ControlBox property**

| Value | Description |
|-------|-------------|
| -1 | True - Enables the display of the control box |
| 0 | False - Prevents the display of the control box |

**Table 4.3 Possible values of ControlBox property**

## Example Syntax

```
Sub SetColor (FormName As Form)
    If FormName.ControlBox=0 Then          'Tests for disabled control box on the
                                           'indicated form
        FormName.BackColor=RGB(192,192,192) 'Form's background changes to gray
    Else
        FormName.BackColor=RGB(0,128,0)    'Form's background changes to green
    End If
End Sub
```

## Description

The ControlBox property manages the user's access to a drop-down command menu that contains options for sizing, closing, or moving the window. The control to access the menu can be selected with the mouse or keyboard. The control box is in a form's upper left corner, as shown in Figure 4.2. A form's ControlBox property can only be set at design time. Any attempt to change the ControlBox property of a form at run time will generate an error. You can, however, use the ControlBox property as a reference at run time. In the example syntax, a subfunction named SetColor uses the ControlBox property setting to decide the background color of a form.

### BorderStyle, MaxButton, and MinButton Properties

The commands displayed on the control box include the familiar Restore, Move, Size, Minimize, Maximize, Close, and Switch To. Several properties affect the display of the control box when the ControlBox property is True. When the BorderStyle property of the form is 0 (none), the control box will not be displayed. If the MaxButton and MinButton properties of that form are False, then those commands will not appear on the ControlBox. When the BorderStyle property of a form is 1 (fixed single) or 3 (fixed double), Size does not appear in the control box. As long as the ControlBox property of a form is True, both the Restore and Move commands will appear on the control box.

## Example

The Setup project at the end of this section shows the difference between a form with and without the control box. The Setup form's ControlBox property begins with the default value of True; the Display form's ControlBox property is False, removing the representation of the control box from the screen. As a form's ControlBox property may not be changed at run time, this is the only way to visually display this difference.

## Comments

Notice that the control box can always be seen on a form at design time. It is only at run time that you can see when a ControlBox property is False. This is to provide easy manipulation of the forms at design time, but has no effect on the final appearance of the forms.

# Hide Method

## Objects Affected

| Check | Clipboard | Combo | Command | Dbug |
|-------|-----------|-------|---------|------|
| Dir | Drive | File | ▶ Form | Frame |
| Label | List | Menu | Option | Picture |
| Printer | Screen | Scroll | Text | Timer |

## Purpose

The Hide method makes an active and visible form disappear from the screen and is the same as setting the form's Visible property to False (0). Hidden forms reside in the operating memory of the computer. A form's Visible property changes to False when the form is hidden with the Hide Method. This method disconnects the form from user input. A hidden form can still respond to coded events and any resulting property changes or DDE (Dynamic Data Exchange) communication. For example, a law firm's client data entry system could begin with the primary name and address form visible and the case detail form hidden. Events could place the information the user enters (such as a name) into the corresponding fields of the hidden data entry form. Table 4.4 summarizes the FormName argument of the Hide method.

## General Syntax

```
[form.]Hide
```

| Argument | Description |
|----------|-------------|
| form | Identifies the form to be hidden |

Table 4.4 Argument of the Hide method

## Example Syntax

```
Sub Form1_Load ()
    Form2.Hide                        'Hide form2
    Form2.BackColor = RGB(0,255,0)    'Set background color of form2 to light green
    Form2.ForeColor = RGB(0,0,255)    'Set the text color of form2 to blue
    MsgBox "Press Ok to see form2"    'Display msgbox indicating press ok to see form2
    Form2.Show                        'Unhide Form2
End Sub
```

## Description

The Hide method is a useful way of reducing clutter by removing a form from the screen without removing it from memory. Any forms that are not initially needed can be loaded and hidden until desired. The Show method displays a hidden form on the screen. Hidden forms take a little more time to load at program startup, but reduce the load time when needed. For example, a personal information manager might load up the address book, scheduler, and to-do list at program startup. This allows the user to switch quickly between the information found in each form. With this approach, each form displays in a fraction of the time necessary to load it.

### The Show Method

The Hide method shares an inverse relationship with the Show method. Hide removes the form from sight and Show restores it. In the example syntax, the two methods work together to make a form invisible while its colors change. After making modifications, the Show method restores it to view. This technique also could be used for a warning dialog box that displays different messages depending on the situation.

### The Visible Property

When the Hide method makes a form invisible, the Visible property of the form becomes False. The difference between using the Hide method and directly changing the setting of the Visible property lies in the types of objects affected. The Hide method can only be used on a form. In contrast, the Visible property can be used on any of the controls or forms in Visual Basic. This difference can be used in generic functions and procedures to limit an effect to forms.

## Example

The Setup project at the end of this section demonstrates the Hide method several times. When the user presses the SetMode command button on the Setup form, the SetMode_Click event removes this form from the screen. A Hide method expression keeps the Setup form in memory while taking it out of the user's view. The Hide method also keeps the Display form in memory. In this case, the Hide method is better than the Unload statement because it saves time putting the Display form on screen when needed again.

## Comments

A hidden form or control can still have its properties changed or referenced. Forms disappear off the screen as quickly as the computer's processor allows. The amount of available operating memory determines the number of forms that can be hidden.

# Load Event

## Objects Affected

| Check | Clipboard | Combo | Command | Dbug |
|-------|-----------|-------|---------|------|
| Dir | Drive | File | ▶ Form | Frame |
| Label | List | Menu | Option | Picture |
| Printer | Screen | Scroll | Text | Timer |

## Purpose

The Load event is a very important built-in procedure that specifies what actions will be taken when a form loads. A loaded form is in memory but cannot be seen by the user. A form's Load event takes place in three ways. First, any forms loaded at program startup initiate a Form_Load event. Second, Visual Basic generates a Form_Load event if a form loads using a Form_Load statement. Third, any change or reference made to a property of an "unloaded" control or form triggers the Form_Load event. For example, a calculator could have a Form_Load event that changes the Text property of the readout text box to 0. When the user presses a command button labeled Tape, a second form could be loaded below the calculator on the screen. This second form's Load event places the last few calculations made in its display text window.

## General Syntax

```
Sub Form_Load ()
```

## Example Syntax

```
Sub Form_Load ()
    Dir1.Path = "\WinWord"   'Sets the initial path to the Winword directory
    File1.Path = Dir1.Path   'Makes File box's path same as Directory box
    File1.FileName = "*.DOC"  'Limits the types of files displayed to the "DOC" extension
    Text1.Text = File1.Path  'Displays current path in the text window
End Sub
```

## Description

The Form_Load event is a subroutine for initializing the form and any related variables. Text boxes may have their initial information inserted. List and combo boxes can be given their lists for the user to choose from. A letter-writing program might prompt the user to select a name from its database. Any option or check box controls may be set to their initial values. The drive, directory, and file boxes get their default Path and FileName properties in the Form_Load event of the example syntax. This relieves the user of the necessity of changing to the correct drive and directory. In the example syntax, the File1 file box displays only files with the DOC extension. Figure 4.3 shows what this form and its controls might look like.

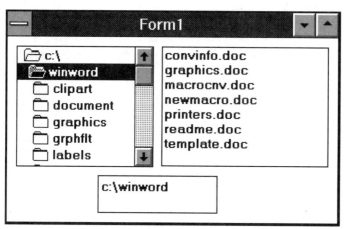

Figure 4.3 Appearance of example syntax

### The Load, Resize, Paint, and GotFocus Events

If more than one event is attached to a particular control, they are processed in the following order: Load, Resize, Paint, and GotFocus. This is an important point to keep in mind if any of the actions that take place in one event depend upon actions in another event. For example, a data entry form for an address book would have problems if the Load event disables the Address1 text box, and the GotFocus event tries to use it.

### The Unload Event

The Load event shares an inverse relationship with the Unload event. While the Load event affects the form when opened, the Unload event takes place when it is closed. Both events can depend on each other. For example, the Load event might set up the form to initiate some action. The Unload event could either restore the form to its preloaded settings or process the actions that took place. The address book, for example, might use the Load event to insert into the edit screen the last accessed information. An Unload event might save the information entered into the fields to the database.

## Example

The Setup project at the end of this section demonstrates the Load event. When the Setup form loads at program startup, the Load event defines the current contents of the program variables and loads the Display form into memory. This initialization works best here, because the Load event is always the first event to be processed when more than one event is called at the same time. The other event that occurs when the form loads is the Resize event. This event's expressions depend upon the variables defined in the Load event.

## Comments

Again, keep in mind that the Load event is always the first event of a referenced or loaded form to be processed.

# Load Statement

## Objects Affected

| | | | | |
|---|---|---|---|---|
| ▶ Check | Clipboard | ▶ Combo | ▶ Command | Dbug |
| ▶ Dir | ▶ Drive | ▶ File | ▶ Form | Frame |
| ▶ Label | ▶ List | Menu | ▶ Option | ▶ Picture |
| Printer | Screen | Scroll | ▶ Text | ▶ Timer |

## Purpose

The Load statement directly places a form or control into memory without making it visible to the user. The single argument used for this statement is the object. An object argument can be the CtlName property of a form, control, or control array. A form or control remains in memory until taken out by an Unload statement or until the program or parent form closes. In the example syntax, a warning dialog box loads into memory when the Warning form is needed. When the user leaves the Text1 text box blank, the Warning box dis-

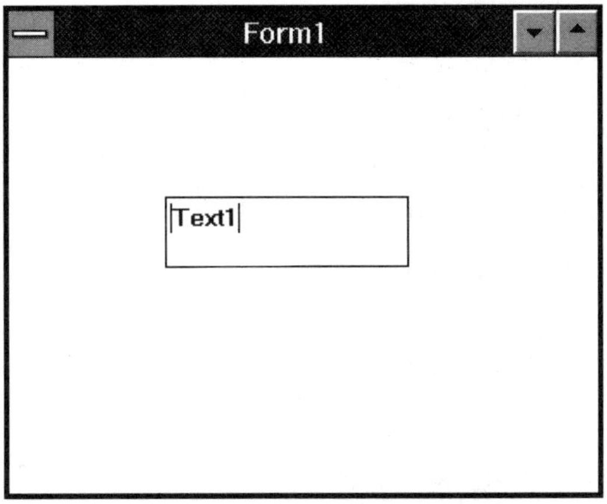

Figure 4.4 Example syntax shows "Loaded" form

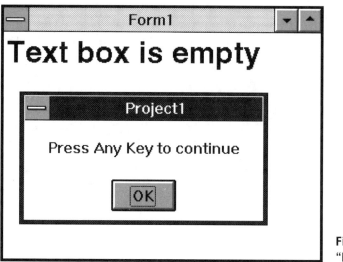

Figure 4.5 Example syntax shows "Loaded" warning form

plays to tell the user that the text box is blank. Figures 4.4 and 4.5 show what these two forms might look like. Table 4.5 summarizes the meaning of the object argument.

## General Syntax

Load object

| Argument | Description |
|----------|-------------|
| object | FormName or CtlName property of the item to be loaded |

Table 4.5 Argument of the Load statement

## Example Syntax

```
Sub Text1_Change ()
    Load WarningForm                         'Place WarningForm in memory
    If Text1.Text = "" Then                  'Check if Text box is empty
        WarningForm.AutoRedraw = -1          'Ensures that printed text is not erased
        WarningForm.FontSize = 20            'Change text size to 20
        WarningForm.Print "Text box is empty" 'Print message on form
        WarningForm.Show                     'Display Warning Form
        MsgBox "Press Any Key to continue"
    End If
    Unload WarningForm
    Form1.Show
End Sub

Sub Form_Load ()
    Automobile_Option(0).Caption = "General Motors"    'Uses control array to
                                                       'create two new
```

```
     Automobile_Option(0).Top = 500          'option button and displays these option
     Load Automobile_Option(1)               'buttons on the screen.
     Automobile_Option(1).Caption = "Ford"
     Automobile_Option(1).Top = 1500
     Load Automobile_Option(2)
     Automobile_Option(2).Caption = "Chrysler"
     Automobile_Option(2).Top = 2500
     Automobile_Option(1).Visible = -1
     Automobile_Option(2).Visible = -1
End Sub
```

## Description

The Load statement loads forms and controls into memory without displaying them. Once a form loads into memory, you can quickly unhide it by changing the Visible property of the form or control to True (-1). Another way of doing this is by using the Show method. While a form is in memory, its properties can be accessed and changed. The second example listed in the example syntax uses the Load statement to create new controls for the Automobile_Option control array. Figure 4.6 shows what this form might look like.

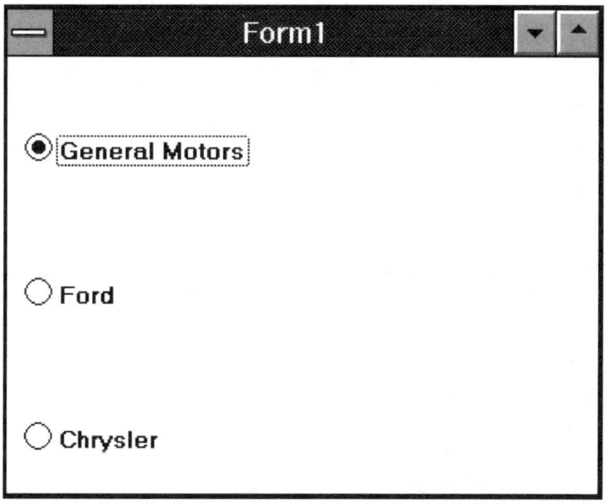

Figure 4.6 Example syntax shows loaded option buttons

### The Show Method

The Load statement and the Show method have very similar functions in Visual Basic, but the difference between them is very important. The Load statement does not directly make the controls or forms that it brings into memory visible to the user. The Show method statement both loads the control or form into memory and makes it visible to the user. A Load statement allows you to pre-load a control or form without displaying it. The amount of time required to bring up new screens can be reduced by loading all the necessary forms early.

## Example

In the Setup project at the end of this chapter, the Load statement loads the Display form into memory at program startup. This Load statement is in the Setup_Load event to ensure that the form can be quickly brought up when needed. In this case, the Load statement is a better choice than a Show method statement, because it does not make the form visible on the screen. This reduces screen clutter and makes it less likely for the user to be confused when confronted with two forms at once.

## Comments

Multiple instances of a particular control can be made visible on a form by setting up a control array and giving each control a unique array number. This is very useful for standardizing the events for a particular type of control. For example, an option box could be set up and loaded initially with a control array. Each instance of the control array could be made visible and have a different label.

# MaxButton Property

## Objects Affected

| | | | | |
|---|---|---|---|---|
| Check | Clipboard | Combo | Command | Dbug |
| Dir | Drive | File | ▶ Form | Frame |
| Label | List | Menu | Option | Picture |
| Printer | Screen | Scroll | Text | Timer |

## Purpose

Like a standard window, a Visual Basic form can be minimized to an icon, restored to its last size, or maximized to full screen size. Sometimes you may not want your forms to be able to do this. The MaxButton property controls whether the maximize icon button will appear in the top right corner of a form at run time. Figure 4.7 shows what the maximize button looks like on a maximized form. Here the button becomes a "restore button" that the user can click on to return the window to its default ("normalized") size. Figure 4.8 displays the maximize button on a normalized form (one that is of default size and can be maximized.) There are two possible settings for the MaxButton property, True (-1) and False (0). True is the default value for all forms. When this property is False, the maximize option disappears from the control box of the form. This property is a useful tool for removing this ability from the user in cases where this would be inappropriate. A situation where it might be inappropriate to let the user maximize a form is in a data entry system. Multiple windows placed in specific positions on the screen could not be maximized. Table 4.6 summarizes the argument of the MaxButton property.

## General Syntax

```
[form.]MaxButton
```

| Argument | Description |
|---|---|
| form | Identifies the FormName property of the referenced form |
| | When no name precedes, the code accesses the MaxButton property of the current form |

**Table 4.6 Argument of the MaxButton property**

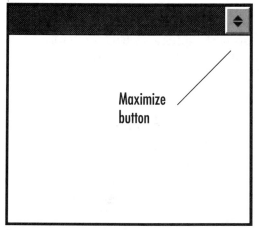

**Figure 4.7 The maximize button of a maximized form**

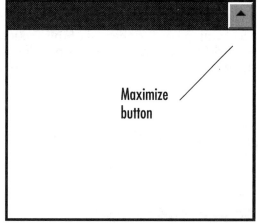

**Figure 4.8 The maximize button of a normal form**

## Example Syntax

```
Sub WindowLoad (FormName As Form)
    If  FormName.MaxButton = -1 Then      'Checks for enabled Maximize button
        FormName.WindowState = 2          'Maximizes the specified form
    Else
        FormName.WindowState = 1          'Normalizes the specified form
End Sub
```

## Description

The MaxButton property of a form controls whether a form can display a maximize button in the top right corner. A form's MaxButton property can only be set at design time. Any attempt to change the MaxButton property of a form at run time will generate an error. You can, however, use the MaxButton property as a reference at run time. The example syntax subfunction called WindowLoad uses a form's MaxButton setting to determine whether to maximize or normalize a form. This is a generic function that can be used on more than one form of a program. This standardizes the way the different types of forms appear on the screen.

### The BorderStyle and WindowState Properties

The BorderStyle property of a form also affects the appearance of the maximize control. If the BorderStyle of a form is either 0 (none) or 3 (fixed double), then the maximize button will *not* be displayed with either setting. With BorderStyle 3, if the MaxButton property is True, then the maximize command will appear in the control box of the form even though there is no maximize button. No matter what the settings of the MaxButton and BorderStyle properties are, you can still maximize a form using the WindowState property, as shown in the example syntax. A form's BorderStyle property has no effect on the form's ability to be maximized.

### Example

The Setup project at the end of this section shows the difference between a form with and without the maximize button. The Display form's maximize button changes to disabled, and the Setup form's maximize button is enabled.

### Comments

Remember that the absence of the maximize button on a form does not prevent the form from being maximized by the user if the maximize option appears in the control box menu.

# MinButton Property

### Objects Affected

| | | | | |
|---|---|---|---|---|
| Check | Clipboard | Combo | Command | Dbug |
| Dir | Drive | File | ▶ Form | Frame |
| Label | List | Menu | Option | Picture |
| Printer | Screen | Scroll | Text | Timer |

### Purpose

Like a standard window, a Visual Basic form can be minimized to an icon or to its last size, or it can be maximized to be full screen. Sometimes you may not want your forms to be able to do this. The MinButton property controls whether the minimize icon button will appear in the top right corner of a form at run time. Figure 4.9 displays how the minimize button appears on a form. There are two possible settings for the MinButton property, True (-1) and False (0). True is the default value for all forms. The presence of the MinButton control determines whether the user will be able to use the minimize button to reduce the size of the form down to the icon symbol designated for it. The MinButton property is a useful tool for removing this ability from the user in cases where this would be inappropriate. A situation where it might be appropriate to prevent the user from minimizing a window is when you want the user to exit the form with the OK button. Minimizing a window in this case rather than hiding or unloading it

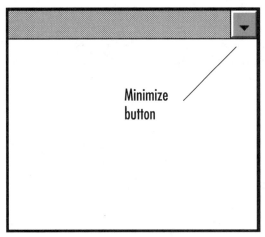

**Figure 4.9 The minimize button of a form**

could cause a problem the next time the program calls that window. There may be no command to normalize the size of the form in that form's Load event. Table 4.7 summarizes the form argument of MinButton property.

## General Syntax

```
[form.]MinButton
```

| Argument | Description |
|----------|-------------|
| form | Identifies the FormName property of the referenced form |
| | If no name precedes an expression, the code references the property of the current form |

**Table 4.7 Argument of the MinButton property**

## Example Syntax

```
Sub FormSize (FormName As Form)                         'Checks the MinButton property
                                                        'setting
    FormName.WindowState = Abs(Form1.MinButton) -1  'and minimizes the form if it is False
End Sub                                                  'otherwise the form is 'normalized.
```

## Description

The MinButton property of a form determines whether a form can display its minimize control button in the top right corner of the form. The BorderStyle property of a form affects the appearance of the minimize button. A form's MinButton property can only be set at design time. Any attempt to change the MinButton property of a form at run time will generate an error. You can, however, use the MinButton property as a reference at run time. The example above uses the setting of the MinButton property of a form to determine whether the form will appear in normal or minimized size. This function is generic so that it can be used for all of the forms of a program to establish a standard setup.

### The BorderStyle and WindowState Properties

The BorderStyle property of a form also affects the appearance of the minimize control. If the BorderStyle of a form is either 0 (none) or 3 (fixed double), then the minimize button will *not* be displayed with either setting. As long as the MinButton Property is True and the BorderStyle of the form is 3 (fixed double), the minimize command will still appear in the control box of a form. No matter what the setting for the MinButton or BorderStyle properties is, a form can still be minimized using the WindowState property, as shown in the example. A form's BorderStyle property has no effect upon the form's ability to be minimized. For example, a form with a MinButton property set to 0 and a BorderStyle of 3 (fixed double), can still be minimized using the statement Form.WindowState = 2.

## Example

The Setup project at the end of this section uses the MinButton property at design time to disable the minimize button of the Display form. This shows the difference between a form with and without the minimize button.

## Comments

Remember that the absence of the MinButton on a form does not prevent the user from minimizing a form if the Minimize command appears in the control box menu.

# Resize Event

## Objects Affected

| | | | | |
|---|---|---|---|---|
| Check | Clipboard | Combo | Command | Dbug |
| Dir | Drive | File | ▶ Form | Frame |
| Label | List | Menu | Option | Picture |
| Printer | Screen | Scroll | Text | Timer |

## Purpose

The Resize event is a built-in procedure that specifies what actions take place when the user resizes a form or when the form is first made visible. This event can be triggered by anything that brings a form into the user's sight or changes its size. When a form is activated, the Resize event is triggered. For example, a form with a Load event that maximizes the form upon loading it up on the screen would initiate a Resize event. In this case, the Resize event would be processed at the time of execution of the code that triggers it, regardless of what code remains to be processed in the Form_Load event. You use the Resize event to process any actions that need to take place when the size of the form changes. Because the Load event always processes prior to the Resize event, the Resize event would be generated and call for the redrawing of the form with a Refresh method statement. In the example syntax, the Resize event of

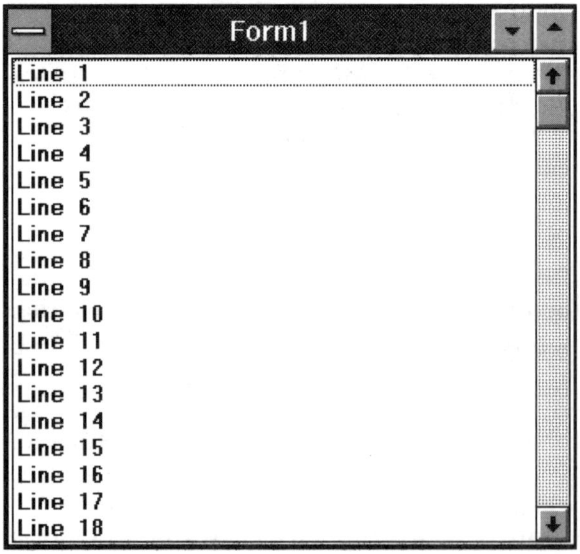

Figure 4.10 Form1 with List1 list box filled in by Resize event

Form1 changes the size of the List1 list box to fill its interior. Figure 4.10 shows what Form1 and the List1 list box might look like.

## General Syntax

```
Sub Form_Resize ()
```

## Example Syntax

```
Sub Form_Load ()
    For i = 1 To 20                            'Generates 20 line items in the
                                               'List1 list box
        List1.AddItem "Line " + str$(i)
    Next i
End Sub

Sub Form_Resize ()
    List1.Move 25,25,ScaleWidth-50,ScaleHeight-25 'Fill Form1 with the List1
                                                  'list box
End Sub
```

## Description

When your program changes the WindowState, Visible, Height, or Width properties of a form, Visual Basic triggers a Resize event. This event is also triggered any time a form loads with the Load or Show statements. The user can also trigger this event by changing the size of the form with the mouse. You can use the Resize event to adjust the position of controls on a form after the form's size has changed. Sometimes changes to the WindowState, Visible, Height, and Width properties make it necessary to adjust the position of controls on the same form. In the syntax example, each time the Form1 form's height or width is changed, the Form_Resize event adjusts the height and width of the List1 list box. This has the effect of filling the surface of the form with the List1 list box. This is an excellent use of the Resize event to ensure that the List1 list box fills the entire form.

### The ScaleWidth and ScaleHeight Properties

The ScaleWidth and ScaleHeight properties of a form serve as references. Each control's size is a fraction of the values of the ScaleWidth and ScaleHeight properties. In the example syntax, the Move statement references these properties to change the size of a control. This is a very basic example of this technique; the Setup project at the end of this section shows this process in further detail.

### The Load, Paint, and GotFocus Events

If there is more than one event attached to a particular control, they are processed in the following order: Load, Resize, Paint, and GotFocus. This is an important point to keep in mind if any of the actions that take place in one event are based upon actions in another event. For example, a data entry form for an address book would have problems if the Form_Load event disables the Address1 text box. If the Form_GotFocus event subsequently attempts to define the Address1 text box's contents, this would create an error.

### Example

The Resize event in the Setup project at the end of this section controls the size and placement of the command button Set Mode on the screen. Whenever the form's size changes, the Resize event adjusts the size and position of the command button. This shows how a form's controls can be adjusted to compensate for changes in the form's size.

### Comments

The Resize event takes place every time a form loads, resizes, or displays on the screen.

# Show Method

### Objects Affected

| | | | | |
|---|---|---|---|---|
| Check | Clipboard | Combo | Command | Dbug |
| Dir | Drive | File | ▶ Form | Frame |
| Label | List | Menu | Option | Picture |
| Printer | Screen | Scroll | Text | Timer |

### Purpose

The Show method loads a form into memory and displays it on the screen. A Show method statement can begin with the CtlName of the form. If Show does not specify a form, then the current form appears. A Show method has either a modeless or modal style. The default setting is modeless. Modal forms block the execution of any code until you remove a form from sight. (This also has the effect of preventing the user from changing the focus to another form.) Forms shown in modeless style will not prevent any other code from running. Table 4.8 summarizes the arguments of the Show method.

### General Syntax

```
[form.]Show[style%]
```

| Argument | Description |
|---|---|
| form | Identifies the FormName property of the form to display |
| style% | Value representing whether to load the form in modal or modeless format |

**Table 4.8 Arguments of the Show method**

### Example Syntax

```
Sub Command1_Click ()
    DataForm.Show 0              'Display DataForm
    Text1.Text = ""             'Change text property of Text1 to blank
    DataForm.Hide               'Hide DataForm
    Warning.Show 1              'Show Modal version of Warning form
    End
End Sub
```

```
Sub Warning_Click ()
    Warning.Hide              'Hide Warning form
End Sub
```

## Description

The Show method lets you load and display a form on the screen, or display an already loaded form. (A form remains in memory until it is removed using an Unload statement or until the program ends.) For example, a data entry program could load all of its secondary forms into memory when the program starts. Later, the program's main menu could use the Show method to quickly display a needed form.

### Modeless vs. Modal Style

A Show method statement has the optional argument style%. This value determines whether the form is to be loaded in modeless (0) or modal (1) style. When an expression does not contain a number, the form displays in modeless style. If you don't use this argument, the form will be modeless. Modal forms will not permit the execution of any code until they are removed with either a Hide method or an Unload statement. A modal form also prevents the processing of code that follows the modal Show method expression. With this mode, you can display a message to the user without specifically interrupting the code. The program will continue where it left off when hidden or unloaded. Most forms load using this style. Table 4.9 summarizes the settings of the style% argument.

| style% | Description |
|--------|-------------|
| 0 | Modeless - Code after the Show method runs normally |
| 1 | Modal - Code after the Show method runs after the form closes |

Table 4.9 Possible settings of the style% argument of the Show method

### The Visible Property

Placing a form on the screen with the Show method changes its Visible property to True (-1). The difference between using the Show method and directly changing the setting of the Visible property lies in the types of objects affected. The Show method can only be used on a form. In contrast, the Visible property can be used on any Visual Basic controls or forms. You can use this difference in generic functions and procedures if you want to limit the types of objects affected by forms.

### The Load Statement

The Load statement and Show method are very similar, but the difference between them is very important. Load brings controls or forms into memory, but it does not directly make them visible to the user. The Show method makes the control or form visible to the user, loading it if necessary. You can use these functions together to help your program run more smoothly. First, use the Load statement to load your forms into memory at the beginning of the program. Then use the Show method to quickly display the forms.

## Example

In the Setup project at the end of this section, the Show method displays both the Display and Setup forms. During the demonstration, the Setup form displays in two different modes of operation, modal and modeless. When the form is put on the screen in modeless style, the user's input is not stopped and any events that follow take place without being stopped. In contrast, when the form appears on a screen in modal style, no code that follows will be processed until it is closed.

## Comments

The Show method only loads a form if it is not already in memory.

# UnLoad Event

## Objects Affected

| | | | | |
|---|---|---|---|---|
| Check | Clipboard | Combo | Command | Dbug |
| Dir | Drive | File | ▶ Form | Frame |
| Label | List | Menu | Option | Picture |
| Printer | Screen | Scroll | Text | Timer |

## Purpose

The Unload event is a built-in procedure that specifies what actions will be taken when a form is unloaded. An Unload statement or the end of a program triggers the Unload event. You can use the Unload event to handle any tasks that must be taken care of prior to closing a form. For example, an Unload event for a data entry form could automatically enter unsaved data into the database.

## General Syntax

```
Sub Form_UnLoad (Cancel As Integer)
```

## Example Syntax

```
Sub Form_UnLoad (Cancel As Integer)
    Const YES = 6, No = 7                    'This routine asks the user if he
    Ans% = MsgBox("Are you sure that you wish to exit?",4)  'or she really
                                             'wishes to exit. A
    If Ans% = Yes Then                       'yes response closes the program.
        End                                  'A negative response displays the
    ElseIf Ans% = No Then                    'Form1 form
        Form1.Show
    End If
End Sub
```

## Description

The Form Unload event specifies what actions take place when a form is closed. All forms close automatically at the end of the program. An Unload statement can also close a form. One use of this event is to reset the information on the form before removing it from memory. Another use of the Unload event can be to give the user a final chance to prevent ending the program. In the example syntax, a MsgBox statement in the Unload event asks the user if he or she really wishes to exit.

There is an advantage to placing certain routines in an Unload event rather than linking them to a command button. Using an Unload event provides the user with a safety net that will prevent the user from forgetting to save a file or forgetting to enter important information in a data entry field. If save routines are only in command buttons and the user forgets to select the button prior to exiting, the information entered would be lost. (In some cases, however, such code might be better attached to an OK button: for example, if you want the user to confirm changes being made to a database.)

### The Load Event

The Unload event shares an inverse relationship with the Load event. While the Load event affects the form when it is initially opened, the Unload event executes when the form is closed. Both events can depend on each other. For example, the Load event might set up the form to initiate some action. The Unload event could then either restore the form to its preloaded settings or process the actions that took place. An address book might use the Load event to insert the last accessed information into the edit screen. This form's Unload event might ensure that the information entered into the fields is saved to the database.

### Example

The Setup project at the end of this section uses an Unload event for the Display form. This event presents a message box asking whether the user wishes to exit the program.

### Comments

The Unload event does not occur when a form is simply hidden.

# UnLoad Statement

### Purpose

The Unload statement removes a form or control from memory. This statement takes an object for its argument. The object can be the CtlName property of a form, control, or control array. Use the Unload statement to clear forms that are no longer needed. This statement also will reduce the memory being used if a program has a large number of forms. For example, a text editor with a large number of files open simultaneously could use the Unload statement to close files the user no longer needs. Table 4.10 summarizes the meaning of the object argument of the Unload statement.

### General Syntax

```
Unload object
```

| Argument | Description |
|----------|-------------|
| object | FormName or CtlName property of the item to be unloaded |

**Table 4.10 Argument of the Unload statement**

## Example Syntax

```
Sub Command1_Click
    If Text1.Text = "" Then        'Checks if Text box is blank
        Unload Form2               'Removes Form2 from display
    Else
        Form2.Hide                 'Removes Form2 from sight but leaves in memory
    End If
End Sub
```

## Description

The Unload statement unloads forms and controls both from the display and memory. A form remains out of memory unless the program references one of its properties. If this happens, the form will be loaded back into memory, although it won't appear on the screen. Since multiple Load and Unload statements take up a lot of processing time, we recommend you use the corresponding Hide and Show method statements for frequently used forms. In the example syntax, the form is unloaded only if the Text box is blank.

### The Hide Method

The Unload statement and Hide method have similar functions in Visual Basic, but the difference between them is very important. Unload removes a form from memory as well as from the user's view. A Hide method statement only takes the form out of view. This difference gives you the flexibility to remove forms that are no longer needed with Unload but to only hide forms that will be used again.

## Example

In the Setup project at the end of this section, the Unload statement removes the Display form from memory. This occurs when the user presses the Unload Display command button. The Unload statement generates the Unload event, which asks whether the user wishes to leave the program.

## Comments

The Unload statement may be used to remove a control of a control array created with the Load statement.

# WindowState Property

## Objects Affected

| Check | Clipboard | Combo | Command | Dbug |
|-------|-----------|-------|---------|------|
| Dir | Drive | File | ▶ Form | Frame |
| Label | List | Menu | Option | Picture |
| Printer | Screen | Scroll | Text | Timer |

## Purpose

The WindowState property determines or changes the size of a form window at run time. There are three possible settings for this property: normal (0), minimized (1), and maximized (2). Normal is the default. A maximized form fills the screen; a normal form returns a maximized or minimized form to its previous size. An icon replaces a minimized form on the screen. You can assign a unique icon to a form at design time by changing the form's Icon property. If no specific icon is chosen, the default Visual Basic icon appears. Tables 4.11 and 4.12 summarize the meaning of the form and state% arguments of the WindowState property.

## General Syntax

```
[form.]WindowState[ = state%]
```

| Argument | Description |
|----------|-------------|
| form | FormName property of the form whose size is being changed |
| state% | Value indicates what size to make the form |

**Table 4.11 Arguments of the WindowState property**

| state% | Description |
|--------|-------------|
| 0 | Normal - Restores the form to the previous size |
| 1 | Minimize - Reduces the form to an icon |
| 2 | Maximize - Fills the screen with the form |

**Table 4.12 Possible state% settings of the WindowState property**

## Example Syntax

```
Sub FormLoad (FormName As Form)          'Defines a New Sub Function
    Select Case FormName.MaxButton       'Defines the Maximum Button property
                                         'as the case setting
        Case -1
            Form1.WindowState = 2        'Maximize the form
        Case 0
            Form1.WindowState = 1        'Minimize the form
    End Select
End Sub
```

## Description

The WindowState property determines the appearance of a form on the screen. A form's WindowState property is initialized at design time but can be changed at run time. This expression begins with the name of the affected form. In the above example, a generic function changes the size of the form based on the MaxButton property. The state% argument indicates the new size of the form. A value of 2 (maximize) will fill the entire screen and 0 (normal) restores the form to the previous size.

A state% value of 1 minimizes the form into an icon. If an icon isn't chosen at design time, the Visual Basic icon appears on the screen. To assign an icon to a form on Visual Basic's programming screen, select the Icon property and click on the ellipsis

(...) at the right-hand side of the settings bar. Find the desired icon in the file list box and double-click on its file name to select it. Visual Basic comes with several icons, or you may create your own. (see the discussion of the Icon Property in Chapter 5, *Designing the Application's Appearance.*

### The MaxButton and MinButton Properties

The MaxButton and MinButton properties of the same form have no effect on a form's WindowState property. These properties control whether the maximize and minimize buttons appear in the top right corner of a form. The WindowState property can be used to change the size of a form no matter what the setting of the MaxButton and MinButton properties are. For example, a form with both the MaxButton and MinButton properties set to False could still be minimized by simply changing the WindowState property.

### The Resize Event

A change in the WindowState property triggers a Resize event. You can use the Resize event in this case to adjust the controls on the screen based on the new size. Use the ScaleWidth, ScaleHeight, ScaleTop, and ScaleLeft properties to specify the size and location of the controls on the screen. For example, a text editor could use the Resize event to adjust the text box to fill the form. This event would take place each time the form size is changed so that the text box always fills the entire form.

## Example

The Setup project at the end of this section uses the WindowState property three times. Each of the upper command buttons on the Display form controls one of the different states of this property. By setting the WindowState of the Display form to 2, the form is maximized. When the WindowState of the Display form is set to 1, the form is minimized to an icon. Finally, the Display form is restored to its former size and shape when 0 is used. Notice that the settings of the MaxButton and MinButton properties of the form have no effect on the WindowState of a form.

## Comments

The commands available on the control box of a form have no effect on the WindowState property of a form.

# Setup Project

## Project Overview

This Setup project demonstrates the setup of a Visual Basic form. This example shows how to use the properties, events, methods, and statements that directly control a form's basic appearance.

This project has two forms, the Setup form and the Display form. Each form's setup is broken down into three sections: assembly, figure display, and source code. Please refer to the figures to see where the forms' elements should be placed.

## Assembling the Project:  Setup Form

1. Begin a new project by selecting the File menu and the New project option. Make a new form (the Setup form) with the objects and properties shown in Table 4.13.

| Object | Property | Setting |
|---|---|---|
| Form | Caption | Setup |
| | ControlBox | True |
| | Icon | \VB\ICONS\COMPUTER\KEY06.ICO |
| | FormName | Setup |
| | MaxButton | True |
| | MinButton | True |
| Command button | Caption | Show Modeless Form |
| | CtlName | SetMode |

**Table 4.13 Elements of the Setup form**

2. Size the objects on the screen, as shown in Figure 4.11.

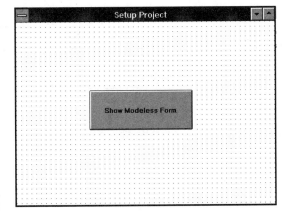

**Figure 4.11 What the Setup form should look like when completed**

3. Enter the following code in the General Declarations section. This code declares the variables that define the dimensions of the form's command button.

```
Dim ConvertHeight As Integer
Dim ConvertWidth As Integer
Dim OldFormHeight As Integer
```

```
Dim OldFormWidth As Integer
Dim OldHeight As Integer
Dim NewHeight As Integer
Dim OldWidth As Integer
Dim NewWidth As Integer
Dim OldLeft As Integer
Dim NewLeft As Integer
Dim OldTop As Integer
Dim NewTop As Integer
```

4. Enter the following code in the Form_Load event. This routine saves the form's current dimensions and loads the Display form.

```
Sub Form_Load ()
   OldFormHeight = Setup.Height
   OldFormWidth = Setup.Width
   OldHeight = SetMode.Height
   OldWidth = SetMode.Width
   OldLeft = SetMode.Left
   OldTop = SetMode.Top
   Load Display
End Sub
```

5. Enter the following code in the Form_Resize event. This code is triggered when the form's size is changed. This event sets the dimensions of a command button as a fraction of the size of the form.

```
Sub Form_Resize ()
StartHere:
   On Error GoTo 0
   ConvertHeight = OldFormHeight / Setup.ScaleHeight
   ConvertWidth = OldFormWidth / Setup.ScaleWidth
   NewHeight = OldHeight - ((OldFormHeight - Setup.Height) * ConvertHeight)
   NewWidth = OldWidth - ((OldFormWidth - Setup.Width) * ConvertWidth)
   NewTop = OldTop - ((OldTop - Setup.Top) * ConvertHeight)
   NewLeft = OldLeft - ((OldLeft - Setup.Left) * ConvertWidth)
   On Error GoTo Off
   SetMode.Move NewLeft, NewTop, NewWidth, NewHeight
   Exit Sub
Off:
   MsgBox "Control positioned out of area"
   Setup.Height = OldFormHeight
   Setup.Width = OldFormWidth
   Resume StartHere
End Sub
```

6. Enter the following code in the SetMode_Click event. This code triggers when the user presses the command button SetMode. This event toggles the mode of the Display form between modeless and modal and changes the corresponding caption on the command button.

```
Sub SetMode_Click ()
   If SetMode.Caption = "Show Modeless Form" Then
      Setup.Hide
```

```
        SetMode.Caption = "Show Modal Form"
        Display.Show 0
        MsgBox "This is a Modeless Form"
        Display.Hide
        Setup.Show 0
    Else
        Setup.Hide
        SetMode.Caption = "Show Modeless Form"
        MsgBox "The next form is a Modal Form"
        Display.Show 1
        Setup.Show 0
    End If
End Sub
```

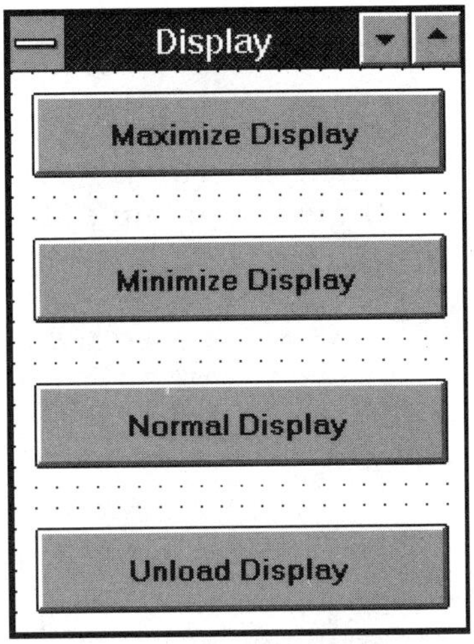

## Assembling the Project - Display Form

1. Create a new form using the specifications in
Table 4.14 by again selecting the File menu and
then choosing New form. Make the New form in
the shape of a vertical rectangle in the center of
the Setup form.

Figure 4.12 What the Display form
should look like when completed

| Object | Property | Setting |
|--------|----------|---------|
| Form | Caption | Display |
| | ControlBox | False |
| | FormName | Display |
| | MaxButton | False |
| | MaxButton | False |
| Command button | Caption | Maximize Display |
| | CtlName | Max_Display |
| Command button | Caption | Minimize Display |
| | CtlName | Min_Display |
| Command button | Caption | Normal Display |
| | CtlName | Normal_Display |
| Command button | Caption | Unload Display |
| | CtlName | Remove_Form |

Table 4.14 Elements of the Display form

2. Size the objects on the screen as shown in Figure 4.12.

3. Enter the following code in the Max_Display_Click event. This code is triggered when the user presses the Maximize Display button. This event maximizes the Display form's size.

```
Max_Display_Click ()
```

```
    Display.WindowState 2
End Sub
```

4. Enter the following code in the Form_Unload event. This code is triggered when the form is removed from the computer's memory. With this code, the user is prompted to be sure he or she wishes to exit the program.

```
Sub Form_UnLoad ()
    Const YES = 6, NO = 7
    Ans% = MsgBox("Are you sure that you wish to exit?", 4)
        If Ans% = YES Then
            End
    End If
End Sub
```

5. Enter the following code in the Min_Display_Click event. This code is triggered when the user presses the Minimize Display command button. This event minimizes the Display form to an icon on the screen.

```
Sub Min_Display_Click ()
    Display.WindowState 1
End Sub
```

6. Enter the following code in the Normal_Display_Click event. This code is triggered when the user presses the Normal Display command button. This event normalizes the Display form on the screen.

```
Sub Normal_Display_Click ()
    Display.WindowState 0
End Sub
```

7. Enter the following code in the RemoveForm_Click event. This code is triggered when the user presses the RemoveForm command button. This event removes the Display form from the screen.

```
Sub RemoveForm_Click ()
    Unload Display
End Sub
```

## How It Works

The Setup project displays a command button on the Setup form. Inititially, the command button reads "Show Modal form." When the user presses the command button, the Setup form is hidden and the Display form appears on the screen with a message box, which calls it a Modal form. After the user presses the OK button on the message box, the Display form disappears and the Setup form reappears. Now the command button on the Setup form reads "Show Modeless form."

The next time the user presses this command button, the Display form is displayed in Modeless form. To maximize the form, the user presses the command button labeled Maximize form. In order to minimize the form, the user presses the command button labeled Minimize form. To restore the Display form on the screen, the user presses the command button labeled Normalize form. To exit the program, the user presses the command button labeled Unload Display.

### Startup

The Setup project first sets the program's variables, opens the forms, and processes the Resize event. The Setup form's Form_Load event saves the form's dimensions and loads the Display form. There is no need for a Load statement for the Setup form. The Resize event uses the form's dimensions together with the Scale properties to position the command button on the screen.

### Running the Setup Project

When all these tasks are completed, the user sees a form with a Show Modeless Form command button in the center. Now is a good time to adjust the form's size to see how the Resize event works. Notice that the program will prevent the user from manipulating the Setup form too drastically. Pay particular attention to the correct use of the line names Start Here and Off. These labels allow an On Error statement to trap any errors resulting from extreme changes to the form's size.

Press the command button on this form to see the effects of a Modeless Show method statement. This command removes the Setup form from sight with a Hide method, and then changes the caption of the command button to Show Modal Form. This demonstrates that the properties of a form can be modified when the form is not on the screen. Next, a Show method brings the Display form up on the screen and a MsgBox statement tells the user that this is a modeless form. Notice that the line of code that places the message box on the screen comes *after* the Show method statement. This demonstrates that a modeless form does not prevent the code that follows it from being processed. When the user presses the OK button, a Hide method removes the Display form from the screen and a Modeless Show statement restores the Setup form. (A Resize event is triggered here, but since the form's size has not changed, nothing happens.)

Now the command button reads "Show Modal Form." Press the button again. This time the Caption property will be changed back to Show Modeless Form. A message box tells the user that the next form is a modal form, and then the Display form appears on the screen. Notice that the Modal Show method statement prevents the next line of code from being processed until the form is taken off the screen. This is the reason why the code needed to display the message box is placed before the Show method statement.

The Display form has the four command buttons. Each of the top three command buttons have Click events attached to them. These events provide examples of the different settings of the WindowState property of a form. The top button, Maximize Display, will fill the screen with the Display form. If the user presses the next button, Minimize Display, then the form moves to the bottom of the screen, represented by an icon. The Normal Display command button returns the form to its original shape and size. Notice that the MaxButton and MinButton properties of this form have been changed to False so that neither of these buttons are shown at run time. This makes it clear that these properties do not affect whether a form can be minimized or maximized.

After you have tried all of these buttons, press the Unload Display button. This button uses an Unload statement to generate an Unload event that asks whether the user wishes to exit the program now. If the user responds "yes," an End statement stops the program immediately. Otherwise, the program continues normally. At this point, the Display form is unloaded from memory and a Modeless Show method makes the Setup form visible again. Note: This line must be placed here, because a modeless form cannot be made visible while a modal form is still visible. To exit the program, press the control box at the top right corner of the Setup form and choose Close.

# Designing the Application's Appearance

T he appearance of an application affects the way the user feels about it and reacts to it. Poorly designed screens impair the overall usefulness of even the most cleverly written program. A screen with clashing colors is one example of poor design Command buttons placed in haphazard fashion can confuse and frustrate users. Unnecessarily complex control arrangements also create difficulties. Users always notice these kinds of problems. Such problems reduce the chance that people will bother to work with a program. A user does not see cleverly written code; a user reacts to the way the program looks.

Since DOS itself did not include tools for creating user interfaces, traditional DOS programs each provided their own idiosyncratic assortment of interface elements. Since Windows *does* provide menus, dialog boxes, and windows that operate in a standard way, Windows programs usually have a common look and feel. The Microsoft Windows environment thus represents an attempt to simplify the operation of computers and computer software. Windows provides a universal interface that a user can theoretically apply to new programs. When you've learned how to use one DOS program, you've learned how to use one DOS program. But when you've learned how to use one Windows program, you've learned most of what you need to know to operate *any* Windows program.

Windows reduces the amount of training time needed to teach people new programs by making at least some of the parts of new programs familiar. Unfortunately, a universal interface is not enough. The appearance of the program must receive first priority. Windows programmers must build upon that common store of functionality to tailor the interface to the needs of the particular application. Decisions must be made about the colors, types, styles, and positions of the controls to be used.

## Screen Design in Visual Basic

Microsoft Visual Basic is revolutionary in the way that it addresses this screen design problem. Traditionally, you make decisions about a program's appearance after you write the underlying code. This process concentrates upon the code first and the forms and controls second. Visual Basic reverses this process and allows you to design the screens before you write the underlying code. This is an important change in emphasis that reflects a crucial difference between Visual Basic and other languages.

Visual Basic gives screen design top priority in the program design process. Each of the forms and controls first appears visually on the screen, then you connect your code to the different elements on the screen. In other languages, written code produces the forms and controls on the screen. This system makes it necessary to run the program to find out how the forms and controls appear. Screens produced with written code must also be modified with written code. In Visual Basic, changing the appearance of forms and controls is an easy process of screen manipulation.

## Color

People respond to the color of the elements on the screen. For example, objects with a red coloring can represent danger or warning. If the background of a warning box is red, then it gets more attention. This is a powerful tool that augments the appearance of forms and controls on the screen. In designing a form interactively with Visual Basic, you can use the on-screen color palette to make color choices (see Figure 5.1).

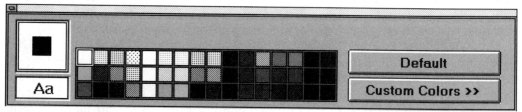

**Figure 5.1 Color palette**

In Visual Basic, the BackColor and ForeColor properties control an object's color. Colors are represented by a 4-byte integer number that indicates a mixture of the three electronic primary colors: blue, red, and green. One way to set a color value is to set this number directly. The first byte of this number is ignored. The second, third, and fourth bytes represent how much blue, red and green, respectively, will be used in the color mixture. Each color can be assigned a value between 0 and 255 (or 0 to FF in hexadecimal notation), which indicates that color's intensity in the mixture. You can also assign a color value with the RGB function. This function lets you supply a decimal number for each electronic primary color, and returns a color number based on these values. A number between 0 and 255 represents each primary color. Still another way to assign a color value is to use the QBColor function. This function lets you select one of 16 colors from a palette in a way familar to QuickBASIC programmers.

## Appearance of Screen Objects

Forms have four possible border styles: none, sizable, fixed single, and fixed double. The BorderStyle property of a form determines which type of border appears around it. A form with no border also has no maximize button, minimize button, or control box. This border style is a popular choice for warning boxes, which usually do not need these options. The user can change the size of sizable forms with the mouse, just as the name suggests. Both the fixed single and fixed double borders disable the mouse's ability to change their sizes. However, the user can still maximize or minimize the form.

Each object has a height and width. The number representing the object's height and width depends on the type of measurement. A height's number is different if expressed in inches or centimeters (although the object's actual height does not change). Objects that are 1 inch in height are also 2.54 centimeter high. Visual Basic determines the height and width of objects with the Height and Width properties of the object. These properties contain the current height and width of the object expressed in the measure set in the ScaleMode property.

Each object on the screen is a certain distance from the edges of another object. A control on a form positions itself in terms of the left and top edges of the form, whereas forms on the screen locate themselves in terms of the left and top edges of the screen. The number that shows the distance of an object from the edge is different if calculated in inches rather than in centimeters (the object's actual distance does not change). Visual Basic returns the distance from the left and top edges with the Left and Top properties of the object. These properties include the current distance expressed in the measure type set in the ScaleMode property.

### Icons and Pointers

A minimized form becomes an icon that represents the form. This icon serves to remind the viewer that the form is still in the operating memory of the computer. Visual Basic permits the modification of this icon either at run or design time. At design time, the properties bar provides a list of the icons available. Access this list by selecting the Icon property on the properties bar and clicking the ellipsis (...). Figure 5.2 shows what the properties bar and list look like in the default Visual Basic setup. For a listing of the icons that shipped with Microsoft Visual Basic, look in the Microsoft *Visual Basic Programmer's Guide,* pages 400-409.

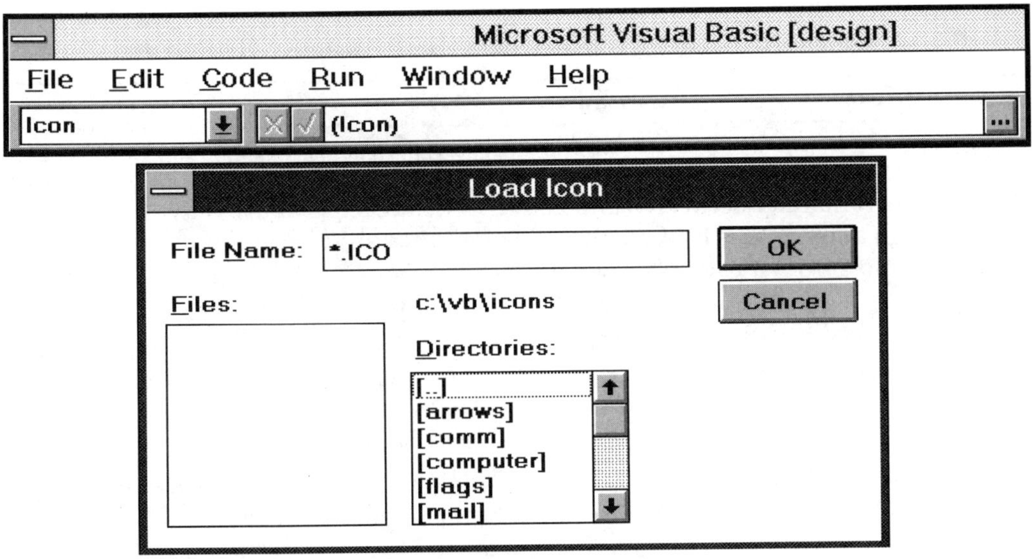

**Figure 5.2 Properties bar (above) and icon load screen**

You can also change the icon of the mouse pointer to reflect the current function of the program. Some pointer shapes have become traditonal for Windows programs. When activity takes place in the background such that the user must wait before continuing work, an hourglass can replace the normal arrow. If the cursor is over a text box, the cursor can change to an I-beam so the user can manipulate the text box's contents. In Visual Basic, the MousePointer property determines the type of cursor that appears over an application's forms and controls.

Finally, an object's visibility determines whether or not the user sees it on the screen. (Don't confuse an invisible object with one that is covered by another window or application.)

## Properties That Determine Appearance

A set of 11 properties governs the way a form or control appears to the user. These properties affect the color (BackColor and ForeColor) of a form or control. With these two properties, the standard Windows colors can be modified from the default to whatever the programmer or user wishes. Both of these properties can be adjusted at design time or run time. Each of the dimensions (Height, Width, Left, and Top) of a form or control can be changed at design time. None of these properties may be changed at run time. By using the Caption Property of a form or control, the text that appears on the object may be modified either at run time or design time. A form's BorderStyle property may be modified to display a different kind of surrounding edge to the form. Another icon may be chosen for a form in the Icon property. This icon is displayed when the form is minimized, and permits you to differentiate between minimized forms. An icon other than the normal arrow may also be chosen for the mouse pointer when it is over the control or form. Finally, a form or control may be removed from the screen with the Visible property. This gives you a great deal of control over a form's appearance, allowing you to create special looks for individual types of forms and controls. In this way, you can have a special setup for particular types of forms.

Table 5.1 summarizes the properties that affect the appearance of forms and controls.

| Use or Set This... | | To Do This... |
|---|---|---|
| BackColor | Property | Adjust the background color of a form or control |
| BorderStyle | Property | Adjust the edges of a form at design time |
| Caption | Property | Indicate what text will appear on a form or control |
| ForeColor | Property | Adjust the color of the text of a form or control |
| Height | Property | Adjust the vertical size of a form or control at design time |
| Icon | Property | Determine the icon to display for a minimized form |
| Left | Property | Adjust the position of a form in relation to the left edge of screen or a control in relation to the left edge of the form. You can only set this value at design time |
| MousePointer | Property | Determine the icon to display when a mouse is over a form or control |
| Top | Property | Adjust the position of a form in relation to the top edge of screen or a control in relation to the top edge of the form. You can only set this value at design time |

| | | |
|---|---|---|
| Visible | Property | Determine whether a form is visible to the user |
| Width | Property | Adjust the horizontal size of a form or control at design time |

**Table 5.1 Properties dealing with the general appearance of a form or control**

The following pages investigate these properties in detail. At the end of this section, step-by-step directions describe how to assemble the Appearance project, which demonstrates these properties.

# BackColor Property

## Objects Affected

▶ Check    Clipboard    ▶ Combo    ▶ Command    Dbug
▶ Dir    ▶ Drive    ▶ File    ▶ Form    ▶ Frame
▶ Label    ▶ List    Menu    ▶ Option    ▶ Picture
▶ Printer    Screen    Scroll    ▶ Text    Timer

## Purpose

The BackColor property defines or determines the background color of a form or control. This value can be the hexadecimal code from the Visual Basic color menu or an expression using the RGB function. The values passed to the RGB function identify the red, green, and blue components that make up the color you want. When an object's BackColor property does not end in a new color choice, it serves as a reference for the current background color of the object. For example, a program might start with a Form_Resize event that changes the color of the form based on its size. A maximized form has a white BackColor property, RGB(0,0,0). Normalized forms have their BackColor property set to blue, RGB(0,0,255). Whenever another form loads, the new form bases its BackColor property on the first form. Table 5.2 summarizes the arguments of the BackColor property.

## General Syntax

```
[form.]BackColor[= color&]
[control.]BackColor[=color&]
```

| Argument | Description |
|---|---|
| form | FormName property of the form. Changes or references current form with no name |
| control | CtlName property of the control |
| color& | Value of the color defined with hexadecimal number, RGB function, or QBColor function |

**Table 5.2 Arguments of the BackColor property**

## Example Syntax

```
Sub Form_Resize
    If WindowState = 2 Then              'If the window is maximized
        BackColor = RGB(0,0,255)         'Changes the background to blue
    Else
        BackColor = RGB(255,255,255)     'Changes the background to white
    End If
End Sub
```

## Description

With the BackColor property you can change the Windows environment's default settings for the background color of a form or control. (The default setting of the BackColor of a form is the color chosen in the control panel for the Windows background.) Each BackColor property expression begins with the name of the object whose background is being changed. The CtlName property uniquely identifies its control, whereas a form's FormName property uniquely identifies a form. If no name precedes an expression, the code references or changes the BackColor property of the current form. The color& argument of a BackColor expression must be a hexadecimal value. Either an explicit hexadecimal number, the RGB function, or the QBColor function defines the hexadecimal value of color&. In the example syntax, the background color of the form changes according to its present size. The background of a maximized form is blue. Otherwise, the background of the form is white. Notice that the RGB function defines the color& argument. Both the QBColor function and the hexadecimal number produce exactly the same results.

## RGB and QBColor Functions

The BackColor property of an object returns a hexadecimal value obtained in one of three different ways. The simplest method is to use the hexadecimal number of the color needed. A valid hexadecimal value ranges from 0 to 16,777,215 (&HFFFFFF). Table 5.3 provides the hexadecimal values of some of the most common colors. You may also obtain the hexadecimal value of any of the sixteen standard Windows colors with the QBColor function by specifying the integer color number as used in Quick BASIC (and other versions of Microsoft BASIC). A value returned by an RGB function also provides the definition for the BackColor property of an object. In the first three columns of Table 5.3, the red, green, and blue values define an RGB function in the form of RGB (Red, Green, Blue). Customized colors result from the adjustment of the values of these three variables. Either setting will work. For example, the BackColor property of a form becomes blue with either the statement BackColor = RGB(0,0,255) or BackColor = &HFF000&. See Appendix A, *Visual Basic Language Summary,* for additional details about the RGB and QBColor functions.

| Color | Red Value | Green Value | Blue Value | Hexadecimal | QBColor |
|-------|-----------|-------------|------------|-------------|---------|
| Black | 0 | 0 | 0 | &H0 | 0 |
| Red | 255 | 0 | 0 | &HFF | 4 |

| Green | 0 | 255 | 0 | &HFF00 | 2 |
| Yellow | 0 | 255 | 255 | &HFFFF | 6 |
| Blue | 0 | 0 | 255 | &HFF0000 | 1 |
| Magenta | 255 | 0 | 255 | &HFF00FF | 5 |
| Cyan | 0 | 255 | 255 | &HFFFF00 | 3 |
| White | 255 | 255 | 255 | &HFFFFFF | 15 |
| Light Gray | 192 | 192 | 192 | &H00C0C0C0 | 7 |
| Dark Gray | 128 | 128 | 128 | &H00808080 | 8 |

**Table 5.3 Values of common colors in RGB, QBColor, and hexadecimal format**

### The ForeColor Property

The BackColor and ForeColor properties of a form combine to produce the colors that you see when the form displays. Whenever you change one of these properties, you should consider how the new color combination will work together. If the foreground and background colors contrast, it may make your program harder to use and may detract from its usefulness. For example, setting the BackColor property to blue and the ForeColor property to red is objectionable to most users.

## Example

In the Appearance project at the end of this section, the BackColor property of the Appear and Warning forms is gray (&H00C0C0C0). You will set this property at design time to simplify the process. Notice how the BackColor property of the form has no effect on the setting of the control's background color. Each control has its own separate BackColor property independent of the settings of the form's BackColor property.

## Comments

The BackColor property of a form or control is an effective way to highlight certain controls to attract the user's attention or to make something more visible. For instance, to emphasize list boxes on a form with a gray background, set the BackColor property of the list boxes to white.

# BorderStyle Property

## Objects Affected

| | | | | |
|---|---|---|---|---|
| Check | Clipboard | Combo | Command | Dbug |
| Dir | Drive | File | ▶ Form | Frame |
| ▶ Label | List | Menu | Option | ▶ Picture |
| Printer | Screen | Scroll | ▶ Text | Timer |

## Purpose

The BorderStyle property determines the appearance of a border for a form, label, picture box, or text box. This property is modifiable at design time only. This feature lets you change the borders of the different elements of a program to reflect their function. With the border style of a form, you determine whether a form can be resized or moved. For example, a communications program might give all alert boxes a fixed double border, configuration screens a fixed single border, and the default sizeable border for the main communications window. In this way, the user quickly sees the function of a form by looking at the appearance of its border. Tables 5.4 and 5.5 summarize the different settings of the BorderStyle property's arguments.

## General Syntax

```
[form.]BorderStyle[= setting%]
[control.]BorderStyle[=setting%]
```

| Argument | Description |
|----------|-------------|
| form | FormName property of the form |
| control | CtlName property of the text box, label, or picture box |
| setting% | Value representing the type of border |

Table 5.4 Arguments of the BorderStyle property

| setting% | Description |
|----------|-------------|
| 0 | None (no border, control box, maximize button, or minimize button) |
| 1 | Fixed Single (sizeable with maximize or minimize buttons or WindowState property) |
| 2 | Sizeable (sizeable border). This is the default setting |
| 3 | Fixed double (non-sizeable border without minimize or maximize buttons) |

Table 5.5 Settings for the BorderStyle property

## Example Syntax

```
Sub SetBackground (FormName As Form)            'Set Background Function
    Select Case FormName.BorderStyle            'Obtains border of indicated form
        Case 0                                  'No border
            FormName.BackColor = RGB(0,0,255)   'Blue Background
            FormName.ForeColor = RGB(255,255,255) 'White Text
        Case 1                                  'Fixed Single border
            FormName.BackColor = RGB(255,255,255) 'White Background
            FormName.ForeColor = RGB(0,0,255)   'Blue Text
        Case 2                                  'Sizeable Border
            FormName.BackColor = RGB(0,0.255)   'Blue Background
            FormName.ForeColor = RGB(255,255,0) 'Yellow Text
        Case 3                                  'Fixed Double Border
            FormName.BackColor = RGB(0,255,255) 'Cyan Background
            FormName.ForeColor = RGB(0,0,0)     'Black Text
```

```
    End Select
End Sub
```

## Description

Use the BorderStyle property at design time to set the appearance of the edges of a form, text box, label, or picture box. The border chosen at design time affects a form's control box, maximize button, and minimize buttons. (At design time, the control box, maximize button, and minimize button are always visible). Additionally, the BorderStyle property of a form affects the user's ability to change the form's size. When the BorderStyle property of a text box, picture box, or label changes, the single border line around the object appears or disappears.

### Sizeable Border

The default setting for the BorderStyle property of a form is 2 (sizeable). A sizeable border has no effect upon the display of the control box, maximize button, and minimize controls. Figure 5.3 displays how a form with a sizeable border appears on the screen. Corresponding values for these properties (ControlBox, MaxButton, MinButton) are True (-1) by default. Changing to one of these properties is independent of the other two properties. For example, setting a form's ControlBox property to False (0) prevents it from displaying. When a form retains the default border style, the user can change the size of the form at run time.

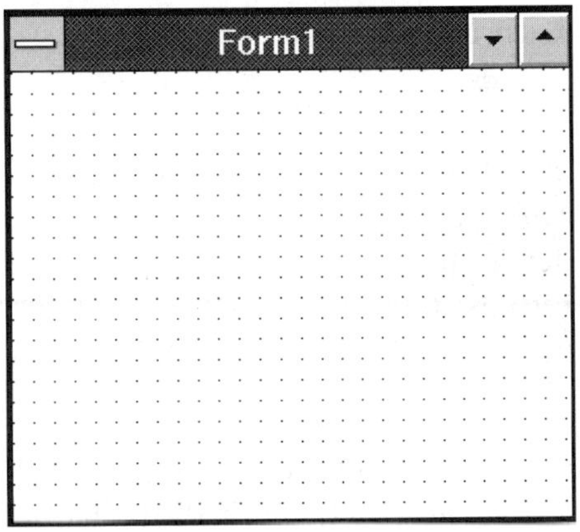

**Figure 5.3 Form with sizeable border allows the user to resize it ( note thickness of border)**

### No Border

A form with the BorderStyle set to 0 will not have a border or any of the objects normally associated with a border. For this reason, the maximize button, minimize button, and control box will not appear on the form, regardless of the settings of the ControlBox, MaxButton, or MinButton properties. The title bar of the form will also not appear. When a form's BorderStyle property is 0, the form may not be resized or minimized. You may use this property, for example, to set the BorderStyle of a word processor's configuration form to 0 to prevent the user from resizing the form and inadvertently hiding some of the controls. This would also have the effect of preventing the user from exiting the form without using the exit button. Figure 5.4 shows what a form with no border looks like.

### Fixed Single Border

If the BorderStyle of a form is 1 (fixed single), then the border is a single line around the form. Figure 5.5 demonstrates the appearance of a form with a fixed single border.

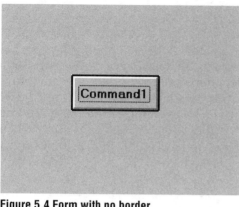

Figure 5.4 Form with no border

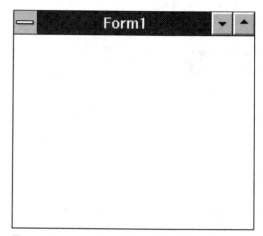

Figure 5.5 Form with a fixed single border

The maximize button, minimize button, and control box may appear on the form, depending on the setting of the MaxButton, MinButton, and ControlBox properties. A form with this border style may have its size changed only by maximizing or minimizing it. The user maximizes or minimizes this kind of form with either the command options on the control box or the icon buttons. This is the only way a user can adjust the borders of a form with this border style. Any changes in the WindowState property of a form produce the same kind of results. For example, you can position some of the entry fields of an employee database so that they are not initially visible. On the basis of the information the user enters, the form expands to maximized format when the user provides the password.

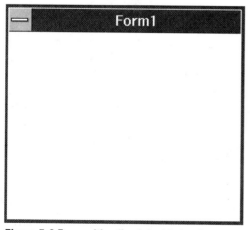

Figure 5.6 Form with a fixed double border

### Fixed Double Border

When a form's BorderStyle property is 2 (fixed double), the border is a thick line around the form. This border does not include the maximize and minimize buttons, regardless of the settings of the MaxButton and MinButton properties. A control box appears on the form, provided that the ControlBox property is True. Both the maximize and minimize command buttons will be options on the control box unless the MaxButton and MinButton properties are False. Users may not adjust the size of the form at run time by dragging the borders with the mouse. Only the

WindowState property—or the maximize, minimize, or restore options on the control box—may change the size of a form with this kind of border style. Figure 5.6 shows what a form with a fixed double border looks like on the screen.

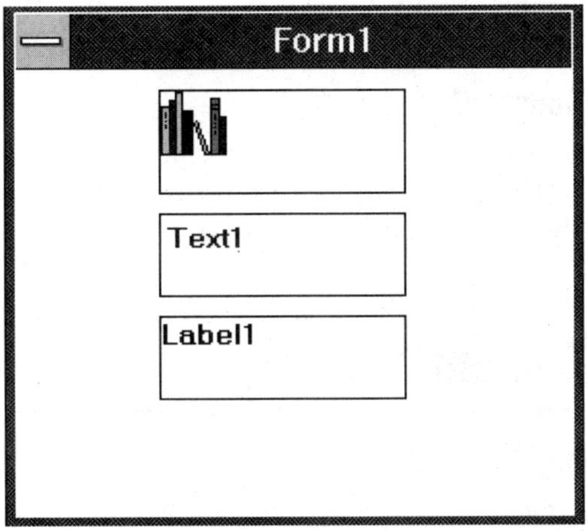

### Text Boxes, Labels, and Picture Boxes

Every label, text box, and picture box also has a BorderStyle property. Figure 5.7 demonstrates the appearance of the border around each of these controls. Unlike the setting of a form's property, the BorderStyle property of a label, text box, or picture box has an effect only if there is a border. This border appears around the indicated label, text box, or picture box. If the value of this property is True, then a single line appears around the bounds of the text box, picture box, or label. A border does not appear around one of these controls with a False (0) BorderStyle property. Table 5.6 shows the default settings of the setting% argument of the BorderStyle property.

**Figure 5.7 Border around picture box, text box, and label**

| Setting | Description |
|---------|-------------|
| 0 | None (default for label) |
| 1 | Fixed single (default for text and picture box) |

**Table 5.6 The effects of the BorderStyle property on labels, text boxes, and picture boxes**

### Example

In the Appearance project at the end of this section, the BorderStyle property removes the border of the warning form. This removes the control box, maximize button, and minimize button from the user's view. As a result, the only means for exiting the Warning form is the Cancel command button. Forms with this border style restrict the command options to either the ReDial or Cancel command buttons.

The BorderStyle property of both the label boxes on the Warning forms remains at the default value of 0. As a result, no border appears around either of these labels. This has the effect of displaying only the text of the Caption property of the label box. Since the BackColor property of these labels is also white (default), only the text appears.

The Appear form begins with its border style set to fixed single (1). The form is minimizable but not sizeable. The default sizeable border style is inappropriate in this case, because the user should not be able to change the size of the form and accidentally hide some of its controls. The double fixed (3) border is not suitable, as the user must be able to minimize the form to see its initial Icon property.

## Comments

Make sure to choose the correct border for each form in a program. The default sizeable setting is not always appropriate. In many cases, giving the user the ability to change the size of the form may cause errors.

# Caption Property

## Objects Affected

| | | | | |
|---|---|---|---|---|
| ▶ Check | Clipboard | Combo | ▶ Command | Dbug |
| Dir | Drive | File | ▶ Form | ▶ Frame |
| ▶ Label | List | ▶ Menu | ▶ Option | Picture |
| Printer | Screen | Scroll | Text | Timer |

## Purpose

The Caption property indicates what text will appear to label a control or form. A form's Caption property appears in its title bar. This title bar is between the control box and the minimize and maximize buttons. Text in a Caption property of a label or command button appears on the control. Option buttons or check boxes place the contents of their Caption property to the right of the control. This text helps to identify the control's function. A frame's Caption property displays on the top right corner of the frame. All of these controls' Caption properties are modifiable either at design or run time. Do not use the Caption property of a form or control to identify it in the code (use the CtlName property for that.) Each control's Caption property contains a text string or text variable. For example, both "Text String" and TextString$ are acceptable definitions for this property at run time. Table 5.7 summarizes the arguments of the Caption property.

## General Syntax

```
[control.]Caption[= textstring$]
[form.]Caption[=textstring$]
```

| Argument | Description |
|---|---|
| form | FormName property of the form |
| control | CtlName property of the control |
| textString$ | Text to place in or on the control or form indicated |

**Table 5.7 Arguments of the Caption property**

## Example Syntax

```
Sub Commmand1_Click
    If  Command1.Caption = "Print" Then     'This routine alternates between dis
                                            'playing the word
            Command1.Caption = "Display"    'Display and Print each time the user
                                            'presses the Command1
    Else                                    'command button.
            Command1.Caption = "Print"
    End If
End Sub
```

## Description

The Caption property defines or determines the text that appears on a command button, option box, check box, frame, label, menu, or form. You can set this property at
design time with the properties bar on Visual Basic's control bar. You can also set the
caption property of a form or control at run time. A Caption property expression begins with the CtlName property of the control or FormName property of the form.
When no name appears in an expression, the form's Caption property changes. The
TextString$ argument contains the string of text to redefine the Caption property
with. If the TextString$ argument is blank, then the text on the form or control is
blank. In the example, the Caption property of the Command1 command button
changes with each clicking of the command button.

### Forms

When the Caption property of a form
changes, the contents of this property
display at the top of the form in the title
bar. The title bar is the region between
the control box and the minimize and
maximize buttons. If the BorderStyle of
a form is 0 (no border), then the title bar
is no longer at the top of the form and
the Caption property (if any) is ignored.
Remember that the Caption property of
a form is for visual and not identification purposes. (You may use the same
name for the FormName property, however.) Figure 5.8 shows where the Caption property of the Form1 form
appears at the top of the form.

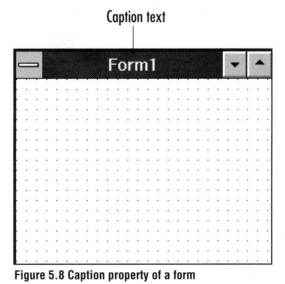

**Figure 5.8 Caption property of a form**

### Labels

With the Caption property of a label, the text entered displays on the form. A label's
Caption property is alterable either at design time or run time. If the label's AutoSize

Caption text

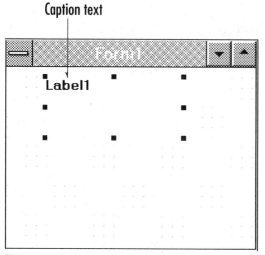

**Figure 5.9 Caption property of a label**

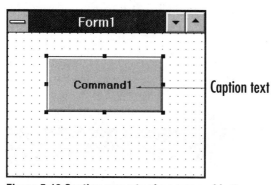

**Figure 5.10 Caption property of a command button**

property is True (-1), then the label's size automatically increases or decreases to fit with each change. For example, the label below a picture box containing a trashcan icon changes from Delete to Disabled whenever the user turns the delete feature off. In this case, the AutoSize property directs the expansion of the width of the label box to accommodate the larger word Disabled. Figure 5.9 displays where the Caption property of the Label1 label box appears on the label control.

### Command Buttons

The first command button created on a form will begin with the Caption property set to Command1. Each new command button caption property receives the next incremented number. In this way, the next command button is Command2, then Command3, and so on. No doubt you will want to change these caption values to appropriate descriptions of the commands the buttons are to execute. A command control's Caption property is modifiable either at design time or run time. You can also use the Caption property to assign an access key to a command button. To do so, place an ampersand (&) before the letter in the caption that you wish to make the access key. For example, the P key would become the access key for a command button with a Caption property of &Print. The user can then hold down the Alt key and press P to trigger the command button's Click event. This change appears in text on the command button shown with the access letter underlined. Figure 5.10 indicates the location where the Caption property displays on the Command1 command button.

### Option Buttons and Check Boxes

Option buttons and check boxes have their Caption property contents placed on the right of the graphic objects. These properties are modifiable at both design and run time, but do not possess the AutoSize feature of the label box. For this reason, make sure you provide enough space for any changes to the captions of these controls. Figure 5.11 demonstrates the place where the Caption properties of the Option1 option box and Check1 check boxes appear on the screen.

## Example

In the Appearance project at the end of this section, the Caption property of the Appear form changes for identification purposes. The initial Caption property of the first form is Form1. Since this label isn't descriptive, Form1 becomes Appearance project. Notice that when the Appear form displays on the screen, this text appears at the top of the form. The Caption property serves as a way of identifying which form is presently being displayed.

Each time the Dial command button is pressed, the Caption property of the Appear form changes to Dialing and the phone number. This demonstrates that the Caption property is modifiable at run time. When the Appear form minimizes, this is also the message displayed below the icon representing the form.

The Caption properties of the Dial and Results Label boxes on the Warning form change each time the ReDial command button is pressed. In this case, the Caption property serves as both a reference and a means of changing the text in the label box. This sends a series of messages to the user.

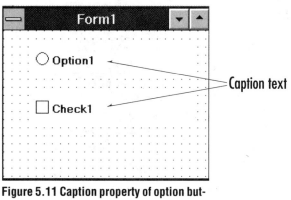

Figure 5.11 Caption property of option buttons and check boxes

## Comments

A form's Caption property does not appear when the form's BorderStyle is 0.

---

# ForeColor Property

## Objects Affected

| | | | | |
|---|---|---|---|---|
| ▶ Check | Clipboard | ▶ Combo | ▶ Command | Dbug |
| ▶ Dir | ▶ Drive | ▶ File | ▶ Form | ▶ Frame |
| ▶ Label | ▶ List | Menu | ▶ Option | ▶ Picture |
| ▶ Printer | Screen | Scroll | ▶ Text | Timer |

## Purpose

The ForeColor property defines or determines the foreground color of a form or control. This value can be the hexadecimal code from the Visual Basic color menu or an expression using the RGB function, or the value returned from the QBColor function. The values passed to the RGB function identify the red, green, and blue components that make up the desired color. When an object's ForeColor property does not end in a new color choice, it serves as a reference for the current foreground color of the object. For example, a program might start with a Form_Resize event that changes the color of the form based on its size. While the form is maximized, the ForeColor property is white, RGB(0,0,0). When the form is normalized, the form's ForeColor property is blue, RGB(0,0,255). Whenever another form loads, the new form would then base its ForeColor property on the first form. Table 5.8 lists the values to use to set the Fore-Color of a form to various common settings.

## General Syntax

```
[form.]ForeColor[= color&]
[control.]ForeColor[=color&]
```

| Argument | Description |
|----------|-------------|
| form | FormName property of the form. No name means the current form |
| control | CtlName property of the control |
| color& | Value of the color defined with hexadecimal number, RBG function, or QBColor function |

Table 5.8 Arguments of the ForeColor property

## Example Syntax

```
Sub Form_Load ()
    If ForeColor = RGB(0,0,0) Then
        BackColor = RGB(255,255,255)
    End If
End Sub
```

## Description

The ForeColor property enables you to change the Windows environment's default settings for the foreground color of a form or control. (The default setting of the ForeColor property of a form is the color chosen in the control panel for the Windows text.) Any time you are changing a form's foreground color, you can check the default background color to make sure the colors are different so that the form will still be visible.

### RGB and QBColor Functions

The ForeColor property of an object returns a hexadecimal value obtained in three different ways. The simplest method is to use the hexadecimal number of the color needed. A valid hexadecimal value ranges from 0 to 16,777,215 (&HFFFFFF). Table 5.9 displays the hexadecimal values of some of the most common colors. You may obtain the hexadecimal value of any of the sixteen standard Windows colors with the QBColor function. RGB functions provide the hexadecimal values for ForeColor expressions. In Table 5.9 the first three columns, labeled red, green, and blue, contain the values for an RGB function. In order to use these values, they appear in the form of

RGB(Red,Green,Blue). To produce customized colors, adjust the values of these three variables. Either setting will work. For example, the ForeColor of a form becomes blue with either the statement ForeColor = RGB(0,0,255) or ForeColor = &HFF000&.

| Color | Red Value | Green Value | Blue Value | Hexadecimal | QBColor |
|-------|-----------|-------------|------------|-------------|---------|
| Black | 0 | 0 | 0 | &H0 | 0 |
| Red | 255 | 0 | 0 | &HFF | 4 |
| Green | 0 | 255 | 0 | &HFF00 | 2 |
| Yellow | 0 | 255 | 255 | &HFFFF | 6 |
| Blue | 0 | 0 | 255 | &HFF000 | 1 |
| Magenta | 255 | 0 | 255 | &HFF00FF | 5 |
| Cyan | 0 | 255 | 255 | &HFFFF00 | 3 |
| White | 255 | 255 | 255 | &HFFFFFF | 15 |
| Light Gray | 192 | 192 | 192 | &H00C0C0C0 | 7 |
| Dark Gray | 128 | 128 | 128 | &H00808080 | 8 |

Table 5.9 Values of common colors in RGB, QBColor, and hexadecimal format

The QBColor function can also be used to return a value for setting the ForeColor property. Call this function with the appropriate integer color number (0-15) as used by programmers in QuickBASIC or other versions of Microsoft BASIC.

See Appendix A, *Visual Basic Language Summary*, for more information about the RGB and QBColor functions.

### The BackColor Property

The BackColor and ForeColor properties of a form interact effectively. Whenever you change one of these properties, you should consider how the new color combination will work. If the foreground and background colors contrast, it will make your program harder to use and will detract from its usefulness. For example, setting the BackColor to blue and the ForeColor to red is objectionable to most users.

## Example

In the Appearance Project at the end of this section, the ForeColor property of the Appear and Warning forms is changed to blue (&HFF000). This property change occurs at design time for both forms to simplify the process. Modifications are also possible at run time.

## Comments

The ForeColor property of a form or control is an effective means of highlighting certain controls to get the user's attention or to make it easier for the user to see something. For instance, red text on an otherwise black and white screen will draw the user's attention to a command button.

# Height Property

## Objects Affected

| | | | | |
|---|---|---|---|---|
| ▶ Check | Clipboard | ▶ Combo | ▶ Command | Dbug |
| ▶ Dir | ▶ Drive | ▶ File | ▶ Form | ▶ Frame |
| ▶ Label | ▶ List | Menu | ▶ Option | ▶ Picture |
| ▶ Printer | ▶ Screen | ▶ Scroll | ▶ Text | Timer |

## Purpose

The Height property defines or determines the vertical size of a form or control on the screen, form, picture box, or Printer object. Forms, Printer objects, and Screen objects are always measured in twips. A control's size uses the units of measurement set in the ScaleMode property of the current form or picture box. The default unit of measurement for a control is twips (1 twip = 1/20 point; 1 inch = 72 points; 1440 twips = 1 inch). Except for the dimensions of the height setting of a Printer object, which is defined at run time, the Height property of an object is available at both design and run time. To manually adjust the Height property of a command button at design time, click on one of its edges and resize it. You can also adjust the height by entering the desired measurement into the properties bar. Table 5.10 summarizes the arguments of the Height property, and Table 5.11 outlines measurement types.

## General Syntax

```
[form.]Height[=height!]
[control.]Height[=height!]
Printer.Height[=height!]
Screen.Height[=height!]
```

| Argument | Description |
|---|---|
| form | FormName of the form |
| control | CtlName of the control |
| Printer | Printer object |
| Screen | Screen object |
| height! | Vertical height of the object |

Table 5.10 Arguments of the Height property

| Measurement | Size |
|---|---|
| Twip | 1440 twips = 1 inch |
| Point | 72 points = 1 inch |
| Pixels | Varies depending on system being used |
| Characters | 12 characters horizontally and 6 vertically |
| Millimeters | 254 millimeters = 1 inch |
| Centimeters | 2.54 centimeters = 1 inch |

Table 5.11 Possible measurement types in relation to 1 inch

## Example Syntax

```
Sub Form_Load
    Form1.Height = (Command1.Height * 5)  'Defines height and width of the form as 5
    Form1.Width = (Command1.Width * 5)    'times the height and width of command button.
End Sub
```

## Description

The Height property of an object measures the vertical height of a form, screen, or picture box. You can enter this value at design time by manually sizing the object with the mouse or by entering the value at the properties bar. You can modify the Height property of a control or form either at design or run time. In contrast, you can only set the Height properties of the Printer and Screen objects at run time. A setting must be between 0 and a maximum value specified by the system itself. Visual Basic automatically adjusts itself to the resolution of the screen or printer. You should ensure that your objects are not too large for the most common 640x480 and 800x600 resolution screens to display.

### Left, Top, Width, and Height Properties

When you create a form or control in Visual Basic, the Left, Top, Width, and Height properties display in the far right side of the properties bar. Figure 5.12 shows what the properties bar looks like on the screen. The first two numbers, separated by a comma, represent the left and top position of the control or form. A form's Height property provides the maximum height for the

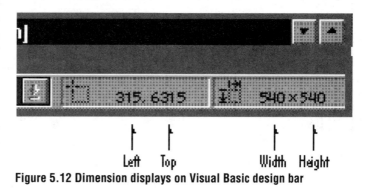

Figure 5.12 Dimension displays on Visual Basic design bar

controls placed on it. Similarly, the value of the Height property of the screen sets the maximum value of a form's property. This varies from system to system, according to the resolution of the monitor. The width and the height of the object appear to the right of these numbers, separated by an "x." If the object is a control, then the numbers shown are in the units of measurement specified by the ScaleMode property of the current form. A form's Height property is measured in twips. This difference allows for variances in the resolution of screens used for each computer. For example, a system with an 800x600 display shows more on the screen than a 640x480 display.

### Screen and Printer

On the basis of the computer screen and printer being used, the Height property returns the height of the screen or page available. The Height property of the screen and printer objects is not available at design time and is read-only at run time.

### Scale Mode

The ScaleMode property of a form directly controls the meaning of the value of the Height property. When the ScaleMode property changes at design time from one measurement to another, Visual Basic recalculates the value of the Height property in this new type of measurement. As the ScaleMode property is not modifiable at run time, the meaning of the value of the Height property does not change while the program is running. For example, no matter what size a command box becomes based on changes in the size of the parent form, the Height property will remain the same.

### ScaleHeight Property

The ScaleHeight property divides the height of a form, picture box, or Printer object into the number of units set in the property. For example, when a form's ScaleHeight property changes to 100 on the properties bar, the height of the form is divided into 100 equal units. (Changing the ScaleHeight property of the form to a new value does not change the actual size of the control.) This unit changes in size as the form's height changes. In this way, increasing the height of the form has the effect of increasing the size of one of these units (the height remains divided into 100 units that are now larger in size). These units define the upper and lower limits of the possible height of controls on this form. With the Move statement, the size of the control adjusts based on the changes in height to the form. For example, a Resize event might adjust the Height property

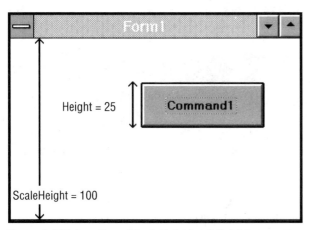

**Figure 5.13 Interaction of ScaleHeight and Height properties**

of a command box of a form by triggering a move statement that always ensures that the command box is one-fourth the size of the form. In this example the ScaleHeight property of the form is 100, and the Height property of the Command1 command button is 25 (one-fourth the height of the form). Figure 5.13 displays this concept visually.

### Measurements in the CONSTANT.TXT File

The CONSTANT.TXT file found in the main Visual Basic Directory, contains the suggested constant values to use in your Visual Basic applications. In order to use the CONSTANT.TXT file, load it into the project's global module. To do this, open Visual Basic's Project window and double-click on the global module. This will load the global module into the Code window. Then open Visual Basic's Code menu and choose the Load Text option. This brings up a dialog box. Select the CONSTANT.TXT file and click on the Merge button. This will read the file into the global module. The following listing shows the applicable variables in the CONSTANT.TXT file:

```
' ScaleMode (form, picture box, Printer)
Global Const USER = 0              ' 0 – User
Global Const TWIPS = 1             ' 1 – Twip
Global Const POINTS = 2            ' 2 – Point
Global Const PIXELS = 3            ' 3 – Pixel
Global Const CHARACTERS = 4        ' 4 – Character
Global Const INCHES = 5            ' 5 – Inch
Global Const MILLIMETERS = 6       ' 6 – Millimeter
Global Const CENTIMETERS = 7       ' 7 – Centimeter
```

## Example

In the Appearance project at the end of this section, set the Height property of the forms and controls at design time. This is done either by dragging the control's edges with the mouse, or by entering the value into the properties bar.

## Comments

Remember that changes to the ScaleHeight property of a form only alter the value of the Height property of a control and not the actual height.

# Icon Property

## Objects Affected

| Check | Clipboard | Combo | ▶ Command | Dbug |
|-------|-----------|-------|-----------|-------|
| Dir | Drive | File | ▶ Form | Frame |
| Label | List | Menu | Option | Picture |
| Printer | Screen | Scroll | Text | Timer |

## Purpose

The Icon property defines the icon displayed on the screen when a form is in a minimized window state. This property is only available for a form and the file must be in the standard icon format (ICO Extension), such as the format used for the icons that ship with Visual Basic. The Icon property of a newly created form is automatically set to the default Visual Basic icon. By using different icons for different forms, each element of the program displays in another way. For example, a communications program might use a telephone icon to represent the program when it is in minimized format. An excellent choice to use when the communications program dialing the number in the background might be attached to the phone with the receiver off the hook.

## General Syntax

[form.]Icon

| Argument | Description |
|----------|-------------|
| form | FormName of the form |

Table 5.12 Argument of the Icon property

## Example Syntax

```
Sub Form_Resize ()
    If WindowState = 0 Then                           'Checks if form is minimized
        If Form1.Caption = "Dialing Number" Then     'Checks if form reads this text
            Form1.Icon = LoadPicture("\VB\ICONS\COMM\PHONE04.ICO"  'Changes icon
                                                                    'to open phone
        ElseIf Form1.Caption = "Hanging Up" Then     'Checks if form reads this text
            Form1.Icon = LoadPicture("\VB\ICONS\COMM\NET3.ICO")   'Changes icon
                                                                    'to knife cutting
        Else
            Form1.Icon = LoadPicture("\VB\ICONS\COMM\PHONE01.ICO") 'Changes icon to
                                                                    'phone
        End If
    End If
End Sub
```

## Description

A form's Icon property defines the default icon to display when a form appears minimized on the screen. Table 5.12 explains the Form argument of the Icon property. At creation time, a form's Icon property defaults to the Visual Basic Icon. A form's Icon property is modifiable either at design or run time. In this way, you may temporarily change an icon at run time to reflect changes in the functioning of the program. In the example above, the main form of a communications program's Icon property changes for different functions. An open phone symbol appears for a dialing operation, a knife cutting a cable for a phone hang up operation, and a phone for an inactive program.

### Design Time Setting

At design time, you can choose an icon on the properties bar. Select the Icon property and click on the ellipsis (...) on the right side of the settings bar. Use the file list box to find the directory containing the icon you want, and then select the icon. Any of the icons included with the Visual Basic package will work well for this property. For a listing of the icons that came with Visual Basic, look in the Microsoft *Visual Basic Programmer's Guide,* pages 400-49.

### The LoadPicture Function

Use the LoadPicture function to change the Icon property of a form at run time. In the example above, the original setting for the form's Icon property is the PHONE01.ICO icon. This displays if the text on the communications program is neither Dialing Number nor Hanging Up.

## Example

In the Appearance project at the end of this section, the Icon property of the Appear form begins as PHONE01.ICO. This is the icon that appears at the bottom of the screen when the dialer is not running. The minimize button is on the Appear form so that the user may take a look at this default icon.

Pressing the Dial command button activates the DialCommand_Timer, which uses the LoadPicture function to change the Appearance form's Icon property to the PHONE04.ICO icon. The program then minimizes the Appear form and the user sees an icon with the receiver off the hook at the bottom of the computer screen.

After pressing the Cancel command button, the Icon property of the Appear form becomes the former icon. This is a graphic means of indicating the completion of the dialing operation. In this way, the icons constantly inform the user what operations (if any) are taking place.

## Comments

Do not forget to give every form that can be minimized a different kind of icon rather than leaving the default icon. This enables the user to differentiate between the icons at the bottom of the screen.

# Left Property

## Objects Affected

| | | | | |
|---|---|---|---|---|
| ▶ Check | Clipboard | ▶ Combo | ▶ Command | Dbug |
| ▶ Dir | ▶ Drive | ▶ File | ▶ Form | ▶ Frame |
| ▶ Label | ▶ List | Menu | ▶ Option | ▶ Picture |
| Printer | Screen | ▶ Scroll | ▶ Text | Timer |

## Purpose

The Left property defines or determines the distance of a form or control from the left edge of the form or picture box. A control's distance measures in the units indicated by the ScaleMode property of the current form or picture box. For forms, this distance is always measured in twips. The default unit of measurement for controls is twips (1 twip = 1/20 point; 1 inch = 72 points; 1440 twips = 1 inch). The Left property of an object is available either at design and run time. For example, the Left property of a form on a screen adjusts by clicking on the titlebar of the form and moving it or inputting the exact desired measurement in the properties bar. Tables 5.13 and 5.14 summarize the different arguments of the Left property and the possible measurement types.

## General Syntax

```
[form.]Left[=left!]
[control.]Left[=left!]
```

| Argument | Description |
|---|---|
| form | FormName of the form |
| control | CtlName of the control |
| left! | Horizontal left distance of the object |

Table 5.13 Arguments of the Left property

| Measurement | Size |
|---|---|
| Twip | 1440 twips = 1 inch |
| Point | 72 points = 1 inch |
| Pixels | Varies depending on system being used |
| Characters | 12 characters horizontally and 6 vertically |
| Millimeters | 254 millimeter = 1 inch |
| Centimeters | 2.54 centimeters = 1 inch |

Table 5.14 Possible measurement types in relation to 1 inch

## Example Syntax

```
Sub LeftDistance (Ctl As Control,FormName As Form)'New function LeftDistance
    'All of the following values equal one inch    'Note for programmer
    Select Case FormName.ScaleMode               'Based on Control's ScaleMode
        Case 0                                    'User-Defined Measurement
            Ctl.Left = Ctl.ScaleLeft              'Distance equals ScaleLeft
        Case 1                                    'Measure in twips
            Ctl.Left = 1440
        Case 2                                    'Measure in Points
            Ctl.Left = 72
        Case 3                                    'Measure in Pixels
            Ctl.Left = 1000
        Case 4                                    'Measure in Characters
            Ctl.Left = 12
        Case 5                                    'Measure in Inches
            Ctl.Left = 1
        Case 6                                    'Measure in Millimeters
            Ctl.Left = 254
        Case 7                                    'Measure in Centimeters
            Ctl.Left = 2.54
    End Select
End Sub
```

## Description

The Left property of an object measures the horizontal distance from the left of a form, screen, or picture box. You can enter this value at design time by manually moving the object with the mouse, or by entering the value at the properties bar. You can modify the Left property of a control or form either at design time or at run time. A setting must be between 0 and a maximum value specified by the system itself. Visual Basic automatically adjusts itself to the resolution of the screen. You should ensure that your objects are not too far from the edges for the most common 640x480 and 800x600 resolution screens to display.

The example syntax outlines a Sub function named LeftDistance, which sets a control's distance from the left side of the screen. This change references the ScaleMode property of the form. This is another excellent example of the use of a generic function that applies to more than one control in a program.

### Left, Top, Width, and Height Properties

When you create a form or control in Visual Basic, the Left, Top, Width, and Height properties display in the far right side of the properties bar. See the discussion of the properties bar in the Height property entry in this chapter. A form's Left property is measured in twips.

### The ScaleMode Property

The ScaleMode property of a form directly controls the meaning of the value of the Left property. When the ScaleMode property changes from one measurement to another at design time, Visual Basic recalculates the value of the Left property in this new type of measurement. As the ScaleMode property is not modifiable at run time, the meaning of the value of the Left property does not change while the program is running. For example, no matter what size a command box becomes based on changes in the size of the parent form, the Left property will remain the same.

### Measurements in the CONSTANT.TXT File

The CONSTANT.TXT file, found in the main Visual Basic Directory, contains the suggested constant values to use in your Visual Basic applications. In order to use the CONSTANT.TXT file, load it into the project's global module. To do this, open Visual Basic's Project window and double-click on the global module. This will load the global module into the Code window. Then open Visual Basic's Code menu, and choose the Load Text option. This brings up a dialog box. Select the CONSTANT.TXT file and click on the Merge button. This will read the file into the global module. The following listing displays the applicable variables in the CONSTANT.TXT file.

```
' ScaleMode (form, picture box, Printer)
Global Const USER = 0              ' 0 - User
Global Const TWIPS = 1            ' 1 - Twip
Global Const POINTS = 2          ' 2 - Point
Global Const PIXELS = 3          ' 3 - Pixel
Global Const CHARACTERS = 4      ' 4 - Character
Global Const INCHES = 5          ' 5 - Inch
Global Const MILLIMETERS = 6     ' 6 - Millimeter
Global Const CENTIMETERS = 7     ' 7 - Centimeter
```

### Example

In the Appearance project at the end of this section, set the Left property of the forms and controls at design time. This is done either by dragging the control's edges with the mouse, or by entering the value into the properties bar.

### Comments

Remember that changes to the ScaleLeft property of a form only alter the value of the Left property of a control and not the actual distance.

# MousePointer Property

## Objects Affected

| | | | | |
|---|---|---|---|---|
| ▶ Check | Clipboard | ▶ Combo | ▶ Command | Dbug |
| ▶ Dir | ▶ Drive | ▶ File | ▶ Form | ▶ Frame |
| ▶ Label | ▶ List | Menu | ▶ Option | ▶ Picture |
| Printer | ▶ Screen | ▶ Scroll | ▶ Text | Timer |

## Purpose

The MousePointer property of a form or control indicates what cursor pointer to display when the mouse pointer is over the object. Set this property either at design time or run time. A mouse pointer can take many forms including arrow, hourglass, and I-beam. Normally, the type of cursor chosen bases its setting on the present function of the program running. For example, the Click event of a command button changes the MousePointer property of the current form to an hourglass to tell the user to wait. When this activity is over, restore the MousePointer property. In this way, you can alert the user when there is activity taking place that forces the user to wait. Table 5.15 shows the different settings of the MousePointer property.

## General Syntax

```
[form.]MousePointer[=setting%]
[control.]MousePointer[=setting%]
Screen.MousePointer[=setting%]
```

| Value | Mouse Pointer Cursor |
| --- | --- |
| 0 | Assumes the outline of the control |
| 1 | Arrow |
| 2 | Cross-hair pointer |
| 3 | Text entry I-beam |
| 4 | Square within a square |
| 5 | Four-directional cross with arrows facing up, down, left, and right |
| 6 | Two-directional arrow pointing diagonally (upper arrow to the right and lower arrow to the left) |
| 7 | Two-directional arrow pointing up and down |
| 8 | Two-directional arrow pointing diagonally (upper arrow to the left and lower arrow to the right) |
| 9 | Two-directional arrow pointing left and right |
| 10 | Arrow pointing up |
| 11 | Hourglass |
| 12 | No drop |

Table 5.15 Possible values for the MousePointer property

## Example Syntax

```
Sub Command1_GotFocus ()
    Form1.MousePointer = 11        'Changes the mousepointer to an hourglass
End Sub

Sub Command1_LostFocus ()
    Form1.MousePointer = 0         'Makes the mousepointer of the form an arrow
End Sub
```

## Description

The MousePointer property determines what cursor to display on the screen when the mouse pointer is over a control or form. Set this property for either the entire form or for individual controls. Any form or control may have its MousePointer property changed at run time. When you modify the Screen object's MousePointer property, the mouse pointer modifies for all the objects on the screen. When you modify a form's MousePointer property, any special settings for individual controls on the form similarly alter. To restore the settings for individual forms or controls, set the MousePointer property of the screen or form to 0. For example, when the user clicks the command button labeled Print, the mouse pointer of the screen becomes an hourglass. The cursor will remain an hourglass until the property restores to the default value of 0.

### Mouse Pointer Types in the CONSTANT.TXT File

The CONSTANT.TXT file, found in the main Visual Basic Directory, contains the suggested constant values to use in your Visual Basic applications. In order to use the CONSTANT.TXT file, you must load it into the project's global module. To do this, you open Visual Basic's Project window and double-click on the global module. This will load the global module into the Code window. Then open Visual Basic's Code menu, and choose the Load Text option. This brings up a dialog box. Select the CONSTANT.TXT file and click on the Merge button. This will read the file into the global module. The following listing displays the applicable variables in the CONSTANT.TXT file.

```
' MousePointer (form, controls)
Global Const DEFAULT = 0           ' 0 - Default
Global Const ARROW = 1             ' 1 - Arrow
Global Const CROSSHAIR = 2         ' 2 - Cross
Global Const IBEAM = 3             ' 3 - I-Beam
Global Const ICON_POINTER = 4      ' 4 - Icon
Global Const SIZE_POINTER = 5      ' 5 - Size
Global Const SIZE_NE_SW = 6        ' 6 - Size NE SW
Global Const SIZE_N_S = 7          ' 7 - Size N S
Global Const SIZE_NW_SE = 8        ' 8 - Size NW SE
Global Const SIZE_W_E = 9          ' 9 - Size W E
Global Const UP_ARROW = 10         ' 10 - Up Arrow
Global Const HOURGLASS = 11        ' 11 - Hourglass
Global Const NO_DROP = 12          ' 12 - No drop
```

### Outline Pointer

Every control begins with the outline of itself as the default mouse pointer. This mouse pointer only appears on the screen during a mouse operation such as a drag operation. You can use this outline to guide the user during a drag operation. Since this property is the default value for a control, it is not necessary to change it for a drag operation. Figure 5.14 shows what the outline mouse pointer looks like.

### Arrow Pointer

One of the most familiar mouse pointers is the left-pointing arrow cursor. Figure 5.15 shows how the arrow mouse pointer appears on the screen. This is the cursor most frequently used in Windows to select items and activate programs. When a form's

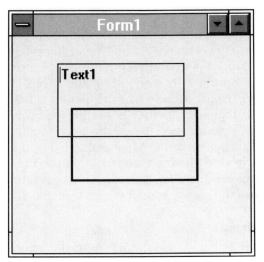

Figure 5.14 Outline mouse pointer

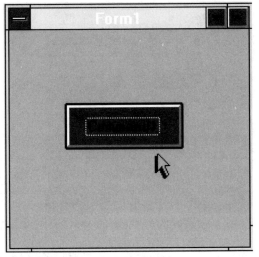

Figure 5.15 Arrow mouse pointer

MousePointer property has this value, the user can easily select command buttons, check boxes, and option boxes by placing the arrow's small point directly on the desired object. The horizontal and vertical scroll bars also function well with the arrow mouse pointer. This mouse cursor permits the user either to click on the bar to change the position of the selector box, or to click and drag the selector box to the desired location. Similarly, when the arrow is over a drive list box, directory list box, or combo box, it serves as a selector cursor.

### I-Beam Cursor

The I-beam cursor gives the user a guide in selecting and entering text on the screen. Figure 5.16 shows how the I-Beam cursor appears over a text box. The I-beam mouse pointer allows easy manipulation of the different points within a text box on the screen. By changing to this cursor, the cursor on the screen is easier to move in between different characters on the screen for editing. Additionally, the I-beam mouse pointer locates quickly in a particular point of the text and then drags over the selected text just as easily as for the arrow mouse pointer. In this case, the I-beam mouse pointer is a better choice than the arrow mouse pointer, because the I-beam mouse pointer works best with text.

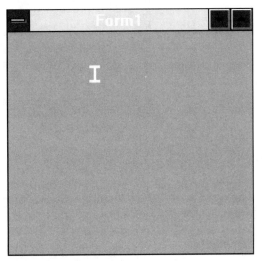

Figure 5.16 I-beam cursor

**Figure 5.17 Hourglass mouse pointer**

### Hourglass Cursor

An hourglass is also a familiar symbol to the Windows user. Figure 5.17 shows an hourglass cursor. This cursor normally reminds the user that the computer is working on the effects of the user's last action, and that the user must wait before interacting further with the program. When you plan to stop the user from taking further actions, change the MousePointer property of the screen to the hourglass cursor. In this case, the cursor will not change no matter which form or control the mouse pointer moves over.

### Sizing Cursors

All of the sizing cursors, which have the values between five and nine, are also familiar to Windows users. Each of these cursors displays in Figure 5.18. These cursors appear when the user changes the size of a window on the screen. Each cursor consists of arrows pointing toward the parts of the window that the window's resizing changes.

**Figure 5.18 Mouse sizing cursors**

### Example

In the Appearance project at the end of this section, the MousePointer property of the screen changes when the user clicks either the Dial command button on the Appear form or the Redial command button on the Warning form. This signifies to the user that no other actions may take place while the dial operation is underway. The MousePointer property of the screen overrides the settings of the various controls of both the Appear and Warning forms. Until the MousePointer property returns to 0, the only MousePointer that displays is the hourglass.

At design time, the default settings of the command buttons of each form and the ListBox of the Appear form are changed to the arrow.

### Comments

The hourglass mouse pointer is an excellent way to indicate to the user that the computer is busy, and that the user must wait before going on to the next task.

# Top Property

## Objects Affected

| | | | | |
|---|---|---|---|---|
| ▶ Check | Clipboard | ▶ Combo | ▶ Command | Dbug |
| ▶ Dir | ▶ Drive | ▶ File | ▶ Form | ▶ Frame |
| ▶ Label | ▶ List | Menu | ▶ Option | ▶ Picture |
| Printer | Screen | ▶ Scroll | ▶ Text | Timer |

## Purpose

The Top property defines or determines the distance of a form or control from the top edge of the form or picture box. A control's distance measures in the units indicated by the ScaleMode property of the current form or picture box. This distance is always in twips for forms. The default unit of measurement is twips (1 twip = 1/20 point; 1 inch = 72 points; 1440 twips = 1 inch). The Top property of an object is available both at design time and run time. For example, to maintain a text box's top distance from the edge of the form at one-eighth the distance, the Resize event uses the Move method to always place it at one-eighth of that distance. Tables 5.16 and 5.17 summarize the different arguments of the Top property and the possible measurement types.

## General Syntax

```
[form.]Top[=top!]
[control.]Top[=top!]
```

| Argument | Description |
|---|---|
| form | FormName of the form |
| control | CtlName of the control |
| top! | Vertical top distance of the object |

**Table 5.16 Arguments of the Top property**

| Measurement | Size |
|---|---|
| Twip | 1440 twips = 1 inch |
| Point | 72 points = 1 inch |
| Pixels | Varies depending on system being used |
| Characters | 12 characters horizontally and 6 vertically |
| Millimeters | 254 millimeters = 1 inch |
| Centimeters | 2.54 centimeters = 1 inch |

**Table 5.17 Possible measurement types in relation to 1 inch**

## Example Syntax

```
Sub ResetForm (FormName As Form)
    If FormName.ScaleMode <> 0 Then          'Checks if ScaleMode is set to user-defined
        FormName.Top = 1                      'Form's distance from top placed at 1
        FormName.Left = 1                     'Form's distance from left placed at 1
    Else
        FormName.Top = FormName.ScaleTop      'Form's distance from left and top made equal
        FormName.Left = FormName.ScaleLeft    'to the value of the ScaleLeft &
                                              'ScaleTop properties
    End If
End Sub
```

## Description

The Top property of an object measures the vertical distance from the top of a form, screen, or picture box. You can enter this value at design time by manually moving the object with the mouse or by entering the value at the properties bar. The Top property of a control or form is modifiable either at design time or run time. A setting must be between 0 and a maximum value specified by the system itself. Visual Basic automatically adjusts itself to the resolution of the screen. You should ensure that your objects are not too far from the edges for the most common 640x480 and 800x600 resolution screens to display.

The example syntax outlines a Sub function named ResetForm, which sets a form's distance from the left and top sides of the screen. If the ScaleMode property is user-defined, the Left and Top properies are set to the values of the ScaleLeft and ScaleTop properties. This is another excellent example of the use of a generic function to apply to all of the forms in a program.

### Left, Top, Width, and Height properties

When you create a form or control in Visual Basic, the Left, Top, Width, and Height properties display in the far right side of the properties bar. See the discussion of the properties bar in the Height property entry in this chapter. A form's Top property begins with a measurement in twips.

### The Scale Mode Property

The ScaleMode property of a form directly controls the meaning of the value of the Top property. When this property changes at design time from one measurement to another, Visual Basic recalculates the value of the Top property in this new type of measurement. As the ScaleMode property is not modifiable at run time, the meaning of the value of the Top property does not change while the program is running. For example, no matter what size a command box becomes based on changes in the size of the parent form, the Top property will remain the same.

### Measurements in the CONSTANT.TXT File

The CONSTANT.TXT file, found in the main Visual Basic Directory, contains the suggested constant values to use in your Visual Basic applications. In order to use the CONSTANT.TXT file, you must load it into the project's global module. To do this, open Visual Basic's Project window and double-click on the global module. This will load the global module into the Code window. Then open Visual Basic's Code menu and choose the Load Text option. This brings up a dialog box. Select the CONSTANT.TXT file and click on the Merge button. This will read the file into the global module. The following listing displays the applicable variables in the CONSTANT.TXT file.

```
' ScaleMode (form, picture box, Printer)
Global Const USER = 0          ' 0 - User
Global Const TWIPS = 1         ' 1 - Twip
Global Const POINTS = 2        ' 2 - Point
Global Const PIXELS = 3        ' 3 - Pixel
Global Const CHARACTERS = 4    ' 4 - Character
Global Const INCHES = 5        ' 5 - Inch
Global Const MILLIMETERS = 6   ' 6 - Millimeter
Global Const CENTIMETERS = 7   ' 7 - Centimeter
```

## Example

In the Appearance project at the end of this section, set the Top property of the forms and controls at design time. This is done either by dragging the control's edges with the mouse, or by entering the value into the properties bar.

## Comments

Remember that changes to the ScaleTop property of a form only alter the value of the Top property of a control and not the actual distance.

# Visible Property

## Objects Affected

| | | | | |
|---|---|---|---|---|
| ▶ Check | Clipboard | ▶ Combo | ▶ Command | Dbug |
| ▶ Dir | ▶ Drive | ▶ File | ▶ Form | ▶ Frame |
| ▶ Label | ▶ List | ▶ Menu | ▶ Option | ▶ Picture |
| Printer | Screen | ▶ Scroll | ▶ Text | Timer |

## Purpose

The Visible property defines whether a form or control is visible to the user. Many programs start by loading all of their different elements into memory. A temporarily unnecessary form is hidden by setting the Visible property to False (0). This reduces the amount of time necessary for bringing forms up on the screen later. Tables 5.18 and 5.19 summarize the arguments of the Visible property.

## General Syntax

```
[form.]Visible[=boolean%]
[control.]Visible[=boolean%]
```

| Argument | Description |
|---|---|
| form | FormName property of the form |
| control | CtlName property of the control |
| boolean% | Indicates whether the object is visible or invisible to the user |

**Table 5.18 Arguments of the Visible property**

| Boolean | Effect |
|---|---|
| 0 | Removes the object from the view of the user |
| -1 | (Default) Makes an object visible by the user |

**Table 5.19 Available settings for the Visible property**

## Example Syntax

```
Sub Form_Load ()
    Load "AddressBook"            'Places an invisible form in memory
    Personal_Data.Show            'Places a visible form in memory
    Personal_Data.Visible = 0     'Changes the form's visible property to
                                  'false which removes
End Sub                          'it from the users view.

Sub Change (ControlName As Form, Control) 'New function with Control as argument
    If ControlName.Visible = 0 Then       'Checks if the indicated control  is visible
        ControlName.Visible = -1          'Makes indicated control visible
    Else
        ControlName.Visible = 0           'Makes indicated control invisible
    End If
End Sub
```

## Description

The Visible property lets you show or hide a control or form on the screen. There are two possible settings for the Visible property of a form or control: True (-1) and False (0). A form or control with a False Visible property disappears from the sight of the user. While its Visible property is False, a form or control remains in memory and quickly returns to the screen when needed. When the Visible property of a form or control is True (-1), the form or control is visible to the user. A Show method, Hide method, or Load statement directly affects this value; see the next descriptions for details. In the example syntax, the Form_Load event changes the Visible property of the Personal_Data text box to False.

### The Show Method

When a Show method brings a form up on the screen, it automatically sets the Visible property of the form to True. The Show method loads the form into memory if necessary. Setting a form's Visual property directly also loads the form into memory and makes it visible. The main difference is that the Show method has two modes of operation. A form opened with the Modeless Show method will behave in the same way as a form opened by setting the Visible property directly. However, if a form loads with a Modal Show method, then the form has full control of the program until hidden or unloaded from memory. Any code that follows a Modal Show method executes only after the hiding or closing of the Modal form.

### The Hide Method

The Hide method changes the Visible property of a form to False and removes it from view. Unlike the Show method, this element of the language is indistinguishable from the Visible property if applied to a form. Unlike the Hide and Show methods, the Visible property is available for either a form or a control. This makes it flexible for more generic functions. In the example function above, any kind of control or form can be made visible or invisible.

### The Load Statement

A Load statement brings a form into memory and sets its Visible property to False. Using this statement differs from setting the Visible property directly in only one way. The Visible property works on both controls and forms and the Load statement will only work on forms. Table 5.20 outlines the different ways that the Hide method, Show method, and Load statement interact with the Visible property.

| Element | Effect on | Visible property | Differences |
|---|---|---|---|
| Show method | Changes | Visible property to True (-1) | Modal mode |
| Hide method | Changes | Visible property to False (0) | Affects only forms |
| Load statement | Changes | Visible property to False (0) | Affects only forms |

Table 5.20 The effects and differences of various language elements on the Visible property

## Example

In the Appearance project at the end of this section, the Visible property removes the Results label box from view. This keeps the contents of the Caption property available for reference for the next time that the next pressing of the ReDial command button. In this way, the Results label box disappears from the user's sight to prevent confusion about what is presently taking place in the program. If the Results label box were not hidden in this fashion, then the user might be confused with the contents of that box when it is no longer needed.

## Comments

The Visible property will work on either a form or a control. For this reason, it is a more flexible element of the language than the Hide and Show methods, which may only be used on forms.

# Width Property

## Objects Affected

| | | | |
|---|---|---|---|
| ▶ Check | Clipboard | ▶ Combo | ▶ Command | Dbug |
| ▶ Dir | ▶ Drive | ▶ File | ▶ Form | ▶ Frame |
| ▶ Label | ▶ List | Menu | ▶ Option | ▶ Picture |
| ▶ Printer | ▶ Screen | ▶ Scroll | ▶ Text | Timer |

## Purpose

The Width property defines or determines the horizontal size of a form or control on the screen, form, picture box, or Printer object. Forms, Printer objects, and Screen objects are always measured in twips. A control's size uses the units of measure indicated by the ScaleMode property of the current form or picture box. The default unit of measurement for a control is twips (1 twip = 1/20 point; 1 inch = 72 points; 1440 twips = 1 inch). Except for the dimensions of the width setting of a Printer object, which is defined at run time, the Width property of an object is available at both design time and run time. To manually adjust the Width property of a picture box at design time, click on one of its edges and resize it by dragging. You can also adjust the width by entering the desired measurement into the properties bar. Table 5.21 summarizes the different arguments of the Width property; Table 5.22 summarizes the possible measurement settings of the Width property.

## General Syntax

```
[form.]Width[=width!]
[control.]Width[=width!]
Printer.Width[=width!]
Screen.Width[=width!]
```

| Argument | Description |
|---|---|
| form | FormName of the form |
| control | CtlName of the control |
| Printer | Printer object |
| Screen | Screen object |
| width! | Vertical width of the object |

Table 5.21 Arguments of the Width property

| Measurement | Size |
|---|---|
| Twip | 1440 twips = 1 inch |
| Point | 72 points = 1 inch |
| Pixels | Varies depending on system being used |
| Characters | 12 characters horizontally and 6 vertically |
| Millimeters | 254 millimeters = 1 inch |
| Centimeters | 2.54 centimeters = 1 inch |

**Table 5.22 Possible measurement types in relation to 1 inch**

## Example Syntax

```
Sub Form_Resize
    Form.1.Width = (Picture1.Width * 2)    'Width and height of form are made
    Form1.Height = (Picture1.Height * 2)   'twice the size of the width and height
    Picture1.Top = ((Form1.Height / 2) - ((Picture1.Height) / 2)) 'of the
                                            'Picture1 picture box. Picture
    Picture1.Left = ((Form1.Width / 2) - ((Picture1.Width) / 2))   'appears in
                                            'center of the form.
End Sub
```

## Description

The Width property of an object measures the horizontal width of a form, screen, or picture box. You can enter this value at design time by manually moving the object with the mouse, or by entering the value at the properties bar. You can modify the Width property of a control at run time or design time. In contrast, you can set the Width properties of both the Printer and

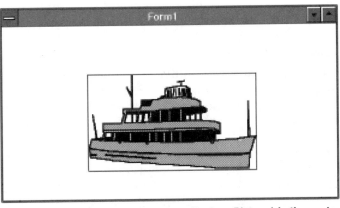

**Figure 5.19  Form1's Width property displays Picture1 in the center the form**

Screen objects at run time. A setting must be between 0 and a maximum value specified by the system itself. Visual Basic automatically adjusts itself to the resolution of the screen or printer. You should ensure that your objects are not too large for the most common 640x480 and 800x600 resolution screens to display.

In the example syntax, the Form1 form's Width property is twice the size of the setting of the Picture1 picture box. This demonstrates the ways in which this property serves as a basis for changes to the measurements of other objects. Figure 5.19 shows what this example might look like.

### The Left, Top, Width, and Height Properties

When you create a form or control in Visual Basic, the Left, Top, Width, and Height properties display in the far right side of the properties bar. See the discussion of the properties bar in the Height property entry in this chapter. A form's Width property begins with a value that represents a measurement in twips.

### Screen and Printer

On the basis of the computer screen and printer being used, the Width property returns the width of the screen or page available. With this property, the code determines the amount of usable space available on the printed page or screen. The Width property of the Screen and Printer objects is not available at design time and is read-only at run time. For this reason, the value of this property normally serves as a reference and is not changeable at run time.

### Scale Mode

The ScaleMode property of a form directly controls the meaning of the value of the Width property. When the ScaleMode property changes at design time from one measurement to another, Visual Basic recalculates the value of the Width property in this new type of measurement. As the ScaleMode property is not modifiable at run time, the meaning of the value of the Width property does not change while the program is running. For example, no matter what size a command box becomes based on changes in the size of the parent form, the Width property will remain the same.

### The ScaleWidth Property

The ScaleWidth property divides the width of a form, picture box, or Printer object into the number of units set in the property. When a form's ScaleWidth property changes to 100 on the properties bar, the width of the form is divided into 100 equal units. (Changing the ScaleWidth property of the form to a new value does not change the actual size of the control.) This unit changes in size as the form's height changes. In this way, increasing the width of the form has the effect of increasing the size of one of these units. (The width remains divided into 100 units that are now larger in size.) These units define the upper and lower limit of the possible width of controls on this form. With the Move statement, the size of the control adjusts based on the changes in width to the form. For example, a Resize event might adjust the Width property of a command box of a form by triggering a move statement that always ensures that the command box is one-fourth the size of the form. In this example, the ScaleWidth property of the form is 100, and the Width property of the Command1 command button is 25 (one-fourth the width of the form). Figure 5.20 displays this concept visually.

### Measurements in the CONSTANT.TXT File

The CONSTANT.TXT file, found in the main Visual Basic Directory, contains the suggested constant values to use in your Visual Basic applications. In order to use the

CONSTANT.TXT file, you must load it into the project's global module. To do this, open Visual Basic's Project window and double-click on the global module. This will load the global module into the Code window. Then open Visual Basic's Code menu and choose the Load Text option. This brings up a dialog box. Select the CONSTANT.TXT file and click on the Merge button. This will read the file into the global module. The following listing displays the applicable variables in the CONSTANT.TXT file.

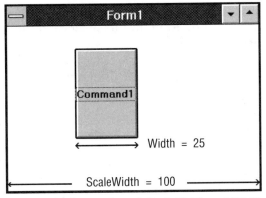

**Figure 5.20 Interaction of ScaleWidth and Width properties**

```
' ScaleMode (form, picture box,
Printer)
Global Const USER = 0          ' 0 — User
Global Const TWIPS = 1         ' 1 — Twip
Global Const POINTS = 2        ' 2 — Point
Global Const PIXELS = 3        ' 3 — Pixel
Global Const CHARACTERS = 4    ' 4 — Character
Global Const INCHES = 5        ' 5 — Inch
Global Const MILLIMETERS = 6   ' 6 — Millimeter
Global Const CENTIMETERS = 7   ' 7 — Centimeter
```

## Example

In the Appearance project at the end of this section, set the Width property of the forms and controls at design time. This is done either by dragging the control's edges with the mouse or by entering the value into the properties bar.

## Comments

Remember that changes to the ScaleWidth property of a form only alter the value of the Width property of a control and not the actual width.

# The Appearance Project

## Project Overview

The Appearance project demonstrates the properties of the Visual Basic language that influence the appearance of a program's forms and controls. By assembling the different forms and functions of this project, you will learn how to change the appearance of forms and controls on the screen. This project has three sections. The first section assembles the Appear form and its associated functions. The second section constructs the Warning form and its associated functions. The third section discusses how the project works.

## Assembling the Project: The Appear Form

1. Make a new form (The Appear form) with the objects and properties in Table 5.23.

| Object | Property | Setting |
|---|---|---|
| Form | BackColor | RGB(192,192,192), &H00C0C0C0 |
| | BorderStyle | 1 - Fixed single |
| | Caption | Appearance project |
| | ForeColor | RGB(0,0,255), &HFF000 |
| | FormName | Appear |
| | Icon | ..\VB\ICONS\COMM\PHONE01.ICO |
| | MaxButton | False |
| Listbox | CtlName | PhoneList |
| | MousePointer | 1 |
| | Sorted | True |
| Command button | Caption | Dial |
| | CtlName | Dial |
| | MousePointer | 1 |
| Command button | Caption | Exit |
| | CtlName | Exit_Program |
| | MousePointer | 1 |
| Timer | CtlName | DialCommand |
| | Enabled | False |
| | Interval | 1000 |

**Table 5.23 Settings for the Appear Form in the Appearance project**

2. Size the objects on the screen, as shown in Figure 5.21. Figure 5.22 shows what the Appear form will look like when running.

3. Enter the following code in the Form_Load event subroutine. This code adds the items to the phone list and disables the timer.

```
Sub Form_Load ()
    DialCommand.Enabled = 0
    PhoneList.AddItem "John Doe          517-555-1212"
    PhoneList.AddItem "Jane Doe          908-789-8901"
    PhoneList.AddItem "John Smith        313-531-7909"
    PhoneList.AddItem "Allen Goodson     206-908-8973"
End Sub
```

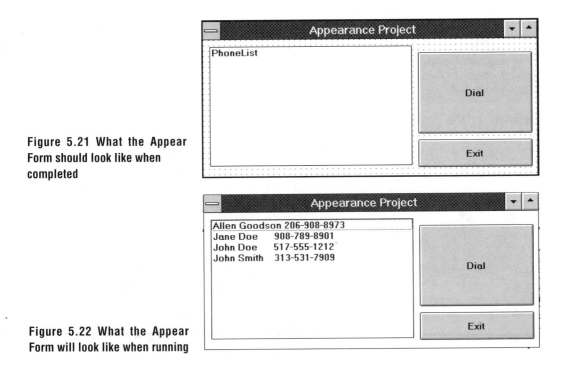

**Figure 5.21 What the Appear Form should look like when completed**

**Figure 5.22 What the Appear Form will look like when running**

4. Enter the following code in the Dial_Click event subroutine. This code is executed when the user clicks the Dial command button. The mouse pointer is changed to an hourglass, the caption is modified to tell the user which number is dialing, and the DialCommand dialer is initiated.

```
Sub Dial_Click ()
    Screen.MousePointer = 11
    Appear.Caption = "Dialing " + PhoneList.List(PhoneList.ListIndex)
    DialCommand.Enabled = -1
End Sub
```

5. Enter the following code in the DialCommand_Timer event subroutine. This code changes the minimize icon of the form and then minimizes the form. The Warning form is displayed as a modal form, and the Caption is restored to the original Appearance project. Finally, the screen's mouse pointer is returned to the default value and the DialCommand timer is disabled.

```
Sub DialCommand_Timer ()
    Appear.Icon = LoadPicture("\VB\ICONS\COMM\PHONE04.ICO")
    Appear.WindowState = 1
    Warning.Show 1
    Appear.Caption = "Appearance Project"
    Screen.MousePointer = 0
    DialCommand.Enabled = 0
End Sub
```

6. Enter the following code in the Exit_Program_Click event subroutine. This closes all forms and exits.

```
Sub Exit_Program_Click ()
    End
End Sub
```

## Assembling the Project: Warning Form

1. Make a new form (the Warning form) with the objects and properties in Table 5.24.

| Object | Property | Setting |
|---|---|---|
| Form | Caption | Warning |
| | ForeColor | &H80000008& |
| | FormName | Warning |
| | ControlBox | False |
| | MinButton | False |
| | MaxButton | False |
| | BorderStyle | 0 - None |
| Label | Caption | "" |
| | CtlName | Dial |
| Label | Caption | "" |
| | CtlName | Results |
| Command button | Caption | ReDial |
| | CtlName | ReDial |
| | MousePointer | 1 |
| Command button | Caption | Cancel |
| | CtlName | Cancel |
| | MousePointer | 1 |
| Timer | CtlName | DialTimer |
| | Enabled | False |
| | Interval | 1000 |
| Timer | CtlName | DialResults |
| | Enabled | False |
| | Interval | 1000 |

**Table 5.24 Settings for the Warning form in the Appearance project**

2. Size the objects on the screen, as shown in Figure 5.23.

3. Enter the following code in the Cancel_Click event subroutine. The user activates this event by clicking the Cancel button. This routine unloads the Warning form and displays the Appear form.

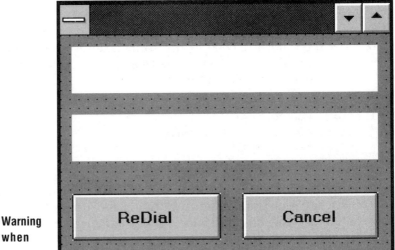

**Figure 5.23 What the Warning form should look like when completed**

```
Sub Cancel_Click ()
    Unload Warning
    Appear.Icon = LoadPicture("\VB\ICONS\COMM\PHONE01.ICO")
    Appear.WindowState = 0
End Sub
```

4. Enter the following code in the DialResults_Timer event subroutine. This code displays the results of the dial attempt. The text of this message is based on the results of any previous dial attempt(s).

```
Sub DialResults_Timer ()
    Results.Visible = -1
    If Results.Caption = "" Then
        Results.Caption = "No Response"
    ElseIf Results.Caption = "No Response" Then
        Results.Caption = "Sorry, No Response"
    ElseIf Results.Caption = "Sorry, No Response" Then
        Results.Caption = "Sorry, Still No Response"
    Else
        Results.Caption = "Hey what do you expect? This is a demonstration"
    End If
    Screen.MousePointer = 0
    DialResults.Enabled = 0
End Sub
```

5. Enter the following code in the DialTimer_Timer event subroutine. This code disables the DialTimer timer and enables the DialResults timer.

```
Sub DialTimer_Timer ()
    DialTimer.Enabled = 0
```

```
        DialResults.Enabled = -1
     End Sub
```

6. Enter the following code in the Form_Load event subroutine. When the
Warning form is first loaded, the DialTimer event is enabled and the caption is changed to DialingNumber.

```
Sub Form_Load ()
   DialTimer.Enabled = -1
   Dial.Caption = "Dialing Number"
   DialResults.Enabled = 0
End Sub
```

7. Enter the following code in the Redial_Check event subroutine. This code
changes the mouse pointer to an hourglass, displays the next dial message
in the dial label box, and enables the DialTimer.

```
Sub Redial_Click ()
   Screen.MousePointer = 11
   Results.Visible = 0
   If Dial.Caption = "Dialing Number" Then
       Dial.Caption = "Redialing Number"
   ElseIf Dial.Caption = "Redialing Number" Then
       Dial.Caption = "Redialing Number Again!"
   Else
       Dial.Caption = "Redialing Number one more time!"
   End If
   DialTimer.Enabled = -1
End Sub
```

Figure 5.24 shows what the Warning form will look like when it is running.

## How It Works

The Appearance project opens by displaying a list of phone numbers in a list box on
the Appear form. When the user selects one of these numbers from the list and presses
the Dial command button, the Warning form displays on the screen. While the Warning form appears on the screen, the Appear form is minimized at the bottom of the
screen. The Warning form displays the results of the attempt to dial. (Note: This example does not actually dial the number.) Each time the user presses the Redial button
on the Warning form, new messages appear on the screen. The user presses the Cancel
command button to exit the Warning form.

### Running the Appearance Project

When the user selects a number from the phone list and clicks the dial command
button, the Dial_Click event is triggered. The screen's mouse pointer is changed to an
hourglass to reflect that the program is busy. The MousePointer property settings of all
of the other controls and forms are overridden while the screen's mouse pointer is set
to an hourglass.

Next, the Caption property of the Appear form is modified to read Dialing and show the contents of the PhoneList item. The Caption is displayed in the title bar of the Appear form. This is an excellent method for informing the user what is taking place.

The DialClick event ends by enabling the DialCommand timer event. This routine in turn changes the Icon property of the Appear form to a picture of a phone with the receiver off the new hook. The DialCommand timer then minimizes the appear form and displays the Warning form. Since the Warning form is shown in Modal mode, the next lines of code are not executed until that form is unloaded from memory.

The Warning form's Load event changes the Dial label box's Caption property to Dialing Number. This demonstrates how the Caption property of a control can be modified at run time. Changing this property shows

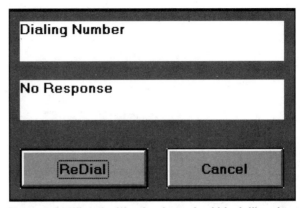

**Figure 5.24 What the Warning form should look like when running**

the user the actions of the program as they take place.

At this point, the DialTimer_Timer and DialResults_Timer events are triggered. The DialResults event makes the Results label box (which is below the Dial box) visible to the user, and then changes its message based on the current setting. Next, the screen's MousePointer property is restored to the default value of 0, which restores the mouse pointer settings of the controls and forms of the program. In this case, the hourglass is changed back to the standard arrow.

Each time the Redial command button is clicked, the screen's mouse pointer is changed back to an hourglass and the Dial label box's caption is changed. This command button has the important effect of changing the messages on the label boxes to reflect how many times that the Redial command button has been pressed. The Redial routine then triggers the DialTimer_Timer event, which in turn triggers the DialResults_Timer event.

When the user clicks the Cancel button, the Warning form is unloaded from memory and the Icon property of the Appear form is changed back to its original setting with a LoadPicture function. This displays a hung-up phone briefly on the bottom of the screen, until the Appear form is placed back up on the screen.

Notice that the last portion of the DialCommand_Timer event is processed as soon as the Warning form is removed. This changes the Appear form's Caption property back to the original Appearance Project text. If the Warning form had been shown in modal mode, this code would have been executed earlier. To exit the program, press the command button labeled Exit.

# Using Forms and Controls
# in Program Code

I n Chapters 2 through 5 of the *Visual Basic SuperBible*, we have been concerned mainly with the visual design of screen objects (forms and controls). If you have read these chapters, however, you have seen numerous code examples showing ways in which forms and controls are referred to in Visual Basic code. In this chapter, we will take a systematic look at how forms and controls are used in your program code.

## Referring to Objects in Code

Objects are referred to using their appropriate name properties. The FormName property serves as the reference name for forms. It is often followed by a period (.) and the name of a particular property to be set or changed. For example, you can set the WindowState property of the the form "Form1" as follows:

```
Form1.WindowState = 2   ' Maximizes Form1
```

A control is referenced by its CtlName property. The general syntax for the CtlName is the same as for a form. For example, the following statement assigns the text "My dog has fleas" to the text property of the textbox "MyBox":

```
MyBox.Text = "My dog has fleas"
```

### References to Events

A reference to an event begins with the CtlName or FormName of the object that triggers the indicated event, followed by an underscore (_) and the name of the event:

```
Sub MyBox_Change ()
```

Here we have begun the definition of a Sub procedure that deals with the Change event for the form MyBox. (See Appendix A, *Visual Basic Language Summary*, for information on Sub procedures and other language elements.) An underscore (_) appears between the object's CtlName or FormName and the event name. Functions, statements, and methods place the CtlName or FormName either before or after the property name. Exactly where the name appears depends upon the syntax of each individual expression, as shown in its reference entry.

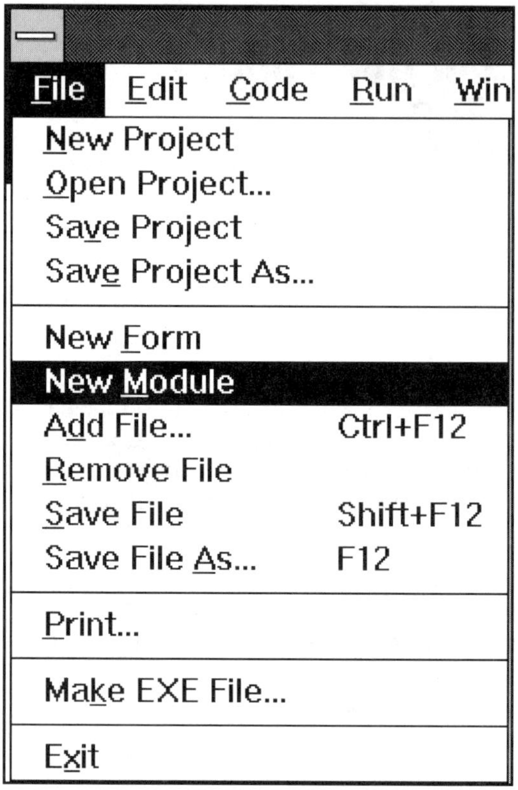

## Modules

Code that references the controls and properties of more than one form calls for the creation of a new module. To create a new module, select the New Module command on the Visual Basic File menu (see Figure 6.1). This module includes any functions that reference or affect the controls or properties of more than one form. In order to create a Sub procedure function in this module, simply type the code into its General Declarations section. Modules allow you to define common behavior for a number of different forms without duplicating code.

## More About Referencing

The "active object" is the currently selected form or control on the screen. Active controls have an outline around them. Visual Basic permits the identification of the currently active control without its CtlName property through the ActiveControl property. Windows differentiates between active and inactive forms with the colors of their title bars and borders (set these colors in the color section of the Windows control panel). When the name of a form is not available, the ActiveForm property may be substituted. This technique can be useful for writing general-purpose procedures to deal with whatever object is active at a particular time.

Figure 6.1 Creating a new module

As noted earlier, each form or control in a program has a name that identifies it in the code. This name is a 40-character text string that must begin with an alphabetical letter. The same rules apply to both the FormName and CtlName properties.

A control array is a group of one or more controls that share the same CtlName. Each control in an array has an index value that distinguishes it from the other controls in the control array. The first control in a control array has an index value of 0. Each new control in the control array receives a successively higher index value. In this way, the next control has an index value of 1, the next 2, and so on. This value appears in between parentheses after the CtlName of the control array. For example, if you have an array of text boxes, you can specify the loading of the "nth" text box as follows:

```
Load TextBoxes(n)
```

In Visual Basic, every control is on one of the program's forms. This form is the parent form of the control, meaning that it is the form that the control is on. Each control has a Parent property at run time that identifies its parent form. This property enables the code to reference the properties of the parent form without its FormName property.

Sometimes there is a need for special tags on the controls and forms of an application. The Tag property provides a means of identifying forms and controls with descriptive text. Changing a form or control's Tag property has no direct effect on its appearance. The Tag property is for identification purposes only.

Table 6.1 lists the seven properties that are involved in referencing forms or controls in Visual Basic.

| Use or Set This... | | To Do This... |
|---|---|---|
| ActiveControl | Property | Access the attributes of the active control |
| ActiveForm | Property | Access the attributes of the active form |
| CtlName | Property | Word that identifies a control in the code |
| FormName | Property | Word that identifies a form in the code |
| Index | Property | Identify a control in a control array |
| Parent | Property | Identify the form that a form is positioned on |
| Tag | Property | Identify a control of a form with a unique text string |

**Table 6.1 Properties dealing with the referencing of forms and controls**

The following pages investigate these properties in detail. At the end of this section, step-by-step directions explain how to assemble the Reference Project, which illustrates a variety of techniques for referencing objects in code.

# ActiveControl Property

## Objects Affected

| | | | | |
|---|---|---|---|---|
| Check | Clipboard | Combo | Command | Dbug |
| Dir | Drive | File | Form | Frame |
| Label | List | Menu | Option | Picture |
| Printer | ▶ Screen | Scroll | Text | Timer |

## Purpose

The ActiveControl property returns the currently active control on the screen, and thus begins with a reference to the Screen object, as shown in the general syntax below. The active control is the control that has the focus and will receive subsequent user input. You can examine or change a property of the active control by referring to "Screen.ActiveControl[.property]," as shown in the example syntax, which references

the Caption property of the three command buttons on the form with differing results. Here the background color of the form changes to the color indicated by the
selected command button. By referencing the selected command button, one statement embodies all the changes in the background color. Table 6.2 summarizes the
arguments of the ActiveControl property.

## General Syntax

```
Screen.ActiveControl[.property]
```

| Argument | Description |
| --- | --- |
| Screen | Refers to the active control on the screen (must appear or an error generates) |
| property | Name of the property to reference |

**Table 6.2 Arguments of the ActiveControl property**

## Example Syntax

```
Sub Form_Click ()
    Select Case Screen.ActiveControl.Caption  'Checks active control's Caption property
        Case "Command1"
            Form1.BackColor = RGB(255, 0, 0)  'Changes form's background to red
        Case "Command2"
            Form1.BackColor = RGB(0, 255, 0)  'Changes form's background to green
        Case "Command3"
            Form1.BackColor = RGB(0, 0, 255)  'Changes form's background to blue
    End Select
End Sub

Sub CheckControl ()
    If TypeOf Screen.ActiveControl Is CommandButton Then 'Checks if control is a command
                                                         'button
        Screen.ActiveControl.Visible = 0                 'Makes command button invisible
    ElseIf TypeOf Screen.ActiveControl Is TextBox        'Checks if control is a  text box
        StoredText$ = Screen.ActiveControl.Text          'Stores contents of text box
    End If
End Sub
```

## Description

The ActiveControl property substitutes for the name of the control on the screen that
has the focus. A control has the focus when selected on the screen by the user. This
property is only accessible at run time and will not work at design time. When the
ActiveControl property accesses the control with the focus, the control's control type
and properties serve as a basis for a property change or action. In the example syntax,
a select case statement determines the background color of the form based on which
command button has the focus.

### Ineligible Controls

You cannot use the ActiveControl property to reference controls that are ineligible for focus. A control may be ineligible for receiving focus for a number of reasons. When a control's Visible property is False, that control may not have the focus or be referenced with the ActiveControl property. Both the Timer control and the label control are ineligible for the focus. In contrast, controls with False TabStop properties cannot receive the focus with the Tab key. These controls are still accessible with the ActiveControl property. This is possible because a control is still selectable with a mouse while its TabStop property is False.

### The Tag Property

When none of a control's properties are appropriate for use in an ActiveControl expression, the Tag property serves as an excellent method for differentiating between the various controls of a form. The Tag property of a control can be assigned a unique text string that you can use to refer to the control when necessary. For example, each of the controls on a data entry form can receive a unique Tag property text string in the Form_Load event of the form. This string becomes a method of identifying the affected controls with subsequent actions through the use of the Tag property. This process involves first checking the Tag value of the active control. You could also assign Tag properties that identify the type of form involved. In

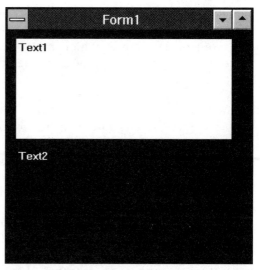

**Figure 6.2 Active control with its background changed to white**

the next example, the GotFocus event of the Text1 text box calls upon a generic function that only changes the background color of text boxes. Figure 6.2 shows how this might look on the screen.

```
Sub ChangeBackground
    If Screen.ActiveControl.Tag <> "Text" Then      'Checks the control's tag property
        Screen.ActiveControl.BackColor = RGB(0,0,0)  'Changes control's background white
    End If
End Sub

Sub Text1_GotFocus
    ChangeBackground                                 'Accesses the ChangeBackground
                                                     'sub function
End Sub
```

## Example

In the Reference project at the end of this section, the program accesses the ActiveControl property at several points in the code. The ActiveControl property acts as a means of referencing the control with the focus. This is a means of referencing a control by its present state rather than by its CtlName.

The GotFocus event of the Letter_Type control array references the active control to change the ForeColor and BackColor properties of the control on the screen. This "Selected" function modifies the color changes. When one of the Letter_Type controls receives the focus, the newly selected control's background changes to black and the text is yellow.

A Select Case statement in the GotFocus event of the Letter_Type control array references the Index value of the active control. In this way, the index value of the current control determines which part of the Select Case statement to process. This example shows the method of accessing an active control's property without changing the property.

When one of the check boxes of the Letter_Options control array is selected, the Letter_Options_Click event determines which control is active with the ActiveControl property. Two If-Then statements reference the active control's Value and Tag properties. The first If-Then statement checks the Value property of the active control. If the Value property is 1, then the actions triggers. The second If-Then statement compares the contents of the Tag property. When the Tag property is Address_Option, the action triggers. This demonstrates the powerful ability to use the ActiveControl property and If-Then statement together.

Finally, the ActiveControl property serves as a direct method of referencing a change to the property of controls in particular parts of the Reference Project. In the Letter_Options_Click event, the forecolor of the top member of the Letter_Options control array changes to black when checked. The Letter_Type_GotFocus event defines the TypeIndex global variable with the index value of the current control.

## Comments

The word Screen must appear before the ActiveControl name or an error will be generated.

# ActiveForm Property

## Objects Affected

| | | | | |
|---|---|---|---|---|
| Check | Clipboard | Combo | Command | Dbug |
| Dir | Drive | File | Form | Frame |
| Label | List | Menu | Option | Picture |
| Printer | ▶ Screen | Scroll | Text | Timer |

## Purpose

The ActiveForm property references the currently active form on the screen: that is, the form that has been selected for the next input. At run time, this property may determine the setting of the active form's indicated property. This property may serve as the basis of a statement that then influences the properties of other forms or controls. For example, a file management program with two file directory forms might utilize a function in an external module to position the forms on the screen based upon which is the active form. In this way, two side-by-side forms appear on the screen, with the active form always displayed on the left side of the screen. Table 6.3 summarizes the arguments of the ActiveForm property.

## General Syntax

```
Screen.ActiveForm[.property]
```

| Argument | Description |
| --- | --- |
| Screen | Refers to the active form on the screen (Must appear or an error generates) |
| property | Name of the property to reference |

**Table 6.3 Arguments of the ActiveForm property**

## Example Syntax

```
Sub FormPosition (FormName As Form)          'Function of new Module
    Screen.ActiveForm.Height = Screen.Height  'Make form's height equal screen
    Screen.ActiveForm.Width = (Screen.Width / 2) 'Make form's width half of screen
    Screen.ActiveForm.Top = 0                 'Place form at top
    Screen.ActiveForm.Left = 0                'Place form on left margin
    FormName.Height = Screen.Height           'Make form's height equal screen
    FormName.Width = (Screen.Width / 2)       'Make form's width half of screen
    FormName.Top = 0                          'Place form at top
    FormName.Left = FormName.Width            'Make form fill half of screen
End Sub

Sub Form_Click ()
    FormPosition Form2                        'Calls FormPosition function
End Sub
```

## Description

The ActiveForm property defines the form on the screen that has the focus. A form has the focus when it is the selected or active form on the screen. This property is accessible at run time and will not work at design time. When the ActiveForm property accesses the control with the focus, the form's properties serve as a basis for a property change or action. In the example syntax, the active form's dimensions determine those of the inactive form. With the ActiveForm property, the process of defining the dimensions of the forms is a simple matter of placing the active form on the left side of the screen and the inactive form on the right side.

### Ineligible Forms

The ActiveForm property cannot reference forms that are ineligible for focus. A form may be ineligible for receiving focus for a number of reasons. When a form's Visible property is False, that control may not have the focus or reference it with the ActiveForm property. If the unselected form is hidden when the other is selected, then the dimensions of the form are unadjustable. In order to change the size of both the selected and unselected forms in the example syntax, access it with an alternate reference, such as its FormName.

### The Tag Property

When none of a form's properties are appropriate for use in an ActiveForm expression, the Tag property serves as an excellent method for differentiating between the various forms of a program. The Tag property of a control can be assigned a unique text string that you can use to refer to the control when necessary. A Select Case statement might then be set up to determine the Tag property of the active form. In this way, the active form's background color changes from white to blue.

```
Sub ChangeBackground ()                             'New Module
    Select Case Screen.ActiveForm.Tag              'Checks Tag Property of form
        Case "Main Form"
            Screen.ActiveForm.BackColor = RGB(255,255,255)   'White background
        Case "Secondary Form"
            Screen.ActiveForm.BackColor = RGB(0,0,255)       'Blue background
    End Select
End Sub

Form_Resize ()
    ChangeBackground                                'Accesses sub function
        ChangeBackground
End Sub
```

## Example

In the Reference project at the end of this section, the Print_Letter_Click event uses the ActiveForm property to print the letter on the Letter form. The ActiveForm property determines which form in the LetterGen function prints the contents of the letter. Notice that the ActiveForm is the Letter form and not the Reference form. Even though the Print_Letter_Click event is a subroutine of the Reference form, the active form is the one currently selected on the screen.

## Comments

The word Screen must precede each ActiveForm property statement or it will not work properly. Notice that the subfunction FormPosition must be a part of a new module so that all of the forms of the program may use it. This is very important; if it is not done, the example above will not work properly.

# CtlName Property

## Objects Affected

| | | | | |
|---|---|---|---|---|
| ▶ Check | Clipboard | ▶ Combo | ▶ Command | Dbug |
| ▶ Dir | ▶ Drive | ▶ File | Form | ▶ Frame |
| ▶ Label | ▶ List | ▶ Menu | ▶ Option | ▶ Picture |
| Printer | Screen | ▶ Scroll | ▶ Text | ▶ Timer |

## Purpose

The CtlName property identifies the name to use when referencing a control in a program. This property is only modifiable at design time. A control's CtlName property may be up to 40 characters in length and must begin with a letter of the alphabet. Be careful not to use a reserved name, or an error will result. A newly created control's default CtlName property is the name of the control type and an integer. For example, the default CtlName for a text box is Text1. With each addition of another control of the same type, the integer at the end of the CtlName is incremented by 1. As a result, the second list box on a form has a CtlName property of List2. Table 6.4 summarizes the argument of the CtlName property.

## General Syntax

`[ctlName.]Property`

| Argument | Description |
|---|---|
| CtlName | Name used to identify the control in the code |

**Table 6.4 Argument of the CtlName property**

## Example Syntax

```
Sub Form1_Click
    If TextBox(0).Text = "Background is blue" Then      'This subroutine checks the
        Form1.BackColor = RGB(255,255,255)             'contents of the first part of
        Form1.ForeColor = RGB(0,0,255)                 'the TextBox Control array for
        TextBox(0).Text = "Background is white"        'which color to set the
        TextBox(1).Text = "Foreground is blue"         'foreground and background of
    ElseIf TextBox(0).Text = "Background is white" Then 'the form. 'Clicking' the form
        Form1.BackColor = RGB(0,0,255)                 'changes background and
        Form1.ForeColor = RGB(255,255,255)             'foreground form blue to white.
        TextBox(0).Text = "Background is blue"
        TextBox(1).Text = "Foreground is white"
    End If
End Sub
```

## Description

A control's CtlName property contains the name at design time that determines what word to use when referencing it. This name is either the default setting or a user-defined choice. The CtlName of a control normally serves as a part of any expression that directly affects the control. In an expression, the CtlName property acts as a reference for which control to affect. Each of the expressions in the example syntax begins with either Form1 for the form or TextBox for the text box. Without either the CtlName or FormName property in these expressions, an error occurs. This is because the code needs to know which object's property to access. When there is no error, the property of the form itself changes.

### The ActiveControl Property

The ActiveControl property substitutes for the CtlName of whatever control is currently active (selected). This is the one exception to the usual need for the CtlName property of the control. In this case, the ActiveControl property identifies the control with the focus. For example, a function can change the BackColor and ForeColor property of the selected control. This enables the program to show the user the selected control visually.

### Control Arrays

When more than one control of the same type has the same CtlName, these controls are part of a control array. At design time, Visual Basic asks if this is what you wish to do in order to prevent the accidental creation of a control array. Any number of controls may belong to a control array, provided that they are the same control type. Each control has a unique index property number in the order of creation. This number helps to reference that control. This number appears in parentheses after the shared CtlName. For example, the second control of the Assist control array appears as Assist(1).

### The Index Property

If a control is part of a control array, then the control will have a unique index number. The first member of a control array has an index value of 0. The next control has an index value of 1, the next becomes 2, and so on. This property is changeable at design time. This number becomes a part of the CtlName of the control (TextBox(0).Text). When these properties work together, they serve as an excellent method for consolidating code for similar controls. In the example syntax, the Form1_Click event references the two members of the TextBox control array, TextBox(0) and TextBox(1).

## Example

All of the controls of the Reference Project receive names that identify them during the program's operation. These names are in the CtlName property of each control and serve as a reference. The CtlName properties are changeable at design time and simplify the process of finding the control's name.

The Reference Project directly accesses the different controls at two places in the code. The Letter_Type_GotFocus event enables and disables the Letter_Options array controls based upon their CtlName property. When the OK_Button_Click event triggers, it references the CtlName property of the textbox that contains the user-entered text.

## Comments

Do not reference the CtlName property directly in the code. An If-Then statement that uses the CtlName property of the active control to determine the background color of a form generates an error. In this case, the Tag property may provide a workable alternative.

# FormName Property

## Objects Affected

| | | | | |
|---|---|---|---|---|
| Check | Clipboard | Combo | Command | Dbug |
| Dir | Drive | File | ▶ Form | Frame |
| Label | List | Menu | Option | Picture |
| Printer | Screen | Scroll | Text | Timer |

## Purpose

The FormName property is the reference name of a form in a program. This property only changes at design time. A form's FormName property contains up to 40 characters and must begin with a letter of the alphabet. Be careful not to use a reserved name, or an error will result. A newly created form's default FormName property is the word Form and an integer. For example, the default FormName for a form is Form1. With each creation of another form, the integer at the end of the FormName increments by 1. As a result, the second form has a FormName property of Form2. Table 6.5 summarizes the argument of the FormName property.

## General Syntax

[FormName.]Property

| Argument | Description |
|---|---|
| formname | Name used to identify the form in the code |

Table 6.5 Argument of the FormName property

## Example Syntax

```
Sub Form1_GotFocus
    If Form2.Icon = "\VB\MISC\FACE01.ICO" Then   'Checks icon property of form2
        Form1.WindowState = 2                    'Maximizes form1 on the screen
        Form2.WindowState = 1                    'Minimizes form2 on the screen
    Else
        Form1.WindowState = 2                    'Maximizes form1 on the screen
        Form2.Hide                               'Hides form2
    End If
End Sub
```

## Description

A form's FormName property receives a name at design time that determines its reference name. This name is either the default setting or a user-defined choice. In an expression, the FormName property acts as a reference for the affected form. The example syntax demonstrates this concept. Each time the setting of the form's icon property is checked, the expression begins with the FormName property. Without the FormName in these expressions, the code refers to the parent form.

### The ActiveForm Property

The ActiveForm property substitutes for the FormName of the active (selected) form. This is the one exception to the rule that an expression affecting a form's properties must utilize its FormName to identify it. In this case, the ActiveForm property serves as a means of identifying the form as the one with the focus. For example, a module sub-function can be set up to change the size of the form selected. This enables the program to standardize the appearance of the forms that appear on the screen.

## Example

All of the forms of the Reference project have names that identify them during the running of the program. These names are in the FormName property of each form and serve as a reference. The FormName properties are changeable at design time to simplify the process of finding the form's name needed for each part of the project's operation.

## Comments

Do not reference the FormName property directly in the code. An If-Then statement that uses the FormName property of the active form to determine the foreground color of the form will generate an error. The Tag property may provide a workable alternative in such cases.

# Index Property

## Objects Affected

| | | | | |
|---|---|---|---|---|
| ▶ Check | Clipboard | ▶ Combo | ▶ Command | Dbug |
| ▶ Dir | ▶ Drive | ▶ File | Form | ▶ Frame |
| ▶ Label | ▶ List | ▶ Menu | ▶ Option | ▶ Picture |
| Printer | Screen | ▶ Scroll | ▶ Text | ▶ Timer |

## Purpose

The Index property determines the referenced element of a control array. When a control is not part of a control array, its Index property has no value. Controls that are part of a control array may have index values of 0 to 32,767. This value is manually adjustable at design time and is not accessible at run time. Any reference to a control in a control array must include its index property value. In the example syntax, the controls of the control array Printer_Choices appear in the code, with the index number in parentheses. Table 6.6 summarizes the arguments of the Index property.

## General Syntax

```
[control][i%].Index
```

| Argument | Description |
|----------|-------------|
| control | Shared CtlName of the control array |
| i% | Index value of the control |

Table 6.6 Arguments of the Index property

## Example Syntax

```
Sub Printer_Choices_Click ()
    Select Case Printer_Choices.Index       'Sets up Control array as Index Value
        Case 0                              'Control Printer_Choices(0)
            PrinterText.Text = "HP LaserJet IIP"
        Case 1                              'Control Printer_Choices(1)
            PrinterText.Text = "HP LaserJet II
        Case 2                              'Control Printer_Choices(2)
            PrinterText.Text = "HP LaserJet III"
    End Select
End Sub
```

## Description

The Index property identifies the specific part of a control array referenced. An Index expression normally consists of the control's CtlName property followed by the value of the index placed in parentheses. Programs with multiple forms require the inclusion of the FormName of the form. Forms never receive an index property value. This property is modifiable at design time only and may not be referenced at run time.

### Option and Check Box Controls

The Index property of an option box or check box control sets up a logical connection between these controls. Each control's index property differentiates it from the other controls in the control array. All of the code in a control array is common to each of the controls. In the example above, a select case statement uses the index property of the control array Printer_Choices to indicate what name will appear in the text box PrinterText. This is an excellent example of the use of the index value in a program to differentiate between the different members of a control array.

### The Load and Unload Statements

When used in conjunction with the Load and Unload statements, the index property of a control array allows the creation of new controls. First, create a single control with an index value of 0. Next, change its Visible property to False (0). At run time, load a new member of the control array using an unused index value. When no longer needed, you can disable these controls with the unload statement. For example, create an option control box with an index value of 0. Each time that another option box becomes necessary, load it with the load statement.

## Example

The Reference project at the end of this section sets the Index property for each of the three control arrays in this program. On the Reference form, the control arrays are Letter_Type and Letter_Options. The Data_Entry form has the TextBox control array. You can either allow Visual Basic to define the index value of the controls in creation order, or change the values manually.

The Index property serves as a reference at several points in the Reference Project. In the Letter_Type_GotFocus event, the index property determines which part of the code to process. The identification of the Letter_Options array control to be enabled or disabled includes its index property in this event subroutine. The Letter_Op–tions_Click event uses the index property to indicate exactly which control the user pressed. Its Index property also determines whether to change the text of the control to black.

## Comments

A new control in a control array has a default index property value that is equal to the lowest available number.

# Parent Property

## Objects Affected

| | | | |
|---|---|---|---|
| ▶ Check | Clipboard | ▶ Combo | ▶ Command | Dbug |
| ▶ Dir | ▶ Drive | ▶ File | Form | ▶ Frame |
| ▶ Label | ▶ List | ▶ Menu | ▶ Option | ▶ Picture |
| Printer | Screen | ▶ Scroll | ▶ Text | ▶ Timer |

## Purpose

Each control belongs to a form. A control's Parent property identifies the control's form. Each Parent property expression must contain the CtlName of the control being accessed. This property is not available at design time and is not modifiable at run time (thus you cannot permanently move a control from one form to another at run time). This property enables the construction of generic functions that work for various controls on one or more forms. (A function for more than one form must be part of an additional module). In the example syntax, a new module contains the RestorePointer function. This function uses the TYPEOF keyword to identify the type of control, and then uses the Parent property to reference and change the control's form. In this way, the mouse pointer of the entire form changes to one of three choices based upon the type of control indicated. Table 6.7 summarizes the argument of the Parent property.

## General Syntax

```
[control.]Parent
```

| Argument | Description |
| --- | --- |
| control | CtlName property of the control |

Table 6.7 Argument of the Parent property

## Example Syntax

```
Sub RestorePointer (Source As Control)        'Define New Module
    If TypeOf Source Is TextBox Then          'Checks if control is a text box
        Source.Parent.MousePointer = 3        'I-Bar Mouse Pointer
    Else If TypeOf Source Is PictureBox Then  'Checks if control is picture box
        Source.Parent.MousePointer = 4        'Icon Mouse Pointer
    Else                                      'All other controls are given an
        Source.Parent.MousePointer = 1        'arrow for a mouse pointer
    End If
End Sub

Sub Form_Load
    RestorePointer Form1.Text1                'Calls RestorePointer function
    RestorePointer Form2.Picture1             'for each of the indicated controls.
    RestorePointer.Form3.Check1
End Sub
```

## Description

The Parent property of a control makes its form's properties available. The control argument identifies the CtlName of the control. In this way, the Parent property can be set up in a subfunction that can affect the different controls of several forms. Accomplish this with the use of a separate module that holds the function. This allows the referencing of any control on any form in a program from one function. In the example syntax, the function RestorePointer changes the MousePointer property of the form to a special type based upon the named control in the expression. As a result, the Parent property serves as a reference to the control and form.

### The ActiveControl Property

When the ActiveControl property substitutes for a specific control with the Parent property, a generic function applies directly to a number of controls. The ActiveControl property references the control with the focus. Depending on which type of control has the focus, different actions may be initiated on the properties of the Parent form. The next example changes the Icon property of the form based on the selected control. This pairing of the ActiveControl and Parent property works best when placed within a separate module, so that the subfunction or routine operates on more than one form.

```
'This subfunction must be placed as part of a new module which can then be
'accessed by more than one form. Notice that the form's icon changes based
'upon which type of control is active on the screen.

Sub ChooseIcon ()
 If TypeOf Screen.ActiveControl Is TextBox Then
  Screen.ActiveControl.Parent.Icon=LoadPicture("C:\VB\MISC\FACE02.ICO")
 ElseIf Screen.ActiveControl Is CommandButton Then
  Screen.ActiveControl.Parent.Icon=LoadPicture("C:\VB\MISC\FACE01.ICO")
 End If
End Sub


Sub Form_Resize ()
    ChooseIcon                    'Invokes the ChoseIcon subfunction.
End Sub
```

### Control Arrays and the Index Property

Another method of referencing controls on a Parent form uses the Index property
value of a control array. With the Index property, the Parent form's appearance is
modifiable based on the selected member of a control array. In the next example, the
index property of the controls of a control array determines what action to take on the
form. This subfunction will work with more than one form or control array with the
use of the ActiveControl property. Notice how ActiveControl replaces the CtlName of
the control array.

```
Sub CheckArray ()                                         'Create New Module
    If  Screen.ActiveControl.Index = 0 Then               'Index Property = 0
       Screen.ActiveControl.Parent.BackColor = RGB(0,0,255) 'Blue Background
    ElseIf Screen.ActiveControl.Index = 1 Then            'Index Property = 1
       Screen.ActiveControl.Parent.ForeColor = RGB(255,255,255) 'White foreground
       Screen.ActiveControl.Parent.BackColor = RGB(0,0,255) 'Blue Background
    ElseIf Screen.ActiveControl.Index = 2 Then            'Index Property = 2
       Screen.ActiveControl.Parent.BackColor = RGB(0,0,0)  'White Background
    End If
End Sub

Sub Form_Load ()
    CheckArray                 'Runs function CheckArray
End Sub
```

## Example

In the Reference Project at the end of this section, the Selected and DeSelected functions use the Parent property to find the BackColor property of the active control's
form. This method allows these subfunctions to differentiate between active controls,
and to initiate a color change for the control based on which form that the control is
on. When the BackColor of the form is gray, the control's Foreground property
changes to yellow with Selected, and the normal blue with DeSelected. The BackColor
property changes to Black for Selected, and White for DeSelected. If the form's
BackColor is white, then the control's Foreground property toggles between the normal black with Selected and blue with DeSelected.

## Comments

The Parent property works best when placed within an external module, but also works within a form's subroutines.

# Tag Property

## Objects Affected

| | | | | |
|---|---|---|---|---|
| ▶ Check | Clipboard | ▶ Combo | ▶ Command | Dbug |
| ▶ Dir | ▶ Drive | ▶ File | ▶ Form | ▶ Frame |
| ▶ Label | ▶ List | ▶ Menu | ▶ Option | ▶ Picture |
| Printer | Screen | ▶ Scroll | ▶ Text | ▶ Timer |

## Purpose

The Tag property stores a unique text string to a form or control. The other properties of a form or control are unaffected by the text string setting of its Tag property. This property is changeable at either design time or run time and has a default empty string. In the example syntax, the Tag property of a form changes when the size of the form alters. Note that a Resize event processes the first time that a form loads. Table 6.8 summarizes the arguments of the Tag property.

## General Syntax

```
[form.]Tag[=string$]
[control.]Tag[=string$]
```

| Argument | Description |
|---|---|
| form | FormName of the form |
| control | CtlName of the control |
| string$ | Contains the identifying string of text |

Table 6.8 Arguments of the Tag property

## Example Syntax

```
Sub Form_Resize ()
    If Form1.Tag = "" Then            'Checks if the form's tag property is
                                      'blank
        Form1.Tag = "Loaded"          'Changes tag property to "Loaded"
    ElseIf Form1.Tag = "Loaded" Then  'Checks if the form's tag property is
                                      '"Loaded"
        Form1.Tag = "Changed"         'Changes tag property to "Changed"
    End If
End Sub
```

## Description

The Tag property serves as an excellent method for differentiating between the various controls of a form. Tag property expressions begin with the CtlName of the control or the FormName of the form affected. A form or control's Tag property receives a unique text string (string$) that refers to the form or control necessary. This property also serves as a means of indicating that some kind of action has occurred. In the example syntax, the Tag property of a form changes to reference when modifications take place to the size of the form.

## Example

In the Reference project at the end of this section, the Tag property of the Letter_Options control array determines whether the ForeColor property of the control should change. This is a method of only allowing the color change to take place for the top two controls of the array, Return Address and Addressee, which both have a Tag property of Address_Option. Notice how this property works without changing the properties of the control.

## Comments

The Tag property of a form or control must be a text string and will not work with a numeric value.

# The Reference Project

## Project Overview

The Reference project demonstrates the properties of the Visual Basic Language used to access a program's controls and forms. All of these properties appear in the setup and operation of the Reference Project. By following the examples of the different forms and subroutines of this project, you will learn how to reference forms and controls in Visual Basic.

The Reference project consists of three forms: Reference, Letter, and Data_Entry. The first section deals with the assembly of the controls and subroutines of the Reference form. The next section outlines the construction of the controls and subroutines of the Letter form. The final section discusses the controls and subroutines of the Data_Entry form. Each section includes step-by-step instructions on how to put the form and its controls together. A table lists the different elements of the form's controls, along with a picture of how the form looks with these controls. This is followed by a list of the code subroutines to enter for this form. The final setup section explains the setup of the Reference Global Module and Refer Module. Finally, there is a discussion of the actual operation of the project. Please read this information carefully and use the pictures of the forms as guides in putting this project together.

## Assembling the Project

1. Make a new form (the Reference form) with the objects and properties in Table 6.9. Notice that all of the CheckBox controls have the same CtlName property, Letter_Options. Similarly, all of the OptionBox controls share the CtlName property, Letter_Type. The second control that you create with the same name generates a message. This message asks you if you wish to create a control array. Please respond "Yes." If you wish to avoid this, simply change the first control's index property to 0.

| Object | Property | Setting |
|---|---|---|
| Form | BackColor | Grey, RGB(192,192,192), &H00C0C0C0 |
|  | BorderStyle | 1 - Fixed Single |
|  | Caption | Reference Project |
|  | ForeColor | Blue, RGB(0,0,255), &HFF0000 |
|  | FormName | Reference |
|  | Icon | ..\VB\ICONS\MAIL\MAIL10.ICO |
| Frame | Caption | Letter Type |
|  | CtlName | Letter_Type_Options |
| OptionBox | Caption | Introduction Letter |
|  | CtlName | Letter_Type |
|  | Index | 0 |
|  | TabIndex | 0 |
| OptionBox | Caption | Acceptance Letter |
|  | CtlName | Letter_Type |
|  | Index | 1 |
|  | TabIndex | 1 |
| OptionBox | Caption | General Letter |
|  | CtlName | Letter_Type |
|  | Index | 2 |
|  | TabIndex | 2 |
| Frame | Caption | Letter_Options |
|  | CtlName | Letter_Options |
|  | Index | 0 |
|  | TabIndex | 3 |
| CheckBox | Caption | Return Address |
|  | CtlName | Letter_Options |
|  | Index | 0 |
|  | TabIndex | 3 |
|  | Tag | Address_Option |
|  | Value | 0 - Uncheck |

*Table 6.9 (continued)*

| Object | Property | Setting |
|---|---|---|
| CheckBox | Caption | Addressee |
| | CtlName | Letter_Options |
| | Index | 1 |
| | TabIndex | 4 |
| | Tag | Address_Option |
| | Value | 0 - Unchecked |
| CheckBox | Caption | Greeting |
| | CtlName | Letter_Options |
| | Index | 2 |
| | TabIndex | 5 |
| | Value | 0 - Unchecked |
| CheckBox | Caption | Closing |
| | CtlName | Letter_Options |
| | Index | 3 |
| | TabIndex | 6 |
| | Value | 0 - Unchecked |
| CheckBox | Caption | Body |
| | CtlName | Letter_Options |
| | Index | 4 |
| | TabIndex | 7 |
| | Value | 0 - Unchecked |
| CheckBox | Caption | Enclosure List |
| | CtlName | Letter_Options |
| | Index | 5 |
| | TabIndex | 8 |
| | Value | 0 - Unchecked |
| CheckBox | Caption | Carbon Copy List |
| | CtlName | Letter_Options |
| | Index | 6 |
| | TabIndex | 9 |
| | Value | 0 - Unchecked |
| Command button | Caption | Print Letter |
| | CtlName | Print_Letter |
| | TabIndex | 10 |
| Command button | Caption | Exit |
| | CtlName | Exit_Program |
| | TabIndex | 11 |

**Table 6.9 Settings for Reference form in the Reference project**

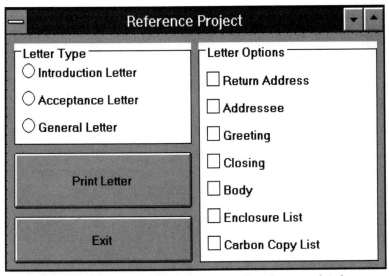

**Figure 6.3 What the Reference form should look like when completed**

2. Size the objects on the screen, as shown in Figure 6.3.

3. Enter the following code in the Form_Load event subroutine. This code modifies the background and foreground of the form. These property changes ensure that their settings are correct.

```
Sub Form_Load ()
    BackColor = RGB(192, 192, 192)
    ForeColor = RGB(0, 0, 255)
End Sub
```

4. Enter the following code in the Letter_Options_Click event subroutine. Notice that this event is for all of the option boxes of this control array. This subroutine triggers when the user clicks one of the Letter_Option check boxes. Clicking on one of the first two check boxes causes the text's color to change. When the check box has an X in it, the text is black. On an unchecked check box, the text appears normally. This subroutine displays the Data_Entry form when the check box contains an X.

```
Sub Letter_Options_Click (Index As Integer)
    If Screen.ActiveControl.Value = 1 Then
        If Screen.ActiveControl.Tag = "Address_Option" Then
            Screen.ActiveControl.ForeColor = RGB(0, 0, 0)
        End If
```

```
            On Error GoTo 0
            Title$ = "Reference Project"
            CurrentIndex = Screen.ActiveControl.Index
            Data_Entry.Show
        ElseIf Screen.ActiveControl.Value = 0 Then
            If Screen.ActiveControl.Tag = "Address_Option" Then
                Screen.ActiveControl.ForeColor = RGB(0, 0, 255)
            End If
        End If
    End If
End Sub
```

5. Enter the following code in the Letter_Type_GotFocus event subroutine. This code executes when one of the Letter_Type control array option boxes receives the focus. At that point, the color of the control changes to yellow on black using the Selected function. Next, each of the Letter_Option check boxes are enabled or disabled. The DeSelected function changes the appearance of the unchosen members of the Letter_Type control array to normal. Finally, the global variable TypeIndex changes to the index property of the current control.

```
Sub Letter_Type_GotFocus (Index As Integer)
    Selected Screen.ActiveControl
    Select Case Screen.ActiveControl.Index
        Case 0
            Letter_Options(2).Enabled = 0
            Letter_Options(3).Enabled = 0
            Letter_Options(4).Enabled = 0
            Letter_Options(5).Enabled = 0
            Letter_Options(6).Enabled = 0
            DeSelected Letter_Type(1)
            DeSelected Letter_Type(2)
        Case 1
            Letter_Options(2).Enabled = -1
            Letter_Options(3).Enabled = -1
            Letter_Options(4).Enabled = 0
            Letter_Options(5).Enabled = 0
            Letter_Options(6).Enabled = 0
            DeSelected Letter_Type(0)
            DeSelected Letter_Type(2)
        Case 2
            Letter_Options(2).Enabled = -1
            Letter_Options(3).Enabled = -1
            Letter_Options(4).Enabled = -1
            Letter_Options(5).Enabled = -1
            Letter_Options(6).Enabled = -1
            DeSelected Letter_Type(0)
            DeSelected Letter_Type(1)
    End Select
    TypeIndex = Screen.ActiveControl.Index
End Sub
```

6. Enter the following code in the Print_Letter_Click event subroutine. Pressing the command button Print_Letter triggers this event. This code hides the Reference form and calls the LetterGen function, which generates the letter on the screen based on the user's previous entries. After pressing the OK button on the message box, the letter disappears and the Reference form reappears on the screen.

```
Sub Print_Letter_Click ()
   Reference.Hide
   Letter.Show
   LetterGen Screen.ActiveForm
   Message$ = "Here is your letter, Press OK to exit"
   MsgBox Message$, 0, "Reference Project"
   Unload Letter
   Reference.Show
   Body = ""
End Sub
```

7. Enter the following code in the Exit_Program_Click event. Pressing the command button Exit_Program triggers this event. This code exits the program and closes all the open forms.

```
Sub Exit_Program_Click ()
   End
End Sub
```

**The Letter Form**

1. Make a new form with the objects and properties in Table 6.10.

| Object | Property | Setting |
|--------|----------|---------|
| Form | BackColor | White, RGB(255,255,255), &HFFFFFF |
| | BorderStyle | 1 - Fixed Single |
| | Caption | "" |
| | ControlBox | False |
| | ForeColor | Blue, RGB(0,0,255), &HFF0000 |
| | FormName | Letter |
| | MaxButton | False |
| | MinButton | False |
| TextBox | BorderStyle | 0 - None |
| | CtlName | BodyText |
| | Index | 0 |
| | MultiLine | True |
| | Visible | False |

**Table 6.10 Settings for Letter form in the Reference project**

2. Size the objects on the screen, as shown in Figure 6.4 .

### The Data_Entry Form

1. Make a new form with the objects and properties in Table 6.11.

Figure 6.4 What the Letter form should look like in the design mode

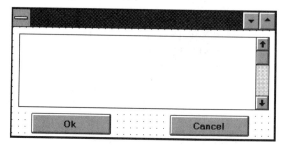

Figure 6.5 What the Data_Entry form should look like

| Object | Property | Setting |
|---|---|---|
| Form | BackColor | White, RGB(255,255,255), &HFFFFFF |
| | BorderStyle | 1 - Fixed Single |
| | Caption | "" |
| | ControlBox | False |
| | CtlName | Data_Entry |
| | ForeColor | Blue, RGB(0,0,255), &FF0000 |
| | MaxButton | False |
| | MinButton | False |
| TextBox | CtlName | Entry_Text |
| | Index | 0-6 |
| | MultiLine | True |
| | ScrollBar | 2 - Vertical |
| | TabIndex | 0-6 |
| | Text | "" |
| | Visible | False |
| Command button | Caption | OK |
| | CtlName | OK_Button |
| | Default | False |
| | TabIndex | 7 |
| Command button | Caption | Cancel |
| | CtlName | Cancel_Button |

| | |
|---|---|
| Default | False |
| TabIndex | 8 |

**Table 6.11 Settings for the Data_Entry form in the Reference project**

2. Size the objects on the screen, as shown in Figure 6.5.

3. Enter the following code in the Cancel_Button event subroutine. The user activates this event when the user presses the Cancel command button. This prevents whatever is in the text box from being saved.

```
Sub Cancel_Button_Click ()
    Unload Data_Entry
    Reference.Show
End Sub
```

4. Enter the following code in the Cancel_Button_GotFocus event subroutine. This event generates when the user selects the Cancel button. The Selected function changes the foreground color of the button to blue.

```
Sub Cancel_Button_GotFocus ()
    Selected Cancel_Button
End Sub
```

5. Enter the following code in the Cancel_Button_LostFocus event subroutine. This event triggers when the user unselects the Cancel button. The DeSelected function restores the foreground color of the button to normal.

```
Sub Cancel_Button_LostFocus ()
    DeSelected Cancel_Button
End Sub
```

6. Enter the following code in the Form_Load event subroutine. This code processes when the form loads. The background and foreground colors of the form are white and blue. Based on the current setting of the CurrentIndex global variable, a text box becomes visible on the screen.

```
Sub Form_Load ()
    BackColor = RGB(255, 255, 255)
    ForeColor = RGB(0,0,255)
    WindowState = 0
    Select Case CurrentIndex
        Case 0
            Data_Entry.Caption = "Enter the Return Address"
            Entry_Text(0).Text = Return_Address
            Entry_Text(0).Visible = -1
        Case 1
            Data_Entry.Caption = "Enter the Addressee's Address"
            Entry_Text(1).Text = Addressee
            Entry_Text(1).Visible = -1
        Case 2
            Data_Entry.Caption = "Enter the Greeting"
```

```
            Entry_Text(2).Text = Greeting
            Entry_Text(2).Visible = -1
        Case 3
            Data_Entry.Caption = "Enter the closing"
            Entry_Text(3).Text = Closing
            Entry_Text(3).Visible = -1
        Case 4
            Data_Entry.Caption = "Enter the body of the letter"
            Entry_Text(4).Text = Body
            Entry_Text(4).Visible = -1
        Case 5
            Data_Entry.Caption = "Enter the Enclosure List"
            Entry_Text(5).Text = Enclosure
            Entry_Text(5).Visible = -1
        Case 6
            Data_Entry.Caption = "Enter the Carbon Copy List"
            Entry_Text(6).Text = CCList
            Entry_Text(6).Visible = -1
        End Select
    End Sub
```

7. Enter the following code in the OK_Button_Click event subroutine. This event triggers when the user presses the OK button. The appropriate global variable changes the contents of the text box.

```
Sub OK_Button_Click ()
    If CurrentIndex = 0 Then
        Return_Address = Entry_Text(0).Text
    ElseIf CurrentIndex = 1 Then
        Addressee = Entry_Text(1).Text
    ElseIf CurrentIndex = 2 Then
        Greeting = Entry_Text(2).Text
    ElseIf CurrentIndex = 3 Then
        Closing = Entry_Text(3).Text
    ElseIf CurrentIndex = 4 Then
        Body = Entry_Text(4).Text
    ElseIf CurrentIndex = 5 Then
        Enclosure = Entry_Text(5).Text
    ElseIf CurrentIndex = 6 Then
        CCList = Entry_Text(6).Text
    End If
    Entry_Text(CurrentIndex).Visible = 0
    Unload Data_Entry
    Reference.Show
End Sub
```

8. Enter the following in the OK_Button_GotFocus event subroutine. This event activates with the selection of the OK button. The Selected function changes the foreground color of the button to blue.

```
Sub OK_Button_GotFocus ()
    Selected OK_Button
End Sub
```

9. Enter the following code in the OK_Button_LostFocus event subroutine. This event processes when the OK button is unselected. The DeSelected function restores the foreground color of the button to normal.

```
Sub OK_Button_LostFocus ()
   DeSelected OK_Button
End Sub
```

## Modules

1. Enter the following code in the Global Module and save the file as REFERENC.BAS. This defines the global variables used in the Reference Project.

```
Global CurrentIndex As Integer
Global TypeIndex As Integer
Global Return_Address As String
Global Addressee As String
Global Greeting As String
Global Closing As String
Global Body As String
Global Enclosure As String
Global CCList As String
```

2. Make a new module and save it as REFER.BAS. This module contains the functions available to all of the forms of the Reference project.

3. Enter the following code in the DeSelected function of the Refer module. This code changes the color of the indicated control's background and foreground.

```
Sub DeSelected (ControlName As Control)
   If ControlName.Parent.BackColor = RGB(192, 192, 192) Then
      ControlName.BackColor = RGB(255, 255, 255)
      ControlName.ForeColor = RGB(0, 0, 255)
   ElseIf ControlName.Parent.BackColor = RGB(255, 255, 255) Then
      ControlName.ForeColor = RGB(0, 0, 0)
   End If
End Sub
```

4. Enter the following code in the LetterGen function of the Refer module. This code generates the letter on the Letter form with the user's inputted information.

```
Sub LetterGen (FormName As Form)
         FormName. Cls
         FormName. ScaleHeight = 100
         FormName. ScaleWidth = 100
         FormName. Print Return_Address,
         LineFeed   FormName
         FormName. Print Addressee,
         LineFeed   FormName      If Greeting = "" Then
```

```
            Greeting = "To Whom it may concern"
        End If
        FormName.Print Greeting,
        LineFeed FormName
        If Body = "" Then
            If TypeIndex = 0 Then
                Body = "I would like to take this opportunity to"
                Body = Body + " Introduce myself."
            ElseIf TypeIndex = 1 Then
                Body = "I accept your kind offer."
            Else
                Body = ""
            End If
        End If
        Load FormName.BodyText(1)
        FormName.BodyText(1).Left = 0
        FormName.BodyText(1).Top = FormName.CurrentY
        FormName.BodyText(1).Height = 10
        FormName.BodyText(1).Width = 100
        FormName.BodyText(1).Visible = -1
        FormName.BodyText(1).Text = Body
        FormName.CurrentY = FormName.CurrentY + 11
        FormName.Print Closing,
        LineFeed FormName
        If Enclosure <> "" Then
            FormName.Print "Enclosures:",
            LineFeed FormName
            FormName.Print Enclosure,
            LineFeed FormName
        End If
        If CCList <> "" Then
        FormName.Print "CC:",
            FormName.Print
            FormName.Print
            FormName.Print CCList,
            FormName.Print
        End If
    End Sub
```

5. Enter the following code in the LineFeed function of the Refer module. This code inserts a line on the form.

```
Sub LineFeed (FormName As Form)
    FormName.Print
    FormName.Print
End Sub
```

6. Enter the following code in the Selected function of the Refer module. This code changes the indicated control's background and foreground.

```
Sub Selected (ControlName As Control)
    If ControlName.Parent.BackColor = RGB(192, 192, 192) Then
        ControlName.BackColor = RGB(0, 0, 0)
```

```
        ControlName.ForeColor = RGB(255, 255, 0)
    ElseIf ControlName.Parent.BackColor = RGB(255, 255, 255) Then
        ControlName.Parent.ForeColor = RGB(0, 0, 255)
    End If
End Sub
```

## How It Works

The Reference project demonstrates referencing through the creation of different kinds of letters. When the project opens, the user sees a list of the possible types of letters to create: introduction letter, acceptance letter, and general letter. Once the user chooses the type of letter, he or she selects the different letter options to include in the letter from the check boxes in the Letter options frame. Each time the user selects one of these check boxes, Visual Basic asks for the required information. Once the user has selected all of the required options and entered the information, he or she presses the Print Letter command button to display the letter on the screen.

### Startup

All of the elements of the Reference project receive identification names referenced throughout the program. Each form has its FormName changed to the more descriptive choices of Reference, Letter, and Data_Entry. The default settings of each control change to reflect their function. These names change to simplify the process of finding the reference name needed for each part of the project.

When the program starts, the Reference form displays on the screen, triggering the Form_Load event. This event contains two property expressions that alter the background and foreground colors of the form. In this case, the name of the form is not necessary for the property changes. All subroutine expressions that do not begin with either the CtlName or FormName property deal with the form.

The first line of the Letter_Type_GotFocus event triggers when the Letter_Type control array receives the focus. This event directs the "Selected" function to change the currently active control's foreground and background properties. An ActiveControl property expression indicates that the "Selected" function affects the control with the current focus. This demonstrates the indirect method of referencing a specific control. Instead of referencing the control by its CtlName property, this usage identifies the control with the current focus. This is also an excellent way of creating a generic function or subroutine that works for more than one control in the array.

After identifying the control to be affected, the Selected function changes the appearance of the control using the FormName argument name. This is another form or indirect reference that involves defining the argument FormName by the phrase that follows the function name. Otherwise, the ActiveControl property would need to be in each statement of this function. In this case, the BackColor property of the control becomes black and the ForeColor property yellow. This has the affect of highlighting the control on the screen.

A SelectCase statement uses the ActiveControl property to find the index value of the currently selected control. The index value of the currently selected control determines which of the members of the Letter_Options control array are enabled. Each element of the Letter_Options control array appears with its index value placed between parentheses. In this case, the CtlName of the control demonstrates a direct reference. Each of the BackColor and ForeColor properties of the other two members of the Letter_Type control array changes to normal with another direct reference using the index value and the DeSelect function.

Saving the index value to the global variable TypeIndex demonstrates another form of indirect reference. Storing the value of the currently selected control allows access to this control's properties in other forms and modules. This value is available even when another control has the focus.

Selecting one element of the Letter_Options array triggers the Letter_Options_Click event. This event uses the tag property to determine whether to modify the text color of the check box. Only the upper two controls, labeled Return Address and Addressee, have Tag properties that equal the required Address_Option. As a result, the text of only these two controls changes to black when checked. This is a method for directly referencing a control with a qualifying requirement that must be True for the statement to process.

Depending on which of the check boxes of the Letter_Options control array the user presses, the index value of the active control stores to the global variable and the Data_Entry form displays. This process involves calling the Data_Entry form on the screen with its FormName property name as part of a Show method statement. This is the direct method for referencing a form.

The Form_Load event of the Data_Entry form normalizes the form on the screen and sets its colors. In this case, the WindowState, BackColor, and ForeColor properties of the form change when no reference name appears. With no reference name provided in the expression, the form's properties change.

A Select Case statement determines the present value of the global variable CurrentIndex and displays the appropriate text box on the screen. Seven possible text boxes are part of the TextBox control array. Each text box is in the same location on the form and invisible. The setting of the CurrentIndex global variable determines which text box to make visible on the screen. Notice the use of the direct method of naming the control to access.

### Running the Reference Project

At this point in the program, the user enters the text into the text box and presses the OK or Cancel button when completed. Both of these command buttons have GotFocus and LostFocus events, which change their ForeColor property. The Selected and DeSelected functions and the direct referencing of the command buttons make these changes. Notice how the outline on the command button changes.

Pressing the OK command button activates the OK_Button_Click event which accesses the CurrentIndex global variable again. With the value returned, the event saves the contents of the text box to the appropriate global variable. This takes place with the direct use of the CtlName and Index properties of the text box on the screen.

When all of the active check boxes have been marked, indicating that information has been entered, click on the Print Letter button. After hiding the reference form with a direct reference, the Letter form displays on the screen. The ActiveForm calls the LetterGen function. This function determines that the Letter form is active. This is an important point, because although the code of the Reference form is still running, the currently active form is the Letter form.

The argument of the LetterGen is the FormName that is the ActiveForm property for the purposes of this project. FormName serves as the reference name throughout this function that generates the text on the Letter form. This is an excellent method of reducing the size of the lines by replacing the Screen.ActiveForm reference with FormName.

When the text box appears on the screen, a Load statement generates a new part of the control array BodyText. Notice that this control array did not exist prior to this generation. This ability permits the creation and manipulation of multiple instances of a particular control. Press the OK button on the message box after viewing the letter on the screen. Choose the Exit command button to leave the Reference project.

# Responding to Changes in Properties

Almost every object in Visual Basic has one primary property that can change as a direct result of the user's actions. Often your program needs to be informed of any changes to an object's primary property as soon as the changes are made. For example, if the user types some text into a text box, the new contents of this control trigger a Change event. Code you write for this event could, for example, save the text to facilitate an Undo feature. This chapter covers the Change event and how it is used with each object. The Change event is explained in detail, with a separate description for each object that has a Change event. The Change project at the end of the chapter demonstrates how the Change event can be used with a Text box to maintain a count of the characters entered in the box.

## Change Event

### Objects Affected

| | | | | |
|---|---|---|---|---|
| Check | Clipboard | ▶ Combo | Command | Debug |
| ▶ Dir | ▶ Drive | File | Form | Frame |
| ▶ Label | List | Menu | Option | ▶ Picture |
| Printer | Screen | ▶ Scroll | ▶ Text | Timer |

### Purpose

The Change event initiates an action when the user changes the value of an object's primary property, such as by making a selection or entering data.

### General Syntax

```
Sub CtlName_Change ([Index As Integer])
```

Table 7.1 summarizes the arguments used with this syntax.

| Arguments | Description |
|---|---|
| Form | FormName of the parent form |
| CtlName | CtlName of the control |
| Index | An integer that uniquely identifies an element of a control array |

Table 7.1 Arguments of the Change event

## Example Syntax

```
Global ThisText As String

Sub Text1_Change ()
    ThisText = Text1.Text      'Update ThisText any time the text in Text1 is changed
End Sub
```

## Description

Many of the objects in Visual Basic are based on one primary property. For instance, the text box control's primary property is the Text property. When an object's primary property is modified, you may wish your program to react to any changes that have been made to the property. The Change event occurs any time an object's primary property is modified. This event occurs regardless of the manner in which the property is changed. In other words, the event is initiated if the property is changed by the user, the program's code, or DDE events.

Table 7.2 lists all the objects that use the Change event, and the properties upon which it is based.

| Use Change with This Object... | To React to a Change in This Property... |
| --- | --- |
| Combo | Text |
| Dir | Path |
| Drive | Drive |
| Label | Caption |
| Picture | Picture |
| Scroll | Value |
| Text | Text |

Table 7.2 Objects that activate the Change event, and their primary properties

If you assign a value to an object's primary property that is the same as its current setting, the Change event will not be initiated. However, because the Change event occurs any time an object's primary property is modified, you need to be careful not to code circular Change events. In other words, you should avoid placing code in two or more object's Change events that modify each other's primary properties. For instance, imagine a program has two labels, with the following Change events:

```
Sub Label1_Change ()
    Dim Temp As Integer

    Temp = Val(Label1.Caption)
    Label2.Caption = Str(Temp + 1)
End Sub

Sub Label2_Change ()
    Dim Temp As Integer
```

```
    Temp = Val(Label2.Caption)
    Label1.Caption = Str(Temp + 1)
End Sub
```

The Label1_Change event modifies the Caption property of the Label2 object. This causes Label2's Change event to occur. That event modifies Label1's Caption property, which will again cause its Change event to occur. As you can see, this will result in both events calling each other endlessly.

### Combo Boxes

When used with the combo box object, the Change event occurs when any change is made to the box's Text property. The Text property only applies when a Combo box's Style property is set to 0 or 1 (drop-down or simple combo); therefore, the Change event can only occur with these styles. If a combo box's Style property is set to 2, no Change event could ever be initiated.

The user may change the Text property of a combo box by doing one of two things. First, if the user types any text in the edit portion of a combo box, a Change event will occur. Since the text is changed with each keystroke, the Change event will occur every time the user presses a key that generates an ASCII character. For example, if the user types the word "HELLO," the Change event will be called five times, once for each keystroke. Second, the user can change this property by selecting any of the list entries in the combo box. A list entry is selected any time the user presses the up or down arrow keys, or clicks on one of the entries with the mouse.

Setting the combo box's Text property within a program's code also causes the Change event to occur. For instance:

```
Combo1.Text = "Hello"
```

In the above line of code, the Text property of a combo box is set to "Hello." After this is performed, Visual Basic initiates the combo box's Change event. When that event has finished, execution will resume at the line following this one.

### Directory List Box

The primary property for the directory list box is the Path property. The Change event will occur any time this property is changed. The user may change this property by double-clicking on any entry listed in the directory box. This sets the Path property to the path specified by the entry chosen by the user. Setting the Path property to a new value within a program's code also causes the Change event to occur.

Chapter 19, *Managing Files in Drive, Directory, and File List Boxes*, contains an example of the Change event with the Directory list box object.

### Drive List Box

The primary property for the drive list box is the Drive property. This property can be changed by choosing a new drive letter from the object's drop down list, or by assigning a value to the property within the program's code.

Chapter 19, *Managing Files in Drive, Directory, and File List Boxes*, contains an example of the Change event with the Drive list box object.

### File List Box

The File list box has two primary properties: Path and Pattern. Because of this, it also has two Change events: PathChange and PatternChange. The PathChange event occurs when the Path property of a file list box has been changed. The PatternChange property occurs when its Pattern property has been modified. Both of these events are explained in detail in Chapter 19, *Managing Files in Drive, Directory, and File List Boxes*.

### Label

The primary property for the Label object is the Caption property. The Caption property can be changed by assigning it a string value within your program's code, or as the result of a Dynamic Data Exchange (DDE) operation. Please refer to Chapter 25, *Transferring Data with Dynamic Data Exchange*, for more on DDE.

### Picture Boxes

The primary property for the Picture object is the Picture property. The Picture property can be changed by assigning it a value within your program's code, or as the result of a Dynamic Data Exchange (DDE) operation. Please refer to Chapter 25, *Transferring Data with Dynamic Data Exchange*, for more on DDE.

### Scroll Bars

The primary property for the Scroll bars object is the Value property. This property indicates the relative position of a scroll bar's button on the bar. The Value property of a scroll bar can be changed in four ways. First, the user can click on either arrow. This causes the Value property to be incremented or decremented by the amount indicated by the bar's SmallChange property. Second, clicking the grey area of the scroll bar causes the Value property to be affected in a similar manner as clicking an arrow, but the amount of change is indicated by the bar's LargeChange property. Third, the user can click and drag the button to a specific position on the bar. This causes the Value property to be set according to the position of the button on the bar. Finally, the Value property can be set in the program's code.

Chapter 20, *Operating Scroll Bars*, uses the Change event with the scroll bars object in its example project.

### Text Boxes

When used with the Text box object, the Change event occurs when any change is made to the box's Text property.

If the user types any text in the text box, a Change event will occur. Since the text is changed with each keystroke, the Change event will occur every time the user presses a key that generates an ASCII character. For example, if the user types the word "HELLO," the Change event will be called five times, once for each keystroke. Also, assigning a string value to this property within your program will initiate a Change event. Text boxes can also be changed as a result of a DDE conversation. The Change event will also occur when this happens.

Chapter 13, *Getting User Input with Text Boxes*, uses the Change event along with the Text box object.

### Control Array

The Index argument is only used if the related control is part of a control array. This Index specifies which element of the array is the one that activated the event. When referencing the control, the element being referenced must be specified by placing the index number between parentheses just after the control name, and before the property name (that is, CtlName(Index).Property).

## Comments

Although some objects do not have an associated Change event, you may code your program to react to a change in these object's primary properties by using other events for the same purpose. For example, the Click event may be used to react to a change in the Check box, Option button, and List box objects.

# Change Project

## Project Overview

The Change project demonstrates the use of the Change event. In this project, you will create a form with a text box control and a label control. The text box's Change event will be used to display the number of characters in the box. Although this project uses only one of the controls that have a Change event, the concept behind using the Change event is similar for all other controls.

## Assembling the Change Project Form

1. Create a new form (the Change form) and place on it the controls specified in Table 7.3.

| Object | Property | Setting |
|--------|----------|---------|
| Form | Caption | Change Project |
| | ScaleMode | Twip |
| | ScaleHeight | 1845 |
| | ScaleWidth | 3195 |
| Text Box | BorderStyle | 0 - None |
| | CtlName | Text1 |
| | Height | 1605 |
| | Left | 0 |
| | MultiLine | True |
| | ScrollBars | 2 - Vertical |

*Table 7.3 (continued)*

| Object | Property | Setting |
|--------|----------|---------|
|  | Text | (no text) |
|  | Top | 0 |
|  | Width | 3195 |
| Label | BackColor | &H00C0C0C0 |
|  | BorderStyle | 1 - Fixed Single |
|  | Caption | no characters |
|  | CtlName | NoOfCharacters |
|  | Height | 255 |
|  | Left | 0 |
|  | Top | 1620 |
|  | Width | 3255 |

**Table 7.3 Property settings for the Change project**

2. Check the appearance of your form against Figure 7.1.

3. Enter the following code into the Text1_Change event. In this event, the number of characters that reside in the text box is determined with the Len function.

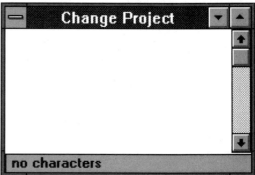

**Figure 7.1 How the Change project form should look when complete**

```
Sub Text1_Change ()
    Dim CharCount As Integer
    Dim CountMsg As String

    CharCount = Len(Text1.Text)
    CountMsg = "characters"
    Select Case CharCount
    Case 0
        CountMsg = " no characters"
    Case 1
        CountMsg = " one character"
    Case Else
        CountMsg = Format$(CharCount, " ### ")
        CountMsg = CountMsg + "characters"
    End Select
    NoOfCharacters.Caption = CountMsg
End Sub
```

## Running the Change Project

When the user enters some text in the text box, the Change event is triggered. The Caption property of the NoOfCharacters label control is set in the Text_Change event's code, based on the number of characters found. Because this event occurs any time a change is made to the text in Text1, the label caption is updated immediately.

# PART THREE
# DRAWING GRAPHICS

# Setting Up Graphical Objects

N ot long ago, most programs showed only text without any pictures. Today, however, most programs (especially those written for Windows) incorporate graphic images. Graphics can be simple lines, circles, or boxes. Graphics can also include bitmaps and icons loaded from disk. In addition to making programs more attractive, graphics help the user recognize and interact with the features of the program. For instance, a form with a picture of a printer represents the printer and any actions relating to this device.

## Graphics in Visual Basic

Visual Basic enables the easy creation, display, and manipulation of graphic images, whether simple drawn graphics or complex bitmap images. This flexibility makes the process of generating special effects on the screen an easier task than in many other languages. With a program that uses graphics on its screens, the user sees a visual interface that connects the various actions of the program with pictures that remind the user of the action. Visual Basic also allows the creation of special effects that can produce animated actions, simulations, or games.

### Graphics and the Picture Box

When the form is an inappropriate location for drawn graphics, a picture box is an alternative. Picture boxes are controls that contain graphics or pictures. Graphics placed on a picture box behave in the same way as those on a form. The main difference lies in the fact that a picture box has the ability to display files in icon (*.ICO), Windows metafile (*.WMF), or bitmap (*.BMP) format. Use the tool bar to create a picture box on a form at design time. Figure 8.1 shows which icon on the tool bar to choose.

Picture box

Figure 8.1
Tool bar
with picture
box icon

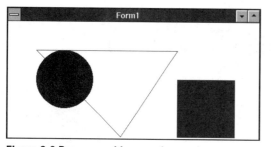

**Figure 8.2 Drawn graphics on a form**

### Drawn Graphics

Drawn graphics are any shapes produced with the Circle, Line, or PSet methods. The Circle method creates curved objects, including circles, ellipses (ovals), and arches. The Line method generates lines or box objects, including straight lines, squares, rectangles, and triangles. The PSet method makes spots of varying sizes and colors. Each of these methods produces graphics at run time. Graphics drawn with these methods can appear on either forms or picture boxes. Figure 8.2 displays a drawn circle, triangle, and box.

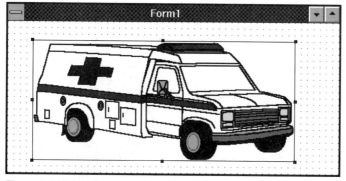

**Figure 8.3 Picture box showing a bitmap file**

### Pictures and Picture Files

A picture is any object loaded into a picture box with its Picture property. A loaded object must be a file in icon (*.ICO), Windows metafile (*.WMF), or bitmap (*.BMP) format. To display a file in a picture box, select the picture box on the form. Choose the Picture property on the properties bar. Press the ellipsis (...) on the right side of the properties bar. Select the file from the directory and press enter to display it on the screen. Figure 8.3 shows a picture box displaying the contents of a file. Save any changes made to a file with the SavePicture statement.

The contents of a picture box are normally set at design time and the loaded file becomes a part of the executable file of the program. This is inconvenient when the file loaded changes during program execution. Visual Basic provides the LoadPicture function for needs like these, allowing special graphics to load at run time.

Sometimes the need arises to remove graphics from a form or picture box. Loaded pictures disappear when the Picture property is an empty LoadPicture function. The Cls method removes any drawn graphics from a form or picture box. (Note: The Cls method has no effect on loaded pictures.) This is an important capability to keep in mind when manipulating graphic images.

### The Use of Color

Color defines the ways people respond to the elements on the screen. Objects with a red coloring tend to represent danger or warning. If the background of a warning box is red, then it gets more attention. Do not underestimate this ability to use color to affect people's responses. This is a powerful tool that augments the appearance of forms and controls on the screen. Each Visual Basic color has unique hexadecimal codes. Finding a particular color's code involves two possible methods. The color palette aids the setting of these properties at design time. Figure 8.4 shows what the color palette looks like. Objects' colors change at runtime, with the RGB and QBColor functions providing the necessary settings for the BackColor and ForeColor properties. Chapter 5, *Designing the Application's Appearance,* discusses the use of these functions and properties in detail.

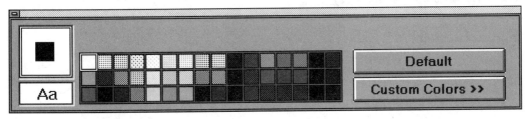

**Figure 8.4 Color palette**

Two elements of the Visual Basic Language determine the effects of changing the appearance of a form or picture box: the AutoRedraw property and the Paint event. When the size of a form or picture box resizes to a smaller or larger size, these properties indicate what occurs. These elements also determine what happens when the graphics on a form become temporarily obscured. Minimized forms containing graphics display them based upon the contents of the AutoRedraw property and Paint event. Graphics drawn while the AutoRedraw property is True reappear in these instances. When the AutoRedraw property is false, graphics do not reappear. The exception is if the actions that produced the graphics are in the Paint event. This event triggers each time a form loads or changes its appearance.

Table 8.1 summarizes the three properties, three methods, three functions, one statement, and one event that influence the basic display of graphics in Visual Basic.

| Use or Set This... | | To Do This... |
|---|---|---|
| AutoRedraw | Property | Determine whether a drawn object redisplays after uncovering it |
| Cls | Method | Wipe the surface of a picture box or form of all drawn objects |
| Image | Property | Determine the Microsoft Windows handle name assigned to an object |
| LoadPicture | Function | Change the graphics contents of a picture box or form |
| Paint | Event | Trigger when a portion of a form or picture box uncovers |
| Picture | Property | Determine the graphics object that initially appears in a form or picture box |
| Point | Method | Discover the RGB colors of a particular point on a form or picture box |
| PSet | Method | Change the RGB colors of a particular point on a form or picture box |
| QBColor | Function | Determine the RGB values of a specified color |
| RGB | Function | Define the RGB values of an object in an expression |
| SavePicture | Statement | Save any graphical object on a form or picture box to a specified file name |

**Table 8.1 Methods, properties, event, functions, and statement dealing with graphics**

The following pages investigate these methods, properties, event, functions, and statement in detail. At the end of this section, step-by-step directions explain how to assemble the Graphics Project.

# AutoRedraw Property

## Objects Affected

| | | | | |
|---|---|---|---|---|
| Check | Clipboard | Combo | Command | Dbug |
| Dir | Drive | File | ▶ Form | Frame |
| Label | List | Menu | Option | Picture |
| Printer | Screen | Scroll | Text | Timer |

## Purpose

The AutoRedraw property indicates whether the drawn graphical objects on a form or picture box redisplay when uncovered. A drawn object is an object produced with the Circle, Line, or PSet methods. Forms need the AutoRedraw property when other forms are first placed over them and then uncover them. When a hidden form redisplays, the AutoRedraw property determines whether to redraw the form's graphics. A form's AutoRedraw property setting determines the effects of resizing it between normal and minimized. Graphics drawn while the AutoRedraw property is True (-1) are unaffected by any of these changes. Any of these changes prevent the restoration of the graphics drawn while the AutoRedraw property is False (0). In this way, the AutoRedraw property determines whether or not the graphics reappear on a form or picture box. Tables 8.2 and 8.3 summarize the arguments of the AutoRedraw property.

## General Syntax

```
[form.]AutoRedraw[=boolean%]
[picturebox.]AutoRedraw[=boolean%]
```

| Argument | Description |
|---|---|
| form | FormName of the form |
| picture box | CtlName of the picture box |
| boolean% | Value indicating the property's new setting |

Table 8.2 Arguments of the AutoRedraw property

| boolean% | Description |
|---|---|
| False (0) | Default. Any objects that are drawn on the screen while this is the setting will not be redrawn |
| True (-1) | Any objects that are drawn on the screen while this is the setting will be redrawn |

Table 8.3 Available values of the boolean argument of the AutoRedraw property

## Example Syntax

```
Sub Form_Click ()
    ScaleMode = 5              'Displays a circle while the AutoRedraw property is
                              'True and a
    AutoRedraw = -1           'triangle while the AutoRedraw property is False.
                              'If the form is
    FillStyle = 0             'minimized and then restored on the screen, only the
                              'triangle
    FillColor = RGB(0, 0, 255) 'reappears.
    Circle (1, 1), .5
    AutoRedraw = -0
    ForeColor = RGB(255, 0, 0)
    Line (0.5 , 0.5)-(2, 1)
    Line -(2, 2)
    Line -(0.5, 0.5)
End Sub
```

## Description

The AutoRedraw property specifies whether a drawn object on a form or picture box redraws after being uncovered on the screen. There are two possible settings for this property, True (-1) and False (0). This is the boolean argument in the general syntax. AutoRedraw is changeable at either design time or run time. An AutoRedraw property expression begins with the name of the picture box or form affected. If a Redraw property expression does not begin with the name of the picture box or form, then the form's property changes. The example syntax demonstrates this difference between the two settings of the AutoRedraw property. First, the Circle method draws a circle with the AutoRedraw property set to True (-1). Next, three Line method expressions create a triangle with the AutoRedraw property set to False (0). Figure 8.5 shows what this example should look like. Minimizing and normalizing the form results in the erasure of the triangle and restoration of the circle. Figure 8.6 shows what Form1 looks like without the triangle.

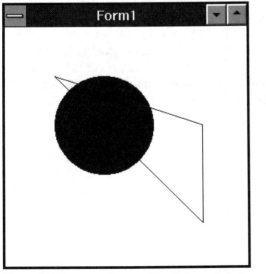

**Figure 8.5 Drawn syntax graphics before minimizing the form**

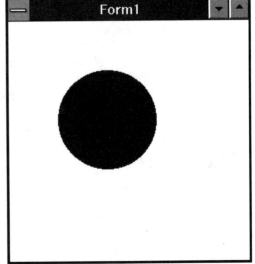

**Figure 8.6 Drawn syntax graphics after minimizing and normalizing the form**

The example syntax provides no name for the object being drawn on. With no other name indicated, the circle and triangle appear on the form and the AutoRedraw of the form changes property.

### The Cls method and BackColor Property

The Cls method and BackColor property of a form or picture box have similar or dissimilar effects depending on the setting of the AutoRedraw property. If all of the graphics appear while the AutoRedraw property is False (0), then both have the effect of removing all of the graphics. If graphics are created with the AutoRedraw property at True (-1), only changes to the BackColor property will remove the graphics. In situations where some of the graphics on the form or picture box were created with the AutoRedraw property at False and some at True, changes to the BackColor property will work in the same way. The Cls method will remove only the graphics generated with the AutoRedraw property of the picture box or form set to False (0).

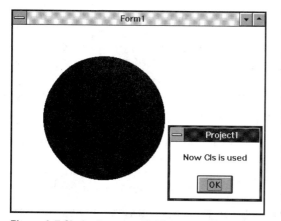

**Figure 8.7 Circle drawn on the form with code in the Form_Load and Form_Paint events**

### The Paint Event

The Paint event of a form and AutoRedraw property of a form or picture box have similar effects. Both indicate what happens with the normalizing, maximizing, or uncovering of a form or picture box. The next example draws a circle on the form with each display, uncovering, or resizing of the form. When the Cls method removes this circle from the screen, the circle remains undrawn until the Paint event triggers again. The effect is different if the same actions are within the Form_Load event with the AutoRedraw property set to True. In this case, the Cls method statement has no effect on the drawn circle, because the AutoRedraw property setting prevents the graphic from being removed. In programming, it is important to remember the difference between these two elements of the language. Figure 8.7 shows what both examples might look like.

```
Sub Form_Click ()
    AutoRedraw = -1                 'Objects will be redrawn after uncovered
    ScaleMode = 5                   'Sets the measurement type to inches
    FillStyle = 0                   'Objects will be solid
    FillColor = QBColor(0)          'Objects will be black
    Circle (1.5, 1.5), 1            'Draws a black circle
    MsgBox ("Now Cls is used")      'Displays a message box
    Cls                             'Removes the circle from the form
End Sub

Sub Form_Paint ()
```

```
        ScaleMode = 5              'Sets the measurement type to inches
        FillStyle = 0             'Objects will be solid
        FillColor = QBColor(0)    'Objects will be black
        Circle (1.5, 1.5), 1      'Draws a black circle
        MsgBox ("Now Cls is used") 'Displays a message box
        Cls                       'Removes the circle from the form
End Sub
```

### The Refresh Method

When a form's AutoRedraw property is False, the Refresh method has the effect of clearing whatever graphics are on the screen. If the AutoRedraw property is True, then the Refresh property only removes those elements of the screen generated while the AutoRedraw property was False.

## Example

The Graphics project at the end of this section adjusts the AutoRedraw property of the picture box Blanker_Icon and Graphics and Screen_Blanker forms. The AutoRedraw property of both the Graphics form and the picture box Blanker_Icon changes to True. This allows any graphics placed on either the Graphics form or the picture box Blanker_Icon to be redisplayed after being temporarily obscured. In order to allow periodic removal of the graphics on the Screen_Blanker form, the Screen_Blanker's AutoRedraw property is False (0).

By setting the AutoRedraw property of the Screen_Blanker form to False, the effects of the Cls method on the Form_Click event changes. Since the Cls method only affects drawn graphical objects produced while the AutoRedraw property is True (-1), the Cls method clears the Screen_Blanker form when called. If the AutoRedraw property of the Screen_Blanker form had been True (-1), then any spots, circles, squares, or lines would not disappear.

## Comments

Keep in mind that the AutoRedraw property is only available for forms and picture boxes.

---

# Cls method

## Objects Affected

| | | | | |
|---|---|---|---|---|
| Check | Clipboard | Combo | Command | Dbug |
| Dir | Drive | File | ▶ Form | Frame |
| Label | List | Menu | Option | ▶ Picture |
| Printer | Screen | Scroll | Text | Timer |

## Purpose

The Cls method removes drawn graphics or text from an object on the screen. The object must be either a form or a picture box. This method clears all the drawn objects off the indicated form or picture box. The Cls method has no effect on a form's controls and their contents. Loaded pictures do not disappear when the Cls method removes the drawn graphics on a form or picture box. Similarly, a Cls statement directed to the form has no effect on graphics placed on a picture box. Using the Cls method on a picture box has no effect on the graphics on the picture box's form. Table 8.4 summarizes the object argument of the Cls method.

## General Syntax

```
[object.]Cls
```

| Argument | Description |
|----------|-------------|
| object | FormName of form or CtlName of picture box |

**Table 8.4 Object argument of the Cls method**

## Example Syntax

```
Sub Form_Click ()
    FillStyle = 6                   'Objects placed on the screen will contain cross
                                    'hatch lines
    FillColor = QBColor(4)          'Color inside a drawn object will be red
    X = ScaleWidth / 2              'X and Y place the circle in the center of the form
    Y = ScaleHeight / 2
    Radius = ScaleWidth / 4         'Radius defined as one quarter of width of form
    Print "Demo Text"               'Prints this text on screen
    Circle (X, Y), Radius           'Draws Circle
    Select Case AutoRedraw          'Displays a message based upon the setting of the
                                    'AutoRedraw property
        Case -1
            MsgBox "Effects of Cls with AutoRedraw set to True."
            AutoRedraw = 0
        Case 0
            MsgBox "Effects of Cls with AutoRedraw set to False."
        AutoRedraw = -1
    End Select
    Cls                             'Clears the form
End Sub
```

## Description

The Cls method clears drawn text and graphics on a form or picture box. An object argument of a Cls method expression is either the CtlName property of a picture box or FormName property of a form. If a Cls method begins with the CtlName of a picture box, only the contents of the indicated picture box change. When Cls method expressions begin with no name or the FormName of the form, they only affect the contents of a form. In the example syntax, the form's graphics clear without naming the form's FormName. This occurs because the Cls method changes the form's graphics when no name precedes a Cls method expression. (See Figures 8.8 and 8.9 for a look at what the example syntax should produce).

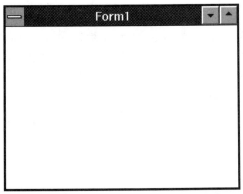

**Figure 8.8 Results of example syntax with Auto-Redraw property set to False**

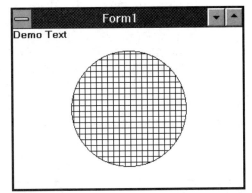

**Figure 8.9 Results of example syntax with Auto-Redraw property set to True**

### The CurrentX and CurrentY Properties

The Cls method changes the CurrentX and CurrentY properties of a form or picture box to 0. Graphics created on a form or picture box with the AutoRedraw property set to True (-1) remain unaffected. In this case, the Cls method works well as a means of easily resetting these coordinates.

### The Picture Property

The use of the Cls method has no effect on a picture box's Picture property. The Cls method only affects drawn graphics. As a result, the Cls method does not work on the contents of a picture box that contains a loaded picture. However, the Cls method clears any drawn graphics within a picture box that also has a loaded picture.

### The BackColor Property and the AutoRedraw Property

The Cls method and the BackColor property of a form or picture box have similar or dissimilar effects, depending upon the setting of the AutoRedraw property. These Visual Basic elements produce the same results on graphics drawn while the AutoRedraw property is False (0). The Cls method removes the graphics (AutoRedraw = 0) from the screen. Changes to the BackColor property of the form or object have the same effect. Drawn graphics with the AutoRedraw property at True (-1) only disappear when the BackColor property changes. In situations where some of the graphics appeared with the AutoRedraw property at False and some at True, changes to the BackColor property work in the same way. The Cls method only removes the graphics produced with the AutoRedraw property of the picture box or form set to False (0).

## Example

In the Graphics project at the end of this section, the Cls method clears the Screen_Blanker form of all drawn graphics. Within the Form_Click event of the Screen_Blanker event, the Cls method triggers when the user answers "Yes," he or she wishes to stop the current blanker. As a result, the form clears with the Cls method. Notice that the BackColor of the form changes manually with the selection of the Blank Screen option. This is because the Cls method has no effect on the BackColor property of the form. Also notice that the AutoRedraw property is False (0). If the AutoRedraw property changes to True (-1), then the Cls method has no effect on the drawn graphics.

## Comments

Using the Cls method does not clear the background or foreground color of a form or picture box.

# Image Property

## Objects Affected

| | | | | |
|---|---|---|---|---|
| Check | Clipboard | Combo | Command | Dbug |
| Dir | Drive | File | ▶ Form | Frame |
| Label | List | Menu | Option | ▶ Picture |
| Printer | Screen | Scroll | Text | Timer |

## Purpose

The Image property defines the value that Microsoft Windows automatically gives to an image on a picture box or form. This property identifies a drawn graphics image on the screen. Microsoft Windows sets the value returned by the Image property. This value is not manually changeable at run time and is not accessible at design time. An Image property value serves as identification for the entire contents of an indicated form or picture box. This value can be used in appropriate API calls (see Appendix C, *Using the Windows API*). In the example syntax, both the red circle and the blue circle appear on the first form. Table 8.5 summarizes the form argument of the Image property.

## General Syntax

```
[form]Image
[picturebox.]Image
```

| Argument | Description |
|---|---|
| form | FormName property of the affected form |

Table 8.5 Argument of the Image property

## Example Syntax

```
Sub Command1_Click ()
    AutoRedraw = -1          'Makes form1's AutoRedraw property True
    FillStyle = 0            'Defines the object to be drawn as solid
```

```
FillColor = QBColor(4)              'Defines the object to be drawn as red
ScaleMode = 5                       'Defines dimensions as being measured in inches
Print "This is a red circle"        'Prints test in top left corner of window
Circle (1, 1), .5                   'Draws a red circle on the form
FillColor = QBColor(1)              'Defines the object to be drawn as blue
Circle (3, 1), .5                   'Draws a blue circle on the form
Form2.Show                          'Displays second form on the screen
Form2.AutoRedraw = -1               'Makes Form2's AutoRedraw property True
Form2.Picture = Form1.Image         'Gives Form2 the same images as Form1
End Sub
```

## Description

The Image property provides the value that Microsoft Windows uses to identify the text and generated graphics on a form or picture box. This value references all of the graphics and text that appear on a screen. In the example syntax, the Image property transfers all of the graphics on Form1 to Form2 by setting Form2's Picture property to equal Form1's Image property. This shows that the Image property identifies all of the graphics on a form and not just one individual part of the graphics. As the Windows environment sometimes

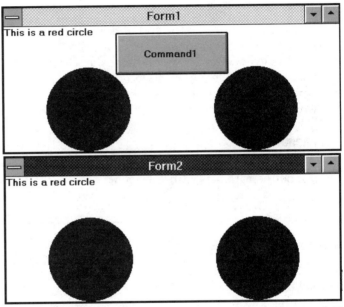

**Figure 8.10 What Form1 and Form2 of the example syntax might look like**

changes the value returned by the Image property, another variable should never store this value for later reference. Figure 8.10 shows what Form1 and Form2 might look like on the screen.

### The Picture Property

The Picture property of a form or picture may be defined as equal to the Image property of another form or picture. This has the effect of reproducing the same graphics on both forms and picture boxes. In the example syntax, the Picture property of Form2 alters to equal the Image property of Form1. By making Form2's Picture property equal to Form1's Image property, the same graphics appear on both forms. Notice that this change has no effect upon the other properties of Form2. As a result, the actual image that appears on Form1 appears on Form2 without changes to Form2's ScaleMode, FillColor, and FillStyle properties.

### The AutoRedraw Property and Paint Event

Both the AutoRedraw property and the Paint event of a form or picture box display the effects of an Image property expression. In the example syntax, the subroutine contains statements that change the AutoRedraw property of both Form1 and Form2. These property changes are necessary to ensure the immediate display of the new contents of Form2's Picture property. Another method of accomplishing this is to move the listed actions in the example syntax into a Paint event. This would ensure that the results of this change occur immediately on the screen.

### Example

In the Graphics project at the end of this section, the Image property serves as a means of saving the current graphics image on the screen. When the user clicks the form, the Form_Click event asks the user if he or she wishes to save the current image to a file. If the user responds "Yes," then the SavePicture statement accesses the Image property of the Screen_Blanker form to determine the Windows handle value. The code uses this value to save the current contents of the screen to the bitmap file TEST.BMP.

### Comments

The Image property of a form or picture box may change during program execution. Do not define variables with this value.

# LoadPicture Function

### Purpose

The LoadPicture function places pictures on forms and picture boxes. Table 8.6 summarizes the stringexpression$ argument of the LoadPicture function.

### General Syntax

```
LoadPicture([stringexpression$])
```

| Argument | Description |
|---|---|
| stringexpression$ | Path and filename of the graphics to load |

**Table 8.6 Argument of the LoadPicture function**

### Example Syntax

```
Sub Picture1_MouseDown (Button As Integer, Shift As Integer, X As Single, Y As Single)
    Picture1.Picture = LoadPicture("\VB\ICONS\OFFICE\FILES03B.ICO")
                                    'Displays an open file cabinet in
    Picture1.DragIcon = LoadPicture("\VB\ICONS\OFFICE\FILES04.ICO")
                                    'Picture1 and hand taking file out
    Picture1.Drag 1                 'of a file cabinet in Picture2. when
```

```
Form2.Icon = LoadPicture("\VB\ICONS\MISC\FACE03.ICO")
                                'the user presses the mouse down.
Form2.WindowState = 1
                        'Form2 minimizes to a happy face
End Sub
```

## Description

A picture loads into a form or picture box with the LoadPicture function. The loaded picture must be in bitmap (*.BMP), icon (*.ICO), or Windows metafile (*.WMF) format. If the LoadPicture expression does not end in a stringexpression$ argument, the specified picture clears of any settings. A stringexpression$ is the name with or without the extension of the picture file. If the file is in the current search path or the same directory, then the extension is not necessary. In the example syntax, the icons appear with their full paths because none of the icons are in the path and they would otherwise generate an error. (Note: If you did not use the default directories when you installed Visual Basic, these paths may need to change.)

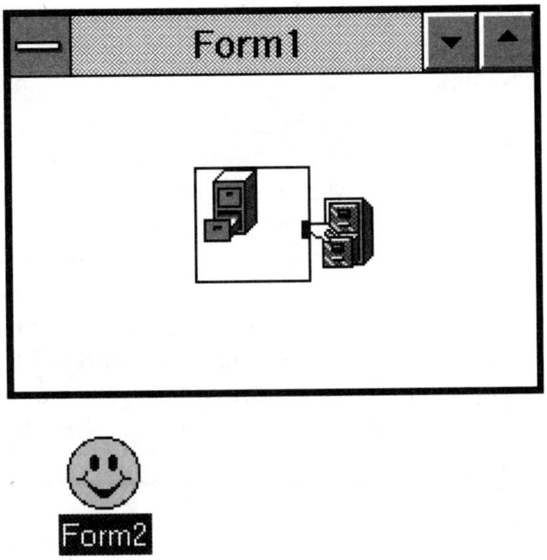

**Figure 8.11 Picture of example syntax**

The Icon, DragIcon, and Picture properties are all definable at run time with this function. This function overrides the initial setting of these properties.

In the example syntax, the LoadPicture function redefines all three types of properties to signify the beginning of a drag operation. This is a graphical method of displaying the current action by changing the Picture property of the picture box. The picture box becomes an open file cabinet to signify the beginning of a drag operation. See Figure 8.11 for a picture of what the example syntax should look like.

### The DragIcon Property

Define the DragIcon of a control at run time with a LoadPicture function similar to the one in the example syntax. This icon displays from when a drag operation begins until the drag operation ends. This permits the program to signify to the user the type of operation taking place. For example, the DragIcon changes to an open file folder or a diskette to signify when a file or an entire disk copies from one place to another.

### The Icon Property

Define the Icon property of a control at run time with a LoadPicture function similar to the one used in the example syntax. This icon represents a minimized form. By changing the Icon property of a form, the program specifies the type of operation taking place. For example, a communications program changes the icon property of a dialer directory form to a phone off the hook when the dialer dials a number.

### The Picture Property

The LoadPicture function defines the Picture property of a form or picture box at run time in the same way as the example syntax. Either the AutoRedraw of the form or the Picture must be True, or the changes must occur within a Paint event for it to be immediately apparent. For example, the icon displayed in the Picture1 control box does not change unless the AutoRedraw property is True.

### Example

In the Graphics project at the end of this section, the LoadPicture function defines the picture box Blanker_Icon with other icons that define the type of blanker option currently selected. When the program starts, the topmost control of the Blanker_Options control array receives the focus, triggering the Blanker_Options_GotFocus event. This event uses a Select Case statement to determine the index property of the currently active control. Based on the Index property value, the Picture property of the picture box Blanker_Icon changes to the icon MOON01.ICO. In this case, the LoadPicture function redefines the Picture property of the picture box to another icon based on the selected Blanker_Options control. Notice that no file indicates when the active control is the one labeled Squares. This has the effect of instructing the Picture property not to display an image on the screen.

### Comments

A LoadPicture function expression without the name of a graphics file has the effect of blanking the contents of the Picture, Icon, or DragIcon properties of an object.

# Paint Event

## Objects Affected

| | | | | |
|---|---|---|---|---|
| Check | Clipboard | Combo | Command | Dbug |
| Dir | Drive | File | ▶ Form | Frame |
| Label | List | Menu | Option | ▶ Picture |
| Printer | Screen | Scroll | Text | Timer |

## Purpose

The Paint event defines what actions take place with the uncovering of a previously obscured part of a form or picture box. Either restoring a minimized form or uncovering an obscured form triggers a Paint event. This event only applies to generated graphics and does not affect the appearance of the controls on a form. Table 8.7 summarizes the arguments of the Paint event.

## General Syntax

```
Sub Form_Paint ()
Sub CtlName_Paint ([Index As Integer])
```

| Argument | Description |
|----------|-------------|
| CtlName | CtlName property of the affected picture box |
| FormName | FormName property of the affected form |

**Table 8.7 Possible arguments of the Paint event**

## Example Syntax

```
Sub Form_Click ()
    Refresh                              'Triggers the paint event
End Sub

Sub Form_Paint ()
    Static Num As Integer                'Define Num as static variable
    X = ScaleWidth / 2                   'Define X as half of width of form
    Y = ScaleHeight / 2                  'Define Y as half of height of form
    Radius = ScaleWidth / 4              'Define Radius as 1/4 of width of form
    FillStyle = 0                        'Objects drawn will be solid
    Num = Num + 1                        'Increment the variable Num
    Select Case Num
        Case 1                           'Num = 1
            FillColor = QBColor(0)       'FillColor is black
            Circle (X, Y), Radius, , -6.283, -1.571  'Draw part of a circle
        Case 2                           'Num = 2
            FillColor = QBColor(1)       'FillColor is blue
            Circle (X, Y), Radius, , -1.571, -3.142  'Draw part of a circle
        Case 3                           'Num = 3
            FillColor = QBColor(2)       'FillColor is green
            Circle (X, Y), Radius, , -3.142, -4.713  'Draw part of a circle
        Case 4                           'Num = 4
            FillColor = QBColor(3)       'FillColor is Cyan
            Circle (X, Y), Radius, , -4.713, -6.283  'Draw part of a circle
        Case 5                           'Num = 5
            FillColor = QBColor(4)       'FillColor is red
            Circle (X, Y), Radius        'Draw a red circle
        Case 6                           'Num = 6
            Num = 0                       'Reset Num for the drawing of the
                                         'next
    End Select                           'series of circles
End Sub
```

## Description

The Paint event may contain actions that place graphics objects on the screen. A Paint event triggers when the form loads, at the uncovering of a form, or when a minimized form changes to normalized or maximized style. This event normally reproduces the same graphic image or images on a form or picture box. In some cases, however, it can produce a totally new graphics image. In the example syntax, triggering the paint event by each click on the form produces a new portion of a circle on the screen. This example demonstrates the flexibility of the paint event, which allows for changes in the graphical images appearing on a screen. Figure 8.12 displays what the example syntax might look like on the screen.

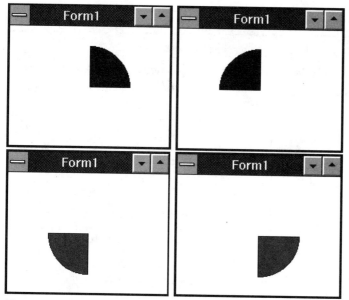

**Figure 8.12 Graphics displayed in example syntax**

### Graphics from the Circle, Line, PSet, and Print Methods

The Paint event directly affects the production of the graphics and text effects produced by the Circle, Line, PSet, and Print methods. With the AutoRedraw of a form or picture box set to False, the Paint event reproduces any expressions that place graphics or text upon the form or picture box. Otherwise, hidden portions of drawn graphics on forms and controls do not reappear when uncovered.

### The AutoRedraw Property

The AutoRedraw property and Paint event share similar tasks. Both determine what happens to a form when loaded or uncovered. The example syntax demonstrates one very important difference. A form with its AutoRedraw property set to True (-1) only reproduces the portions of the screens drawn while that property was True. This is in direct contrast to the example syntax showing that the Paint event can process actions that produce entirely different graphics with each triggering of the Paint event.

### The Refresh Method

The Refresh method triggers the Paint event of a form. This method represents a means of activating a paint event when it is necessary without the normal criteria for generating one. In the example syntax, the Refresh method is in the Form_Click event so that the Paint event triggers with each clicking of the form. With this setup, the image on the form changes under the control of the user.

### The Load, Resize, Paint, and GotFocus Events

If there is more than one event attached to a particular control, they process in the following order: Load, Resize, Paint, and GotFocus. This is an important point to keep in mind if any of the actions that take place in one event depend on actions in another event. For example, a data entry form for an address book would cause an error if the Load event disables the Address1 text box and the GotFocus event tries to use it.

## Example

The Graphics project at the end of this section demonstrates the operation of the Paint event as part of the Screen_Blanker form. When the Form_Click event triggers, the

Refresh method activates the Paint event of the Screen_Blanker form. The Paint event resets the BackColor property of the form to white. This demonstrates the triggering of the Paint event with the Refresh method. This also shows that the activation of a timer has the effect of disabling the Paint event. Normally, the Paint event triggers when a form loads. The Timer event prevents this from taking place.

## Comments

Both the Paint event and the AutoRedraw property produce the same type of results on a specific form. Try not to use them both together.

# Picture Property

## Objects Affected

| | | | | |
|---|---|---|---|---|
| Check | Clipboard | Combo | Command | Dbug |
| Dir | Drive | File | ▶ Form | Frame |
| Label | List | Menu | Option | ▶ Picture |
| Printer | Screen | Scroll | Text | Timer |

## Purpose

The Picture property indicates what image appears on a form or picture box. This property is definable at either design time or run time, and defaults to display nothing. A picture box contains run time drawn graphics or a loaded picture file. Tables 8.8 and 8.9 summarize the different arguments and choices of the Picture property.

## General Syntax

```
[form.]Picture[=picture]
[picturebox.]Picture[=picture]
```

| Argument | Description |
|---|---|
| form | FormName of the form |
| picturebox | CtlName of the picture box |
| picture | Picture property setting |

Table 8.8 Arguments of the Picture property

| Picture | Effect |
|---|---|
| None | No picture (Default setting) |
| Picture | Contains the name and path of the graphic file to display on the form or picture box |

Table 8.9 Picture property choices

## Example Syntax

```
Sub Picture1.Click
    Picture1.AutoRedraw = -1              'Objects redrawn when uncovered
    X = Picture1.ScaleWidth /2           'X equals width of picture box
    Y = Picture1.ScaleHeight / 2         'Y equals height of picture box
    Radius = Picture1.ScaleWidth /4      'Radius equals picture box's width
    Picture1.FillStyle = 0               'Solid fillstyle
    Picture1.Fillcolor = QBColor(4)      'Fill color is red
    If Command1.Caption = "Icon" Then    'If the caption is "Icon"
        Picture1.Picture = LoadPicture("\VB\ICONS\MISC\FACE03.ICO")
                                         'Picture is a smiling face
        Command1.Caption = "Circle"
    ElseIf Command1.Caption = "Circle" Then   'If the caption is "Circle"
        Picture1.Circle (X, Y),Radius    'Draw a circle
        Command1.Caption = "Square"
    ElseIf Command1.Caption = "Square" Then   'If the caption is "Square"
        Picture1.Line(500,500) - Step (1000,1000), , BF      'Draw a square
        Command1.Caption = "Other"
    ElseIf Command1.Caption = "Other" Then    'If the caption is "Other"
        Picture2.Picture = Picture1.Image     'Makes the Picture2 box the same
        Command1.Caption = "Icon"             'as the Picture1 picture box
    End If
End Sub
```

## Description

The Picture property determines the graphic image that displays on a form or picture box. A loaded picture must be in bitmap (*.BMP), icon (*.ICO), or Windows metafile (*.WMF)

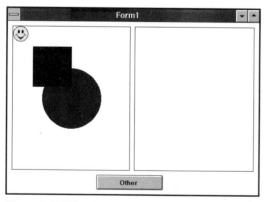

format. A Picture property contains the picture file, with or without its extension. If the file is in the current search path or the same directory, then the extension is not necessary. In the example syntax, the picture box displays a circle, a square, or an icon with each clicking of the picture. This demonstrates the full range of graphics that may be displayed on a picture box or form. Figure 8.13 shows what the example syntax might look like on the screen.

The example syntax defines the Picture property with the name and path of the FACE03.ICO.

**Figure 8.13 What the example syntax might look like**

### The LoadPicture Function

The LoadPicture function redefines the Picture property of a form or picture box. This image file overrides the default setting. Picture boxes contain graphics files in bitmap (*.BMP), icon (*.ICO), or Windows metafile (*.WMF) format. The LoadPicture function is unnecessary at design time. As shown in the example syntax, the LoadPicture function works as a simple definition expression.

### The Image Property

In order to place the same picture in one picture box as in another, redefine the Picture property of a picture box with the Image property of another. Microsoft Windows gives every graphic image in Visual Basic a unique value returned by the Image property of a picture box or form. In the example syntax, the Picture property of Picture2 equals the Image property of Picture1. This has the effect of reproducing all of the graphic images of Picture1 in the Picture2 picture box.

### Example

In the Graphics project at the end of this section, the Picture property of the picture box Blanker_Icon changes according to the currently selected blanker option on screen. The initially selected control of the control array Blanker_Options is the option control labeled Blank Screen. For this reason, the Picture property of the Blanker_Icon picture box changes to \VB\ICONS\MISC\MOON01.ICO.

When the program starts, the Graphics form displays on the screen. The topmost control of the Blanker_Options control array receives the focus triggering the Blanker_Options_GotFocus event. This event determines the currently active control. The Picture property of the picture box Blanker_Icon changes to the icon MOON01.ICO. In this case, the LoadPicture function redefines the Picture property of the picture box to another icon based on the Blanker_Options control selected. While the active control is the one labeled Squares, the Blanker_Icon Picture property changes to nothing. In this way, the Blanker_Icon picture box displays nothing on the screen.

### Comments

The Picture property can display both a graphics file and drawn graphics images at the same time.

# Point Method

### Objects Affected

| | | | | |
|---|---|---|---|---|
| Check | Clipboard | Combo | Command | Dbug |
| Dir | Drive | File | ▶ Form | Frame |
| Label | List | Menu | Option | ▶ Picture |
| Printer | Screen | Scroll | Text | Timer |

### Purpose

The Point method returns the RGB hexidecimal value of the color of a specified point on a form or picture box. This method only works at run time. The x! and y! coordinates of the point on the form or picture box appear in every Point method expression. If no object name precedes the Point name, then it returns the color of the current point on the form. Table 8.10 summarizes the arguments of the Point method.

## General Syntax

```
[object.]Point(x!,y!)
```

| Argument | Description |
|----------|-------------|
| object | FormName of form or CtlName of picture box |
| x! | Horizontal coordinate of the point on the object |
| y! | Vertical coordinate of the point on the object |

Table 8.10 Arguments of the Point method

## Example Syntax

```
Sub Form_Click ()
    AutoRedraw = -1              'Sets form's AutoRedraw property to True
    FillStyle = 0               'Sets drawn object to solid
    FillColor = QBColor(0)      'Sets drawn object to black
    X = ScaleWidth / 2          'Sets X equal to half of the width of the form
    Y = ScaleHeight / 2         'Sets Y equal to half of the height of the form
    Radius = ScaleWidth / 4     'Sets radius equal to 1/4 of the width of the form
    Circle (X, Y), Radius       'Draws a circle on the form
End Sub

Sub Command1_Click
    BackColor = Point (CurrentX,CurrentY)   'Changes the background color to circle's
                                            'color
End Sub
```

## Description

The Point method indicates the RGB hexidecimal color of a place on a form or picture box. This value defines the color of other portions of a form or picture box. An object indicated must be either the CtlName of a picture box or the FormName of a form. Both the x and y coordinates must be single variable values. These variables may represent values of measurements according to the ScaleMode measurement type for a variable. Otherwise, these values appear as fractions of the ScaleHeight and ScaleWidth properties.

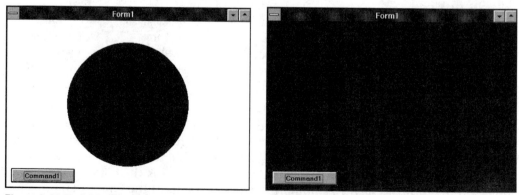

Figure 8.14 Circle drawn on the form          Figure 8.15 Black background on form

In the example syntax, the background color of the form changes to black when the user presses the Command1 command button. The Point method finds the color of the current coordinates on the form in the center of the black circle. This results in changing the background color of the form to black. With no CtlName or FormName provided, the color of the form changes. Figures 8.14 and 8.15 show the pictures of the form before and after the user presses the Command1 command button.

### The CurrentX and CurrentY Properties

The combination of the Point method and the CurrentX and CurrentY properties provides the color of the current coordinates on a form or picture box. The current coordinates begin in the upper left corner of the form or picture box. Each drawn object changes the coordinates based on where the object appears. As shown in the example syntax, the CurrentX and CurrentY properties directly define the x and y coordinates of a Point method. Since the CurrentX and CurrentY coordinates are already in the center of the drawn circle, the coordinates do not change. This returns the color of the circle in the center of the form. In this way, the BackColor of the entire form changes to blue, effectively removing the circle from view.

## Example

In the Graphics project at the end of this section, the Blank_Timer event uses the Point method to reset the BackColor property of the Screen_Blanker form. This is done with a Point method expression that uses the CurrentX and CurrentY coordinates to determine the color of the current point on the form. Since the BackColor property of the form is already white, the background remains white. Although there is no change to the color of the background of the form, the redefinition of the BackColor of the form has the effect of erasing all of the graphics images on the screen. If the AutoRedraw property of the form is True, then the graphics image is unaffected.

## Comments

The Point method will generate an error if the coordinates are not specified.

# PSet Method

## Objects Affected

| | | | | |
|---|---|---|---|---|
| Check | Clipboard | Combo | Command | Dbug |
| Dir | Drive | File | ▶ Form | Frame |
| Label | List | Menu | Option | ▶ Picture |
| ▶ Printer | Screen | Scroll | Text | Timer |

## Purpose

The PSet method sets the RGB hexadecimal value of the color of a point on a form, picture box, or printer object. The DrawWidth property of the form, picture box, or printer object determines the size of this point. This method only works at run time. A point's coordinates must be provided. If no object name precedes the Point name, then the point of color appears on the form. In this way, points of differing colors can be displayed on a form or picture box. Table 8.11 summarizes the arguments of the PSet method.

## General Syntax

```
[object.]PSet[Step](x!,y!),[,color&]
```

| Argument | Description |
|----------|-------------|
| object | FormName of form, ControlName of control, or Printer for printer object |
| Step | X and Y coordinates measure distance from the current coordinates on the object |
| x!,y! | Horizontal and vertical distance from upper left corner of the object or the current coordinates |
| color& | Hexadecimal value representing the created point's color |

**Table 8.11 Arguments of the PSet method**

## Example Syntax

```
'This subroutine will draw a point on the screen at the interval specified for the timer
'(Must be other than 0).

Sub Timer1_Timer ()
    Static Color As Integer
    X = Int((ScaleWidth - (ScaleWidth / 20)) * Rnd + (ScaleWidth / 20))
    Y = Int((ScaleHeight - (ScaleHeight / 20)) * Rnd + (ScaleHeight / 20))
    DrawWidth = 20
    PSet (X, Y), QBColor(Color)
    If Color <> 15 Then
        Color = Color + 1
    Else
        Color = 0
    End If
End Sub
```

### Description

The PSet method places a point of color (in RGB hexadecimal format) on a specified point of a form, picture box, or Printer object. An object is a picture box's CtlName, or a form's FormName, or Printer for the printer object. If there is no specified object, then the point of color appears upon the current form. This method requires both the x! and y! coordinates in single value format. When the Step option is in a PSet expression, the coordinates given are in relation to the current position of the horizontal and vertical screen coordinates. Normally, the x! and y! coordinates measure the distance from the upper left corner of the object. In the example syntax, the PSet method places points with differing colors at random locations on the screen. See Figure 8.16 for a picture of this example.

## The RGB and QBColor Functions

Set the color of a PSet method expression with either the RGB or QBColor functions. For specialized color combinations, use the RGB function. The RGB function provides the ability to set the red, green, and blue elements of a color to produce its hexadecimal value. If one of the standard colors is acceptable, then the QBColor function provides a means of setting the color with one value. Set a QBColor function with a value between 0 and 15, as used in Quick BASIC and other versions of Microsoft BASIC. The example syntax uses the QBColor function to redefine the color of the point with each generation of the Timer1 event. A static variable named Color keeps the last value in the QBColor function between each generation of the Timer1 event. This value increments by one with each execution of the Timer1 event until it reaches 15. In this way, each generated spot is in a different color.

## The Rnd Function and Timer Event

For the purposes of the example syntax, the Rnd function and Timer event produce points of color on the screen. The Rnd function produces random values for the X and Y coordinates of the PSet method. These expressions use a formula that ensures that the value returned is always between the maximum and mini-

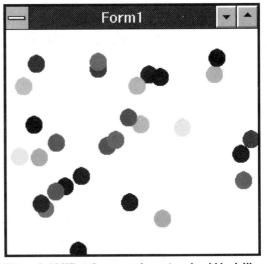

**Figure 8.16 What the example syntax should look like**

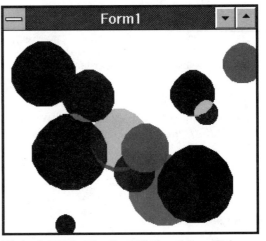

**Figure 8.17 What the DrawWidth and DrawMode examples should look like**

mum values. In this case, the total width and height of the form sets the maximum and minimum values. This ensures that the points of color do not generate off the visible portions of the form. The Timer event triggers at intervals set at design time at the designer's discretion (try 1000 first).

## The DrawMode and DrawWidth Properties

The PSet method also produces points of varying sizes and colors with changes to DrawMode and DrawWidth properties. These properties control the size and effect of the graphics generated with the PSet method. By using the formula used for the X and Y coordinates to set the boundaries of random numbers, the DrawMode property's setting randomly changes to produce different types of colored dots. The next example also varies the size of the circles by scaling DrawWidth to a random value. Figure 8.17 shows what this example might look like.

```
'This event draws points of varying size and color on the form at the interval
'set at design time.
Sub Timer1_Timer ()
    Static Color As Integer
    X = Int((ScaleWidth - (ScaleWidth / 20)) * Rnd + (ScaleWidth / 20))
    Y = Int((ScaleHeight - (ScaleHeight / 20)) * Rnd + (ScaleHeight / 20))
    DrawMode = Int((16 - (1)) * Rnd + (1))
    DrawWidth = Int((100 - (20)) * Rnd + (20))
    PSet (X, Y), QBColor(Color)
    If Color <> 15 Then
        Color = Color + 1
    Else
        Color = 0
    End If
End Sub
```

### The CurrentX and CurrentY Properties

The CurrentX and CurrentY properties are excellent replacements for the x! and y! arguments of the PSet method. These properties return the current horizontal and vertical position on the form, picture box, or printer object (see Chapter 24, *Sending Data to the Printer*). When a form loads, the default position is in the upper right corner of the form, picture box, or printer object. This position changes with the use of the Circle, Line, PSet, and Cls methods according to the new coordinates that they set. In this way, the point appears at the present horizontal and vertical position on the screen.

## Example

In the Graphics project at the end of this section, the PSet method generates spots of color on the screen with the Spots option selected on the Graphics form. On the basis of the random setting of the X and Y coordinate variables and the Color variable, a spot of color appears on the screen. The random setting of the DrawWidth property determines the size of the spot. In this way, a series of color spots of random size appears on the screen at random locations. This is an excellent demonstration of the possible uses of the PSet method.

## Comments

The shape of a point on a form made with the PSet method is a circle.

# QBColor Function

## Purpose

The QBColor function helps to define the color of an object on the screen. An object defined with this function is one of 16 possible colors. Every color is a combination of RGB color values that make up its hexadecimal value. In the example syntax, all the possible color choices appear in a 16-box grid. Each color displays in numerical order from left to right and top to bottom. Table 8.12 summarizes the color returned in QBColor, with the values defined.

## General Syntax

QBColor(qbcolor%)

| qbcolor% | Color |
|----------|-------|
| 0 | Black |
| 1 | Blue |
| 2 | Green |
| 3 | Cyan |
| 4 | Red |
| 5 | Magenta |
| 6 | Yellow |
| 7 | White |
| 8 | Gray |
| 9 | Light Blue |
| 10 | Light Green |
| 11 | Light Cyan |
| 12 | Light Red |
| 13 | Light Magenta |
| 14 | Light Yellow |
| 15 | Bright White |

Table 8.12 List of the colors returned in QBColor with the values defined

## Example Syntax

```
Sub Form_Click ()
    AutoRedraw = -1                'Sets form AutoRedraw property to True
```

```
    Cls                             'Clears the screen
    ScaleHeight = 4                 'Divides height of form into four parts
    ScaleWidth = 4                  'Divides width of form into four parts
    Color% = 0                      'Defines Color variable as 0
    For H% = 0 To 3                 'Draw a grid of 16 colors
        For W% = 0 To 3
            Line (W%, H%)-(W% + 1, H% + 1), QBColor(Color%), BF
            Color% = Color% + 1
        Next W%
    Next H%
End Sub
```

## Description

The QBColor function defines the RGB hexadecimal color code of a specified number. Each number specified in a QBColor function must be between 0 and 15. These numbers represent preset color combinations of RGB values displayed on the screen by setting the BackColor, ForeColor, or FillColor properties of a form, picture box, or Printer object. The QBColor function sets the color of the Circle and Line methods. In the example syntax, the QBColor function provides the colors of the boxes drawn with the Line method.

### The FillColor, BackColor, and ForeColor Properties

The QBColor function provides the hexadecimal color for the FillColor, BackColor, and ForeColor properties. In the next example, the background color of a form changes to blue. The code references the new property setting with the next clicking of the form to change the color back to white.

```
Sub Form_Click
    If BackColor = QBColor(15)          'Checks if BackColor is white
        BackColor -=QBColor(1)          'BackColor is blue
    ElseIf BackColor = QBColor(1)       'Checks if BackColor is blue
        BackColor = QBColor(15)         'BackColor is white
    End If
End Sub
```

## Example

In the Graphics project at the end of this section, the QBColor function sets the BackColor and ForeColor properties of the forms and the color of spots, circles, squares, and lines. The Form_Click and Form_Paint events of Screen_Blanker forms reset their BackColor property to white. This demonstrates the common use of the QBColor function as a way of setting a color for an object.

Each QBColor definition has the variable Color placed in the parentheses that follow the QBColor name. This variable increases by one each time that the timer event processes until the value reaches 15. Every value represents a color that displays in the indicated spot, circle, square, or line on the screen. At that point, the Color variable changes to 0 and the process repeats. Either the QBColor function or RGB function would work in the places where the QBColor function appears in the code. The QBColor function is better here because it makes the process of changing the colors easier, with only one variable to increment.

## Comments

The QBfunction returns a hexadecimal code contained by a variable when made equal to this value.

# RGB Function

## Purpose

The RGB function provides a means of defining the color of an object on the screen. RGB functions only change the colors of objects within the context of FillColor, BackColor, and ForeColor property expressions. When the RGB function is in an expression, the color of the indicated object changes. An object's color changes through the setting of three variables: red, green, and blue. Each value in an RGB function expression represents the amount of red, green, and blue contained in the displayed color. In the example syntax, the RGB function provides the color of the BackColor and ForeColor properties of a form. The code also references the color as a test for which color change to make. Table 8.13 summarizes the values of common colors in RGB, QBColor, and hexadecimal formats.

## General Syntax

```
RGB(red%,green%,blue%)
```

| Color | Red Value | Green Value | Blue Value | Hexadecimal | QBColor |
|-------|-----------|-------------|------------|-------------|---------|
| Black | 0 | 0 | 0 | &H0 | 0 |
| Red | 255 | 0 | 0 | &HFF | 4 |
| Green | 0 | 255 | 0 | &HFF00 | 2 |
| Yellow | 0 | 255 | 255 | &HFFFF | 6 |
| Blue | 0 | 0 | 255 | &HFF000 | 1 |
| Magenta | 255 | 0 | 255 | &HFF00FF | 5 |
| Cyan | 0 | 255 | 255 | &HFFFF00 | 3 |
| White | 255 | 255 | 255 | &HFFFFFF | 15 |
| Light Gray | 192 | 192 | 192 | &H00C0C0C0 | 7 |
| Dark Gray | 128 | 128 | 128 | &H00808080 | 8 |

Table 8.13 Values of common colors in RGB, QBColor, and hexadecimal formats

## Example Syntax

```
Sub Form_Load ()
    BackColor = RGB(255,255,255)          'Defines BackColor as white
    ForeColor = RGB(0, 0, 255)            'Defines ForeColor as blue
End Sub
```

```
Sub Form_Click ()
    If BackColor = RGB(255,255,255) Then        'Checks if BackColor is white
        BackColor = RGB(0, 0, 255)              'Defines BackColor as blue
        ForeColor = RGB(255,255,255)            'Defines ForeColor as white
    ElseIf BackColor = RGB(0, 0, 255) Then      'Checks if BackColor is blue
        BackColor = RGB(255,255,255)            'Defines BackColor as white
        ForeColor = RGB(0, 0, 255)              'Defines ForeColor as blue
    End If
End Sub
```

## Description

The RGB function returns the hexadecimal value of the combination of three color values. Each of the numbers in an RGB function is between 0 and 255. Each number represents a preset color combination of Red, Green, and Blue values. This color displays on the screen when it appears in the color argument of the BackColor, ForeColor, or FillColor properties. The RGB function also provides the color of objects drawn with the Circle and Line methods. In the example syntax, the RGB function defines the color argument of the Line method expression that generates the squares of colors on the screen. This demonstrates the use of the RGB function to change and reference the color of an object. Initially, the background and foreground colors of the form change to white and blue, respectively, in the Form_Load event.

### The FillColor, BackColor, and ForeColor Properties

The RGB function provides the hexadecimal color for the FillColor, BackColor, and ForeColor properties. In the example syntax, the background and foreground colors of the form are initially blue and white. The next clicking of the form references the BackColor property to change these two properties back to white and blue.

## Example

The Graphics project at the end of this section uses the RGB function with the selection of the option box labeled Blank Screen. In this case, the Blanker_Timer event changes the BackColor of the form to black with an RGB function definition. For the purposes of this color definition, the color does not change with each processing of the Blanker_Timer event.

## Comments

The RGB function is not definable using the QBColor function.

# SavePicture Statement

## Objects Affected

| Check | Clipboard | Combo | Command | Dbug |
|-------|-----------|-------|---------|------|
| Dir | Drive | File | ▶ Form | Frame |
| Label | List | Menu | Option | ▶ Picture |
| Printer | Screen | Scroll | Text | Timer |

## Purpose

The SavePicture statement saves a file or drawn object on a picture box or form to a new file. Any drawn objects on a picture box or form save as a bitmap (*.BMP). Identify the graphics to save with the Image property of the form or picture box. A file that loads into the Picture property of a form or picture box saves in the same format as the original file. Place the name of the file name to save to in the stringexpression$. Table 8.14 summarizes the arguments of the SavePicture statement.

## General Syntax

`SavePicture picture, stringexpression$`

| Argument | Description |
|---|---|
| picture | Image property of form or picture box that the graphics are on |
| stringexpression$ | Path and filename of the file to save |

Table 8.14 Arguments of the SavePicture statement

## Example Syntax

```
Sub Command1_Click ()
    AutoRedraw = -1        'Ensures that graphics remain on the form
    ScaleWidth = 4         'Draws a square on the screen and saves it to the
    ScaleHeight = 4        'file SQUARE.BMP in the Visual Basic directory.
    X = 1
    Y = 1
    Line (X, Y)-(X + 2, Y + 2), QBColor(1), BF
    SavePicture Image, "C:\VB\SQUARE.BMP"
End Sub
```

## Description

The SavePicture statement saves the current contents of a picture box or form to a file. When the picture to save is a loaded file, this statement saves the file in its original format. Loaded files saved with the SavePicture must be in one of the following formats: icon (*.ICO), bitmap (*.BMP), and Windows metafile (*.WMF). In this case, a SavePicture statement includes the name of the file with its extension. The path of the file is optional. This statement also provides a means of saving the graphics on a form or picture box. A SavePicture statement's picture argument identifies exactly which graphics to save with the Image property of the form or

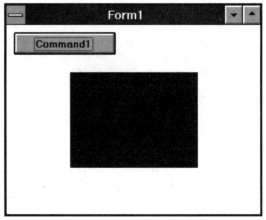

Figure 8.18 Square drawn by pressing Command1 command button

picture box. The example syntax saves the current contents of the form to the file SQUARE.BMP. Figure 8.18 shows what the square might look like on the form.

## Example

In the Graphics project at the end of this section, the SavePicture statement saves the drawn graphics on the screen. Until the user clicks the form with the mouse, the screen either remains black or keeps generating spots, circles, squares, or lines. Clicking the form causes the display of a message box that asks if the user wishes to save the current image on the screen to a file. If the user responds "Yes," then the SavePicture statement accesses the Image property of the Screen_Blanker form to determine the Windows handle value. Using this value, the SavePicture statement saves the current picture to the bitmap file TEST.BMP. This process demonstrates the use of the SavePicture statement and Image property.

## Comments

The SavePicture statement works with either a form or a picture box only and does not include any of the controls on the form.

# Graphics Project

## Project Overview

The Graphics project demonstrates the properties of the Visual Basic Language that affect basic graphics on a form or picture box. This project shows the operation of the properties, methods, functions, statement, and event that manipulate graphics. All of these elements appear in the setup and operation of the Graphics project. By following the examples of the different forms and subroutines of this project, you will learn how to change basic graphics on a picture box or form.

The first section deals with the assembly of the controls and subroutines of the Graphics form. The next section discusses the construction of the controls and subroutines of the Screen_Blanker form. Each of these sections includes step-by-step instructions on how to put together the form and its controls. A section on how the program works follows these two sections. Please read this information carefully, and use the pictures of the forms as guides in the assembling of this project.

## Assembling the Project

1. Make a new form (the Graphics form) with the objects and properties listed in Table 8.15. Notice that all of the OptionBox controls have the CtlName property of Blanker_Options. The second control created with the same name generates a message asking you if you wish to create a control array. Please respond "Yes." If you wish to avoid this, simply change the first control's Index property to 0. This has the effect of creating a control array without the message.

| Object | Property | Setting |
|--------|----------|---------|
| Form | AutoRedraw | True |
| | BackColor | White, RGB(255,255,255), &H00FFFFFF |

|  | BorderStyle | 1 - Fixed Single |
|  | Caption | Graphics Project |
|  | ControlBox | False |
|  | ForeColor | Blue, RGB(0, 0, 0), &HFF000 |
|  | FormName | Graphics |
|  | Icon | ..\VB\ICONS\MISC\MOON01.ICO |
|  | MaxButton | False |
|  | MinButton | True |
| Frame | Caption | Blanker Options |
|  | CtlName | Blanker_Frame |
| OptionBox | Caption | Blank Screen |
|  | CtlName | Blanker_Options |
|  | Index | 0 |
|  | TabIndex | 0 |
| OptionBox | Caption | Color Spots |
|  | CtlName | Blanker_Options |
|  | Index | 1 |
|  | TabIndex | 1 |
| OptionBox | Caption | Circles |
|  | CtlName | Blanker_Options |
|  | Index | 2 |
|  | TabIndex | 2 |
| OptionBox | Caption | Squares |
|  | CtlName | Blanker_Options |
|  | Index | 3 |
|  | TabIndex | 3 |
| OptionBox | Caption | Lines |
|  | CtlName | Blanker_Options |
|  | Index | 4 |
|  | TabIndex | 4 |
| Picture | AutoRedraw | True |
|  | AutoSize | True |
|  | BackColor | White, RGB(255,255,255), &H00FFFFFF |
|  | BorderStyle | None |
|  | CtlName | Blanker_Icon |
|  | Picture | ..\VB\ICONS\MISC\MOON01.ICO |
| Command button | Caption | Activate Blanker |
|  | CtlName | Activate_Blanker |
| Command button | Caption | Quit |
|  | CtlName | Quit_Program |

Table 8.15 Properties and controls of the Graphics form in the Graphics project

2. Size the objects on the screen, as shown in Figure 8.19.

3. Enter the following code in the Activate_Blanker_Click event subroutine. This code triggers when the user presses the command button labeled Activate Blanker. This routine hides the Graphics form from the user's view and displays the Screen_Blanker form on the screen.

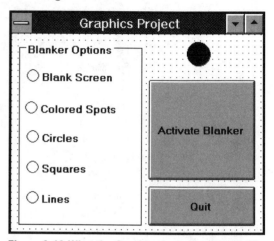

```
Sub Activate_Blanker_Click ()
    Graphics.Hide
    Screen_Blanker.Show
End Sub
```

**Figure 8.19 What the Graphics form should look like when completed**

4. Enter the following code in the Blanker_Options_GotFocus event subroutine. This routine activates when one of the controls of the control array Blanker_Options receives the focus. Based on the active control, the Picture property of the picture box Blanker_Icon changes to the indicated icon. Unless the control option labeled Squares is the active control, the BackColor of the picture box is white; otherwise, it is black.

```
Sub Blanker_Options_GotFocus (Index As Integer)
    Select Case Screen.ActiveControl.Index
        Case 0
            Blanker_Icon.Picture = LoadPicture("\VB\ICONS\MISC\MOONO1.ICO")
            Blanker_Icon.BackColor = QBColor(15)
        Case 1
            Blanker_Icon.Picture = LoadPicture("\VB\ICONS\MISC\MOONO5.ICO")
            Blanker_Icon.BackColor = QBColor(15)
        Case 2
            Blanker_Icon.Picture = LoadPicture("\VB\ICONS\MISC\MISC38.ICO")
            Blanker_Icon.BackColor = QBColor(15)
        Case 3
            Blanker_Icon.Picture = LoadPicture()
            Blanker_Icon.BackColor = QBColor(0)
        Case 4
            Blanker_Icon.Picture = LoadPicture("\VB\ICONS\MISC\MISC22.ICO")
            Blanker_Icon.BackColor = QBColor(15)
    End Select
    CurrentIndex = Screen.ActiveControl.Index
    Icon = Blanker_Icon.Picture
End Sub
```

5. Enter the following code in the Program_Quit event subroutine. This code triggers when the user presses the command button labeled Quit. When this is done, the End statement closes the program.

```
Sub Quit_Program_Click ()
    End
End Sub
```

### The Screen_Blanker Form

1. Make a new form with the objects and properties listed in Table 8.16.

| Object | Property | Setting |
|--------|----------|---------|
| Form | AutoRedraw | False |
| | BackColor | White, RGB(255,255,255), &H00FFFFFF |
| | BorderStyle | 0 - None |
| | Caption | "" |
| | ControlBox | False |
| | FormName | Screen_Blanker |
| | MaxButton | False |
| | MinButton | False |
| | MousePointer | 11 - Hourglass |
| Timer | CtlName | Blanker |
| | Enabled | False |
| | Interval | 100 |

**Table 8.16 Objects and properties of the Screen_Blanker 2 form**

2. Size the objects on the screen, as shown in Figure 8.20.

3. Enter the following code in the General Declarations section of the Screen_Blanker form. This code defines the variable Color, which is used to set the colors of the graphics objects drawn on the screen.

```
Dim Color As Integer
```

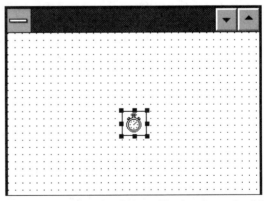

**Figure 8.20 What the Screen_Blanker form should look like**

4. Enter the following code in the Blanker_Timer event subroutine. This routine triggers when the Enabled property of the Blanker timer changes to True and processes at intervals of 100 milliseconds. Depending on the selected option box on the Graphics form, a blank screen or a series of colored spots, circles, squares, or lines appears on the screen. These graphics continue to generate on the screen until the user clicks the form.

```
Sub Blanker_Timer ()
   X = Int((ScaleWidth - (ScaleWidth / 20)) * Rnd + (ScaleWidth / 20))
   Y = Int((ScaleHeight - (ScaleHeight / 20)) * Rnd + (ScaleHeight / 20))
   DrawWidth = Int((100 - (20)) * Rnd + (20))
   Select Case CurrentIndex
      Case 0
         Screen_Blanker.BackColor = RGB(0, 0, 0)
      Case 1
         Screen_Blanker.PSet (X, Y), QBColor(Color)
      Case 2
         Radius = Int((ScaleWidth / 2 - (ScaleWidth / 20)) * Rnd + (ScaleWidth / 20))
         Circle (X, Y), Radius, QBColor(Color)
      Case 3
         X1 = Int((ScaleWidth - (ScaleWidth / 20)) * Rnd + (ScaleWidth / 20))
         Y1 = Int((ScaleHeight - (ScaleHeight / 20)) * Rnd + (ScaleHeight / 20))
         Line (X, Y)-(X1, Y1), QBColor(Color), BF
      Case 4
         X1 = Int((ScaleWidth - (ScaleWidth / 20)) * Rnd + (ScaleWidth / 20))
         Y1 = Int((ScaleHeight - (ScaleHeight / 20)) * Rnd + (ScaleHeight / 20))
         Line (X, Y)-(X1, Y1), QBColor(Color)
   End Select
   If CurrentIndex <> 0 Then
      If Color <> 15 Then
         Color = Color + 1
      Else
         Color = 0
         BackColor = Point(CurrentX, CurrentY)
      End If
   End If
End Sub
```

5. Enter the following code in the Form_Click event subroutine. This routine processes when the user clicks the form with the mouse. This asks the user if he or she wishes to save the bitmap on the screen. The user is also asked if he or she wishes to exit this blanker.

```
Sub Form_Click ()
   Blanker.Enabled = 0
   Screen_Blanker.Refresh
   Msg$ = "Would you like to save this image?"
   Title$ = "Graphics Project"
   Ans% = MsgBox(Msg$, 4, Title$)
   If Ans% = 6 Then
      SavePicture Image, "C:\VB\TEST.BMP"
   End If
   Screen_Blanker.Refresh
   Msg$ = "Would you like to stop this blanker?"
   Ans% = MsgBox(Msg$, 4, Title$)
   If Ans% = 7 Then
      Blanker.Enabled = -1
   Else
      Select Case CurrentIndex
         Case 0
```

```
            BackColor = QBColor(15)
        Case 1, 2, 3, 4
            Cls
    End Select
    Unload Screen_Blanker
    Graphics.Show
  End If
End Sub
```

6. Enter the following code in the Form_Load event subroutine. This code triggers when the Screen_Blanker form displays on the screen. This code maximizes the form on the screen and changes the Blanker Timer's Enabled property to True.

```
Sub Form_Load ()
   WindowState = 2
   Blanker.Enabled = -1
End Sub
```

7. Enter the following code in the Form_Paint event subroutine. This code activates when the Refresh method in the Form_Click event triggers it. The background of the Screen_Blanker form changes to white with this event.

```
Sub Form_Paint ()
   BackColor = QBColor(15)
End Sub
```

## Modules

1. Enter the following code in the global module and save the file as GRAPHICS.BAS. This code defines the global variables used in the Graphics project.

```
Global CurrentIndex As Integer
Global Background As Integer
```

## How It Works

The Graphics project opens with a configuration form that allows the user to select which kind of blanker to display on the screen (see Figures 8.21, 8.22, 8.23, and 8.24). Each time the user selects a new option from the list of options boxes, a new icon appears on the configuration screen. This icon represents the type of blanker chosen by the user. To display the blanker on the screen, the user presses the Activate Blanker command button. The chosen graphics continue to display on the screen until the user clicks the screen with the mouse. At this point, the system asks the user whether to stop the program and whether to save the current graphics on the screen. Press the Quit button on the configuration screen to exit.

### Startup

The AutoRedraw properties of the picture box Blanker_Icon and Graphics and Screen_Blanker forms receive initial adjustments at design time. The AutoRedraw

Figure 8.21. Graphics drawn with the line option selected on the Graphics form

Figure 8.22. Graphics drawn with the circle option selected on the Graphics form

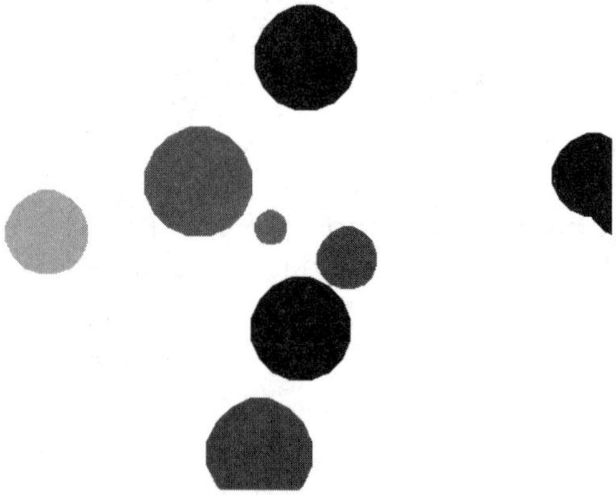

Figure 8.23. Graphics drawn with the spots option selected on the Graphics form

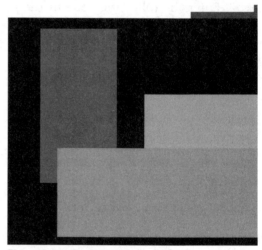

Figure 8.24. Graphics drawn with the squares option selected in the Graphics form

property of both the Graphics form and the picture box Blanker_Icon changes to True. This allows any graphics placed on either the Graphics form or the picture box Blanker_Icon to redisplay every time they are obscured and revealed. In order to allow the periodic removal of drawn graphics on the Screen_Blanker form, the Screen_Blanker's AutoRedraw property is False.

The Picture property of the picture box Blanker_Icon receives an initial setting at design time. As the initially selected control of the array Blanker_Options is Blank Screen, the icon for this choice begins with the Picture property of this picture box. For this reason, the Picture property of the Blanker_Icon picture box is \VB\IC-ONS\MISC\MOON01.ICO.

When the program starts, the Graphics form displays on the screen. The topmost control of the Blanker_Options control array receives the initial focus, triggering the Blanker_Options_GotFocus event. This event uses a Select Case statement to determine the index property of the currently active control. Based on the Index property value, the Picture property of the picture box Blanker_Icon changes to the icon MOON01.ICO. In this case, the LoadPicture function redefines the Picture property of the picture box to another icon based on the selected the control in the Blanker_Options control array. Notice that no file is specified when the active control is the one labeled Squares. When no file name appears, the code instructs the Picture property not to display an image on the screen.

After determining the icon to display in the picture box Blanker_Icon, the Icon property of the Graphics Form becomes the same icon. A simple expression makes the Icon property equal to Blanker_Icon.Picture. In this way, the Picture property of the picture box defines the same property of another element of the project. This demonstrates the definition the graphics properties (Icon or DragIcon) with the picture property of a form or picture box.

### Running the Graphics Project

Pressing the command button Activate Blanker triggers the Blanker Timer event on the Screen_Blanker form. This event displays a series of graphics images on the form in colors defined with the RGB and QBColor functions. These functions are in different points in the Blanker Timer event.

The RGB function in the Blanker_Timer event changes the BackColor of the form to black. For the purposes of this color definition, the color does not change with each processing of the Blanker_Timer event.

The QBColor function sets the color of each of the spots, circles, squares, and lines that appear on the screen. Each QBColor definition has the variable Color placed in the parentheses that follow the QBColor name. This variable increments by one each time that the Timer event triggers until the value reaches 15. The value represents a color displayed in the indicated spot, circle, square, or line. At that point, the Color variable changes to 0 and the process begins again.

Following the resetting of the variable Color to 0, the background of the Screen_Blanker form changes to white. This is done with the Point method, which uses the CurrentX and CurrentY coordinates to determine the color of the current point on the form. Since the BackColor of the form is already white, the background remains white. Although there is no change to the color of the background of the form, the redefinition of the BackColor of the form has the effect of erasing all of the graphic images on the screen.

The PSet method draws spots of differing sizes and colors on the screen. Based on the random setting of the X and Y coordinate variables and the Color variable, a spot of color appears on the screen. The DrawWidth property determines the size of the spot on the form. In this way, a series of spots of random size and color appear on the screen. This is an excellent demonstration of a possible use of the PSet method.

Until the user clicks the form with the mouse, the screen keeps generating the indicated graphics. Clicking the form displays a message that asks the user if he or she wishes to save the current image on the screen to a file. If the user responds "Yes," then the SavePicture statement accesses the Image property of the Screen_Blanker form to determine the Windows handle value. Using this value, the code saves the current contents of the screen to the bitmap file TEST.BMP.

Clicking the form activates the Paint event of the Screen_Blanker form with the Refresh method in the Form_Click event. The Paint event resets the BackColor property of the form to white. This demonstrates the manual activation of the Paint event with the Refresh method. This also shows that the activation of a timer has the effect of disabling the Paint event. Normally, the Paint event triggers when a form loads. The Timer event prevents this from taking place.

The program asks the user if he or she wishes to stop the screen blanker. If the answer is "Yes," the form clears with the Cls method. Notice that the BackColor property of the form changes manually with the selection of the Blank Screen option. This is because the Cls has no effect on the BackColor property of the form.

# Designing with the Coordinate System

One of the strengths of the Windows environment is that it supports many video cards and monitors of varying types, resolutions, and manufacturers. Windows supports all the most common monitor types: EGA, VGA, and Super VGA. Each of these monitor types will display the same program differently. Windows supports many different monitor resolutions. The most common current resolutions are 640x350 (EGA), 640x480 (VGA), 800x600 (Super VGA), and 1024x768 (Super VGA). Windows supports the monitors produced by many manufacturers, using drivers that they supply. Monitors with different manufacturers and resolutions display the same programs differently. While Windows does a good job of providing basic functionality with any and all supported video hardware, the possible effects of these differences need to be taken into account for programs that run in Windows.

This enormous variety of monitor types creates the challenge of setting up applications that will work on as many monitors as possible. Each of these monitor types supports a set number of colors that limit the number of colors your programs can use. EGA monitors support the simultaneous display of 16 colors. VGA and Super VGA monitors can display up to 256 colors simultaneously. To avoid unpleasant surprises, it is often best to not change the colors of your programs and instead allow the Windows environment to define your program's colors.

Monitors with different resolutions display the same forms slightly differently. The higher the resolution, the larger the forms that display on it may appear. Since many monitors are still only capable of displaying 640x480 resolution, be careful to ensure that a form will fit on the lower-resolution screens. Figures 9.1 and 9.2 show the difference between a form displayed on an 800x600 display and a 640x480 display. Each form's dimensions are identical on the properties bar (upper right corner). The form displayed on the 800x600 monitor (Figure 9.1) appears larger than the form on the 640x480 monitor (Figure 9.2), but this is an illusion. A closer look at the position of the form in Figures 9.1 and 9.2 reveals that the one on the 640x480 display is proportionally larger than the other items on the screen. Notice that the Figure 9.1 form is smaller than the white properties bar labeled Form1 above it. The form in Figure 9.2 uses a substantially larger amount of space.

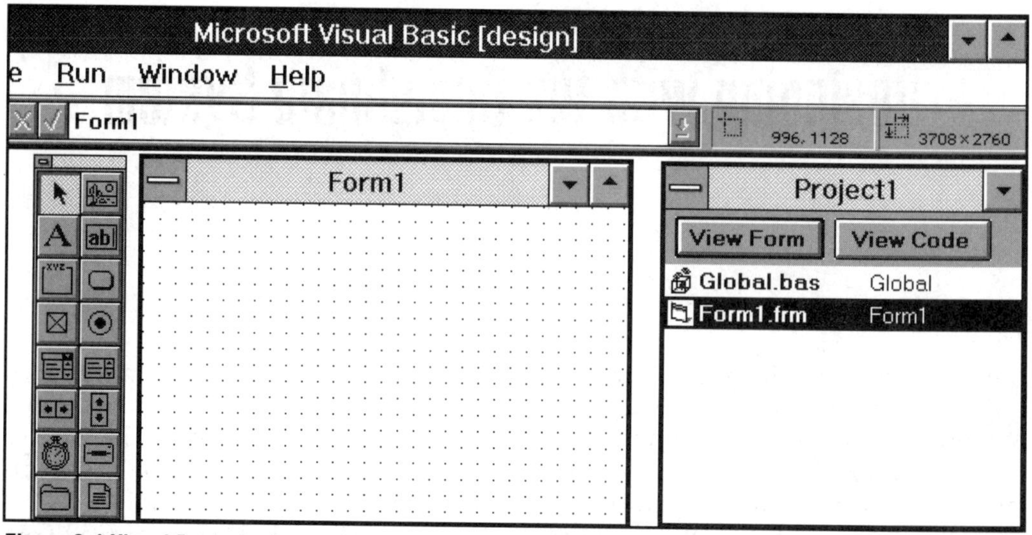

Figure 9.1 Visual Basic design screen on 800x600 resolution display

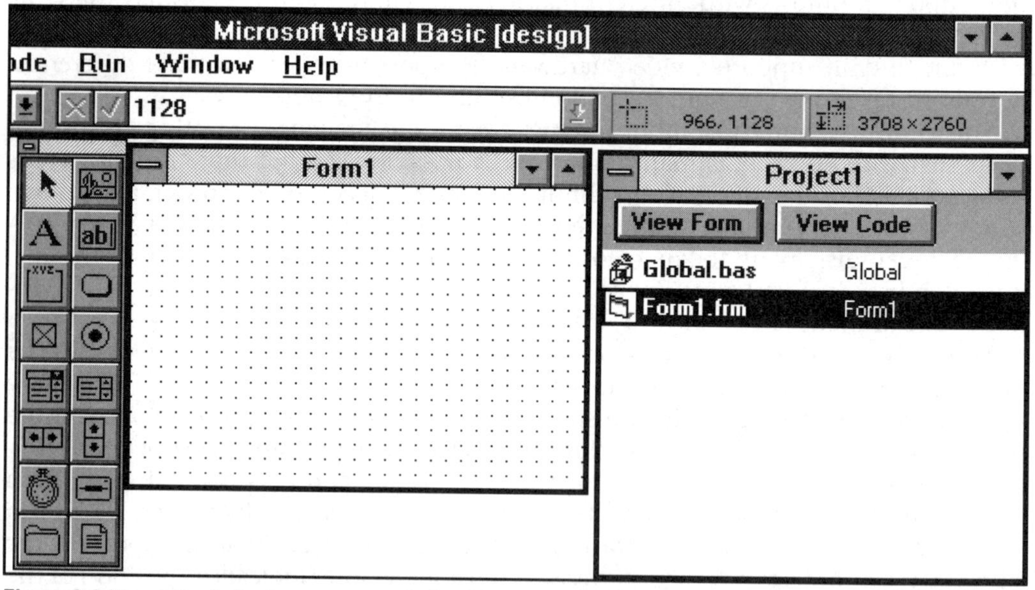

Figure 9.2 Visual Basic design screen on 640x480 resolution display

Visual Basic measures the position and size of the forms on these monitors in the twip unit of measure. Unfortunately, twips are not always an acceptable unit of measure for every program. A drawing program works better when the unit of measure is pixels, which measures the very smallest dot on a screen. Some word processing applications require precise measurements for where the text will appear. In cases like these, the point measure unit works best. The solution to this need lies in setting up a coordinate system for the objects and text that appear on the form.

## What Is the Coordinate System?

The coordinate system indicates where an object appears on the screen or the printer. An object's coordinates measure its distance from the top left corner of the screen, form, picture box, or Printer object. The Left and Top properties contain the coordinates of a form, control, or Printer object. Figure 9.3 shows the Left and Top properties of a command button control. A form's coordinates measure the distance in twips. Controls measure the distance in the unit of measure set by their forms. Similarly, graphics drawn on a form or picture box with the Circle, Line, PSet, or Print methods use the form or picture box's unit of measure. The ScaleMode property of a form, picture box, or Printer object determines its internal unit of measure. This is the unit of measure that objects placed on a form, picture box, or Printer object must use.

Visual Basic supports several types of units of measure, as summarized in Table 9.1. An object's ScaleMode property sets the internal unit of measure.

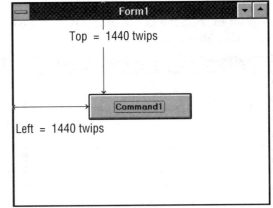

**Figure 9.3 Left and Top properties of the Command1 command button**

Any object placed on a form, picture box, or Printer object must use the unit of measure defined in this property. The default unit of measure for each form, picture box, or Printer object is twips. Visual Basic imposes no restrictions on the available units of measure choices for the screen and printer. Under normal circumstances, reserve characters and points for the printer and pixels for the screen.

| Unit of Measure | Description |
|---|---|
| Twip | 1440 twips = 1 inch, 20 twips = 1 point |
| Point | 72 points = 1 inch, 1 point = 20 twips |
| Pixel | Size of the screen's resolution dots |
| Character | X axis: 120 twips = 1 character, Y axis: 240 twips = 1 character |
| Inch | 1 inch = 1440 twips, 1 inch = 72 points |
| Millimeter | 254 millimeters = 1 inch, 5.67 twips = 1 millimeter |
| Centimeter | 2.54 centimeters = 1 inch, 567 twips = 1 centimeter |

**Table 9.1 Available units of measure in Visual Basic**

The default unit of measure for any object in Visual Basic is twips. If the ScaleMode property of an object does not change, the measurements shown on the properties bar are in twips. Unless there is a specific reason for changing to another unit of measure, leave the ScaleMode property at this default setting. Twips always measure the positions of forms on the screen.

Each object has a height and width expressed in terms of a given unit of measure. The number representing the same object's height and width changes with each new unit of measure. A height's number is different if expressed in inches than centimeters (although of course the object's height does not change). For example, a 1-inch-high object is actually 2.54 units high in centimeters. Visual Basic determines the height and width of objects with the Height and Width properties of the object. These properties contain the current height and width of the object expressed in the unit of measure set in the ScaleMode property. Notice that Form1's Height and Width properties, shown in Figure 9.4, include the title bar at the top of the form and the borders.

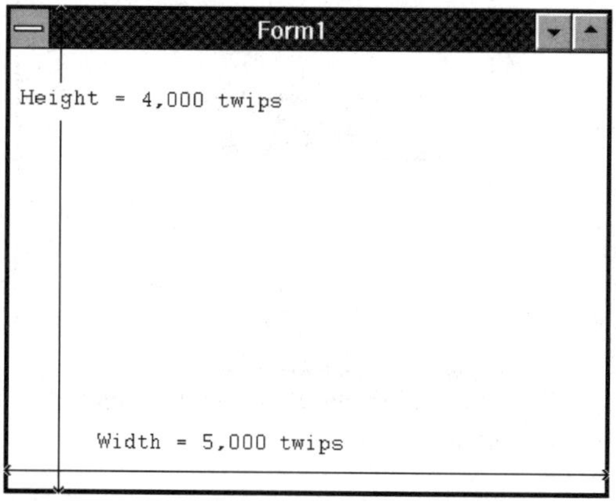

**Figure 9.4 Height and width of a form**

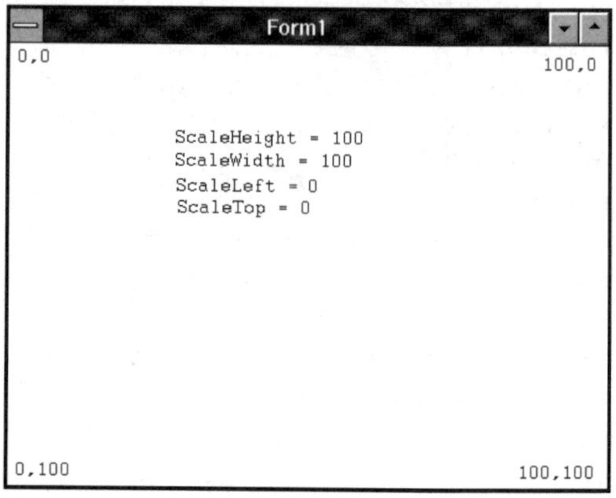

**Figure 9.5 ScaleHeight, ScaleWidth, ScaleLeft, and ScaleTop properties**

Figures 9.3 and 9.4 show that a form's Height, Width, Left, and Top properties include the borders and title bars. The ScaleHeight, ScaleWidth, ScaleLeft, and ScaleTop properties do not include these parts of a form. These properties provide the dimensions of the usable surface of a form. Figure 9.5 shows the usable surface of a form with its dimensions set in the ScaleHeight, ScaleWidth, ScaleLeft, and ScaleTop properties. Setting the ScaleLeft and ScaleTop properties to 0 and the ScaleHeight and ScaleWidth properties to 100 divides the form into 100 equal units. An object in the upper left corner is at the coordinates 0,0. Objects in the lower right corner have the coordinates 100,100. Notice that these measurements are independent of the actual unit size of the form on the screen.

The unmodified ScaleHeight and ScaleWidth properties of a form, picture box, or Printer object measure the height and width of the form without the border and title bar. These measure the surface in the unit of measure set by the ScaleMode property of the form, picture box, or Printer object. Each form, picture box, or Printer object begins with the ScaleLeft and ScaleTop properties set to 0. These properties define the coordinates of the upper left corner.

Changing the settings of the ScaleHeight, ScaleWidth, ScaleLeft, and ScaleTop properties has no effect upon an object's size and location. Any modifications only change the scale or unit of measure that objects must use inside this object. Notice that Figures 9.6 and 9.7 are the same size even though the values of the ScaleHeight and ScaleWidth properties are different. Alterations to these properties have the effect of

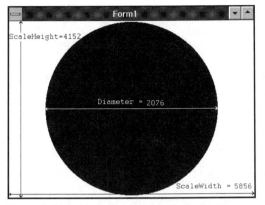

**Figure 9.6 Circle drawn on a form using twip measurements**

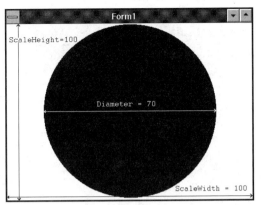

**Figure 9.7 Circle drawn on a form with custom scale**

changing the ScaleMode property to user-defined (0). The value of the ScaleHeight and ScaleWidth properties of a form, picture box, or Printer object represents the new unit of measure. In this way, the vertical height and horizontal width of the object divides into 100 units each. Thus it makes sense to use such a custom scale when you are concerned about the *relative* size and position of screen elements rather than their *absolute* physical measurements.

The screen coordinates on a form, picture box, or Printer object begin in the top left corner. Every time a Circle, PSet, Line, or Print method places graphics or text on an object, these screen coordinates change. Coordinates measure the distance from the top left corner of the object using the unit of measure set by the object's ScaleMode property. Using the Circle method changes the current coordinates to the center of the circle. Each Line method modifies the current screen coordinates to the second set of coordinates of the drawn line or box. PSet methods alter the screen coordinates to the center of the drawn spot of color. A Print method expression changes the screen coordinates to the end of the line of text. The CurrentX and CurrentY properties of the form, Printer object, and picture box define exactly where the current screen coordinates presently are on it.

Table 9.2 displays the one method and 11 properties that determine the position of controls and graphics objects on a form, picture box, or Printer object.

| Use or Set This... | | To Do This... |
|---|---|---|
| CurrentX | Property | Set the horizontal position of a drawn object within a form, picture box, or Printer object |
| CurrentY | Property | Set the vertical position of a drawn object within a form, picture box, or Printer object |
| Height | Property | Set the vertical length of an object |
| Left | Property | Set the horizontal distance from the left edge of a form, picture box, or Printer object |
| Scale | Method | Set the limits of the horizontal and vertical coordinates for a form, picture box, or Printer object |

Table 9.2 (continued)

| Use or Set This... | | To Do This... |
|---|---|---|
| ScaleHeight | Property | Set the vertical coordinate of the lower right corner of an object |
| ScaleLeft | Property | Set the horizontal coordinate of the top left corner of an object |
| ScaleMode | Property | Determine which unit of measure to use for a form, picture box, or Printer object |
| ScaleTop | Property | Set the vertical coordinate of upper left corner of an object |
| ScaleWidth | Property | Set the horizontal coordinate of the lower right corner of an object |
| Top | Property | Set the vertical distance from the top edge of a form, picture box, or Printer object |
| Width | Property | Set the horizontal length of an object |

**Table 9.2 Method and properties dealing with the Visual Basic coordinate system**

Table 9.2 investigates the method and properties covered in detail in the following pages. The Coordinates project at the end of this section provides step-by-step instructions on how to assemble it.

# CurrentX and CurrentY Properties

## Objects Affected

| | | | | |
|---|---|---|---|---|
| Check | Clipboard | Combo | Command | Dbug |
| Dir | Drive | File | ▶ Form | Frame |
| Label | List | Menu | Option | ▶ Picture |
| ▶ Printer | Screen | Scroll | Text | Timer |

## Purpose

The CurrentX and CurrentY properties provide the horizontal (CurrentX) and vertical (CurrentY) coordinates on a form, picture box, or Printer object. A value in a CurrentX or CurrentY property represents a measurement of the distance from the top or left edges of the form, picture box, or Printer object. This value is in the units of measure set by the ScaleMode property of the form, picture box, or Printer object. When a form loads, the coordinates set in the ScaleLeft and ScaleTop properties are the default values for the CurrentX and CurrentY properties. This means that the CurrentX and CurrentY properties begin with the coordinates of the upper left corner of the Form, Picture Box, or Printer object (normally 0,0). Every use of a Circle, Line, PSet, Cls, Printer, or NewPage method modifies the values set in the CurrentX and CurrentY properties. Table 9.3 summarizes the different arguments of the CurrentX and CurrentY properties.

## General Syntax

```
[form.]CurrentX[=x!]
[picturebox.].CurrentX[=x!]
Printer.CurrentX[=x!]
[form.]CurrentY[=y!]
[picturebox.].CurrentY[=y!]
Printer.CurrentY[=y!]
```

| Arguments | Description |
|-----------|-------------|
| form | FormName of the form |
| picturebox | CtlName of picture box |
| Printer | Identifies Printer object |
| x!,y! | Current horizontal and vertical positions on the object |

Table 9.3 Arguments of the CurrentX and CurrentY properties

## Example Syntax

```
Sub Form_MouseDown (Button As Integer, Shift As Integer, X As Single, Y As Single)
    Form1.WindowState = 2          'Maximizes the window on screen
    X = CurrentX + 1000            'Defines horizontal and vertical coordinates
    Y = CurrentY + 1000            'the current setting + 1000 units
    Const PI = 3.14159265          'Define Constant PI
    FillStyle = 0                  'Make the color of object drawn black
    Circle (X, Y), 1000, , -PI / 1, -PI / 2 'Draw a circle with a 90-degree slice removed
End Sub
```

## Description

The CurrentX and CurrentY properties indicate the current position on a form, picture box, or Printer object. Each CurrentX and CurrentY property expression must begin with the name of the form, picture box, or Printer object (FormName of form, CtlName of picture box, or Printer for Printer object). If no name appears in an expression, the current form's properties are assumed. A CurrentX or CurrentY property expression ends with its value (if none appears, the code references the property's current value). These properties begin with the values set in the ScaleLeft and ScaleTop properties of the form, picture box, or Printer object. Whenever a drawn object appears on a form, picture box, or Printer object, the current screen coordintes change (a drawn object is anything produced with the Circle, Line, PSet, or Print methods). Table 9.4 lists the different methods that affect the values in the CurrentX and CurrentY properties of an object.

In the example syntax, the circle with a 90-degree slice removed appears at the coordinates set by values in the CurrentX and CurrentY properties of the form. Each time the user presses the mouse, the program increments the CurrentX and CurrentY properties. This causes a second circle to appear 1000 units lower and further to the right of the last circle drawn (remember that we are using twips, the default measure, and that thousands of twips fit on the screen). This demonstrates how the CurrentX and CurrentY properties change with the use of the Circle method. Figure 9.8 shows how this circle might appear on the screen.

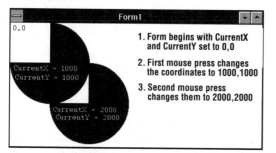

**Figure 9.8 What the example syntax might look like**

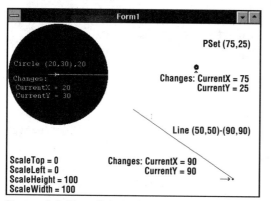

**Figure 9.9 The effects of graphics methods on CurrentX and CurrentY properties**

### Effect of the Circle, Cls, Line, Print, PSet, and NewPage methods

The Circle, Cls, Line, Print, PSet, and NewPage methods change the current coordinates on the screen or Printer object. This has the effect of changing the values in the CurrentX and CurrentY properties of the form, picture box, or Printer object. Drawing a circle on an object changes the CurrentX and CurrentY properties to the center of the circle. Placing a line on an object moves the CurrentX and CurrentY properties to the second point on the line (see Figure 9.9). Putting a point of color on an object modifies the CurrentX and CurrentY properties to the center of the spot of color. Using the Cls method restores the CurrentX and CurrentY properties to the coordinates of the upper left corner. Each print method alters the CurrentX and CurrentY properties to the end of the line of text if the expression ends in a semicolon, or one character width away if the expression ends in a comma. The NewPage method advances to the next page of the Printer object and restores the CurrentX and CurrentY properties to this new page's upper left corner. Table 9.4 summarizes the effects of these methods on the CurrentX and CurrentY properties.

| Method | Effect on CurrentX property |
| --- | --- |
| Circle | Changes the coordinates inside the form, picture box, or Printer object to the center of the circle |
| Cls | Restores the coordinates within a form, picture box, or Printer object to the upper left corner |
| Line | Changes the coordinates inside the form, picture box, or Printer object to the end of the line |
| Print | Changes the coordinates to the next print position in a Printer object |
| PSet | Places the coordinates of the form, picture box, or Printer object to the point drawn |
| NewPage | Advances to the next page on the Printer object in the upper left corner |

**Table 9.4 Effect of other elements of languages on CurrentX and CurrentY properties**

### Example

In the Coordinates project at the end of this section, the CurrentX and CurrentY properties provide the positions of circles and lines. Pressing the mouse button down triggers the ShowDisplay_MouseDown event that draws the circle on the Coordinate form or ShowDisplay picture box. On the ShowDisplay picture box, each time the user presses the mouse button, a new circle appears 0.5 inches lower and further to the right of the previous circle. Graphics on the coordinate form appear 20 units lower and further to the right using the user-defined scale set in the ScaleHeight and ScaleWidth properties of the form.

When the user presses the ChangePicture command button, the text on the command button changes from Circle to Line. After this change, each time the user clicks the screen with the mouse, lines appear on the screen instead of circles. These lines start at points that are 0.5 inches further to the right and lower than the end point of the previous line. Each time a line appears on the screen, the CurrentX and CurrentY properties of the form automatically change to the end point of the line.

## Comments

Be careful not to confuse the CurrentX and CurrentY properties with the Left and Top properties of a control. The CurrentX and CurrentY properties do not affect the positions of controls. Set a control's position on the form with its Top and Left properties.

# Height Property

## Objects Affected

| | | | | |
|---|---|---|---|---|
| ▶ Check | Clipboard | ▶ Combo | ▶ Command | Dbug |
| ▶ Dir | ▶ Drive | ▶ File | ▶ Form | ▶ Frame |
| ▶ Label | ▶ List | Menu | ▶ Option | ▶ Picture |
| ▶ Printer | ▶ Screen | ▶ Scroll | ▶ Text | Timer |

## Purpose

The Height property defines or determines the vertical size of a form or control on the screen, form, picture box, or Printer object. Forms, Printer objects, and Screen objects are always measured in twips. A control's size uses the units of measurement set in the ScaleMode property of the current form or picture box. The default unit of measurement for a control is twips (1 twip = 1/20 point; 1 inch = 72 points; 1440 twips = 1 inch). Except for the dimensions of the height setting of a Printer object, which is defined at run time, the Height property of an object is available at both design time and run time. To manually adjust the Height property of a command button at design time, click on one of its edges and resize it. You can also adjust the height by entering the desired measurement into the properties bar. Tables 9.5 and 9.6 summarize the different arguments of the Height property.

## General Syntax

```
[form.]Height[=height!]
[control.]Height[=height!]
Printer.Height[=height!]
Screen.Height[=height!]
```

| Argument | Description |
|---|---|
| form | FormName of the form |
| control | CtlName of the control |
| Printer | Printer object |
| Screen | Screen object |
| height! | Vertical height of the object |

Table 9.5 Arguments of the Height property

| Measurement | Size |
|---|---|
| Twip | 1440 twips = 1 inch |
| Point | 72 points = 1 inch |
| Pixels | Varies depending upon the system being used |
| Characters | 12 characters horizontally and 6 vertically |
| Millimeters | 254 millimeters = 1 inch |
| Centimeters | 2.54 centimeters = 1 inch |

Table 9.6 Possible measurement types in relation to 1 inch

## Example Syntax

```
Sub Form_Load
    Form1.Height = (Command1.Height * 5) 'Defines the height and width of the form as 5
    Form1.Width = (Command1.Width * 5)    'times the height and width of the command button.
End Sub
```

## Description

The Height property of an object measures the vertical height of a form, screen, or picture box. You can enter this value at design time by manually sizing the object with the mouse or by entering the value at the properties bar. You can modify the Height property of a control or form either at design or run time. In contrast, you can only set the Height properties of the Printer and Screen objects at run time. A setting must be between 0 and a maximum value specified by the system itself. Visual Basic automatically adjusts itself to the resolution of the screen or printer. You should ensure that your objects are not too large for the most common 640x480 and 800x600 resolution screens to display.

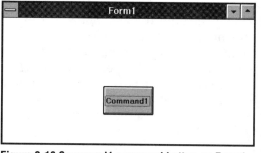

Figure 9.10 Command1 command button on Form1

In the example syntax, the Form_Load event defines the height and width of Form1 as five times the height and width of the Command1 command button. Figure 9.10 shows what this form might look like.

### The Left, Top, Width, and Height Properties

When you create a form or control in Visual Basic, the Left, Top, Width, and Height properties display in the far right side of the properties bar. Figure 9.11 shows what the properties bar looks like on the screen. The first two numbers, separated by a comma, represent the left and top position of the control or form. A form's Height property provides the maximum height for the controls placed upon it. Similarly, the value of the Height property of the screen sets the maximum value of a form's property.

**Figure 9.11 Dimension displays on Visual Basic design bar**

This varies from system to system according to the resolution of the monitor. The width and the height of the object appear to the right of these numbers, separated by an "x." If the object is a control, then the numbers shown are in the units of measurement specified by the ScaleMode property of the current form. A form's Height property is measured in twips. This difference allows for variances in the resolution of screens used for each computer. For example, a system with an 800x600 display shows more on the screen than a 640x480 display.

### Screen and Printer

In reference to the computer screen and printer being used, the Height property returns the height of the screen or page available. The Height property of the screen and Printer objects is not available at design time and is read-only at run time.

### The Scale Mode

The ScaleMode property of a form directly controls the meaning of the value of the Height property. When the ScaleMode property changes at design time from one measurement to another, Visual Basic recalculates the value of the Height property in this new type of measurement. As the ScaleMode property is not modifiable at run time, the meaning of the value of the Height property does not change while the program is running. For example, no matter what size a command box becomes based on changes in the size of the parent form, the Height property will remain the same.

### The ScaleHeight Property

The ScaleHeight property divides the height of a form, picture box, or Printer object into the number of units set in the property. For example, when a form's ScaleHeight property changes to 100 on the properties bar, the height of the form is divided into 100 equal units. (Changing the ScaleHeight property of the form to a new value does not change the actual size of the control.) This unit changes in size as the form's height changes. In this way, increasing the height of the form has the effect of increasing the size of one of these units (the height remains divided into 100 units that are now larger in size). These units define the upper and lower limit of the possible height of controls on this form.

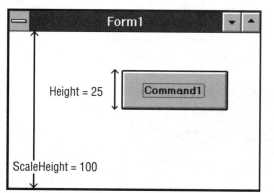

**Figure 9.12 Interaction of ScaleHeight and Height properties**

With the Move statement, the size of the control adjusts based on the changes in height to the form. For example, a Resize event might adjust the Height property of a command box of a form by triggering a move statement that always ensures that the command box is one-fourth the size of the form. In this example, the ScaleHeight property of the form is 100, andthe Height property of the Command1 command button is 25 (one-fourth the height of the form). Figure 9.12 displays this concept visually.

### Scale Mode Values in the CONSTANT.TXT File

The CONSTANT.TXT file, found in the main Visual Basic Directory, contains the suggested names for constant values to use in your Visual Basic applications. In order to use the CONSTANT.TXT file, you must load it into the project's global module. To do this, open Visual Basic's Project window and double-click on the global module. This will load the global module into the Code window. Then open Visual Basic's Code menu and choose the Load Text option. This brings up a dialog box. Select the CONSTANT.TXT file and click on the Merge button. This will read the file into the global module. The following listing displays the applicable values in the CONSTANT.TXT file.

```
' ScaleMode (form, picture box, Printer)
Global Const USER = 0          ' 0 - User
Global Const TWIPS = 1         ' 1 - Twip
Global Const POINTS = 2        ' 2 - Point
Global Const PIXELS = 3        ' 3 - Pixel
Global Const CHARACTERS = 4    ' 4 - Character
Global Const INCHES = 5        ' 5 - Inch
Global Const MILLIMETERS = 6   ' 6 - Millimeter
Global Const CENTIMETERS = 7   ' 7 - Centimeter
```

## Example

The Height properties of the ShowDisplay and PictureView command buttons change at design time to make them fit on the screen as desired. Make design time adjustments to these properties by manually dragging them with the mouse, or changing their values on the properties bar.

## Comments

Remember that changes to the ScaleHeight property of a form only alter the value of the Height property of a control and not the actual height.

# Left Property

## Objects Affected

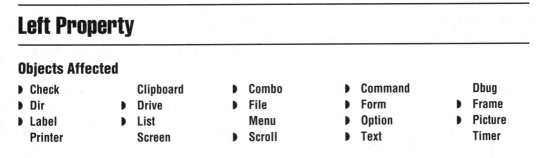

| | | | | |
|---|---|---|---|---|
| ▶ Check | Clipboard | ▶ Combo | ▶ Command | Dbug |
| ▶ Dir | ▶ Drive | ▶ File | ▶ Form | ▶ Frame |
| ▶ Label | ▶ List | Menu | ▶ Option | ▶ Picture |
| Printer | Screen | ▶ Scroll | ▶ Text | Timer |

## Purpose

The Left property defines or determines the distance of a form or control from the left edge of the form or picture box. A control's distance measures in the units indicated by the ScaleMode property of the current form or picture box. For forms, this distance is always measured in twips. The default unit of measurement for controls is twips (1 twip = 1/20 point; 1 inch = 72 points; 1440 twips = 1 inch). The Left property of an object is available either at design time or at run time. For example, the Left property of a form on a screen adjusts by clicking on the title bar of the form and moving it or inputting the exact desired measurement in the properties bar. Tables 9.7 and 9.8 summarize the different arguments of the Left property and the possible measurement types.

## General Syntax

```
[form.]Left[=left!]
[control.]Left[=left!]
```

| Argument | Description |
|---|---|
| form | FormName of the form |
| control | CtlName of the control |
| left! | Horizontal left distance of the object |

Table 9.7 Arguments of the Left property

| Measurement | Size |
|---|---|
| Twip | 1440 twips = 1 inch |
| Point | 72 points = 1 inch |
| Pixels | Varies depending uponthe  system being used |
| Characters | 12 characters horizontally and 6 vertically |
| Millimeters | 254 millimeters = 1 inch |
| Centimeters | 2.54 centimeters = 1 inch |

Table 9.8 Possible measurement types in relation to 1 inch

## Example Syntax

```
Sub LeftDistance (Ctl As Control,FormName As Form)    'New function LeftDistance
                                                      'All of the following values equal
                                                      'one inch
                                                      'Note for programmer
        Select Case FormName.ScaleMode                'Based on Control's ScaleMode
            Case 0                                    'User-Defined Measurement
                Ctl.Left = Ctl.ScaleLeft              'Distance equals ScaleLeft
            Case 1                                    'Measure in twips
                Ctl.Left = 1440
            Case 2                                    'Measure in Points
                Ctl.Left = 72
            Case 3                                    'Measure in Pixels
                Ctl.Left = 1000
            Case 4                                    'Measure in Characters
                Ctl.Left = 12
            Case 5                                    'Measure in Inches
                Ctl.Left = 1
            Case 6                                    'Measure in Millimeters
                Ctl.Left = 254
            Case 7                                    'Measure in Centimeters
                Ctl.Left = 2.54
        End Select
End Sub
```

## Description

The Left property of an object measures the horizontal distance from the left of a form, screen, or picture box. You can enter this value at design time by manually moving the object with the mouse or by entering the value at the properties bar. You can modify the Left property of a control or form either at design time or at run time. A setting must be between 0 and a maximum value specified by the system itself. Visual Basic automatically adjusts itself to the resolution of the screen. You should ensure that your objects are not too far from the edges for the most common 640x480 and 800x600 resolution screens to display.

The example syntax outlines a subfunction named LeftDistance, which can set a control's distance from the left side of the screen using the available type of measurements. The subfunction references the ScaleMode property of the form to determine what measure to set. This is another excellent example of the use of a generic function that applies to more than one control in a program.

### The Left, Top, Width, and Height Properties

When you create a form or control in Visual Basic, the Left, Top, Width, and Height properties display in the far right side of the properties bar. See Figure 9.11 and the discussion in the chapter under the Height property.

## The Scale Mode

The ScaleMode property of a form directly controls the meaning of the value of the Left property. When the ScaleMode property changes from one measurement to another at design time, Visual Basic recalculates the value of the Left property in this new type of measurement. As the ScaleMode property is not modifiable at run time, the meaning of the value of the Left property does not change while the program is running. For example, no matter what size a command box becomes based on changes in the size of the parent form, the Left property will remain the same.

### Scale Mode Values in the CONSTANT.TXT File

The CONSTANT.TXT file, found in the main Visual Basic Directory, contains the suggested names for constant values to use in your Visual Basic applications. In order to use the CONSTANT.TXT file, you must load it into the project's global module. To do this, open Visual Basic's Project window and double-click on the global module. This will load the global module into the Code window. Then open Visual Basic's Code menu and choose the Load Text option. This brings up a dialog box. Select the CONSTANT.TXT file and click on the Merge button. This will read the file into the global module. The following listing displays the applicable values in the CONSTANT.TXT file.

```
' ScaleMode (form, picture box, Printer)
Global Const USER = 0            ' 0 - User
Global Const TWIPS = 1           ' 1 - Twip
Global Const POINTS = 2          ' 2 - Point
Global Const PIXELS = 3          ' 3 - Pixel
Global Const CHARACTERS = 4      ' 4 - Character
Global Const INCHES = 5          ' 5 - Inch
Global Const MILLIMETERS = 6     ' 6 - Millimeter
Global Const CENTIMETERS = 7     ' 7 - Centimeter
```

## Example

The Left properties of the ShowDisplay and PictureView command buttons are set at design time to position them on the screen. Make design time adjustments to these properties by manually dragging them with the mouse, or changing their value on the properties bar.

## Comments

Remember that changes to the ScaleLeft property of a form only alter the value of the Left property of a control and do not change the actual distance.

# Scale Method

## Objects Affected

| | | | | |
|---|---|---|---|---|
| Check | Clipboard | Combo | Command | Dbug |
| Dir | Drive | File | ▶ Form | Frame |
| Label | List | Menu | Option | ▶ Picture |
| ▶ Printer | Screen | Scroll | Text | Timer |

## Purpose

The Scale method defines the boundaries of a form, picture box, or Printer object. This method defines all four of the ScaleHeight, ScaleWidth, ScaleTop, and ScaleLeft properties in one expression instead of four. Two groups of numbers, (x1!,y1!) and (x2!,y2!), define the boundaries of the form, picture box, or Printer object. The first set of numbers sets the coordinates of the upper left corner of the object (x1!,y1!). An object's coordinates in the lower right corner appear in the second set of numbers (x2!,y2!). Table 9.9 summarizes the definition of each of the coordinates of the scale method.

## General Syntax

[object.]Scale[(x1!,y1!)-(x2!,y2!)]

| Argument | Description |
|---|---|
| object | FormName of form, CtlName of picture box, or Printer for Printer object |
| x1! | Sets ScaleLeft property |
| y1! | Sets ScaleTop property |
| x2! | Sets ScaleWidth property |
| y2! | Sets ScaleHeight property |

Table 9.9 Arguments of the Scale method

## Example Syntax

```
Sub Form_MouseDown (Button As Integer, Shift As Integer, X As Single, Y As Single)
    Form1.Scale (0,0)-(100,100)              'Defines the form's coordinate parameters
    Form1.WindowState = 2                    'Maximizes the window on screen
    For I% = 1 to 5
        X = CurrentX + 10                    'Defines horizontal & vertical coordinates
        Y = CurrentY + 10                    'the current setting + 10 units
        Const PI = 3.14159265                'Define Constant PI
        FillStyle = 0                        'Make the color of object drawn black
        Circle (X, Y), 10, , -PI / 1, -PI / 2 'Draw a circle with a 90-degree slice
```

```
    Next I%
End Sub

Sub Form1_Resize
    Form1.Scale (0, 0)-(500, 500)              'Defines coordinate parameters for
                                              'form
    Text1.Move 0, 0, ScaleWidth, (ScaleHeight/2)   'Text1 window fills upper half of form
    Text2.Move 0, 251, ScaleWidth, (ScaleHeight/2)'Text2 window fills lower screen
End Sub
```

## Description

The Scale method determines the limits of the coordinates used on a form, picture box, or Printer object. Each Scale method must begin with the CtlName of the form or control being modified. If there is no object name, the coordinate system of the parent form changes. In the first set of numbers (x1!,y!) are the horizontal and vertical coordinates of the upper left corner of the object (ScaleLeft,ScaleTop). The numbers in the next set of numbers (x2!,y2!) represent the lower right corner of the same object (ScaleWidth,ScaleHeight). Any coordinates that are given within this object must be between these coordinates. This method has no effect upon the positioning and size of current controls on the screen.

In the first example syntax, the boundaries of usable coordinates are between 0 and 100, which permits the programmer to easily figure out where to put controls or objects. In the first example syntax, the ScaleMethod defines a picture box that fills the entire space of a form with the coordinates 0,0-100,100. Any objects placed within this picture box use coordinates between 0 and 100. In this way, setting coordinates becomes easier through the establishment of a system of easily calculated coordinates. With previous coordinates, the center of the picture box would be 50,50. In the example syntax, the Scale method defines the scale of Form1, which the Circle method uses to draw a circle on the screen. The For statement then generates a series of circles displaced increasingly toward the lower right corner of the form. Figure 9.13 shows what the series of circles will look like.

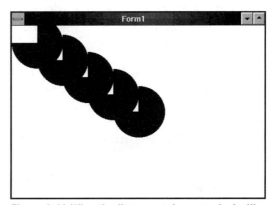

**Figure 9.13 What the first example syntax looks like**

ScaleMode expressions that do not provide new coordinates change the ScaleMode property to the default of twips measurement units. In the second example above, the Scale method provides the scale that the Form1_Resize event uses to ensure that the Text1 text box remains in the upper half of Form1, and the Text2 text box stays in the lower half. Figure 9.14 shows what these controls should look like on Form1.

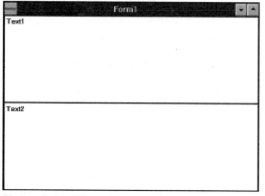

**Figure 9.14 What the second example syntax looks like**

### The CurrentX and CurrentY Properties

The Scale method works well when combined with the CurrentX and CurrentY properties of a form, picture box, or Printer object. Setting a custom scale with the Scale method removes a great deal of confusion that arises from positioning and sizing an object on a form, picture box, or Printer object. Working with numbers between 0 and 100 makes it easier to discover the center of an object than when working with numbers like 0 and 2848. This simplifies the process of drawing objects on the screen.

### Example

The Coordinate project at the end of this section uses the Scale method to create a user-defined scale for the Printer object. Instead of individually changing the ScaleLeft, ScaleTop, ScaleWidth, and ScaleHeight properties, the Scale method changes them all in one line. The ScaleLeft, ScaleTop, ScaleWidth, and ScaleHeight properties of the Coordinate form all change in the Form_Load event to the same coordinates as those for the Printer object. However, the change for the form takes four lines of code and the change for the Printer object only takes one. This is an excellent way to reduce the amount of code necessary for creating user-defined dimensions.

# ScaleHeight Property

## Objects Affected

| | | | | |
|---|---|---|---|---|
| Check | Clipboard | Combo | Command | Dbug |
| Dir | Drive | File | ▶ Form | Frame |
| Label | List | Menu | Option | ▶ Picture |
| ▶ Printer | Screen | Scroll | Text | Timer |

## Purpose

The ScaleHeight property sets or determines the usable height of a form, picture box, or Printer object (usable height excludes the title bar and borders of an object). An object's size is measured in the units indicated by the setting of the ScaleMode property of the form. Twips are the default unit of measure. When the ScaleMode property of the form is 0 (user specified), the ScaleHeight property value represents a proportional scale. This proportional scale divides the usable height of the object into a number of units equal to the value of the ScaleHeight property. If the object's size changes, then the value of the ScaleHeight remains the same while the size of each unit of the proportional scale grows larger or smaller. For example, a text box with a height equal to the ScaleHeight would fill the entire vertical space of the form. If this same form's ScaleHeight property changes to 100, then the text box's Height property would also be 100 to fill the entire vertical surface of the form. When this text box only needs to fill half of the space of a form, it would have a Height property equal to 50. Table 9.10 summarizes the arguments of the ScaleHeight property.

## General Syntax

```
[form.]ScaleHeight[=scale!]
[picturebox.]ScaleHeight[=scale!]
[Printer.]ScaleHeight[=scale!]
```

| Argument | Description |
|---|---|
| form | FormName of the form |
| picture box | CtlName of the picture box |
| Printer | Printer object |
| Scale! | Vertical length of the object |

Table 9.10 Arguments of the ScaleHeight property

## Example Syntax

```
Sub Form_Resize ()
    ScaleHeight = 100      'Sets the coordinate scale to 100
    ScaleWidth = 100       'for both the height and width
    Command1.Height = 25   'Makes the command button's height 1/4 of height of form
    Command1.Width = 25    'Makes the command button's width 1/4 of width of form
End Sub
```

## Description

The ScaleHeight property measures the usable height of a form, picture box, or Printer object, excluding the border or title bar of the object. Each ScaleHeight property expression begins with the name of the affected object (CtlName of the picture box, FormName property of the picture box, or Printer for Printer object). In the default value, this number reflects the height of the form, picture box, or Printer object without the border or title bar. You can change this value either at design time or run time. A new value becomes the user-defined proportional measurement of the form, picture box or Printer object. Table 9.10 lists the arguments of the ScaleHeight property. The height of any control or graphics object is a fraction of the height of the object it is on.

In the example syntax, the Form_Resize event changes the ScaleHeight and ScaleWidth property of Form1 to 100. With this new scale, the Command1 command button's height and width becomes one-fourth that of Form1 by changing them to 25. These settings do not determine the actual size of either the control or the form, but the proportional

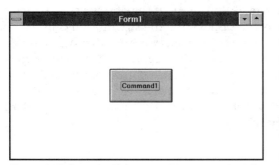

**Figure 9.15 Command1 command button on Form1**

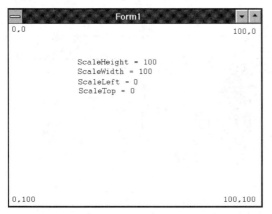

**Figure 9.16 The ScaleHeight, ScaleWidth, ScaleTop, and ScaleLeft properties**

difference. For this reason, the actual size of the Command1 button becomes larger when the form is larger and smaller when the form is smaller. Figure 9.15 shows what this example might look like.

### The ScaleHeight, ScaleWidth, ScaleTop, and ScaleLeft Properties

The ScaleHeight, ScaleWidth, ScaleTop, or ScaleLeft properties provide the boundaries of possible settings for objects placed upon a form, picture box, or Printer object. Each object's ScaleTop and ScaleLeft properties indicate the coordinates of the upper left corner. The ScaleWidth and ScaleHeight properties provide the coordinates of the lower right corner of an object. A visible control or object on a form, picture box, or Printer object must be between the upper and lower boundaries set by these properties. As shown in the example syntax, changes can be initiated with the definitions of the width of controls as fractions of the ScaleHeight of the current form. This is very useful for helping to ensure that controls are not obscured when a form's size changes. If this routine is in the Resize event of the form in question, then every time the form's size changes, the controls also change. Figure 9.16 shows the relationship between these properties

### Example

The ScaleHeight property appears in the Form_Resize event of the Coordinates Project. By setting the ScaleHeight and ScaleWidth properties to 100, the size of each of the distances that these properties represent divides into 100 equal units. Referencing these properties in the move method allows the ShowDisplay picture box to fill the lower four-fifths of the Coordinate form. Each time the Coordinate form's size changes, the ShowDisplay picture adjusts to fill it.

### Comments

Remember that the ScaleHeight property does not measure the entire height of a form, picture box, or Printer object. The ScaleHeight property does not include the title bar at the top of a form or the border around an object.

# ScaleLeft Property

## Objects Affected

| | | | | |
|---|---|---|---|---|
| Check | Clipboard | Combo | Command | Dbug |
| Dir | Drive | File | ▶ Form | Frame |
| Label | List | Menu | Option | ▶ Picture |
| ▶ Printer | Screen | Scroll | Text | Timer |

## Purpose

The ScaleLeft property sets or determines the left coordinate of the upper left corner of a form, picture box, or Printer object. This property has no influence over the Left property of a form, picture box, or Printer object; it only defines the lower limit of possible coordinates on an object. A newly created form, picture box, or Printer object begins with its ScaleLeft property set to 0. This property may be a higher value than 0, but should be set to a value lower than those of the ScaleHeight and ScaleWidth properties. Table 9.11 summarizes the arguments of the ScaleLeft property.

## General Syntax

```
[form.]ScaleLeft[=scale!]
[picturebox.]ScaleLeft[=scale!]
[Printer.]ScaleLeft[=scale!]
```

| Argument | Description |
|---|---|
| form | FormName of the form |
| picture box | CtlName of the picture box |
| Printer | Printer object |
| scale! | Left coordinate of an object |

Table 9.11 Arguments of the ScaleLeft property

## Example Syntax

```
Sub Form_Resize ()
    ScaleLeft = 100                        'Upper left corner coordinates
    ScaleTop = 100                         'become 100,100
    ScaleWidth = 200                       'lower right corner coordinates
    ScaleHeight = 200                      'become 200,200
    Command1.Move ScaleLeft, ScaleTop      'Move command button to upper left corner
End Sub
```

## Description

The ScaleLeft property provides the usable left coordinate of a form, picture box, or Printer object, excluding the border or title bar of the object. Each ScaleLeft property

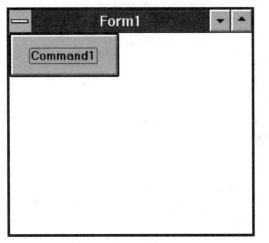

**Figure 9.17 Command1 command button in upper left corner of form**

expression begins with the name of the affected object (CtlName of the picture box, FormName property of the picture box, or Printer for Printer object). In the default value, this number reflects the left coordinate of the form, picture box, or Printer object without the border or title bar.

In the example syntax, the ScaleLeft property defines the horizontal value of the upper left corner as 100. With this new scale, the Command1 command button's height and width become one-fourth that of Form1 by changing them to 25. When the coordinates of the Command1 command button change value, the command button appears in the upper left corner of the form. Figure 9.17 shows what this might look like on the screen.

### The ScaleWidth, ScaleHeight, ScaleTop, and ScaleLeft Properties

The ScaleHeight, ScaleWidth, ScaleTop, or ScaleLeft properties provide the boundaries of possible settings for objects placed upon a form, picture box, or Printer object. Each object's ScaleTop and ScaleLeft properties indicate the coordinates of the upper left corner. The ScaleWidth and ScaleHeight properties provide the coordinates of the lower right corner of an object. A visible control or object on a form, picture box, or Printer object must be between the upper and lower boundaries set by these properties. See Figure 9.16 for the relationship between these properties.

### Example

The ScaleLeft property appears in the Form_Resize event of the Coordinates Project at the end of this section. The Coordinate form's ScaleLeft property changes to 0 as part of the redefinition of the form's coordinate system. This changes the range of possible coordinates on the form to between 0 and 100.

# ScaleMode Property

## Objects Affected

| | | | | |
|---|---|---|---|---|
| Check | Clipboard | Combo | Command | Dbug |
| Dir | Drive | File | ▶ Form | Frame |
| Label | List | Menu | Option | ▶ Picture |
| ▶ Printer | Screen | Scroll | Text | Timer |

## Purpose

The ScaleMode property indicates what unit of measure to use for the form, picture box, or Printer object. This property's default setting is twip (1 inch = 1440 twips). Unless the ScaleMode property is zero (0) (user-defined), all of the dimensions of the forms, controls, and graphical objects use this measurement. Selecting the User-Defined option for this property changes the unit of measure to the range set by the ScaleWidth, ScaleHeight, ScaleTop, and ScaleLeft properties. Tables 9.12 and 9.13 summarize the different arguments and measurement types of the ScaleMode property.

## General Syntax

```
[form.]ScaleMode[=mode%]
[picturebox.]ScaleMode[=mode%]
[Printer.]ScaleMode[=mode%]
```

| Argument | Description |
|----------|-------------|
| form | FormName of the form |
| picture box | CtlName of the picture box |
| Printer | Printer object |
| mode% | Current unit of measure |

Table 9.12 Arguments of the ScaleMode property

| Mode% | Measure Type |
|-------|--------------|
| 0 | User-Defined. Automatically changed to this setting when the ScaleHeight, ScaleWidth, ScaleLeft, and ScaleTop properties change |
| 1 | Twip (1 Inch = 1440 twips). This is the default value for this property |
| 2 | Point (1 Inch = 72 points) |
| 3 | Pixel (Smallest point on a monitor determined by its resolution) |
| 4 | Character (horizontal width = 120 twips/Unit) (vertical width = 240 twips/Unit) |
| 5 | Inch |
| 6 | Millimeter |
| 7 | Centimeter |

Table 9.13 The different measurement types of the ScaleMode property

## Example Syntax

```
Sub Form_Resize ()
    Static i As Integer          'Defines i as a static variable
    ScaleLeft = 500              'Upper left corner coordinates become
    ScaleTop = 500               '500,500
    ScaleWidth = 1000            'Lower right corner coordinates become
    ScaleHeight = 1000           '1000,1000
```

```
    List1.Move ScaleLeft, ScaleTop, ScaleWidth,ScaleHeight
                                  'Fills screen with list box
    For i = i To (i + 15)         'Displays list on screen
        List1.AddItem "List " + Str$(i)
    Next i
End Sub

Sub Form_Load ()
    Form1.WindowState = 2         'Maximizes the form on the screen
    Form1.ScaleMode = 5           'Defines the form's measure as inches
    Text1.Move 1,1,3,3            'Defines dimensions and position of Text box
End Sub
```

## Description

The ScaleMode property defines the measurement unit to use for a form, picture box, or Printer object. Every ScaleMode property expression begins with the name of the object affected (CtlName of Control, FormName of form, and Printer for Printer object). If a ScaleMode property expression does not provide the name, then the form's ScaleMode property changes. ScaleMode property expressions must be one of the values listed in Table 9.13.

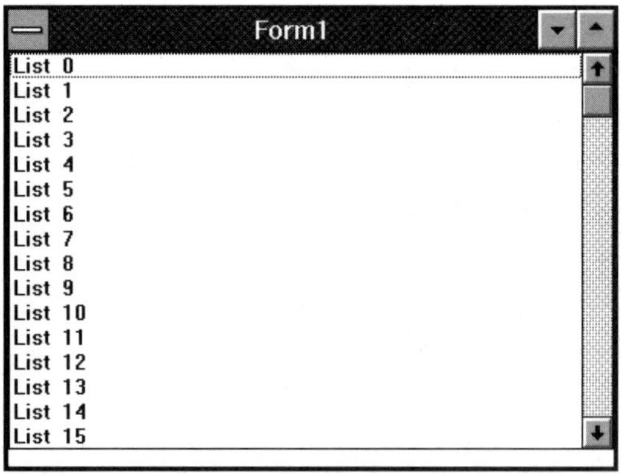

Figure 9.18 List box displayed on Form1

### The ScaleLeft, ScaleTop, ScaleWidth, and ScaleHeight Properties

In the example syntax, the ScaleMode property of the form affects the size and position of the controls positioned on them. The first example does not even contain a ScaleMode property line in the code. The ScaleMode property automatically changes to 0 (user-defined) when the ScaleLeft, ScaleTop, ScaleWidth, and ScaleHeight properties change. With this example, the size and position of the List1 list box appears in relation to the size and position of Form1 (see Figure 9.18).

### The Move Method

The second example shows the use of the ScaleMode property to initially adjust the position and shape of the text box on the form. In this case, the ScaleMode property value of 5 sets the unit of measurement to inches. The Move method uses this setting to define the upper left corner of the Text1 text box and the lower right corner of the Text1 text box (see Figure 9.19).

## Example

The ScaleMode property sets the unit of measurement to inches. All the measurements inside the ShowDisplay picture box must be in inches. All of the measurements on the ShowDisplay picture box are in inches. The manual setting of the ScaleHeight, ScaleWidth, ScaleTop, and ScaleLeft properties of the ShowDisplay picture box automatically change the ScaleMode property to 0 (user-defined).

## Comments

One important point to remember is whether you desire to affect the settings of a form, picture box, or Printer object. Unless the form's ScaleMode property is what you wish to change, remember to begin a ScaleMode property expression with the name of the object affected.

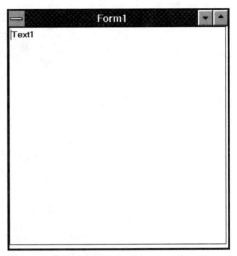

Figure 9.19 Text box displayed on Form1

---

# ScaleTop Property

## Objects Affected

| | | | | |
|---|---|---|---|---|
| Check | Clipboard | Combo | Command | Dbug |
| Dir | Drive | File | ▶ Form | Frame |
| Label | List | Menu | Option | ▶ Picture |
| ▶ Printer | Screen | Scroll | Text | Timer |

## Purpose

The ScaleTop property sets or determines the top coordinate of the upper top corner of a form, picture box, or Printer object. This property has no influence over the Top property of a form, picture box, or Printer object. It only defines the lower limit of possible coordinates on an object. A newly created form, picture box, or Printer object begins with its ScaleTop property set to 0. This property may be a higher value than 0, but should be set to a value lower than those of the ScaleHeight and ScaleWidth properties. Table 9.14 summarizes the arguments of the ScaleTop property.

## General Syntax

```
[form.]ScaleTop[=scale!]
[picturebox.]ScaleTop[=scale!]
[Printer.]ScaleTop[=scale!]
```

| Argument | Description |
|---|---|
| form | FormName of the form |
| picture box | CtlName of the picture box |
| Printer | Printer object |
| scale! | Top coordinate of an object |

**Table 9.14 Arguments of the ScaleTop property**

## Example Syntax

```
Sub Form_Resize ()
    ScaleLeft = 100                              'Upper left corner coordinates
    ScaleTop = 100                               'become 100,100
    ScaleWidth = 400                             'Lower right corner coordinates
    ScaleHeight = 400                            'become 400,400
    Command1.Move ScaleLeft * 2, ScaleTop * 2    'Command button changes position
End Sub
```

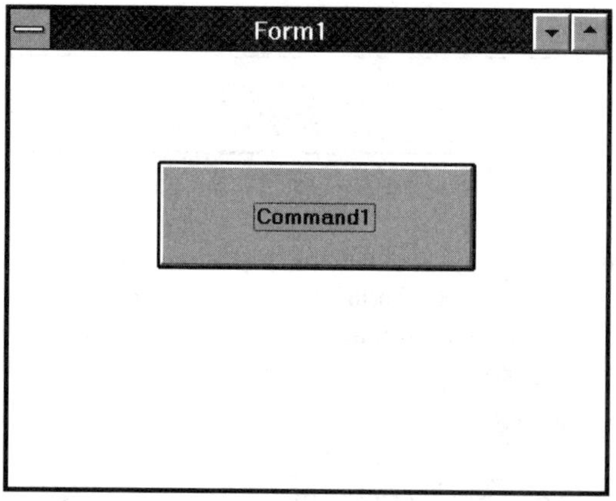

**Figure 9.20 Command1 command button on Form1**

## Description

The ScaleTop property provides the usable top coordinate of a form, picture box, or Printer object, excluding the border or title bar of the object. Each ScaleTop property expression begins with the name of the affected object (CtlName of the picture box, FormName property of the picture box, or Printer for Printer object). In the default value, this number reflects the top coordinate of the form, picture box, or Printer object without the border or title bar.

In the example syntax, the ScaleTop property changes to 100. This change redefines the range of possible coordinates on the form to 100-400 for both the horizontal and vertical coordinates. Figure 9.20 shows what the Command1 command button might look like on Form1.

### The ScaleWidth, ScaleHeight, and ScaleLeft Properties

The ScaleHeight, ScaleWidth, ScaleTop, or ScaleLeft properties provide the boundaries of possible settings for objects placed upon a form, picture box, or Printer object. Each object's ScaleTop and ScaleLeft properties indicate the coordinates of the upper left corner. The ScaleWidth and ScaleHeight properties provide the coordinates of the lower right corner of an object. A visible control or object on a form, picture box, or

Printer object must be between the upper and lower boundaries set by these properties. See Figure 9.16 for the relationship between these properties.

## Example

The ScaleTop property appears in the Form_Resize event of the Coordinates project at the end of this section. The Coordinate form's ScaleTop property changes to 0 as part of the redefinition of the form's coordinate system. This changes the range of possible coordinates on the form to between 0 and 100.

# ScaleWidth Property

## Objects Affected

| | | | | |
|---|---|---|---|---|
| Check | Clipboard | Combo | Command | Dbug |
| Dir | Drive | File | ▶ Form | Frame |
| Label | List | Menu | Option | ▶ Picture |
| ▶ Printer | Screen | Scroll | Text | Timer |

## Purpose

The ScaleWidth property sets or determines the usable width of a form, picture box, or Printer object (usable width excludes the title bar and borders of an object). An object's size is measured in the units indicated by the setting of the ScaleMode property of the form. Twips are the default unit of measure. When the ScaleMode property of the form is 0 (user-specified), the ScaleWidth property value represents a proportional scale. This proportional scale divides the usable width of the object into a number of units equal to the value of the ScaleWidth property. If the object's size changes, then the value of the ScaleWidth remains the same, while the size of each unit of the proportional scale grows larger or smaller. Table 9.15 summarizes the arguments of the ScaleWidth property.

## General Syntax

```
[form.]ScaleWidth[=scale!]
[picturebox.]ScaleWidth[=scale!]
[Printer.]ScaleWidth[=scale!]
```

| Argument | Description |
|---|---|
| form | FormName of the form |
| picture box | CtlName of the picture box |
| Printer | Printer object |
| scale! | Horizontal size of an object |

Table 9.15 Arguments of the ScaleWidth property

## Example Syntax

```
Sub Form_Load ()
    ScaleWidth = 100                          'Lower right corner coordinates become
    ScaleHeight = 100                         '100,100
    List1.Move 0,0,ScaleWidth,ScaleHeight/2   'Moves top of list box
                                              'to middle point of form
End Sub
```

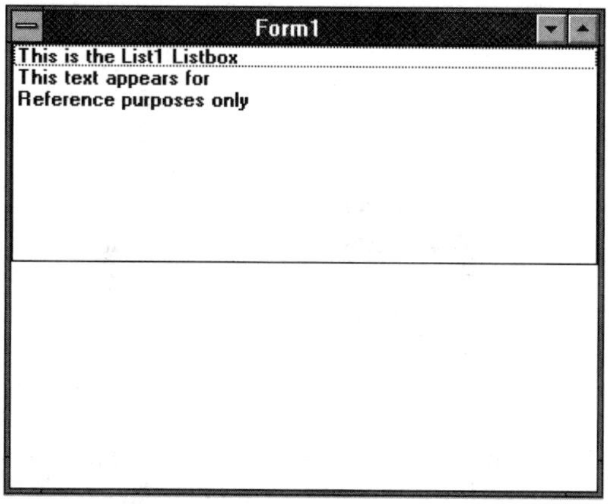

**Figure 9.21 List1 list box on Form1**

## Description

The ScaleWidth property measures the usable width of a form, picture box, or Printer object, excluding the border or title bar of the object. Each ScaleWidth property expression begins with the name of the affected object (CtlName of the picture box, FormName property of the picture box, or Printer for the Printer object). In the default value, this number reflects the width of the form, picture box, or Printer object, without the border or title bar. You can change this value either at design time or at run time. A new value becomes the user-defined proportional measurement of the form, picture box or Printer object. The width of any control or graphics object is a fraction of the width of the object it is on.

In the example syntax, the ScaleWidth property of Form1 changes to 100. This allows the List1 list box to fill the entire width of Form1 when the width portion of the Move method expression moves the list box. Figure 9.21 shows how this might look on the screen.

### The ScaleHeight, ScaleWidth, ScaleTop, and ScaleLeft Properties

The ScaleHeight, ScaleWidth, ScaleTop, or ScaleLeft properties provide the boundaries of possible settings for objects placed on a form, picture box, or Printer object. Each object's ScaleTop and ScaleLeft properties indicate the coordinates of the upper left corner. The ScaleWidth and ScaleHeight properties provide the coordinates of the lower right corner of an object. A visible control or object on a form, picture box, or Printer object must be between the upper and lower boundaries set by these properties. As shown in the example syntax, changes can be initiated with the use of a Move method that makes the definitions of the width of controls fractions of the ScaleWidth of the current form. This is very useful for helping ensure that controls are not obscured when a form's size changes. If this routine is in the Resize event of the form in question, then every time the form's size changes, the controls also change. See Figure 9.16 for the relationship between these properties.

### Example

The ScaleWidth property appears in the Form_Resize event of the Coordinates project at the end of this section. By setting the ScaleHeight and ScaleWidth properties to 100, the size of each of the distances that these properties represent divides into 100 equal units. Referencing these properties in the move method allows the ShowDisplay picture box to fill the lower four-fiifths of the Coordinate form. Each time the Coordinate form's size changes, the ShowDisplay picture adjusts to fill it.

# Top Property

### Objects Affected

| | | | | |
|---|---|---|---|---|
| ▶ Check | Clipboard | ▶ Combo | ▶ Command | Dbug |
| ▶ Dir | ▶ Drive | ▶ File | ▶ Form | ▶ Frame |
| ▶ Label | ▶ List | Menu | ▶ Option | ▶ Picture |
| Printer | Screen | ▶ Scroll | ▶ Text | Timer |

### Purpose

The Top property defines or determines the distance of a form or control from the top edge of the form or picture box. A control's distance measures in the units indicated by the ScaleMode property of the current form or picture box. This distance is always in twips for forms. The default unit of measurement is twips (1 twip = 1/20 point; 1 inch = 72 points; 1440 twips = 1 inch). The Top property of an object is available at both design time and run time. Tables 9.16 and 9.17 summarize the different arguments of the Top property and the possible measurement types.

### General Syntax

```
[form.]Top[=top!]
[control.]Top[=top!]
```

| Argument | Description |
|---|---|
| form | FormName of the form |
| control | CtlName of the control |
| top! | Vertical top distance of the object |

Table 9.16 Arguments of the Top property

| Measurement | Size |
|---|---|
| Twip | 1440 twips = 1 inch |
| Point | 72 points = 1 inch |
| Pixels | Varies depending upon the system being used |
| Characters | 12 characters horizontally and 6 vertically |
| Millimeters | 254 millimeters = 1 inch |
| Centimeters | 2.54 centimeters = 1 inch |

**Table 9.17 Possible measurement types in relation to 1 inch**

## Example Syntax

```
Sub ResetForm (FormName As Form)
    If FormName.ScaleMode <> 0 Then          'Checks if ScaleMode is set to user-defined
        FormName.Top = 1440                   'Form's distance from top placed at 1440
        FormName.Left = 1440                  'Form's distance from left placed at 1440
    Else
        FormName.Top = FormName.ScaleTop      'Form's distance from left and top made equal
        FormName.Left = FormName.ScaleLeft   'to the value of the ScaleLeft & ScaleTop
    End If                                     'properties
End Sub
```

## Description

The Top property of an object measures the vertical distance from the top of a form, screen, or picture box. You can enter this value at design time by manually moving the object with the mouse or by entering the value at the properties bar. The Top property of a control or form is modifiable either at design time or at run time. A setting must be between 0 and a maximum value specified by the system itself. Visual Basic automatically adjusts itself to the resolution of the screen. You should ensure that your objects are not too far from the edges for the most common 640x480 and 800x600 resolution screens to display.

The example syntax outlines a subfunction named ResetForm, which sets a form's distance from the left and top sides of the screen. If the ScaleMode property is user-defined, the Left and Top properties are set to the values of the ScaleLeft and ScaleTop properties. Otherwise, the ResetForm function places the form 1440 twips from the edge of the screen. This is another example of the use of a generic function to apply to all of the forms in a program.

### The Left, Top, Width, and Height Properties

When you create a form or control in Visual Basic, the Left, Top, Width, and Height properties display in the far right side of the properties bar. See Figure 9.11 and the discussion under the Height property in this chapter.

### The Scale Mode

The ScaleMode property of a form directly controls the meaning of the value of the Top property. When this property changes at design time from one measurement to another, Visual Basic recalculates the value of the Top property in this new type of measurement. As the ScaleMode property is not modifiable at run time, the meaning of the value of the Top property does not change while the program is running. For example, no matter what size a command box becomes based on changes in the size of the parent form, the Top property will remain the same.

### Measurement Values in the CONSTANT.TXT File

The CONSTANT.TXT file, found in the main Visual Basic Directory, contains the names of constants to use in your Visual Basic applications. In order to use the CONSTANT.TXT file, you must load it into the project's global module. To do this, open Visual Basic's Project window and double-click on the global module. This will load the global module into the Code window. Then open Visual Basic's Code menu and choose the Load Text option. This brings up a dialog box. Select the CONSTANT.TXT file and click on the Merge button. This will read the file into the global module. The following listing displays the applicable values in the CONSTANT.TXT file.

```
' ScaleMode (form, picture box, Printer)
Global Const USER = 0           ' 0 – User
Global Const TWIPS = 1          ' 1 – Twip
Global Const POINTS = 2         ' 2 – Point
Global Const PIXELS = 3         ' 3 – Pixel
Global Const CHARACTERS = 4     ' 4 – Character
Global Const INCHES = 5         ' 5 – Inch
Global Const MILLIMETERS = 6    ' 6 – Millimeter
Global Const CENTIMETERS = 7    ' 7 – Centimeter
```

## Example

In the Coordinates project at the end of this section, set the Top property of the forms and controls at design time. This is done either by dragging the control's edges with the mouse or by entering the value into the properties bar.

## Comments

Remember that changes to the ScaleTop property of a form only alter the value of the Top property of a control and do not alter the actual distance.

# Width Property

## Objects Affected

| | | | | |
|---|---|---|---|---|
| ▶ Check | Clipboard | ▶ Combo | ▶ Command | Dbug |
| ▶ Dir | ▶ Drive | ▶ File | ▶ Form | ▶ Frame |
| ▶ Label | ▶ List | Menu | ▶ Option | ▶ Picture |
| ▶ Printer | ▶ Screen | ▶ Scroll | ▶ Text | Timer |

## Purpose

The Width property defines or determines the horizontal size of a form or control on the screen, form, picture box, or Printer object. Forms, Printer objects, and Screen objects are always measured in twips. A control's size uses the units of measure indicated by the ScaleMode property of the current form or picture box. The default unit of measurement for a control is twips (1 twip = 1/20 point; 1 inch = 72 points; 1440 twips = 1 inch). Except for the dimensions of the width setting of a Printer object, which is defined at run time, the Width property of an object is available at both design time and run time. To manually adjust the Width property of a picture box at design time, click on one of its edges and resize it by dragging. You can also adjust the width by entering the desired measurement into the properties bar. Table 9.10 summarizes the arguments of the Width property, and the Table 9.19 lists the possible measurement settings.

## General Syntax

```
[form.]Width[=width!]
[control.]Width[=width!]
Printer.Width[=width!]
Screen.Width[=width!]
```

| Argument | Description |
|---|---|
| form | FormName of the form |
| control | CtlName of the control |
| Printer | Printer object |
| Screen | Screen object |
| width! | Vertical width of the object |

Table 9.18 Arguments of the Width property

| Measurement | Size |
|---|---|
| Twip | 1440 twips = 1 inch |
| Point | 72 points = 1 inch |
| Pixels | Varies depending on the system being used |
| Characters | 12 characters horizontally and 6 vertically |
| Millimeters | 254 millimeters = 1 inch |
| Centimeters | 2.54 centimeters = 1 inch |

**Table 9.19 Possible measurement types in relation to 1 inch**

## Example Syntax

```
Sub Form_Load ()
    Form.1.Width = (Picture1.Width * 2)   'Width and height of the form are made twice the size
    Form1.Height = (Picture1.Height * 2) 'of the width and height of picture box.
End Sub
```

## Description

The Width property of an object measures the horizontal width of a form, screen, or picture box. You can enter this value at design time by manually moving the object with the mouse or by entering the value at the properties bar. You can modify the Width property of a control at run time or design time. In contrast, you can set the Width properties of both the Printer object and Screen object at run time. A setting must be between 0 and a maximum value specified by the system itself. Visual Basic automatically adjusts itself to the resolution of the screen or printer. You should ensure that your objects are not too large for the most common 640x480 and 800x600 resolution screens to display.

**Figure 9.22 Picture1 picture box on Form1**

In the example syntax, the Form1 form's Width property is twice the size of the setting of the Picture1 picture box, as shown in Figure 9.22. This demonstrates the ways in which this property serves as a basis for changes to the measurements of other objects.

### The Left, Top, Width, and Height Properties

When you create a form or control in Visual Basic, the Left, Top, Width, and Height properties display in the far right side of the properties bar. See Figure 9.11 and the discussion under the Height property in this chapter.

### Screen and Printer

In reference to the computer screen and printer being used, the Width property returns the width of the screen or page available. With this property, the code determines the amount of usable space available on the printed page or screen. The Width property of the Screen and Printer objects is not available at design time and is read-only at run time. For this reason, the value of this property normally serves as a reference and is not changeable at run time.

### The Scale Mode

The ScaleMode property of a form directly controls the meaning of the value of the Width property. When the ScaleMode property changes at design time from one measurement to another, Visual Basic recalculates the value of the Width property in this new type of measurement. As the ScaleMode property is not modifiable at run time, the meaning of the value of the Width property does not change while the program is running. For example, no matter what size a command box becomes based on changes in the size of the parent form, the Width property will remain the same.

### The ScaleWidth Property

The ScaleWidth property divides the width of a form, picture box, or Printer object into the number of units set in the property. When a form's ScaleWidth property changes to 100 on the properties bar, the width of the form is divided into 100 equal units. (Changing the ScaleWidth property of the form to a new value does not change the actual size of the control.) This unit changes in size as the form's height changes. In this way, increasing the width of the form has the effect of increasing the size of one of these units (the width remains divided into 100 units that are now larger in size). These units define the upper and lower limit of the possible width of controls on this form. With the Move statement, the size of the control adjusts based on the changes in width to the form. For example, a Resize event might adjust the Width property of a command box of a form by triggering a move statement that always ensures that the command box is one-fourth the size of the form. In this example, the ScaleWidth property of the form is 100, and the Width property of the Command1 command button is 25 (one-fourth the width of the form). Figure 9.23 displays this concept visually.

### Measurement Values in the CONSTANT.TXT File

The CONSTANT.TXT file, found in the main Visual Basic Directory, contains the names to use for constant values in your Visual Basic applications. In order to use the CONSTANT.TXT file, you must load it into the project's global module. To do this, open Visual Basic's Project window and double-click on the global module. This will load the global module into the Code window. Then open Visual Basic's Code menu and choose the Load Text option. This brings up a dialog box. Select the CONSTANT.TXT file and click on the Merge button. This will read the file into the global module. The following listing gives the applicable variables in the CONSTANT.TXT file.

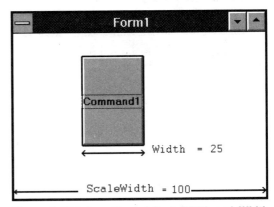

**Figure 9.23 Interaction of ScaleWidth and Width properties**

```
' ScaleMode (form, picture box, Printer)
Global Const USER = 0              ' 0 - User
Global Const TWIPS = 1             ' 1 - Twip
Global Const POINTS = 2            ' 2 - Point
Global Const PIXELS = 3            ' 3 - Pixel
Global Const CHARACTERS = 4        ' 4 - Character
Global Const INCHES = 5            ' 5 - Inch
Global Const MILLIMETERS = 6       ' 6 - Millimeter
Global Const CENTIMETERS = 7       ' 7 - Centimeter
```

## Example

The Width properties of the ShowDisplay and PictureView command buttons change at design time to make them fit on the screen as desired. Make design time adjustments to these properties by manually dragging them with the mouse or changing their values on the properties bar.

## Comments

Remember that changes to the ScaleWidth property of a form only alter the value of the Width property of a control and do not alter the actual width.

# Coordinates Project

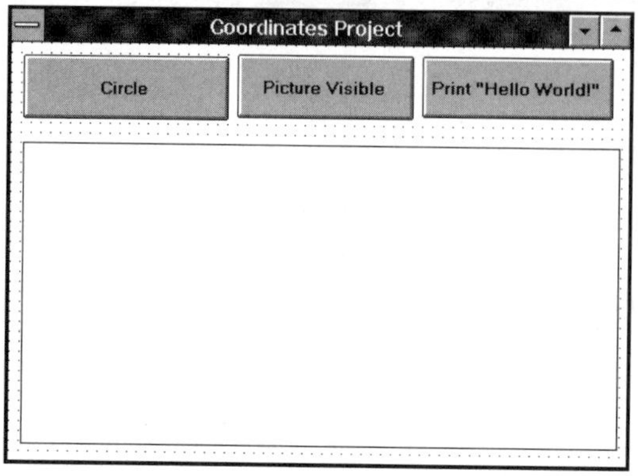

Figure 9.24 What the Coordinates form should look like when completed

## Project Overview

The Coordinates project demonstrates the concepts of the coordinate system in Visual Basic. This project shows the functioning of the method and properties that control the position of controls and placement of graphics objects on a form, picture box, or Printer object. By following the examples of the different elements of this project, you will learn how to place controls and graphical objects. The first part of this section explains the assembly of the project. Please refer to Figure 9.24 for the placement of the different elements of each form. Following these assembly instructions is a discussion of the operation of the Coordinates project.

## Assembling the Project

1. Make a new form (the Coordinates form) with the objects and properties listed in Table 9.20.

| Object | Property | Setting |
|---|---|---|
| Form | AutoRedraw | True |
| | FormName | Coordinate |
| | Caption | Coordinates Project |
| | FillStyle | 0 - Solid |
| | ScaleMode | 0 - User defined |
| Command button | Caption | Circle |
| | CtlName | ChangePicture |
| Command button | Caption | Picture VIsible |
| | CtlName | PictureView |
| Command button | Caption | Print "Hello World!" |
| | CtlName | Print_Hello |
| Picture box | CtlName | ShowDisplay |
| | ScaleMode | 5 - Inches |
| | FillStyle | 0 - Solid |

Table 9.20 Settings for the Coordinates project

2. Size the objects on the screen, as shown in Figure 9.30.

3. Enter the following code in the Form_Click event subroutine. This code triggers each time with each clicking of the form with the mouse. When the user clicks the form with the mouse, this code produces a circle or a line on the form. A circle displays when the word Circle is on the command button ChangePicture, and a line when the word Line appears.

```
Sub Form_Click ()
    If PictureView.Caption = "Picture Hidden" Then
        If ChangePicture.Caption = "Circle" Then
            X = CurrentX + 20
            Y = CurrentY + .20
            Circle (X, Y), 20
        Else
            X = CurrentX + 20
            Y = CurrentY + 20
            Line (X,Y)-(X+20,Y+20)
        End If
    End If
End Sub
```

4. Enter the following code in the Form_DblClick event subroutine. Rapidly clicking the left mouse button twice triggers this event. This code clears the form of all graphics and restores the CurrentX and CurrentY properties to the coordinates 0,0.

```
Sub Form_DblClick ()
    Cls
End Sub
```

5. Enter the following code in the Form_Load event subroutine. This codeschanges the ScaleTop, ScaleLeft, ScaleHeight, and ScaleWeight properties of the form to a user-defined scale between 0 and 100. These changes take place when the Coordinates form loads at program startup.

```
Sub Form_Load ()
    ScaleTop = 0
    ScaleLeft = 0
    ScaleHeight = 100
    ScaleWidth = 100
End Sub
```

6. Enter the following code in the Form_Resize event subroutine. This code triggers when the form loads at program startup and every time the form's size changes. Each time this happens, the size of the ShowDisplay picture box changes to fill the lower four-fifths of the form.

```
Sub Form_Resize ()
    ShowDisplay.Move 0, 20, ScaleWidth, ScaleHeight
End Sub
```

7. Enter the following code in the ChangePicture_Click event subroutine. Pressing the ChangePicture command button triggers this code. This code alternates the words on the ChangePicture command button between Circle and Line.

```
Sub ChangePicture_Click ()
    If ChangePicture.Caption = "Circle" Then
        ChangePicture.Caption = "Line"
    Else
        ChangePicture.Caption = "Circle"
    End If
End Sub
```

8. Enter the following code in the ShowDisplay_DblClick event subroutine. Rapidly clicking the left mouse button twice triggers this event. This code clears the ShowDisplay picture box of all graphics and restores its CurrentX and CurrentY properties to the coordinates 0,0.

```
Sub ShowDisplay_DblClick ()
    ShowDisplay.Cls
End Sub
```

9. Enter the following code in the ShowDisplay_Click event subroutine. The ShowDisplay_Click event triggers with each clicking of the mouse. This draws a circle or a line on the ShowDisplay picture box. A circle displays when the word Circle is on the command button ChangePicture and a line when the word Line appears.

```
Sub ShowDisplay_Click ()
    ShowDisplay.FillColor = RGB(0, 0, 0)
    If ChangePicture.Caption = "Circle" Then
        X = ShowDisplay.CurrentX + 0.5
        Y = ShowDisplay.CurrentY + 0.5
        ShowDisplay.Circle (X, Y), 0.5
    Else
        X = ShowDisplay.CurrentX + 0.5
        Y = ShowDisplay.CurrentY
        ShowDisplay.Line (X, Y)-(X + 1, Y + 1)
    End If
End Sub
```

10. Enter the following code in the PictureView_Click event subroutine. Each clicking of the PictureView command button triggers this event. This code alternates the words on the PictureView command button from Picture Visible to Picture Hidden.

```
Sub PictureView_Click ()
    If PictureView.Caption = "Picture Visible" Then
        PictureView.Caption = "Picture Hidden"
        ShowDisplay.Visible = 0
    Else
        PictureView.Caption = "Picture Visible"
        ShowDisplay.Visible = -1
    End If
End Sub
```

11. Enter the following code in the Print_Hello_Click event subroutine. Each clicking of the Print_Hello command button triggers this event. This code sends the words "Hello World!" to the printer.

```
Sub Print_Hello_Click ()
  Printer.CurrentX = 40
  Printer.CurrentY = 48
  Printer.Print "Hello World!"
  Printer.EndDoc
End Sub
```

## How It Works

The Coordinates project displays a screen with three command buttons along the top and a picture box that covers the lower four-fifths of the form. Whenever the user clicks the picture box with the mouse, a line or a circle appears on the picture box. If the user presses the middle button labeled Picture Visible, then the text changes to Picture Hidden and the picture box disappears. When the user clicks the mouse over the form, lines and circles appear on the form. Whether circles or lines appear when the user presses the mouse depends upon whether the far left command button reads Circle or Line. To clear the form or the picture box of all graphics, the user must rapidly click the mouse twice.

The button on the far right of the Coordinates form reads "Print Hello World." When the user presses this command button, the printer will print the words "Hello World!" The printer must be on and ready to accept a printout for this to work properly.

### Startup

The Form_Load event subroutine is triggered when the Coordinates form loads at program startup. This event changes the unit of measure settings of the Coordinates form and Printer object to user-defined. The settings of the ScaleHeight and ScaleWidth properties change to 100, and the ScaleLeft and ScaleTop properties become 0. A single line of code changes each property value for the coordinate form. In contrast, a Scale method expression. Both set up the same proportional scale from 0 to 100. The measurement unit on the form and Printer object becomes 1/100 of their dimensions.

The Form_Resize event processes next with a Move method expression. Based upon the settings of the ScaleHeight, ScaleWidth, ScaleTop, and ScaleLeft properties, a Move method adjusts the shape of the Picture box named ShowDisplay to fit the space of the form below the ChangePicture, Print_Hello, and PictureView command buttons. Each of the dimensions in the Move method uses the Scale properties of the Coordinates form ShowDisplay to adjust the ShowDisplay picture box to fit under the command buttons.

### Running the Coordinates Project

The Change_Picture event activates when the user clicks the right Change_Picture command button. If the caption is Circle, then the property changes to Line. Otherwise, the caption changes to Circle.

Clicking the right mouse button while the mouse arrow is over the picture box triggers the ShowDisplay_Click event. When this command button reads Circle, clicking the Coordinates form or ShowDisplay picture box produces circles. If this command button reads Line, then clicking the Coordinates form or ShowDisplay picture box displays lines.

The circles and lines drawn within the ShowDisplay picture box appear at the coordinates of the CurrentX and CurrentY properties of the picture box. Each pressing of the right mouse button generates a circle or line that is a little lower and further to the right than the previous circle or line. This may carry the circle or line off the screen. Note: If the form is maximized, only the portions of the lines and circles that were visible when the form was smaller display.

Pressing the command button that reads Picture Visible changes its caption to Picture Hidden and hides the ShowDisplay picture box. A circle or line appears on the form with every clicking of the form, depending upon whether the ChangePicture command button reads Circle or Line. To clear the form, press the mouse rapidly twice to trigger the Cls method in the Form_DblClick event.

# Drawing Shapes

S hapes are images drawn on the surface of a form, picture box, or Printer object. You can draw with curved lines to produces arcs, circles, and ellipses. Drawn straight lines make up lines, squares, rectangles, and triangles. A drawn shape may contain any combination of curved or straight lines. You can define a color and/or pattern to fill solid (enclosed) shapes. The lines that make up a shape can be solid, dashed, or dotted. You can make the line around a shape invisible. When an image appears, it can cover or be covered by the other objects on the screen.

The methods, statements, properties, and functions explained in Chapter 8, *Setting Up Graphical Objects,* affect the appearance of shapes on the screen. Although an understanding of the use of these elements of Visual Basic is not required for this chapter, the concepts discussed in that chapter can help give you a complete picture of how drawn graphics work. You may wish to read or review that chapter.

## The Appearance of Shapes in Visual Basic

Visual Basic provides several properties for specifying the appearance of shapes on a form, picture box, or Printer object. The Circle method places a curved shape on the indicated portion of a screen. The Line method produces any kind of shape that consists of straight lines.

Once you have a shape, there are a number of ways you can alter its appearance. The FillColor property determines the color to place within an enclosed shape (or you can make it transparent). You can also use the FillStyle property to specify a pattern to fill a shape; a shape can have both a pattern and a fill color. Setting the DrawMode property of a form or control affects how the shape's colors interact on the screen. This property indicates whether a newly drawn shape covers the existing graphic objects on the screen. Some settings of this property change all of the graphics objects to black or white.

Shapes are also tied to the characteristics of their form or control. Each form or control determines the width of the line around a shape with the DrawWidth property. The DrawStyle property indicates the format of the line that surrounds a shape (solid, dashed, dotted, or even nonexistent.) Table 10.1 summarizes these five properties and two methods.

| Use or Set This... | | To Do This... |
|---|---|---|
| Circle | Method | Draw a circle, ellipsis, or arc on the form, picture box, or Printer object |
| DrawMode | Property | Define the appearance of drawn shapes |
| DrawStyle | Property | Define the outside line around a shape |
| DrawWidth | Property | Define the width of the line on the edge of a shape |
| FillColor | Property | Set the color to fill circles and boxes created with Line and Circle Methods |
| FillStyle | Property | Set the pattern to fill circles and boxes |
| Line | Method | Draw a line, square, or rectangle on a form, picture box, or Printer object |

**Table 10.1 Methods and properties dealing with drawing shapes**

The properties and methods in Table 10.1 are investigated in detail in the following pages. Step-by-step directions for assembling the Drawing project are described at the end of this chapter.

# Circle Method

## Objects Affected

| | | | | |
|---|---|---|---|---|
| Check | Clipboard | Combo | Command | Dbug |
| Dir | Drive | File | ▶ Form | Frame |
| Label | List | Menu | Option | ▶ Picture |
| ▶ Printer | Screen | Scroll | Text | Timer |

## Purpose

The Circle method generates a curved shape on an indicated object on the screen or printer. This method can create a variety of curved objects including circles, ellipses (ovals), and arches. The object on the screen to be drawn on is a form, picture box, or Printer object. Curved shapes appear in relation to the top left corner of the form, picture box, or Printer object. Shapes drawn on a form have no affect on the controls placed on the form. If a shape is in the same position as a control on a form, the image displays behind the control. Table 10.2 summarizes the arguments of the Circle method.

## General Syntax

```
[object.]Circle[Step](x!,y!),radius![,[color&][,[start!][,[end!][,aspect!]]]]
```

| Argument | Description |
|---|---|
| object | FormName of the form or CtlName of the picture box or Printer object that the shape is to be drawn on. If no object is given, then the form is assumed |
| Step | Changes the effects of the coordinates given as being relative to the current coordinates returned by the CurrentX and CurrentY properties. Normally, the coordinates are given in relation to the top left corner of the object being drawn on |
| (x!,y!) | The horizontal and vertical distance of the center of the curved shape from the edge of the object. The value of this shape is a single-precision value in a unit of measure specifed by the ScaleMode property |
| radius! | A single-precision value that measures the distance from the center to the edge of a circle. The value of this shape is measured in units indicated by the ScaleMode property |
| color& | The RGB color of the outline of a curved shape. This argument is either a long integer value or may be defined with either the RGB or QBColor functions. The absence of this argument indicates that the ForeColor property is to be used |
| start!, end! | Indicates the begining and ending position of a partial circle or arc. This argument is a single-precision value with a default value of 0 and ranges between -6.283 radians and 6.283 radians |
| aspect! | A single-precision value that defaults to 1.0 (Circle) and produces a horizontally elongated circle (ellipse) as the aspect value is made larger. As the aspect is reduced, the circle becomes vertically elongated |

**Table 10.2 Arguments of the Circle method**

## Example Syntax

```
'Draws a circle with a slice taken out.
'This slice grows larger each time the user
'presses the Command1 command button.
Sub Command1_Click ()
    Static Start As Double          'Defines a static variable
    Cls                             'Clears the form
    Aspect! = 1                     'Defines the Aspect
    FillColor = QBColor(7)          'Changes color to white
    FillStyle = 0                   'Makes all objects solid
    X! = ScaleWidth / 2             'Defines x as half scalewidth.
    Y! = ScaleHeight / 2            'Defines y as half scaleheight.
    R = ScaleWidth / 3              'Defines r as 1/3 scalewidth.
    If Abs(Start) > 6.283 Then      'Checks if Start is greater than 6.283.
        Start = 0                   'Defines Start as 0
    End If
    Circle (X!, Y!), R, QBColor(0), Start, -6.283, Aspect!
    Start = Start - .785            'Reduces Start value
End Sub
```

## Description

The Circle method produces a curved shape on a form, picture box, or Printer object, with several arguments that modify the shape's appearance. The object argument indicates whether to place the curved shape on a form, picture box, or Printer object (using the FormName of the form, CtlName of the picture box, or Printer for the Printer object). If the keyword STEP follows the word Circle, then the x! and y! coordinates are set in relation to the current values of the CurrentX and CurrentY properties. Omitting the word STEP changes the meaning of the x! and y! coordinates to being in relation to the top left corner of the object. The values of each of the x! (horizontal) and y! (vertical) coordinates define the position of the shape. A curved shape's radius is in the radius! argument. The ScaleMode property defines the unit of measure used by the x!, y!, and radius! arguments. The color& argument sets the color of the line that surrounds a curved shape and defaults to the ForeColor property when it is left blank. Define this argument with either an RGB hexadecimal number, RGB function, or QBColor function. To skip an argument in the middle of the syntax, include the comma (,) for each argument excluded. Don't end a Circle method with a comma.

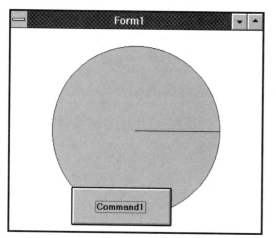

**Figure 10.1 Example syntax circle**

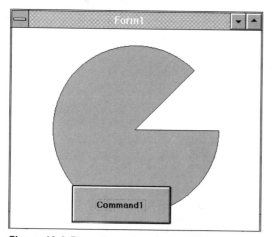

**Figure 10.2 Example syntax circle with slice taken out**

### Using PI

A circle is a line whose points are all the same distance from a point on a surface. The distance between the line and the point is the radius. To find the distance of the line around the point, multiply 2 by PI by the radius of the circle (2*PI*Radius). This formula produces the circumference or distance of the line around a point. PI is a constant with an approximate value of 3.141592654. Find this value by multiplying 4 by the arctangent of 1 (4*Atn(1)). If you do not know what an arctangent is, then do not worry, as it is not crucial to using the Circle method. In the example syntax, PI is the basis for the definition of the visible portion of the partial circle. Table 10.3 shows the different formulas used with circles.

| Formula | Description |
|---------|-------------|
| 2*PI*Radius | Finds the circumference of a circle |
| 4*Atn(1) | Finds the value of PI |

**Table 10.3 Circle formulas**

### The Start! and End! Arguments

The start! and end! arguments of the Circle method define the dimensions of a partial circle or arch. Each partial circle's start! and end! arguments are expressed in terms of PI and the formula (degrees *(PI/180)). This formula returns a value between 0 and 6.283 representing the degrees of a circle from 1 to 360 degrees. All start! and end! arguments have a value between these two values of 0 and 6.283. Zero is not a valid value for either argument. In Visual Basic, the 360-degree point on a circle is at the three o'clock position on the circle. Table 10.4 displays the values to use for possible positions on a circle from 45 degrees to 360 degrees at intervals of 45 degrees. Figure 10.3 visually displays these positions on a circle.

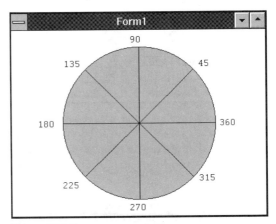

**Figure 10.3 Degrees on a circle**

In the example syntax, the end! argument changes each time that the command button is pressed to reflect a larger and larger slice removed from the circle. Note that the circles drawn by the pressing of the Command1 command button appear behind the button, since drawn graphics are always placed under existing controls. This has the effect of obscuring any parts of the circles that are in the same position as the command button. Figures 10.1 and 10.2 show what this example might look like

| Degrees | Approximate Value | Formula |
|---------|-------------------|---------|
| 360 | 6.283 | (360*(PI/180)) |
| 315 | 5.498 | (315*(PI/180)) |
| 270 | 4.712 | (270*(PI/180)) |
| 225 | 3.927 | (225*(PI/180)) |
| 180 | 3.142 | (180*(PI/180)) |
| 135 | 2.356 | (135*(PI/180)) |
| 90 | 1.571 | (90*(PI/180)) |
| 45 | 0.785 | (45*(PI/180)) |

**Table 10.4 Approximate values for start! and end! positions on a circle**

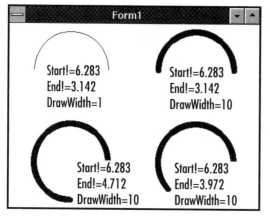

**Figure 10.4 Arcs**

## Partial Circles and Arcs

Using the start! and end! arguments in a Circle method produces partial circles on forms, picture boxes, or Printer objects. Each start! and end! argument contains a value obtained by multiplying the degree desired by PI divided by 180. The part of the circle displayed appears between the boundaries of the degrees indicated. When the values of the start! and end! arguments are negative numbers, a line appears between the center of the circle and the edge of the drawn partial circle. Figure 10.4 displays some example arcs. In the example syntax, the end! argument reduces in size with each pressing of the Command1 command button. This produces a smaller visible portion of the circle on the screen.

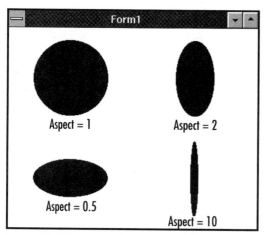

**Figure 10.5 Demonstration of the effects of aspect**

## Ellipses

The value of the Aspect argument of a Circle method defines whether a circle is a perfect circle or elongated. When the aspect argument is one, both the horizontal and vertical distance from the edge of the circle to the center is equal to the radius. If the value is less than 1, then the circle is elongated horizontally. Setting the aspect argument to a value greater than 1 has the effect of creating a vertical ellipse. A value specified in the aspect argument defines the ratio of difference between the horizontal and vertical dimensions of the circle. Figure 10.5 shows the effects of aspect on the drawing of a circle.

## The FillColor and FillStyle properties

The FillColor and FillStyle properties affect the contents of a shape drawn with the Circle method. A shape contains the color indicated by the FillColor property of the form, picture box, or Printer object. Depending on the setting of the FillStyle property, the shape contains a solid or pattern form of the color set in the FillColor property.

## The DrawWidth Property

The width of a line that surrounds a shape drawn with the Circle method is defined by the setting of the DrawWidth property. If the start! and end! arguments of the Circle method have positive values, then the DrawWidth property defines the width of the line drawn to the center of the circle. This combination is an excellent means of placing an arch of a desired width on the screen.

## Example

In the Shape project at the end of this section, the Circle method serves as a means of drawing circles on the Draw picture box. Pressing the command button labeled Circle produces a circle on the Draw picture box. This circle uses the settings chosen in properties represented in the menus of the Shape form. This code is within the Draw_Circle_Click event subroutine connected to the Draw_Circle command button. The circle varies in size and appears at a random location within the picture box. Each of the settings of the DrawMode, DrawWidth, DrawStyle, FillStyle, and FillColor properties determines how the circle displays on the Shape form.

## Comments

A curved shape may only be filled with a color or pattern when completely bounded by a line on all sides. Otherwise, the shape is empty no matter what the settings of the properties that affect a shape's interior.

# DrawMode Property

## Objects Affected

| | | | | |
|---|---|---|---|---|
| Check | Clipboard | Combo | Command | Dbug |
| Dir | Drive | File | ▶ Form | Frame |
| Label | List | Menu | Option | ▶ Picture |
| ▶ Printer | Screen | Scroll | Text | Timer |

## Purpose

The DrawMode property determines what happens to a shape's colors when the shape appears on the screen. You can use this property to determine how new and existing graphics on the screen will interact visually. This property modifies the colors of the FillColor, ForeColor, and BackColor properties of a form, picture box, or Printer object to produce differing results on the screen. In its default setting, the DrawMode property has no effect on the color of a drawn shape. With some settings, the actual color produced is the opposite or inverse of the normal color indicated by the corresponding property. Some DrawMode property settings combine the colors of the ForeColor, FillColor, and BackColor properties to produce a new color. The settings of each of the FillColor, ForeColor, and BackColor properties remain unchanged by the setting of the DrawMode property. Table 10.5 summarizes the arguments of the DrawMode property; Table 10.6 lists the effects of the different settings of the DrawMode property.

## General Syntax

```
form.DrawMode [= mode%]
picturebox.DrawMode [= mode%]
Printer.DrawMode = [= mode%]
```

| Argument | Description |
|----------|-------------|
| form | FormName property of form |
| control | CtlName property of picture box |
| Printer | Printer object |
| mode% | Value representing the appearance of new shapes |

Table 10.5 Arguments of the DrawMode property

| mode% | Description | Effect |
|-------|-------------|--------|
| 1 | Blackness | All shapes are black |
| 2 | Not Merge Pen | Colors are the inverse of Merge Pen |
| 3 | Mask Not Pen | Colors are a mixing of the BackColor and inverse of the FillColor |
| 4 | Not Copy Pen | Colors are the inverse of the FillColor |
| 5 | Mask Pen Not | Colors are a mixing of the FillColor and the inverse of the BackColor |
| 6 | Invert | Ouput isthe inverse of the BackColor property |
| 7 | Xor Pen | Colors are a mixing of the FillColor and BackColor. Restores the previous colors below a shape when the next shape appears. This removes the previous shape and gives an illusion of movement |
| 8 | Not Mask Pen | Colors are the inverse of Mask Pen |
| 9 | Mask Pen | Colors are the common ones between the BackColor and FillColor |
| 10 | Not Xor Pen | Colors are the inverse of the Xor Pen colors |
| 11 | Nop | Output remains unmodified |
| 12 | Merge Not Pen | Colors are a mixing of BackColor and inverse of FillColor |
| 13 | Copy Pen | (Default) FillColor |
| 14 | Merge Pen Not | Colors are a mixing of the Fill Color and inverse of BackColor |
| 15 | Merge Pen | Colors are a mixing of the FillColor and BackColor |
| 16 | Whiteness | All Shapes are white |

Table 10.6 Possible settings and effects of the DrawMode property

## Example Syntax

```
Sub DisplayColor (Num As Integer, Con As Control)
     If Num = 0 Then Con.Text = "Black"      'Text box changed to read Black
     If Num = 1 Then Con.Text = "Blue"       'Text box changed to read Blue
     If Num = 2 Then Con.Text = "Green"      'Text box changed to read Green
     If Num = 3 Then Con.Text = "Cyan"       'Text box changed to read Cyan
```

```
    If Num = 4 Then Con.Text = "Red"              'Text box changed to read Red
    If Num = 5 Then Con.Text = "Magenta"          'Text box changed to read Magenta
    If Num = 6 Then Con.Text = "Yellow"           'Text box changed to read Yellow
    If Num = 7 Then Con.Text = "White"            'Text box changed to read White
    If Num = 8 Then Con.Text = "Gray"             'Text box changed to read Gray
    If Num = 9 Then Con.Text = "Light Blue"       'Text box changed to read Light Blue
    If Num = 10 Then Con.Text = "Light Green"     'Text box changed to read Light Green
    If Num = 11 Then Con.Text = "Light Cyan"      'Text box changed to read Light Cyan
    If Num = 12 Then Con.Text = "Light Red"       'Text box changed to read Light Red
    If Num = 13 Then Con.Text = "Light Magenta"   'Text box changed to read Light Magenta
    If Num = 14 Then Con.Text = "Light Yellow"    'Text box changed to read Light Yellow
    If Num = 15 Then Con.Text = "Bright White"    'Text Box changed to read Bright White
End Sub

Sub Form_Click ()
    Static Color As Integer             'Defines temporary variable
    Cls                                 'Clears screen of graphics
    FillColor = QBColor(Color)          'Defines the color
    FillStyle = 0                       'Graphics are solid
    DrawWidth = 5                       'Drawn lines are 5 pixels in width
    ForeColor = QBColor(1)              'ForeColor is blue
    If DrawMode = 16 Then               'Checks if DrawMode is 16
        DrawMode = 1                    'Changes DrawMode to 1
    Else
        DrawMode = DrawMode + 1         'Increments DrawMode by 1
    End If
    Text1.Text = Str$(DrawMode)         'Display the current DrawMode setting
    DisplayColor Color, Text2           'Calls sub function DisplayColor
    X = ScaleWidth / 2                  'Defines X as half the width of screen
    Y = ScaleHeight / 2                 'Defines Y as half the height of screen
    R = ScaleWidth / 4                  'Detines R as 1/4 the width of screen
    Circle (X, Y), R                    'Draws a circle
    If Color = 15 Then                  'Checks if Color is 15
        Color = 0                       'Changes Color to black
    Else
        Color = Color + 1               'Increments Color by 1
    End If
    FillColor = QBColor(Color)          'Changes FillColor
    DisplayColor Color, Text3           'Calls sub function DisplayColor
    X = 2 * ScaleWidth / 3              'Defines X as 2/3 the width of screen
    Y = 2 * ScaleHeight / 3             'Defines Y as 2/3 the width of screen
    Circle (X, Y), 1000                 'Draws a circle
End Sub
```

## Description

The DrawMode property affects the color of shapes drawn on the screen. Each DrawMode property expression begins with either the FormName of the form, CtlName of the picture box, or Printer for the Printer object. When the DrawMode property does not refer to a name, the form's DrawMode property changes. This property contains a variable labeled Mode% in the general syntax. This variable refers to the value given to the DrawMode property. Each object starts with a default DrawMode property set to 13. With this setting, the shape is drawn normally. Notice that each of the values in Table 10.6 indicates what kind of change to make to a shape's normal colors.

The example syntax demonstrates each of these settings with each click of the form. Notice that sometimes nothing displays. Try changing the BackColor property to another color and see how this affects each of these settings.

As noted earlier, the ForeColor and BackColor properties remain unchanged. Although the FillColor property changes, this alteration is independent of the settings of the DrawMode property.

### Example

In the Shape project at the end of this section, the DrawMode property determines how the indicated colors display on the Draw picture box. The Pen menu lists the possible settings of the DrawMode property of the Draw picture box. The form loads with the default choice set to Copy Pen on the Pen menu. This option indicates that the colors set in the FillColor, ForeColor, and BackColor properties of the Draw picture remain unmodified. Another selection on the Pen menu changes the colors of the next shapes drawn according to the DrawMode property setting. If the DrawMode property of the Draw picture box changes to Whiteness or Blackness, the shapes appear in white or black. In cases where the color of the shape matches the color of the background of the form, the shape does not appear. If the border is a different color, only the border appears.

### Comments

This property does not affect previously drawn shapes, unless they are covered by a newly drawn shape.

# DrawStyle Property

### Objects Affected

| | | | | |
|---|---|---|---|---|
| Check | Clipboard | Combo | Command | Dbug |
| Dir | Drive | File | ▶ Form | Frame |
| Label | List | Menu | Option | ▶ Picture |
| ▶ Printer | Screen | Scroll | Text | Timer |

### Purpose

The DrawStyle property controls the appearance of the line surrounding a drawn shape on a form, picture box, or Printer object. An object's DrawStyle property defaults to producing a solid line. Using the other possible settings of the DrawStyle property, the line is changeable to a dashed line, dotted line, dash-dot line, or dash-dot-dot line. When the DrawStyle property is invisible, the line around a shape does not appear. This property only affects a shape when it is actually on the screen. Any changes made to this property have no effect on those images that have already been drawn. Table 10.7 summarizes the arguments for the DrawStyle property, and Table 10.8 summarizes the possible values for this property.

## General Syntax

```
form.DrawStyle[=style%]
picturebox.DrawStyle[=style%]
Printer.DrawStyle[=style%]
```

| Argument | Description |
|----------|-------------|
| form | FormName property of form |
| control | CtlName property of picture box |
| Printer | Printer object |
| style% | Value representing the appearance of lines around shapes |

Table 10.7 Arguments of the DrawStyle property

| style% | Description |
|--------|-------------|
| 0 | Solid (Default) |
| 1 | Dash |
| 2 | Dot |
| 3 | Dash-dot |
| 4 | Dash-dot-dot |
| 5 | Invisible |
| 6 | Inside solid |

Table 10.8 Possible settings of the DrawStyle property

## Example Syntax

```
'Displays the different settings of the
'DrawStyle property in a circle.
Sub Form_Click ()
    Static C As Integer              'Defines Static variable C
    If C = 0 Then                    'Checks current setting of C
        C = 3                        'Defines Variable as C
    ElseIf C < 12 Then               'Checks if C is less than 12
        C = C + 1                    'Increments C by one
        DrawStyle = DrawStyle + 1    'Increments DrawStyle by one
    Else
        Exit Sub                     'Exit the subroutine
    End If
    X = ScaleWidth / 2               'Defines X as half the width of form
    Y = ScaleHeight / 2              'Defines Y as half the height of form
    R = ScaleWidth / C               'Defines R as a fraction of width of form
    Circle (X, Y), R                 'Draws a circle
End Sub
```

## Description

The DrawStyle property sets the type of line placed around a shape. Each DrawStyle prop-

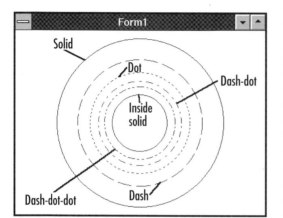

**Figure 10.6 Different settings of DrawStyle property**

erty expression begins with the name of the affected object (FormName of the form, CtlName of the picture box, or Printer for Printer object). When a DrawStyle expression does not include a name, the DrawMode property of the current form changes. This property includes a variable labeled style% in the general syntax. The style% variable refers to the value given to the DrawStyle property. Each object starts with a default DrawStyle property set to solid (0). With this setting, the line around a shape displays as a solid line.

The example syntax shows results of each of the possible settings of the style% variable inside the circle. Each of these line patterns displays on the screen in successively smaller circles. Figure 10.6 displays what this example might look like on your screen.

### The DrawWidth Property

The DrawWidth property defines the thickness of the line around a drawn shape. Changing the value of the DrawWidth property to greater than 1 pixel in width has the effect of making the line around the shape solid when the DrawStyle property is a solid line, dash line, dot line, dash-dot line, or dash-dot-dot line (values 0 through 4). When this happens, the actual setting of the DrawStyle property remains unchanged. If the DrawWidth property of the form in the example syntax changes to a value greater than 1, the first settings produce 4 circles with solid lines. This demonstrates the interaction of the DrawWidth and DrawStyle properties.

### Example

In the Shape project at the end of this section, the DrawStyle property determines the appearance of the lines around a shape. The default setting of the DrawStyle property for any form, picture box, or Printer object is 0. The Solid item on the Line menu represents the solid line setting. While this property remains at this setting, all lines appear as a solid line. Selecting another number on the Line menu changes the line around the next drawn shapes to another format. Invisible indicates that the line will not appear around a shape. If the DrawWidth property of the Draw picture box changes to a value other than one, Visual Basic ignores the setting of the DrawStyle property between 1 and 4 and draws a solid line.

### Comments

Remember that the ForeColor property sets the color of the line around a shape.

# DrawWidth Property

## Objects Affected

| | | | | |
|---|---|---|---|---|
| Check | Clipboard | Combo | Command | Dbug |
| Dir | Drive | File | ▶ Form | Frame |
| Label | List | Menu | Option | ▶ Picture |
| ▶ Printer | Screen | Scroll | Text | Timer |

## Purpose

The DrawWidth property sets the width of lines drawn on a form, picture box, or Printer object. A value given to the DrawWidth property represents the thickness of the line in pixels. When this property's value increases, the border around a drawn shape such as a circle or square thickens. On an object with a larger DrawWidth property, a line drawn with the Line method produces a thick line. With a DrawWidth property set larger than one, the PSet method produces brushlike effects which are the width set by the DrawWidth property. Table 10.9 summarizes the arguments of the DrawWidth property.

## General Syntax

```
form.DrawWidth[=size%]
picturebox.DrawWidth[=size%]
Printer.DrawWidth[=size%]
```

| Argument | Description |
|---|---|
| form | FormName property of form |
| control | CtlName property of picture box |
| Printer | Printer object |
| size% | Value representing the width of lines around shapes in pixels |

Table 10.9 Arguments of the DrawWidth property

## Example Syntax

```
'Shows the widths of the different settings
'of the DrawWidth property by drawing lines
'with successively higher settings.
Sub Form_Click ()
    Static X As Integer         'Defines the static variable X
    Static Y As Integer         'Defines the static variable Y
    CX = ScaleWidth / 500       'Defines CX as 1/500 of form's width
    CY = ScaleHeight / 10       'Defines CY as 1/10 of form's height
    DrawWidth = DrawWidth + 1   'Increments the DrawWidth by 1
    X = CX                      'Defines X as CX
```

```
      Y = Y + CY              'Increments Y by CY
      For L = 1 To 499        'Run this statement 499 times
         X = X + CX           'Increments X by CX
         PSet (X, Y)          'Draws a point on a form
      Next L                  'Run the For statement again
      X = 0                   'Sets X to zero
   End Sub
```

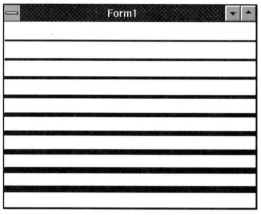

**Figure 10.7 DrawWidth property in the example syntax**

## Description

The DrawWidth property sets the thickness of a line drawn on a form, picture box, or Printer object. Every DrawWidth property expression begins with the name of the affected object (FormName of the form, CtlName of the picture box, or Printer for Printer object). When a DrawWidth property expression has no name, the form's DrawWidth property changes. This property includes a variable labeled size% in the general syntax. The size% variable refers to the value given to the DrawWidth property. Each object begins with a default DrawWidth property set to 1. With this value, any lines drawn are 1 pixel thick. Additionally, every increase in this value represents that number of pixels for any lines drawn.

In the example syntax, the DrawWidth property of the form increases by 1 with each click of the form. Notice that the line created by the PSet method is successively thicker. Figure 10.7 shows what this example might look like on your screen.

### The Circle, Line, and PSet Methods

When the DrawWidth property of a form, picture box, or Printer object changes from the default value of 1, it affects the output of the Circle, Line and PSet methods. With a larger DrawWidth property setting, any circles displayed have enlarged borders. The Line method produces a line with a thickness set by the DrawWidth property. Using the PSet method, a point appears in the size indicated by the DrawWidth property. In the example syntax, the PSet method acts in conjunction with the DrawWidth property to draw a series of spots that make up a line on the screen.

### The DrawStyle Property

If the DrawWidth property changes to greater than 1, a DrawStyle property less than or equal to 4 has no effect on the appearance of a drawn line, which will be solid. With the DrawWidth property set to 1, the DrawStyle property changes the line or lines in a drawn shape from a solid line to dashes, dots, or a combination of the two depending on that property's value. When the DrawWidth property is larger than 4, a line drawn by either the Circle or Line method is solid. This does not affect the actual setting of the DrawStyle property.

## Example

In the Shape project at the end of this section, the DrawWidth property of the Draw picture box determines the thickness of the lines and border around a shape. When the Width menu is selected on the Shape form, the user sees a list of the numbers 1 through 10. At program startup, the checked number is the number 1, representing the thickness in pixels of lines drawn on the Draw picture box. Selecting another number on the Width menu causes the next shapes to have lines with that thickness. The DrawWidth property sets the thickness of lines. Each new number selected from the Width menu changes the DrawWidth property of the Draw picture box. The possible settings of the DrawWidth property are not limited to between 1 and 10.

## Comments

The DrawWidth property does not affect the setting of the DrawStyle property.

# FillColor Property

## Objects Affected

| Check | Clipboard | Combo | Command | Dbug |
|-------|-----------|-------|---------|------|
| Dir | Drive | File | ▶ Form | Frame |
| Label | List | Menu | Option | ▶ Picture |
| ▶ Printer | Screen | Scroll | Text | Timer |

## Purpose

The FillColor property sets the color of the interior of circles and boxes drawn on a form, picture box, or Printer object. An object's FillColor property is defined with the hexadecimal value of the color desired either directly (with a hexadecimal number), or with the QBColor or RGB functions. Any changes made to the FillColor property have no effect on the colors of previously drawn shapes already on the object. This property works in conjunction with the FillStyle property to choose what will fill the interior of circles and boxes. When the FillStyle property remains at its default setting of transparent, the FillColor property does not affect the appearance of drawn circles and boxes. If the FillColor property remains unchanged and the FillColor property is not transparent, then the interior of circles and boxes is black. Table 10.10 summarizes the arguments of the FillColor property.

## General Syntax

```
form.FillColor[=color&]
picturebox.FillColor[=color&]
Printer.FillColor[=color&]
```

| Argument | Description |
|----------|-------------|
| form | FormName property of form |
| control | CtlName property of picture box |
| Printer | Printer object |
| color& | Value representing the interior color of drawn shapes |

Table 10.10 Arguments of the FillColor property

## Example Syntax

```
Sub Form_Click ()
    AutoRedraw = -1               'Sets the form's AutoRedraw property to True
    Cls                           'Clears the form
    ScaleWidth = 4                'Divides the width of the form into four parts
    ScaleHeight = 4               'Divides the height of the form into four parts
    DrawWidth = 5                 'Defines thickness as 5 pixels
    FillStyle = 0                 'Defines FillStyle as solid
    ForeColor = QBColor(0)        'Defines the ForeColor property as black
    Color% = 0                    'Defines the color variable as 0
    For H% = 0 To 3               'Draws 16 colored boxes on the screen with the
        For W% = 0 To 3           'FillColor property and Line method.
            FillColor = QBColor(Color%)
            Line (W%, H%)-(W% + 1, H% + 1), , B
            Color% = Color% + 1
        Next W%
    Next H%
End Sub
```

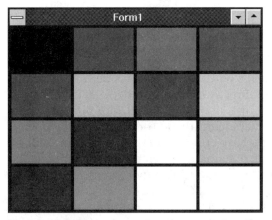

Figure 10.8 Example syntax demonstrates the FillColor property

## Description

The FillColor property defines the interior color of drawn circles and boxes on forms, picture boxes, or Printer objects. Every FillColor property expression begins with the name of the affected object (the FormName of the form, CtlName of the picture box, or Printer for Printer object). If a FillColor property expression does not include the object's name, then the current form's FillColor property changes. This property includes the variable labeled color& in the general syntax. Each form, picture box, and Printer object begins with the FillColor property set to black. The color& variable refers to the Long value given to the FillColor property. This integer must be in hexadecimal form. For example, HFF000 is the hexadecimal value for blue. You can set this property with either the RGB or QBColor functions.

In the example syntax, the FillColor property changes for each drawing of a box on the screen, incrementing the value used with the QBColor function by 1 to get the next color. This results in the division of the form into 16 equal parts, in which any one of the 16 possible colors of the QBColor function may appear. Figure 10.8 shows what this example might look like.

### The RGB and QBColor Functions

Both the RGB and QBColor functions provide a means of defining the color of the FillColor property without using the confusing hexadecimal RGB codes. If standard colors like red, green, blue, and cyan are acceptable, then the QBColor function works very well. When a special mix of RGB values is necessary, the RGB function allows the setting of specialized colors. Be careful not to give this property a color that matches the background color of the form or picture box. In cases where the FillColor property is the same as the BackColor property, shapes won't be visible. Table 10.11 lists the most common settings of the RGB and QBColor functions. In the example syntax, the QBColor function serves as a means of defining the color of each of the boxes as they appear on the screen. Notice that the color of each square is unaffected by the changes made to the FillColor property for the next squares. Once a shape appears on the screen or printer, its attributes are permanent.

| Color | Red Value | Green Value | Blue Value | Hexadecimal | QBColor |
|---|---|---|---|---|---|
| Black | 0 | 0 | 0 | &H0 | 0 |
| Red | 255 | 0 | 0 | &HFF | 4 |
| Green | 0 | 255 | 0 | &HFF00 | 2 |
| Yellow | 0 | 255 | 255 | &HFFFF | 6 |
| Blue | 0 | 0 | 255 | &HFF000 | 1 |
| Magenta | 255 | 0 | 255 | &HFF00FF | 5 |
| Cyan | 0 | 255 | 255 | &HFFFF00 | 3 |
| White | 255 | 255 | 255 | &HFFFFFF | 15 |
| Light Gray | 192 | 192 | 192 | &H00C0C0C0 | 7 |
| Dark Gray | 128 | 128 | 128 | &H00808080 | 8 |

**Table 10.11 Values of common colors in RGB, QBColor, and hexadecimal formats**

### The FillStyle Property

The FillStyle property works in conjunction with the FillColor property to define the pattern and color inside drawn circles and boxes. If the FillStyle of a form, picture box, or Printer object is left at the default value of 1 (transparent), then any drawn objects appear empty. When the FillStyle property is 0 (solid), the drawn circles and boxes contain the color indicated by the FillColor property. Since the default value of the FillColor property is 0 (black), the default output is a black circle or box (provided the

FillStyle property is set to solid). With the FillStyle property set to a value between 2 and 7 inclusive, the FillColor property determines what color to give the patterns drawn inside the circle or box. In the example syntax, the FillStyle property is 0 to indicate that each of the boxes drawn contain solid styles of the colors indicated by the FillColor property.

## Example

In the Shape project at the end of this section, the FillColor property indicates the color of drawn shapes. The Form_Load event sets the FillColor property of the Draw picture box on the Shape form at program startup. A QBColor function defines the FillColor property as black. Any changes made to the default menu choices on the Shape form affect the other properties of the Shape form. The user can select a new QBColor value (between 0 and 15) on the color menu.

## Comments

Remember to change the FillStyle property from the default setting of 1, or the FillColor property will not affect any shapes drawn with the Line or Circle methods.

# FillStyle Property

## Objects Affected

| | | | | |
|---|---|---|---|---|
| Check | Clipboard | Combo | Command | Dbug |
| Dir | Drive | File | ▶ Form | Frame |
| Label | List | Menu | Option | ▶ Picture |
| ▶ Printer | Screen | Scroll | Text | Timer |

## Purpose

The FillStyle property defines the appearance of the interior of a drawn shape on a form, picture box, or Printer object. An object's FillStyle property is a value between 0 and 7 inclusive. Any changes made to the FillStyle property do not affect shapes already on the screen. This property works in conjunction with the FillColor property to specify what fills the interior of circles and boxes. When the FillStyle property remains at its default setting of transparent, the FillColor property does not affect the appearance of the next circles and boxes drawn. If the FillColor property remains unchanged and the FillStyle property is not transparent, any circles and boxes are black. Table 10.12 summarizes the arguments of the FillStyle property, and Table 10.13 lists this property's possible settings.

## General Syntax

```
form.FillStyle[=style%]
picturebox.FillStyle[=style%]
Printer.FillStyle[=style%]
```

| Argument | Description |
|---|---|
| form | FormName property of form |
| control | CtlName property of picture box |
| Printer | Printer object |
| style% | Value representing the style to place in the interior of drawn shapes |

**Table 10.12 Arguments of the FillStyle property**

| style% | Description |
|---|---|
| 0 | Solid |
| 1 | Transparent (Default) |
| 2 | Horizontal Line Pattern |
| 3 | Vertical Line Pattern |
| 4 | Upward Diagonal Pattern |
| 5 | Downward Diagonal Pattern |
| 6 | Cross |
| 7 | Diagonal Cross |

**Table 10.13 List of possible settings of the FillStyle property**

## Example Syntax

```
Sub Timer1_Timer ()
    AutoRedraw = -1                  'Sets the form's AutoRedraw property to True
    Cls                              'Clears the form
    ScaleWidth = 4                   'Divides the width of the form into four parts
    ScaleHeight = 4                  'Divides the height of the form into four parts
    Color% = 0                       'Defines the color variable as 0
    For H% = 0 To 3                  'Draws 16 colored boxes on the screen with the
        For W% = 0 To 3              'FillColor property and Line method.
            FillColor = QBColor(Color%)
            Line (W%, H%)-(W% + 1, H% + 1), , B
            Color% = Color% + 1
        Next W%
    Next H%
    If FillStyle = 7 Then            'When the last possible setting of FillStyle is
        FillStyle = 0                'reached, reset.
    Else
        FillStyle = FillStyle + 1    'Increment the present setting by one.
    End If
End Sub
```

## Description

The FillSyle property defines the interior style of drawn circles and boxes on forms, picture boxes, or Printer objects. Every FillStyle property expression begins with the name of the affected object (FormName of the form, CtlName of the picture box, or printer for Printer object). If a FillStyle property expression does not include the object's name, then the current form's FillStyle property changes. This property includes the variable labeled style% in the general syntax. Each form, picture box, and Printer objectbegins with the

FillColor property set to transparent. This integer must be one of the possible settings listed in Table 10.13. With its default transparent setting at 1, the FillStyle property prevents the display of the color set in the FillColor property. Setting the FillStyle property to 0 produces the solid color indicated by the FillColor property.

In the example syntax, the FillStyle property increases by 1 at intervals of 1000 to display the different possible settings of the FillStyle property with different colors. This results in the successive display of 16 boxes of colors or patterns (set Timer1's Interval property to 1000). Notice that the first display contains lines with no colors. This is because the default setting of this property is transparent. Figures 10.9 through 10.16 display different fill styles on the screen.

### The FillColor Property

The FillStyle property works in conjunction with the FillColor property to define the pattern and color inside drawn circles and boxes. If the FillStyle of a form, picture box, or Printer object is left at the default value of 1 (transparent), then any drawn objects appear empty. When the FillStyle property is 0 (solid), the drawn circles and boxes

| | |
|---|---|
| **Figure 10.9 Transparent fill style** | **Figure 10.10 Horizontal fill style** |

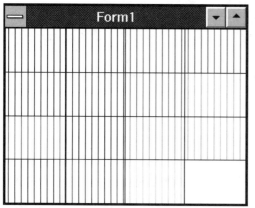

**Figure 10.11 Vertical line fill style**

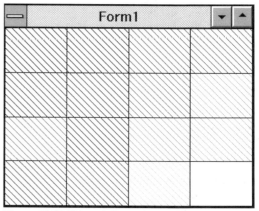

**Figure 10.12 Upward diagonal fill style**

contain the color indicated by the FillColor property. Since the default value of the FillColor property is 0 (black), the default output is a black circle or box (provided the FillStyle property is set to solid). With the FillStyle property set to a value between 2 and 7 inclusive, the FillColor property determines what color to give the patterns drawn inside the circle or box. In the example syntax, the FillStyle property increases by 1 for each triggering of the timer event.

## Example

In the Shape project at the end of this section, the FillStyle property determines whether a shape is empty or contains a solid color or pattern. The FillStyle property of the Draw picture box is 0 in the Form_Load event subroutine. Setting the Draw picture box's FillStyle property to solid indicates that the interiors of the next shapes will be solid. Any changes made to the default menu choices on the Shape form affect the other properties of the Shape form. The user can select a new fill style (between 0 and 7) on the pattern menu.

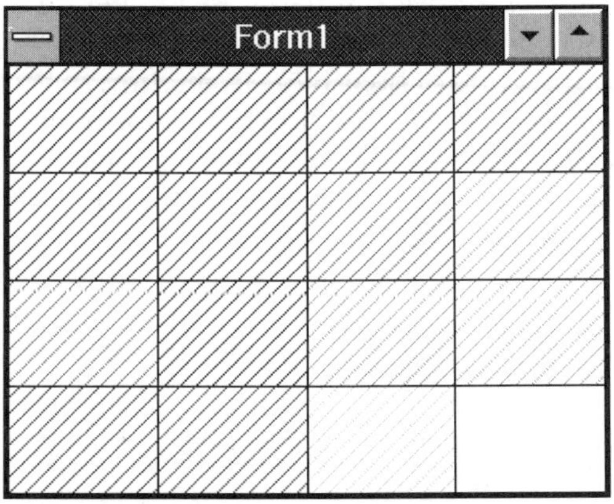

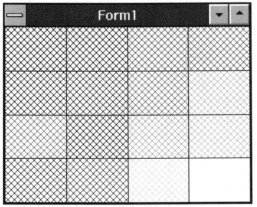

Figure 10.13 Downward diagonal fill style

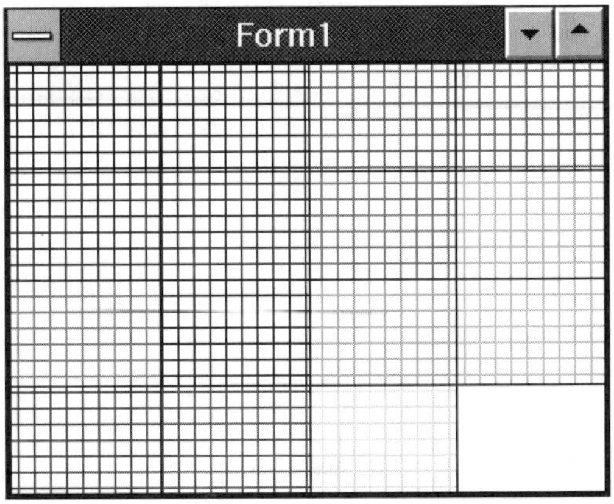

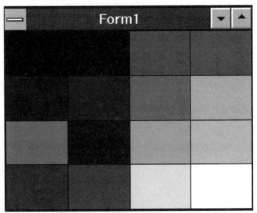

Figure 10.14 Cross fill style

Figure 10.15 Diagonal cross fill style

Figure 10.16 Solid fill style

## Comments

The FillColor property's setting is independent of the setting of the FillStyle property.

# Line Method

## Objects Affected

| | | | | |
|---|---|---|---|---|
| Check | Clipboard | Combo | Command | Dbug |
| Dir | Drive | File | ▶ Form | Frame |
| Label | List | Menu | Option | ▶ Picture |
| ▶ Printer | Screen | Scroll | Text | Timer |

## Purpose

The Line method draws a line or box shape on an object on the screen or printer. This method creates a number of shapes, including straight lines, squares, rectangles, and triangles. The object on the screen to be drawn on must be a form, picture box, or Printer object. A line method expression positions a line or box shape in relation to the top left corner of the form, picture box, or Printer object. Shapes drawn on a form have no effect on the controls placed on the form. If a shape is in the same position as a control, the image appears behind the control. Table 10.14 summarizes the different arguments of the Line method.

## General Syntax

```
[object.]Line[[Step](x1!,y1!)]-[Step](x2!,y2!)[,[color&],B[F]]]
```

| Argument | Description |
|---|---|
| object | FormName of the form or CtlName of the picture box or Printer object |
| Step | Changes coordinates given as being relative to the current coordinates in the CurrentX and CurrentY properties. Normally the coordinates are in relation to the top left corner |
| x1!,y1! | The position of the starting point for a line, square, or rectangle. The value of this argument is a single-precision value (between -3.37E+38 and 3.37E+38) in a unit of measure specifed by the ScaleMode property. If the coordinates are omitted, the line begins at the position indicated by the CurrentX and CurrentY properties |
| Step | This indicates that the end point coordinates are relative to the line starting point |
| x2!,y2! | The horizontal and vertical position of the end point for a line, square, or rectangle. The value of this argument is a single-precision value (between -3.37E+38 and 3.37E+38) in a unit of measuure specified by the ScaleMode property. These coordinates are required |
| color& | The RGB color of the outline of a shape. This argument is either a hexadecimal value or may be defined with either the RGB or QBColor functions |

| B | This argument creates a box with the indicated coordinates serving as the opposite corners |
| F | This argument fills the box with the color specified by the color& argument. If the color& argument does not appear, the box fills with the color and style set in the FillColor and FillStyle properties. The F argument cannot appear without the B argument |

**Table 10.14 Arguments of the Line method**

## Example Syntax

```
Sub Picture1_Click ()
    Static Num As Integer                              'Defines Integer Num
    Static Color As Integer                            'Defines Integer Color
    Picture1.Cls                                       'Clear picture
    Picture1.ScaleWidth = 5                            'Divides picture's width into 5
                                                       'parts
    Picture1.ScaleHeight = 5                           'Divides picture's height into
                                                       '5 parts
    If Num = 0 Then                                    'Checks the value of Num
        Picture1.Line (1, 1)-(4, 4), QBColor(Color)    'Draws a line
        Num = 1
    ElseIf Num = 1 Then
        Picture1.Line (1, 1)-(4, 4), QBColor(Color), B 'Draws a box.
        Num = 2
    ElseIf Num = 2 Then
        Picture1.Line (1, 1)-(4, 4), QBColor(Color), BF 'Draws a filled in box
        Num = 3
    ElseIf Num = 3 Then
        Picture1.Line (3, 1)-(4, 4), QBColor(Color)    'Draws a triangle
        Picture1.Line (4, 4)-(1, 3), QBColor(Color)
        Picture1.Line (1, 3)-(3, 1), QBColor(Color)
        Num = 0
    End If
    Picture1.DrawWidth = Picture1.DrawWidth + 1        'Increases the size of the
                                                       'DrawWidth.
    If Color = 15 Then                                 'Increments Color until it
                                                       'reaches 15.
        Color = 0
    Else
        Color = Color + 1
    End If
End Sub
```

## Description

A Line method produces a line or box on a form, picture box, or Printer object. Several arguments affect the appearance of objects drawn with the Line method. Every Line method expression begins with the name of the affected object (FormName of the form, CtlName of the picture box, or printer for Printer object). When a Line method expression does not include the object's name, the shape appears on the current form. The Line method coordinates (x1!,y1!) and (x2!,y2!) represent the positions of the two points on a line or the upper left and lower right corners of a box. Each of the x1!, x2! coordinates represents a horizontal position. The y1! and y2! coordinates define the vertical positions. If the STEP keyword precedes either the first (x1!,y1!) or second (x2!,y2!) set of coordinates, then the coordinates are set in relation to the current values of the CurrentX and CurrentY properties. When the word STEP does not appear, the coordinates outline a position in relation to the top left corner of the object. The color& argument sets the color of the line surrounding the shape and defaults to the ForeColor property. This argument contains a hexadecimal number, an RGB function, or a QBColor function. You may skip an argument in the middle of the syntax, but must include the comma (,) for each argument excluded. Don't end a Line method with a comma. Look at the Line method expressions in the example syntax for some examples.

In the example syntax, the Line method draws a line, square, filled-in square, and triangle. Each Line method expression demonstrates the proper operation of this method with different results. The creation of the triangle involves the integration of three different line method expressions. Figures 10.17, 10.18, 10.19, and 10.20 show what each of these shapes looks like on the screen.

### The B and F Arguments

When the B and F arguments are in a Line method expression, a box appears instead of a line. In this case, the start point (x1!,y1!) coordinates represent the top left corner of the box and the end point (x2!,y2!) defines the bottom right corner. If the F argument appears, the interior of the box is the color indicated by the color& argument. Both the FillColor and FillStyle properties affect the interior of a box when the color& argument does not appear. With the FillStyle set to the default setting of 1 (transparent), the F argument has no apparent effect. In the example syntax, the B argument and then the B & F arguments produce a square on the picture box. Notice that when the B argument is alone, an unfilled square displays. With both the B and F arguments, a square appears filled with the color specified by the color& argument.

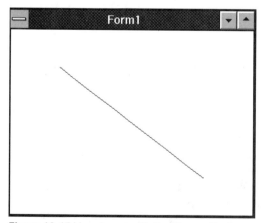

**Figure 10.17 Line drawn with the Line method**

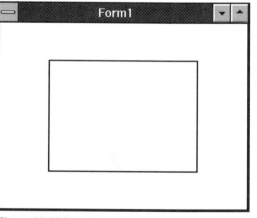

**Figure 10.18 Box drawn with the Line method**

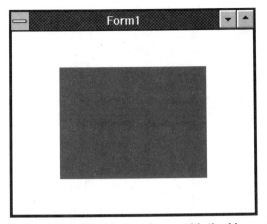

**Figure 10.19 Filled-in box drawn with the Line method**

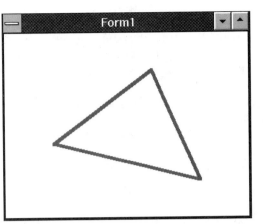

**Figure 10.20 Triangle drawn with three Line methods**

### The ScaleMode Property

The ScaleMode property determines the unit of measure used by objects placed on a form, picture box, or Printer object. In its default setting, objects on a form, picture box, or Printer object measure their sizes and positions in twips (1 inch = 1440 twips). Each Line method expression's coordinates measure the distance from the upper left corner of the form, picture box, or Printer object to the current coordinates set in the CurrentX and CurrentY properties. Any changes made to the ScaleHeight, ScaleWidth, ScaleTop, or ScaleLeft properties of the object change the ScaleMode property to 0 (user-dcfincd). In the example syntax, all the coordinates are set in relation to the user-defined scales defined for the ScaleHeight and ScaleWidth properties. The coordinates 0,0 place object in the upper left corner and 5,5 puts 1 in the lower right corner. In this way, each of the objects drawn with the Line method uses this scale in the coordinates set. Figure 10.21 shows how the unfilled box appears on the screen.

### Example

In the Shape project at the end of this section, the Line method serves as a means of drawing lines, squares, rectangles, and triangles on the Draw form. The command buttons labeled Line, Square, Rectangle, and Triangle all contain Line methods to produce the indicated object on the Draw picture box. When the Line method appears without the B or F arguments in the

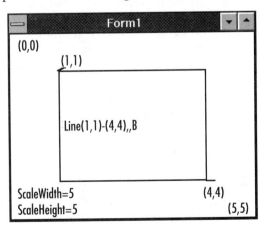

**Figure 10.21 Coordinate system of the Line method**

Draw_Line_Click event, a line is drawn between the randomly indicated points. By adding the B argument to the Line method in the Draw_Rectangle_Click event, a rectangle of varying size and location displays instead of a line. In this case, the two indicated points serve as the upper left and lower right corners of the rectangle. With the B argument in the Draw_Square_Click event, a square of varying size and location appears. This is accomplished by making the second point of the square the same distance for the X and Y coordinates. Three Line methods work together in the Draw_Triangle_Click event to produce the three sides of the triangle on the Draw picture box.

## Comments

The Line method can create triangles or any other type of straight-line shape by making the starting point of one line begin at another line's end point. It is easier to create squares or rectangles by specifying the B option, however.

# The Shape Project

## Project Overview

The Shape project demonstrates the methods and properties that directly affect the appearance of drawn shapes on forms, picture boxes, and Printer objects. This example shows the process of drawing a graphical shape on an object. Using the Line and Circle methods, the Shape project places circles, lines, squares, rectangles, and triangles on the picture box. By manipulating the settings of the FillColor, FillStyle, DrawMode, DrawStyle, and DrawWidth properties, the Shape project visually displays how these properties affect the interaction between different drawn shapes.

The following pages discuss the assembly and operation of the Shape project. The first section deals with the assembly of the controls on the Shape form. Following this is a discussion that shows and briefly explains the contents of the subroutines of this project. Finally, there is a discusion of the operation of the project. Please read this information carefully and use the pictures on the form as guides in the process of assembling the project.

## Assembling the Project

1. Make a new form (the Shape form) with the objects and properties in Table 10.15.

| Object | Property | Setting |
|--------|----------|---------|
| Form | BorderStyle | 1 - Fixed Single |
| | Caption | Shape Project |
| | ControlBox | True |
| | FormName | Shape |
| | Icon | \VB\ICONS\WRITING\PEN02.ICO |
| | MaxButton | False |

| | | |
|---|---|---|
| Picture Box | CtlName | Draw |
| | TabIndex | 5 |
| Command button | Caption | Circle |
| | CtlName | Draw_Circle |
| | TabIndex | 0 |
| Command button | Caption | Line |
| | CtlName | Draw_Line |
| | TabIndex | 1 |
| Command button | Caption | Square |
| | CtlName | Draw_Square |
| | TabIndex | 2 |
| Command button | Caption | Rectangle |
| | CtlName | Draw_Rectangle |
| | TabIndex | 3 |
| Command button | Caption | Triangle |
| | CtlName | Draw_Triangle |
| | TabIndex | 4 |

**Table 10.15 Elements of the Shape form**

2. Size the objects on the screen, as shown in Figure 10.22

3. Open the Menu Design window from the Window option on the Visual Basic control bar. Create the following menus for the Shape form: Width, Color, Pattern, Pen, and Line. Tables 10.16, 10.17, 10.18, 10.19, and 10.20 represent the different menus on the Shape form. Indented options on these tables represent options under the indicated menu.

Figures 10.23, 10.24, 10.25, 10.26, and 10.27 show how the respective menus look when opened.

| Menu | CtlName | Index | Checked |
|---|---|---|---|
| Width | Width_Choice | | |
| 0 | Width_Format | 0 | Yes |
| 1 | " | 1 | No |
| 2 | " | 2 | No |
| 3 | " | 3 | No |
| 4 | " | 4 | No |
| 5 | " | 5 | No |
| 6 | " | 6 | No |
| 7 | " | 7 | No |
| 8 | " | 8 | No |
| 9 | " | 9 | No |

**Table 10.16 Menu options of the Width menu on the Shape form**

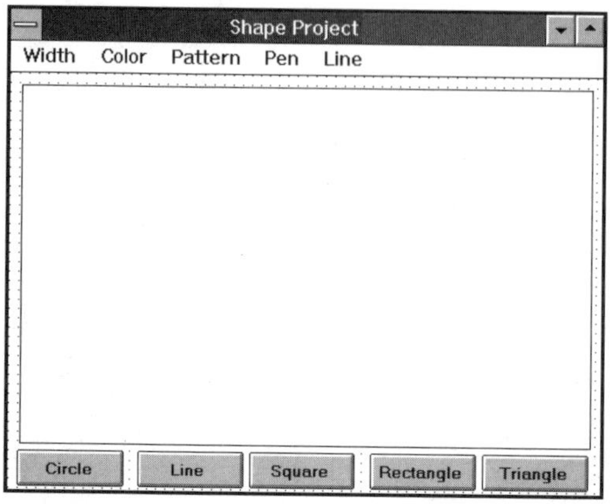

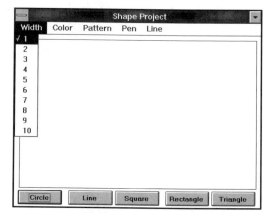

Figure 10.22 What the Shape form should look like when completed

Figure 10.23 Width menu on the Shape form

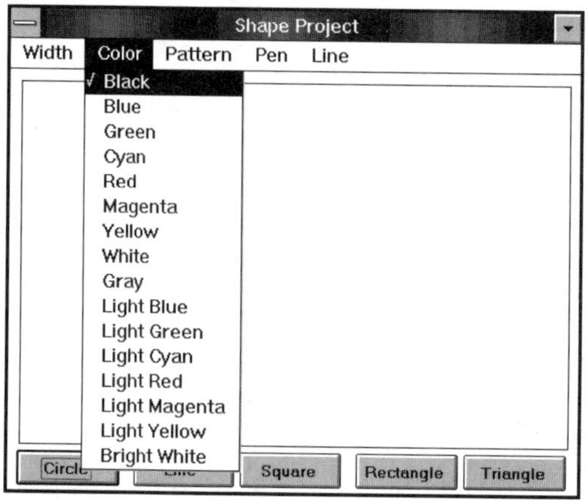

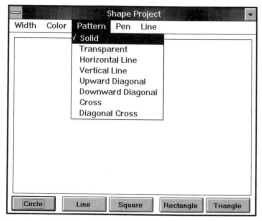

Figure 10.24 Color menu on the Shape form

Figure 10.25 Pattern menu on the Shape form

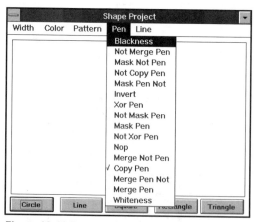

Figure 10.26 Pen menu on the Shape form

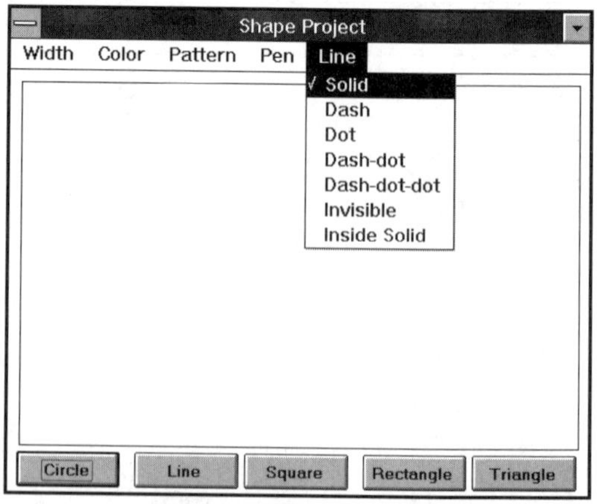

Figure 10.27 Line menu on the Shape form

| Menu | CtlName | Index | Checked |
|------|---------|-------|---------|
| Color | Color_Choice | | |
| Black | Color | 0 | Yes |
| Blue | " | 1 | No |
| Green | " | 2 | No |
| Cyan | " | 3 | No |
| Red | " | 4 | No |
| Magenta | " | 5 | No |
| Yellow | " | 6 | No |
| White | " | 7 | No |
| Gray | " | 8 | No |
| Light Blue | " | 9 | No |
| Light Green | " | 10 | No |
| Light Cyan | " | 11 | No |
| Light Red | " | 12 | No |
| Light Magenta | " | 13 | No |
| Light Yellow | " | 14 | No |
| Bright White | " | 15 | No |

Table 10.17 Menu options of the Color menu on the Shape form

| Menu | CtlName | Index | Checked |
|------|---------|-------|---------|
| Pattern | Pattern_Choice | | |
| Solid | Pattern | 0 | Yes |
| Transparent | " | 1 | No |
| Horizontal Line | " | 2 | No |
| Vertical Line | " | 3 | No |
| Upward Diagonal | " | 4 | No |
| Downward Diagonal | " | 5 | No |
| Cross | " | 6 | No |
| Diagonal Cross | " | 7 | No |

Table 10.18 Menu options of the Pattern menu on the Shape form

| Menu | CtlName | Index | Checked |
|------|---------|-------|---------|
| Pen | Pen_Choice | | |
| Blackness | Pen | 1 | No |

*Table 10.19 (continued)*

| Menu | CtlName | Index | Checked |
|---|---|---|---|
| Not Merge Pen | " | 2 | No |
| Mask Not Pen | " | 3 | No |
| Not Copy Pen | " | 4 | No |
| Mask Pen Not | " | 5 | No |
| Invert | " | 6 | No |
| Xor Pen | " | 7 | No |
| Not Mask Pen | " | 8 | No |
| Mask Pen | " | 9 | No |
| Not Xor Pen | " | 10 | No |
| Nop | " | 11 | No |
| Merge Not Pen | " | 12 | No |
| Copy Pen | " | 13 | Yes |
| Merge Pen Not | " | 14 | No |
| Merge Pen | " | 15 | No |
| Whiteness | " | 16 | No |

**Table 10.19 Menu options of the Pen menu on the Shape form**

| Menu | CtlName | Index | Checked |
|---|---|---|---|
| Line | Line_Choice | | |
| Solid | Line_Format | 0 | Yes |
| Dash | " | 1 | No |
| Dot | " | 2 | No |
| Dash-dot | " | 3 | No |
| Dash-dot-dot | " | 4 | No |
| Invisible | " | 5 | No |
| Inside solid | " | 6 | No |

**Table 10.20 Menu options of the Line menu on the Shape form**

4. Enter the following code in the Color_Click event subroutine. This code triggers when the user selects a new color on the Color menu. When this code activates, the Checked property of each of the menu options unchecks and then the new color receives the check mark. Finally, the Draw form's FillColor property changes to the new color.

```
Sub Color_Click (Index As Integer)
   Color(0).Checked = 0
   Color(1).Checked = 0
   Color(2).Checked = 0
   Color(3).Checked = 0
   Color(4).Checked = 0
   Color(5).Checked = 0
   Color(6).Checked = 0
   Color(7).Checked = 0
   Color(8).Checked = 0
   Color(9).Checked = 0
   Color(10).Checked = 0
   Color(11).Checked = 0
   Color(12).Checked = 0
   Color(13).Checked = 0
   Color(14).Checked = 0
   Color(15).Checked = 0
   Color(Index).Checked = -1
   Draw.FillColor = QBColor(Index)
End Sub
```

5. Enter the following code in the Draw_Click event subroutine. This code triggers when the user presses a mouse key while the mouse pointer is over the Draw picture box. When this happens, the Draw picture box clears of all the drawn shapes.

```
Sub Draw_Click ()
   Draw.Cls
End Sub
```

6. Enter the following code in the Draw_Circle_Click event subroutine. When the user clicks the Circle command button, this code draws a circle of random length and location.

```
Sub Draw_Circle_Click ()
   X = Int((100 - (1)) * Rnd + (1))
   Y = Int((100 - (1)) * Rnd + (1))
   R = Int((25 - (1)) * Rnd + (1))
   Draw.Circle (X, Y), R
End Sub
```

7. Enter the following code in the Draw_Line_Click event subroutine. When the user clicks the Line command button, this code draws a line of random length and location.

```
Sub Draw_Line_Click ()
   X1 = Int((100 - (1)) * Rnd + (1))
   Y1 = Int((100 - (1)) * Rnd + (1))
   X2 = Int((100 - (1)) * Rnd + (1))
   Y2 = Int((100 - (1)) * Rnd + (1))
   Draw.Line (X1, Y1)-(X2, Y2)
End Sub
```

8. Enter the following code in the Draw_Rectangle_Click event subroutine. When the user clicks the Rectangle command button, this code draws a rectangle of random size and location.

```
Sub Draw_Rectangle_Click ()
    X1 = Int((75 - (1)) * Rnd + (1))
    Y1 = Int((75 - (1)) * Rnd + (1))
    X2 = Int((50 - (1)) * Rnd + (1))
    Y2 = Int((50 - (1)) * Rnd + (1))
    Draw.Line (X1, Y1)-Step(X2, Y2), , B
End Sub
```

9. Enter the following code in the Draw_Square_Click event subroutine. When the user clicks the Square command button, this code draws a square of random size and location.

```
Sub Draw_Square_Click ()
    X1 = Int((50 - (1)) * Rnd + (1))
    Y1 = Int((50 - (1)) * Rnd + (1))
    X2 = Int((50 - (1)) * Rnd + (1))
    Y2 = X2
    Draw.Line (X1, Y1)-Step(X2, Y2), , B
End Sub
```

10. Enter the following code in the Draw_Triangle_Click event subroutine. When the user clicks the Triangle command button, this code draws a triangle of random size and location.

```
Sub Draw_Triangle_Click ()
    X1 = Int((100 - (1)) * Rnd + (1))
    Y1 = Int((100 - (1)) * Rnd + (1))
    X2 = Int((100 - (1)) * Rnd + (1))
    Y2 = Int((100 - (1)) * Rnd + (1))
    X3 = Int((100 - (1)) * Rnd + (1))
    Y3 = Int((100 - (1)) * Rnd + (1))
    Draw.Line (X1, Y1)-(X2, Y2)
    Draw.Line (X2, Y2)-(X3, Y3)
    Draw.Line (X3, Y3)-(X1, Y1)
End Sub
```

11. Enter the following code in the Form_Load event subroutine. This code processes when the program starts. At that time, the code sets the default values of the Draw Picture box.

```
Sub Form_Load ()
    Draw.ScaleHeight = 100
    Draw.ScaleWidth = 100
    Draw.FillColor = QBColor(0)
    Draw.FillStyle = 0
    Draw.AutoRedraw = -1
End Sub
```

12. Enter the following code in the Line_Format_Click event subroutine. When the user clicks one of the options on the Line menu, all of the options are first unchecked and then the new selection is checked. The Index

value of the chosen option on the menu redefines the setting of the DrawStyle property of the Draw picture box.

```
Sub Line_Format_Click (Index As Integer)
  Line_Format(0).Checked = 0
  Line_Format(1).Checked = 0
  Line_Format(2).Checked = 0
  Line_Format(3).Checked = 0
  Line_Format(4).Checked = 0
  Line_Format(5).Checked = 0
  Line_Format(6).Checked = 0
  Line_Format(Index).Checked = -1
  Draw.DrawStyle = Index
End Sub
```

13. Enter the following code in the Pattern_Click event subroutine. When the user selects an option on the Pattern menu, the new option is checked and the FillStyle property of the Draw picture box changes to the new setting.

```
Sub Pattern_Click (Index As Integer)
  Pattern(0).Checked = 0
  Pattern(1).Checked = 0
  Pattern(2).Checked = 0
  Pattern(3).Checked = 0
  Pattern(4).Checked = 0
  Pattern(5).Checked = 0
  Pattern(6).Checked = 0
  Pattern(7).Checked = 0
  Pattern(Index).Checked = -1
  Draw.FillStyle = Index
End Sub
```

14. Enter the following code in the Pen_Click event subroutine. When the user selects an option on the Pen menu, the new option is checked and the DrawMode property of the Draw picture box changes to the new setting.

```
Sub Pen_Click (Index As Integer)
  Pen(0).Checked = 0
  Pen(1).Checked = 0
  Pen(2).Checked = 0
  Pen(3).Checked = 0
  Pen(4).Checked = 0
  Pen(5).Checked = 0
  Pen(6).Checked = 0
  Pen(7).Checked = 0
  Pen(8).Checked = 0
  Pen(9).Checked = 0
  Pen(10).Checked = 0
  Pen(11).Checked = 0
  Pen(12).Checked = 0
  Pen(13).Checked = 0
  Pen(14).Checked = 0
  Pen(15).Checked = 0
  Pen(Index).Checked = -1
  Draw.DrawMode = (Index + 1)
End Sub
```

15. Enter the following code in the Width_Format_Click event subroutine.
When the user selects an option on the Width menu, a new option is
checked and the DrawWidth property changes to the new setting.

```
Sub Width_Format_Click (Index As Integer)
 Width_Format(0).Checked = 0
 Width_Format(1).Checked = 0
 Width_Format(2).Checked = 0
 Width_Format(3).Checked = 0
 Width_Format(4).Checked = 0
 Width_Format(5).Checked = 0
 Width_Format(6).Checked = 0
 Width_Format(7).Checked = 0
 Width_Format(8).Checked = 0
 Width_Format(9).Checked = 0
 Width_Format(Index).Checked = -1
 Draw.DrawWidth = (Index + 1)
End Sub
```

## How It Works

The Shape project displays a form with a picture box with several command buttons
along the form's bottom edge. Each time the user presses one of these command buttons, a graphics image of random size appears in a random location on the picture box.
The text on the command button determines what type of graphics appears. For example, a circle appears when the user presses the command button labeled Circle.

To change the way the graphics are drawn with these command buttons, the user
selects a new option on one of the Shape form's menus. These menus represent the
settings of the properties that affect the appearance of graphics. By changing the settings of these menus, the user clearly sees how these properties interact.

### Startup

When the program starts, certain properties of the Draw picture box on the Shape
form change in the Form_Load event to ensure the proper operation of the Shape
project. Both the ScaleHeight and ScaleWidth properties of the Draw picture box are
100 each. This divides the available space on the Draw picture box into 100 equal
units. The AutoRedraw property of the Draw picture box is True to ensure that any
shapes do not erase when the Shape form minimizes or becomes obscured by another
form on the screen. These settings ensure the proper operation of the program and
match the settings of the menu items checked.

The Form_Load event sets the FillColor property of the Draw picture box on the
Shape form at program start up. Using the QBFunction to find the hexadecimal value
of the color black, the FillColor property sets to black. This means that any shapes
drawn on the Draw picture box fill with the color black. If any of the menu choices
change, then the appearance of the shape may change subject to the effects of the
other properties of the Shape form. In this way, the black color serves as the default
color to use until the color changes on the Color menu by selecting another color. The
FillColor property of the Draw picture box also changes when the selection on the

Color menu changes. Notice that in both cases, the color changes with the setting of the QBColor function between 0 and 15, representing the chosen color.

The FillStyle property of the Draw picture form is 0 in the Form_Load event subroutine. This completely fills all the shapes drawn on the Draw picture form with the color indicated by the FillColor property. If nothing changes after the program starts, then the combination of the FillColor and FillStyle properties produces black circles, squares, and rectangles. When the checked item Solid on the Pattern menu changes to another choice, this changes the contents of the next drawn shapes. The FillStyle property of the Draw form redefines the value of the newly indicated pattern. In this way, the FillStyle property becomes equal to the current value of the index variable that represents the selected item on the menu.

### Running the Shape Project

Selecting the Width menu on the Shape form displays a list of the numbers 1 through 10. At program startup, the checked number is the number 1, representing the thickness in pixels of lines. Since the value of this property has not changed up to this point, the default value is 1. Selecting another number on the Width menu changes the thickness of the lines on the next shapes. Even though the list of possible widths for this demonstration is between 1 and 10, the possible setttings are not limited to these values.

The default setting of the DrawStyle property for any form, picture box, or Printer object is 0. The checked item Solid on the Line menu represents this setting. While this property remains at this setting, all lines are solid lines. Since the value of this property has not changed up to this point, the default value is 0. Another selected number on the Line menu changes the appearance of the line around the next shapes drawn. Invisible indicates that the line does not appear around a shape. If the DrawWidth property of the Draw picture box changes to a value other than 1, Visual Basic ignores the setting of the DrawStyle property between 1 and 4 and draws a solid line.

The Pen menu lists the possible settings of the DrawMode property of the Draw picture box. Since the setting is unmodified, the default choice of Copy Pen is checked on the Pen menu. This option indicates that the colors in the FillColor, ForeColor, and BackColor properties of the Draw picture remain unmodified to produce shapes. Another selected number on the Pen menu changes the colors of the next shapes according to the effects of the new setting of the DrawMode property. If the DrawMode property of the Draw picture box changes to Whiteness or Blackness, the shapes appear in white or black. In cases where the color of the shape matches the color of the Background of the form, the shape appears not to be drawn. Sometimes the empty border appears.

Pressing command button labeled Circle produces a circle on the Draw picture box. This circle uses the settings chosen in properties represented in the menus of the Shape form. This code is within the Draw_Circle_Click event subroutine connected to the Draw_Circle command button. The circle varies in size and appears at a random location within the picture box. Each of the settings of the DrawMode, DrawWidth, DrawStyle, FillStyle, and FillColor properties determines how the circle displays on the Shape form.

The command buttons labeled Line, Square, Rectangle, and Triangle all contain Line methods to produce the indicated object on the Draw picture box. When the Line method appears without the B or F arguments in the Draw_Line_Click event, a line is drawn between the randomly indicated points. By adding the B argument to the Line method in the Draw_Rectangle_Click event, a rectangle of varying size and location displays instead of a line. In this case, the two indicated points serve as the upper left and lower right corners of the rectangle. With the B argument in the Draw_Square_Click event, a square of varying size and location appears. This is accomplished by making the second point of the square the same distance for the X and Y coordinates. Three Line methods work together in the Draw_Triangle_Click event to produce the three sides of the triangle on the Draw picture box.

# PART FOUR
# DISPLAYING FONTS AND TEXT

# Displaying Text with Objects

Text strings can be placed directly on a form, picture box, or Printer object. The font properties of forms, picture boxes, and Printer objects define the font, size, and appearance of text strings. Drawing text on an object in this way produces graphics rather than text. After a text string prints on an object, it becomes part of the background of the object that may be saved to a graphics file. For this reason, text strings drawn on a form, picture box, or Printer object are not editable. Once a text string is on an object, this text behaves in the same ways as other graphics on the object.

## Drawing Text in Visual Basic

Because text in Windows can be in a variety of fonts and point sizes, you cannot assume that all text will have the same size characters. Your program must be able to dynamically scale and position text according to the font, size, and object being used.

### Fonts and Text Styles

Chapter 12, Defining and Using Fonts, discusses several properties that affect the appearance of text strings. An object's FontName property sets the font style to format text strings. The FontSize property of the object sets the size of a text string. The FontBold, FontStrikeThru, and FontUnderline properties of the object cause the actual appearance of the text to change to bold, strikethrough, or underlined, respectively. The FontTransparent property of the object can be used either to make the text string overwrite, or to show the graphics placed under it.

### Methods for Scaling and Displaying Text

Visual Basic provides three methods that control the display of text on forms, picture boxes, and Printer objects. The TextHeight method returns the amount of vertical space needed to display a specified text string. With the TextWidth method, you can obtain the amount of horizontal space necessary to show the text string. Each text string is actually placed on a form, picture box, or printer object with the Print method. Table 11.1 displays the three methods that are used to place text on a form, picture box, or Printer object.

| Use or Set This... | | To Do This... |
|---|---|---|
| Print | Method | Places a text string on a form, picture box, or Printer object |
| TextHeight | Method | Determine the amount of vertical space needed for an indicated string in the units set by the ScaleMode Property of a form, Picture box, or Printer object |
| TextWidth | Method | Determine the amount of horizontal space needed for an indicated string in the units set by the ScaleMode Property of a form, Picture box, or Printer object |

**Table 11.1 Methods dealing with drawing text**

The following pages investigate the methods in Table 11.1 in detail. The Text project at the end of this section includes step-by-step directions for assembling this demonstration of drawing text.

# Print Method

## Objects Affected

| | | | | |
|---|---|---|---|---|
| Check | Clipboard | Combo | Command | ▶ Dbug |
| Dir | Drive | File | ▶ Form | Frame |
| Label | List | Menu | Option | ▶ Picture |
| ▶ Printer | Screen | Scroll | Text | Timer |

## Purpose

The Print method places a text string on a form, picture box, or Printer object. Each text string prints at the position on the object indicated by the CurrentX and CurrentY properties (current screen or printer coordinates). Since there is no text wrap feature, any strings that are larger than the space allowed will be cut short on the right. A text string displays on the screen in the font and point size set in the FontName and FontSize property. The form, picture box, or Printer object's ForeColor property determines the text's color. Once a text string prints on an object with the Print method, the content and format of the text cannot be changed. Table 11.2 summarizes the arguments of the Print method.

## General Syntax

```
[object.]Print[expressionlist][{;|,}]
```

| Argument | Description |
|---|---|
| object | Either the FormName property of the Form, the CtlName property of the Control, or Printer for the Printer object indicating the object that the Expressionlist string is printed on |

| | |
|---|---|
| expressionlist | A number or text string for the Print method to print on the object |
| , | Places the text cursor one character in width away from the end of the text string |
| ; | Places the text cursor at the end of the text string |

Table 11.2 Arguments of the Print method

## Example Syntax

```
Sub Timer1_Timer ()
    AutoRedraw = -1                     'Turns on redraw.
    Static Color As Integer             'Defines Color as a static variable.
    Display$ = "Warning"                'Stores text string.
    FontName = "Helv"                   'Indicates Helvetica font.
    FontSize = 30                       'Indicates 30pt. font.
    X = TextWidth(Display$) / 2         'Defines X as half of Text width.
    Y = TextHeight(Display$) / 2        'Defines Y as half of Text height.
    CurrentX = (ScaleWidth / 2) - X     'Sets current position so that
    CurrentY = (ScaleHeight / 2) - Y    'the text appears in the center.
    If Color% = 0 Then                  'Alternates the color between black
        Color% = 4                      'and red with the triggering of the
    ElseIf Color% = 4 Then              'timer event.
        Color% = 0
    End If
    ForeColor = QBColor(Color%)
    Print Display$                      'Prints warning on the form.
End Sub
```

## Description

The Print method puts a string of text at an object's current position. Each Print method identifies the object to place the string on by preceding it with the FormName property of the form, CtlName property of the picture box, or Printer for the Printer object. If a Print method does not include a name, the text prints on the current form. In order for something to be printed on an object, it must be a character string and not a numeric value (if it is a numeric value, an error generates). Print method expressions that end with a comma change the current screen or printer coordinates to the next print zone away from the displayed text. A print zone is 14 character widths in the current font and point size. Print method expressions that end in semicolons change the current screen or printer coordinates to directly after the text. The current screen or printer position determines where the next text appears on a form, picture box, or Printer object. In the example syntax, the print method places the text string Display$ on the form in the color, point size, and font indicated by the property settings of the form.

In the example syntax, the Print method places the text string containing the string "Warning" in the center of the form. Notice that the CurrentX and CurrentY properties control the actual position where the print method puts the text string modified by the values calculated by the TextHeight and TextWidth methods. Figure 11.1 shows what this example might look like on the screen.

### Positioning Text with the the TextWidth and TextHeight Methods

The TextWidth and TextHeight methods calculate the amount of horizontal and

Figure 11.1 Example syntax demonstrating text string printed on a form

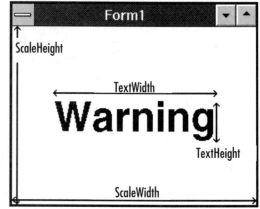

Figure 11.2 Positioning text in the example syntax

vertical space necessary to display the specified text string in the currently set font and point size. Values returned by these methods are measured in the units indicated by the ScaleMode property of the form, picture box, or Printer object. These values serve as a reference for positioning the text on the form, picture box, or Printer object. In the example syntax, the TextWidth and TextHeight methods change the current position to print the text in the center of the form.

### Positioning Text with the CurrentX, CurrentY, ScaleWidth, and ScaleHeight Properties

The CurrentX and CurrentY properties work well with the ScaleWidth and ScaleHeight properties to determine where a text string prints on a form, picture box, or Printer object. The ScaleWidth and ScaleHeight properties provide the usable horizontal and vertical surface of an object (height and width less the borders and title bar). By defining the CurrentX and CurrentY properties as fractions of the ScaleWidth and ScaleHeight properties, the text prints in the current position. In the example syntax, these properties find the center of the form by dividing the ScaleWidth and ScaleHeight properties by half and defining the CurrentX and CurrentY properties with the returned values. Figure 11.2 illustrates this procedure.

### Example

In the Text project at the end of this section, the Print method fills the form with the message entered by the user. Notice that this Print method ends with a semicolon. The semicolon ensures that the next text entry follows directly after the previous text printed on the same line. If the semicolon is changed to a comma, each print method places the text at the next print zone, 14 columns to the right. (This behavior is similar to that of the PRINT statement in regular BASIC.)

### Comments

Visual Basic treats text produced with the Print method as graphics. For this reason, the text is then subject to the normal effects of graphics operations.

# TextHeight and TextWidth Methods

## Objects Affected

| | | | | |
|---|---|---|---|---|
| Check | Clipboard | Combo | Command | Dbug |
| Dir | Drive | File | ▶ Form | Frame |
| Label | List | Menu | Option | ▶ Picture |
| ▶ Printer | Screen | Scroll | Text | Timer |

## Purpose

The TextHeight and TextWidth methods help you position text on a form, picture box, or Printer object by telling you what the height and width of the text string would be if displayed using the current font and point size. Each object's FontName property determines the name of the font type used to display a string. The FontSize property of the object indicates the character size in points. A value returned by the TextHeight and TextWidth methods represents the size of the text string using the unit of the measure in the ScaleMode property. Both of these methods are available at run time only. Table 11.3 summarizes the arguments of the TextWidth and TextHeight methods.

## General Syntax

```
[object.]TextHeight(stringexpression$)
[object.]TextWidth(stringexpression$)
```

| Argument | Description |
|---|---|
| object | FormName of the form, CtlName of the Picture box, or Printer for the Printer object representing the object drawn on |
| stringexpression$ | Text string to determine the width or height necessary to display |

Table 11.3 Arguments for the TextHeight and Text Width methods

## Example Syntax

```
Sub Form_Click ()
    Cls
    AutoRedraw = -1                      'Redraws graphics when uncovered.
    ForeColor = QBColor(0)               'Makes text black.
    BackColor = QBColor(15)              'Makes background white.
    FontName = "Helv"                    'Defines the font.
    FontSize = 8.25                      'Defines the point size.
    Display$ = "Demonstration"           'Defines text variable.
    X = TextWidth(Display$)              'Defines X and Y as the space needed to display
    Y = TextHeight(Display$)             'the Display$ text string.
    EndX = Abs(ScaleWidth / X) + 1       'indicates the number of times that the string
    EndY = Abs(ScaleHeight / Y) + 1      'is displayed horizontally and vertically.
    For H = 1 To EndY                    'Fill the form with the text string.
        For W = 1 To EndX
            Print Display$;
        Next W
        CurrentY = CurrentY + Y
        CurrentX = 0
    Next H
End Sub
```

## Description

The TextHeight and TextWidth methods determine the amount of space needed to display the stringexpression$ on an object. An object consists of the CtlName property of the picture box, FormName property of the form, or Printer for the Printer object. Each stringexpression$ must be a string variable and may not be a numeric value (a numeric value generates an error).

In the example syntax, the TextHeight and TextWidth methods are used to calculate the amount of vertical and horizontal space needed to display the text string "Demonstration" such that it is repeated enough times to fill the screen. Figure 11.3 shows what this example might look like on the screen.

### Text and the Print Method

The Print method places an indicated text string on a form, picture box, or Printer object at the current position on the object. Unless it changes, the default position on a form, picture box, or Printer object is in the top left corner. The values returned by the TextHeight and TextWidth methods serve as a reference for positioning the same string printed on an object. In the example syntax, the Print method places the word "Demonstration" at the current position until the words fill the entire form. Notice that the semicolon follows the print method to ensure that the next text is placed directly after it.

### Positioning with the ScaleHeight and ScaleWidth Properties

Both the ScaleHeight and ScaleWidth properties serve as a means of determining where a text string appears on a form, picture box, or Printer object. Since the ScaleHeight and ScaleWidth properties return the current height and width of the object, fractions of these properties work as excellent ways of positioning text on an object. For example, to place the letter T in the center of a form, change the values of the CurrentX property to half the ScaleWidth and of the CurrentY property to half the ScaleHeight property. Then modify the resulting values with those provided by the TextHeight and TextWidth methods. This places the letter T in the center of the form. In the example syntax, the ScaleHeight and ScaleWidth properties work in conjunction with the TextWidth and TextHeight methods to determine how many times that the text will appear if printed from top to bottom and left to right.

### The AutoRedraw Property

The AutoRedraw property determines whether printed text stays on a form, picture box, or Printer object after it is covered and uncovered. When the AutoRedraw property is at the default setting of False, the text does not reappear after being covered by another form. If the AutoRedraw property is True, then text redraws after being uncovered. In the example syntax, the AutoRedraw property is True to ensure that the text redraws on the form if minimized or covered and then uncovered. Note: This setting is important; without it, the example might not work properly. If the AutoRedraw property is False, then minimizing and maximizing the form erases the text on it.

## Example

In the Text Project at the end of this section, the TextHeight and TextWidth methods determine the size of the user's entered text. The values returned by the TextHeight and TextWidth methods provide the number of times that this message may appear horizontally and vertically on the form. Dividing the Scale-Width and ScaleHeight properties by the value returned by the TextHeight and TextWidth methods provides the number of times to run the Print method. In order to ensure that the form is completely filled with this text, 1 is added to the returned value, thus showing the partial message at the end of each line.

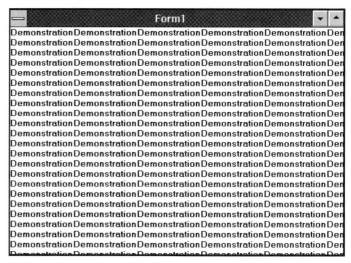

**Figure 11.3 Example syntax fills the screen**

# The Text Project

## Project Overview

The Text project shows how text prints on an form, picture box, or Printer object. These methods calculate the amount of space needed to place the indicated text on the form. This information provides the number of times that the message can print on the form, and controls how many times that the Print method generates.

The following pages discuss the assembly and operation of the Text project. The first section deals with the assembly of the Text form. Next, there is a listing and explanation of the contents of the subroutines of this project. Finally, there is a discussion of how the code operates. Please read this information carefully and use the pictures of the form to check your results.

## Assembling the Project

1. Make a new form (the Text form) with the objects and properties listed in Table 11.4.

| Object | Property | Setting |
|---|---|---|
| Form | BorderStyle | 2 - Sizeable |
| | Caption | Text Project |
| | FormName | Text |

**Table 11.4 Elements of the Text form**

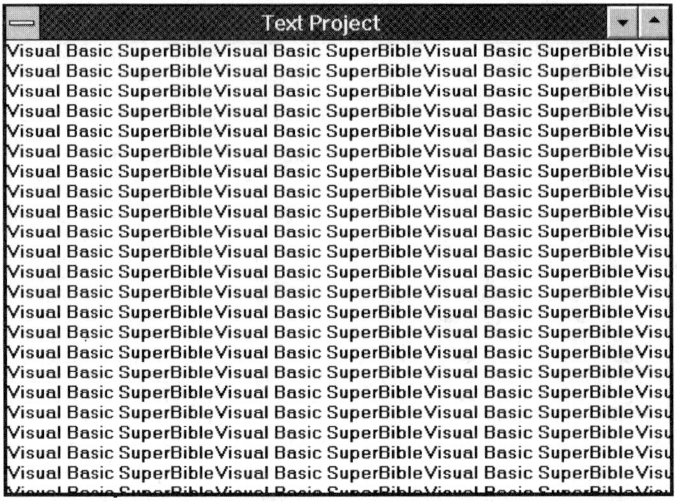

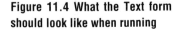

Figure 11.4 What the Text form should look like when running

2. Size the form to approximately this size and shape. Notice how the form should appear with the default text shown in Figure 4.4.

3. Enter the following code in the General Declarations section.

```
Dim Mess$ As String
```

4. Enter the following code in the General Declarations section. This has the effect of creating a new subfunction with the name Draw. When this code triggers, the background of the form fills with the indicated message string.

```
Sub Draw (S As String)
    Cls
    X = TextWidth(S$)
    Y = TextHeight(S$)
    EndX = Abs(ScaleWidth / X) + 1
    EndY = Abs(ScaleHeight / Y) + 1
    For H = 1 To EndY
        For W = 1 To EndX
            Print S$;
        Next W
        CurrentY = CurrentY + Y
        CurrentX = 0
    Next H
End Sub
```

5. Enter the following code in the Form_Click event subroutine. When the user clicks the form, the code prompts the user for the text string to print. The form then fills with this text using the Draw subfunction.

```
Sub Form_Click ()
    Cls
    T$ = "Text Project"
    M$ = "Enter the message you would like to appear"
```

```
      M$ = M$ + " on the background of the form."
      Mess$ = InputBox$(M$, T$, "Visual Basic SuperBible")
      If Mess$ = "" Then End
      Draw Mess$
   End Sub
```

6. Enter the following code in the Form_Load event subroutine. This code is triggered at program startup. It defines the different properties of the form and asks the user for what text to display. The form then fills this text with the Draw subfunction.

```
Sub Form_Load ()
   AutoRedraw = -1
   ForeColor = QBColor(0)
   BackColor = QBColor(15)
   FontName = "Helv"
   FontSize = 8.25
   T$ = "Text Project"
   M$ = "Enter the message you would like to appear"
   M$ = M$ + " on the background of the form."
   Mess$ = InputBox$(M$, T$, "Visual Basic SuperBible")
   If Mess$ = "" Then End
   Draw Mess$
End Sub
```

7. Enter the following code in the Form_Resize event subroutine. This code is activated whenever the size of the form changes. The Draw subfunction processes again to fill the entire contents of the form.

```
Sub Form_Resize ()
   Draw Mess$
End Sub
```

## How It Works

This project displays a form on the screen that is filled with the text that the user enters when the program starts. This is similar to the operation of the example syntax for the TextHeight and TextWidth methods, with the addition of the ability to fill the screen with any text specified by the user. The default text that prints on the form is "Visual Basic SuperBible." If the user presses the OK button without changing the text, this is the text that appears on the form. The user can change the text on the form by clicking the form with the mouse. When this happens, the system prompts the user to enter the new text to print on the form.

The Draw subfunction utilizes both the TextHeight and TextWidth methods to determine the size of the user's entered text. The values returned by the TextHeight and TextWidth methods provide the number of times that this message may appear horizontally and vertically on the form. Dividing the ScaleWidth and ScaleHeight properties by the value returned by the TextHeight and TextWidth methods provides the number of times to run the Print method. In order to ensure that the form is completely filled with this text, 1 is added to the returned value. This shows the partial message at the end of each line.

In the Draw subfunction, the Print method fills the form with the message entered by the user. Notice that this Print method ends with a semicolon. The semicolon is at the end of the Print method instead of the comma to ensure that the next text prints directly after the previous text printed.

You may wish to experiment by entering text with varying fonts and point sizes into the form.

# Defining and Using Fonts

**A** specific character style name, or font, determines the overall appearance of characters of text. Windows comes with a standard set of fonts, and additional fonts can be obtained from a variety of sources. Windows is designed to make all installed fonts available "transparently" to each program, but there are some limitations. The printer connected to the computer usually has a limited selection of fonts stored in the printer hardware (or plugged in as cartridges). For example if an unmodified Hewlett Packard LaserJet IIP printer is connected to a computer, then text printed with this printer may use either the Courier or LinePrinter font. Most traditional DOS programs do not allow you to see the formatted text on the screen prior to printing it. In the Microsoft Windows environment, however, printer fonts are displayed on the screen in roughly the same way that they will appear on the printed page. This "WYSIWYG" (What You See Is What You Get) feature is one of the greatest advantages provided by Windows 3.0.

## Screen Fonts and Printer Fonts

There are two general types of fonts in Microsoft Windows: screen fonts and printer fonts. Screen fonts affect the appearance of text on the screen. The Microsoft Windows environment is shipped with several screen fonts, which include Helv (Helvetica), Tms Roman (Times Roman), and System. Other environments may have more screen fonts, depending on the printer. Printer fonts control the look of text outputted by a printer. A printer font can be either a resident or a soft font. Resident fonts are those character styles that are contained in the printer. Soft fonts are typefaces that are located in the computer. These fonts are sent from the computer to the connected printer. They allow printers such as the HP Laserjet to produce a variety of fonts.

In Microsoft Windows, screen and printer fonts may be generated "on the fly." The Adobe Type Manager third-party product replaces many of the default Windows printer and screen fonts. This product provides fonts in clearer styles that are easier to read both on the screen and on paper. Several other popular products produce screen and printer fonts in this same way.

The point size of a font indicates how large or small a text string is on a screen or printed page. Each increase in the point size of a text string makes it larger. Decreasing the point size of a text string makes it grow smaller. With the Adobe Type Manager, for example, a string of text can be displayed or printed in any size between 6 and 48 points.

The typestyle of a font modifies its overall appearance. Examples of typestyles include boldface and italics.

### Fonts in Visual Basic

In Visual Basic, the appearance of the text on the screen or the printer can be set to any available font and point size. Both the FontName and FontSize properties determine the typestyle and size of text on a form, control, or Printer object. The Fonts and FontCount properties provide the number and names of the fonts available for the screen or the printer. Each of the FontBold, FontItalic, FontStrikethru, FontTransparent, and FontUnderline properties adds typestyle effects to text on a form, control, or Printer object.

Table 12.1 summarizes the properties that affect the appearance of text on a form, control, or Printer object.

| Use or Set This... | | To Do This... |
|---|---|---|
| FontBold | Property | Display a darker (boldface) font on the printer or screen |
| FontCount | Property | Return the number of fonts available for the screen or active printer |
| FontName | Property | Set or indicate the name of the current font |
| Fonts | Property | Return the names of the fonts available for the screen or active printer |
| FontSize | Property | Set or indicate the point size of the font |
| FontStrikeThru | Property | Indicate whether text should have a line drawn through it |
| FontTransparent | Property | Indicate whether text includes the background graphics |
| FontUnderline | Property | Indicate whether text should have a line drawn under it |

**Table 12.1 Properties dealing with fonts**

The properties in Table 12.1 are investigated in detail in the following pages. Step-by-step directions assembling the Fonts project are described at the end of this section.

# FontBold Property

## Objects Affected

| | | | | |
|---|---|---|---|---|
| ▶ Check | Clipboard | ▶ Combo | ▶ Command | Dbug |
| ▶ Dir | ▶ Drive | ▶ File | ▶ Form | ▶ Frame |
| ▶ Label | ▶ List | Menu | ▶ Option | ▶ Picture |
| ▶ Printer | Screen | Scroll | ▶ Text | Timer |

## Purpose

The FontBold property determines whether the text on a form, control, or Printer object appears as boldface type. When it is boldface, the text appears thicker and darker in color. This property may be modified at either design or run time. Any changes made to the FontBold property of a form or Printer object only affect the appearance of text drawn after the alteration. Once a string of text is printed on a form or Printer object, any changes to this property have no effect on it. A control's FontBold property always changes the appearance of any existing text on the control. Table 12.2 summarizes the arguments of the FontBold property; Table 12.3 summarizes its settings.

## General Syntax

```
form.FontBold[=state%]
control.FontBold[=state%]
Printer.FontBold[=state%]
```

| Arguments | Description |
|-----------|-------------|
| form | FormName of the form |
| control | CtlName of the control |
| Printer | Printer object |
| state% | Current setting of FontBold property |

**Table 12.2 Arguments of the FontBold property**

| state% | Description |
|--------|-------------|
| True (-1) | Text on the indicated object is bold |
| False (0) | Text on the indicated object is normal |

**Table 12.3 Settings of the state% variable of the FontBold property**

## Example Syntax

```
Sub Form_Load ()
    AutoRedraw = -1                    'Property is redrawn each time it is uncovered
    FontSize = 8                       'Initial setting of text is 8 pt
    ForeColor = QBColor(0)             'Black text
    BackColor = QBColor(15)            'White background
    For I = 1 To 10                    'Generate the following code 10 times
        FontBold = Abs(FontBold) - 1   'Toggle the FontBold property
        If FontBold = 0 Then           'Checks if FontBold is False
            T$ = "Normal"              'Defines text string
            FontSize = FontSize + 1.8  'Increments point size by 1.8
        Else
            T$ = "Bold"                'Defines text string
        End If
        Mess$ = "This is " + FontName + " " 'Displays the text on the screen
        Mess$ = Mess$ + Str$(FontSize)
        Mess$ = Mess$ + "pt " + T$
        Print Mess$
    Next I
End Sub
```

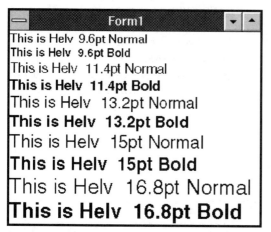

**Figure 12.1 Sample font listing on a form**

## Description

The FontBold property affects the appearance of the text on an object. An object's name is the first part of a FontBold property expression. The object may be identified using the FormName property of a form, the CtlName property of a control, or the name Printer for the Printer object. When no object is given, the parent form is assumed to be the object addressed. The FontBold expression ends with an integer value of either 0, representing False, or 1, standing for True. This property defaults to False. False means that the text placed on the object is not changed by this property. True can have two possible effects. On forms and Printer objects, the True setting makes only new text bold. All of the previously entered text strings are unaffected on a form or Printer object. Text on controls is immediately affected by changes made to its FontBold property.

In the example syntax, text is printed on the form in both normal and bold format, demonstrating the difference between bold and normal. Figure 12.1 shows approximately what should display on your screen.

### FontItalic, FontStrikethru, FontTransparent, and FontUnderline

There are four other special effect font properties in Visual Basic: FontItalic, FontStrikethru, FontTransparent, and FontUnderline. More than one of these properties may be set to the same object, combining the indicated effects. When the FontItalic and FontBold properties are both True, the text on the object is in bold italics. Similarly, the FontBold property can be combined with the other special effects. (This assumes that the font indicated in FontName has a bold italics font. Some fonts may not include all typestyles.)

### The FontName Property

The FontName property determines whether the FontBold property has any effect upon the text on a form, control, or Printer object. Some system configurations do not have a bold version of the font chosen in the FontName property. In cases like this, the appearance of the text on the object is unaffected by the setting of the FontBold property.

## Example

The Font project at the end of this section demonstrates the use of the FontBold property. Clicking on the check box labeled Bold triggers the Font_Bold_Click event. Each time this event is processed, the text on the Display_Text text box is switched from bold to normal and normal to bold.

## Comments

Notice that a bold text string needs a larger display space. Be careful to provide enough space for bold as well as normal text. See Chapter 11, *Displaying Text with Objects*, for information on font positioning and scaling.

# FontCount Property

## Objects Affected

| | | | | |
|---|---|---|---|---|
| Check | Clipboard | Combo | Command | Dbug |
| Dir | Drive | File | Form | Frame |
| Label | List | Menu | Option | Picture |
| ▶ Printer | ▶ Screen | Scroll | Text | Timer |

## Purpose

The FontCount property indicates the number of printer or screen fonts available, depending on whether you specify the Screen or Printer object. If the screen is indicated, then the number of screen fonts is returned. For screen fonts, the value returned encompasses all of the Windows screen fonts. For the printer, the value specifies the number of fonts that may be placed upon a printer object, including all resident and soft fonts. You may only access the FontCount property at run time, not design time. Used together, the FontCount and Fonts properties produce a list of the names of the possible fonts. Table 12.4 summarizes the arguments of the FontCount property.

## General Syntax

```
Printer.FontCount
Screen.FontCount
```

| Arguments | Description |
|---|---|
| Printer | Printer object |
| Screen | Screen object |

Table 12.4 Arguments of the FontCount property

## Example Syntax

```
Sub Form_Load ()
    S$ = Str$(Screen.FontCount)                             'Finds the current number of
    P$ = Str$(Printer.FontCount)                            'screen and printer fonts
    Text1.Text = "There are " + S$ + " Screen fonts"       'Prints number of fonts
    Text2.Text = "There are " + P$ + " Printer fonts"      'Prints number of fonts
End Sub
```

## Description

The FontCount property indicates the number of fonts available for the present configuration. If a FontCount property is preceded by the word Screen, then this property provides the number of screen fonts. With the word Printer, the value calculated by the FontCount property includes all of the resident and soft fonts. This property is only available for reference at run time and will only be changed if fonts are removed. Some configurations will provide a different number of available fonts for the screen and printer.

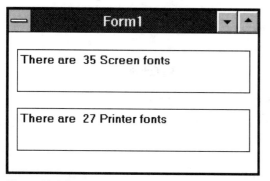

**Figure 12.2 Sample screen and printer font counts**

In the example syntax, the FontCount property provides the number of fonts available for the screen and the printer. These numbers are then printed in the Text1 and Text2 text boxes. Figure 12.2 shows what this form might look like on the screen. (The actual number of fonts depends on your setup. Notice that the numbers may not match.)

### The Fonts Property

Using the Fonts and FontCount properties together provides a list of the names of the available fonts. The FontCount property provides the maximum value that may be set for the Fonts property. Each value between 1 and the FontCount property will provide the name of one of the fonts available for the display or printer. Remember not to use the results from both the screen and the printer, or the list may not be accurate.

## Example

In the Font project at the end of this section, the FontCount property generates a list of the fonts available on the system. The FontCount property works with the Fonts property to provide the names of the fonts in string format. At program startup, these properties function together to fill the contents of the Font_Name combo list box. Pressing the command button labeled Screen Fonts produces a list of the system fonts on the FontList form.

## Comments

With some configurations, a list of screen or printer fonts may include more than one entry for a particular font.

# FontItalic Property

## Objects Affected

| | | | | |
|---|---|---|---|---|
| ▶ Check | Clipboard | ▶ Combo | ▶ Command | Dbug |
| ▶ Dir | ▶ Drive | ▶ File | ▶ Form | ▶ Frame |
| ▶ Label | ▶ List | Menu | ▶ Option | ▶ Picture |
| ▶ Printer | Screen | Scroll | ▶ Text | Timer |

## Purpose

The FontItalic property specifies whether the text on a form, control, or Printer object appears in italic type. If the FontItalic property is changed to italics, then the text becomes scriptlike in format. This property may be modified at either design time or run time. Any changes made to the FontItalic property of a form or Printer object only affect the appearance of text drawn after the change. Once a string of text is printed on a form or printer object, any subsequent changes to this property have no effect on it. A control's FontItalic property always changes the appearance of the existing text on it. Table 12.5 and 12.6 summarize the arguments and settings of the FontItalic property.

## General Syntax

```
form.FontItalic[=state%]
control.FontItalic[=state%]
Printer.FontItalic[=state%]
```

| Arguments | Description |
|-----------|-------------|
| form | FormName of the form |
| control | CtlName of control |
| Printer | Printer object |
| state% | Current setting of FontItalic property |

Table 12.5 Arguments of the FontItalic property

| state% | Description |
|--------|-------------|
| True | Text on the indicated object is in italics |
| False | Text on the indicated object is normal |

Table 12.6 Settings of the state% variable of the FontItalic property

## Example Syntax

```
Sub Form_Load ()
    Static S As Integer      'Defines static variable S
    AutoRedraw = -1          'Property is redrawn each time it is uncovered
    FontSize = 8             'Initial setting of text is 8 pt
    ForeColor = QBColor(0)   'Black text
    BackColor = QBColor(15)  'White background
    For I = 1 To 15          'Runs this code 15 times
        Select Case S        'Select case statement prints the current font
            Case 0           'in normal, bold, italic, and bolditalics format
                FontBold = 0
                FontItalic = 0
                T$ = "Normal"
                FontSize = FontSize + 1.8
                S = S + 1
            Case 1
                FontBold = -1
                T$ = "Bold"
                S = S + 1
```

```
        Case 2
            FontBold = 0
            FontItalic = -1
            T$ = "Italics"
            S = S + 1
        Case 3
            FontBold = -1
            T$ = "Bold Italics"
            S = 0
    End Select
    Mess$ = "This is " + FontName + " "  'Displays the text on the screen
    Mess$ = Mess$ + Str$(FontSize)
    Mess$ = Mess$ + "pt " + T$
    Print Mess$
    Next I
End Sub
```

```
┌─────────────────────────────────────┐
│ ─          Form1            ▼ │ ▲ │
├─────────────────────────────────────┤
│ This is Helv  9.6pt Normal           │
│ This is Helv  9.6pt Bold             │
│ This is Helv  9.6pt Italics          │
│ This is Helv  9.6pt Bold Italics     │
│ This is Helv  11.4pt Normal          │
│ This is Helv  11.4pt Bold            │
│ This is Helv  11.4pt Italics         │
│ This is Helv  11.4pt Bold Italics    │
│ This is Helv  13.2pt Normal          │
│ This is Helv  13.2pt Bold            │
│ This is Helv  13.2pt Italics         │
│ This is Helv  13.2pt Bold Italics    │
│ This is Helv  15pt Normal            │
│ This is Helv  15pt Bold              │
│ This is Helv  15pt Italics           │
└─────────────────────────────────────┘
```

**Figure 12.3 The Helvetica typeface in normal, bold, italics, and bold italics**

## Description

The FontItalic property changes the appearence of the text on an object. A FontItalic expression begins with the name of the object affected. You identify the object with the FormName property of a form, CtlName property of a control, or Printer for the Printer object. When no object is given, the parent form is assumed to be the object being addressed. Every FontItalic property statement ends with an integer value of either 0, representing False, or 1, standing for True. This property defaults to False. False means that the text placed on the object is not changed by this property. True can have two possible effects. On forms and printer objects, the True setting only changes new text to italics. All of the previously entered text strings are unaffected on a form or Printer object. Existing text as well as subsequent text on controls is immediately affected by changes made to its FontItalic property.

The example syntax provides a listing of the default system's font in normal, italics, bold, and bold italics format. Figure 12.3 shows what this might look like on your system. (Note: "Helv" is not every system's default font, so your results may vary.)

### The FontBold, FontStrikethru, FontTransparent, and FontUnderline Properties

There are four other font typestyle properties in Visual Basic: FontBold, FontStrikethru, FontTransparent, and FontUnderline. More than one of these properties may be set to the same object, combining the effects indicated. For example, when the FontItalic and FontBold properties are both True, the text on the object is bold italics. (This is only true if the font indicated in FontName has a Bold Italics font. Not all typestyles are necessarily available for each font.)

### The FontName Property

The FontName property determines whether the FontItalic property affects the text on a form, control, or Printer object. With some system configurations, the font chosen in the FontName property does not have an italics version. In cases like this, the appearance of the text on the object is unaffected by the setting of the FontItalic property. Try out the example with different fonts by changing the FontName property of the form to determine if the italic and bold italic properties are available for that particular font.

## Example

The Font project at the end of this section demonstrates the FontItalic property. Clicking the check box labeled Italic with the mouse triggers the Font_Bold_Click event. This event changes the setting of the FontItalic property of the Display_Text text box. Each time this event is processed, the text on the Display_Text text box is switched between italic and normal.

## Comments

Some fonts, such as the Script font shipped with Windows 3.0, are unaffected by the FontItalic property.

# FontName Property

## Objects Affected

| | | | | |
|---|---|---|---|---|
| ▶ Check | Clipboard | ▶ Combo | ▶ Command | Dbug |
| ▶ Dir | ▶ Drive | ▶ File | ▶ Form | ▶ Frame |
| ▶ Label | ▶ List | Menu | ▶ Option | ▶ Picture |
| ▶ Printer | Screen | Scroll | ▶ Text | Timer |

## Purpose

The FontName property specifies the name of the current font of a form, control, or Printer object. Any text that is placed upon one of these objects is formatted with the font selected in the object's FontName property. This property may be accessed at design time or run time. Each individual system's configuration controls the default setting of the FontName property. A system's display device and active printing device directly affect the default setting of the FontName property. Third-party font generators, such as the Adobe Type Manager, can also affect the default setting of the FontName property. Table 12.7 summarizes the arguments of the FontName property.

## General Syntax

```
form.FontName [=font$]
control.FontName [=font$]
Printer.FontName [=font$]
```

| Arguments | Description |
|-----------|-------------|
| form | FormName of the form |
| control | CtlName of the control |
| Printer | Printer object |
| font$ | Text string that represents certain font |

**Table 12.7 Arguments of the FontName property**

## Example Syntax

```
Sub Form_Load ()
    For I = 0 To (Printer.FontCount - 1)        'Adds each of the font names to
        Combo1.AddItem Printer.Fonts(I)         'the combo list
    Next I
    Combo1.Text = Text1.FontName                'Displays the current font
End Sub

Sub Combo1_Click ()
    Text1.FontName = Combo1.Text                'Changes the current font
    Text2.Text = Combo1.Text                    'Displays the new current font
End Sub
```

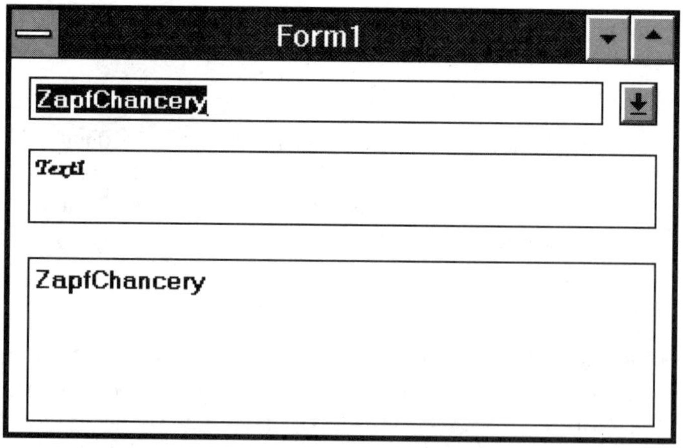

**Figure 12.4 Example syntax on the screen**

## Description

The FontName property provides the name of the currently selected font for an object. A FontName property statement begins with the FormName property of a form, the CtlName property of a control, or Printer for a Printer object. Each object has its own separate font setting that may be different from the choices for the other objects in a program. If no object name is provided, the FontName property of the parent form is accessed or modified. When a FontName property expression is made equal to a text string, the current font changes to this new font. Any text string used in an expression must be a valid font for the current system. This property may also be referenced as a means of obtaining the name of the selected font.

In the example syntax, the fonts provided by the Adobe Type Manager are included in the Combo1 combo list box. Notice how the FontName property of the Text1 text box is defined with the font name chosen in the Combo1 combo list box. Figure 12.4 shows what this example might look like on your screen.

### The Fonts and FontCount properties

The Fonts and FontCount properties give the exact spelling of the valid font names of a system. The Fonts property uses a number between 1 and the value of the FontCount property to provide the font's name. This combination returns a text string that may be utilized to define the FontName property of an object. In the example, the Fonts and FontCount properties are accessed to list the available fonts in the Combo1 combo list box. Changing the Sorted property to True changes the generated list to alphabetical order.

### Example

In the Font project at the end of this section, the FontName property modifies the appearance of an object's text. Selecting a new font name from the combo list box Font_Name, the Font_Name_Click event accesses the FontName property of the Display_Text text box. This changes the text on the text box to the new font. Pressing the command button labeled Screen Fonts changes the FontName property of the FontList form for each line of the font list. In this way, each name of the list appears and prints out in the font type named.

### Comments

With some system configurations, a list of screen or printer fonts may include more than one entry for a particular font.

# Fonts Property

## Objects Affected

| Check | Clipboard | Combo | Command | Dbug |
| --- | --- | --- | --- | --- |
| Dir | Drive | File | Form | Frame |
| Label | List | Menu | Option | Picture |
| ▶ Printer | ▶ Screen | Scroll | Text | Timer |

## Purpose

The Fonts property provides the name of one of the available fonts of the screen or printer, depending on which of these objects you specify and which font number you use. Exactly which value stands for which font is determined by the system. This property is modified whenever the active printer is changed to another printing device with different fonts. A combination of the FontCount and Fonts properties produces a list of the names of the possible fonts. Table 12.8 summarizes the arguments of the Fonts Property.

## General Syntax

```
Printer.Fonts(index%)
Screen.Fonts(index%)
```

| Arguments | Description |
|-----------|-------------|
| Printer | Printer object |
| Screen | Screen object |
| index% | Value that represents a screen or printer font |

**Table 12.8 Arguments of the Fonts property**

## Example Syntax

```
Sub Form_Load ()
    AutoRedraw = -1 'Turns on autoredraw
    For I = 0 To (Screen.FontCount - 1)      'Displays all of the fonts
        FontName = Screen.Fonts(I)           'Changes font
        Print Screen.Fonts(I)                'Prints the font name
    Next I
End Sub
```

**Figure 12.5 List of available fonts**

## Description

The Fonts property provides the names of an available system font specified by the index number, which must be between 0 and the value of the FontCount property, which indicates the total number of fonts available. If a Fonts property is begun with the word Screen, then this property provides the name of an indicated screen font. With the word Printer, the Fonts property returns the name of a resident or soft font in the printer. This property is only available for reference at run time and will only change when fonts are removed from the system. Some configurations will provide a different font for the same number with the screen and printer objects.

In the example syntax, the Fonts property serves as a means of printing the names of the available screen fonts on the form. A For loop controls the repeated invocation of the Fonts property for each font number from 0 to one less than the value of the FontCount property. These font names are printed in the font indicated by the font name. Figure 12.5 shows what this list might look like. If the Screen object is changed to Printer, this list may be different.

### The FontCount Property

Using the Fonts and FontCount properties together provides a list of the names of the available fonts. The FontCount property provides the maximum value that may be set for the Fonts property. Each value between 1 and the FontCount property will provide the name of one of the fonts available for the display or printer. Remember not to use the results from both the screenand the printer, or the list may not be accurate. In the example, the number of the font name to provide with the Fonts property is obtained with the FontCount property.

### Example

In the Font project at the end of this section, the Fonts property gives a list of the names of the fonts available on the system. The FontCount property works with the Fonts property to provide the names of the fonts in string format. At program startup, these properties function together to fill the contents of the Font_Name combo list box. Pressing the command button labeled Screen Fonts produces a list of the system fonts on the FontList form.

### Comments

With some system configurations, a list of screen or printer fonts may include more than one entry for a particular font.

# FontSize Property

## Objects Affected

| | | | | |
|---|---|---|---|---|
| ▶ Check | Clipboard | ▶ Combo | ▶ Command | Dbug |
| ▶ Dir | ▶ Drive | ▶ File | ▶ Form | ▶ Frame |
| ▶ Label | ▶ List | Menu | ▶ Option | ▶ Picture |
| ▶ Printer | Screen | Scroll | ▶ Text | Timer |

## Purpose

The FontSize property sets the point size of the current font of a form, control, or Printer object. Any text subsequently placed on one of these objects will be formatted with the point size selected in the object's FontSize property. This property may be accessed at design time or run time. Each system's configuration controls the default setting of the FontSize property. A system's display device and active printing device directly affect the default setting of the FontSize property. Third-party font generators, such as the Adobe Type Manager, can also change the default setting of the FontSize property. Table 12.8 summarizes the arguments of the FontSize property.

## General Syntax

```
form.FontSize[=points%]
control.FontSize[=points%]
Printer.FontSize[=points%]
```

| Arguments | Description |
|-----------|-------------|
| form | FormName of the form |
| control | CtlName of control |
| Printer | Printer object |
| points% | Value that represents the size of the letters on an object |

**Table 12.9 Arguments of the FontSize property**

## Example Syntax

```
Sub Form_Click ()
    Text1.Text = "This is " + str$(Text1.FontSize) + " pt"   'Prints current font size
    Text1.FontSize = Text1.FontSize + 2                       'Increments font size
End Sub
```

## Description

The FontSize property of an object changes the size of text. An object's name is the first part of a FontSize property expression. You identify the object with the FormName prop-

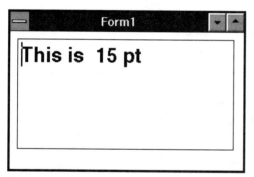

erty of a form, the CtlName property of a control, or Printer for the Printer object. When no object is given, the parent form is assumed to be the object being addressed. FontSize expressions are defined with an integer value that represents the size of text on the screen. When no value is given, the FontSize property serves as a reference.

In the example syntax, the FontSize property of the Text1 text box is incremented by 2 each time the form is clicked with the mouse. Notice how the text gets progressively larger with each click.

**Figure 12.6  Example syntax prints the current font size**

### The FontName Property

The FontName property of an object determines exactly which font is used to format the text on it. Each font has certain point sizes it may be displayed in. In this way, the FontName and FontSize properties work together to produce text on a form, control, or Printer object. Notice that the example ignores any limits set by the normal point sizes of the default font set in the FontName property. This is because Microsoft Windows allows fonts to be displayed in arbitrary point sizes.

## Example

In the Font project at the end of this section, the FontSize property modifies the size of an object's text. When a new point size is chosen from the combo list box Font_Size, the Font_Size_Click event accesses the FontSize property of the Display_Text text box. This has the effect of changing the text on the text box to the new size.

## Comments

Any changes to the FontSize property of an object affect the existing text on a control. This means all of the text on a control must be the same point size.

# FontStrikethru Property

## Objects Affected

| | | | | |
|---|---|---|---|---|
| ▶ Check | Clipboard | ▶ Combo | ▶ Command | Dbug |
| ▶ Dir | ▶ Drive | ▶ File | ▶ Form | ▶ Frame |
| ▶ Label | ▶ List | Menu | ▶ Option | ▶ Picture |
| ▶ Printer | Screen | Scroll | ▶ Text | Timer |

## Purpose

The FontStrikethru property determines if the text on a form, control, or printer object is formatted with a line through it. Strikethrough text is often used in legal documents to indicate superceded or eliminated language, or to indicate editorial deletion. This property may be changed at either design time or run time. Any changes made to the FontStrikethru property of a form or printer object only affect the appearance of text drawn after the change. A control's FontStrikethru property is not affected by the limitations of forms and printer objects. Table 12.10 summarizes the arguments of the FontStrikethru property. Table 12.11 summarizes its possible settings.

## General Syntax

```
form.FontStrikethru[=state%]
control.FontStrikethru[=state%]
Printer.FontStrikethru[=state%]
```

| Arguments | Description |
|---|---|
| form | FormName of the form |
| control | CtlName of the control |
| Printer | Printer object |
| state% | Current setting of the FontStrikethru property |

Table 12.10 Arguments of the FontStrikethru property

| state% | Description |
|--------|-------------|
| True | Text on the indicated object is strikethru |
| False | Text on the indicated object is normal |

**Table 12.11 Settings of the state% variable of the FontStrikethru property**

## Example Syntax

```
Sub Form_Click ()
    M$ = "Please Enter your message here"      'Asks for the word to display in the
    T$ = "Visual Basic SuperBible"             'Text1 text box and displays this
    A$ = InputBox$(M$, T$, Text1.Text)         'text with a line through it.
    Text1.FontStrikethru = Abs(Text1.FontStrikethru) - 1
    Text1.Text = A$
End Sub
```

## Description

The FontStrikethru property controls whether to place a horizontal line through the text on an object. Either the FormName property of a form, the CtlName property of a control, or Printer for the Printer object identifies the object. If an object name is not provided, the parent form is assumed. Each FontStrikethru property statement ends with an integer value of either 0, representing False, or 1, standing for True. This property defaults to False. False indicates that the text placed on the object is not changed by this property. True can have two possible effects. On forms and printer objects, the True setting only places a line through new text. All of the previously entered text strings are unaffected on a form or printer object. Text on controls, however, is immediately affected by changes made to its FontStrikethru property.

In the example syntax, since a control (text box) is specified, the text immediately reflects the change in the Font-Strikethru property. Figure 12.7 displays what this might look like on the screen.

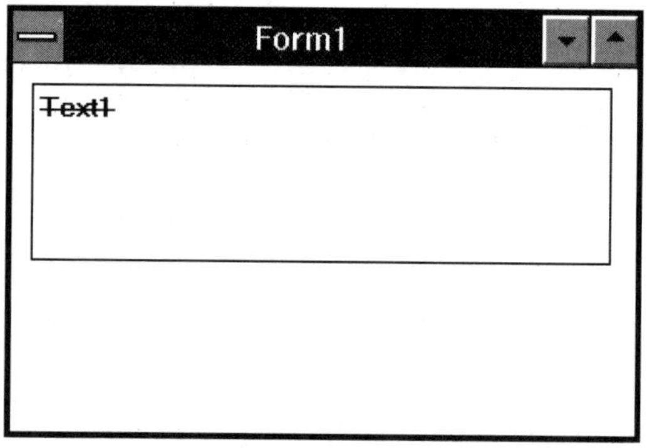

**Figure 12.7 Strikethrough text**

### The FontBold, FontItalic, FontTransparent, and FontUnderline Properties

Visual Basic provides four other special effects for controlling the appearance of text: FontBold, FontItalic, FontTransparent, and FontUnderline. If more than one of these properties is changed from its default False setting, then the effects are combined.

## Example

The Font project at the end of this section demonstrates the FontStrikethru property. Clicking the check box labeled Strikethru with the mouse triggers the Font_Strikethru_Click event. This event changes the setting of the FontStrikethru property of the Display_Text text box. Each time this event is processed, the text on the Display_Text text box is switched from strikethru to normal and normal to strikethru.

## Comments

Remember that all of the text on a control is affected by any changes to the FontStrikethru property.

# FontTransparent Property

## Objects Affected

| | | | | |
|---|---|---|---|---|
| Check | Clipboard | Combo | Command | Dbug |
| Dir | Drive | File | ▶ Form | Frame |
| Label | List | Menu | Option | ▶ Picture |
| ▶ Printer | Screen | Scroll | Text | Timer |

## Purpose

The FontTransparent property indicates how the text on a form, control, or Printer object interacts with the graphics beneath it. When it is made transparent, the text is surrounded by the underlying graphics. Otherwise, a block in the background color surrounds the text, obscuring portions of the graphics beneath. This property may be modified at either design time or run time. Any changes made to the FontTransparent property of a form or printer object only affect the appearance of text drawn after the change. Table 12.2 summarizes the arguments of the FontTransparent property; Table 12.13 summarizes its settings.

## General Syntax

```
form.FontTransparent[=state%]
picturebox.FontTransparent[=state%]
Printer.FontTransparent[=state%]
```

| Arguments | Description |
|---|---|
| form | FormName of the form |
| control | CtlName of the control |
| Printer | Printer object |
| state% | Current setting of the FontTransparent property |

Table 12.12 Arguments of the FontTransparent property

| state% | Description |
|---|---|
| True | Text on the object is surrounded by the underlying graphics |
| False | Underlying graphics are obscured by the space around the text |

Table 12.13 Settings of the state% variable of the FontTransparent property

## Example Syntax

```
Sub Form_Click ()
    FillColor = QBColor(1)                          'Sets FillColor to Blue
    FillStyle = 0                                   'Sets FillStyle to solid
    ForeColor = QBColor(0)                          'Sets text color to black
    X = ScaleWidth / 2                              'Defines X as half width of form
    Y = ScaleHeight / 2                             'Defines Y as half height of form
    R = ScaleWidth / 3                              'Defines R as one third width of form
    Circle (X, Y), R                                'Draws a circle on the form
    CurrentX = R                                    'Changes the current position
    FontTransparent = Abs(FontTransparent) - 1      'Toggles the setting
    FontSize = 30                                   'Sets the font size to 30.
    Print "This is a circle"                        'Prints message on the form
End Sub
```

## Description

The FontTransparent property determines what happens when graphics and text share the same space on a form or Printer object. Each FontTransparent property expression begins with either Printer for the Printer object, the FormName property for the form, or the CtlName property of a picture box. If an object name is not provided, the parent form is assumed. A FontTransparent property statement ends with an integer value of either 0, representing False, or 1, standing for True. This property defaults to False. False indicates that the text placed on the object is not changed by this property. True can have two possible effects. On forms, picture boxes, and Printer objects, the True setting only changes the appearance of new text. Previously entered text strings are unaffected on a form, picture box, or Printer object.

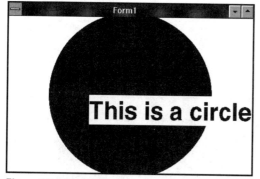

**Figure 12.8 Text that obscures underlying graphics**

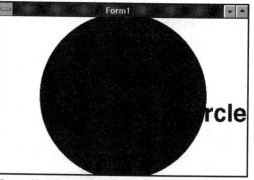

**Figure 12.9 Text that is part of underlying graphics**

In the example syntax, the text either obscures or becomes part of the underlying graphics each time the user clicks the form. Figure 12.8 shows what text that obscures the underlying graphics looks like, and Figure 12.9 displays text that is transparent to the graphics.

### The FontBold, FontItalic, FontStrikethru, and FontUnderline Properties

Visual Basic provides four other special effects for controlling the appearance of text. These properties are FontBold, FontItalic, FontStrikethru, and FontUnderline. If more than one of these properties is True, then the effects are combined.

## Example

The Font project at the end of this section demonstrates the FontTransparent property's effects. The Display_Font_Click event draws a circle on the FontList form, which interacts with the list of fonts. Each time the command button labeled Screen Fonts is pressed, the FontTransparent property is changed. When the FontTransparent property is changed to True, the circle surrounds the text of the font list. If the FontTransparent property is False, then a bar around the text appears, obscuring the circle where they intersect. In the first displayed list, the FontTransparent property is True.

## Comments

The FontTransparent property controls the appearance of the background around the text, not the text itself.

# FontUnderline Property

## Objects Affected

| | | | | |
|---|---|---|---|---|
| ▶ Check | Clipboard | ▶ Combo | ▶ Command | Dbug |
| ▶ Dir | ▶ Drive | ▶ File | ▶ Form | ▶ Frame |
| ▶ Label | ▶ List | Menu | ▶ Option | ▶ Picture |
| ▶ Printer | Screen | Scroll | ▶ Text | Timer |

## Purpose

The FontUnderline property indicates whether the text on a form, control, or Printer object is underlined. When it is underlined, the text has a line placed under it. This property may be modified at either design time or run time. Any changes made to the FontUnderline property of a form or printer object only affect the appearance of text drawn after the alteration. Once a string of text is printed on a form or printer object, any changes to this property have no effect. A control's FontUnderline property, on the other hand, always changes the appearance of the text on it. Table 12.14 summarizes the argument of the FontUnderline property; Table 12.15 summarizes its settings.

## General Syntax

```
form.FontUnderline[=state%]
control.FontUnderline[=state%]
Printer.FontUnderline[=state%]
```

| Arguments | Description |
|---|---|
| form | FormName of the form |
| control | CtlName of the control |
| Printer | Printer object |
| state% | Current setting of the FontUnderline property |

**Table 12.14 Arguments of the FontUnderline property**

| state% | Description |
|--------|-------------|
| True | Text on the indicated object is underlined |
| False | Text on the indicated object is normal |

**Table 12.15 Settings of the state% variable of the FontUnderline property**

## Example Syntax

```
Sub Form_Click ()
    M$ = "Please Enter your message here"      'Asks for the word to display in the
    T$ = "Visual Basic SuperBible"             'Text1 text box and displays this
    A$ = InputBox$(M$, T$, Text1.Text)         'text with an underline.
    Text1.FontUnderline = Abs(Text1.FontUnderline) - 1
    Text1.Text = A$

                                               End Sub
```

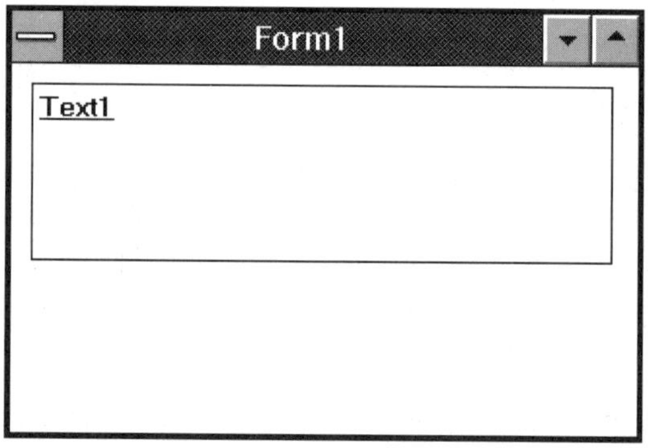

**Figure 12.10 Underlined text**

## Description

The FontUnderline property determines whether a line is placed under the text on an object. An object's name is the first part of a FontUnderline property expression. This can be the FormName property of a form, the CtlName property of a control, or Printer for the Printer object. When no object is given, the parent form is assumed to be the object addressed. Each FontUnderline property expression ends with an integer value of either 0, representing False, or 1, standing for True. This property defaults to False. False means that the text placed on the object is not changed by this property. True can have two possible effects. On forms and printer objects, the True setting only underlines new text. All of the previously entered text strings are unaffected on a form or Printer object. Text on controls is immediately affected by changes made to its FontUnderline property.

In the example syntax, each click of the mouse button changes the FontUnderline property of the text box control Text1. Notice that the FontUnderline property affects all of the text entered on the text box.

### The FontBold, FontItalic, FontStrikethru, and FontTransparent Properties

Visual Basic provides four other special effects for controlling the appearance of text: FontBold, FontItalic, FontStrikethru, and FontTransparent. If more than one of these properties is changed from its default False setting, then the effects are combined.

## Example

The Font project at the end of this section demonstrates the FontUnderline property. Clicking the check box labeled Underline triggers the Font_Underline_Click event. This event changes the setting of the FontUnderline property of the Display_Text text box. Each time this event is processed, the text on the Display_Text text box is switched from underlined to normal and normal to underlined.

## Comments

The FontUnderline property places a line under all characters, including blank spaces, on the object.

# The Font Project

## Project Overview

The Font Project demonstrates the properties that affect the appearance of text in Visual Basic. This example will show the interaction of the properties affecting the text's appearance. By manipulating the different controls of this project, you will see all of the fonts available for your system. Exactly what you will see depends on what fonts you have installed in your system.

This project has two sections, corresponding to the two forms that comprise the Font project. The first section deals with the assembly of the controls and subroutines of the Font form. The next section explains the FontList form's subroutine. Each of these sections include step-by-step instructions on how to put the form and its controls together using Table 12.16, listing the different elements of code to enter. After both forms are explained, there is a guide to the operation of the project. Please read this information carefully and use the pictures of the forms as guides in the process of assembling this project.

## Assembling the Project

1. Make a new form (the Font form) with the objects and properties shown in Table 12.16.

| Object | Property | Setting |
|---|---|---|
| Form | BorderStyle | 1 - Fixed Single |
| | Caption | Font Project |
| | ControlBox | False |
| | FormName | Font_Project |
| | MaxButton | False |
| Text box | CtlName | Display_Text |
| | FontBold | False |
| | FontItalic | False |
| | FontStrikethru | False |
| | FontTransparent | False |
| | FontUnderline | False |

*Table 12.16 (continued)*

| Object | Property | Setting |
|---|---|---|
| Combo box | CtlName | Font_Name |
| | Sorted | True |
| Combo box | CtlName | Font_Size |
| Frame | Caption | Special Effects |
| | CtlName | Spl_Effects |
| Option box | Caption | Bold |
| | CtlName | Bold_Font |
| | Value | 0 - Unchecked |
| Option box | Caption | Italic |
| | CtlName | Italic_Font |
| | Value | 0 - Unchecked |
| Option box | Caption | Strikethru |
| | CtlName | Strikethru_Font |
| | Value | 0 - Unchecked |
| Option box | Caption | Underline |
| | CtlName | Underline_Font |
| | Value | 0 - Unchecked |
| Command button | Caption | Screen Fonts |
| | CtlName | Display_Fonts |
| Command button | Caption | Exit |
| | CtlName | Program_Exit |

**Table 12.16 Elements of the Font form**

2. Size the objects on the screen, as shown in Figures 12.11 and 12.12.

3. Enter the following code in the Bold_Font event subroutine. This code is triggered when the user clicks the check box labeled Bold. When there is an "x" in the check box, the text in the text box Display_Text is changed to bold. Otherwise, the text in the text box is normal.

```
Sub Bold_Font_Click ()
   Display_Text.FontBold = Abs(Display_Text.FontBold) - 1
End Sub
```

4. Enter the following code in the Display_Fonts_Click event subroutine. This code is activated when the user presses the Display_Fonts command button. After the user presses this button, the Font_Project form is hidden and the FontList is displayed. Notice that each time that the user presses the command button, the transparent property of the Font_List form is turned on or off.

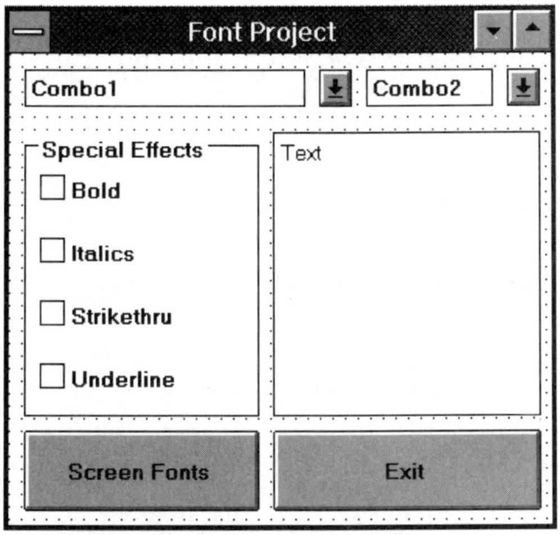

**Figure 12.11 What the Font form should look like when completed**

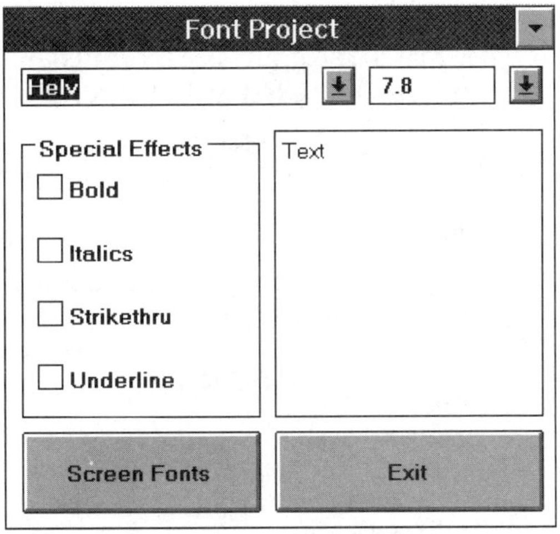

**Figure 12.12 What the Font form will look like when running**

```
Sub Display_Fonts_Click ()
    Font_Project.Hide
    Load FontList
    FontList.AutoRedraw = -1
    FontList.ForeColor = QBColor(0)
    FontList.BackColor = QBColor(15)
    FontList.Show
    FontList.FontSize = 10
    FontList.FontTransparent = (Abs(FontList.FontTransparent) - 1)
End Sub
```

5. Enter the following code in the Exit_Program_Click event subroutine. This code is processed when the command button Exit is pressed. At this point, the program is closed.

```
Sub Exit_Program_Click ()
    End
End Sub
```

6. Enter the following code in the Font_Name_Click event subroutine. This code is triggered when the user selects another choice in the combo list box Font_Name. The FontName property of the Display_Text text box is modified to match the font selected in the combo list box. This routine changes the font style of the text displayed in the Display_Text text box.

```
Sub Font_Name_Click ()
    Display_Text.FontName = Font_Name.Text
End Sub
```

7. Enter the following code in the Font_Size_Click event subroutine. This code is activated when the user changes the number displayed in the Font_Size

combo list box. The FontSize property of the Display_text text box changes to match the point size indicated in the combo list box. This routine changes the size of the letters in text displayed in the Display_Text text box.

```
Sub Font_Size_Click ()
   Display_Text.FontSize = Val(Font_Size.Text)
   Font_Size.Text = Str$(Display_Text.FontSize)
End Sub
```

8. Enter the following code in the Form_Load event subroutine. The Form_Load event is processed at program startup. This code places the names of all of the fonts available in the present system into the Font_Name combo list box. The Font_Size combo list box displays a list of the possible point sizes between 8 and 26.

```
Sub Form_Load ()
   For F% = 0 To (Printer.FontCount - 1)
      Font_Name.AddItem Printer.Fonts(F%)
   Next F%
   N% = 6
   For P% = 1 To 10
      N% = N% + 2
      Font_Size.AddItem Str$(N%)
   Next P%
   Font_Name.Text = Display_Text.FontName
   Font_Size.Text = Str$(Display_Text.FontSize)
End Sub
```

9. Enter the following code in the Italic_Font_Click event subroutine. This code is triggered when the user clicks the check box labeled Italic. When there is an "x" in the check box, the text in the text box Display_Text is changed to italics. Otherwise, the text in the text box is normal.

```
Sub Italic_Font_Click ()
   Display_Text.FontItalic = Abs(Display_Text.FontItalic) - 1
End Sub
```

10. Enter the following code in the Strikethru_Font_Click event subroutine. This code is triggered when the user clicks the check box labeled Strikethru. When there is an "x" in the check box, the text in the text box Display_Text has a line placed through it. Otherwise, the text in the text box is normal.

```
Sub Strikethru_Font_Click ()
   Display_Text.FontStrikethru = Abs(Display_Text.FontStrikethru) - 1
End Sub
```

11. Enter the following code in the Underline_Font_Click event subroutine. This code is triggered by the clicking of the check box labeled Underline. When there is an "x" in the check box, the text in the text box Display_Text is underlined. Otherwise, the text in the text box is normal.

```
Sub Underline_Font_Click ()
   Display_Text.FontUnderline = Abs(Display_Text.FontUnderline) - 1
End Sub
```

**The FontList Form**

1. Make a new form, with the objects and properties listed in Table 12.17.

| Object | Property | Setting |
|--------|----------|---------|
| Form | BorderStyle | 2 - Sizeable |
| | Caption | Font List |
| | ControlBox | False |
| | FormName | FontList |
| | MaxButton | True |
| | MinButton | True |

**Table 12.17 Elements of the FontList form**

2. Size the objects on the screen as shown in Figure 12.13, which also shows what the form will look like when running.

3. Enter the following code in the Form_Click event subroutine. When the user clicks the mouse button over the FontList form, the FontList form is hidden and the Font_Project form is displayed.

```
Sub Form_Click ()
   FontList.Hide
   Font_Project.Show
End Sub
```

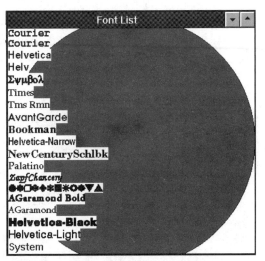

**Figure 12.13 What the FontList form should look like when running**

4. Enter the following code in the Form_GotFocus event subroutine. This code is triggered when the FontList form displays on the screen. This draws a circle on the form, along with all the names of the screen fonts.

```
Sub Form_GotFocus ()
   Screen.MousePointer = 11
   Cls
   X = ScaleWidth / 2
   Y = ScaleHeight / 2
   R = ScaleWidth / 2
   FillStyle = 0
   FillColor = QBColor(2)
   Circle (X, Y), R
   CurrentX = 0
   CurrentY = 0
   For I = 0 To (Abs(Screen.FontCount) - 1)
```

```
        FontName = Screen.Fonts(I)
        Print Screen.Fonts(I)
    Next I
    Screen.MousePointer = 0
End Sub
```

## How It Works

This program provides a form that allows the user to see how the different fonts of a system look. The text displayed in the Display_Text text box changes according to the settings of the Font_Name and Font_Size combo list boxes. Each of the check boxes, labeled Bold, Italics, Strikethru, and Underline, defines whether the text appears with these special effects. Pressing the command button labeled Screen Fonts produces a list of the available system screen fonts.

When the program loads, the Form_Load event uses the FontCount property to find how many fonts are available in the system. The FontCount property and Fonts property provide the values needed to place the names of the system's fonts in the Font_Name combo list box. Notice that the Sorted property changes the order in which the names appear in this combo box. This is necessary because the list returned by the multiple use of the Fonts property is not in alphabetical order.

The Fonts property provides the name of each of the fonts available in the current system. Each font of the system is identified with a value between 0 and the value provided by the FontCount property minus 1. The text string provided by each Font's property expression appears in the combo list box Font_Name. Notice that the Sorted property changes the order in which the font list appears. This is necessary because the list returned by the multiple use of the Fonts property is not in alphabetical order.

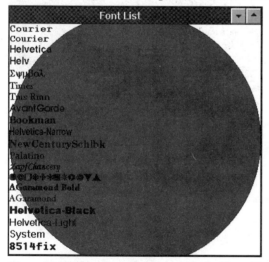

**Figure 12.14 What the FontList form looks like with FontTransparent set to True**

The FontSize property is the default setting of the Font_Size combo list box. This shows the point size of the text in the Display_Text text box. If this is not done, then the combo list box Font_Size would be initially blank. Notice that many of the values of the FontSize property are fractions.

### Running the Program

The settings of the check boxes marked Bold, Italic, Strikethru, and Underline reflect the appearance of the Display_Text text box. When a check box is checked, the format of the text in the Display_Text text box changes. These instructions are contained within the Click event subroutine of each check box.

Each time the user selects a new font or point size, the text in the text box is changed to this new setting. This shows the ways in which the point size and font interact with each other.

The Fonts, FontCount, and FontName properties are all accessed to display a list of fonts when the user presses the command button Screen Fonts. This list prints on the background of the FontList form, which is displayed by the Display_Font_Click event. Each font name appears in the format of the font it names. In some cases, this makes the font name unreadable. One good example of this is when the Zapf Dingbat font is displayed.

The Display_Font_Click event draws a circle on the FontList form, which interacts with the list of fonts. Each time the command button labeled Screen Fonts is pressed, the FontTransparent property is changed. When the FontTransparent property is changed to True, the circle surrounds the text of the font list (see Figure 12.14). If the FontTransparent property is False, then a bar around the text appears obscuring the circle where it appears (see Figure 12.13).

# Getting User Input with Text Boxes

**A**lmost every program you write will need some sort of mechanism for getting text input from the user. In other languages, this would usually mean you'd need to write a routine for accepting keyboard input, and then appending that input to a string variable. Of course, your routine would need to take into account any special editing keys, such as the right or left direction arrow, Home, or End keys. If you wanted to get really fancy, you might even write into the routine the ability to cut and paste text from other areas of the application. In Visual Basic, all this is taken care of with the text box control.

The text box control is a rectangle in which the user may enter or edit text. When a text box control receives the focus, an insertion point appears in the box. The insertion point is a slim flashing vertical line that indicates where new text will be entered within the box. This cursor can be moved by using the direction keys or the Home and End keys, or by clicking at the desired position in the text box with the mouse pointer.

The text box's primary property is the Text property. This property is a string value that contains any text that has been entered into the text box. The value of the Text property can be modified in one of three ways: user input, your program's code, or DDE messages. Any time the Text property is changed, the text box's Change event occurs (see Chapter 7, *Responding to Changes in Properties*).

## Editing in a Text Box

A Visual Basic text box gives the user full editing capabilties. It automatically inherits all the conventions of a standard Windows text box, including the ability to cut, copy, and paste to and from the Windows clipboard area. A user can select text for these functions by holding down the shift key and pressing the right or left direction arrows, or by clicking and dragging the mouse cursor over the desired text. This causes the selected text to become reverse highlighted. Once text has been selected, the user may perform several operations on it. Pressing the Delete key causes the selected text to be deleted from the text box. Pressing Shift+Delete will copy the selected text to the clipboard, and then delete it from the text box. This is commonly called "cutting" text. The user can also copy selected text to the clipboard without deleting it by pressing the Ctrl+Insert key combination. Pressing Shift+Insert will cause any text that is currently being stored on the clipboard to be "pasted" into the text box at the position specified by the text box's insertion point. These functions can also be controlled and emulated by your program by using the SelText, SelStart, and SelLength properties. For more information on how to interact with the Windows clipboard, please see Chapter 23, *Using the Windows Clipboard*.

### Multiline Text Boxes

By default, a text box consists of only one line of text. You may allow the user to enter more than one line of text by setting the MultiLine property. If you've set the MultiLine property to True, you may also wish to set the ScrollBars property. This allows you to place scroll bars on the left and bottom edges of the text box. This allows the user to quickly scroll through any text with the mouse.

### Text Boxes and Combo Boxes

The combo box control has two styles, drop-down combo and simple combo, which include an edit area that is very similar to the text box control. Because of this, these two styles of combo boxes share the SelLength, SelStart, SelText, and Text properties. Please refer to Chapter 18, *Using List and Combo Boxes,* for more information on these controls.

Table 13.1 lists the properties that relate to the text box control, and their uses.

| Use or Set This... | | To Do This... |
| --- | --- | --- |
| MultiLine | Property | Set up a text box to accept multiple-line input |
| SelLength | Property | Set or read the length of the currently selected text (if any) |
| SelStart | Property | Set or read the starting position of the currently selected text (if any) |
| SelText | Property | Replace or read the currently selected text string |
| ScrollBars | Property | Set up horizontal or vertical scroll bars (or both) for a text box |
| Text | Property | Set or read the text contained in a text box |

**Table 13.1 The properties that govern the appearance and behavior of a text box control**

Each of these properties is explained in detail in this chapter. At the end of the chapter, an example project demonstrates the usage of all of these elements combined.

# MultiLine Property

### Objects Affected

| | | | | |
| --- | --- | --- | --- | --- |
| Check | Clipboard | Combo | Command | Debug |
| Dir | Drive | File | Form | Frame |
| Label | List | Menu | Option | Picture |
| Printer | Screen | Scroll | ▶ Text | Timer |

### Purpose

The MultiLine property is used to set up a text box control for entry of multiple lines of text. Although this property can only be set at design time, your program can read its value at run time. Table 13.2 summarizes the arguments used with the MultiLine property.

## General Syntax

`[Form.]CtlName.MultiLine`

| Arguments | Description |
|-----------|-------------|
| Form | FormName of the parent form |
| CtlName | CtlName of the control |

Table 13.2 Arguments of the MultiLine property

## Example Syntax

`MultiLineStatus = Text1.MultiLine`

## Description

By default, this property is set to False (0), causing the associated text box to be a single-line text box. However, you may wish to set this property to True (-1) at design time to create a multiple-line text box. A multiple-line text box allows the user to enter more than one line in the text box.

If the ScrollBars property is set to 0 (none) or 2 (vertical only), a multiple-line text box will automatically wrap text over to the next line when it exceeds the width of the box. Otherwise, it is up to the user to create new lines. If there is no button on the same form with its Default property set to true, the user can create new lines by pressing the Enter key. If there is a default button on the form, the user must use the Ctrl+Enter key combination to create a new line.

The example syntax reads the value of the MultiLine property for the text box "Text1." It could be used in an If statement to determine whether to format multiline text.

## Example

In the TextBox project, the edit area of the mini-text editor is a multiple-line text box.

# ScrollBars Property

## Objects Affected

| | | | | |
|--------|-----------|--------|-----------|---------|
| Check | Clipboard | Combo | Command | Debug |
| Dir | Drive | File | Form | Frame |
| Label | List | Menu | Option | Picture |
| Printer | Screen | Scroll | ▶ Text | Timer |

## Purpose

The ScrollBars property is set at design time to determine what types of scroll bars, if any, will appear at the edges of a text box. Scroll bars allow the user to read or position text that is too wide (or has too many lines) to fit in the window. This property is read only at run time. The arguments for the ScrollBars property are summarized in Table 13.3

## General Syntax

```
[Form.]CtlName.ScrollBars
```

| Arguments | Description |
|-----------|-------------|
| Form | FormName of the parent form |
| CtlName | CtlName of the control |

Table 13.3 Arguments of the ScrollBars property

## Example Syntax

```
ScrollBarStatus = Text1.ScrollBars
```

## Description

The ScrollBars property is referenced using the name of a control. This property is only useful when the MultiLine property is set to True (-1). If used when MultiLine is False (0), this property has no effect.

Scroll bars are graphic objects that consist of a bar with arrows at each end and a button between the arrows. Scroll bars give the user the ability to quickly scroll through text with the mouse. There are two types of scroll bars: vertical and horizontal.

The scroll bar's button indicates the relative position of the insertion point within the text box's text. The user can move this button by clicking and dragging it, by clicking on the bar itself, or by clicking on one of the arrows at either end of the scroll bar. Moving the button on the scroll bar causes the text within the text box to be scrolled in proportion to the amount it is moved.

The example syntax stores the current value of the ScrollBars property of form Text1 in the variable ScrollBarStatus. It could be used in an If statement to test for the presence of scroll bars.

Table 13.4 lists the possible values for this property, and their effects.

| Value | Effect of Setting |
|-------|-------------------|
| 0 | The text box will have no scroll bars, and text will wrap automatically. This is the default setting |
| 1 | A horizontal scroll bar appears at the bottom edge of the text box, and no word wrapping will occur |
| 2 | A vertical scroll bar appears at the right edge of the text box, and text will wrap automatically |
| 3 | Vertical and horizontal scroll bars appear at the edges of the text box, and no word wrapping will occur |

Table 13.4 Possible settings for the ScrollBars property

If the ScrollBars property is set to 0 (none) or 2 (vertical only), a multiple-line text box will automatically wrap text over to the next line when it exceeds the width of the box.

Otherwise, it is up to the user to create new lines. If there is no button on the same form with its Default property set to True, the user can create new lines by hitting the Enter key. If there is a default button on the form, the user must use the Ctrl+Enter key combination to create a new line.

### Example

In the TextBox project, the ScrollBars property for the edit portion of the mini-text editor is set to 2 (vertical scroll bars) at design time.

# SelLength Property

### Objects Affected

| | | | | |
|---|---|---|---|---|
| Check | Clipboard | ▶ Combo | Command | Debug |
| Dir | Drive | File | Form | Frame |
| Label | List | Menu | Option | Picture |
| Printer | Screen | Scroll | ▶ Text | Timer |

### Purpose

The SelLength property sets or returns the number of selected characters within a text or combo box. Characters can be selected (reverse highlighted) by the user, usually for an editing operation. Your program can also select a portion of the text in the text box. This property can be set and read at run time only. Table 13.5 summarizes the arguments of the SelLength property.

### General Syntax

[Form.]CtlName.SelLength [= NumberOfChars&]

| Arguments | Description |
|---|---|
| Form | FormName of the parent form |
| CtlName | CtlName of the control |
| NumberOfChars | A long integer that can be assigned to the property to select text from within the program's code |

Table 13.5 Arguments of the SelLength property

### Example Syntax

SaveSelLength& = Text1.SelLength          'Save the length of the selected text

### Description

This property is used in conjunction with the SelStart and SelText properties for working with text that has been selected by the user in a text or combo box. A user can select text for these properties by holding down a Shift key and pressing the right or left direction arrows, or by clicking and dragging the mouse cursor over the desired text. This causes the selected text to become reverse highlighted. Your program can then read the settings of these properties in order to perform operations on the selected text. The SelStart property determines the starting point of the selected text within a text or combo box. The SelLength property determines the number of characters selected. SelText is a string property that contains the selected text.

The SelLength property is specified using the name of a control. The SelLength property is a long integer that is used to set or return the number of selected characters in the text. If no characters are selected, this property returns 0.

This property can also be set within a program's code. Doing so has no effect unless its text box has the focus when the property is set. If the text box does have the focus, assigning this property a value causes that number of characters to be selected in the text box, starting at the position indicated by the SelStart property. If the program assigns this property a value that indicates a number of characters that exceed the length of the text in the text box, only the existing characters are selected, and the SelLength property is adjusted to reflect this. Setting this property to a value less than 0 causes an "Invalid property value" error to occur during run time.

The example syntax saves the length of the current text selection to a variable for future use.

### Example

In the TextBox project, the SelLength and SelStart properties are saved in the Text1_KeyDown event. This is done to enable the Undo function of the mini-text editor.

### Comments

This property also applies to combo boxes whose Style property has been set to 0 (dropdown combo) or 1 (simple combo). When used on the combo box control, it behaves in the same manner as described above.

# SelStart Property

### Objects Affected

| | | | | |
|---|---|---|---|---|
| Check | Clipboard | ▶ Combo | Command | Debug |
| Dir | Drive | File | Form | Frame |
| Label | List | Menu | Option | Picture |
| Printer | Screen | Scroll | ▶ Text | Timer |

### Purpose

The SelStart property sets or returns the starting position of selected text within a text or combo box. Text may be selected by the user or the program, and appears in reverse highlighting in the text box. If there is no selected text, this property sets or returns the position of the box's insertion point. The arguments for the SelStart property are summarized in Table 13.6

## General Syntax

[Form.]CtlName.SelStart [= StartPos&]

| Arguments | Description |
| --- | --- |
| Form | FormName of the parent form |
| CtlName | CtlName of the control |
| StartPos& | An long integer that can be assigned to the property to set the position of the insertion point |

Table 13.6 Arguments of the SelStart property

## Example Syntax

SaveSelStart& = Text1.SelStart

## Description

This property is used in conjunction with the SelLength and SelText properties for working with text that has been selected in a text or combo box by the user. A user can select text for these properties by holding down a Shift key and pressing the right or left direction arrows, or by clicking and dragging the mouse cursor over the desired text. This causes the selected text to become reverse highlighted (see Figure 13.1). Your program can then read the settings of these properties in order to perform operations on the selected text. The SelStart property determines the starting point of the selected text within a Text or Combo box. SelLength determines the number of characters selected. SelText is a string property that contains the selected text.

The SelStart property is invoked using the name of a control. The SelStart property is a long integer value that indicates the starting position of the selected characters in a text or combo box. The value of SelStart is

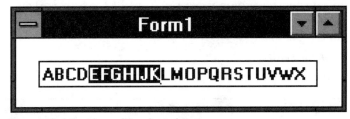

Figure 13.1 Text box with selected text

zero-based. This means the first selected character is the position after the value of SelStart. For instance, if the value of SelStart is 1, and the value of SelLength is 2, the second and third characters in the text are selected. If there is no text currently selected, SelStart will return the position of the text box's insertion point.

You may set the SelStart property by assigning a long integer value to it. This value must be a non-negative number, or an "Invalid property value" error will occur during run time. If this value is greater than the length of the text in the text or combo box, SelStart is set to a value equal to the length of the text. Assigning a value to the SelStart property automatically sets the SelLength property to 0, and moves the insertion point in the text box to the specified position.

The example syntax saves the starting position of the selected text in a variable for future use.

## Example

In the TextBox project, the SelLength and SelStart properties are saved in the Text1_KeyDown event. This is done to enable the Undo function of the mini-text editor.

## Comments

This property also applies to combo boxes whose Style property has been set to 0 (drop-down combo) or 1 (simple combo). When used on the combo box control, it behaves in the same manner as described above.

# SelText Property

## Objects Affected

| | | | | |
|---|---|---|---|---|
| Check | Clipboard | ▶ Combo | Command | Debug |
| Dir | Drive | File | Form | Frame |
| Label | List | Menu | Option | Picture |
| Printer | Screen | Scroll | ▶ Text | Timer |

## Purpose

The SelText property replaces or returns the currently selected text within a text or combo box. Users can select text (typically by dragging with the mouse), or text may be selected by program action. Table 13.7 summarizes the arguments of the SelText property.

## General Syntax

`[Form.]CtlName.SelText [= NewText$]`

| Arguments | Description |
|---|---|
| Form | FormName of the parent form |
| CtlName | CtlName of the control |
| NewText$ | A string that can be placed at the text box's insertion point. NewText$ replaces any selected text |

Table 13.7 Arguments of the SelText property

## Example Syntax

```
Clipboard.SetText Text1.SelText      'Send the selected text to the clipboard
Text1.SelText = ""                   'Delete the selected text (set it to null)
```

## Description

This property is used in conjunction with the SelLength and SelStart properties for working with text that has been selected in a text or combo box by the user. A user can select text for these properties by holding down a Shift key and pressing the right or left direction arrows, or by clicking and dragging the mouse cursor over the desired text. This causes the selected text to become reverse highlighted. Your program can then read the settings of these properties in order to perform operations on the selected text. The SelStart property determines the starting point of the selected text within a Text or Combo box. SelLength determines the number of characters selected. SelText is a string property that contains the selected text.

The SelText property is specified beginning with the name of the control. You can optionally assign a string of text to replace the selection or to be inserted at the current insertion point. The SelText property returns a string copy of the selected characters from the text box or combo box. This string can be used by your programs to cut and paste to the Windows clipboard. If no characters are currently selected, this property will return a null string.

Assigning a string value to this property can cause one of two things to happen. If there is any text selected when the assignment is done, the selected text in the text box, or combo box is replaced by the assigned text. If no text is selected, the new text is inserted into the text or combo box's text at the the box's insertion point.

Figure 13.1 displayed a text box with some selected text. In this example, the value of the SelStart property would be 4, SelLength would be 7, and SelText would be "EFGHIJK."

The example syntax copies the selected text to the clipboard by assigning the value of the SelText property of the text box to the SetText method of the clipboard. The SelText property is then assigned an empty (null) string, deleting the selected text.

## Comments

This property also applies to combo boxes whose Style property has been set to 0 (drop-down combo) or 1 (simple combo). When used on the combo box control, it behaves in the same manner as described above.

# Text Property

## Objects Affected

| | | | | |
|---|---|---|---|---|
| Check | Clipboard | ▶ Combo | Command | Debug |
| Dir | Drive | File | Form | Frame |
| Label | ▶ List | Menu | Option | Picture |
| Printer | Screen | Scroll | ▶ Text | Timer |

## Purpose

The Text property is used to read the text contained in a text box or the selected item in a list or combo box. When used with a text box or control, this property can also be set at design or run time. This is also true when the Text property is used with a combo box whose Style property is set to 0 (drop-down combo), or 1 (simple combo). Table 13.8 summarizes the arguments of the Text property.

## General Syntax

`[Form.]CtlName.Text [= TextString$]`

| Arguments | Description |
|---|---|
| Form | FormName of the parent form |
| CtlName | CtlName of the control |
| TextString$ | A string that can be assigned to this property, and thereby replaces all text in the text box |

Table 13.8 Arguments of the Text property

## Example Syntax

```
Text1.Text = TxtBeforeChange$        'Assigns a string to the text box Text1
SelectedItem$ = List1.Text           'Assigns the value of a list box's selected
                                     'item to a string
```

## Description

The Text property is a string that allows your program to access the contents of the edit area of a text box or combo box. It also can represent a chosen item in a list box. Specify the name of the control involved. You can optionally assign a string as the value for this property.

The Text property also allows you to access and manipulate the text inside a text box. This property is a string representation of the contents of the box, and can be manipulated by any of Visual Basic's string functions and statements such as Left$, Mid$, and Right$. Any operations performed on this property are reflected by the text inside a text box.

You may assign a string to the Text property. This causes the text in the box to be replaced by the assigned string. The user can also directly edit the text represented by the Text property. Any time a box's Text property is modified, it causes the box's Change event to occur.

This property can theoretically contain a string up to 65,535 characters in length. However, assigning large numbers of characters to this property greatly degrades the performance of the box. In other words, the longer the value of the Text property, the slower the text box will react to user input.

The first example syntax assigns a string to the Text property of text box Text1. This text will now appear in the box. The second example syntax assigns the text in list box List1 to a string for future use.

## Example

In the TextBox project, a multiline text box is used to edit text. The Text property of this box is manipulated in several procedures. The length of the Text property is determined in the Change event for the text box, so the number of characters typed can be displayed. In the FileNew_Click event, the Text property is set to a null string. In the Text1_KeyDown event, the value of the Text property is saved in a string variable so that it can be restored by the user. When the Undo option is chosen from the Edit menu, the EditUndo_Click event occurs. This event assigns the value of the previously saved string variable to the Text property, thereby restoring its original state.

### Combo and List Boxes

The Text property is also used with the combo and list box controls. When used on the drop-down (Style = 0) and simple (Style = 1) combo box styles, this property works in the same manner as described above. When used with the list box control or a drop-down list (combo box with Style set to 2), the Text property is read-only, and returns the string value of the selected item in the list. Please refer to Chapter 18, *Using List and Combo Boxes,* for more information on these controls.

# Textbox Project

## Project Overview

The TextBox project, outlined in the following pages, demonstrates the concepts behind the text box control. This project uses each of the properties covered in this chapter, and demonstrates how they work together. By following the examples in this project, you should be able to get a firm grasp on the concepts behind dealing with text boxes.

This project makes use of the KeyDown event, which occurs when the user presses any key on the keyboard. More information on the KeyDown event can be found in Chapter 16, *Handling Keyboard Input.*

There are also some methods used with the Clipboard object in this project. These methods send or receive text from the clipboard area of Windows. Please refer to Chapter 23, *Using the Windows Clipboard,* for more on this subject.

## Assembling the Project

1. Create a new form (the TextBox form) and place on it the following controls. Use Table 13.9 to set the properties of the form and each control.

| Object | Property | Setting |
|--------|----------|---------|
| Form | FormName | TextBox |
| | Caption | Text Box Project |
| | ScaleHeight | 4500 |
| | ScaleWidth | 7365 |
| | Left | 1035 |
| | Top | 1140 |
| Label | CtlName | Number_Of_Characters |
| | Caption | " 0 Characters" |
| | Height | 255 |
| | Left | 0 |
| | Top | 4260 |
| | Width | 7365 |
| Text box | CtlName | Text1 |
| | Text | "" (Null) |
| | Height | 4250 |
| | Left | 0 |
| | Mulitline | True (-1) |
| | ScrollBars | 2 - Vertical |
| | Top | 0 |
| | Width | 7365 |

**Table 13.9 Elements of the TextBox form**

2. Using the Menu Design window, create a menu with the settings in Table 13.10 (choose the Menu Design window option from Visual Basic's Window menu).

| Caption | CtlName | Indent |
|---------|---------|--------|
| &File | FileMenu | No |
| &New | FileNew | Once |
| - | FileNothing | Once |
| E&xit | FileExit | Once |
| &Edit | EditMenu | No |
| &Undo | EditUndo | Once |
| - | EditNothing | Once |
| Cu&t | EditCut | Once |
| &Copy | EditCopy | Once |
| &Paste | EditPaste | Once |
| &Delete | EditDelete | Once |

**Table 13.10 Menu settings for the TextBox project**

3. Check the appearance of your form with Figure 13.2.

4. Enter the following code into the general declarations area of the form. This code sets up constants for true and false values. Also, three variables are created for later use in the program. If the user changes the text in the box, these variables will save the contents of the text box just prior to the changes. This information can then be used to later restore the text box to its value before the changes were made.

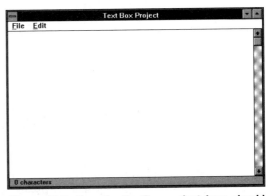

**Figure 13.2  How the TextBox project form should look**

```
Const True = -1
Const False = 0
Dim TxtBeforeChange As String
Dim PosBeforeChange As Integer
Dim LenBeforeChange As Integer
```

5. Enter the following code into the Form_Resize event. This event occurs when the user changes the size of the form. Its purpose is to adjust the size of the edit area to match the size of the form.

```
Sub Form_Resize ()
    Text1.Height = Form1.ScaleHeight - 250
    Text1.Width = Form1.ScaleWidth
    Number_Of_Characters.Top = Text1.Height
    Number_Of_Characters.Height = 250
    Number_Of_Characters.Width = Form1.ScaleWidth
End Sub
```

6. Enter the following code into the Text1_Change event. This event determines the number of characters in the text box, and displays that information by assigning a string to the Caption property of the label control named Number_Of_Characters.

```
Sub Text1_Change ()
    Dim Temp As String

    Temp = Format$(Len(Text1.Text), " ##,###,##0")
    Temp = Temp + " Character"
    If Len(Text1.Text) <> 1 Then Temp = Temp + "s"
    Number_Of_Characters.Caption = Temp
End Sub
```

7. Enter the following code into the FileNew_Click event. This event is used to clear the text box for new text input.

```
Sub FileNew_Click ()
    Text1.Text = ""
End Sub
```

8. Enter the following code into the FileExit_Click event. This event ends the program by unloading the main form from memory, and executing the End statement.

```
Sub FileExit_Click ()
   Unload Form1
   End
End Sub
```

9. Enter the following code into the Edit_Click event. This event occurs when the user clicks the Edit menu. The code in this event is executed just prior to opening the menu. As its first task, it disables all of the Edit menu options. It then checks the status of several items; based on what it finds, it may enable the related Edit menu option. The first item it checks is the string variable TxtBeforeChange. If this string is not null, the Undo option is enabled. The SelLength property is then checked to see if the user has selected any text in the text box. If so, the Cut, Copy, and Delete menu options are enabled. Finally, it checks to see if there is any text stored in the Windows clipboard area, and enables the Paste option if there is.

```
Sub Edit_Click ()
   EditUndo.Enabled = False
   EditCut.Enabled = False
   EditCopy.Enabled = False
   EditPaste.Enabled = False
   EditDelete.Enabled = False
   If Len(TxtBeforeChange) > 0 Then EditUndo.Enabled = True
   If Text1.SelLength > 0 Then
       EditCut.Enabled = True
       EditCopy.Enabled = True
       EditDelete.Enabled = True
   End If
   If Clipboard.GetFormat(1) Then EditPaste.Enabled = True
End Sub
```

10. Enter the following code into the EditUndo_Click event. This event occurs when the user chooses the Undo option from the Edit menu. This can only be done if the option has been enabled in the Edit_Click event. This event sets the Text, SelStart and SelLength properties to values that have been previously saved in the Text1_KeyDown event. This has the effect of undoing the last change that was made to the text in the text box.

```
Sub EditUndo_Click ()
   Text1.Text = TxtBeforeChange
   Text1.SelStart = PosBeforeChange
   Text1.SelLength = LenBeforeChange
End Sub
```

11. Enter the following code into the EditCut_Click event. This event occurs when the user chooses the Cut option from the Edit menu. This can only be done if the option has been enabled in the Edit_Click event. The pur-

pose of this event is to copy the selected text to the Windows clipboard area, and then delete the selected text. This is done by using the SelText property as the argument to the Clipboard.SetText method (for more on the SetText method, please refer to Chapter 23, *Using the Windows Clipboard*), and then assigning a null string to the SelText property.

```
Sub EditCut_Click ()
  Clipboard.SetText Text1.SelText
  Text1.SelText = ""
End Sub
```

12. Enter the following code into the EditCopy_Click event. This event occurs when the user chooses the Copy option from the Edit menu, which can only be done if the option has been enabled in the Edit_Click event. The purpose of this event is to copy the selected text to the Windows clipboard area. This is done by assigning the SelText property as the argument to the Clipboard.SetText method (for more on the SetText method, please refer to Chapter 23, *Using the Windows Clipboard*).

```
Sub EditCopy_Click ()
  Clipboard.SetText Text1.SelText
End Sub
```

13. Enter the following code into the EditPaste_Click event. This event occurs when the user chooses the Paste option from the Edit menu, which can only be done if the option has been enabled in the Edit_Click event. The purpose of this event is to copy text from the Windows clipboard area into the text box. This is done by assigning the text returned by the clipboard.GetText method (for more on the GetText method, please refer to Chapter 23, *Using the Windows Clipboard*) to the SelText property. The text is inserted into the text box at the position of the box's insertion point. Any selected text in the text box is replaced by the text that is copied from the clipboard.

```
Sub EditPaste_Click ()
  Text1.SelText = Clipboard.GetText(1)
End Sub
```

14. Enter the following code into the EditDelete_Click event. This event occurs when the user chooses the Delete option from the Edit menu, which can only be done if the option has been enabled in the Edit_Click event. The purpose of this event is to delete the text that is currently selected. This is done by assigning a null string to the SelText property.

```
Sub EditDelete_Click ()
  Text1.SelText = ""
End Sub
```

15. Enter the following code into the Text1_KeyDown event. This event is used to save the current settings of the text box before changes are made. The values of the Text, SelStart, and SelLength properties are assigned to

the variables that were defined in the General Declarations area of the form. The Shift argument is tested to determine whether the user has pressed the Ctrl or Alt keys. The properties are only saved if the Shift argument indicates these have not been pressed. More information can be found on the KeyDown event in Chapter 16, *Handling Keyboard Input*.

```
Sub Text1_KeyDown (KeyCode As Integer, Shift As Integer)
  If Shift < 2 Then
      TxtBeforeChange = Text1.Text
      PosBeforeChange = Text1.SelStart
      LenBeforeChange = Text1.SelLength
  End If
End Sub
```

## How It Works

The program created by this project is a simple text editor. It has four main controls: Text1 (a text box), Number_Of_Characters (a label), File (a menu control), and Edit (another menu control).

The Text1 control is the text entry area of the form. This control is a multiple-line (MultiLine = True) text box with a vertical scroll bar (ScrollBars = 2) on the right edge of the text area. The user can edit text in this control. Portions of text may be selected with a Shift+direction key, or by dragging the mouse cursor over the text. The selected text may be cut (Shift+Delete), or copied (Ctrl+Insert) to the clipboard, or may be deleted (Delete), or may be replaced by text from the clipboard (Shift+Insert).

Choosing the New option from the File menu causes the text edit area of the window to be cleared. Choosing Exit causes the program to end.

The Edit menu provides the editor with an Undo option. The Undo option restores the text in the text box to the state it was in before the last time it was changed. For instance, if the user selects and deletes some text, the Undo option can be used to restore the text to its value before the delete was performed.

The rest of the Edit options provide alternate methods for working with the Clipboard. The Cut, Copy, and Delete options are all disabled unless the user has selected some text in the text box. The Cut and Delete options both remove the selected text from the text box. However, Cut copies the selected text to the clipboard before removing it. The Copy option copies any selected text to the clipboard.

The Paste option on the Edit menu copies any text that resides on the Clipboard object into the text box. This option is only enabled if the clipboard contains text.

# PART FIVE
# MOUSING, DRAGGING, AND KEY PROCESSING

# Responding to Mouse Events

The mouse device is an integral part of the Windows environment. Depending on the application, it allows the user to easily select items (such as buttons or menu options), to move objects (such as icons or the insertion point), to edit text, and to perform drawing functions.

The mouse can perform three basic tasks. First, moving the mouse changes the position of the mouse pointer on the screen. Second, a button on the mouse can be pressed. And finally, a pressed button on the mouse can be released.

Visual Basic provides five events to handle these three tasks; Click, DblClick, MouseDown, MouseMove, and MouseUp. The Click event is generated when the left button on the mouse has been pressed and then released. The DblClick event occurs when the left button on the mouse has been pressed and then released twice in quick succession. The MouseDown event occurs when any button on the mouse (left, center, or right) is pressed. The MouseMove event is generated when the mouse is moved. Finally, the MouseUp event occurs when any button on the mouse is released.

Table 14.1 details the five mouse-related events and their purposes.

| Use This... | | To Do This... |
| --- | --- | --- |
| Click | Event | React to the user clicking the left mouse button |
| DblClick | Event | React to the user clicking the left mouse button twice |
| MouseDown | Event | React to the user pressing any mouse button |
| MouseMove | Event | React to any mouse movement |
| MouseUp | Event | React to the user releasing any mouse button |

Table 14.1 Events dealing with mouse operations

Each of these events is explained in detail within this chapter. At the end of this chapter, the Mouse project demonstrates the use of all these events combined.

## The Mouse and CONSTANT.TXT

Some of the examples below use constant declarations that are included in the CONSTANT.TXT file that came with the Visual Basic compiler. These are given in the following listing:

```
Global Const SHIFT_MASK = 1
Global Const CTRL_MASK = 2
Global Const ALT_MASK = 4
Global Const LEFT_BUTTON = 1
Global Const RIGHT_BUTTON = 2
Global Const MIDDLE_BUTTON = 4
```

In order to use the CONSTANT.TXT file, it must be loaded into the project's global module. To do this, open Visual Basic's Project window, and double-click on the global module. This will load the global module into the Code window. Then open Visual Basic's Code menu and choose the Load Text option. This brings up a dialog box. Select the CONSTANT.TXT file and click on the Merge button. This will read the file into the global module.

# Click Event

## Objects Affected

| | | | | |
|---|---|---|---|---|
| ▶ Check | Clipboard | ▶ Combo | ▶ Command | Debug |
| ▶ Dir | Drive | ▶ File | ▶ Form | Frame |
| ▶ Label | ▶ List | ▶ Menu | ▶ Option | ▶ Picture |
| Printer | Screen | Scroll | Text | Timer |

## Purpose

The Click event is called when the user presses and releases the left button on the mouse. A user will usually click on a command button to activate whatever function is associated with the button. Clicking on a form, or any of the other types of controls, generally means the user is selecting that control or form. For instance, the Click event associated with a Menu control is generated when a user selects that menu item by clicking on it. The arguments used in defining a Click event are summarized in Table 14.2.

## General Syntax

```
Sub Form_Click()
Sub CtlName_Click([Index As Integer])
```

| Arguments | Description |
|---|---|
| Form | FormName of the parent form |
| CtlName | CtlName of the control |
| Index | Uniquely identifies an element of a control array |

**Table 14.2 Arguments of the Click event**

## Example Syntax

```
Sub Form_Click()
    Label1.Caption = "The form has been clicked" 'Sets Label1's caption when the user
                                                 'clicks on the form

End Sub

Sub Label2_Click(Index As Integer)
    Dim Message As String

    Message = "This is index number "           'Set up a message string indicating
                                                 'the index number of the
    Message = Message + Format$(Index, "###")    'element of the label control array on
                                                 'which the user clicked
    Message = Message + " of the Label2 control array."
    Label2(Index).Caption = Message
End Sub
```

## Description

The Click event is defined in a Sub procedure starting with the name of the control or parent form, followed by an underscore and Click(). If the referenced control is part of a control array, the word Click is followed by an index variable within parentheses, as in the second syntax example.

The Click event is generated when a user places the mouse pointer over a form or an enabled control, and then presses and releases the left mouse button once. If a control's Enabled property is set to False (0), the Click event is passed to its parent form. Depending on the control, the Click event can also be generated by certain keyboard actions, or by changing the setting of the control's Value property. Table 14.3 lists the actions that may activate a Click event.

| With This Object... | These Actions Will Activate a Click Event... |
|---|---|
| All eligible controls | Placing the mouse pointer on the form or control and clicking the left mouse button |
| check box | Pressing the space bar when the check box has the focus |
| | Changing the setting of the check box's Value property |
| Command Button | Pressing the Enter key when the button's Default property is True (-1) and no other button has the focus |
| | Pressing the Escape key when the button has its Cancel property set to True (-1) |
| | Pressing the space bar or Enter key when the button has the focus |
| | Setting the button's Value property to true |
| Combo Box, Directory List Box, File List Box, and List Box | Pressing an up or down cursor key on the keyboard when the list box has the focus |
| Form | Placing the mouse pointer on any disabled control on the form and clicking the left mouse button |
| Option Button | Giving the focus to an option button whose Value property was previously false |
| | Setting the button's Value property to true |

**Table 14.3 Actions that activate the Click event**

The first syntax example simply puts a message in the form's caption when the mouse is clicked on the form. The second example references an array of label controls. The Click event's code inserts the index number of the label that was clicked into the message displayed.

### Event Order

With certain objects, clicking the mouse button causes more than one event to occur. On forms, file list boxes, labels, list boxes, and picture boxes, the following events in this order are activated every time the left mouse button is clicked once: MouseDown, MouseUp, Click. For all other eligible controls, only the Click event is activated. See the entry on DblClick for more information on the event order when the left mouse button is clicked more than once.

### Control Arrays

The Index argument is only used if the related control is part of a control array. This Index specifies which element of the array is the one that activated the event. When referencing the control, the element being referenced must be specified by placing the index number between parentheses just after the control name, and before the property name (that is, CtlName(Index).Property).

## Example

In the Mouse project, there are two command buttons (ClearButton, and ExitButton) that use the Click event. The ClearButton_Click event will clear the canvas when the user clicks on the Clear button. The ExitButton_Click event simply ends the program when the user clicks on the Exit button.

The ColorPalette control array is an array of picture controls that activates the ColorPalette_Click event when the user clicks on any of the elements in the control array. This event changes the foreground color of the canvas.

## Comments

By default, the left mouse button is the one associated with this event. However, Windows lets the user swap the functions of the left and right mouse buttons via the Mouse settings in the Control Panel program. If this has been done, this event will respond to the right mouse button.

# DblClick Event

## Objects Affected

| | | | | |
|---|---|---|---|---|
| Check | Clipboard | ▶ Combo | Command | Debug |
| Dir | Drive | ▶ File | ▶ Form | Frame |
| ▶ Label | ▶ List | Menu | ▶ Option | ▶ Picture |
| Printer | Screen | Scroll | Text | Timer |

## Purpose

The DblClick event responds to the user pressing the left mouse button twice in quick succession, which is known as a "double-click." A user will usually double-click on a form or control in order to initiate a default action. Depending on the design of the application, a double-click on a form or control could be an alternative to clicking on an OK button or pressing Enter to execute the default action. The arguments used in defining a DblClick event are summarized in Table 14.4.

## General Syntax

```
Sub Form_DblClick()
Sub CtlName_DblClick([Index As Integer])
```

| Arguments | Description |
|-----------|-------------|
| Form | FormName of the parent form |
| CtlName | CtlName of the control |
| Index | Uniquely identifies an element of a control array |

**Table 14.4 Arguments of the DblClick event**

## Example Syntax

```
Sub Form_DblClick()                    'When the mouse button is pressed twice on the
                                       'form
    ChangeColors                       'Calls a routine to change the form's colors
End Sub

Sub List1_DblClick(Index As Integer)   'Automatically clicks OK button when a list item
    Call OK_Button_Click               'is double-clicked on
End Sub
```

## Description

The DblClick event is defined in a Sub procedure named starting with the name of the control or parent form, followed by an underscore and DblClick(). If the referenced control is part of a control array, the word DblClick is followed by an index variable within parentheses, as in the second syntax example.

The DblClick event occurs when the user presses and releases the left mouse button twice in quick succession. The period of time in which two clicks must occur in order to be considered a double-click is defined in the mouse settings area of the Window's Control Panel. If the mouse is clicked twice, but not in the time defined by the Control Panel, two separate Click events occur.

This event is also activated if the FileName property of a File List Box is changed to a name that is the same as an existing DOS file.

When used with a combo box, this event is only called if the Style property is set to 1 (simple combo), and the double-click occurs when the mouse pointer is over one of the list items.

The first syntax example calls a routine to change the color of the form when the user double-clicks on it (this could be used to highlight the fact that the user has selected the form). The second example syntax calls the Click event for the OK button whenever any list box in the control array is double-clicked. This allows double-clicking to be an alternative way for the user to provide the confirmation represented by the OK button.

### Event Order

With certain objects, clicking the mouse button causes more than one event to occur. On forms, file list boxes, labels, list boxes, and picture boxes, the following events in this order are activated every time the left mouse button is double-clicked: MouseDown, MouseUp, Click, DblClick, MouseUp. For all other eligible controls, the event order is Click, DblClick.

### Control Array

The Index argument is only used if the related control is part of a control array. This Index specifies which element of the array is the one that activated the event. When referencing the control, the element being referenced must be specified by placing the index number between parentheses just after the control name, and before the property name (for example, CtlName(Index).Property).

## Example

In the Mouse project, the ColorPalette control array responds to a double-click by activating the ColorPalette_DblClick event. This event sets the background color of the canvas.

## Comments

By default, the left mouse button is the one associated with this event. However, Windows lets the user swap the functions of the left and right mouse buttons via the Mouse settings in the Control Panel program. If this has been done, this event will respond to the right mouse button.

Although indicated otherwise by the Microsoft Visual Basic Language reference, there is no DblClick event associated with the directory list box control. However, double-clicking on a path in the directory list box does cause the Path property of the box to change to the selected path.

# MouseDown Event

## Objects Affected

| | | | | |
|---|---|---|---|---|
| Check | Clipboard | Combo | Command | Debug |
| ▶ Dir | Drive | ▶ File | ▶ Form | Frame |
| ▶ Label | ▶ List | Menu | Option | ▶ Picture |
| Printer | Screen | Scroll | Text | Timer |

## Purpose

The MouseDown event occurs when any button—left, center, or right—on the mouse is pressed. Depending on circumstances, the press of a mouse button may indicate selection of an item, pressing a button control, or beginning a drag. (Dragging triggers its own event, as discussed in Chapter 15, *Managing the Dragging Event*). Unlike the Click event, the MouseDown event can be used to determine not only that a mouse button has been pushed, but *which* button was pushed. You can also determine whether the Shift, Ctrl, or Alt key was being held down when the mouse button was clicked. This can allow for a variety of different kinds of interaction with your application. Table 14.5 summarizes the arguments of the MouseDown event.

## General Syntax

```
Sub Form_MouseDown(Button As Integer, Shift As Integer, X As Single, Y As Single)
Sub CtlName_MouseDown([Index As Integer, ]Button As Integer, Shift As Integer, X As ⇐
                Single, Y As Single)
```

| Arguments | Description |
|---|---|
| Form | FormName of the parent form |
| CtlName | CtlName of the control |
| Index | Uniquely identifies an element of a control array |
| Button | Integer variable returning number of button pressed |
| Shift | Integer variable returning status of Shift, Alt, and Ctrl keys at time of button press |
| X, Y | Single-precision variables returning coordinates of mouse pointer location when button was pushed |

Table 14.5 Arguments of the MouseDown event

## Example Syntax

```
Sub Form_MouseDown(Button As Integer, Shift As Integer, X As Single, Y As Single)
    If Button = 1 Then          'If the left button is pressed
        StartX = X              'Save the current co-ordinates of the mouse pointer
        StartY = Y              'on the form
    End If
End Sub

Sub Picture_MouseDown(Index As Integer, Button As Integer, Shift As Integer, X As ⇐
                Single, Y As Single)
    If Button = 1 Then          'If the left button is pressed
        StartX(Index) = X       'Save the current co-ordinates of the mouse pointer
        StartY(Index) = Y       'on the picture control
    End If
End Sub
```

## Description

The MouseDown event is defined in a Sub procedure named using the control name (or name of the parent form) and variables representing the button number, shift status, and X and Y mouse position coordinates. An index variable precedes the other variables if the Sub procedure is written to handle a control array.

The MouseDown event is initiated when the user presses down on any of the three buttons on the mouse. It supplies four arguments, which indicate the status of the mouse at the time the event is called.

The Button argument is an integer variable that indicates which button has been pressed. Its value is set to 1 for the left button, 2 for the right button, and 4 for the center button. For this event, the Button argument will indicate the status of only one button at a time.

The Shift argument is an integer variable that indicates the status of the Shift, Alt, and Ctrl keys at the time the event was called. Each shift key is assigned a value: 1 for Shift, 2 for Ctrl, and 4 for Alt. When any of these keys is pressed, its value is added to the Shift argument. The easiest way to test the Shift argument is with logical (bitwise) operators. Table 14.6 lists logical equations that return a non-0 value if a certain shift key is pressed.

| When the... | This Will Return Non-0 | Or, if CONSTANT.TXT is Loaded Into the Global Module |
|---|---|---|
| Shift key is pressed | (Shift And 1) | (Shift And SHIFT_MASK) |
| Ctrl key is pressed | (Shift And 2) | (Shift And CTRL_MASK) |
| Alt key is pressed | (Shift And 4) | (Shift And ALT_MASK) |

Table 14.6 Logical equations for testing the status of the shift parameter

The X and Y arguments are single-precision variables that correspond to the mouse pointer's position within the related form or control at the time the event was called. X is the horizontal coordinate, and Y is the vertical coordinate. These arguments are expressed in the measurements defined for the form or control with the ScaleMode, ScaleHeight, ScaleWidth, and other Scale properties. See Chapter 5, *Designing with the Coordinate System,* for more info about these properties.

Once a mouse button is pressed while the mouse pointer is over a form or control, that form or control "owns" all the successive mouse events until a MouseUp event is processed, even if the mouse pointer leaves the area of the form or object. This could cause some mouse events to receive X and Y arguments that are not on the form or control.

The first example syntax saves the current mouse pointer coordinates when the left button (button 1) is pressed. The second example syntax uses an array of picture boxes. When the left mouse button is clicked on a picture, the current X and Y pointer coordinates are saved in the corresponding elements of the StartX and StartY arrays.

### Control Array

The Index argument is only used if the related control is part of a control array. This Index specifies which element of the array is the one that activated the event. When referencing the control, the element being referenced must be specified by placing the index number between parentheses just after the control name, and before the property name (that is, CtlName(Index).Property).

## Example

In the Mouse project, the Canvas picture control initiates the Canvas_MouseDown event when the mouse pointer is over it and any button on the mouse is pressed. This event turns on the DrawOn flag, which tells the Canvas_MouseMove event to start drawing. It also saves the current coordinates of the mouse pointer for future reference.

## Comments

If the program is halted while inside this event, a corresponding MouseUp event may not be called when the mouse button is released. This can happen if a Stop statement is executed or a breakpoint is set inside this event.

# MouseMove Event

## Objects Affected

| | | | | |
|---|---|---|---|---|
| Check | Clipboard | Combo | Command | Debug |
| ▶ Dir | Drive | ▶ File | ▶ Form | Frame |
| ▶ Label | ▶ List | Menu | Option | ▶ Picture |
| Printer | Screen | Scroll | Text | Timer |

## Purpose

The MouseMove event defines the actions to be taken when the user moves the mouse pointer. You can find out where the mouse pointer was when it was moved, what button (if any) was down, and whether the Shift, Ctrl, or Alt key was being held down. The arguments and variables of the MouseMove event are summarized in Table 14.7.

## General Syntax

```
Sub Form_MouseMove(Button As Integer, Shift As Integer, X As Single, Y As Single)
Sub CtlName_MouseMove([Index As Integer, ]Button As Integer, Shift As Integer, X As ⇐
          Single, Y As Single)
```

| Arguments | Description |
|---|---|
| Form | FormName of the parent form |
| CtlName | CtlName of the control |
| Index | Uniquely identifies an element of a control array |
| Button | Integer variable returning number of button pressed during move |
| Shift | Integer variable returning status of Shift, Ctl, or Alt keys during move |
| X, Y | Single-precision variables returning X, Y coordinates of mouse pointer position at start of move |

Table 14.7 Arguments of the MouseMove event

## Example Syntax

```
Sub Form_MouseMove(Button As Integer, Shift As Integer, X As Single, Y As Single)
    If Shift And SHIFT_MASK Then
        Line (LastX, LastY) - (X, Y)
    End If
End Sub

Sub Picture1_MouseMove(Index As Integer, Button As Integer, Shift As Integer, X As ⇐
                 Single, Y As Single)
    If Shift And SHIFT_MASK Then
        Picture1(Index).Line (LastX, LastY) - (X, Y)
    End If
End Sub
```

## Description

The MouseMove event is defined in a Sub procedure named using the control name (or name of the parent form) and variables representing the button number, shift status, and X and Y mouse position coordinates. An index variable precedes the other variables if the Sub procedure is written to handle a control array.

This event is initiated when the user moves the mouse pointer. It supplies four arguments, which indicate the status of the mouse at the time the event is called.

The Button argument is an integer variable that indicates which button or buttons are currently pressed. Each button is assigned a value: 1 for left, 2 for right, and 4 for center. When any of these buttons is pressed, its value is added to the Button argument. The easiest way to test the Button argument is with logical (bitwise) operators. Table 14.8 lists logical equations that return a non-0 value if a certain button is pressed.

| When the... | This Will Return Non-zero | Or, if CONSTANT.TXT is Loaded Into the Global Module |
|---|---|---|
| Right is pressed | (Button And 1) | (Button And LEFT_BUTTON) |
| Left is pressed | (Button And 2) | (Button And RIGHT_BUTTON) |
| Center is pressed | (Button And 4) | (Button And MIDDLE_BUTTON) |

Table 14.8 Logical equations for testing the status of the mouse buttons

The Shift argument is an integer variable that indicates the status of the Shift, Alt, and Ctrl keys at the time the event was called. Each shift key is assigned a value: 1 for Shift, 2 for Ctrl, and 4 for Alt. When any of these keys is pressed, its value is added to the Shift argument. See Table 14.6 in the MouseDown entry for details on how to test the Shift argument for a specific value.

The X and Y arguments are single-precision variables that correspond to the mouse pointer's position within the related form or control at the time the event was called. X is the horizontal coordinate, and Y is the vertical coordinate. These arguments are expressed in the measurements defined for the form or control with the ScaleMode, ScaleHeight, ScaleWidth, and other Scale properties.

Once a mouse button is pressed while the mouse pointer is over a form or control, that form or control "owns" all the successive mouse events until a MouseUp event is processed, even if the mouse pointer leaves the area of the form or object. This could cause the MouseUp event to receive X and Y arguments that are not on the form or control.

The first example syntax checks whether the shift key is down when the mouse pointer is moved. If so, a line is drawn from the previously saved pointer position to the current pointer X,Y coordinates (that is, where the mouse was at the time the event was triggered.) The second example syntax does the same thing, except that it is used with an array of picture boxes.

### Control Array

The Index argument is only used if the related control is part of a control array. This Index specifies which element of the array is the one that activated the event. When referencing the control, the element being referenced must be specified by placing the index number between parentheses just after the control name, and before the property name (for examples, CtlName(Index).Property).

### Example

In the Mouse project, the Canvas picture control calls the Canvas_MouseMove event whenever the mouse pointer is moved over its surface. If the DrawOn flag is set to true, it will then perform a drawing operation based on which button is pressed, and the status of the Shift argument.

### Comments

If the program is halted while inside this event, the MouseUp event may not be called when the mouse button is released. This can happen if a Stop statement is executed or a breakpoint is set inside this event.

# MouseUp Event

## Objects Affected

| | | | | |
|---|---|---|---|---|
| Check | Clipboard | Combo | Command | Debug |
| ▶ Dir | Drive | ▶ File | ▶ Form | Frame |
| ▶ Label | ▶ List | Menu | Option | ▶ Picture |
| Printer | Screen | Scroll | Text | Timer |

## Purpose

The MouseUp event occurs when any button—left, center, or right—on the mouse is released. You can also find out where the mouse pointer was when the button was released. You can also determine whether the Shfit, Ctrl, or Alt key was being held down when the mouse button was released. Table 14.9 summarizes the arguments of the MouseUp event.

## General Syntax

```
Sub Form_MouseUp(Button As Integer, Shift As Integer, X As Single, Y As Single)
Sub CtlName_MouseUp([Index As Integer, ]Button As Integer, Shift As Integer, X As ⇐
            Single, Y As Single)
```

| Arguments | Description |
|-----------|-------------|
| Form | FormName of the parent form |
| CtlName | CtlName of the control |
| Index | Uniquely identifies an element of a control array |
| Button | Integer variable returning number of button pressed |
| Shift | Integer variable returning status of Shift, Alt, and Ctrl keys when mouse buttonis pushed |
| X, Y | Single-precision variables that return the X, Y coordinates of the mouse pointer at the time the mouse button was released |

**Table 14.9 Arguments of the MouseUp event**

## Example Syntax

```
Sub Form_MouseUp(Button As Integer, Shift As Integer, X As Single, Y As Single)
    If Button = 1 Then          'If the left button was released
        EndX = X                'Save the current co-ordinates of the mouse pointer
        EndY = Y                'on the form
    End If
End Sub

Sub Picture_MouseUp(Index As Integer, Button As Integer, Shift As Integer, X As ⇐
            Single, Y As Single)
    If Button = 1 Then          'If the left button was released
        EndX(Index) = X         'Save the current co-ordinates of the mouse pointer
        EndY(Index) = Y         'on the picture control
    End If
End Sub
```

## Description

The MouseUp event is defined in a Sub procedure named using the control name (or name of the parent form) and variables representing the button number, shift status, and X and Y mouse position coordinates. An index variable precedes the other variables if the Sub procedure is written to handle a control array.

This event is initiated when the user releases any of the three buttons on the mouse. It supplies four arguments, which indicate the status of the mouse at the time the event is called.

The Button argument is an integer variable that indicates which button has been pressed. Its value is set to 1 for the left button, 2 for the right button, and 4 for the center button. For this event, the Button argument will indicate the status of only one button at a time.

The Shift argument is an integer variable that indicates the status of the Shift, Alt, and Ctrl keys at the time the event was called. Each shift key is assigned a value: 1 for Shift, 2 for Ctrl, and 4 for Alt. When any of these keys is pressed, its value is added to the Shift argument. The Shift argument is a combination of these values. See Table 14.6 in the MouseDown entry for details on how to test the Shift argument for a specific value.

The X and Y arguments are single-precision variables that correspond to the mouse pointer's position within the related form or control at the time the event was called. X is the horizontal coordinate, and Y is the vertical coordinate. These arguments are expressed in the measurements defined for the form or control with the ScaleMode, ScaleHeight, ScaleWidth, and other Scale properties.

Once a mouse button is pressed while the mouse pointer is over a form or control, that form or control "owns" all the successive mouse events until a MouseUp event is processed. This remains true even if the mouse pointer leaves the area of the form or object. This could cause the MouseUp event to receive X and Y arguments that are not on the form or control.

In the first example syntax, the current mouse position in the form is saved if the left mouse button was released. The second example performs the same service, but for an array of picture box controls.

### Control Array

The Index argument is only used if the related control is part of a control array. This Index specifies which element of the array is the one that activated the event. When referencing the control, the element being referenced must be specified by placing the index number between parentheses just after the control name, and before the property name (for example, CtlName(Index).Property).

## Example

The Canvas_MouseUp event in the Mouse project sets the DrawOn flag to False and clears the coordinates that were saved by the Canvas_MouseDown event.

## Comments

If the program is halted after a mouse button has been pressed, but before it has been released, this event may not be called when the mouse button is released. This can happen if a Stop statement is executed or a breakpoint is set inside the MouseDown or MouseMove events.

# The Mouse Project

## Project Overview

The Mouse project demonstrates the use of the five mouse-related events: Click, DblClick, MouseDown, MouseMove, and MouseUp. Each of these events is used at least once in the operation of this project. By following the examples in this project, you should be able to learn the principles behind using these events.

## Assembling the Project

1. Create a new form (the Mouse form) and place on it the following controls as specified in Table 14.10. Please note there is a group of five picture controls that share the CtlName of "ColorPalette." These picture controls are part of a control array. As soon as you create a second picture control with the CtlName of "ColorPalette," Visual Basic will ask if you wish to create a control array. Please click the "Yes" button.

| Object | Property | Setting |
|---|---|---|
| Form | FormName | Mouse |
| | BackColor | Dark Grey, RGB(128, 128, 128), &H00808080& |
| | Caption | Mouse Project |
| | Height | 5475 |
| | Width | 6000 |
| Picture Box | CtlName | Canvas |
| | ScaleMode | Twip |
| | Height | 3315 |
| | Left | 60 |
| | Top | 90 |
| | Width | 5685 |
| Command Button | CtlName | ClearButton |
| | Caption | Clear |
| | ScaleMode | Twip |
| | Height | 435 |
| | Left | 60 |
| | Top | 3540 |
| | Width | 1155 |

| Command Button | CtlName | ExitButton |
| --- | --- | --- |
| | Caption | Exit |
| | ScaleMode | Twip |
| | Height | 435 |
| | Left | 1290 |
| | Top | 3540 |
| | Width | 1155 |
| Label | CtlName | CurrentColor |
| | Alignment | 2 - Center |
| | BorderStyle | 1 - Fixed Single |
| | Caption | A |
| | ScaleMode | Twip |
| | Height | 435 |
| | Left | 2820 |
| | Top | 3540 |
| | Width | 435 |
| Picture | CtlName | ColorPalette |
| | BackColor | Bright White, RGB(255, 255, 255), &HFFFFFF& |
| | BorderStyle | 1 - Fixed Single |
| | Caption | A |
| | ScaleMode | Twip |
| | Height | 435 |
| | Index | 0 |
| | Left | 3630 |
| | Top | 3540 |
| | Width | 435 |
| Picture | CtlName | ColorPalette |
| | BackColor | Black, RGB(000, 000, 000), &H000000& |
| | BorderStyle | 1 - Fixed Single |
| | Caption | A |
| | ScaleMode | Twip |
| | Height | 435 |
| | Index | 1 |
| | Left | 4050 |
| | Top | 3540 |
| | Width | 435 |

*Table 14.10 (continued)*

| Object | Property | Setting |
|--------|----------|---------|
| Picture | CtlName | ColorPalette |
| | BackColor | Red, RGB(255, 000, 000), &H0000FF& |
| | BorderStyle | 1 - Fixed Single |
| | Caption | A |
| | ScaleMode | Twip |
| | Height | 435 |
| | Index | 2 |
| | Left | 4470 |
| | Top | 3540 |
| | Width | 435 |
| Picture | CtlName | ColorPalette |
| | BackColor | Blue, RGB(000, 000, 255), &HFF0000& |
| | BorderStyle | 1 - Fixed Single |
| | Caption | A |
| | ScaleMode | Twip |
| | Height | 435 |
| | Index | 3 |
| | Left | 4890 |
| | Top | 3540 |
| | Width | 435 |
| Picture | CtlName | ColorPalette |
| | BackColor | Bright Yellow, RGB(255, 255, 000), &H00FFFF& |
| | BorderStyle | 1 - Fixed Single |
| | Caption | A |
| | ScaleMode | Twip |
| | Height | 435 |
| | Index | 4 |
| | Left | 5310 |
| | Top | 3540 |
| | Width | 435 |

**Table 14.10 Property settings for the mouse project**

2. Check the appearance of your form against Figure 14.1.

3. Load the CONSTANT.TXT file into the global module. To do this, open Visual Basic's Project window, and double-click on the global module. This

will load the global module into the Code window. Then open Visual Basic's Code menu, and choose the Load Text option. This brings up a dialog box. Select the CONSTANT.TXT file and click on the Merge button. This will read the file into the global module.

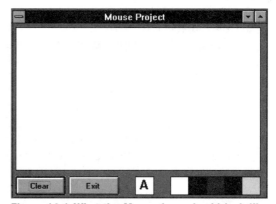

4. Enter the following code in the General Declarations area of the Mouse form.

```
Const True = -1
Const False = 0
Dim DrawOn As Integer
Dim StartX As Single
Dim StartY As Single
Dim LastX As Single
Dim LastY As Single
Dim SaveColor As Single
```

**Figure 14.1 What the Mouse form should look like when complete**

5. Enter the following code in the ClearButton_Click event. This code uses the Cls method to clear the Canvas picture control when the Clear button is clicked.

```
Sub ClearButton_Click ()
    Canvas.Cls
End Sub
```

6. Enter the following code into the ExitButton_Click event. This event ends the program when the Exit button is clicked.

```
Sub ExitButton_Click ()
    End
End Sub
```

7. Enter the following code into the Canvas_MouseDown event. This event is activated when the user presses down any of the buttons on the mouse while the mouse pointer is over the Canvas picture control. It sets the DrawOn flag to True (-1), and saves the current mouse pointer coordinates. These coordinates are later used in the Canvas_MouseMove event.

```
Sub Canvas_MouseDown (Button As Integer, Shift As Integer, X As Single, Y As Single)
    DrawOn = True
    StartX = X
    StartY = Y
End Sub
```

8. Enter the following code into the Canvas_MouseMove event. When the user moves the mouse pointer across the surface of the Canvas picture con-

trol, this routine checks to see if the DrawOn flag is set. If so, it then checks
to see if the left or right button is currently pressed. If the left button is
pressed, it draws a line from the last known position of the mouse pointer to
the current position of the mouse pointer. If the right button is pressed, it
draws a line from the coordinates saved by the Canvas_MouseDown event
to the current mouse pointer coordinates. If the user is also holding the
Shift key down while pressing the right mouse button, a box is drawn whose
opposite corners match the coordinates saved by the Canvas_MouseDown
event, and the current mouse pointer position. As a last step, this event
saves the current mouse pointer position so it has a reference point for the
next time it is called with the left mouse button pressed.

```
Sub Canvas_MouseMove (Button As Integer, Shift As Integer, X As Single, Y As⇐
                 Single)
    If DrawOn Then
        If Button = LEFT_BUTTON Then              'Is the left button pressed?
            Canvas.Line (LastX, LastY)-(X, Y)     'Draw a line
        ElseIf Button = RIGHT_BUTTON Then         'Is the right button pressed?
            Canvas.Line (StartX, StartY)-(X, Y)   'Continue drawing a sun
            If (Shift And SHIFT_MASK) Then 'Is the shift key pressed?
                Canvas.Line (StartX, StartY)-(X, Y), , B draw boxes
            End If
        End If
    End If
    LastX = X
    LastY = Y
End Sub
```

9. Enter the following code into the Canvas_MouseUp event. This event occurs when the user releases the mouse button. It sets the DrawOn flag to
   False (0), and zeros out the starting mouse pointer position.

```
Sub Canvas_MouseUp (Button As Integer, Shift As Integer, X As Single, Y As⇐
                 Single)
    DrawOn = False
    StartX = 0
    StartY = 0
End Sub
```

10. Enter the following code into the ColorPalette_Click event. This event oc-
    curs when the user clicks on one of the elements of the ColorPalette pic-
    ture control array. This event changes the foreground color of the Canvas
    picture control to the same color as the element that was clicked. The
    CurrentColor ForeColor property is also changed, so the user can see what
    the current color selections are. This event also happens when the user double-
    clicks on the element. This is why the current ForeColor property for the
    Canvas picture control is saved. This allows us to restore the ForeColor prop-
    erty to its original value if the event is activated by a double-click.

```
Sub ColorPalette_Click (Index As Integer)
  SaveColor = Canvas.Forecolor
  Canvas.Forecolor = ColorPalette(Index).BackColor
  CurrentColor.Forecolor = ColorPalette(Index).BackColor
End Sub
```

11. Enter the following code into the ColorPalette_DblClick event. This event is activated when the user double-clicks one of the elements of the ColorPalette picture control array. This event changes the background color of the Canvas picture control to the same color as the element that was clicked. The CurrentColor BackColor property is also changed, so the user can see what the current color selections are. Because this event is triggered after the Click event, we must first restore the ForeColor property of the Canvas picture control to its original state.

```
Sub ColorPalette_DblClick (Index As Integer)
  Canvas.Forecolor = SaveColor
  CurrentColor.Forecolor = SaveColor
  Canvas.BackColor = ColorPalette(Index).BackColor
  CurrentColor.BackColor = ColorPalette(Index).BackColor
End Sub
```

## How It Works

The application developed in the Mouse project is a crude drawing program. When the program is started, the Mouse form appears with a blank canvas. The user can then use the mouse to draw on the canvas.

Pressing and holding down the left mouse button, and moving the mouse while the mouse pointer is over the canvas, causes the program to draw a line on the canvas. The Canvas_MouseDown event is called first, and, because there is a button pressed, it sets the DrawOn flag to True (-1) and saves the current coordinates of the mouse pointer. Then, the Canvas_MouseMove event is called. In this event, a line is drawn from the last known mouse pointer position to the current mouse pointer position. This causes the line to follow the mouse pointer around the canvas until the user releases the left button.

Pressing and holding down the right mouse button also draws lines on the canvas. The Canvas_MouseDown event is called first. Because there is a button pressed, it sets the DrawOn flag to True (-1) and saves the current coordinates of the mouse pointer. Then the Canvas_MouseMove event is called. In this event, the coordinates of the saved mouse position are used along with the coordinates of the current mouse pointer position to draw the line. This causes several lines to be drawn, all originating at the same point.

If the Shift key is held down along with the right mouse button, a box is drawn around each line generated. This creates an interesting effect.

When the mouse buttons are released, the Canvas_MouseUp event is called. This event turns the DrawOn flag off (sets it to False), and clears the saved mouse position coordinates.

The foreground color of the canvas may be changed by clicking on any of the elements of the ColorPalette array. This causes the ColorPalette_Click event to occur. Because a Click event is always called just prior to the DblClick event, it saves the current foreground color of the canvas before changing it. This allows the DblClick event to restore it, if need be. The ColorPalette_Click event then changes the foreground color of the canvas to the same color as the background of the ColorPalette element that was clicked. These changes are also performed on the CurrentColor label control. This control displays to the user which colors are currently selected.

The background color of the canvas may be changed by double-clicking on any of the elements of the ColorPalette array. This causes the ColorPalette_DblClick event to occur. The first task performed by this event is to restore the foreground color of the canvas. It then sets the background color of the canvas to the same color as the background of the ColorPalette element that was double-clicked. These changes are also performed on the CurrentColor label control, which shows the user which colors are currently selected.

# Managing the Dragging Event

Your program may need to let the user drag an object with the mouse. Dragging means moving an object (such as icon or graphic image) from one position on the screen to another. For example file managers often allow you to copy or move files between directories by dragging a filename or icon from one directory area to another.

To drag an object, select it by pointing at it with your mouse or other pointing device. Press the mouse button (click) on the object and—without releasing the mouse button—move the object to a new location on the screen. When you drag an object, you will see an icon representing the object. The icon is usually an outline of the object. To set the object in its new location, release the mouse button.

A drag-and-drop operation involves two possible objects: source and target. The source is the object that the user clicks with the mouse. When a drag-and-drop operation ends, the object that the drag icon is over is the target. If a drag-and-drop operation does not end over another object, then there is no target object. An example of a drag-and-drop operation including a source and a target is when the user clicks and drags an icon representing a file to the icon symbol of a printer to print a file. Such a process would involve an event connected with the target. Any kind of action that follows the dropping of the source over the target is part of the target.

Drag mode determines how a drag operation begins. There are two settings for drag mode: automatic and manual. In automatic drag mode, dragging operations begin when the user clicks the mouse. This process takes place without the use of any code. Manual drag mode prevents the starting of a drag operation with only the clicking of the mouse. The only way to begin a drag operation on an object with its drag mode set to manual is with a statement in the code of the program.

## Dragging in Visual Basic

In Visual Basic, an object's DragMode property indicates its drag mode setting: manual or automatic. The only way to begin a drag operation on an object with a manual DragMode property is with the Drag method. Each manual drag operation begins and ends with DragMode method expressions. The DragIcon property of the object determines whether the outline of the object or another icon appears on the screen during a drag operation. The DragDrop event contains the actions that take place when a drag operation terminates over an object. The DragOver event contains the actions that take place when the user drags an object over another object.

Table 15.1 displays the Visual Basic properties, events, and methods that determine the means and results of a drag operation.

| Use or Set This... | | To Do This... |
| --- | --- | --- |
| Drag | Method | Begin or ends manual dragging |
| DragDrop | Event | Initiate an action when a dragged control is dropped onto a form or control |
| DragOver | Event | Initiate an action when a dragged control is over a form or control |
| DragMode | Property | Choose automatic or manual drag mode |
| DragIcon | Property | Select the icon to display when the control is part of a drag operation |

Table 15.1 Methods, properties, and events involved in a drag operation

The following pages discuss each of the methods, events, and properties in Table 15.1 in detail. The Drag project at the end of this section includes step-by-step directions on how to create a Visual Basic project that uses them all.

# Drag Method

## Objects Affected

- Check        Clipboard    ▶ Combo       ▶ Command     Dbug
  Dir          Drive        ▶ File          Form        ▶ Frame
- Label        ▶ List       Menu          ▶ Option     ▶ Picture
  Printer      Screen       ▶ Scroll       ▶ Text       Timer

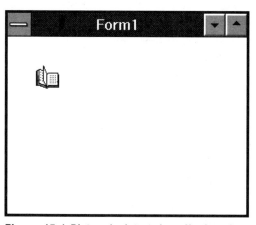

Figure 15.1 Picture1 picture box displayed on screen

## Purpose

The Drag method initiates or ends a dragging operation. With this method, you can manipulate objects on the screen when a control's DragMode property is manual. A Drag method statement typically appears in the MouseDown event of the control to be dragged. This has the effect of beginning a drag operation when the user presses the mouse button. Dragging operations begun with this method normally end with another Drag method expression. Another Drag method expression normally appears in the MouseUp event subroutine of the same control. The drag operation ends when the user releases the mouse button. This triggers the DragDrop event of the

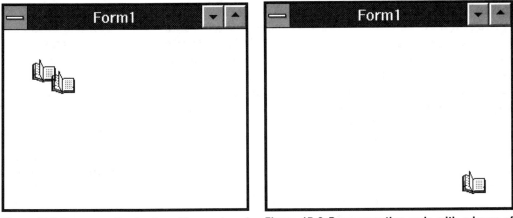

**Figure 15.2 Drag operation begins with pressing of mouse button**

**Figure 15.3 Drag operation ends with release of mouse button**

form that moves the icon to the new location. In the example syntax, the Drag method moves the Picture1 picture box from one portion of the screen to another. Figures 15.1, 15.2, and 15.3 show the icon on Picture1 both before, during, and after a drag operation. Tables 15.2 and 15.3 summarize the arguments and possible values of the Drag method.

## General Syntax

```
control[index%].Drag [action%]
```

| Argument | Description |
|----------|-------------|
| control | CtlName of the control that is affected by the drag operation |
| index% | Index value of a control if it is part of a control array |
| action% | Value that indicates what dragging operation to take |

**Table 15.2 Arguments of the Drag method**

| action% | Description |
|---------|-------------|
| 0 | Cancels a dragging operation |
| 1 | Begins a dragging operation |
| 2 | Ends a dragging operation |

**Table 15.3 Possible values of the action% argument**

## Example Syntax

```
Sub Picture1_MouseDown (Button As Integer, Shift As Integer, X As Single, Y As Single)
    Picture1.Drag              'Begins a drag operation.
End Sub

Sub Form_DragDrop (Source As Control, X As Single, Y As Single)
    Source.Move X, Y           'Moves the picture box to the new location.
End Sub
```

## Description

A Drag method statement consists of three possible elements. Each Drag method expression begins with the CtlName property of the control being dragged. This is normally the control whose event contains the Drag method, but it can be any other control. If the control is part of a control array, then the value of the index property follows the CtlName of the control. Finally, a Drag method statement ends with a value that represents what type of drag operation to take.

There are three possible settings for the action% parameter: 0, 1, and 2. A value of 0 cancels a dragging operation. This prevents the triggering of any events normally associated with the ending of a drag operation. Using a value of 1 begins a drag operation. Drag operations end with a value of 2. This triggers the DragDrop event of the form or control that the drag icon is over. The default for action% is 1. This value is used when no other value is specified or the action% argument is omitted.

### The DragMode property

The DragMode property of a control indicates whether the Drag method is necessary to initiate a drag operation. When the DragMode property of a control remains at its default value of 0 (manual), the Drag method is the only way to initiate a drag operation. If the DragMode property changes to 1 (automatic), then the Drag method is not necessary. In this case, a drag operation is started when the user presses a mouse button while the mouse pointer is over the control. With the example syntax, the Picture1 picture box's DragMode property remains at its default setting of manual. If you were to change the DragMode property to automatic and remove the Drag method statement from the MouseDown event, there would be no change in the operation of the example.

### The DragIcon Property

The DragIcon property indicates the icon that appears during a drag operation to show where to move the Picture1 picture box. This property's default setting is a gray outline of the dragged control. This outline is a guide for where the control appears when the drag operation is completed. In the example syntax, the DragIcon property is the same icon as the one displayed in the Picture1 picture box. Figure 5.2 displays two icons, representing the icon in the Picture1 picture box, and the DragIcon.

### The Move Method

The user can move a control to a new location on the screen with a Move method expression. By placing a Move method expression in the DragDrop event of the form, the control moves to the new location at the end of a drag operation. In the example syntax, the Move method places the Picture1 picture box in a new location on the screen. The X and Y values returned by the DragDrop event of the form provide the new coordinates of the Picture1 picture box.

### The DragDrop Event

The DragDrop event contains the actions that occur when the user releases the mouse button while the drag icon is over another control or form. This event is unaffected by whether the drag operation began with a Drag method expression or mouse click. In the example syntax, releasing the mouse button over a portion of the form triggers the DragDrop event. Notice that there is no need for another Drag method statement to terminate the drag operation. The user triggers a DragDrop event by releasing the mouse button.

## Example

In the Drag project at the end of this section, the Drag method is used several times. The Drag method initiates a dragging operation on the selected file in the Icon_List file list box. In the Icon_List_Click event, the Drag method processes when the user selects a file. The DragOver event of ClearPicture demonstates the setting of action% to 0 (to cancel drag). This drag operation ends when the user clicks on the left mouse button and drags the picture from the Display_Icon picture box to the ClearPicture picture box.

# DragDrop Event

## Objects Affected

| | | | | |
|---|---|---|---|---|
| ▶ Check | Clipboard | ▶ Combo | ▶ Command | Dbug |
| ▶ Dir | ▶ Drive | ▶ File | ▶ Form | ▶ Frame |
| ▶ Label | ▶ List | Menu | ▶ Option | ▶ Picture |
| Printer | Screen | ▶ Scroll | ▶ Text | Timer |

## Purpose

A DragDrop event contains the actions that occur at the completion of a drag-and-drop operation over another object. Drag-and-drop operations terminate with either a Drag method expression or the release of a mouse button. When the user releases the mouse button while the mouse pointer is over an object, this is known as the drop part of a drag-and-drop operation. Table 15.4 summarizes the arguments and variable of the DragDrop event.

## General Syntax

```
Sub FormName_DragDrop (Source as Control, X as Single, Y as Single)
Sub CtlName_DragDrop ([Index as Integer,] Source as Control, X as Single, Y as Single)
```

| Arguments | Description |
|---|---|
| CtlName | Identifies the control that the dragged control is dropped on |
| FormName | Identifies the form that the dragged control is dropped on |
| Index | Identifies a control in a control array |
| Source | The control that is dropped over this object |
| x,y | Current horizontal (x) and vertical (y) coordinates of the mouse pointer |

**Table 15.4 Arguments and variables of the DragDrop event**

## Example Syntax

```
Sub Form_Load ()
    Picture1.Picture = LoadPicture("\VB\ICONS\MISC\MISC04.ICO") 'Defines Picture1
    Picture1.DragMode = 1                          'Sets automatic Drag
    Picture1.DragIcon = Picture1.Picture           'Defines DragIcon property
End Sub

Sub Picture2_DragDrop (Source As Control, X As Single, Y As Single)
    Picture2.Picture = Source.Picture              'Changes Picture2 to
                                                   'display same picture as
Picture1
End Sub
```

## Description

A DragDrop event triggers when the user drops a dragged control over another control or form. Each DragDrop event uses the FormName and CtlName properties to indicate exactly which control or form that the control is dropped over. X and Y coordinates define the location of the dragged control in relation to the control being dragged. These coordinates measure the horizontal and vertical distance in units defined by the ScaleMode property. The Source argument identifies the dragged-and-dropped control that caused the event. Source replaces the CtlName property of the dragged control in expressions where the user can drag-and-drop more than one object over a control.

In the example syntax, an automatic drag operation triggers when the mouse pointer is over the Picture1 picture box (which is the Source control) and the user presses the mouse button. The DragDrop event redefines the Picture property of the Picture2 picture box with the Picture property of the dragged control. Figures 15.4 and 15.5 illustrate how the contents of the Picture2 picture box change to match that of Picture1 after the drag-and-drop operation.

### Control Arrays

If the control designated in a drag-and-drop operation is a member of a control array, then Visual Basic will provide an Index property value. This Index value defines which

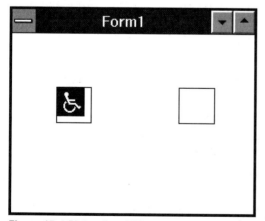

**Figure 15.4 Picture1 and Picture2 before the drag-and-drop operation**

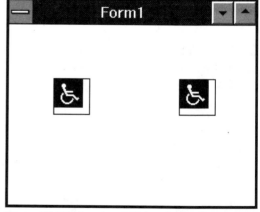

**Figure 15.5 Picture1 and Picture2 after the drag-and-drop operation**

item of the control array was dropped on the object. This is useful in situations where there is a need to have different actions for different items of the same control array.

### Example

The Drag project at the end of this section uses the DragDrop event of the Picture1 picture box. This subroutine triggers when the user selects the file name of an icon from the list of icons (displayed in Icon_List) and drops it on top of the Display_Icon picture box that displays the icon chosen.

# DragOver Event

## Objects Affected

| | | | | |
|---|---|---|---|---|
| ▶ Check | Clipboard | ▶ Combo | ▶ Command | Dbug |
| ▶ Dir | ▶ Drive | ▶ File | ▶ Form | ▶ Frame |
| ▶ Label | ▶ List | Menu | ▶ Option | ▶ Picture |
| Printer | Screen | ▶ Scroll | ▶ Text | Timer |

## Purpose

A DragOver event contains the actions that take place when a drag operation moves the mouse pointer over an object. These actions do not necessarily terminate a drag-and-drop operation, but the DragOver event can serve this purpose. In the example syntax, the DragOver event triggers up to three separate times. The DragOver event occurs each time the object enters, is over, and exits the space above the Picture2 picture box. Notice how this one event changes the appearance of the Picture2 picture box. Figures 15.6, 15.7, and 15.8 display what the screen looks like before, during, and after a DragOver event. Table 15.5 summarizes the arguments and variables of the DragOver event.

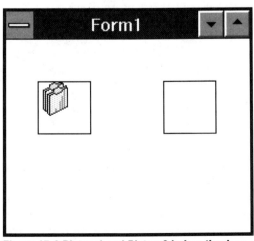

Figure 15.6 Picture1 and Picture2 before the drag-and-drop operation

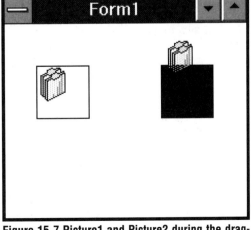

Figure 15.7 Picture1 and Picture2 during the drag-and-drop operation

## General Syntax

```
Sub FormName_DragOver (source as Control, x as Single, y as Single, State as ⇐
                       Integer)
Sub CtlName_DragOver ([index as Integer,] source as Control, x as Single, y as ⇐
                       Single, state as Integer)
```

| Arguments | Description |
|---|---|
| CtlName | CtlName property of the control that the drag-and-drop operation terminates over |
| FormName | FormName property of the Form that the drag-and-drop operation terminates over |
| index | Identifies a control in a control array |
| source | The dragged and dropped control |
| x,y | Current horizontal (x) and vertical (y) coordinates in relation to the present location of the dragged and dropped control |
| state% | Whether the dragged control is entering, over, or exiting the space above another control |

**Table 15.5 Arguments and variables of the DragOver event**

## Example Syntax

```
Sub Form_Load ()
    Picture1.Picture = LoadPicture("\VB\ICONS\MISC\MISC04.ICO")   'Defines Picture1
    Picture1.DragMode = 1                        'Sets automatic Drag
    Picture1.DragIcon = Picture1.Picture         'Defines DragIcon property
End Sub

Sub Picture2_DragOver (Source As Control, X As Single, Y As Single, State As Integer)
    Select Case State                            'Checks the current state of object
                                                 'over it
        Case 0, 2                                'Checks if the object is over it
            Picture2.BackColor = QBColor(0)      'Changes backcolor to black
        Case 1                                   'Checks if the object is no longer over it
            Picture2.BackColor = QBColor(15)     'Changes backcolor to white
    End Select
End Sub

Sub Picture2_DragDrop (Source As Control, X As Single, Y As Single)
    Picture2.BackColor = QBColor(15)             'Changes Background to white
    Picture2.Picture = Picture1.Picture          'Places icon in picture box
End Sub
```

## Description

A DragOver event is activated when the user drags an object over another control or form. Each DragOver event uses the FormName and CtlName properties to indicate exactly which control or form the user drags an object over. x and y coordinates define the location of the dragged control in relation to the control being dragged. These coordinates measure the horizontal and vertical distance in units defined by the ScaleMode property. The source argument identifies the dragged control that caused the event. source replaces the CtlName property of the dragged control in expressions where more than one object can be dropped and dragged to a control.

As the example syntax shows, the Form_Load Sub procedure is normally used to set up the picture(s) and the dragging mode and to set up the icon to be used to indicate the picture being dragged (in this case, the dragged icon is the same as the original picture).

The DragOver event for Picture2 determines what happens if another control (Picture1 in this case) is dragged over it. Here the background of Picture2 is changed to black while being dragged over (see Figure 15.7), and changes back to white as soon as the dragged control crosses back over Picture2's boundaries. The DragDrop event for Picture2 controls what happens if the mouse button is released while another control is over the

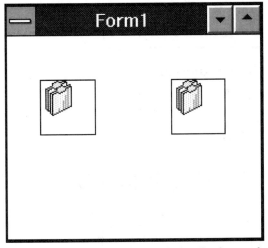

**Figure 15.8 Picture1 and Picture2 after the drag-and-drop operation**

picture (that is, the other control is being "dropped on" Picture2). When this happens, Picture2's background is changed to white and the contents of Picture2 are changed to those of Picture1, in effect dropping a copy of Picture1 on Picture2 (see Figure 15.8). Notice that if the user drops the icon, the DragDrop event must have a line of code that changes the background of the Picture2 picture box to white. This is necessary because the state% argument is never 1 in a drag-and-drop operation.

### The State Variable

The state% variable returns the three possible ways that a control may be dragged over an object. A control's DragOver event is first triggered when an object enters the space above it. When this happens, the state% variable returns a value of 0. While a dragged control is a over control or form, the state% variable returns the value of two (2). After a dragged control leaves the space above a control or form, the DragOver event triggers one last time and gives a value of 1. The values of the state% variable are summarized in Table 15.6.

| State% | Description |
|--------|-------------|
| 0 | Object enters the space above another object |
| 1 | Object exits the space above another object |
| 2 | Object is over the space above another object (executes once) |

**Table 15.6 Values of the state% variable**

### Example

In the Drag project at the end of this section, the DragOver event clears the icon displayed in the Display_Icon picture box. When the user drags that icon over to the ClearPicture picture box, the State% argument of the DragOver event returns the value of 0. The resulting code changes the Picture property of Display_Icon to blank.

# DragIcon Property

## Objects Affected

| | | | | |
|---|---|---|---|---|
| ▶ Check | Clipboard | ▶ Combo | ▶ Command | Dbug |
| ▶ Dir | ▶ Drive | ▶ File | ▶ Form | ▶ Frame |
| ▶ Label | ▶ List | Menu | ▶ Option | ▶ Picture |
| Printer | Screen | ▶ Scroll | ▶ Text | Timer |

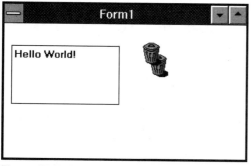

**Figure 15.9 Picture1 and Text1 before the drag-and-drop operation**

## Purpose

The DragIcon property indicates what icon will be used as a pointer during a drag operation. This property is a useful way to indicate what type of drag operation is being initiated. If used with the DragOver and DragDrop events, this property can be used to change the pointer icon during a drag operation. In the example syntax the drag icon changes to a trashcan when it is over the Picture1 picture box. This graphically shows the user the results of completing the drag-and-drop operation. Notice that when the user drops the control, the text is erased from the Text1 text box. Figures 15.9, 15.10, and 15.11 show what the screen looks like before, during and after a drag-and-drop operation. Table 15.7 summarizes the arguments of the DragIcon property.

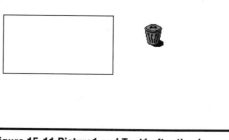

**Figure 15.10 Picture1 and Text1 during the drag-and-drop operation**

**Figure 15.11 Picture1 and Text1 after the drag-and-drop operation**

## General Syntax

```
control[(index%)] .DragIcon [= icon]
form[(index%)].DragIcon[=icon]
```

| Argument | Description |
|----------|-------------|
| control | CtlName property of the control |
| form | FormName property of the form |
| index% | Identifies a control in a control array |
| icon | Path and file name of the icon |

**Table 15.7 Arguments of the DragIcon property**

## Example Syntax

```
Sub Form_Load ()
    Picture1.Picture = LoadPicture("\VB\ICONS\COMPUTER\TRASH01.ICO")
                                    'Defines Picture1
    Picture1.DragMode = 1           'Sets automatic Drag
    Text1.Text = "Hello World!"     'Defines Text property
    Text1.DragIcon = LoadPicture("\VB\ICONS\MAIL\MAIL01A.ICO")    'Defines DragIcon
                                    'property
    Text1.DragMode = 1              'Drag mode will activate with click
End Sub                             'of the mouse

Sub Picture1_DragOver (Source As Control, X As Single, Y As Single, State As
    Integer)
    Select Case State               'Checks the current state of object over it.
        Case 0, 2                   'Checks if the object is over it
            Text1.DragIcon = Picture1.Picture           'Redefines DragIcon
                                    'property
        Case 1                      'Checks dragged control's location
            Text1.DragIcon = LoadPicture("\VB\ICONS\MAIL\MAIL01A.ICO")'Redefines Icon
    End Select
End Sub

Sub Picture1_DragDrop (Source As Control, X As Single, Y As Single)
    Source.Text = ""                'Blanks the text
    Source.DragIcon = LoadPicture("\VB\ICONS\MAIL\MAIL01A.ICO")    'Restores DragIcon of
                                    'Text1
End Sub
```

## Description

A DragIcon property identifies what icon to display in place of the mouse pointer during a drag operation. The CtlName property of the control or FormName property of the form identify which object's DragIcon property to change. When no name appears, the DragIcon property of the form is changed. In cases where a control is part of a control array, the index property must also be included.

### Using Icons

The DragIcon can be specified at both design time and run time. At design time, the programmer selects the DragIcon by choosing the DragIcon property on the properties bar and clicking on the ellipsis (...) at the right-hand side of the settings bar. The programmer selects the file name of the icon by double-clicking on the icon in the file list box. To set the DragIcon property at run time, use the LoadPicture function, including the icon's filename and path. Table 5.8 shows the possible settings of the DragIcon property.

| Icon | Description |
|---|---|
| None | Default. The drag icon is the point indicated by the MousePointer property. This is normally the outline of the control |
| Icon | Includes the path and name of the icon to display. This file must have an "ICO" extension and format |

**Table 15.8 Possible settings of Icon argument of DragIcon property**

In the example syntax, the DragIcon property is changed in the DragOver event. In the example syntax, the Form_Load Sub procedure loads the picture for Picture1, sets the drag mode to the icon that will be used to indicate that dragging is in progress (the trash can in this case). The DragOver event must check that the source control is no longer over the destination: Here, if the source control moves away without being dropped, DragIcon is restored to the original. In the DragDrop event, the DragIcon is also changed back to the original, indicating that a drag-and-drop operation has been completed.

## Example

The Drag project at the end of this section uses the DragIcon property for the Display_Icon picture box and Icon_List file list box. For the Icon_List file list box, the DragIcon specifies what icon to use when dragging the icon file to be displayed in the Display_Icon picture box. In the Display_Icon picture box, the DragIcon property is set at run time to the icon displayed.

## Comments

Even on color displays, the icon for dragging will only be shown in monochrome.

# DragMode Property

## Objects Affected

| | | | | |
|---|---|---|---|---|
| ▶ Check | Clipboard | ▶ Combo | ▶ Command | Dbug |
| ▶ Dir | ▶ Drive | ▶ File | Form | ▶ Frame |
| ▶ Label | ▶ List | Menu | ▶ Option | ▶ Picture |
| Printer | Screen | ▶ Scroll | ▶ Text | Timer |

## Purpose

The DragMode property of a control indicates whether it may be dragged in a drag operation without the use of a Drag method expression. Every control has an initial setting of manual. This indicates that the control may not normally be dragged. A drag operation may only be begun on a control with a manual setting by using the Drag method. With a control's DragMode property set to automatic, a drag operation begins when the user presses and holds down a mouse button over the object. Both of these settings are demonstrated in the example. When the user clicks the Command1 command button with the mouse, the DragMode property is changed to automatic. After this property changes, the automatic DragMode enables you to move the command button on the form. Notice that the control cannot be dragged when it reads manual. Figures 15.12 and 15.13 show what the example syntax might look like on the screen. Tables 15.9 and 15.10 summarize arguments and possible settings of the DragMode property.

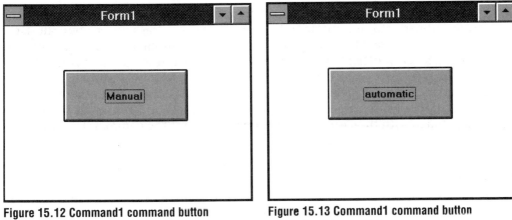

Figure 15.12 Command1 command button displaying "manual"

Figure 15.13 Command1 command button displaying "automatic"

## General Syntax

```
control[(index%)].DragMode[=mode%]
```

| Argument | Description |
|----------|-------------|
| control | CtlName of the control |
| index% | Identifies the control in the control array |
| mode% | DragMode setting |

Table 15.9 Arguments of the DragMode property

| Mode% | Description |
|-------|-------------|
| 0 | Manual (Default). Drag method is required for a drag operation |
| 1 | Automatic. User pushing the mouse button over a control creates a drag operation |

Table 15.10 Possible settings of the DragMode property

## Example Syntax

```
Sub Command1_Click ()
    Command1.Caption = "automatic"     'Changes text on command button
    Command1.DragMode = 1              'Changes DragMode to automatic
End Sub

Sub Form_DragDrop (Source As Control, X As Single, Y As Single)
    Source.Move X, Y                   'Moves the picture box to the new location
    Command1.Caption = "manual"        'Changes text on command button
    Command1.DragMode = 0              'Changes DragMode to manual
End Sub
```

## Description

The initial value of any newly created control is manual (0). A value of 1 changes the DragMode property to automatic. Controls cannot be dragged without the Drag method unless the DragMode property is changed to automatic. While a control is being dragged, no other mouse actions (Click,Double Click, MouseDown, MouseMove, MouseUp, GotFocus) will function. If the control's DragMode property is set to automatic, none of the events generated by mouse actions will function during a drag operation. In the example syntax, both the manual and automatic DragModes are demonstrated with the Command1 command button. The command button Command1 can only be moved when it reads "automatic."

### The Drag Method

While the DragMode property of a control is set to manual, the control may not normally be dragged until it is changed to automatic. If the MouseDown event of the control contains a Drag method expression, however, then this will have the same effect as changing the control's DragMode property to automatic.

## Example

In the Drag project at the end of this section, the majority of the controls remain in manual DragMode. The Display_Icon picture box can be changed from manual to automatic DragMode to demonstrate the effects of the modes on dragging icons to the ClearPicture icon.

# The Drag Project

## Project Overview

This Drag project demonstrates dragging in Visual Basic. This example shows how to use the properties, events, and methods that directly effect dragging.

This project has one form, the Dragging form. The Dragging form's setup is broken down into three sections: assembly, source code, and how it works.

## Assembling the Project

1. Make a new form (the Dragging form) with the objects and properties listed in Table 15.11.

| Object | Property | Setting |
|---|---|---|
| Form | BackColor | Gray, RGB(192,192,192), &H00C0C0 |
| | BorderStyle | 1 - Fixed Single |
| | Caption | Icon Viewer |
| | ControlBox | False |
| | Icon | \VB\ICONS\MISC\MISC02.ICO |
| | FormName | Dragging |
| | MaxButton | False |
| | MinButton | True |
| Drive List box | CtlName | Drive_List |
| Directory list box | CtlName | Directory_List |
| File List box | CtlName | Icon_List |
| | DragIcon | \VB\ICONS\COMPUTERS\DISK06.ICO |
| | Pattern | *.ICO |
| | Tag | Icon_List |
| Picture box | CtlName | Display_Icon |
| | DragIcon | \VB\ICONS\COMPUTERS\DISK06.ICO |
| | DragMode | 0 - Manual |
| Picture box | BackColor | Gray, RGB(192,192,192), &H00C0C0 |
| | CtlName | ClearPicture |
| | Picture | \VB\ICONS\COMPUTER\TRASH01.ICO |
| Command button | Caption | Manual |
| | CtlName | ClearMode |
| Command button | Caption | Exit |
| | CtlName | Program_End |
| Label | Caption | Clear |
| | CtlName | Label1 |

**Table 15.11 Elements of the Dragging form**

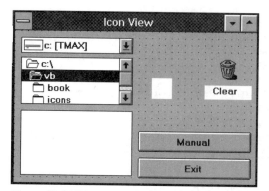

Figure 15.14 What the Dragging form should look like when completed

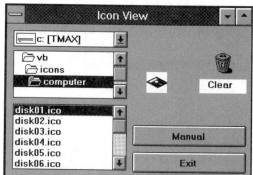

Figure 15.15 What the Dragging form should look like when running

2. Size the objects on the screen, as shown in Figures 15.14 and 15.15.

3. Enter the following code in the Drive_List_Change event subroutine. This code is triggered when the user chooses another drive in the Drive_List drive box. When this code changes, the path of the Directory_List directory box is changed to display the directories of the new drive chosen.

```
Sub Drive_List_Change ()
    Directory_List.Path = Drive_List.Drive
End Sub
```

4. Enter the following code in the Directory_List_Change event subroutine. This code is activated when the user selects another directory in the Directory_List directory list box. Another way of triggering this code is to change the drive selected in the Drive_List drive box. After this happens, the contents of the Icon_List are modified to display the icons in the indicated directory.

```
Sub Directory_Change ()
    Icon_List.Path = Directory_List.Path
    ChDir Icon_List.Path
    Icon_List.SetFocus
End Sub
```

5. Enter this code in the Icon_List_MouseDown event subroutine.This code is activated when the user presses a mouse button over an icon listed in the "Icon_List" box. This routine begins a drag operation.

```
Sub Icon_List_MouseDown (Button As Integer, Shift As Integer, X As Single, Y⇐
                         As Single)
    Icon_List.Drag 1
End Sub
```

6. Enter this code in the Display_Icon_DragDrop event subroutine. This code is triggered when the user releases a mouse button while the drag icon is

over the Icon_Display picture box. After checking to make sure that the file dragged is from the Icon_List file list box, this routine displays the icon.

```
Sub Display_Icon_DragDrop (Source As Control, X As Single, Y As Single)
    If Source.tag = "Icon_List" Then
        Display_Icon.Picture = LoadPicture(Source.List(Source.ListIndex))
    End If
    Display_Icon.DragIcon = Display_Icon.Picture
End Sub
```

7. Enter this code in the ClearPicture_DragOver event subroutine. This code is activated when the user drags the drag icon over the ClearPicture. When this happens, this routine terminates the drag operation and erases the icon in Display_Icon picture box.

```
Sub ClearPicture_DragOver (Source As Control, X As Single, Y As Single, State ⇐
                           As Integer)
    Source.Drag 2
    Display_Icon.Picture = LoadPicture()
End Sub
```

8. Enter this code in the ClearMode_Click event subroutine. This code is triggered when the user presses the ClearMode command button. The caption on the command button changes from manual to automatic and automatic to manual. In this way, the caption on the command button indicates the type of DragOperation that will take place.

```
Sub ClearMode_Click ()
    If ClearMode.Caption = "Clear = manual" Then
        ClearMode.Caption = "Clear = automatic"
        Display_Icon.DragMode = 1
    Else
        ClearMode.Caption = "Clear = manual"
        Display_Icon.DragMode = 0
    End If
End Sub
```

9. Enter this code in the Program_End_Click event subroutine. This code is activated when the user presses the command button labeled "Exit." This routine closes down the Drag project.

```
Sub Program_End_Click ()
    End
End Sub
```

## How It Works

This project shows a list of the icon files available on a system. The user selects a file from this list and drags it to the Display_Icon picture box. When the user releases the mouse button while the dragged icon is over the Display_Icon picture box, the icon of that file displays. To erase this icon from the Display_Icon picture box, the user drags it to the trashcan. This erases the icon from the Display_Icon picture box.

The MouseDown event of the Icon_List file list box contains a Drag method statement. This is necessary because the DragMode property of the Icon_List file list is set to manual. This demonstrates the only way to start a drag operation when the DragMode property is set to manual.

All of the controls in the Drag Project start with a default setting of manual (0). When the user presses the ClearMode command button, the Display_Icon picture box's DragMode property changes. The text on the command button reflects whether the picture box's property is manual or automatic. The icon displayed in the Display_Icon picture box cannot be dragged to the trashcan icon when the ClearMode command button reads manual. This demonstrates that a drag operation will not work without a Drag method when a control's DragMode is set to manual.

When the user drags a file from the Icon_List file list box, the Picture property of the Display_Icon picture box changes to the file dragged. This happens when the user releases the mouse button while the mouse pointer is over the Display_Icon picture box. By releasing the button in this way, the DragDrop event of the Display_Icon picture box is triggered. This code changes the Picture property of the Display_Icon to contain the icon of the dragged file.

While the command button ClearMode reads automatic, the DragOver event is demonstrated. When the user drags a file to the Clear_Picture picture box, the DragDrop event terminates the drag operation with a Drag method statement. Then, the icon displayed in the Display_Icon picture box is erased.

# Handling Keyboard Input

lthough the mouse is a very useful tool, the keyboard continues to be the main method for entering data into computer programs. Programming environments must therefore provide the necessary facilities for dealing with the user's keyboard input. The text box control in Visual Basic can handle keyboard input in most situations, but sometimes you need a little more direct control over keyboard input—such as when handling special keys and key combinations. For these situations, Visual Basic provides two properties, three events, and one statement, which allow you to get down to the nitty-gritty when dealing with the keyboard.

Even though using the mouse to select objects on the screen is a visually intuitive method, sometimes removing a hand from the keyboard slows the user down. The Default and Cancel properties help to remedy this situation. These properties are used to directly link the Enter or Escape keys to the Click event of an existing command button. When the default property of a command button is set to True (-1), hitting the Enter key will activate that button's Click event. The same relationship is shared by the Escape key and Cancel property. In general, it's a good idea for your application to provide keyboard alternatives to the mouse wherever possible.

## Reading the Keyboard

Simply put, a keyboard can perform only two tasks. First, it can tell a program when a key is currently pressed. Second, it can tell a program when a pressed key is released. Visual Basic has three events for handling these tasks: KeyDown, KeyPress, and KeyUp. The KeyDown event is activated every time any key on the keyboard is pressed down. This includes shift keys, such as Shift, Ctrl, and Alt. The KeyPress event is activated when a key corresponding to a valid ASCII character (not a shift key) is pressed and released. The KeyUp event is the inverse of the KeyDown event. It is activated when any currently pressed key, including any of the shift keys, is released.

Finally, Visual Basic provides the SendKeys statement. This statement is used to simulate keyboard activity. It can send keystrokes to the same program that issues the statement, or any other Windows program that is currently running. This statement can be useful for automatic program testing or (to a limited extent) communication between programs.

Table 16.1 details these six elements and their purposes.

| Use or Set This... | | To Do This... |
|---|---|---|
| Cancel | Property | Link the Escape key to a command button's Click event |
| Default | Property | Link the Enter key to a command button's Click event |
| KeyDown | Event | Intercept a keystroke when it is pressed |
| KeyPress | Event | Intercept an ASCII character keystroke |
| KeyUp | Event | Intercept a keystroke when it is released |
| SendKeys | Statement | Simulate keyboard input from within the program |

**Table 16.1 Properties, events, and statement that deal with the keyboard**

### Constant Values in the CONSTANT.TXT File

Some of the examples below use constant declarations that are included in the CONSTANT.TXT file that came with the Visual Basic compiler.

In order to use the CONSTANT.TXT file, it must be loaded into the project's global module. To do this, open Visual Basic's Project window and double-click on the global module. This will load the global module into the Code window. Then open Visual Basic's Code menu and choose the Load Text option. Select the CONSTANT.TXT file from the dialog box and click on the Merge button. This will read the file into the global module.

# Cancel Property

## Objects Affected

| | | | | |
|---|---|---|---|---|
| Check | Clipboard | Combo | ▶ Command | Debug |
| Dir | Drive | File | Form | Frame |
| Label | List | Menu | Option | Picture |
| Printer | Screen | Scroll | Text | Timer |

## Purpose

The Cancel property enables the Escape key to execute the Click event of a command button. Use the Cancel property when one button on the form is set up to initiate a cancel action, and you want the user to be able to use the Escape key as an alternative way to cancel an action. This property can be set at design time, and set or read at run time. Table 16.2 summarizes the arguments of the Cancel property.

## General Syntax

```
[form.]commandbutton.Cancel[ = boolean%]
```

| Arguments | Description |
|-----------|-------------|
| form | FormName of the parent form |
| commandbutton | CtlName of the control |
| boolean | A True (-1) or False (0) value that can be used to set the property within the program's code |

**Table 16.2 Arguments of the Cancel property**

## Example Syntax

```
Sub Form_Load ()
    ClearButton.Cancel = -1              'Links the Clear button to the Escape key
End Sub
```

## Description

Sometimes it is necessary to provide the user with a command button with which to back out of, or cancel, an operation. The Cancel property allows you to assign that cancel action to the Escape key. This property can either be set to True (-1), or False (0) by you at design time, or by the application during run time. Because only one button on a form may be the cancel button, setting this property to True for one button automatically sets it to False for all the other buttons on the same form.

To set the Cancel property, begin with the name of the button control to be activated by the Escape key.

In order to make a button on a form the cancel button, the Cancel, Enabled, and Visible properties must all be set to True (-1). Also, the button's parent form must be the active form on the screen. If all these conditions are met, the cancel button's Click event will be executed when the user presses the Escape key.

Although the Click event for the cancel button is executed when the Escape key is pressed, the focus is not shifted to the cancel button. Unless the cancel button's Click event sets the focus to another control, it stays at the control that originally had the focus when the Escape key was pressed.

In the example syntax the Cancel property of the ClearButton control is set to -1. Now if the user presses the Escape key, the effect will be the same as clicking on ClearButton, except that the focus will not shift to the button.

## Example

In the Keys project at the end of this chapter, the Cancel property of the ClearButton control is set to True (-1) at design time. This setting causes the ClearButton control's click event to occur if the user presses the Escape key.

## Comments

The KeyDown, KeyPress, and KeyUp events, which are usually activated when a user presses a key on the keyboard, are bypassed when the Escape key is pressed to activate a cancel button's Click event.

# Default Property

## Objects Affected

| | | | | |
|---|---|---|---|---|
| Check | Clipboard | Combo | ▶ Command | Debug |
| Dir | Drive | File | Form | Frame |
| Label | List | Menu | Option | Picture |
| Printer | Screen | Scroll | Text | Timer |

## Purpose

The Default property enables the Enter key to execute the Click event of a command button. This is used when one button on the form will initiate a default action, and you want the user to be able to press the Enter key as an alternative way to say, "OK, do it." This property can be set at design time, and set or read at run time. Table 16.3 summarizes the arguments of the Default property.

## General Syntax

```
[form.]commandbutton.Default[ = boolean%]
```

| Arguments | Description |
|---|---|
| form | FormName of the parent form |
| commandbutton | CtlName of the control |
| boolean | A True (-1) or False (0) value that can be used to set the property within the program's code |

Table 16.3 Arguments of the Default property

## Example Syntax

```
Sub Form_Load ()
    OkButton.Default = -1                'Links the OkButton to the Enter key
End Sub
```

## Description

In most cases, a form has one command button that is used to perform the default action for that form. The Default property allows you to assign that default action to the Enter key. This property can either be set to True (-1), or False (0) by you at design time, or by the application during run time. Because only one button on a form may be the default, setting this property to True for one button automatically sets it to False for all the other buttons on the same form.

To set the Default property, begin with the name of the button control to be activated by the Enter key.

In order to make a button on a form the default, the Default, Enabled, and Visible properties must all be set to True (-1). Also, the button's parent form must be the active form on the screen. If all these conditions are met, and no other button currently has the focus, the default button's Click event will be executed when the user hits the Enter key.

Although the Click event for the default button is executed, the focus is not shifted to the default button when the user hits the Enter key. Unless the default button's Click event sets the focus to another control, it stays at the control that originally had the focus when the Enter key was pressed.

The example syntax sets the Default property of the OKButton to -1 (True). Pressing Enter will now be equivalent to clicking on the OKButton, except the focus will not shift to the button.

## Example

In the Keys project at the end of this chapter, the Default property of the SendButton control is set to True (-1) at design time. This setting causes the SendButton control's click event to occur if the user presses the Enter key.

## Comments

The KeyDown, KeyPress, and KeyUp events, which are usually activated when a user presses a key on the keyboard, are bypassed when the Enter key is pressed to activate a default button's Click event.

# KeyDown Event

## Objects Affected

| | | | | |
|---|---|---|---|---|
| ▶ Check | Clipboard | ▶ Combo | ▶ Command | Debug |
| ▶ Dir | ▶ Drive | ▶ File | ▶ Form | Frame |
| Label | ▶ List | Menu | ▶ Option | ▶ Picture |
| Printer | Screen | ▶ Scroll | ▶ Text | Timer |

## Purpose

The KeyDown event is used for low-level keyboard handling. It reports the current status of the keyboard when a key is pressed and this event's control has the focus. The arguments of the KeyDown event are summarized in Table 16.4.

## General Syntax

```
Sub Form_KeyDown (KeyCode As Integer, Shift As Integer)
Sub CtlName_KeyDown ([Index As Integer, ]KeyCode As Integer, Shift As Integer)
```

| Arguments | Description |
|-----------|-------------|
| form | FormName of the parent form |
| ctlname | CtlName of the control |
| index | Uniquely identifies an element of a control array |
| KeyCode | Integer variable returning the scan code of the key pressed |
| Shift | Integer variable indicating the status of the Ctrl, Alt, and Shift keys |

Table 16.4 Arguments of the KeyDown event

## Example Syntax

```
Sub Form_KeyDown (KeyCode As Integer, Shift As Integer)
    Beep                'Beep any time a user tries to type on an empty form.
End Sub

Sub Text1_KeyDown (Index As Integer, KeyCode As Integer, Shift As Integer)
    Dim AltOn As Integer
    Dim CtrlOn As Integer
    Dim ShiftOn As Integer

    If Shift And ALT_MASK Then AltOn = 1        'If one of the shift keys
    If Shift And CTRL_MASK Then CtrlOn = 1      'is on, turn on its corresponding
    If Shift And SHIFT_MASK Then ShiftOn = 1    'check box

    Alt_Check.Value = AltOn
    Ctrl_Check.Value = CtrlOn
    Shift_Check.Value = ShiftOn
End Sub
```

## Description

Each time a user presses a key on the keyboard, including the Shift, Ctrl, or Alt keys, the KeyDown event is initiated for the control that currently has the focus. Forms also have a KeyDown event, but it will occur only if the form contains no active controls.

Because it does not ignore the non-character-based keys, this event lets the program react to the user pressing function keys (F1 through F12), or any unusual key combinations such as (Ctrl+Shift+key). This event supplies two arguments, KeyCode and Shift, that tell the program which key or keys pressed caused the event to occur. To define the KeyDown event, use the name of the affected control, followed by an Index variable if you are using a control array.

The KeyCode argument supplies a number that uniquely identifies the key pressed. This number corresponds to the physical key on the keyboard, not the character that the key generates. For instance, if the user holds down the shift key and presses "A," the KeyCode argument will contain the same value as when the user presses the "A" key alone, even though the character generated will be different. The CONSTANT.TXT file lists the possible values for the KeyCode argument.

The Shift argument is an integer variable that indicates the status of the Shift, Alt, and Ctrl keys at the time the event was called. Each of the three special shift keys is assigned a value: 1 for Shift, 2 for Ctrl, and 4 for Alt. When any of these keys is pressed, its value is added to the Shift argument. The easiest way to test the Shift argument is with logical (bitwise) operators. Table 16.5 lists logical equations that return a non-zero value if a certain shift key is pressed.

| When the... | This Logical Equation Will return Non-Zero | Or, if CONSTANT.TXT is Loaded Into the Global Module |
|---|---|---|
| Shift key is pressed | (Shift And 1) | (Shift And SHIFT_MASK) |
| Ctrl key is pressed | (Shift And 2) | (Shift And CTRL_MASK) |
| Alt key is pressed | (Shift And 4) | (Shift And ALT_MASK) |

**Table 16.5 Logical equations for testing the Shift status**

Keep in mind that this event is called when any key on the keyboard is pressed. Therefore, if the user presses any Shift+key combination, the event occurs for as many keys as are in the combination. For instance, if the user presses Ctrl+Shift+A, this event will occur three times. The first time, the KeyCode argument will be 11 (the code for the Ctrl key), and the Shift argument will be 2 (the shift code for Ctrl). The second time KeyCode will be 10 (the code for the Shift key), and the Shift argument will be 3 (the shift code for Ctrl plus the shift code for Shift). Finally, on the third call, KeyCode will be 41 (the code for the "A" key), and Shift will again be 3.

The first example syntax produces a beep whenever a key is pressed. The second example syntax uses the logical relationships in Table 16.5 to store the status of the Alt, Ctrl, and Shift keys in variables.

### Control Arrays

The Index argument is only used if the related control is part of a control array. This Index specifies which element of the array is the one that activated the event. When When the...referencing the control, the element being referenced must be specified by placing the index number between parentheses just after the control name, and before the property name (for example, CtlName(Index).Property).

## Example

In the Keys project at the end of this chapter, the Key_Down event is used to count the number of times a key is pressed. It is also used to set the values of the check boxes that indicate whether the Alt, Ctrl, and Shift keys are pressed.

## Comments

Pressing and holding a key down will cause this event to be activated repeatedly until the key is released.

The only time the KeyDown event for a form will be executed is when there are no controls on the form, or all controls on the form are disabled.

# KeyPress Event

## Objects Affected

| | | | | |
|---|---|---|---|---|
| ▶ Check | Clipboard | ▶ Combo | ▶ Command | Debug |
| ▶ Dir | ▶ Drive | ▶ File | ▶ Form | Frame |
| Label | ▶ List | Menu | ▶ Option | ▶ Picture |
| Printer | Screen | ▶ Scroll | ▶ Text | Timer |

## Purpose

The KeyPress event intercepts ASCII keystrokes when this event's control has the focus. This lets the program audit the user's input, byte by byte. This can be useful for validating data input and alerting the user as soon as an invalid character is entered. Table 16.6 summarizes the arguments of the KeyPress event.

## General Syntax

```
Form_KeyPress(KeyAscii As Integer)
CtlName_KeyPress([Index As Integer], KeyAscii As Integer)
```

| Arguments | Description |
|---|---|
| form | FormName of the parent form |
| ctlname | CtlName of the control |
| index | Uniquely identifies an element of a control array |
| KeyAscii | An integer number representing the ASCII code of the character whose key was pressed |

Table 16.6 Arguments of the KeyPress event

## Example Syntax

```
Text1_KeyPress(Index As Integer, KeyAscii As Integer)
    Dim Char As String * 1

    Char = Chr$(KeyAscii)           'Change the code to a character
    Char = UCase$(Char)             'Change the character to upper case
    KeyAscii = Asc(Char)            'Replace the character code
End Sub
```

## Description

This event is called every time the user presses a key that corresponds to a valid ASCII character. Visual Basic considers the following as valid ASCII keystrokes:

| Valid Character | KeyASCII Code |
|---|---|
| Any printable keyboard character | ASCII code of the character |
| Ctrl+"A" through Ctrl+"Z" | 1 through 26 |
| Enter, and Ctrl+Enter | 13, and 10 |
| Backspace, and Ctrl+Backspace | 8, and 127 |
| Tab | 9 |

**Table 16.7 Possible values for the KeyASCII argument**

Define the KeyPress event starting with the name of the affected control and an Index variable (if using a control array). If the value of KeyAscii is modified within this event, the modification is passed on to the control. This allows you to audit the text being entered. For instance, if you only want uppercase letters to be entered in a text box, you can use the KeyPress event for that control to change each character to uppercase as it's entered. This is done in the example syntax by first getting the character code from the KeyAscii event by applying Basic's chr$ function, then using the Basic UCase$ function to change the character to its uppercase equivalent. Finally, assigning the uppercase character back to the KeyAscii event has the effect of changing the character just entered to uppercase (if it had been lowercase.)

### Control Array

The Index argument is only used if the related control is part of a control array. This Index specifies which element of the array is the one that activated the event. When referencing the control, the element being referenced must be specified by placing the index number between parentheses just after the control name and before the property name (for example, CtlName(Index).Property).

### Example

In the Keys project at the end of this chapter, the KeyPress event is also used to change any lowercase input to uppercase.

# KeyUp Event

## Objects Affected

| | | | | |
|---|---|---|---|---|
| ▶ Check | Clipboard | ▶ Combo | ▶ Command | Debug |
| ▶ Dir | ▶ Drive | ▶ File | ▶ Form | Frame |
| Label | ▶ List | Menu | ▶ Option | ▶ Picture |
| Printer | Screen | ▶ Scroll | ▶ Text | Timer |

## Purpose

The KeyUp event is used for low-level keyboard handling. It reports the current status of the keyboard when a key is released and this event's control has the focus. Table 16.8 summarizes the arguments of the KeyUp event.

## General Syntax

```
Sub Form_KeyUp (KeyCode As Integer, Shift As Integer)
Sub CtlName_KeyUp ([Index As Integer, ]KeyCode As Integer, Shift As Integer)
```

| Arguments | Description |
|-----------|-------------|
| form | FormName of the parent form |
| ctlname | CtlName of the control |
| index | Uniquely identifies an element of a control array |
| KeyCode | An integer number representing the scan code of the key released |
| Shift | An integer number indicating the status of the Ctrl, Alt, and Shift keys |

**Table 16.8 Arguments of the KeyUp event**

## Example Syntax

```
Sub Form_KeyUp (KeyCode As Integer, Shift As Integer)
    Beep                                        'Beep any time a user tries
                                                'to type on an empty form.
End Sub

Sub Text1_KeyUp (KeyCode As Integer, Shift As Integer)
    Label1.Caption = Format$(KeyCode, "###")    'Show last key released
End Sub
```

## Description

This is the compliment to the KeyDown event. Everytime a user releases a pressed key on the keyboard, including the Shift, Ctrl, or Alt keys, this event is inititated for the object that currently has the focus. Forms also have a Keydown event, but it will only occur if the form contains no active controls. Before this event occurs, a KeyDown event will occur at least once, with an identical KeyCode value. Where the KeyDown event may be executed several times when a user holds a combination of keys down, the KeyUp event is only executed once per keystroke, when the user releases the key. This makes this event perfect for low-level keyboard handlers when you wish to disable the automatic repetition of keys on the keyboard.

Define the KeyUp event by beginning with the name of the affected control. Add an index variable if you are using a control array.

The KeyCode argument returns a number that uniquely identifies the key released. This number corresponds to the physical key on the keyboard, not the character that the key generates. For instance, if the user holds down the Shift key and then presses and releases "A," the KeyCode argument will contain the same value as when the user presses and releases the "A" key alone, even though the character generated will be different. The CONSTANT.TXT file that comes with Visual Basic lists the possible values for the KeyCode argument.

The Shift argument is an integer variable that indicates the status of the Shift, Alt, and Ctrl keys at the time the event was called. Each shift key is assigned a value: 1 for Shift, 2 for Ctrl, and 4 for Alt. When any of these keys is pressed, its value is added to the Shift argument. The easiest way to test the Shift argument is with logical (bitwise) operators. See Table 16.5 in the entry for KeyDown for more information on testing the value of the Shift argument.

Keep in mind the KeyUp event is called when any key on the keyboard is released. Therefore, if the user presses and then releases any shift-key combination, the event occurs for as many keys as are in the combination. For instance, if the user presses Ctrl+Shift+A, and then releases them in reverse order, the KeyUp event will occur three times. The first time, KeyCode will be 41 (the code for the "A" key), and Shift will be 3 (the shift code for Ctrl plus the shift code for Shift). The second time KeyCode will be 10 (the code for the Shift key), and the Shift argument will again be 3. Finally, on the third call the KeyCode argument will be 11 (the code for the Ctrl key), and the Shift argument will be 2 (the shift code for Ctrl).

The first example syntax simply beeps when any key is released. The second example syntax formats the keycode for the key just released and displays it by assigning it to the control's Caption property.

### Control Array

The Index argument is only used if the related control is part of a control array. This Index specifies which element of the array activated the event. When referencing the control, the element being referenced must be specified by placing the index number between parentheses just after the control name, and before the property name (for example, CtlName(Index).Property).

### Example

In the Keys project at the end of this chapter, the Key_Up event is used to count the number of times a key is released. It is also used to set the values of the check boxes which indicated whether the Alt, Ctrl, and Shift keys were pressed.

### Comments

The only time a the KeyUp event for a form will be executed is when there are no controls on the form, or all controls on the form are disabled.

# SendKeys Statement

## Purpose

The SendKeys statement allows your program to simulate keyboard input. The keystrokes created by the program go to whatever application is running in the active window. Only Windows programs can receive these characters. This statement is very useful for controlling a program that does not support DDE (Dynamic Data Exchange), and can also be used to test programs automatically with sample input. Table 16.9 summarizes the arguments of the SendKeys statement.

## General Syntax

```
SendKeys Keystrokes$[, Pause%]
```

| Arguments | Description |
|-----------|-------------|
| Keystrokes$ | A string of keystrokes and commands that simulate keystrokes |
| Pause | A True (-1) or False (0) value indicating whether to wait for the keystrokes to be processed before continuing |

Table 16.9 Arguments of the SendKeys statement

## Example Syntax

```
Sub Command1_Click ()
    Text1.SetFocus    'Set the focus to the text box so the characters go there
    SendKeys "This is simulated keyboard input{ENTER}", -1
End Sub
```

## Description

The Keystrokes$ argument specifies the keyboard characters being sent, and must be a string expression. When used in the KeyStrokes$ argument, Visual Basic assigns special meanings to certain characters, as shown in Table 16.10.

| Character | Meaning |
|-----------|---------|
| % | Alt key press - The string "%F" generates an Alt+"F". The string "%(ABC)" is Alt+A  Alt+B  Alt+C |
| ^ | Ctrl key press - The string "^C" generates a Ctrl+"C". The string "^(AB)" is Ctrl+A Ctrl+B |
| + | Shift key press - The string "+D" generates a Shift+"D". The string "+(AB)" is Shift+A Shift+B |
| { | Beginning of a special code |
| } | Ending of a special code |
| () | Parentheses are used to group characters that are being SHIFTed, CTRLed, or ALTed |
| [] | Brackets cause an "Illegal function call"; use {[}, and {]} if you wish to send these characters |

Table 16.10 Special characters and their meanings with the SendKeys statement

If you wish to send any of the characters that have a special meaning, you need to place braces around the character. For instance, if you wish to send the addition sign, you need to specify this string: "{+}"

Non-printable keystrokes (such as function keys) may be sent by using one of the symbolic codes listed in Table 16.11.

| | | |
|---|---|---|
| {BACKSPACE} | {BKSP} (for backspace) | {BS} (for backspace) |
| {BREAK} | {CAPSLOCK} | {CLEAR} |
| {DELETE} | {DEL} (for delete) | {DOWN} |
| {END} | {ENTER} or ~ | {ESCAPE} or {ESC} |
| {HELP} | {HOME} | {INSERT} |
| {LEFT} | {NUMLOCK} | {PG DN} (page down) |
| {PG UP} (page up) | {PRTSC} (print screen) | {RIGHT} |
| {SCROLLOCK} | {TAB} | {F1} (function key) |
| {F2} (function key) | {F3} (function key) | {F4} (function key) |
| {F5} (function key) | {F6} (function key) | {F7} (function key) |
| {F8} (function key) | {F9} (function key) | {F10} (function key) |
| {F11} (function key) | {F12} (function key) | {F13} (function key) |
| {F14 (function key) | {F15 (function key) | {F16 (function key) |

**Table 16.11 Non-printable keystroke codes for the SendKeys statement**

You may also specify that a character be repeated by placing the character and a number specifying the number of repetitions together inside braces. For instance, in the following examples, the {RIGHT} code and the character "A" are both sent 25 times:

```
SendKeys {Right 25}
SendKeys {A 25}
```

The Pause% argument is a boolean value that specifies whether to wait for the program to process the characters or not. This only has an effect if the program receiving the keystrokes is not the one issuing the SendKeys statement. If the value of Pause% is True (-1), the next statement in the sending program will not be executed until the receiving program has processed the characters. If Pause% is False (0), or omitted, execution continues as soon as the keystrokes are sent.

The example syntax shows one way to put specified characters into a text box. Notice that the focus must first be set to the text box so that the string used with the SendKeys statement is sent there as input.

## Example

In the Keys project the SendButton_Click event uses the SendKeys statement to send text to the Windows NotePad program. The first SendKeys statement sends an Alt+Space "X" combination to open the NotePad's control box and maximize its window. Then the text in the text box of the Keys project form is sent to the NotePad.

## Comments

If the program in the active window is the one sending the keystrokes, it will also be the one receiving the keystrokes. When this is the case, the Pause% argument has no effect. Therefore, it is generally a good idea to follow each SendKeys statement with a DoEvents() function call so the program can process the keystrokes.

# Keys Project

## Project Overview

This Keys project explores the use of the two properties, two events, and one statement covered in this section. Each of these is used at least once in the following project. By following the examples here, you should develop a good understanding of the subjects covered in this chapter.

## Assembling the Project

1. Create a new form (the Keys form) and place the following controls on it. Use Table 16.12 to set the properties of the form and each control.

| Object | Property | Setting |
|--------|----------|---------|
| Form | Caption | Keys Project |
| | FormName | Keys |
| | Height | 4110 |
| | Icon | \VB\ICONS\COMPUTER\KEY04.ICO |
| | Width | 5265 |
| Command | CtrlName | SendButton |
| | Caption | &Send |
| | Default | True (-1) |
| | Left | 240 (twips) |
| | Height | 495 (twips) |
| | Top | 3000 (twips) |
| | Width | 1335 (twips) |
| Command | CtrlName | ClearButton |
| | Caption | &Clear |
| | Cancel | True (-1) |
| | Left | 1800 (twips) |
| | Height | 495 (twips) |
| | Top | 3000 (twips) |
| | Width | 1335 (twips) |

| Check Box | CtlName | Alt_Check |
| | Caption | Alt Key |
| | Height | 255 (twips) |
| | Left | 3480 (twips) |
| | Top | 2520 (twips) |
| | Width | 1095 (twips) |
| Check Box | CtlName | Ctrl_Check |
| | Caption | Ctrl Key |
| | Height | 255 (twips) |
| | Left | 3480 (twips) |
| | Top | 1920 (twips) |
| | Width | 1095 (twips) |
| Check Box | CtlName | Shift_Check |
| | Caption | Shift Key |
| | Height | 255 (twips) |
| | Left | 3480 (twips) |
| | Top | 3120 (twips) |
| | Width | 1095 (twips) |
| Label | CtlName | Label1 |
| | Caption | Keys Pressed |
| | Height | 255 (twips) |
| | Left | 3480 (twips) |
| | Top | 240 (twips) |
| | Width | 1455 (twips) |
| Label | CtlName | Label2 |
| | Caption | Keys Released |
| | Height | 255 (twips) |
| | Left | 3480 (twips) |
| | Top | 1080 (twips) |
| | Width | 1455 (twips) |
| Label | CtlName | DownCtr |
| | Caption | 0 |
| | Alignment | 1 - Right Justify |
| | BorderStyle | 1 - Fixed Single |
| | FontName | Courier |
| | FontSize | 9.75 |
| | Height | 255 (twips) |
| | Left | 3480 (twips) |
| | Top | 480 (twips) |
| | Width | 1455 (twips) |

*Table 16.12 (continued)*

| Object | Property | Setting |
|--------|----------|---------|
| Label | CtlName | UpCtr |
| | Caption | 0 |
| | Alignment | 1 - Right Justify |
| | BorderStyle | 1 - Fixed Single |
| | FontName | Courier |
| | FontSize | 9.75 |
| | Height | 255 (twips) |
| | Left | 3480 (twips) |
| | Top | 1320 (twips) |
| | Width | 1455 (twips) |
| Test Box | CtlName | Text1 |
| | Height | 2655 (twips) |
| | Left | 240 (twips) |
| | Text | |
| | Top | 240 (twips) |
| | Width | 2895 (twips) |

**Table 16.12  Controls and property settings for the Keys project**

2. Check the appearance of your form against Figure 16-1.

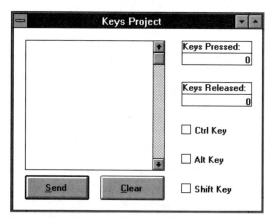

**Figure 16.1  What the Keys project form should look like when completed**

3. Load the CONSTANT.TXT file into the global module. To do this, open Visual Basic's Project window and double-click on the global module. This will load the global module into the Code window. Then open Visual Basic's Code menu and choose the Load Text option. This brings up a dialog box. Select the CONSTANT.TXT file and click on the Merge button. This will read the file into the global module.

4. Enter the following code into the General Declarations area of the Keys form.

```
Dim KeysPressed As Long
Dim KeysReleased As Long
```

5. Enter the following code into the Text1_KeyDown event. This routine counts the number of key presses. It also sets the Ctrl, Alt, and Shift check boxes.

```
Sub Text1_KeyDown (KeyCode As Integer, Shift As Integer)
   Dim AltStatus As Integer
   Dim CtrlStatus As Integer
   Dim ShiftStatus As Integer

   KeysPressed = KeysPressed + 1
   DownCtr.Caption = Format$(KeysPressed, "########0")

   If Shift And ALT_MASK Then AltStatus = 1
   If Shift And CTRL_MASK Then CtrlStatus = 1
   If Shift And SHIFT_MASK Then ShiftStatus = 1
   Alt_Check.Value = AltStatus
   Ctrl_Check.Value = CtrlStatus
   Shift_Check.Value = ShiftStatus
End Sub
```

6. Enter the following code into the Text1_KeyUp event. This routine counts the number of key releases. It also sets the Ctrl, Alt, and Shift check boxes.

```
Sub Text1_KeyUp (KeyCode As Integer, Shift As Integer)
   Dim AltStatus As Integer
   Dim CtrlStatus As Integer
   Dim ShiftStatus As Integer

   KeysReleased = KeysReleased + 1
   UpCtr.Caption = Format$(KeysReleased, "########0")

   If Shift And ALT_MASK Then AltStatus = 1
   If Shift And CTRL_MASK Then CtrlStatus = 1
   If Shift And SHIFT_MASK Then ShiftStatus = 1
   Alt_Check.Value = AltStatus
   Ctrl_Check.Value = CtrlStatus
   Shift_Check.Value = ShiftStatus
End Sub
```

7. Enter the following code into the Text1_KeyPress event. This event converts each character that is typed in the Text1 text box to an uppercase character.

```
Sub Text1_KeyPress (KeyAscii As Integer)
   Dim Char As String * 1

   Char = UCase$(Chr$(KeyAscii))
   KeyAscii = Asc(Char)
End Sub
```

8. Enter the following code into the ClearButton_Click event. Depending on the value of the text in Text1, this event will do one of two things; If there is text in the Text1 text box, this event will clear the text to a null string. If there is no text to clear, the program is ended.

```
Sub ClearButton_Click ()
   If Text1.Text = "" Then
      End
   Else
      Text1.Text = ""
   End If
End Sub
```

9. Enter the following code into the SendButton_Click event. This event sends text to the NotePad program. It first tries to activate the program. If the NotePad program is not currently running, an error is generated, and the error handling routine will execute it. Otherwise, an Alt+Space+"X" key sequence is sent to the program, thereby maximizing it. The text from Text1 is then sent to the NotePad, and the program waits for the NotePad to process it.

```
Sub SendButton_Click ()
    Dim Tries As Integer

    On Error GoTo Load_NotePad
    AppActivate "NotePad - (untitled)"
    On Error GoTo 0

    SendKeys "%{ }x"
    SendKeys Text1.Text, -1
Exit Sub

Load_NotePad:
    If Tries > 0 Then
        MsgBox "Cannot Load NotePad"
        Exit Sub
    Else
        Tries = Shell("NotePad")
    End If
Resume

End Sub
```

## How It Works

This program does several things. First it has a text box control, Text1, which accepts input from the user. However, the coding in the Text1_KeyPress event forces all the alphabetic input to be uppercase characters.

The Text1_KeyDown and Text1_KeyUp events count the number of times the user presses and releases keys, as well as monitor the status of the Ctrl, Alt, and Shift keys. In both events, if any of those shift keys are currently pressed, the value of the corresponding check box is set to 1; otherwise, it is set to 0. This causes each check box to immediately reflect the status of its shift key. These events display the number of keys pressed and released by updating the Caption property of the labels DownCtr and UpCtr each time they're called.

The SendButton control is used to send text to the Windows NotePad program. Because this button has its Default property set to true, the SendButton_Click event can be executed when the user presses the Enter key. Doing so causes the NotePad program to become activated via the AppActivate statement. It is then maximized, because the Alt+Space+"x" key stroke combination is sent to it. Finally, the SendButton_Click event sends the text in the Text1 text box control to the NotePad. The NotePad stays active until the user exits it or switches to another program.

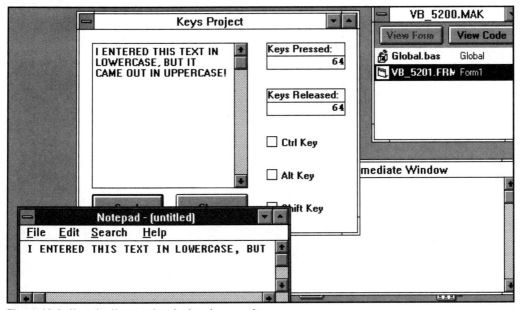

**Figure 16.2. How the Keys project looks when running**

The ClearButton control performs one of two actions. First, if there is text in the Text1 text box control, the ClearButton_Click event will set it to a null string. If it's already null, this event ends the program. Because the Cancel property for the ClearButton control is set to True, the user can execute this Click event by pressing the Escape key.

Figure 16-2 shows the Keys project running. The text was entered in lowercase and converted to uppercase, and the Send button has been clicked to send the text to Notepad. (We resized the Notepad window to make it visible.)

# PART SIX
# DESIGNING DIALOG, LIST, AND COMBO BOXES

# Creating and Using Dialog Boxes

In most applications, there is one main window from which the user directs the program to perform its tasks. Although the user will spend most of his or her time working within this window, some of a program's tasks require that the user make a decision or input some information that is not part of the main window. When this situation occurs, most programs will open another window on top of the main window. This window will generally display a message that tells the user that the program needs some information. It will also contain one or more objects, such as text boxes or command buttons, with which the user can respond to the program's request or make additional settings. This child window will retain the focus until the user performs an action to close it. For instance, within the Visual Basic environment, you load a project onto the desk top by selecting Open Project from the File menu. When you do this, Visual Basic needs to determine which project file you wish to open. In order to get your input, Visual Basic displays a new window, where you can select a project file. Once you've selected your file, the window disappears and you are returned to the main area of the Visual Basic environment. When a window is used in this manner, it is called a dialog box.

## Types of Dialog Boxes

There are three basic styles of dialog boxes. The first style is the simple message box. This type of dialog box simply displays a message and waits for the user to close the box by clicking on a button. The simple message dialog box is used to notify the user of certain information. For instance, when a run time error occurs in a Visual Basic program, a simple message dialog box is displayed telling you which error caused the program to halt. You can use a simple message box when you need to tell the user what has happened, but don't require anything from the user other than the acknowledgment implied in clicking on the OK button.

The second style of dialog box also displays a simple message. However, more than one command button is displayed on the dialog box so the user can make a choice of several options. In most Windows programs, if you attempt to exit a program, this type of dialog box appears and asks if you want to save the files before exiting. Generally, such a dialog box will have Yes, No, and Cancel buttons. How the program acts when the dialog box is closed is based on the button that you choose.

The final style of dialog box actually asks the user to enter information. This type of box generally has one or more controls for entering text or choosing a listed item. The example of the File Open dialog box mentioned previously is such a box.

## Creating Dialog Boxes in Visual Basic

In Visual Basic, a dialog box is simply a specialized type of form. You can create dialog boxes by adding new forms to your program, and placing appropriate controls (such as Yes or OK, No, or Cancel buttons) on them. Of course, you also have to write program code to react to the user's actions when the dialog box is displayed, with code attached to each button control, text box, and so on. If your dialog box requires the user to enter text into more than one text box, or if you need to design a fairly complex dialog box, this is the only way to go.

However, if the dialog box you need is fairly simple and you're willing to forego customization, you can take advantage of the statements and functions Visual Basic provides for creating standard dialog boxes. In other words, if all you need to do is display a message, or get a simple decision, or have the user input one line of text, you do not have to create a new form to display the dialog box.

Three commands allow you to create dialog boxes "on the fly": the MsgBox statement, and the MsgBox and InputBox$ functions. The MsgBox statement displays a message in a dialog box along with an OK button. Once the user clicks on the OK button, the box goes away without any value being returned to the program. The MsgBox function also displays a message and one or more buttons, and waits for the user to click on one of them. Additionally, the MsgBox function returns a numeric value to your program that indicates which button the user chose. The InputBox$ function includes a text box, an OK button, and a Cancel button. The user can then enter a line of text into the text box on the dialog. When the user clicks either of the buttons, the InputBox$ function returns the text from the text box.

Table 17.1 details these elements of the Visual Basic language and their respective uses.

| Use This... | | To Do This... |
|---|---|---|
| InputBox | Function | Display a box with a message that returns a line of text from the user |
| MsgBox | Function | Display a message in a box that returns a button choice from the user |
| MsgBox | Statement | Display a message in a box |

Table 17.1 The two functions and one statement that create dialog boxes

This chapter discusses these functions and statement in detail. At the end of the chapter, the Dialog project demonstrates the use of these elements of Visual Basic.

## Using the CONSTANT.TXT File

Some of the examples below use constant declarations that are included in the CONSTANT.TXT file that comes with the Visual Basic compiler. In order to use the

CONSTANT.TXT file, it must be loaded into the project's global module. To do this, open Visual Basic's Project window and double-click on the global module. This will load the global module into the Code window. Then open Visual Basic's Code menu, and choose the Load Text option. This brings up a dialog box. Select the CONSTANT.TXT file and click on the Merge button. This will read the file into the global module.

# InputBox$ Function

## Purpose

The InputBox$ function displays a dialog box with a message and a text box in which the user may enter some text. It returns a string containing the text entered by the user. The InputBox$ function is thus an alternative to designing a form with a text box for simple text input. Table 17.2 sumarizes the arguments for the InputBox$ function.

## General Syntax

```
InputBox$(Prompt$ [, BoxName$][, DefaultText$][, Left%, Top%])
```

| Arguments | Description |
|-----------|-------------|
| Prompt$ | A string expression containing instructions for the user |
| BoxName$ | A string expression that will be used for the title of the dialog box |
| DefaultText$ | A string expression that specifies a default entry in the dialog's text box |
| Left%, Top% | Integer values that indicate the placement of the dialog box on the screen |

Table 17.2 Arguments of the InputBox$ function

## Example Syntax

```
Title$ = "Greetings"
Prompt$ = "What is your name?"
Default$ = ""
X% = 2000
Y% = 4000
N$ = InputBox$(Prompt$, Title$, Default$, X%, Y%)
```

## Description

You use the InputBox$ function when you want get a simple line of text from the user. InputBox$ displays a dialog box that contains an OK button and a Cancel button, a text box for user input, and the text specified by the Prompt$ argument. The Prompt$ argument may be any string expression of up to approximately 255 characters (the exact number of characters allowed is determined by the width of the characters used). If this string is too long to fit on one line in the dialog box, the text will automatically wrap around to the next line. You may force a new line by inserting a carriage return/ line feed pair (Chr$(13) + Chr$(10)) in the prompt string.

The BoxName$ argument specifies the text to be displayed in the title area of the dialog box. If this argument is not used, the title bar will be empty.

When the dialog box is displayed, the text specified by the DefaultText$ argument is automatically placed in the dialog's text box. This argument specifies a default entry in the text box; normally, this is what you anticipate will be the most frequently used response. This text is selected, so any new entry will replace it unless the user presses the Home, End, right or left direction keys, or clicks on the text box with the mouse. If this argument is not used, the text box will be empty when the dialog box is initially displayed. Note that you can either define an optional argument as an empty string ("") and name it in the function call, or put a comma in place of the omitted argument.

The Left% and Top% arguments are used to specify the position of the dialog box on the screen. They must both be used or both be omitted. These are integer numbers expressed in twips. A twip is a measurement equal to 1/1440 of a printed inch. When used, the Top% argument indicates the distance between the top of the screen and the top of the dialog box. The Left% argument specifies the distance between the left edge of the screen and the left edge of the dialog box. If these arguments are omitted, the box will be centered horizontally, and placed one-third of the way from the top of the screen. (See Chapter 5, *Designing the Application's Appearance,* for more about screen measurements and positioning objects.)

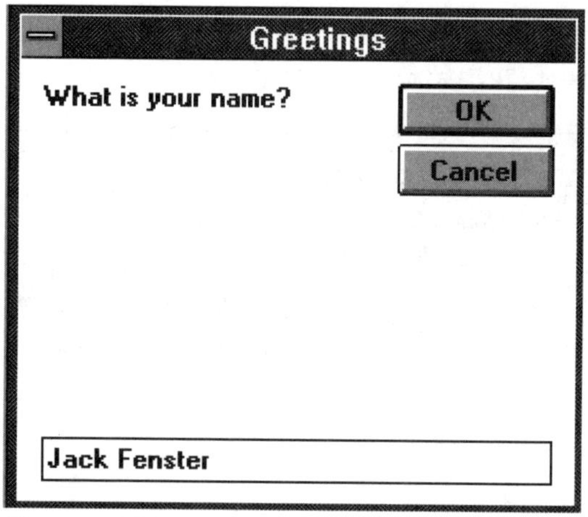

While the dialog box is displayed, the user can type text in its text box. When the user clicks on the OK button, or presses the enter key, the dialog box will disappear and return the string in the text box. Optionally, the user can click on the Cancel button, or hit the [ESC] (escape) key. This also causes the dialog box to disappear, but the string returned is null ("").

The example syntax displays a dialog box with the title "Greetings" asking for the user's name, as shown in Figure 17.1.

**Figure 17.1 Dialog box produced by the example syntax**

## Example

In the Dialog project at the end of this chapter, an InputBox$ function is used to get some text from the user. The returned text is assigned to a string variable for use later in the program.

# MsgBox Function

## Purpose

The MsgBox function displays a dialog box with a message and an optional icon. Your program instructs the function to display one or more sets of predefined command buttons on the dialog box. When the user selects one of these buttons, this function returns a number based on the selected button.

## General Syntax

MsgBox(Message$[, Options%][, BoxName$])

| Arguments | Description |
|---|---|
| Message$ | A string expression containing a message to the user |
| Options% | An integer value specifying which icon (if any) and button set will be used with the dialog box |
| BoxName$ | A string expression that will be used for the title of the dialog box |

Table 17.3 Arguments of the MsgBox function

## Example Syntax

ButtonPressed = MsgBox("Disk Error", 2, "Cannot Open File")

## Description

The MsgBox function displays a message in a dialog box with an optional icon. Your program specifies a set of buttons to display on the dialog box, and the function returns a value that indicates which button the user clicked on. You use this function to get a decision from the user. Figure 17.2 shows a typical use of the MsgBox function.

The message displayed is specified by the Message$ argument. This must be a string expression of up to 1024 characters. Any characters past the 1024-character limit will be truncated. The message will automatically word wrap at the right edge of the box. However, this word wrapping requires that spaces appear somewhere within the text. If no spaces are present, the displayed string is truncated at the 255th character. You may force a new line by inserting a carriage return/line feed pair (Chr$(13) + Chr$(10)) in the message string.

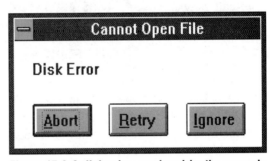

Figure 17.2 A dialog box produced by the example syntax

The Options% argument determines the appearance of the dialog box. The value of this argument controls three things: the icon displayed, if any, the command buttons displayed, and which command button will be the default.

The MsgBox function has six predefined sets of buttons that may be displayed on its dialog box. The Options% argument specifies which of these sets are used. Each set provides a group of possible answers to a specific type of question. For instance, one set displays Abort, Retry, and Ignore buttons. You can use this set to give the user a choice of actions to take when the program encounters some sort of hardware error. Another set displays Yes, No, and Cancel buttons. A good use for this set is to ask the user if he or she wishes to save any open files before exiting a program. Table 17.4 summarizes the six sets of buttons available to the MsgBox function. If no button set is specified, the dialog box displays one OK button.

| Button Value | CONSTANT.TXT Value | Meaning of Value |
|---|---|---|
| 0 | MB_OK | Display an OK button only |
| 1 | MB_OKCANCEL | Display OK and Cancel buttons |
| 2 | MB_ABORTRETRYIGNORE | Display Abort, Retry, and Ignore buttons |
| 3 | MB_YESNOCANCEL | Display Yes, No, and Cancel buttons |
| 4 | MB_YESNO | Display Yes and No buttons |
| 5 | MB_RETRYCANCEL | Display Retry and Cancel buttons |

**Table 17.4 Values for the buttons displayed with the MsgBox function and statement**

The default button on the dialog box is the button whose value will be returned if the user presses the Enter key. Normally, the-left most button on the dialog box is set as the default button. However, you may change the default to another button by setting the Options% argument to one of the values defined in Table 17.5. On a similar note, if a dialog box displays a Cancel button, the Cancel button's value will be returned if the user presses the Escape key.

| Default Value | CONSTANT.TXT Value | Meaning of Value |
|---|---|---|
| 0 | MB_DEFBUTTON1 | Sets first button as default |
| 256 | MB_DEFBUTTON2 | Sets second button as default |
| 512 | MB_DEFBUTTON3 | Sets third button as default |

**Table 17.5 Values for the default button setting with the MsgBox function and statement**

Placing an icon on the dialog box helps the user to understand the nature of the dialog box. For example, suppose the user has instructed your program to delete a file. Knowing that users can make mistakes, you might want to display a message in a dialog box and make the user confirm the action. Displaying the familiar stop sign in the dialog box is a good visual tool to let the user know that a critical operation is about to be performed (see Figure 17.3). Your program uses the Options% argument to specify one of several predefined icons. Table 17.6 summarizes the types of icons available and their values.

**Figure 17.3 A message box with a stop sign icon**

| Icon Value | CONSTANT.TXT Value | Meaning of Value |
|---|---|---|
| 16 | MB_ICONSTOP | Displays a red STOP sign, used for critical messages |
| 32 | MB_ICONQUESTION | Displays a question mark within a green circle, used for queries |
| 48 | MB_ICONEXCLAMATION | Displays a red circle with an exclamation mark, used for warnings |
| 64 | MB_ICONINFORMATION | Displays the letter "i" within a blue circle, used for information |

**Table 17.6 Values for the icons displayed with the MsgBox function and statement**

You specify a combination of the above settings by using the logical or operator. For instance, if you wished to display a critical error dialog box with Yes, No, and Cancel buttons, and you wanted the Cancel button to be the default, your code could look something like this (keep in mind that this example uses constants that are declared by placing the CONSTANT.TXT file in the program's global module):

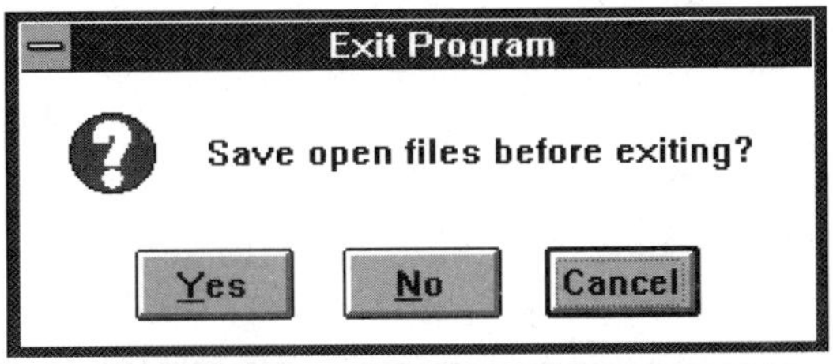

**Figure 17.4 A dialog box that combines values for the Options% argument**

```
Dim MB_Options As Integer
Dim ButtonPressed As Integer

MB_Options = MB_YESNOCANCEL Or MB_DEFBUTTON3 Or MB_ICONQUESTION

ButtonPressed = MsgBox("Save open files before exiting?", MB_Options)
```

Figure 17.4 shows the resulting dialog box.

When the user chooses a button, the dialog box will disappear and the function will return a value indicating which button was chosen. Table 17.7 summarizes the possible values returned by this function.

| Return Value | CONSTANT.TXT Value | Meaning of Value |
|---|---|---|
| 1 | IDOK | Indicates the OK button was pressed |
| 2 | IDCANCEL | Indicates the Cancel button was pressed |
| 3 | IDABORT | Indicates the Abort button was pressed |
| 4 | IDRETRY | Indicates the Retry button was pressed |
| 5 | IDIGNORE | Indicates the Ignore button was pressed |
| 6 | IDYES | Indicates the Yes button was pressed |
| 7 | IDNO | Indicates the No button was pressed |

**Table 17.7 Values returned by the MsgBox function**

Finally, you may specify a title for the dialog box using the BoxName$ argument. This argument must be a string expression, and will be displayed in the title area of the dialog box. If this argument is omitted, the name of the project is displayed. For instance, if your project is named "Project1," that is what will be displayed. The arguments for the MsgBox function are summarized in Table 17.3.

### Example

In the Dialog project at the end of this chapter, a call to the MsgBox function is made to display a box asking whether the user wishes to continue running the program and entering text.

# MsgBox Statement

### Purpose

The MsgBox statement displays a dialog box with a message, an OK button, and an optional icon. The only user action is acknowledging the message by clicking on the OK button. No value is returned to the program.

### General Syntax

MsgBox Message$[, Options%][, BoxName$]

NOTE: Unlike the MsgBox function, the syntax for this statement does not call for parentheses around its arguments.

| Arguments | Description |
|-----------|-------------|
| Message$ | A string expression containing a message to the user |
| Options% | An integer value specifying which icon, if any, and button set will be used with the dialog box |
| BoxName$ | A string expression that will be used for the title of the dialog box |

Table 17.8 Arguments of the MsgBox statement

### Example Syntax

MsgBox "Greetings!", 48

### Description

The MsgBox statement is used to display a message in a dialog box. The message displayed is specified by the Message$ argument. This must be a string expression up to 1024 characters long. Any characters past the 1024-character limit will be truncated. The message will automatically word wrap at the right edge of the box. However, this word wrapping requires that spaces appear somewhere within the text. If no spaces are present, the displayed string is truncated at the 255th character. You may force a new line by inserting a carriage return/line feed pair (Chr$(13) + Chr$(10)) in the message string.

The Options% argument determines the appearance of the dialog box. The value of this argument controls three things: the command buttons to be displayed, which command button will be the default, and which icon (if any) will be displayed. This argument is used in the same manner as the Options% argument of the MsgBox function. Its possible values are defined in Tables 17.4, 17.5, and 17.6 in the preceding entry. Just as with the MsgBox function, you can use this argument to define a specific set of buttons to place on the dialog box. However, because the MsgBox statement returns no value, there is no way for your program to determine which button the user chose. Therefore, it is useless to specify that any buttons aside from the OK button be displayed on the MsgBox statement's dialog box.

You may specify a title for the dialog box using the BoxName$ argument. This argument must be a string expression, and will be displayed in the title area of the dialog box. If this argument is omitted, the name of the project is displayed. For instance, if your project is named "Project1," that is what will be displayed. The arguments for the MsgBox statement are summarized in Table 17.8.

The example syntax creates a box that displays the message "Greetings" together with the exclamation mark icon, as shown in Figure 17.5.

Figure 17.5 A dialog box produced by the MsgBox statement

## Example

In the Dialog project that follows, the MsgBox statement is used to display text previously entered by the user.

# Dialog Project

## Project Overview

This project is a little different from all the other projects in this book, as it is not based on a form. Instead, the main logic is controlled from a code module. A code module is much like a form without any visual properties. This project involves one simple procedure that demonstrates the use of the InputBox function and MsgBox function and statement. When you have finished with this project, you should have a fair grasp of the purposes and use of these Visual Basic elements.

## Setting Up the Program

1. Because this program has no base form, we must first get rid of any forms currently loaded. Load up the Visual Basic environment, and choose the New Project option from the File menu. Single click on Form1.Frm in the Project window. Then unload this form by choosing the Remove File option from the File menu.

2. Create a code module by selecting the New Module option from the File menu. This should bring up the Code window.

3. Load the CONSTANT.TXT file into the global module. To do this, open Visual Basic's Project window, and double-click on the global module. This will load the global module into the Code window. Then open Visual Basic's Code menu, and choose the Load Text option. This brings up a dialog box. Select the CONSTANT.TXT file and click on the Merge button. This will read the file into the global module.

4. Enter the following text into the General Declarations area of the module. This procedure is the entire program.

```
Sub Main ()
    Dim Msg As String
    Dim CRLF As String * 2
    Dim BoxTitle As String
    Dim Response As Integer
    Dim MB_Options As Integer

    CRLF = Chr$(13) + Chr$(10)
    Do
        BoxTitle = "Dialog Project - Input Box"
        Msg = InputBox$("Please enter a line of text", BoxTitle)

        Msg = "This is the text you entered: " + CRLF + CRLF + Msg
        MB_Options = MB_ICONINFORMATION
        BoxTitle = "Dialog Project - Message Box Statement"
        MsgBox Msg, MB_Options, BoxTitle

        MB_Options = MB_YESNO Or MB_ICONQUESTION
        BoxTitle = "Dialog Project - Message Box Function"
        Response = MsgBox("Enter another line of text?", MB_Options, BoxTitle)
    Loop Until Response = IDNO
End Sub
```

5. Set the startup form to the procedure Main(). Do this by choosing the Set Startup Form option from Visual Basic's Run menu, and selecting the entry for Sub Main. Click the OK button.

## How It Works

This is a simple program that reads a line of text input by the user, displays the text entered in a message box, and then asks if the user wishes to enter another line of text. Since you set the procedure Sub Main as the startup form, Visual Basic begins execution there. After declaring and initializing some variables, the program enters a Do...Loop structure.

The first task in this loop is to retrieve a line of text from the user. This is done with the InputBox function. A string constant is used to specify the prompt displayed, and a title is indicated by the string variable BoxTitle. This displays a dialog box with an OK, a Cancel button, and a text box (see Figure 17.6). If the user enters text into the text box, and either clicks on the OK button or hits the Enter key, the entered text is assigned to the string variable Msg. Otherwise Msg is assigned a null string.

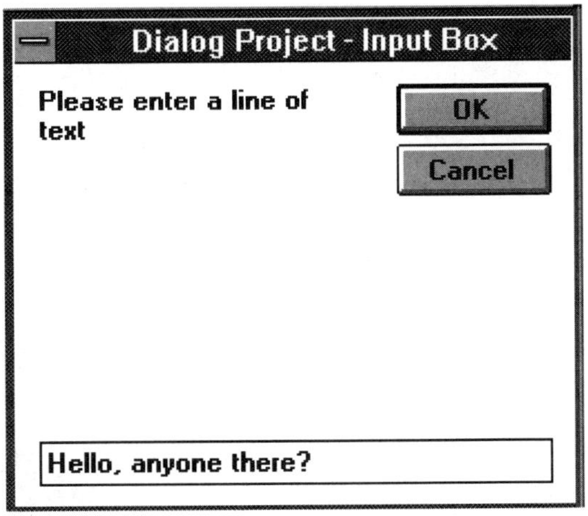

The Msg variable is then modified to become the prompt for the upcoming MsgBox statement. A string constant is concatenated with two carriage return/line feed pairs along with the original value of Msg. When this variable is displayed in the MsgBox statement, it will display the text entered in the previous InputBox function, two lines below the string constant.

The integer variable MB_Options is set to the value indicated by the constant MB_ICONINFORMATION. This causes the MsgBox statement to display a blue circle with the letter "i" in it (see Figure 17.7).

When the user clicks the OK button, the dialog box created by the MsgBox statement disappears.

The MB_Options and BoxTitle variables are then set up for the MsgBox function. MB_Options is set to a value that is

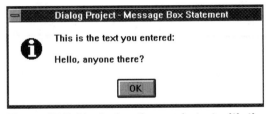

**Figure 17.6 Getting text from the user via the Input-Box function**

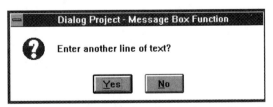

**Figure 17.7 Displaying the user's text with the MsgBox statement**

**Figure 17.8 The MsgBox function can be used to ask the user whether to continue**

the logical or of the constants MB_YESNO and MB_ICONQUESTION. This instructs the MsgBox function to display a dialog box with a Yes button, a No button, and a question mark icon in a green circle. If the user clicks the No button, the value returned by the MsgBox function will equal the constant IDNO, and the program will end. Otherwise, execution continues with the statement following the Do keyword. The box displayed by the MsgBox function is shown in Figure 17.8.

# Using List and Combo Boxes

**M**any programs ask users to make selections from lists. The drive, directory, and file list boxes discussed in the next chapter are specialized for presenting lists used for navigating around the file system, and load their selections automatically. But Visual Basic also provides a more generic facility for presenting lists from which users can choose options, such as colors, styles, fonts, or even data records. With these lists, you supply the options (and can revise the list by inserting or deleting items). Selection lists can even be combined with text input to give the user the choice of selecting a listed item or typing in the name of some other choice. One style of list box and three styles of combo boxes provide you with a variety of tools for presenting a list of choices to the user.

## List Boxes

The list box is a simple box that contains a list of items that have been defined by the program. The user may choose an item from a list box by clicking on it, or by using the up and down arrow keys to move the reverse highlight to the desired item and then pressing Enter. If there are more items in the list than can be displayed in the list box, Visual Basic will automatically add a scroll bar on the right edge of the list box. The user can then scroll up and down the list quickly with the mouse or the PgUp and PgDown keys.

## Combining Lists and Text Input

Combo boxes, as the name implies, provide a combination of the list box and the text box objects. All combo boxes have an edit area and a list area. The currently selected item from the list is always displayed in the edit area of a combo box. The list area appears below the edit area, and when visible, acts in the same manner as a list box. There are three styles of combo boxes; the drop-down combo, the simple combo, and the drop-down list.

   The drop-down combo box displays the currently selected item in an edit area similar to that of a text box. A down arrow is displayed to the right of the edit area. The list portion of this combo box stays hidden until the user clicks the down arrow. This causes the list of items to "drop-down." The user may either choose an item from the list, or type an entry in the edit area.

The simple combo box also has an edit area in which the currently selected item is displayed. The list portion of this combo box is always visible under the edit area. As with the drop-down combo, the user may either choose an item from the list, or type an entry in the edit area.

The drop-down list box is similar in structure to the drop-down combo box. As with the drop-down combo, the list area stays hidden until the user clicks on the down arrow. However, the user cannot edit the text in the edit area, but can only choose an item from the list portion of the drop-down list.

The types of list and combo boxes are summarized in Table 18.1.

| Use This Type of Box... | To Do This... |
|---|---|
| simple list box | Present a list of items for selection |
| drop-down combo | Allow user to type in a selection, or open a list from which to make a selection |
| simple combo | Allow user to type in a selection, or select from a list that is always visible |
| drop-down list box | Allow user to accept the displayed selection, or open a list to make a different selection |

**Table 18.1 Types of list and combo boxes**

## Managing Lists

When you first create a list or combo box, there are no items in the control's list. Items need to be added to a control's list from within your program's code. This is done with the AddItem method. Visual Basic keeps track of how many items have been added to a list, and places that number in the ListCount property. Items may be deleted from a list with the RemoveItem method. When this is done, the ListCount property is automatically updated to reflect that an item has been removed.

The lists of these controls are quite similar to one-dimensional string arrays. Each entry is assigned an index number when it is added to the list. Your program can specify the index number of an item when it is added, or Visual Basic can automatically assign the index number. The string value of each listed entry can be read by your program with the List property. Your program supplies an index number to this property, which returns a string copy of the listed item specified by the index.

The whole idea of using a list or combo box is so your program can determine the user's choice from a list of items. The ListIndex and Text properties are used to determine which item in the list that the user has selected. The ListIndex property returns the index number of the selected item, while the Text property returns a string copy of the selected item.

Table 18.2 displays the two methods, one event, and six properties that influence the settings and effects of the list and combo boxes.

| Use or Set This... | | To Do This... |
|---|---|---|
| AddItem | Method | Add items to the list or combo box |
| DropDown | Event | Initiate an action when a drop-down box is opened |
| List | Property | Set or return the text in a list entry |
| ListCount | Property | Return the number of items in a list |
| ListIndex | Property | Set or return the index number of the selected list item |
| Sorted | Property | Sort the items in a list or combo box |
| Style | Property | Set the style of a combo box |
| Text | Property | Return the selected item in a list or combo box |
| RemoveItem | Method | Remove an item from a list or combo box |

**Table 18.2 Methods, event, and properties dealing with list and combo boxes**

The following pages describe the use of the methods, event, and properties that enable you to set up and manage the various types of list and combo boxes. The ListBox project at the end of the chapter demonstrates how these list management techniques are used together.

# AddItem Method

## Objects Affected

| | | | | |
|---|---|---|---|---|
| Check | Clipboard | ▶ Combo | Command | Debug |
| Dir | Drive | File | Form | Frame |
| Label | ▶ List | Menu | Option | Picture |
| Printer | Screen | Scroll | Text | Timer |

## Purpose

The AddItem method adds an item to the list of a list box or combo box. Table 18.3 summarizes the arguments of the AddItem method.

## General Syntax

`[Form.]CtlName.AddItem Item$[, Index%]`

| Arguments | Description |
|---|---|
| Form | FormName of the control's parent form |
| CtlName | The CtlName name of the List or Combo box |
| Item$ | A string expression containing the value that is being added to the list |
| Index% | An optional index number specifying the placement of the new item in the list |

**Table 18.3 Arguments of the AddItem method**

## Example Syntax

```
Sub Form_Load ()
    List1.AddItem "Red"        'Add color names to a list box
    List1.AddItem "Blue"
    List1.AddItem "Green"
End Sub
```

## Description

When the list box and combo box objects are defined, no items are assigned to the list. Therefore, you must use the AddItem method to create list entries. To specify the AddItem method, begin with the name of the control (list or combo box). When the AddItem method is executed, the value of the string expression specified by the Item$ argument is added to the list.

You can specify the exact placement of the new item in the list by providing the index argument. If you supply the index number, Visual Basic will add one to the index number of the item that currently holds the specified index, and all those items that follow it. The new item is then added to the list at the specified index (see Figure 18.1). In other words, supplying an index number inserts the new item at that position in the list. It does not replace the item that is currently at that position.

If you supply the index number, it must be no less than 0 and no greater than the value of the ListCount property. If the index specified is not in this range, Visual Basic will issue an Illegal function call error.

The index numbering of the list is 0-based. Therefore, if a list contains five items, the first item is index number 0, and the highest

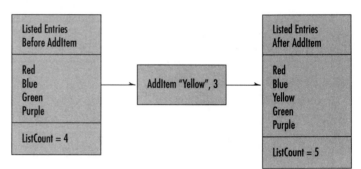

**Figure 18.1 Specifying an index with the AddItem method**

index number is 4. Most often, the AddItem method is used in the Form_Load event of the parent form to initialize the list entries. This ensures the list is loaded before the user has access to the List or Combo box.

If you omit the index argument, Visual Basic assigns the next available index number to the new item. In other words, if there are five items in the list, the highest index number will be four. Therefore, the next available index number will be 5.

The example syntax adds three color names to a list box. Assuming nothing was added previously, "Red" will have index 0, "Blue" index 1, and so on.

## Example

The Form_Load event in the ListBox project uses the AddItem method to initialize the list box with color names. In the Combo0_DropDown, Combo2_DropDown, and MoveButton_Click events, the AddItem method is used to copy list entries from one List or Combo box to another.

## Comments

It is not recommended that the index argument of the AddItem method be used with a List or Combo box that has the Sorted property set to True. This may cause the sort order of the list to be corrupted.

# DropDown Event

## Objects Affected

| | | | | |
|---|---|---|---|---|
| Check | Clipboard | ▶ Combo | Command | Debug |
| Dir | Drive | File | Form | Frame |
| Label | List | Menu | Option | Picture |
| Printer | Screen | Scroll | Text | Timer |

## Purpose

The DropDown event is a built-in procedure that specifies what actions will be taken when the user opens the list portion of a drop-down combo or drop-down list box. This provides your program with an opportunity to tailor the list entries based on information that may not have been available at an earlier time, such as the activity the user is performing or preferences previously expressed by the user. Table 18.4 summarizes the arguments of the DropDown event.

## General Syntax

```
Sub CtlName_DropDown()
Sub CtlName_DropDown([Index As Integer])
```

| Arguments | Description |
|---|---|
| CtlName | The CtlName of the control |
| Index | A unique number that identifies a specific element in a control array |

Table 18.4 Arguments of the DropDown event

## Example Syntax

```
Sub Title_DropDown()
    If UserSecurity > 100 then          'If this is a high level user
        If Title.ListCount = 4 then
            Title.AddItem "Manager"     'Add Manager title to the list if
                                        'it does not yet exist
        End if
    End If
End Sub
```

## Description

The box control used with the DropDown event must be either a drop-down combo box (Style = 0) or drop-down list box (Style = 2). In drop-down boxes the list portion of the control is not visible until the user opens it by clicking on its scroll arrow. When this happens, the control's DropDown event is triggered. The code in this event is executed before the user can choose from the items in the list.

Define the DropDown event Sub procedure by starting with the name of the box control to be affected. Add the index argument if the box is part of a control array.

The example syntax adds an item (the title "manager") to the list box if the user's security level is high enough. This is an example of how the DropDown event can be used to tailor the choices offered by the program to the circumstances of the user.

### Control Array

The Index argument is only used if the related control is part of a control array. This Index specifies which element of the array is the one that activated the event. When referencing the control, the element being referenced must be specified by placing the index number between parentheses just after the control name, and before the property name (that is, CtlName(Index).Property).

## Example

Combo0_DropDown and Combo2_DropDown are both DropDown events in the ListBox project. These events are used to copy list entries from another list or combo box.

# List Property

## Objects Affected

| | | | | |
|---|---|---|---|---|
| Check | Clipboard | ▶ Combo | Command | Debug |
| ▶ Dir | ▶ Drive | ▶ File | Form | Frame |
| Label | ▶ List | Menu | Option | Picture |
| Printer | Screen | Scroll | Text | Timer |

## Purpose

The List property has two functions. First, it can set the value of a list entry in a list or combo box—that is, specify an item to be displayed on a list. Second, it can read the current value (contents) of a list entry from a list or combo box. This property cannot be set at design time.

The List property is also used with the drive, directory and file list box controls. For a description of how this property is used with these controls, please refer to Chapter 19, *Managing Files in Drive, Directory, and File List Boxes*.

Table 18.5 summarizes the arguments of the List property.

## General Syntax

```
[Form.]CtlName.List(Index%) [= Value$]
```

| Arguments | Description |
|-----------|-------------|
| form | FormName of the control's parent form |
| CtlName | CtlName of the List or Combo box |
| Index% | The index number of the desired list entry |
| Value$ | A string expression that can be assigned to the list entry |

**Table 18.5 Arguments of the List property**

## Example Syntax

```
List1.List(1) = "Hello there"          'Assigns the string to list entry #1
FirstItem$ = List1.List(0)             'Assigns the value of the first listed
                                       'item to a string
```

## Description

The List property sets or returns a list's contents in a manner similar to accessing values from and assigning values to an array. The List property begins with the name of the affected list or combo box control. It is followed by an index number in parentheses, which identifies which list entry is being referenced. Optionally an equals sign and a value can be added to assign the specified value to the list entry.

The index numbering of the list is 0-based. Therefore, if a list contains five items, the first item is index number 0, and the highest index number is 4. The number of items in a list can be determined by using the ListCount property.

When using the List property to assign text to a list entry, the program must use an index number that references an item currently in the list. For instance, if a list has five items in it, the program can only use an index number from 0 to 4 when assigning a value to a list entry, or an "Invalid property array index" error will occur. Your program can determine the highest current index number by subtracting 1 from the value of the ListCount property.

When using the List property to read list entries, the contents of the list entry specified by the index are returned. Specifying an index that is out of the range of added entries will return a null string.

In the example code, the first statement assigns the string "Hello there" to item 1 in the list for box List1. Note that 1 is actually the second item in the list. The second statement assigns the value of the first item listed in the list (which is index 0) to the string variable FirstItem$.

## Example

In the ListBox project, the List property is used in the Combo0_DropDown and Combo2_DropDown events to specify the source string when items are being added to the Combo0 and Combo2 boxes.

# ListCount Property

## Objects Affected

| | | | | |
|---|---|---|---|---|
| Check | Clipboard | ▶ Combo | Command | Debug |
| ▶ Dir | ▶ Drive | ▶ File | Form | Frame |
| Label | ▶ List | Menu | Option | Picture |
| Printer | Screen | Scroll | Text | Timer |

## Purpose

The ListCount property is read at run time to determine the number of listed items in a list or combo box. This is a read-only property, and cannot be set by the program at design time or run time.

The ListCount property is also used with the drive, directory and file list box controls. For a description of how this property is used with these controls, please refer to Chapter 19, *Managing Files in Drive, Directory, and File List Boxes*.

Table 18.6 summarizes the arguments of the ListCount property.

## General Syntax

[Form.]Ctlname.ListCount

| Arguments | Description |
|---|---|
| Form | FormName of the parent form |
| CtlName | CtlName of the List or Combo box |

Table 18.6 Arguments of the ListCount property

## Example Syntax

```
Do While Combo0.ListCount        'Remove all the items in the list
    Combo0.Remove Item 0         'until the ListCount property is zero.
Loop
```

## Description

The ListCount property returns the number of items that have been added to a list it invoked by using the name of the affected simple combo, drop-down combo, or drop-down list box. Each time the AddItem method is used on a list control, this property is incremented. Using the RemoveItem method decrements it.

The ListCount property is most commonly used for bounds checking. In other words, when working with a list or combo box, you can check possible Index values against this property to make sure your program does not reference a list entry that does not exist. Keep in mind, however, that the index numbering of a list is 0-based, and that the value of the ListCount property is not the same as the highest index number. In other words, if a list has five items in it, the value of ListCount will be 5, while the highest index number in that list will be 4. Thus you could have a test like this:

```
If Index > MyBox.ListCount - 1 ' Bounds error, index too large for list
```

The example syntax uses a While loop to remove items from the list as long as ListCount is greater than 0.

## Example

In the ListBox project at the end of this chapter, the ListCount property is used in the Combo0_DropDown event as an indicator for when to stop removing items from the Combo0 list. It is also used in the same event to determine how many items there are in the List1 list box, so the procedure knows when to stop adding items to Combo0's list. The Combo2_DropDown event also uses this property in a similar fashion.

# ListIndex Property

## Objects Affected

| | | | | |
|---|---|---|---|---|
| Check | Clipboard | ▶ Combo | Command | Debug |
| ▶ Dir | ▶ Drive | ▶ File | Form | Frame |
| Label | ▶ List | Menu | Option | Picture |
| Printer | Screen | Scroll | Text | Timer |

## Purpose

The ListIndex property returns the index number of the selected item in a list. The selected item is the one that has been previously set by the program, or highlighted by the user using the arrow keys or by clicking on the item. Assigning a value to the ListIndex property changes the selected item to the entry at the specified index. This property cannot be set at design time.

The ListIndex property is also used with the drive, directory, and file list box controls. For a description of how this property is used with these controls, please refer to Chapter 19, *Managing Files in Drive, Directory, and File List Boxes*.

Table 18.7 summarizes the arguments of the ListIndex property.

## General Syntax

```
[Form.]CtlName.ListIndex [= Index%]
```

| Arguments | Description |
|---|---|
| Form | FormName of the parent form |
| CtlName | CtlName of the List or Combo box |
| Index% | An index number of an item that is currently in the list |

**Table 18.7 Arguments of the ListIndex property**

## Example Syntax

```
List1.ListIndex = 0      'Sets the selected item in List1 to the first entry
L% = List1.ListIndex     'Assigns to L% the index number of the selected item in List1
```

## Description

Specify the ListIndex property by beginning with the name of the list box or combo box control to be affected. When read, this property returns the index number of the currently selected item in a list. If no item is currently selected, a -1 is returned. If the user enters text in the edit area of the simple or drop-down combo box, and that text does not match a listed item, this property will also return a ListIndex value of -1.

The program may also change the currently selected item of a list by setting this property. When using the ListIndex property to set the currently selected list entry, the program must use an index number that references an item currently in the list. For instance, if a list has five items in it, the an index number from 0 to 4 must be used or an "Invalid property array index" error will occur.

The first statement in the example syntax sets the selected item on List1 to the item with the index value 0: that is, the first item on the list. In the second statement, the ListIndex property returns the index number of the currently selected item in List1, and assigns it to the variable L%.

## Example

The MoveButton_Click event in the ListBox project uses the ListIndex property to determine the currently selected item in the List1 list control. This item is then added to Combo1's list, and deleted from List1's list.

## Comments

When used with list and combo boxes, using the statement CtlName.List(ListIndex) gives the same result as CtlName.Text.

# RemoveItem Method

## Objects Affected

| | | | | |
|---|---|---|---|---|
| Check | Clipboard | ▶ Combo | Command | Debug |
| Dir | Drive | File | Form | Frame |
| Label | ▶ List | Menu | Option | Picture |
| Printer | Screen | Scroll | Text | Timer |

## Purpose

The RemoveItem method deletes an item from the list in a list or combo box. Table 18.8 summarizes the arguments of the RemoveItem method.

## General Syntax

`[Form.]CtlName.RemoveItem Index%`

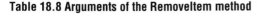

| Arguments | Description |
|---|---|
| Form | FormName of the parent form |
| CtlName | CtlName of the list or combo box |
| Index% | An integer value specifying the index number of the list item to be removed |

**Table 18.8 Arguments of the RemoveItem method**

## Example Syntax

```
Do While List1.ListCount          'Remove all the items in the List1 list
    List1.RemoveItem 0
Loop
```

## Description

The RemoveItem method is the complement to the AddItem method. The RemoveItem method deletes from a list or combo box's list the entry indicated by the Index% argument. Begin the specification of the RemoveItem method with the name of the list or combo box to be affected.

When an item is re-

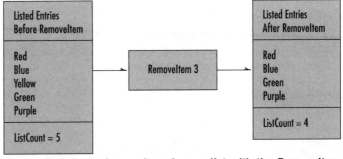

**Figure 18.2 Removing an item from a list with the RemoveItem method**

moved from the list, the index number of each entry in the list that followed the removed item is decremented. The ListCount property for the control is also decremented. Figure 18.2 graphically illustrates this process.

Care should be taken when removing items from a list. If your program specifies an index value that is greater than that of the highest current item, Visual Basic will issue an "Illegal function call" error. To be safe, always check the ListCount property before using the RemoveItem method. The index numbering of the list is 0-based. If a list contains five items, the first item has an index of 0, and the highest index number is 4. Therefore, the value of supplied index should always be less than the value of the ListCount property.

The example code uses a Do While loop to check the current number of items in the list, using the ListCount property. As long as items remain, item 0 is removed. Each time item 0 is removed, the other items' indexes are decremented, moving the next item up into the "0" position.

## Example

The ListBox project demonstrates the use of the RemoveItem method in the Combo0_DropDown, Combo2_DropDown, and MoveButton_Click events. In the DropDown events, RemoveItem is used to clear all the list entries before copying entries from another List or Combo box. In the MoveButton event, RemoveItem deletes entries from the List1 list box.

# Sorted Property

## Objects Affected

| | | | | |
|---|---|---|---|---|
| Check | Clipboard | ▶ Combo | Command | Debug |
| Dir | Drive | File | Form | Frame |
| Label | ▶ List | Menu | Option | Picture |
| Printer | Screen | Scroll | Text | Timer |

## Purpose

The Sorted property specifies at design time whether or not the items in the list or combo box are to be automatically sorted by Visual Basic. Table 18.9 summarizes the arguments of the Sorted property.

## General Syntax

[Form.]CtlName.Sorted

| Arguments | Description |
|---|---|
| Form | FormName of the parent form |
| CtlName | CtlName of the List or Combo box |

Table 18.9 Arguments of the Sorted property

## Example Syntax

```
If Combo1.Sorted = True then          'If the items in the Combo box are sorted
    Call BinarySearch(Search$)         'Use a binary search
Else
    Call LinearSearch(Search$)         'Otherwise search one item at a time
End If
```

## Description

The Sorted property is perhaps the best feature of list and combo boxes. When you set the Sorted property to True (-1), Visual Basic automatically attends to all the chores associated with keeping the list sorted alphabetically. If this property is set to False, no sorting of any kind is performed on the list. This property may only be set at design time, but it may be checked during run time as a boolean value.

Specify the Sorted property starting with the name of the list or combo box control to be affected. In order to keep items sorted, Visual Basic changes the index numbers of the items in a list as necessary. Because of this, Visual Basic needs absolute control over how the index numbers are assigned when items are added. Therefore, using the index argument of the AddItem method is not recommended for a list or combo box that has the Sorted property set to True.

The example syntax checks the Sorted property of the box Combo1 to determine whether to do a binary search (which is very fast but works only on a sorted list) or a linear search (which is much slower, but can work on an unsorted list.)

### Example

Combo0 and Combo1 in the example ListBox project have their Sorted property set to True.

# Style Property

### Objects Affected

| | | | | |
|---|---|---|---|---|
| Check | Clipboard | ▶ Combo | Command | Debug |
| Dir | Drive | File | Form | Frame |
| Label | List | Menu | Option | Picture |
| Printer | Screen | Scroll | Text | Timer |

### Purpose

The Style property sets the style of a combo box. A combo box can be one of three styles: drop-down combo, simple combo, or drop-down list. Table 18.10 summarizes the arguments of the style property.

### General Syntax

`[Form.]CtlName.Style`

| Arguments | Description |
|---|---|
| Form | FormName of the parent form |
| CtlName | CtlName of the list or combo box |

**Table 18.10 Arguments of the Style property**

### Example Syntax

```
If Combo1.Style = 0 then Text1.Text = "Drop down Combo"
If Combo1.Style = 1 then  Text1.Text = "Simple Combo"
If Combo1.Style = 2 then  Text1.Text = "Drop Down List"
```

## Description

Three settings are available for the Style property: 0 for drop-down combo, 1 for simple combo, and 2 for drop-down list. This property can only be set at design time, but it may be checked at run time as an integer value.

Specify the Style property starting with the name of the combo box control to be affected. The example code simply determines what type of combo box Combo1 is, and sets the text accordingly.

### Drop-Down Combo Box

The drop-down combo box consists of three areas: the edit area, the down arrow, and the list area. The edit area allows the user to enter text in the same manner as a text box. The down arrow is displayed just to the right, but separated from, the edit area. The list area of the drop-down combo box stays hidden from view until the user clicks on the down arrow associated with the box. Alternately, the list area is also opened when the user presses the down cursor key while simultaneously holding down the Alt key. Either action causes the list area to drop-down below the edit area. The list area closes as soon as the user selects an item. Because the user can enter text, or choose from a list of items, this style provides a useful tool for data entry fields that may have some often used values, yet cannot be restricted to a limited number of choices.

### Simple Combo Box

The simple combo box is much like a drop-down combo box that has its list area always open. Again, its value can be set by user input in the edit area, or by the user clicking on the desired list item. The default setting for the Height property of this object will display only the edit area. Therefore, it's a good idea to increase the Height property at design time in order to let the items in the list be viewed. Because the list area of this style is constantly open, it uses more screen space than the drop-down combo box.

### Drop-Down List Box

The drop-down list box is almost identical to the drop-down combo. The major functional difference is that the drop-down list box requires the user to choose an item from the list area. While the selected item appears in the edit area, nothing can be typed there by the user. This style is used for data entry fields that have a limited number of valid values.

## Example

The ListBox Project has one of each style of combo box. Combo0 is a drop-down combo (Style 0), Combo1 is a simple combo (Style 1), and Combo2 is a drop-down list (Style 2).

## Comments

In styles 0 and 1, if the user enters text in the edit area of the combo box that does not match any items in the control's list, the value of that combo box's ListIndex will be -1.

# Text Property

## Objects Affected

| | | | | |
|---|---|---|---|---|
| Check | Clipboard | ▶ Combo | Command | Debug |
| Dir | Drive | File | Form | Frame |
| Label | ▶ List | Menu | Option | Picture |
| Printer | Screen | Scroll | ▶ Text | Timer |

## Purpose

The Text property is used to read the text of the selected item in a list or combo box. Additionally, the Text property can be used to set the selected item in combo boxes whose Style property is set to 0 (Drop-Down combo) or 1 (simple combo). Table 18.11 summarizes the arguments of the Text property when used with a list box or combo box.

## General Syntax

```
[Form.]CtlName.Text [= TextString$]
```

| Arguments | Description |
|---|---|
| Form | FormName of the parent form |
| CtlName | CtlName of the list or combo box |
| TextString$ | A string expression that can be assigned to the edit area of the drop-down and simple combo box styles |

Table 18.11 Arguments of the Text property when used with a list box or combo box

## Example Syntax

```
SelectedItem$ = List1.Text      'Assigns the value of a list box's selected item to a string
Combo1.Text = "Hello"           'Assigns a string to the edit area of a simple combo box
```

## Description

Specify the Text property starting with the name of the list or combo box to be affected. You can optionally assign a text string to become the new value of the selected item.

When used with list and combo boxes, the Text property returns a string copy of the currently selected item in the control's list. If no item has yet been selected, this property will return a null string.

This is an alternative to using the List and ListIndex properties together. For instance, in most cases the following two lines of code are functionally equivalent:

```
A$ = List1.List(ListIndex)
A$ = List1.Text
```

The only difference between these two examples occurs when the user has not yet selected an item in the list. When this is the case, the first line in the example would generate an error (because ListIndex would have a value of -1.) The second line of code would not. Instead, the variable A$ would be assigned a null value.

In the example syntax the first statement stores the text of the currently selected item for List1 in the string variable SelectedItem$. The second statement assigns the string "Hello" to the selected item in Combo1: This causes the word "Hello" to appear in the edit area of this combo box.

### Drop-Down and Simple Combos

As discussed in the introduction to this chapter, the drop-down combo and simple combo box styles allow the user to edit text in the edit area of the control. Because of this, the Text property takes on a somewhat different meaning when used with these combo box styles.

When used on drop-down or simple combo boxes, the Text property is a string representation of the contents of the edit area of the control. By default, this is the selected item from the list; thus in the default case, the Text property has the same meaning as with non-combo list boxes. However, since the user can type text into the edit area of a combo box, the Text property can sometimes contain such an input item, probably not matching any item on the list.

You can manipulate the contents of the edit area by assigning it a value, or by using it as an argument with any of Visual Basic's string functions and statements such as Left$, Mid$, and Right$. Any operations performed on this property are reflected by the text inside the edit area.

You may assign a string to the Text property. This causes the text in the box to be replaced by the assigned string. The user can also directly edit the text represented by the Text property. Any time a combo box's Text property is modified, it causes the combo box's Change event to occur.

### Example

The Text property is used in the MoveButton_Click event of the ListBox project at the end of this chapter. When the user clicks on the move button, the item that is selected in the List1 list box is added to the Combo1 combo box. The Text property is used with List1 as the argument to the AddItem method.

# ListBox Project

### Project Overview

The ListBox Project in the following pages demonstrates the concepts relating to the list and combo boxes. By following the steps in this project, you will learn to create a list box and one of each style of combo box, to add and remove items from each object's list, and to determine and react to the current values in each object's list.

## Assembling the Project

1. Create a new form (the ListBox form) and place on it the objects and properties specified in Table 18.12. In the table, all values for the Left, Height, Top and Width properties are in twips.

| Object | Property | Setting |
| --- | --- | --- |
| Form | Caption | List box project |
| | FormName | ListBox |
| | Height | 4425 |
| | Width | 7485 |
| Label | CtlName | List1 |
| | Caption | List box |
| | Height | 255 |
| | Left | 120 |
| | Top | 120 |
| | Width | 1455 |
| Label | CtlName | Combo0 |
| | Caption | DropDown Combo |
| | Height | 255 |
| | Left | 1800 |
| | Top | 120 |
| | Width | 1695 |
| Label | CtlName | Combo1 |
| | Caption | Simple Combo |
| | Height | 255 |
| | Left | 3720 |
| | Top | 120 |
| | Width | 1455 |
| Label | CtlName | Combo2 |
| | Caption | DropDown List |
| | Height | 255 |
| | Left | 5400 |
| | Top | 120 |
| | Width | 1815 |
| List box | CtlName | List1 |
| | Sorted | False (0) |
| | Height | 2565 |
| | Left | 120 |
| | Top | 600 |
| | Width | 1575 |

*Table 18.12 (continued)*

| Object | Property | Setting |
|--------|----------|---------|
| Combo box | CtlName | Combo0 |
| | Sorted | False (0) |
| | Style | 0 - DropDown Combo |
| | Height | 300 |
| | Left | 1800 |
| | Top | 600 |
| | Width | 1695 |
| Combo box | CtlName | Combo1 |
| | Sorted | True (-1) |
| | Style | 1 - Simple Combo |
| | Height | 2580 |
| | Left | 3720 |
| | Top | 600 |
| | Width | 1575 |
| Combo box | CtlName | Combo2 |
| | Sorted | True (-1) |
| | Style | 0 - DropDown list |
| | Height | 300 |
| | Left | 5400 |
| | Top | 600 |
| | Width | 1815 |
| Command Button | CtlName | MoveButton |
| | Caption | Move —> |
| | Height | 735 |
| | Left | 1800 |
| | Top | 2160 |
| | Width | 1695 |

**Table 18.12 Property settings for the ListBox project**

2. Compare the appearance of your form with Figure 18.3.

3. Enter the following code into the Form_Load event. This event uses the AddItem method to initialize the contents of the List1 list box control and sets the current list item index to 0.

```
Sub Form_Load ()
   List1.AddItem "Red"
   List1.AddItem "Blue"
   List1.AddItem "Yellow"
```

```
        List1.AddItem "Black"
        List1.AddItem "White"
        List1.AddItem "Purple"
        List1.AddItem "Orange"
        List1.AddItem "Cyan"
        List1.AddItem "Pink"
        List1.AddItem "Magenta"
        List1.AddItem "Green"
        List1.AddItem "Chartreuse"
        List1.AddItem "Brown"
        List1.AddItem "Lavender"
        List1.ListIndex = 0
    End Sub
```

4. Enter the following code into the Combo0_DropDown event. This event occurs when the user clicks on the down arrow to the right of the text area for this list. It deletes any items currently listed in the Combo0 DropDown combo box with the RemoveItem method. It then retrieves each item from the List1 list box's list, and adds them to Combo0's list with the AddItem method.

```
Sub Combo0_DropDown ()
    Do While Combo0.ListCount
        Combo0.Remove Item 0
    Loop
    L% = List1.ListCount
    Do While L%
        L% = L% - 1
        Combo0.AddItem List1.List(L%)
    Loop
End Sub
```

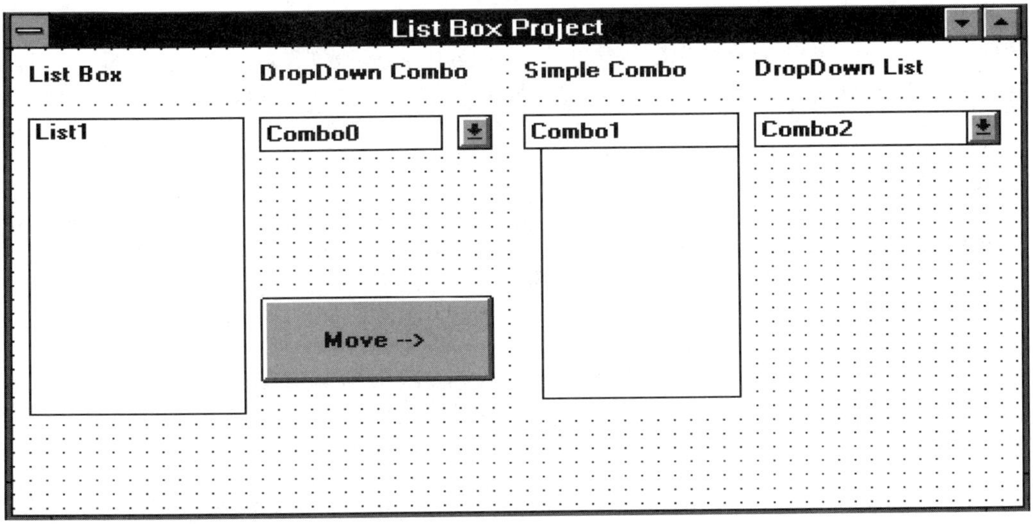

Figure 18.3 How the ListBox project form should look when completed

5. Enter the following code into the Combo2_DropDown event. This event occurs when the user clicks on the down arrow to the right of the text area for this list. When activated, it deletes any items currently listed in Combo2's list. It then retrieves each item from Combo1's list, and adds them to Combo2's list with the AddItem method.

```
Sub Combo2_DropDown ()
    Do While Combo2.ListCount
        Combo2.Remove Item 0
    Loop
    L% = Combo2.ListCount
    Do While L%
        L% = L% - 1
        Combo2.AddItem Combo1.List(L%)
    Loop
End Sub
```

6. Enter the following code into the MoveButton_Click event. This event is activated when the user clicks on the MoveButton command button. It uses the AddItem and RemoveItem methods to move the selected entry from List1's to Combo1's list.

```
Sub MoveButton_Click ()
    If List1.ListCount Then
        L% = List1.ListIndex
        Combo1.AddItem List1.Text
        List1.RemoveItem L%
        If (List1.ListCount - 1) < L% then L% = List1.ListCount - 1
        List1.ListIndex = L%
    End If
End Sub
```

## How It Works

The ListBox project begins in the Form_Load event. Here, AddItem is used to load List1 with a list of colors. The event also sets List1's ListIndex to 0, so when the form is displayed, the first item in the list will be reverse highlighted. The three Combo boxes remain unloaded until the user performs some sort of action on them. Figure 18.4 shows the ListBox project after the form has been loaded.

Clicking on the down arrow of the DropDown Combo box causes the Combo0_DropDown event to be executed. This subprogram performs three tasks. First, it displays an information box to the user indicating that it is about to copy the list items from the List1 list box. Second, it deletes all items that may currently be loaded in Combo0's list. This is done by checking Combo0's ListCount property. As long as Combo0's ListCount property is not zero, the first item on the list (index 0) is deleted using the RemoveItem method. The final task in this event is to load Combo0's list with the items in List1's list. This is done by loading an integer variable with the number of items in List1's list. Each of Combo0's list entries are then set by using the AddItem method and the List() property. Notice the index variable L% is decremented

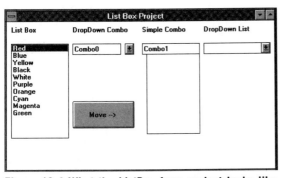

**Figure 18.4 What the ListBox form project looks like when loaded**

before the AddItem method is used. As you may recall, the index argument of the List() property is 0-based, therefore the highest index is always one less than the ListCount property. Because L% is based on the ListCount property, it must be decremented before being used as an index for the List() property.

Clicking on the "Move" button causes the MoveButton_Click event to execute. This event copies the currently selected item from List1's list to Combo1's list, and then deletes the item from List1. First, the event checks the ListCount property of List1 to see if there are truly any items in the list. If there are items in the list, and index variable (L%) is set using the ListIndex property. List1's Text property is used to place the new item in Combo1's list with the AddItem method. The item is then deleted from List1's list using the RemoveItem method. List1's ListIndex property is then reset using the ListCount property and the earlier created index variable (L%).

Clicking on the down arrow of the drop-down list box causes the Combo2_DropDown event to be executed. This subprogram performs the same tasks as those in the Combo0_DropDown event, but it copies Combo1's list items instead.

# Managing Files in Drive, Directory, and File List Boxes

With most applications, users must load 1 or more files, work with them, and then save them to disk. There is thus a need to organize and keep track of files. With older DOS programs, users often had to use relatively arcane DOS commands to manage their files. On a typical hard disk with many directories, subdirectories, and files, file management can mean keeping track of complicated pathnames that specify just where files are located on the disk.

Windows, however, provides an easier way to handle files. The user can select the disk drive to work with, view directories and their files in scrolling lists, and simply select files of interest with the keyboard and mouse. Many Windows users can now do all of their file management without working directly with DOS at all. Windows users will expect your application to provide that same easy access to the file system through point-and-click navigation. Recognizing this, Visual Basic packages the needed file system navigation tools for you, saving tedious coding.

Visual Basic provides the drive, directory, and file list boxes for you to use in providing the interface that lets the user move around the logical structure of the DOS files system. These controls take most of the work dealing with selecting drives, directories, and files away from you, and let you concentrate on the main work of the application.

## File-Oriented List Boxes

For the user and the programmer, the list boxes that present the file system work much like the list box and combo box controls described in Chapter 18, *Using List and Combo Boxes*. In fact, the file-related list boxes share the List, ListCount, and ListIndex properties with the list and combo boxes. These properties are discussed again in this chapter because there are some differences that need to be taken into account when they're used with the file-related list boxes. Here, however, your program does not have to add or remove items from the lists of the file-related list boxes. Visual Basic automatically reads the structure of the disk, builds the lists of directories and files, and updates the list when the user adds or removes files.

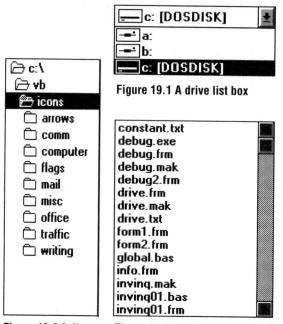

**Figure 19.1 A drive list box**

**Figure 19.2 A directory list box**

**Figure 19.3 A file list box**

### The Drive List Box

The drive list box is like a drop-down list box that lets the user choose from any of the available drives on the user's system. Visual Basic automatically explores the user's system, and adds all of the floppy, fixed, and network drives to the list. Drive list items that reflect local fixed disks will also display that disk's label with the drive letter. For network drives, the network name is displayed. Figure 19-1 shows a drive list box with the drop-down list open.

### The Directory List Box

The directory list box is like a simple list box that lets the user choose a directory on a disk drive (see Figure 19.2). Clicking once on any of the listed directories moves the selection bar; double-clicking on a directory entry changes the current directory for the directory list box.

### The File List Box and File Attributes

The file list box is like a simple list box that lets the user choose a file within a directory (see Figure 19.3). Unlike the directory list box, a simple click selects a list entry.

In the DOS file system, each entry for a file in a directory includes a special area called the attribute byte. Four of the bits in this byte are used to indicate certain settings for the file to which the directory entry is related. The bits are called the archive, hidden, system, and read-only bits. If an attribute bit is on (set to a binary value of 1), that indicates that the related file falls into the catagory defined by that bit. For instance, if a file's read-only bit is set on, that file is a read-only file.

The file list box has several properties that allow you to select which files are displayed in the box based on the settings of these bits. These are the Archive, Hidden, Normal, ReadOnly, and System properties. When the file list box control scans a directory, it selects files for display based on the settings of these properties. If more than one of these properties is set on, then the files selected will reflect a combination of the set properties.

In this chapter, we will be discussing the twelve properties, two events, and one method that are specific to these file-related controls. They are summarized in Table 19.1. At the end of the section, the Drive project demonstrates the use of each of these controls and their properties, events, and methods.

| Use or Set This... | | To Do This... |
|---|---|---|
| Archive | Property | Set or read whether archive files are shown in a file list box |
| Drive | Property | Set or read the current drive selected in a drive list box |
| FileName | Property | Set or read the current file selected in a file list box |
| Hidden | Property | Set or read whether hidden files are shown in a file list box |
| List | Property | Return an item from a drive, dir, or file list box's list |
| ListCount | Property | Return the number of items in a drive, dir, or file list box's list |
| ListIndex | Property | Return the index of the selected item in a drive, dir, or file list |
| Normal | Property | Set or return whether normal files are displayed in a file list box |
| Path | Property | Set or return the current path for a directory or file list box |
| PathChange | Event | Initiate an action when the Path property of a file list box is changed |
| Pattern | Property | Set or return the current file pattern for a file list box |
| PatternChange | Event | Initiate an action when a file list box's Pattern property is changed |
| ReadOnly | Property | Set or return whether read-only files are displayed in a file list box |
| Refresh | Method | Reset the list entries in a drive, dir, or file list box. |
| System | Property | Set or return whether System files are displayed in a file list box |

**Table 19.1  The properties, events, and method that pertain to drive, directory, and file list boxes**

# Archive Property

## Objects Affected

| | | | | |
|---|---|---|---|---|
| Check | Clipboard | Combo | Command | Debug |
| Dir | Drive | ▶ File | Form | Frame |
| Label | List | Menu | Option | Picture |
| Printer | Screen | Scroll | Text | Timer |

## Purpose

The Archive property sets or returns a value that determines whether or not files with their archive bit set on will be displayed in a file list box.  Files with the archive bit set have been copied by the DOS XCOPY or BACKUP commands, or similar programs. Setting this property to false will thus suppress the display of files that have been backed up, which can be helpful for file management. The Archive property can be set at design time, and set or read at run time. Table 19.2 summarizes the arguments of the Archive property.

## General Syntax

```
[form.]ctlname.Archive [= boolean%]
```

| Arguments | Description |
|-----------|-------------|
| form | FormName of the parent form |
| ctlname | CtlName of the file list box |
| boolean% | A True (-1) or False (0) indicating whether archive files will be selected |

**Table 19.2 Arguments of the Archive property**

## Example Syntax

```
Sub ArchiveCheck_Click ()
    File1.Archive = -ArchiveCheck.Value        'Sets the Archive property of
End Sub                                         'File1


Sub Form_Load ()
    Dim ArchiveBit

    ArchiveBit = abs(File1.Archive)             'Read the Archive property setting
    ArchiveCheck.Value = ArchiveBit             'Set the check box to reflect it
End Sub
```

## Description

The DOS file system sets aside 1 byte in the directory entry of each file for attribute information. Five properties can select files for display in a file list box based on the setting of this attribute byte. These are the Archive, Hidden, Normal, ReadOnly, and System properties. The set of files that are displayed in a file list box is based on the combination of these properties.

One of the bits in the attribute byte is the archive bit. This bit is set on automatically by DOS every time a file is modified. Certain programs (such as XCOPY, and BACKUP) can then set this bit off when a file is backed up. This allows the system to make incremental backups based on whether a file has been modified since the last backup.

The Archive property is used to select files based on the setting of the archive bit. Specify this property by starting with the name of the file list box control to be affected. This property has two possible values: True (-1) or False (0).

### Interaction of the Archive Property and Other Properties

The files selected when the Archive property is True are a subset of the files selected by the Normal property. In other words, setting this property to True has no effect unless the Normal property is set to False. In that case, any files whose archive bit is set on will be selected for display, regardless of the setting of the read-only bit. However, if a file's archive bit is on, but its hidden or system bits are also set on, it will not be selected unless the Hidden or System properties are also True.

Table 19.3 lists all the possible combinations for the attribute byte, and which of those combinations will be displayed when the Archive property is True. This table lists only the files that will be selected with the archive bit as the basis. Other files may be selected for the same file list box by setting the ReadOnly, Hidden, or System properties. The A, H, R, and S in the Attribute Value column designate a set status for the archive, hidden, read-only, and system bits, respectively.

| Attribute Value | Select This File? |
| --- | --- |
| none set | No - the archive bit is not set |
| A | Yes |
| AH | No - the hidden bit is set |
| AHR | No - the hidden bit is set |
| AHRS | No - both the hidden and system bits are set |
| AHS | No - both the hidden and system bits are set |
| AR | Yes |
| ARS | No - the system bit is set |
| AS | No - the system bit is set |
| H | No - the archive bit is not set |
| HR | No - the archive bit is not set |
| HRS | No - the archive bit is not set |
| HS | No - the archive bit is not set |
| R | No - the archive bit is not set |
| RS | No - the archive bit is not set |
| S | No - the archive bit is not set |

Table 19.3 Displayed files when the Archive property is set

If this property is not changed at design time, its value will be True (-1) when the program begins.

## Example

In the Drives, Dirs, and Files project, the Archive property is first read in the Form_Load event. The value returned is used to set the ArchiveCheck check box. In the ArchiveCheck_Click event, this property is set to reflect the status of the check box. When the check box is checked, the Archive property is set to True (-1). This code is also shown in the example syntax. Note that the abs() function must be used to change the True value (-1) to the value of 1 needed to set a check box. A false (0) value is of course not affected.

# Drive Property

## Objects Affected

| | | | | |
|---|---|---|---|---|
| Check | Clipboard | Combo | Command | Debug |
| Dir | ▶ Drive | File | Form | Frame |
| Label | List | Menu | Option | Picture |
| Printer | Screen | Scroll | Text | Timer |

## Purpose

The Drive property is used to set or return the selected drive for a drive list box. Files on the selected drive will be recognized and displayed by an associated file list box. This property is also helpful for responding when the user changes the current drive. The arguments for the Drive property are summarized in Table 19.4.

## General Syntax

[form.]ctlname.Drive [= drive]

| Arguments | Description |
|---|---|
| form | FormName of the parent form |
| ctlname | CtlName of the drive list box |
| drive | A string whose first letter is that of a valid DOS drive |

Table 19.4 Arguments of the Drive property

## Example Syntax

```
Sub Drive1_Change ()
    Dir1.Path = CurDir$(Drive1.Drive)      'Uses the Drive property to set
                                           'the Dir box pat
End Sub

Sub Set_Drive
    Drive1.Drive = "A:\"                    'Sets the selected drive for the Drive list
                                           'to A:
End Sub
```

## Description

The Drive property can be read at run time to find out which is the selected drive for a drive list box. For all types of drives, a 2-byte drive designation string is returned with the letter of the drive followed by a colon (for example,"d:"). When the selected drive is a local fixed disk, the 2-byte drive string is followed by the drive's label, if any. For instance, if the fixed disk "C:" has the label "MASTER," this property will return the string "c: [MASTER]." Network drives return the name of the network connection for this drive. For instance, if the shared drive "\\SERVER\MAIN" is mounted as logical drive "D:", this property will return the string "d: [\\SERVER\MAIN]."

Specify the Drive property by starting with the name of the drive list box control to be affected. You can set the value for this property by assigning a string with a drive letter to it. Only the first character of the string is used. For instance in the example above, although the supplied string is three characters long, only the character "A" is used to set the Drive property. The balance of the string is ignored. The supplied character must reflect a valid drive on the system, otherwise an error occurs. The arguments for the Drive property are summarized in Table 19.4.

When the Drive property is used to set the selected drive in a Drive list box, it refreshes the list and activates the Drive_Change event. You can include code for this event to do such things as setting a new default path.

If this property is not set at design time, it is set to the current default drive as recognized by DOS.

The first Sub procedure in the example syntax reacts to a change in the current drive by using the CurDir$ function together with the Drive property to get the current directory for the new drive. This directory path is then used to set the current path for the Dir1 directory list box. The second example Sub procedure simply sets the current drive for drive list box Drive1 to "A:\".

### Example

In the Drives, Dirs, and Files project, the Drive property is set in the Form_Load event to the current drive. In the Drive1_Change event, the Drive property is used to set the Path property of the Dir1 directory list box control.

### Comments

The Refresh method can be used with the Drive list box to update any network drive changes.

# FileName Property

## Objects Affected

| | | | | |
|---|---|---|---|---|
| Check | Clipboard | Combo | Command | Debug |
| Dir | Drive | ▶ File | Form | Frame |
| Label | List | Menu | Option | Picture |
| Printer | Screen | Scroll | Text | Timer |

## Purpose

The FileName property allows your program to read the currently selected filename for a file list box, or to set a new current filename. This property can only be set or read at run time. It cannot be set at design time. Table 19.5 summarizes the arguments of the FileName property.

## General Syntax

```
[form.]ctlname.FileName [= path]
```

| Arguments | Description |
|-----------|-------------|
| form | FormName of the parent form |
| ctlname | CtlName of the file list box |
| path | A string containing a path or file name pattern |

Table 19.5 Arguments of the FileName property

## Example Syntax

```
Sub File1_Click ()
    SelectedFile.Text = File1.FileName         'Set the text box to the currently
                                               'selected file
End Sub

Sub OKButton_Click ()
    Old_FileName$ = File1.FileName             'Change the selected file to the
                                               'name specified
    On Error Resume Next                       'in the SelectedFile text box
    File1.FileName = SelectedFile.Text
    If Err > 0 Then MsgBox "Invalid File Name Specified", 48
End Sub
```

## Description

To specify the FileName property, begin with the name of the file list box to be affected. When you don't specify a path or pattern to set this property, a string is returned that specifies the name of the file that is currently selected in the file list box. The string returned does not specify the drive or path of the file. Use the Path property to determine that information. If no file is selected, a null string is returned.

When setting this property in your program, you can use a drive, path, and file name. The file name can contain wildcard characters (* and ?). When your program supplies the drive or path, the file list box's Path property gets changed to the drive and path specified and a PathChange event occurs. If the supplied file name contains wildcard characters, the file list box's Pattern property gets changed to the file pattern specified and a PatternChange event occurs. This makes the FileName property perfect for allowing the user to change the path and file search pattern by using a text box.

The first Sub procedure in the example syntax is activated when the user clicks on the file list box "SelectedFile." When this happens, the Text property for the box is set to the currently selected file returned by the FileName property. This makes the selected filename appear in the text box, which is the typical behavior for this control. The second Sub procedure, activated when the user clicks on the OK button, sets the FileName property to whatever text is in the text box and then checks for any error involving the filename. This procedure can thus handle the user typing in a filename not on the current list.

## Example

In the Drives, Dirs, and Files project, the FileName property is read to set the Text property of the SelectedFile text box control in the File1_PathChange, File1_PatternChange, and File1_Click events. In the OKButton_Click event, the FileName property is set to the value of the Text property of the SelectedFile text box control.

## Comments

When setting this property, make sure to audit the setting so it specifies a valid drive and path.

# Hidden Property

## Objects Affected

| | | | | |
|---|---|---|---|---|
| Check | Clipboard | Combo | Command | Debug |
| Dir | Drive | ▶ File | Form | Frame |
| Label | List | Menu | Option | Picture |
| Printer | Screen | Scroll | Text | Timer |

## Purpose

The Hidden property sets or returns a value that determines whether or not files with their hidden bit on will be displayed in a File list box. (Under DOS, hidden files are not normally displayed in directory listings.) This property can be set at design time, and set or read at run time. Table 19.6 summarizes the arguments of the Hidden property.

## General Syntax

```
[form.]ctlname.Hidden [= boolean%]
```

| Arguments | Description |
|---|---|
| form | FormName of the parent form |
| ctlname | CtlName of the file list box |
| boolean% | A True (-1) or False (0) indicating whether hidden files will be selected |

Table 19.6 Arguments of the Hidden property

## Example Syntax

```
Sub HiddenCheck_Click ()
    File1.Hidden = -HiddenCheck.Value        'Sets the Hidden property of File1
End Sub

Sub Form_Load ()
    Dim HiddenBit

    HiddenBit = abs(File1.Hidden)            'Read the Hidden property setting
    HiddenCheck.Value = HiddenBit            'Set the check box to reflect it
End Sub
```

## Description

The DOS file system sets aside 1 byte in the directory entry of each file for attribute information. Five possible properties select files for display in a File list box based on the setting of this attribute byte. These are the Archive, Hidden, Normal, ReadOnly, and System properties. The set of files displayed in a file list box is based on the combination of these properties.

One of the bits in this attribute byte is the hidden bit. This bit is used to hide files from the user. When this bit is set on, the related file is invisible to DIR (except with DIR /A or DIR /A:H in DOS 5.0), COPY, and most other DOS commands, as well as most programs. This provides a limited security scheme for certain files.

The Hidden property is used to select files based on the setting of the hidden attribute bit. Specify this property by beginning with the name of the file box control to be affected. This property has two possible values: True (-1) or False (0). Setting this property to True (-1) selects files with their hidden bit set on to be displayed, regardless of the setting of the archive and read-only bits. However, if a file also has its system bit set on, it will only be displayed if the System property is also set to True. Setting this property to False prevents all files whose hidden bit is set on from being excluded from the File list box, regardless of the settings of the other four attribute properties. Omitting the setting returns the current value of the Hidden property.

Table 19.7 lists all the possible combinations for the attribute byte, and which of those combinations will be displayed when the Hidden property is True. This table only lists those files that will be selected with the hidden bit as the basis. Other files may be selected for the same file list box by setting the Archive, Normal, ReadOnly, or System properties. The A, H, R, and S in the Attribute Value column designate a set status for the archive, hidden, read-only, and system bits, respectively.

| Attribute Value | Select This File? |
| --- | --- |
| none set | No - the hidden bit is not set |
| A | No - the hidden bit is not set |
| AH | Yes |
| AHR | Yes |
| AHRS | No - the system bit is set |
| AHS | No - the system bit is set |
| AR | No - the hidden bit is not set |
| ARS | No - the hidden bit is not set |
| AS | No - the hidden bit is not set |
| H | Yes |
| HR | Yes |
| HRS | No - the system bit is set |
| HS | No - the system bit is set |
| R | No - the hidden bit is not set |
| RS | No - the hidden bit is not set |
| S | No - the hidden bit is not set |

**Table 19.7 Displayed files when the Hidden property is set**

If this property is not changed at design time, its value will be False (0) when the program begins.

## Example

In the Drives, Dirs, and Files project, the Hidden property is first read in the Form_Load event. The value returned is used to set the HiddenCheck check box. In the HiddenCheck_Click event, this property is set to reflect the status of the check box. When the check box is checked, the Hidden property is set to True (-1). This code is also shown in the example syntax given earlier. Note the abs() function must be used to change the True value (-1) to the value of 1 needed to set a check box. A false (0) value is of course not affected.

# List Property

## Objects Affected

| | | | | |
|---|---|---|---|---|
| Check | Clipboard | ▶ Combo | Command | Debug |
| ▶ Dir | ▶ Drive | ▶ File | Form | Frame |
| Label | ▶ List | Menu | Option | Picture |
| Printer | Screen | Scroll | Text | Timer |

## Purpose

The List property can be used with a drive, directory, or file list box to read the name of a drive designation, directory name, or file name, respectively. The designation or name to be read is specified using an index to its position in the list. This property is read-only, which cannot be set at design time or run time. Table 19.8 summarizes the arguments for the List property.

## General Syntax

```
[form]ctlname.List(Index%)
```

| Arguments | Description |
|---|---|
| form | FormName of the parent form |
| ctlname | CtlName of the control |
| Index% | An integer that identifies a particular list entry |

**Table 19.8 Arguments of the List property**

## Example Syntax

```
ThisFile$ = File1.List(1)          'Assigns the second file name in the list to
                                   'ThisFile$
```

## Description

The List property works in the same general way with drive, directory, and file list boxes, differing only in the meaning of the item retrieved. (Note that directory boxes use a different index numbering system than other types of list boxes; see below.)

Specify the List property starting with the name of the drive, directory, or file list box to be affected. The List property is followed by an index number in parentheses, designating the position of the item in the list to be read.

Note that the List property is also used with generic list and combo boxes. See Chapter 18, *Using List and Combo Boxes,* for details.

### Drive List Boxes

A drive box's List property can be read at run time to determine which drives are in the list and thus presumably available for use. The desired list item is specified by referencing the List property with an index number in a manner similar to using an array. The drives are listed in alphabetical order, and the index numbering starts at 0. So if a system has drives A:, B:, C:, and D:, drive A: has an index number of 0, and drive D: has an index number of 3. If the supplied index is greater than the highest list item's index number, a null string is returned.

For all types of drives, a 2-byte drive designation string is returned with the letter of the drive followed by a colon (for example, "d:"). When the listed drive is a local fixed disk, the 2-byte drive string is followed by the drive's label, if any. For instance, if the fixed disk "C:" has the label "MASTER," this property will return the string "c: [MASTER]". Network drives return the name of the network connection for this drive. For instance, if the shared drive \\SERVER\MAIN is mounted as logical drive D:, this property will return the string d: [\\SERVER\MAIN].

### Directory List Boxes

A directory box's List property can be read to determine the names of all the directories that are currently being displayed in the directory list box. The desired list item is specified by referencing the List property with an index number in a manner similar to using an array.

The current open directory is set to index number -1. The index number is incremented once for each subdirectory under the current directory, and

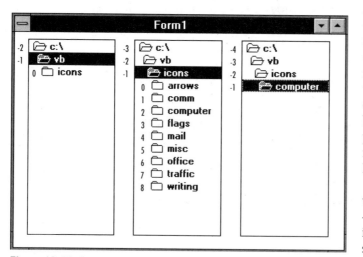

**Figure 19.4 Index number assignment for directory list boxes**

decremented for each parent directory over it. For instance, Figure 19.4 shows three directory list boxes, all with different current directories in the same directory tree.

In the first directory box, the range for the index numbers in the list is -2 to 0. The current open directory is "vb," therefore it is assigned an index value of -1. The "c:\" directory is 1 above it, so it's assigned index -2. The "icons" directory is assigned index 0, since it is the first subdirectory under the first-level vb directory. The second directory box begins the index assignment at the "icons" directory, giving it an index of -1. The directories "vb" and "c:\" are assigned index numbers -2 and -3, respectively. As you can probably now guess, the range of index numbers in the third directory box is -4 to -1.

The string returned when the List property is used with the directory box contains the full path name from the root directory to the directory in the specified list item.

### File List Boxes

A file list box's List property can be read at run time to find out all the files that match the current Archive, Hidden, Normal, Pattern, ReadOnly, and System properties. The file name returned by this property does not include the file's full path. The latter can be obtained using the Path property with the file list box.

The desired list item is specified by referencing the List property with an index number in a manner similar to using an array. The first file in the list is index 0. The last file has an index number equal to the number of files in the list minus 1. If the supplied index is greater than the highest list item's index number, a null string is returned.

The example syntax assigns the name of the second file in the file list to the variable ThisFile$. Notice that the meaning of the index value 1 would be different if a directory list box were used: in that case 1 would mean the second file name listed *below* the current directory.

# ListCount Property

## Objects Affected

| Check | Clipboard | ▶ Combo | Command | Debug |
|---|---|---|---|---|
| ▶ Dir | ▶ Drive | ▶ File | Form | Frame |
| Label | ▶ List | Menu | Option | Picture |
| Printer | Screen | Scroll | Text | Timer |

## Purpose

The ListCount property is read at run time to determine the number of listed items in a drive, directory, or file list box. This is a read-only property, and cannot be set at design time or run time. Table 19.9 summarizes the arguments of the ListCount property.

## General Syntax

```
[form.]Ctlname.ListCount
```

| Arguments | Description |
|-----------|-------------|
| form | FormName of the parent form |
| ctlname | CtlName of the control |

**Table 19.9 Arguments of the ListCount property**

## Example Syntax

```
NumberOfFiles% = File1.ListCount
NumberOfSubDirs% = Dir1.ListCount
```

## Description

When used with drive and file list boxes, the ListCount property returns the number of of items in the list. When used with a directory list box, the property returns the number of subdirectories under the current directory entry.

Specify the ListCount property beginning with the name of the drive, directory, or file list control to be affected.

The example syntax uses the ListCount property to obtain the number of files and subdirectories, respectively. These numbers are assigned to variables for future use.

Note that the ListCount property is also used with generic list and combo boxes. See Chapter 18, *Using List and Combo Boxes*, for details.

## Example

The ListCount property is used in several of the events in the Drives, Dirs, and Files project at the end of this chapter. In each of these events, the File1.ListCount property is used to update the Caption property of the FileCount label. This label displays to the user the number of files contained in the File list box.

## Comments

The property returns the number of items in a list, not the index number of the last listed item. Because the index numbers in a list are 0 based, the index number of the last listed item is always ListCount - 1.

# ListIndex Property

## Objects Affected

| | | | | |
|---|---|---|---|---|
| Check | Clipboard | ▶ Combo | Command | Debug |
| ▶ Dir | ▶ Drive | ▶ File | Form | Frame |
| Label | ▶ List | Menu | Option | Picture |
| Printer | Screen | Scroll | Text | Timer |

## Purpose

The ListIndex property returns or sets the index number of the selected item in a drive, directory, or file list box. This property cannot be set at design time. Table 19.10 summarizes the arguments of the ListIndex property.

## General Syntax

```
[form.]ctlname.ListIndex [= Index%]
```

| Arguments | Description |
|-----------|-------------|
| form | FormName of the parent form |
| ctlname | CtlName of the control |
| index | Identifies a particular entry in the control's list |

Table 19.10 Arguments of the ListIndex property

## Example Syntax

```
File1.ListIndex = 0        'Sets the selected item to the first item in the
                           'list

L% = File1.ListIndex       'Assigns L% the index of the selected item in
                           'File1
```

## Description

The ListIndex property can be used to read the index number of the selected item in a drive, directory, or file list box. Begin the specification of this property with the name of the drive, directory, or list box to be affected. Specifying an index sets the currently selected item to the item in that position on the list, keeping in mind that the first item is referenced with index number 0.

When the program begins, the ListIndex for a drive list box is assigned the value that corresponds to the current default drive. For a directory list box, the program begins with ListIndex set to -1, indicating the current open directory. For file list boxes, the ListIndex property begins at -1, indicating that no file has been selected yet. When used on a directory list box, keep in mind that the selected directory can be different from the current directory in the box. Clicking on a directory entry once selects it, double-clicking an entry opens it. In order to determine the current open directory entry, use the List property with a -1 index value.

The ListIndex property can also be assigned a value in order to change the selected item in a drive, directory, or file list box. The value assigned to the ListIndex property must be within the range of the list or a "Invalid property array index" error will occur.

The first statement in the example syntax sets the currently selected file in file list box File1 to the first item on the displayed list. The second example statement saves the index number of the currently selected file in file list box File1 in the variable L%.

# Normal Property

## Objects Affected

| | | | | |
|---|---|---|---|---|
| Check | Clipboard | Combo | Command | Debug |
| Dir | Drive | ▶ File | Form | Frame |
| Label | List | Menu | Option | Picture |
| Printer | Screen | Scroll | Text | Timer |

## Purpose

The Normal property sets or returns a value that determines whether or not normal files will be displayed in a File list box. Normal files are those that do not have the hidden or system attribute set: these files are not normally displayed in DOS directory listings. This property can be set at design time, and set or read at run time. Table 19.11 summarizes the arguments of the Normal property.

## General Syntax

```
[form.]ctlname.Normal [= boolean%]
```

| Arguments | Description |
|---|---|
| form | FormName of the parent form |
| ctlname | CtlName of the file list box |
| boolean% | A True (-1) or False (0) indicating whether normal files will be selected |

Table 19.11 Arguments of the Normal property

## Example Syntax

```
Sub NormalCheck_Click ()
    File1.Normal = -NormalCheck.Value    'Sets the Normal property of File1
End Sub

Sub Form_Load ()
    Dim NormalBit

    NormalBit = abs(File1.Normal)        'Read the Normal property setting
    NormalCheck.Value = NormalBit        'Set the check box to reflect it
End Sub
```

## Description

The DOS file system sets aside 1 byte in the directory entry of each file for attribute information. Five properties select files for display in a file list box based on the setting of this attribute byte: the Archive, Hidden, Normal, ReadOnly, and System properties.

The set of files displayed in a file list box is based on the combination of these properties. Normal files are defined as all files whose hidden and system bits are not set on, regardless of the settings of the archive and read-only bits.

Begin the specification of the Normal property with the name of the file list box to be affected. The Normal property has two possible values: True (-1) or False (0). Setting this property to True selects all files whose hidden and system bits are set off, regardless of the settings of the archive and read-only bits. In essence, this makes normal files a superset of the files selected with the Archive and ReadOnly properties, combined with all files that have no attribute bits set on. When this property is set to False, the file list box excludes any files that have none of the attribute bits set on. Any other files may be selected by setting the other four attribute properties.

Table 19.12 lists all the possible combinations for the attribute byte, and which of those combinations will be selected when the Normal property is True. This table lists only those files that will be selected when the hidden and system bits are off. Other files may be selected by setting the Hidden and System properties. The A, H, R, and S in the Attribute Value column designate a set status for the archive, hidden, read-only, and system bits, respectively.

| Attribute Value | Select This File? |
| --- | --- |
| none set | Yes |
| A | Yes |
| AH | No - the hidden bit is set |
| AHR | No - the hidden bit is set |
| AHRS | No - both the hidden and system bits are set |
| AHS | No - both the hidden and system bits are set |
| AR | Yes |
| ARS | No - the system bit is set |
| AS | No - the system bit is set |
| H | No - the hidden bit is set |
| HR | No - the hidden bit is set |
| HRS | No - both the hidden and system bits are set |
| HS | No - both the hidden and system bits are set |
| R | Yes |
| RS | No - the system bit is set |
| S | No - the system bit is set |

**Table 19.12  Displayed files when the Normal property is set**

If the Normal property is not changed at design time, its value will be True (-1) when the program begins.

## Example

In the Drives, Dirs, and Files project, the Normal property is first read in the Form_Load event. The value returned is used to set the NormalCheck check box. In the NormalCheck_Click event, this property is set to reflect the status of the check box. When the check box is checked, the Normal property is set to True (-1). This code is also shown in the example syntax above. Note that the abs() function must be used to turn a regular True value (-1) into the one value needed to set a check box.

# Path Property

## Objects Affected

| | | | | |
|---|---|---|---|---|
| Check | Clipboard | Combo | Command | Debug |
| ▶ Dir | Drive | ▶ File | Form | Frame |
| Label | List | Menu | Option | Picture |
| Printer | Screen | Scroll | Text | Timer |

## Purpose

The Path property is used to set or read the currently opened directory path in a directory list box, or the current directory in a file list box. At design time, this property is set to the current default directory, and cannot be changed. However, this property can be set or read at run time. Table 19.13 summarizes the arguments of the path property.

## General Syntax

```
[form.]ctlname.Path [= path]
```

| Arguments | Description |
|---|---|
| form | FormName of the parent form |
| ctlname | CtlName of the file or directory list box |
| path | A string containing a valid path name |

Table 19.13 Arguments of the Path property

## Example Syntax

```
Sub Dir1_Change ()                      'Read the Dir list box Path to set the
    File1.Path = Dir1.Path              'File list box Path property and
    ChDir Dir1.Path                     'change the current directory.
End Sub

Sub File1_PathChange ()
    Dir1.Path = File1.Path             'Change the Dir list box Path to the
    Drive1.Drive = File1.Path          'Path from the File list box
End Sub
```

## Description

Specify the Path property by beginning with the name of the directory or file list box to be affected. To set this property, specify a string containing a valid path name.

The operation of the Path property for directory list boxes is somewhat different than in file list boxes, so the two controls will be discussed separately.

### Directory List Boxes

A user can select a directory entry in a directory list box by clicking on it. However, this does not open the directory; it merely moves the highlight bar to it and changes the ListIndex property to reflect the selected directory. When a user double-clicks on a directory entry, that entry is opened, and any subdirectories underneath it are displayed.

The Path property returns the directory path of the currently open directory in a directory list box. The full path is returned, including the drive letter.

You can also assign a string to this property from within your program's code. This string must contain the valid path name of an existing directory on the system on which your program is run. This causes the open directory in the directory list box to be changed to the path specified in the string.

Any time the Path property of a directory list box is changed, either by the user or by the program, the directory list box's Change event is triggered.

### File List Boxes

The Path property of the file list box control specifies the directory from which the box is to select its files. Reading this property returns the full path of the file list box's current directory, including the drive letter.

You can change the current directory path for a file list box by assigning a string to this property from within your program's code. This string must contain the valid path name of an existing directory on the system on which your program is run. This causes the current directory of a file list box to be changed to the path specified in the string.

Any time the Path property of a file list box is changed, the File list box's PathChange event is triggered.

## Example

The Path property for the File1 list box is set in the Form_Load and Dir1_Change events. For the Dir1 list box, it is set in the Form_Load and File1_PathChange events. Whenever the user changes the path in the directory list or file list box, the other's property is set to reflect the change. This code is also shown in the example syntax above.

## Comments

Some sort of validity checking should be in place to ensure the string being assigned to the Path property is a valid existing drive and path. If the path is not valid, an error will occur.

# PathChange Event

## Objects Affected

| | | | | |
|---|---|---|---|---|
| Check | Clipboard | Combo | Command | Debug |
| Dir | Drive | ▶ File | Form | Frame |
| Label | List | Menu | Option | Picture |
| Printer | Screen | Scroll | Text | Timer |

## Purpose

The PathChange event is a built-in procedure that specifies the actions that will be taken when the current path of a file list box is changed. The arguments for the PathChange event are summarized in Table 19.14.

## General Syntax

```
Sub File1_PathChange ([Index As Integer])
End Sub
```

| Arguments | Description |
|---|---|
| File1e | CtlName of the file list box |
| index | Uniquely identifies an element of a control array |

Table 19.14 Arguments of the PathChange event

## Example Syntax

```
Sub File1_PathChange ()
   Dir1.Path = File1.Path          'When the File list box's path is changed,
   Drive1.Drive = File1.Path       'change the path in the Dir & Drive list
                                   'boxes
End Sub
```

## Description

The PathChange event is activated anytime the current path for a file list box is changed. This can happen by assigning a new value to the Path property, or by assigning a value that includes a path to the FileName property of the file list box.

   This event is mostly used so the program can change the Path and/or Drive properties for any directory and/or drive list boxes that are on the same form.

   Specify the PathChange event starting with the name of the file list box to be affected.

### Control Array

The Index argument is only used if the related control is part of a control array. This Index specifies which element of the array is the one that activated the event. When referencing the control, the element being referenced must be specified by placing the index number between parentheses just after the control name, and before the property name (for example, CtlName(Index).Property).

The example syntax shows how to update the path for a drive and a directory list box when a file box's path is changed somewhere in the code.

## Example

In the Drives, Dirs, and Files project, the Path property of the directory list box control, Dir1, can be changed by the user when a directory entry is clicked on. This causes the Dir1_Change event to occur. In this event, The Path property of Dir1 is assigned to the Path property of the file list box control, File1. This causes the current directory for File1 to be changed to the directory opened by the user. When File1.Path is assigned the value of Dir1.Path, the listed entries in File1 are updated to reflect the files in the opened directory.

## Comments

Directory list boxes do not have a PathChange event. This function is covered by using their Change event.

# Pattern Property

## Objects Affected

| | | | | |
|---|---|---|---|---|
| Check | Clipboard | Combo | Command | Debug |
| Dir | Drive | ▶ File | Form | Frame |
| Label | List | Menu | Option | Picture |
| Printer | Screen | Scroll | Text | Timer |

## Purpose

The Pattern property is used to set or read the currently selected file matching pattern in a file list box. Only files that match the Pattern property are displayed in the file list box. This property can be set at design time, and set or read at run time.

## General Syntax

```
[form.]ctlname.FileName [= pattern]
```

| Arguments | Description |
|---|---|
| form | FormName of the parent form |
| ctlname | CtlName of the file list box |
| pattern | A string containing a full or partial file name pattern |

**Table 19.15 Arguments of the Pattern property**

## Example Syntax

```
File1.Pattern = "*.DAT"
```

## Description

The setting of the Pattern property determines which files will be displayed in the file list box. Begin the specification of this property with the name of the file list box to be affected. Follow the property name with an equals sign and a string containing a valid DOS file pattern. The pattern can have no more than eight characters for a name, a period, and up to three characters for the extension. The wildcard characters (* and ?) can be (and most often are) used in the pattern. The "?" wildcard matches all characters that share the same position in the file name. The "*" wildcard matches all files that share the same pattern up to the position held by it. The Pattern property cannot specify a drive or path. When this property is changed by a program it activates the PatternChange event for that File list box.

When the Pattern property is read, it returns the current pattern setting for the specified file list box.

The example code assigns the string "*.DAT" to the Pattern for the File1 file list box. The list will change to show only those files that end in the .DAT extension. (What is displayed is also subject to the settings of the attribute properties.)

## Example

In the Drives, Dirs, and Files project, the Pattern property for the File1 list box is set at design time to display all the files (*.*).

## Comments

Some sort of validity checking should be in place to ensure the string being assigned to the Pattern property is a valid pattern. If the pattern is not valid, an error will occur.

# PatternChange Event

## Objects Affected

| | | | | |
|---|---|---|---|---|
| Check | Clipboard | Combo | Command | Debug |
| Dir | Drive | ▶ File | Form | Frame |
| Label | List | Menu | Option | Picture |
| Printer | Screen | Scroll | Text | Timer |

## Purpose

The PatternChange event is a built-in procedure that specifies the actions that will be taken when the Pattern property of a file list box is changed. The Pattern property specifies a pattern (possibly including DOS wildcards) that specifies which filenames will be listed in a file list box. The arguments for the PatternChange event are summarized in Table 19.16.

## General Syntax

```
Sub ctlname_PatternChange ([Index As Integer])
End Sub
```

| Arguments | Description |
|-----------|-------------|
| ctlname | CtlName of the file list box |
| index | Uniquely identifies an element of a control array |

Table 19.16 Arguments of the PatternChange property

## Example Syntax

```
Sub File1_PatternChange ()
   Pattern.Text = File1.Pattern
End Sub
```

## Description

The PatternChange event is activated anytime the display pattern for a file list box is changed. This will happen when a new value is assigned to the Pattern property or the FileName property of the file list box.

Specify the PatternChange event by beginning a Sub procedure definition with the name of the file list box to be affected.

The example syntax responds to a change in the file pattern by assigning the new pattern to the text for the Pattern text box, displaying it as the default text in the text entry area.

### Control Array

The Index argument is only used if the related control is part of a control array. This Index specifies which element of the array is the one that activated the event. When referencing the control, the element being referenced must be specified by placing the index number between parentheses just after the control name, and before the property name (for example, CtlName(Index).Property).

## Example

In the Drives, Dirs, and Files project at the end of this chapter, the PathChange event for file list box File1 is coded so that it shows the number of matching files in the box's caption, and also updates the display of the selected file in the SelectedFile text box.

## Comments

Directory list boxes do not have a PathChange event. This function is covered by using the Change event.

# ReadOnly Property

## Objects Affected

| | | | | |
|---|---|---|---|---|
| Check | Clipboard | Combo | Command | Debug |
| Dir | Drive | ▶ File | Form | Frame |
| Label | List | Menu | Option | Picture |
| Printer | Screen | Scroll | Text | Timer |

## Purpose

The ReadOnly property sets or returns a value that determines whether or not files with their read-only bit on will be displayed in a file list box. Read-only files cannot be changed or deleted, but only examined. Making files read-only thus offers a measure of protection for important files. The ReadOnly property can be set at design time, and set or read at run time. The arguments for the ReadOnly property are summarized in Table 19.17.

## General Syntax

```
[form.]ctlname.ReadOnly [= boolean%]
```

| Arguments | Description |
|---|---|
| form | FormName of the parent form |
| ctlname | CtlName of the File list box |
| boolean% | A True (-1) or False (0) indicating whether read-only files will be selected |

Table 19.17 Arguments of the ReadOnly property

## Example Syntax

```
Sub ReadOnlyCheck_Click ()
    File1.ReadOnly = -ReadOnlyCheck.Value      'Sets the ReadOnly property of File1
End Sub

Sub Form_Load ()
    Dim ReadOnlyBit

    ReadOnlyBit = abs(File1.ReadOnly)          'Read the ReadOnly property setting
    ReadOnlyCheck.Value = ReadOnlyBit          'Set the check box to reflect it
End Sub
```

## Description

The DOS file system sets aside 1 byte in the directory entry of each file for attribute information. Five properties can select files for display in a File list box based on the setting of this attribute byte: the Archive, Hidden, Normal, ReadOnly, and System properties. The set of files displayed in a file list box is based on the combination of these properties.

One of the bits in this attribute byte is the read-only bit. When this bit is set on, DOS allows the related file to be read from, but not written to or deleted. This prevents users from inadvertently changing or erasing sensitive files.

The ReadOnly property is used to select files based on the setting of the read-only bit. Begin the specification of this property with the name of the file list box to be affected. You can assign a value to the ReadOnly property, or obtain the current value of this attribute.

The ReadOnly property has two possible values: True (-1) or False (0). The files selected when this property is True are a subset of the files selected by the Normal property. In other words, setting this property to True has no effect unless the Normal property is set to False. In that case, any files whose read-only bit is set on will be selected for display, regardless of the setting of the archive bit. However, if a file's read-only bit is on, but its hidden or system bits are also set on, it will not be selected unless the Hidden or System properties are also True.

Table 19.18 lists all the possible combinations for the attribute byte, and which of those combinations will be displayed when the ReadOnly property is True. This table lists only the files that will be selected with the ReadOnly bit as the basis. Other files may be selected for the same File list box by setting the Archive, Hidden, or System properties. The A, H, R, and S in the Attribute Value column designate a set status for the archive, hidden, read-only, and system bits, respectively.

| Attribute Value | Select This File? |
| --- | --- |
| none set | No - the read-only bit is not set |
| A | No - the read-only bit is not set |
| AH | No - the read-only bit is not set |
| AHR | No - the hidden bit is set |
| AHRS | No - both the hidden and system bits are set |
| AHS | No - both the hidden and system bits are set |
| AR | Yes |
| ARS | No - the system bit is set |
| AS | No - the read-only bit is not set |
| H | No - the read-only bit is not set |
| HR | No - the hidden bit is set |
| HRS | No - both the hidden and system bits are set |
| HS | No - both the hidden and system bits are set |
| R | Yes |
| RS | No - the system bit is set |
| S | No - the read-only bit is not set |

Table 19.18 Displayed files when the ReadOnly property is set

If the ReadOnly property is not changed at design time, its value will be True (-1) when the program begins.

### Example

In the Drives, Dirs, and Files project, the ReadOnly property is first read in the Form_Load event. The value returned is used to set the ReadOnlyCheck check box. In the ReadOnlyCheck_Click event, this property is set to reflect the status of the check box. When the check box is checked, the ReadOnly property is set to True (-1). This is also shown in the example syntax. Note that the abs() function must be used to turn a True (-1) value into the value of 1 needed to set the checkbox.

# Refresh Method

### Objects Affected

| | | | | |
|---|---|---|---|---|
| ▶ Check | Clipboard | ▶ Combo | ▶ Command | Debug |
| ▶ Dir | ▶ Drive | ▶ File | ▶ Form | ▶ Frame |
| ▶ Label | ▶ List | Menu | ▶ Option | ▶ Picture |
| Printer | ▶ Screen | ▶ Scroll | ▶ Text | Timer |

### Purpose

The Refresh method forces any changes affecting a control to be reflected in its status or display immediately. Table 19.19 summarizes the arguments for the Refresh property.

### General Syntax

```
[form.]ctlname.Refresh
```

| Arguments | Description |
|---|---|
| form | FormName of the parent form |
| ctlname | CtlName of the control |

Table 19.19 Arguments of the Refresh method

### Example Syntax

```
File1.Refresh
```

### Description

The Refresh method is useful in two situations. First, because Windows is a multitasking program, it is possible to make a change to a control that is not reflected on the screen because background processing is in progress. Using the Refresh method causes any changes to the specified control to be reflected immediately.

Second, the Refresh method can be used to cause the drive, directory, and file list boxes to update their lists. These controls only read their information from the disk when the user chooses an item from their list. This can cause problems if the files or directories have changed since the information was read. For instance, if a program uses the file list box to delete a file, unless the Refresh method is invoked, that file name stays in the File list box after the user deletes it. These controls may also need to be refreshed on a regular basis if the user is working in a networked environment, where the file information can change without notice.

Specify the Refresh method by beginning with the name of the control (such as a drive, directory, or file list box) to be affected.

In the example syntax, the control File1 (presumably a file list box) is refreshed. Any files that have been added to or deleted from the directory displayed by the file list box (perhaps by another running process on a network) will now be reflected in the file list.

### Example

In the Drives, Dirs, and Files project, the Refresh method is used in the File1_Click event. This causes any changes that have been made to the drive and file information by any other programs to be updated in this program.

### Comments

Other than the file-related list boxes, most controls will automatically refresh as fast as needed without using the Refresh method.

# System Property

### Objects Affected

| Check | Clipboard | Combo | Command | Debug |
|---|---|---|---|---|
| Dir | Drive | ▶ File | Form | Frame |
| Label | List | Menu | Option | Picture |
| Printer | Screen | Scroll | Text | Timer |

### Purpose

The System property sets or returns a value that determines whether or not files with their system bit set on will be displayed in a File list box. The System bit is used by DOS to designate files that are of special importance to the system, and thus should be hidden from sight and protected from deletion. The System property can be set at design time, and set or read at run time. Table 19.20 summarizes the arguments of the System property.

## General Syntax

```
[form.]ctlname.System [= boolean%]
```

| Arguments | Description |
|---|---|
| form | FormName of the parent form |
| ctlname | CtlName of the file list box |
| boolean% | A True (-1) or False (0) indicating whether system files will be selected |

**Table 19.20 Arguments of the System property**

## Example Syntax

```
Sub SystemCheck_Click ()
    File1.System = -SystemCheck.Value    'Sets the System property of File1
End Sub

Sub Form_Load ()
    Dim SystemBit

    SystemBit = abs(File1.System)        'Read the System property setting
    SystemCheck.Value = SystemBit        'Set the check box to reflect it
End Sub
```

## Description

The DOS file system sets aside 1 byte in the directory entry of each file for attribute information. Five properties can select files for display in a file list box based on the setting of this attribute byte: the Archive, Hidden, Normal, ReadOnly, and System properties. The set of files displayed in a file list box is based on the combination of these properties.

The system attribute bit normally designates a file as one of the DOS kernal or BIOS files. However, this bit can be set for other non-system files. As with the read-only attribute bit, files with the system bit set cannot be deleted.

The System property is used to select files based on the setting of the system attribute bit. This property has two possible values: True (-1) or False (0). Setting this property to True (-1) selects files with their system bit set on to be displayed, regardless of the setting of the archive and read-only bits. However, if a file also has its hidden bit set on, it will only be displayed if the Hidden property is also set to True. Setting this property to False prevents all files whose system bit is set on to be excluded from the File list box, regardless of the settings of the other four attribute properties.

Table 19.21 lists all the possible combinations for the attribute byte, and which of those combinations will be displayed when the System property is True. This table only lists those files that will be selected with the system bit as the basis. Other files may be selected for the same file list box by setting the Archive, Hidden, Normal, or ReadOnly properties. The A, H, R, and S in the Attribute Value column designate a set status for the archive, hidden, read-only, and system bits, respectively.

| Attribute Value | Select This File? |
|---|---|
| none set | No - the system bit is not set |
| A | No - the system bit is not set |
| AH | No - the system bit is not set |
| AHR | No - the system bit is not set |
| AHRS | No - the hidden bit is set |
| AHS | No - the hidden bit is set |
| AR | No - the system bit is not set |
| ARS | Yes |
| AS | Yes |
| H | No - the system bit is not set |
| HR | No - the system bit is not set |
| HRS | No - the hidden bit is set |
| HS | No - the hidden bit is set |
| R | No - the system bit is not set |
| RS | Yes |
| S | Yes |

Table 19.21  Displayed files when the System property is set

If the System property is not changed at design time, its value will be False (0) when the program begins.

## Example

In the Drives, Dirs, and Files example project, the System property is first read in the Form_Load event. The value returned is used to set the SystemCheck check box. In the SystemCheck_Click event, this property is set to reflect the status of the check box. When the check box is checked, the System property is set to True (-1). This code is also shown in the example syntax. Note that the abs() function must be used to turn the -1 (True) value into the value of 1 needed to set the check box.

# Drives, Dirs, and Files Project

## Project Overview

This project creates a program that lets the user explore the drives, directories and files on a system. It uses each of the properties and events discussed in this chapter. By following the examples in this project, you should be able to learn the principles of Drive, Directory, and List boxes.

## Assembling the Project

1. Create a new form (the Drives, Dirs, and Files form), and place on it the following controls. Use Table 19.22 to set the properties of the form and each control.

| Object | Property | Setting |
|---|---|---|
| Form | Caption | Drives, Dirs, and Files Project |
| | FormName | Drives |
| | Height | 4425 |
| | Icon | \VB\ICONS\COMPUTER\DRIVE01.ICO |
| | Width | 6735 |
| Check Box | CtrlName | Archive_Check |
| | Caption | Archive |
| | Height | 255 (Twips) |
| | Left | 5280 (Twips) |
| | Top | 1440 (Twips) |
| | Width | 1215 (Twips) |
| Check Box | CtrlName | Hidden_Check |
| | Caption | Hidden |
| | Height | 255 (Twips) |
| | Left | 5280 (Twips) |
| | Top | 1920 (Twips) |
| | Width | 1215 (Twips) |
| Check Box | CtrlName | Normal_Check |
| | Caption | Normal |
| | Height | 255 (Twips) |
| | Left | 5280 (Twips) |
| | Top | 2400 (Twips) |
| | Width | 1215 (Twips) |
| Check Box | CtrlName | ReadOnly_Check |
| | Caption | Read Only |
| | Height | 255 (Twips) |
| | Left | 5280 (Twips) |
| | Top | 2880 (Twips) |
| | Width | 1215 (Twips) |
| Check Box | CtrlName | System_Check |
| | Caption | System |
| | Height | 255 (Twips) |
| | Left | 5280 (Twips) |
| | Top | 3360 (Twips) |
| | Width | 1215 (Twips) |

| | | |
|---|---|---|
| TextBox | Ctlname | SelectedFile |
| | Text | *.* |
| | Height | 285 (Twips) |
| | Left | 120 (Twips) |
| | Top | 120 (Twips) |
| | Width | 2415 (Twips) |
| File List Box | Ctlname | File1 |
| | Height | 2955 (Twips) |
| | Left | 120 (Twips) |
| | Pattern | *.* |
| | Top | 480 (Twips) |
| | Width | 2415 (Twips) |
| Label | Ctlname | FileCount |
| | Height | 255 (Twips) |
| | Left | 120 (Twips) |
| | Top | 3480 (Twips) |
| | Width | 2415 (Twips) |
| Drive List Box | Ctlname | Drive1 |
| | Height | 315 (Twips) |
| | Left | 2760 (Twips) |
| | Top | 120 (Twips) |
| | Width | 2295 (Twips) |
| Directory List Box | Ctlname | Dir1 |
| | Height | 3255 (Twips) |
| | Left | 2760 (Twips) |
| | Top | 480 (Twips) |
| | Width | 2295 (Twips) |
| Command Button | Ctlname | OKButton |
| | Default | True (-1) |
| | Height | 495 (Twips) |
| | Left | 5280 (Twips) |
| | Top | 120 (Twips) |
| | Width | 1215 (Twips) |
| Command Button | Ctlname | ExitButton |
| | Height | 495 (Twips) |
| | Left | 5280 (Twips) |
| | Top | 720 (Twips) |
| | Width | 1215 (Twips) |

**Table 19.22  Property settings for the Drives, Dirs, and Files project**

2. Check the appearance of your form against Figure 19.5.

3. Enter the following code into the Form_Load event. This event uses the CurDir$ function to set the starting paths for the Drive1, Dir1, and File1 list boxes. It also reads the default attribute settings from the File1 file list box control, and sets the values of the Archive_Check, Hidden_Check, Normal_Check, ReadOnly_Check, and System_Check check box controls. Check boxes are set on with a value of 1, while the attribute properties of a file list box return a 0 or a -1. Therefore, the Abs() (absolute value) function is used to change the -1 to a 1.

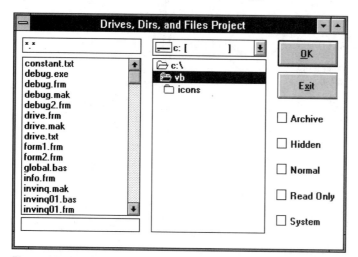

**Figure 19.5 What the form should look like for the Drives, Dirs, and Files project**

```
Sub Form_Load ()
   Drive1.Drive = CurDir$
   Dir1.Path = CurDir$
   File1.Path = CurDir$
   Archive_Check.Value = Abs(File1.Archive)
   Hidden_Check.Value = Abs(File1.Hidden)
   Normal_Check.Value = Abs(File1.Normal)
   ReadOnly_Check.Value = Abs(File1.ReadOnly)
   System_Check.Value = Abs(File1.System)
   SelectedFile.Text = ParseFileName()
End Sub
```

4. Enter the following code into the click events for the check boxes. Each of these events uses the value of its check box control Value setting to set the corresponding attribute property of the File1 file list box. They also update the label FileCount to reflect the number of files displayed in the File1 file list box.

```
Sub Archive_Check_Click ()
   File1.Archive = -Archive_Check.Value
   FileCount.Caption = Format$(File1.ListCount, "##,###") + " Files"
End Sub
```

```
Sub Hidden_Check_Click ()
   File1.Hidden = -Hidden_Check.Value
   FileCount.Caption = Format$(File1.ListCount, "##,###") + " Files"
End Sub

Sub Normal_Check_Click ()
   File1.Normal = -Normal_Check.Value
   FileCount.Caption = Format$(File1.ListCount, "##,###") + " Files"
End Sub

Sub ReadOnly_Check_Click ()
   File1.ReadOnly = -ReadOnly_Check.Value
   FileCount.Caption = Format$(File1.ListCount, "##,###") + " Files"
End Sub

Sub System_Check_Click ()
   File1.System = -System_Check.Value
   FileCount.Caption = Format$(File1.ListCount, "##,###") + " Files"
End Sub
```

5. Enter the following code into the Dir1_Change event. This event does two things. First it updates the Path property of the File1 file list box to reflect the change made to this directory's path. If the new path is different from the old, doing this also causes the File1_PathChange event to be activated. Second, it changes the current directory to the one specified by the new path.

```
Sub Dir1_Change ()
   File1.Path = Dir1.Path
   ChDir Dir1.Path
End Sub
```

6. Enter the following code into the File1_Change event. This event first updates the Path property of the Dir1 directory list box. If the new path is different from the old, doing this also causes the Dir1_Change event to occur. It also sets the Drive property of the Drive1 drive list box. Again, if this changes the current Drive setting, the Drive1_Change event will be activated. The event then updates the text in the SelectedFile text box control by making a call to the ParseFileName function. Finally, the number of files displayed in the File1 file list box is updated.

```
Sub File1_PathChange ()
   Dir1.Path = File1.Path
   Drive1.Drive = File1.Path
   SelectedFile.Text = ParseFileName()
   FileCount.Caption = Format$(File1.ListCount, "##,###") + " Files"
End Sub
```

7. Enter the following code into the File1_PatternChange event. This event occurs when the user changes the FileName property by editing the text in the SelectedFile text box.

```
Sub File1_PatternChange ()
   FileCount.Caption = Format$(File1.ListCount, "##,###") + " Files"
   SelectedFile.Text = ParseFileName()
End Sub
```

8. Enter the following text into the Drive1_Change event. This event sets the Path property of the Dir1 directory list box. If this changes the current path for the directory list box, the Dir1_Change event will be initiated.

```
Sub Drive1_Change ()
   Dir1.Path = CurDir$(Drive1.Drive)
End Sub
```

9. Enter the following code into the File1_Click event. Clicking on a file places its name in the SelectedFile text box.

```
Sub File1_Click ()
   SelectedFile.Text = File1.FileName
End Sub
```

10. Enter the following text for the command buttons. The OKButton_Click event sets the FileName property of the File1 file list box to the text that is in the SelectedFile text box control. If this text specifies a path or pattern that is different than that currently in use by the File1 file list box, it causes the File1_PathChange, and/or File1_Pattern_Change events to occur.
    The ExitButton_Click event simply ends the program.

```
Sub OKButton_Click ()
   File1.FileName = SelectedFile.Text
End Sub

Sub ExitButton_Click ()
   End
End Sub
```

11. Enter the following code in the general declarations area of the form. Once the first line is complete (Function...) Visual Basic will give this function its own window. This function reads the current File1.Path and File1.FileName properties and, based on these, parses together the full path and file name of the selected file(s).

```
Function ParseFileName () As String
   Dim TempFile As String
   Dim Temp_Dir As String

   Temp_Dir = File1.Path
   TempFile = File1.Pattern
   If TempFile = "" Then TempFile = "*.*"
   If Right$(Temp_Dir, 1) <> "\" Then TempFile = "\" + TempFile
   ParseFileName = Temp_Dir + TempFile
End Function
```

## How It Works

This very simple program allows the user to explore the disk drives, directories, and files on the system on which it is run. The user can select drives, directories, and files by clicking or double clicking on the desired lists. Clicking on the attribute (Archive, Hidden, Normal, Read Only, and System) check boxes causes the selection of the files in the File1 file list box to be limited to those that match the checked boxes.

The selected files for display in the File1 file list box can also be modified by entering a new path or pattern in the SelectedFile text box control, and clicking the OK button (or pressing the Enter key, since the Default property of the OKButton control is set to True). For instance, placing the text "*.EXE" will cause only the files in the selected directory that have an extension of "EXE" to be displayed in the file list box.

Regardless of where a change is made, that change is reflected by all the related controls. For instance, if the current directory is changed by double clicking on the Dir1 directory list box, the files in the File1 file list box are updated.

Clicking the Exit button ends the program.

# Operating Scroll Bars

Scroll bars are a ubiquitous feature of Windows programs. The most common use of scroll bars is, of course, to let the user move around in a piece of text that is too large to fit in the window. Any desired portion of the text can be brought into view by clicking on the scroll bar with the mouse or dragging the button. Scroll bars can also be used for positioning a graphic image that is too large for the window. For example, the window may be made to represent a 100-square-mile portion of a large map, and the scroll bars can then be used to change the part of the map being viewed.

Scroll bars can also be used to allow the user to enter a value graphically. In other words, instead of having the user enter an ambiguous or hard to understand number in a text box, and then having the program check to see if the number is in the correct range, you can set up a visual tool on the screen with which the user can manipulate the value. In this case the scroll bar acts like a sliding control, such as that found on some radio and audio equipment.

## Operating the Scroll Bar

Scroll bars are controls that consist of a bar with arrows at each end and a button between the arrows. There are two types of scroll bars: vertical and horizontal.

The button's position within the scroll bar is directly related to the value represented by the scroll bar. For horizontal scroll bars, the button is in the leftmost position when the value of the scroll bar is at its minimum setting, and at the rightmost when the value is at its maximum. A minimum value on a vertical scroll bar places the button at the top, while the maximum value places the button at the bottom. Any value in between places the button on the bar in a position proportional to the value represented by the bar.

The value represented by a scroll bar can be changed in four ways. First, the user can click on either arrow. This causes the value represented by the scroll bar to be incremented or decremented by a small amount in the direction of the selected arrow. Second, the user may click the scroll bar on one side of the button or the other. This causes the scroll bar's value to be affected in a manner similar to clicking an arrow, but the amount of change is greater. The user can also click and drag the button to a specific position on the bar. This causes the value of the scroll bar to be set according to the position of the button. Finally, the value of a scroll bar can be set in the program's code.

Table 20.1 summarizes the five properties that control the operation of scroll bars.

| Use or Set This... | | To Do This... |
|---|---|---|
| LargeChange | Property | Set or return the amount changed when the user clicks on the bar |
| Max | Property | Set or return the maximum value represented by the scroll bar |
| Min | Property | Set or return the minimum value represented by the scroll bar |
| SmallChange | Property | Set or return the amount changed when the user clicks on an arrow |
| Value | Property | Set or return the value represented by the scroll bar |

**Table 20.1 Properties that affect the operation of a scroll bar**

These five properties are explored in this section. Following the discussion on all the properties is the Scroll Bars project, which demonstrates their use.

# LargeChange Property

## Objects Affected

| | | | | |
|---|---|---|---|---|
| Check | Clipboard | Combo | Command | Debug |
| Dir | Drive | File | Form | Frame |
| Label | List | Menu | Option | Picture |
| Printer | Screen | ▶ Scroll | Text | Timer |

## Purpose

The LargeChange property sets or returns the amount of change that occurs when the user clicks on the bar portion of a scroll bar. This property can be set at design time, and set or read at run time. The arguments for the LargeChange property are summarized in Table 20.2.

## General Syntax

```
[form.]CtlName.LargeChange [= amount%]
```

| Arguments | Description |
|---|---|
| form | FormName of the parent form |
| ctlname | CtlName of the scroll bar control |
| amount% | An integer value indicating the amount of change made when the user clicks on the bar |

**Table 20.2 Arguments of the LargeChange property**

## Example Syntax

```
HScroll1.LargeChange = 100        'The value of the scroll bar will be changed in
                                  'increments of 100

L% = VScroll1.LargeChange         'Assigns the LargeChange value to L%
```

## Description

One of the ways for the user to change the value of a scroll bar is to click on the bar between the button and one of the arrows. This adjusts the Value property of the scroll bar by whatever amount is defined by the LargeChange property. For instance, if the LargeChange property is set to 100, clicking below the button on the bar portion of a vertical scroll bar will add 100 to the scroll bar's Value property.

Begin the specification of this property with the name of the scroll bar control to be affected. Any value you assign to this property must be an integer whose value is within the range defined by the Min and Max properties of the same control. If the program tries to assign a value that is not in this range, an "Invalid property value" error will occur.

The first statement in the example syntax sets the LargeChange value for the scroll bar control HScroll1 to 100. This is the amount by which the scroll bar's Value property will change when the user clicks on the bar between the button and one of the arrows. The second statement simply saves the LargeChange property of the scroll bar VScroll1 into the integer variable L%.

## Example

In the Scroll Bars project, the LargeChange property is set to 100 at design time. This causes the control Picture2 to be scrolled 100 twips at a time.

## Comments

The SmallChange property defines a smaller amount of change for when the user clicks one of the arrows at either end of the bar.

# Max Property

## Objects Affected

| | | | | |
|---|---|---|---|---|
| Check | Clipboard | Combo | Command | Debug |
| Dir | Drive | File | Form | Frame |
| Label | List | Menu | Option | Picture |
| Printer | Screen | ▶ Scroll | Text | Timer |

## Purpose

The Max property sets or returns the maximum value of a scroll bar. This property can be set at design time, and set or read at run time. Table 20.3 summarizes the arguments of the Max property.

## General Syntax

```
[form.]CtlName.Max [= value%]
```

| Arguments | Description |
|-----------|-------------|
| form | FormName of the parent form |
| ctlname | CtlName of the scroll bar control |
| value% | An integer expression indicating the value at the high end of the scroll bar |

Table 20.3 Arguments of the Max property

## Example Syntax

```
HScroll1.Max = 1000 'Sets the maximum value for the scroll bar to 1000
```

## Description

The Max property defines the value represented by a vertical scroll bar when the button is at its bottommost position, or by a horizontal scroll bar when its button is at its rightmost position. This is an integer value that must be in the range -32768 to 32767. Along with the Min property, Max defines the acceptable range of values for a scroll bar. By default, this property is set to 32767.

Specify the Max property by beginning with the name of the scroll bar control to be affected. To set the Max property, assign it an integer value within the proper range.

One would expect the Max property to always be a value greater than the Min property. However, this is not always true. Visual Basic will accept a Max property that is less than the Min property for the same control. This causes changes to the value of the scroll bar to be effected in an opposite manner than normal. For instance, if the Max property is less than the Min property, clicking on the top arrow of a vertical scroll bar would add to the scroll bar's value instead of subtracting.

The example syntax sets the maximum value for scroll bar HScroll1 to 1000. Since this is a horizontal scroll bar, it will have the value 1000 when the button is all the way to the right.

## Example

In the Scroll Bars project, the Max property of the horizontal and vertical Scroll Bars is set in the Form_Load event. The value placed in the Max property is an arithmetic equation that figures out what values for the Picture2.Top and Picture2.Left properties would allow the right and bottom edges of the control Picture2 to be displayed.

# Min Property

## Objects Affected

| | | | | |
|--------|-----------|--------|---------|---------|
| Check | Clipboard | Combo | Command | Debug |
| Dir | Drive | File | Form | Frame |
| Label | List | Menu | Option | Picture |
| Printer | Screen | ▶ Scroll | Text | Timer |

## Purpose

The Min property sets or returns the minimum value of a scroll bar. This property can be set at design time, and set or read at run time. Table 20.4 summarizes the arguments of the Min property.

## General Syntax

```
[form.]CtlName.Min [= value%]
```

| Arguments | Description |
|-----------|-------------|
| form | FormName of the parent form |
| ctlname | CtlName of the scroll bar control |
| value% | An integer expression indicating the value at the low end of the scroll bar |

**Table 20.4 Arguments of the Min property**

## Example Syntax

```
HScroll1.Min = 100   'Sets the minimum value for the scroll bar to 100
```

## Description

The Min property defines the value represented by a vertical scroll bar when the button is at its topmost position, or by a horizontal scroll bar when the button is at its leftmost position. This is an integer value that must be in the range of from -32768 to 32767. Along with the Max property, Min defines the acceptable range of values for a scroll bar. By default, this property is set to 0.

Specify the Min property by beginning with the name of the scroll bar control to be affected. To set the Min property, assign it an integer value within the proper range.

One would expect the Min property to always be a value less than the Max property. However, this is not always true. Visual Basic will accept a Min property that is greater than the Max property for the same control. This causes changes to the value of the scroll bar to be effected in an opposite manner than normal. For instance, if the Min property is greater than the Max property, clicking on the top arrow of a vertical scroll bar would add to the scroll bar's value instead of subtracting.

In the example syntax, the minimum value of the horizontal scroll bar HScroll1 is set to 100. This is the value the scroll bar will have when the button is all the way to the left.

## Example

In the Scroll Bars example project, the Min property of the horizontal and vertical scroll bars is set to 0 in the Form_Load event.

# SmallChange Property

## Objects Affected

| | | | | |
|---|---|---|---|---|
| Check | Clipboard | Combo | Command | Debug |
| Dir | Drive | File | Form | Frame |
| Label | List | Menu | Option | Picture |
| Printer | Screen | ▶ Scroll | Text | Timer |

## Purpose

The SmallChange property sets or returns the amount of change that occurs when the user clicks on one of the arrows at either end of a scroll bar. This property can be set at design time, and set or read at run time. Table 20.5 summarizes the arguments of the SmallChange property.

## General Syntax

```
[form.]CtlName.SmallChange [= amount%]
```

| Arguments | Description |
|-----------|-------------|
| form | FormName of the parent form |
| ctlname | CtlName of the scroll bar control |
| amount% | An integer value indicating the amount of change made when the user clicks on one of the bar's arrow icons |

Table 20.5 Arguments of the SmallChange property

## Example Syntax

```
HScroll1.SmallChange = 10      'The value of the will be changed in increments of 10

L% = VScroll1.SmallChange      'Assigns the SmallChange value to L%
```

## Description

One of the ways the user can change the value of a scroll bar is to click on one of the arrows at either end of it. When this occurs, the value of the scroll bar is adjusted by whatever amount is defined by the SmallChange property.

The SmallChange property is an integer whose range must be between the values defined by the Min and Max properties of the same control. If the program tries to assign a value that is not in this range, an "Invalid property value" error will occur.

Specify the SmallChange property by beginning with the name of the scroll bar control to be affected. To set the SmallChange property, assign it an integer value within the proper range.

In the example syntax, the SmallChange property for the HScroll1 scroll bar is set to 10. This is the amount by which the value of the scroll bar will increase or decrease when the user clicks on the arrows at the ends of the scroll bar.

## Example

In the Scroll Bars project, the SmallChange property is set to 10 at design time. This causes the control Picture2 to be scrolled 10 twips at a time when the user clicks an arrow.

## Comments

The LargeChange property defines a larger amount of change for when the user clicks on the scroll bar itself.

# Value Property

## Objects Affected

| | | | | |
|---|---|---|---|---|
| ▶ Check | Clipboard | Combo | ▶ Command | Debug |
| Dir | Drive | File | Form | Frame |
| Label | List | Menu | ▶ Option | Picture |
| Printer | Screen | ▶ Scroll | Text | Timer |

## Purpose

The Value property sets or returns the value currently represented by a scroll bar. This property can be set at design time, and set or read at run time. The arguments for the Value property are summarized in Table 20.6.

## General Syntax

```
[form.]CtlName.Value [= value%]
```

| Arguments | Description |
|---|---|
| form | FormName of the parent form |
| ctlname | CtlName of the scroll bar control |
| value% | An integer expression indicating a position on the scroll bar |

Table 20.6 Arguments of the Value property

## Example Syntax

```
V% = VScroll1.Value 'Assigns the value from the scroll bar to V%
```

## Description

The Value property contains a value that is proportional to the current postion of the button on the scroll bar. This value is in relation to the values specified by the Min and Max properties. For instance, if the button is three-quarters across a horizontal scroll bar, and the Min and Max properties are set to 0 and 100, respectively, the Value property will have a value of 75. Conversely, if the Value property for the same scroll bar is set to 25, the button will be moved to a position one-fourth of the distance across the bar.

Specify the Value property by beginning with the name of the scroll bar control to be affected. To set the Value property, assign it an integer value within the proper range.

If the program sets this property, it must be within the range defined by the Min and Max properties, or an "Invalid property value" error will occur. When read, this property returns an integer in the same range. The maximum range for Min and Max is -32768 to 32767, so the Value property for a scroll bar control is always within this range.

This property can be changed in four ways. First, the user can click on the arrow at either end of the Scroll Bar. This causes the Value property to be incremented or decremented by the amount defined by the SmallChange property in the direction of the selected arrow. Second, the user may click the scroll bar on one side of the button or the other. This causes the Value property to be affected in a manner similar to clicking an arrow, but the amount of change is that defined by the LargeChange property. The user can also click and drag the button to a specific position on the bar. This causes the Value of the scroll bar to be set according to the position of the button in proportion to the Min and Max properties. Finally, the value of a scroll bar can be set in the program's code.

The example syntax saves the current value of the scroll bar VScroll1 in the integer variable V%.

### Example

In the Scroll Bars project, the Value property is read in the HScroll1_Change and VScroll1_Change events. In these events, this property is used to set the position of Picture2.

This property is set by each of the Click events for all the buttons on the form. By setting the Value property, each of these buttons positions Picture2 at a different corner.

### Comments

The Value property is also used for the check box, command button, and option button controls. For command and option buttons, the possible values for the Value property are True (-1) and False (0), meaning the button is or is not selected. Check boxes can have the values 0 (not checked), 1 (checked), or 2 (dimmed). For more information on these items, see the appropriate entry in Chapter 3, *Programming with Objects*.

# Scroll Bars Project

### Project Overview

The project outlined in the following pages demonstrates the concepts behind the use of scroll bars. By following the examples in this project, you will learn how to use the LargeChange, Min, Max, SmallChange, and Value properties as they relate to the scroll bar controls.

### Assembling the Project

1. Create a new form (the Scroll Bars form) and place on it the following controls. Use Table 20.7 to set the properties of the form and each control.

Note: When you create the Picture2 control, first make sure Picture1 has the focus. Then double-click on the picture control icon. This creates Picture2 as a child of Picture1, which is necessary for this program to operate correctly.

| Object | Property | Setting |
|--------|----------|---------|
| Form | FormName | Scroll |
| | Caption | Scroll Bars Project |
| | Height | 5610 |
| | Left | 975 |
| | Top | 1350 |
| | Width | 7740 |
| Picture | CtlName | Picture1 |
| | Height | 3855 |
| | Left | 10 |
| | Top | 10 |
| | Width | 7335 |
| Picture | CtlName | Picture2 |
| | Autosize | True (-1) |
| | Left | 0 |
| | Picture | (Bitmap) \WINDOWS\CHESS.BMP |
| | Top | 0 |
| Command | CtlName | BotLeft |
| | Caption | Bottom Left |
| | Height | 975 |
| | Left | 1980 |
| | Top | 4140 |
| | Width | 1425 |
| Command | CtlName | BotRight |
| | Caption | Bottom Right |
| | Height | 975 |
| | Left | 4020 |
| | Top | 4140 |
| | Width | 1425 |
| Command | CtlName | TopLeft |
| | Caption | Top Left |
| | Height | 975 |
| | Left | 30 |
| | Top | 4140 |
| | Width | 1425 |

*Table 20.7 (continued)*

| Object | Property | Setting |
|---|---|---|
| Command | CtlName | TopRight |
| | Caption | Top Right |
| | Height | 975 |
| | Left | 6150 |
| | Top | 4140 |
| | Width | 1425 |
| Horizontal Scroll | CtlName | HScroll1 |
| | Height | 255 |
| | LargeChange | 100 |
| | Left | 10 |
| | SmallChange | 10 |
| | Top | 4170 |
| | Width | 1425 |
| Vertical Scroll | CtlName | VScroll1 |
| | Height | 3855 |
| | LargeChange | 100 |
| | Left | 7350 |
| | SmallChange | 10 |
| | Top | 10 |
| | Width | 255 |

**Table 20.7 Property settings for the Scroll Bars project**

2. Check the appearance of your form with Figure 20.1.

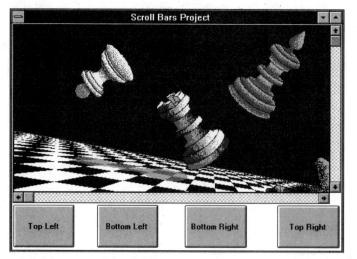

Figure 20.1 How the Scroll Bars form should look when complete

3. Enter the following code into the HScroll1_Change and VScroll1_Change events. These events set the coordinates for the upper left hand corner of Picture2.

```
Sub HScroll1_Change ()
    Picture2.Left = -HScroll1.Value
End Sub

Sub VScroll1_Change ()
    Picture2.Top = -VScroll1.Value
End Sub
```

4. Enter the following code into the Form_Load event. This event sets the minimum and maximum values for the HScroll1 and VScroll1 scroll bar controls.

```
Sub Form_Load ()
    HScroll1.Max = (Picture2.Width - Picture1.Width)
    VScroll1.Max = (Picture2.Height - Picture1.Height)
    HScroll1.Min = 0
    VScroll1.Min = 0
End Sub
```

5. Enter the following code into the Click events for the four buttons. These routines set the coordinates for the Picture2 picture control. By choosing one of these buttons, the picture gets set to the respective corner.

```
Sub TopLeft_Click ()
    HScroll1.Value = HScroll1.Min
    VScroll1.Value = VScroll1.Min
End Sub

Sub TopRight_Click ()
    HScroll1.Value = HScroll1.Max
    VScroll1.Value = VScroll1.Min
End Sub

Sub BotLeft_Click ()
    HScroll1.Value = HScroll1.Min
    VScroll1.Value = VScroll1.Max
End Sub

Sub BotRight_Click ()
    HScroll1.Value = HScroll1.Max
    VScroll1.Value = VScroll1.Max
End Sub
```

## How It Works

This project creates a program that displays the CHESS.BMP bitmap picture that comes with Windows. However, the area for displaying the picture is smaller than the picture itself. Therefore, we need to provide a method for the user to scroll the picture to the left and right, and up and down.

The picture control Picture1 defines the viewing area for the bitmap. Picture2 is placed as a child of Picture1, with its AutoSize property set to True (-1). Although Picture2 is larger than Picture1, because it is a child the displayed portion of Picture2 cannot overlap the area defined by Picture1.

We can now determine which portion of Picture2 is displayed by changing its Left and Top properties. Initially, the Left and Top properties are set to 0. These properties are changed in the HScroll1_Change and VScroll1_Change events, which occur whenever the user changes the value of either the horizontal or vertical scroll bars. The minimum and maximum values for the scroll bars are defined in the Form_Load event. In this event, the minimum for each bar is set to 0, while the maximum is set to a value that will reflect the Left and Top values of Picture2 when the bottom right hand corner of the picture is being displayed.

Each of the Click routines set the Value property of the scroll bars. Doing so also causes the Change events for the scroll bars to occur, thereby changing the Top and Left coordinates of Picture2.

# PART SEVEN
# MANAGING DATA FLOW

# Establishing and Controlling Focus

I n Windows, the control or form that is currently active and will be able to respond to a mouse click or keypress is said to "have the application focus." In designing an application, it is important to know how the focus can be changed by your program and by the user. Depending on circumstances, it may be quite acceptable to allow the user to move the focus freely from one form or control to another, providing flexibility in using your application. Sometimes, however, you may wish to prevent the focus from being moved. For example, there may be an action (such as a file update) that should be completed before other actions can be permitted. The Visual Basic features discussed in this chapter will enable you to establish and control the focus as necessary.

## What Happens When the Focus Changes?

How does the focus change in an application? First, the user can establish the focus on a control using the Tab key or mouse. The user can press the Tab (or Shift-Tab) key until the control is graphically outlined. More commonly, he or she can move the mouse to a control and press its left button to select that control. If available, the user can press a command button that uses the SetFocus method to automatically select the control.

Once a new control is chosen, the code you provide generates any actions created by giving focus to the control. Your code then processes any user input based upon the type of control that has the focus. Finally, when the focus is removed from the control following input, the code initiates any actions triggered when the focus is changed to another control.

## Focus In Visual Basic

Several tools in Visual Basic influence the setting of the focus and its effects. The AppActivate statement gives the focus to another Windows application. A form or control within the application can be given the focus with the SetFocus method. The GotFocus event contains any actions that occur when a form or control receives the focus. Actions in the LostFocus event take place when a form or control loses the focus. A control's Enabled property indicates whether it is eligible or ineligible for receiving the focus. The TabIndex property determines the order in which the user can access the controls on a form with the Tab key. A control's TabStop property indicates whether a control is accessible with the Tab key.

Table 21.1 displays the one statement, one method, two events, and three properties that influence the setting and effects of focus in Visual Basic.

| Use or Set This... | | To Do This |
|---|---|---|
| AppActivate | Statement | Select an application window |
| Enabled | Property | Indicate whether a control or form can respond to events |
| GotFocus | Event | Initiate an action when a control or form is given the focus |
| LostFocus | Event | Initiate an action when a control or form gives up the focus |
| SetFocus | Method | Give the focus to the indicated control or form |
| TabIndex | Property | Set or discover a control's place in the Tab order |
| TabStop | Property | Determine whether a control is accessible with the Tab key |

**Table 21.1 Statement, method, properties, and events dealing with the Focus**

The statements, methods, events, and properties in Table 21.1 are investigated in detail in the following pages. You'll find step-by-step directions to assemble the Focus project at the end of the chapter.

# AppActivate Statement

## Purpose

When there are multiple Windows applications on your screen, the AppActivate statement gives a particular application the focus. An application keeps the focus until it is closed or another form or control receives the focus. This is useful for accessing and controlling or obtaining information from another active Windows application from your Visual Basic program without using DDE links. DDE, a means of establishing data links between Windows applications, is discussed in Chapter 25, *Transferring Data with Dynamic Data Exchange*. Table 21.2 summarizes the argument of the AppActivate statement.

## General Syntax

```
AppActivate titletext$
```

| Argument | Description |
|---|---|
| titletext$ | The text that appears in the title bar of an application |

**Table 21.2 Argument of AppActivate statement**

## Example Syntax

```
Sub Command1_Click ()
    On Error GoTo OpenFileMan                'Specifies to go to the OpenFileMan if an error
                                             'occurs
    AppActivate "File Manager"               'Attempts to give the focus to File Manager
    SendKeys "%{ }{Down 4}{Enter}", -1       'SendKeys maximizes File Manager
    MsgBox "File Manager is now active"      'Displays Message with OK button
    SendKeys "%{ }{Down 5}{Enter}", -1       'SendKeys directs File Manager to close itself down
    SendKeys "{Enter}", -1                   'SendKeys sends enter confirming the close. order
    GoTo PEnd                                'Goto End of Program
OpenFileMan:
    x = Shell("\Windows\WinFile.exe", 2)     'Open File Manager
    Resume                                   'Return to the statement generating the error
PEnd:
End Sub
```

## Description

The AppActivate statement has only one argument, titletext$, which specifies what program receives the focus. The titletext$ argument can be a text string between quotation marks or a previously defined text variable. This argument contains only the text found in the program bar at the top of the application that is to receive the focus. In the example syntax, the title bar of the program reads File Manager.

There are several limits to using the AppActivate statement to shift the focus of an application. If the text is not exactly the same as that shown in the application's title bar, then an error will be generated. While the host program is still in control, all of the commands that are sent to the application with the focus must be done using SendKeys. AppActivate does not establish a DDE connection.

In the example syntax, AppActivate works in conjunction with SendKeys to open the Windows File Manager application. Figure 21.1 shows the screen with the File Manager window open. Notice how the SendKeys statement is used to send the specific keystrokes to the File Manager that are needed first to maximize, and then to close, that application. (The SendKeys statement is discussed in Chapter 16, *Handling Keyboard Input*. In that chapter, you will learn how to specify special keys as well as regular ASCII characters.)

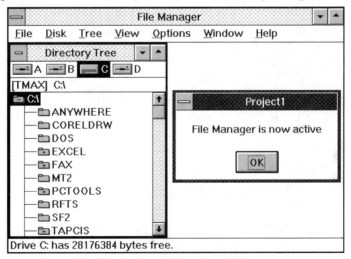

**Figure 21.1 File Manager opened via the AppActivate statement**

## Example

In the Focus project, the AppActivate statement gives the focus to the Envelope form when the user presses the Create Envelope button on the Focus project form. The Envelope form is made visible by making the Visible property True, and then it receives the focus.

AppActivate is used a second time in the same way when the user presses the OK button on the Envelope form. In this case, the Envelope form is made invisible by making the Visible property False and then AppActivate restores the focus to the Focus project form.

## Comments

If there is more than one instance of the same program specified in memory, then the AppActivate statement activates one of them at random.

# Enabled Property

## Objects Affected

| | | | | |
|---|---|---|---|---|
| ▶ Check | ▶ Clipboard | ▶ Combo | ▶ Command | Dbug |
| ▶ Dir | ▶ Drive | ▶ File | ▶ Form | ▶ Frame |
| ▶ Label | ▶ List | ▶ Menu | ▶ Option | ▶ Picture |
| Printer | Screen | ▶ Scroll | ▶ Text | ▶ Timer |

## Purpose

Use the Enabled property to indicate whether a control can respond to user input. There are two possible settings for this property, True or False. This property is extremely useful for making certain controls or forms inaccessible or unchangeable while they are still visible on the screen. For example, a check box with a False Enabled property will not accept a mouse click. This is an effective method for preventing events associated with a control from being triggered at the wrong time. If the user tries to Tab to a disabled control, the control will be skipped and the next control will receive the focus. The default value of this property is True. Table 21.3 summarizes the arguments of the Enabled property, and Table 21.4 summarizes its boolean values.

## General Syntax

```
[form.] Enabled[=boolean%]
[control.] Enabled[=boolean%]
```

| Argument | Description |
|---|---|
| form | FormName of the form |
| control | CtlName of the control |
| boolean% | Value represents whether the control is enabled or disabled |

**Table 21.3 Arguments of the Enabled property**

| boolean% | Description |
|----------|-------------|
| 0 | False - Control or form is disabled |
| -1 | True - Control or form is enabled |

Table 21.4 Boolean values of the Enabled property

## Example Syntax

```
Sub CityStateZip_Change
    Frame1.Enabled = 0                        'Disables the frame
    If Name.Text <> "" Then                   'If the Name, Address, and CityStateZip
        If Address.Text <> "" Then            'text boxes are all blank, this routine
                                              'enables
            If CityStateZip.Text <> "" Then   'the frame they are placed upon so that they
                Frame1.Enabled = -1           'can be edited.
            End If
        End If
    End If
End Sub


Sub Drive1_Change
    If Text1.Text = "Password" Then           'Disables the drive box when the user has not
        Dir1.Path = Drive1.Drive              'entered the correct password in the text box.
        File1.Path = Dir1.Path
    Else
        Drive1.Enabled = 0
        File1.Path = Dir1.Path
        Drive1.Drive = "C:"
    End If
End Sub


Sub Check1_Change
    If Check1.Value = -1 Then                  'This routine enables the command
                                               'button, option box,
        CommandDelete.Enabled = -1             'and picture boxes when the check box is
                                               'checked.

        OptionConfirm.Enabled = -1
        MenuDelete.Enabled = -1
        TrashcanPicture.Enabled =-1
    Else
        CommandDelete.Enabled = 0              'This routine disables the command
                                               'button, option box,
        OptionConfirm.Enabled = 0              'and picture boxes when the check box is
                                               'unchecked.

        MenuDelete.Enabled = 0
        TrashcanPicture.Enabled = 0
    End If
End Sub


Sub Report_Type_Option_Click (Index As Integer)
    Select Case Report_Type_Option            'Enables the indicated control when the
                                              'user selects the
        Case 0                                'option box on the screen.
```

```
            List1.Enabled = -1
            Text1.Enabled = 0
            Combo1.Enabled = 0
        Case 1
            List1.Enabled = 0
            Text1.Enabled = -1
            Combo1.Enabled = 0
        Case 2
            List1.Enabled = 0
            Text1.Enabled = 0
            Combo1.Enabled = -1
    End Select
End Sub

Sub CommandSnooze_Click                  'Timer is "toggled". If the timer is
    Timer1.Enabled = Abs(Timer1.Enabled)-1  'presently running, it is turned off. If
End Sub                                  'it is off it is turned on.
```

## Description

There are only two possible settings for the Enabled property: True (-1) and False (0). Using a variable makes it possible to control the Enabled property of several controls at once. With this kind of setup, entire groups of controls can be enabled and disabled by modifying only one variable. Specify the Enabled property by beginning with the name of the form or control to be affected. This property can be changed at either design or run time.

The Enabled property can be used with both forms and controls. A control that has been disabled will turn grey on a color monitor (it will turn a lighter shade of grey or reverse video on monochrome). For example, the OK button on a data entry form could be disabled until the user finishes an entry session.

When its Enabled property is set to False, a control will not recognize any input. Focus may never be given to a disabled control. Mouse events (Click, DoubleClick, MouseDown, MouseMove, MouseUp, and GotFocus) will not effect a disabled control. No matter what place it has in a form's TabIndex order, the user will be unable to access a control using the Tab key.

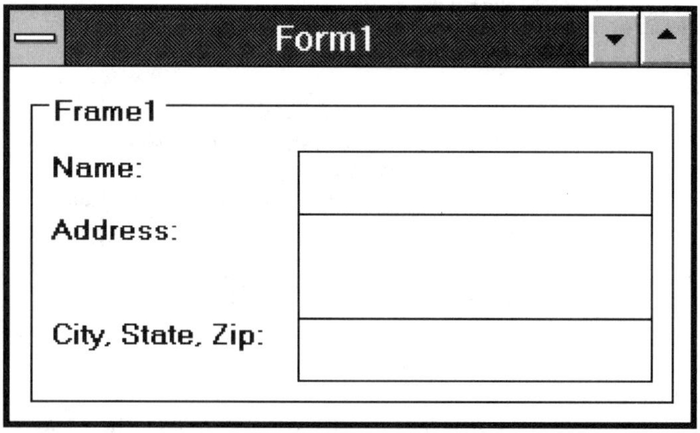

### Forms and Frames

A frame is a grouping of controls within a form. Forms and frames respond to the Enabled property in the same ways. When the Enabled property of a frame or form is False, all of the controls within are

**Figure 21.2 Example syntax frame with its text boxes**

also effectively disabled. Even though a control will not respond to user input or mouse events when its parent form or frame is set to False, the actual value of the control's Enabled property remains unchanged. In the first Sub procedure in the example syntax, the CityStateZip function checks if the data entry text boxes named Name, Address, and CityStateZip are empty. If they are all empty, then the function enables the Frame1 frame that these controls are within so that the user can enter data in them. When the text boxes contain information, the Frame1 frame remains disabled so that they cannot be changed. Figure 21.2 shows what this might look like on the screen.

### Drive, Directory, and File Boxes

Drive, directory, and file list box controls give the user access to the files on a computer. If the Enabled property of one of these controls is false, then access to the files on the computer is restricted. In the second Sub procedure in the example syntax, a user without the password cannot access the files on other drives. When the

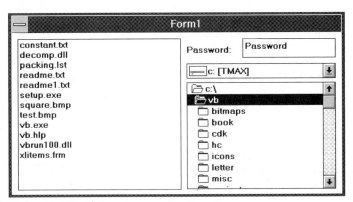

**Figure 21.3 Example syntax password system**

word Password does not appear in the Text1 text box, the Drive1 drive box's Enable property is changed to False. Figure 21.3 shows what this example might look like on the screen.

### Option, Check, Command, Picture, and Menu

Enabling and disabling the Enabled property of the option, check, or command button, or the picture box or Menu controls, prevents the user from using these controls. This is a way of removing choices from the user. Option and Check boxes that do not

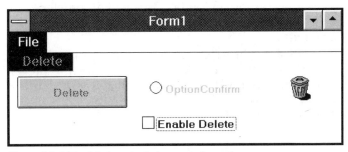

**Figure 21.4 Disabled controls in example syntax**

apply to a particular situation can be removed by changing their Enable property to False. Command and menu controls can be turned off so that the user does not initiate inapplicable actions. The third Sub procedure in the example syntax restricts the user's access to the other controls on the form while the Check1 check box remains unmarked. Figure 21.4 shows what this example might look like.

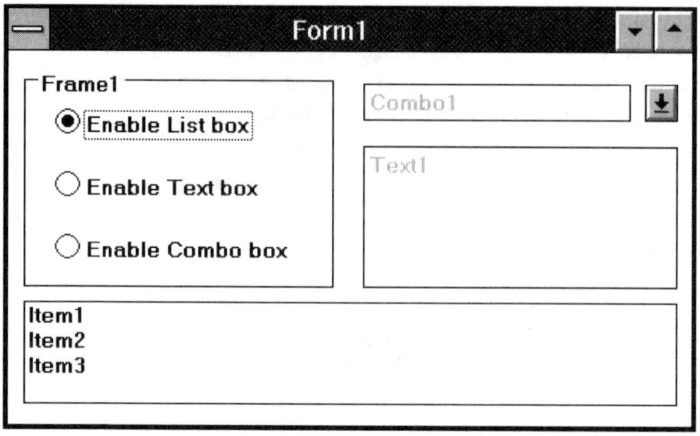

**Figure 21.5 Disabled text and combo boxes**

### List, Combo, and Text Boxes

Enabling and disabling the Enabled property of a list, combo, or text box prevents the user from changing the information in these controls. In the fourth Sub procedure in the example syntax, the option box chosen in Form1 determines the accessible control on the form. The text on a disabled list, combo, or text box appears gray. It is a lighter gray or reverse video on monochrome monitors. Figure 21.5 shows how this example might look on the screen.

### Timer

The Enabled property of the Timer control turns it on and off. This is useful for stopping previously scheduled events from taking place. In the fifth Sub procedure in the example syntax, a snooze button for an alarm program postpones or terminates the upcoming alarm from sounding by changing the timer control's Enable property to False. This change suspends the timer event's operation.

### Example

The Focus project at the end of this section uses the Enabled property to enable and disable the Return_Address text box. At program startup, the Return_Address text box is initially disabled. While the user leaves the option box labeled Permanent selected, the Return_Address text box remains disabled. To edit the Return_Address text box, the user selects the option box labeled Edit or New.

### Comments

Notice that a control that has the Enabled property set to False cannot be accessed with either the mouse or the keyboard. If you wish to prevent Tab key access to a control, then setting the TabStop property will accomplish this without needing to disable the control itself. When the TabStop property of a control is set to False, the control can still be accessed or given the focus using the mouse or the SetFocus method.

# GotFocus Event

## Objects Affected

| | | | | |
|---|---|---|---|---|
| ▶ Check | Clipboard | ▶ Combo | ▶ Command | Debug |
| ▶ Dir | ▶ Drive | ▶ File | ▶ Form | Frame |
| Label | ▶ List | Menu | ▶ Option | ▶ Picture |
| Printer | Screen | ▶ Scroll | ▶ Text | Timer |

## Purpose

The GotFocus event is a built-in procedure that specifies what actions will be taken when a control or form receives the focus. A control or form receives the focus either by user action (Tab keypress or mouse click) or by code using the SetFocus method. A form may only be given the focus when all of the visible controls are disabled using the Enable property. For example, a form with several hidden controls can have a Got_Focus event that will make these controls visible. This can keep the screen from looking cluttered by providing auxiliary controls only when they are needed. Another common use of the GotFocus event is to display context-sensitive help messages on a status bar at the bottom of the screen as the user moves from one control or form to another. Table 21.5 summarizes the arguments of the GotFocus event.

## General Syntax

```
Sub Form_GotFocus ()
Sub CtlName_GotFocus (Index As Integer)
```

| Argument | Description |
|----------|-------------|
| form | FormName property of the form with the focus |
| control | CtlName property of the control with the focus |
| Index | Index value of the control in a control array |

**Table 21.5 Arguments of the GotFocus event**

## Example Syntax

```
Sub Form_GotFocus (Index As Integer)
    Command2.Visible = -1          'Command button control made visible
    Text1.Visible = -1             'Text control made visible
    Picture1.Visible = -1          'Picture control made visible
    Array_Option(0).Visible = -1   'First option control of array made visible
    Array_Option(1).Visible = -1   'Second option control of array made visible
    Command1.Enable = -1           'Second command button control enabled
End Sub
```

## Description

The GotFocus event is triggered when the focus shifts to a form or control. There are several ways a control or form can get the focus. A user may select a new form or control with the mouse or by moving through the controls on a form with the Tab key. Begin the specification of the GotFocus event with the name of the form or control to be affected. If you are working with a control array, add an index variable in parentheses at the end of the statement.

Forms and controls can receive the focus with the SetFocus method. When a form or control receives the focus, you may use the GotFocus event to change the properties of the object with the focus. In the first example, the Enable properties of the controls on Form1 change to True when the form receives the focus.

The example syntax responds to a form's receiving the focus by making a variety of controls visible. This is done by setting the Visible property of each control to -1 (True). Notice that two of the controls specified are part of an array of option buttons.

### The Load, Resize, Paint, and GotFocus Events

If more than one event is attached to a particular control, the events are processed in the following order: Load, Resize, Paint, and GotFocus. This is an important point to keep in mind if any of the actions that take place in one event depend upon actions in another event. For example, a data entry form for an address book would cause errors if the Load event disables the Address1 text box and the GotFocus event tries to use it.

### Control Arrays

If the control with the focus is part of a Control Array, then the Index argument indicates which part of the array has the focus. The index number specifies the affected part of the control array and appears between parentheses between the control's CtlName property and the property in the form of Control(#).property.

## Example

In the Focus project at the end of this section, the GotFocus event is used in the control array of the Return Address option box to trigger the enabling and disabling of the Return Address text box. If the user selects the control labeled either Edit or New, the Return Address text box's Enable property changes to True. Otherwise, the Enable property of the Return Address text box remains False.

This event is also used for the Return Address and Addressee text boxes to erase any previous address. For the Return Address, this will allow erasure only if the user selects the control option labeled New.

## Comments

As a control will not function with the Enabled and Visible properties set to False, the GotFocus event will not work until they are both True. Labels and frames are not eligible to receive the focus.

# LostFocus Event

## Objects Affected

| | | | | |
|---|---|---|---|---|
| ▶ Check | ▶ Clipboard | ▶ Combo | Command | Dbug |
| ▶ Dir | ▶ Drive | ▶ File | ▶ Form | Frame |
| Label | ▶ List | Menu | ▶ Option | ▶ Picture |
| Printer | Screen | ▶ Scroll | ▶ Text | Timer |

## Purpose

The LostFocus event is a built-in procedure that specifies what actions will be taken when a control or form loses the focus either because the user selected another object or the code reassigned the focus. Although a LostFocus event is attached to a specific control, its effect can be on any other control or form as well as the original control. For this reason, LostFocus can even be used to determine which control will receive the focus next, by using a SetFocus method expression which reassigns the focus to another control. Table 21.6 summarizes the arguments of the LostFocus event.

## General Syntax

```
Sub Form_LostFocus ()
Sub CtlName_LostFocus ([Index As Integer])
```

| Argument | Description |
|----------|-------------|
| form | FormName property of the form losing focus |
| control | CtlName property of the control losing focus |
| index | Index value of the control in a control array |

Table 21.6 Arguments of the LostFocus event

## Example Syntax

```
Sub Form_LostFocus ()
    AppActivate "Program Manager"              'Gives focus to Program Manager
    SendKeys "%{ }{Down 4}{Enter}", -1         'SendKeys maximizes Program Manager
End Sub

Sub Text1_GotFocus ()
    Command1.ForeColor = H00FF0000&            'The text turns blue in the text box
                                               'when the text
End Sub                                        'box loses the focus.
```

## Description

The LostFocus event is triggered when the focus is changed from the current control or form to another control or form. This could occur in several ways. A user may choose another control with the use of a mouse, or by moving through the controls on a form with the Tab key. A SetFocus method can also give the focus to another control. (In the first Sub procedure in the example syntax, an AppActivate statement is used to give the focus to another application, the Program Manager.)

Begin the definition of a LostFocus event with the name of the form or control to be affected. If a control in a control array is to be referenced, end the statement with an index variable in parentheses.

When a control loses the focus, you may want to change the properties of some other control or form. The LostFocus event can contain actions that may change the appearance of controls or forms to signify that this control has lost the focus. Certain other controls or forms may have their Enabled property changed to True or False. In the second Sub procedure in the example syntax, the color of the text on the Command1 command button changes to blue when the Text1 text box loses the focus.

### Control Arrays

If the control with the focus is part of a control array, then the Index argument indicates which part of the array has the focus. The index number specifies the affected part of the control array and appears between parentheses between the control's CtlName property and the property in the form of Control(#).property.

### Example

The Focus project at the end of this section uses the LostFocus event for the Return_Address text box. After the user enters the new return address in the Return_Address text box, the LostFocus event of the text box shifts the focus to the Return_Address option box. The user triggers a LostFocus event by pressing the Tab key. This LostFocus event resets the TabStop properties of each of the options boxes in the Return_Address frame. This routine removes both of the option boxes labeled Edit and New from the TabIndex order by changing their TabStop properties False. The TabStop property of the option box, labeled Permanent, is made True. These actions ensure that only the first option, labeled Permanent, may be accessed by pressing the Tab key. No matter whether the user uses the mouse to select another control or the Tab key, the LostFocus event forces the control to pass to the first option box in the Return_Address frame.

### Comments

As a control will not function with the Enabled and Visible properties set to False, the LostFocus event will not work until they are both True.

# SetFocus Method

### Objects Affected

| | | | | |
|---|---|---|---|---|
| ▶ Check | Clipboard | ▶ Combo | ▶ Command | Dbug |
| ▶ Dir | ▶ Drive | ▶ File | ▶ Form | Frame |
| Label | ▶ List | Menu | ▶ Option | ▶ Picture |
| Printer | Screen | ▶ Scroll | ▶ Text | Timer |

### Purpose

The SetFocus method gives the focus to the specified control or form. Any form or control may receive the focus in this way, provided that its Enabled and Visible properties are both True. SetFocus is the direct way to establish focus under program control. Table 21.7 summarizes the arguments for the SetFocus method.

### General Syntax

```
control.SetFocus
form.SetFocus
```

| Argument | Description |
|---|---|
| Form | FormName property of form receiving the focus |
| Control | CtlName property of control receiving the focus |

Table 21.7 Arguments of the SetFocus method

## Example Syntax

```
Sub CommandEdit_Click ()
    If CommandSave.Enabled = 0 Then      'If CommandSave button is disabled
        Text1.SetFocus                   'set the focus to the Text1 box
    Else
        CommandSave.SetFocus             'Set the focus to the CommandSave button
    End If
End Sub
```

## Description

The SetFocus method gives a control or form the focus. The control and form arguments of a SetFocus operation must be the FormName property of a form or the CtlName property of a control. Only those controls and forms with Enabled properties set to True may actually be given the focus. There is no difference in effect between setting the focus in the code or with user input. In the example syntax, the user could also give the focus to the Text1 text box with the mouse or by pressing the Tab key. The other way to change the focus is to activate the SetFocus method expression by pressing the CommandEdit command button.

There are several effects of changing the focus with the SetFocus method. Changing the focus to another control or form triggers the LostFocus event for the form or control that loses the focus. The GotFocus event of

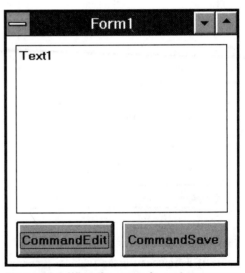

Figure 21.6 What the example syntax program looks like

the form or control that receives the focus triggers when the SetFocus method gives it the focus. In the example syntax, pressing the CommandEdit command button shifts the focus to either the Text1 text box or CommandSave command button depending upon whether the CommandSave button is enabled or disabled. Figure 21.6 displays what this example might look like on the screen.

## Example

The Focus project at the end of this section uses the SetFocus method to shift the focus from the Return_Address text box back to the Return_Address option box. This

Return_Address text box's LostFocus event automatically generates this SetFocus method expression. The SetFocus method moves the focus to the option box labeled Permanent in the Return_Address frame. This action takes place regardless of which control the user clicks with the mouse or what control is next in the TabIndex order.

## Comments

Labels and frames are not eligible to receive the focus.

# TabIndex Property

## Objects Affected

| | | | | |
|---|---|---|---|---|
| ▶ Check | Clipboard | ▶ Combo | ▶ Command | Dbug |
| ▶ Dir | ▶ Drive | ▶ File | Form | ▶ Frame |
| ▶ Label | ▶ List | Menu | ▶ Option | ▶ Picture |
| Printer | Screen | ▶ Scroll | ▶ Text | Timer |

## Purpose

The TabIndex property sets the order in which the user can access the controls on a form by pressing the Tab key. The control with the lowest TabIndex value (usually 0) is normally the control that receives the focus when the form opens. This property is modifiable at either run time or design time. The arguments of the TabIndex property are summarized in Table 21.8.

## General Syntax

[Control.]TabIndex[=index%]

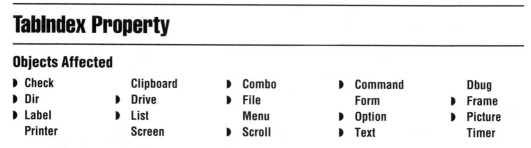

| Argument | Description |
|---|---|
| control | CtlName property of the control |
| index% | Index value of the control in a control array |

Table 21.8 Arguments of the TabIndex property

## Example Syntax

```
Sub Command1_Click ()          'Changes the tab order of the controls on the form
    Text1.TabIndex = 3         'Run into a new order when the user presses the
                               'Command1
    Command1.TabIndex = 0      'Run in command button.
    Text2.TabIndex = 1
    Text3.TabIndex = 2
End Sub
```

## Description

To specify the TabIndex property, begin with the name of the control to be affected. If the control is part of a control array, end the statement with an index variable in parentheses.

The TabIndex property can be changed in three possible ways. At design time, you may choose to change the order of controls to meet a special need. The TabIndex property of a particular control may also be changed at run time.

Changing the TabIndex property of a control may cause a change in that property for other controls on the form. For example, if a control with a lower TabIndex property is deleted at design time, then all the controls with higher values will have their TabIndex value reduced by 1. At run time, altering a control's TabIndex property value to a lower value (for example, changing 2 to 0) changes the TabIndex property value of the other controls to higher values (0 becomes 1, and 1 becomes 2). Changing the TabIndex number of a control to a higher value (such as 0 to 2) reduces the value of the TabIndex property of the other controls (1 becomes 0, and 2 becomes 1).

The TabIndex property of a control can be one of a range of values equal to the number of controls on a form. The first control of a Form has a TabIndex property value of 0. By default, Visual Basic sets the value of each control in the order in which you create the controls. The first control created on a form thus has an initial TabIndex property value of 0.

The example syntax changes the TabIndex (and thus the order of access) of specified controls when the button Command1 is clicked on. Note that a control with a TabIndex property of 0 is not always the first control with the focus when the form is opened. In the example syntax, the Command1 command button does not begin with the focus because its Visible property is False. In fact, the control would not even appear on the screen.

### Effects of the Visible, TabStop, and Enabled Properties

Changing the Visible, TabStop, or Enabled property of a control to False has no affect on its TabIndex property value. However, while any of these properties of a control is False, the control is inaccessible with the Tab key. In the example syntax, the Command1 command button would not receive the focus when the form loads if any of these properties were False. The command button retains its TabIndex property value of 0, however.

## Example

The TabIndex property order of the controls in the example at the end of this section is set at design time. By setting the TabIndex property of each control to the order in which it will be needed, this reduces the number of times that the SetFocus method must be used. Since some of the controls might be created in a different order than the order in which they are needed in the Focus Project, the TabIndex properties need to be adjusted. By setting the TabIndex properties of each control at design time, you avoid writing SetFocus method expressions to move the focus in a way that does not coincide with the control's creation order.

## Comments

All controls on a form have a Tab order value except for menus and timers.

# TabStop Property

## Objects Affected

| | | | | |
|---|---|---|---|---|
| ▶ Check | Clipboard | ▶ Combo | ▶ Command | Dbug |
| ▶ Dir | ▶ Drive | ▶ File | Form | Frame |
| Label | ▶ List | Menu | ▶ Option | ▶ Picture |
| Printer | Screen | ▶ Scroll | ▶ Text | Timer |

## Purpose

The TabStop property indicates whether a control is accessible with the Tab key. The two possible values for this property are True (-1) and False (0). True is the default setting. The TabStop property of a particular control does not affect whether a control can be selected with the mouse or accept user input from the mouse or keyboard. A control with a True TabStop property cannot be accessed with the Tab key if the Enabled or Visible properties of the control are False. Table 21.9 summarizes the arguments of the TabStop property, and Table 21.10 summarizes its boolean values.

## General Syntax

[Control.] TabStop[=boolean%]

| Argument | Description |
|---|---|
| control | CtlName of control |
| boolean% | Value represents whether the control is accessible or inaccessible with the Tab key |

Table 21.9 Arguments of the TabStop property

| boolean% | Description |
|---|---|
| 0 | False - Control is inaccessible with the Tab key |
| -1 | True - Control is accessible with the Tab key |

Table 21.10 Boolean values of the TabStop property

## Example Syntax

```
Sub Text1.GotFocus ()
    Text2.TabStop = 0        'Text2 text box becomes inaccessible when the Text1
                             'text box receives the focus
    Text3.TabStop = -1       'and the Text1 text box remains accessible.
End Sub
```

## Description

Specify the TabStop property by starting with the name of the control to be affected. The TabStop property of a control possesses a value of -1 (True) or 0 (False). All controls are originally set to True and are accessible with the Tab key. If the control's TabStop property is False, then it becomes inaccessible with the Tab key. In this case, the control can still be given the focus with either the SetFocus method or the mouse. This is different from setting the Enabled property false, which makes the control completely ineligible for the focus.

In the example syntax, the TabStop property of the Text2 and Text3 text boxes changes when the Text1 text box receives the focus. The Text2 text box becomes inaccessible with the Tab key and the Text3 text boxes become accessible.

### Effects of the Visible and Enabled Properties

Changing the Visible or Enabled property of a control to False has no effect on its TabStop property value. While either of these properties of a control is False, however, the control is also inaccessible with the Tab key. Even when a control's TabStop property is False, it can still receive the focus as long as the control is both Enabled and Visible. In the example syntax, both the Text2 and Text3 text boxes remain eligible for the focus.

## Example

The Focus project at the end of this section changes the TabStop property of the unchosen options of the control array Return_Address to false. This makes these controls inaccessible with the Tab key. This is done to eliminate unnecessary tab keystrokes and still keep the other options available.

# Focus Project

## Project Overview

The Focus project outlined in the following pages demonstrates the concept of Focus in Visual Basic. This example is designed to demonstrate the properties, events, method, and statement that directly affect focus. By following the examples of the different elements of this project, you will learn how to establish and remove focus from controls and forms.

There are two assembly phases to this project, one for each of the project's two forms. Each of these phases consists of three sections: assembly, figure display, and source code. The first phase involves the setup of the main Focus form and the second, the Envelope form. Please refer to the figures for the placement of the different elements of each form.

## Assembling the Project

1. Make a new form (the Focus form) with the objects and properties listed in Table 21.11.

| Object | Property | Setting |
|---|---|---|
| Form | BackColor | Gray, H00C0C0C0, RGB(192,192,192) |
| | Caption | Focus Project |
| | FormName | Focus |
| Frame | Caption | Return Address |
| | CtlName | Return_Address_Frame |
| Option box | Caption | Permanent |
| | CtlName | Ret_Add_Option |
| | Index | 0 |
| | TabIndex | 0 |
| | TabStop | True |
| Option box | Caption | Edit |
| | CtlName | Ret_Add_Option |
| | Index | 1 |
| | TabIndex | 1 |
| | TabStop | False |
| Option box | Caption | New |
| | CtlName | Ret_Add_Option |
| | Index | 2 |
| | TabIndex | 2 |
| | TabStop | False |
| Text | CtlName | Return_Address |
| | MultiLine | True |
| | TabIndex | 3 |
| | TabStop | True |
| | Text | "" |
| Text | CtlName | Addressee |
| | MultiLine | True |
| | TabIndex | 4 |
| | TabStop | True |
| | Text | "" |

| Label | BackColor | Gray, &H00C0C0C0, RGB(192,192,192) |
|---|---|---|
| | BorderStyle | 0-None |
| | Caption | Return_Address |
| | CtlName | Return_Address_Label |
| Label | BackColor | Gray, &H00C0C0C0, RGB(192,192,192) |
| | BorderStyle | 0-None |
| | Caption | Addressee |
| | CtlName | Addressee_Label |
| Command button | Caption | Print Envelope |
| | CtlName | Create_Envelope |
| Command button | Caption | Exit |
| | CtlName | Exit_Program |

**Table 21.11 Objects and properties of the Focus form**

2. Size the objects on the screen, as shown in Figure 21.7.

3. Enter the following code in the General Declarations section. This code defines the Current variable.

```
Dim Current As Integer
```

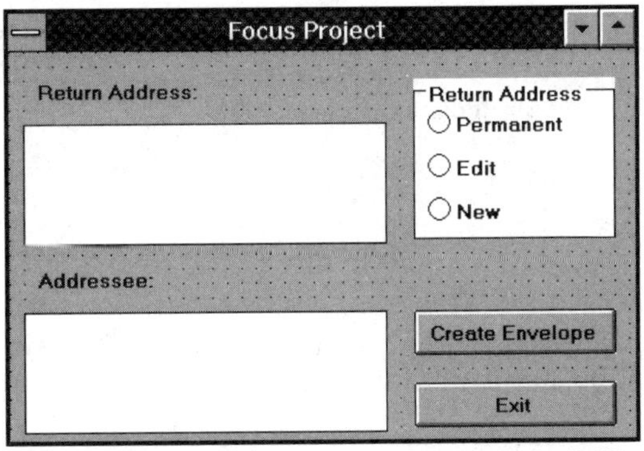

**Figure 21.7 What the Focus form should look like when completed**

4. Enter the following code in the Form_Load event subroutine. This code is triggered when the Focus form is first loaded. The variables are defined and the interface is set up for data entry.

```
Sub Form_Load ()
    Return_Address.Text = "Address Line 1"
    Addressee.Text = "Address Line 1"
    Return_Address.Enabled = 0
    Ret_Add_Option(1).Enabled = 0
End Sub
```

5. Enter the following code in the Address_Change event subroutine. This event is triggered whenever the user changes the text in the Addressee text box. This code defines the global variable Select_Address as being equal to the present contents of the Addressee text box.

```
Sub Address_Change ()
    Select_Address = Addressee.Text
End Sub
```

6. Enter the following code in the Addressee_GotFocus event subroutine. This event is triggered each time that the user selects the Addressee text box. If the user selects the option box labeled Permanent, then this routine blanks the Addressee text box's Text property.

```
Sub Addressee_GotFocus ()
    If Ret_Add_Option(Current).Index = 0 Then
        Addressee.Text = ""
    End If
End Sub
```

7. Enter the following code in the Create_Envelope_Click event subroutine. This event is triggered when the user presses the Print_Envelope command button. This routine makes the Envelope form visible and gives it the focus.

```
Sub Create_Envelope_Click ()
    Envelope.Visible = -1
    AppActivate "Envelope"
End Sub
```

8. Enter the following code in the Program_Exit_Click event subroutine. This event is triggered when the user presses the Exit command button. This closes the program down.

```
Sub Program_Exit_Click
    End
End Sub
```

9. Enter the following code in the Ret_Add_Option_GotFocus event subroutine. This event is triggered when the user chooses another option in the Ret_Add_Option control array. This routine enables and disables the Return_Address text box based on which option the user chooses.

```
Sub Ret_Add_Option_GotFocus ()
    Select Case Index
        Case 0
            Return_Address.Enabled = 0
        Case 1, 2
            Return_Address.Enabled = -1
    End Select
End Sub
```

10. Enter the following code in the Ret_Add_Option_LostFocus event subroutine. This event is triggered when one of the Ret_Add_Option option boxes loses the focus. This routine stores the index value of the currently selected control in that array to the global variable Current. The global variable Current serves as a reference for the selected control in the Ret_Add_Option control array.

```
Sub Ret_Add_Option_LostFocus ()
  Current = Ret_Add_Option(Index).Index
End Sub
```

11. Enter the following code in the Return_Address_Change event subroutine. This event is triggered when the user enters or changes the text in the Return_Address text box. This routine stores the current contents of the Return_Address text box to the global variable Select_Return. The global variable Select_Return provides the Return address of the envelope to print on the screen. When this is done, this routine enables the option box labeled Permanent so the new address can remain on the screen.

```
Sub Return_Address_Change ()
  Select_Return = Return_Address.Text
  Ret_Add_Option(1).Enabled = -1
End Sub
```

12. Enter the following code in the Return_Address_GotFocus event subroutine. This event is triggered when the Return_Address text box receives the focus. If the Ret_Add_Option control labeled Edit is not selected, whatever text is there is blanked.

```
Sub Return_Address_GotFocus ()
  If Ret_Add_Option(Current).Index > 1 Then
      Return_Address.Text = ""
  End If
End Sub
```

13. Enter the following code in the Return_Address_LostFocus event subroutine. This event is triggered when the Return_Address text box loses the focus. When the Return_Address text box loses the focus, the Ret_Add_Option control labeled Permanent receives the focus.

```
Sub Return_Address_LostFocus ()
  Ret_Add_Option(0).TabStop = -1
  Ret_Add_Option(1).TabStop = 0
  Ret_Add_Option(2).TabStop = 0
  Ret_Add_Option(0).SetFocus
End Sub
```

14. Enter the following code in the GLOBAL.BAS module and save the module as FOCUS.BAS. This code stores the global variables for the Focus project. These global variables store the addresses to display on the Envelope form.

```
Global Select_Return As String
Global Select_Address As String
```

## Assembling the Envelope Form

1. Make a new form (the Envelope form) with the objects and properties in Table 21.12.

| Object | Property | Setting |
|---|---|---|
| Form | Caption | Envelope |
| | ControlBox | False |
| | FormName | Envelope |
| | MaxButton | False |
| | MinButton | False |
| | Visible | False |
| Text box | BorderStyle | 0 - None |
| | Caption | "" |
| | CtlName | Env_Return |
| | MultiLine | True |
| Text box | BorderStyle | 0 - None |
| | Caption | "" |
| | CtlName | Env_Address |
| | MultiLine | True |
| Picture | BorderStyle | 0 - None |
| | Picture | "..VB\ICONS\MAIL\MAIL18.ICO" |
| Command button | Caption | OK |
| | CtlName | OK-Button |

**Table 21.12 Objects and properties of the Envelope form**

2. Size the objects on the screen, as shown in Figure 21.8.

3. Enter the following code in the Form_Load event subroutine. This code is triggered when the form is initially loaded. In this event, the Text properties of the text boxes Env_Return and Env_Address are made equal to the global variables Select_Return and Select_Address.

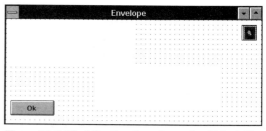

**Figure 21.8 What the Envelope form should look like when completed**

```
Sub Form_Load ()
   Env_Return.Text = Select_Return
   Env_Address.Text = Select_Address
End Sub
```

4. Enter the following code in the OK_Button_Click event subroutine. This code is triggered when the OK command button is pressed. The Focus form is given the focus and the Envelope form is hidden but not removed from memory.

```
Sub OK_Button_Click ()
   AppActivate "Focus Project"
   Envelope.Hide
End Sub
```

## How It Works

The Focus project displays a form with two text boxes, three option buttons, and two command buttons. The user enters a return address in the text box labeled Return Address by selecting the option button either labeled New or Edit. To enter the addressee information, the user chooses the text box labeled Adressee with the mouse or Tab key. Once the user enters both addresses, pressing the command button labeled Create Envelope generates an envelope on the screen. To exit the program, the user presses the command button labeled Exit.

### Startup

The Focus Project begins with a series of setup procedures and variable definitions that prepare the demonstration program for use. After the variables are set, the Load_Form procedure of the Focus form is triggered by being opened. Each of the Text properties of the Return_Address and Addressee text boxes is set to Address Line 1. This change to both text boxes generates the Change event for each. The Return_Address_Change event results in redefining the global variable Select_Return as being equal to the contents of the Return_Address text box. The Enabled property of the option button, labeled Edit, Ret_Add_Option(1), is also set to False. The Addressee_Change event redefines the global variable Select_Return as being equal to the contents of the Return_Address text box. The Form_Load procedure finishes by setting the Enabled property of the option box labeled Edit to False.

Once the initial settings and events of the project have been processed, focus is given to the control with the lowest TabStop property, the option box labeled Permanent. This initiates the GotFocus event for the control array Ret_Add_Option, which includes all three of the option boxes, Permanent, Edit, and New. The Ret_Add_Option_GotFocus event tests the present setting of the option boxes and disables the Return_Address Text box by changing that control's Enabled property to False.

## Running the Focus project

In order to proceed with the demo, the user must now move the focus from the Permanent option box to the New option box by pressing the Tab key or selecting it with the mouse. This triggers the GotFocus event again, which determines that the third control is now set and enables the Return_Address text box by setting its Enabled property to True. Once this is done, the user can select the Return_Address text box by pressing the Tab key or using the mouse again.

When the Return_Address text box receives the focus, the LostFocus event for the control array Ret_Add_Option and GotFocus for the Return_Address text box are started. The Ret_Add_Option_LostFocus event sets the variable Current to the present value of the Ret_Add_Option index. The Return_Address_GotFocus event checks to see if the Current has a value indicating an Edit or New operation with an If-Then statement. Since the Ret_Add_Option is presently set to New, the statement is True and the contents of the Return_Address text box are blanked.

Next, the user must enter the Return_Address and Addressee information. Simply enter the Return_Address lines for the envelope as you wish to see them into the text box (pressing return after each line). When the data entry is complete, press the Tab key. The LostFocus event for the Return_Address resets the TabStop property of the Permanent option box to True and the Edit and New option boxes to False and uses a SetFocus method expression to give the focus to the first Permanent option. This triggers the GotFocus event of that control as explained previously, which disables the Return_Address text box. Press the Tab key or select the Addressee text box to enter the address of the individual this envelope is being sent to. The GotFocus event of the Addressee text box blanks its contents. Enter the address and move to the Create Envelope button by pressing the Tab key or using the mouse.

Click on the Create Envelope command button to trigger the Click event. This makes the Envelope form visible and uses the AppActivate statement to give the focus to it. The text boxes display the return address and address information that you previously entered. Press OK to exit.

# Timing and Time Information

Some Visual Basic applications need to keep track of time. Visual Basic provides ways to determine the time at which something happened, or should be made to happen. In testing your program, you may also want to determine how long your code takes to perform a particular action. Visual Basic provides information about the current time in a variety of formats.

## Time in Visual Basic

Visual Basic divides time into units of measure that are familiar to the user, such as the date and time of day. The date uses the month, day, and year to pinpoint a specific day in time. Each date may be further defined by the exact hours, minutes, and seconds in which the moment took place. These units of measure allow a time to be referenced in the code for the triggering of actions. In this context, timing is a means of determining when an action or actions will take place based upon the passage of time.

### Time and the Serial Number

In Visual Basic, the date and time may be expressed with a serial number that can represent both the date and time of day of a specified moment. In this serial number, the digits to the left of the decimal point represent the total days elapsed since December 31, 1899. The supplied serial number must represent a date in the range between January 1, 1753 and December 31, 2078. For example, the serial number 33631 represents that many days elapsed since December 31, 1899, which works out to January 28, 1992. The digits to the right of the decimal point represent the total seconds elapsed since 12:00 midnight of the current day, expressed as a decimal fraction of a day. Thus in the serial number 33631.0648842593, the time portion corresponds to approximately 1:33 AM.

### The Timer Control

In order for a set of actions to be governed by time, those actions must be connected to a timer control on a Visual Basic form. This ability endows the programmer with the option of bypassing the normal operation of a program with actions based upon time rather than user input. Unless the timer control is disabled, the actions of the timer control will be processed each time that the specified time interval is reached. Although a Visual Basic application may have as many timer controls as needed, no more than 16 timer controls may be active at the same time. This is a limitation of the Windows environment and not Visual Basic. Remember that the timer control is only visible at design time. Timer controls are not visible at run time.

### Visual Basic Tools for Timing

Visual Basic provides several tools that influence the display and manipulation of time. The Interval property of the timer control indicates how much time must pass before triggering the actions in the Timer event. The Timer event contains exactly what actions take place when the designated time is set in the Interval property. The Timer function uses 12:00 midnight as a timing reference point. The current setting of the time and date in the computer is obtainable with the Date$ and Time$ functions. A computer's date and time settings are modifiable with the Date$ and Time$ statements. The date and time in integer format are convertible to serial values with the DateSerial and TimeSerial functions. The DateValue and TimeValue functions change the date and time in string format to serial format. A serial number is convertible to normal format with the Month, Day, and Year functions. Each of the Hour, Minute, and Second functions converts a time serial number to normal format. Table 22.1 displays the statement, property, event, and functions that affect Timing within a Visual Basic application.

| Use or Set This... | | To Do This |
|---|---|---|
| Date$ | Function | Return the system date set in the computer |
| Date$ | Statement | Set the system date |
| DateSerial | Function | Return the serial number that represents an indicated date in integer format |
| DateValue | Function | Return the serial number of an indicated date in string format |
| Day | Function | Return an integer between 1 and 31 that represents the day of the month of the indicated serial number |
| Hour | Function | Return an integer between 0 and 23 that represents the hour of the day of an indicated date and time serial number |
| Interval | Property | Determine the interval of time for which an active control must pause before processing the Timer event |
| Minute | Function | Return an integer between 0 and 59 that represents the minute of the day of an indicated time serial number |
| Month | Function | Return the integer between 1 and 12 that represents the number of the month of a year indicated by the serial number |
| Now | Function | Return a serial number for the current date and time |
| Second | Function | Return the integer between 0 and 59 that represents the second of the minute in an indicated time serial number |
| Time$ | Function | Return the current system time |
| Time$ | Statement | Set the system time |

| Timer | Event | Determine actions that take place when the Interval of a Timer Control has passed |
|---|---|---|
| Timer | Function | Return the number of seconds since midnight |
| TimeSerial | Function | Return the serial number for the indicated time |
| TimeValue | Function | Covert a time in string format to a serial number |
| WeekDay | Function | Return an integer between 1 and 7 that represents the day of the week |
| Year | Function | Return an integer between 1753 and 2078 that represents the year of a serial number |

Table 22.1 The property, event, and functions that affect Timing in Visual Basic applications

The following pages investigate the features summarized in Table 22.1 in detail. Step-by-step directions at the end of this section describe how to assemble the Timing project.

# Date$ Function

## Purpose

The Date$ function provides your computer's current system date when used in a Visual Basic application. As the returned date is in string format, it may appear directly in text strings without modification. This eliminates the need for the Format$ function to convert the current date to a string that can be included in the text property of a text box or another place where a string is necessary.

## General Syntax

```
Date$
```

## Example Syntax

```
Sub Form_Load ()
    Msg$ = "This is today's date: " + Date$
    If Date$ = "07-04-92" Then
        Msg$ = "Today is the fourth of July :" + Date$
    ElseIf Format$(Now,"mm-dd") = "12-25" Then
        Msg$ = "Today is Christmas " + Format$(Now,"mm-dd-yyyy")
    End If
    MsgBox Msg$
End Sub
```

## Description

A Date$ function returns a string of 10 characters that represents the computer's current system date. The function has no arguments. The character string returned by the Date$ function is presented in the form of mm-dd-yyyy. In this form, the mm part of

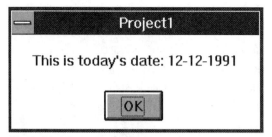

**Figure 22.1 Date displayed on a message box**

the string stands for the current month, which must be between 0 and 12, for the 12 months of the year. The dd portion of the returned string is the day of the current day of the month and must be between 1 and 31. This string ends with the yyyy that returns the current year that must be between 1980 and 2099. Table 22.2 lists the meaning of the characters returned by the Date$ function.

In the example syntax, an If-Then statement checks the current date of the computer to determine which message to display on the screen. With this example, the Date$ function produces the same results as the Format$ function to display the current date at the end of the indicated message. Figure 22.1 shows what the message box should look like on the screen.

| Date | Settings Range |
|------|----------------|
| Month (mm) | A number between 1 and 12 inclusive |
| Day (dd) | A number between 01 and 31 inclusive |
| Year (yyyy) | A year between 1980 and 2099 inclusive |

**Table 22.2 Possible returned settings of Date$ function**

### The Format$ Function

The Format$ function, used with the current date returned by the Now function, and the Date$ function produce the same results. In some cases, however, the Date$ function is a better choice for a particular situation, while others work better with the Format$ function. With the example syntax, the Date$ function checks if the day is July 4, 1992, and the Format$ function looks to see whether the day is December 25. Notice that the Date$ function requires less space in the code to display the date, but the Format$ function will work on its date for any year, while the other only operates for the year 1992. This example demonstrates the tradeoff between the flexibility of the Format$ function and the shorter required size of the Date$ function.

## Example

In the Time project at the end of this section, the Date$ function serves as a means of displaying the time on the screen. When the Default_Date_Timer event is triggered, the Date$ function provides the current date to display in the Current_Date label box. This function serves as a means of saving the current date to an indicated variable in string format. With this event, the Date$ function directly defines the Caption property of the Current_Date label box. In this way, the label box shows the date in the format defined by the international section of the WIN.INI file. If this format is acceptable for a particular application, then this function is a good way to display the date with very little code.

## Comments

Use the Date$ statement to change the current system date of the computer.

# Date$ Statement

## Purpose

The Date$ statement allows the user to change the system date of a computer within a Visual Basic application. This date may or may not change the system date permanently on your computer depending on your configuration. Most computers today have a battery that saves the date each time the user shuts off the computer. Computers without a battery or some other means of saving the date will not keep the date that the user enters with this function. For all other computers, the change that you make to the system date is normally a permanent change. In the example syntax, the Date$ statement serves as a means of changing the system date that the user enters. Figures 22.2 and 22.3 show what this example might look like on the screen. Table 22.3 summarizes the argument of the Date$ statement, and Table 22.4 summarizes the possible acceptable contents of the datestring argument.

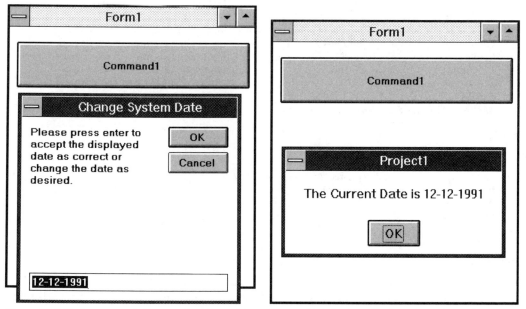

Figure 22.2 System prompts the user to enter a date    Figure 22.3 System displays the entered date

## General Syntax

Date$ = datestring$

| Argument | Description |
|----------|-------------|
| datestring$ | String that represents the date |

**Table 22.3 Argument of Date$ statement**

| datestring$ | Possible Settings |
|-------------|-------------------|
| mm | A number between 1 and 12 inclusive |
| dd | A number between 1 and 31 inclusive |
| yy | A number between 00 and 99 inclusive |
| yyyy | A date between 1980 and 2099 inclusive |

**Table 22.4 Possible acceptable contents of the datestring$ argument**

## Example Syntax

```
Sub Command1_Click ()
Start:
    On Error Goto BadFormat                     'Sets Error Checking.
    Msg$ = "Please press enter to accept the "  'Defines String Msg$.
    Msg$ = Msg$ + "displayed date as correct "
    Msg$ = Msg$ + "or change the date as desired."
    Title$ = "Change System Date"               'Defines String Title$.
    Current$ = Date$                            'Obtains current date.
    New$ = InputBox$(Msg$, Title$, Current$)    'Gets the user entered date.
    CurDate# = DateValue(Current$)              'Gets serial number of date.
    NewDate# = DateValue(New$)                  'Gets serial number of entered date.
    If CurDate# <> NewDate# Then                'Checks the serial numbers.
        Date$ = New$                            'Changes the date to the entered date.
    End If
    MsgBox "The Current Date is " + Date$       'Displays the new date.
    Exit Sub
BadFormat:
    Msg$ = "You have entered the date in an incorrect "
    Msg$ = Msg$ + "format. Please reenter the date in "
    Msg$ = Msg$ + "mm-dd-yy, mm-dd-yyyy, mm/dd/yy, or "
    Msg$ = Msg$ + "mm/dd/yyyy format."
    MsgBox Msg$
    Resume Start
End Sub
```

## Description

The argument for the Date$ statement must be a string containing a valid date. The valid date formats that the Date$ statement will accept are mm-dd-yy, mm-dd-yyyy, mm/dd/yy, and mm/dd/yyyy. A datestring$ must be a string variable, or the system will generate an error. In this form, the mm part of the string stands for the current month that must be between 0 and 12, for the 12 months of the year. The dd portion of the returned string is the day of the current day of the month and must be between 1 and 31. This string ends with the yyyy that returns the current year, which must be between 1980 and 2099. Strings that end in yy represent the last two digits of the familiar year, with 1992 being expressed as 92.

The example syntax gives the user the opportunity to change the system date with an input box whose contents provide the new definition of the date. Notice that if the user enters a date in any format other than those shown, the system generates an error. Also notice that variables used for storing and comparing numeric dates should be double precision (as indicated by the # symbol), or comparisons may not work correctly.

## Example

In the Time project at the end of this section, the Date$ statement serves as a means of setting the system date of the computer. After the user presses the command button labeled Enter Date, an input box prompts the user for a new date by the triggering of the Enter_Date_Click event. If the user has changed the date, then the date returned by the Inputbox defines the Date$ statement and modifies the computer system's date. This makes the Date$ equal to the New$ string returned by the Inputbox. Notice that the Date$ statement must be defined with a string to function properly and that it works in conjunction with the DateValue function that checks if a change has been made by the user.

## Comments

Try changing your system date with the example program before turning off your computer (after exiting windows) to determine if the Date$ statement affects your computer's date setting. If the date remains unchanged, then it does not affect the date of your computer.

Remember that while 31 is the maximum date for a month, not all months have 31 days.

# DateSerial Function

## Purpose

The DateSerial function converts the values of an indicated date to a Visual Basic serial number. With this function, the elements of a date, including the year, month, and day, may be converted to a universal format of numbers. These numbers are for reference or date calculation purposes. A serial number produced by a DateSerial function might serve as a reference for some actions that take place based on the value of the serial number. By using expressions instead of the values, the DateSerial function determines a date based upon the user's entered information. Table 22.5 summarizes the arguments for the DateSerial function.

## General Syntax

```
DateSerial(year%, month%, day%)
```

| Argument | Description |
|----------|-------------|
| year% | A year between 1753 and 2078 inclusive |
| month% | A number between 1 and 12 inclusive |
| day% | A number between 01 and 31 inclusive |

**Table 22.5 Possible arguments for the DateSerial function**

## Example

```
Sub Command1_Click ()
Start:
    On Error GoTo NotDate              'Takes the date entered in Text box 1 and
    If Text1.Text = "" Then GoTo EnterDate   'adds the figures entered in the other text
    BeginDate = DateValue(Text1.Text)  'boxes to the Year, Month, and Day of the
    BeginMonth = Month(BeginDate)      'entered date to obtain a new date.
    EndMonth = Val(Text3.Text)
    BeginDay = Day(BeginDate)
    EndDay = Val(Text4.Text)
    BeginYear = Year(BeginDate)
    EndYear = Val(Text2.Text)
    EndDate = DateSerial(BeginYear + EndYear, BeginMonth + EndMonth, BeginDay + ⇐
                  'EndDay)
    Label1.Caption = Format$(EndDate, "mm-dd-yyyy")
    Exit Sub
EnterDate:
    MsgBox "Please Enter a value in each box."
    Exit Sub
NotDate:
    If BeginYear + EndYear > 2078 Then
        MsgBox "Please enter a lower value for the year."
        Text2.Text = ""
    ElseIf BeginMonth + EndMonth > 12 Then
        MsgBox "Please enter a lower value for the month."
        Text3.Text = ""
    ElseIf BeginDay + EndDay > 31 Then
        MsgBox "Please enter a lower value for the day."
        Text4.Text = ""
    Else
        MsgBox "Please enter a valid date."
        Text1.Text = ""
    End If
    Resume Start
End Sub
```

## Description

The DateSerial function returns a serial number that represents the month, day, and year of a date on the calendar, as discussed in the introduction to this chapter. Each of the three arguments of this function represents the numerical values of a date in time.

With the year% variable, the year of a date is a 4-digit number between 1753 and 2078 inclusive. Any value between 0 and 178 represents a year between 1900 and 2078. Month% stands for the month of a date between 1 and 12, with January being represented by 1 and December by 12. Date% represents the day of a month between 01 and 31. This variable is subject to the number of days actually in a month (a day in the month of February may not have a day% variable that equals 31).

In the example syntax, the numbers entered into the text boxes below the date increase the year, month, and day of the entered date to produce a new date based upon the amount specified in each text box. Figure 22.4 shows what this example might look like on the screen. An error-checking system enforces the limits of each of these variables, forcing the user to enter a valid number in each text box.

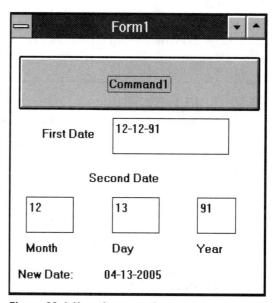

Figure 22.4 How the example syntax looks on the screen

### The Month, Day, and Year Functions

The Month, Day, and Year functions are the logical choices to use to obtain the variables for a DateSerial function. In the example syntax, each of these functions provides the necessary values of the date entered by the user. Notice how each function only returns the value that represents the month, day, or year, respectively, of the date. Each function ignores all of the other values in the date. The Year function provides only the number of the current year.

## Example

In the Time project at the end of this section, the DateSerial function determines the serial number of the provided month, day, and year variables. The Calc_Date_Click event uses the DateSerial function to find the date that lies approximately the same amount of time between two user-entered dates. The user enters both dates in the input boxes. The results are then stored to variables that are each separated into hours, minutes, and seconds. This function calculates the date that lies approximately between the two entered dates. The DateSerial function provides for the separation of the month, day, and year portions of the date. The average of each portion is immediately stored to a variable that displays in a message box. Notice that the DateSerial function returns a serial number that must first be converted to a string with the format function prior to being displayed.

## Comments

The DateSerial function's greatest value lies in its ability to quickly calculate the serial number of a calculated date, such as in the example syntax.

# DateValue Function

## Purpose

The DateValue function converts a date in the form of a string into a Visual Basic serial number. This function changes differently formatted dates to a universal numerical form. The serial number is a reference for calculation purposes. A serial number produced by a DateValue function might serve as a reference for some actions that take place based on the value of the serial number. This same serial number may also be used to calculate a date based upon an expression with another serial number. Table 22.6 summarizes the argument of the DateValue function, and Table 22.7 summarizes the valid DateValue formats.

## General Syntax

```
DateValue(datestring$)
```

| Argument | Description |
|----------|-------------|
| datestring$ | String that represents a date for the DateValue function to convert |

**Table 22.6 Argument of DateValue function**

| Valid datestring$ Formats |
|---------------------------|
| 01/01/1991 |
| 01/01/91 |
| January 1, 1991 |
| Jan 1, 1991 |
| 01-Jan-1991 |
| 01 January 90 |

**Table 22.7 Valid DateValue Formats**

## Example Syntax

```
Sub Command1_Click ()
Start:
    On Error GoTo NotDate                'Sets error trap to NotDate.
    If Text1.Text = "" Then GoTo EnterDate  'Checks if Text box is blank.
```

```
        If Text2.Text = "" Then GoTo EnterDate   'Checks if Text box is blank.
        FirstDate = DateValue(Text1.Text)        'Finds serial number of entered date.
        EndDate = DateValue(Text2.Text)          'Finds serial number of entered date.
        Text1.Text = Str$(FirstDate)             'Displays the serial number.
        Text2.Text = Str$(EndDate)               'Displays the serial number.
        Days = Abs(EndDate - FirstDate)          'Finds number of days between date.
        Label1.Caption = Str$(Days) + " Days"    'Displays the number of days.
        Exit Sub                                 'Exits subroutine.
EnterDate:
        MsgBox "Please Enter a date in each box."
        Exit Sub
NotDate:
        MsgBox "Please enter a date only"
        Resume Start
End Sub
```

## Description

The DateValue function converts a date string to a serial number that represents the month, day, and year of a date on the calendar. There are a number of acceptable date formats for the order of appearance of the month, day, and year in the datestring$. The international section of the WIN.INI file defines the default order of the month, day, and year. If a datestring$ contains the actual name of a month in long or abbreviated form, the DateValue function will also be able to convert it to a serial number. In addition to recognizing 01/01/1991 and 01/01/91, the DateValue function will also be able to convert January 1, 1991, Jan 1, 1991, 01-Jan-1991, and 01 January 91. If the year portion of a datestring$ is omitted, the current year is assumed. All of these combinations will work in the example, so try them out with different date formats for each text box. This demonstrates the conversion of date strings of differing formats to serial numbers. The same equation produces a result that reflects the difference in days between the two dates.

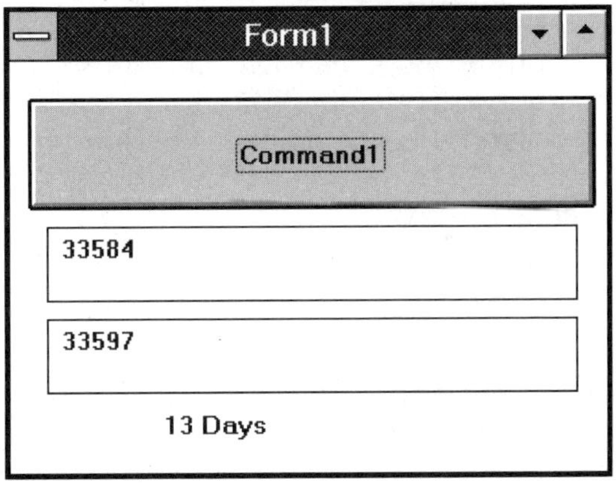

**Figure 22.5 What the example syntax looks like on the screen**

In the example syntax, the DateValue function finds the serial number of the two dates that the user enters in the Text1 and Text2 text boxes. The difference between the two serial numbers provides the number of days that are between the two entered dates. Figure 22.5 shows what this example might look like on the screen.

## Example

In the Time project at the end of this section, the TimeValue function changes a text date to a serial number. The user must press the command button labeled Enter Date to change the date displayed on the screen. The Enter_Date_Click event prompts the user for the new date, displaying the current date as the default in the input box. In order for the date to be set properly, the DateValue function changes the returned string to a serial number. Notice that the DateValue checks the date stored in the Current$ variable rather than just utilizing the Now function for comparison.

## Comments

Although DateValue will not display time information that might be in the text string, invalid time information (such as 89;98) will cause Visual Basic to generate an error. Negative numbers in the date string represent dates prior to December 31, 1899.

# Hour, Minute, and Second Functions

## Purpose

The Hour, Minute, and Second functions convert a serial number to these familiar elements of time. The Hour function returns an integer that is between 0 (12:00AM) and 23 (11:00PM) inclusive. Using the Minute and Second functions on a serial number results in an integer between 0 and 59 inclusive representing the minute or second portion of the time. These functions give the programmer the ability to display or return a serial number's hour, minute, and second on the indicated day. Table 22.8 summarizes the argument of the Hour, Minute, and Second functions.

## General Syntax

```
Hour(serial#)
Minute(serial#)
Second(serial#)
```

| Argument | Description |
|----------|-------------|
| serial# | Serial number of the date to find the hour, minute or second |

**Table 22.8 Argument of the Hour, Minute, and Second functions**

## Example Syntax

```
Sub Timer1_Timer ()
    Timer1.Interval = 1000                      'Sets Interval to 1 Second
    If Hour(Now) > 12 Then                      'Checks if time is AM or PM
        NormalTime = Hour(Now) - 12             'Changes 24hour to 12hour time
        DayTime$ = " PM"                        'Sets Daytime string to PM
    Else
        DayTime$ = " AM"                        'Sets Daytime string to AM
        NormalTime = Hour(Now)                  'Finds the current hour
    End If
    Current$ = Str$(NormalTime) + " :"          'Defines variable as the current hour
    Current$ = Current$ + Str$(Minute(Now)) + " :" 'minute, and seconds separated by
```

```
Current$ = Current$ + Str$(Second(Now))    'colons.
Current$ = Current$ + DayTime$
Text1.Text = Current$                      'Displays the current time in Text1
                                           'text box

End Sub
```

## Description

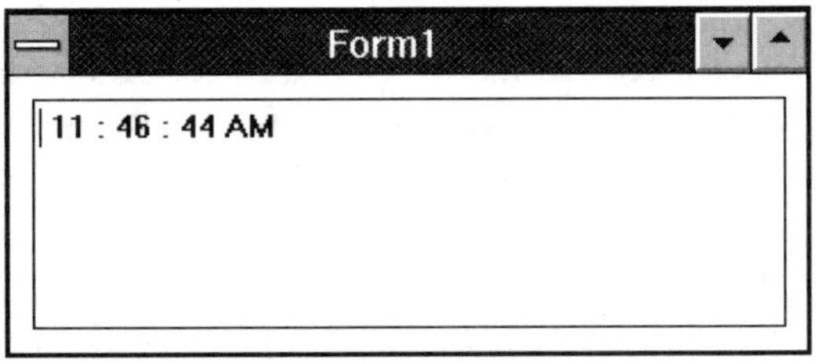

The serial# argument of an Hour, Minute, or Second function may represent a date and time between January 1, 1753 and December 31, 2078 inclusive. In a serial number, the digit to the right of the decimal point returns the time of the day. Only the right side of the serial number is necessary for the Hour, Minute, and Second functions to produce the time of the day. The part of the serial number on the left side of the decimal point is the date and has no effect upon the value returned for the Hour, Minute, and Second functions.

**Figure 22.6 Time displayed in the Text1 text box**

In the example syntax, the Hour, Minute, and Second functions work together to display the current time in the Text1 text box on the form. The text AM and PM also follows the time displayed on the screen.

### Current Time and the Now Function

The Now function provides the serial number of the current system date and time. When this function works with the Hour, Minute, and Second functions, the result is a value that defines the hour, minute, and second. In the example syntax, the Now function serves this purpose of providing the serial number for the Hour, Minute, and Second functions to provide the time to display in the text box. Notice that a space is left for the unseen 0 when the number is a single digit.

### The Timer Event and Interval Property

When the Timer event and Interval property are used along with the Hour, Minute, Second, and Now functions, the time may be obtained at intervals specified by the Interval property of the timer control. The accuracy of the time displayed on the screen depends on the Interval property. If you watch the seconds change in the example syntax, you will notice that sometimes certain seconds are skipped. In order to keep this problem from happening, reduce the interval to one half the needed accuracy. For the example, this may be avoided by changing the interval from 1000 milliseconds (1 second) to 500 milliseconds (1/2 second).

## Example

In the Time project at the end of this section, the Hour, Minute, and Second functions provide the data for displaying the time on the screen. When the user presses the command button labeled 24Hr Time, the Clock24 Timer is disabled and the Clock12

Timer is enabled. The Clock12_Timer event is triggered by the enabling of the Clock12 timer control. This has the effect of displaying the time in the Caption property of the Current_Time label box in 12-hour format. The Hour, Minute, and Second functions work with the Now function to produce the time in 12-hour form. If the value is greater than 12, then the displayed hour has 12 subtracted from it. Additionally, the time ends with AM when the value returned by the Hour function is less than or equal to 12, and PM when it is greater than 12. It is not necessary to modify the results of either the Minute or Second functions to display 12-hour time. Although this method for displaying the time is substantially longer than the Time$ function, it is more flexible about how the time appears on the screen.

## Comments

The time obtained is only as accurate as the setting of the system clock.

# Interval Property

## Objects Affected

| | | | | |
|---|---|---|---|---|
| Check | Clipboard | Combo | Command | Dbug |
| Dir | Drive | File | Form | Frame |
| Label | List | Menu | Option | Picture |
| Printer | Screen | Scroll | Text | ▶ Timer |

## Purpose

The Interval property of a timer control indicates the length of time to wait before processing the Timer event. Once a timer control is activated, the actions listed in the Timer event are triggered each time that the time indicated in the interval has passed. Unless the interval is changed or the control is disabled, the Timer event will continue to be processed at this interval of time until the program ends. This property is changeable either at design time or run time. Each timer control's Interval property is independent of the Interval properties of other timer controls on the same form. Table 22.9 summarizes the arguments of the Interval property of a timer control, and Table 22.10 summarizes its possible settings.

## General Syntax

```
timer.Interval = milliseconds&
```

| Argument | Description |
|---|---|
| timer | CtlName property of the timer control being affected |
| milliseconds& | Amount of time that must pass between the processing of the Timer event (as a long integer) |

**Table 22.9 Arguments of the Interval property of a Timer control**

| milliseconds& | Effect |
|---|---|
| 0 | Disables the timer (default) |
| 1-65,767 | If the enable property is set to True, then the Timer event is activated after the amount of time specified by the value of this property. This property represents the interval in milliseconds |
| | The Timer event is run each time that the interval is reached until the Timer is disabled |

**Table 22.10 Possible settings of the Interval property of a Timer control**

## Example Syntax

```
Sub Timer1_Timer ()
    Timer1.Interval = 1000                           'Sets Interval to 1 Second.
    Current$ = Str$(Hour(Now)) + ":"                 'Defines variable as the current
    Current$ = Current$ + Str$(Minute(Now)) + ":"   'hour,minute, and seconds separated by
                                                     'colons.
    Current$ = Current$ + Str$(Second(Now))
    Text1.Text = Current$                            'Defines text box as the string
                                                     'current
End Sub

Sub Timer1_Timer ()
    Timer1.Interval = 1000                           'Sets Interval to 1 Second.
    Current$ = Str$(Hour(Now)) + ":"                 'Defines variable as the current
    Current$ = Current$ + Str$(Minute(Now)) + ":"   'hour,minute, and seconds separated by
                                                     'colons.
    Current$ = Current$ + Str$(Second(Now))
    Text1.Text = Current$                            'Defines text box as the string
                                                     'current

    If Timer >= 21600 Then                           'Checks if time is 6:00 or greater.
        Beep                                         'Beep a warning to the user.
    EndIf
End Sub
```

## Description

Each Interval property expression begins with the CtlName property of the timer control and ends with the milliseconds& argument. The milliseconds& argument, an Interval property expression, may be any number between 0 and 65,767 milliseconds (64.8 seconds). Even though the measurements are in milliseconds, the system measures the passage of time with 18 ticks per second. For this reason, the interval can not be guaranteed to pass exactly on time, making it necessary to reference the system clock.

In the example syntax for this property, the interval property displays the hour, minute, and seconds of the time from the system clock. If you watch the changing time carefully, you will notice that the seconds listed will sometimes miss a number. This problem is caused by the differences in the way that the system calculates the time with 18 ticks per second instead of milliseconds. To prevent this, change the Interval property of the timer to half of the needed accuracy— that is, 500.

### The Enabled Property

If the Interval property of a timer control is set to 0, then the timer control is disabled and will not process the Timer event. The Enabled property of a timer control indicates whether the control is active or inactive. When the Enabled property of a timer control is False (0), it is disabled, and the Timer event connected to the timer control is not waiting to be processed. For this reason, if either the Enabled property or the Interval property is disabled in this way, the timer control stays inactive until its Interval property is a non-0 value and the Enabled property is True (-1). In the example syntax, the Enabled property is changed at design time to allow the timer control to activate immediately when the program is started.

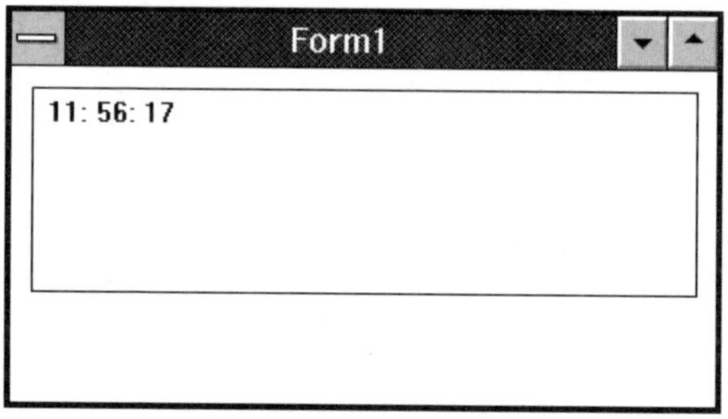

In this example, the Timer event will be processed every 1000 milliseconds or 1 second. Since the timer is enabled when the form is loaded, the timer will keep on displaying the time until the form is closed. This provides a very simple clock. Figure 22.7 shows what this clock might look like on the screen.

**Figure 22.7 Time generated from first example syntax**

### The Timer Function

Since the Interval property has a maximum possible length of 65,767 milliseconds (64.8 seconds), the Timer function must be used to generate actions that require longer lengths of time before they are triggered. A timer event could be set up on a form to check the amount of time since midnight with the Timer function until the timer returns an amount that is greater that the time specified for the event to take place. In the second syntax example, an alarm triggers after 6:00 AM each time the form is started.

## Example

In the Time project at the end of this section, the Interval property of each of the timer controls is the amount of time appropriate for that timer. When the Time project starts, the Form_Load event subroutine starts both the Default_Date and Clock24 timer controls. These controls are activated by changing their Enabled properties to True and Interval properties to 1000 (Default_Date) and 500 (Clock24) milliseconds. Both of these property changes are necessary to ensure that the Timer events of both controls are processed. If the Enabled property of a timer control is False, then the Timer event will not work. Similarly, the Timer event will not function with the Interval property of the timer control set to a 0 value.

## Comments

Although the Interval property of one timer control has no effect on another timer control, Windows has a limit of no more than 16 active timer controls at a time. Please be sure that you do not exceed this limit, or an error will be generated.

# Now Function

## Purpose

The Now function provides the serial number for the current date and time of the computer's system clock-calendar. Most computers today have a battery that saves the date and maintains the time each time that user turns off the computer. Computers without a battery or some other means of saving the date and time must have these items set correctly for the Now function to produce the correct information.

## General Syntax

Now

## Example Syntax

```
Sub Timer1_Time ()
    Timer1.Interval = 100                                'Sets timer interval.
    Text1.Text = Str$(Now)                               'Displays serial number.
    Text2.Text = Format$(Now,"mmmm-dd-yy hh:mm:ss")      'Displays current date and
                                                         'time.
End Sub
```

## Description

The Now function has no arguments. The serial number returned by the Now function represents the system date and time at the moment that the code is run. This serial number's digits to the left of the decimal point represent the date and digits to the right stand for the time, as explained in the introduction to this chapter.

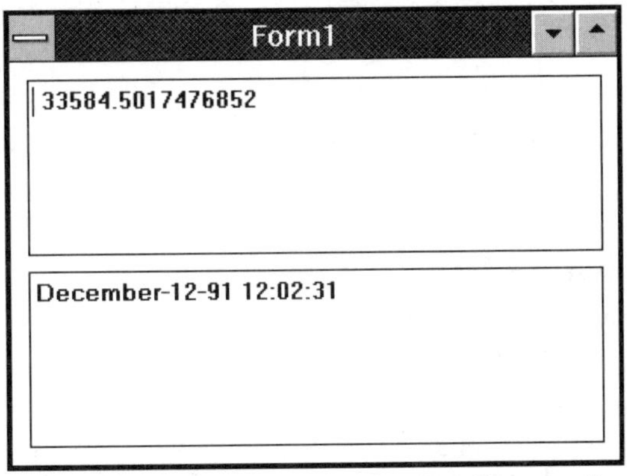

In the example syntax, the Now function serves as a means of displaying the date, time, and serial number on the screen. With this example, the time and date are shown in the Text2 text box

**Figure 22.8 Serial number and date/time on the screen**

and the serial number that produces this information, rerturned by the Now function, is placed in the text1 text box. Notice that in both cases, the serial number must be converted to a string prior to defining the Text property of the text1 and text2 text boxes. Figure 22.8 shows what this example might look like on the screen.

## Example

In the Time project at the end of this section, the Now function provides the serial number of the current time and date. The Special_Date_Timer event uses the Now function to define the Month, Day, and Year functions. Every time that the

Clock24_Timer event is processed, the code checks if either the current hour or minute are 0. In the Clock12_Timer event, the Now function provides the details of the time to display in the Current_Time label box. Notice the serial number returned by the Now function determines both time and date attributes.

# Time$ Function

## Purpose

The Time$ function provides your computer's current system time when used in a Visual Basic application. As the returned time is in string format, it may be used directly in text strings without modification. This eliminates the need to use the Format$ function to convert the current time to a string. Table 22.11 summarizes the possible returned settings of the Time$Function.

## General Syntax

Time$

| Time | Description |
|------|-------------|
| Hour (hh) | A number between 00 and 23 inclusive |
| Minute (mm) | A number between 00 and 59 inclusive |
| Second (ss) | A number between 00 and 59 inclusive |

Table 22.11 Possible returned settings of the Time$ function

## Example Syntax

```
Sub Timer1_Timer ()
    If Now < TimeValue("08:00:00") Then          'Checks the time.
        MsgBox "You are early for work! " + Time$ 'Displays message and time.
    ElseIf Now <= TimeValue("08:30:00") Then     'Checks the time.
        MsgBox "Welcome to work " + Time$         'Displays message and time.
    ElseIf Now > TimeValue("08:30:00") Then      'Checks the time.
        MsgBox "You are late for work " + Time$   'Displays message and time.
    ElseIf Now > TimeValue("12:00:00") Then      'Checks the time.
        MsgBox "Time for lunch! " + Time$         'Displays the time.
    ElseIf Now > TimeValue("17:30:00") Then      'Checks the time.
        MsgBox "Time to go home! " + Format$(Now,"hh:mm") 'Displays the time.
    End If
End Sub
```

## Description

The Time$ function has no arguments. This function returns a string of 8 characters that represents the computer's current system time. This function's returned character string is in the form of hh:mm:ss. In this form, the hh part of the string stands for the current hour that must be between 0 and 23, for the 24 hours of the day. The mm portion of the returned string is the minute of the current day and must be between 00 and 59. This string ends with the ss that returns the current second that must be between 00 and 59.

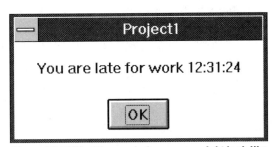

Figure 22.9 What the reminder screen might look like

The example syntax checks the current time of the computer to determine which message to display on the screen. With this example, the Time$ function works in the same way as the Format$ function to display the current time at the end of the indicated message. Figure 22.9 shows what this example might look like on the screen.

## The Format$ Function

The Format$ function and Time$ function produce the same results when the Format function converts the current time to the hh:mm:ss format. In some cases, the Time$ function is a better choice for a particular situation while other applications work better with the Format$ function. In the example syntax, the Time$ and Format$ functions provide the date to display in the message on the screen. Notice that the Time$ function requires less space in the code to display the time. The Format$ function provides a way to display only the hour and minute of the current time. This example demonstrates the tradeoff between the flexibility of the Format$ function and the shorter required size of the Time$ function.

## Example

In the Time project at the end of this section, the Time$ function provides the means of finding the current time and returning the time in string format. The Clock24_Timer event displays the current time in the Current_Time label box with the Time$ function. In this case, the Time$ function serves as a direct definition of the Caption property of the Current_Time label box. As a result, the time is displayed in the label box in 24-hour format hh:mm:ss (hh = hour, mm = minutes, ss = seconds). If the 24-hour format serves the needs of a particular situation, this function is an excellent method for displaying the time with a minimum amount of lines of code.

## Comments

Use the Time$ statement to change the current system time of the computer.

# Time$ Statement

## Purpose

The Time$ statement allows the user to change the system time of a computer within a Visual Basic application. This time may or may not change the system time permanently on your computer, depending upon its configuration. Most computers today have a battery that saves the time on each occasion the user turns off the computer. Computers without a battery or some other means of saving the time will not keep the time that the user enters with this function. For all other computers, the change that you make to the system date is normally a permanent change. Table 22.12 summarizes the argument of the Time$ statement, and Table 22.13 summarizes the possible acceptable contents of the TimeString$ of a Time$ statement.

## General Syntax

```
Time$ = timestring$
```

| Argument | Description |
| --- | --- |
| timestring$ | Time in string format for the function to convert to a serial number |

**Table 22.12 Argument of the Time$ statement**

| timestring$ | Possible Settings |
| --- | --- |
| hh | A number between 00 and 23 inclusive |
| mm | A number between 00 and 59 inclusive |
| ss | A number between 00 and 59 inclusive |

**Table 22.13 Possible acceptable contents of the TimeString$ of a Time$ statement**

## Example Syntax

```
Sub Command1_Click ()
Start:
    On Error Goto BadFormat                      'Sets Error Checking.
    Msg$ = "Please press enter to accept the "   'Defines String Msg$.
    Msg$ = Msg$ + "displayed time as correct "
    Msg$ = Msg$ + "or change the time as desired."
    Title$ = "Change System Time"               'Defines String Title$.
    Current$ = Time$                            'Obtains current time.
    New$ = InputBox$(Msg$, Title$, Current$)    'Gets the user entered time.
    CurTime# = TimeValue(Current$)              'Gets serial number of time.
    NewTime# = TimeValue(New$)                  'Gets serial number of entered date.
    If CurTime# <> NewTime# Then                'Checks the serial numbers.
        Time$ = New$                            'Changes the date to the entered date.
    End If
    MsgBox "The Current Time is " + Time$       'Displays the new time.
    Exit Sub
BadFormat:
    Msg$ = "You have entered the time in an incorrect "
    Msg$ = Msg$ + "format. Please reenter the time in "
    Msg$ = Msg$ + "hh:mm:ss, 1:30PM, or 13:30."
    MsgBox Msg$
    Resume Start
End Sub
```

## Description

The user must input any changes to the system time in a format that the Time$ statement will recognize as a time. The valid time formats that the Time$ statement will accept are hh, hh:mm, and hh:mm:ss. The timestring$ argument must be a string variable or the system generates an error. In this form, the hh part of the string stands for the current hour, which must be between 00 and 23. These values represent the 24 hours of the day. The mm portion of the returned string is the minute of the current day, and must be between 00 and 59. This string may end with ss that returns the current seconds. The seconds must be between 0 and 59. For strings that do not end in mm or ss, these settings represent 0.

The example syntax gives the user the opportunity to change the system time with an input box whose contents may then be given as the new definition of the time. Notice that if the user enters a time in any format other than those shown, the system generates an error. If the time entered is valid, the Time$ statement changes the system time to the time entered by the user. Figures 22.10 and 22.11 show what this example might look like on the screen.

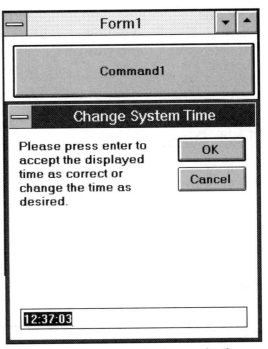

**Figure 22.10 The screen asks the user for the new time**

## Example

In the Time project at the end of this section, the Time$ statement sets the computer time. After the user presses the command button labeled Enter Time, an input box prompts the user for a new time by the triggering of the Enter_Time_Click event. If the user changes the time, the Time$ statement

**Figure 22.11 The screen displays the current time**

uses the user-entered time to modify the computer's time. This makes the Time$ statement equal to the New$ string returned by the input box. Notice that a string defines the Time$ statement.

## Comments

Try changing your system time with the example program before turning off your computer (after exiting Windows) to determine if the Time$ statement affects your computer's date setting. If the time remains the same as it was before, the system's time remains unaffected.

# Timer Event

## Objects Affected

| | | | | |
|---|---|---|---|---|
| Check | Clipboard | Combo | Command | Dbug |
| Dir | Drive | File | Form | Frame |
| Label | List | Menu | Option | Picture |
| Printer | Screen | Scroll | Text | ▶ Timer |

## Purpose

The Timer event contains the actions that take place when the interval value of the timer control has elapsed. This event takes place every time that the interval of time elapses until the timer control is disabled. A timer control is disabled by setting its Enabled property to False, by setting its Interval property to 0, or by unloading the form. Table 22.14 summarizes the arguments of the Timer event.

## General Syntax

```
Sub CtlName_Timer ([Index As Integer])
```

| Argument | Description |
|---|---|
| CtlName | CtlName property of the timer |
| Index | This argument serves as a reference for the part of a control array addressed |

Table 22.14 Arguments of the Timer event

## Example Syntax

```
Sub Timer1_Timer ()
    Cls                              'Clear the form.
    Const PI = 3.14159265            'Define Constant PI.
    Static Num As Double             'Define Static Variable
    FillColor = QBColor(1)           'Sets form's fillcolor.
    FillStyle = 0                    'Sets form's fillstyle to solid.
    X% = ScaleWidth / 2              'Defines as half width of screen.
    Y% = ScaleHeight / 2             'Defines as half height of screen.
    Radius% = ScaleWidth / 4         'Defines as 1/4 of width of screen.
    Circle (X%, Y%), Radius%, , Num, -6.283  'Draws partial circle on screen.
```

```
    Num = Num - ((2 * PI) / 60)    'Reduces value of variable.
    Text1.Text = Str$(Num)         'Displays setting of variable.
    If Abs(Num) >= 6.283 Then      'Checks value of variable.
        Num = 0                    'Redefines variable as zero.
        Timer1.Enabled = 0         'Disables Timer.
        Cls                        'Clears screen.
    End If
End Sub
```

## Description

Begin the definition of the Timer event with the name of the timer control to be affected. Add an index variable in parentheses at the end of the statement. Note that since all the controls of a control array share the same Timer event, the Index value has nothing to do with the Timer event. The index argument is for reference purposes only.

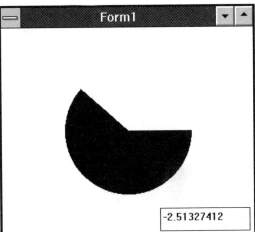

In the example syntax, the Timer event is triggered when the form is loaded. This Timer event displays a circle on the screen with a line drawn from the center of the circle to the right

**Figure 22.12 Partial circle generated by Timer events**

edge of the circle. Each time the event runs, it draws a circle with a larger and larger slice removed. When the circle disappears from the screen, the timer control's Enable property is changed to False, ending the timing. Figure 22.12 shows what this example might look like on the screen.

### The Interval Property

The Interval property of a timer control indicates how frequently to process the Timer event. This property is measured in milliseconds and may range in value from 0 to 65,676 (64.8 seconds). No matter what the setting of this property, if the Enabled property is False, the Timer event will not be processed. The example syntax sets the Interval property of the Timer1 control to 1000 to allow for the processing of the Timer event at once per second. By setting up the Interval property in this way, the circle graphically displays the amount of time left in the minute since the form was loaded.

### The Enabled Property

The Enabled property of a timer control determines whether the control is active or inactive. When the timer control's Enabled property is True, the code processes the Timer event at the intervals specified by the Interval property. While the timer control's property is False, the control remains disabled. If the Interval property is 0, then the Timer event is not processed. In the example syntax, the Enabled property of the timer control must be True to trigger the Timer event at the loading of the form. This property automatically changes back to False when the circle has disappeared off the screen.

## Example

In the Time project at the end of this section, the Timer event produces regular actions that display the time and date on the screen. The Timer events of both controls trigger after the Form_Load event enables both the Default_Date and Clock24 Timer controls. The Clock24 Timer contains code that displays the current time in the Current_Time label box and triggers every 500 milliseconds (half second). Code in Default_Date timer control shows the date in the Current_Date label box. Notice that the Default_Date has an Interval property of 1000 milliseconds, but is not run at intervals, because its Enabled property is False each time it is run.

# Timer Function

## Purpose

The Timer function provides the number of seconds that have elapsed since 12:00 midnight. This function may serve as a reference for determining the number of seconds elapsed between two different uses of the Timer function on the same day.

## General Syntax

```
Timer
```

## Example Syntax

```
Sub Timer1_Timer ()
    Timer1.Interval = 500                         'Sets Timer Interval.
    Static ProgStart As Double                    'Defines static variable.
    Msg$ = " Elapsed seconds since Midnight"      'Defines message.
    Midnight = Int(Timer)                         'Stores current seconds.
    ST$ = Str$(Midnight)                          'Converts to text.
    Text1.Text = ST$ + Msg$                       'Displays seconds since midnight.
    T$ = Format$(Now, "hh:mm:ss")                 'Stores current time.
    If ProgStart = 0 Then                         'If ProgStart has not been set,
        ProgStart = Midnight                      'sets ProgStart.
    End If
    Msg$ = Str$(Int(Midnight - ProgStart))        'Stores seconds since startup.
    Msg$ = Msg$ + " Seconds since program start"  'Stores message.
    Text2.Text = Msg$                             'Displays seconds since startup.
    Text3.Text = T$                               'Displays current time.
End Sub
```

## Description

The Timer function returns the value that represents the number of seconds elapsed since midnight. This function has no argument, and returns a value between 0 and

86,400 (the number of seconds in one day). For this reason, the difference between two values gained on different days will not return the number of seconds between the two moments in time.

The example syntax uses the Timer function to store and display the current number of seconds since midnight and program startup. It finds the difference between the variables produced at program startup and now and then provides the number of elapsed seconds since program startup. Figure 22.13 shows what the example should look like on the screen.

## Example

In the Time project at the end of this section, the Timer function returns a serial number that represents the number of seconds elapsed since midnight. After the user presses the Stop Watch command button, the Timer function serves as a part of the StopWatch_Timer event to generate the circle and digital count on the form. In this event, the Timer function acts both as a reference and increments the time since the user pressed the command button. When the user presses the Stop Watch command button, the code stores the serial number to the Start# static variable. Each triggering of the StopWatch_Timer event displays the number of hours, minutes, and seconds that have elapsed. This is done by displaying the difference between the current Timer result and the Start# variable. Notice that this event only works when comparing times on the same day, because the Timer function only deals with time since midnight.

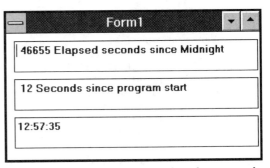

Figure 22.13 What the Timer function example should look like

# TimeSerial Function

## Purpose

The TimeSerial function converts the values of an indicated time to a Visual Basic serial number. This function converts the elements of time (hours, minutes, and seconds) to a universal numeric format that may then be used for reference or time calculation purposes. A serial number produced by a TimeSerial function might serve as a reference for some actions that take place based on the value of the serial number. By using expressions instead of the values, the TimeSerial function determines a time based upon the user's entered information. Table 22.15 summarizes the arguments of the TimeSerial function.

## General Syntax

```
TimeSerial(hour%, minute%, second%)
```

| Argument | Description |
|----------|-------------|
| hour% | A number between 00 and 23 inclusive |
| minute% | A number between 00 and 59 inclusive |
| second% | A number between 00 and 59 inclusive |

**Table 22.15 Possible arguments for the TimeSerial function**

## Example Syntax

```
Sub Command1_Click ()
Start:
    On Error GoTo NotTime                    'Takes the time entered in Text box 1 and
    If Text1.Text = "" Then GoTo EnterTime   'adds the figures entered in the other text
    BeginTime = TimeValue(Text1.Text)        'boxes to the Hour, Minute, and Second of the
    BeginHour = Hour(BeginTime)              'entered Time to obtain a new time.
    EndHour = Val(Text2.Text)
    BeginMinute = Minute(BeginTime)
    EndMinute = Val(Text3.Text)
    BeginSecond = Second(BeginTime)
    EndSecond = Val(Text4.Text)
    EndTime = TimeSerial(BeginHour + EndHour, BeginMinute + EndMinute, BeginSecond⇐
                   + EndSecond)
    Label1.Caption = Format$(EndTime, "hh:mm:ss")
    Exit Sub
EnterTime:
    MsgBox "Please Enter a value in each box."
    Exit Sub
NotTime:
    If BeginSecond + EndSecond > 60 Then
        MsgBox "Please enter a lower value for the Second."
        Text2.Text = ""
    ElseIf BeginHour + EndHour > 24 Then
        MsgBox "Please enter a lower value for the Hour."
        Text3.Text = ""
    ElseIf BeginMinute + EndMinute > 60 Then
        MsgBox "Please enter a lower value for the Minute."
        Text4.Text = ""
    Else
        MsgBox "Please enter a valid Time."
        Text1.Text = ""
    End If
    Resume Start
End Sub
```

## Description

The TimeSerial function returns a serial number that represents the hour, minutes, and seconds of a time on the clock. Each of the three arguments of this function represent the numerical values of time. The hour% argument provides the hour of a day expressed as a 2-digit number between 01 and 23 inclusive. The minute% argument stands for the minutes of time between 0 and 59. The second% argument represents the second of a day between 0 and 59.

In the example syntax, the numbers entered into the text boxes below the date increase the hour, minutes, and seconds of the entered time to produce a new time based on the amount specified in each text box. Figure 22.14 shows what this might look like on the screen.

An error-checking system in the example syntax enforces the limits of each of these arguments. This forces the user to enter a number in each text box that does not exceed the bounds of the numbers entered for the hour, minute, and second.

### The Hour, Minute, and Second Functions

The Hour, Minute, and Second functions are the logical choices to use to obtain the variables for the TimeSerial function. The example syntax uses each of these functions to obtain the necessary values of the time entered by the user. Notice that the function only returns the value of the item specified by the function. For example, the Hour function only provides the value of the hour portion of the time.

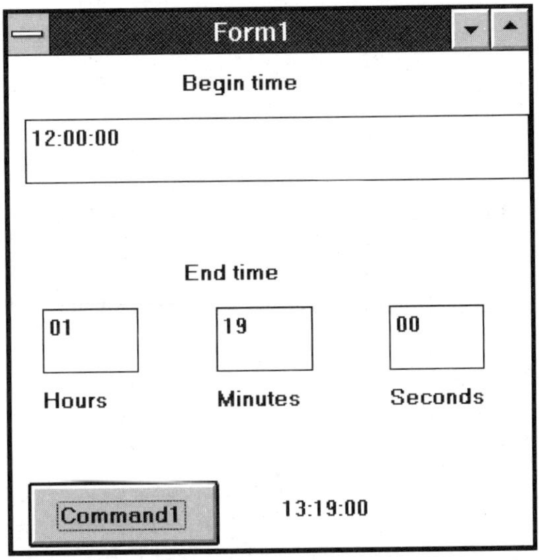

## Example

In the Time project at the end of this section, the TimeSerial function finds the serial number of individual hours, minutes, and seconds. The Calc_Time_Click event subroutine uses the TimeSerial function

**Figure 22.14 What the TimeSerial example looks like on the screen**

to find the number of hours, minutes, and seconds between two times that the user enters. The user enters both times in the input boxes. Each of the entered dates is stored in a variable separated into hours, minutes, and seconds. This function permits the calculation of the difference between the two entered times. The TimeSerial function provides for the separation of the hour, minute, and second portions of the time. This difference between each portion is immediately stored to a variable. Notice that the TimeSerial function returns a serial number that must first be converted to a string with the format function prior to being displayed.

## Comments

The TimeSerial function's greatest value lies in its ability to quickly calculate the serial number of a calculated time such as in the example syntax.

# TimeValue Function

## Purpose

The TimeValue function converts a time in the form of a string into a Visual Basic serial number. This function changes times in differing formats to a universal numerical form. The resulting serial number is usable as a reference for calculation purposes. A serial number produced by a TimeValue function might serve as a reference for some actions that take place based on the value of the serial number. This same serial number can also be used to calculate a time based on an expression with another serial number. Table 22.16 summarizes the argument of the TimeValue function.

## General Syntax

```
TimeValue(timestring$)
```

| Argument | Description |
|---|---|
| timestring$ | Text string to convert to a time serial number |

**Table 22.16 Argument of the TimeValue function**

## Example Syntax

```
Sub Command_Click ()
Start:
    On Error GoTo NotTime              'Sets error trap to NotTime.
    If Text1.Text = "" Then GoTo EnterTime   'Checks if Text box is blank.
    If Text2.Text = "" Then GoTo EnterTime   'Checks if Text box is blank.
    FirstTime = TimeValue(Text1.Text)  'Finds serial number of entered Time.
    EndTime = TimeValue(Text2.Text)    'Finds serial number of entered Time.
    Text1.Text = Str$(FirstTime)       'Displays the serial number.
    Text2.Text = Str$(EndTime)         'Displays the serial number.
    T = EndTime - FirstTime            'Finds the difference between Times.
    Seconds$ = Str$(Int(T * 86400))    'Finds the number of seconds.
    Label1.Caption = Seconds$ + " seconds"  'Displays the number of seconds.
    Exit Sub      'Exits subroutine.
EnterTime:
    MsgBox "Please Enter a Time in each box."
    Exit Sub
NotTime:
    MsgBox "Please enter a Time only"
    Text1.Text = ""
    Text2.Text = ""
    Resume Start
End Sub
```

## Description

A TimeValue function converts a time string to a serial number that represents the hour, minutes, and seconds of a time on the clock. There are a number of acceptable time formats for the order of appearance of the hour, minutes, and seconds in the timestring$. The time setting of the international section of the WIN.INI defines the default order of the hour, minutes, and seconds.

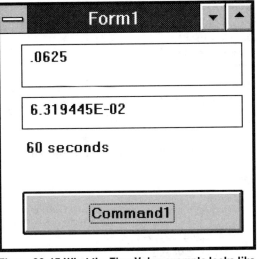

The example syntax demonstrates how to convert date strings of differing formats to serial numbers. The TimeValue function is used to find the serial number of the two times that the user enters in the Text1 and Text2 text boxes. When the code finds the difference between the two serial numbers, the result is the number of days between the two entered times. Figure 22.15 shows what this example might look like on the screen.

**Figure 22.15 What the TimeValue example looks like on the screen**

### Example

In the Time project at the end of this section, the TimeValue function changes a time string to a serial number. When the user wishes to correct the time displayed on the screen, he or she presses the command button labeled Enter Time. The Enter_Time_Click event prompts the user for the new time, displaying the current time as the default. An input box returns the string entered by the user. In order for the time to be set properly, the TimeValue function converts the returned string to a serial number. Notice that the string returned by TimeValue function stores in the Current$ variable rather than using the Now function for comparison. Otherwise, the time might have changed since the Enter_Time_Click event was triggered.

### Comments

In the example, the serial number returned by finding the number of seconds between the two entered times is not exact and requires the use of an Int function to round the number off.

# Weekday, Month, Day, and Year Functions

### Purpose

The Weekday, Month, Day, and Year functions convert a serial number to these familiar elements of the date. These values can be used to construct or format a date in the usual terms, such as "December 15, 1993." Table 22.17 summarizes the argument of the Weekday, Month, Day, and Year functions.

## General Syntax

```
Month(serial#)
Day(serial#)
Minute(serial#)
WeekDay(serial#)
```

| Argument | Description |
|----------|-------------|
| serial# | Serial number to display in month, day, year, or weekday format |

**Table 22.17 Argument of the Weekday, Month, Day, and Year functions**

## Example Syntax

```
Sub Form_Load ()
    CMonth% = Month(Now)              'Stores current month number.
    CDay% = Day(Now)                  'Stores current day number.
    CYear% = Year(Now)               'Stores current year number.
    Week% = Weekday(Now)              'Stores current weekday number.
    If CYear% < 2000 Then             'Checks if current year is less than 2000.
        If CYear% > 1899 Then         'Checks if current year is greater than 1899.
            Yr$ = Format$(CYear%, "yy")  'Stores last two digits of year.
        Else
            Yr$ = Str$(CYear%)        'Stores all four digits of year.
        End If
    End If
    Select Case CMonth%               'Checks month number for which month name to
        Case 1                        'store to the M$ string variable.
            M$ = "Jan"
        Case 2
            M$ = "Feb"
        Case 3
            M$ = "March"
        Case 4
            M$ = "April"
        Case 5
            M$ = "May"
        Case 6
            M$ = "June"
        Case 7
            M$ = "July"
        Case 8
            M$ = "August"
        Case 9
            M$ = "Sept"
        Case 10
            M$ = "Oct"
        Case 11
            M$ = "Nov"
        Case 12
            M$ = "Dec"
    End Select
    Select Case Week%                 'Checks the week number for which week name
```

```
        Case 1                          'to store to the W$ string variable.
            W$ = "Sunday "
        Case 2
            W$ = "Monday "
        Case 3
            W$ = "Tuesday "
        Case 4
            W$ = "Wednesday "
        Case 5
            W$ = "Thursday "
        Case 6
            W$ = "Friday "
        Case 7
            W$ = "Saturday "
    End Select
    Text1.Text = W$ + M$ + "-" + Str$(CDay%) + "-" + Str$(CYear%)
End Sub
```

## Description

The Weekday, Month, Day, and Year functions each take a Visual Basic date serial number (a double precision value) and return the appropriate numeric value for that element of the date.

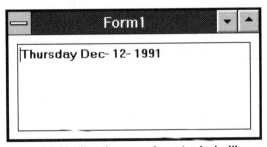

The Weekday function returns an integer between 1 (Sunday) and 7 (Saturday). The Month function returns the month as an integer between 1 and 12. January is represented by 1 and December by 12. With the Day function, an integer is returned between 1 and 31

**Figure 22.16 What the example syntax looks like on the screen**

inclusive. Since not every month has 31 days in it, the month of a serial number can reduce the range of possible days. The Year function returns an integer between 1753 and 2078 that stands for the date. If the serial number is negative, then it represents a year prior to 1900. These functions thus give the programmer the ability to display or return the weekday, month, day, and year of a serial number.

As explained in the introduction to this chapter, the numbers to the left of the decimal point in a serial number represent the date, while the fractional part to the right of the decimal represents the time. Only the left side of the serial number is necessary for producing the day of the month. The part of the serial number on the right side has no effect upon the value returned for the Month, Day, and Year functions.

In the example syntax, the serial number produced by the Now function works with each of these functions to find the values that represent the present date stored in the computer. With a Select Case statement that examines the current value returned by the WeekDay and Year functions, the month and weekday names for the displayed date are determined. All of this resulting information combines to display the weekday and date in the Text1 textbox. Figure 22.16 shows what this example might look like on the screen.

## Example

In the Time project at the end of this section, the Weekday, Month, Day, and Year functions provide the date to display on the screen. After the user presses the command button labeled Normal Date, the code disables the Default_Date Timer and enables the Special_Date Timer. The code triggers the Special_Date_Timer event by the enabling of the Special_Date timer control. This has the effect of displaying the date in the Caption property of the Current_Date label box in mixed words and numbers. In this way, 01-01-92 becomes January 1, 1992. Rather than using the Date$ function, the Month, Day, and Year functions are used with the Now function to produce the date. A Select Case statement checks the value returned by the pairing of the Month and Now functions to define the first part of the date displayed as the name of the current month. The Day and Now functions return the day number to place after the current month. The Year and Now functions provide the year.

Both the Default_Date_Timer and Clock24_Timer events use the WeekDay function to determine the current day of the week. The value returned by the WeekDay function serves as part of a Select Case statement that displays the name of the corresponding week day in the Day_Name label box. This defines the Caption property of the Day_Name label box as the name represented by the value returned. Notice that the serial number required for this function is obtained with the Now function that provides the serial number for the current date and time.

## Comments

A negative serial number represents a year prior to 1899 and has no effect on the value returned by the Day function. An integer returned by this function does not represent the total amount of days contained within a serial number, only the date's day of the month.

# The Time Project

## Project Overview

The Time project outlined in the following pages demonstrates the concept of time in Visual Basic. This example is designed to demonstrate the property, event, functions, and statements that directly affect time. By following the examples of the different elements of this project, you will learn how these elements of the language work in Visual Basic.

The following pages discuss the assembly and operation of the Time project. The first section deals with the assembly of the Time form. Next, there is a listing and explanation of the contents of the subroutines of this project. Finally, a guide to the operation of the project discusses the operation of the code. Please read this information carefully and use the pictures of the form to check your results.

## Assembling the Project

1. Make a new form (the Time form) with the objects and properties listed in Table 22.18.

| Object | Property | Setting |
|---|---|---|
| Form | BorderStyle | 1 - Fixed Single |
| | Caption | Time Project |
| | ControlBox | False |
| | FormName | Time |
| | Icon | \VB\ICONS\MISC\CLOCK04.ICO |
| | MaxButton | False |
| | MinButton | True |
| Label box | Caption | "" |
| | CtlName | Current_Time |
| | FontSize | 18 |
| Label box | Caption | "" |
| | CtlName | Current_Date |
| | FontSize | 18 |
| Label box | Caption | "" |
| | CtlName | Day_Name |
| | FontSize | 18 |
| Label box | Caption | "" |
| | CtlName | StopWatch_Time |
| | FontSize | 18 |
| Timer | CtlName | Clock24 |
| | Enabled | False |
| | Interval | 500 |
| Timer | CtlName | Clock12 |
| | Enabled | False |
| | Interval | 500 |
| Timer | CtlName | StopWatch |
| | Enabled | False |
| | Interval | 500 |
| Timer | CtlName | Default_Date |
| | Enabled | False |
| | Interval | 100 |
| Timer | CtlName | Special_Date |
| | Enabled | False |
| | Interval | 100 |
| Command button | Caption | Enter Time |
| | CtlName | Enter_Time |
| | TabIndex | 0 |

*Table 22.18 (continued)*

| Object | Property | Setting |
|---|---|---|
| Command button | Caption | Enter Date |
| | CtlName | Enter_Date |
| | TabIndex | 1 |
| Command button | Caption | 24Hr Time |
| | CtlName | Format_Time |
| | TabIndex | 2 |
| Command button | Caption | Normal Date |
| | CtlName | Format_Date |
| | TabIndex | 3 |
| Command button | Caption | Stop Watch |
| | CtlName | Stop_Watch |
| | TabIndex | 4 |
| Command button | Caption | Exit |
| | CtlName | Exit_Program |
| | TabIndex | 5 |
| Picture | CtlName | Count_Down |
| | TabStop | False |

**Table 22.18 Elements of the Time form**

2. Size the objects on the screen, as shown in Figure 22.17

3. Enter the following code in the Calc_Date_Click event subroutine. This code is triggered when the user presses the command button labeled Calc Date. Two input boxes prompt the user for two dates. Both input boxes default to today's date. After the user enters, a message box is displayed that indicates the date that lies approximately the same number of days between both of the entered dates.

```
Sub Calc_Date_Click ()
    Msg$ = "Please Enter the first of two dates that you "
    Msg$ = Msg$ + "would like to find the month, day, "
    Msg$ = Msg$ + "and year that lie between."
    Title$ = "First Date"
    EnteredDate$ = InputBox$(Msg$, Title$, Date$)
    BeginDate = DateValue(EnteredDate$)
    BM = Month(BeginDate)
    BD = Day(BeginDate)
    BY = Year(BeginDate)
    Msg$ = "Please Enter the second of two dates that you "
    Msg$ = Msg$ + "would like to find the month, day, "
    Msg$ = Msg$ + "and year that lie between."
    Title$ = "Second Date"
    EnteredDate$ = InputBox$(Msg$, Title$, Date$)
    EndTime = DateValue(EnteredDate$)
```

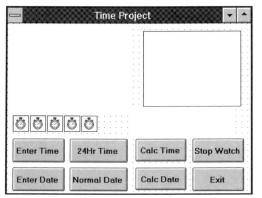

**Figure 22.17 What the Time form should look like when completed**

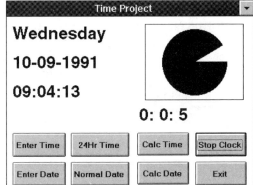

**Figure 22.18 What the Time form should look like when running**

```
    EM = Month(EndDate)
    ED = Day(EndDate)
    EY = Year(EndDate)
    Difference = DateSerial(((BM + EM) / 2), ((BD + ED) / 2), ((BY + EY) / 2))
    New$ = Format$(Difference, "mm-dd-yyyy")
    MsgBox "The date that lies between these dates is " + New$
End Sub
```

4. Enter the following code in the Calc_Time_Click event subroutine. This code is triggered when the user presses the command button labeled Calc Time. Two input boxes prompt the user for two times. The time shown in each input box is the current time. After the user enters both times, a message box displays the difference between them in hours, minutes, and seconds.

```
Sub Calc_Time_Click ()
    Msg$ = "Please Enter the first of two times that you "
    Msg$ = Msg$ + "would like to find the hours, minutes, "
    Msg$ = Msg$ + "and seconds that lie between."
    Title$ = "First Time"
    EnteredTime$ = InputBox$(Msg$, Title$, Time$)
    BeginTime = TimeValue(EnteredTime$)
    BH = Hour(BeginTime)
    BM = Minute(BeginTime)
    BS = Minute(BeginTime)
    Msg$ = "Please Enter the second of two times that you "
    Msg$ = Msg$ + "would like to find the hours, minutes, "
    Msg$ = Msg$ + "and seconds that lie between."
    Title$ = "Second Time"
    EnteredTime$ = InputBox$(Msg$, Title$, Time$)
    EndTime = TimeValue(EnteredTime$)
    EH = Hour(EndTime)
    EM = Minute(EndTime)
    ES = Second(EndTime)
    Difference = TimeSerial(Abs(BH - EH), Abs(BM - EM), Abs(BS - ES))
    New$ = Format$(Difference, "hh:mm:ss")
    MsgBox "The difference between these times is " + New$
End Sub
```

5. Enter the following code in the Clock12_Timer event subroutine. This code is triggered when the user presses the command button labeled 12Hr Time. This routine generates12hr formatted time on the screen. This event continues to process at half-second intervals until the user presses the command button again or the Timer Project ends.

```
Sub Clock12_Timer ()
    If Hour(Now) > 12 Then
        H$ = LTrim$(Str$(Hour(Now) - 12))
        D$ = "PM"
    ElseIf Hour(Now) <= 12 Then
        H$ = LTrim$(Str$(Hour(Now)))
        D$ = "AM"
    End If
    If Minute(Now) < 10 Then
        M$ = "0" + LTrim$(Str$(Minute(Now)))
    Else
        M$ = LTrim$(Str$(Minute(Now)))
    End If
    If Second(Now) < 10 Then
        S$ = "0" + LTrim$(Str$(Second(Now)))
    Else
        S$ = LTrim$(Str$(Second(Now)))
    End If
    CurTime$ = H$ + ":" + M$ + ":" + S$ + D$
    Current_Time.Caption = CurTime$
    If Hour(Now) = 0 Then
        If Minute(Now) > 0 Then
            Exit Sub
        Else
            If Format_Date.Caption = "Normal Date" Then
                Default_Date.Interval = 1000
                Default_Date.Enabled = -1
            ElseIf Format_Date.Caption = "Special Date" Then
                Special_Date.Interval = 1000
                Special_Date.Enabled = -1
            End If
        End If
    End If
End Sub
```

6. Enter the following code in the Clock24_Timer event subroutine. This code is triggered when the Enabled property of the Clock24 timer control changes to True and the Interval property to 500. The Clock12_Timer event updates the screen at half-second intervals until the user presses the command button again or the Time project ends.

```
Sub Clock24_Timer ()
    Current_Time.Caption = Time$
    If Hour(Now) = 0 Then
        If Minute(Now) > 0 Then
            Exit Sub
        Else
            Default_Date.Enabled = -1
```

```
        End If
    End If
End Sub
```

7. Enter the following code in the Default_Date_Timer event subroutine. This code is triggered when the Enabled property of the Default_Date timer control changes to True. This places the current name of the week on the form.

```
Sub Default_Date_Timer ()
    Current_Date.Caption = Date$
    DayName% = Weekday(Now)
    If DayName% = 1 Then Day_Name.Caption = "Sunday"
    If DayName% = 2 Then Day_Name.Caption = "Monday"
    If DayName% = 3 Then Day_Name.Caption = "Tuesday"
    If DayName% = 4 Then Day_Name.Caption = "Wednesday"
    If DayName% = 5 Then Day_Name.Caption = "Thursday"
    If DayName% = 6 Then Day_Name.Caption = "Friday"
    If DayName% = 7 Then Day_Name.Caption = "Saturday"
    Default_Date.Enabled = 0
End Sub
```

8. Enter the following code in the Enter_Date_Click event subroutine. This code is triggered when the user presses the command button labeled Enter Date. An input box prompts the user to change the date displaying the current date as the default text. In this way, the Time project allows the user to change the system date.

```
Sub Enter_Date_Click ()
Startup:
    On Error GoTo BdFormat
    Msg$ = "Please press enter to accept the "
    Msg$ = Msg$ + "displayed date as correct "
    Msg$ = Msg$ + "or change the date as desired."
    Title$ = "Change System Date"
    Current$ = Date$
    New$ = InputBox$(Msg$, Title$, Current$)
    CurDate# = DateValue(Current$)
    NewDate# = DateValue(New$)
    If CurDate# <> NewDate# Then
        Date$ = New$
    End If
    Exit Sub
BdFormat:
    Msg$ = "You have entered the date in an incorrect "
    Msg$ = Msg$ + "format. Please reenter the date in "
    Msg$ = Msg$ + "mm-dd-yy, mm-dd-yyyy, mm/dd/yy, or "
    Msg$ = Msg$ + "mm/dd/yyyy format."
    MsgBox Msg$
    Resume Startup
End Sub
```

9. Enter the following code in the Enter_Time_Click event subroutine. This code is triggered when the user presses the command button labeled Enter

Time. An input box prompts the user to change the time, displaying the current time as the default choice. In this way, the Time project allows the user to change the system time.

```
Sub Enter_Time_Click ()
Start:
   On Error GoTo BadFormat
   Msg$ = "Please Press enter to accept the"
   Msg$ = Msg$ + "displayed time as correct"
   Msg$ = Msg$ + "or change the time as desired."
   Title$ = "Change System Time"
   Current$ = Time$
   New$ = InputBox$(Msg$, Title$, Current$)
   CurTime# = TimeValue(Current$)
   NewTime# = TimeValue(New$)
   If CurTime# <> NewTime# Then
       Time$ = New$
   End If
   Exit Sub
BadFormat:
   Msg$ = "You have entered the time in an incorrect"
   Msg$ = Msg$ + "format. Please reenter the time in"
   Msg$ = Msg$ + "hh:mm:ss, 1:30PM, or 13:30"
   MsgBox Msg$
   Resume Start
End Sub
```

10. Enter the following code in the Exit_Program_Click event subroutine. This code is activated when the user presses the command button labeled Exit. With this subroutine, the program ends.

```
Sub Exit_Program_Click ()
   End
End Sub
```

11. Enter the following code in the Form_Load event subroutine. This routine triggers when the program first loads into memory. This displays the current time, date, and day of the week on the form.

```
Sub Form_Load ()
   Clock24.Interval = 500
   Clock24.Enabled = -1
   Default_Date.Interval = 1000
   Default_Date.Enabled = -1
End Sub
```

12. Enter the following code in the Format_Date_Click event subroutine. This code is triggered when the user presses the command button labeled Normal Date. This changes the text on this command button to Special Date or vice versa. The format of the date displayed on the screen changes from one format to another.

```
Sub Format_Date_Click ()
  If Format_Date.Caption = "Normal Date" Then
      Current_Date.Caption = ""
      Current_Date.FontSize = 13.8
      Special_Date.Interval = 100
      Special_Date.Enabled = -1
      Format_Date.Caption = "Special Date"
  ElseIf Format_Date.Caption = "Special Date" Then
      Current_Date.Caption = ""
      Current_Date.FontSize = 18
      Default_Date.Interval = 100
      Default_Date.Enabled = -1
      Format_Date.Caption = "Normal Date"
  End If
End Sub
```

13. Enter the following code in the Format_Time_Click event subroutine. This code is activated when the user presses the command button labeled Format_Time. The text changes from 24Hr Time to 12Hr Time and vice versa. In this way, the command button toggles between displaying the time in the form shown on this command button.

```
Sub Format_Time_Click ()
  If Format_Time.Caption = "24Hr Time" Then
      Clock24.Enabled = 0
      Clock12.Interval = 500
      Clock12.Enabled = -1
      Format_Time.Caption = "12Hr Time"
  ElseIf Format_Time.Caption = "12Hr Time" Then
      Clock12.Enabled = 0
      Clock24.Interval = 500
      Clock24.Enabled = -1
      Format_Time.Caption = "24Hr Time"
  End If
End Sub
```

14. Enter the following code in the Special_Date_Timer event subroutine. This code is triggered when the user presses the command button labeled Normal Date. This changes the text on the button to Special Date and enables the Special_Date timer control. The present date is expressed in terms of the month's name followed by the day number with the normal suffix (st, nd, rd, th) and the year.

```
Sub Special_Date_Timer ()
  CM = Month(Now)
  Select Case CM
      Case 1
          M$ = "January "
      Case 2
          M$ = "February "
      Case 3
```

```
            M$ = "March "
        Case 4
            M$ = "April "
        Case 5
            M$ = "May "
        Case 6
            M$ = "June "
        Case 7
            M$ = "July "
        Case 8
            M$ = "August "
        Case 9
            M$ = "September "
        Case 10
            M$ = "October "
        Case 11
            M$ = "November "
        Case 12
            M$ = "December "
    End Select
    CD = Day(Now)
    Select Case CD
        Case 1, 21, 31
            D$ = Str$(CD) + "st,"
        Case 2, 22
            D$ = Str$(CD) + "nd,"
        Case 3, 23
            D$ = Str$(CD) + "rd,"
        Case Else
            D$ = Str$(CD) + "th,"
    End Select
    Y$ = Str$(Year(Now))
    Current_Date.Caption = M$ + D$ + Y$
    DayName% = Weekday(Now)
    If DayName% = 1 Then Day_Name.Caption = "Sunday"
    If DayName% = 2 Then Day_Name.Caption = "Monday"
    If DayName% = 3 Then Day_Name.Caption = "Tuesday"
    If DayName% = 4 Then Day_Name.Caption = "Wednesday"
    If DayName% = 5 Then Day_Name.Caption = "Thursday"
    If DayName% = 6 Then Day_Name.Caption = "Friday"
    If DayName% = 7 Then Day_Name.Caption = "Saturday"
    Special_Date.Enabled = 0
End Sub
```

15. Enter the following code in the Stop_Watch_Click event subroutine. This code is started when the user presses the command button labeled Stop Watch. Its caption changes from Stop Watch to Stop Clock or vice versa. In this way, the stopwatch is started when the user presses the command button the first time, and disabled when he or she presses it a second time.

```
Sub Stop_Watch_Click ()
    If Stop_Watch.Caption = "Stop Watch" Then
        Stop_Watch.Caption = "Stop Clock"
        StopWatch.Interval = 1000
        StopWatch.Enabled = -1
```

```
ElseIf Stop_Watch.Caption = "Stop Clock" Then
    Stop_Watch.Caption = "Stop Watch"
    StopWatch.Enabled = 0
    StopWatch_Time.Caption = ""
    Count_Down.Cls
End If
End Sub
```

16. Enter the following code in the StopWatch_Timer event subroutine. This code is triggered when the user presses the command button labeled Stop Watch. When this happens, a graphic circle counts down the seconds of each minute.

```
Sub StopWatch_Timer ()
 Count_Down.Cls
 Static Start As Double
 Static M As Integer
 Static S As Integer
 Static Num As Double
 Const PI = 3.14159265
 If Start# = 0 Then
     Start# = Timer
 End If
 T% = Int(Timer) - Int(Start#)
 H% = Int(T% / 3600)
 Count_Down.FillColor = QBColor(1)
 Count_Down.FillStyle = 0
 X% = Count_Down.ScaleWidth / 2
 Y% = Count_Down.ScaleHeight / 2
 Radius% = Count_Down.ScaleWidth / 3
 Count_Down.Circle (X%, Y%), Radius%, , Num, -6.283
 Num = Num - ((2 * PI) / 60)
 Watch$ = Str$(H%) + ":" + Str$(M%) + ":" + Str$(S%)
 S% = S% + 1
 StopWatch_Time.Caption = Watch$
 If Abs(Num) >= 6.283 Then
     Num = 0
     If S% = 60 Then
         S% = 0
     End If
     If M% = 60 Then
         M% = 0
     Else
         M% = M% + 1
     End If
     Count_Down.Cls
 End If
End Sub
```

## How It Works

The Time project displays the calendar date and time on the screen when it first loads on the screen. The user can change the date and time displayed by pressing the command buttons labeled Enter Date and Enter Time. The user starts a stopwatch by pressing the command button labeled Stop Watch. While the stopwatch is running, a graphic circle displays on the screen, representing the ticks of each second of a minute. The Calc Time and Calc Date command buttons enable the user to quickly find the amount of time between two time periods or the date between two dates. To exit the program, press the command button labeled Exit.

### Startup

When the Time project begins, the Form_Load event subroutine starts both the Default_Date and Clock24 timer controls. These controls activate when their Enabled properties change to True and Interval properties become 1000 (Default_Date) and 500 (Clock24) milliseconds. Both of these property changes are necessary to ensure that the Timer events of both controls process properly. If the Enabled property of a timer control is False, then the Timer event will not work. Similarly, the Timer event will not function with the Interval property of the timer control set to a 0 value.

After the Form_Load event enables both the Default_Date and Clock24_Timer controls, the Timer events of both controls are triggered. The Clock24 timer contains code which displays the current time in the Current_Time label box and is processed every 500 milliseconds (half-second). With the code in the Default_Date timer control, the date displays in the Current_Date label box. This event is only triggered when the Time project is initially loaded. Notice that the Default_Date has an Interval property of 1000 milliseconds, but is not run at intervals because its Enabled property is set to False each time it is run.

### Running the Time Project

The Clock24_Timer event displays the current time in the Current_Time label box with the Time$ function. This function provides the current time to store in the indicated variable in string format. In this case, the Time$ function serves as a direct definition of the Caption property of the Current_Time label box. As a result, the time appears in the label box in the 24-hour format hh:mm:ss (hh = hour, mm = minutes, ss = seconds). If the 24-hour format serves the needs of a particular situation, this function is an excellent method for displaying the time with a minimum amount of lines of code.

When the Default_Date_Timer event is triggered, the current date displays in the Current_Date label box with the Date$ function. This function saves the current date to an indicated variable in string format. With this event, the Date$ function defines the Caption property of the Current_Date label box. In this way, the date displays in the label box in the format defined by the international section of the WIN.INI file. If this format is acceptable for a particular application, then this function is a good way to display the date with very little code.

Both the Default_Date_Timer and Clock24_Timer events use the Weekday function to determine the current day of the week. The value returned by the Weekday function is part of a Select Case statement that displays the name of the corresponding weekday in the Day_Name label box. This defines the Caption property of the Day_Name label box as the name representing the value returned. Notice that the Now function provides the serial number required for this function.

The Now function determines the serial number of the current date and time. Every time the Clock24_Timer event is processed, two If-Then statements check if either the current hour or minute are 0. This is done with the Hour, Minute, and Now functions, which wait until the returned hour and minute are both 0. In the Hour and Minute functions, the Now function provides the needed serial number to determine whether both the hour and minute are 0. Each time both of these criteria match, the Default_Date_Timer event uses the Now function to determine the weekday, as described in the previous section. Notice the serial number returned by the Now function helps to determine both the time and date attributes.

When the user presses the command button labeled 24Hr Time, the code disables the Clock24_Timer and enables the Clock12_Timer. The Clock12_Timer event is triggered by the enabling of the Clock12_Timer control. This has the effect of displaying the time in the Caption property of the Current_Time label box in 12-hour format. The Hour, Minute, and Second functions work with the Now function to produce the time in 12-hour form. If the value is greater than 12, then the displayed hour has 12 subtracted from it before displaying. Additionally, the time is followed by AM when the value returned by the Hour function is less than or equal to 12, and PM when it is greater than 12. Neither the Minute nor Second functions need to be modified to display 12-hour time. Although this method for displaying the time is substantially longer than the Time$ function, it is more flexible about how the time appears on the screen.

After the user presses the command button labeled Normal Date, the code disables the Default_Date Timer and enables the Special_Date Timer. The Special_Date_Timer event is triggered by the enabling of the Special_Date timer control. This has the effect of displaying the date in the Caption property of the Current_Date label box in mixed words and numbers. In this way, 01-01-92 becomes January 1st, 1992. Rather than using the Date$ function, the Month, Day, and Year functions are used with the Now function to produce the date. This routine checks the value returned by the pairing of the Month and Now functions to define the first part of the date displayed as the name of the current month. The Now function provides the year.

The user presses the command button labeled Enter time to correct the time displayed on screen. The Enter_Time_Click event prompts the user for the new time displaying the current time as the default. This is done with the input box which returns a string. In order for the time to be set properly, the TimeValue function converts the returned string to a serial number. With the resulting serial number, the code checks if the time has changed. Notice that the TimeValue is used on the time stored in the Current$ variable rather than just utilizing the Now function for comparison. Otherwise, the time might have changed since the Enter_Time_Click event was triggered.

After the user presses the command button labeled Enter Time, an input box prompts the user for the new time by the triggering of the Enter_Time_Click event. If the user changed the time, then the time returned by the input box defines the Time$ statement and modifies the computer system's time. This is done by making the Time$ equal to the New$ string returned by the input box.

The user presses the command button labeled Enter Date to correct the date displayed on the screen. The Enter_Date_Click event prompts the user for the new date with the current date as the default. In order for the date to be set properly, the DateValue function changes the returned string to a serial number. Using the resulting serial number, the code checks if the date changed. Notice that the DateValue works with the date stored in the Current$ variable rather than the Now function.

After the user presses the command button labeled Enter Date, an input box prompts the user for a new date by the triggering of the Enter_Date_Click event. If the user changed the date, then the date returned by the input box defines the Date$ statement and modifies the computer system's date. This is done by making the Date$ equal to the New$ string returned by the input box. Notice that the Date$ statement must be defined with a string to function properly, and that it is used in conjunction with the DateValue function, which checks if the user made a change.

Following the pressing of the command button labeled Stop Watch, the Timer function serves as a part of the StopWatch_Timer event that generates the circle and digital count on the form. In this event, the Timer function acts both as a reference and as a means of incrementing the time. When the user presses the Stop Watch command button, the serial number is stored to the Start# static variable. Each time that the StopWatch_Timer event is triggered, the current seconds since midnight are compared to the value of the Start# variable to display the number of hours, minutes, and seconds that have elapsed. This is done by displaying the difference between the current Timer result and the Start# variable. Notice that this event only works when comparing times on the same day because the Timer function only deals with time since midnight.

The TimeSerial function is used in the Calc_Time_Click event subroutine to find the number of hours, minutes, and seconds between two times the user enters. Both times are entered by the user in InputBoxes. These results are then stored to variables, which are each separated into hours, minutes, and seconds. This function is used to permit the calculation of the difference between the two entered times. Since the TimeSerial function provides for the separation of the hour, minute, and second portions of the time, the results of differences between each portion may be immediately stored to a variable, which may then be displayed in a message box. Notice that the TimeSerial function returns a serial number, which must first be converted to a string with the format function prior to being displayed.

The DateSerial function is used in the Calc_Date_Click event subroutine to find the date that lies approximately the same amount of time between two user-entered dates. Both dates are entered by the user in InputBoxes. These results are then stored to variables, which are each separated into hours, minutes, and seconds. This function is used to permit the calculation of the date that lies approximately between the two entered dates. Since the DateSerial function provides for the separation of the month, day, and year portions of the date, the results of the average of each portion may be immediately stored to a variable, which may then be displayed in a message box. Notice that the DateSerial function returns a serial number, which must first be converted to a string with the format function prior to being displayed.

# Using the Windows Clipboard

One of the advantages of using the Windows operating environment is that all Windows programs can copy and retrieve text and graphics to and from an area in the environment called the clipboard. The clipboard is a temporary holding area for data that has been cut or copied from your application, or any other Windows application.

Windows provides a program called clipboard that allows the user to view the clipboard area. These two objects should be distinguished. Even though the clipboard program is not active all the time, the clipboard area is always accessible as long as Windows is running.

## What You Can Do with the Clipboard

Generally, the clipboard can hold three types of items. First, it can hold text. Text is any combination of letters, numbers, or characters that can be represented by ASCII codes. Second, it can hold graphics. Windows lets the user cut and paste pictures as well as text. However, unlike the case with cutting, copying, and pasting text, each individual program must define how graphics are to be handled. Finally, the clipboard can hold DDE messages being sent from one program to another. For more information on this type of messaging, see Chapter 25, *Transferring Data with Dynamic Data Exchange*.

It is important to realize that the clipboard is a *temporary* storage location. The clipboard may hold one item of each of these data types. When a program copies an item to the clipboard, it replaces any item of the same type that previously resided there. Also, anything on the clipboard disappears when you exit Windows, although you can use the clipboard program to save the clipboard's contents to a file.

The Windows environment automatically gives the user a way to select text and send it to the clipboard. To select text in any Windows application, hold down the Shift key and press one of the cursor movement keys. Alternately, you can click and hold the left mouse button and drag it over the text to be selected. Selected text is reverse highlighted. Once text is selected, press the Control+Insert key combination to send the text to the clipboard. Press Shift+Delete to send the text to the clipboard and delete it from the screen. Data that is held in the clipboard area can be retrieved by pressing the Shift+Insert key combination.

Again, all these key combinations and their functions are handled by the Windows environment, so you don't need to program these routines into your Visual Basic application youself. However, you may want to provide the user with alternate methods for cutting, copying, and pasting data to and from the clipboard. Visual Basic gives you the tools you will need to clear the clipboard, copy data or text to it, determine the type of data currently stored on it, or retrieve text or data from it.

## Visual Basic and the Clipboard Object

The Clear method is the simplest of the clipboard methods. As you may guess by its name, it clears any data that currently resides on the clipboard. The GetData and GetText methods (used for graphic information and for text, respectively) are used to retreive information from the clipboard. These methods must specify a particular type of information that they are requesting. Before either of these methods are executed, you can use the GetFormat method to determine whether the desired type of information is currently being held on the clipboard. There are also two methods, SetData (for graphics) and Set Text (for text), which can be used to send information to the clipboard.

Table 23.1 lists the methods that affect the Clipboard object.

| Use or Set This... | | To Do This... |
|---|---|---|
| Clear | Method | Clear the contents of the clipboard area |
| GetData | Method | Retrieve graphic data from the clipboard area |
| GetFormat | Method | Return True if the specified data type is stored in the clipboard area |
| GetText | Method | Retrieve text from the clipboard area |
| SetData | Method | Send graphic data to the clipboard area |
| SetText | Method | Send text to the clipboard area |

**Table 23.1 Methods that affect the Clipboard object**

### Constants in the CONSTANT.TXT File

Some of the examples in this chapter make use of constant declarations that are included in the CONSTANT.TXT file that comes with the Visual Basic compiler. These constants and their respective values and meanings are shown in Table 23.2.

| Constant Name | Value of Constant | Meaning of Constant |
|---|---|---|
| CF_LINK | &HBF00 | Clipboard is holding a DDE link |
| CF_TEXT | 1 | Clipboard is holding text |
| CF_BITMAP | 2 | Clipboard is holding a bitmap graphic |
| CF_METAFILE | 3 | Clipboard is holding a Windows metafile graphic |
| CF_DIB | 8 | Clipboard is holding a device independent bitmap graphic |

**Table 23.2 Constant declarations in the CONSTANT.TXT file**

In order to use the CONSTANT.TXT file, it must be loaded into the project's global module. To do this, open Visual Basic's Project window, and double-click on the global module. This will load the global module into the Code window. Then open Visual Basic's Code menu and choose the Load Text option. This brings up a dialog box. Select the CONSTANT.TXT file, and click on the Merge button. This will read the file into the global module.

# Clear Method

## Objects Affected

| | | | | |
|---|---|---|---|---|
| Check | ▶ Clipboard | Combo | Command | Debug |
| Dir | Drive | File | Form | Frame |
| Label | List | Menu | Option | Picture |
| Printer | Screen | Scroll | Text | Timer |

## Purpose

Clears the contents of the Clipboard.

## General Syntax

Clipboard.Clear

## Example Syntax

Clipboard.Clear

## Description

The Clear method, which has no arguments, clears any and all text and graphics that may be currently stored in the clipboard area. After this is done, nothing can be retrieved from the clipboard until some text or graphic information is sent to it.

The example syntax clears the clipboard. Anything that had been stored in the clipboard is no longer retrievable.

## Example

In the Clipboard project, the command button ClearClipboard invokes this method to clear the clipboard.

# GetData Method

## Objects Affected

| | | | | |
|---|---|---|---|---|
| Check | ▶ Clipboard | Combo | Command | Debug |
| Dir | Drive | File | Form | Frame |
| Label | List | Menu | Option | Picture |
| Printer | Screen | Scroll | Text | Timer |

## Purpose

Retrieves graphic information (pictures) from the clipboard area. Table 23.3 summarizes this arguments of the GetData method.

## General Syntax

`Clipboard.GetData([format%])`

| Argument | Description |
|----------|-------------|
| format% | An integer expression indicating the desired data format |

**Table 23.3 Argument of the GetData method**

## Example Syntax

```
Picture1.Picture = Clipboard.GetData(CF_BITMAP)      'Gets a bitmap from the
                                                     'Clipboard
```

## Description

The GetData method copies the specified type of graphic data from the clipboard into the specified object. The type of data requested is specified by the format% parameter. This parameter is an integer with the value of 2, 3, or 8. Table 23.5 details possible values and their meanings.

| Value | If CONSTANT.TXT is used... | Meaning |
|-------|----------------------------|---------|
| 2 | CF_BITMAP | Requesting a bitmap graphic |
| 3 | CF_METAFILE | Requesting a metafile graphic |
| 8 | CF_DIB | Requesting a device independent bitmap graphic |

**Table 23.4 Data formats for the GetData method**

If the format is not specified, it will default to 2 (CF_BITMAP).

The example syntax retrieves a bitmapped graphic from the clipboard and assigns it to the Picture property of Picture1, in essence pasting it into the picture box.

## Example

In the Clipboard project, the GetData method is used in the RetrieveData_Click event. This event copies any bitmap information that may be in the clipboard to the Picture1 picture control.

## Comments

If no data of the requested type is being stored on the clipboard, nothing is returned.

# GetFormat Method

## Objects Affected

| | | | | |
|---|---|---|---|---|
| Check | ▶ Clipboard | Combo | Command | Debug |
| Dir | Drive | File | Form | Frame |
| Label | List | Menu | Option | Picture |
| Printer | Screen | Scroll | Text | Timer |

## Purpose

The GetFormat method returns an integer value (True or False) indicating whether the requested data type is stored in the clipboard. Table 23.5 summarizes the arguments of the GetFormat method.

## General Syntax

```
Clipboard.GetFormat(format%)
```

| Argument | Description |
|---|---|
| format% | An integer expression indicating the desired data format |

Table 23.5 Argument of the GetFormat method

## Example Syntax

```
TextStored = GetFormat(CF_TEXT)          'Returns True if text is stored on Clipboard
```

## Description

The GetFormat method tests the contents of the clipboard and returns True (-1) if the requested data type is stored on it or False (0) if not. The type of data requested is specified by the format% parameter. This parameter is an integer, and must be one of the values specified in Table 23.6.

The example syntax determines whether any text is currently residing in the clipboard. The answer, which will be True (-1) or False (0), is stored in the variable TextStored.

| Value | If CONSTANT.TXT is used... | Meaning |
|---|---|---|
| &HBF00 | CF_LINK | Returns True (-1) if a DDE link is stored on the clipboard |
| 1 | CF_TEXT | Returns True (-1) if text is stored on the clipboard |
| 2 | CF_BITMAP | Returns True (-1) if a bitmap graphic is stored on the clipboard |
| 3 | CF_METAFILE | Returns True (-1) if a metafile graphic is stored on the clipboard |
| 8 | CF_DIB | Returns True (-1) if a device independent bitmap graphic is stored |

Table 23.6 Data formats for the Getformat method

## Example

The GetFormat method is used in the RetrievePicture_Click and RetrieveText_Click events of the Clipboard project. The value returned by the GetFormat method is used to determine whether to copy the data from the clipboard, or to print a message informing the user of the lack of the requested data.

# GetText Method

## Objects Affected

| | | | | |
|---|---|---|---|---|
| Check | ▶ Clipboard | Combo | Command | Debug |
| Dir | Drive | File | Form | Frame |
| Label | List | Menu | Option | Picture |
| Printer | Screen | Scroll | Text | Timer |

## Purpose

The GetText method retrieves text information from the clipboard. Table 23.7 summarizes the arguments of the GetText method.

## General Syntax

```
Clipboard.GetText([format%])
```

| Argument | Description |
|---|---|
| format% | An integer expression indicating the desired data format |

Table 23.7 Argument of the GetText method

## Example Syntax

```
Text1.Text = Clipboard.GetText(CF_TEXT) 'Gets text from the Clipboard
```

## Description

The GetText method copies the specified type of text from the clipboard into the specified object. The type of data requested is specified by the format% parameter. This parameter is an integer with a value of 1 or &HBF00. Table 23.8 summarizes the data formats for the GetText method.

| Value | If CONSTANT.TXT is used... | Meaning |
|---|---|---|
| &HBF00 | CF_LINK | Requesting a DDE link |
| 1 | CF_TEXT | Requesting text information |

Table 23.8 Data formats for the GetText method

The format value CF_LINK (&HBF00) can be used to set up a Dynamic Data Exchange (DDE) link. DDE is discussed in Chapter 25, *Transferring Data with Dynamic Data Exchange*. If the format is not specified, it will default to 1 (CF_TEXT).

The example syntax copies any text stored on the clipboard to the text box Text1. Assigning the text returned by the GetText method to the Text property of the text box causes the text to be displayed in the text area of the box.

### Example

In the Clipboard project, the GetText method is used in the RetrieveText_Click event. This event copies any text information that may be in the clipboard to the Text1 text box control.

### Comments

If the requested data type is not being stored on the clipboard, a null string is returned.

# SetData Method

### Objects Affected

| | | | | |
|---|---|---|---|---|
| Check | ▶ Clipboard | Combo | Command | Debug |
| Dir | Drive | File | Form | Frame |
| Label | List | Menu | Option | Picture |
| Printer | Screen | Scroll | Text | Timer |

### Purpose

The SetData method places graphic information in the clipboard object. Table 23.9 summarizes the arguments of the SetData method.

### General Syntax

```
Clipboard.SetData graphic%[, format%]
```

| Argument | Description |
|---|---|
| graphic% | An integer number that is the handle of the graphic image (Picture or Image properties) |
| format% | An integer expression indicating the data format of the graphic image |

**Table 23.9 Argument of the SetData method**

### Example Syntax

```
Clipboard.SetData Picture1.Picture, CF_BITMAP   'Copies a bitmap to the 1Clipboard
Clipboar1d.SetData Pictur1e2.Picture, CF_METAFILE 'Copies a metafile to the Clipboard
Clipboard.SetData Picture3.Picture, CF_DIB
                                                 'Copies a device independent bitmap
                                                 'to the Clipboard
```

## Description

The SetData method is the complement to the GetData method. It copies the specified graphic to the clipboard in the specified format. The type of data being sent to the clipboard is specified by the format% parameter. This parameter is an integer with the value of 2, 3, or 8. Table 23.10 details its possible values and their meanings.

| Value | If CONSTANT.TXT is used... | Meaning |
|---|---|---|
| 2 | CF_BITMAP | Sending a bitmap graphic |
| 3 | CF_METAFILE | Sending a metafile graphic |
| 8 | CF_DIB | Sending a device independent bitmap graphic |

**Table 23.10 Data formats for the SetData method**

If the format is not specified, it will default to 2 (CF_BITMAP).

The example syntax gives statements showing how the three kinds of graphics listed in Table 23.10 can be copied from a picture box to the clipboard. Of course executing all three statements in succession would result in only the last picture being kept in the clipboard, since the clipboard can hold only one graphic at a time.

## Example

In the Clipboard project, this method is used in the SendPicture_Click event. When this event is executed, the bitmap in the picture control Picture1 is copied to the clipboard.

# SetText Method

## Objects Affected

| | | | | |
|---|---|---|---|---|
| Check | ▶ Clipboard | Combo | Command | Debug |
| Dir | Drive | File | Form | Frame |
| Label | List | Menu | Option | Picture |
| Printer | Screen | Scroll | Text | Timer |

## Purpose

The SetText method places text information in the Clipboard object. Table 23.11 summarizes the arguments of the SetText method.

## General Syntax

```
Clipboard.SetText Text$[, format%]
```

| Argument | Description |
|----------|-------------|
| Text$ | A string expression containing the text to be sent to the clipboard |
| format% | An integer expression indicating the data format of the text |

**Table 23.11 Arguments of the SetText method**

## Example Syntax

```
Clipboard.SetText Text1.Text   'Copies the text from the text box to the Clipboard
```

## Description

The SetText method is the complement of the GetText method. It copies the specified text information to the clipboard in the specified format. The type of data being sent to the clipboard is specified by the format% parameter. This parameter is an integer with the value of 1 or &HBF00. Table 23.12 details its possible values and their meanings.

| Value | If CONSTANT.TXT is used... | Meaning |
|-------|---------------------------|---------|
| &HBF00 | CF_LINK | Sending a DDE link |
| 1 | CF_TEXT | Sending text information |

**Table 23.12 Data formats for the SetText method**

The format value CF_LINK (&HBF00) can be used to set up a Dynamic Data Exchange (DDE) link. DDE is discussed in Chapter 25, *Transferring Data with Dynamic Data Exchange*.

If the format is not specified, it will default to 1 (CF_TEXT) as in the example syntax, which copies the text in text box Text1 to the clipboard.

## Example

In the Clipboard project, this method is used in the SendText_Click event. When this event is executed, the text in the text box control Text1 is copied to the clipboard.

# The Clipboard Project

## Project Overview

The project outlined on the following pages demonstrates the use of each of the elements of Visual Basic discussed in this chapter. When you have finished with this project, you should feel comfortable with the concepts behind using the Clear, GetData, GetFormat, GetText, SetData, and SetText methods.

## Assembling the Project

1. Create a new form (the clipboard form), and place on it the controls specified in Table 23.13.

| Object | Property | Setting |
|---|---|---|
| Form | FormName | Clip |
| | Caption | Clipboard Project |
| | Height | 3258 |
| | Width | 6255 |
| Picture | CtlName | Picture1 |
| | Height | 3262 |
| | Left | 120 |
| | Picture | \WINDOWS\CHESS.BMP |
| | Top | 120 |
| | Width | 5895 |
| Text Box | CtlName | Text1 |
| | Height | 375 |
| | Left | 120 |
| | Top | 3000 |
| | Width | 5895 |
| Command Button | CtlName | ClearClipboard |
| | Caption | ClearClipboard |
| | Height | 375 |
| | Left | 120 |
| | Top | 3960 |
| | Width | 5895 |
| Command Button | CtlName | RetrievePicture |
| | Caption | Picture <— Clipboard |
| | Height | 375 |
| | Left | 3240 |
| | Top | 2520 |
| | Width | 2775 |
| Command Button | CtlName | RetrieveText |
| | Caption | Text <— Clipboard |
| | Height | 375 |
| | Left | 3240 |
| | Top | 3480 |
| | Width | 2775 |

| Command Button | CtlName | SendPicture |
| --- | --- | --- |
| | Caption | Picture —> Caption |
| | Height | 375 |
| | Left | 120 |
| | Top | 2520 |
| | Width | 2775 |
| Command Button | CtlName | SendText |
| | Caption | Text —> Caption |
| | Height | 375 |
| | Left | 120 |
| | Top | 3480 |
| | Width | 2775 |

**Table 23.13 Controls and property settings for the clipboard project**

2. Check the appearance of your form against Figure 23.1.

3. Load the CONSTANT.-TXT file into the global module. To do this, open Visual Basic's Project window and double-click on the global module. This will load the global module into the Code window. Then, open Visual Basic's Code menu, and choose the Load Text option. This brings up a dialog box. Select the CONSTANT.TXT file and click on the Merge button. This will read the file into the global module.

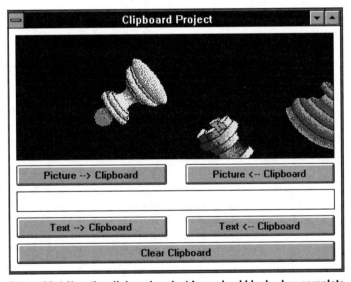

**Figure 23.1 How the clipboard project form should look when complete**

4. Enter the following code into the Form_Load event. This event activates the Window's clipboard program, which displays the current contents of the clipboard area.

```
Sub Form_Load ()
   On Error Resume Next
   AppActivate "Clipboard"
   If Err > 0 Then A% = Shell("C:\Windows\ClipBrd", 1)
End Sub
```

5. Enter the following code into the SendPicture_Click event. This event occurs when the user clicks on the SendPicture command button, and sends
the bitmap in the Picture1 picture control to the clipboard.

```
Sub SendPicture_Click ()
    ClipBoard.Clear
    ClipBoard.SetData Picture1.Picture
End Sub
```

6. Enter the following code into the SendText_Click event. This event occurs
when the user clicks on the SendPicture command button. When it occurs,
any text in the Text1 text box control that is selected gets sent to the clipboard. If no text is selected, a null string is sent to the clipboard.

```
Sub SendText_Click ()
    Dim ClipText As String

    ClipText = Mid$(Text1.Text, Text1.SelStart + 1, Text1.SelLength)
    ClipBoard.SetText ClipText
End Sub
```

7. Enter the following code into the Clearclipboard_Click event. When the
user clicks the ClearClipboard button, this event clears the clipboard of all
text and graphic information.

```
Sub ClearClipboard_Click ()
    ClipBoard.Clear
End Sub
```

8. Enter the following code into the RetrievePicture_Click and Retrieve-
Text_Click events. Each event first checks the clipboard to see if the desired
type of information is stored there. If it is, that data is copied to Picture1 or
Text1 (depending on the button clicked). If not, a message is displayed informing the user of this.

```
Sub RetrievePicture_Click ()
    If ClipBoard.GetFormat(CF_BITMAP) = TRUE Then
        Picture1.Line (0, 0)-(Picture1.Width, Picture1.Height),
Picture1.BackColor, BF
        MsgBox "About to copy Clipboard"
        Picture1.Picture = ClipBoard.GetData(CF_BITMAP)
    Else
        MsgBox "There are no Bitmaps in the Clipboard"
    End If
End Sub

Sub RetrieveText_Click ()
    If ClipBoard.GetFormat(CF_TEXT) = TRUE Then
        MsgBox "About to copy Clipboard"
        Text1.SelText = ClipBoard.GetText(CF_TEXT)
    Else
        MsgBox "There is no text in the Clipboard"
    End If
End Sub
```

## How It Works

This program copies graphic and text information to and from the Windows environment clipboard. When the program begins, the Form_Load event activates the clipboard viewing program if it is already running. If the clipboard viewer isn't running, the Form_Load event executes it. (This program works best if the clipboard viewer and the clipboard project windows are arranged so that both can be seen at the same time.)

Clicking the button with the caption "Picture —> Clipboard" will send the picture in the Picture1 control to the clipboard.

Clicking the button with the caption "Picture <— Clipboard" will retrieve a bit map from the clipboard and place it in the Picture1 picture control.

Clicking the button with the caption "Text1 —> Clipboard" will send any selected text in the Text1 text box control to the clipboard. Text can be selected with the mouse or the keyboard. To select text with the mouse, click on the text box and drag the mouse cursor over the desired text. To select text using the keyboard, hold the Shift key down and use the cursor direction keys.

Clicking the button with the caption "Text <— Clipboard" will retrieve any text from the clipboard and place it in the Text1 text box control.

When the user clicks the ClearClipboard button, this event clears the clipboard of all text and graphic information.

# Sending Data to the Printer

**M**any programs need the capability to create some sort of printed hard copy output. Because the Windows environment (rather than individual applications) handles all printer output, Visual Basic has included the predefined Printer object. This object sends printer output commands from your program to the Windows routines, which in turn send the output to the printer.

When working in other languages (such as QuickBASIC), the printer is usually treated as a sequential output device. Once an item is written to the printer, the print position advances and there can be no going back. With Visual Basic, however, this is not true.

You can think of the Printer object as a form that cannot be viewed until the Visual Basic program tells Windows to print it. This "form" represents one page of printed output. In most cases, until your program instructs Windows to print it, anything can be done to a page of printer output. This is advantageous, as it allows the program to move the print position anywhere on a page, regardless of where it currently resides. This makes outputting graphics and special printing effects to the printer very easy.

## Coordinate Systems and the Printer Object

In order to control the placement of text and graphics on the printer page, the Printer object uses a coordinate system in the same manner as a form. (Coordinates for forms and controls are discussed in Chapter 5, *Designing with the Coordinate System*, which makes good background reading for this chapter.) The only difference between a form's coordinate system and that of the printer object is that the height and width of a form can be changed. The height and width of the Printer object's page is fixed as long as it represents the same brand of printer.

Any point on the printer page can be referred to by specifying that point's position in the format X, Y, where X is the horizontal position, and Y is the vertical position. The coordinates of the upper left-hand corner of the printer page can be determined by reading the values of the Printer object's ScaleTop and ScaleLeft properties. Usually, these properties are set to 0 (meaning the upper left-hand corner is coordinate 0, 0). However, you are allowed to set up your own coordinate system, and in doing so to assign different values to these properties. The bottom right-hand corner can be determined by reading the Printer object's properties ScaleHeight and ScaleWidth. These properties return the height and width of the usable page area. The ScaleMode property determines the unit of measurement that is used for the values returned by the

ScaleHeight and ScaleWidth properties. It also determines the unit of measurement that is used for the coordinate system of the printer page. Any methods that specify a coordinate on the printer page do so using that unit of measurement. By default, the ScaleMode property is set to twips. A twip is equal to 1/1440 of an inch. However, the ScaleMode property can be set to several other types of measurement.

When a method is executed on the Printer object, its placement on the page is determined by either the coordinates specified in the method, or by the coordinates of the current print position. You can use the CurrentX and CurrentY properties of the Printer object to read or set the current print position on the page. CurrentX represents the horizontal position, while CurrentY represents the vertical position. Again, both of these properties reflect values that represent the unit of measurement specified by the ScaleMode property.

## The Printer Object's Methods and Properties

When creating a printed document, the program works one page at a time. All the output for a specific page is first set up by using many of the same methods that work on a form. These include the Circle, Line, Print, PSet, TextHeight, and TextWidth methods. (Graphics methods such as Circle and Line are also discussed in Chapter 10, *Drawing Shapes*. Methods for scaling text are also discussed in Chapter 11, *Displaying Text with Objects*.) Each of these methods works in exactly the same manner as on a form, except when the printer has no color capabilities (such as with the majority of printers in use today). In that case, if a color parameter is used for a method, it is ignored and the output is always black.

Visual Basic keeps track of the current page number via the Page property, which is specific to the Printer object. Each time a new page is generated, the value of this property is incremented. You can use this property to place page numbers on your printed output.

A new page is generated by executing the NewPage method. This method ends output to the current page, and saves its image in memory. NewPage then increments the value of the Page property, and begins a new blank page. When your program has finished generating its printer output, it needs to send the output to the Windows printing routines. This is accomplished with the EndDoc method. EndDoc sends all the printer pages that have been saved in memory to the Windows printing routines, and then clears them from memory. Also, if any methods had been executed on the Printer object since the last NewPage method was executed, EndDoc will automatically generate a new page.

Visual Basic also supplies the PrintForm method. When executed on a form, this method sends a copy of the form to the printer. All graphics, text, and controls (with the exception of the menu control) on the form are printed.

When outputting text to the printer, changing font styles and sizes can be done with the Font... properties. These properties and their uses are covered in detail in Chapter 12, *Designing and Using Fonts*.

Table 24.1 details the methods and properties that affect the operation of the Printer object.

| Use or Set This... | | To Do This... |
| --- | --- | --- |
| Circle | Method | Generate a circle on the current page |
| CurrentX | Property | Set or return the current horizontal print position |
| CurrentY | | Set or return the current vertical print position |
| EndDoc | Method | Send generated output to the Windows printer routines |
| Line | | Generate a line or box on the current page |
| NewPage | | End the current page and start a new blank page |
| Page | Property | Return the current page number |
| Print | Method | Generate text output to the current page |
| PrintForm | | Send a copy of a Visual Basic form to the Windows printer routines |
| PSet | | Generate a pixel on the current page |
| ScaleLeft | Property | Set or return the left most horizontal position on the printer page |
| ScaleHeight | | Set or return the height of a page in units defined by ScaleMode |
| ScaleMode | | Set or return the unit of measurement for the coordinate system |
| ScaleTop | | Set or return the top most vertical position on the printer page |
| ScaleWidth | | Set or return the width of a page in units defined by ScaleMode |
| TextHeight | Method | Calculate the height of text as it would be output to the printer |
| TextWidth | | Calculate the width of text as it would be output to the printer |

**Table 24.1 Methods and properties that affect the Printer object**

The rest of this chapter discusses these methods and properties in detail. At the end of the chapter, the Printer project demonstrates the use of each of these elements of Visual Basic.

## Comments

The Printer object is designed to send output to the default printer specified by Windows. Unfortunately, since there can only be one default printer at a time, there is no documented method for a Visual Basic program to be able to access multiple printers simultaneously. However, there is a way to work around this. Because Windows runs on top of DOS, the DOS devices LPT1:, LPT2:, and LPT3: can be opened as a sequential output file, and text can be sent to them by the Print # and Write # statements. This technique will work using Windows 3.0 and Visual Basic 1.0, but there are no guarantees it will continue to perform properly with later versions of these packages. Using this technique could also cause your printer output to conflict with printer output from the Windows print spooler.

# Circle Method

## Objects Affected

| | | | | |
|---|---|---|---|---|
| Check | Clipboard | Combo | Command | Debug |
| Dir | Drive | File | ▶ Form | Frame |
| Label | List | Menu | Option | ▶ Picture |
| ▶ Printer | Screen | Scroll | Text | Timer |

## Purpose

The Circle method generates a circle, ellipse, or arc on the current page. The arguments for the Circle method are summarized in Table 24.2.

## General Syntax

```
Printer.Circle [Step](X_Pos!, Y_Pos!), Radius![, Color&][, Start!][, End!][,
Aspect!]
```

| Argument | Description |
|---|---|
| Step | Indicates X_Pos! and Y_Pos! are relative to the current position |
| X_Pos!, Y_Pos! | Single-precision expressions indicating the placement of the graphic on the print page |
| Radius! | Single-precision expression indicating size of graphic |
| Start! | Single-precision expression indicating starting radian |
| End! | Single-precision expression indicating ending radian |
| Color& | Long integer expression indicating print color. Has no effect on black and white printers |
| Aspect! | Single-precision expression indicating shape of graphic (circle or ellipse) |

Table 24.2 Arguments of the Circle method

## Example Syntax

```
Printer.Circle (1000, 1000), 1000          'Prints a circle with a 1000 Twip radius

Printer.Circle Step (100, 100), 50         'This circle's center is relative to the
                                           'current position
```

## Description

The Circle method can be used with the Printer object to print whole circles, portions of circles (arcs), or whole or partial ellipses (flattened circles). The Step, X_Pos!, and Y_Pos! parameters specify the center of the circle, ellipse, or arc to be printed. If the STEP keyword is used, X_Pos! and Y_Pos! indicate a position relative to the current print position (see the entries for CurrentX and CurrentY in this chapter). If the STEP keyword is omitted, X_Pos! and Y_Pos! indicate an absolute position on the current print page. In either case, the position specified should fall into the range defined by the Printer.ScaleHeight and Printer.ScaleWidth properties.

The Radius! parameter specifies the size of the circle, ellipse or arc. This value is expressed in the units defined by the Printer.ScaleMode property. By default, this property is set to Twips.

When this method is used on a printer without color capabilities, the Color& parameter is ignored. All output occurs in black, regardless of the color specified.

When only a partial circle is desired, the Start! and End! parameters define the size and angle of the arc. These parameters are expressed in radians. The three o'clock position of a circle is defined as 0 radians. The Circle method begins drawing at the radian specified by the Start! parameter, and stops drawing at the radian defined by the End! parameter.

The Aspect! parameter is used to create an ellipse. By default, the aspect of the shape is 1, which will create a circle. If Aspect! is greater than 1, or a negative value, a vertical ellipse is created. If Aspect! is between 0 and 1, a horizontal ellipse is drawn.

When finished, the Circle method leaves the CurrentX, and CurrentY properties for the Printer object set to the coordinates specified by the Step, X_Pos!, and Y_Pos! parameters.

If anyone of the optional parameters is not used, but one or more of the following parameters is, commas must be used to hold the place of the unused parameter. For instance, if the aspect is to be specified, but all other optional settings are not, the statement would read:

```
Circle (100, 100), 100,,,,2
```

This would draw a vertical ellipse. Because the Aspect! parameter is used, commas must hold the places of the Color&, Start!, and End! parameters.

The first example syntax statement prints a circle at an absolute location (X = 1000, Y = 1000) with a radius of 1000. The second example statement centers the circle at a point X = 100, Y = 100, *relative* to the current print position.

## Example

In the Printer project, the Circle method is used in PrintCircle procedure. This procedure is called from the FilePrintGraphics_Click event, which occurs when the user clicks the Print Graphics option on the project's File menu. PrintCircle prints the supplied string and then uses the Circle method to draw a circle around it. The placement and radius of the circle are figured using the TextHeight and TextWidth methods and the CurrentX and CurrentY properties.

## Comments

This method is covered in greater detail in Chapter 10, *Drawing Shapes*. However, it has been included again in this chapter to demonstrate its use with the printer object.

# CurrentX Property

## Objects Affected

| | | | | |
|---|---|---|---|---|
| Check | Clipboard | Combo | Command | Debug |
| Dir | Drive | File | ▶ Form | Frame |
| Label | List | Menu | Option | ▶ Picture |
| ▶ Printer | Screen | Scroll | Text | Timer |

## Purpose

The CurrentX property sets or returns the current horizontal print position on the current page. The argument of the CurrentX property is summarized in Table 24.3.

## General Syntax

```
Printer.CurrentX [= horizontalposition!]
```

| Argument | Description |
|---|---|
| horizontalposition | Single-precision expression indicating a horizontal coodinate on the print page |

**Table 24.3 Argument of the CurrentX property**

## Example Syntax

```
X! = Printer.CurrentX              'Places the current horizontal print
                                   'position into X!

Printer.CurrentX = Printer.ScaleWidth  'Sets the print position to the right edge
                                       'of printing area
```

## Description

The CurrentX property is used to read or set the horizontal position on the current print page. It is a single-precision value that is in the range defined by the Printer object's ScaleWidth property. Each of the methods that output to the Printer object can do so in relation to the current print position. The CurrentX property, along with its complementary property CurrentY, defines that print position. One good use for these properties is to read their settings prior to a print operation, so that the print position can be restored afterwards.

A Visual Basic program can change the current print position by assigning a value to this property. The value assigned should be between 0 and the value of the Printer.ScaleWidth property. Unfortunately, Visual Basic does not check to see if the value being assigned to the CurrentX property is in this range. If it is not, no output to this print position will be printed. However, because CurrentX is an integer data type, it cannot be set to a value less than -32768 or greater than 32767, or an "Overflow" error will occur.

The first statement in the example syntax stores the current X (horizontal) print position in the integer variable X1. The second statement sets the CurrentX property to the value of the ScaleWidth property. Since the latter represents the width of the page, the effect of this statement is to move the print position to the right edge of the printing area.

### Example

The CurrentX property is used throughout the Printer example project. In most cases, it is used to set the positioning of the next print operation. In the graphics printing routines, it is used to save the current print position, so that it may be restored for the next operation.

### Comments

This property is covered in greater detail in Chapter 9, *Designing with the Coordinate System*.

# CurrentY Property

### Objects Affected

| | | | | |
|---|---|---|---|---|
| Check | Clipboard | Combo | Command | Debug |
| Dir | Drive | File | ▶ Form | Frame |
| Label | List | Menu | Option | ▶ Picture |
| ▶ Printer | Screen | Scroll | Text | Timer |

### Purpose

The CurrentY property sets or returns the current vertical print position on the current page. Table 24.4 summarizes the arguments of the CurrentY property.

### General Syntax

```
Printer.CurrentY [= verticalposition!]
```

| Argument | Description |
|---|---|
| verticalposition | Single-precision expression indicating a vertical coodinate on the print page |

Table 24.4 Argument of the CurrentY property

### Example Syntax

```
Y! = Printer.CurrentY                        'Places the current vertical print
                                             'position into Y!

Printer.CurrentY = Printer.ScaleHeight       'Sets the print position to the
                                             'bottom of the printing area
```

## Description

The CurrentY property is used to read or set the vertical position on the current print page. It is a single-precision value that should be in the range defined by the Printer object's ScaleHeight property. Each of the methods that output to the Printer object can do so in relation to the current print position. This property, along with its complementary property CurrentY, defines that print position. One good use for these properties is to read their settings prior to a print operation, so that the print position can be restored afterward.

A Visual Basic program can change the current print position by assigning a value to this property. The value assigned should be between 0 and the value of the Printer.ScaleHeight property. Unfortunately, Visual Basic does not check to see if the value being assigned to the CurrentY property is in this range. If it is not, no output to this print position will be printed. However, because CurrentY is an integer data type, it cannot be set to a value less than -32768 or greater than 32767, or an "Overflow" error will occur.

The first statement in the example syntax stores the current Y (vertical) print position in the integer variable Y!. The second statement sets the CurrentY position to the value of the ScaleHeight property. Since the ScaleHeight property represents the height of the page, the effect is to move the print position to the bottom edge of the printing area.

## Example

The CurrentY property is used throughout the Printer project. In most cases, it is used to set the positioning of the next print operation. In the graphics printing routines, it is used to save the current print position, so that it may be restored for the next operation.

## Comments

This property is covered in greater detail in Chapter 9, *Designing with the Coordinate System*.

# EndDoc Method

## Objects Affected

| | | | | |
|---|---|---|---|---|
| Check | Clipboard | Combo | Command | Debug |
| Dir | Drive | File | Form | Frame |
| Label | List | Menu | Option | Picture |
| ▶ Printer | Screen | Scroll | Text | Timer |

## Purpose

The EndDoc method ends the current document, and sends output to the Windows printing routines.

## General Syntax

```
Printer.EndDoc
```

## Example Syntax

```
Printer.EndDoc
```

## Description

A "document" in Visual Basic is a set of pages that have been created on the Printer object but not yet output. Remember that in Visual Basic, printing statements do not result in immediate output to the printer but become part of the current page, which is completed by using the NewPage method. The latter method starts a new page but does not output the previous page.

The EndDoc method is used when all printing for a document has been completed. This method has no arguments. It causes several thing to happen. First, if any methods that output to the Printer object have been executed since the last time the NewPage method was used, EndDoc will perform all the same tasks as NewPage. This includes advancing to the next page and setting the CurrentX and CurrentY properties to 0 (top of page). It also sends all output that has been generated by the Printer object to the Windows printing routines. Windows in turn sends this output to the printer (if Print Manager, or another print spooler, is active for this printer, it will intercept the output). EndDoc also sets the value of the Page property back to 1.

The example syntax simply executes the EndDoc method and carries out all applicable procedures discussed above.

## Example

The EndDoc method is used in two places in the Printer project. First, it is used at the end of the FilePrintGraphics_Click event. When used there, the graphics that have been generated are sent to the Windows printer routines. The EndDoc method in this routine sends the printer a form feed since a NewPage method hasn't been used yet.

In the FilePrintText_Click event, the EndDoc method is executed soon after a NewPage method is executed, and therefore it does not send a form feed. In this case, the EndDoc method sends all the text that has been generated by this event.

## Comments

Because Visual Basic keeps all output to the Printer object in memory until the EndDoc method is used, it's a good idea to use this method as often as possible.

# Line Method

## Objects Affected

| | | | | |
|---|---|---|---|---|
| Check | Clipboard | Combo | Command | Debug |
| Dir | Drive | File | ▶ Form | Frame |
| Label | List | Menu | Option | ▶ Picture |
| ▶ Printer | Screen | Scroll | Text | Timer |

## Purpose

The Line method generates a line or a box on the current print page. The arguments for the Line method are summarized in Table 24.5.

## General Syntax

```
Printer.Line [Step](StartX!, StartY!)-(EndX!, EndY!)[,Color&][,B | BF]
```

| Argument | Description |
| --- | --- |
| Step | Indicates StartX! and StartY! are relative to the current position |
| StartX!, StartY! | Coordinates of beginning point of the line |
| EndX!, EndY! | Coordinates of ending point of the line |
| Color& | Long integer expression indicating print color. Has no effect on black-and-white printers |
| B | Draws a box with StartX!, StartY! as the upper left corner & EndX!, EndY! as the bottom right |
| BF | Draws a box that is filled in with the color specified by Color& (or black if printer has no color capability) |

**Table 24.5 Arguments of the Line method**

## Example Syntax

```
Printer.Line (100, 100)-(200, 200)          'Draws a line with a 45-degree angle

Printer.Line (100, 100)-(200, 200), , B     'Draws a box whose top left corner is
                                            'position 100, 100, and bottom right
                                            'corner is position 200, 200
```

## Description

The Step, StartX!, and StartY! parameters for the Line method specify the beginning point of the line, or the upper left-hand corner of the box to be printed. If the STEP keyword is used, StartX! and StartY! indicate a position relative to the current print position (see the entries for CurrentX and CurrentY in this chapter). If the STEP keyword is omitted, StartX! and StartY! indicate an absolute position on the current print page. In either case, the position specified should fall into the range defined by the Printer.ScaleHeight and Printer.ScaleWidth properties.

The EndX!, and EndY! parameters specify the ending point of the line, or the bottom right-hand corner of the box to be printed. Again, the position specified should fall into the range defined by the Printer.ScaleHeight and Printer.ScaleWidth properties.

When this method is used on a printer without color, the Color& parameter is ignored. All output occurs in black, regardless of the color specified.

The final parameter indicates whether or not a box is drawn, and if it is to be filled. If this parameter is omitted, a simple line is generated. If a "B" is specified, an empty box is generated. Finally, if a "BF" is specified, a filled box is generated.

The first statement in the example syntax draws a line between the coordinates 100, 100 and 200, 200. The line moves from upper left to lower right at a 45-degree slope. The second statement uses the same coordinates, but because of the B parameter the coordinates are considered to be the upper left and lower right corners of a box.

## Example

The Line method is used in two procedures in the Printer project. In the PrintBox procedure, the Line method draws a box around a supplied string. In the PrintLine procedure the Line method strikes out a line of text. In both cases, the placement and dimensions of the box or line are figured using the TextHeight and TextWidth methods and the CurrentX and CurrentY properties.

## Comments

This method is covered in greater detail in Chapter 10, *Drawing Shapes*. However, it has been included again in this chapter to demonstrate its use with the Printer object.

# NewPage Method

## Objects Affected

| Check | Clipboard | Combo | Command | Debug |
|-------|-----------|-------|---------|-------|
| Dir | Drive | File | Form | Frame |
| Label | List | Menu | Option | Picture |
| ▶ Printer | Screen | Scroll | Text | Timer |

## Purpose

The NewPage method ends output for the current page and sets up the next page for subsequent output.

## General Syntax

```
Printer.NewPage
```

## Example Syntax

```
Printer.NewPage
```

## Description

The NewPage method, which has no arguments, is the Visual Basic equivalent to issuing a form feed. The current print page is saved, and will be output when the program ends or the EndDoc method is executed. The work area for the print page is then cleared, and the CurrentX and CurrentY properties are set to 0 to set up a new page. Also, executing this method causes the Page property to be incremented.

Execute this method when all printing on a page is complete. After this method is used, the program can then begin print operations for the next page. If the NewPage method has not been used since the last time data was output to the Printer object, executing the EndDoc method will also cause a new page operation.

The example syntax executes the NewPage event with the effects just described.

### Example

The Printer project uses the NewPage method to generate a new page just after a footer has been printed for the FilePrintText_Click event. When this occurs, the current page is saved in memory, the Page property is incremented, and the page work area is cleared. The CurrentX and CurrentY properties are also set to 0.

# Print Method

### Objects Affected

| | | | | |
|---|---|---|---|---|
| Check | Clipboard | Combo | Command | Debug |
| Dir | Drive | File | ▶ Form | Frame |
| Label | List | Menu | Option | ▶ Picture |
| ▶ Printer | Screen | Scroll | Text | Timer |

### Purpose

The Print method sends text to the Printer object. Table 24.6 summarizes the argument of the Print method.

### General Syntax

```
Printer.Print [expression-list]
```

| Argument | Description |
|---|---|
| expression-list | A list of values, string or numeric, that will be printed |

**Table 24.6 Argument of the Print method**

### Example Syntax

```
Printer.Print "Hello "; Person$; ", how are you?"
                                    'Sends the string literals and
                                    'variable to the Printer object
```

### Description

The Print method prints the text specified by the expression list. The expression list contains one or more expressions of any data type (Integer, Long, Single, Double, Currency, or user defined). Each expression can be separated by a semicolon or a comma (if neither is used, semicolons are automatically inserted by Visual Basic). Using a semicolon to separate expressions prints each expression as if it were all one concatenated string. Using commas, however, causes the expressions that follow a comma to be printed at the next "print zone." A print zone is every 14 columns, where a column is equal to the average width of every character in the current font and font size for the Printer object.

If a comma or semicolon trails the last expression in the list, the CurrentX and CurrentY properties are set to the point following the last character printed. However, if both are omitted from the end of the list, the CurrentX property is set to 0 and CurrentY is set to the next print line. This is the equivalent of doing a carriage return/ line feed on a traditional printer.

If executing a Print method will cause the specified text to be printed below the position defined by Printer.ScaleHeight, a new page is automatically generated. However, if executing a Print method will cause the specified text to be printed beyond the position defined by Printer.ScaleWidth, no new line is generated. The text is merely truncated. Take care not to cause this method to print past position 32767, as this will cause an "Overflow" to occur.

The example syntax sends the literal strings "Hello" and "how are you" to the print page. (The quote marks themselves are not sent). Between these items, the contents of the string variable Person$ is also sent. If Person$ had been set to "Bryon," then the resulting output will look something like this:

```
Hello Bryon, how are you?
```

Notice that any spaces between strings must be included in one or the other of the strings. Semicolons rather than commas are used to separate strings, so that output is not moved to the next print zone.

## Example

The Print method is used throughout all portions of the Printer project. It is most heavily used in the procedures that relate to the FilePrintText_Click event. This event occurs when the user clicks the Print Text option on the File menu of the Printer project. This event reads the file CONSTANT.TXT, and uses the Print method to generate a hard copy of the first two pages of the file.

## Comments

This method is covered in greater detail in Chapter 11, *Displaying Text with Objects*. However, it has been included in this chapter to demonstrate its use with the Printer object.

# PrintForm Method

## Objects Affected

| | | | | |
|---|---|---|---|---|
| Check | Clipboard | Combo | Command | Debug |
| Dir | Drive | File | Form | Frame |
| Label | List | Menu | Option | Picture |
| ▶ Printer | Screen | Scroll | Text | Timer |

## Purpose

The PrintForm method sends a copy of a Visual Basic form to the Windows printing routines. This can be an easy way to take advantage of Visual Basic's form design capabilities in creating printed forms, and to format printed output so that it is identical to what is shown on the screen. The Table 24.7 summarizes the arguments of the PrintForm method.

## General Syntax

`[form.]PrintForm`

| Argument | Description |
|---|---|
| form | FormName of the form to be printed |

Table 24.7 Argument of the PrintForm method

## Example Syntax

`AddressForm.PrintForm`

## Description

This very useful method allows you to design an output form that can be sent to the printer. The only argument used is the name of the form to be printed. If not explicitly specified, the form with the focus will be printed.

All controls on the form will also be printed, with the exception of the menu controls.

If any graphics have been added to the form, or any picture on the form, they will only be printed if the AutoReDraw property for that form or picture was set to True (-1) at that time.

Although the form to be printed does have to be loaded into memory when this method is executed, it does not need to be visible. This makes it easy to design complicated forms for printing, without having to code complex procedures in your program. You can design an output form in the same manner as a form for the screen. Picture controls can be used for letterhead and other similar features, while labels can be used for any text that will be printed on the form. When it comes time to print the form, all the program has to do is set the caption property of any labels that represent changed data, and execute the PrintForm method. Note that the PrintForm method sends the form directly to the Windows printing routines. It does not use the printer object or the system of pages and documents used by most other printing techniques.

The example syntax sends a copy of AddressForm to the printer.

## Example

In the Printer project, this method can be found in the FilePrintForm_Click event. This event is activated when the user chooses the Print Form option on the File menu of the Printer project. This event uses the PrintForm method to send a copy of the current form to the printer.

# PSet Method

## Objects Affected

| | | | | |
|---|---|---|---|---|
| Check | Clipboard | Combo | Command | Debug |
| Dir | Drive | File | ▶ Form | Frame |
| Label | List | Menu | Option | ▶ Picture |
| ▶ Printer | Screen | Scroll | Text | Timer |

## Purpose

The PSet method draws a dot on the current print page. The Table 24.8 summarizes the arguments of the PSet method.

## General Syntax

```
Printer.PSet [Step](X_Pos!, Y_Pos!)[,Color&]
```

| Argument | Description |
|---|---|
| Step | Indicates X_Pos! and Y_Pos! are relative to the current position |
| X_Pos!, Y_Pos! | Single-precision expressions indicating the placement of the dot |
| Color& | Long integer expression indicating print color. Has no effect on black-and-white printers |

**Table 24.8 Argument of the PSet method**

## Example Syntax

```
Sub Shade (Text As String)              'This sub procedure uses the PSet method
   OldX = Form1.CurrentX                'to shade a line before it is printed
   OldY = Form1.CurrentY                'Save current co-ordinates
   NewX = OldX + Form1.TextWidth(Text)
   NewY = OldY + Form1.TextHeight(Text)
   For Y = OldY To NewY Step 50         'For every 50 vertical positions
      For X = OldX To NewX Step 50      'For every 50 horizontal positions
         Form1.PSet (X, Y)
                                        'Print a dot
      Next
   Next
   Form1.CurrentX = OldX
   Form1.CurrentY = OldY
End Sub
```

## Description

The PSet method generates a dot on the current print page at the position specified. The Step, X_Pos!, and Y_Pos! parameters specify where the point is to be generated. If the STEP keyword is used, X_Pos! and Y_Pos! indicate a position relative to the current print position (see the entries for CurrentX and CurrentY in this chapter). If the STEP keyword is omitted, X_Pos! and Y_Pos! indicate an absolute position on the current print page. In either case, the position specified should fall into the range defined by the Printer.ScaleHeight and Printer.ScaleWidth properties.

If this method is used on a printer without color capabilities, the Color& parameter is ignored. All output occurs in black, regardless of the color specified.

### Example

In the Printer project, the PSet method is used in the PrintBox procedure. If PrintBox's Shaded parameter is True, it shades the contents of the box. This shading is done by using the PSet method to generate a dot every 50 positions horizontally and vertically. This technique is also shown in the example syntax.

### Comments

This method is covered in greater detail in Chapter 8, *Setting Up Graphical Objects*. However, it has been included in this chapter to demonstrate its use with the Printer object.

# ScaleHeight Property

### Objects Affected

| | | | | |
|---|---|---|---|---|
| Check | Clipboard | Combo | Command | Debug |
| Dir | Drive | File | ▶ Form | Frame |
| Label | List | Menu | Option | Picture |
| ▶ Printer | Screen | Scroll | Text | Timer |

### Purpose

The ScaleHeight property sets or returns the height of a printer page in units defined by the ScaleMode property. Table 24.9 summarizes the argument of the ScaleHeight property.

### General Syntax

```
Printer.ScaleHeight [= setting]
```

| Argument | Description |
|---|---|
| setting | A single-precision expression indicating a programmer defined coordinate system for the printer page |

Table 24.9 Argument of the ScaleHeight property

### Example Syntax

```
SpaceLeft = Printer.ScaleHeight — Printer.CurrentY  'Vertical space left on the page
```

### Description

The absolute height of a print page can be determined by using the Height property with the Printer object. Unfortunately, the print page of most printers has a border in which printing is impossible. The Height property does not take this into account. However, the ScaleHeight property returns the print page's usable height (the height of the area inside the borders).

The ScaleHeight property is measured in the units defined by the Printer object's ScaleMode property. By default, this property is measured in twips. This, however, can be changed in two ways. First, if the ScaleMode property is changed, ScaleHeight units will reflect the change. Also, if the ScaleHeight property is explicitly set at design time or by a program, ScaleMode is automatically set to 0 (user-defined scaling). To define your own scale, specify the page height in your own coordinate system using the setting argument.

The ScaleHeight property is used mainly to help determine the printing position on a page. It can be used in conjunction with the TextHeight method to calculate when an end of a page is going to occur. For instance, in the following code, if the value of SpaceLeft is less than three print lines, a footer is generated:

```
SpaceLeft = Printer.ScaleHeight - Printer.CurrentY    'Vertical space lefton page
If SpaceLeft < Printer.TextHeight("Page:") *3 Then PrintFooter
```

The example syntax uses the same method to determine the amount of vertical space remaining on the page.

## Example

In the Printer project, the ScaleHeight property is mainly used in the FilePrint-Text_Click event. There, it calculates how close the program is to the bottom of the print page. This is used to determine when to print a footer on the page.

## Comments

This property is covered in greater detail in Chapter 9, *Designing with the Coordinate System*. However, it has been included in this chapter to demonstrate its use with the Printer object.

# ScaleLeft Property

## Objects Affected

| | | | | |
|---|---|---|---|---|
| Check | Clipboard | Combo | Command | Debug |
| Dir | Drive | File | ▶ Form | Frame |
| Label | List | Menu | Option | Picture |
| ▶ Printer | Screen | Scroll | Text | Timer |

## Purpose

The ScaleLeft property sets or returns the leftmost horizontal position on the printer page. This property can be set at design time, and set or read during run time. Table 24.10 summarizes the argument of the ScaleLeft property.

## General Syntax

```
Printer.ScaleLeft [= setting]
```

| Argument | Description |
|----------|-------------|
| setting | A single-precision expression indicating a programmer-defined coordinate system for the printer page |

Table 24.10 Argument of the ScaleLeft property

## Example Syntax

```
CurrentX = ScaleLeft          'Set current print position to left edge of page
```

## Description

In order to control the placement of text and graphics on a printer page, the Printer object uses a coordinate system in which any point on a printer page can be specified in the format X, Y; where X is the horizontal position, and Y is the vertical position. By default, the upper left-hand corner of the printer page is coordinate 0, 0. However, by using this property along with the ScaleTop property, you can define a custom system in which the coordinates of the upper left-hand corner have a different value.

Assigning a value to this property does one of two things. First, the leftmost horizontal position on the printer page will be referred to by the assigned value. Second, if the ScaleMode property has not yet been set to 0 (user defined), setting the ScaleLeft property will also set ScaleMode to 0. In other words, assigning a value to the ScaleLeft property automatically sets the ScaleMode property to reflect a programmer-defined coordinate system. However, the values of the ScaleHeight and ScaleWidth properties remain the same (please see the entries for ScaleHeight, ScaleMode, and ScaleWidth in this chapter, and in Chapter 9, *Designing with the Coordinate System*).

The ScaleLeft property can be read in order to ascertain the coordinate value of the leftmost horizontal position on the printer page. If the value of the ScaleMode property is other than 0 (for example, the coordinate system is not programmer-defined), this property will always return 0.

The example syntax sets the horizontal print position (reflected in the CurrentX property) to the value of the ScaleLeft property. The result is that the print position is moved to the left edge of the page.

## Comments

This property is covered in greater detail in Chapter 9, *Designing with the Coordinate System*. However, it has been included in this chapter to demonstrate its use with the Printer object.

# ScaleMode Property

## Objects Affected

| | | | | |
|---|---|---|---|---|
| Check | Clipboard | Combo | Command | Debug |
| Dir | Drive | File | ▶ Form | Frame |
| Label | List | Menu | Option | ▶ Picture |
| ▶ Printer | Screen | Scroll | Text | Timer |

## Purpose

The ScaleMode property sets the unit of measurement to be used for the Printer object's coordinate system. This property can be both read and set at design time or run time. Table 24.11 summarizes the setting argument for the ScaleMode property.

## General Syntax

```
Printer.ScaleMode [= mode%]
```

| Argument | Description |
|----------|-------------|
| setting | A single-precision expression indicating the coordinate system for the printer page |

Table 24.11 Argument of the ScaleMode property

## Example Syntax

```
Printer.ScaleMode = 1          'Set the scale mode to twips
```

## Description

The Printer object's coordinate system is used to specify the placement of text and graphics methods on the printer page. This placement is specified by supplying the position in the format X, Y; where X is the horizontal position and Y is the vertical position on the page. The ScaleMode property determines the unit of measurement that the values in X and Y represent.

The default for the ScaleMode property is twips, which equate to 1/1440 inch. This is generally adequate; however, Visual Basic allows you to choose from several other units of measurement, as well as define your own system. Table 24.12 shows the possible values for the property.

| Setting | Unit Used | Description |
|---------|-----------|-------------|
| 0 | User defined | This occurs when you assign a value to the printer's ScaleHeight or ScaleWidth properties. Doing so creates your own coordinate system |
| 1 | TWIP | Equal to 1/1440 inch |
| 2 | Point | Equal to 1/72 inch |
| 3 | Pixel | Smallest dot possible on the printer. The number of pixels per page is different for each brand of printer |
| 4 | Character | A character's height is 1/6 inch, its width is 1/12 inch |
| 5 | Inch | Standard inch |
| 6 | Millimeter | Metric millimeter |
| 7 | Centimeter | Metric centimeter |

Table 24.12 Settings for the ScaleMode property

The example syntax sets the unit of measurement for the Printer object to twips. Since this is the default, you would not have to make this setting unless your application sometimes uses other units.

## Comments

This property is covered in greater detail in Chapter 9, *Designing with the Coordinate System*. However, it has been included in this chapter to demonstrate its use with the Printer object.

# ScaleTop Property

## Objects Affected

| | | | | |
|---|---|---|---|---|
| Check | Clipboard | Combo | Command | Debug |
| Dir | Drive | File | ▶ Form | Frame |
| Label | List | Menu | Option | Picture |
| ▶ Printer | Screen | Scroll | Text | Timer |

## Purpose

The ScaleTop property sets or returns the topmost vertical position on the printer page. This property can be set at design time, and set or read during run time. The setting argument for the ScaleTop property is summarized in Table 24.13.

## General Syntax

```
Printer.ScaleTop [= setting]
```

| Argument | Description |
|---|---|
| setting | A single-precision expression indicating a programmer-defined coordinate system for the printer page |

Table 24.13 Argument of the ScaleTop property

## Example Syntax

```
CurrentY = ScaleTop    'Set current print position to top of page
```

## Description

In order to control the placement of text and graphics on a printer page, the Printer object uses a coordinate system in which any point on a printer page can be specified in the format X, Y; where X is the horizontal position, and Y is the vertical position. By default, the upper left-hand corner of the printer page is coordinate 0, 0. However, by using this property, along with the ScaleLeft property, you can custom define a system in which the coordinates of the upper left-hand corner have a different value.

Assigning a value to this property does one of two things. First, the topmost vertical position on the printer page will be referred to by the assigned value. Second, assigning a value to the ScaleTop property will also set ScaleMode to 0 (programmer-defined coordinate system). However, the values of the ScaleHeight and ScaleWidth properties remain the same. (Please see the entry for ScaleHeight, ScaleMode, and ScaleWidth in this chapter, and in Chapter 9, *Designing with the Coordinate System.*)

The ScaleTop property can also be read by your program in order to ascertain the coordinate value of the topmost vertical position on the printer page. If the value of the ScaleMode property is any value other than 0 (that is, the coordinate system is not programmer-defined), this property will always return 0.

The example syntax sets the vertical print position to the value of the ScaleTop property, thus moving the print position to the top of the page.

## Comments

This property is covered in greater detail in Chapter 9, *Designing with the Coordinate System.* However, it has been included in this chapter to demonstrate its use with the Printer object.

# ScaleWidth Property

## Objects Affected

| | | | | |
|---|---|---|---|---|
| Check | Clipboard | Combo | Command | Debug |
| Dir | Drive | File | ▶ Form | Frame |
| Label | List | Menu | Option | Picture |
| ▶ Printer | Screen | Scroll | Text | Timer |

## Purpose

The ScaleWidth property sets or returns the width of a printer page in units defined by the ScaleMode property. Table 24.14 summarizes the argument of the ScaleWidth property.

## General Syntax

```
Printer.ScaleWidth [= setting]
```

| Argument | Description |
|---|---|
| setting | A single-precision expression indicating a programmer-defined coordinate system for the printer page |

Table 24.14 Argument of the ScaleWidth property

## Example Syntax

```
SpaceLeft = Printer.ScaleWidth - Printer.CurrentX
                        'Horizontal space left on line
```

## Description

The absolute width of a print page can be determined by using the Width property with the Printer object. Unfortunately, the print pages of most printers have a border in which printing is impossible. The Width property does not take this nonprinting border into account. However, the ScaleWidth property returns the print page's usable Width (the width of the area inside the unprintable borders).

The ScaleWidth property is measured in the units defined by the Printer object's ScaleMode property. By default, this property is set to twips. This, however, can be changed in two ways. First, if the ScaleMode property is changed, ScaleWidth units will reflect the change. Also, if the ScaleWidth property is set by the program, ScaleMode is automatically set to 0 (user-defined scaling). Finally, you can use the setting argument to set a width value that establishes your own scale for the page measurements.

This property is used mainly to help determine the printing position on a page. It can be used in conjunction with the TextWidth method to calculate when an end of a print line is going to occur. For instance, in the following code, if the value of SpaceLeft is less than the width of the text to be printed, it will advance to the next line.

```
SpaceLeft = Printer.ScaleWidth - Printer.CurrentX
'Horizontal space left on line
If SpaceLeft < Printer.TextWidth(Text$) Then Printer.Print " "
```

The example syntax also uses this technique.

The ScaleWidth and TextWidth properties are also useful for centering or right justifying text on a print page. To right justify text, set the Printer object's CurrentX property to the value of the ScaleWidth minus the TextWidth of the text to be printed. To center text, calculate the same CurrentX value as right justification, and then divide it by 2.

## Example

In the Printer project, the ScaleWidth property is used in several procedures. Its main task in this program is to provide information so the program can calculate the correct positioning for centering and right justifying text on the page.

## Comments

This method is covered in greater detail in Chapter 9, *Designing with the Coordinate System*. However, it has been included in this chapter to demonstrate its use with the Printer object.

# TextHeight Method

## Objects Affected

| Check | Clipboard | Combo | Command | Debug |
|---|---|---|---|---|
| Dir | Drive | File | ▶ Form | Frame |
| Label | List | Menu | Option | ▶ Picture |
| ▶ Printer | Screen | Scroll | Text | Timer |

## Purpose

The Textheight method returns the height of the supplied text as it will be output on the printer. This is helpful for properly positioning and scaling printed output or for adding special effects such as shading and strikeout. The string argument used is summarized in Table 24.15.

## General Syntax

```
Printer.TextHeight(text$)
```

| Argument | Description |
|----------|-------------|
| text$ | A string expression whose text height will be returned |

**Table 24.15 Argument of the TextHeight method**

## Example Syntax

```
Sub Shade (Text As String)          'This sub procedure uses the PSet method
   OldX = Form1.CurrentX            'to shade a line before it is printed
   OldY = Form1.CurrentY            'Save current co-ordinates
   NewX = OldX + Form1.TextWidth(Text)
   NewY = OldY + Form1.TextHeight(Text)   'We need to find out how high to make the shading
   For Y = OldY To NewY Step 50
      For X = OldX To NewX Step 50
         Form1.PSet (X, Y)
      Next
   Next
   Form1.CurrentX = OldX
   Form1.CurrentY = OldY
End Sub
```

## Description

The TextHeight method examines the supplied string and returns a value that equals the height of the string as it will be printed in the current font and font size for the Printer object. The number returned is expressed in the format specified by the Printer.ScaleMode property. By default, this property is set to twips.

This method is useful when trying to add special effects to printed text, such as shading and strikeout. It can also be used before a Print method in order to determine whether printing a line of text will cause a new page to be generated. For instance, before using the Print method, the value returned from TextHeight can be added to CurrentY and compared to ScaleHeight. If Scale.Height is less, the program can anticipate a new page.

The example syntax uses the value returned by the TextHeight method to determine the height of the area to be shaded.

## Example

The TextHeight method is used throughout the Printer project. In the graphics printing procedures, it is used to help calculate the coordinates of the graphics that are being printed. In the FilePrintText_Click event, it is used along with the ScaleHeight property to determine when a footer will be printed.

## Comments

This method is also covered in Chapter 13, *Getting User Input with Text Boxes*. However, it has been included in this chapter to demonstrate its use with the Printer object.

# TextWidth Method

## Objects Affected

| | | | | |
|---|---|---|---|---|
| Check | Clipboard | Combo | Command | Debug |
| Dir | Drive | File | ▶ Form | Frame |
| Label | List | Menu | Option | ▶ Picture |
| ▶ Printer | Screen | Scroll | Text | Timer |

## Purpose

The TextWidth method returns the width of the supplied text as it will be output on the printer. This is helpful for properly positioning and scaling printed output or for adding special effects such as shading and strikeout. Table 24.16 summarizes the argument of the TextWidth method.

## General Syntax

```
Printer.TextWidth(text$)
```

| Argument | Description |
|---|---|
| text$ | A string expression whose text width will be returned |

Table 24.16 Argument of the TextWidth method

## Example Syntax

```
Sub Shade (Text As String)           'This sub procedure uses the PSet method
   OldX = Form1.CurrentX             'to shade a line before it is printed
   OldY = Form1.CurrentY             'Save current co-ordinates
   NewX = OldX + Form1.TextWidth(Text)  'We need to find out how wide to make the shading
   NewY = OldY + Form1.TextHeight(Text)
   For Y = OldY To NewY Step 50
      For X = OldX To NewX Step 50
         Form1.PSet (X, Y)
      Next
   Next
   Form1.CurrentX = OldX
   Form1.CurrentY = OldY
End Sub
```

## Description

The TextWidth method examines the supplied string arguments, and returns a value that equals the width of the string as it will be printed in the current font and font size for the Printer object. The number returned is expressed in the format specified by the Printer.ScaleMode property. By default, this property is set to twips.

This method is useful when trying to add special effects to printed text such as shading and strikeout. It can also be used to determine the correct position for centering or flushing text to the right. For instance, in the example code below, Header$ will be centered on its line while PageNo$ will be right flushed.

```
CurrentY = Printer.ScaleWidth - Printer.TextWidth(Header$) / 2
Printer.Print Header$
CurrentY = Printer.ScaleWidth - Printer.TextWidth(PageNo$)
Printer.Print PageNo$;
```

The example syntax uses the TextWidth method to determine the width of the text area to be shaded.

## Example

The TextWidth method is used throughout the Printer project. In the graphics printing procedures, it is used to help calculate the coordinates of the graphics that are being printed. In the FilePrintText_Click event, it is used along with the ScaleWidth property to determine the correct print positioning when the program wishes to center or right justify text.

## Comments

This method is also covered in Chapter 13, *Getting User Input with Text Boxes*. However, it has again been included in this chapter to demonstrate its use with the Printer object.

# Printer Project

## Project Overview

The following project details the use of the Printer object and its related methods and properties. After you have completed this project, you should have a firm understanding of the concepts behind the Printer object. By following the examples outlined in this project, you will learn how to print Visual Basic forms, output text, and output graphics to the printer.

## Assembling the Project

1. Create a new form (the Printer form) and place on it the controls, specified in Table 24.17.

| Object | Property | Setting |
|---|---|---|
| Form | CtlName | Form1 |
| | Caption | Printer Project |
| | Height | 2850 |
| | Icon | \VB\ICONS\WRITING\NOTE12.ICO |
| | Left | 2460 |
| | Top | 1995 |
| | Width | 3855 |
| Label | CtlName | Label1 |
| | Caption | Name: |
| | Height | 255 |
| | Left | 120 |
| | Top | 120 |
| | Width | 735 |
| Label | CtlName | Label2 |
| | Caption | Address: |
| | Height | 255 |
| | Left | 120 |
| | Top | 600 |
| | Width | 735 |
| Text Box | CtlName | Text1 |
| | Height | 375 |
| | Left | 960 |
| | Text | |
| | Top | 120 |
| | Width | 2655 |
| Text Box | CtlName | Text2 |
| | Height | 1215 |
| | Left | 960 |
| | Text | |
| | Top | 600 |
| | Width | 2655 |

**Table 24.17 Controls and property settings for the Printer project**

2. Use the Menu Design window (choose the Menu Design window option from Visual Basic's Window menu) to create a menu with the settings given in Table 24.18.

| Caption | CtlName | Indent |
|---------|---------|--------|
| &File | FileMenu | No |
| Print &Form | FilePrintForm | Yes |
| Print &Graphics | FilePrintGraphics | Yes |
| Print &Text file | FilePrintText | Yes |
| - | FileNothing | Yes |
| E&xit | FileExit | Yes |

**Table 24.18 Menu settings for the Printer project**

3. Check the appearance of your form against Figure 24.1.

4. Enter the following code into the FilePrintGraphics_Click event. This event occurs when the user chooses Print Graphics from the File menu.

```
Sub FilePrintGraphics_Click ()
    Form1.MousePointer = 11
    PrintBox "This text is in a box", 0
    PrintBox "This text is in a shaded box", -1
    PrintLine "This text is crossed out"
    PrintCircle "This text is in a circle"
    Printer.EndDoc
    MsgBox "Done Printing Graphics"
    Form1.MousePointer = 0
End Sub
```

5. Enter the following code into the General Declarations area of the form. This procedure is called from the FilePrintGraphics_Click event. PrintBox prints the supplied string, and then uses the Line method to draw a box around it.

If the Shaded parameter is True, it shades the contents of the box. This shading is done by using the PSet method to generate a dot every 50 positions horizontally and vertically.

The placement and dimensions of the box are figured using the Text-Height and TextWidth methods and the CurrentX and CurrentY properties.

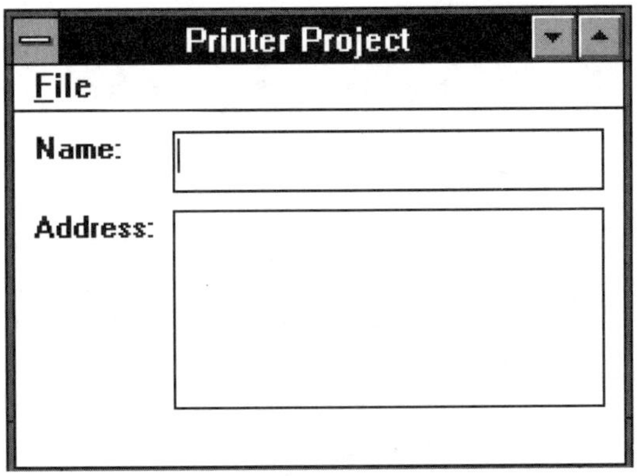

Figure 24.1 How the Printer project form should look when complete

```
Sub PrintBox (Msg As String,
Shaded As Integer)
    Dim Left_X As Single
    Dim Right_X As Single
    Dim Top_Y As Single
    Dim Bottom_Y As Single
```

```
        Left_X = Printer.CurrentX                'Figure box coordinates
        Top_Y = Printer.CurrentY
        Right_X = Printer.CurrentX + Printer.TextWidth(Msg) + 200
        Bottom_Y = Printer.CurrentY + Printer.TextHeight(Msg) + 200
        Printer.CurrentX = Printer.CurrentX + 100
        Printer.CurrentY = Printer.CurrentY + 100
        Printer.Print Msg                         'Print the message
        Printer.Line (Left_X, Top_Y)-(Right_X, Bottom_Y), , B
        If Shaded = -1 Then
            For Y_Pos = Top_Y To Bottom_Y Step 50
                For X_Pos = Left_X To Right_X Step 50
                    Printer.PSet (X_Pos, Y_Pos)
                Next
        Next
        End If
        Printer.CurrentX = 0
        Printer.CurrentY = Bottom_Y + 100
    End Sub
```

6. Enter the following code into the General Declarations area of the form. This procedure is called from the FilePrintGraphics_Click event. PrintLine prints the supplied string, and then uses the Line method to strike it out. The placement and length of the strikeout line are figured using the Text-Height and TextWidth methods and the CurrentX and CurrentY properties.

```
Sub PrintLine (Msg As String)
    Dim X_Start As Single
    Dim X_End As Single
    Dim Y_Pos As Single

    Y_Pos = (Printer.TextHeight(Msg) / 2) + Printer.CurrentY
    X_Start = Printer.CurrentX
    X_End = X_Start + Printer.TextWidth(Msg)
    Printer.Print Msg
    Printer.Line (X_Start, Y_Pos)-(X_End, Y_Pos)
    Printer.CurrentX = 0
    Printer.CurrentY = Printer.CurrentY + 100
End Sub
```

7. Enter the following code into the General Declarations area of the form. This procedure is called from the FilePrintGraphics_Click event. PrintCircle prints the supplied string and then uses the Circle method to draw a circle around it. The placement and radius of the circle are figured using the Text-Height and TextWidth methods and the CurrentX and CurrentY properties.

```
Sub PrintCircle (Msg As String)
    Dim X_Pos As Single
    Dim Y_Pos As Single
    Dim Radius As Single

    Radius = (Printer.TextWidth(Msg) / 2) + 100
    X_Pos = Printer.CurrentX + Radius
    Y_Pos = Printer.CurrentY + Radius
    Printer.CurrentX = Printer.CurrentX + 100
    Printer.CurrentY = Printer.CurrentY + Radius
    Printer.Print Msg
    Printer.Circle (X_Pos, Y_Pos), Radius
```

```
   Printer.CurrentX = 0
   Printer.CurrentY = Y_Pos + Radius + 100
End Sub
```

8. Enter the following code in the FilePrintForm_Click event. This event is activated when the user chooses the Print Form option on the File menu of the Printer project. This event sends a copy of the current form to the printer.

```
Sub FilePrintForm_Click ()
   PrintForm
End Sub
```

9. Enter the following code into the FilePrintText_Click event. This event occurs when the user clicks the Print Text option on the File menu of the Printer project. This event reads and generates the first two pages of the file CONSTANT.TXT. When the document is finished, the EndDoc statement sends the output to the Windows printing routines.

NOTE: The file CONSTANT.TXT must be in the \VB directory on the default drive, or the Open statement will generate a "File not found" error.

```
Sub FilePrintText_Click ()
   Dim FileName As String
   Dim InputLine As String
   Dim SpaceLeft As Single
   Dim Shading As Integer
   Dim FileNumber As Integer

   FileNumber = FreeFile
   FileName = "\VB\CONSTANT.TXT"
   Open FileName For Input As #FileNumber

   Form1.MousePointer = 11
   Do
       If Printer.CurrentX = 0 And Printer.CurrentY = 0 Then PrintHeader
FileName
       Line Input #FileNumber, InputLine
       Printer.Print InputLine
       SpaceLeft = Printer.ScaleHeight - Printer.CurrentY
       If SpaceLeft < (3 * Printer.TextHeight("Page:")) Then PrintFooter
   Loop Until EOF(FileNumber) Or Printer.Page = 3
   Close FileNumber
   Printer.EndDoc
   Form1.MousePointer = 0
End Sub
```

10. Enter the following code into the General Declarations area of the form. This procedure is called from the FilePrintText_Click event. It prints a header at the top line of the page. It uses the ScaleWidth, CurrentX, and CurrentY properties together with the TextWidth method to center the file name and right justify the page number on the top line.

```
Sub PrintHeader (Header As String)
   Dim PageNo As String

   Printer.CurrentX = 0
   Printer.Print Date$;
```

```
        Printer.CurrentX = (Printer.ScaleWidth - Printer.TextWidth(Header)) / 2
        Printer.Print Header;
        PageNo = "Page: " + Format$(Printer.Page, "###")
        Printer.CurrentX = Printer.ScaleWidth - Printer.TextWidth(PageNo)
        Printer.Print PageNo
        Printer.Print " "
    End Sub
```

11. Enter the following code into the general declarations area of the form. This procedure is called from the FilePrintText_Click event. It prints a footer at the bottom line of the page. It uses the ScaleWidth, CurrentX, and CurrentY properties together with the TextWidth method to center the page number. It also uses the NewPage method to end the current page and clear the page work area.

```
    Sub PrintFooter ()
        Dim PageNo As String

        Printer.Print
        PageNo = "Page: " + Format$(Printer.Page, "###")
        Printer.CurrentX = (Printer.ScaleWidth - Printer.TextWidth(PageNo)) / 2
        Printer.Print PageNo;
        Printer.NewPage
    End Sub
```

12. Enter the following code into the FileExit_Click event. This event unloads the current form from memory. Because this is the only form in memory, this causes the program to end.

```
    Sub FileExit_Click ()
        Unload Form1
    End Sub
```

## How It Works

This example program sets up a simple data entry form that has a menu with four choices: Print Form, Print Graphics, Print Text, and Exit.

The user can choose simply to print the form by opening the file menu and clicking on the Print Form option. This causes the FilePrintForm_Click event to occur, which uses the PrintForm method to send a copy of the form, and any text that is visible in the Name and Address text boxes, to the printer.

If the user chooses the Print Graphics option, the FilePrintGraphics_Click event is executed. This event calls three Sub procedures that demonstrate the use of the graphics methods on the Printer object.

The first of the three procedures is the PrintBox procedure. This prints a box around the text that is supplied by one of its arguments. This is done by using the Line method. The dimensions and placement of the box are figured using the CurrentX, and CurrentY properties along with the TextHeight and TextWidth methods. PrintBox also has the Shaded argument, which indicates whether or not the text inside the box will be shaded. If this argument is true, the PSet method generates a dot every 50 positions inside the box.

The next procedure, PrintLine, prints its supplied text argument, and then proceeds to draw a line through it. Again, the position of the line is determined by the CurrentX and CurrentY properties in conjunction with the TextHeight method. The TextWidth method is used to calculate the length of the strikeout line.

In the last of the three procedures, the PrintCircle method is used to generate a circle with the supplied text argument centered within it. The placement and radius of the circle are figured using the TextHeight and TextWidth methods and the CurrentX and CurrentY properties.

If the user chooses the Print Text File option, the FilePrintText_Click event is executed. This event opens the CONSTANT.TXT file, and reads and prints the first two pages. It checks the CurrentX and CurrentY properties for 0. If they are both 0 (indicating that the routine is at the top of a new page), it executes the PrintHeader procedure. This procedure prints a header at the top line of the page. It uses the ScaleWidth, CurrentX, and CurrentY properties together with the TextWidth method to center the file name and right justify the page number on the top line. Execution then returns to the FilePrintText_Click event.

FilePrintText_Click then reads and prints the next line. After this has been accomplished, it uses the ScaleHeight and TextHeight methods to determine if it is at the bottom of a page. If so, the PrintFooter procedure is called. This procedure prints a centered page number, and executes the NewPage method. Doing so causes the Printer.Page property to be incremented, CurrentX and CurrentY to be set to 0, and the page work area to be cleared. Upon returning to the FilePrintText_Click event, the Page property is checked. If it equals 3, we have finished printing the first two pages and the file is no longer read.

# Transferring Data with Dynamic Data Exchange (DDE)

**D**ynamic Data Exchange is a means of communication between two Microsoft Windows applications. A DDE conversation establishes a temporary or permanent link between two Windows applications. This link acts as a conduit for the exchange of data between the connected applications. The data exchanged may either be information, which is copied from one application to another, or commands or keystrokes for the other application to process. Links may not be established with applications that do not support DDE communication. Check your application's documentation to see if it supports DDE. The Windows 3.0 File Manager does not support DDE, so a link may not be established between this version of File Manager and a Visual Basic application.

In a DDE conversation, the application that creates the link is known as the client application and the application that responds is known as a server application. Any application that supports DDE can serve as either a server or a client. One application can serve as both a client and a server with several other applications at the same time. Only one active DDE link should be established between a Visual Basic control or form and another application. For example, a link between a Microsoft Excel spreadsheet cell and a text control is acceptable as long as the parent form does not already have a link with the same cell. Such a situation creates an infinite loop of updates.

## Elements of a DDE Link

A DDE conversation between two applications requires an application name, topic, and item. The application name is the unique name that identifies the application in Windows. Every DDE link has a topic, which indicates what type of data is being addressed by the link. The item specifically identifies the data being exchanged by the two applications. Neither the application name nor the topic are modifiable once a DDE link has been established or the DDE connection will be broken. In contrast, the item of a DDE conversation may be changed as many times as necessary.

All of the applications in Windows have a name that identifies them in a DDE link. This name is normally the filename of the executable file used to start the program. The application name of a Visual Basic program is always the filename of the executable file. In a DDE conversation, the client application must have the name of the server in order to establish a link. Table 25.1 contains the application names of some common Windows applications that support DDE.

| Windows Application | FileName | Application Name |
|---|---|---|
| Microsoft Excel | EXCEL.EXE | Excel |
| Microsoft Word | WINWORD.EXE | WinWord |
| Pioneer Q+E | QE.EXE | QE |
| Polaris Packrat | PACKRAT.EXE | Packrat |

**Table 25.1 Application names of common Windows applications**

A DDE link also must indicate the part of the server application with which to establish the connection. The available topics vary from application to application, but one choice is virtually universal to all DDE supporting applications: System. With the System topic, a DDE link can obtain the other topics that the application supports as well as information about the application, such as the data formats that it supports. In Microsoft Excel, Microsoft Word, and Pioneer Q+E, the path and filename may serve as a topic in a DDE link. Visual Basic applications can define the topic using the LinkTopic property.

The actual data transferred through a DDE link is called the item. In Visual Basic applications, the item is defined with the LinkItem property. An item in a Visual Basic application may be a text box, label, or picture on a form. When the topic of a DDE link is a spreadsheet, the item may be a cell reference such as R1C1 on an Excel spreadsheet. If a link is established with a WinWord document, the item might be a glossary name.

## Types of Links

Two basic types of links may be established between two applications: hot and cold. A hot link updates the data to the other application every time that the data changes. A cold link updates the data only when the data is specifically requested. A link, whether hot or cold, is either a server or a client link, depending on the direction in which the data is passed. Server links involve situations where the data passes from the server to the client. With client links, the data is transferred from the client to the server.

A server link may be established between a form or control in a Visual Basic application and another Windows application that supports DDE communication. In a server link, the client (initiating application) obtains information from the server (responding application). When this transfer of information takes place depends on the type of server link created. If this is a cold server link, then the transfer takes place only when requested. Data transfers in hot server links take place every time that the control or form changes.

The client link may be set up between a form or control in a Visual Basic application and another Windows application that supports DDE communication. In a client link, the server (initiating application) requests information from the client (responding application). When this request for information takes place depends on the type of client link. When this is a cold client link, then the request takes place only when requested. Data transfers in hot client links take place every time that the application's specified information changes.

## DDE in Visual Basic

Visual Basic provides several tools that influence the operation of DDE links with other applications. Any actions tied to the opening or closing of a link appear in the LinkOpen and LinkClose events. The LinkError event provides for actions that take place when problems with links occur. A client controls a server by sending the server's macro commands through the link with the LinkExecute method. Any actions that need to take place in the Visual Basic application when a LinkExecute method is used may be placed in the LinkExecute event. Both the item and the topic of a DDE conversation may be determined with the LinkItem and LinkTopic properties. Whether a DDE link is hot or cold may be set with the LinkMode property. When information needs to be moved from the client to the server, it may be accomplished with the LinkPoke method. Cold DDE links may transfer information manually with the LinkRequest method. All of the contents of a Visual Basic application's picture box may be transferred to another application with the LinkSend method. The LinkTimeout property determines how long a control will wait for a response from the other application.

Table 25.2 displays the four properties, three methods, and four events that affect DDE communication with other Windows applications that support this protocol.

| Use or Set This... | | To Do This... |
|---|---|---|
| LinkClose | Event | Indicate the actions that take place when a DDE link is closed |
| LinkError | Event | Indicate the actions that take place when a DDE link produces an error |
| LinkExecute | Event | Send a command to another application |
| LinkItem | Property | Indicate the item to use with a DDE link |
| LinkMode | Property | Determine whether a control's DDE link is hot or cold or off or indicates if a form is set to server or off |
| LinkOpen | Event | Indicate the actions that take place when a DDE link is opened |
| LinkPoke | Method | Send information from the client to the server |
| LinkRequest | Method | Ask for and obtain information from another application |
| LinkSend | Method | Transfer contents of picture box to a connected application |
| LinkTimeout | Property | Determine the time that a control will wait for a response from an application |
| LinkTopic | Property | Indicate the Topic to use with a DDE link |

**Table 25.2 Properties, methods, and events dealing with the referencing of forms and controls**

The following pages investigate the properties, methods, and events in detail. The DDE project at the end of this section includes step-by-step instructions to assemble the project.

# LinkClose Event

## Objects Affected

| | | | | |
|---|---|---|---|---|
| Check | Clipboard | Combo | Command | Dbug |
| Dir | Drive | File | ▶ Form | Frame |
| ▶ Label | List | Menu | Option | ▶ Picture |
| Printer | Screen | Scroll | ▶ Text | Timer |

## Purpose

The LinkClose event processes any actions that occur when the DDE link between a form, label, picture box, or text box and another program terminates. Changing the LinkMode property of the object to none (0) results in the termination of a DDE link. Attempting to change the LinkTopic property of an object also closes a DDE link. The LinkClose event contains any of the actions that occur when a link terminates. Table 25.3 summarizes the arguments of the LinkClose event.

## General Syntax

```
Sub form_LinkClose()
Sub ctlname_LinkClose (index As Integer)
```

| Argument | Description |
|---|---|
| form | FormName property of form |
| ctlname | CtlName property of control |
| index | Identifies control in a control array |

**Table 25.3 Arguments of the LinkClose event**

## Example Syntax

```
Sub Form_LinkClose ()
    If LinkMode <> 0 Then              'Checks if LinkMode is currently at none
        LinkMode = 0                   'Changes LinkMode to none
        MsgBox "DDE link closed prematurely"  'Displays message on the screen
    Else If LinkMode = 0 Then          'Checks if LinkMode is currently at none
        MsgBox "DDE Link closed normally"     'Displays LinkMode to none
    End If
End Sub
```

## Description

The LinkClose event contains any actions that occur when a DDE link closes. Specify the LinkClose event starting with the name of the control involved in the link, or the name of its parent form. Add the index argument in parentheses at the end of the statement if a control array is involved.

A DDE link terminates in several ways. Any attempt to modify the topic of a link results in the termination of the link. A form or control's link ends when its LinkMode property changes to 0. Keep each of these methods in mind when setting up a LinkClose event. In the example syntax, the routine checks the current setting of the LinkMode property of the form. The code determines if the link closed with the LinkMode or another method.

### The LinkMode Property

Changing the LinkMode property of an object initiates or terminates a link with another application. The LinkClose event triggers when the LinkMode property closes a link. In the example syntax, the LinkClose event checks to determine if a change to the LinkMode property terminated the link.

### The LinkTopic Property

The contents of a LinkTopic are part of the unique identifying characteristics of a DDE link. The other characteristics are the application name and topic. A link's topic identifies the element of the other application being linked. Neither of these characteristics is modifiable on an active link or the link will close, triggering the LinkClose event. In the example syntax, the routine checks the present setting of the LinkMode property to determine if the link was closed without a change to the LinkMode property. The abnormal message displays if the LinkClose event was triggered by an attempted change of the topic while the link was active.

### Control Arrays

When there is a DDE link between a control in a control array and another application, the index property must be provided. In this case, such a link involves a specific control in the control array and does not involve the contents or settings of the other controls in the control array. In order to access all of the controls of a control array, the link must be established with the form.

## Example

In the DDE project at the end of this section, the LinkClose events check the setting of each control's LinkMode property when the link with that control closes. Each DDE link's Visual Basic element triggers before the program closes. In this case, each LinkClose event calls the subfunction CheckLink. The CheckLink subfunction checks if the LinkMode property of the control is 0. If the Link property is not 0, then this subfunction changes it to 0. This ensures that when a link closes, the LinkMode property of the control reflects this status.

## Comments

Since the item of a DDE link is modifiable while the link is active, changes to the item do not trigger the LinkClose event.

# LinkError Event

## Objects Affected

| | | | | |
|---|---|---|---|---|
| Check | Clipboard | Combo | Command | Dbug |
| Dir | Drive | File | ▶ Form | Frame |
| ▶ Label | List | Menu | Option | ▶ Picture |
| Printer | Screen | Scroll | ▶ Text | Timer |

## Purpose

The LinkError event is triggered when a DDE link conversation produces an error. This error can never be caused by Visual Basic code and may only be the result of problems with the connected application, the link itself, or the Windows environment. For this reason, this event returns a value you can use to determine what action to take based upon the error that occurred. Table 25.4 summarizes the valid arguments of the LinkErr event.

## General Syntax

```
Sub form_LinkError (LinkErr As Integer)
Sub ctlname_LinkError ([index As Integer,]linkErr As Integer)
```

| Argument | Effect |
|---|---|
| form | FormName property of form |
| ctlname | CtlName property of control |
| index | Indentifying value of the control in a control array |
| LinkErr | The LinkErr Value returned |

Table 25.4 Valid arguments of the LinkError event

## Example Syntax

```
Sub TextBox(0)_LinkError (Index As Integer, LinkErr As Integer)
    Select Case LinkErr
        Case 1
            Msg$ = "Microsoft Excel asked for data in an incompatible format."
        Case 2
            Msg$ = "Microsoft Excel asked for data without an established link."
        Case 3
            Msg$ = "Microsoft Excel attempted a DDE operation without establishing
            a DDE link."
        Case 4
            Msg$ = "Microsoft Excel attempted to modify the Item in a DDE link that
            wasn't established."
        Case 5
            Msg$ = "Microsoft Excel attempted to Poke data without establishing a
            DDE link."
        Case 6
            Msg$ = "Microsoft Excel attempted a DDE operation after the Link was closed."
```

```
        Case 7
            Msg$ = "There are too many active DDE links established."
        Case 8
            Msg$ = "Some of the data sent through the link was lost, because it was too long."
        Case 9
            Msg$ = "The index value of a nonexistent control in a control array was
            specified."
        Case 10
            Msg$ = "An unexpected DDE operation was sent from the other application."
        Case 11
            Msg$ = "There is not enough memory available for a DDE link."
        Case 12
            Msg$ = "Microsoft Excel tried to perform an operation reserved for
            Client Applications."
    End Select
    MsgBox Msg$
End Sub
```

## Description

The LinkError event serves as a means of providing information about the nature of problems when they occur. Specify this event starting with the name of the control involved in the link, or the name of its parent form. The LinkError event contains actions that respond to the problem. Any actions in this event mainly serve as a warning that something is wrong. Table 25.5 lists the possible errors that would trigger this event. In the example syntax, the LinkError event informs the user what kind of problem has occurred. Since the Excel application's actions cause the error, changes must be made to that application before the link may be successfully processed. Errors of this type typically require recoding in the connected application.

| LinkErr Value | Problem |
| --- | --- |
| 1 | The linked application asked for data in an incompatible format |
| 2 | An application asked for data without an established link |
| 3 | An application attempted a DDE operation without establishing a DDE link |
| 4 | An application attempted to modify the item in a DDE link that has not been established |
| 5 | An application attempted to poke data without establishing a DDE link |
| 6 | An application attempted a DDE operation after the server form's LinkMode was set to None (0) |
| 7 | There are too many active DDE links established |
| 8 | Some of the data sent through the link was lost because it was too long |
| 9 | The index value of a nonexistent control in a control array was specified in a DDE link |
| 10 | An unexpected DDE operation was sent from the other application |
| 11 | There is not enough memory available for a DDE link |
| 12 | The server application tried to perform an operation reserved for client applications |

**Table 25.5 Causes of the link error values returned in the LinkErr variable**

In the example syntax, the LinkError event's LinkErr value is used to display a message to inform the user of the error.

### Control Array

When there is a DDE link between a control in a control array and another application, the index property must be provided. In this case, such a link involves a specific control in the control array and does not involve the contents or settings of the other controls in the control array. In order to access all of the controls of a control array, the link must be established with the form.

### Example

In the DDE project at the end of this section, the LinkError event informs another application of problems with an existing DDE link. This event is only applicable to DDE links that occur when the form is the server in a DDE link. Since WinWord is the only application that communicates with this form in this project, each of the error messages is directed at WinWord. These error messages may only be generated by the actions of the other applications; they have no effect upon the DDE link itself. Read these messages carefully to get an idea of what kinds of problems can occur in a DDE link between another application and a Visual Basic form.

### Comments

The LinkError event LinkErr values have no effect on the value of the Err variable in Err functions.

# LinkExecute Event

## Objects Affected

| | | | | |
|---|---|---|---|---|
| Check | Clipboard | Combo | Command | Dbug |
| Dir | Drive | File | ▶ Form | Frame |
| Label | List | Menu | Option | Picture |
| Printer | Screen | Scroll | Text | Timer |

## Purpose

The LinkExecute event contains a Visual Basic application's responses to command strings sent through a DDE link. A LinkExecute event is only triggered when the form is the server of a DDE link. The client application transmits a command through a DDE link to the server application. Forms with no code in the LinkExecute event will ignore any commands sent through the link from the client application. Source code in a LinkExecute event must respond to specific commands. If another application sent the word "wait" to a Visual Basic application with the LinkExecute event in the example syntax, the command would have no effect because the word "wait" does not appear in that event. Table 25.6 summarizes the arguments of the LinkExecute event.

## General Syntax

```
Sub Form_LinkExecute (Cmdstr As String, Cancel As Integer)
```

| Argument | Effect |
|----------|--------|
| CmdStr | Contents of the command string are transmitted through a DDE link from a client application |
| Cancel | Indicates whether the command string was accepted or rejected. If 0 is returned, then the command was accepted. Any value greater than 0 indicates that the command was rejected |

Table 25.6 Arguments of the LinkExecute event

## Example Syntax

```
Sub Form_LinkExecute (CmdStr As String, Cancel As Integer)
    Cancel = 0                       'Defines Cancel to return that command was
                                     'accepted
    Select Case UCase$(CmdStr)       'Format text of cmdstr in all uppercase characters
        Case "SETUP"                 'Checks if cmdstr equals "SETUP"
            WindowState = 2          'Maximize window
            Cls                      'Clear screen and reset CurrentX and CurrentY
                                     'coordinates
            BackColor = QBColor(1)   'Make the background blue
        Case "DATE" 'Checks if cmdstr equals "DATE"
            Print Date$,             'Prints the date on the form
            Print                    'Puts a space after the date
            Print                    'Puts a space after the date
        Case "TIME" 'Checks if cmdstr equals "TIME"
            Print Time$,             'Prints the time on the form
            Print                    'Puts a space after the time
            Print                    'Puts a space after the time
        Case "CLOSE"                 'Checks if cmdstr equals "CLOSE"
            Hide                     'Hides the current form on the screen
        Case "SHOW" 'Checks if cmdstr equals "SHOW"
            Form1.Show               'Displays the form on the screen
        Case Else                    'Otherwise
            Cancel = -1              'The Cancel variable changed to indicate that
    End Select                       'command isn't accepted
End Sub
```

## Description

The LinkExecute event contains a library of possible commands that may be sent to this form through a DDE link. There are two possible arguments for this event, CmdStr and Cancel. Any command sent through a link is stored to the text string CmdStr and may then be accessed to determine what kind of action should take place. When the command string sent does not match any of the criteria listed in a LinkExecute event, the Cancel variable changes to 1 to indicate that the command was rejected. This informs the sending application that the command was not valid for this application.

In the example syntax, the LinkExecute event contains a list of commands that may be sent to its parent form. Any commands that are sent to the form through a DDE link will be checked to see if they match any of the acceptable commands. If a match is made, then the command is processed. Otherwise, the Cancel variable changes to 1 and the sending application is informed that the sent commands were rejected.

### Example

In the DDE project, the LinkExecute event of the DDE form defines which command strings may be sent to that form through a DDE link. In this case, the only valid command string is GRAPH. The GRAPH command string is sent by the picture field on Document1 of Word for Windows. This command obtains the contents of the Graph Picture box with the LinkSend method connected to the GRAPH command string. Every time WinWord sends the command string GRAPH, this routine updates the picture field on Document1.

### Comments

The actions listed in the LinkExecute event of a form have no effect on the use of the LinkExecute method in the same form.

# LinkExecute Method

### Objects Affected

| | | | | |
|---|---|---|---|---|
| Check | Clipboard | Combo | Command | Dbug |
| Dir | Drive | File | Form | Frame |
| ▶ Label | List | Menu | Option | ▶ Picture |
| Printer | Screen | Scroll | ▶ Text | Timer |

### Purpose

The LinkExecute method transmits commands to another application through a DDE link. This method permits the client application in a DDE link conversation to control the behavior of the server application. Commands sent with the LinkExecute method have the same effect as if the user entered them. Table 25.7 summarizes the arguments of the LinkExecute method.

### General Syntax

```
control.LinkExecute cmdstr$
```

| Argument | Effect |
|---|---|
| control | Text box, picture box, label control's CtlName property |
| CmdStr | Command string for the client application to send to the server application to process |

Table 25.7 Arguments of the LinkExecute method

## Example Syntax

```
Sub Form_Load ()
Startup:
    On Error GoTo OpenWinWord              'Sets error trap to OpenWinWord
    Text1.LinkTimeout = -1                 'Turns off Timeout error
    Text1.LinkMode = 0                     'Sets LinkMode property to none
    Text1.LinkTopic = "WinWord|System"     'Sets the Topic for the DDE link
    Text1.LinkMode = 2                     'Opens a cold link with Winword
    Text1.LinkExecute "[FileClose 2]"      'Closes the current file without
                                           'saving it
    Text1.LinkExecute "[FileNew 0,""Letter""]" 'Opens new file with Letter Template
    AppActivate "Microsoft Word - Document2" 'Gives the focus to Word
    End                                    'Ends program
                                           'OpenWinWord:
    If Err = 282 Then                      'Checks if WinWord wasn't in memory
                                           'causing
        x = Shell("Winword.exe", 3)        'the error making it necessary to start
        Resume Startup                     'Winword. Returns to the program's
                                           'beginning
    Else
        Error Err                          'Forces display of error message.
    End If
End Sub
```

## Description

A LinkExecute method consists of two arguments that identify the DDE links. The link is identified by the CtlName of the text box, picture box, or label that is connected to the other application. Any commands that are sent through the link will be contained in the CmdStr string of a LinkExecute method.

The example syntax contains a routine connected to the Text1 text box that sends a series of commands to Microsoft Word for Windows through a DDE link. These commands result in the opening of a new file based upon the Letter template. When this form opens Word for Windows, the user no longer has to press File, New, and then choose Letter from the list of templates. The program does this automatically and then exits.

### The LinkTopic Property

In order for a LinkExecute method to be processed, a link must first be established with the other application. A control or form's LinkTopic property provides the name of the other application along with the topic, which is normally the file name. In this case, the System Topic is used instead of the file name, because the first command sent by the LinkExecute method closes the open file. As a result, the link is maintained with WinWord without being dependent on which document is open at the time. This is a very useful technique to use when dealing with multiple documents in WinWord or any other DDE-supporting Windows application.

### The LinkTimeout Property

The LinkExecute method requires the proper setting of the LinkTimeout property of the control or form. The LinkTimeout property determines the amount of time that a control will wait for a response from the other application. When the value of the LinkTimeout property is set to -1, the control or form will wait indefinitely until the user presses the Alt key on the keyboard or the application responds. In the example syntax, the LinkTimeout property is set to -1 to prevent any delays in execution from generating an error.

### The LinkMode Property

The LinkMode property determines what type of link is to be established. Since a form may not serve as a client in a DDE link, the LinkExecute method requires a link between a control and another application. In some cases, the link may only be established with a particular type of control. For example, picture files (*.PCX, *.TIF, and so on) would only be linkable into picture boxes. Sometimes, the other application may only support a cold link (2). With the example syntax, the link may not be established with a picture box instead of a text box. WinWord 1.1 only supports cold (2) links, making it necessary to specify only this kind of link when sending LinkExecute methods to WinWord 1.1 (the new version of WinWord, Word for Windows 2.0, now supports hot links).

### Error Trapping

The Err function, Error Statement, and On Error Statement are an important part of the operation of a DDE link subroutine. Through the use of the On Error statement On Error Goto WinWord, the code provides for the possibility that WinWord is not loaded when this program is run. If WinWord is not running, an error is generated and code in the OpenWinWord section is processed. This routine checks if the error regards the absence of WinWord. If WinWord is not present, then the Shell function loads Winword into memory. After WinWord has been loaded, the link is established and the LinkExecute command strings are transmitted. An error message displays on the screen when an unanticipated error occurs. These error-related functions and statements are summarized in Appendix A, *Visual Basic Language Summary*.

## Example

The LinkExecute method is used extensively in the DDE project at the end of this section. When the DDE and Sales_Display forms are loaded, the subfunction SetupExcel utilizes the LinkExecute method to set up Excel's Sheet1 with data and generates a graph with Excel's own macro language. After the user presses the command button Create Report, the Create_Report_Click event generates a report on Document1 of WinWord by sending its own macro commands through the DDE link with the LinkExecute method.

## Comments

Notice that the commands sent in the LinkExecute method in the example are placed between square brackets, and any quotation marks placed within them are modified to double quotation marks. This is a requirement for sending macro commands to Microsoft Word and Excel for Windows.

# LinkItem Property

## Objects Affected

| | | | | |
|---|---|---|---|---|
| Check | Clipboard | Combo | Command | Dbug |
| Dir | Drive | File | Form | Frame |
| ▶ Label | List | Menu | Option | ▶ Picture |
| Printer | Screen | Scroll | ▶ Text | Timer |

## Purpose

The LinkItem property references the data transmitted through a DDE link from the client application to the server application. This property corresponds to the Item argument of a DDE link and may be changed without closing down an active link. When a Visual Basic form is the server in a DDE link, the LinkItem property of the form contains the CtlName of the control identified in the item of the DDE link. Table 25.8 summarizes the arguments of the LinkItem property.

## General Syntax

[form.]{label|picturebox|textbox}.LinkItem[=stringexpression$]

| Argument | Description |
|---|---|
| form | FormName of the form |
| label | CtlName of the label box |
| picture | CtlName of the picture box |
| textbox | CtlName property of the text box |
| stringexpression$ | Identifies the item of a DDE link |

Table 25.8 Arguments of the LinkItem property

## Example Syntax

```
Sub Form_Load ()
Startup:
    On Error GoTo OpenQE                'Sets Error trap to OpenQE
    Text1.LinkTimeout = -1              'Turns off Timeout error
    Text1.LinkMode = 0                  'Sets LinkMode to none
    Text1.LinkTopic = "QE|System"       'Sets the Topic for DDE link
    Text1.LinkItem = "ALL"              'Sets the Item for DDE Link
    Text1.LinkMode = 2                  'Opens a cold link with Q+E
    Text1.LinkExecute "[Open('C:\EXCEL\QE\EMP.DBF')]"  'Opens Data file
    Text1.LinkExecute "[Open.Index('C:\EXCEL\QE\EMPLNAME.NDX',TRUE)]"
                                        'Opens index file
    Text1.LinkExecute "[SAVE.QUERY.AS('C:\EXCEL\QE\EMP.QEF')]"'Saves settings to query
                                        'file
    Text1.LinkMode = 0                  'Closes link with Q+E.
    Text1.LinkTopic = "QE|C:\EXCEL\QE\EMP.DBF" 'Changes Topic for DDE link.
    Text1.LinkItem = "C:\EXCEL\QE\EMP.QEF" 'Changes Item for DDE link.
    Text1.LinkMode = 2                  'Opens a cold link with Q+E.
```

```
        Text1.LinkExecute "[Open('C:\EXCEL\QE\EMP.QEF')]"  'Opens Query file.
        End                                    'Closes program.
OpenQE:
        If Err = 282 Then                      'Checks if Q+E wasn't in memory causing
            x = Shell("QE.exe", 3)             'the error making it necessary to start
            Resume Startup                     'Q+E. Returns to the program's beginning
        Else
            Error Err                          'Forces display of error message
        End If
End Sub
```

## Description

Begin the specification of the LinkItem property with the name of the control (which must be a text box, picture box, or label). A LinkItem property's Stringexpression$ argument contains a string expression depending on which application is being linked with the Visual Basic application. This value must be a string expression of up to 255 characters.

In the example syntax, the LinkItem of the text box Text1 is defined with two text strings. In the first link, the LinkItem is defined as All. This is a Q+E specification for DDE items, which include the entire database file listed in the topic. In the second link, the LinkItem is defined with the path and name of the Q+E query file EMP.QEF. Notice that the file still needs to be loaded, even though a link has been established with the query file.

Details of the DDE link will vary with the application being linked with. For example, links with Microsoft Excel may define the LinkItem property with the location of the cells that contain the appropriate data. In links with Pioneer Q+E, the topic may be the entire data base specified in the topic by defining the LinkItem property as All or the appropriate query file name. These settings are used in the following example to display the contents of the EMP.DBF file on the screen.

### The LinkTopic Property

The LinkTopic property defines which items may be chosen for a DDE link. The available items also depend on which application you are linking to the Visual Basic application. When the DDE link's topic is set to System, the LinkItem may be set to any available part of the application. In the example syntax, the LinkItem is set at All when the LinkTopic property is System. After the LinkTopic is changed to C:\EXCEL\QE\EMP.DBF, the list of available items is reduced to its query files. For this reason, the newly created query file C:\EXCEL\QE\EMP.QEF is specified.

### The LinkMode Property

The LinkMode property determines what type of link is to be established. Since a form may not serve as a client in a DDE link, the LinkExecute method requires a link between a control and another application. In some cases, the link may only be established with a particular type of control. For example, picture files (*.PCX, *.TIF, and so on) would only be linkable to picture boxes. Sometimes the other application may only support a cold link (2). With the example syntax, the link may not be established with a picture box instead of a text box. Q+E 3.0 only supports cold (2) links in this particular setup. This makes it necessary to specify only this kind of link when sending LinkExecute method expressions to Q+E 3.0.

## Error Trapping

The Err function, Error Statement, and On Error Statement are important parts of the operation of a DDE link subroutine. These error-related functions and statements are summarized in Appendix A, *Visual Basic Language Summary*. Through the use of the On Error Statement On Error Goto OpenQE, the code provides for the possibility that Q+E is not loaded when this program is run. If Q+E is not running, an error is generated and code in the OpenQE section is processed. This routine checks if the error involves the absence of Q+E. If Q+E is not present, then the Shell function loads Q+E into memory. After Q+E has been loaded, the link is established and the LinkExecute command strings are transmitted. An error message displays on the screen when an unanticipated error occurs.

## WinWord System Items

Three items may be used with the topic System in Microsoft Word for Windows: SysItems, Topics, and Formats. The SysItems item produces a list of the possible items that may be used with the System topic. The Topics item provides a list of the open documents that includes the path names. A Formats item returns a list of all of the Clipboard formats supported by Word for Windows. This is very important information to keep in mind when setting up a link with WinWord. Use Table 25.9 as a reference for obtaining information about Microsoft WinWord.

| Item | Description |
| --- | --- |
| SysItems | Returns a list of the available Items that may be used with the System topic |
| Topics | Returns a list of available open documents in WinWord |
| Formats | Returns a list of available Clipboard formats supported by WinWord |

**Table 25.9 List of possible items for the topic System with Microsoft Word for Windows**

## Excel System Items

There are seven items that may be used with the topic System in Microsoft Excel for Windows. They are SysItems, Topics, Status, Formats, Selection, Protocols, and EditEnvItems. The SysItems item produces a list of the possible items that may be used with the System topic. The Topics item provides a list of the available topics and the path and file names of the open spreadsheets. The Status item returns the text Ready when the Excel application is not busy with an operation of some kind. A Formats item returns a list of all of the Clipboard formats supported by Excel for Windows. The Selection item indicates the reference location of the currently active cell or cells, including the name of the spreadsheet. Protocols items display the types of DDE link protocols that Excel supports, including StdFileEditing and Embedding. The items are summarized in Table 25.10.

| Item | Description |
|------|-------------|
| SysItems | Returns a list of the available Items that may be used with the System Topic |
| Topics | Returns a list of the available Topics, which includes the presently open spreadsheets in Excel |
| Status | Returns the text Ready when Excel is not processing a DDE link action |
| Formats | Returns a list of the Clipboard formats supported by Excel |
| Selection | Returns the reference of the currently active cell or cells on a spreadsheet |
| Protocols | Returns the DDE protocols that Excel supports: StdFileEditing and Embedding |
| EditEnvItems | StdHostNames, StdTargetDevice, and StdDocDimensions |

**Table 25.10 List of possible Items for the topic System with Microsoft Excel for Windows**

### Q+E System Items

Eight items may be utilized with the topic  System  in Pioneer Q+E for Windows. They are SysItems, Topics, Formats, Status, LogOn, LogOff, Sources, and Tables. The SysItems item produces a list of the items that may be used with the System topic. The Topics item provides a list of the available topics and the path and file names of the open database files. The Formats item returns a list of all of the Clipboard formats supported by Excel for Windows. The Status item returns the text Ready when Q+E is not busy with an operation of some kind. Both the LogOn and LogOff Items provide information about whether Q+E is presently connected to a SQL server. The Sources item returns the database formats that Q+E supports. These items are summarized in Table 25.11.

| Item | Description |
|------|-------------|
| SysItems | Returns a list of the available items that may be used with the System topic |
| Topics | Returns a list of the available topics, which includes the presently open files in Q+E |
| Formats | Returns a list of the Clipboard formats supported by Q+E |
| Status | Returns the text Ready when Q+E is not processing a DDE link action |
| LogOn | Returns if Q+E is logged into a SQL server |
| LogOff | Returns if Q+E is not logged into a SQL server |
| Sources | Returns the data base formats that Q+E supports and can import |

**Table 25.11 List of possible items for the topic System with Pioneer Q+E for Windows**

## Example

In the DDE project at the end of this section, the LinkItem property is used to specify to what cell on Sheet1 of Excel one of the text boxes on the Sales_Display form is connected. When the Sales_Display form is first loaded, the LinkItem of each text box is set to the default cell references. This property changes when the user presses the command button labeled Display Figures. Depending upon which of the option boxes of the control array Sales_Figures is selected, the Display_Figures_Click event determines which cell to link each text box to. No matter how many times during the operation of the program the LinkItem property changes, the DDE link remains open and simply changes its focus to the newly designated cell. Notice that the LinkTopic of each text box Excel|Sheet1 remains the same.

## Comments

The example displayed in this section was written with the version of Q+E 3.0 that is shipped with Microsoft Excel and uses the EMP.DBF and EMPLNAME.NDX files that were shipped with it. This example may not work with other versions of Q+E.

# LinkMode Property

## Objects Affected

| | | | | |
|---|---|---|---|---|
| Check | Clipboard | Combo | Command | Dbug |
| Dir | Drive | File | ▶ Form | Frame |
| ▶ Label | List | Menu | Option | ▶ Picture |
| Printer | Screen | Scroll | ▶ Text | Timer |

## Purpose

The LinkMode property determines the type of DDE link to establish and then creates this type of link with the application, topic, and item specified in the LinkTopic and LinkItem properties. When the LinkMode property of a form is changed, the form's LinkMode property indicates whether a DDE link may or may not be established with the form. If the LinkMode of a form is modified, then the setting of the control's LinkMode property creates either a hot or a cold link with another application, or an open link is closed. Table 25.12 summarizes the arguments of the LinkMode property. Tables 25.13 and 25.14 summarize the values and effects of the LinkMode property.

## General Syntax

`[form.][control.]LinkMode[=mode%]`

| Argument | Description |
|---|---|
| form | FormName property of the form |
| control | CtlName property of the control |
| mode% | Current status of the LinkMode property |

**Table 25.12 Arguments of the LinkMode property**

| mode% | Effect |
|-------|--------|
| 0 | None (Default). No DDE Link established |
| 1 | Hot. The control is updated each time the linked data changes |
| 2 | Cold. The control is updated only when the LinkRequest method is used |

**Table 25.13 Values and effects of the LinkMode property of a text box, picture box, or label**

| mode% | Effect |
|-------|--------|
| 0 | No DDE links may be established with this form |
| 1 | Server (default). Permits any text box, picture box, or labels on the form to be specified as the LinkItem so that they may supply data to the client application |

**Table 25.14 Values and effects of the LinkMode property of a form**

## Example Syntax

```
Sub Form_Load ()
Startup:
    On Error GoTo OpenXL                                      'Sets Error trap to OpenXL
    Text1.LinkMode = 0                                        'Sets LinkMode to none
    Text1.LinkTopic = "Excel|Sheet1"                          'Sets Text1's Topic
    Text1.LinkItem = "R1C1"                                   'Sets Text1's Item
    Text1.LinkMode = 2                                        'Opens Cold DDE link
    Text1.LinkExecute "[Select(""R1C1"")]"                    'Selects first cell
    Text1.LinkExecute "[Formula(1)]"                          'Inserts value in first cell
    Text1.LinkExecute "[Select(""R1C2:R1C4"")]"              'Selects cells
    Text1.LinkExecute "[Formula.Fill(""=RC[-1]+1"")]"        'Inserts formula in cells
    Text1.LinkExecute "[Select(""R2C1:R10C1"")]"            'Selects cells
    Text1.LinkExecute "[Formula.Fill(""=R[-1]C+100"")]"     'Inserts formula in cells
    Text1.LinkExecute "[Select(""R2C2:R10C2"")]"            'Selects cells
    Text1.LinkExecute "[Formula.Fill(""=R[-1]C+R[-1]C"")]"  'Inserts formula in cells
    Text1.LinkExecute "[Select(""R2C3:R10C3"")]"            'Selects cells
    Text1.LinkExecute "[Formula.Fill(""=R[-1]C*2"")]"       'Inserts formula in cells
    Text1.LinkExecute "[Select(""R2C4:R10C4"")]"            'Selects cells
    Text1.LinkExecute "[Formula.Fill(""=R[-1]C*2"")]"       'Inserts formula in cells
    Text1.LinkExecute "[Select(""R1C1:R10C4"")]"            'Selects all the cells
    Text1.LinkExecute "[New(2,3)]"                            'Creates a new chart
    Picture1.LinkMode = 0                                     'Sets Picture1's LinkMode
    Picture1.LinkTopic = "Excel|Chart1"                       'Sets Picture1's Topic
    Picture1.LinkMode = 1                                     'Opens Hot link
    Form1.Show                                                'Displays Form1
    Exit Sub                                                  'Exits subroutine OpenXL:
    If Err = 282 Then                                         'Checks if Excel wasn't in
                                                              'memory causing
        x = Shell("Excel.exe", 3)                             'the error making it necessary
                                                              'to start
        Resume Startup                                        'Excel. Returns to the
                                                              'program's beginning
    Else
        Error Err                                             'Forces display of error
                                                              'message
    End If
```

## Description

The LinkMode property controls whether a DDE link exists and what type of link it is, if it does exist. This property may be changed at run time or design time. The value of the LinkMode property determines whether a form may be part of a DDE link. The LinkMode property establishes the presence or absence of an active link as well as the type of the link. When there is no link, the value is 0 (none). An active link may be either hot (1) or cold (2). Begin the LinkMode specification with the name of the control (which must be a label, text box, or picture box) or the name of its parent form.

The example syntax demonstrates the two types of LinkMode links, hot and cold, in establishing a link to an Excel spreadsheet, which is shown and updated in the picture box. Note that the contents of the Text1 text box are never updated because the LinkRequest method is not used to update the cold link. Each time the data on the Excel spreadsheet is changed, the chart on Picture1 is changed automatically by the hot link.

### Using the LinkTopic and LinkItem Properties with Forms

The LinkMode property works with the LinkTopic and LinkItem properties of the form. With a form, the LinkTopic property determines the name for a client application to use in order to establish a DDE link. A form's LinkItem specifies which control on the form will be connected to the client application through a DDE link. This property contains the CtlName property of this indicated control. In this way, the server form has some control of the behavior of links that are established by other applications. The LinkTopic property of an active DDE link may not be changed. In contrast, the LinkItem property may be changed as many times as necessary.

### Using the LinkTopic and LinkItem Properties with Controls

The LinkMode property functions with the help of the settings of the LinkTopic and LinkItem properties of the same control. With the LinkTopic property, the control, the application name, and topic (usually the file name or System) provide the information needed to establish a DDE link. A control's LinkItem property indicates which part of the server application the control will be connected to. In the example syntax, the first link's LinkTopic (Text1 text box) is Excel|Sheet1 and the LinkItem is R1C1. Notice that the second link changes to the picture box and that the LinkTopic is Excel|Chart1 with no LinkTopic. Neither of these links has an effect on the other settings in regard to their LinkTopic and LinkItem properties.

### The LinkError Event

The LinkError event specifies what happens when a client application initiates an action that generates an error. The LinkError event returns the error in the ErrLink variable which may then be used to specify what the difficulty is. This is an excellent method for handling errors generated by applications with their DDE LinkMode properties set to server (1).

## Example

In the DDE project at the end of this chapter, the LinkMode property of each control establishes a DDE link with other applications and determines whether the link is hot or cold. At program startup, Excel is loaded into memory and a cold DDE links established between the label box First Quarter and the Excel spreadsheet. When the DDE and Sales_Display forms are loaded into memory at program startup, each of the text boxes on the Sales_Display form links to places on the Sheet1 spreadsheet of Excel. By changing the LinkMode property of each control to 2, a cold link is created between the text box and the cell on the spreadsheet indicated by the LinkItem of the text box. After the user presses the command button labeled Create Report, the Create_Report_Click event sets up a cold DDE link with WinWord. These examples demonstrate the creation and operation of cold DDE links.

When the DDE form is loaded into memory, the Load_Form event establishes a hot link between the Graph picture box and the Graph1 Sheet of Excel. This is done by setting the LinkMode property of the picture box to 1, which indicates a hot DDE link. With this hot Link, the Graph picture box will be updated each time a change is made to the Chart1 sheet.

## Comments

In some situations, a hot link may not be possible even though the application supports this kind of link.

# LinkOpen Event

## Objects Affected

| | | | | |
|---|---|---|---|---|
| Check | Clipboard | Combo | Command | Dbug |
| Dir | Drive | File | ▶ Form | Frame |
| ▶ Label | List | Menu | Option | ▶ Picture |
| Printer | Screen | Scroll | ▶ Text | Timer |

## Purpose

The LinkOpen event processes any actions that take place when a DDE link opens between a form, label, picture box, or text box and another program. A link may be opened by either a Visual Basic application or an external application. The LinkOpen event of the form triggers when another application establishes a DDE link. Tables 25.15 and 25.16 summarize the arguments and variables of the LinkOpen event.

## General Syntax

```
Sub form_LinkOpen (Cancel As Integer)
Sub ctlname_LinkOpen ([Index As Integer,]Cancel As Integer)
```

| Argument | Description |
|---|---|
| form | FormName property of the form |
| ctlname | CtlName property of the control |

**Table 25.15 Arguments of the LinkOpen event**

| Variable | Description |
|----------|-------------|
| index | Index value of the control in a control array with which the link is established |
| cancel | The value returned by this event determines whether or not a link is created. Any non-0 value results in the prevention of the activation of the DDE link. When the Cancel variable is not defined or is defined as 0, the link is permitted to be established |

**Table 25.16 Predefined variables of the LinkOpen event**

## Example Syntax

```
Sub Command1_Click ()
    Text1.LinkTimeout = -1                     'Turns off Timeout Error
    Text1.LinkMode = 0                         'Sets LinkMode to none
    Text1.LinkTopic = "Excel|System"          'Sets Topic
    Text1.LinkMode = 2                         'Opens a Cold Link
    Text1.LinkExecute "[File.Close(FALSE)]"   'Closes presently open file in Excel
    Text1.LinkMode = 0                         'Cuts the link with Excel
    End                                        'End Program
End Sub

Sub Text1_LinkOpen (Cancel As Integer)
    If Text1.Text = "No" Then                  'Checks the contents of Text box
        Cancel = 1                             'Indicates that DDE link is not
                                               'established
        Exit Sub                               'Exits the subroutine
    Else
        x = Shell("Excel",3)                   'Opens Excel
        Cancel = 0                             'Indicates that DDE link is established
    End If
End Sub
```

## Description

The LinkOpen event controls whether a link may be created between either a Visual Basic control and another application or another application and a Visual Basic form. Each LinkOpen event returns a value in the Cancel variable that permits or refuses a DDE link. When the LinkOpen event contains no code or the Cancel variable is 0, the link is permitted. If the Cancel variable is a non-0 value, the link is not established. Begin the specification of this event with the name of the control involved in the link, or the name of its parent form.

In the example syntax, the LinkOpen event of the text box tests whether the Text property contains the word No. As long as the Text box does not contain this word, the link is established. Notice that the expressions that are placed after the LinkMode property change are processed after the LinkOpen event is run.

### The LinkMode Property

When a DDE Link is created by setting the LinkMode property of a picture box, text box, or label to 1 (hot) or 2 (cold), the LinkOpen event of that control triggers. Do not place any commands that depend upon the link such as the LinkExecute, LinkRequest, and LinkPoke methods in the LinkOpen event. The actual link is not set up until the

LinkOpen event is finished processing. In cases where the Cancel variable is a non-0 value and the link is not created, any expressions that depend upon the link will result in an error. This is why the End Statement is placed after the definition of Cancel as 0 in the example syntax. Otherwise, the code that follows the LinkMode setting would generate an error.

### Access by an External Application

If the LinkMode property of a form is 1 (server), an external application may establish a DDE link with any text box, picture box, or label on the form. Any actions in the LinkOpen event process before the link is established. The Cancel value returned by the LinkOpen event indicates whether the link is permitted or denied. If the Cancel value is 0, the link is permitted. If the Cancel value is a non-0 value, the link is denied, generating an error message.

## Example

In the DDE project at the end of this section, the LinkOpen event determines if a DDE link will be opened and what happens prior to the opening of a DDE link. When the DDE link opens between the Graph picture box on the DDE form and the Chart1 sheet of Excel, the LinkOpen event of the picture box is processed. This event changes the MousePointer of the screen to an arrow and confirms that the link may be opened by setting the Cancel variable to 0.

## Comments

Any actions that depend on the link must wait until after the LinkOpen event is processed or an error will generate. This is because the link is not actually established with another application until the Cancel value is returned at the end of the LinkOpen event. If the event contains no actions, then the link is established normally. Otherwise, the definition of Cancel as any non-0 value prevents the link.

# LinkPoke Method

## Objects Affected

| | | | | |
|---|---|---|---|---|
| Check | Clipboard | Combo | Command | Dbug |
| Dir | Drive | File | Form | Frame |
| ▶ Label | List | Menu | Option | ▶ Picture |
| Printer | Screen | Scroll | ▶ Text | Timer |

## Purpose

The LinkPoke method inserts the contents of a Visual Basic client control into the item specified in the server application. This method temporarily reverses the flow of information. A normal link transfers data from the server to the client when the link is hot or the LinkRequest method is utilized. With the LinkPoke method, the client provides information to the server. This change in the passage of data is only temporary and has no effect on the normal operation of the link either before or after the LinkPoke method. Table 25.17 summarizes the argument of the LinkPoke method.

## General Syntax

```
control.LinkPoke
```

| Argument | Description |
|----------|-------------|
| control | CtlName property of the control |

**Table 25.17 Argument of the LinkPoke method**

## Example Syntax

```
Sub Command1_Click ()
Startup:
    On Error Goto OpenXL              'Sets Error trap to OpenXL
    Text1.Text = "Data Transfered"    'Defines Text property of Text box
    Text1.LinkTopic = "Excel|Sheet1"  'Defines Topic
    Text1.LinkItem = "R1C1"           'Defines Item
    Text1.LinkTimeout = -1            'Turns off Timeout error
    Text1.LinkMode = 2                'Opens a cold link
    Text1.LinkPoke                    'Inserts information into "R1C1"
    Text1.LinkMode = 0                'Closes the link
    Exit Sub                          'Exits the subroutine
OpenXL:
    If Err = 282 Then                 'Checks if Excel wasn't in memory causing
        x = Shell("Excel.exe", 3)     'the error making it necessary to start
        Resume Startup                'Excel. Returns to the program's beginning
    Else
        Error Err                     'Forces display of error message
    End If
End Sub
```

## Description

A LinkPoke method transfers the contents of the control in the control argument to the item identified by the linked application. Exactly which control is affected by this expression is determined by the Control argument of the LinkPoke method and the control that establishes the link. The Control argument is the CtlName property of the control involved in the DDE link. When the specified control is a picture box, the contents of the Picture property are transferred to the item. If the control is a text box, the contents of the Text property are moved to the item. With a label box, the Caption property is transmitted to the item.

In the example syntax, the LinkPoke method places the contents of the text box Text1 into the Excel spreadsheet's R1C1 cell when the user presses the command button.

### The LinkTopic Property

Each LinkPoke method requires that the LinkTopic property contain the name of the application and the topic into which the data is being inserted. The application must support DDE links. The topic is normally the name of the file. In the example syntax, the LinkTopic is defined as Excel|Sheet1. This indicates that the data will be placed somewhere on Excel's default Sheet1.

### The LinkItem Property

The LinkItem property of the control determines the exact destination of the data that the LinkPoke method inserts in the Topic. A LinkItem may be changed at run time so that each LinkPoke method can place data in a new location in the topic. Without the LinkItem property of the control, the LinkPoke method will generate an error. In the example syntax, the data is placed in the R1C1 cell of the Sheet1 spreadsheet identified by the LinkItem property of the Text1 text box. This setting ensures that the words "Data Transferred" will be copied to the R1C1 cell.

### The LinkModeProperty

A LinkPoke method will work when the LinkMode property is set to hot (1) or cold (2). Even though a valid link is established with the LinkMode property, the LinkPoke method will not work unless both the LinkTopic and LinkItem properties are set to valid elements of the other application that may receive the contents of the indicated control. For example, if two Visual Basic applications are linked through a picture box on the client and a text box on the server, an error will occur.

### Example

In the DDE project at the end of this section, the LinkPoke method appears in the Change events of the text boxes on the Sales_Display form. This method ensures the correct display of any changes made by the user to the figures shown.

# LinkRequest Method

### Objects Affected

| | | | | |
|---|---|---|---|---|
| Check | Clipboard | Combo | Command | Dbug |
| Dir | Drive | File | Form | Frame |
| ▶ Label | List | Menu | Option | ▶ Picture |
| Printer | Screen | Scroll | ▶ Text | Timer |

### Purpose

The LinkRequest method updates a cold link between a Visual Basic control and another application. Hot DDE links between applications do not require this method, as this data is updated automatically. Table 25.18 summarizes the argument of the LinkRequest method.

### General Syntax

```
control.LinkRequest
```

| Argument | Description |
|---|---|
| control | CtlName property of the control |

Table 25.18 Argument of the LinkRequest method

## Example Syntax

```
Sub Command1_Click ()
Startup:
    On Error GoTo OpenWinWord                'Sets error trap to OpenWinWord
    Text1.LinkTimeout = -1                   'Turns off Timeout error
    Text1.LinkMode = 0                       'Sets LinkMode property to none
    Text1.LinkTopic = "WinWord|System"       'Sets the Topic for the DDE link
    If Text1.Text <> "Text1" Then            'Checks if Text box has default text
        Text1.LinkItem = "SysItems"          'Sets the Item for the DDE link
    ElseIf Text1.LinkItem = "SysItems" Then  'Checks the setting of LinkItem
        Text1.LinkItem = "Topics"            'Sets the Item for the DDE link
    ElseIf Text1.LinkItem = "Topics" Then    'Checks the setting of LinkItem
        Text1.LinkItem = "Formats"           'Sets the Item for the DDE link
    End If
    Text1.LinkMode = 2                       'Opens a cold link with Winword
    Text1.LinkRequest                        'Updates the Text1 text box
    End                                      'Ends program
OpenWinWord:
    If Err = 282 Then                        'Checks if WinWord wasn't in memory causing
        x = Shell("Winword.exe", 3)          'the error making it necessary to start
        Resume Startup                       'Winword. Returns to the program's beginning
    Else
        Error Err                            'Forces display of error message
    End If
End Sub
```

## Description

A LinkRequest method transfers an item's contents to a control in a linked application. Exactly which control is affected by this expression is determined by the Control argument of the LinkRequest method and the control with which the link is established. The Control argument is the CtlName property of the control involved in the DDE link. When the control is a picture box, the Picture property is updated by the item. If the control is a text box, the contents of the Text property change to match the item. With a label box, the Caption property is modified to contain the item's text.

In the example syntax, the LinkRequest method displays a list of the available items for a DDE conversation with the System topic when the user presses the Command1 command button. If the user presses the command button a second time, the LinkRequest method returns the name and path of the open documents in WinWord. When the user presses the Command1 command button a third time, the LinkRequest method returns the clipboard formats supported by Word for Windows.

### The LinkTopic Property

The LinkTopic property of a control indicates the topic to use for the DDE link. Each topic serves as a unique identifier along with the name of the application with which the link is being established. This topic may not be changed while the link is active. In the example syntax, the topic is set to System so that the different items available for that topic may be displayed in the text box with the LinkRequest method.

### The LinkItem Property

The LinkItem property of the control determines exactly where the LinkRequest method obtains the data to insert into the control. A LinkItem may be changed at run time so that each time that a LinkRequest method is triggered, the contents of another source are inserted in the control. Without the setting of the LinkItem property of the control, the LinkRequest method will generate an error. In the example syntax, the LinkItem is changed twice, reflecting the current contents of the Text property of the Text1 text box.

### The LinkMode Property

You establish a cold link between a control and another application for two possible reasons. If the other application is only capable of supporting a cold DDE link, then this is the only means of establishing this kind of link. The other reason to set up a cold link with another application is to indicate when the link will be updated and when it will not. These are the purposes for which the LinkRequest method was designed. In this way, the LinkMode property determines whether the LinkRequest method will be necessary by setting up hot (1) or cold (2) links.

### Example

In the DDE project at the end of this section, the LinkRequest method updates the contents of the text boxes on the Sales_Display form. Since there is a cold DDE link between the text boxes and the cells on Excel's Sheet1 spreadsheet, the LinkRequest method is needed to display the contents of the indicated cells. When the user presses the command button labeled Display Figures, the LinkRequest method changes the contents of the text boxes to the contents of the cell indicated by the LinkItem property.

### Comments

Use the System topic with the items listed in Tables 25.9, 25.10, and 25.11 to discover what items are available for the LinkRequest method to obtain information from.

# LinkSend Method

## Objects Affected

| | | | | |
|---|---|---|---|---|
| Check | Clipboard | Combo | Command | Dbug |
| Dir | Drive | File | Form | Frame |
| Label | List | Menu | Option | ▶ Picture |
| Printer | Screen | Scroll | Text | Timer |

## Purpose

The LinkSend method transfers the contents of a picture box on a form to another application. This method is only useful when the DDE link is established by another application that functions as the client. The form that the picture box is on acts as the server. This method is necessary for updating the client application, no matter whether the link created is hot or cold. Table 25.19 summarizes the argument of the LinkSend method.

## General Syntax

```
control.LinkSend
```

| Argument | Description |
|----------|-------------|
| control | CtlName property of control |

Table 25.19 Argument of the LinkSend method

## Example Syntax

```
Sub Form_LinkExecute (CmdStr As String, Cancel As Integer)
    Cancel = 0                          'Expression returns that command was accepted
    Select Case UCase$(cmdStr)          'Makes all of the text of command upper case
        Case "[UPDATE]"                 'Checks if command string is UPDATE
            Picture1.LinkTimeout = -1   'Turns off timeout error
            Picture1.LinkSend           'Updates the contents of other application
        Case Else                       'Otherwise
            Cancel = 1                  'Expression returns that command wasn't
                                        'accepted
    End Select
End Sub
```

## Description

The LinkSend method transfers the contents of the picture box control to the linked client application. The control argument of the LinkSend method identifies the picture box with its CtlName property.

In the example syntax, the LinkSend method updates the linked application that sends the Update command through the DDE link. The item on the client application receives the updated picture. This is an important possible use of this method that determines when a picture on another application needs updating.

### The LinkExecute Event

The LinkExecute event is an excellent location for the LinkSend method to update the picture on a client application. In the example syntax, the word UPDATE resets the contents of the picture on the client application that sends the command. This is a good method for allowing the other application to indicate when the picture on it needs to be updated.

## Example

In the DDE project at the end of this section, the LinkSend method updates the picture field on the Document1 file of WinWord. Each time an application sends the word GRAPH to the DDE form, the LinkExecute event of the DDE form finds this word and uses the LinkSend method to update the linked picture field in WinWord. Notice that the LinkSend method is necessary for displaying the picture in the WinWord document.

## Comments

Whether a hot or cold link is established with a form has no effect on the updating of a picture, as this depends on a picture box control.

# LinkTimeout Property

## Objects Affected

| | | | | |
|---|---|---|---|---|
| Check | Clipboard | Combo | Command | Dbug |
| Dir | Drive | File | Form | Frame |
| ▶ Label | List | Menu | Option | ▶ Picture |
| Printer | Screen | Scroll | ▶ Text | Timer |

## Purpose

The LinkTimeout property of a picture box, text box, or label indicates how long a Visual Basic application needs to wait for a response from another application involved in a DDE link. A control's LinkTimeout property only affects the operation of a DDE link in which the control is the client and the other application is the server. Table 25.20 summarizes the arguments of the LinkTimeout property.

## General Syntax

[form.][label|picturebox|textbox].LinkTimeout[=Duration%]

| Argument | Description |
|---|---|
| control | The CtlName property of the picture box, text box, or label control |
| form | The FormName of the form being affected |
| duration% | The interval specified for the Timeout property |

**Table 25.20 Arguments of the LinkTimeout property**

## Example Syntax

```
Sub Form_Load ()
Startup:
    On Error GoTo OpenWinWord          'Sets error trap to OpenWinWord
    Label1.LinkTimeout = 50            'Sets Timeout interval to 100 seconds
    Label1.LinkMode = 0                'Sets LinkMode property to none
    Label1.LinkTopic = "WinWord|System" 'Sets the Topic for the DDE link
    Label1.LinkMode = 2                'Opens a cold link with Winword
    Label1.LinkTimeout = -1            'Turns off timeout interval
    Label1.LinkExecute "[FileClose 2]" 'Closes the current file without saving it
    Label1.LinkExecute "[FileOpen]"    'Opens the file open dialog box
    End                                'Ends program
OpenWinWord:
    If Err = 282 Then                  'Checks if WinWord wasn't in memory causing
        x = Shell("Winword.exe", 3)    'the error making it necessary to start
        Resume Startup                 'Winword. Returns to the program's beginning
    Else
        Error Err                      'Forces display of error message.
    End If
End Sub
```

## Description

The LinkTimeout property of a picture box, text box, or label sets the length of time that a link remains open without a response from the other application. The control argument of a LinkTimeout property expression contains the CtlName property of the control.

A control's LinkTimeout property is adjustable up or down according to the time that the other application needs to process the commands sent through the link for it to process. Increases in the value of the Timeout property increase the amount of time that the control will wait. Decreases in the value of the Timeout property shorten the time an application waits for a response. An error generates if there is no response from the other application in the time specified by the LinkTimeout property of the control.

A control's LinkTimeout property duration% argument defines the amount of time to wait. The duration is measured in tenths of a second, so the default value of 50 represents 5 seconds. Changing the duration% variable to -1 ensures that the control will wait indefinitely for the other application to respond. The example syntax changes the Timeout property of the label control both before and after establishing the link. First, the value is increased from 50 to 100. Next, the Timeout property is modified to -1, disabling the timeout error.

In the example syntax, the Timeout property is initially 100. This routine turns off the timeout error by changing the LinkTimeout property to -1. This prevents the display of any errors created by the opening of the FileOpen dialog box if the visual basic application is not closed quickly enough.

### The On Error Statement

The On Error Statement sets up an error-detection system to trap any errors generated at run time. An error-trapping system may be designed to trap specific errors or general errors. For example, your program can anticipate an error when a LinkMode property change attempts to create a link with an unloaded application. In the example syntax, the first line in the Form_Load event directs any errors to the label OpenWinWord. If an error was caused by the fact that WinWord was not loaded in memory, the error trap loads WinWord. If the error is not recognized, the Error Err results in the display of the error message on the screen. See Appendix A, *Visual Basic Language Summary*, for a summary of the On Error Statement and other error-related features.

### The LinkExecute Method

When the LinkExecute method sends commands through the link to the server application, the value of the Timeout property determines how long the client application will wait for a response from the server application. In cases where the server application needs extra time to process the commands sent to it with the LinkExecute method, increase the LinkTimeout property setting to reflect this need. The example syntax completely disables the LinkTimeout property by setting it to -1. This prevents the timeout error from being generated and allows the processing of the End Statement. This is necessary because WinWord's FileOpen command displays a dialog box that normally prevents the processing of the commands that follow the LinkExecute command.

## Example

In the DDE project at the end of this section, the LinkTimeout property of each form and control has a direct affect on the operation of the established DDE links. At design time, all of these properties remain at their default settings. If there are any problems with the amount of time allowed for each control, then increase the number until enough time is provided for the DDE link operations listed for that control. On some slower machines, this may be necessary or an error will be generated if the other application fails to respond in the specified amount of time.

## Comments

The Timeout property of one control is unaffected by the Timeout property of another control.

# LinkTopic Property

## Objects Affected

| | | | | |
|---|---|---|---|---|
| Check | Clipboard | Combo | Command | Dbug |
| Dir | Drive | File | ▶ Form | Frame |
| ▶ Label | List | Menu | Option | ▶ Picture |
| Printer | Screen | Scroll | ▶ Text | Timer |

## Purpose

The LinkTopic property defines the application name and subject that uniquely identify a DDE link between a form, picture box, text box, or label and another application. A server form's LinkTopic specifies the topic name that another application must use to create a DDE link with the form. If this topic is not used, then any attempt to establish a link with the form will result in an error. When the control is the client of a DDE link, the LinkTopic determines the server application and topic of the link. Since a DDE link is uniquely identified by the application name and the topic, the LinkTopic property may not be changed on an active link. Table 25.21 summarizes the arguments of the LinkTopic property.

## General Syntax

```
[form.]LinkTopic[=Link$]
[label.]LinkTopic[=Link$]
[picturebox.]LinkTopic[=Link$]
[textbox.]LinkTopic[=Link$]
```

| Argument | Description |
|---|---|
| form | FormName property of the form |
| label | CtlName property of the label box |
| picture box | CtlName property of the picture box |
| text box | CtlName property of the text box |
| link$ | Application name and topic of a DDE link |

Table 25.21 Arguments of the LinkItem property

## Example Syntax

```
Sub Command1_Click ()
Startup:
    On Error Goto OpenApp
    If Text1.Text = "Winword" Then          'Checks the current contents of textbox
        Text1.LinkTopic = "Winword|System"  'Changes the DDE link Topic
        App$ = "Winword.exe"                'Defines App$ Text variable
    ElseIf Text1.Text = "Q+E" Then          'Checks the current contents of textbox
        Text1.LinkTopic = "QE|System"       'Changes the DDE link Topic
        App$ = "QE.exe"                     'Defines App$ Text variable
    ElseIf Text1.Text = "Excel" Then        'Checks the current contents of textbox
        Text1.LinkTopic = "Excel|System"    'Changes the DDE link Topic
        App$ = "Excel.exe"                  'Defines App$ Text variable
    Else
        End                                 'Ends Program
    End If
StartLink:
    Text1.LinkItem = "SysItems"             'Changes the DDE link Item
    Text1.LinkMode = 2                      'Establishes a link with the application
    Text1.LinkRequest                       'Updates the Text1 text box
OpenApp:
    If Err = 282 Then                       'Checks the err value
        x = Shell(App$, 3)                  'If the application was not in memory, then
        Resume StartLink                    'load the application
    Else
        Error Err                           'Forces display of error message
    End If
End Sub
```

## Description

Begin the specification of the LinkTopic property with the name of the control involved in the link (which must be a text box, picture box, or label) or the name of its parent form.

There are two possible definitions of the link$ string argument in a LinkTopic property expression. A form's LinkTopic property sets the application name that another application must use to establish a DDE link. A form's LinkTopic property's link$ argument must be a text string. The LinkTopic property of a picture box, text box, or label includes the application name and the topic. These two elements are separated from each other by a vertical line (character code 124). There is a limit of 255 characters for the LinkTopic definition.

In the example syntax, the LinkTopic consists of the application name followed by the topic System. This has the effect of establishing a DDE link with the indicated application which is not dependent upon any particular file. Additionally, the other application (WinWord, Excel, or Q+E) may be polled for the acceptable topics for a DDE link.

### The LinkItem Property

The LinkItem property of the control determines the exact destination of the general information entered in the LinkTopic property. Unlike the LinkTopic property, the LinkItem property may be changed while a link is active. Some applications will allow the creation of a DDE link without a specific LinkItem. When the System topic is used, the LinkItem may be set to a variety of settings that are dependent upon the application on the other side of the link. The example syntax sets the LinkItem property to SysItems, which returns all of the possible items that may be chosen with the System topic. Please refer to Tables 25.9, 25.10, and 25.11 in the LinkItem property section of this chapter.

### The LinkMode Property

A LinkTopic property will work when the LinkMode property is set to hot (1) or cold (2). Even though the LinkMode property establishes a valid link, the link will not work unless both the LinkTopic and LinkItem properties are set to valid elements of the other application. In the example syntax, the LinkMode property is a cold link so the programer controls when to update the information to the text box with a LinkRequest method.

### The Client Control

The LinkTopic property identifies the portion of a DDE link that may not be changed without severing the link between the control and another application. An application name is normally the file name of the executable program without the extension. The LinkTopic property of a form identifies a Visual Basic application with the FormName property as the default setting. Each of the available Topics may be obtained by setting the LinkTopic to "System" and the LinkItem to "Topics." Normally, the LinkTopic indicates the path and filename of the data file being accessed through the link.

| Argument | Description |
|---|---|
| Application Name | The name of the application's execution file without the .EXE extension |
| Topic | The general location of the data in the application like the filename |

Table 25.22 Two parts of the link$ argument of the LinkTopic property for a client control

### The Server Form

A form's LinkTopic property determines the name that another application needs to establish a DDE link with this form. This is the name of the Visual Basic project (*.MAK) or executable (*.EXE) file without the extension, as summarized in Table 25.23. This property has no effect on the operation of a link in which one of the controls on the form establishes a DDE link with another application.

| Argument | Description |
|---|---|
| Topic | The name of the application's project file (*.MAK) or execution file (*.EXE) without the extension |

Table 25.23 Link$ argument of LinkTopic property for a server form

## Example

In the DDE project at the end of this section, the LinkTopic serves as a means of identifying the application and file that the DDE link will be established with. At program startup, the LinkTopic property of the text boxes on the Sales_Display form is indicated to be Excel|Sheet1, which identifies the application as Microsoft Excel and the file name as Sheet1. The LinkTopic property of the Graph picture box on the DDE form is Excel|Chart1 to identify Microsoft Excel and the Chart1 file. Before the DDE link can be created between WinWord and the WordLink label box of the DDE form, the LinkTopic of the label box must be WinWord|System.

## Comments

Be careful that multiple DDE links between the same application do not create an infinite loop of updates. An example of this problem is if a server form is linked to another application and the text box on the same form is part of a client link to the same application. A hot link setup in both directions results in an infinite loop.

# The DDE Project

## Project Overview

The DDE project demonstrates the properties, methods, statements, and events that affect the operation of DDE links with Visual Basic applications. This example shows the process of establishing and maintaining DDE links between two applications. The Visual Basic application is both a client and a server. Both Microsoft Excel and Word for Windows are required for this example. Since every application may not function in the same way, the techniques used in this project may not work exactly the same with other applications. However, this project should give you an understanding of how DDE links operate.

Two forms and two modules comprise the DDE project. This section has four parts, one for each of these elements. The first part deals with the assembly of the controls and subroutines of the DDE form. The next part discusses the Sales_Display form's controls and subroutines. Each of the first two sections includes step-by-step instructions on how to put the form and its controls together. The following part lists the contents of the DDE global module. The final part outlines the subroutines of the DDE Link module. After all four of these sections, there is a guide to the operation of the project. Please read this information carefully and use the pictures of the forms as guides in the process of assembling this project.

## Assembling the Project

1. Make a new form (the DDE form) with the objects and properties in Table 25.24. Notice that all the OptionBox controls have a CtlName property of Sales_Figures. The second control that you create with the same name will generate a message asking you if you wish to create a control array. Please respond "Yes." Another way to create a control array is to set the first control's Index property to 0.

| Object | Property | Setting |
|---|---|---|
| Form | BorderStyle | 1 - Fixed Single |
| | Caption | DDE Project |
| | ControlBox | False |
| | Icon | \VB\OFFICE\GRAPH01.ICO |
| | LinkMode | 1 - Server |
| | LinkTopic | DDEForm |
| | MaxButton | False |
| | MinButton | True |
| | MousePointer | 1 - Arrow |
| | FormName | DDE |
| Frame | CtlName | Sales_Figures_Frame |
| | TabIndex | 0 |
| Option box | Caption | Quarterly Gross Sales |
| | CtlName | Sales_Figures |
| | Index | 0 |
| | TabIndex | 1 |
| Option box | Caption | Quarterly Cost of Goods Sold |
| | CtlName | Sales_Figures |
| | Index | 1 |
| | TabIndex | 2 |
| Option box | Caption | Quarterly Net Sales |
| | CtlName | Sales_Figures |
| | Index | 2 |
| | TabIndex | 3 |
| Command button | Caption | Display Figures |
| | CtlName | Display_Figures |
| | TabIndex | 4 |
| Command button | Caption | Create Report |
| | CtlName | Create_Report |
| | TabIndex | 5 |
| Command button | Caption | Exit Program |
| | CtlName | Exit_Program |
| | TabIndex | 6 |
| Picture box | AutoRedraw | True |
| | CtlName | Graph |
| | LinkMode | 0 |
| | LinkTopic | "" |
| | TabIndex | 7 |
| | TabStop | False |

| Label | Caption | "" |
|---|---|---|
| | CtlName | WordLink |
| | LinkMode | 0 |
| | LinkTopic | WinWord\|System |
| | TabIndex | 8 |

**Table 25.24 Elements of the DDE form**

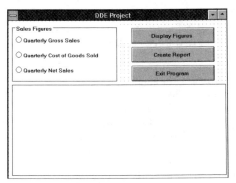

**Figure 25.1 What the DDE form should look like when completed**

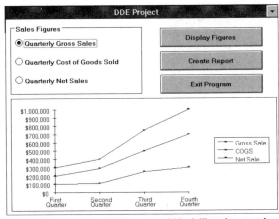

**Figure 25.2 What the DDE form should look like when running**

2. Size the objects on the screen, as shown in Figures 25.1 and 25.2.
3. Enter the following code in the Create_Report_Click event subroutine. This code is triggered when the user presses the command button labeled Create Report. This routine loads Word For Windows into memory and establishes two DDE links. The first link allows macro commands to be sent to WinWord and the second places the contents of the picture box graph on the WinWord document.

```
Sub Create_Report_Click ()
Startup:
   On Error GoTo OpenWord
   Screen.MousePointer = 11
   WordLink.LinkTopic = "Winword|System"
   DDE.Hide
   WordLink.LinkMode = 2
   AppActivate "Microsoft Word - Document1"
   WordLink.LinkTimeout = 1000
   WordLink.LinkExecute "[InsertField .Field = ""dde DDE DDEForm GRAPH""]"
   WordLink.LinkExecute "[InsertPara]"
   WordLink.LinkExecute "[ParaDown]"
   WordLink.LinkExecute "[FormatParagraph 3,0,0,0,2]"
   WordLink.LinkExecute "[Insert ""These are the year's sales figures""]"
   DDE.Show
   Exit Sub
OpenWord:
   If Err = 282 Then
       x = Shell("WinWord.exe", 3)
       Resume Startup
   Else
       Error Err
   End If
End Sub
```

4. Enter the following code in the Display_Figures_Click event. This event is

activated when the user presses the command button labeled Display Figures. This routine checks the value of the global variable Displayed% to find the selected Sales_Figures option box. The selected option box indicates which parts of the Excel spreadsheet with which to establish a link. These figures provide the quarterly figures of the appropriate section (Gross Sales, COGS, or Net Sales).

```
Sub Display_Figures_Click ()
    DDE.Hide
    Select Case Displayed%
        Case 0
            Sales_Display.First_Quarter_Figures.LinkItem = "R2C2"
            Sales_Display.First_Quarter_Figures.LinkRequest
            Sales_Display.Second_Quarter_Figures.LinkItem = "R2C3"
            Sales_Display.Second_Quarter_Figures.LinkRequest
            Sales_Display.Third_Quarter_Figures.LinkItem = "R2C4"
            Sales_Display.Third_Quarter_Figures.LinkRequest
            Sales_Display.Fourth_Quarter_Figures.LinkItem = "R2C5"
            Sales_Display.Fourth_Quarter_Figures.LinkRequest
        Case 1
            Sales_Display.First_Quarter_Figures.LinkItem = "R3C2"
            Sales_Display.First_Quarter_Figures.LinkRequest
            Sales_Display.Second_Quarter_Figures.LinkItem = "R3C3"
            Sales_Display.Second_Quarter_Figures.LinkRequest
            Sales_Display.Third_Quarter_Figures.LinkItem = "R3C4"
            Sales_Display.Third_Quarter_Figures.LinkRequest
            Sales_Display.Fourth_Quarter_Figures.LinkItem = "R3C5"
            Sales_Display.Fourth_Quarter_Figures.LinkRequest
        Case 2
            Sales_Display.First_Quarter_Figures.LinkItem = "R4C2"
            Sales_Display.First_Quarter_Figures.LinkRequest
            Sales_Display.Second_Quarter_Figures.LinkItem = "R4C3"
            Sales_Display.Second_Quarter_Figures.LinkRequest
            Sales_Display.Third_Quarter_Figures.LinkItem = "R4C4"
            Sales_Display.Third_Quarter_Figures.LinkRequest
            Sales_Display.Fourth_Quarter_Figures.LinkItem = "R4C5"
            Sales_Display.Fourth_Quarter_Figures.LinkRequest
        Case 3
            Sales_Display.First_Quarter_Figures.LinkItem = "R5C2"
            Sales_Display.First_Quarter_Figures.LinkRequest
            Sales_Display.Second_Quarter_Figures.LinkItem = "R5C3"
            Sales_Display.Second_Quarter_Figures.LinkRequest
            Sales_Display.Third_Quarter_Figures.LinkItem = "R5C4"
            Sales_Display.Third_Quarter_Figures.LinkRequest
            Sales_Display.Fourth_Quarter_Figures.LinkItem = "R5C5"
            Sales_Display.Fourth_Quarter_Figures.LinkRequest
    End Select
    Sales_Display.Show
End Sub
```

5. Enter the following code in the Exit_Program_Click event subroutine. This code will be run when the user presses the command button labeled Exit Program. The End statement ends the program and closes all of the open

DDE links. This has the effect of activating any LinkClose events connected to any of the controls and forms that are part of these links.

```
Sub Exit_Program_Click ()
    End
End Sub
```

6. Enter the following code in the Form_LinkError event subroutine. If WinWord encounters a problem when attempting to establish a DDE link with the DDE form, this routine prints the appropriate error message on the screen.

```
Sub Form_LinkError (LinkErr As Integer)
    Select Case LinkErr
        Case 1
            Msg$ = "WinWord asked for data in an incompatible format."
        Case 2
            Msg$ = "WinWord asked for data without an established link."
        Case 3
            Msg$ = "WinWord attempted a DDE operation without establishing a DDE link."
        Case 4
            Msg$ = "WinWord attempted to modify the Item in a DDE link that
            wasn't established."
        Case 5
            Msg$ = "WinWord attempted to Poke data without establishing a DDE
            link."
        Case 6
            Msg$ = "WinWord attempted a DDE operation after the link was closed."
        Case 7
            Msg$ = "There are too many active DDE links established."
        Case 8
            Msg$ = "Some of the data sent through the link was lost, because it
            was too long."
        Case 9
            Msg$ = "The index value of a nonexistent control in a control array
            was specified."
        Case 10
            Msg$ = "An unexpected DDE operation was sent from the other application."
        Case 11
            Msg$ = "There is not enough memory available for a DDE link."
        Case 12
            Msg$ = "WinWord tried to perform an operation reserved for Client
            Applications."
    End Select
    MsgBox Msg$
End Sub
```

7. Enter the following code in the Form_LinkExecute event subroutine. This code is activated when another application attempts to establish a DDE link with the DDE form. If the command sent was GRAPH, then the link updates the picture box in WinWord. Otherwise this routine informs the other application that the command was not accepted.

```
Sub Form_LinkExecute (cmdStr As String, Cancel As Integer)
    Cancel = 0
```

```
      Select Case UCase$(cmdStr)
          Case "[GRAPH]"
              Graph.LinkSend
          Case Else
              Cancel = 1
      End Select
End Sub
```

8. Enter the following code in the Form_LinkOpen event subroutine. This event is triggered when Winword establishes a DDE link with the DDE form. This routines changes the screen's mouse pointer to an arrow

```
Sub Form_LinkOpen (Cancel As Integer)
    Screen.MousePointer = 1
End Sub
```

9. Enter the following code in the Form_Load event subroutine. This code runs at program startup when the DDE form is loaded on the screen. The hourglass displays to indicate that the system is busy. Then this routine establishes a DDE link with the Chart1 file of Excel.

```
Sub Form_Load ()
    Screen.MousePointer = 11
    Load Sales_Display
    Graph.LinkTopic = "Excel|Chart1"
    Graph.LinkMode = 1
End Sub
```

10. Enter the following code in the Graph_LinkClose event subroutine. When the DDE form is closed at the end of this program, this subroutine is activated. Using the CheckLink subfunction, the code ensures that the Graph picture box's LinkMode property is properly set to 0 when the link is closed.

```
Sub Graph_LinkClose ()
    CheckLink Graph
End Sub
```

11. Enter the following code in the Graph_LinkOpen event subroutine. This code is activated when a WinWord opens a link between the WinWord picture field and the picture box Graph on the DDE form. The Cancel value indicates that the link may be created and the screen's mouse pointer returns to an arrow.

```
Sub Graph_LinkOpen (Cancel As Integer)
    Cancel = 0
    Screen.MousePointer = 1
End Sub
```

12. Enter the following code in the Sales_Figures_GotFocus event subroutine. Any changes made to the selected option in the Sales_Figures option box triggers this event. This routine saves the index property value into the global variable Delayed%.

```
Sub Sales_Figures_GotFocus (Index As Integer)
  Displayed% = Screen.ActiveControl.Index
End Sub
```

13. Enter the following code in the WordLink_LinkClose event subroutine.
Closing the DDE link between the WordLink label box and WinWord triggers this event. Using the CheckLink subfunction, the code ensures that the label's LinkMode property is properly set to 0.

```
Sub WordLink_LinkClose ()
  CheckLink WordLink
End Sub
```

## The Sales_Display Form

1. Make a new form (the Sales_Display form) with the objects and properties in Table 25.25.

| Object | Property | Setting |
|--------|----------|---------|
| Form | BorderStyle | 1 - Fixed Single |
| | Caption | Display Form |
| | ControlBox | False |
| | FormName | Sales_Display |
| | LinkMode | 0 - None |
| | LinkTopic | "" |
| | MaxButton | False |
| | MinButton | False |
| Label | Caption | First Quarter |
| | CtlName | First_Quarter |
| | TabIndex | 5 |
| Label | Caption | Second Quarter |
| | CtlName | Second_Quarter |
| | TabIndex | 6 |
| Label | Caption | Third Quarter |
| | CtlName | Third_Quarter |
| | TabIndex | 7 |
| Label | Caption | Fourth Quarter |
| | CtlName | Fourth_Quarter |
| | TabIndex | 8 |
| Text box | CtlName | First_Quarter_Figures |
| | TabIndex | 0 |
| | LinkItem | "" |
| | LinkMode | 0 - None |
| | LinkTimeout | 50 |
| | MousePointer | 3 - I-Beam |
| | Text | "" |

*Table 25.25 (continued)*

| Object | Property | Setting |
|---|---|---|
| Text box | CtlName | Second_Quarter_Figures |
| | TabIndex | 1 |
| | LinkItem | "" |
| | LinkMode | 0 - None |
| | LinkTimeout | 50 |
| | MousePointer | 3 - I-Beam |
| | Text | "" |
| Text box | CtlName | Third_Quarter_Figures |
| | TabIndex | 2 |
| | LinkItem | "" |
| | LinkMode | 0 - None |
| | LinkTimeout | 50 |
| | MousePointer | 3 - I-Beam |
| | Text | "" |
| Text box | CtlName | Fourth_Quarter_Figures |
| | TabIndex | 3 |
| | LinkItem | "" |
| | LinkMode | 0 - None |
| | LinkTimeout | 50 |
| | MousePointer | 3 - I-Beam |
| | Text | "" |
| Command button | Caption | OK |
| | CtlName | OK_Button |
| | TabIndex | 4 |

**Table 25.25 Objects and properties of the Sales_Display form in the DDE project**

2. Size the objects on the screen, as shown in Figures 25.3 and 25.4.

3. Enter the following code in the General Declarations section to create the SetupExcel subfunction. The Form_Load event of the Sales_Display form calls this function. This routine loads Microsoft Excel into memory and establishes a DDE link. Then, this routine enters all the data needed for this project into the spreadsheet and graphs it on Chart1. Finally, this routine closes the DDE link.

```
Sub SetupExcel (Textbox As Control)
   Textbox.LinkTopic = "Excel|Sheet1"
   Textbox.LinkItem = "R1C1"
   Textbox.LinkMode = 2
   Textbox.LinkExecute "[Select(""R1C1"")]"
   Textbox.LinkExecute "[Select(""R[1]C"")]"
```

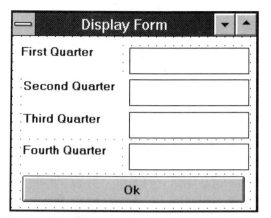

**Figure 25.3 What the Sales_Display form should look like when completed**

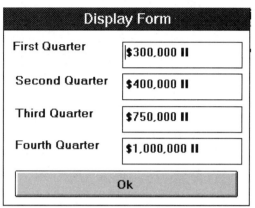

**Figure 25.4 What the Sales_Display form should look like when running**

```
Textbox.LinkExecute "[Formula.Fill(""Gross Sales"")]"
Textbox.LinkExecute "[Select(""R[1]C"")]"
Textbox.LinkExecute "[Formula.Fill(""COGS"")]"
Textbox.LinkExecute "[Select(""R[1]C"")]"
Textbox.LinkExecute "[Formula.Fill(""Net Sales"")]"
Textbox.LinkExecute "[Select(""R[-3]C[1]"")]"
Textbox.LinkExecute "[Formula.Fill(""First Quarter"")]"
Textbox.LinkExecute "[Select(""R[1]C"")]"
Textbox.LinkExecute "[Formula.Fill(""300000"")]"
Textbox.LinkExecute "[Select(""R[1]C"")]"
Textbox.LinkExecute "[Formula.Fill(""100000"")]"
Textbox.LinkExecute "[Select(""R[1]C"")]"
Textbox.LinkExecute "[Formula.Fill(""=Sum(R[-2]C-R[-1]C)"")]"
Textbox.LinkExecute "[Select(""R[-3]C[1]"")]"
Textbox.LinkExecute "[Formula.Fill(""Second Quarter"")]"
Textbox.LinkExecute "[Select(""R[1]C"")]"
Textbox.LinkExecute "[Formula.Fill(""400000"")]"
Textbox.LinkExecute "[Select(""R[1]C"")]"
Textbox.LinkExecute "[Formula.Fill(""110000"")]"
Textbox.LinkExecute "[Select(""R[1]C"")]"
Textbox.LinkExecute "[Formula.Fill(""=Sum(R[-2]C-R[-1]C)"")]"
Textbox.LinkExecute "[Select(""R[-3]C[1]"")]"
Textbox.LinkExecute "[Formula.Fill(""Third Quarter"")]"
Textbox.LinkExecute "[Select(""R[1]C"")]"
Textbox.LinkExecute "[Formula.Fill(""750000"")]"
Textbox.LinkExecute "[Select(""R[1]C"")]"
Textbox.LinkExecute "[Formula.Fill(""250000"")]"
Textbox.LinkExecute "[Select(""R[1]C"")]"
Textbox.LinkExecute "[Formula.Fill(""=Sum(R[-2]C-R[-1]C)"")]"
Textbox.LinkExecute "[Select(""R[-3]C[1]"")]"
Textbox.LinkExecute "[Formula.Fill(""Fourth Quarter"")]"
Textbox.LinkExecute "[Select(""R[1]C"")]"
Textbox.LinkExecute "[Formula.Fill(""1000000"")]"
Textbox.LinkExecute "[Select(""R[1]C"")]"
Textbox.LinkExecute "[Formula.Fill(""300000"")]"
Textbox.LinkExecute "[Select(""R[1]C"")]"
```

```
   Textbox.LinkExecute "[Formula.Fill(""=Sum(R[-2]C-R[-1]C)"")]"
   Textbox.LinkExecute "[Select(""R1C1:R4C5"")]"
   Textbox.LinkExecute "[Column.Width(,,,3)]"
   Textbox.LinkExecute "[Select(""R2C2:R4C5"")]"
   Textbox.LinkExecute "[FORMAT.NUMBER(""$#,##0_);($#,##0)"")]"
   Textbox.LinkExecute "[SELECT(""R1C1:R4C5"")]"
   Textbox.LinkExecute "[NEW(2,1)]"
   Textbox.LinkExecute "[FORMAT.MAIN(4,1,,,FALSE,FALSE,FALSE)]"
   Textbox.LinkExecute "[LEGEND(TRUE)]"
   Textbox.LinkExecute "[FULL(TRUE)]"
   Textbox.LinkMode = 0
End Sub
```

4. Enter the following code in the First_Quarter_Figures_Change event subroutine. Any change to the contents of the First_Quarter_Figures text box
   triggers this event. This routine transfers the current contents of the text
   box to the Excel cell indicated by the LinkItem property of the text box.

```
Sub First_Quarter_Figures_Change ()
   First_Quarter_Figures.LinkPoke
End Sub
```

5. Enter the following code in the First_Quarter_Figures_LinkClose event subroutine. Closing the DDE link between the First_Quarter_Figures text box
   and Excel triggers this event. Using the CheckLink subfunction, the code
   ensures that the text box's LinkMode property is properly set to 0.

```
Sub First_Quarter_Figures_LinkClose ()
   CheckLink First_Quarter_Figures
End Sub
```

6. Enter the following code in the Form_Load event subroutine. Loading the
   Sales_Display form into memory at program startup triggers this event. If
   Excel is not in memory, this subroutine loads it. This routine then establishes DDE links between the text boxes on the Sales_Display form and cells
   on the Sheet1 spreadsheet.

```
Sub Form_Load ()
Startup:
   On Error GoTo OpenExcel
   First_Quarter_Figures.LinkTopic = "Excel|Sheet1"
   First_Quarter_Figures.LinkItem = "R2C2"
   First_Quarter_Figures.LinkMode = 2
   Second_Quarter_Figures.LinkTopic = "Excel|Sheet1"
   Second_Quarter_Figures.LinkItem = "R2C3"
   Second_Quarter_Figures.LinkMode = 2
   Third_Quarter_Figures.LinkTopic = "Excel|Sheet1"
   Third_Quarter_Figures.LinkItem = "R2C4"
   Third_Quarter_Figures.LinkMode = 2
   Fourth_Quarter_Figures.LinkTopic = "Excel|Sheet1"
   Fourth_Quarter_Figures.LinkItem = "R2C5"
   Fourth_Quarter_Figures.LinkMode = 2
   Exit Sub
OpenExcel:
```

```
      If Err = 282 Then
          x = Shell("Excel.exe", 3)
          SetupExcel First_Quarter
          Resume Startup
      Else
          Error Err
      End If
End Sub
```

7. Enter the following code in the Form_Unload event subroutine. This code is activated when the Sales_Display form is removed from memory. When this happens, this subroutine cuts any existing links between Excel and the text boxes of the Sales_Display form.

```
Sub Form_Unload (Cancel As Integer)
   First_Quarter_Figures.LinkMode = 0
   Second_Quarter_Figures.LinkMode = 0
   Third_Quarter_Figures.LinkMode = 0
   Fourth_Quarter_Figures.LinkMode = 0
End Sub
```

8. Enter the following code in the Fourth_Quarter_Figures_Change event subroutine. This code is activated when the user changes the contents of the Fourth_Quarter_Figures text box. This routine transfers the current contents of the text box to the Excel cell indicated by the LinkItem property of the text box.

```
Sub Fourth_Quarter_Figures_Change ()
   Fourth_Quarter_Figures.LinkPoke
End Sub
```

9. Enter the following code in the Fourth_Quarter_Figures_LinkClose event subroutine. This code is triggered by the closing of the DDE link between the Fourth_Quarter_Figures text box and Excel. Using the CheckLink subfunction, the code checks to ensure that the text box's LinkMode property is properly set to 0 when the link is closed.

```
Sub Fourth_Quarter_Figures_LinkClose ()
   CheckLink Fourth_Quarter_Figures
End Sub
```

10. Enter the following code in the OK_Button_Click event subroutine. This code is triggered when the the user presses the command button labeled OK. This routine hides the Sales_Display and remains in memory while the DDE form appears on the screen.

```
Sub OK_Button_Click ()
  Sales_Display.Hide
  DDE.Show
End Sub
```

11. Enter the following code in the Second_Quarter_Figures_Change event subroutine. This code is activated whenever the user changes the contents of

the Second_Quarter_Figures text box. This routine transfers the current contents of the text box to the Excel cell indicated by the LinkItem property of the text box.

```
Sub Second_Quarter_Figures_Change ()
  Second_Quarter_Figures.LinkPoke
End Sub
```

12. Enter the following code in the Second_Quarter_Figures_LinkClose event subroutine. Closing the DDE link between the Second_Quarter_Figures text box and Excel triggers this event. This routine uses the CheckLink subfunction to ensure that the text box's LinkMode property is properly set to 0.

```
Sub Second_Quarter_Figures_LinkClose ()
  CheckLink Second_Quarter_Figures
End Sub
```

13. Enter the following code in the Third_Quarter_Figures_Change event subroutine. This code is activated when the user changes the contents of the Third_Quarter_Figures text box. This routine transfers the current contents of the text box to the Excel cell indicated by the LinkItem property of the text box.

```
Sub Third_Quarter_Figures_Change ()
  Third_Quarter_Figures.LinkPoke
End Sub
```

14. Enter the following code in the Third_Quarter_Figures_LinkClose event subroutine. Closing the DDE link between the Third_Quarter_Figures text box and Excel triggers this event. This routine uses the CheckLink subfunction to ensure that the text box's LinkMode property is properly set to 0.

```
Sub Third_Quarter_Figures_LinkClose ()
  CheckLink Third_Quarter_Figures
End Sub
```

### The DDE Global Module

1. Enter the following code into the global module and save it under the name DDE by choosing the Save option on the File menu. This code defines the Displayed variable as global.

```
Global Displayed As Integer
```

## Assembling the Project - DDELink Module

1. Create a new module by selecting the New Module option on the File menu. Save the new module as DDELink by selecting the Save File option on the File menu. Enter the following code into the module to make the global subfunction CheckLink.

```
Sub CheckLink (CtlLink As Control)
   If CtlLink.LinkMode <> 0 Then
      CtlLink.LinkMode = 0
   End If
End Sub
```

## How It Works

The DDE project is a very simple program that does most of the work for the user. When the Sales_Display form appears on the form, all of the links already exist with Excel. The graph created by the data entered in Excel appears on the form. To create the link with WinWord, the user presses the command button labeled Create Report. By selecting one of the different options in the option box, the user gets another set of figures to adjust on the Excel spreadsheet to produce a different graph on the screen. The user presses Exit to leave the program.

### Startup

At design time, the LinkMode properties of the forms and controls are modified to their default settings. Each of the control's' LinkMode properties remain at the default value of 0. The DDE form's LinkMode Property stays at 1, which means that it may act as a server in a DDE link conversation. In contrast, the Sales_Display form's LinkMode Property is modified to 0 to remove it from being linked to another application within a DDE conversation. Even though this property may be modified at run time, the property of the Sales_Display form is modified at this point to prevent any need for a change later. This is a way to identify which parts of the program will be eligible for DDE conversations and which ones will not.

The DDE form's LinkTopic Property is changed to DDEForm at design time to define what name that another application must indicate to establish a DDE link with it. This property has no effect on the operation of DDE links between this form's controls and other applications in which the control acts as the client. When a DDE link is established between the Graph Picture box and the Chart1 sheet of Excel, the link is unaffected by the LinkTopic Property setting of the form.

### Running the DDE Project

When the Sales_Display form is loaded into memory, the LinkTopic and LinkItem properties of the text boxes are set in the Form_Load event. Each text box's LinkTopic property is defined as Excel|Sheet1. In the first part, the name of the application to be linked to is given as Excel, which is the name for Microsoft Excel for Windows. Sheet1 identifies the name of the file that contains the data to be accessed. The exact location on the spreadsheet Sheet1 is given in the LinkItem of each text box as the coordinates of the specific cell that contains the data being linked. These coordinates are in Excel's R1C1 format which indicates a cell's distance from the top left corner of the spreadsheet in terms of the number of cells from the top (C#) and the left (R#).

As each text box's LinkTopic and LinkItem properties are set, the DDE link outlined by these two properties is established by the modification of the LinkMode property of the same control to 2. This creates a cold link between the indicated cell of Sheet1.

Since the link is a cold link, it does not automatically update the text box with the contents of the cell referenced in the LinkItem property. While the link is set to 2, the text box's Text property may only be changed with a LinkRequest method. In this way, the text box contents may be controlled by when the LinkRequest is actually utilized.

The first time that the LinkMode property is changed to 2, an error is generated because Excel has not been loaded into memory. This error is trapped by the On Error statement On Error Goto OpenExcel, which directs the code to process the contents of the OpenExcel section of the subroutine. Using an If-Then statement to determine the value of the generated error, the Shell command loads Excel into memory. If the error is not created by the absence of Excel in memory, the second part of the If-Then statement places the error message on the screen.

When the error is caused by the absence of Excel, the SetupExcel subfunction is called before the cold link may actually be established between the First_Quarter_Figures text box and the R2C2 cell of the Sheet1 spreadsheet. This subfunction creates a table of sales figures on Excel's Sheet1 with the LinkExecute method utilizing Excel's own macro language. Notice that each macro command that is sent to Excel must be placed between square brackets and that any quotation marks placed between these brackets are doubled. If you do not do this, the macro command will generate an error.

After the cold links are established between Excel and the Sales_Display form's text boxes, the Form_Load event of the DDE form adjusts the settings of the Graph picture box's LinkTopic and LinkMode properties. The LinkTopic of the picture box is changed to Excel|Chart1 to create a link with Microsoft Excel and the newly created Chart1 sheet. When the LinkMode property of the picture box is changed to 1, the graph displayed on Chart1 is duplicated within the Graph picture box. This demonstrates the operation of a DDE link with a picture box.

By setting the LinkMode Property of the Graph picture box on the DDE form to 1, a hot DDE link is established with the Chart1 sheet of Microsoft Excel. This hot link ensures that no matter what changes are made to the graph on Chart1, these changes are updated to the Graph picture box as soon as they are made. If a cold link were set up instead of a hot link, then a LinkRequest method would need to be used to reflect any changes made to the graph on the Excel Chart1 sheet. In this case, the hot link is better because each time the numbers that the graph is based on on Sheet1 are modified, the change is reflected immediately.

When the DDE link is opened between the Graph picture box and the Chart1 sheet of Excel, the LinkOpen event of the Graph picture box is triggered. The screen's MousePointer is modified to its previous setting of arrow from the hourglass to reflect that the calculations are completed. Since the Cancel variable is returned as 0, the link may then be opened. This demonstrates one use of the LinkOpen event and shows how the setting of the Cancel variable to the value of 0 allows a DDE link to be established. If the value of Cancel had been set to a non-0 value, then the link would not have been permitted to be made.

At this point, the DDE form displays on the screen showing the graph from the Excel Chart1 Sheet in the picture box. Up to this point, the text boxes of the Sales_Display form have not been updated because they are linked to the Excel Sheet1 with cold DDE links. This makes it necessary to transfer the contents of the cells of the

Excel Sheet1 spreadsheet to the indicated text boxes on the Sales_Display form. When the command button labeled Display Figures is pressed, a Select Case statement uses the global variable to determine which of the option boxes on the DDE form is presently selected. Based on this setting, the LinkItem of each text box is changed to a cell on the Sheet1 and the LinkRequest method updates the contents of the indicated text box. In this way, the Sales_Display form is shown on the screen with the quarterly figures that match the option box chosen on the DDE form.

When the contents of the text boxes on the Sales_Display form are changed, the Change event of each text box is activated. The Change event utilizes the LinkPoke method to update the linked cell on Excel's Sheet1 to include any changes made to the contents of the text box. In this way, the user is given the ability to modify the contents of the spreadsheet on Sheet1 and the graph on Chart1 that is based upon it. Notice that if the figures displayed in the text boxes are changed, the graph is modified also when the DDE form is shown again. This demonstrates the operation of the LinkPoke method, which reverses the normal flow of information from the client to the server instead of the normal server to client.

When the user presses the command button labeled Create Report, Word For Windows is opened and a cold DDE link is established with the Label box WordLink. This link serves as a means of setting up a picture field in the default Document1 file using a LinkExecute method. The field references the Graph picture box on the DDE form and creates a DDE link with this picture box. In this case, the DDE form acts as the server of a DDE link. Notice that the WinWord field utilizes the LinkTopic DDEForm to identify the DDE form. With this information for general reference, the final word GRAPH corresponds to the word GRAPH placed in the Select Case Statement of the LinkExecute event. The GRAPH option updates the contents of the picture on WinWord's Document1. If any other word is sent by the other application besides GRAPH, then the error message is returned to the sending application. As a result, this part of the DDE project demonstrates a possible use for the LinkExecute event of a form.

The field picture on the Document1 file of WinWord is updated with the use of the LinkSend method within the LinkExecute event of the DDE form. In this case, the LinkSend method allows a picture on a client application to be updated by the server application. With the DDE project, this is achieved every time that the client application sends the GRAPH command to the DDE form. As a result, the LinkSend updates any changes to the image on the Document1 file when the command word GRAPH is sent to the DDE form.

The DDE form is set up with a special error-trapping system for applications attempting to perform DDE operations with it. This event is only applicable to DDE links that occur when the form is acting as a server to a client application. Since WinWord is the only application that communicates with this form in this project, each of the error messages is directed at WinWord. These error messages may only be generated by the actions of the other applications and are for informational purposes only. Read these messages carefully to get an idea of what kinds of problems can occur in a DDE link between another application and a Visual Basic form.

When the command button labeled Program_Exit is pressed, all of the links between the forms of the DDE project and other applications are closed. This has the effect of triggering the LinkClose event of each DDE link. Each DDE link's Visual Basic element is triggered before the program can be closed. In this case, the subfunction CheckLink in the DDELink module is called by each LinkClose event. The CheckLink subfunction uses an If-Then statement to check if the LinkMode Property of the control has been changed to 0. If the LinkProperty is not set to 0, then this subfunction changes it to 0. This ensures that when a link is closed, the LinkMode Property of the control reflects this status.

# Appendix A
# Visual Basic Language Tutorial

As the name suggests, Visual Basic consists of two parts: a visual interface with many built-in functions, and a version of the BASIC language. As you know, to program in Visual Basic you design objects and then specify the behavior of each object when a particular event happens to it. You specify an object's behavior using the statements and functions of the BASIC language.

This appendix is an overview and tutorial introduction to the elements of the Visual BASIC language and to some commonly used programming techniques. We will break down the language elements of Visual Basic into functional categories. Each category pertains to a particular area of the language and lists the statements and functions that relate to that area along with some tutorial information about how to use those commands.

We do not have space here to cover many of the generic features of the BASIC language that are included in Visual Basic. If you do not have much experience with BASIC programming, we suggest that you look at some of the books on BASIC programming listed in Appendix E, *Further Reading*.

Appendix B, *Visual Basic Language Reference*, provides a concise alphabetical reference to each statement and function used in Visual Basic. Use this reference to find out more about the exact rules for using each statement or function, examples of usage, and other details.

## Strings

Each character that can be displayed on the screen, or printed on a printer, is represented by a 1-byte numeric value called an ASCII code. For instance, the ASCII code for the character "A" is 65, the code for "B" is 66, and so on. The ASCII character set consists of 127 character codes. The first 31 codes represent characters that cannot be displayed, but are used for special purposes. For example, the end of a text file is determined by the placement of an "end of file" character, which is ASCII code 26. The remaining codes represent all the printable characters such as upper- and lower-case letters, numerals, spaces, and punctuation. When one or more of these ASCII codes are arranged together to represent text in your program, it is called a string.

In Visual Basic, there are two types of strings: variable and fixed length. As the names imply, variable length strings shrink and grow depending on the length of the data that has been assigned to them. Fixed length strings never change size. If a fixed length string is assigned a value that is longer than the string, any extra characters are ignored. (Another way to say this is that the string is "truncated" to the number of characters allowed for in the variable.) If it is assigned a value that is shorter than it, the balance of a fixed length string is padded with spaces.

One of Visual Basic's strongest assets is its string handling capabilities. Visual Basic has inherited from previous BASIC languages a rich and powerful array of functions and statements designed to make even the most complicated string operations a snap to perform. Table A.1 lists Visual Basic's string handling commands.

| Use This... | | To Do This... |
|---|---|---|
| Asc | Function | Determine the ASCII value of a string character |
| Chr$ | Function | Translate an ASCII value into a string character |
| Format$ | Function | Translate a date or time serial or a number into a formatted string |
| Instr | Function | Find the position of one string within another |
| LCase$ | Function | Translate all upper-case characters in a string to lower-case |
| Left$ | Function | Return a portion of a string starting from the leftmost character |
| Len | Function | Determine the length of a string or other variable type |
| LSet | Function | Left justify a value in a string or a programmer-defined type |
| LTrim$ | Function | Truncate any leading spaces from a string |
| Mid$ | Function | Return a portion of a string |
| Mid$ | Statement | Assign a value to a portion of a string |
| Right$ | Function | Return a portion of a string starting from the rightmost character |
| RSet | Function | Right justify a value in a string or a programmer-defined type |
| RTrim$ | Function | Truncate any following spaces from a string |
| Space$ | Function | Return a specified number of spaces |
| Str$ | Function | Translate a numeric value into an unformatted string |
| String$ | Function | Return a string of characters repeated a specified number of times |
| UCase$ | Function | Translate all lower-case characters of a string into upper-case |

**Table A.1 Functions and statements that affect strings**

### String Literals and Assigning Values to a String

A string literal is a method of representing a string by specifying an actual string of characters. Most often, string literals are used to assign a value to a string variable. This is done by placing a string variable to the left of the assignment operator, and a literal to the right. For example:

```
H$ = "Hello, world!"
```

This example assigns the value "Hello, world!" to the variable H$.

You can also control how a string will be justified when it is assigned. Justification refers to the alignment of the characters—for example, left justification means that the characters start at the leftmost position, while right justification means that the last character is in the rightmost position. You can specify the justification of a string assignment by using the LSet and RSet statements. Lset will left justify the source string within the destination string. Conversely, RSet will right justify. Both LSet and RSet treat the destination string as if it were a fixed length string, regardless of how it was originally declared. Therefore, the length of the destination string will never be affected by the LSet or RSet statements. If the destination string is shorter than the source string, any extra characters are truncated. If the destination is longer than the source, it will be padded with spaces.

```
Dim RJust As String * 15      'Define a fixed length string of 15 characters length
LJust$ = RJust                'Create a variable length string LJust$, and make it 15 characters long
RSet RJust = "Hello, world!"  'Right justify "Hello, World!" into fixed length string RJust
LSet LJust$ = "Hello, world!" 'Left justify "Hello, World!" into variable length string LJust$
```

In the example above, two string variables are created; one as a fixed length string and one as a variable length string. After being assigned the string literal, the variable RJust will have a value of "Hello, world!" and LJust$ will have a value of "Hello, world!".

Two strings may be combined into one by using string concatenation. You indicate concatenation with the addition sign (+).

```
A$ = "Hello"
B$ = "world"
C$ = A$ + ", " + B$
```

In this example, the values of A$, the literal string ", ", and B$ are combined and assigned to C$. This sets the value for C$ to "Hello, world".

### Determining the Length of a String

Because strings in Visual Basic can be of variable length, you may sometimes need a way to determine how long a string actually is before you can process it correctly. This is done with the Len function. Len returns the number of bytes that are assigned to a string.

```
ThisDate$ = "01-01-1992"
StrLen% = Len(ThisDate$)
```

In the above example, the variable StrLen% will be assigned a value of 10, which is the length of the string ThisDate$. Len also can be used to measure the length of any other data type, including programmer-defined data types. For instance:

```
Type PersonType
    Name As String * 10
    SSN As Long
End Type

Dim Person As PersonType

PersonLen% = Len(Person)
```

This will assign a value of 14 to the variable PersonLen%, because the programmer-defined type contains a string that is 10 bytes in length, and a long integer which is 4 bytes in length.

### Translating a Number into a String

When Visual Basic stores a numeric value in memory, it does so in a manner in which the value cannot be directly displayed on the screen. If you wish to display a number, you need to translate the numeric value to a string before doing so. The simplest way to do this is with the Str$ function. This function translates any numeric value into an unformatted string:

```
X% = 100
Y% = -100
XNum$ = Str$(X%)
YNum$ = Str$(Y%)
```

This example translates the numeric values contained in the integer variables X% and Y% into displayable strings. The Str$ function always reserves a character for the sign of the numeric value it is translating. If the value is positive, the leading character of the returned string will be a space. If it is negative, the leading character will be a dash. Therefore, in the example above, the value of XNum$ will be "100" and YNum$ will be "-100".

While the Str$ function presents a workable solution, it is not very elegant because it does not allow you to easily control the format of the returned string. For this purpose, Visual Basic provides the Format$ function. The Format$ function requires two arguments: the numeric value to be translated and an edit pattern upon which the format of the returned string will be based. For instance:

```
X! = 234.9
Num1$ = Str$(X!)
Num2$ = Format$(X!, "###.00")
```

In this example, Num1$ is assigned the value " 234.9", while Num2$ is assigned the value "234.90".

There are many different formatting options you may apply to the translation of a number with the Format$ function (see Appendix B for details). This function is also used to translate a date/time serial number into a readable date and/or time (please see the section on Date and Time later in this appendix).

### String Size and Font Size

Displaying strings is more complicated in Visual Basic than in traditional BASIC languages because Windows has several different fonts, and most of these fonts are proportional. Therefore, two strings that contain the same number of characters may be of different lengths when displayed. Because of this, if you wish to display several numbers on a form so that they all line up at their decimal point, you must take several steps other than just translating them with the same edit pattern. The easiest way around this problem is to use label controls to display numbers. When you create these controls, set the FontName property to a non-proportional font. Also, set the Alignment property to 1 (right justify).

### Finding One String within Another

Another useful string-related function is Instr. This function will search inside one string for the occurrence of another string pattern. It will then return the position within the source string at which the desired pattern was found. For instance:

```
Source$ = "This is a dog."
SearchPattern$ = "is"
FoundPos% = Instr(Source$, SearchPattern$)
```

In this example, the string variable Source$ is searched for the first occurrence of the string pattern "is". FoundPos% is assigned the value 3, because "is" is found at the third character position in Source$. You may also specify where in the source string you wish the search to begin by optionally using an argument to indicate a start position:

```
Source$ = "This is a dog."
SearchPattern$ = "is"
FoundPos% = Instr(4, Source$, SearchPattern$)
```

This example begins its search at the fourth character position in Source$. FoundPos% is then assigned the value 6, which is where the next occurrence of the string pattern "is" is found.

If the desired string is not found within the source string, a 0 is returned.

### Getting at Parts of a String

Although a string is a self-contained unit, you may wish to get at only a portion of it (for example, to change the order of a name or address). Visual Basic has three functions that allow you to read only a portion of a string. These are the Left$, Mid$, and Right$ functions. As you may guess, the Left$ function returns a number of characters from the left end of a string; Mid$ returns characters from the middle of a string; and Right$ returns characters from the right end of a string. Both the Left$ and Right$ functions require only two arguments: the source string and the number of characters desired. The Mid$ function requires an extra argument which indicates the starting position of the first desired character.

```
FullName$ = "James Thomas Espinoza"
EndOfFirstName% = Instr(FullName$, " ")        'Find the first space character indicating end of
                                               'first name
```

```
StartOfMidName% = EndOfFirstName% + 1        'Middle name starts at next character
EndOfMidName% = Instr(StartOfMidName%, FullName$, " ")  'Find the next space character indicating end of middle
                                             'name

FirstNameLen% = EndOfFirstName% - 1          'Figure lengths of names
MidNameLen% = EndOfMidName% - StartOfMidName%
LastNameLen% = Len(FullName$) - EndOfMidName%

FirstName$ = Left$(FullName$, FirstNameLen%)    'Extract the names
MidName$ = Mid$(FullName$, StartOfMidName%%, MidNameLen%)
LastName$ = Right$(FullName$, LastNameLen%)
```

This example uses the Left$, Mid$, and Right$ functions to separate the first, middle, and last names from a string containing all three. The separate strings can now be rearranged as desired—for example, you could change a name from "First, Middle, Last" order to "Last, First, Middle" and then alphabetize by last name.

There is also a Mid$ *statement*. The difference between a statement and a function is that a function returns a value, while a statement does not. The statement form of Mid$ is used to change the specified portion of an existing string to some other set of characters. Because this is a statement rather than a function, the keyword MID$ appears to the left of the assignment operator:

```
T$ = "This car is red"
Mid$(T$, 6, 3) = "bat"
```

This example changes the value of T$ to "This bat is red".

### Working with the ASCII Character Set

Although it is not required that you memorize which characters are represented by which ASCII codes, it is sometimes useful to be able to determine the ASCII code of a character, or to translate an ASCII code into a character. These tasks are performed by the Asc and Chr functions.

The Asc function returns the ASCII code for the supplied character. Conversely, the Chr function returns a 1-byte string containing the character that is represented by the supplied ASCII code.

```
ThisDate$ = "01-01-1992"
DateLen% = Len(ThisDate%)
DashValue% = Asc("-")
SlashValue% = Asc("/")
For CharPos% = 1 To DateLen%
    ThisChar$ = Mid$(ThisDate$, CharPos%, 1)
    CharVal% = Asc(ThisChar$)
    If CharVal% = DashValue% Then
        ThisChar$ = Chr$(SlashValue%)
        Mid$(ThisDate$, CharPos%, 1) = ThisChar$
    End If
Next
```

In the above example, the variable ThisDate$ holds a formatted date string. This routine examines the ASCII values of each character in the string, and if it comes upon a dash character (-), translates it to a slash (/).

### Comparing Strings

Strings are compared using the same operators (such as =, <, or >) that are used with numbers. With strings, a statement such as:

```
If A$ = B$ Then PRINT "They are equal"
```

checks to see whether A$ and B$ are equal. But although two strings may seem equal to you, Visual Basic may not agree. For instance:

```
A$ = "Hello"
B$ = "Hello "
If A$ = B$ Then C% = 1 Else C% = 2
```

Even though the strings A$ and B$ are essentially the same, Visual Basic will not consider them equal, because B$ has a following space while A$ does not. To combat this, Visual Basic has two functions, LTrim$ and RTrim$, which examine and return a copy of a string with extra spaces removed. The LTrim$ function will remove any spaces from the left side of the source string, while RTrim$ removes spaces from the right.

```
A$ = "Hello"
B$ = "Hello "
If  BTrim$(A$) = BTrim$(B$) Then C% = 1 Else C% = 2

Function BTrim$(T$)
    Temp$      = LTrim$(T$)
    BTrim$     = RTrim$(Temp$)
End Function
```

This example uses the programmer-defined function BTrim$ to trim both leading and following spaces from a string. BTrim$ uses the Visual Basic functions LTrim$ and RTrim$ to do this.

Another situation that can interfere with the comparison of two strings is capitalization. If two strings that are otherwise identical are capitalized differently, Visual Basic will not view them as equal.

```
A$ = "HELLO"
B$ = "Hello"
If A$ = B$ Then C% = 1 Else C% = 2
```

In this example, A$ and B$ will not be equal because they are capitalized differently. You can control the case of letters within a string with the LCase$ and UCase$ functions. Both functions return a copy of the source string with the case of all letters changed. LCase$ converts the letters to lower-case, while UCase$ converts them to upper-case.

```
A$ = LCase$("HELLO")
B$ = LCase$("Hello")
If A$ = B$ Then C% = 1 Else C% = 2
```

In this example, A$ and B$ will be equal.

In comparing strings, the > (greater than) and < (less than) symbols ask whether one string is later or earlier in the alphabet than the other. For example:

```
If "Dog" > "Cat" Then Print "Greater than"
```

is true because "D" comes after "C" in the alphabet. Note however that comparison is made using the ASCII character sequence. The expression:

```
"Dog < "cat"
```

is actually true, because lower-case letters come after upper-case ones in the ASCII character sequence. Thus you should usually convert strings to all upper-case (with UCase$) or all lower-case (with LCase$) before making any comparisons.

### Creating a Series of Characters

Suppose you want to create a string that is 20 bytes long and contains 20 asterisks. (This can be useful for filling in the amount on a check.) To do this, you could assign a string literal of 20 asterisks to a string variable:

```
Asters$ = "********************"
```

While this works, it is not very elegant. What if you need a 200-byte-long string? You certainly wouldn't want to sit and type 200 asterisks! Or suppose, as with printing checks, you need to be able to print a *variable* number of asterisks on demand? A better alternative is to use the String$ function. This function allows you to create strings of repeated characters by supplying two arguments that indicate the number and type of character desired. For example:

```
Asters$   = String$(200, "*")
Fill$     = String$(Remain%, "*")
```

The first line of code assigns 200 asterisks to the variable Asters$, while the second statement uses the value of the variable Remain% to determine how many asterisks will be stored in Fill$.

The Space$ function works in the same manner as the String$ function, except that it always returns spaces.

```
Blanks$ = Space$(100)
```

This line of code assigns 100 spaces to the variable Blank$.

## Arithmetic and Numbers

One of the primary functions of computers is to relieve the user of the drudgery of having to manually perform mathematical calculations. Fortunately, Visual Basic does a good job of relieving the programmer of these tasks as well. Included in its array of commands are not only the standard math functions, such as addition and subtraction, but several more advanced functions for handling trigonometry, logarithms, and random number generation. Table A.2 lists Visual Basic's arithmetic commands.

| Use This... | | To Do This... |
|---|---|---|
| Abs | Function | Return the absolute value of a numeric expression |
| Atn | Function | Return the arctangent of a numeric expression |
| CInt | Function | Translate a numeric expression into integer format |
| CLng | Function | Translate a numeric expression into long integer format |
| CSin | Function | Translate a numeric expression into single-precision format |
| CDbl | Function | Translate a numeric expression into double-precision format |
| CCur | Function | Translate a numeric expression into currency format |
| Cos | Function | Return the cosine of a numeric expression |
| Exp | Function | Raise the natural logarithmic base ($e$) to the specified power |
| Fix | Function | Truncate the fractional part of a number and convert it to integer format |
| Hex$ | Function | Return a string that represents a number in hexadecimal (base 16) |
| Int | Function | Return the largest integer that is less than or equal to a number |
| Log | Function | Return the natural logarithm of a numeric expression |
| Oct$ | Function | Return a string that represents a number in octal (base 8) notation |
| Randomize | Statement | Seed the random number generator |
| Rnd | Function | Return a randomly generated number between 0 and 1 |
| Sgn | Function | Determine the sign of a numeric expression |
| Sin | Function | Return the sine of a numeric expression |
| Sqr | Function | Return the square root of a number |
| Tan | Function | Return the tangent of a number |
| Val | Function | Return the numeric value of a string |

**Table A.2 Functions and statements that affect numbers and numeric variables**

### Working with a Number's Sign

Visual Basic has two functions that work with the sign of a numeric value. First, the Abs function returns a numeric value that is the absolute value of the supplied argument. The absolute value of a number disregards the sign. This is handy when you need to determine the relation of two numbers.

```
A% = 5
B% = 10
C% = Abs(A% - B%)
D% = Abs(B% - A%)
```

In this example, the difference between the values in A% and B% are computed by subtracting B% from A%. Because the Abs function is used, this difference will always be a positive value. In other words, both C% and D% will contain the same value: 5.

The second function that deals with the sign of a numeric value is the Sgn function. This function very simply returns a value based on the sign of a number.

```
If Sgn(A%) = 1 Then B$ = "A% is a positive value"
If Sgn(A%) = 0 Then B$ = "A% is 0"
If Sgn(A%) = -1 Then B$ = "A% is a negative value"
```

In this example, the value of B$ is set depending on the sign of the variable A%.

### Hexadecimal and Octal Notation

By default, numeric values in Visual Basic are decimal (base 10) numbers. However, you can use hexadecimal (base 16) or octal (base 8) notation to specify values. These two forms of notations are sometimes used because they more readily translate to the internal workings of a computer. References to addresses in memory are therefore usually given in hexadecimal. Hexadecimal notation is indicated by preceding a hexadecimal number with the prefix "&H". Octal numbers are preceded by an "&O". For instance:

```
Num1% = &H100 'Assign hexadecimal 100 to Num1% (hexadecimal 100 = decimal 256)
Num2% = &0100 'Assign octal 100 to Num2% (octal 100 = decimal 64)
```

Visual Basic also provides a way to translate decimal numbers for display in hexadecimal or octal format with the Hex$ and Oct$ functions. Each of these functions require a numeric argument and return a string which is the value of the argument in the respective notation.

```
HexNum$ = Hex$(256)
OctNum$ = Oct$(64)
```

In this example, the string variable HexNum$ will have a value of "100" and OctNum$ will also have a value of "100."

### Converting from One Type of Number to Another

Visual Basic has five different numeric formats: Integer, Long, Single, Double, and Currency. (See Appendix B for more information on how the different types of numbers can be declared.) Each format is stored in memory in a different manner. There are times in a program when variables of one type must be converted to another type before they can be accurately used. For instance, when a Sub procedure is called with arguments, any values passed to the procedure must be of the same type as the Sub procedure is expecting. If the value you need to pass is not in the correct format, it must be converted before it is passed. If you assign a value to a variable, Visual Basic will automatically handle any conversion needed. Therefore:

```
B# = 200.22
A! = B#
Call Test(A!)
```

In this example, the value is automatically converted to single-precision format before it is assigned to the variable A!. However, if the only reason we are doing this assignment is to pass the value to a Sub procedure or Function, it adds an extra line of code to your program and it creates an extra variable that is otherwise not needed. A better solution is to use one of the numeric conversion functions: CInt, CLng, CSin, CDbl, CCur. Each of these functions convert a numeric value from any other type to the type indicated by the function. Using a conversion function eliminates the extra line of code and the extra variable used in the above example:

```
B# = 200.22
Call Test( CSin(B#) )
```

Two more functions are used to convert numeric values. These are the Int and Fix functions. Like the CInt function, these functions convert a numeric value (such as a single- or double-precision decimal) to integer format. Both of these differ slightly from the CInt function in how they treat the fractional portion of the supplied argument. While CInt will round the fractional portion to the nearest whole number, Int returns the next lowest integer value and Fix simply truncates the fractional portion without doing any rounding, as shown in Table A.3.

| Value | Int(Value) | Fix(Value) | Cint(Value) |
|-------|------------|------------|-------------|
| 2.7   | 2          | 2          | 3           |
| 2.2   | 2          | 2          | 2           |
| 2     | 2          | 2          | 2           |
| -2    | -2         | -2         | -2          |
| -2.2  | -3         | -2         | -2          |
| -2.7  | -3         | -2         | -3          |

**Table A.3 Return values for Fix, Int, and CInt functions**

Notice that for a negative number such as -2.7, Fix returns -2 because that is the next lower integer, while Cint returns -3 because that is the *closest* integer.

The final conversion function converts a string into a numeric value. This is done with the Val function. Val accepts one string argument, and if that argument contains a readable number, it will return that number's value. Val does this by examining the supplied string from left to right. It begins its translation as soon as it encounters a character that is not a space. The translation is ended as soon as it encounters a non-numeric character. For example:

```
A$ = " 1234 Street"
B$ = " ThisTown, Ca, 92122"
ValA! = Val(A$)
ValB! = Val(B$)
```

In this example, ValA! will be assigned a value of 1234. Because the Val function encounters non-numeric characters before any numeric characters in B$, ValB! will be assigned a value of 0.

### Trigonometric Functions

Trigonometry is a branch of mathematics that involves the measurement of the sides and angles of a right triangle. Through the use of trigonometric functions, you can determine the length of all sides and the size of all angles in a right triangle with limited information.

Trigonometry depends on two concrete facts about a right triangle. First, by definition the size of one of the angles in a right triangle is always 90 degrees. Second, the sum of all the angles in a triangle is 180 degrees. Using this information, you can determine the measurements of all sides and angles of a right triangle if you know: (a) the length of two of the sides, or (b) the length of one side and the size of one angle (other than the right angle). Figure A.1 shows a right triangle with the parts labeled. We will refer to this triangle throughout the following discussion.

Visual Basic has four trigonometric functions: Tan, Atn , Sin, and Cos. In order to provide the highest accuracy possible, each of these functions treat angle measurements as radians. Therefore, if your angles are measured in units of degrees, you will need to convert your measurements. You can convert degrees to radians with the following function definition:

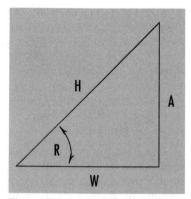

```
CONST PI = 3.14159265358979

Function Deg2Rad(Degrees)
    Deg2Rad = Degrees * (PI / 180)
End Function
```

**Figure A.1  A right triangle whose width is W, altitude is A, hypotenuse is H, and angle is R**

The first of the four functions is Tan. This function is based on the trigonometric function tangent. The tangent of an angle is equal to the altitude of the triangle divided by the width. Therefore:

```
Tan(R) = A / W    or    W = Tan(R) * A    or    A = W / Tan(R)
```

The following two lines of code use the Tan function to figure the length of the width and altitude of a triangle:

```
Altitude = Width / Tan(Angle)
Width = Tan(Angle) * Altitude
```

The Atn function is used for the trigonometric arctangent function, which is the inverse of the tangent function. It returns the angle, for which the supplied argument is the tangent. This allows you to determine the size of the angle when you know the lengths of the width and altitude:

```
Atn(A / W) = R
```

Therefore, the following line of code would determine the angle:

```
Angle = Atn(Altitude / Width)
```

The Sin function is based on the trigonometric sine function. The sine of an angle is equal to the altitude divided by the hypotenuse (the hypotenuse is the side that is opposite the right angle). Therefore:

```
Sin(R) = A / H    or    A = Sin(R) * H    or    H = A / Sin(R)
```

The following two lines of code use the Sin function to figure the length of the hypotenuse and altitude of a triangle:

```
Hypotenuse = Altitude / Sin(Angle)
Altitude = Hypotenuse * Sin(Angle)
```

Finally, the Cos function is used for the trigonometric cosine function. The cosine of an angle is equal to the width divided by the hypotenuse. Therefore:

```
Cos(R) = W / H    or    W = Cos(R) * H    or    H = W / Cos(R)
```

The following two lines of code use the Cos function to figure the length of the hypotenuse and width of a triangle:

```
Hypotenuse = Width / Sin(Angle)
Width = Hypotenuse * Sin(Angle)
```

By using one or more of these functions, your programs can determine the measurements for all sides and angles of a right triangle with only limited information.

## Logarithms

There is a way to reverse the effect of almost every mathematical operation. For example, you can reverse 3 * 4 = 12 as 12 / 4 = 3. This is a fairly simple operation when applied to addition or multiplication; however, when the arithmetic gets a bit more advanced, reversing the operations gets more complicated.

One of the areas where this applies is in exponentiation. Given the formula: $X = Y^z$; you probably know this means: multiply Y by itself the number of times indicated by Z and assign the value to X. So far no problem. But what if you have values for X and Y, and need to determine the value of Z?

This is where logarithms come in. Simply put, a logarithm is the exponent required to raise a certain base number so that it matches the target number. In other words, the logarithm of X is Z, as long as the logarithmic base is agreed upon as being Y.

There are two common types of logarithms: common and natural. Common logarithms have a base of 10. Therefore, using the above equation, Y would equal 10, and Z (the logarithm of X) would be the value needed to raise Z so it matched X. Natural logarithms have a base of approximately 2.71828182845905 (referred to as $e$). Natural logarithms can be used to calculate the logarithm of a number when the desired base is other than 10 or $e$.

Visual Basic provides two functions that deal with logarithms: Log and Exp. Both of these functions assume a logarithmic base of $e$ (natural log). The Log function returns the natural logarithm of the supplied numeric value. Exp is the inverse of Log. It raises $e$ to the specified power. The following two lines of code are functionally equivalent:

```
A! = Exp(5)
A!=2.718282 ^ 5
```

You can use the Log function to return the logarithm of any base. This is done by dividing the natural log of the desired number by the natural log of the desired base. The following function performs this task:

```
Function AnyLog(LogBase, Number)
    AnyLog = Log(Number) / Log(LogBase)
End Function
```

## Random Numbers

In most languages, random number generation is usually left up to the programmer. In Visual Basic, however, this task is handled quite nicely by the Randomize statement and Rnd function.

In computers, random numbers are not truly random. A series of random numbers must start with a seed number on which to base its number generation. This is performed by the Randomize statement. By default, the Randomize statement uses the system timer (which holds the number of seconds elapsed since midnight) as the seed. However, you can optionally specify any other number in the range -32768 to 32767. It's usually best to use the default, as this creates the closest thing to truly random numbers. If you use a specific number as a seed, the series of random numbers generated will always be the same. This may be suitable for some statistical procedures, but would not make for good games.

Randomize must be used before the Rnd function is used. Although it can be used several times throughout a program it is best if it is used only once. Therefore, the Randomize statement should be placed in the Load event of the main form or module of a program.

The Rnd function returns random numbers (based on the seed provided by the Randomize statement) in a range between 0 and 1. It is often more convenient to return random numbers in some other specified range. The following function assumes that the Randomize statement has already been executed:

```
Function Random(LoVal!, HiVal!)
    Range! = 1 + (HiVal! - LoVal!)
    Random = (Rnd * Range!) + LoVal!
End Function
```

In the above example, the programmer-defined function Random generates a random number that falls into the range defined by the arguments LoVal! and HiVal! (You could use the Int function to produce random integers.)

## Date and Time

One of the best built-in features that distinguishes Visual Basic from other BASIC languages are its date and time handling capabilities. In Visual Basic, a double-precision number called a date/time serial is used to represent dates and times. Using a date/time serial, you can store any date between January 1, 1753, and December 31, 2078, inclusive; and any time, accurate up to the second, between 00:00am (midnight) and 11:59pm. This serial number consists of two parts: one for the date, and one for the time. (See Chapter 22, *Timing and Time Information,* for more information on the use of time and timing in Visual Basic programs.)

The whole number portion of the serial number represents the date. This value is the number of days that have elapsed between December 30, 1899, and the represented day. For instance, the date serial for January 1, 1992, is 33,604. Dates previous to 12-30-1899 are represented by a negative number.

The fractional portion of the serial represents a time. This number is equal to what fraction of the day has passed between midnight and the represented time. For instance, the time serial for 12:00 noon is 0.5, because at noon half the day has elapsed.

Along with the date/time serial, Visual Basic also has functions for retrieving and setting the current system date and time using a string format.

Table A–4 lists Visual Basic date and time handling functions.

| Use This... | | To Do This... |
| --- | --- | --- |
| Date$ | Function | Return a formatted string representing the current system date |
| Date$ | Statement | Set the current system date |
| DateSerial | Function | Return a date serial based on supplied day, month, and year values |
| DateValue | Function | Translate a formatted date string into a date serial |
| Day | Function | Return the day of the month based on a date serial (1-31) |
| Format$ | Function | Return a formatted date or time string based on a supplied serial |
| Hour | Function | Return the hour of the day based on a time serial (0-23) |
| Minute | Function | Return the minute of the hour based on a time serial (0-59) |
| Month | Function | Return the month of the year based on a date serial (1-12) |
| Now | Function | Return a serial number representing the current system date and time |
| Second | Function | Return the second of the minute based on a time serial (0-59) |
| Time$ | Function | Return a formatted string representing the current system time |
| Time$ | Statement | Set the current system time |
| Timer | Function | Return the number of seconds that have elapsed since midnight |
| TimeSerial | Function | Return a time serial based on the supplied hour, minute, and second |

| | | |
|---|---|---|
| TimeValue | Function | Return a time serial based on a formatted time string |
| WeekDay | Function | Return the day of the week based on a date serial (1-7) |
| Year | Function | Return the year based on a date serial (1753 to 2078 ) |

**Table A.4 Functions and statements that deal with date and time**

### Getting the Current Date and Time

The simplest form of date and time handling come from the Date$ and Time$ functions. These functions return the current system date and time in a formatted string. The following lines of code read the current system date and time and assign those values to the Caption property of two labels:

```
Label1.Caption = Date$
Label2.Caption = Time$
```

While the Date$ and Time$ functions return formatted strings, the Now function returns a date/time serial number that represents the current date and time. As described above, this serial is a double-precision number that holds the date on the left of its decimal point and the time on the right. The following example uses the Now function to retrieve the current system date and time:

```
A# = Now
```

### Setting the System Date and Time

Your program can also set the system date and time with the Date$ and Time$ statements. Both of these statements take a formatted string as an argument:

```
Time$ = "12:20:30"        'Set the system time to 12:20:30
Date$ = "01-01-1992"      'Set the system date to Jan 1, 1992
```

### Translating between Formatted Strings and Date/Time Serials

Although the date/time serial is an efficient method for storing and working with dates and times, the number itself holds little meaning to an end user. Therefore, we need a way to translate back and forth between the serial and a readable string.

Translating from a formatted date or time string to the corresponding serial number requires the use of the DateValue and TimeValue functions. Both of these functions take a formatted string as an argument and return a serial number that represents it. Each of these functions returns only the portion of the serial that pertains to their function. In other words, the value returned by the DateValue function does not have the digits to the right of the decimal that represent time. Conversely, the TimeValue function returns a serial with no digits to the left of the decimal. The following example is a programmer-defined function that uses the DateValue and TimeValue functions to return a combined date/time serial.

```
Function DateTimeValue (InDate$, InTime$) As Double
    DateTimeValue# = DateValue(InDate$) + TimeValue(InTime$)
End Function
```

Translating a date/time serial into a readable string involves the use of the Format$ function. This function requires two arguments: the date/time serial and an edit pattern. Format$ is a very powerful function that provides several options for formatting the date and time, including the ability to print a full or abbreivated name of the month or day. The examples below use the Format$ function to assign formatted date and time strings to the Caption properties of two label controls:

```
Serial# = Now                                    'Get current system date
Label1.Caption = Format$(Serial#, "mmmm dd, yyyy")   'Display date in format
                                                 'Monthname day, year
Label2.Caption = Format$(Serial#, "hh:mm")       'Display hours and minutes, no seconds
```

### Creating a Date / Time Serial from Separate Parts

Sometimes you have all the separate parts of a date or time in numeric format and need to combine these parts into a date/time serial. For example, imagine your program has three variables that all hold a different piece of date information: YearVal%, MonthVal%, and DayVal%. There may be a need in your program for combining these values into one date serial. This can be done with the DateSerial function. DateSerial requires three integer arguments which specify the year, month, and day and return a date serial that represents those values. The TimeSerial function performs a similar task for time serials.

### Extracting Information from a Date/Time Serial

At other times it may be necessary to break a date/time serial into its component parts—days, month, years, hours, minutes, and seconds. When working with a date serial, you can use the Day (day of month), WeekDay (day of week), Month (month of year), and Year functions. For working with time serials, Visual Basic includes the Hour, Minute, and Second functions. Each of these functions takes a date/time serial as an argument and returns a specific piece of data about the date/time represented by the serial.

The following programmer-defined function uses the Day and WeekDay functions to return a number that corresponds to the week of the month represented by a date/time serial:

```
Function WeekOfMonth (Serial#) As Integer
    WorkMonth% = Month(Serial#)                            'Get the working month and year
    WorkYear% = Year(Serial#)
    WorkSerial# = DateSerial(WorkYear%, WorkMonth%, 0)  'Get the date serial for the first day of the month
    FirstWeekDay% = Weekday(FirstDayOfMonth#)              'On what week day did the fist day of the month occur?
    DayOfMonth% = Day(Serial#) + FirstWeekDay%            'Get the working day of month and factor w/first day
    Week% = (DayOfMonth% - 1) \ 7                          'Week% = 0 to 4 depending on DayOfMonth%
    WeekOfMonth = Week% + 1                                'WeekOfMonth = 1 to 5
End Function
```

### Performing Math with Dates and Times

The biggest advantage of working with date/time serials is that they allow you to easily perform math functions on dates and times. This is very useful for applications such as accounting programs that need to figure the number of days between periods. The following example figures out the number of days until Christmas:

```
XMasYear% = Year(Now)   'Get this year
XMasDate# = DateSerial(XMasYear%, 12, 25)              'Get date serial for this year's XMas
If Now > XMasDate# Then 'Has XMas already past this year?
    XMasYear% = XMasYear% + 1                          'Next XMas is next year
    XMasDate# = DateSerial(XMasYear%, 12, 25)          'Get date serial for next year's XMas
End If
DaysUntilXMas# = XMasDate# - Now
```

## Process Control

One of the reasons computers are more than just advanced calculators is that they have the ability to control the order and flow of the execution of their operations. This control over execution is called process control. Process control can be broken down into three main elements: branching, iteration, and conditional execution.

Branching is the most basic of the process control elements. It involves simply jumping from one area of code to another. In Visual Basic there are two types of branching. The first of the two merely jumps to another part of your program. It does nothing to help you return to your original starting point. The second type saves its place in the program's code before branching. This allows the program to return to where it came from once its task is finished.

Iteration involves the repetition of program instructions. There will be many times in your programs when you will wish to execute a set of instructions a number of times, or continually while (or until) a certain condition exists. Visual Basic provides three techniques for performing iteration.

Conditional execution allows your programs to execute a set of instructions only if a certain condition is true. This gives your programs the ability to make decisions based on the values of data.

Table A-5 lists the statements that perform process control tasks.

| Use This... | | To Do This... |
|---|---|---|
| Do...Loop | Statements | Repeat a group of instructions until or while a condition is True |
| Exit... | Statement | Exit from a specific block of code |
| For...Next | Statements | Repeat a group of instructions a specified number of times |
| GoSub...Return | Statements | Branch to a subroutine then return |
| GoTo | Statement | Branch without return to a portion of code |
| If...Then...Else... | (single-line If) | Perform a simple conditional execution of code |
| If...Then...Elself... | (multiple-line If) | Perform a complex conditional execution of code |
| On...Gosub | Statements | Branch based on a supplied numeric value, then return |
| On...GoTo | | Branch based on a supplied numeric value without return |
| Select Case... | | Perform conditional execution based on the value of one expression |
| Stop | Statement | Halt execution for debugging |
| While...Wend | | Repeat a group of instructions while a condition is True |

**Table A.5 Statements that perform process control**

### Branching

Visual Basic has two statements that perform branching: GoTo and GoSub. The GoTo statement branches to the specified label. It does not save its place before branching, so once it has branched, there can be no going back. Because of this, the GoTo statement is generally considered an un-structured command, and its use is frowned upon by many who consider themselves to be structured programmers.

The GoSub statement also branches to a specified label, but it saves its place before doing so. Your program can then return to its original position in the code by executing a Return statement.

Both GoTo and GoSub must specify a label that exists in the same procedure as the branching instruction. A label is a unique name that ends with a colon. For example:

```
Goto Error:
```

jumps execution to the part of the program that begins with the label Error:

(Visual Basic also allows you to use line numbers instead of labels. Line numbers are a cumbersome feature of early versions of BASIC, and are seldom used today.)

### Loops

There are three styles of loop instructions you can use to perform iteration in Visual Basic. These are: For...Next, Do...Loop, and While...Wend. Each kind of loop has its own features and is useful in particular circumstances.

### The For...Next Loop

For...Next loop performs a block of instructions for a set number of times. You specify as arguments to the For statement a starting value, an ending value, and a numeric variable name that will be used as a counter. When the For statement is first encountered, the counter variable is initialized to the starting value. The block of code is then executed until the counter variable exceeds the ending value. Figure A.2 shows the flow of a For...Next loop. The following statements:

```
Total = 0
For N% = 1 To Num%
     Total = Total + N%
Next N%
```

count from 1 to the value of Num%, summing the numbers in between.

Note that you can specify that the counter be incremented by a number other than 1, by using the Step keyword. The following loop:

```
For N% = Num% To 1 Step -1
```

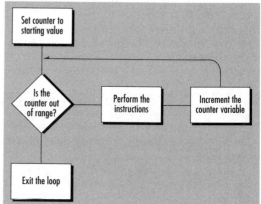

**Figure A.2 The flow of a for-next loop**

counts *downward* from the value of Num% to 1.

### Varieties of the Do...Loop Structure

The Do...Loop is the most versatile and hence the most useful loop structure in Visual Basic. The statements that comprise a Do...Loop allow you to repeat a block of code as long as a certain condition (which is defined by you) exists, or until a certain condition becomes true. It also lets you specify whether to check the condition at the top or bottom of the loop. Essentially, this gives you four unique styles of loops:

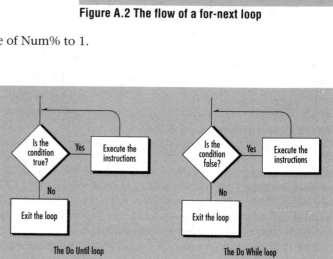

**Figure A.3 The flow of the Do Until and Do While loops**

Do While, Do Until, Loop While, and Loop Until.

Both the Do While and Do Until loops check the condition at the top of the loop. This means that if the exit condition is met before the loop is entered, the instructions within the Do...Loop will not execute. The following are examples of the Do While and Do Until loops:

```
Open "TEST.DAT" For Input As #1
Do Until EOF(1)
     Line Input #1, A$
Loop

Open "TEST.DAT" For Input As #1
Do While NOT EOF(1)
     Line Input #1, A$
Loop
```

These two loops are actually equivalent: both make sure that the end of the file has not been reached *before* attempting to input any data. Since reading beyond the end of a file generates an error, it is important that checking be done at the top of the loop. Figure A.3 shows the flow of processing in the Loop Until and Loop While loops. Notice that the only difference is that the Loop Until loop checks whether the condition is true, and the Loop While loop checks whether the condition is false.

The Loop While and Loop Until loops check the exit condition at the end of the loop. Therefore, the statements within the loop are always executed at least once. The following are examples of these styles of loops:

```
Do                                                      'This is a Loop Until loop
    Person$ = InputBox$("Please enter your name")       'The block of code within the loop will repeat until
    Person$ = LTrim$(Person$)                           'the user enters something into the input box
    Person$ = RTrim$(Person$)
Loop Until Person$ > ""
```

```
Do                                                      'This is a Loop While loop
    Person$ = InputBox$("Please enter your name")       'The block of code within the loop will repeat as long
    Person$ = LTrim$(Person$)                           'as the variable Person$ is null
    Person$ = RTrim$(Person$)
Loop While Person$ = ""
```

The flow of these loops is illustrated in Figure A.4. Notice that here, too, the only difference between the loops is that Loop Until checks whether the condition is true, while the Loop While loop checks whether it is false. In both cases, the code is executed once before the check is made, since at least one iteration is needed for the user to enter the data.

### The While...Wend Loop

The final of the three types of loops is the While...Wend loop. This loop structure is left over from older BASIC languages. Basically, it performs the same function in the same manner as the Do While loop discussed above:

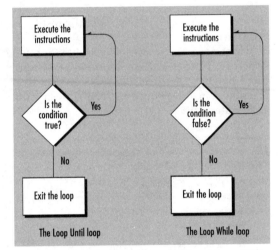

**Figure A.4 The flow of the Loop Until and Loop While loops**

```
Open "TEST.DAT" For Input As #1
While NOT EOF(1)
    Line Input #1, A$
Wend
```

### Conditional Execution

Conditional execution is used to define a set of instructions that will only be executed if a certain condition (defined by you) is true. In other words, conditional execution allows your program to make decisions and perform specific tasks based on the outcome of these decisions.

The most simple of Visual Basic's decision making statements is the single-line If statement. This statement simply says: If the condition is true, do a task. Optionally, you can also specify a second task for the If statement to perform when the condition is false: If the condition is true, do a task; otherwise, do a different task. The following is an example of a single-line If statement:

```
CONST True = -1
CONST False = 0
If A% = B% Then C% = True Else C% = False
```

The single-line If statement is limited to one line of instructions. In other words, if you need to execute a whole block of instructions based on the outcome of a condition, this statement will not work well. When this is the case, it is better to use a multiple-line If statement. Along with allowing you to define blocks of code that will be executed depending on a condition, the multiple-line If statement lets you group seemingly unrelated tests in the same If statement:

```
If GarmentColor = Green Then
    GreenShirts = GreenShirts + 1
    Cost = Cost + 1
ElseIf GarmentSize = Large Then
    LargeShirts = LargeShirts + 1
End If
```

In this example, the variable GarmentColor is tested to see if it equals the value in Green. If it does, the block of code under the test is executed. If it does not, the GarmentSize variable is tested.

If you need to test a single variable for several different values, you can use the Select Case structure. The Select Case structure very simply makes many tests on the same value. Structured programmers prefer to use Select Case over a multiple-line If because they feel it is more readable. The following examples show a multiple-line If statement and the equivalent Select Case statement:

```
If ThisColor = Blue Then
    CtrBlue = CtrBlue + 1
ElseIf ThisColor = Red OR ThisColor = Green Then
    CtrNotBlue% CtrNotBlue% + 1
Else
    CtrOther = CtrOther + 1
End If

Select Case ThisColor
    Case Blue
        CtrBlue = CtrBlue + 1
    Case Red, Green
        CtrNotBlue% CtrNotBlue% + 1
    Case Else
        CtrOther = CtrOther + 1
End Select
```

Both of the above examples are functionally equivalent. However, the Select Case is clearer and easier to understand.

The final two conditional statements in Visual Basic are the On GoTo and On GoSub statements. These statements put a twist on the branching commands GoTo and GoSub that we discussed earlier. Instead of specifying one label as the target of the branch operation, you supply these statements with a numeric value and a list of labels. Depending on the value supplied, the program will branch to one of the listed labels:

```
On A% GoSub First, Second, Third
    :
    :
First:
    B$ = "Your horse won!"
Return

Second:
```

```
        B$ = "Your horse placed!"
Return

Third:
        B$ = "Your horse showed!"
Return
```

Note that the On GoSub and On GoTo statements automatically assign sequential integers to the specified variable. That is, in the above example, when A% is 1, the instructions at the label First: are executed, when A% is 2 the instructions at Second: are executed, and so on. On GoTo works in the same way except that there is no return from the branch.

## Programmer-Defined Functions and Procedures

One of the main elements of structured programming involves defining and using self-contained areas of a program called procedures. Most often, these procedures are designed to perform a single task. Such a procedure can be called any number of times from within a program to perform that task. Coding in this manner provides three distinct advantages. First, once the procedure is coded and debugged, it can be used any number of times without having to recode it. Second, using separate procedures makes a program modular, organizing the code to match the functional structure of the program. Therefore, it is easier to track down and eliminate any logic errors in an application. Finally, because these procedures are entirely self-contained, any variables declared within a procedure become local variables that cannot be changed from outside the procedure. This eliminates any logic errors that might occur if the programmer inadvertently uses the same variable name for two different purposes in different areas of a program.

For many years, the BASIC languages did not have the ability to define or use procedures. Fortunately, that is no longer the case. As a matter of fact, all of the events that are linked to objects in Visual Basic are procedures. Visual Basic, along with some other modern BASIC languages, includes two types of procedures: Functions and Sub procedures. Both Functions and Sub procedures are used to perform a specific task defined by the programmer. Functions have an added feature in that along with performing their task, they can return a value.

Table A.6 lists the statements used to define and use programmer-defined Functions and Sub procedures.

| Use This... | | To Do This... |
| --- | --- | --- |
| Call | Statement | Execute a programmer-defined or DLL Sub procedure |
| Declare | Statement | Inform Visual Basic of external DLL procedures |
| Exit | Statement | Exit a programmer-defined Sub procedure or Function |
| Function... | Statements | Define a programmer-defined function |
| End Function | | |
| Sub...End Sub | Statements | Define a subprocedure |

**Table A.6 Statements that control functions and procedures**

### Scope of Functions and Sub Procedures

Much like variables, Functions and Sub procedures have a scope. The scope of a Function or Sub procedure defines that procedure's accessibility to other portions of your program. Functions and Sub procedures can be placed in the code area of a form or inside a module. Any Functions or Sub procedures that are defined in the code area of a form are local to that form. In other words, the procedure cannot be called from another form. Procedures defined in a module are global throughout the application. This means they can be called from any form or module.

### Defining and Using Programmer-Defined Sub Procedures

Before a Sub procedure can be used, you must define it. You do this with the Sub and End Sub statements. These statements surround the code inside the Sub procedure and define the beginning and end of the procedure. One of the nicest things about using Sub procedures is that you can define them so that they accept arguments that provide information to act on. The following is an example of a Sub procedure:

```
Sub SinIncrement (A!)
    A! = A! + 1
End Sub
```

In this example, we have defined a Sub procedure that accepts one single-precision argument. This Sub procedure increments (adds 1 to) the argument and then exits. Once the procedure has been designed, it can then be executed by calling it as follows:

```
Dim C as Single
Call SinIncrement(C)
```

Alternatively, you can omit the Call keyword and simply have:

```
SinIncrement C
```

When you omit the word Call you must also omit the parentheses around the procedure arguments.

As you can see, when the Sub procedure is defined, it uses a variable called A! as its argument. However, when we called it, we used a variable named C. When the call to the Sub procedure is made, Visual Basic substitutes the value C for its argument A!. The only thing you need to make sure of is that the parameters passed to a Sub procedure are of the same variable type as the argument that the procedure is expecting. In other words, if you define a procedure so that it expects a single-precision argument, you must use a single-precision value when you call it.

### Defining and Using Programmer-Defined Functions

As stated above, a Function is very similar to a Sub procedure. The big difference is that a Function returns a value, while a Sub procedure does not. Functions are defined in a similar manner as a Sub procedure. Instead of using Sub and End Sub statements, however, Functions are defined with Function and End Function statements. An extra step is also involved in defining a Function. Because Functions return a value, you need to specify what type of value (single-precision, integer, string, and so on) the Function is to return. You also need to tell the Function exactly what value to return before exiting. This example shows a function definition:

```
Function BTrim$ (T$)
    Temp$    = T$
    Temp$    = LTrim$(Temp$)
    Temp$    = RTrim$(Temp$)
    Btrim$   = Temp$
End Function
```

In this example, we've defined a function that accepts one string argument. Because the function name (BTrim$) ends in a type declaration character ($), we know that it will return a string value. The purpose of this function is to return a copy of its passed argument with both leading and following spaces removed. Notice that the function's code ends with the statement Btrim$ = Temp$. Assigning a value to the function name (BTrim$) gives the function its return value.

### The Operating Environment

Regardless of the purpose of the application, chances are it will need to interact with the operating environment in some manner. The operating environment on a computer is the main interface between an application and the hardware present on the system. Because of the existence of the operating environment, your applications will rarely need intimate information about a hardware device in order to use it. Instead, your programs make general requests of the operating environment, and it handles the down and dirty details of accessing the hardware involved.

Visual Basic provides several useful commands for accessing portions of the operating environment. These commands include the ability to navigate through the DOS file system, to load and execute others applications, and to read and react to special commands and environment variables.

Table A.7 lists the Visual Basic commands that deal with the operating environment.

| Use This... | | To Do This... |
| --- | --- | --- |
| AppActivate | Statement | Give the focus to a running Windows application |
| Beep | Statement | Sound a tone on the system speaker |
| ChDir | Statement | Change the current working directory |
| ChDrive | Statement | Change the default working drive |
| Command$ | Function | Retrieve command line parameters used to launch the program |
| CurDir$ | Function | Retrieve the current working directory |
| Dir$ | Function | Retrieve a directory entry that matches a specified file name pattern |
| Environ$ | Function | Retrieve entries from DOS's environment variable table |
| Kill | Statement | Remove a file from the disk |
| MkDir | Statement | Create a subdirectory |
| Name | Statement | Rename a file on the disk |
| RmDir | Statement | Remove a subdirectory |
| Shell | Function | Initiate execution of a program |

**Table A.7 Functions and statements that deal with the operating environment**

### The DOS File System: Drives, Directories, and Files

In Chapter 19, we discussed how you can use the Visual Basic Drive, Directory, and File list boxes to visually navigate the DOS file system. The Visual BASIC language also includes several commands for performing similar tasks from within your program without using those objects. To start with, you can use the ChDrive and ChDir statements to change the default drive and working sub-directory. You can also use the CurDir$ function to determine the current default drive and directory.

Visual Basic also has three commands that work with DOS files. The first and most powerful of the three is the Dir$ function. This function returns file names in the current default directory that match a specified pattern, much in the way that the DIR command in DOS does. The following example reads all file names with an extension of "DAT" into a list box:

```
A$ = Dir$("*.DAT")
Do Until Len(A$) = 0        'When A$ is null, all file names have been read
   List1.AddItem A$         'Add the file name to the list box
   A$ = Dir$
Loop
```

The other two commands are the Kill and Name statements. The Kill statement erases files from a disk in a way similar to the DEL command in DOS. The Name statement is used to change the name of a file (similar to the REN command in DOS).

### Command-Line Parameters and Environment Variables

The command line is the text used to launch an application from the Windows environment. It always includes the path and name of the program's executable file. This command line can also include one or more parameters that, when read by the application, direct it to behave in a certain manner upon startup. The syntax and meaning of these parameters, sometimes called switches, are defined by the application that reacts to them. You can design your programs to react to command line switches by reading the string returned by the Command$ function. This function returns all text that appears on the command line following the program's executable file name.

One common use for the Command$ function is to specify the name of a file that is to be automatically loaded when the program starts up. The following example reads the string returned by the Command$ function, and if a valid file name is specified, calls a procedure to load it:

```
FileName$ = Command$                                  'Get the command line parameter
If Len(FileName$) > 0 Then FileName$ = Dir$(FileName$)  'If file is specified, check to see if it exists
If Len(FileName$) > 0 Then Call LoadFile(FileName$)     'If FileName$ is not null, it exists. Load it.
```

Another useful function for obtaining information from the system is the Environ$ function. DOS contains an internal table that holds miscellaneous strings. These strings are called environment variables and most often hold information regarding the set up of the particular system upon which your programs are run.

Environment variables follow a specific format. The name of the environment variable precedes an equal sign, which is then followed by the value of the variable, as in:

```
variable_name=variable_value
```

The Visual Basic Environ$ function lets your programs read these variables in one of two possible ways. First, you can read a variable by specifying its name in the Environ$ function:

```
A$ = Environ$("TEMP")
```

This will copy the value of the TEMP variable to the string variable A$. (If this variable does not exist, A$ will be given a null value.) The second method for retrieving environment variables involves using a number to indicate the position of the desired variable in the environment table. When this method is used, the variable name as well as its value is returned. This example reads all of a system's environment variables into a list box:

```
Ctr% = 1                              'Initialize counter variable
Do   List1.AddItem Environ$(Ctr%)     'Add environment variable name and value Doto list box
     Ctr% = Ctr% + 1                  'Point to next environment variable
Loop Until Len(Environ$(Ctr%)) = 0    'When Environ$ returns a null string, all DoDovariables have been read
```

Environment variables are set with the DOS SET command. Each computer system will probably have a different set of environment variables with different values. As a matter of fact, it's a fair bet that no two computers have exactly the same group of environment variable settings. However, there are a few environment variables that can be found on most computers. One of these variables is the "PATH" variable. This variable lists all drives and directories that should be searched when trying to locate an executable file. Another is the "COMSPEC" variable. This variable lists the drive and path in which the DOS command line processor (COMMAND.COM) can be found. Finally, when Windows starts, it adds its own variable called "windir". Unlike all other environment variable names, which are in uppercase letters, this entry is in lower-case. The "windir" variable contains the path to the Windows directory.

### Executing Other Programs

The Shell function is used to execute other programs. Using this function, you specify the path and file name of the executable file you wish to run. This file can be a DOS command (such as CHKDSK) or some other program on the disk. You can also specify the status of the program when it begins. In other words, you can control whether the new program will be run in windowed or full screen mode, and whether it will immediately receive the focus. Shell automatically searches the DOS path for the executable file. If the file is found and it executes without error, the Shell function will return the Windows task ID of the executing program.

You can also use the AppActivate statement to direct Windows to give the focus to a specific application. This application must already be running before the AppActivate statement is executed. (The concept of the application focus is covered in detail in Chapter 21, *Establishing and Controlling the Application Focus*.)

## Working with Data Files

Computers would be of little use if they did not have a way in which to store data in a fairly permanent manner. Could you imagine what it would be like if each time you needed a computer to process a large amount of information someone had to enter all the raw data first? Obviously, it would be a time-consuming, tedious task. Fortunately, this is not the case. Computers these days have fast high-capacity disk drives on which to store data.

Visual Basic puts a complete set of file-manipulating commands at your disposal. About the only thing missing from Visual Basic's collection of features is an indexed or keyed file format. Hopefully, this will come in later versions of the language or in third-party add-ons.

Table A.8 lists the file-related functions and statements in Visual Basic.

| Use This... | | To Do This... |
|---|---|---|
| Close | Statement | Terminate processing of an open file |
| EOF | Function | Determine if the end of a sequential access file has been reached |
| FileAttr | Function | Retrieve system information about an open file |
| FreeFile | Function | Retrieve an unused file number |
| Get | Statement | Read data from a binary or random access file |
| Input | Statement | Read data from a sequential access input file |
| Input$ | Function | Read a specified number of bytes from a file |
| Line Input | Function | Read one line of data from a sequential access input file |
| Loc | Function | Retrieve the current location of the file pointer in a file |
| Lock...UnLock | Statements | Restrict multiple-user access to a portion of a file |
| LOF | Function | Retrieve the length (in bytes) of an open file |
| LSet | Statement | Copy data to a record variable |
| Open | Function | Initiate processing of a file |
| Print | Statement | Write undelimited data to a sequential access output file |
| Put | Statement | Write data to a binary or random access file |
| Reset | Statement | Close all open files |
| Seek | Function | Return the actual position of the file pointer |
| Seek | Statement | Move the file pointer to a specified position in a file |
| Type...End Type | Statements | Define a record variable for random access files |
| Width | Statement | Define the width of a sequential access output file |
| Write | Statement | Write delimited data to a sequential access output file |

**Table A.8 Functions and statements that file operations**

## Opening a File

The Open statement is used to initiate processing on a file. A file must be opened before you can do anything else with it. Using this statement tells Visual Basic the path and name of the file you wish to open, how you wish to process the file, and what number you wish to use in order to refer to this file in subsequent operations. This is an example of a typical open statement:

```
Open "TEST.DAT" For Random As #1 Len = 128
```

This example opens the file TEST.DAT, and specifies that is will be processed in random input/output mode. This file is opened as file number 1. The file number is how this particular file will be referenced by other file operations as long as it is open. No two open files can use the same file number simultaneously. If you wish, you can let Visual Basic keep track of which file numbers are currently in use, and which are available with the FreeFile function. Use the FreeFile function to assign the next available unused file number to a variable. Then you use that variable to reference the file in all subsequent file operations:

```
Dim TestFile As Integer              'Place in the Global module so Testfile can be accessed
                                     'from anywhere in the program
    :
    :
TestFile = FreeFile                  'Get next available unused file number
Open "TEST.DAT" For Random As #TestFile Len = 128  'Open the file
```

### Sequential Access Files

Sequential files are processed from beginning to end in a line-by-line manner. When opened, the file pointer is placed at the beginning of the file (except when opened for Append, which places the pointer at the end of the file). Each read or write moves the file pointer forward. Under normal circumstances, the file pointer never goes back, it only moves forward.

Sequential files can be opened in one of three modes: Output, Append, or Input. When you open a sequential output file, Visual Basic searches the specified directory. If the file name you specified in the open statement does not exist, it will be created. If it does exist, the current file is erased, and a new one is created. You can then write data to the file with the Print # and Write # statements. Both of these statements write ASCII characters to the file. The difference between the two is that the Print # statement does no formatting of the data, while the Write # statement adds comma delimiters between each value written to the file.

When you open a sequential append file, Visual Basic searches the specified directory for the specified file name. If the file is not found, an error occurs. However, if the file is found, the file pointer is placed at the end of the file. From that point on, the file is treated as if it was a sequential output file, and the data you write is added to the file.

When you open a sequential input file, Visual Basic searches the specified directory for the specified file name. If the file is not found, an error occurs. If the file is found, you may use the Input #, Input$, and Line Input # statements to read data from the file. You must be careful not to read past the end of the file, as this causes an error to occur. You can prevent this by using the EOF function to test for the end of the file. The following example reads a sequential file a line at a time until the end is reached:

```
Open "TEST.DAT" For Input As #TestFile
Do Until EOF(TestFile)
    Line Input #TestFile, A$
Loop
```

### Random Access Files

Random access files are both input and output files. Random access files are record based. In other words, they are made up of a group of the same size records. The size of a random access record is defined in the file's Open statement with the Len clause. Unlike sequential files, this type of access mode allows you to move directly to any record position in the file.

Records are read with the Get # statement. The Get # statement allows you to specify which record you wish to read, and a record variable as the target of the operation. Visual Basic will read data from the indicated record and copy it to the record variable. Each time a read is done, a full record is read, regardless of the size of the record variable used. In other words, if you specify a record length of 128 bytes in the open statement, then 128 bytes will be read with each Get # statement, no matter how large or small the record variable is. Records are most often defined with the Type...End Type structure:

```
                                    'This code appears in the global module
Type NameAndAddress
    First As String * 25            'First name
    Middle As String * 1            'Middle initial
    Last As String * 25 'Last name
    Street As String * 25           'Street name
    City As String * 25             'City name
    State As String * 2             'State abbreviation
    Zip As Long                     'Zip code
    Filler As String * 21           'Filler to make it a 128 byte record
End Type

                                    'This code appears in your program
Dim NaddrsRecord As NameAndAddress  'Declare record variable

RecordLen% = Len(NaddrsRecord)      'Get length of record
NaddrsFile% = FreeFile              'Get a file number
Open "NADDRS.DAT" For Random As #NaddrsFile% Len = RecordLen%    'Open the file
Get #NaddrsFile%, 100, NaddrsRecord
```

This example opens the random file NADDRS.DAT and reads record number 100 into the record variable NaddrsRecord. This record is declared as the user-defined NameAndAddress type. Once you have read a record you can access its individual parts by referring to the name of the record file and the name of the field you are interested in. For example, NaddrsRecord.Last refers to the last name field, which is a string of 25 characters. (If the actual name is shorter than 25 characters, the remaining characters will be blanks. You can get rid of the blanks with the RTrim$ function.)

The LSet statement can be used to copy the contents of one record variable to another. For example:

```
Dim Person1, Person2 As NameAndAddress
LSet Person1= Person2
```

copies all the information for Person2 into the Person1 record. Note that if the two records are of different user-defined types only the number of bytes contained in the shorter of the two record types will be copied.

Writing records to a random file is very similar to reading them. Instead of the Get statement, you use the Put statement. Just as in the Get statement, you can specify a record number on which the operation will take place. Again, the record size indicated by the open statement dictates how many bytes are written to the file.

```
Put #NaddrsFile%, 100, NaddrsRecord
```

## Binary Files

Like Random files, binary files are also input/output files. However, while random files are record-oriented, binary files are byte-oriented. This means that the records in a binary file can be of variable size. Binary files also use the Get # and Put # statements to read and write to files. Instead of specifying a record position in the file, however, when used on binary files these statements specify a byte position. The length of the read or write is determined by the length of the record variable used.

## Getting Information About an Open File

Visual Basic provides several commands that report on the current condition of an open file. One of these is the FileAttr function. Depending on which you request, this function returns one of two pieces of information. The first of the two is a code which indicates which mode the file was opened under: Input, Output, Append, Random, or Binary. This function can also return a value which equals the DOS file handle that was assigned to this file by the operating system. This number is sometimes needed in order to access this file from a DLL (Dynamic Link Library). The following example uses both aspects of the FileAttr function:

```
VB_OpenMode% = FileAttr(1, 1)
DOS_Handle% = FileAttr(1, 2)
```

Another useful function is the LOF (length of file) function. This function returns the length of a file in bytes. It is most useful for determining the end of a binary file or the number of records in a random file. The following example figures the number of 128-byte-length records in a random file that was opened using file number 1:

```
NumberOfRecords& = LOF(1) / 128
```

The Seek function returns a value that indicates the current position of the file pointer. When used on random files, the value returned by this function indicates a record number. With all other file types, this value represents a byte position within the file. You can also use Seek as a statement to move the file pointer to a specific position in a file.

The final function that returns file information is the Loc function. This function is very similar to the Seek function. While the Seek function returns the current position of the file pointer, Loc returns the position of the file pointer at the time of the last read or write. For random files, the value returned is a record number. For binary files, the value is a byte position. For sequential files, the value is current byte position divided by 128. This makes Loc just about useless with sequential files.

## Working in a Networked Environment

When working in a networked environment, special attention must be paid to how files are accessed. Because several users may have access to the same data in the same file simultaneously, you need to write your programs so they prevent any possible corruption of data. Most often, this is done by restricting multiple accesses to the file or portions of the file at specific times.

To start with, the Open statement has two clauses that control the access to a file. These are the access and lock clauses. The access clause tells the operating system what type of access your program is requesting from the file. You can request read, write, or read and write privileges. The success or failure of the file open depends on the access you request and any restrictions other users have previously placed on the file.

The lock clause tells the operating system what privileges your program will allow other users once it has opened the file. Your program can specify that other users be allowed full access, or it can restrict read access, write access, or both read and write access.

Requesting access and restricting privileges in the Open statement are file locking measures. In other words, such measures affect the entire file. However, if several users need simultaneous access to a file, you should not restrict access to the entire file. Instead, you should only restrict access to those portions of the file that are currently being worked on by your program. This is done with the Lock and UnLock statements. With the Lock statement, you specify a portion of a file (one or more records for random files, or one or more bytes for binary files) to which no other users may have access. This restriction stays in effect until you reverse it with the UnLock statement.

This concludes our brief tour of the elements of the Visual Basic language.

# Appendix B
# Visual Basic Language Reference

This appendix provides a concise but complete reference to all the statements and functions that make up the BASIC language used by Visual Basic. We will first review the language elements that you use to construct Visual Basic program statements. These elements include variables, constants, built-in and programmer-defined data types, and operators. The bulk of the appendix is an alphabetical reference that describes each of Visual Basic's keywords—both those that form statements (such as Dim and If) and those that represent built-in functions that process data (such as Abs and Format$). Each entry details the purpose and syntax of the statement or function and gives an example and a description illustrating its use.

If you don't have much experience with BASIC programming, we recommend that you explore one or more of the books listed in Appendix E, *Further Reading*. If you are familiar with BASIC but want to review some important aspects of the language and learn about some of the special features of Visual Basic's implementation of the BASIC language, we suggest that you read Appendix A, *Visual Basic Language Tutorial*.

## Elements of the Visual Basic Language

Visual Basic has many unique features with its objects, properties, methods, and events. The main purpose of these special features is to provide you with a quick and easy way to give your programs an intuitive graphic user interface. However, these features do not give your programs the tools to do the actual processing tasks that are the core of any application. For this reason Visual Basic comes complete with a powerful set of language commands that allow you to write complex programs to handle just about any chore. We will now briefly summarize the language elements of Visual Basic.

## Variables

Variables are how a programming language refers to the various types of data that can be held in the computer's memory. To use variables successfully you must know how you can name a variable, what types of data a variable can represent, and how to assign and use the value of a variable.

### Variable Names

Visual Basic has some rules regarding how you may set up a variable name. These rules help Visual Basic tell the difference between your variables and other elements of the language. These rules are:

1. A variable name may not be longer than 40 characters.

2. The first character of a variable name must be a letter (A through Z). This letter can be uppercase or lowercase.

3. The remaining characters can be letters (A through Z or a through z), numbers (0 through 9), or underscores (_).

4. The last character can be one of these type declaration characters (explained later): %, &, !, #, @, $

5. The variable name cannot be a Visual Basic reserved word. Reserved words include Visual Basic properties, events, methods, operators, statements, and functions.

Variable names in Visual Basic are not case-sensitive. That is, Visual Basic makes no distinctions between upper- and lowercase characters in a variable name. In the code fragment below, all three lines refer to the same variable.

```
invoicetotal = 100
INVOICETOTAL = 100
InvoiceTotal = 100
```

When declaring and using variable names, it is helpful to use a name that is easily read and describes the purpose of the data that it contains, rather than a cryptic abbreviation such as N or T1. This makes it much easier for you to understand how a program works. Proper use of capitalization can help make variable names more readable. For instance, although the three lines in the example above refer to the same variable, the third format is much easier to read and understand because the first letter of each word in the variable name is capitalized. You can also use the underscore chartacter (_) to help make a variable more readable. For example:

```
Invoice_Total = 100
```

This variable name is is made more readable because the underscore character is used to seperate different words in the variable name.

### Variable Types

In most languages variables not only represent the value of data but the type as well. Each type of variable views its contents in a different way. In Visual Basic there are six simple variable types: string, integer, long integer, single-precision, double-precision, and currency. String variables represent data as ASCII characters. The other five variable types each represent a different method for storing a numeric value. The numeric type you choose determines the range of the values you can place in that variable, and how accurately they can be stored.

String variables are used to hold text or alphanumeric information. Strings can be of fixed or variable lengths. A fixed-length string is assigned a specific length when it is created, and that length cannot be changed. Variable-length strings continually shrink and grow as values are assigned to them. Theoretically, a string can be up to 65,535 characters long. However, strings require overhead in memory (4 bytes per string) for some control information, so the actual maximum length is a little less than that.

The integer variable type is the simplest kind of numeric data. This variable type requires 2 bytes of memory for storage, and can hold any whole number in the range of from -32768 to +32767. Because integers can only store whole numbers, any fractional portion of a number is rounded off to the nearest whole number when it is assigned to an integer variable.

The long integer variable type is closely related to the integer. The long type, however, uses 4 rather than 2 bytes of storage. Because of this, its range is much greater than the integer variable, allowing you to store whole numbers from -2,147,483,648 to +2,147,483,647.

Both the single-precision and double-precision variable types are used to store numbers that might have a fractional portion. These variables store values in a floating point number format. Representing numbers in floating point format is very much like using scientific notation. Like scientific notation, floating point numbers have a sign, a mantissa, and an exponent. The main difference between the two is that scientific notation is a base 10 system (decimal), and floating point numbers work on a base 2 (binary) system. The advantage of representing a number in this fashion is that it allows the variables to store a fairly large range of numbers in a limited amount of memory. However, there are disadvantages to using floating point numbers. Along with the limits on range, a floating point number is also limited to the number of digits it can represent accurately. As a result of this, rounding floating point numbers sometimes produces a result that may be insufficiently precise for your application. Finally, math operations on a floating point number are not as fast as when performed on an integer or long integer variable.

A single-precision variable requires 4 bytes of storage, and has a range of from -3.37E+38 to +3.37E+38. It can accurately hold numbers up to seven digits long. The double-precision variable uses 8 bytes of memory. It can represent numbers from -1.67D+308 to +1.67D+308—a huge range of values, with an accuracy of 16 digits.

The currency variable type is a modified integer. What sets it apart from an integer is that it has an implied decimal point. This allows numbers represented by a currency variable to have up to 4 digits to the right of the decimal point. Because it is stored as an 8-byte integer, math operations are faster on it than on floating point numbers. The range of a currency variable is from -9.22E+14 to +9.22E+14, and it can accurately represent any number of digits that fall into that range.

Table B.1 lists Visual Basic's variable types, and the range, if any, that can be held in that type.

| Variable Type | Storage Required | Range of Variable |
|---|---|---|
| String | Length of string + 4 | Up to almost 65,535 characters |
| Integer | 2 bytes | -32,768 to +32,767 |
| Long | 4 bytes | -2,147,483,648 to +2,147,483,647 |
| Single | 4 bytes | -3.402823E+38 to -1.401298E+45 and, |
| | | +1.401298E-45 to +3.402823E+38 |
| Double | 8 bytes | -1.797693134862315D+308 to -4.94066D-324 and, |
| | | +4.94066D-324 to +1.797693134862315D+308 |
| Currency | 8 bytes | -922337203685477.5808 to |
| | | +922337203685477.5807 |

**Table B.1 Types and ranges of variables in Visual Basic**

### Variable Scope

When a variable is declared in Visual Basic, the placement of its declaration determines how accessible that variable will be to certain portions of the program. The visibility of a variable to the program is referred to as a variable's scope.

The coding area of Visual Basic is set up in a tiered format. Each tier has associated with it rules that govern how variables declared within it can be accessed. These tiers are set up in a hierarchical manner.

The broadest of these tiers is called the global module. Variables declared in this area are accessible by all portions of a program. As a matter of fact, the sole purpose of the global module is to define items that can be seen by all areas of a program. No "executable" commands may be placed in the global module. When a variable is declared in this area, it is referred to as a "global" variable.

On the next level down are the coding areas of forms and modules. As you already know, a form is the object on which controls can be drawn. Each form has attached to it an area that holds program code. Modules are very much like forms without any visual elements. Instead, modules are simply areas in which to place code. Both forms and modules have an area called the General Declarations area. Variables that are declared in this area are available to any routines that are in the same form or module. These variables cannot be accessed by any routines in a different form or module. Variables declared in this area are called "form-level" or "module-level" variables. Like the global module, the General Declarations area of a form or module is reserved for declaring items. No "executable" commands may be placed there.

The last and lowest level tier contains Visual Basic procedures. Visual Basic procedures are contained inside a form or module. These include the predefined event procedures that are attached to objects, as well as programmer-defined Sub procedures and functions. Because they can only be accessed locally within a procedure, variables that are declared inside a procedure are called "local" variables.

If you have trouble figuring out the scope of a variable, draw yourself a hierarchy chart of your program. Make a box for the global module at the top of the chart, and place one box for each of the forms and modules in your program below it. Draw a line from the global module box to each of the boxes that represent a form or module. Underneath each form and module, place a box for each procedure inside that form or module. Again, draw a line from the form or module box to each of the boxes that represent a procedure inside the form or module. Inside each box, list the variables that have been declared in the area of your program represented by the box. It is now an easy task to examine the scope of the variables in your program. If you have a question about whether a variable can be accessed by a procedure, simply find that procedure's box, and follow the lines upward. Each box you encounter on your way up to the global module will list variables that are available to the procedure in question.

Figure B.1 shows an example hierarchy chart based on a program with two forms and one module, each with at least one procedure.

### Declaring Variables

So far we've discussed that you can assign a name and a type to an area of storage and refer to that memory location by its assigned name. The actual practice of assigning a name and type to an area of memory is called "declaring" a variable. In most languages, a variable must be declared in a program before it can be used. This is done because most compilers need to know how memory will be set up before it can begin compiling the executable code of a program. Although, like other languages, Visual Basic allows you to formally declare a variable before using it, this is not required. Variables in Visual Basic can be declared either implicitly or explicitly. Implicitly declared variables are variables that have been declared "on the fly"—that is, no code

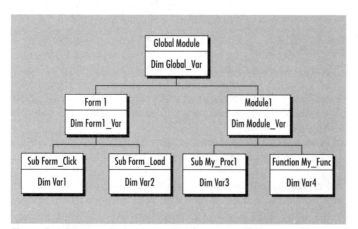

**Figure B.1 An example hierarchy chart showing variable scope**

needs to be written to specifically set up a memory location for the variable before it is used in the program. An explicitly declared variable is formally declared before it is used in the program. When you explicitly declare a variable, you include code in your program for the express purpose of informing Visual Basic that memory is to be allocated for a variable.

### Implicitly Declared Variables

In order to implicitly declare a variable in Visual Basic, you just use it in a line of code. For instance, in the following line of code, a value is assigned to a numeric variable.

```
MyVar = 1
```

If the variable MyVar had not yet been declared, Visual Basic would create storage for that variable. Because assigning a value to a variable is an executable command, implicitly defined variables can only be defined within a procedure. Therefore, all implicit variables are local variables; they cannot be accessed outside of the procedure in which they are used.

By default, when you use a variable that has not been formally declared, Visual Basic assumes that it will be a single-precision variable. However, there are two ways you can control the variable type of an implicitly declared variable. First, by appending a type declaration character to the end of the variable name, you can force Visual Basic to use a specific variable type. If you append a type declaration to a variable name, it becomes part of the variable name and must always be used to refer to that variable. For instance, in the code below, three implicit variables are assigned the numeric value of -1. Each one will store this value differently, based on the type declaration character at the end of its variable name.

```
Var1% = -1
Var2! = -1
Var3# = -1
```

In this example, Var1% is an integer variable, Var2! is a single-precision variable, and Var3# is a double-precision variable.

When strings are declared in an implicit manner, they are always declared as variable length strings. See Table B.2 for a list of the type declaration characters and the variable types with which they are used.

As mentioned previously, if you do not include a type declaration character, Visual Basic assumes an implicit variable is single-precision. This can be modified, however, with the Deftype statements. This statement is used in the General Declarations area of a form or module to define a range of letters that indicate a specific variable type. If the first letter of an implicit variable falls within this defined range, that variable will be assigned the data type specified by the Deftype statement. For instance:

```
DefInt A-F
```

In the example above, Visual Basic will assign the integer variable type to any variable that is implicitly declared in the same form or module, as long as the first letter of the variable's name falls into the range A through F. Table B.2 lists the six Deftype statements and the variable types with which they are used.

| Variable Type | Declaration Character | Deftype Statement |
|---|---|---|
| String | $ | DefStr |
| Integer | % | DefInt |
| Long | & | DefLng |
| Single | ! | DefSng |
| Double | # | DefDbl |
| Currency | @ | DefCur |

**Table B.2 Declaration characters and Deftype statements used to implicitly declare variable types**

Because you can declare variables implicitly simply by using them, Visual Basic does not generate an error when it comes across a variable name it has not yet encountered. Instead it allocates storage for that variable and proceeds normally. This can cause logic errors in your programs if you are not careful. One of the most frustrating and hard-to-find bugs that can occur in a Visual Basic program is the one that is caused by the programmer accidently mistyping a variable name. For instance, in the following code fragment, the program is supposed to figure the square root of the number 128, and place it into the variable SqrRoot.

```
This_Number = 128
SqrRoot = Sqr(ThisNumber)    'Sqr is a Visual Basic function that returns the square root of a number
```

Chances are, the variable SqrRoot is not going to be assigned the expected value. Instead, it will probably be assigned a value of 0. Why? Because the variable assigned the value of 128 is not the same as the variable used in the Sqr function. One variable name has an underscore, and the other does not. In this small code fragment, the error is fairly easy to spot. However, in larger, more complicated programs, such errors are harder to track down.

### Explicitly Declared Variables

Visual Basic also allows you to declare variables explicitly. Explicitly declared variables are assigned a variable name and data type before they are used. This is the preferred manner of declaring variables, because it makes your programs more readable. In Visual Basic you explicitly declare variables by using the Dim, Static, or Global statements. These statements have different implications for the visibility of the declared variable.

The Global statement is used when you wish to declare a variable in the global module. Variables declared using this statement are declared as global variables. That is to say, these variables are visible to all procedures in the program.

The Dim statement can be used to declare module-level variables in the General Declarations area of a form or module. Module-level variables are accessible to all procedures that are contained in the same form or module as the variable declaration.

The Dim statement can also be used inside a procedure to declare local variables. Local variables are limited in scope to the procedure in which they are declared. They cannot be accessed by other procedures. When the Dim statement is used to declare a local variable, that variable is allocated each time the procedure is entered, and de-allocated when it is exited. In other words, when Visual Basic begins to execute a procedure, it scans the procedure for Dim statements. If there are any, it will allocate memory for the variables specified by the Dim statement. When Visual Basic is through executing the procedure, it will de-allocate any memory that was assigned to a variable in the procedure with the Dim statement. This frees the memory up for other variables. However, it also means that variables declared with the Dim statement do not retain their value between procedure calls. (This sort of variable is sometimes called an "automatic variable").

The Static statement, like the Dim statement, is used to allocate storage for local variables. Local variables created with the Static statements are often called "static" variables. Unlike local variables that have been declared with the Dim statement, static variables are allocated once, and are not de-allocated until the program terminates. This means that static variables retain their value between procedure calls.

To explicitly declare a simple variable, use one of the following syntaxes:

```
Global variable_name As type    'Use this to declare a global variable
Dim variable_name As type       'Use this to declare a module-level, or local variable
Static variable_name As type    'Use this to declare a static local variable
```

In the variable_name parameter, supply a unique name that complies with the rules that apply to variable names listed earlier. Specify the type as Integer, Long, Single, Double, Currency, String or String * length (for fixed-length strings). For example:

```
Dim IntegerVar As Integer        'Declares an integer variable named IntegerVar
Dim LongVar As Long              'Declares a long integer variable named LongVar
Dim SingleVar As Single          'Declares a single-precision variable named SingleVar
Dim DoubleVar As Double          'Declares a double-precision variable named DoubleVar
Dim CurrencyVar As Currency      'Declares a currency variable named CurrencyVar
Dim StringVar As String          'Declares a string variable named StringVar
Dim FixedVar As String * 10      'Declares a 10-byte-long fixed-length string variable named FixedVar
```

## Constants: The "Read Only" Variables

Visual Basic allows you to set up a special type of variable called a constant. Constants are variables whose value is assigned either in the global module, or in the General Declarations area of a form or module, and cannot be changed. The syntax for declaring a constant is:

```
[Global] Const constant_name = value
```

The GLOBAL keyword is used if the constant is being defined in the global module. The constant_name parameter is a unique name you will use in place of the defined value in your program.

Constants are used in your programs to give a meaningful name to a value that might otherwise be ambiguous or hard to remember. For instance, colors in Visual Basic are represented by a long integer number. This number represents a mixture of the electronic primary colors: red, green, and blue. You could set the background color of an object by assigning a color's number to its BackColor property:

```
Text1.BackColor = &hFFFF
```

While this works fine, and causes no confusion to Visual Basic, it can cause you a little extra work in deciphering that the hex value FFFF is the color number for yellow. A better, more readable way to do this is to create a constant with a descriptive name, and assign the color number to it:

```
Global Const YELLOW = &hFFFF
```

In the example above, we have created a constant with the name YELLOW, which holds the value of the color number for yellow. We have placed the constant definition in the global module, so we need to proceed the Const statement with the GLOBAL keyword. We can then use the constant anywhere in our program:

```
Text1.BackColor = YELLOW
```

Constants can represent string or numeric values. It is a common practice to capitalize all the letters in a constant's name. This makes identifying a constant in your source code easier.

See the entry for Const in the alphabetical reference in this appendix for more information on this statement.

NOTE: The Visual Basic package comes with a file named CONSTANT.TXT, which contains constant declarations for color numbers, true and false values, and other system related information. You can use these declarations by loading this file directly into the global module of your programs.

## Programmer-Defined Variable Types

Visual Basic provides all the simple variable types needed to write just about any application. However, when a variable is declared, its type is specified by a keyword that only indicates the type of data the variable will represent. It says nothing about how the variable will be used. For instance, as you saw in the preceding example, Visual Basic represents colors with a long integer number. Suppose, before changing the BackColor property of a control, we wish to save its current color setting. This can be done by assigning the value of the control's BackColor property to a long integer variable.

```
Dim SaveBack As Long
SaveBack = Text1.BackColor
Text1.BackColor = YELLOW
```

This example will work fine, as long as you remember that the colors need to be stored in a long integer, and declare any variables that will be assigned a color number accordingly. If for some reason you use the wrong variable type, an improper value will be stored. As a solution to sometimes absent-minded programmers, Visual Basic allows you to set up your own variable types in the global module. You can assign meaningful names to these programmer-defined types, and then use them to declare variables anywhere in your program. Programmer-defined variables are set up with the Type...End Type statement. Let's rework the above example using Type...End Type. In the global module, we will define a variable type named ColorNumber. Inside the type definition, we will specify that this data type will have one element named Color of the long integer variable type:

```
Type ColorNumber
        Color As Long
End Type
```

Now, anywhere in our program, we can define a variable as type ColorNumber.

```
Dim SaveBack As ColorNumber
SaveBack.Color    = Text1.BackColor
Text1.BackColor   = YELLOW
```

As you can see, the variable SaveBack was defined as type ColorNumber. However, when we assigned a value to the variable, a period was added to SaveBack, which was followed by the element name Color. This indicates that SaveBack is a variable that was declared using a programmer-defined variable type, and that the value is being assigned to the Color element of that variable. You need to specify the element name because Visual Basic allows you to define variable types with more than one element. This is very useful because it allows you to refer to a group of variables with one name. For instance, suppose we wished to store people's names and social security numbers. Instead of using several variables to do this, we could set up a variable type that would hold all the information we need:

```
Type Name_And_SS
    FirstName As String      * 25
    LastName As String       * 25
    SocialSecurity As Long
End Type
```

We can then assign this type to variables. This lets us refer to all elements as one variable:

```
Dim Person1 As Name_And_SS
Dim Person2 As Name_And_SS

Person1.FirstName = "Nick"
Person1.LastName = "Scott"
Person1.SocialSecurity = 000000000
Person1 = Person2
```

As you can see, in the last line of the example, the value of one programmer-defined variable is assigned to another. This copies the contents of all the elements in one programmer-defined variable to the corresponding elements in the other. However, this can only be done when both programmer-defined variables are of the same type. (See the entry for LSet for a way to copy some programmer-defined variables of differing lengths.)

## Arrays

The basic function of an array is to store an entire series of the same type of variables and reference them by the same variable name. This is very useful when you are working on several pieces of data that all have the same variable type and purpose.

For example, suppose you need to keep track of an inventory of cars, and you need to separate them by color. You could set up a separate variable for each color, such as RedCars, BlueCars, WhiteCars, and BlackCars. Each of these variables would be declared as an integer. The purpose of each variable is the same: to hold the number of cars that are that color. This presents two problems, however. First, all the cars cannot be referenced by the same name. Therefore, if we need to determine the number of all the cars, we have to add all the variables: AllCars = RedCars + BlueCars + WhiteCars + BlackCars. This makes referring to all the cars an awkward process. Second, if a new color is added, we have to create a new variable to handle it. This means each time a new color is added, you need to modify the program and recompile it.

A better solution is to use an array to hold the data. Using an array allows you to set up one variable name, Cars, that has a separate storage area for each color. Each of these areas is referred to as an element of the array. When you work with an array, you use an index number (called the subscript) to tell Visual Basic which element you are referencing. To create an array, use the Global, Dim, or Static statements. These statements declare an array's name, variable type, and size. For instance:

```
Dim Cars(100) As Integer
Dim Colors(100) As String
```

These statements declare two arrays. The first array, Cars, is an integer array. This array can be used to store the number of cars per color. The second array, Colors, is a string array. It can be used to store the names of each of the possible colors.

The argument inside the parentheses of the array declaration specifies the number of the first and last elements in the array. In the example above, only the number of the last element in the array is specified, so Visual Basic will assume the starting array element is number 0. Therefore, both arrays will have 101 elements, numbered from 0 to 100. An integer array can have up to 65,535 elements in all. (While Visual Basic doesn't directly provide for larger arrays, Microsoft has made available a dynamic link library (DLL) that uses a Windows API call to support "huge" arrays.)

The starting element number of an array can be changed in two ways. First, you may place an Option Base statement in the General Declarations area of a form or module. This allows you to set the default starting element number to 0 or 1 when an array is declared. Second, you can specify the starting element in the array declaration:

```
Dim WorkHours(800 To 1700) As String
```

This statement declares an array whose lowest available element is 800, and highest is 1700.

After an array is declared, you need some technique for referencing elements in the array. This is done by specifying the desired element number, or subscript, in parentheses following the array name. For instance, this code fragment assigns a color name to element number 5 of the Colors array:

```
Colors(5) = "Red"
```

Not only can you define the number of elements in an array, but you can also define the number of dimensions. Up to this point, the examples we've used have all been one-dimensional arrays. You can think of one-dimensional arrays in a linear manner. For instance, the Cars array from the example above can be visualized:

```
Cars(0)  Cars(1)  Cars(2)         Cars(98) Cars(99) Cars(100)
```

However, Visual Basic allows you to set up multidimensional arrays. Multidimensional arrays have more than one set of subscript elements. For instance, by creating a two-dimensional array, you define that the array has both length and width. This lets us set up data in a tabular format. For example, the following statement sets up a two-dimensional array.

```
Dim Tbl(1 To 10, 1 To 10) As Integer
```

In order to reference an element in a multidimensional array, you need to supply a subscript for each dimension in the array. If you were to visualize the Tbl array, it might look something like this:

```
Tbl(1,1)  Tbl(2,1)  Tbl(3,1)  Tbl(4,1)  Tbl(5,1)  Tbl(6,1)  Tbl(7,1)  Tbl(8,1)  Tbl(9,1)  Tbl(10,1)
Tbl(1,2)  Tbl(2,2)  Tbl(3,2)  Tbl(4,2)  Tbl(5,2)  Tbl(6,2)  Tbl(7,2)  Tbl(8,2)  Tbl(9,2)  Tbl(10,2)
Tbl(1,3)  Tbl(2,3)  Tbl(3,3)  Tbl(4,3)  Tbl(5,3)  Tbl(6,3)  Tbl(7,3)  Tbl(8,3)  Tbl(9,3)  Tbl(10,3)
Tbl(1,4)  Tbl(2,4)  Tbl(3,4)  Tbl(4,4)  Tbl(5,4)  Tbl(6,4)  Tbl(7,4)  Tbl(8,4)  Tbl(9,4)  Tbl(10,4)
Tbl(1,5)  Tbl(2,5)  Tbl(3,5)  Tbl(4,5)  Tbl(5,5)  Tbl(6,5)  Tbl(7,5)  Tbl(8,5)  Tbl(9,5)  Tbl(10,5)
Tbl(1,6)  Tbl(2,6)  Tbl(3,6)  Tbl(4,6)  Tbl(5,6)  Tbl(6,6)  Tbl(7,6)  Tbl(8,6)  Tbl(9,6)  Tbl(10,6)
Tbl(1,7)  Tbl(2,7)  Tbl(3,7)  Tbl(4,7)  Tbl(5,7)  Tbl(6,7)  Tbl(7,7)  Tbl(8,7)  Tbl(9,7)  Tbl(10,7)
Tbl(1,8)  Tbl(2,8)  Tbl(3,8)  Tbl(4,8)  Tbl(5,8)  Tbl(6,8)  Tbl(7,8)  Tbl(8,8)  Tbl(9,8)  Tbl(10,8)
Tbl(1,9)  Tbl(2,9)  Tbl(3,9)  Tbl(4,9)  Tbl(5,9)  Tbl(6,9)  Tbl(7,9)  Tbl(8,9)  Tbl(9,9)  Tbl(10,9)
Tbl(1,10) Tbl(2,10) Tbl(3,10) Tbl(4,10) Tbl(5,10) Tbl(6,10) Tbl(7,10) Tbl(8,10) Tbl(9,10) Tbl(10,10)
```

Adding a third dimension would give the array depth, as well as length and width. However, you do not have to stop at just three dimensions. Visual Basic allows you to create arrays that have as many as 60 dimensions. Although this is a neat feature, your mind can get a little boggled when the number of dimensions in an array exceeds three. Large multidimensional arrays can also consume prodigious amounts of memory.

### Dynamic Arrays

Dynamic arrays are arrays that can be allocated and deallocated at run time. This allows you to make your programs more flexible by creating arrays whose size is determined by factors that are unknown at design time, such as the size of a data file.

Dynamic arrays are allocated using the ReDim statement and deallocated with the Erase statement. The most efficient way to set up a dynamic array is to declare it twice. The first declaration is performed in either the global module with the Global statement, or in the General Declarations area of a form or module with the Dim statement. However, declare the array without any entries inside its parentheses:

```
Dim Cars() As Integer
Dim Colors() As String
```

This tells Visual Basic that you want to declare an array, but you do not yet know how many dimensions or elements it will contain. You can then place the ReDim statement inside a procedure to define the number of dimensions and elements:

```
Sub LoadColors (LastColor As Integer)
    ReDim Colors(LastColor) As String
    ReDim Cars(LastColor) As Integer
    :
    [Place your code here]
    :
End Sub
```

You are not required to use the Global or Dim statements to originally declare a dynamic array. However, when Visual Basic allocates storage for a dynamic array at run time, the use of these statements allows it to do so faster and more efficiently. Also, the array's scope will reflect the placement of the original declare (that is, if the array was first declared in the global module, its elements will all be global variables.) However, using this method has the disadvantage of limiting a dynamic array to eight dimensions. While eight is usually enough dimensions for any application, some programs will require that an array have more.

If you wish to declare a dynamic array with more than eight dimensions, or wish it to be a local array (not accessible by any other procedure), do not include a Global or Dim statement for the array.

After a dynamic array has been declared, you can again use the ReDim statement any number of times to change the number of elements in the array. Take care when doing this, as redimensioning an array will erase the current contents of the array. The number of dimensions in an array, however, cannot be changed once it has been set.

## Operators

Operators are symbols that tell Visual Basic to manipulate data in some specified way. For example, the assignment operator (=) can store a value in a variable, while the addition operator (+) adds two quantities together. There are also operators that compare values, returning a True or False value as the result.

### The Assignment Operator

In Visual Basic the assignment operator is used to place values into a variable or property. The assignment operator is the equal sign (=). This operator is used by placing a variable or property to the left of the operator, and an expression to the right. This causes the value of the expression to be assigned to the variable or property. For example:

```
Height% = 100
Area! = PI * Radius ^ 2
MyBox.Text = MyPrompt$
```

The first example assigns the numeric literal value 100 to the integer variable Height%. In the second example, the value of the expression PI * Radius ^ 2 is assigned to the single-precision variable Area!. The last example assigns the string MyPrompt$ to the Text property of the object MyBox.

As you can see, the assignment operator is used to assign values to both numeric and string variables and properties. If your program assigns a numeric value of one data type to a numeric variable or property of a different data type, Visual Basic will automatically convert the value to the type of the receiving variable or property. For instance, if your program assigns an integer value to a single-precision variable, the value will be converted to a single-precision value before it is assigned to the variable. However, if the value is not within the allowable range for the type of the result data item, an overflow error will occur. For example, your program will cause an error if it assigns a value greater than 32767 or less than -32768 to an integer variable. You cannot assign a string value to a numeric variable or property. This causes a Type Mismatch error. By the same token, you cannot assign a numeric value to a string variable or property. Visual Basic provides the Str$ and Val functions for converting numeric values to strings and strings to numeric values.

### Arithmetic Operators

The arithmetic operators are used to perform math functions on numeric values. The familiar addition, subtraction, multiplication, and division operators need no discussion, but there are additional operators that perform other arithmetic functions. The exponentiation operator (^) causes the number on the left of the operator to be raised by the power indicated by the number on the right of the operator. You can change the sign of a numeric value with the negation operator (-). Positive numbers become negative, and negative numbers become positive. The integer division (\) and modulo arithmetic (Mod) operators perform integer math. Integer division divides one value by another, and returns the result with any fractional portion truncated. Modulo arithmetic returns the remainder of an integer division. For instance, in the following code:

```
A% = 5 \ 2
B% = 5 Mod 2
```

The value of A% will be 2 (5 divided by 2 is 2.5, truncate the .5, and you get 2), and the value of B% will be 1 (5 divided by 2 is 2, with a remainder of 1).

Visual Basic assigns an order of precedence to its arithmetic operators. When more than one operator is used in an expression, the precedence of the operators determines in which order the operations occur. For example:

```
A! = 2 * 4 - 5
```

In this example, the variable A! will be assigned a value of 3. This is because the multiplication operator has a higher precedence than the subtraction operator. Therefore, Visual Basic evaluates this expression in this order:

1. Multiply 2 and 4, getting a result of 8
2. Subtract 5 from the result (8), getting a new result of 3
3. Assign the new result (3) to A!

The precedence of an expression can be modified by surrounding an operation with parentheses. This causes the operations inside the parentheses to be executed before any operations outside them. For instance, if we place parentheses around part of the equation used above, a different value will be assigned to the variable:

```
A! = 2 * (4 - 5)
```

In this example, Visual Basic evaluates this expression in this order:

1. Subract 5 from 4, getting a result of -1
2. Multiply that result (-1) by 2, getting a new result of -2
3. Assign the new result (-2) to A!

Several sets of parenthesies may be used to control the precedence of a complex expression. The arithmetic operators are listed in Table B.3 in order of precedence.

| Use This... | To Perform... | Example |
|---|---|---|
| ^ | Exponentiation | A! = 3^4 |
| - | Negation | A! = -1 |
| *, / | Multiplication & Division | A! = B! * C! A! = B! / C! |
| \ | Integer Division | A% = B% \ C% |
| Mod | Modulo Arithmetic | A% = B% Mod C% |
| +, - | Addition & Subtraction | A% = B% + C% A% = B% - C% |

**Table B.3 Arithmetic operators in order of precedence**

### Relational Operators

Relational operators are used to compare two expressions and determine their relationship. Using the relational operators, your programs can determine if the values of two expressions are equal, if one is greater than the other, or if one is less than the other. Relational operators all share the same precedence, and unless modified by parentheses, their operations are performed after any arithmetic operations in the same expression. The values in a relational expression are examined from left to right. The relational operators available in Visual Basic are listed in Table B.4.

| Use This... | To Test For... | Example | |
|---|---|---|---|
| = | Equality | A% = B% | True if the values of A% and B% are equal |
| <> | Non-equality | A% <> B% | True if the value of A% is not equal to B% |
| > | Greater than | A% > B% | True if the value of A% is greater than that of B% |
| < | Less than | A% < B% | True if the value of A% is less than that of B% |

| >= | Greater than or equal to | A% >= B% | True if the value of A% is not less than that of B% |
| <= | Less than or equal to | A% <= B% | True if the value of A% is not greater than that of B% |

**Table B.4 Relational operators**

Most commonly, relational operators are used to help your programs make decisions. When used in this fashion, relational operators are very often used in the parameters of an If, Do...Loop, Select Case, or While...Wend statement. For instance, in the following code fragment, the values of two variables are tested for equality:

```
If A% = B% Then Label1.Caption = "A% and B% are equal"
```

In this example, the values of the integer variables A% and B% are compared. If they are equal, the Caption property of a label control is set.

Relational operators return a value that represents the result of the test. If the tested expression is true, a value of -1 is returned. If the expression is false, a value of 0 is returned. You can actually assign the results of a relational test to a numeric variable. For example:

```
C% = (A% > B%)
```

If the values of the integer variables A% and B% are equal, the value of C% will be set to -1. Otherwise, C% is assigned a value of 0.

## Logical (Bitwise) Operators

If every decision we made were based on only one factor, the world would be a much simpler place to live in. Unfortunately for us and our programs, this is not the case. Each decision made in a lifetime, and in a program, is based on several determining factors. For instance, let's talk about when to eat lunch. To start off with, you could say: "If I'm hungry, I'll eat lunch." But what if you don't have the time to eat lunch? This needs to be taken into account, so the decision on when to eat lunch is modified: "If I'm hungry, and I have time, I'll eat lunch." You could have lunch delivered, and that would save you the time you need, so your new decision would be: "If I'm hungry, and I have time or the food is delivered, I'll eat lunch." Modifying decisions in this manner is a prime example of how logical operators are used. For instance, you can use logical operators to write a line of code in a program that mirrors our lunch example:

```
If Hungry% = True And (FreeTime% > 30 Or Delivery% = True) Then Call Do_Lunch
```

Logical operators are used to combine two or more numeric values. Since the result of a relational operation is a numeric value, the most common use for logical operators is to combine relational expressions. This lets you build complex decisions from several simple decisions. Unless modified by parentheses, logical operations occur after all arithmetic and relational operations in the same expression. Like arithmetic operators, logical operators are assigned precedence. It is not a bad idea to use parentheses liberally when using logical operators. This ensures your program will reflect the exact order of precedence you desire. It also makes your code much more readable. Table B.5 lists the logical operators available in Visual Basic in their order of precedence.

| Use this... | For... | Example |
| --- | --- | --- |
| Not | Logical negation | If Not (A% = B%)... |
| And | Logical and | If (A% = B%) And (C% = D%)... |
| Or | Inclusive or | If (A% = B%) Or (C% = D%)... |
| Xor | Exclusive or | If (A% = B%) Xor (C% = D%)... |
| Eqv | Logical equivalence | If (A% = B%) Eqv (C% = D%)... |
| Imp | Implication | If (A% = B%) Imp (C% = D%)... |

**Table B.5 Logical operators in order of precedence**

Much like relational operators, an expression with logical operators actually returns a numeric value. This value is based on the bit values of the numeric expressions supplied to the logical operator. The logical operators examine these values bit by bit. Based on the settings of the bits, logical operators set a corresponding bit in the result value. Because they actually perform bit operations, logical operators are sometimes referred to as "bitwise" operators.

### Logical Negation (the Not Operator)

The logical negation operator, Not, is the only operator that has a single operand. This operator examines each bit in the supplied operand, and sets the corresponding bit in the result value to the exact opposite. In other words, if the bit in the operand is on, the bit in the result will be set off, and vice versa. Table B.6 lists the possible settings of the result bit when the Not operator is used.

| Operand Bit | Resulting Bit |
| --- | --- |
| 1 | 0 |
| 0 | 1 |

**Table B.6 Truth table for the Not operator**

### Logical And (the And Operator)

The logical and operator, And, compares the bits of its operands. If both bits are set on, the corresponding bit in the result is set on; otherwise, the result bit is set off. Table B.7 lists the possible settings of the result bit when the And operator is used.

| First Operand Bit | Second Operand Bit | Resulting Bit |
| --- | --- | --- |
| 1 | 1 | 1 |
| 0 | 1 | 0 |
| 1 | 0 | 0 |
| 0 | 0 | 0 |

**Table B.7 Truth table for the And operator**

### Inclusive Or (the Or Operator)

The inclusive or operator, Or, compares the bits of the two operands. If one or both of the bits is on, it sets the corresponding result bit on. The only time the result bit is set off is when both bits in the operands are off. Table B.8 lists the possible settings of the result bit when the Or operator is used.

| First Operand Bit | Second Operand Bit | Resulting Bit |
| --- | --- | --- |
| 1 | 1 | 1 |
| 0 | 1 | 1 |
| 1 | 0 | 1 |
| 0 | 0 | 0 |

**Table B.8 Truth table for the Or operator**

### Exclusive Or (the Xor Operator)

The exclusive or operator, Xor, compares the bits of its two operands. If only one of the two bits are on, it sets the corresponding result bit on. If both bits in the operands are on, or both bits are off, the result bit is set off. Table B.9 lists the possible settings of the result bit when the Xor operator is used.

| First Operand Bit | Second Operand Bit | Resulting Bit |
|---|---|---|
| 1 | 1 | 0 |
| 0 | 1 | 1 |
| 1 | 0 | 1 |
| 0 | 0 | 0 |

Table B.9 Truth table for the Xor operator

### Logical Equivalence (the Eqv Operator)

The logical equivalence operator, Eqv, tests the equality of the bits in the two operands. If both bits are on, or both bits are off, the corresponding result bit is set on. If one bit is on and the other is off, the result bit is set off. Table B.10 lists the possible settings of the result bit when the Eqv operator is used.

| First Operand Bit | Second Operand Bit | Resulting Bit |
|---|---|---|
| 1 | 1 | 1 |
| 0 | 1 | 0 |
| 1 | 0 | 0 |
| 0 | 0 | 1 |

Table B.10 Truth table for the Eqv operator

### Implication (the Imp Operator)

The implication operator, Imp, is perhaps the strangest one in the bunch. This operator sets its result based on whether the bit in the first operand "implies" the value of the bit in the second operand, according to rules of logic beyond the scope of this book. If the bit in the first operand is on, the implied value for the second operand is also on. However, if the bit in the first operand is off, the implied value for the second operand can be on or off. Therefore, the only time this operator sets its result bit to off is when the bit in the first operand is on, and the bit in the second operand is False. Table B.11 lists the possible settings of the result bit when the Imp operator is used.

| First Operand Bit | Second Operand Bit | Resulting Bit |
|---|---|---|
| 1 | 1 | 1 |
| 0 | 1 | 1 |
| 1 | 0 | 0 |
| 0 | 0 | 1 |

Table B.11 Truth table for the Imp operator

### An Overview of Visual Basic's Statements and Functions

There are three ways to perform tasks in your Visual Basic programs. First, you can use methods to effect a change on a Visual Basic object. Second, you can use operators to return or assign a value, or make a decision based on the value of one or more expressions. Finally, you can use statements and functions to process information. Up to this point, we have covered the methods and operators available in Visual Basic. In the following reference entries, we will explore the statements and functions you can use in your Visual Basic programs.

Statements and functions are very similar. Both are used to perform a specific task in your programs. Depending on the particular statement or function, both can be supplied with, and react to information in the form of passed parameters. The difference between the two is that functions return a value, while statements do not.

For more information on the format of these reference entries, please see Chapter 1, *Using the Visual Basic SuperBible.*

# Abs - Function

### Purpose
The Abs function returns the absolute value of a number.

### General Syntax
`Abs(numeric-expression)`

### Usage
`A! = Abs(B!)`
This statement places the absolute value of the variable B! into the variable A!.

### Description
Abs returns the unsigned value of the supplied numeric expression. For instance, both Abs(-299) and Abs(299) return the value of 299.

# AppActivate - Statement
### See Also: Shell

### Purpose
The AppActivate statement activates a running Windows program, and gives it the current focus. This statement cannot affect whether the target application is maximized or minimized.

### General Syntax
`AppActivate programtitle`

### Usage
`AppAcitvate "Paintbrush - (Untitled)"`
Assuming the Paintbrush application is already running, and it has no file loaded, this example will give it the focus. Note that the exact title as it appears in the program's window must be used, with the same spacing, although case is disregarded.

### Description
This statement is explained in detail in Chapter 21, *Establishing and Controlling the Application Focus.*

# Asc - Function
### See Also: Chr$

### Purpose
The Asc function returns the numeric ASCII code of a character.

### General Syntax
`Asc(string-expression$)`

### Usage
`A% = Asc("Hello")`
This example places the value 72 (the ASCII code for the character "H") in the variable A%.

### Description
The Asc function returns the numeric ASCII value of the first character in the supplied string.

# Atn - Function

**See Also:  Cos, Sin, Tan**

## Purpose
The Atn function returns the arctangent of a numeric expression.

## General Syntax
```
Atn(numeric-expression)
```

## Usage
```
A! = Atn(B!)
```
This example places the arctangent of the value of B! in the variable A!.

## Description
Atn is a trigonometric function that returns the arctangent of the supplied expression. The arctangent is the inverse of tangent. Therefore, the arctangent of a number gives the size of the angle for which the number is the tangent. The angle returned by the Atn function is in radians. If the supplied numeric expression is an integer, or single-precision variable, the returned value will be single-precision. Otherwise, Atn returns a double-precision value.

# Beep - Statement

## Purpose
The Beep statement causes the computer's speaker to produce a short tone.

## General Syntax
```
Beep
```

## Usage
```
If ErrorNumber% > 0 then Beep
```
This example "beeps" the speaker if the variable ErrorNumber is set.

## Description
The Beep statement causes the computer to send a short tone to the speaker. You can control neither the tone nor the duration; however, issuing several beep commands consecutively can create the effect of a longer beep.

The effect of the Beep statement is disabled if sound is turned off in the sound section of the Windows Control Panel application.

# Call - Statement

**See Also:  Declare, Sub**

## Purpose
The Call statement executes a Visual Basic Sub procedure or a Windows Dynamic Link Library (DLL) procedure.

## General Syntax
```
Call procedure-name [(argument1[, argument2 ])...
procedure-name [argument1[, argument2 ]] ...
```

## Usage
```
Call ManyBeeps (12)
```
This example transfers control to the Sub procedure ManyBeeps, and passes the value of 12 to it as an argument.
```
SortArray Colors%()
```

The preceding statement transfers execution to the Sub procedure SortArray, and passes the integer array Colors% to the procedure. The Call keyword and parentheses around the argument list have been omitted.

### Description

The Call statement is used to transfer control to a Visual Basic Sub procedure, or to a procedure in a Windows DLL. The call may be followed by a list of arguments, which are passed to the Sub procedure. There are two methods for executing the Call statement. The first requires the use of the Call keyword, and the use of parentheses around the group of arguments (if any). The second method allows you to omit the Call keyword, but requires the surrounding parentheses to be omitted as well. In any case, if the argument being passed is an entire array, the array name must be followed by empty parentheses.

If not specified otherwise, variables passed to the Sub procedure are passed "by reference." This allows the Sub procedure to modify the actual contents of the variable being passed. Alternatively, you can enclose a passed variable in parenthesies, which causes Visual Basic to make a duplicate of the variable, and to pass the address of the duplicate instead. This will prevent the Sub procedure from making changes to the original passed variable. Sometimes a Windows DLL routine will require that an argument be passed "by value." This means the routine is expecting the value of the argument rather than its address to be pushed onto the stack. This is accomplished by using the ByVal keyword in the Declare statement for this routine (see the entry for the Declare statement in this appendix).

## C<Type> (Numeric Conversion Functions)

### Purpose

Functions whose names have the form C<Type> convert a numeric expression from any numeric data type into the specified data type. The actual functions used for different data types are given below.

### General Syntax

```
CCur(numeric-expression)
CDbl(numeric-expression)
CInt(numeric-expression)
CLng(numeric-expression)
CSng(numeric-expression)
```

### Usage

```
A@ = CCur(B#)      'Convert from Double to Currency
B# = CDbl(C%)      'Convert from Integer to Double
C% = CInt(D&)      'Convert from Long to Integer
D& = CLng(E!)      'Convert from Single to Long
E! = CSng(A@)      'Convert from Currency to Single
```

The above examples demonstrate the use of the five data type conversion functions.

### Description

There are five numeric data type conversion functions in Visual Basic. These are CCur (convert to currency), CDbl (convert to Double), CInt (convert to Integer), CLng (convert to Long), and CSng (convert to single). Each method converts a numeric expression from any data type to the type specified by the function. The same effect can be achieved by assigning a numeric expression to a variable of the desired data type. These functions can be used to ensure the correct data type is being passed to a Visual Basic Sub procedure or a Windows Dynamic Link Library (DLL).

With the CInt function, the numeric expression parameter must be within the range of from -32,768 and 32,767 inclusive. The range for CLng is -2,147,438,648 to +2,147,438,647 inclusive. If the parameter is not within the correct range, Visual Basic will issue an overflow error.

## ChDir - Statement

**See Also:  ChDrive, CurDir$, MkDir, RmDir**

### Purpose

The ChDir statement changes the current working directory on the specified drive.

## General Syntax

```
ChDir path$
```
path$ must be a string in the format of [drive:][\]dir[\subdir][\subdir…]

## Usage

```
ChDir "D:\MyDir"
```
This statement changes the current working (default) directory on drive "D:" to "MyDir".

```
DirName$ = "\Main\MailBox"
ChDir DirName$
```
The above statements change the default directory on the default drive to "\Main\MailBox"

## Description

The ChDir statement affects the operation of file-related commands such as Open and Kill. Those commands do not require the drive or path of a file name to be fully specified in order to perform their duties. When the drive and/or directory is not specified, those commands will use the current working, or default, drive and directory. It is thus very important to set the correct working directory before issuing commands that do not specify full pathnames.

The setting of the defualt directory can be changed with the ChDir statement. In this statement, the path$ parameter must be a valid directory on the drive specified, and may be no longer than 128 characters. If not, Visual Basic will issue a "Path not found error." If no drive is specified in the path parameter, the default drive is used. If a drive other than the current drive is specified, Visual Basic only changes the default directory on that drive; it does not change the default drive to the one in the path parameter. Use the ChDrive statement to change the default drive.

---

# ChDrive - Statement

**See Also:  ChDir, CurDir$, MkDir, RmDir**

## Purpose

The ChDrive statement changes the current default drive.

## General Syntax

```
ChDrive Drive$
```

## Usage

```
ChDrive "A"

DriveSpec$ = "C:"
ChDrive DriveSpec$
```

## Description

The ChDrive statement changes the default working drive for Visual Basic's file-related statements such as Open and Kill. Those commands do not require the drive or path of a file name to be fully specified in order to perform their duties. When the drive and/or directory is not specified, those commands will use the current working, or default, drive and directory.

The ChDrive statement is used to change the current default drive setting. The drive argument must be a string whose first character corresponds to the letter of a valid DOS drive. If the drive argument is a null string, no action is taken.

---

# Chr$ - Function

**See Also:  Asc**

## Purpose

The Chr$ function returns the character that corresponds to the supplied ASCII code.

## General Syntax

```
Chr$(Ascii-Code%)
```

### Usage

```
A$ = Chr$(65)
```
The above example places the character "A" in the variable A$.

### Description

The Chr$ function is the complement to the Asc function. It returns the character whose ASCII code is specified as its argument. The ASCII-Code argument must be in the range of from 0 to 255. This function is useful for specifying characters that you cannot type at the keyboard, such as special control codes for the printer. Another good use for this function is generating double quote marks in strings. Because Visual Basic uses double quotes to delimit strings, you cannot include a double quote mark in a string directly. You can, however, use Chr$(34) to produce a double quote mark within a string.

# Close - Statement

### Purpose

Closes an open file channel.

### General Syntax

```
Close [#][filenumber%][, [#]filenumber%]
```

### Usage

```
Close
```
Closes all open files.

```
Close #1
```
Closes the file opened as file number 1.

```
Close 1, 5, 10
```
Closes the files opened as file number 1, 5 and 10. Notice that the # sign is optional.

### Description

The Close statement closes a file that has previously been opened by the Open statement. The Close statement also flushes the buffers associated with the file and writes any remaining data in them to disk. If the filenumber supplied is not a currently open file, Visual Basic will ignore this statement, and continue with the next statement. Although Visual Basic will automatically close all open files at program termination, it is good programming practice to close each open file before the program ends.

Once a file has been closed, the file number cannot be referenced by any other file-related statements (such as Get or Put) until an Open statement has been issued with the file number.

# Command$ - Function

### Purpose

The Command$ function returns a string that contains any command-line parameters that were used when Visual Basic or a the Visual Basic environment program was started.

### General Syntax

```
Command$
```

### Usage

```
Params$ = Command$
```
Stores command-line parameters for the current program into the string Params$.

### Description

When associated with the launching of the Visual Basic environment, this function returns any text that followed the /CMD parameter on the command line. The string returned by the Visual Basic environment can be modified by choosing the <u>M</u>odify Command$... option from the <u>R</u>un menu. When used with a Visual Basic program, Command$ returns any text which followed the executable file name on the command line. This function is useful for providing a way for the user to set up different options at run time. (Note that unlike the case with DOS command-line parameters, the name of the program file is not included in the parameter string.)

# Const - Statement

**See Also: Deftype, Dim, Global**

## Purpose

The Const statement assigns a meaningful symbolic name to a constant value.

## General Syntax

```
[Global] Const name = expression [,name = expression]...
```

## Usage

```
TRUE = -1
FALSE = 0
```

In this example, the Const statement assigns the constant value -1 to the name "TRUE", and 0 to the name "FALSE".

## Description

The Const statement provides a way for you to set up a symbolic name to represent a constant value. Creating named constants makes for good programming practice, because the code is more readable. Also, if a program uses the same value in several places, using a constant lets you make changes to the value in only one place when necessary. Finally, Visual Basic protects you against inadvertantly changing a constant's value by issuing an error message if any such attempt is made.

A constant must be defined before it is used. If not, Visual Basic generates a "Duplicate definition" error at compile time. It is not uncommon to use all capital letters in a constant's name. This makes recognizing constants in a program easier.

If a constant is defined in the global module, the Global keyword may precede the Const statement. This declares the constant as global throughout the project, and may be used by all procedures in all modules. If a constant is defined in the General Declarations area of a module, that constant may be used by all procedures in that module, but is inaccessible to other modules. A Const can also be used within a Visual Basic Sub procedure or Function, making the constant local to that Sub or Function.

There are some restrictions on what can be assigned to a constant. A constant may be assigned a numeric or a string literal. A string literal is any string that is bracketed by double quotes. A numeric literal is simply a number, such as 1 or 564.34. Constant assignments may include arithmetic and/or logical operators. The exception to this rule is the exponentiation operator (^), which causes Visual Basic to generate an "Illegal function call" error. Another constant may be used in the assignment of a constant (see the example above), but a variable cannot. A constant cannot be assigned a value from a built-in or programmer-defined function. String concatenation may not be used.

You may specify the data type of the constant by using a type declaration character at the end of the constant name. However, further references to the constant need not include the type declaration character. For instance, in the following code, a constant is set up that specifies the integer data type, yet the declaration character is not used thereafter:

```
Const MAX_LOOPS% = 10

x% = 0
Do
    x% = x% + 1
Loop Until x% > MAX_LOOPS
```

If no type declaration character is used in the Const statement, Visual Basic will automatically assign a data type to the constant. If you assign a string to a constant, Visual Basic will set the constant up as a string. If the constant is assigned a numeric value, Visual Basic will check the size of the number being assigned to the constant and assign it the simplest possible data type. The data type assigned to a constant is not affected by the use of the DeEFtype statements.

# Cos - Function

**See Also: Atn, Sin, Tan**

### Purpose
The Cos function returns the cosine of an angle.

### General Syntax
Cos(angle)
angle is expressed in radians.

### Usage
A! = Cos(4.93)
The cosine of 4.93 is assigned to the variable A!.

### Description
The Cos function is used to determine the cosine of an angle. The function expects the angle to be expressed in radians; therefore, if the angle is in degrees, it must first be converted using the formula radians = degrees * pi/180.

If angle is supplied as an integer or a single-precision value, Cos will return a single-precision value; otherwise, it returns a double-precision value.

# CurDir$ - Function

**See Also: ChDir, ChDrive, MkDir, RmDir**

### Purpose
The CurDir$ function returns the current default directory for the specified drive.

### General Syntax
CurDir[(drive$)]

### Usage
Default$ = CurDir$
A$ = CurDir$("A")
C$ = CurDir$("C:")
The first example assigns a string containing the default directory path from the default drive to the variable Default$. The second example assigns the default directory on drive A:, while the third example assigns the default directory path on drive C:.

### Description
DOS always maintains a default directory for each drive in the system. The default directory is the one that will be searched first for a filename if no path is specified. The CurDir$ function returns the default directory of the specified drive. If a drive designation is supplied, only the first character is used. The drive letter can be upper or lowercase, and must be a valid drive letter ("A" through *n*, where *n* is specified by the Lastdrive parameter in the CONFIG.SYS file, or "E" if not specified). If the letter is not a valid drive, a "Device unavailable" error occurs. If the first character of the drive parameter is not a letter, Visual Basic generates an "Illegal function call" error. If no drive is specified, or the drive parameter is a null string, the default drive is used.

Since the path returned by CurDir$ includes the drive letter, this function is also useful for determining which drive is currently the default drive.

# Date$ - Function and Statement

**See Also: DateValue, Now, Time$**

### Purpose
The Date$ function returns the current system date, and the Date$ statement sets it.

## General Syntax

Function:
```
Date$
```

Statement:
```
Date$ = date-string$
```

## Usage

```
Today$ = Date$
```
Assigns a string containing the current system date to the variable Today$

```
Date$ = "01-01-1996"
```
Sets the current system date to January 1, 1996.

## Description

Date$ can be used as a function, to return the current system date; or as a statement, to set the current system date. When used as a function, Date$ returns a string with the current system date in the format mm-dd-yyyy. As a statement, the system date may be set by using a string in a valid date format. The valid date string formats are:

mm-dd-yyyy
mm-/dd/yyyy
mm-dd-yy
mm/dd/yy

The date can be set to any date between January 1, 1980 and December 31, 2099 inclusive. If the date is not in this range, or the format of the date string is not one of those above, Visual Basic issues an "Illegal function call" error.

If the date is set using the Date$ statement, its permanence is dependent on the type of system and version of DOS being used. Generally, if the system has a CMOS memory and is running under DOS 3.3 or greater, the date will be retained in the CMOS. Otherwise, the date may be lost when the system is powered down.

## Comments

In the above descriptions, mm refers to the month, dd to the day, yy to a two-digit year, and yyyy to a four-digit year.

# DateSerial - Function

### See Also: DateValue, Day, Month, Now, Year

## Purpose

The DateSerial function returns a double-precision serial number based on the supplied year, month, and day.

## General Syntax

```
DateSerial(year%, month%, day%)
```

## Usage

```
MyDate# = DateSerial(1921, 02, 26)
```
Places a double-precision serial number representing the date February 26, 1921 into the variable MyDate#.

## Description

The DateSerial function is used to return a double-precision serial number representing a date in the range of from January 1, 1753 to December 31, 2078, inclusive. If the date requested is not in this range, Visual Basic issues an "Illegal function call" error. The serial number represents the number of days since December 30, 1899. Therefore, January 01, 1900 has a serial number of 2, while January 1, 1753 has a negative serial number of -53688.

The most useful aspect of this function is its ability to return a serial number based on the desired date's relation to another date. In other words, if the year, month, and day of January 02, 1996, are plugged into this function, the value 35066 is returned. However, if we subtract 30 from the day parameter;

```
D# = DateSerial(1996, 01, 02 - 30)
```

the value 35036 is returned (30 days before January 2, 1996). The serial number representing the date December 03, 1995 is 35036.

# DateValue - Function

**See Also: Date$, DateSerial, Day, Month, Now, Weekday, Year**

## Purpose
The DateValue function returns a double-precision serial number that represents the date of the supplied string.

## General Syntax
```
DateValue(date-string)
```

## Usage
```
D# = DateValue("01-01-1996")
```
Assigns a double-precision serial number representing the date January 1, 1996 to the variable D#.

## Description
The DateValue function is used to return a double-precision serial number representing a date in the range of from January 1, 1753 to December 31, 2078, inclusive. If the date requested is not in this range, Visual Basic issues an "Illegal function call" error. The serial number represents the number of days since December 30, 1899. Therefore, January 01, 1900 has a serial number of 2, while January 1, 1753 has a negative serial number of -53688.

DateValue can translate any numeric date string that is in the same format as the "sShortDate=" entry in the Win.Ini file. Therefore, if that entry is set up as "mm/dd/yyyy", DateValue can translate the string "08/06/1995". However, if the sShortDate entry is set up differently than the supplied numeric date string, an "Illegal function call" error will be generated. The DateValue function can also successfully translate several other date formats. For instance, the following dates can be understood and translated:

August 06, 1995,
Aug 06, 1995
06 August, 1995
06 Aug, 1995

# Day - Function

**See Also: DateSerial, DateValue, Now, Weekday**

## Purpose
The Day function returns an integer representing the day of the month based on the supplied serial number.

## General Syntax
```
Day(serial#)
```

## Usage
```
Today# = DateValue(Date$)
DayOfMonth% = Day(Today#)
```
Returns today's day of month from serial number returned by DateValue and Date$ functions.

## Description
This function uses a double-precision serial number representing a date to return an integer value representing the day of the month. The supplied serial number represents the number of days since December

30, 1899. Therefore, January 01, 1900 has a serial number of 2, while January 1, 1753, has a negative serial number of -53688. The supplied serial number must represent a date in the range of from January 1, 1753 to December 31, 2078, inclusive. If the date requested is not in this range, Visual Basic issues an "Illegal function call" error.

# Declare - Statement

### See Also: Call

### Purpose
The Declare statement informs Visual Basic that you will be using external procedures in Dynamic Link Libraries (DLLs). Declare is also used to specify certain Visual Basic functions for use without parentheses.

### General Syntax
```
Declare Sub procname Lib libname$ [Alias aliasname$][(arg-list)]
```
```
Declare Function procname [Lib libname$] [Alias aliasname$][(arg-list)][As type]
```

### Usage
```
Declare Sub Scramble Lib "Puzzle" (ByVal Pieces As Integer)
```
This example declares the DLL procedure "Scramble" with one integer parameter (to be passed by value to Visual Basic).

```
Declare Function No_Of_Pieces Lib "Puzzle" alias "_NOP" As Integers
```
This declares the DLL integer function "_NOP" to be referenced as No_Of_Pieces.

```
Declare Function ErrorStatus As Integer
```
This declares a Visual Basic function for use without parentheses.

### Description
Use the Declare statement to set up the use of Sub procedcures and Functions contained in a DLL. The Declare statement can only be used in a global module, or in the declarations section of a module or form. DLL routines that are declared in a form's declarations section are available to that form only; otherwise the DLL routines are available to all procedures in all modules.

The procname is the name by which the Visual Basic program will reference the DLL procedure. This name must follow the same rules as a Visual Basic variable name. If the name of the procedure in the DLL does not conform to Visual Basic's naming conventions, you must use the Alias keyword to specify the name of the procedure as it appears in the DLL.

Including a data type declaration character at the end of a function name declares the type of data that function will return. This can also be done by using the As type clause, where type is Integer, Long, Single, Double, Currency, or String.

The libname parameter specifies the DOS filename of the Dynamic Link Library. You must specify the full path name if the library is not in the default directory on the default drive.

Declaring the arguments for an external procedure can sometimes be a tricky process. Several arguments can be declared one after another, separated by commas. The format for declaring arguments is as follows:

```
([ByVal]variablename[As type][,[ByVal]variablename[As type] ])
```

Sometimes a DLL procedure will require that an argument be passed "by value." This means the routine is expecting the value of the argument rather than its address to be pushed onto the stack. You set the ByVal keyword to specify that an argument's value rather than its address is to be provided to the called procedure.

If no type declaration character is used at the end of the argument's variable name, you may use the As type clause to specify the type of variable being passed. Type can be Integer, Long, Single, Double, Currency, String, Any, Form, Control, or any programmer-defined type. The Any type is used to override data type checking for that argument. The type "Any" cannot be used on arguments that are being passed by value. The Form and Control data types are used only when a form or control is being passed to the external procedure.

An additional use of the Declare statement is to allow your program to call a function that takes no arguments, without having to use empty parentheses in the function call. Thus, in the third example above, your program can now have a statement such as:

```
ErrNo = ErrorStatus
```

rather than:

```
ErrNo = ErrorStatus()
```

This facility is useful mainly in converting older BASIC programs that do not provide parentheses when calling such functions. You can make such declarations only at the module (not global or form) level.

# Def<type> - Statement

## Purpose

Statements of the form Def<type> can be used to set the default data type for variables and functions in forms and modules. The <type> part of the keyword actually stands for the types specified in the keywords below.

## General Syntax

```
DefCur firstletter-lastletter[, firstletter-lastletter]
DefDbl firstletter-lastletter[, firstletter-lastletter]
DefInt firstletter-lastletter[, firstletter-lastletter]
DefLng firstletter-lastletter[, firstletter-lastletter]
DefSng firstletter-lastletter[, firstletter-lastletter]
DefStr firstletter-lastletter[, firstletter-lastletter]
```

## Usage

```
DefCur A-D    'Sets default type to Currency for variables starting with A,    B, C, or D
DefDbl E-H    'Sets default type to Double for variables starting with E, F,    G, or H
DefInt I-L    'Sets default type to Integer for variables starting with I,      J, K, or L
DefLng M-P    'Sets default type to Long for variables starting with M, N,      O, or P
DefSng Q-T    'Sets default type to Single for variables starting with Q, R,    S, or T
DefStr U-X    'Sets default type to String for variables starting with U, V,    W, or X
```

## Description

The Def<type> statements are used in the declarations section of a form or module. They allow you to define the default data type for variables based on the first letter of the variable's name. The firstletter-lastletter parameters define the range of letters that will be affected by this Deftype statement. The letter range is not case-sensitive, therefore g-M is the same as G-M. If the letter range is specified backwards (for example, Z-M instead of M-Z), Visual Basic will transpose the letter range, in order to process it alphabetically.

The Deftype statement affects only the module or form in which it appears. Even if it is used in the global module of a program, only those variables defined in the global module are affected.

Once a range has been established with a Deftype statement, that range cannot be redefined. If a redefinition is attempted, Visual Basic issues a "Duplicate Deftype" error. The use of the Dim, Static, or Global statements overrides the type assigned by Deftype, as does the use of a type declaration character.

# Dim - Statement

## See Also: Global, Option Base, ReDim, Static, Type

## Purpose

The Dim statement allocates storage for, and establishes the data type of, Visual Basic variables or arrays in a module or procedure.

## General Syntax

For declaring the data type of a simple variable
```
Dim [Shared] name [As type][, name [As type]]
```

For declaring an array:
```
Dim [Shared] name[(suscript-range)][As type][, name[(subscript-range)][As type]
```

## Usage

```
Dim A as Integer          'Declares the variable A as an integer
Dim B!(100) As Single     'Declares single-precision array B, with 100 elements, numbered 0 to 100
Dim C$(-30 to 60)         'Declares string array C$, with 91 elements numbered -30 to +60
```

## Description

The Dim statement is used to declare storage and data types for simple and array variables. When the Dim statement is used in the declarations section of a form or module, the variable or array declared by that statement is available to all procedures in that form or module. Using the Dim statement inside a procedure allocates a local simple variable which cannot be seen by any other procedure. Dim cannot be used to allocate storage for an array within a procedure. The Static and ReDim commands are used to do this. To declare a variable or array that is accessible globally (across modules and forms), use the Global statement in the declarations section of the global module, rather than using Dim.

The Dim statement is used along with the As type clause to explicitly declare the data type of a simple variable. For instance,

```
Dim MyVar As Integer
```

creates a storage for an Integer variable named MyVar. This is an alternate method to using the Visual Basic type declaration characters (!, @, #, $, %, &). This also allows you to assign your own data types (created with the Type statement) to a variable, as in the following code:

```
Type Rolodex
    Name as String * 20
    Number as Long
    Address as String * 100
End Type

Dim Cards as Rolodex
```

The most frequently used purpose for the Dim statement is to allocate storage for an array and to specify its dimensions and range of subscripts. Arrays provide a method for creating an entire series of variables and referencing them by the same variable name. An index number (called the subscript) is used to determine which particular element in an array is being referenced. A more detailed discussion on the concept of arrays can be found in the tutorial in Appendix A.

The dimensions of an array are defined by the entry in the subscript-range portion of the Dim statement. The subscript-range follows this format:

```
[lo-element To] hi-element[,[lo-element To] hi-element]
```

The lo-element parameter lets you define the range of the subscripts as well as the number of elements in the array. If lo-element is not used, the lowest valid subscript will be 0 (unless the default has been changed using Option Base), and the supplied number will be the highest valid subscript. The number of elements allowed in an array depends on the desired data type for that array. Visual Basic allows approximately 64K of data space for each array declared (not to exceed installed memory, of course). Therefore, an Integer array (which is 2 bytes long per element) may have up to 32,767 elements, while a Long or a Single precision (4 bytes per element) array may have half that.

Dim initializes all elements of variable-length string arrays to null strings. All other arrays are initialized to 0s (including fixed-length strings and user-defined types).

At times it may be useful to have a multidimensional array. To declare such an array, include as many sets of subscripts as needed, separated by commas.

```
Dim MultiArray (1 To 100, 50 To 60, -100 to 100) As Integer
```

The example above declares an array with three dimensions of 100, 11, and 201 elements, respectively. The first dimension can be referenced by subscripts from 1 to 100, the second may have subscripts ranging from 50 to 60, and the third from -100 to +100. Visual Basic allows arrays to have as many as 60 dimensions.

Leaving the parentheses empty in a Dim statement declares a dynamic array. The number of dimensions and elements in a dynamic array is defined within a procedure by the ReDim statement. Dynamic arrays are allocated at runtime, and may have the number of elements redefined at any time. However, once set, the number of dimensions in a dynamic array cannot be changed. See the entry for ReDim in this appendix for more discussion of dynamic arrays.

# Dir$ - Function

**See Also: CurDir$, ChDir, ChDrive**

### Purpose
The Dir$ function returns a file name that matches the supplied pattern.

### General Syntax
For the first call to Dir$ for a pattern:
```
Dir$(pattern$)
```

For each successive call for the same pattern:
```
Dir$
```

### Usage
```
Docs$ = Dir$("*.DOC")         'Returns the first directory entry that matches "*.DOC"
Do until Docs$ = ""
    Docs$ = Dir$              'Returns each successive directory entry that matches "*.DOC"
Loop
```

### Description
The first time Dir$ is called, the pattern$ parameter must be included, or Visual Basic issues an "Illegal function call" error. Pattern$ refers to a string expression that represents a potential file name. It can include a drive specifier, a file path, and a file name. Wildcard characters (? and *) can be used in the file name, following the usual rules used by DOS. If the drive and/or path is not specified, Dir$ will use the default drive and/or path. When pattern$ is supplied, Dir$ returns the first directory entry that matches the supplied pattern. Dir$ can then be called with no argument to retrieve each successive directory entry that matches the original pattern. The directory entry returned by Dir$ includes only the file name and extension. When all directory entries have been retrieved, Dir$ returns a null string. When this happens, the next call to Dir$ must again supply a pattern or suffer an "Illegal function call" error.

It is not necessary to call Dir$ until a null string is returned before a new pattern is used.

### Comments
Visual Basic does not check to see if the supplied pattern parameter is a valid DOS file name. If the pattern supplied is not a valid file name, Dir$ just returns a null string. If the pattern specified a drive that does not exist, a "Device unavailable" error will be returned.

# Do...Loop - Statements

**See Also: Exit, For...Next, While...Wend**

### Purpose
The Do... Loop statements repeat a group of program instructions until a condition is met or while a condition exists.

### General Syntax
To test the condition at the top of a loop:
```
Do [{While | Until} condition]
    [statements]
    [Exit Do]
    [statements]
Loop
```

To test the condition at the bottom of the loop:
```
Do
    [statements]
    [Exit Do]
    [statements]
Loop [{While | Until} condition]
```

## Usage

```
Do
    A% = MsgBox("Please click Yes button", 3)
Loop Until A% = 6
```

This example repeatedly displays a message box until the user clicks on the "Yes" button.

## Description

The Do...Loop statement executes a block of statements while a specified condition is True, or until a condition becomes True. The Microsoft Visual Basic Language Reference documents a "condition" as any expression that can evaluate to a True (-1) or False (0) value. However, the Do...Loop structure considers the condition met if it evaluates to any non-0 numeric value. The condition may be tested at either the beginning or end of the loop. In effect, this provides you with five styles of looping: Do While, Do Until, Loop While, Loop Until, and the infinite Do...Loop.

The Do While...Loop first checks the condition before executing any statements within the statement block. If the condition tests out as a non-0 value, the statement block is executed. When execution reaches the Loop keyword, the program will branch back up to the Do, and the condition will be checked again. The execution of this statement block will repeat until the condition evaluates as a False (0) value.

The Do Until...Loop also first checks the condition before executing any statements within the statement block. If the condition tests out as a False (0) value, the statement block is executed. When execution reaches the Loop keyword, the program will branch back up to the Do, and the condition will be checked again. The execution of this statement block will repeat until the condition evaluates as a Non-False (non-0) value.

The Do...Loop While will execute all the statements in the block once before checking the condition. When execution reaches the Loop keyword, the condition is checked. If it evaluates as a True (non-0) value, the program branches back to the Do and the statement block is again executed. The execution of this statement block will repeat until the condition evaluates as a False (0) value.

The Do...Loop Until will execute all the statements in the block once before checking the condition. When execution reaches the Loop keyword, the condition is checked. If it evaluates as a False (0) value, the program branches back to the Do and the statement block is again executed. The execution of this statement block will repeat until the condition evaluates as a Non-False (non-0) value.

The final style consists of the infinite loop. Because the Do...Loop's conditional statement is optional, you can create a loop that will execute continuously, without end. Generally, this type of loop is used to perform background-oriented tasks. If you write a program with an infinite loop, you should provide a way for the operating system to continue to perform any needed tasks. Most often, this is done with the DoEvents function (see the entry for the DoEvents function in this appendix). Since there is rarely a case in which you would desire to write a true infinite loop, you should provide some sort of trigger that will either end the program, or exit the loop. The most common way to exit an infinite loop is to use the Exit Do statement. This command skips any commands between it and the Loop keyword, exits the loop, and continues execution with the next instruction following the Loop keyword. See the tutorial in Appendix A for further discussion and examples of the Do...Loop constructs.

# DoEvents - Function

## Purpose

The DoEvents function temporarily surrenders control to the operating environment (Windows) so that programs running in the background may execute any needed tasks. This function returns the number of open windows created by your Visual Basic application. It is most commonly used in idle loops, in conjunction with the SendKeys statement, or during Dynamic Data Exchange conversations.

## General Syntax

```
DoEvents()
```

## Usage

```
Offset = MaxRow% \ 2
DO WHILE Offset > 0
```

```
        Limit = MaxRow% - Offset
        DO
            Switch = FALSE
            FOR Row = 1 TO Limit
                IF SortArray#(Row) > SortArray#(Row + Offset) THEN
                    SWAP SortArray#(Row), SortArray#(Row + Offset)
                    Switch = Row
                END IF
            NEXT Row
            Limit = Switch - Offset
        LOOP WHILE Switch
        Offset = Offset \ 2
        A% = DoEvents%           'Place DoEvents here to give the operating system some time
    LOOP
```

In this example, the DoEvents function is used at the bottom of a loop that controls a sorting algoritm. Since the sort may take a while, we wish to give the operating system a chance to complete some of its tasks while we are sorting.

### Description

There are two methods for creating a multitasking environment: preemptive and non-preemptive. Preemptive environments give each running program a certain amount of processing time. If the program does not complete its task in its allotted time, the operating environment will interrupt it and put it on hold. It will then allow the next program to execute until its allotted time has expired. The operating environment continually performs this switching from program to program, thereby performing multitasking.

Windows is a non-preemptive environment. Programs that run under Windows wait for events to occur, and when a waited-for event happens, the program then executes an event handler to react to it. In Visual Basic, all of the events that are related to an object are event handlers. Because they are not actually executing code, several programs can reside together within the Windows environment while waiting for an event to occur. However, once one program begins to execute an event handler, it has full control of the operating environment and prevents other programs from performing any tasks at all until the handler is finished processing. This usually is not a problem, because most events handlers are written to perform their tasks quickly. Even so, some method must be in place so that large and slower processing handlers may temporarily yield to the operating environment and allow other programs to check for events. In Visual Basic, the DoEvents function performs this task.

There are three common uses for the DoEvents function. First, this function is used to create an idle loop in your programs. Sometimes your program will have a set of instructions that need to be performed repeatedly in a Do...Loop, For...Next, or While...Wend loop, but you do not wish this loop to monopolize the operating environment. Such a loop is an idle loop. In these cases, you may place a DoEvents function somewhere within the loop so other programs in the environment may process any events that have occurred since the loop began (or the last DoEvents was executed). For instance, suppose your program needed to sort a large array. You know that such a sort may take a while, so including a DoEvents function within the sort routine will allow the sort to act as if it is being performed in the background.

Second, DoEvents can be used to pause your program so a SendKeys statement may be processed. Normally, SendKeys is used to send simulated keystrokes to an application. SendKeys has an argument that instructs it to pause until the destination program processes the sent keystrokes. However, this argument is ineffective if the source and destination programs are the same. In this case, you can follow the SendKeys statement with a DoEvents function, which will pause processing long enough for the application to process the keystrokes. For more on the SendKeys statement, please see Chapter 16, *Handling Keyboard Input*.

Finally, the DoEvents function can be used during Dynamic Data Exchange (DDE) conversations. As mentioned above, when your Visual Basic program has control of the environment, no other programs can respond to events. Therefore, if your program initiates a DDE conversation with another application, it must allow that application to respond to the DDE events. Because of this, it is a good practice to follow each DDE Link... operation (or small groups of operations) with a DoEvents function call. For more on DDE, please refer to Chapter 25, *Transferring Data with Dynamic Data Exchange*.

### Comments

Care should be taken so that the DoEvents function is not called recursively. This means you need to make sure that the event that executes the DoEvents function does not get executed a second time before the DoEvents function returns control to your program. Recursive calls to this function can easily cause

Windows to run out of resources. For instance, imagine your application has a command button that performs a time-consuming task when the user clicks on it. You'd probably want to include a DoEvents function call in the routine, so other applications could respond to events while yours performed its task. Your button's click event might look something like this:

```
Sub Command1_Click ()
    Dim Done As Integer

    Done = FALSE
    Do
        :
        [this is where your code would appear]
        :
        A% = DoEvents()             'Place this here so other programs can do their thing
    Loop Until Done
End Sub
```

At first, it looks as if this routine would perform as wished. However, what happens if the user clicks on the same button while the DoEvents function is executing? Your Visual Basic program would react to the click by again initiating the Command1_Click event, thereby causing two instances of the routine to be executing concurrently.

The best way to prevent this from occurring is to disable the control whose event executes the DoEvents function. For instance, we could add two lines to the above click event:

```
Sub Command1_Click ()
    Dim Done As Integer

    Command1.Enabled = 0        'Disable the button so it cannot execute this event again
    Done = FALSE
    Do
        :
        [this is where your code would appear]
        :
        A% = DoEvents()         'Place this here so other programs can do their thing
    Loop Until Done
    Command1.Enabled = -1       'Enable the button so it can now be clicked upon
End Sub
```

In this example, the button this event is associated with gets disabled before the time-consuming portion of its task is executed. It stays disabled until the task is complete.

# End - Statement

**See Also: Function, If...Then...Else, Select Case, Stop, Sub, Type**

### Purpose
The End statement specifies the end of a program or of a block of statements such as a Sub procedure or function.

### General Syntax
```
End [Function | If | Select | Sub | Type]
```

### Usage
```
Sub Hello
    Print Hello
End Sub
```

### Description
The End statement is used to end a program, or, when accompanied by another keyword, to terminate one of several types of statement blocks.

End by itself terminates program execution, closes all files, clears all variables, and erases all forms and modules from memory. Executing the End statement does not cause the Form_UnLoad event to activate.

"End Function" signifies the end of a Function definition. An End Function must terminate every Function block. It is not generally necessary to type this statement in, as Visual Basic automatically adds it when the Function keyword is used.

"End If" terminates a multiple-line If...Then...Else block. If an If...Then...Else statement is in multiple-line format, the End If must be used to terminate the block. Not doing so results in a "Block If without End If" error at compile time.

"End Select" ends a Select Case block. Not using the End Select will generate a "Select Case without End Select" error at compile time.

"End Sub" signifies the end of a Sub procedure definition. An End Sub must terminate every Sub block. It is not generally necessary to type this statement in, as Visual Basic automatically adds it when the Sub keyword is used.

"End Type" marks the end of a programmer-defined type definition. End Type must be used with the Type keyword, or a "Statement invalid in Type block" error will result.

# Environ$ - Function

## Purpose
The Environ$ function returns settings from the operating system's environment table.

## General Syntax
```
Environ$({entry-name$ | entry-position%})
```

## Usage
```
A$ = Environ$("Path")
```
Places the current path into the variable A$.

```
A$ = Eviron$(1)
```
Places the current setting for the first environment table entry into the variable A$

## Description
DOS and some other operating systems maintain a table of strings called "environmental variables." Values in the environment table typically store information about such things as the current drive and path, the location of the command processor, or special settings needed by various programs.

The Environ$ function allows the program to read the current setting of the operating system's environment table. Entries in the environment table are set by using the DOS command syntax SET entry-name=entry-value. See a DOS reference manual for more information on the SET command. Environ$ allows you to specify either the name, or position of the entry to be retrieved.

If you specify a table entry name, it must match exactly (including capitalization) one of the entry names in the environment table, or a null string is returned. If the supplied string does match an entry name, Environ$ returns only the text assigned to that entry.

You can also specify an entry number as the parameter to Environ$. This number corresponds to the position of an entry in the environment table. For example, if a numeric argument of 2 is used, Environ$ returns the second line in the environment table. If the number specified is 0, Visual Basic generates an "Illegal function call" error. If the number specified is greater than the number of lines in the table, a null string is returned. Using a valid numeric argument causes the entire corresponding entry to be returned in the format entry-name=entry-value.

# EOF - Function

## See Also: Close, Get, Input #, Line Input #, Loc, LOF, Open

## Purpose
The EOF function returns the end of file status of an open file. It is important to check the end of file status so as to avoid reading past the end of a file, which causes an error.

## General Syntax
```
EOF(file-number)
```

## Usage
```
Do
    Line Input #1, A$
Loop Until EOF(1)
```

## Description

For sequential files, the EOF function returns True (-1) if the last Input, or Line Input, statement caused the program to reach the end of the file. For random access and binary files, this function returns True (-1) if the last Get attempted to read a record that was beyond the length of the file.

The file number specified as the argument must be the number used in the Open statement of a currently open file. If not, Visual Basic generates a "Bad file name or number" error.

# Erase - Statement

**See Also: Dim, ReDim**

## Purpose

The Erase statement deallocates space reserved for dynamic arrays. Erase also reinitializes the elements in a static array.

## General Syntax

```
Erase arrayname [, arrayname]
```

## Usage

```
Erase AddressCards
```

## Description

Erasing a static array merely reinitializes the contents of the array. If the array is a variable length string array, all the elements are set to null strings. Otherwise, all elements in the array are set to 0.

Erasing a dynamic array actually frees up the memory that the array is using. The program can now use the Dim statement to create a new dynamic array with the same name as the old one. Note that it is not necessary to Erase an array before redeclaring it with ReDim.

# Erl - Function

**See Also: Err, Error, Error$, On Error Goto, Resume**

## Purpose

Returns the line number of the statement that caused an error.

## General Syntax

```
Erl
```

## Usage

```
BadLine& = Erl
```

## Description

The Erl function is used only if line numbers are useful in the program. It does not work with line labels or procedure names. If the line that caused the error does not have a line number, this function will return the number of the line previous to it that does have a number. if no lines in the program have line numbers, 0 is returned. Visual Basic treats line numbers greater than 65,529 as labels, therefore Erl ignores them.

Erl will be set to 0 if a Resume Next, On Error Goto, or On Error Resume Next statement is executed. Also, it is not guaranteed that the value of Erl will remain unchanged when calling a Visual Basic Sub procedure or Function.

# Err - Function and Statement

**See Also: Erl, Error, Error$, On Error Goto, Resume**

## Purpose

As a function, Err returns the error code of the most recent error. As a statement, Err allows you to set the error code.

### General Syntax

As a function:
```
Err
```

As a statement:
```
Err = code%
```

### Usage

```
Err = 100
```
Set the error code to 100.

```
If Err > 0 Then
    ErrorNumber% = Err
    Call ErrorRoutine(ErrorNumber%)
End if
```
If an error has occured, save the error number and call an error-handling routine with that number as argument.

### Description

The Err keyword is both a function and a statement. As a function, it returns the error code of the most recent error. As a statement, it allows the program to set the value of the error code. The value of Err is set whenever Visual Basic encounters an error, when the program sets it via the Err statement, or when a Resume Next, On Error Goto, or On Error Resume Next statement is executed. Resume Next, On Error Goto, and On Error Resume Next set the error code to 0. It is not guaranteed the value of Err will remain unchanged when calling a Visual Basic Sub procedure or Function.

# Error - Statement

See Also: **Erl, Err, Error$, On Error Goto, Resume**

### Purpose

The Error function simulates the occurrence of an error. You can use it as an aid to testing or debugging a program.

### General Syntax

```
Error errorcode%
```

### Usage

```
Error 5
```
This generates an "Illegal function call" error.

### Description

The errorcode% specified must be in the range of from 1 to 32,767. This statement is very useful for debugging error handling routines. Using this statement, you can cause a specific error to occur, and then see if the error-handling code works properly. You can also use error codes greater than those used by Visual Basic. This allows you to define custom error codes.

# Error$ - Function

See Also: **Erl, Err, Error, On Error Goto, Resume**

### Purpose

The Error$ function returns the error message that corresponds to the supplied error code.

### General Syntax

```
Error$[(errorcode%)]
```

### Usage

```
Msg$ = Error$(5)
```
This places the text "Illegal function call" into the variable Msg$.

## Description

The Error$ function is used to retrieve Visual Basic's message for a particular error. The errorcode% parameter specifies the desired error message, and must be in the range of from 1 to 32,767. If an error number is not used by Visual Basic, the message "user-defined error" will be returned. If errorcode% is omitted, the message returned will be that of the most recent error. If no error has occurred, Visual Basic returns a null string.

When the errorcode% parameter is used, some of the error messages returned by this function may seem incomplete. This is because they depend on internal variables that are set only when an error has actually occurred. When the errorcode% parameter is used, no error has occurred, so the internal variables have not been set. For instance, Error$(382) will return the following message:

```
' ' property cannot be set at run time
```

Because this error has not occurred, there is no object for it to reference. The single quotes denote the place in the message the object's name would be inserted.

# Exit - Statement

**See Also:  Do...Loop, For...Next, Function, Sub**

## Purpose

The Exit statement provides an alternate exit for statement blocks such as a Do...Loop, For...Next, Sub, or Function.

## General Syntax

```
Exit Do
Exit For
Exit Function
Exit Sub
```

## Usage

```
Function Fruit$(FruitNo as Integer)
    Dim F as String
    If FruitNo = 0 then Exit Function
    If FruitNo = 1 then F = "Apple"
    If FriutNo = 2 then F = "Grape"
    Fruit$ = F
End Function
```

This example causes the Fruit$() function to terminate if the value of the passed argument FruitNo is 0.

## Description

The Exit Do statement exits a Do...Loop and continues execution with the instruction following the Loop instruction. The Exit For statement exits a For...Next loop and continues execution with the instruction following the Next instruction. The Exit Function statement exits a Function and continues execution at the instruction following invocation of the Function. Similarly the Exit Sub statement exits a Sub procedure and continues execution at the instruction following the call to the procedure. The type of Exit used must match the type of statement block it is being used in (for example, Exit Sub cannot be used to exit a For...Next loop).

# Exp - Function

**See Also:  Log**

## Purpose

The Exp function raises the natural logarithmic base $e$ to the specified power. (The natural logarithm, which has a base of about 2.718, should not be confused with the common logarithm, whose base is 10.)

## General Syntax

```
Exp(power)
```

## Usage

```
A! = 14
B! = Exp(A!)
```
Returns a single-precision number that represents the natural logarithmic base raised to the power of 14.

```
C# = 14
D# = Exp(C#)
```
Returns a double-precision number that represents the natural logarithmic base raised to the power of 14.

## Description

If the power is supplied as an integer or single-precision number, Exp will return a single-precision value. If any other data type is used, a double-precision number is returned. If supplied as an integer or single-precision number, the power parameter must not exceed 88.02969. If supplied as any other data type, it must not exceed 709.782712893. Doing so will cause an "Overflow" error to occur.

The logarithm of a number is the power to which the logarithmic base must be raised in order to achieve that number. The natural logarithmic base is referred to by the symbol $e$, and has an approximate value of 2.718282. Exp performs the inverse operation of a natural logarithm. It raises $e$ to the power specified by the power parameter.

# FileAttr - Function

### See Also: Open

## Purpose

The FileAttr function returns system information about an open file.

## General Syntax

```
FileAttr(filenumber%, infotype%)
```

## Usage

```
Open "Test" for input as #1
VB_OpenMode% = FileAttr(1, 1)
DOS_Handle% = FileAttr(1, 2)
```

## Description

The filenumber parameter refers to the number that was used when the file was open. If filenumber does not refer to a currently opened file, Visual Basic issues a "Bad file name or number" error.

The infotype% parameter indicates the type of information that is being requested. If infotype% is 1, FileAttr returns a number that refers to the mode the file was opened under. Table B.12 lists the open modes, and the codes returned.

| Open Mode | Return Value |
|-----------|--------------|
| Input | 1 |
| Output | 2 |
| Random | 4 |
| Append | 8 |
| Binary | 32 |

**Table B.12 Return values for the FileAttr function**

When infotype% is 2, FileAttr returns the DOS file handle that has been assigned to this file.

# Fix - Function

### See Also: CInt, Int

## Purpose

The Fix function truncates the fractional part of a numeric expression and converts it to an integer.

## General Syntax

```
Fix(numeric-expression)
```

## Usage

```
B! = 54.72
A% = Fix(B!)
```

This assigns the value 54 to the variable A%.

## Description

The Fix function returns the whole number portion of a numeric-expression. All digits to the right of the decimal are truncated. No rounding is performed. Use the CInt or CLng functions to convert to an integer with rounding.

The Int function performs the same operation as Fix when the argument is positive, or when there are no digits to the right of the decimal. The difference between the two is how they handle negative values. Int will return the next whole negative number that is less than the argument. Fix returns the next whole negative number that is greater than the argument. Table B.13 compares the effects of Fix vs Int and Cint.

| Value | Fix(value) | Int(value) | Cint(value) |
|-------|-----------|-----------|-------------|
| 2.7 | 2 | 2 | 3 |
| 2.2 | 2 | 2 | 2 |
| 2 | 2 | 2 | 2 |
| -2 | -2 | -2 | -2 |
| -2.2 | -2 | -3 | -2 |
| -2.7 | -2 | -3 | -3 |

Table B.13 Return values for Fix, Int, and CInt functions

# For...Next - Statements

## See Also: Do...Loop, Exit, While...Wend

## Purpose

The For and Next statements are used to repeat the execution of a block of statements for a specified number of times.

## General Syntax

```
For counter = startvalue To endvalue [Step increment]
     [statements]
     [Exit For]
     [statements]
Next [counter][, counter]
```

## Usage

```
A% = 0
For X% = 1 to 10
     A% = A% + X%
Next
```

This loop sums the digits from 1 through 10. Each time the loop runs, it adds the next digit in the counter (X%) to the variable A%, which accumulates the total. The final value of A% is thus 1+2+3+4+5+6+7+8+9+10, or 55.

```
For X% = 10 to 1 Step -1
     A% = A% + X%
Next
```

This loop uses the Step keyword with a negative value, so the counter (X%) starts at 10, and decrements on each pass until it reaches 0.

## Description

The For...Next loop structure allows you to set up a group of statements that will be executed a specified number of times. The counter parameter is used to count the iterations of the loop, and must be a simple variable of any numeric data type. It cannot be an array element or a record element. The parameter's startvalue and endvalue indicate the starting and ending values that will be assigned to the counter. They may be any numeric expression of any data type. Increment indicates the amount the counter is changed each time the loop is executed. If not explicitly indicated, increment defaults to one. The variable name of counter can follow the keyword Next, but it is not necessary. If counter is omitted, Visual Basic will match the Next keyword with the most recent For keyword.

When a For...Next loop is encountered, Visual Basic first assigns to the counter the value of startvalue. It then compares counter to endvalue. If increment is positive, and counter is greater than endvalue, the loop is exited. If increment is negative, and counter is less than endvalue, the loop is exited. If counter is within the range indicated by startvalue and endvalue, the statement block between the For and Next keywords is executed. When execution reaches the Next keyword, increment is added to counter. Visual Basic again compares the counter to endvalue. If increment is positive, and counter is greater than endvalue, the loop is exited. If increment is negative, and counter is less than endvalue, the loop is exited. Otherwise the statement block is again executed.

The Exit For statement can also be used inside the statement block to cause the loop to end immediately, and execution then jumps to the statement following the Next keyword.

You can nest several loops within each other. This is useful for setting or getting at the contents of a multi-dimensional array. Nested loops must be closed in the reverse order in which they were opened. If counter variables are not being used alongside the Next keyword, this is handled automatically, and all you have to do is make sure there is one Next for each For. Visual Basic allows you to use one Next keyword for all the loops by specifying several counter variables. For instance, these two loops are identical:

```
For x% = 1 to 10
    For y% = 1 to 10
        For z% = 1 to 10
            B% = x% + y% + z%
        Next z%
    Next y%
Next x%

For x% = 1 to 10
    For y% = 1 to 10
        For z% = 1 to 10
            B% = x% + y% + z%
Next z%, y%, x%
```

If Visual Basic encounters a For statement, and cannot find a matching Next, it generates a "For without Next" error. If it encounters a Next before encountering a For, a "Next without For" error is issued. This error is also caused when the counter variable alongside the Next keyword does not appear in reverse order of the counter in the For statement. For instance, the following code will generate a "Next without For" message:

```
For t1% = 1 To 10
    For t2% = 1 To 10
        For t3% = 1 To 10
            B% = x% + y% + z%
Next t1%, t2%, t3%
```

# Format$ - Function

### See Also: DateSerial, Now, Str$, TimeSerial

### Purpose
The Format$ function converts a numeric expression, date serial or time serial into a formatted string.

### General Syntax
```
Format$(numeric-expression,edit-pattern)
```

### Usage
```
N! = 545.3
Label1.Caption = Format$(N!, "###.00")
```
Sets the Caption property of Label1 to "545.30"

```
D# = DateValue("08/22/1964")
Label2.Caption = Format$(D#, "dddd, mmmm dd, yyyy")
```
Sets the Caption property of Label2 to "Saturday, August 22, 1964"

```
T# = TimeValue("01:02:45")
Label3.Caption = Format$(T#, "h:mm")
```
Sets the Caption property of Label3 to "1:02"

## Description

Any number can be converted to a formatted string. For a number, the edit pattern can have one of three styles. The first style supplies one edit pattern, and all numbers are converted using that pattern. The second style has two edit patterns separated by a semicolon. Non-negative numbers will be formatted according to the first edit pattern, and negative numbers will use the second. The final style has three edit patterns, all separated by semicolons. The first pattern is used to format positive numbers, the second for negative, and the third for 0.

Table B.14 details the numeric formatting characters, and their uses.

| Symbol | Effect of symbol |
|--------|------------------|
| 0 | Zero-digit place holder. If the number has fewer digits than the edit pattern, the empty digits are 0-filled. |
| # | Null digit place holder. If the number has fewer digits than the edit pattern, the empty digits become null. This place holder does not blank fill. Therefore, the resultant string may be shorter than the original edit pattern. |
| % | Percentage place holder. This symbol returns the result of the number multiplied by 100, and appends a % to it. |
| . | Decimal place holder. Indicates where the decimal point is to be placed in the edit string. |
| , | Thousands separator. This is used to separate every three digits to the left of the decimal to make a long number more readable. Two commas adjacent to each other cause the three digits that would be between them to be ignored. The same effect is created when a comma is used just to the left of the decimal place holder. |
| E-, e- | Returns the number in scientific format. This requires that a digit place holder (0 or #) be placed to the immediate left of the E or e, or an "Illegal function call" error will occur. An appropriate number of digit place holders should be placed to the right of the - in order to display the exponent. A minus sign will be inserted next to any negative exponents. |
| E+, e+ | Returns the number in scientific notation. Works the same as E- and e-, but a + sign is inserted next to any positive exponents as well as a - sign next to negative exponents. |
| -, +, $, (, ) | These characters will be returned literally and do not affect the format of the number. |
| \char | This symbol returns the character specified by char. The backslash is not returned. |
| "string" | Enclosing a string in quotes will return that string literally. Quotation marks can only be inserted into an edit pattern via the use of Chr$(34) and string concatenation. |

**Table B.14 Numeric format symbols**

### Date Serials

Date serials can be converted to a string with a variety of date formats. The supplied date serial number must be in the range of from -53688 to 65380, inclusive. This range represents a range of dates from 01/01/1753 to 12/31/2078.

Table B.15 details the date string formatting symbols, and what is returned when a serial number for the date 06/01/1991 is used.

| Symbol | Example | Effect of Symbol |
|--------|---------|------------------|
| / | / | Date separator |
| - | - | Date separator |
| d | 1 | Returns the day of the month, omitting any leading 0. |
| dd | 01 | Returns the day of the month with a leading 0, if needed. |

*Table B.15 (continued)*

| Symbol | Example | Effect of Symbol |
|--------|---------|------------------|
| ddd | Sat | Returns the abbreviated day of the week. |
| dddd | Saturday | Returns the full name of the day of the week. |
| ddddd | 06/01/1991 | Returns the full date string in the format specified by the Win.Ini file's entry "sShortDate". If there is no "sShortDate" entry, it defaults to the format "mm/dd/yyyy". This entry can be changed via the International settings in the Window's Control Panel. |
| m | 6 | Returns the number of the month of the year, without a leading 0. |
| mm | 06 | Returns the number of the month of the year, with a leading 0. |
| mmm | Jun | Returns the abbreviated name of the month. |
| mmmm | June | Returns the full name of the month. |
| yy | 91 | Returns the 2-digit year. |
| yyyy | 1991 | Returns the 4-digit year. |

**Table B.15 Date serial format symbols**

## Time Serials

While the whole portion of a serial represents a date, the fractional part can represent a time, which is stored as a fraction of a day. The time returned will be in 24-hour format unless one of the AM/PM format symbols is used. Time serials can be formatted with the symbols shown in Table B.16 (the examples are based on a time of 1:05:31 AM):

| Symbol | Example | Effect of symbol |
|--------|---------|------------------|
| : | : | Time separator |
| h | 1 | Returns the hour, without a leading 0. |
| hh | 01 | Returns the hour, with a leading 0, if needed. |
| m | 5 | Returns the minute, without a leading 0. This must be used immediately following an "h" or an "hh", or the number of the current month will be returned instead. |
| mm | 05 | Returns the minute, with a leading 0. This must be used immediately following an "h" or an "hh", or the number of the current  month will be returned instead. |
| s | 31 | Returns the second, without a leading 0. |
| ss | 31 | Returns the minute, with a leading 0. |
| ttttt | 01:05:31 | Returns the time in the format specified by the entry "sTime" in the Win.Ini file. This entry can be changed via the International settings in the Window's Control Panel. |
| AM/PM, am/pm | | Returns "AM" for any hour before noon, and "PM" for any hour after (in the specified case). |
| A/P, a/p | | Returns "A" for any hour before noon, and "P" for any hour after (in the specified case). |
| AMPM | | Uses the AM/PM format specified by the "s1159" and "s2359" entries in the Win.Ini file. These entries can be changed via the International settings in the Windows Control Panel. |

**Table B.16 Time serial format symbols**

# FreeFile - Function

## See Also:  Open

## Purpose

The FreeFile function returns an unused file number that you can use to open a file.

## General Syntax

```
FreeFile
```

## Usage

```
FileNo% = FreeFile
Open "Test.Dat" For Random As #FileNo% Len = 32
```

## Description

When opening a file, you must supply a number (in the range of from 1 to 255) by which the file will be referenced throughout the program. Visual Basic will issue a "File already open" error if you attempt to open a file using a file number that is assigned to an already open file. FreeFile eliminates the need for you to keep track of which file numbers have and have not been used.

The number returned by the FreeFile function does not change until you open a file with the returned number. Therefore, it is a good idea to open a file with the returned number immediately after using this function. For instance:

```
File1% = FreeFile
File2% = FreeFile

Open "file1.dat" For Random As #File1% Len = 128
Open "file2.dat" For Random As #File2% Len = 128
```

In the example code above, Visual Basic will issue a "File already open" error. This will happen because no file was opened after FreeFile was used to assign a value to File1%. Therefore both variables File1% and File2% will have the same value. Instead, always immediately follow the file number assignment with a file open:

```
File1% = FreeFile
Open "file1.dat" For Random As #File1% Len = 128

File2% = FreeFile
Open "file2.dat" For Random As #File2% Len = 128
```

# Function...End Function - Statements

### See Also:  End, Exit, Sub

## Purpose

The Function and End Function statements declare and define a Visual Basic procedure that can receive arguments and return a value of a specified data type.

## General Syntax

```
[Static] Function function-name[(arguments)][As type]
     [Static var[,var] ]
     [Dim var[,var] ]
     [statements]
     [Exit Function]
     [statements]
     function-name = expression
End Function
```

## Usage

```
Function TrimStr(ByVal I as String) As String
     Ltrim(I)
     RTrim(I)
     TrimStr = I
End Function

B$ = " Hello "
A$ = TrimStr(B$)
```

This Function combines the effects of the Visual Basic Functions LTrim and RTrim. Because the ByVal keyword is used, the supplied argument is passed by value, and cannot be changed by the Function. The result of the Function assigns the string "Hello" to the variable A$, with the leading and trailing spaces trimmed off.

## Description

Although Visual Basic has many useful predefined Functions, it is sometimes necessary to create a custom Function that suits a specific need for a program. The Function..End Function block allows you to do just that. A call to a programmer-defined Function is made in the same manner as a call to a Visual Basic Function. The Function name can be placed on the right side of an assignment, or can be used as an argument in another function or Sub procedure call. The following examples are both correct calls to a Function:

```
A$ = TrimStr(B$)
C$ = UCase$(TrimStr(B$))
```

The data type of the returned value must be declared in the Function definition. This can be done by appending a data type declaration character (!, @, #, $, %, &) to the end of the Function name. Alternatively, the As type parameter may be used. Only one of these two methods may be used in a particular Function definition.

The allocation of local variables (variables that are accessible only to this Function) is performed by using either the Dim or Static statements. Variables that are allocated with the Dim statement are deallocated when the Function is exited. Therefore, they do not retain their value between calls to the Function. To guarantee that a variable keeps its value between calls, it should be declared with the Static statement. If you want to have all local variables retain their value between calls, the Function definition should begin with the optional Static keyword.

Arguments may be passed to the Function in order to modify its behavior, or to give it information to act upon. The format for declaring arguments is as follows:

```
([ByVal]variablename[As type][,[ByVal]variablename[As type] ])
```

The variablename indicates the name by which the argument will be referred to from within the Function. It may end in a type declaration character, or the As type parameter may be used to declare the data type of the incoming argument. The type may be Integer, Long, Single, Double, Currency, or String. By default, the arguments are passed by reference. This means the address of the variable is passed instead of the actual value. This allows the Function to make changes to the passed arguments. In order to prevent this from happening, the ByVal keyword may be used to force the arguments to be passed by value instead. If a Function has no arguments, empty parentheses must accompany the Function name (unless the function has been declared with the Declare statement).

The Function is normally exited when execution reaches the End Function keywords. However, an alternate exit may be forced by using the Exit Function statement. This causes the Function to be immediately terminated, and execution returns to the instruction following the call to the Function. Before the Function is exited, it must be assigned the value that it will be returning. This is done by assigning the desired return value to the Function name just prior to exiting the Function.

Visual Basic Functions can be called recursively. This means that a Function can call itself.

# Get - Statement

### See Also: Lof, Open, Put, Type

### Purpose
The Get statement reads a block of data from a disk file into a predefined record buffer.

### General Syntax
```
Get [#]filenumber%,[position&], recordbuffer
```

### Usage
```
Type Rolodex
    Name as String * 20
    Number as Long
    Address as String * 100
End Type

Dim PhoneCard as Rolodex
Open "Cards.Dat" For Random As #1 Len = 128

Get #1, 129, PhoneCard
```
This example opens a file for random access, and reads the 129th record into the user-defined variable PhoneCard. The size of the data read is 128 bytes, as defined by the LEN keyword in the open statement.

Because PhoneCard is only 124 bytes long, and the file was opened for random access, the extra bytes read are discarded.

```
Type Rolodex
     Name as String * 20
     Number as Long
     Address as String * 100
End Type

Dim PhoneCard as Rolodex
Open "Cards.Dat" For Binary As #1

Get #1, 129, PhoneCard
```

This example opens a file for binary access, and reads the file beginning at the 129the byte. Because the file was opened for bunary access, the length of the data read is 124 bytes, as defined by the length of the PhoneCard variable.

### Description

The Get statement is used to read data from a disk file into a previously defined record area. The filenumber parameter indicates which file is to be read from. This number must be from 1 to 255, and match the number used in the Open statement of a currently open file. If the file number used does not match a currently opened file, a "Bad file name or number" error is generated. The file must have been opened in either Random access or Binary mode. If not, Visual Basic will issue a "Bad file mode" error.

If the position parameter is omitted, the commas must still be used. If position specifies an area that is beyond the length of the file, the record buffer will be empty. Visual Basic does no checking to see if a Get is being attempted past the length of the file. This task is left to you. Use the Lof function to determine the length of an open file.

The recordbuffer parameter refers to the area in which the data from the read will be stored. It can be of any data type. Most often, it is of a type defined by you (using the Type statement) whose fields match those of the file's record structure.

### Reading Random Access Files

The position parameter for random access files represents the desired record number. If this parameter is omitted, the next record in the file is read. For instance, if no records have been read, a Get without the position specified will read record number 1. The next Get will read record number 2, etc. The largest possible valid record number is 2,147,483,647.

The variable used for the recordbuffer must be of a length that is less than or equal to the length specified in the Open statement. Using a variable whose length is too long results in a "Bad record length" error.

### Reading Binary Files

The position parameter for binary files refers to the byte position in the file where reading is to start. The first byte in the file is position 1, the second is 2, and so on.

The size of the read is determined by the size of the record buffer. This allows a file to have variable record lengths.

# Global - Statement

### See Also:  Const, Dim, Option Base, Static

### Purpose

The Global statement is used in the global module to declare and allocate storage for simple variables and arrays that will be accessible to all modules and forms.

### General Syntax

For declaring the data type of a simple variable
```
Global name [As type][, name [As type]]
```

For declaring an array:
```
Global name[(suscript-range)][As type][, name[(subscript-range)][As type]
```

## Usage

```
Global Num1 As Integer, Num2 As Single
```
Declares two variables, Num1 and Num2, as types Integer and Single, respectively.

```
Global MyArray(1 to 100) As Integer
Global YourArray(-10 to 10) As String
```
Declares the arrays MyArray and YourArray. MyArray contains 100 integer elements that can be accessed by using a subscript with a value from 1 to 100. YourArray contains 21 string elements that can be accessed using a subscript with a value of -10 to +10.

## Description

Variables declared with the Global statement can be accessed from any form, module, or procedure in a program. This statement must be used in the global module; using it anywhere else generates an "Invalid outside global module" error.

The data type of the variable can be specified by either appending a data type declaration character (!, @, #, $, %, &) to the end of the variable name, or by using the As type clause. The type may be Integer, Long, Single, Double, Currency, String (for variable length strings), String * length (for fixed length strings), or a programmer-defined type.

Arrays may also be declared with the Global statement. Arrays provide a method for creating an entire series of variables, and referencing them by the same variable name. An index number (called the subscript) is used to determine which particular element in an array is being referenced. A more detailed discussion on the concept of arrays can be found in Appendix A, *Visual Basic Language Tutorial*.

The dimensions of an array are defined by the entry in the subscript-range portion of the Global statement. The subscript range follows this format:

```
[lo-element To] hi-element[,[lo-element To] hi-element]
```

The lo-element parameter lets you define the range of the subscripts, as well as number of elements in the array. If lo-element is not used, the lowest valid subscript will be 0 (unless the default has been changed using Option Base), and the supplied number will be the highest valid subscript. The number of elements allowed in an array depends on the desired data type for that array. Visual Basic allows approximately 64K of data space for each array declared (not to exceed installed memory, of course). Therefore, an Integer array (which is 2 bytes long per element) may have up to 32767 elements, while a Long or a Single precision (4 bytes per element) array may have half that.

Global initializes all elements of variable length string arrays to null strings. All other arrays are initialized to 0s (including fixed length strings and programmer-defined types).

At times, it is necessary to have a multidimensional array. To declare such an array, include as many sets of subscripts as needed, separated by commas.

```
Global MultiArray (1 To 100, 50 To 60, -100 to 100) As Integer
```

The example above declares an array with three dimensions of 100, 11, and 201 elements, respectively. The first dimension can be referenced by subscripts from 1 to 100, the second may have subscripts ranging from 50 to 60, and the third, from -100 to +100. Visual Basic allows arrays to have as many as 60 dimensions.

Leaving the parentheses empty in a Global statement declares a dynamic array. The number of dimensions and elements in a dynamic array is then defined within a procedure by the ReDim statement. Dynamic arrays are allocated at runtime, and may have the number of elements redefined at any time. However, once set, the number of dimensions in a dynamic array cannot be changed. See the entry for ReDim in this appendix for more on dynamic arrays.

# Gosub...Return - Statements

**See Also: On...Gosub, Sub**

## Purpose

The Gosub statement directs the program to branch to a subroutine. Within the subroutine, the Return statement returns execution to the main program. The subroutine must be contained within the same Visual Basic Function or Sub procedure as the initiating Gosub.

## General Syntax

```
Gosub {linelabel | linenumber}

{linelabel: | linenumber}
    :
    [statement-block]
    :
Return
```

## Usage

```
Gosub DoIt

DoIt:
    A$ = "Now I've done it!"
Return
```

When the Gosub is executed, the program branches to the label "DoIt:". When the Return is executed, the program will return to the instruction following the Gosub.

## Description

The Gosub statement is left over from earlier days, when the BASIC languages did not have Sub procedures or Functions. It has been retained in Visual Basic to provide a bit of backward compatibility. The Gosub causes execution to branch to the specified line label or number. The program will then execute from there until it reaches a Return statement. It will then return to the instruction following the Gosub. The specified line label or number must reside in the same procedure, or Visual Basic issues a "Label not defined" error.

Because a subroutine is not a self-contained procedure like a Sub or a Function, there is the possibility that execution can just fall into it. For instance, in the following code, the program will begin executing a subroutine without a Gosub:

```
Sub Test(A As Integer)

If A > 100 then Gosub SquareIt

SquareIt:
    A = A ^ 2
Return
End Sub
```

In this example, the program will fall into the subroutine SquareIt even when the test in the If statement is false. Doing so causes execution to reach a Return statement without having executed a Gosub. Visual Basic issues a "Return without gosub" error when this happens. To prevent this, place an Exit statement before any subroutines in a procedure:

```
Sub Test(A As Integer)

If A > 100 then Gosub SquareIt
Exit Sub

SquareIt:
    A = A ^ 2
Return
End Sub
```

It is generally good practice to avoid the use of Gosub...Return. Whenever possible, use the Function and Sub definitions instead.

# GoTo - Statement

## Purpose

The Goto statement branches unconditionally, and without return, to a line number or label in a procedure.

## General Syntax

```
GoTo {linenumber | linelabel}
```

## Usage

```
GoTo BadPractice
```
Branches to the label "BadPractice."

## Description

The GoTo statement is another relic of early versions of BASIC. The GoTo statement sends execution to the line number or label specified. The line number or label must be in the same procedure as the GoTo. Execution continues at the line specified, and no return address is saved.

GoTo is a highly unstructured command, and should be used with caution, if at all. It is much better programming practice to use the Do...Loop, For...Next, Function, or Sub statements.

# Hex$ - Function

## See Also: Oct$

## Purpose

The Hex$ function converts a decimal numeric expression to a string that represents the value of the numeric expression in hexadecimal format.

## General Syntax

```
Hex$(numeric-expression)
```

## Usage

```
A% = 100
B$ = Hex$(A%)
```
Places a string with the hexidecimal value "64" into the variable B$.

## Description

Hexadecimal notation is a way of counting using 16 digits. The digits in hexadecimal include 0 through 9, and A through F. A hexadecimal "A" equals a decimal 10, "B" equals 11, and so on. Hexadecimal is often used to display memory addresses because it easily converts back and forth from binary. The Hex$ function provides a method of converting a decimal number into hexadecimal.

The supplied numeric-expression is rounded to the nearest whole number before conversion is begun. If numeric-expression is an integer, the string returned by Hex$ will be 4 or fewer bytes long. Otherwise, the return string can be up to 8 bytes long.

# Hour - Function

## See Also: Now, TimeSerial, TimeValue

## Purpose

The Hour function returns the hour of the day as an integer from 0 (Midnight) to 23 (11 pm), based on the supplied time serial.

## General Syntax

```
Hour(timeserial#)
```

## Usage

```
A% = Hour(Now)
```
This example uses the Now function to get the current hour of the day.

## Description

The hour is returned as an integer in the range of from 0 (12 midnight) to 23 (11 pm).

The time serial is a double-precision number created by using the TimeValue, or TimeSerial functions. Date serials and time serials can be combined, because the date serial is stored on the left side of the decimal point, and the time serial is stored on the right.

# If...Then...Else - Statement

**See Also:** If...Then...Elseif...End If, Select Case

## Purpose
The If, Then, and Else statements provide a one-line structure for conditional execution.

## General Syntax
```
If condition Then action1 [Else action2]
```

## Usage
```
If A% > B% Then C% = A% Else C% = B%
```
This example places the higher of the values A% and B% into the variable C%

## Description
Your program will need to make many decisions and, based on those decisions, take one course of action or another. One of the ways you can instruct your program to make such a decision is with the If statement. Visual Basic has two styles of the If... statement. The style described in this entry involves a simple one-line format, and is generally used where only one or two instructions depend on the condition being tested. There is also a muliple-line If statement, which is described in the next entry.

In the single-line If statement, the value of the condition determines if an action is to take place. If the condition evaluates to non-0, the statement(s) in action1 will be executed. If the condition evaluates to 0, execution will continue with the next instruction, unless the Else keyword has been used. In that case, the statement(s) specified in action2 will be executed.

The condition can be any expression that evaluates to a 0 or non-0 value. You can also test the type of an object by using the following syntax in place of condition:

```
TypeOf objectname is objecttype
```

where objectname is the object being tested, and objecttype is any of the objects below.

| | | | | |
|---|---|---|---|---|
| CheckBox | ComboBox | CommandButton | DirListBox | DriveListBox |
| FileListBox | Frame | HScrollBar | Label | ListBox |
| Menu | OptionButton | PictureBox | TextBox | TImer |
| VScrollBar | | | | |

The objecttype must match exactly the spelling of one of the objects above. This is used when you wish to test what type of object a specific control represents. For instance, in the following code, if the tested object is a text box control, the object's ForeColor property is set:

```
Sub ChangeColor (ThisObject As Control)
    If TypeOf ThisObject is TextBox Then ThisObject.ForeColor = RED
End Sub
```

More than one statement may be specified for action1 or action2, as long as the statements are separated by colons. However, this is not suggested practice. The multiple-line If... construct handles this type of task much better.

# If...Then...Elseif...End If - Statements

**See Also:** If...Then...Else, Select Case

## Purpose
The If, Then, ElseIf, and End If statements provide a multiple-line structure for conditional execution.

## General Syntax
```
If condition-1 Then
    :
    [actions-1]
    :
```

```
[ElseIf condition-2 Then]
    :
    [actions-2]
    :
[ElseIf condition-n Then]
    :
    [actions-n]
    :
[Else]
    :
    [else-actions]
    :
End If
```

## Usage

```
If PlantType$ = "Tree" Then
    Message$ = "Is this an Oak, or an Elm?"
    PlantName$ =  InputBox$(Message$)
ElseIf PlantHeight% > 20 Then
    Message$ = "Only trees grow this high"
    MsgBox Message$
Else
    Message$ = "What kind of a plant is this?"
    PlantType$ = InputBox$(Message$)
End If
```

## Description

The multiple-line If... statement is a very useful construct that provides two functions. First, it allows conditional execution of several statements. It also allows you to test several different values in the same construct, having each successive condition dependent on the result of the previous conditions.

If condition-1 evaluates to non-0, the instructions in statement-block-1 will be executed. Visual Basic will then pick up execution at the instruction following the End If clause.

The ElseIf keyword can be used to test more than one condition. Each ElseIf condition is tested only if all the conditions above it have tested false. You may use as many ElseIf conditions as needed.

You may also use the optional Else keyword. The statement block following this keyword will be executed if none of the preceding conditions evaluate as non-0.

The condition-? parameters can be any expression that evaluates to a 0 or non-0 value. You can also test the type of an object by using the following syntax in place of condition-?:

```
TypeOf objectname is objecttype
```

where objectname is the object being tested, and objecttype is any of the objects below.

| | | | | |
|---|---|---|---|---|
| **CheckBox** | **ComboBox** | **CommandButton** | **DirListBox** | **DriveListBox** |
| **FileListBox** | **Frame** | **HScrollBar** | **Label** | **ListBox** |
| **Menu** | **OptionButton** | **PictureBox** | **TextBox** | **Timer** |
| **VScrollBar** | | | | |

The objecttype must match exactly the spelling of one of the objects above. This is used when you wish to test what type of object has a specific control. For instance, in the following code, if the tested object is a text box control, the object's ForeColor and BackColor properties are set:

```
Sub ChangeColor (ThisObject Has Control)
    If TypeOf ThisObject is TextBox Then
        ThisObject.ForeColor = RED
        ThisObject.BackColor = BLACK
    End If
End Sub
```

Nesting of If... statements is allowed, and can be a very useful tool. Be careful to avoid nesting too many If statements, as this makes following the logic of a program difficult. The Select Case statement is a better alternative when more than three separate conditions involving the same expression are to be tested. Also, care must be taken to ensure each multiple-line If has a matching End If.

Visual Basic issues a "Block If without End If" error when there is a missing End If. An "End If without Block If" error is generated when an End If is encountered and cannot be matched to an initiating If.

# Input # - Statement

See Also: **Input$, Line Input#, Write #**

### Purpose
The Input # statement reads data from a sequential access file into variables.

### General Syntax
```
Input #filenumber,var1[,var2]
```

### Usage
```
SeqFile% = FreeFile
Open "Test.Dat" For Input As #SeqFile%
Input #SeqFile%, A$, B%
```
This example reads data from "Test.Dat" into the variables A$ and B%.

### Description
The Input # statement is used to read a sequential file, one variable at a time. The filenumber parameter refers to the number the file was opened with. If the filenumber supplied is not an open file, Visual Basic issues a "Bad file name or number" error. As shown in the preceding example, the FreeFile function can be used to obtain a valid file number for use in opening a file.

The Input # statement assigns the data read from the file to the variables that are specified, one after another, in the statement. The type of variables specified should match the type of data being read. How Visual Basic reads the file is based on the data type of the next variable to be read.

If the next variable to be read is numeric, Visual Basic reads until it reaches a space. This is assumed to be the start of the number. It then reads the file until a comma, a carriage return, a linefeed, the end of file marker, or another space is encountered. If the data that it has read is numeric, the variable is assigned the value of the numeric data. Otherwise, the variable is assigned the value of 0.

If the next variable to be read is a string, the file is read until a non-space character is encountered. This becomes the start of the string. The file is then read until a comma, a carriage return, a linefeed, the end of file marker, or another space is encountered.

Trying to read past the end of a sequential file results in an "Input past end of file" error. This can be prevented by using the EOF function.

# Input$ - Function

See Also: **Input #**

### Purpose
The Input$ function reads a string of characters from a file, assigning no special meaning to carriage returns and line feeds.

### General Syntax
```
Input$(inputlength%,[#]filenumber%)
```

### Usage
```
A$ = Input$(100, 1)
```
Reads 100 characters from the file opened as number 1.

### Description
The Input$ function returns a string of the length specified by inputlength from a data file. The file can be opened under Input, Random or Binary mode. If it is a Random file, the maximum inputlength is the record length specified in the Open statement with the Len parameter. For Input and Binary files, the maximum length is 32,767 bytes. However, any attempt to read past the length of the file will cause an "Input past end of file" error to occur. You should therefore use the Lof function or some other means to check for the end of the file before reading.

Input$ assigns no special meaning to commas, quotes, spaces, carriage returns, or linefeeds. Therefore, the string returned may contain these characters.

# InputBox$ - Function

**See Also:** MsgBox, MsgBox$

## Purpose

The InputBox$ function displays a dialog box with the specified text, and accepts user input.

## General Syntax

```
InputBox$(msg$[,title$][,default-default$,][,xpos%, ypos%]
```

## Usage

```
UserInput$ = InputBox$("Enter some text",,"This is some text")
```

## Description

The InputBox$ function displays a dialog box in which the contents of the string title$ are displayed in the box's title bar, and the string default$ is displayed in the box's text area, usually representing a prompt to the user. The argument xpos% represents the distance of the left side of the dialog box from the left side of the screen, in twips. The ypos% argument represents the distance of the top of the box from the top of the screen, in twips. For more details on the InputBox$ function, see Chapter 17, *Creating and Using Dialog Boxes*.

# InStr - Function

## Purpose

The Instr function searches one string for the occurrence of a second string, and returns a result based on whether or not the second string is found within the first.

## General Syntax

```
InStr([startpos&], string1, string2)
```

## Usage

```
B$ = "Good Bye"
A% = InStr(B$, "Bye")
C% = InStr(7, B$, "Bye")
```

The first example assigns the value 6 to the variable A% because the string "Bye" can be found at the sixth byte position in B$. The second example starts the search at byte position 7, therefore "Bye" cannot be found. The variable C% is assigned a value of 0.

## Description

The parameter string1 is the string that will be searched. String2 is the string that is being searched for. If string2 is found within string1, Instr returns the byte position where the beginning of the search string is found. If the string cannot be found, a 0 is returned. You can optionally use the startpos& parameter. This specifies the position in string1 where you wish the search to start. This is useful for searching one string for multiple occurrences of another. If string2 is a null string, InStr returns the value of startpos& (or 0, if startpos& was not specified).

# Int - Function

**See Also:** CType, Fix

## Purpose

The Int function returns the largest integer that is less than or equal to the supplied numeric expression.

## General Syntax

```
Int(numeric-expression)
```

## Usage

```
A% = Int(-2.86)
B% = Int(2.86)
```

These statements place the value -3 in the variable A%, and the value 2 in the variable B%.

## Description

The Int function essentially rounds a numeric expression to the nearest integer. Int performs the same operation as Fix when the argument is positive, or when there are no digits to the right of the decimal. The difference between the two is how they handle negative values with fractions. Int will return the next whole negative number that is less than the argument. Fix returns the next whole negative number that is greater than the argument. Table B.17 compares the effects of Int, Fix, and Cint.

| Value | Int(Value) | Fix(Value) | Cint(Value) |
|-------|------------|------------|-------------|
| 2.7 | 2 | 2 | 3 |
| 2.2 | 2 | 2 | 2 |
| 2 | 2 | 2 | 2 |
| -2 | -2 | -2 | -2 |
| -2.2 | -3 | -2 | -2 |
| -2.7 | -3 | -2 | -3 |

Table B.17 Return values for Fix, Int, and Cint functions

# Kill - Statement

### See Also:  Name, open

### Purpose

The Kill statement deletes the specified file from the disk.

### General Syntax

```
Kill filename$
```

### Usage

```
FileName$ = File1.List(File1.ListIndex)
Kill FileName$
```
This example erases the file that is currently selected in the FileListBox named File1.

### Description

The Kill statement erases files from a fixed or floppy disk device. The filename parameter specifies the path and file name of the file(s) to be deleted. It may contain the wildcard characters "?" and "*". The "?" wildcard is used to match any single character, and the "*" matches a full file name or extension. If the drive or path are not specified in the filename parameter, the default drive and/or path is used. If the file does not exist on the specified path, or the path itself does not exist, Visual Basic will issue a "File not found" error.

Great care should be taken when using this statement. It is a destructive command that can, if not handled properly, cause oneself huge amounts of grief. Improper use of the Kill statement can cause your programs to inadvertantly delete needed files. To prevent this from happening, when debugging a program that uses this statement, we suggest that you preface this statement with a MsgBox$ function that confirms the action. Then, when you are sure the program is deleting the correct file (or files), remove the MsgBox$ function if desired.

# LBound - Function

### See Also:  UBound

### Purpose

The LBound function returns the value of the smallest usable subscript for the specified dimension of an array.

### General Syntax

```
LBound(arrayname[,dimension%])
```

### Usage

```
Dim Flowers%(1 To 100, -50 To 50)
A% = LBound(Flowers%, 2)
```

The value -50 is assigned to the variable A%, because that is the smallest subscript available in the second dimension of the array Flowers%.

### Description

If the dimension parameter is not specified, the lower bound for the first dimension is returned. LBound is useful in conjunction with UBound for figuring out how many elements a dynamic array has. The number of elements can be found by subtracting the value returned by LBound from the value returned from UBound and adding one.

# LCase$ - Function

### See Also: UCase$

### Purpose

The LCase$ function returns a copy of a string in which all uppercase alphabetic characters have been converted to lowercase.

### General Syntax

```
LCase$(expression$)
```

### Usage

```
C1$ = Command$
C2$ = LCase$(C1$)
```

This example retrieves the command line parameters that were used to start the program, and converts the entries to lowercase.

### Description

The expression$ parameter can be a fixed or variable length string, a string constant, a literal string, the result of any function that returns a string, or any other string expression. The UCase$ function works the same as LCase$, but it converts lowercase to uppercase.

This function is very useful for making a non-case sensitive comparison of two strings. This is helpful when an internal variable is being compared to a user's string input. By using LCase$ (or UCase$), the program can all but ignore the case of the string that has been entered by the user.

# Left$ - Function

### See Also: Mid$, Right$

### Purpose

The Left$ function returns a portion of a string, starting at the first character, of the length specified.

### General Syntax

```
Left$(expression$, length&)
```

### Usage

```
B$ = "Hello, Dolly!"
C$ = Left$(B$, 5)
```

The above example assigns the leftmost five characters from B$ to the variable C$, giving it a value of "Hello".

### Description

The expression$ parameter can be a fixed or variable length string, a string constant, a literal string, the result of any function that returns a string, or any other string expression.

The length& parameter refers to the number of characters to copy. This value may be in the range of from 0 to 65,535. If the length specified is greater than or equal to the full length of the source string,

Left$ returns an exact copy of the source string. If the length is 0, a null string is returned. If length& has a value of less than 0, or greater than 65,535, an "Illegal function call" error is generated.

# Len - Function

## Purpose
The Len function returns the storage length of a variable. It is most commonly used to find the length of a string.

## General Syntax
```
Len(variable-name)
```

## Usage
```
A$ = "Hello"
StrLen% = Len(A$)
```
Because the string "Hello" is 5 bytes long, this places the value 5 into the variable StrLen%.

```
Type UserType
      A1 As String * 10
      A2 As Integer
      A3 As Single
End Type
Dim Test As UserType

TestLen% = Len(Test)
```
This places the length of the programmer-defined variable Test into the variable TestLen%. The value of TestLen% becomes 16; 10 bytes for Test.A1 (Fixed length string), 2 bytes for Test.A2 (Integer), and 4 bytes for Test.A3 (Single precision).

## Description
This very useful function returns the amount of data space needed to store a particular variable. Any type of variable may be used, including user-defined variables. Most commonly, Len is used to get the length of a variable-length string so it can be processed with a loop.

# Let - Statement

## See Also: LSet, RSet

## Purpose
The optional Let statement assigns a value to a variable.

## General Syntax
```
[Let] variablename = expression
```

## Usage
```
A% = 100
B! = Day(Now)
```

## Description
The Let keyword is required in some older versions of BASIC to begin a statement that assigns a value to a variable. The Let keyword is optional in Visual Basic, and rarely used. The data type of variablename must be a string if expression is a string expression. If expression is numeric, and not of the same data type as variablename, Visual Basic will automatically convert the expression to the type indicated by the variable. The expression being assigned a numeric variable must fall into that variable's range, or an "Overflow" error will occur.

   Record variables created with the Type...End Type structure can only use the Let statement if the record variable is being assigned the value of another record variable of the same type. Use the LSet statement to assign a value to a record variable from a different record type.

# Line Input # - Statement

**See Also: Input#, Print #**

### Purpose
The Line Input # statement reads from a sequential file until a carriage return/linefeed pair or the end of the file is reached.

### General Syntax
```
Line Input #filenumber%, variable$
```

### Usage
```
SeqFile% = FreeFile
Open "Notes.Txt" For Input As #SeqFile%
Line Input #SeqFile%, A$
```
This example reads one line of data from "Test.Dat" into the variable A$.

### Description
The filenumber% parameter must be the file number of a currently open file that was opened under the Input mode. If the file number does not match that of a currently open file, Visual Basic issues a "Bad file name or number" error. (The FreeFile function is handy for obtaining a guaranteed legitimate file number that can be used without worrying about its actual value.)

The variable$ parameter must be a string variable. This should normally be a variable length string. If a fixed length string is used, and the length of the data read is shorter than the string, the balance of the variable will be filled with spaces. If the read length is longer than the string, any characters read beyond the length of the string are lost.

Unlike the Input # statement, Line Input # treats commas, spaces, and quotes no differently than any other characters. This makes it useful for reading ASCII files. A read ends when a carriage return/linefeed pair is encountered, resulting in the reading of one complete line of text. The pair is then skipped, and the next read continues from there. A read is also ended when the end of the file is reached.

# Load - Statement

**See Also: Unload**

### Purpose
The Load statement loads a form into memory, or a control into a previously created control array.

### General Syntax
For a form:
```
Load form-name
```

For a control:
```
Load control-name(index)
```

### Usage
```
Load Form1
```
Loads a form into memory without displaying it.

```
Load Text1(1)
```
Loads a text box into a control array.

### Description
This statement loads a form or control into memory. Form-name or control-name represent the name of the form or control to be loaded. If a control is an element of a control array, the index value must be supplied in parentheses following the array name.

Since Visual Basic automatically loads any form or control referenced in code (for example, by the Show method), the Load statement is normally only needed when you want to load a form into memory without showing it. (Sometimes Load is used in order to change one or more properties of a form without immediately displaying the form.)

When a form is loaded, Visual Basic sets all of its properties to their initial (default) values and then executes the Load event procedure for the form.

For more details about the loading and initialization of forms, see Chapter 4, *Setting Up Forms,* and Chapter 6, *Using Forms and Controls in Program Code.*

# LoadPicture - Function

## See Also: SavePicture

## Purpose
Loads a *.BMP, *.ICO, or *.WMF picture from a disk file into, or erases it from, a form or picture box.

## General Syntax
To load a picture into a form or picture box:
```
LoadPicture(picturefile$)
```

To clear a picture from a form or picture box:
```
LoadPicture
```

## Usage
```
Picture = LoadPicture("CHESS.BMP")
```
This example loads the Chess.Bmp bitmap file into the current form.

```
PictureBox1.Picture = LoadPicture("POINT13.ICO")
```
This example loads the icon file Point13.ICO into the picture box named PictureBox1.

```
PictureBox1.Picture = LoadPicture
```
This example clears any picture that has been loaded in the picture box named PictureBox1.

## Description
The LoadPicture statement loads a picture from a specified disk file into a specified form or picture box. The picture file must have the extension .BMP (bitmap), .ICO (icon), or .WMF (Windows metafile). Note that the syntax for loading a picture into a form is different from that for loading a picture into a picture box. In the case of a form, the result of the call to LoadPicture is assigned to "Picture," meaning the Picture property of the form being coded. In the case of a picture box, the Picture property of the picture box is assigned the result of the LoadPicture function.

The LoadPicture function is explained in detail in Chapter 8, *Setting Up Graphical Objects.*

# Loc - Function

## See Also: EOF, LOF, Open

## Purpose
The Loc function returns the current position of the pointer for an open file, which indicates where the next read or write operation will occur. The meaning of the number returned depends on the mode under which the file was opened.

## General Syntax
```
Loc(filenumber%)
```

## Usage
```
A% = Loc(1)
```
This example places a number representing the current position in the file opened as #1 in the variable A%.

## Description
The filenumber% parameter must be the file number of a currently open file. If the file number does not match that of a currently open file, Visual Basic issues a "Bad file name or number" error.

Visual Basic keeps a 128-byte file buffer open for sequential files. When a read or write is done to a sequential file, it does so 128 bytes at a time. Internally, this is much like reading and writing records with

128-byte lengths. Therefore, the value returned by the Loc function for a sequential file is the result of the current byte position divided by 128 (which is the "record number" of the last internal read or write).

For Random access files, this function returns the record number of the last Get or Put statement. If no Get or Put statement has yet been executed, the Loc function returns a 0.

Because Binary files are byte-oriented, the number returned corresponds to the last byte read or written to the file. Again, if no read or write has been performed, Loc returns a 0.

# Lock...UnLock - Statements

### See Also: Get, Put

### Purpose
The Lock statement restricts multi-user access to a specified area of a file. The UnLock statement releases the restrictions placed on an area of a file by a previously issued Lock statement.

### General Syntax
```
Lock [#]filenumber%[,startpos&][ To endpos&]
   :
[statements]
   :
UnLock [#]filenumber%[,startpos&][ To endpos&]
```

### Usage
```
Lock #1
   :
UnLock #1
```
This example restricts other users from access to the entire file. When processing of the file is finished, the restrictions are released with the UnLock statement.

```
Open "Test.Dat" For Random As #1 Len = 32
Lock #1, 100
   :
UnLock #1, 100
```
This example locks and unlocks access to the 100th record in the random access file Test.Dat.

```
Open "Test.Dat" For Binary As #1
Lock #1, 10 To 20
   :
UnLock #1, 10 To 20
```
This example locks and unlocks access to byte positions 10 through 20 of the binary file Test.Dat.

```
Open "Test.Dat" For Binary As #1
Lock #1, To 300
   :
UnLock #1, To 300
```
This example locks and unlocks access to byte positions 1 through 300 of the binary file Test.Dat.

### Description
The Lock and UnLock statements are used for controlling multi-user access to files in a networked or multitasking environment. Because more than one user may have access to the same file simultaneously, such environments present special problems when it comes to maintaining data integrity. For instance, let us suppose two users, Bob and Mary, are on a network working on the same file. Bob reads a record from the file, and a copy of its contents are placed in the memory of his computer. If the program that Bob is using does not restrict access to the record, Mary can also read the record into her own computer's memory. This in itself causes no problems. However, if Bob updates the record, and then Mary also updates the record, Mary's update will be written over Bob's. By using the Lock and UnLock statements, Bob's program could restrict Mary's access to the record until Bob is finished with it. This ensures that when Mary reads the record, it will reflect any changes Bob has made to it.

The filenumber% parameter must be the file number of a currently open file. If the file number does not match that of a currently open file, Visual Basic issues a "Bad file name or number" error.

The area within the file to be locked may be specified with the startpos& and endpos& parameters. If endpos& is omitted, the TO keyword must also be omitted. This will cause the statement to affect only the position specified by startpos&. If the startpos& parameter is not used, the range affected will be from the beginning of the file to the position specified by endpos&. If both parameters ar omitted, the entire file is affected.

When used on a file that has been opened under Random mode, Lock and UnLock affect the records that fall into the range specified by startpos& and endpos&.

For files opened under the Binary mode, these statements affect a range of bytes specified by the startpos& and endpos& parameters.

When used on a file opened under Input or Output modes, the Lock and UnLock statements restrict access to the entire file. If a range has been specified, it is ignored.

Use the UnLock statement to release the restrictions placed on a file by the Lock statement. The parameters in the UnLock statement must match the parameters in the related Lock statement exactly. Not doing so will result in a "Permission Denied" error. Failing to unlock the locked portions of a file before closing it can cause unpredictable results.

When a Lock is placed on a file, the specified portion of the file is not accessible to any other process. This includes other programs that are running on the same computer. If a Visual Basic program tries to read a portion of a file that has been locked by a different process, a "Permission denied" error will occur. This error will also occur if the program attempts to lock a portion of a file that has already been locked by another process.

### Comments
The Lock and UnLock statements depend on the operating system to take care of the details involved with restricting access to files. These capabilities are provided by running SHARE.EXE under a DOS version 3.1 or higher.

## LOF - Function

### See Also: EOF, Loc

### Purpose
The LOF function returns the number of bytes equal to the length of an open file.

### General Syntax
```
LOF([#]filenumber%)
```

### Usage
```
Function NumberOfRecords(FileNo%, RecordLength%) As Long
    Dim FileLength As Integer

    FileLength = LOF(FileNo%)
    NumberOfRecords = FileLength \ RecordLength%
End Function
```
This example uses the LOF function to calculate the number of records in a random access file.

### Description
This function returns the number of bytes in a file, regardless of the mode under which it was opened.

The filenumber% parameter must be the file number of a currently open file. If the file number does not match that of a currently open file, Visual Basic issues a "Bad file name or number" error.

## Log - Function

### See Also: Exp

### Purpose
The Log function returns the natural logarithm of a numeric expression. The natural logarithm, which has a base of approximately 2.718282, should not be confused with the common logarithm, whose base is 10

### General Syntax
```
Log(numeric-expression)
```

## Usage

```
A! = 14
B! = Log(A!)
```
Returns a single-precision number that represents the natural logarithm for 14.

```
C# = 14
D# = Log(C#)
```
Returns a double-precision number that represents the natural logarithm for 14.

## Description

The logarithm of a number is the power to which the logarithmic base must be raised in order to achieve that number. The natural logarithmic base is referred to by the symbol *e,* and has an approximate value of 2.718282.

The supplied numeric expression may be of any numeric format. It must be a non-0 number. If the expression is 0, an "Illegal function call" error will occur.

By default, this function returns a single-precision number. However, if the supplied numeric-expression is in double-precision format, the function will return a double-precision number.

Exp performs the inverse operation of a natural logarithm. It raises *e* to the power specified by the power parameter.

# LSet - Statement

### See Also: Let, RSet, LTrim$

## Purpose

The LSet statement copies one string or user-defined type to another, starting from the left and working to the right. It can also be used to left-justify the contents of a string variable.

## General Syntax

```
LSet result_variable = source_variable
```

## Usage

```
Type NameAndAddress_1
    Name As String * 20
    Number As Long
    Address As String * 75
End Type

Type NameAndAddress_2
    Name As String * 20
    Number As Long
    Street As String * 25
    City As String * 25
    State As String * 20
    Zip As String * 5
End Type

Dim PhoneCard_1 As NameAndAddress_1
Dim PhoneCard_2 As NameAndAddress_2

LSet PhoneCard_2 = PhoneCard_1
```

## Description

The LSet statement assigns to result_variable the value of source_variable. Both variables may be fixed or variable length strings, or a programmer-defined variable type. The assignment performed by the LSet is done byte by byte from the left of source_variable to the right. The assignment cannot change the length of result_variable. If result_variable is shorter than source_variable, the characters that are beyond the length of result_variable are truncated. If result_variable is longer than source_variable, spaces are used to fill out the balance of result_variable.

As can be seen in the example above, this statement allows you to assign one programmer-defined type a value from a different programmer-defined type. However, it does not allow a programmer-defined type to be assigned to a variable or fixed length string. Nor does it allow assignment of different user-defined types when one of those types contains a variable length string.

The LSet statement can also be used with a single variable as both source and result. For example:

```
A$ = " It starts with two spaces"
LSet A$ = "It starts with two spaces"
```

In this case the text in A$ is left-justified: that is, the two spaces at the beginning of the string are removed, the text is moved to the left, and two spaces are added on at the end of the string. The length of the string does not change. This effect is similar to that obtained with the LTrim$ function, except that LTrim$ does not pad the string on the right. The RSet statement performs the same function, except the copy is executed from right to left.

# LTrim$ - Function

## See Also: RTrim$

## Purpose
The LTrim$ function returns a copy of a string with any leading spaces removed.

## General Syntax
```
LTrim$(string-expression)
```

## Usage
```
A$ = LTrim$(" Good Bye ")
```
This example assigns the value "Good Bye " to the variable A$.

## Description
This is the complement of the RTrim$ function. It returns a copy of the supplied string expression without any leading spaces.

The string-expression$ parameter can be a fixed or variable length string, a string constant, a literal string, the result of any function that returns a string, or any other string expression.

# Mid$ - Function

## See Also: Left$, Right$

## Purpose
The Mid$ function copies the specified portion of a string expression.

## General Syntax
```
Mid$(string-expression, start&[, length&])
```

## Usage
```
A$ = "Good bye, Dolly"
B$ = Mid$(A$, 6, 3)
C$ = Mid$(A$, 11)
```
This uses the Mid$ function to assign the value "bye" to the variable B$. In the second example, the length parameter is omitted, so the string returned starts where indicated and continues for the balance of the length of A$. Therefore, the variable C$ is assigned the value "Dolly."

## Description
This function returns the specified substring of a string expression. The string-expression parameter designates the source string and can be a fixed or variable length string, a string constant, a literal string, or the result of any function that returns a string.

The start& parameter specifies the byte position within the source string where the copy will begin. This parameter must be in the range of from 1 to 65535. If not, an "Illegal function call" will occur. If this parameter is greater than the length of the source string, the returned string will be null.

The length& parameter is used to specify how many bytes will be copied. This is an optional parameter. If it is not used, the function will return all the characters from start& to the end of the source string. The length& parameter has a range of from 0 to 65535. If it is not in this range, an "Illegal function call" will occur. If a 0 is specified, a null string is returned. If it specifies a length beyond the end of the source string, only the characters up to the length of the string are returned.

# Mid$ - Statement

## Purpose
The Mid$ statement replaces the specified characters of one string with a string expression.

## General Syntax
```
Mid$(result-string$, start&[, length&]) = string-expression
```

## Usage
```
A$ = "Hello, Dolly"
Mid$(A$, 1, 5) = "Oh my"
Mid$(A$, 8) = "Beck"
```
The first example replaces the "Hello" in A$ with "Oh my." The second example starts at the eighth byte position and replaces whatever text is there with "Beck." Because the length is not specified, the replace is effective for the length of "Beck." This makes A$'s final value "Oh my, Becky."

## Description
This statement copies the supplied string expression into the specified string. The result-string$ parameter must be a variable or fixed length string. This is the string that will receive the characters being copied.

The start& parameter specifies where in the result string the characters are to be placed. This parameter must be greater than 0, and cannot exceed the length of the result string. If it is not in this range, an "Illegal function call" will result.

The length& parameter is optional, and it specifies how many characters will be replaced. If this parameter is omitted, the length will default to the size of string-expression. Regardless of the value in length&, and the length of string-expression, the copy never goes beyond the original length of result-string$.

The string-expression parameter specifies the source of the copy. It can be a fixed or variable length string, a string constant, a literal string, or the result of any function that returns a string.

# Minute - Function

## See Also: Now, TimeSerial, TimeValue

## Purpose
The Minute function returns an integer (with a value of from 0 to 59) that represents the minute of the hour specified by the supplied time serial.

## General Syntax
```
Minute(time-serial#)
```

## Usage
```
A% = Minute(Now)
```
Places the current minute of the hour in the variable A%.

## Description
The minute is returned as an integer in the range of from 0 to 59.

A time serial is a double-precision number that can represent any time of the day. It is a fraction that corresponds to the specified time in proportion to a whole day. Therefore, a time serial for 12:00 noon has a value of .5 (one half of a day), while 6pm has a value of .75 (three quarters of a day). It is created by using the Now, TimeValue, or TimeSerial functions.

Date serials and time serials can be combined, because the date serial is stored on the left side of the decimal point, and the time serial is stored on the right.

# MkDir - Statement

## See Also: ChDir, RmDir

## Purpose
The MkDir statement creates a subdirectory on the specified drive.

### General Syntax
```
MkDir dir-name$
```
dir-name$ must be in the format of [drive:][\]dir[\subdir][\subdir]...

### Usage
```
MkDir "Test"
```
Creates the subdirectory "Test" underneath the default directory on the default drive.

```
MkDir "\Test"
```
Creates the subdirectory "Test" underneath the root directory of the default drive.

```
MkDir "D:\Test"
```
Creates the subdirectory "Test" underneath the root directory of drive D:

### Description
This statement works much like the DOS command of the same name. However, unlike the DOS command, the Visual Basic statement cannot be shortened to MD.

MkDir creates the subdirectory specified by the dir-name$ parameter. Unless the full path name is specified, the new subdirectory is created on the default drive, under the default directory. If a full path name is not indicated, and dir-name$ matches a file or directory that resides on the default drive and directory, a "Path file access error" will occur.

### Comments
Care should be taken when using this statement. Visual Basic allows you to include spaces in the dir-name$ parameter. This will create a subdirectory that cannot be removed by any means other than another Visual Basic or QuickBASIC program.

## Month - Function

### See Also: DateSerial, DateValue, Now

### Purpose
The Month function returns an integer between 1 and 12 representing the month of the year, based on the supplied date serial.

### General Syntax
```
Month(date-serial#)
```

### Usage
```
A% = Month(Now)
```
This places the value of the current month into the integer variable A%.

### Description
This function uses a double-precision serial number representing a date to return an integer value, between 1 and 12, representing the month of the year. The supplied serial number represents the number of days since December 30, 1899. Therefore, January 01, 1900, has a serial number of 2, while January 1, 1753, has a serial number of -53688. The supplied serial number must represent a date in the range of from January 1, 1753, and December 31, 2078, inclusive. If the date requested is not in this range, Visual Basic issues an "Illegal function call" error.

## MsgBox - Function and Statement

### See Also: InputBox$

### Purpose
The MsgBox statement displays a user-defined message in a window with a desired set of command buttons. If used as a function, MsgBox displays the message and also returns an integer that signifies the selected button.

### General Syntax
```
MsgBox(message$[, box-type%][, window-title$])
```

## Usage

`MsgBox("Hello World")`

Displays a window that says "Hello World" and waits for the user to click the OK button.

## Description

The MsgBox statement or function displays the message in message$ in a dialog box. If supplied, window-title$ will be placed on the title bar of the dialog box; box-type% is the sum of up to three values in Table B.18. The values in Table B.18 actually fall into three groups: those that display one or more buttons, those that display a specified icon, and those that determine which button will be considered the default. Thus a box-type% value of 2 + 16 + 0 or 18 would result in the Abort, Retry, and Ignore buttons being displayed, the "Critical Message" icon being shown in the box, and the "Abort" button being the default action.

When used as a function, MsgBox returns an integer that indicates which button was pressed, as shown in Table B.19.

| Value | Effect |
|---|---|
| 0 | Displays OK button |
| 1 | Displays OK and Cancel buttons |
| 2 | Displays Abort, Retry, and Ignore buttons |
| 4 | Displays Yes and No buttons |
| 5 | Displays Retry and Cancel buttons |
| 16 | Displays "Critical Message" icon |
| 32 | Displays "Warning Query" icon |
| 64 | Displays "Information Message" icon |
| 0 | First button is default |
| 256 | Second button is default |
| 512 | Third button is default |

**Table B.18 Values that can be summed in boxtype%**

| Return Value | Meaning |
|---|---|
| 1 | OK button was pressed |
| 2 | Cancel button was pressed |
| 3 | Abort button was pressed |
| 4 | Retry button was pressed |
| 5 | Ignore button was pressed |
| 6 | Yes button was pressed |
| 7 | No button was pressed |

**Table B.19 Meaning of return values of MsgBox function**

Further discussion and examples of use of the MsgBox statement and function can be found in Chapter 17, *Creating and Using Dialog Boxes*.

# Name - Statement

**See Also:  Kill**

## Purpose

The Name statement renames a file or directory, or moves a file to another directory.

## General Syntax

`Name oldname As newname`

### Usage
```
Name "Test_1.Dat" As "Test_2.Dat"
```
This example changes the name of the file Test_1.Dat in the default directory to Test_2.Dat.

### Description
The Name statement is very similar to the RENAME (REN) command in DOS. However, unlike the DOS RENAME, this statement allows the program to rename subdirectories as well as files.

The parameters oldname and newname specify the original and the new path and name of the file. The file specified by oldname must exist. If it does not, a "File not found" error will occur. Conversely, the file specified by newname must not exist or a "File already exists" error is issued. If the drive is specified, the same drive must be used in both oldname and newname, or a "Rename across disks" error will occur. However, Visual Basic does not require the paths of the two parameters to match. This creates the useful side effect of being able to move files from one directory to another. For instance,

```
Name "C:\Temp\Test_1.Dat" As "C:\Test_1.Dat"
```

will move the file "Test_1.Dat" from the "C:\Temp" subdirectory to the root directory.

This statement cannot be used if the file specified by either oldname or newname is currently open. Doing so causes a "File already open" error.

## Now - Function

### See Also: Day, Hour, Minute, Month, Second, WeekDay, Year

### Purpose
The Now function returns a double-precision serial number that corresponds to the current date and time.

### General Syntax
```
Now
```

### Usage
```
A# = Now
```
Places the double-precision date/time serial number for the current system date and time into the variable A#.

### Description
This function returns a double-precision number that is a combined date and time serial number representing the current system time. This provides you with the ability to do math with times and dates easily. This number can also be used with several other Visual Basic date/time functions.

The whole part of the number represents the date and corresponds to the number of days since December 30, 1899. Therefore, January 01, 1900, has a date serial number of 2, while January 1, 1753, has a serial number of -53688.

The fractional part represents the time. This fraction corresponds to the current time in proportion to a whole day. Therefore, a time serial for 12:00 noon has a value of 0.5 (one-half of a day), while 6pm has a value of 0.75 (three-quarters of a day).

## Oct$ - Function

### See Also: Hex$

### Purpose
The Oct$ function returns a string that represents the supplied numeric expression in Octal notation (base 8).

### General Syntax
```
Oct$(numeric-expression)
```

## Usage
```
Octal$ = Oct$(100)
```
This places the octal number 144 into the string variable Octal$.

## Description
Octal notation is a method of counting using only eight digits. This is sometimes used to work with memory addresses because it converts back and forth from binary more easily than decimal, although hexadecimal is more commonly used for this purpose. The Oct$ function provides a method of converting a decimal number into octal.

The supplied numeric-expression is rounded to the nearest whole number before conversion is begun. It cannot exceed the range defined by the long integer data type. If numeric-expression is an integer, the string returned by Oct$ will be 4 or fewer bytes long. Otherwise, the return string can be up to 11 bytes long.

# On Error... - Statement

### See Also: Erl, Err, Error$, Resume

## Purpose
The On Error statement tells the program what to do if an error occurs.

## General Syntax
To enable an error handling routine:
```
On [Local] Error GoTo error-handler

error-handler
    :
    [statements]
Resume [{[0] | Next | {line-number | line-label} }]
```

To cause the Err flag to be set, and then continue with the next statement:
```
On [Local] Error Resume Next
```

To give Visual Basic control of error handling:
```
On [Local] Error GoTo 0
```

## Usage
```
On Error GoTo ErrorTrap
```
This example tells Visual Basic to branch to the label "ErrorTrap" when an error occurs.

```
On Error Resume Next
```
This causes Visual Basic to do little more than set the value of Err, and then resume execution at the next instruction after the statement that caused the error.

```
On Error GoTo 0
```
This deactivates the current error handler and returns all error handling to Visual Basic.

## Description
The On Error statement involves setting up a routine that will be processed when an error occurs. The routine is specified by the errorhandler parameter. This parameter can be a line number or a line label. Because Visual Basic does not allow a GoTo to jump out of a procedure, the line number or label must reside within the same procedure as the On Error... statement. If this is not the case, Visual basic will issue a "Label not defined" error at compile time. The error handling routine should only be exited by using the Resume statement.

The Resume statement is used at the end of the error handling routine after all the error handling tasks have been performed. There are three variations on the Resume statement.

The first involves using the Resume statement with no parameters, or a parameter of 0. This causes execution to resume at the statement that caused the error.

Secondly, the Resume Next statement may be used. This causes execution to pick up at the instruction following the statement that caused the error.

Finally, the Resume keyword may be followed by a line number or line label. This causes execution to continue at the specified line. This is a very unstructured approach, which can lead to "spaghetti code." This variation of the Resume statement should be avoided if possible.

Care should be taken so that the error handling code is not entered inadvertently. Doing so will cause the Resume statement to be executed when no error has occurred. If this happens, Visual Basic will generate a "Resume without error". This can be prevented by placing an Exit Sub or Exit Function just prior to the error handler.

### The On Error Resume Next Statement

This style of the On Error... statement merely sets an error code, and returns control to the statement following the instruction that caused the error. This error code may be obtained with the Err function. Using this style of error processing assumes the program will be checking for errors at strategic places. Failing to do such checking can cause hard to find logic errors in a program. Generally, this type of error processing is used with file I/O. Each time an I/O operation is performed, the Err is checked and reacted upon.

### The On Error GoTo 0 Statement

This statement returns control of error handling to Visual Basic. The same effect is achieved when a procedure with an enabled error handler is exited.

### Comments

The Local keyword has no effect in Visual Basic. It is only used to provide backward compatibility to earlier versions of the BASIC language.

# On...GoSub - Statement

### See Also: On...GoTo, Select Case

### Purpose

The On...GoSub statements transfer execution to a subroutine, based on the value of a numeric expression. When the RETURN keyword is encountered, execution returns to the instruction following the On...GoSub.

### General Syntax

```
On numeric-expression GoSub line_1[, line_2][, line_3] [, line_255]
```

### Usage

```
A% = WeekDay(Now)
On A% GoSub Sunday, Monday, Tuesday, Wednesday, Thursday, Friday, Saturday
```
This example executes a different subroutine based on the current day of the week.

### Description

For the most part, this statement has been kept for backward compatibility to earlier BASIC languages. The Select Case can perform the same functions, and is much more flexible than On...GoSub.

The numeric-expression parameter must be an integer between 0 and 255. If it does not fall into this range, an "Illegal function call" will occur. This parameter determines which routine will be executed.

The line-? parameters are the line labels or numbers of the routines that will be executed. Up to 255 routines may be listed. One or more routines may be listed several times. Line numbers and labels may be mixed in the list.

If numeric-expression equals 1, the first routine listed is executed. If it equals 2, the second is executed, and so on. If the value of numeric-expression is 0, or greater than the number of routines listed, no routines are executed, and the On GoSub... statement is ignored.

# On...GoTo - Statement

### See Also: On...GoSub, Select Case

### Purpose

The On...GoTo statement transfers execution to a line number or label, based on the value of a numeric expression. Execution does not return from the new location.

### General Syntax

```
On numeric-expression GoTo line_1[, line_2][, line_3]...[, line_255]
```

## Usage

```
A% = WeekDay(Now)
On A% GoTo Sunday, Monday, Tuesday, Wednesday, Thursday, Friday, Saturday
```
This example transfers execution to a different label based on the current day of the week.

## Description

For the most part, this statement has been kept for backward compatibility to earlier BASIC languages. The Select Case can perform the same functions, and is much more flexible and structured than On...GoTo. Because there is no return from a GoTo, it is not good programming practice to use this statement.

The numeric-expression parameter must be an integer between 0 and 255. If it does not fall into this range, an "Illegal function call" will occur. This parameter determines to which line number or label execution will be transferred.

The line-? parameters are the line labels or numbers to where execution will be transferred. There may be up to 255 line labels or numbers listed. One or more label or line number may be listed several times. Line numbers and labels may be mixed in the list.

If numeric-expression equals 1, execution is transferred to the first label or line number listed. If it equals 2, execution is transferred to the second, and so on. If the value of numeric-expression is 0, or greater than the number of labels listed, the On GoTo... statement is ignored.

# Open - Statement

### See Also: Close, FreeFile, Get, Input, Input$, Line Input #, Put

## Purpose

The Open statement enables input and output operations on a file.

## General Syntax

```
Open filename$ For mode [Access access] [locktype] As [#]filenumber [Len=recordlength]
```

## Usage

```
Type RecordType
    Type NameAndAddress_1
    Name As String * 20
    Number As Long
    Address As String * 75
End Type

Dim TestRec As RecordType

TestFile% = FreeFile
Open "Test.Dat" For Random Access Read Write Shared As #TestFile% Len = Len(TestRec)
```
This example opens a random access file for reading and writing. The Shared lock parameter allows the file to be opened by other processes. It is opened under the filenumber specified by TestFile%. The LEN keyword is used along with the Len function to define the length of each record.

```
Open "Test.Txt" For Input As #1
```
This statement opens the file Test.Txt for sequential input.

## Description

Before any input or output operations may be performed on a file, it must first be opened. Opening a file causes Visual Basic to allocate a buffer area for the file. Because physically reading from and writing to a file is a slow process, this buffer area is set up, and acts as a way station for the file's data. Generally, Visual Basic reads large blocks of data from a file into this buffer area. When a Get, Input #, Line Input #, or Put statement is executed, the I/O is done from the buffer, not the disk. This reduces the number of physical reads and writes, thereby speeding up file access.

The filename$ parameter can be any type of string expression that contains a valid DOS file name. The drive and path may be specified explicitly. However, if left out, the default drive and/or directory is used.

### The For Clause

There are five different types of files in Visual Basic. Each type behaves a little differently. The type of file being opened is specified by the mode parameter. This parameter must be one of the following: Output, Append, Input, Random, or Binary.

Specifying Output creates the specified file, and gets it ready for sequential output mode. This mode is generally used to write ASCII text files. If a file with the specified name already exists, it is erased, and a new file is created. This mode only allows data to be written to the file via the Print #, and Write # statements. Each write moves the file pointer to the end of the file. Trying to read data from a file opened under this mode causes a "Bad file mode" error to occur.

Specifying Append also causes the specified file to be opened for sequential output. As with the Output mode, if the file does not exist, it will be created. However, unlike the Output mode, if the file already exists it is not erased, but the file pointer is placed at the end of the file. This mode only allows data to be written to the file via the Print #, and Write # statements. Each write moves the file pointer to the end of the file. Trying to read data from a file opened under this mode causes an "Input past end" error to occur. This mode is generally used to add material to ASCII text files.

Opening a file under Input mode opens a sequential file for reading only. As with Output and Append, this mode is mostly used for processing ASCII text files. When opened, the file pointer is placed at the beginning of the file. Reads are performed via the Input #, Input$, and Line Input # instructions. Each read moves the file pointer forward in the file. No writing may be done to a file opened under this mode, or a "Bad file mode" error will occur.

Random is the default file mode. This mode allows both input and output of fixed length records. Reads and writes are performed by the Get and Put statements, respectively. The position of the file pointer may be set in several ways. First, the desired record number may be specified in the Get and Put statements. Second, the file pointer may be set using the Seek statement. Finally, if neither of the two previous methods are used, the file pointer is set to the next record after the most recent operation on this file. This mode is used for files whose records are all of the same or asimilar format, and which all have the same length. The structure of the records is defined by using the Type…End Type statement.

Binary mode also allows both input and output. However, instead of requiring fixed length records, reads and writes may be done at any byte position in the file, for any length. This allows the file to have variable length records. The Get and Put statements are used for reading and writing to the file, and can optionally specify the starting byte position. The Seek statement can also be used to move the file pointer to a desired byte position in the file.

## The Access Clause

When one works in a multiuser or multitasking environment, several processes may have access to the same files. In such an environment, when an open is performed on a file, it is possible that access to that file has been restricted by another process. Because of this, each process must request specific privileges, which define the tasks that need to be performed when it opens a file. The Access clause is used to request the desired privileges for a file. The entry for access must be one of the following keywords; Read, Write, or Read Write.

Access Read requests read-only access to a file. If the open is successful, only read operations may be performed on it. If a write is attempted, a "Permission denied" error will occur. Files opened under Input, Random, or Binary modes may use this access method. A "Syntax error" is generated if this method is used on a file opened under Output, or Append mode.

Access Write requests write-only access. If the open is successful, only write operations may be performed on it. If a read is attempted, a "Permission denied" error will occur. Files opened under Output, Random, and Binary modes may use this access method. Any other modes cause an error to occur.

Access Read Write requests both read and write access to a file. Files opened under Append, Random, and Binary modes may use this access method. Any other modes cause an error to occur.

If the requested access to a file has been restricted by another process, the Open statement will fail, and a "Permission denied" error will occur. The Access clause is only effective when used on a system that is running DOS version 3.1 or higher, and its related SHARE.EXE program. If the DOS version is earlier than 3.1, DOS will issue a "Feature unavailable" error.

## The Locktype Parameter

The locktype parameter is the flip side of the Access clause. This parameter specifies what privileges will be granted to other processes that try to open the file after this open has occurred. By default, when a file is opened, all access to that file by other processes is restricted. However, the default does allow the current process to reopen the file at a subsequent time. This can be changed by setting the locktype parameter to Shared, Lock Read, Lock Write, or Lock Read Write.

Using the Shared keyword places no restrictions on the file. It allows other processes to open it for reading or writing.

Lock Read restricts other processes from opening this file with read access. This type of lock can only be used if no other processes currently have read access to the file. If there are other processes that have read access to the file, this Open issues a "Permission denied" error.

Lock Write restricts other processes from opening this file with write access. This type of lock can only be used if no other processes currently have write access to the file. If there are other processes that have write access to the file, this Open issues a "Permission denied" error.

Lock Read Write restricts other processes from opening this file with read or write access. This type of lock can only be used if no other processes currently have read or write access to the file. If there are other processes that have read or write access to the file, this Open issues a "Permission denied" error. Unlike the default locking scheme, this lock prohibits even the current program from opening this file again.

### The Filenumber Parameter

A numeric-expression between 1 and 255 must be supplied in the filenumber parameter. This is the number that will be used by the Input #, Input$, Line Input #, Get, Put, and other file related statements to reference this file. Only one file at a time can use a particular file number. The best method for keeping track of unused file numbers is to let Visual Basic do it for you via the FreeFile function. Not only does this save you the headache of having to remember which filenumbers are and are not in use, but it also forces the file number to be placed in a variable. If a descriptive variable name is used, it makes the program much more readable.

### The Len Clause

For files opened under Random mode, the recordlength parameter defines the number of bytes that are read or written to the file with each Get or Put statement. If this is omitted, the record length will default to 128 bytes.

For files opened under Input, Append, or Output modes, this parameter defines the size of the read/write buffer. By default, sequential files use a 512-byte buffer. Making the buffer larger will increase the speed of the I/O operations on the file, but will take more memory.

Files opened under Binary mode ignore the Len clause.

In any case, the length specified by the Len clause may be no more than 32767 bytes.

# Option Base - Statement

### See Also: Dim, Global, ReDim

### Purpose

The Option Base statement defines the default lower bound value of an array.

### General Syntax

```
Option Base {0 | 1}
```

### Usage

```
Option Base 1
```

This sets the default value of 1 for the lower bound of any arrays that are defined within the same form or module.

### Description

By default, if an array is created using the Dim, Global, or ReDim statements, and only the highest subscript for an element is defined, the lowest subscript for that element will default to 0. The Option Base statement allows you to change the default lowest subscript from 0 to 1. This statement can only be used in the global module, or in the declarations portion of any module or form. The statement only affects arrays in the same module or form. If it is used, it must appear before any arrays are defined in that module or form.

# Print # - Statement

**See Also: Input #, Write#**

### Purpose

The Print # statement writes unformatted data to a sequential file that has been opened under Output or Append modes.

### General Syntax

```
Print #filenumber, expression-1[{;|,} expression-2][{;|,} expression-3]...
```

### Usage

```
Print #1, "Hello world"
```

This example writes the string literal "Hello world" to the file opened under filenumber 1. A carriage return/line feed pair is then written to the file.

```
Print #1, 100, A$;
```

This example writes the number 100, and the value of A$ to the file. The comma after the number 100 causes A$ to be written at the next print zone. The semicolon after A$ causes Visual Basic to suppress the printing of the carriage return/linefeed pair.

### Description

This statement prints one or more numeric or string expressions to the file indicated by the supplied file number. This is most commonly used to output ASCII text files. If the file number does not match that of a currently open file, Visual Basic issues a "Bad file name or number" error. Also, the file must have been opened under either the Output, or Append modes, or a "Bad file mode" error occurs.

More than one expression may be written at a time. The expressions may be separated by either semicolons or commas. If a semicolon is used, the next expression is written at the very next byte position in the file. If a comma is used, the expression is written at the next print zone. Print zones occur at every 14th byte position in the record.

By default, the Print # statement appends a carriage return/linefeed pair to the end of each record written. This can be suppressed by placing a semicolon after the last expression in the Print # statement.

# Put - Statement

**See Also: Get, Lof, Open, Type**

### Purpose

The Put statement writes data to a file that has been opened under Random or Binary mode.

### General Syntax

```
Put [#]filenumber%,[position&], recordbuffer
```

### Usage

```
Type Rolodex
     Name as String * 20
     Number as Long
     Address as String * 100
End Type

Dim PhoneCard as Rolodex

Open "Cards.Dat" For Random As #1 Len = Len(PhoneCard)
     :
     :
     :
Put #1, 129, PhoneCard
```

This example writes the data that is in the record variable PhoneCard to the 129th record in Cards.Dat.

## Description

The Put statement is used to write data to a disk file from a previously defined record variable. The filenumber parameter indicates the file to which the data is to be written. This number must be from 1 to 255, and match the number used in the Open statement of a currently open file. If the file number used does not match a currently opened file, a "Bad file name or number" error is generated. The file must have been opened in either Random or Binary mode. If not, Visual Basic will issue a "Bad file mode" error.

If the position parameter is omitted, the commas must still be used. If position specifies an area that is beyond the length of the file, the file length is extended to that position. Visual Basic does no checking to see if a Put is being attempted past the current length of the file. This task is left to you. Use the Lof function to determine the length of an open file.

The recordbuffer parameter refers to a variable that contains the data that will be written to the file. It can be of any data type. Most often, it is of a type defined by you (using the Type statement) whose fields match those of the file's record structure.

### Positioning in Random Access Files

The position parameter for random access files specifies the desired record number. If this parameter is omitted, the write occurs at the position currently pointed to by the file pointer. When a Random file is opened, this pointer is set to 1. Each Get or Put sets the file pointer to the next record after the Get or Put. This file pointer may be read using the Seek function, or set by using the Seek statement. The largest valid record number may be 2,147,483,647.

The variable used for the recordbuffer must be of a length that is less than or equal to the length specified in the Open statement. Using a variable whose length is too long results in a "Bad record length" error. If the recordbuffer is a variable length string, a 2-byte string descriptor is also written; therefore, these 2 bytes should be accounted for in the length. If the recordbuffer is shorter than the length specified in the Open statement, only the bytes in the variable will be written.

### Positioning in Binary Files

The position parameter for binary files refers to the byte position in the file where writing is to start. The first byte in the file is position 1, the second is 2, and so on. If this parameter is omitted, the write occurs at the position currently pointed to by the file pointer. When a Binary file is opened, this pointer is set to 1. Each Get or Put sets the file pointer to the next byte position after the Get or Put. This file pointer may be read using the Seek function, or set by using the Seek statement.

The size of the write is determined by the size of the record buffer. This allows a file to have variable record lengths.

# QBColor - Function

## See Also: RGB

## Purpose

The QBColor function converts a color code used in other versions of BASIC to the long integer RGB code used by Visual Basic. The RGB color code is returned in long integer format.

## General Syntax

```
QBColor(color-number%)
```

## Usage

```
Const QB_RED = 4

Red% = QBColor(QB_RED)
```

This places Visual Basic's RGB color number for red into the integer variable Red%.

## Description

Visual Basic represents colors in a manner that corresponds to the Windows environment. This is different than other versions of the BASIC language. The QBColor function provides a method of translating the numeric representations for colors from the other BASICs to the format used by Visual Basic. This number can then be used to set the foreground or background properties of an object. The supplied color-number% must be a number between 1 and 15. Assigning the value to a descriptive constant (as done in the previous example) makes it easier to remember what color is being used. Table B.20 shows the valid color numbers, and the colors they represent.

| Number in QuickBASIC | Number in Visual Basic | Color |
|---|---|---|
| 00 | 00 | Black |
| 01 | 8388608 | Blue |
| 02 | 32768 | Green |
| 03 | 8421376 | Cyan |
| 04 | 128 | Red |
| 05 | 8388736 | Magenta |
| 06 | 32896 | Yellow (actually looks more like brown) |
| 07 | 12632256 | White (looks more like light grey) |
| 08 | 8421504 | Grey |
| 09 | 16711680 | Bright Blue |
| 10 | 65280 | Bright Green |
| 11 | 16776960 | Bright Cyan |
| 12 | 255 | Bright Red |
| 13 | 16711935 | Bright Magenta |
| 14 | 65535 | Bright Yellow |
| 15 | 16777215 | Bright White |

Table B.20 Color codes for QBColor

# Randomize - Statement

**See Also: Rnd, Timer**

### Purpose
The Randomize statement seeds the random number generator, allowing the generation of a new sequence of random numbers.

### General Syntax
```
Randomize [seed%]
```

### Usage
```
Function RndInt(LoNum As Integer, HiNum As Integer) As Integer
    Static Seeded As Integer
    Dim Range As Integer

    If Seeded = 0 Then              'Seed the random number generator if it has not
        Randomize                   'yet been done.
        Seeded = -1
    End If
    Range = HiNum - LoNum + 1
    RndInt = Int(Range * Rnd + LoNum)
End Function
```
This example is a function that uses the Randomize statement and Rnd function to return an integer in the range specified by the integer parameters LoNum and HiNum. No parameter is used for the Randomize statement, so the value from the Timer function is automatically used for the seed.

### Description
The Randomize statement seeds the random number generator. Random numbers can then be returned by the Rnd function. If this statement is not executed before the Rnd function, each time the program is run the numbers generated will be the same. The seed% parameter must be a number in the range of from -32767 to 32767. If it is omitted, Visual Basic will automatically use the value returned by the Timer function as the seed. This default is usually best for games that require an unpredictable random number sequence.

# ReDim - Statement

### See Also: Dim, Erase, Global, Option Base

### Purpose
The ReDim statement defines the number of dimensions and elements in an array, and allocates or reallocates storage.

### General Syntax
```
ReDim [Shared] name[(suscript-range)][As type][, name[(subscript-range)[As type]]
```

### Usage
```
ReDim MyArray(1 to 100) As Integer
ReDim YourArray(-10 to 10) As String
```
Declares the arrays MyArray and YourArray. MyArray contains 100 integer elements that can be accessed by using a subscript with a value of from 1 to 100. YourArray contains 21 string elements that can be accessed using a subscript with a value of from -10 to +10.

### Description
The ReDim statement is used in procedure-level code to perform one of two tasks. First, it can be used to declare and allocate storage for a local dynamic array. The elements in this array may only be accessed within the procedure defined. The ReDim statement can also be used to declare the dimensions and number of elements for a dynamic array that has been declared in the global module, or in the declarations section of the current module or form. Dynamic arrays that are originally declared in the global modules are accessible across all forms and modules. Dynamic arrays that are originally declared in the declarations area of a form or module are accessible only to the procedures within that form or module.

Arrays provide a method for creating an entire series of variables and referencing them by the same variable name. An index number (called the subscript) is used to determine which particular element in an array is being referenced. A more detailed discussion on the concept of arrays can be found in the tutorial in Appendix A.

The dimensions of an array are defined by the entry in the subscript-range portion of the ReDim statement. The subscript-range follows this format:

```
[lo-element To] hi-element[,[lo-element To] hi-element]...
```

The lo-element parameter lets you define the range of the subscripts, as well as the number of elements in the array. If lo-element is not used, the lowest valid subscript will be 0 (unless the default has been changed using Option Base), and the supplied number will be the highest valid subscript. The number of elements allowed in an array is dependent on the desired data type for that array. Visual Basic allows approximately 64K of data space for each array declared (not to exceed installed memory, of course). Therefore, an Integer array (which is 2 bytes long per element) may have up to 32,767 elements, while a long or a single-precision (4 bytes per element) array may have half that.

ReDim initializes all elements of variable length string arrays to null strings. All other arrays are initialized to 0s (including fixed length strings and user defined types).

At times, it is necessary to have a multidimensional array. To declare such an array, include as many sets of subscripts as needed, separated by commas.

```
ReDim MultiArray (1 To 100, 50 To 60, -100 to 100) As Integer
```

The example above declares an array with three dimensions of 100, 11, and 201 elements, respectively. The first dimension can be referenced by subscripts from 1 to 100, the second may have subscripts ranging of from 50 to 60, and the third from -100 to +100. Visual Basic allows arrays to have as many as 60 dimensions.

ReDim allows the program to change the number of elements in an array at will. However, once the number of dimensions has been declared, it cannot be changed. For instance, when the following declaration is used,

```
ReDim TestArray(100, 200)
```

the array TestArray is set up with two dimensions of 101 and 201 elements, respectively. A later ReDim statement can change the number of elements defined for each of the two dimensions, but this array must now always have only two dimensions. Along the same lines, a ReDim statement cannot change the data type that has been assigned to an array.

The Erase statement can be used to de-allocate a dynamic array. This causes any memory that was being used by the array to be freed. If an array is erased, it may not be referred to or a "Subscript out of range" error will occur.

# Rem - Statement

## Purpose
The Rem statement allows you to insert comments in a program.

## General Syntax
```
Rem comment

' comment
```

## Usage
```
Rem This is a comment. The compiler will ignore it.

A% = 20            'This is a comment on the same line as an instruction.
```

## Description
Good programming practice involves the use of comments throughout a program to help explain the logic of the program. When the Rem statement is used, all the text to the right of the statement is ignored by the compiler. The single quote (') character is equivalent to using the Rem statement with a preceding colon. For instance:

```
A% = B% + C% : Rem The rem statement on this line needs a colon to separate it from the instructions
D% = A% ^ 2            'But this line does not need a colon
```

The Rem statement may also be used to temporarily disable certain program instructions. This is sometimes useful in debugging a program. For instance:

```
Do
    A% = A% + 1
    Rem Debug.Print A%      'Remove the "Rem" on this line to send output to the immediate window
Loop Until A% = 10
```

In the code above, if the Rem is removed, the value of the variable A% will be printed in the immediate window. Placing the Rem statement before the instruction causes the compiler to ignore the entire line, thereby disabling it.

# Reset - Statement

## See Also: Close, End

## Purpose
The Reset statement writes all data residing in open file buffers to the appropriate disk files, and then closes all open disk files.

## General Syntax
```
Reset
```

## Usage
```
Reset
```

## Description
This performs the same task as using the Close statement with no parameters. It is not a bad idea to use this statement just prior to ending a program.

# Resume - Statement

**See Also:  On Error...**

## Purpose
The Resume statement releases control from an error handling routine.

## General Syntax
```
Resume [{[0] | Next | {line-number | line-label} }]
```

## Usage
```
Resume
```
Resumes execution at the instruction that caused the error.

```
Resume Next
```
Resumes execution at the instruction after the one that caused the error.

```
Resume TopOfLoop
```
Resumes execution at the label "TopOfLoop."

## Description
The Resume statement is used at the end of an error handling routine that was initiated by the On Error... statement. There are three variations on the Resume statement.

The first involves using the Resume statement with no parameters, or a parameter of 0. This causes execution to resume at the statement that caused the error. Of course, if the conditions that caused the error have not been corrected, control will jump back to the error-handling routine, creating a kind of endless loop.

Second, the Resume Next statement may be used. This causes execution to pick up at the instruction following the statement that caused the error.

Finally, the Resume keyword may be followed by a line number or line label. This causes execution to continue at the specified line. This is a very unstructured approach, which can lead to "spaghetti code." This variation of the Resume statement should be avoided if possible.

For more information on error handling, see the entry for the On Error... statement, and Appendix C, *Debugging*.

# Return - Statement

**See Also:  GoSub, On GoSub**

## Purpose
The Return statement returns control to the next instruction following the originating GoSub or On GoSub statement.

## General Syntax
```
Return
```

## Usage
```
Gosub DoIt

DoIt:
    A$ = "Now I've done it!"
Return
```
When the Gosub is executed, the program branches to the label "DoIt:". When the Return is executed, the program will return to the instruction following the Gosub.

## Description
The Return statement is covered in more detail under the entry for the GoSub statement.

# RGB - Function

**See Also:** QBColor

## Purpose
The RGB function returns a long integer representing the RGB value of a color.

## General Syntax
```
RGB(red%, green%, blue%)
```

## Usage
```
Form1.BackColor = RGB(100, 200, 50)
```
This sets the BackColor property of Form1.

## Description
The parameters red%, green%, and blue% have a value of between 1 and 255, which represents the intensity of each color. If the number supplied for one of these parameters is below 1, an "Illegal function call" error occurs. If a number greater than 255 is used, the value 255 is assumed.

The RGB function mixes the given color values to return a number that represents the color mix.

# Right$ - Function

**See Also:** Left$, Mid$

## Purpose
The Right$ function returns a a portion of a string, starting at the last character, and working to the left, for the length specified.

## General Syntax
```
Right$(expression$, length&)
```

## Usage
```
B$ = "Hello, Dolly!"
C$ = Right$(B$, 6)
```
The above example assigns the rightmost six characters from B$ to the variable C$, giving it a value of "Dolly!".

## Description
The expression$ parameter can be a fixed or variable length string, a string constant, a literal string, the result of any function that returns a string, or any other string expression.

The length& parameter refers to the number of characters to copy. This value may be in the range of 0 to 65,535. If the length specified is greater than or equal to the full length of the source string, Right$ returns an exact copy of the source string. If the length is 0, a null string is returned. If length& has a value of less than 0, or greater than 65,535, an "Illegal function call" error is generated.

# RmDir - Statement

**See Also:** CurDir, MkDir

## Purpose
The RmDir statement removes a subdirectory from a disk.

## General Syntax
```
RmDir dir-name$
```
dir-name$ must be in the format of [drive:][\]dir[\subdir][\subdir]...

## Usage

```
RmDir "Test"
```
Removes the subdirectory "Test" underneath the default directory on the default drive.

```
RmDir "\Test"
```
Removes the subdirectory "Test" underneath the root directory of the default drive.

```
RmDir "D:\Test"
```
Removes the subdirectory "Test" underneath the root directory of drive D:.

## Description

This statement works much like the DOS command of the same name. However, unlike the DOS command, the Visual Basic statement cannot be shortened to RD.

RmDir removes the subdirectory specified by the dir-name$ parameter. If the drive and/or full path name are not specified in dir-name$, the default drive and/or path are used. If the directory to be removed does not exist, a "Path not found" error will occur. The directory specified must be an empty directory, with no child subdirectories. Attempting to remove a directory that is not empty will also generate a "Path not found" error.

# Rnd - Function

### See Also: Randomize

## Purpose

The Rnd function returns a single-precision random number between 0 and 1.

## General Syntax

```
Rnd[(numeric-expression#)]
```

## Usage

```
Function RndInt(LoNum As Integer, HiNum As Integer) As Integer
     Static Seeded As Integer
     Dim Range As Integer

     If Seeded = 0 Then             'Seed the random number generator if it has not
         Randomize                  'yet been done.
         Seeded = -1
     End If
     Range = HiNum - LoNum + 1
     RndInt = Int(Range * Rnd + LoNum)
End Function
```
This example is a function that uses the Randomize statement and Rnd function to return an integer in the range specified by the integer parameters LoNum and HiNum.

## Description

The Randomize statement should be used before the first time the Rnd function is called. This seeds the random number generator. If this is not done, the numbers returned by the Rnd function will be the same every time the program is run.

The numeric-expression# tells the Rnd function what to return. If numeric-expression# is omitted, or has a value greater than 0, the next random number is returned. If numeric-expression# has a value of 0, the previous random number generated is returned. If numeric-expression# has a negative value, the same number is returned for any given numeric-expression#.

The preceding example shows how to convert the value returned by Rnd to a random integer within a specified range.

# RSet - Statement

### See Also: Let, LSet

## Purpose

The RSet statement copies one string into another, byte by byte, starting at the rightmost character in the source string and working to the left.

### General Syntax
```
RSet result_variable = source_variable
```

### Usage
```
Dim NumberBuffer As String * 12
A% = 2003.45
B$ = Format$(A%, "#,###,###.#0")
RSet NumberBuffer = B$
Label1.Caption = NumberBuffer
```
This example uses RSet to right justify the string representation of a number in a label object.

### Description
This statement assigns to result_variable the value of source_variable. Both variables may be fixed or variable length strings. The assignment performed by the RSet is done byte by byte from the right of source_variable to the left. The assignment cannot change the length of result_variable. If result_variable is shorter than source_variable, the characters that are beyond the length of result_variable are not copied. If result_variable is longer than source_variable, spaces are used to fill out the balance of result_variable.

# RTrim$ - Function

### See Also:  LTrim$

### Purpose
The RTrim$ function returns a copy of a string with any following spaces removed.

### General Syntax
```
RTrim$(string-expression)
```

### Usage
```
A$ = RTrim$(" Good Bye ")
```
This example assigns the value " Good Bye" to the variable A$.

### Description
This is the complement of the LTrim$ function. It returns a copy of the supplied string expression without any following spaces.

The string-expression$ parameter can be a fixed or variable length string, a string constant, a literal string, the result of any function that returns a string, or any other string expression.

# SavePicture - Statement

### See Also:  LoadPicture

### Purpose
The SavePicture statement saves a *.BMP, *.ICO, or *.WMF picture from a form or picture box to a disk file.

### General Syntax
```
SavePicture object-name, picturefile$
```

### Usage
```
SavePicture Form1.Picture "CHESS.BMP"
```
This example saves the bitmap from Form1's picture property to the file Chess.Bmp.

### Description
The object-name parameter must be the picture property of the form or control whose picture is to be saved. The string picturefile$ specifies the name of the file into which the picture is to be saved. It should include the appropriate extension (.BMP for bitmaps, .ICO for icons, or .WMF for Windows metafiles). This function is explained in more detail in Chapter 8, *Setting Up Graphical Objects*.

# Second - Function

**See Also: Now, TimeSerial, TimeValue**

## Purpose

The Second function returns an integer (with a value from 0 to 59) that represents the second of the minute specified by the supplied time serial.

## General Syntax

```
Second(time-serial#)
```

## Usage

```
A% = Second(Now)
```

Places the current second of the minute in the variable A%.

## Description

The second is returned as an integer in the range of from 0 to 59.

A time serial is a double-precision number that can represent any time of the day. It is a fraction that corresponds to the specified time in proportion to a whole day. Therefore, a time serial for 12:00 noon has a value of 0.5 (one-half of a day), while 6pm has a value of 0.75 (three-quarters of a day). It is created by using the Now, TimeValue, or TimeSerial functions.

Date serials and time serials can be combined, because the date serial is stored on the left side of the decimal point, and the time serial is stored on the right.

# Seek - Function and Statement

**See Also:  Get, Open, Put**

## Purpose

As a function, Seek returns the current position of the file pointer for any open file. As a statement, Seek moves the file pointer to the specified position in any open file.

## General Syntax

As a function:
```
Seek(filenumber%)
```

As a statement:
```
Seek [#]filenumber%, position&
```

## Usage

```
Open "Test.Dat" For Random As #1 Len = 32
Get #1, 25, TestRec
CurrentRec& = Seek(1)
Seek #1, 100
```

This example first uses the Seek function to save the position of the file pointer after the file is read. This assigns the value 26 (the next record after the Get statement is executed) to the variable CurrentRec&. The Seek statement is then used to move the file pointer to record number 100.

## Description

The filenumber% parameter indicates the file to which Seek is referring. This number must be from 1 to 255, and match the number used in the Open statement of a currently open file. If the file number used does not match a currently opened file, a "Bad file name or number" error is generated.

### The Seek Function

For files opened under Random mode, this function returns the current record number. For all other files, the number returned is the current byte position of the file pointer. The position is returned as a long integer, greater than or equal to 1.

### The Seek Statement

For files opened under Random mode, this statement moves the file pointer to the record number specified by the position& parameter. For all other files, the position& parameter specifies the byte position to move the file pointer to. The position specified must be a number between 1 and 2,147,483,647.

# Select Case - Statement
## See Also: If...ElseIf...Else...End If

## Purpose
The Select Case statement provides a convenient and readable way to base execution on which of several values or conditions an expression satisfies.

## General Syntax
```
Seclect Case expression
     Case condition[, condition][, condition]
          :
          [statements]
          :
     [Case condition[, condition][, condition] ]
          :
          [statements]
          :
     [Case condition[, condition][, condition] ]
          :
          [statements]
          :
     [Case Else]
          :
          [statements]
          :
End Select
```

The condition parameters may be in one of the following formats:

To test for equality:
```
[Is =] expression
```

To test a range of values:
```
lo-expression To hi-expression
```

To test a relation:
```
Is > expression
Is < expression
Is >= expression
Is <= expression
Is <> expression
```

## Usage
```
ThisMonth = Month(Now)
Select Case ThisMonth
     Case 2
          DaysThisMonth = 28
     Case 4, 6, 9, 11
          DaysThisMonth = 30
     Case Else
          DaysThisMonth = 31
End Select
```
This example assigns the number of days for the current month to the variable DaysThisMonth.

```
Select Case UCase$(Fruit$)
     Case "APPLE" To "ORANGE"
          FileIndex$ = "A_TO_O.IDX"
     Case Is > "ORANGE"
          FileIndex$ = "O_TO_Z.IDX"
End Select
```
This example sets up the value of a string based on the value of the variable Fruit$. The UCase$ function is used so we can ignore the alphabetic case of the value in Fruit$.

## Description

The Select Case structure provides you with a method for testing one expression for one or more possible values. Although similar, it offers several enhancements over the If...Then...Else If...Else...End If structure.

The Select Case structure consists of four elements. First, the Select Case clause defines the expression that is being tested. This expression may be any string or numeric variable or expression, literal, constant, or result of a Visual Basic or user defined function.

One or more Case clauses can follow the Select Case clause. The condition parameters of the clause define the test, or group of tests, against the expression in the Select Case clause. The condition parameters can test for a single value, a range of values, or a relation to a value. If the expression in the Select Case clause is numeric, all the condition parameters must be numeric. If the expression in the Select Case clause is a string, all the condition parameter must be strings. As long as those two rules are observed, the condition parameters may be a variable, constant, literal, or the result of a Visual Basic or user-defined function. Several condition parameters may appear in the same Case clause. Each Case clause is followed by a block of statements. This block is executed if any of the condition parameters evaluates true. After a block is executed, the program will branch to the instruction following the End Select clause. This means that only the block for the first "true" expression found will be executed.

The optional Case Else clause allows you to define a block of instructions that will be executed if none of the conditions in any of the Case condition clauses is true.

The End Select clause defines the end if the structure. When a block of statements under any of the Case condition clauses is finished executing, the program will branch to the instruction following this clause.

# SendKeys - Statement

## See Also: DoEvents

## Purpose

The SendKeys statement simulates keyboard input to the active window of your Visual Basic application or of another Windows application. It can be used as a simple way to control other programs that do not support the more powerful and flexible features of Dynamic Data Exchange (DDE).

## General Syntax

```
SendKeys keystrokes$[, wait%]
```

## Usage

```
SendKeys "This input is coming from Visual Basic's SendKeys statement"
```
This example sends the specified string literal to the program in the active window.

## Description

The keystrokes$ parameter represents the actual keystrokes to be sent to the application that has the active window. These keys are received just as if they had been typed by the user. The optional wait% parameter is used only when keystrokes are to be sent to an application other than your Visual Basic application. If set to True (-1), wait% ensures that the keystrokes are processed by the receiving application before the SendKeys statement returns control to your Visual Basic procedure. If False (the default), wait% specifies that SendKeys will resume execution at the next statement as soon as the keystrokes have been sent.

For more details, including an explanation of how to specify nonprinting and other special characters as keystrokes, see Chapter 16, *Handling Keyboard Input*.

# Sgn - Function

## See Also: Abs

## Purpose

The Sgn function evaluates a numeric-expression and returns a value based on whether the numeric-expression is negative, positive, or 0.

### General Syntax
```
Sgn(numeric-expression)
```

### Usage
```
A% = Sgn(100)
```
This example sets the variable A% to 1, indicating the numeric-expression evaluated was positive.

```
B% = Sgn(0)
```
This example sets the variable B% to 0, indicating the numeric-expression evaluated was 0.

```
C% = Sgn(-100)
```
This example sets the variable C% to -1, indicating the numeric-expression evaluated was negative.

### Description
The Sgn function evaluates the supplied numeric-expression, and returns a -1 if it is negative, 1 if it is positive, and 0 if it equals 0.

---

# Shell - Function

### See Also: AppActivate

### Purpose
The Shell function runs a specified *.EXE, *.COM. *.BAT, or *.PIF program.

### General Syntax
```
Shell(program-name$[, mode%])
```

### Usage
```
A% = Shell("WinWord.Exe")
```
This example loads and runs the program file WinWord.Exe. It assumes the file is in the default directory, or in a directory specified by the path statement. Since the mode is not specified, it uses the default mode of 2 (minimized with focus).

```
B% = Shell("C:\Word\WinWord.Exe", 3)
```
This example explicitly declares the drive and path of the program file. The program is executed in mode 3 (maximized with focus).

### Description
The Shell function loads an executable file into the Windows environment, and returns the task ID number that Windows assigns to each running program. The program-name$ parameter must be a string expression that contains a valid executable file name. If the desired program file is not in the default directory on the default drive, or in a directory in the DOS PATH, the drive and path must be specified, or a "File not found" error will occur. Specifying a file that does not have an extension of EXE, COM, BAT, or PIF will cause an "Illegal function call" error.

The mode% parameter determines how the program will be loaded into the Windows environment. It specifies the window style, and whether the program is to receive the focus immediately. Table B.21 details the settings for mode%:

| Mode Value | Window Style | Focus |
|---|---|---|
| 1 | Normal | New program receives focus |
| 2 | Minimized | New program receives focus |
| 3 | Maximized | New program receives focus |
| 4 | Normal | Current program retains focus |
| 7 | Minimized | Current program retains focus |

Table B.21 Shell function values for the mode% parameter

This parameter is optional. If omitted, the new program will be loaded as if mode 2 were specified. The full effect of the mode% parameter can only be taken advantage of by Windows programs. For DOS programs, the mode values 1, 2, and 4 work the same as mode 3.

You could run the DOS command processor by specifying the program "command.com."

# Sin - Function

**See Also: Atn, Cos, Tan**

**Purpose**

The Sin function returns the sine of an angle.

**General Syntax**

```
Sin(angle)
```

**Usage**

```
A! = Sin(4.93)
The sine of 4.93 is assigned to the variable A!.
```

**Description**

Sin is used to determine the sine of an angle. The function expects the angle to be expressed in radians; therefore, if the angle is in degrees it must be converted using the formula radians = degrees * pi/180.

If the angle is supplied as an integer or a single-precision value, Sin will return a single-precision value; otherwise it returns a double-precision value.

# Space$ - Function

**See Also: Spc, String$**

**Purpose**

The Space$ function returns a string containing the specified number of spaces.

**General Syntax**

```
Space$(number-of-spaces&)
```

**Usage**

```
A$ = Space$(5)
```
Gives the variable A$ the value of "      " (five spaces).

**Description**

This function returns a string of the specified number of spaces (ASCII character 32). The number-of-spaces& parameter can be of any numeric type, but it must be a value from 0 to 65535. if it is not in this range, an "Illegal function call" will occur.

# Spc - Function

**See Also: Space$, Tab**

**Purpose**

The Spc function generates spaces for output with the Print method and Print # statement. Unlike Space$, this function respects any settings placed on a file with the Width # statement.

**General Syntax**

```
Spc(number-of-spaces%)
```

**Usage**

```
Print #1, "This bracket -> [" Spc(10) "] <- and this bracket are 10 spaces apart"
```
This example writes the text from the string literals with 10 spaces inserted between the brackets.

**Description**

This function is used for formatting a print line. The number-of-spaces% parameter must be a numeric-expression in the range of from 0 to 32767.

The fundamental difference between this function and the Space$ function is how it behaves when used on a file whose print line width has been defined with the Width # statement. While the Space$ function ignores the defined width, the Spc function does not. This makes the behavior of the Spc function dependent on three factors: the number of spaces requested, the current print position, and the defined width of the print line. This function can react to these factors in one of three ways. First, if the print position plus the number of spaces requested is less than the width of the print line, the number of spaces requested is generated. Second, if the number-of-spaces% parameter is greater than the width defined for the print line, then the spaces generated are equal to the number of spaces requested modulo (MOD) the width of the print line. Finally, if the print position plus the number of spaces requested is greater than the defined width of the print line, spaces will be printed as far as the defined width on the current line, and the balance of the requested spaces will be printed on the next line. Table B.22 gives examples of the Spc function's behavior when a print line is defined by the Width # statement as being 80 characters long.

| Print Position | Spaces Requested | Generated Output |
|---|---|---|
| 01 | 50 | 50 spaces |
| 40 | 50 | 40 spaces, carriage return/linefeed pair, 0 spaces |
| 01 | 100 | 20 spaces (100 MOD 80) |
| 75 | 100 | 5 spaces, carriage return/linefeed pair, 15 spaces (100 MOD 80 returns 20 spaces. As many as possible are printed on the current line, and the balance are printed on the next) |

**Table B.22 Spaces generated by the Spc function**

# Sqr - Function

## Purpose
The Sqr function returns the square root of a number.

## General Syntax
```
Sqr(numeric-expression)
```

## Usage
```
A! = Sqr(72)
```
This example places the square root of 72 into the variable A!, giving it a value of 8.485281.

## Description
This function requires that numeric-expression be a non-negative number of any numeric data type. If numeric-expression is a double-precision value, this function will return a double-precision value. Using any other data type causes Sqr to return a single-precision value.

# Static - Statement

### See Also:  Dim, Global, Option Base, ReDim, Type

## Purpose
The Static statement allocates storage for permanent Visual Basic variables or arrays in a procedure. Unlike the ReDim statement, variables declared with the Static statement do not lose their value between procedure calls.

## General Syntax
For declaring the data type of a simple variable
```
Static name [As type][, name [As type]]
```

For declaring an array:
```
Static name[(suscript-range)][As type][, name[(subscript-range)][As type]
```

## Usage
```
Static A as Integer        'Declares the variable A as an integer
Static B(100) As Single    'Declares single-precision array B, with 101 elements, from 0 to 100
Static C$(-30 to 60)       'Declares string array C$, with 91 elements numbered -30 to +60
```

## Description

The Static statement is used to declare storage and data types for simple and array variables within a Visual Basic Sub or Function. It allocates a local simple variable, or a local array, which cannot be seen by any other procedure. If you wish to declare a variable or array that is accessible globally (across modules and forms), use the Global statement in the declarations section of the global module instead. Variables that are declared with the Static statement do not get deallocated when the procedure which defined them is exited. Therefore, their value is retained between procedure calls.

The Static statement can be used along with the As type clause to explicitly declare the data type of a simple variable. For instance,

```
Static MyVar As Integer
```

creates a storage for an Integer variable named MyVar. This is an alternate method to using the Visual Basic type declaration characters (!, @, #, $, %, &). This also allows you to assign your own data types (created with the Type statement) to a variable, as in the following code:

This code would appear in the global module:

```
Type Rolodex
    Name as String * 20
    Number as Long
    Address as String * 100
End Type
```

This code would appear in the desired procedure:

```
Static Cards as Rolodex
```

Static can also be used to allocate storage for, and define the parameters of, a local array. Arrays provide a method for creating an entire series of variables and referencing them by the same variable name. An index number (called the subscript) is used to determine which particular element in an array is being referenced. A more detailed discussion on the concept of arrays can be found in Appendix A, *Language Tutorial*.

The dimensions of an array are defined by the entry in the subscript-range portion of the Static statement. The subscript-range follows this format:

```
[lo-element To] hi-element[,[lo-element To] hi-element]
```

The lo-element parameter lets you define the range of the subscripts, as well as the number of elements in the array. If lo-element is not used, the lowest valid subscript will be 0 (unless the default has been changed using Option Base), and the supplied number will be the highest valid subscript. The number of elements allowed in an array depends on the desired data type for that array. Visual Basic allows approximately 64K of data space for each array declared (not to exceed installed memory, of course). Therefore, an Integer array (which is 2 bytes long per element) may have up to 32,767 elements, while a Long or a Single-precision (4 bytes per element) array may only have half that.

Static initializes all elements of variable length string arrays to null strings. All other arrays are initialized to 0s (including fixed length strings and user defined types).

At times, it is necessary to have a multidimensional array. To declare such an array, include as many sets of subscripts as needed, separated by commas.

```
Static MultiArray (1 To 100, 50 To 60, -100 to 100) As Integer
```

The example above declares an array with three dimensions of 100, 11, and 201 elements, respectively. The first dimension can be referenced by subscripts from 1 to 100, the second may have subscripts ranging of from 50 to 60, and the third from -100 to +100. Visual Basic allows arrays to have as many as 60 dimensions.

Visual Basic's Sub and Function statements allow for an optional Static keyword. This causes all variables inside that procedure to be declared as static variables, regardless of whether the variable is declared implicitly, with the ReDim, or with the Static statement.

# Stop - Statement

**See Also:** End

### Purpose
The Stop statement stops program execution without closing files or clearing variables. If encountered while in the Visual Basic environment, the Code window is opened and gets the focus. If encountered in a compiled Visual Basic program, the application is unloaded from memory.

### General Syntax
```
Stop
```

### Usage
```
Debug.Print A%
Stop
```
The example prints the value of the integer variable A% in the Immediate window, and then stops execution.

### Description
The Stop statement is used for purposes of debugging a program. It is sometimes advantageous to be able to view the value of a variable, or step through code one statement at a time, while a program is running. This statement allows you to do just that. When the Stop statement is encountered, all program execution is halted. You can then make use of the debugging features of Visual Basic, such as the Immediate window, or several of the options on the Run menu.

# Str$ - Function

**See Also:** Val

### Purpose
The Str$ function converts a numeric expression to a string.

### General Syntax
```
Str$(numeric-expression)
```

### Usage
```
A$ = Str$(100)
B$ = Str$(-100)
```
The value of A$ becomes " 100." A leading space precedes the number where the positive sign is implied. The value of B$ will be "-100." It has no leading space because the negative sign is explicit.

### Description
This function returns an a string which is an unformatted representation of numeric-expression. If formatting is desired, use the Format$ function instead. When a number is converted to a string, the first space of the string is reserved for the sign of the numeric expression. If the numeric expression is positive, the sign is implied, and the string representation of the number is preceded by a space. If it is negative, the string representation of the number is preceded by a minus (-) sign.

# String$ - Function

**See Also:** Space$

### Purpose
The String$ function returns a string containing the specified number of the requested character.

## General Syntax

```
String$(number-of-characters&, ascii-code%)

String$(number-of-characters&, character$)
```

## Usage

```
A$ = String$(10, "*")
B$ = String$(10, 42)
```

Because 42 is the ASCII code for the asterisk character, both of these statements return the same value: "**********".

## Description

This function returns a string of the requested character, for the length specified by number-of-characters&. The number-of-characters& parameter must be in the range of from 0 to 65535, or an "Illegal function call" will occur. You may specify which character to have returned either by supplying the ASCII code of the desired character or by supplying a string whose first character is the desired character.

# Sub...End Sub - Statements

### See Also: Call, End, Exit, Function

## Purpose

The Sub and End Sub statements declare and define a Visual Basic Sub procedure, and its parameters, if any.

## General Syntax

```
[Static] Sub sub-name[(arguments)]
    [Static var[,var]...]
    [Dim var[,var]...]
    [ReDim var[,var]...]
    [statements]
    [Exit Static]
    [statements]
End Sub
```

## Usage

```
Sub SwapInt(Num1 As Integer, Num2 As Integer)
    Dim Temp As Integer

    Temp = Num1
    Num1 = Num2
    Num2 = Temp
End Sub
```

This example defines a procedure that swaps the values of two integer variables.

## Description

The most common use of a Visual Basic Sub procedure is to define the actions of a task that will be performed more than once. This has the effect of reducing the amount of code necessary in a program, because the same task does not have to be recoded. Visual Basic Sub procedures can also be used to break a large task down into several smaller tasks. This makes debugging a program easier, because each particular task is isolated. All of the events caused by Visual Basic controls are Sub procedures. A Sub procedure is executed when Visual Basic encounters a Call statement. The use of the Call keyword is optional. For instance, these two lines will execute identically:

```
Call SwapInt(A%, B%)
SwapInt A%, B%
```

(Notice that when Call is omitted the parentheses around the procedure arguments must also be omitted.) The allocation of local variables (variables that are accessible only to this procedure) is performed by using the Dim, ReDim, or Static statements. Variables that are originally allocated within the procedure using Dim or ReDim statements are de-allocated when the procedure is exited. Therefore, they do not retain their value between calls to the procedure. To guarantee that a variable keeps its value between calls, it should be declared with the Static statement. If it is desired to have all local variables retain their value between calls, the procedure definition should begin with the optional Static keyword.

Arguments may be passed to the procedure in order to modify its behavior, or to give it information to act on. The format for declaring arguments is as follows:

```
([ByVal]variablename[As type][,[ByVal]variablename[As type]...])
```

The variable-name indicates the name that the argument will be referred to as from within the procedure. It may end in a type declaration character, or the As type parameter may be used to declare the data type of the incoming argument. The type may be Integer, Long, Single, Double, Currency, or String. By default, the arguments are passed by reference. This means the address of the variable is passed instead of the actual value. This allows the procedure to make changes to the passed arguments. In order to prevent this from happening, the ByVal keyword may be used to force the arguments to be passed by value instead.

If the expected argument being passed to the procedure is an entire array, the argument is declared as an array by including an empty set of parentheses at the end of the variable name.

The procedure is normally exited when execution reaches the End Sub keywords. However, an alternate exit may be forced by using the Exit Sub statement. This causes the procedure to be immediately terminated, and execution returns to the instruction following the call to the procedure.

Visual Basic procedures can be called recursively. This means that a procedure can call itself. A recursive Sub should not specify the Static keyword in the procedure definition.

# Tab - Function

### See Also: Print #, Spc

### Purpose
The Tab function sets the print position for the Print method or Print # statement.

### General Syntax
```
Tab(column%)
```

### Usage
```
Print #1, Tab(10) "Hello"
```
This prints the string "Hello" in the 10th column of the current line.

### Description
The Tab function is used along with the Print method or Print # statement to set the print position to a specific column in a line.

If the value specified by column% is less than the current print position, column% becomes the new print position. If the current print position is greater than column%, the print position advances to the next line, and then gets set to column%.

If used on a sequential file, the setting of the file's width (via the Width # statement) can affect the behavior of the Tab function. If the value of column% is greater than the width defined for the file, the print position will be calculated as column% modulo (MOD) width.

The print positions on a form are based on the average width of each character in the form's font.

# Tan - Function

### See Also: Atn, Cos, Sin

### Purpose
The Tan function returns the tangent of an angle.

### General Syntax
```
Tan(angle)
```
angle is expressed in radians.

### Usage
```
A! = Tan(4.93)
```
The tangent of 4.93 is assigned to the variable A!.

### Description
Tan is used to determine the tangent of an angle. The function expects the angle to be expressed in radians; therefore, if the angle is in degrees it must be converted using the formula radians = degrees * pi/ 180.

If the angle is supplied as an integer or a single-precision value, Tan will return a single-precision value; otherwise it returns a double-precision value.

# Time$ - Function and Statement

### See Also: Date$, Now, TimeValue

### Purpose
The Time$ function returns the current system time. The Time$ statement is used to set the system time.

### General Syntax
Function:
```
Time$
```

Statement:
```
Time$ = time-string$
```

### Usage
```
T$ = Time$
```
Assigns a string containing the current system date to the variable Today$.

```
Time$ = "12:30:56"
```
Sets the current system time.

### Description
Time$ can be used as a function, to return the current system time, or as a statement, to set the current system time. When used as a function, Time$ returns a string with the current system time in the format hh:mm:ss. As a statement, the system time may be set by using a string in the same format (specifying the seconds is optional).

When using Time$ as a statement, if the format of the time string is not in the correct format, Visual Basic issues an "Illegal function call" error.

If the time is set using the Time$ statement, its permanence depends on the type of system and version of DOS being used. Generally, if the system has a CMOS memory and is running under DOS 3.3 or greater, the date will be retained in the CMOS. Otherwise, the date may be lost when the system is powered down.

### Comments
In the above descriptions, hh refers to the hour, and must be in military format (that is, 01 to 23), mm refers to the minute (00 to 59), and ss to the second (00 to 59).

# Timer - Function

### See Also: Randomize

### Purpose
The Timer function returns the number of seconds since midnight.

### General Syntax
```
Timer
```

### Usage
```
StartTime! = Timer
Call TestProc
```

```
EndTime! = Timer
TimeElapsed! = EndTime! - StartTime!
```
This example uses the Timer function to time how long it takes the procedure TestProc to execute.

## Description
This function is useful for timing how long it takes certain tasks to be performed. It returns a double-precision number that represents the number of seconds that have elapsed since midnight.

# TimeSerial - Function

### See Also: Now, TimeValue

### Purpose
The TimeSerial function returns a time serial based on the integer hour, minutes, and seconds arguments.

### General Syntax
```
TimeSerial(hour%, minutes%, seconds%)
```

### Usage
```
A# = TimeSerial(10, 04, 05)
```
Places a time serial for 10:04:05 in the variable A#.

### Description
A time serial is a double-precision number that can represent any time of the day. It is a fraction that corresponds to the specified time in proportion to a whole day. Therefore, a time serial for 12:00 noon has a value of 0.5 (one-half of a day), while 6pm has a value of 0.75 (three-quarters of a day). The Now and TimeValue functions can also create a time serial.

The most useful aspect of this function is its ability to return a serial number based on the desired time's relation to another time. For instance, the following two statements return the same value:

```
TimeSerial(12, 00 - 15, 00)
TimeSerial(11, 45, 00)
```

The times specified by the arguments must combine to indicate a time between 00:00:00 and 23:59:59, or an "Illegal function call" will occur.

Date serials and time serials can be combined, because the date serial is stored on the left side of the decimal point, and the time serial is stored on the right.

# TimeValue - Function

### See Also: Now, TimeSerial

### Purpose
The TimeValue function returns a double-precision time serial number based on the supplied string.

### General Syntax
```
TimeValue(time-string$)
```

### Usage
```
A# = TimeValue(Time$)
```
Places a time serial for the current system time in the variable A#.

### Description
This function returns a time serial based on the supplied string. TimeValue can translate any time string that is in the same format as the string returned by the Time$ function. It can also translate a time string that includes the "AM" or "PM," such as "1:00AM." If the supplied string includes a recognizable date, the date text is ignored.

A time serial is a double-precision number that can represent any time of the day. It is a fraction that corresponds to the specified time in proportion to a whole day. Therefore, a time serial for 12:00 noon has a value of 0.5 (one-half of a day), while 6pm has a value of 0.75 (three-quarters of a day). The Now and TimeSerial functions can also create a time serial.

Date serials and time serials can be combined, because the date serial is stored on the left side of the decimal point, and the time serial is stored on the right.

## Type...End Type - Statements

**See Also: Dim, Global, ReDim, Static**

### Purpose

The Type and End Type statements declare a programmer-defined variable or record structure.

### General Syntax

```
Type type-name
    element As type
    [element As type]
        :
        :
End Type
```

### Usage

```
Type PhoneCards
    Name As String * 20
    Number As Long
    Address As String * 100
End Type

Dim Cards As PhoneCards
```

### Description

The Type...End Type structure is used in the global module to declare programmer-defined variables, and record variables. Such "custom" variables are generally used to keep several related simple variables together, so they can be addressed by one variable name.

The type-name parameter gives a name to this data type. This name will be used to declare the type of a variable in a later Dim, Global, ReDim, or Static statement.

Each element in the programmer-defined type is then defined. An element is defined by placing the element name followed by an As type clause. The type may be Integer, Long, Single, Double, Currency, String (for a variable length string), String * length (for a fixed length string), or any other user defined type. An element can only be declared as a user defined type if the referenced user defined type has already been declared. An element cannot be declared as an array.

The End Type keyword ends the type definition. Within a program, element names are referred to by placing a period between the name of the variable and the element name. For instance, in order to assign a value to the "Name" element of the "Card" variable in the example above, the following syntax would be used:

```
Cards.Name = "Marika E. Scott"
```

## UBound - Function

**See Also: LBound**

### Purpose

The UBound function returns the value of the largest usable subscript for the specified dimension of an array.

### General Syntax

```
UBound(arrayname[,dimension%])
```

### Usage

```
Dim Flowers%(1 To 100, -50 To 50)
A% = UBound(Flowers%, 2)
```

The value 50 is assigned to the variable A%, because that is the largest subscript available in the second dimension of the array Flowers%.

## Description

If the dimension parameter is not specified, the upper bound for the first dimension is returned. UBound is useful in conjunction with LBound for figuring out how many elements a dynamic array has. The number of elements can be found by subtracting the value returned by LBound from the value returned from UBound, and adding one.

# UCase$ - Function

### See Also: LCase$

## Purpose

The UCase$ function returns a copy of a string in which all lowercase alphabetic characters have been converted to uppercase.

## General Syntax

```
UCase$(expression$)
```

## Usage

```
C1$ = Command$
C2$ = UCase$(C1$)
```

This example retrieves the command line parameters that were used to start the program, and converts the entries to uppercase.

## Description

The expression$ parameter can be a fixed or variable length string, a string constant, a literal string, the result of any function that returns a string, or any other string expression. The LCase$ function works the same as UCase$, but it converts uppercase to lowercase.

This function is very useful for making a non-case sensitive comparison of two strings. This is helpful when an internal variable is being compared to a user's string input. By using UCase$ (or LCase$), the program can all but ignore the case of the string that has been input by the user.

# UnLoad - Statement

### See Also: Load

## Purpose

The Unload statement unloads a form from memory, or a control from a control array.

## General Syntax

```
UnLoad form-name
```

```
UnLoad control-name(index)
```

## Usage

```
UnLoad Form1
```

Unloads a form from memory.

```
UnLoad Text1(1)
```

Unloads a text box from a control array.

## Description

The form-name or control-name represents the name of the form or control to be unloaded from memory. If a control is part of a control array, the appropriate index value must be supplied in parentheses, following the name of the array. This statement is explained in more detail in Chapter 4, *Setting Up Forms*.

# Val - Function

### See Also: Str$

## Purpose

The Val function returns the numeric value of the supplied string expression.

### General Syntax

```
Val(string-expression)
```

### Usage

```
A! = Val("123")
B! = Val("1 2 3")
C! = Val(" 123")
D! = Val("G")
```

The first three lines assign a value of 123 to their respective variables. The fourth example returns 0.

### Description

The Val function is the complement to the Str$ function. It translates the supplied string expression into a double-precision number. Translation begins at the left of the string and works toward the right. Spaces are ignored. Translation ends at the first non-numeric character or at the end of the string, whichever comes first. The first period encountered in a string is translated as a decimal point, but a second period causes the translation to end. Dollar signs and commas are not recognized as numeric characters.

This function is useful for translating the string representation of hexadecimal or octal values into numeric values. For instance, the following code assigns the value of 255 to the variable A%:

```
B$ = Hex$(255)              'Gives B$ the value "FF"
A% = Val("&H" + B$)         'Same as Val("&HFF") which equals 255
```

# WeekDay - Function

### See Also: DateSerial, DateValue, Day, Now

### Purpose

The WeekDay function returns an integer representing the day of the week based on the supplied serial number.

### General Syntax

```
WeekDay(serial#)
```

### Usage

```
DayOfWeek% = WeekDay(Now)
```

Returns today's day of week.

### Description

This function uses a double-precision serial number representing a date to return an integer value representing the day of the week. Sunday returns a value of 1, while Saturday returns a value of 7. The supplied serial number represents the number of days since December 30, 1899. Therefore, January 01, 1900 has a serial number of 2, while January 1, 1753 has a serial number of -53,688. The supplied serial number must represent a date in the range of from January 1, 1753 to December 31, 2078 inclusive. If the date requested is not in this range, Visual Basic issues an "Illegal function call" error.

# While...Wend - Statements

### See Also: Do...Loop

### Purpose

The While and Wend statements repeat a block of instructions while a condition exists.

### General Syntax

```
While condition
    :
    [statements]
    :
Wend
```

### Usage

```
HiElement = UBound(SortArray$)
```

```
Sorting = -1
While Sorting = -1
    Sorting = 0
    For I = 2 To HiElement
        J = I - 1
        If SortArray$(J) > SortArray$(I) Then
            Sorting = -1
            Temp$ = SortArray$(I)
            SortArray$(I) = SortArray$(J)
            SortArray$(J) = Temp$
        End IF
    Next
Wend
```
This example uses the While...Wend structure to bubble sort an array.

### Description
The specified condition is tested. If it is true, the statements in the body of the loop are executed, and the condition is checked again. Since the condition is checked first, the body is never executed if the condition starts out being false. The While...Wend structure works in the same way as the Do Until...Loop structure. It has been retained for compatibility to earlier BASIC languages.

There must be one Wend for every While, and vice-versa. If there is not a one-for-one ratio of While's and Wend's, a "While without Wend" or "Wend without While" error will occur.

# Width # - Statement

### See Also: Print#, Spc, Tab

### Purpose
The Width # statement defines the width of a sequential file's output line.

### General Syntax
```
Width #filenumber, width%
```

### Usage
```
Width #1, 80
```
Sets the output line width for file number 1 to 80 columns.

### Description
When printing to an ASCII text file, it is sometimes necessary to define a maximum output length for each line. This statement defines the width of an output line. The filenumber parameter must be the number of a currently open file that was opened in either Output or Append modes.

The width parameter can be a value of from 0 to 255 columns. Specifying a column width of 0 sets an infinite output width. The default width for a file when it is open is 0.

# Write # - Statement

### See Also: Print #

### Purpose
The Write # statement formats and writes data to a sequential file that has been opened in Output or Append modes.

### General Syntax
```
Write #filenumber[, var1][, var2][, var3]..
```

### Usage
```
Write #1, A$, B%, C!, D#
```
Writes the specified variables to the file opened under number 1. Double quotes are placed around the value in A$, and a comma is written to the file to delimit each variable written. A newline character is written after the value in D# is written.

## Description
This statement writes a comma-delimited list of the supplied variables to the indicated file. Double quotes are placed around any strings, and a newline character is written to the file after each write is finished. If no variables are indicated, only the newline character is written to the file.

# Year - Function

### See Also: DateSerial, DateValue, Now, Weekday

### Purpose
The Year function returns an integer representing a year from 1753 to 2078, based on the supplied serial number.

### General Syntax
```
Year(serial#)
```

### Usage
```
ThisYear% = Day(Now)
```
Returns the current year.

### Description
This function uses a double-precision serial number representing a date to return an integer value representing a year from 1753 to 2078. The supplied serial number represents the number of days since December 30, 1899. Therefore, January 01, 1900, has a serial number of 2, while January 1, 1753, has a serial number of -53,688. The supplied serial number must represent a date in the range of from January 1, 1753 to December 31, 2078, inclusive. If the date requested is not in this range, Visual Basic issues an "Illegal function call" error.

# Appendix C
# Debugging Techniques

In this appendix you will learn how to deal with bugs, or programming errors. Visual Basic provides several useful facilities for finding and fixing bugs. Before we look at these techniques, let us consider the kinds of errors that can occur in programs.

## Programming Errors

There are basically three kinds of programming errors: compilation errors, run-time errors, and logic errors. Of the three, compilation errors are by far the easiest to fix. A compilation error is usually the result of incorrect syntax, such as a mistyped or missing keyword, a missing parenthesis, or a function call that is missing an argument. Visual Basic prevents most syntax errors from becoming compilation errors. It does this by checking the code as you type it, and beeping and displaying an error message as soon as a syntax error is detected. It is, after all, much easier to fix an error at the time you make it than to have to go back and find the errors later. (If you *do* want to be able to enter all your code before dealing with errors, you can go to the Code menu and turn syntax checking off.)

Some compilation errors might not be the result of syntax errors. For example, your program may allocate an object that is larger than the limits defined by Visual Basic. Again, you will receive an explanatory error message.

## Run-time Errors

Run-time errors are usually fairly easy to fix. One common kind of run-time error is the type mismatch, when the kind of data you supply as a Sub procedure or Function argument is different from the kind that the procedure or function expects. For example, the statement

```
N$ = Str$(A$)
```

will cause a run-time error because the Str$ function expects a numeric value, not a string.

Another common run-time error is caused by an attempt to reference a nonexistent array element. If MyArray has 100 elements and the variable Current gets set to 101, then a reference to MyArray(Current) will generate a run-time error. This kind of error sometimes requires a closer examination of your program logic, such as the boundaries defined in a loop.

## Logic Errors

A sometimes sad reality of computers is that they always do what you tell them, even if it's not what you wanted. This is the basis for logic errors. A logic error is caused when a portion of an application, although free of syntax and compilation errors, is not performing in a desired manner. Logic errors are the hardest kind of error to fix, because Visual Basic cannot detect them, and thus cannot give you a helpful error message. You must examine the symptoms, make a diagnosis, fix the problem, and then test your code to make sure you really *have* fixed the problem. The process of locating and repairing logic errors is called "debugging."

The design of a program determines the amount of debugging it will need. When designing an application, remember the five P's: Proper planning prevents poor performance. An application that is well planned from the outset will be much less likely to encounter unexpected results than one that is designed "on the fly." Of course, the more complicated an application, the more chance of a logic error. Therefore, more planning should go into such a project.

Even the best planned project is destined to have some logic errors. Visual Basic provides several tools for ferreting out these errors. Unfortunately, the debugging tools available in Visual Basic are not nearly as comprehensive as in its cousin QuickBASIC. Unlike QuickBASIC, you cannot "watch" variables, set "watchpoints," or "trace" the execution of a program. However, you can set "breakpoints," which allow you to halt execution at a specified point in the program. This allows you to use the Immediate window, or to "step through" the program's code, one line at a time. Visual Basic also features the Debug object, which allows a program to print directly to the Immediate window.

Table C.1 details the tools available to you for debugging your Visual Basic programs.

| Use This... | | To Do This... |
|---|---|---|
| Break | Command | Halt program execution |
| Clear All | Command | Cancel any breakpoints that have been set in the program |
| Debug | Object | Send debug information directly to the Immediate window |
| Immediate Window | Object | Execute Visual Basic functions, statements, and methods in real time |
| Procedure Step | Command | Step through code, treating Sub and Function calls as a single step |
| Set Next Statement | Command | Set the next executing statement to a different line of code |
| Show Next | Command | Display the next executing statement in the code window |
| Single Step | Command | Step through code, branching into Sub and Function calls |
| Stop | Statement | Halt execution from within the program's code |
| Toggle Breakpoint | Command | Set a breakpoint in a program on or off |

**Table C.1 Tools used to debug a Visual Basic program**

## Program Modes

At any given time, Visual Basic is in one of three modes: design mode, run mode, and break mode. As the name suggests, design mode is used for creating screen objects and writing code. When you type in code in design mode, Visual Basic traps syntax errors and gives you appropriate feedback. The debugging tools and features discussed in this appendix are not available in design mode, except you can set breakpoints. (A breakpoint is a place in the code where execution will automatically stop. You can set a breakpoint by selecting Toggle Breakpoint from the Run menu, or by pressing F9.)

Once you run a program (such as by selecting Start or Restart from the Run menu), Visual Basic is said to be in "run mode." During run mode, if a run-time error occurs the program will stop and an appropriate error message is given. You can also suspend program execution by selecting Break from the Run menu (or pressing the Ctrl + Break key combination). Note that the Run menu will not be available if the program is waiting for input (such as in a dialog box.)

When you have executed a break, the program is said to be in break mode. All of the debugging tools described in this chapter are available in break mode. In addition, you can use the Immediate Window to examine data or make changes to code in the code window. You can step through code (executing one statement at a time), continue execution of the program at the next statement, or restart the program from the beginning.

This appendix explores Visual Basic's debugging tools in a reference format. An entry for each of the tools in Table C.1 appears below. Examine these tools, and then try the interactive tutorial to learn how to use most of them. The tutorial includes a sample program that counts the number of characters, words, and lines in an ASCII text file. This program is in its raw state, meaning there are errors in the logic. This tutorial will use most of Visual Basic's debugging tools to solve the logic errors.

# Break

## Purpose
The Break command is used to begin the debugging process. It is used while a program is in run mode to temporarily halt execution so that the program's code and the values of its variables may be examined or modified.

## Selection
The Break command can be selected from the Run menu, or can be executed by pressing the Ctrl and Break keys simultaneously.

## Description
The Break command is what makes all of Visual Basic's debugging commands available. While your program is in run mode, you may select this command to halt the program. When this is done, Visual Basic is placed into break mode, and both the Code and Immediate windows appear. If the program was inactive (waiting for an event to occur), the Immediate window is given the focus. However, if your program was executing code, the Code window is given the focus, and a box is placed around the next line of code to be executed.

While in break mode, you can perform any of the other Debug commands (Toggle Breakpoint, Procedure Step, Set Next Statement, and so on), and you may enter Visual Basic commands into the Immediate window. You can even make changes to your code, thereby changing the way your program executes. In most cases after making a change, you can cause the program to continue where it left off, without having to restart it from the beginning. However, some changes will require that the program be restarted. Visual Basic will inform you of this when you make such a change, and allow you to choose whether you wish to continue with the change and restart the program from the beginning, or to undo the change.

There are three ways to exit the break mode. First, you can choose the Continue option from the Run menu (or press the F5 key). This allows the program to continue at the statement that is surrounded by the box indicating that it is to be the next command to be executed. Second, you can choose the Restart option (or Shift+F5) from the Run menu. This causes the program to restart from the beginning. Finally, you can choose the End option from the Run menu. This causes the program to terminate, and you are returned to design mode.

# Clear All Breakpoints

## Purpose
Clear All Breakpoints is used when all known errors in a program have been found and repaired. This command cancels all breakpoints that have been set throughout a program. Except for those instances in which a halt is coded into the program (such as with the Stop statement), issuing this command allows the program to proceed with no further interruptions.

## Selection
This command is executed by choosing the Clear All Breakpoints option from the run menu.

## Description
Breakpoints are placed in your code with the Toggle Breakpoint command. These are used to halt program execution at specified points in your program. The Clear All Breakpoints command searches your program and cancels any breakpoints that have been set.

# Debug Object

## Purpose

The Debug object is used to send output directly to the Immediate window.

## Selection

The Debug object can only be accessed from within the code of your program. The syntax for using the Debug object is:

```
Debug.Print [expression-list]
```

## Description

The Debug object is used with the Print method to send output directly to the Immediate window (for information on the Print method, please see Chapter 11, *Displaying Text with Objects*). This object provides an alternative technique for setting up "watch" variables. A watch variable is a variable whose value is displayed each time it is changed. The use of watch variables is a very helpful technique, because it allows the programmer to see exactly what is being assigned to a variable and when. Unfortunately, Visual Basic does not provide the ability to set up a true watch variable. Instead, you can use the Debug object in strategic areas in your program, so the value of a variable is printed to the Immediate window at regular intervals. For instance, in the following code fragment, we want to keep tabs on the value of the integer variable ThisVar:

```
Dim ThisVar As Integer  'This variable is declared in the Gen eral Declarations area

Sub Button1_Click ()
    ThisVar = ThisVar + 1
    Debug.Print "ThisVar = "; ThisVar
End Sub
```

In this example, the value of ThisVar will be displayed each time you click on the Command button named Button1. As shown in this example, the best area to place a Debug.Print command is just after the target variable has been changed.

# The Immediate Window

## Purpose

The Immediate window is used to execute Visual Basic functions, statements, and methods in real time, and as an output area for the Debug object.

## Selection

This window automatically appears during run time. It can be selected by clicking the left mouse button while the mouse pointer is over the window. This window can also be selected by choosing the Immediate Window option from Visual Basic's Window menu. However, real time commands can only be entered into this window while the Visual Basic environment is in break mode.

## Description

When you start a program while in the Visual Basic environment, your form appears as the window on the desktop that has the focus. Underneath your form, another window, called the Immediate window, is displayed. When a program is halted due to a Break command, a breakpoint, the execution of a Stop statement, or the occurrence of an untrapped error, this window becomes accessible to you. Before the Immediate window can be used, it must be given the focus. If you have issued a Break command while your program was idle (waiting for an event), the Immediate window will automatically be given the focus. Otherwise, you must give it the focus by selecting it with one of the procedures described above.

While in the Immediate window, you may enter any valid Visual Basic commands. This includes reading and setting the values of any variables that are accessible from the section of the program where execution was halted. In other words, variables that are accessible to the Immediate window are those that have been declared: (1) in the global module, (2) in the General Declarations area of the form with the focus, and (3) in the procedure in which execution was halted. For instance, given the following code:

```
Global GlobalVar As Integer  'This variable is declared in the global routine

Dim ModuleVar As Integer     'This variable is declared in the General Declarations area

Sub Button1_Click ()
    Dim ThisVar1 As Integer

    ThisVar1 = Int(34.54)  'There is a breakpoint at this line
End Sub

Sub Button2_Click ()
    Dim ThisVar2 As Integer

    ThisVar2 = Sqr(254)
End Sub
```

When Visual Basic encounters the line in Button1_Click where the breakpoint is set, execution will halt, and the Immediate window will be given the focus. At that time, you would be able to read and set the values of the variables GlobalVar, ModuleVar, and ThisVar1. However, you would not be able to access ThisVar2, because it is defined in a different procedure from that where execution was halted.

The Immediate window is also used as an output area for the Debug object. This allows you to display information about how a program is running by strategically placing Debug.Print commands in your code. Please see the entry for the Debug object in this chapter.

# Procedure Step

## Purpose
The Procedure Step command is used to step through your code, executing one line at a time. A whole function or procedure is considered to be a single step.

## Selection
This command is executed by choosing the Procedure Step option from the run menu, or by pressing the Shift+F8 key combination.

## Description
It is often useful to be able to execute your program one line at a time, so that you may see exactly which steps are taken throughout the program's execution. This helps you determine where bugs in your program may occur. Portions of your code that you are stepping through may include several calls to functions or procedures that you have written. If you have already debugged these functions and procedures, and know they work correctly, there is no reason for you to have to step through each line in those functions or procedures when they are called. When this is the case, you can use the Procedure Step command. This command will step through code one line at a time. However, when a Procedure Step encounters a function or procedure call, it will execute the entire function or procedure as one step. This saves you the hassle of stepping through all the lines of code in that procedure or function.

## Comment
If you want to step through *every* program statement, including code in procedures or functions, use the Single Step command rather than Procedure Step.

# Set Next Statement

## Purpose
The Set Next Statement command is used while in break mode to inform Visual Basic which is the next line of code to execute.

### Selection

This command is executed by selecting the Set Next Statement option from the Run menu.

### Description

When Visual Basic enters break mode, it places a box around the statement that is to be executed next. You can use the Set Next Statement command to move this box to a different line of code. However, the line of code you choose must reside in the same procedure or function as the original next statement. You set the next statement to be executed by placing the insertion point on the desired line of code, and then selecting the Set Next Statement command.

There are two situations for which this command is most commonly used. First, because Visual Basic allows you to change your code while in break mode, you may wish to immediately test how the changes will execute. This can be done by setting up the first line of your change to be the next statement to be executed. You can then use the Procedure Step or Single Step commands to test how the new coding changes will work.

The second common use for this command is to recover from an untrapped error. Any time an error occurs that you have not trapped in your program's code, the program halts, Visual Basic displays an error message, and the Immediate window is displayed. Sometimes this can happen because of a variable not being set to the correct value. For instance, in the following code fragment, an attempt is made to open a file:

```
FileNumber = Free_File
Open "Test.Dat" For Random As #FileNumber
```

In this example, it seems as though the programmer who wrote this intended to get a free file number from Visual Basic's FreeFile function. Unfortunately, our programmer mistyped the function name, and included an underscore. As a result, Visual Basic creates a variable called Free_File and assigns it the default value of 0. When Visual Basic encounters the line that assigns a value to the variable FileNumber, the assigned value will also be 0. This will cause the Open statement on the next line to issue a "Bad file name or number" error.

When this happens, you can fix the code immediately, by changing the line above the file open. The new code fragment would look like this:

```
FileNumber = FreeFile
Open "Test.Dat" For Random As #FileNumber
```

You would then use the Set Next Statement command to inform Visual Basic to continue execution at the line where the FileNumber variable is assigned a value from the FreeFile function. Not only have you fixed the error, but you have also saved yourself from having to restart the program from the beginning.

## Show Next Statement

### Purpose

The Show Next Statement command locates the next statement that will be executed, and displays it in the Code window.

### Selection

This command is executed by selecting the Show Next Statement option from the Run menu.

### Description

Visual Basic allows you to edit your program's code while in break mode. When Visual Basic enters break mode, the currently executing procedure is displayed in the Code window. However, you can edit other procedures in the program while in break mode. Doing so causes the current procedure to be replaced in the Code window by the procedure you wish to edit. If you need to edit several procedures, it might happen that you forget in which procedure execution was halted. The Show Next Statement command provides a technique for you to quickly load into the Code window the procedure where the program halt occurred. When this command is executed, Visual Basic locates the line of code that is to be the next executed statement, and loads its procedure into the Code window. The next line to be executed will be displayed in the center of the window, with a box around it.

# Single Step

## Purpose

The Single Step command is used to step through your code one line at a time. When a function or procedure call is encountered, this command will load the function or procedure into the Code window, and execute its statements one line at a time.

## Selection

This command is executed by choosing the Single Step option from Visual Basic's Run menu, or by pressing F8.

## Description

It is often useful to be able to execute your program one line at a time, so that you may view exactly which steps are taken throughout the program's execution. This helps you determine where bugs in your program may occur. Portions of your code that you are stepping through may include several calls to functions or procedures that you have written. If you have not yet debugged these functions and procedures, you may wish to step through each line of code in those functions and procedures when they are called. When this is the case, you can use the Single Step command. This command will step through code one line at a time. When a Single Step encounters a function or procedure call, it will load that function or procedure into the Code window, and execute that function's or procedure's code one line at a time. When execution reaches an Exit Function, End Function, Exit Sub, or End Sub statement, it will load into the Code window the parent function or procedure that made the call to the current function or procedure, and continue execution there a step at a time.

## Comment

If you want to step through a main program but not step through the procedures or functions that it calls, use the Procedure Step command instead of Single Step.

# Stop Statement

## Purpose

The Stop statement halts execution of a program.

## Selection

The Stop statement is placed in your code. The syntax for this statement is simply:

```
Stop
```

## Description

The Stop statement is used much like a breakpoint in your code. Unlike a breakpoint, which marks a particular line of code, this command is placed inside your code as an executable statement. The effect of a Stop statement is exactly the same as if you had issued a Break command while executing the line of code with the Stop statement on it. When this command is executed, Visual Basic is placed into break mode. Both the Code and Immediate windows appear, and the Code window will have the focus. Although it will have already been executed, the line of code with the Stop statement will be surrounded with a box, indicating it is the next statement to be executed. However, performing Single Step or Procedure Step at this time will not execute the Stop statement again; it will just set the next statement to the line following the Stop statement.

Most commonly, the Stop statement is used to halt execution when a condition becomes true. For instance, imagine you have a variable in your program that can be set to True or False. For some reason, you may wish to examine the program when that variable becomes False. Using the following line of code, you can cause the program to halt when this is the case:

```
If ThisVar = False Then Stop
```

This has the effect of setting a conditional breakpoint in a program. You must be careful if you use the Stop statement in the debugging of your program. If you do not remove all Stop statements in your program before creating an .EXE file, they will be compiled into the executable version of your program. Then if the executable program comes across a Stop statement, it will terminate, and a "Stop statement encountered" message will be displayed. This is almost guaranteed to make the user of the program very unhappy. Therefore, if you ever place a Stop statement in your program, always do a global search for the word "Stop" and remove every Stop statement before creating an .EXE file.

## Toggle Breakpoint

### Purpose
The Toggle Breakpoint command sets or clears a flag that marks a point in the program where execution will be halted. This command works like a toggle switch. If a line of code is not yet a breakpoint, choosing this command makes it one; otherwise, it cancels the breakpoint for this line of code.

### Selection
This command can be selected by choosing the Toggle Breakpoint option from Visual Basic's Run menu, or by pressing F9.

### Description
A breakpoint is a line of code in your program where you wish execution to be halted. The effect of a breakpoint is exactly the same as if you had issued a Break command while executing the line of code just prior to the breakpoint. In other words, the program is halted before the line with the breakpoint is executed. When a breakpoint is encountered, Visual Basic is placed into break mode. Both the Code and Immediate windows appear, and the Code window will have the focus. The line of code with the breakpoint will be surrounded with a box, indicating it is the next statement to be executed.

Breakpoints are used to halt program execution just prior to a portion of code that you wish to step through, or to examine before it is executed. A breakpoint can also be used to check the results of a particular routine after it has executed.

## The Debug Project

### Overview
The Debug project for Appendix C is actually a brief tutorial that will lead you through some basic steps that can be taken to debug a Visual Basic program. Most of the tools introduced earlier in this appendix are demonstrated in the tutorial.

### Assembling the Project
1. This program depends on the existence of a text file in the Windows directory called DEBUG.TXT. We will build this file using the NotePad program that comes with Windows 3.0 (if you prefer, you may use any other text editor, as long as it saves in ASCII format). Go to the Program Manager, and start the NotePad program. Use this editor to create a text file named DEBUG.TXT that contains the following text:

   ```
   A sometimes sad reality of computers is that they always do what you tell
   them, even if it's not what you wanted. This is the basis for logic errors.
   A logic error is caused when a portion of an application, although free of
   syntax and compilation errors, is not performing in a desired manner. The
   process of locating and repairing logic errors is called "debugging."
   ```

   Because the program we'll be debugging counts lines in a text file, be sure not to add any extra blank lines at the end of the text. Accurate debugging depends on our foreknowledge that the text file has only five lines.

2. Make a form (the Debug form) with the following objects and properties.

| Object | Property | Setting |
| --- | --- | --- |
| Form | FormName | Form1 |
| | Caption | ASCII File Word Counter |
| | Icon | \VB\ICONS\WRITING\NOTE06.ICO |
| Label | CtlName | Label1 |
| | Caption | File Name: |
| Label | CtlName | Label1 |
| | Caption | Lines: |
| Label | CtlName | Label2 |
| | Caption | Words: |
| Label | CtlName | Label3 |
| | Caption | Characters: |
| Label | CtlName | Label4 |
| | Caption | DOS File Length: |
| TextBox | CtlName | FileName |
| | Text | C:\WINDOWS\DEBUG.TXT |
| Label | CtlName | LineCtr |
| | Alignment | 1 - Right Justified |
| | BorderStyle | 1 - Fixed Single |
| | Caption | 0 |
| Label | CtlName | WordCtr |
| | Alignment | 1 - Right Justified |
| | BorderStyle | 1 - Fixed Single |
| | Caption | 0 |
| Label | CtlName | CharCtr |
| | Alignment | 1 - Right Justified |
| | BorderStyle | 1 - Fixed Single |
| | Caption | 0 |
| Label | CtlName | DOS_Len |
| | Alignment | 1 - Right Justified |
| | BorderStyle | 1 - Fixed Single |
| | Caption | 0 |
| Command button | CtlName | CountButton |
| | Caption | &Count |
| | Default | True |
| Command button | CtlName | ExitButton |
| | Caption | E&xit |

**Table C.2 Settings for the Debug project form**

3. Size and place the objects so they match the form shown in Figure C.1.

4. Place the following code in the General Declarations area of the Debug form. This code defines constants for TRUE and FALSE, and sets up an edit pattern for printing formatted numbers.

```
Const TRUE = -1
Const FALSE = 0
Const EditPattern = "#,###,###,##0"
```

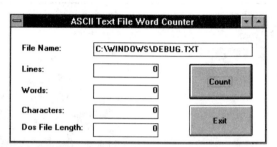

5. Place the following code in the Count-Button_Click event handler. This event is the main procedure for the application. This procedure is invoked when the Count button is clicked. It starts by allocating storage for the counters and other variables. It then opens the file whose name is specified in the FileName text box and assigns the length of the file to the DOS_Len label. At that point, each line in the file is read and the number of characters and words on that line is counted. The values of these counters are then placed in their corresponding labels.

**Figure C.1 What the Debug project form should look like**

```
Sub CountButton_Click ()
    Dim TextFile As Integer
    Dim TextLine As String
    Dim NumberOfLines As Long
    Dim NumberOfWords As Long
    Dim NumberOfChars As Long

    'Get a file number and open the file for input
    TextFile = FreeFile
    Open FileName.Text For Input As #TextFile

    'Set the value of the DOS_Len Label to display the length of the file
    DOS_Len.Caption = Format$(LOF(TextFile), EditPattern)

    'Read the file line by line until the end
    Do Until EOF(TextFile)
        Input #TextFile, TextLine
        NumberOfLines = NumberOfLines + 1
        NumberOfChars = NumberOfChars + Len(TextLine)
        NumberOfWords = NumberOfWords + CountWords(TextLine)
        LineCtr.Caption = Format$(NumberOfLines, EditPattern)
        WordCtr.Caption = Format$(NumberOfWords, EditPattern)
        CharCtr.Caption = Format$(NumberOfChars, EditPattern)
    Loop
End Sub
```

6. Place the following code in the ExitButton_Click event handler. This procedure simply ends the program.

```
Sub ExitButton_Click ()
    End
End Sub
```

7. Enter the following code into the function CountWords(). This function receives a line of text and returns a Long integer that corresponds to the number of words in that line. A word begins with the first alphabetic character (a through z or A through Z) and ends with the first non-alphabetic character.

```
Function CountWords (TextLine As String) As Long
    Dim TextPos As Long
    Dim TextLen As Long
    Dim InWord As Integer
    Dim WordsFound As Integer
    Dim TextChar As String * 1

    InWord = False
    TextPos = 0
    TextLen = Len(TextLine)
    Do Until TextPos = TextLen
        TextPos = TextPos + 1
```

```
        TextChar = Mid$(TextLine, TextPos, 1)
        TextChar = UCase$(TextChar)
        If TextChar < "A" Or TextChar > "Z" Then
            InWord = False
        ElseIf InWord = False Then
            InWord = True
            WordsFound = WordsFound + 1
        End If
    Loop
    CountWords = WordsFound
End Function
```

## The First Run

Once the form is completed, and the program is free of syntax and compilation errors, you can run the application. Close all windows on the workspace except for the Visual Basic menu window. Open the Run menu and choose the Start option, as shown in Figure C.2.

This switches Visual Basic from design mode to run mode (the current mode is always displayed in brackets in the title line of the Visual Basic menu window). This causes two windows to be opened. The first is the Debug form, which is given the focus. The second is the Immediate window. This window is explained a little bit later in this section.

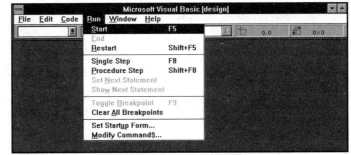

**Figure C.2 Choosing the Start option on the Run menu**

Click on the Count button. This causes the CountButton_Click event to execute. The character, word, and line counts of the DEBUG.TXT file are displayed. However, the program displays that the file has eight lines, when we know it only has five. Time for some debugging. Exit the program by clicking the Exit button.

## Setting Breakpoints

Now that Visual Basic is back in the design mode, bring up the Code window with the Count-Button_Click procedure in it. Place the insertion point on the first line of the procedure. Now, open the Run menu, and choose Toggle Breakpoint, as shown in

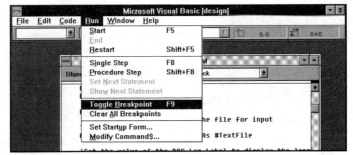

**Figure C.3 How to toggle a breakpoint**

Figure C.3. You will notice that the current line is displayed in boldface text. This line is now a breakpoint in the program. When the program reaches this line, execution will halt just before performing the instructions on the line. However, the program is only paused; all the program information and variables are kept intact. The breakpoint works as a toggle. Keep the insertion point on the first line of the procedure. Again, open the Run menu, and choose Toggle Breakpoint. The line is no longer bold, because the breakpoint has been turned off. If several breakpoints have been set within a program, they may all be turned off at once by using the Clear All Breakpoints option on the Run menu.

A breakpoint may also be toggled with the F9 function key. Find the line in the procedure that matches this one:

```
Input #TextFile, TextLine
```

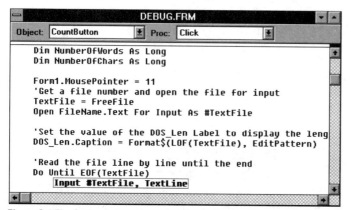

**Figure C.4 The Code window when a breakpoint is encountered**

and press F9. This sets a breakpoint at the line where the text is read.

Although we've not yet fixed the problem, we're going to run the program. This time, execution will stop when we reach the instruction that reads the file. Open the Run menu and choose the Start option (or just press F5). Again, when the Debug project form is displayed, click on the Count button.

Didn't get very far, did we? When the program reaches a breakpoint, it places Visual Basic in break mode. As you can see in Figure C.4, the program stopped, and the Code window opened. The next line of code due to be executed is surrounded by a box. Being in break mode allows us to perform several useful tasks.

### Stepping Through Code

While Visual Basic is in break mode, we can now step through the code. There are two methods for stepping through code: the single step, and procedure step. The single step executes one instruction at a time. If an instruction involves a call to a Visual Basic Function or Sub procedure, that procedure will be loaded into the Code window, and each of its steps will be executed one at a time. A procedure step treats a call to a procedure as one step. Therefore, when a procedure is encountered, all of its instructions are executed without a break.

A single step is executed by opening the Run menu, and choosing the Single Step option (or by pressing F8). Doing so causes the instruction inside the box to be executed, and the box moves to the next instruction.

### Using the Immediate Window

When a program is run under the Visual Basic environment, the Immediate window automatically opens. When in break mode, this window can be used to execute instructions in real time. Any execut-

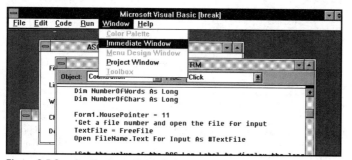

**Figure C.5 Opening the Immediate window**

able Visual Basic statement or function, as well as programmer-defined Sub procedures and Functions, may be run from this window. This makes the window useful for testing procedures, or for viewing the contents of a variable while a program is running. Clicking on the Immediate window gives it the focus. Sometimes this window can get hidden behind the many different windows and forms on the screen. When this

happens, you can bring the Immediate window back to the surface by opening Visual Basic's Window menu and choosing the Immediate Window option, as shown in Figure C.5.

This brings the Immediate window to the forefront and gives it the focus. Instructions can only be entered in the window when Visual Basic is in the break mode.

Now let's go back to our bug hunt. Since we single stepped when the box was around the instruction:

```
Input #TextFile, TextLine
```

we know the first record in the file has been read. We can now use the Immediate window to view the contents of the line that has just been read. Give the Immediate window the focus, and type the following into it:

```
Print TextLine
```

This should print the contents of the string variable TextLine in the Immediate window. You may need to resize the window in order to see the entire line of text. After resizing, the Immediate window should look like Figure C.6.

So far, everything looks OK. The contents of "TextLine" match the first line we entered in the text file.

**Figure C.6 The Immediate window**

### Using the Debug.Print Method

We can now cause the program to continue executing by choosing the Continue option on the Run menu (or by pressing F5). Again, the program halts when it reaches the breakpoint. This time, instead of entering commands in the Immediate window, we're going to use the Print method with the Debug object. (See Chapter 11, *Displaying Text with Objects,* for more information on this method.) Printing to the Debug object sends text directly to the Immediate window. Place the insertion point at the end of the line with the Input # statement, and press Enter. Place the following statement in the blank line that is created:

```
Debug.Print "["; TextLine; "]"
```

Now, position and resize the Code and Immediate windows, so that both are visible on the screen. Single step through the program until the Debug.Print instruction is executed. This instruction sends the contents of the string variable TextLine in brackets to the Immediate window. Your screen should look like Figure C.7.

By looking at the output to the Immediate window, we can see that the string variable TextLine only contains the word "them." For some reason, the rest of the second line did not get read. If we examine the second line of text that should have been read:

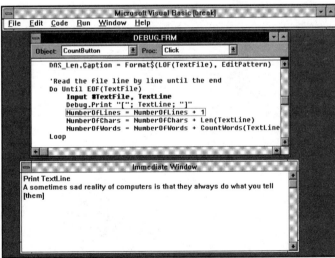

**Figure C.7 Using Debug.Print to send output to the Immediate window**

```
them, even if it's not what you wanted. This is the basis for logic errors.
```

we see that the read stopped when it encountered the comma. We now know that, for some reason, we are not getting an entire line of text every time we read the file. Therefore, we have narrowed our problem down to the following instruction in the CountButton_Click event:

```
Input #FileNumber, TextLine
```

## Fixing the Error

Once the offending line has been isolated, it is generally a good idea to check the statements and functions involved, and see if they're being used properly. In this case, we are trying to input an entire line of text with the Input # statement. This causes a problem, because the Input # statement interprets commas as delimiters, instead of as raw text. For the purposes of this program, the Line Input # statement is more appropriate. Change the offending line to:

```
Line Input #FileNumber, TextLine
```

Now, open the Run menu, and choose the Restart option. This causes the program to start from the beginning. When the form for the Debug project is displayed on the screen, click on the Count button.

Oops! Looks like we forgot about the breakpoint we set. Press F9 to toggle it off. We can also remove the Debug.Print instruction. Now, press F5 to continue.

This time the program runs and gives a correct count of 5 lines, 60 words, and 370 characters. You may notice the number of characters counted differs from the DOS file length. This is because our program does not count the carriage return/linefeed pair at the end of each line as DOS does. If you wish for these two numbers to match, you need to add 2 to the variable NumberOfChars each time a Line Input # is executed.

Congratulations! Using the debugging tools provided by Visual Basic, you have successfully searched out and destroyed the offending logic error. All in all, this was a relatively painless exercise. Of course, as your programs become larger and more complicated, your debugging tasks will become more involved.

# Appendix D
# Using the Windows API

The Microsoft Windows environment defines more than 500 separate functions that programs can use to interact directly with the operating environment. Traditional Windows program development involves making calls to many of these functions, usually from programs written in the C language.

Visual Basic provides built-in features that make it unnecessary to use the API functions in most applications. There may be times, however, when you want to accomplish something that is not directly supplied by Visual Basic. For example, the project at the end of this appendix demonstrates how you can add sound capabilities to a Visual Basic application even though Visual Basic has no built-in object for dealing with the PC speaker and sound system. Visual Basic lets you access any API function directly from your program, putting all of the power of Windows at your disposal.

## Visual Basic and Windows API Functions
In order to make an API function available to a Visual Basic application, the function must be declared in the General procedure section of a form or module. The exact syntax of the code that declares an API function varies for each function. There are several possible sources for each API function that must be identified properly. These sources include the files KERNEL.EXE, GDI.EXE, USER.EXE, COMM.DRV, MOUSE.DRV, KEYBOARD.DRV, and SOUND.DRV. Unfortunately the Windows Programmer's Reference does not list them. This information is provided in the following section along with the syntax to use in Visual Basic applications.

We do not have room in this book to go into details in the reference entries for API functions, and can only provide a brief summary of syntax, arguments, and values used. You can find a complete list of the Windows API functions in *The Waite Group's Windows API Bible* (Waite Group Press, 1992). This reference manual is essential for expanding the capabilities of the Visual Basic language. See Appendix E for other books relating to Windows programming and the API.

---

## Application-execution functions

### LoadModule
This function loads and activates the application named in the lpModuleName argument. If the application is already loaded, then a new version is created.

```
Declare Function LoadModule Lib "Kernel" (ByVal lpModuleName As String, lpParameterBlock As
PARAMETERBLOCK) As Integer
```

| Argument | Description |
|---|---|
| lpModuleName | Null-terminated string containing the file and path of the application to run |
| lpParameterBlock | Points to a data structure that consists of four possible fields |

**Table D.1 Arguments of LoadModule**

| Field | Description |
|---|---|
| wEnvSeg | Segment Address (0 means copy it) |
| lpCmdLine | Null Terminated Command string |
| lpCmdShow | Appearance of application when loaded |
| dwReserved | Null |

Table D.2 Fields of LoadModule

## WinExec

This function executes the Windows or non-Windows application named in the lpCmdLine parameter.

```
Declare Function WinExec Lib "Kernel" (ByVal lpCmdLine As String, nCmdShow As Integer) As Integer
```

| Argument | Description |
|---|---|
| lpCmdLine | Null-terminated string containing the file and path of the application to run |
| nCmdShow | Specifies how a windows application is to be shown. See ShowWindow for possible values |

Table D.3 Arguments of WinExec

| Returned Value | Meaning |
|---|---|
| 0 | Out of memory |
| 2 | File not found |
| 3 | Path not found |
| 5 | Attempt to dynamically link to a task |
| 6 | Library requires separate data segments for each task |
| 10 | Incorrect Windows version |
| 11 | Invalid EXE file |
| 12 | OS/2 application |
| 13 | DOS 4.0 application |
| 14 | Unknown EXE type |
| 15 | Attempt to load a Windows application for an earlier version of Windows |
| 16 | Attempt to load an additional instance of an EXE file |
| 17 | Attempt to load a second instance of an application in a large-frame EMS mode |
| 18 | Attempt to load a protected mode application in real mode |

Table D.4 Returned Values of WinExec

## WinHelp

This function starts the WindowS Help application with the help file identified in the lpHelpFile argument.

```
Declare Function WinHelp Lib "User" (ByVal hWnd As Integer, ByVal lpHelpFile As String, ByVal
wCommand As Integer, dwData As Any) As Integer
```

| Argument | Description |
|---|---|
| hWnd | Identifies window that requested help |
| lpHelpFile | Null-terminated string containing the file and path of the help file |
| wCommand | Indentifies the type of help requested with one of the folllowing values |
| dwData | Identifies the context or keyword of the help requested |

Table D.5 Arguments of WinHelp

### CONSTANT.TXT Variables for WinHelp

| | |
|---|---|
| HELP_CONTEXT | Help for a particular context |
| HELP_HELPONHELP | Displays helpf for using help |
| HELP_INDEX | Displays the index for the help file |
| HELP_KEY | Displays help for a particular keyword |
| HELP_MULTIKEY | Displays help for a keyword of an alternate keyword table |
| HELP_QUIT | Informs the help application that the help file is no longer being used |
| HELP_SETINDEX | Sets the dwData argument as the current index |

### CONSTANT.TXT Global Constant Definitions

Global Const HELP_CONTEXT = &H1
Gbal Const HELP_QUIT = &H2
Global Const HELP_INDEX = &H3
Global Const HELP_HELPONHELP = &H4
Global Const HELP_SETINDEX = &H5
Global Const HELP_KEY = &H101
Global Const HELP_MULTIKEY = &H201

## Atom-management functions

### AddAtom

This function adds the character string in the lpString argument to the atom table.

```
Declare Function AddAtom Lib "Kernel" (ByVal lpString As String) As Integer
```

| Argument | Description |
|---|---|
| lpString | Null terminated character string |

**Table D.6 Argument of AddAtom**

### DeleteAtom

This function deletes the atom identified by the nAtom argument.

```
Declare Function DeleteAtom Lib "Kernel" (ByVal nAtom As Integer) As Integer
```

| Argument | Description |
|---|---|
| nAtom | Identifies the atom and character string to be deleted |

**Table D. 7 Argument of DeleteAtom**

### FindAtom

This function finds the atom table for the character string in the lpString argument.

```
Declare Function FindAtom Lib "Kernel" (ByVal lpString As String) As Integer
```

| Argument | Description |
|---|---|
| lpString | Identifies the character string to search for |

**Table D.8 Argument of FindAtom**

### GetAtomHandle

This function provides the handle of the string in the atom identified by the wAtom argument.

```
Declare Function GetAtomHandle Lib "Kernel" (ByVal wAtom As Integer) As Integer
```

| Argument | Description |
|----------|-------------|
| wAtom | Integer that identifies the atom whose handle is retrieved |

**Table D.9 Argument of GetAtomHandle**

## GetAtomName
This function returns the character string of the nAtom parameter

```
Declare Function GetAtomName Lib "Kernel" (ByVal nAtom As Integer, ByVal lpBuffer As String, ByVal
nSize As Integer) As Integer
```

| Argument | Description |
|----------|-------------|
| nAtom | Identifies the character string to obtain |
| lpbuffer | Indicates the buffer to put the returned character string in |
| nSize | Maximum size of the buffer |

**Table D.10 Argument of GetAtomName**

## GlobalAddAtom
This function creates a global atom for a character string identified by the lpString parameter.

```
Declare Function GlobalAddAtom Lib "Kernel" (ByVal lpString As String) As Integer
```

| Argument | Description |
|----------|-------------|
| lpString | Null-terminated character string to create the atom for |

**Table D.11 Argument of GlobalAddAtom**

## GlobalDeleteAtom
This function reduces the reference count of a global atom by one. If the atom's count is 0, then this removes the string from the atom table.

```
Declare Function GlobalDeleteAtom Lib "Kernel" (ByVal nAtom As Integer) As Integer
```

| Argument | Description |
|----------|-------------|
| nAtom | Specifies the atom affected by this function |

**Table D.12 Argument of GlobalDeleteAtom**

## GlobalFindAtom
This function searches for the global atom connected with a character string.

```
Declare Function GlobalFindAtom Lib "Kernel" (ByVal lpString As String) As Integer
```

| Argument | Description |
|----------|-------------|
| lpString | Null-terminated character string to search for |

**Table D.13 Argument of GlobalFindAtom**

## GlobalGetAtomName
This function copies the character string connected with the atom into a buffer.

```
Declare Function GlobalGetAtomName Lib "Kernel" (ByVal nAtom As Integer, ByVal lpbuffer As String,
ByVal nSize As Integer) As Integer
```

| Argument | Description |
|----------|-------------|
| nAtom | Identifies the character string |
| lpBuffer | Buffer to put the character string into |
| nSize | Maximum size of the buffer |

**Table D.14 Arguments of GlobalGetAtomName**

### InitAtomTable

This function sets up an atom hash table.

```
Declare Function InitAtomTable Lib "Kernel" (ByVal nSize As Integer) As Integer
```

| Argument | Description |
|----------|-------------|
| nSize | Indicates the size of the atom hash table |

**Table D.15 Argument of IntiAtomTable**

# Communications functions

### BuildCommDCB

This function translates the string in the lpDef argument into an appropriate device-control block code. These codes are then placed in the DCB data structure identified by the lpDCB argument

```
Declare Function BuildCommDCB Lib "User" (ByVal lpDef As String, lpDCB As DCB) As Integer
```

| Argument | Description |
|----------|-------------|
| lpDef | DCB control structure |

**Table D.16 Argument of BuildCommDCB**

### ClearCommBreak

This function resets the communication break state of a communications device identified by the nCid argument.

```
Declare Function ClearCommBreak Lib "User" (ByVal nCid As Integer) As Integer
```

| Argument | Description |
|----------|-------------|
| nCid | Communications device |

**Table D.17 Argument of ClearCommBreak**

### CloseComm

This function closes the communications device identified by the nCid argument

```
Declare Function CloseComm Lib "User" (ByVal nCid As Integer) As Integer
```

| Argument | Description |
|----------|-------------|
| nCid | Communications device |

**Table D.18 Argument of CloseComm**

### EscapeCommFunction

This function instructs the communications device identified by the nCid argument to carry out the function in the nFunc argument.

```
Declare Function EscapeCommFunction Lib "User" (ByVal nCid As Integer, ByVal nFunc As Integer) As Integer
```

| Argument | Description |
|----------|-------------|
| nCid | Communications device |
| nFunc | Function for the communications device to carry out |

**Table D.19 Arguments of EscapeCommFunction**

| Name | Meaning |
|------|---------|
| CLRDTR | Clears the data-terminal ready (DTR) signal |
| CLRRTS | Clears the request-to-send (RTS) signal |
| RESETDEV | Resets the device if possible |
| SETDTR | Sends the data-terminal-ready (DTR) signal |
| SETRTS | Sends the request-to-send (RTS) signal |
| SETXOFF | Communications device acts as if an XOFF character is received |
| SETXON | Communications device acts as if an XON character is received |

**Table D.20 Function names and their meanings**

## FlushComm

This function removes all characters from the transmit and receive queue of the communications device identified by the nCid argument. The nQueue argument indicates which queue to flush.

```
Declare Function FlushComm Lib "User" (ByVal nCid As Integer, ByVal nQueue As Integer) As Integer
```

| Argument | Description |
|----------|-------------|
| nCid | Communications device |
| nQueue | Indicates whether to flush the transmit (0) or receive queue (1) |

**Table D.21 Arguments of FlushComm**

## GetCommEventMask

This function obtains the current value of an event and then clears it. The returned value indicates whether the event has taken place.

```
Declare Function GetCommEventMask Lib "User" (ByVal nCid As Integer, ByVal nEvtMask As Integer) As Integer
```

| Argument | Description |
|----------|-------------|
| nCid | Communications device to examine |
| nEnvtMask | Indicates which events are enabled |

**Table D.22 Arguments of GetCommEventMask**

## GetCommState

This function fills the buffer identified by the lpDCB argument with the device control block.

```
Declare Function GetCommState Lib "User" (ByVal nCid As Integer, lpDCB as DCB) As Integer
```

| Argument | Description |
|----------|-------------|
| nCid | Communications device to examine |
| lpDCB | DCB data structure that receives the current device control block |

**Table D.23 Arguments of GetCommState**

## OpenComm

This function activates a commications device and gives it an nCid handle.

```
Declare Function OpenComm Lib "User" (ByVal lpComName As String, ByVal wInQueue As Integer, ByVal wOutQueue As Integer) As Integer
```

| Argument | Description |
|----------|-------------|
| lpCommName | Indicates a string that contains COMn or LPTn |
| wInQueue | Indicates the size of the receive queue |
| wOutQueue | Indicates the size of the transmit queue |

**Table D.24 Arguments of OpenComm**

## ReadComm

This function takes the bytes from the communications device identified in the nCid argument and places them in the buffer set in the lpBuf.

```
Declare Function ReadComm Lib "User" (ByVal nCid As Integer, ByVal lpBuf As String, ByVal nSize As Integer) As Integer
```

| Argument | Description |
|----------|-------------|
| nCid | Communications device to read |
| lpBuf | Buffer to place the received characters into |
| nSize | Indicates the number of characters to be read |

**Table D.25 Arguments of ReadComm**

## SetCommBreak

This function changes the communications device identified by the nCid argument to break state.

```
Declare Function SetCommBreak Lib "User" (ByVal nCid As Integer) As Integer
```

| Argument | Description |
|----------|-------------|
| nCid | Communications device to affect |

**Table D.26 Arguments of SetCommBreak**

## SetCommEventMask

This function activates and obtains the event mask of an identified nCid communications device.

```
Declare Function SetCommEventMask Lib "User" (ByVal nCid as Integer, nEvtMask as Integer) As Long
```

| Argument | Description |
|----------|-------------|
| nCid | Communications device |
| nEvtMask | Indicates which events in the table below to activate |

**Table D.27 Arguments of SetCommEventMask**

| Event | Description |
|-------|-------------|
| EV_BREAK | Determines when a break is found on input |
| EV-CTS | Determines when the clear-to-send (CTS) signal alters state |
| EV-DSR | Determines when the data-set-read (DSR) signal alters state |
| EV_ERR | Determines when a line-status error occurs |
| EV_PERR | Determines when a printer error is found on a parallel device |
| EV_RING | Determines when a ring indicator is detected |
| EV_RLSD | Determines when the receive-line-signal-detect (RLSD) signal alters state |
| EV_RXCHAR | Determines when characters are accepted and moved to the receive queue |
| EV_RXFLAG | Determines when the event character is accepted and put into the receive queue |
| EV_TXEMPTY | Determines when the last character in the transmit queue is sent |

**Table D.28 Event Descriptions for SetCommEventMask**

## SetCommState

This function changes the state of a communications device to the setting indicated by the device control block in the lpDCB argument.

```
Declare Function SetCommState Lib "User" ()
```

| Argument | Description |
|----------|-------------|
| lpDCB | Points to the DCB data structure that contains the communications setting |

**Table D.29 Argument of SetCommState**

## TransmitCommChar

This function places the character identified in the cChar argument at the head of the transmit queue of the communications device specified in the nCid argument.

```
Declare Function TransmitCommChar Lib "User" (ByVal nCid As Integer, ByVal cChar As Integer) As
Integer
```

| Argument | Description |
|----------|-------------|
| nCid | Communications device |
| cChar | Contains the character to transmit |

**Table D.30 Arguments of TransmitCommChar**

## UngetCommChar

This function places the character in the cChar argument into the receive queue of the nCid communications device.

```
Declare Function UngetCommChar Lib "User" (ByVal nCid As Integer, ByVal cChar As Integer) As Integer
```

| Argument | Description |
|----------|-------------|
| nCid | Communications device |
| cChar | Determines the character to place in the receive queue |

**Table D.31 Arguments of UngetCommChar**

## WriteComm

This function transfers the characters in the lpBuf buffer to the nCid communications device.

```
Declare Function WriteComm Lib "User" (ByVal nCid As Integer, ByVal lpBuf As String, ByVal nSize As
Integer) As Integer
```

| Argument | Description |
|----------|-------------|
| nCid | Communications device |
| lpBuf | Identifies the buffer that holds the characters to be sent |
| nSize | Indicates the number of characters to transmit |

**Table D.32 Arguments of WriteComm**

## Communications Variables in CONSTANT.TXT

```
Global Const SETXOFF = 1
Global Const SETXON = 2
Global Const SETRTS = 3
Global Const CLRRTS = 4
Global Const SETDTR = 5
Global Const CLRDTR = 6
Global Const RESETDEV = 7
Global Const LPTx = &H80
Global Const EV_RXCHAR = &H1
```

```
Global Const EV_RXFLAG = &H2
Global Const EV_TXEMPTY = &H4
Global Const EV_CTS = &H8
Global Const EV_DSR = &H10
Global Const EV_RLSD = &H20
Global Const EV_BREAK = &H40
Global Const EV_ERR = &H80
Global Const EV_RING = &H100
Global Const EV_PERR = &H200
Global Const NOPARITY = 0
Global Const ODDPARITY = 1
Global Const EVENPARITY = 2
Global Const MARKPARITY = 3
Global Const SPACEPARITY = 4
Global Const ONESTOPBIT = 0
Global Const ONE5STOPBITS = 1
Global Const TWOSTOPBITS = 2
Global Const IGNORE = 0
Global Const INFINITE = &HFFFF
Global Const CE_RXOVER = &H1
Global Const CE_OVERRUN = &H2
Global Const CE_RXPARITY = &H4
Global Const CE_FRAME = &H8
Global Const CE_BREAK = &H10
Global Const CE_CTSTO = &H20
Global Const CE_DSRTO = &H40
Global Const CE_RLSDTO = &H80
Global Const CE_TXFULL = &H100
Global Const CE_PTO = &H200
Global Const CE_IOE = &H400
Global Const CE_DNS = &H800
Global Const CE_OOP = &H1000
Global Const CE_MODE = &H8000
Global Const IE_BADID = (-1)
Global Const IE_OPEN = (-2)
Global Const IE_NOPEN = (-3)
Global Const IE_MEMORY = (-4)
Global Const IE_DEFAULT = (-5)
Global Const IE_HARDWARE = (-10)
Global Const IE_BYTESIZE = (-11)
Global Const IE_BAUDRATE = (-12)
Global Const EV_RXCHAR = &H1
Global Const EV_RXFLAG = &H2
Global Const EV_TXEMPTY = &H4
Global Const EV_CTS = &H8
Global Const EV_DSR = &H10
Global Const EV_RLSD = &H20
Global Const EV_BREAK = &H40
Global Const EV_ERR = &H80
Global Const EV_RING = &H100
Global Const EV_PERR = &H200
Global Const SETXOFF = 1
Global Const SETXON = 2
Global Const SETRTS = 3
Global Const CLRRTS = 4
Global Const SETDTR = 5
Global Const CLRDTR = 6
Global Const RESETDEV = 7
Global Const LPTx = &H80
```

# Debugging functions

### DebugBreak
This function sends a break to the debugger.

```
Declare Sub DebugBreak Lib "Kernel" ()
```

### FatalExit

This function shows Windows' current state on the debugging monitor and asks the user for instructions. You are prompted with three options: Abort, Break, or Ignore. Choose one of these options according to Table D. 33.

```
Declare Sub FatalExit Lib "Kernel" (ByVal Code As Integer)
```

| Argument | Description |
| --- | --- |
| Code | The error code to show on the screen |

**Table D.33 Argument of FatalExit**

| Response | Description |
| --- | --- |
| A (Abort) | Terminates Windows |
| B (Break) | Emulates a non-maskable interrupt (NMI) to access the debugger |
| I (Ignore) | Ignores the message |

**Table D.34 Responses to FatalExit function**

### OutputDebugString

This function transmits a debugging message to the debugger.

```
Declare Sub OutputDebugString Lib "Kernel" (ByVal lpOutputString As String)
```

| Argument | Description |
| --- | --- |
| lpOutputString | Null-terminated string |

**Table D.35 Arguments of OutputDebugString**

### ValidateCodeSegments

This function discovers if any code segments were changed by random memory overwrites.

```
Declare Sub ValidateCodeSegments Lib "Kernel" ()
```

### ValidateFreeSpaces

This function looks through free segments of memory for valid contents.

```
Declare Function ValidateFreeSpaces Lib "Kernel" () As Long
```

## File I/O functions

### GetDriveType

This function indicates if a disk drive is removable, fixed, or remote. Table D. 37 shows the possible returned values.

```
Declare Function GetDriveType Lib "Kernel" (ByVal nDrive As Integer) As Integer
```

| Argument | Description |
| --- | --- |
| nDrive | Indicates which drive is to be checked by this function where Drive A is 0, Drive B is one (1), Drive C is two (2), and so on |

**Table D.36 Argument of GetDriveType**

| Returned Value | Description |
| --- | --- |
| DRIVE_REMOVEABLE | The disk is removable |
| DRIVE_FIXED | The disk cannot be removed |
| DRIVE_REMOTE | The disk is a network drive |

**Table D.37 Returned value of GetDriveType**

## GetSystemDirectory

This function provides the path of the Windows System subdirectory. The System subdirectory contains the Windows libraries, drives, and screen font files.

```
Declare Function GetSystemDirectory Lib "Kernel" (ByVal lpBuffer As String, ByVal nSize As Integer)
As Integer
```

| Argument | Description |
|----------|-------------|
| lpBuffer | Points to the buffer that will receive the returned pathname string |
| nSize | Maximum size of the buffer |

Table D.38 Arguments of GetSystemDirectory

## GetTempDrive

This function provides the letter of the optimal drive for temporary files.

```
Declare Function GetTempDrive Lib "Kernel" (ByVal cDriveLetter as Integer) As Integer
```

| Argument | Description |
|----------|-------------|
| cDriveLetter | The disk drive letter |

Table D.39 Argument of GetTempDrive

## GetTempFileName

This function creates a temporary filename.

```
Declare Function GetTempFileName Lib "Kernel" (ByVal cDriveLetter as Integer, ByVal lpPrefixString
As String, ByVal wUnique As Integer, ByVal lpTempFileName As String) As Integer
```

| Argument | Description |
|----------|-------------|
| cDriveLetter | Indicates the suggested drive (0 means the default drive) |
| lpPreflxString | Temporary file's prefix filename |
| wUnique | Unique identifying integer |
| lpTempFileName | Buffer that receives the temporary file name |

Table D.40 Arguments of GetTempFileName

## GetWindowsDirectory

This function provides the path of the Windows directory. The Windows directory contains windows applications, initialization, and help files.

```
Declare Function GetWindowsDirectory Lib "Kernel" (ByVal lpBuffer As String, ByVal nSize As Integer)
As Integer
```

| Argument | Description |
|----------|-------------|
| lpBuffer | The buffer that will receive the path |
| nSize | Maximum size of the buffer |

Table D.41 Arguments of GetWindowsDirectory

## _lclose

This function closes the file indicated in the hFile argument.

```
Declare Function lclose Lib "Kernel" Alias "_lclose" (ByVal hFile As Integer) As Integer
```

| Argument | Description |
|----------|-------------|
| hFile | The MS-DOS handle of the file to be closed |

Table D.42 Argument of _lclose

## _lcreat

This function creates a file or opens and truncates an existing file.

```
Declare Function lcreat Lib "Kernel" Alias "_lcreat" (ByVal lpPathName As String, ByVal iAttribute
As Integer) As Integer
```

| Argument | Description |
|----------|-------------|
| lpPathName | Name of the file to open |
| iAttribute | File attributes with one of the values in the next table |

**Table D.43 Arguments of _Lcreate**

| Value | Description |
|-------|-------------|
| 0 | Normal - can be read and written |
| 1 | Read-only - cannot be opened for write |
| 2 | Hidden - invisible to directory search |
| 3 | System - invisible to directory search |

**Table D.44 Values of _lcreate**

## _llseek

This function positions the pointer to a previously opened file named in the hFile argument.

```
Declare Function llseek Lib "Kernel" Alias "_llseek" (ByVal hFile As Integer, ByVal lOffset As Long,
ByVal iOrigin As Integer) As Long
```

| Argument | Description |
|----------|-------------|
| hFile | MS-DOS handle for the file |
| lOffset | Number of bytes to move the pointer |
| iOrigin | Starting position and direction of the pointer. This must one of the values in the following table |

**Table D.45 Arguments of _llseek**

| Value | Description |
|-------|-------------|
| 0 | Place the file pointer lOffset bytes from the beginning of the file |
| 1 | Place the file pointer lOffset bytes from the current position of the file |
| 2 | Place the file pointer lOffset bytes from the end of the file |

**Table D.46 Values of _llseek**

## _lopen

This function opens an existing file named in the lpPathName argument.

```
Declare Function lopen Lib "Kernel" Alias "_lopen" (ByVal lpPathName As String, ByVal iReadWrite As
Integer) As Integer
```

| Argument | Description |
|----------|-------------|
| lpPathName | Name and path of the file |
| iReadWrite | Indicates whether to open the file with read or write access. This must be one of the following values |

**Table D.47 Argument of _lopen**

| Value | Description |
|-------|-------------|
| OF_READ | Read only |
| OF_READWRITE | Read and write |
| OF_SHARE_COMPAT | Compatibility mode |
| OF_SHARE_DENY_NONE | Allows other processes read-write access to the file |
| OF_SHARE_DENY_READ | Refuses other processes read access to the file |
| OF_SHARE_DENY_WRITE | Refuses other processes write access to the file |
| OF_SHARE_EXCLUSIVE | Exclusive mode |
| OF_WRITE | Write only |

Table of D.48 Values of _lopen

### _lread

This function reads the data from a file named in the hFile argument.

```
Declare Function lread Lib "Kernel" Alias "_lread" (ByVal hFile As Integer, ByVal lpBuffer As String,
ByVal wBytes As Integer) As Integer
```

| Argument | Description |
|----------|-------------|
| hFile | MS-DOS handle of the file to read |
| lpBuffer | Buffer to receive the read data |
| wBytes | Number of bytes to read from the file |

Table D.49 Arguments of _lread

### _lwrite

This function writes data to the file named in the hFile argument.

```
Declare Function lwrite Lib "Kernel" Alias "_lwrite" (ByVal hFile As Integer, ByVal lpBuffer As
String, ByVal wBytes As Integer) As Integer
```

| Argument | Description |
|----------|-------------|
| hFile | MS-DOS file handle of the file to be read |
| lpBuffer | Buffer holding the data to be written |
| wBytes | Number of bytes to be written to the file |

Table D.50 Arguments of _lwrite

### OpenFile

This function creates, opens, reopens, or deletes the file named in the lpFileName argument.

```
Declare Function OpenFile Lib "Kernel" (ByVal lpFileName As String, lpReOpenBuff As OFSTRUCT, ByVal
wStyle As Integer) As Integer
```

| Argument | Description |
|----------|-------------|
| lpFileName | Name of the file to open |
| lpReOpenBuff | OFSTRUCT data structure that will receive the information about the file when it is opened |
| wStyle | The action to take. This must be a combination of the values in the following table |

Table D.51 Arguments of OpenFile

| Value | Description |
|---|---|
| OF_CANCEL | Puts a cancel button in the OF_PROMPT dialog box |
| OF_CREATE | Creates a new file |
| OF_DELETE | Deletes the file |
| OF_EXIST | Checks if the file exists |
| OF_PARSE | Puts information about file in the OFSTRUCT data structure |
| OF_PROMPT | Displays a dialog box if Windows could not find the file |
| OF_READ | Read-only file |
| OF_READWRITE | Read-write file |
| OF_REOPEN | Opens file with information in re-open buffer |
| OF_SHARE-COMPAT | Compatibility mode |
| OF_SHARE_DENY_NONE | Other processes may have read and write access to the file |
| OF_SHARE_DENY_READ | Refuses other processes read access |
| OF_SHARE_DENY_WRITE | Refuses other processes write access |
| OF_SHARE_EXCLUSIVE | Exclusive mode |
| OF_VERIFY | Checks the date and time of the file |
| OF_WRITE | Write only |

**Table D.52 Values of OpenFile**

### SetHandleCount

This function modifies the number of handles available to a task.

```
Declare Function SetHandleCount Lib "Kernel" (ByVal wNumber As Integer) As Integer
```

| Argument | Description |
|---|---|
| wNumber | Number of file handles |

**Table D.53 Argument of SetHandleCount**

### File Variable Definitions

```
Global Const DRIVE_REMOVABLE = 2
Global Const DRIVE_FIXED = 3
Global Const DRIVE_REMOTE = 4
Global Const OF_READ = &H0
Global Const OF_WRITE = &H1
Global Const OF_READWRITE = &H2
Global Const OF_SHARE_COMPAT = &H0
Global Const OF_SHARE_EXCLUSIVE = &H10
Global Const OF_SHARE_DENY_WRITE = &H20
Global Const OF_SHARE_DENY_READ = &H30
Global Const OF_SHARE_DENY_NONE = &H40
Global Const OF_PARSE = &H100
Global Const OF_DELETE = &H200
Global Const OF_VERIFY = &H400
Global Const OF_CANCEL = &H800
Global Const OF_CREATE = &H1000
Global Const OF_PROMPT = &H2000
Global Const OF_EXIST = &H4000
Global Const OF_REOPEN = &H8000
```

# Initialization-file functions

### GetPrivateProfileInt

This function provides the integer value of a section from an initialization file.

```
Declare Function GetPrivateProfileInt Lib "Kernel" (ByVal lpApplicationName As String, ByVal
lpKeyName As String, ByVal nDefault As Integer, ByVal lpFileName As String) As Integer
```

| Argument | Description |
|---|---|
| lpApplicationName | Windows Application name that appears in the initialization file |
| lpKeyName | Key Name |
| nDefault | Default value of the key |
| lpFileName | Name and path of the Initialization file |

**Table D.54 Arguments of GetPrivateProfileInt**

## GetPrivateProfileString

This function provides a character string from an initialization file and places it in a buffer.

```
Declare Function GetPrivateProfileString Lib "Kernel" (ByVal lpApplicationName As String, ByVal
lpKeyName As String, ByVal lpDefault As String, ByVal lpReturnedString As String, ByVal nSize As
Integer, ByVal lpFileName As String) As Integer
```

| Argument | Description |
|---|---|
| lpApplicationName | Windows Application name that appears in the initialization file |
| lpKeyName | KeyName |
| lpDefault | Default value of the key |
| lpReturnedString | Buffer that will receive the string |
| nSize | Maximum number of characters to be transmitted to the buffer |
| lpFileName | Name and path of the initialization file |

**Table D.55 Arguments of GetPrivateProfileString**

### GetProfileInt

This function provides the value of an integer key from the Windows initialization file, WIN.INI.

```
Declare Function GetProfileInt Lib "Kernel" (ByVal lpAppName As String, ByVal lpKeyName As String,
ByVal nDefault As Integer) As Integer
```

| Argument | Description |
|---|---|
| lpAppName | Windows Application name that appears in the Windows initialization file |
| lpKeyName | KeyName |
| nDefault | Default value of the key |

**Table D.56 Arguments of GetProfileInt**

## GetProfileString

This function provides a character string from the Windows initialization file, WIN.INI, and places it in a buffer.

```
Declare Function GetProfileString Lib "Kernel" (ByVal lpAppName As String, ByVal lpKeyName As
String, ByVal lpDefault As String, ByVal lpReturnedString As String, ByVal nSize As Integer) As
Integer
```

| Argument | Description |
|---|---|
| lpAppName | Application Name |
| lpKeyName | KeyName |
| lpDefault | Default value of the string |
| lpReturnedString | Buffer that will receive the character string |
| nSize | Number of characters to be transmitted to the buffer |

**Table D. 57 Arguments of GetProfileString**

### WritePrivateProfileString

This function writes the string in the lpString argument under the heading in the specified initialization file.

```
Declare Function WritePrivateProfileString Lib "Kernel" (ByVal lpApplicationName As String, ByVal lpKeyName As String, ByVal lpString As String, ByVal lplFileName As String) As Integer
```

| Argument | Description |
|----------|-------------|
| lpApplicationName | Application heading in initialization file |
| lpKeyName | KeyName |
| lpString | String to place under the KeyName in the initialization file |
| lpFileName | Name and path of the initialization file |

Table D.58 Arguments of WritePrivateProfileString

### WriteProfileString

This function writes the string in the lpString argument under the heading in the Windows initialization file, WIN.INI.

```
Declare Function WriteProfileString Lib "Kernel" (ByVal lpApplicationName As String, ByVal lpKeyName As String, ByVal lpString As String) As Integer
```

| Argument | Description |
|----------|-------------|
| lpApplicationName | Application heading in the WIN.INI file |
| lpKeyName | KeyName |
| lpString | String to place under the KeyName in the initialization file |

Table D.59 Arguments of WriteProfileString

## Memory-management functions

### GetFreeSpace

This function obtains the numbers of bytes available in the global heap.

```
Declare Function GetFreeSpace Lib "Kernel" (ByVal wFlags As Integer) As Long
```

| Argument | Description |
|----------|-------------|
| wFlags | Indicates whether to scan the heap above or below the EMS bank line |

Table D.60 Argument of GetFreeSpace

### GetWinFlags

This function provides the memory configuration of the current system.

```
Declare Function GetWinFlags Lib "Kernel" () As Long
```

**Values in CONSTANT.TXT**

| Returned Value | Description |
|----------------|-------------|
| WF_80x87 | System contains a math coprocessor |
| WF_CPU086 | 8086 CPU |
| WF_CPU186 | 80186 CPU |
| WF_CPU286 | 80286 CPU |
| WF_CPU386 | 80386 CPU |
| WF_CPU486 | 80486 CPU |
| WF_ENHANCED | Enhanced 386 Mode |
| WF_LARGEFRAME | Windows running in EMS Large-frame memory |

| WF_PMODE | Windows running in protected mode |
| WF_SMALLFRAME | Windows running in EMS small-frame memory |
| WF_STANDARD | Standard Mode |

## GlobalAlloc

This function allocates the number of bytes of memory set in the dwBytes argument.

```
Declare Function GlobalAlloc Lib "Kernel" (ByVal wFlags As Integer, ByVal dwBytes As Long) As Integer
```

| Argument | Description |
|---|---|
| wFlags | Sets up one or more flags that indicate how to allocate the memory (see Table D.62) |
| dwBytes | Indicates the number of bytes to be allocated |

**Table D.61 Arguments of GlobalAlloc**

| Value | Meaning |
|---|---|
| GMEM_DDESHARE | Allocates shareable memory for Dynamic Data Exchange |
| GMEM_DISCARDABLE | Allocates discardable memory |
| GMEM_FIXED | Allocates shareable memory |
| LMEM_MOVEABLE | Allocates moveable memory |
| GMEM_NOCOMPACT | Will not compact or discard to satisfy allocation request |
| GMEM_NODISCARD | Will not discard to satisfy allocation request |
| GMEM_NOT_BANKED | Allocates non-banked memory |
| GMEM_NOTIFY | Initiates notification routine if memory object is not discarded |
| GMEM_ZEROINIT | Initializes memory to 0 |

**Table D.62 Values of GlobalAlloc**

## GlobalCompact

This function provides the number of free bytes of global memory indicated in the dwMinFree argument. The GlobalCompact function will compact or discard memory if necessary.

```
Declare Function GlobalCompact Lib "Kernel" (ByVal dwMinFree As Long) As Long
```

| Argument | Description |
|---|---|
| dwMinFree | Number of free bytes needed |

**Table D.63 Argument of GlobalCompact**

## GlobalFlags

This function provides the information about the global memory block in the hMem argument.

```
Declare Function GlobalFlags Lib "Kernel" (ByVal hMem As Integer) As Integer
```

| Argument | Description |
|---|---|
| hMem | The global memory block |

**Table D.64 Argument of GloblaFlags**

| Value | Description |
|---|---|
| GMEM_DDESHARE | The block can be shared in Dynamic Data Exchange (DDE) |
| GMEM_DISCARDABLE | This block may be discarded |
| GMEM_DISCARDED | This block has been discarded |
| GMEM_NOT_BANKED | This block cannot be banked |

**Table D.65 Values of GlobalFlags**

## GlobalFree

This function frees the memory block named in the hMem argument.

```
Declare Function GlobalFree Lib "Kernel" (ByVal hMem As Integer) As Integer
```

| Argument | Description |
|----------|-------------|
| hMem | The global memory block to free |

Table D.66 Argument of GlobalFree

## GlobalHandle

This function provides the handle of the global memory object with the segment address indicated in the wMem argument.

```
Declare Function GlobalHandle Lib "Kernel" (ByVal wMem As Integer) As Long
```

| Argument | Description |
|----------|-------------|
| wMem | The segment address or selector of the global memory object |

Table D.67 Argument of GlobalHandle

## GlobalLock

This function provides the pointer to the global memory object in the hMem argument

```
Declare Function GlobalLock Lib "Kernel" (ByVal hMem As Integer) As Long
```

| Argument | Description |
|----------|-------------|
| hMem | The global memory block to be locked |

Table D.68 Argument of GlobalLock

## GlobalLRUNewest

This function places the global memory object in the hMem argument into the newest and least recently used (LRU) position in memory.

```
Declare Function GlobalLRUNewest Lib "Kernel" (ByVal hMem As Integer) As Integer
```

| Argument | Description |
|----------|-------------|
| hMem | The global memory object to be moved |

Table D.69 Argument of GlobalRunewest

## GlobalLRUOldest

This function places the global memory object in the hMem argument in the oldest least recently used (LRU) position in memory.

```
Declare Function GlobalLRUOldest Lib "Kernel" (ByVal hMem As Integer) As Integer
```

| Argument | Description |
|----------|-------------|
| hMem | The global memory object to be moved |

Table D.70 Argument of GlobalRuOldest

## GlobalReAlloc

This function increases or decreases the number of bytes of the global memory block in the hMem argument to the amount set in the dwBytes argument.

```
Declare Function GlobalReAlloc Lib "Kernel" (ByVal hMem As Integer, ByVal dwBytes As Long, ByVal
wFlags As Integer) As Integer
```

| Argument | Description |
|---|---|
| hMem | The global memory block to reallocate |
| dwBytes | New size of the global memory block |
| wFlags | The value of this argument indicates how to reallocate the global memory block according to the next table |

**Table D.71 Arguments of GlobalReAlloc**

| Value | Description |
|---|---|
| GMEM_DISCARDABLE | Memory may be discarded |
| GMEM_MODIFY | Memory flags are modified but the global memory is not reallocated |
| GMEM_MOVEABLE | Memory is moveable |
| GMEM_NOCOMPACT | Memory may not be compacted or discarded |
| GMEM_NODISCARD | Memory may not be discarded |
| GMEM_ZEROINIT | If the block is increased in size, additional memory is initialized to 0 |

**Table D.72 Values of GlobalReAlloc**

## GlobalSize

This function finds the current size in bytes of the global memory block named in the hMem argument.

```
Declare Function GlobalSize Lib "Kernel" (ByVal hMem As Integer) As Long
```

| Argument | Description |
|---|---|
| hMem | The global memory block |

**Table D.73 Argument of GlobalSize**

## GlobalUnlock

This function unlocks the global memory block named in the hMem argument.

```
Declare Function GlobalUnlock Lib "Kernel" (ByVal hMem As Integer) As Integer
```

| Argument | Description |
|---|---|
| hMem | The global memory block to be unlocked |

**Table D.74 Argument of GlobalUnlock**

## GlobalUnwire

This function unlocks the global memory segment that was locked with the GlobalWire function.

```
Declare Function GlobalUnWire Lib "Kernel" (ByVal hMem As Integer) As Integer
```

| Argument | Description |
|---|---|
| hMem | The segment to unlock |

**Table D.75 Argument of GlobalUnwire**

## GlobalWire

This function places a segment in low memory and locks it.

```
Declare Function GlobalWire Lib "Kernel" (ByVal hMem As Integer) As Long
```

| Argument | Description |
|----------|-------------|
| hMem | The segment to lock |

**Table D.76 Argument of GlobalWire**

## LimitEMSPages

This function places a limit on the amount of expanded memory that Windows will assign to an application.

```
Declare Sub LimitEmsPages Lib "Kernel" (ByVal dwKbytes As Long)
```

| Argument | Description |
|----------|-------------|
| dwkbytes | The amount of kilobytes of expanded memory that applications may have access to |

**Table D.77 Argument of LimitEMSPages**

## LocalAlloc

This function allocates a number of bytes of memory set in the dwBytes argument.

```
Declare Function LocalAlloc Lib "Kernel" (ByVal wFlags As Integer, ByVal wBytes As Integer) As
Integer
```

| Argument | Description |
|----------|-------------|
| wFlags | Sets up one or more flags that indicate how to allocate the memory (see Table D. 79) |
| dwBytes | Indicates the number of bytes to be allocated |

**Table D.78 Argument of LocalAlloc**

| Value | Meaning |
|-------|---------|
| LMEM_DISCARDABLE | Allocates discardable memory |
| LMEM_FIXED | Allocates shareable memory |
| LMEM_MODIFY | Modifies the LMEM_DISCARDABLE flag |
| LMEM_MOVEABLE | Allocates moveable memory |
| LMEM_NOCOMPACT | Will not compact or discard to satisfy allocation request |
| LMEM_NODISCARD | Will not discard to satisfy allocation request |
| LMEM_ZEROINIT | Initializes memory to 0 |

**Table D.79 Values of LocalAlloc**

## LocalCompact

This function provides the number of free bytes of memory indicated in the dwMinFree argument. The LocalCompact function will compact or discard memory if this is necessary.

```
Declare Function LocalCompact Lib "Kernel" (ByVal wMinFree As Integer) As Integer
```

| Argument | Description |
|----------|-------------|
| dwMinFree | Number of free bytes needed |

**Table D.80 Argument of LocalCompact**

## LocalFlags

This function provides information about the local memory block in the hMem argument.

```
Declare Function LocalFlags Lib "Kernel" (ByVal hMem As Integer) As Integer
```

| Argument | Description |
|----------|-------------|
| hMem | The local memory block |

**Table D.81 Argument of LocalFlags**

| Value | Description |
|-------|-------------|
| LMEM_DISCARDABLE | This block may be discarded |
| LMEM_DISCARDED | This block has been discarded |

**Table D.82 Values of LocalFlags**

## LocalFree

This function frees the local memory block named in the hMem argument.

```
Declare Function LocalFree Lib "Kernel" (ByVal hMem As Integer) As Integer
```

| Argument | Description |
|----------|-------------|
| hMem | The local memory block to free |

**Table D.83 Argument of LocalFree**

## LocalHandle

This function provides the handle of the local memory object with the segment address indicated in the wMem argument.

```
Declare Function LocalHandle Lib "Kernel" (ByVal wMem As Integer) As Integer
```

| Argument | Description |
|----------|-------------|
| wMem | The segment address or selector of the global memory object |

**Table D.84 Argument of LocalHandle**

## LocalInit

This function initializes a local heap in the segment set in the wSegment argument.

```
Declare Function LocalInit Lib "Kernel" (ByVal wSegment As Integer, ByVal pStart As Integer, ByVal
pEnd As Integer) As Integer
```

| Argument | Description |
|----------|-------------|
| wSegment | The segment address of the segment that contains the local heap |
| pStart | The starting address of the local heap |
| pEnd | The ending address of the local heap |

**Table D.85 Arguments of LocalInit**

## LocalLock

This function provides the pointer to the local memory object in the hMem argument.

```
Declare Function LocalLock Lib "Kernel" (ByVal hMem As Integer) As Integer '(returns a near pointer)
```

| Argument | Description |
|----------|-------------|
| hMem | The local memory block to be locked |

**Table D.86 Argument of LocalLock**

## LocalReAlloc

This function increases or decreases the number of bytes of the local memory block in the hMem argument to the amount set in the dwBytes argument.

```
Declare Function LocalReAlloc Lib "Kernel" (ByVal hMem As Integer, ByVal wBytes As Integer, ByVal wFlags As Integer) As Integer
```

| Argument | Description |
|----------|-------------|
| hMem | The local memory block to reallocate |
| dwBytes | New size of the local memory block |
| wFlags | The value of this argument indicates how to reallocate the local memory block according to Table D. 88 |

**Table D.87 Arguments of LocalReAlloc**

| Value | Description |
|-------|-------------|
| LMEM_DISCARDABLE | Memory may be discarded |
| LMEM_MODIFY | Memory flags are modified but the local memory is not reallocated |
| LMEM_MOVEABLE | Memory is moveable |
| LMEM_NOCOMPACT | Memory may not be compacted or discarded |
| LMEM_NODISCARD | Memory may not be discarded |
| LMEM_ZEROINIT | If the block is increased in size, additional memory is initialized to 0 |

**Table D.88 Values of LocalReAlloc**

## LocalShrink

This function shrinks the heap named in the hSeg argument to the size in the wSize argument.

```
Declare Function LocalShrink Lib "Kernel" (ByVal hSeg As Integer, ByVal wSize As Integer) As Integer
```

| Argument | Description |
|----------|-------------|
| hSeg | The segment that contains the local heap |
| wSize | The desired size for the local heap |

**Table D.89 Arguments of LocalShrink**

## LocalSize

This function finds the current size in bytes of the local memory block named in the hMem argument.

```
Declare Function LocalSize Lib "Kernel" (ByVal hMem As Integer) As Integer
```

| Argument | Description |
|----------|-------------|
| hMem | The local memory block |

**Table D.90 Argument of LocalSize**

## LocalUnlock

This function unlocks the local memory block named in the hMem argument.

```
Declare Function LocalUnlock Lib "Kernel" (ByVal hMem As Integer) As Integer
```

| Argument | Description |
|----------|-------------|
| hMem | The local memory block to be unlocked |

**Table D.91 Argument of LocalUnlock**

## Locksegment

This function locks the segment identified by its address in the wSegment argument.

```
Declare Function LockSegment Lib "Kernel" (ByVal wSegment As Integer) As Integer
```

| Argument | Description |
|----------|-------------|
| wSegment | The address of the segment to be locked |

**Table D.92 Argument of Locksegment**

## SetSwapAreaSize

This function raises the amount of memory that an application may utilize for its code segments.

```
Declare Function SetSwapAreaSize Lib "Kernel" (ByVal rsSize As Integer) As Long
```

| Argument | Description |
|----------|-------------|
| rsSize | The number of 16-byte paragraphs asked for by the application for use as a code segment |

**Table D.93 Argument of SetSwapAreaSize**

## SwitchStackBack

This function determines the current stack of the task's data segment.

```
Declare Sub SwitchStackBack Lib "Kernel" ()
```

## SwitchStackTo

This function changes the stack of a current task to another data segment.

```
Declare Sub SwitchStackTo Lib "Kernel" (ByVal wStackSegment As Integer, ByVal wStackPointer As
Integer, ByVal wStackTop As Integer)
```

| Argument | Description |
|----------|-------------|
| wStackSegment | Data segment that will contain the stack |
| wStackPointer | The offset of the beginning of the stack |
| wStackTop | The offset of the top of the stack from the beginning of the stack |

**Table D.94 Arguments of SwitchStackTo**

## UnlockSegment

This function unlocks a specified data segment.

```
Declare Function UnlockSegment Lib "Kernel" (ByVal wSegment As Integer) As Integer
```

| Argument | Description |
|----------|-------------|
| wSegment | The segment address |

**Table D.95 Argument of UnlockSegment**

## Memory Management Definitions in CONSTANT.TXT

```
Global Const WF_PMODE = &H1
Global Const WF_CPU286 = &H2
Global Const WF_CPU386 = &H4
Global Const WF_CPU486 = &H8
Global Const WF_STANDARD = &H10
Global Const WF_WIN286 = &H10
Global Const WF_ENHANCED = &H20
Global Const WF_WIN386 = &H20
Global Const WF_CPU086 = &H40
Global Const WF_CPU186 = &H80
Global Const WF_LARGEFRAME = &H100
Global Const WF_SMALLFRAME = &H200
Global Const WF_80x87 = &H400
Global Const GMEM_FIXED = &H0
Global Const GMEM_MOVEABLE = &H2
```

```
Global Const GMEM_NOCOMPACT = &H10
Global Const GMEM_NODISCARD = &H20
Global Const GMEM_ZEROINIT = &H40
Global Const GMEM_MODIFY = &H80
Global Const GMEM_DISCARDABLE = &H100
Global Const GMEM_NOT_BANKED = &H1000
Global Const GMEM_SHARE = &H2000
Global Const GMEM_DDESHARE = &H2000
Global Const GMEM_NOTIFY = &H4000
Global Const GMEM_LOWER = GMEM_NOT_BANKED
Global Const GHND = (GMEM_MOVEABLE Or GMEM_ZEROINIT)
Global Const GPTR = (GMEM_FIXED Or GMEM_ZEROINIT)
Global Const GMEM_DISCARDED = &H4000
Global Const GMEM_LOCKCOUNT = &HFF
Global Const LMEM_FIXED = &H0
Global Const LMEM_MOVEABLE = &H2
Global Const LMEM_NOCOMPACT = &H10
Global Const LMEM_NODISCARD = &H20
Global Const LMEM_ZEROINIT = &H40
Global Const LMEM_MODIFY = &H80
Global Const LMEM_DISCARDABLE = &HF00
Global Const LHND = (LMEM_MOVEABLE+LMEM_ZEROINIT)
Global Const LPTR = (LMEM_FIXED+LMEM_ZEROINIT)
Global Const NONZEROLHND = (LMEM_MOVEABLE)
Global Const NONZEROLPTR = (LMEM_FIXED)
Global Const LNOTIFY_OUTOFMEM = 0
Global Const LNOTIFY_MOVE = 1
Global Const LNOTIFY_DISCARD = 2
```

# Module-management functions

### FreeLibrary

This function reduces the reference count of the loaded library module.

```
Declare Sub FreeLibrary Lib "Kernel" (ByVal hLibModule As Integer)
```

| Argument | Description |
|---|---|
| hLibModule | The loaded library module |

**Table D.96 Argument of FreeLibrary**

### FreeModule

This function reduces the reference count of the loaded module by one.

```
Declare Sub FreeModule Lib "Kernel" (ByVal hModule As Integer)
```

| Argument | Description |
|---|---|
| hModule | The loaded module |

**Table D.97 Argument of FreeModule**

### GetInstanceData

This function tramsmits data from another instance of an application into the data area of the present instance.

```
Declare Function GetInstanceData Lib "Kernel" (ByVal hInstance As Integer, ByVal pData As Integer, ByVal nCount As Integer) As Integer
```

| Argument | Description |
|---|---|
| hInstance | Previous call of the application |
| pData | Buffer in the present instance |
| nCount | Number of bytes to transmit |

**Table D.98 Arguments of GetInstanceData**

### GetModuleFileName

This function finds the full pathname of the executable file from which a module is loaded.

```
Declare Function GetModuleFileName Lib "Kernel" (ByVal hModule As Integer, ByVal lpFilename As
String, ByVal nSize As Integer) As Integer
```

| Argument | Description |
|----------|-------------|
| hModule | The module or instance of the module |
| lpFileName | The buffer to receive the filename |
| nSize | The maximum number of characters to transmit |

**Table D.99 Arguments of GetModuleFileName**

### GetModuleHandle

This function obtains the handle of the module named in the lpModuleName argument.

```
Declare Function GetModuleHandle Lib "Kernel" (ByVal lpModuleName As String) As Integer
```

| Argument | Description |
|----------|-------------|
| lpModuleName | Name of the module |

**Table D.100 Argument of GetModuleHandle**

### GetModuleUsage

This function provides the reference count of an indicated module.

```
Declare Function GetModuleUsage Lib "Kernel" (ByVal hModule As Integer) As Integer
```

| Argument | Description |
|----------|-------------|
| hModule | The Module or instance of the module |

**Table D.101 Argument of GetModuleUsage**

### GetVersion

This function returns the current version of Windows.

```
Declare Function GetVersion Lib "Kernel" () As Integer
```

### LoadLibrary

This function loads the library module indicated by the lpLibFileName argument.

```
Declare Function LoadLibrary Lib "Kernel" (ByVal lpLibFileName As String) As Integer
```

| Argument | Description |
|----------|-------------|
| lpLibFileName | The name of the library to load |

**Table D.102 Argument of LoadLibrary**

## Optimization-tool functions

### ProfClear

This function removes all of the samples in the sampling buffer when the Microsoft Windows Profiler is running.

```
Declare Sub ProfClear Lib "User" ()
```

### ProfFinish

This function stops sampling and flushes the output buffer to disk when the Microsoft Windows Profiler is running.

```
Declare Sub ProfFinish Lib "User" ()
```

## ProfFlush

This function flushes the sampling buffer to disk when the Microsoft Windows Profiler is running.

```
Declare Sub ProfFlush Lib "User" ()
```

## ProfInsChk

This function checks if the Microsoft Windows Profile is running.

```
Declare Function ProfInsChk Lib "User" () As Integer
```

## ProfSampRate

This function determines the rate of code sampling when Microsoft Windows is running.

```
Declare Sub ProfSampRate Lib "User" (ByVal nRate286 As Integer, ByVal nRate386 As Integer)
```

| Argument | Description |
|----------|-------------|
| nRate286 | Indicates the sampling rate of Profiler when the application is running in standard or real mode |
| nRate386 | Indicates the sampling rate of Profiler when the application is running in 386 enhanced mode |

**Table D.103 Arguments of ProfSampRate**

| Value | Sampling Rate |
|-------|---------------|
| 1 | 1.22.070 microseconds |
| 2 | 244.141 microseconds |
| 3 | 488.281 microseconds |
| 4 | 976.562 microseconds |
| 5 | 1.953125 milliseconds |
| 6 | 3.90625 milliseconds |
| 7 | 7.8125 milliseconds |
| 8 | 15.625 milliseconds |
| 9 | 31.25 milliseconds |
| 10 | 62.5 milliseconds |
| 11 | 125 milliseconds |
| 12 | 250 milliseconds |
| 13 | 500 milliseconds |

**Table D.104 Values of ProfSampRate**

## ProfSetup

This function specifies the size of the output buffer when the Microsoft Windows Profiler is running under 386 enhanced mode.

```
Declare Sub ProfSetup Lib "User" (ByVal nBufferSize As Integer, ByVal nSamples As Integer)
```

| Argument | Description |
|----------|-------------|
| nBufferSize | Size of the ouput buffer in kilobytes |
| nSamples | How much sampling data Profiler writes to disk (0 indicates unlimited) |

**Table D.105 Arguments of ProfSetup**

## ProfStart

This function starts sampling when running Microsoft Windows Profiler.

```
Declare Sub ProfStart Lib "User" ()
```

## ProfStop

This function stops sampling when running Microsoft Windows Profiler.

```
Declare Sub ProfStop Lib "User" ()
```

## SwapRecording

If Microsoft Windows Swap is running, then this function begins or ends analyzing swapping behavior.

```
Declare Sub SwapRecording Lib "Kernel" (ByVal wFlag As Integer)
```

| Argument | Description |
|----------|-------------|
| wFlag | Indicates whether to start or stop the Swap analysis |

**Table D.106 Argument of SwapRecording**

| Value | Description |
|-------|-------------|
| 0 | Tells Swap to stop analyzing |
| 1 | Stores Swap calls, discards swap returns |
| 2 | Stores Swap calls, records a large amount of data |

**Table D.107 Values of SwapRecording**

# Resource-management functions

## AccessResource

This function returns the DOS file handle for the file indentified by the hInstance and hResInfo arguments.

```
Declare Function AccessResource Lib "Kernel" (ByVal hInstance As Integer, ByVal hResInfo As Integer)
As Integer
```

| Argument | Description |
|----------|-------------|
| hInstance | Executable file that contains the resource |
| hResInfo | Identifies the resource (handle created with FindResource) |

**Table D.108 Arguments of AccessResource**

## AllocResource

This function identifies the global memory block to allocate for a resource.

```
Declare Function AllocResource Lib "Kernel" (ByVal hInstance As Integer, ByVal hResInfo As Integer,
ByVal dwSize As Long) As Integer
```

| Argument | Description |
|----------|-------------|
| hInstance | Executable file that contains the resource |
| hResInfo | Indentifies a resource |
| dwSize | Minimum size in bytes |

**Table D.109 Arguments of AllocResource**

## FindResource

This function returns the location of a resource file.

```
Declare Function FindResource Lib "Kernel" (ByVal hInstance As Integer, ByVal lpName As String,
ByVal lpType As Any) As Integer
```

| Argument | Description |
|---|---|
| hInstance | Executable file that contains the resource |
| lpName | Null-terminated string that represents the name of the resource |
| lpType | Null-terminated string that stands for the type of resource. Table D. 111 contains predefined types |

**Table D.110 Arguments of FindResource**

| Value | Description |
|---|---|
| RT_ACCELERATOR | Accelerator table |
| RT_BITMAP | Bitmap resource |
| RT_DIALOG | Dialog box |
| RT_FONT | Font resource |
| RT_FONTDIR | Font directory resource |
| RT_MENU | Menu resource |
| RT_RCDATA | User-defined resource |

**Table D.111 Values of FindResource**

## FreeResource

This function returns a boolean value that indicates whether a resource is successfully removed from memory.

```
Declare Function FreeResource Lib "Kernel" (ByVal hResData As Integer) As Integer
```

| Argument | Type | Description |
|---|---|---|
| hResData | Handle | Identifies the resource to be removed from memory |

**Table D.112 Argument of FreeResource**

## LoadAccelerators

This function returns a boolean value that indicates whether an accelerator table is successfully loaded.

```
Declare Function LoadAccelerators Lib "User" (ByVal hInstance As Integer, ByVal lpTableName As String) As Integer
```

| Argument | Type | Description |
|---|---|---|
| hInstance | Handle | Executable file that contains an accelerator table |
| lpTableName | String | Null-terminated string that names an accelerator table |

**Table D.113 Arguments of LoadAccelerators**

## LoadBitmap

This function loads the bitmap resource named by the lpBitmapName contained within the executable file named in hInstance.

```
Declare Function LoadBitmap Lib "User" (ByVal hInstance As Integer, ByVal lpBitmapName As Any) As Integer
```

| Argument | Type | Description |
|---|---|---|
| hInstance | Handle | Executable file that contains the bitmap |
| lpBitmapName | String | Null-terminated string that names a bitmap |

**Table D.114 Arguments of LoadBitmap**

## LoadCursor

This function loads the cursor resource named by the lpCursorName contained within the executable file named in hInstance.

```
Declare Function LoadCursor Lib "User" (ByVal hInstance As Integer, ByVal lpCursorName As Any) As
Integer
```

| Argument | Type | Description |
|----------|------|-------------|
| hInstance | Handle | Executable file that contains the cursor resource |
| lpCursorName | String | Null-terminated string that names the cursor resource |

**Table D.115 Arguments of LoadCursor**

| Value | Description |
|-------|-------------|
| IDC_ARROW | Default arrow cursor |
| IDC_CROSS | Crosshair cursor |
| IDC_IBEAM | Text I-beam cursor |
| IDC_ICON | Empty icon |
| IDC_SIZE | Square with a smaller square inside its lower-right corner |
| IDC_SIZENESW | Double-pointed cursor with arrows pointing northeast and southwest |
| IDC_SIZENS | Double-pointed cursor with arrows pointing north and south |
| IDC_SIZENWSE | Double-pointed cursor with arrows pointing northwest and southeast |
| IDC_SIZEWE | Double-pointed cursor with arrows pointing west and east |
| IDC_UPARROW | Vertical arrow cursor |
| IDC_WAIT | Hourglass cursor |

**Table D.116 Values of LoadCursor**

## LoadIcon

This function loads the icon resource named by the lpIconName contained within the executable file indicated in hInstance.

```
Declare Function LoadIcon Lib "User" (ByVal hInstance As Integer, ByVal lpIconName As Any) As Integer
```

| Argument | Description |
|----------|-------------|
| hInstance | Executable file that contains the icon resource |
| lpIconName | Null-terminated string that names the icon resource |

**Table D.117 Arguments of LoadIcon**

| Value | Description |
|-------|-------------|
| IDI_APPLICATION | Default application icon |
| IDI_ASTERISK | Asterisk |
| IDI_EXCLAMATION | Exclamation point |
| IDI_HAND | Hand-shaped icon |
| IDI_QUESTION | Question mark |

**Table D.118 Values of LoadIcon**

## LoadMenu

This function loads the menu resource named by the lpMenuName contained within the executable file indicated in hInstance.

```
Declare Function LoadMenu Lib "User" (ByVal hInstance As Integer, ByVal lpString As String) As
Integer
```

| Argument | Description |
|----------|-------------|
| hInstance | Executable file that contains the menu resource |
| lpMenuName | Null-terminated string that names the menu resource |

Table D.119 Arguments of LoadMenu

## LoadResource

This function loads the resource identified by the hResInfo argument.

```
Declare Function LoadResource Lib "Kernel" (ByVal hInstance As Integer, ByVal hResInfo As Integer)
As Integer
```

| Argument | Description |
|----------|-------------|
| hInstance | Executable file that contains the resource |
| hResInfo | Identifies the desired resource |

Table D.120 Arguments of LoadResource

## LoadString

This function loads the sting resource identified in the wID argument.

```
Declare Function LoadString Lib "User" (ByVal hInstance As Integer, ByVal wID As Integer, ByVal
lpBuffer As Any, ByVal nBufferMax As Integer) As Integer
```

| Argument | Description |
|----------|-------------|
| hInstance | Executable file that contains the resource |
| wID | Indicates the integer identifier of the string |
| lpBuffer | Buffer to receive the string |
| nBufferMax | Maximum size of the buffer |

Table D.121 Arguments of LoadString

## LockResource

This function retrieves the absolute memory address of the resource identified in the hResData argument.

```
Declare Function LockResource Lib "Kernel" (ByVal hResData As Integer) As Long
```

| Argument | Description |
|----------|-------------|
| hResData | Identifies the desired resource |

Table D.122 Argument of LockResource

## SetResourceHandler

This function sets up a function to load resources.

```
Declare Function SetResourceHandler Lib "Kernel" (ByVal hInstance As Integer, ByVal lpType As Any,
ByVal lpLoadFunc As Any) As Integer
```

| Argument | Description |
|----------|-------------|
| hInstance | Executable file that contains the resource |
| lpType | A short integer that indicates a resource type |
| lpLoadFunc | The procedure-instance address of the application-supplied callback function |

Table D.123 Arguments of SetResourceHandler

## SizeofResource

This function determines the size in bytes of the resource identified in the hInstance argument.

```
Declare Function SizeofResource Lib "Kernel" (ByVal hInstance As Integer, ByVal hResInfo As Integer)
As Integer
```

| Argument | Description |
|----------|-------------|
| hInstance | Executable file that contains the resource |
| hResInfo | Identifies the desired resource |

**Table D.124 Arguments of SizeofResource**

## UnlockResource

This function unlocks the resource named in the hResData argument.

```
Declare Function UnlockResource Lib "Kernel" Alias "GlobalUnlock" (ByVal hMem As Integer) As Integer
```

| Argument | Description |
|----------|-------------|
| hResData | This identifies the global memory block to be unlocked |

**Table D.125 Argument of UnlockResource**

### Resources Definitions in CONSTANT.TXT

```
Global Const RT_CURSOR = 1&
Global Const RT_BITMAP = 2&
Global Const RT_ICON = 3&
Global Const RT_MENU = 4&
Global Const RT_DIALOG = 5&
Global Const RT_STRING = 6&
Global Const RT_FONTDIR = 7&
Global Const RT_FONT = 8&
Global Const RT_ACCELERATOR = 9&
Global Const RT_RCDATA = 10&
Global Const IDC_ARROW = 32512&
Global Const IDC_IBEAM = 32513&
Global Const IDC_WAIT = 32514&
Global Const IDC_CROSS = 32515&
Global Const IDC_UPARROW = 32516&
Global Const IDC_SIZE = 32640&
Global Const IDC_ICON = 32641&
Global Const IDC_SIZENWSE = 32642&
Global Const IDC_SIZENESW = 32643&
Global Const IDC_SIZEWE = 32644&
Global Const IDC_SIZENS = 32645&
Global Const IDI_APPLICATION = 32512&
Global Const IDI_HAND = 32513&
Global Const IDI_QUESTION = 32514&
Global Const IDI_EXCLAMATION = 32515&
Global Const IDI_ASTERISK = 32516&
```

# Segment functions

## AllocDStoCSAlias

This function accepts a data-segment selector and provides a code-segment selector.

```
Declare Function AllocDStoCSAlias Lib "Kernel" (ByVal wSelector As Integer) As Integer
```

| Argument | Description |
|----------|-------------|
| wSelector | The data-segment selector |

**Table D.126 Argument of AllocDstoCSAlias**

## AllocSelector

This function sets up a new selector.

```
Declare Function AllocSelector Lib "Kernel" (ByVal wSelector As Integer) As Integer
```

| Argument | Description |
|---|---|
| hInstance | Executable file that contains the resource |
| hResInfo | The indicated resource |
| dwSize | Identifies the size in bytes to allocate for a resource |

**Table D.127 Arguments of AllocSelector**

## ChangeSelector

This function creates a temporary code selector that corresponds to a specific data selector.

```
Declare Function ChangeSelector Lib "Kernel" (ByVal wDestSelector As Integer, ByVal wSourceSelector
As Integer) As Integer
```

| Argument | Description |
|---|---|
| wDestSelector | A previously allocated selector |
| wSource | The selector to change |

**Table D.128 Arguments of ChangeSelector**

## FreeSelector

This function frees a previously allocated selector.

```
Declare Function FreeSelector Lib "Kernel" (ByVal wSelector As Integer) As Integer
```

| Argument | Description |
|---|---|
| wSelector | The selector to be freed |

**Table D.129 Argument of FreeSelector**

## GlobalFix

This function stops a global memory block from moving in linear memory.

```
Declare Sub GlobalFix Lib "Kernel" (ByVal hMem As Integer)
```

| Argument | Description |
|---|---|
| hMem | The global memory block |

**Table D.130 Argument of GlobalFix**

## GlobalPageLock

This function page-locks the memory connected with a global selector and increases its page-lock count.

```
Declare Function GlobalPageLock Lib "Kernel" (ByVal wSelector As Integer) As Integer
```

| Argument | Description |
|---|---|
| wSelector | The memory selector to be page-locked |

**Table D.131 Argument of GlobalPageLock**

## GlobalPageUnlock

This function reduces the page-lock count for a block of memory.

```
Declare Function GlobalPageUnlock Lib "Kernel" (ByVal wSelector As Integer) As Integer
```

| Argument | Description |
|---|---|
| wSelector | The memory selector to be page-unlocked |

**Table D.132 Argument of GlobalPageUnlock**

## GlobalUnfix

This function unlocks a global memory block.

```
Declare Function GlobalUnfix Lib "Kernel" (ByVal hMem As Integer) As Integer
```

| Argument | Description |
|----------|-------------|
| hMem | The global memory block to be unlocked |

**Table D.133 Argument of GlobalUnfix**

## LockSegment

This function locks a segment in memory.

```
Declare Function LockSegment Lib "Kernel" (ByVal wSegment As Integer) As Integer
```

| Argument | Description |
|----------|-------------|
| wSegment | Address of the segment to be locked |

**Table D.134 Argument of LockSegment**

## UnlockSegment

This function unlocks a segment of memory.

```
Declare Function UnlockSegment Lib "Kernel" (ByVal wSegment As Integer) As Integer
```

| Argument | Description |
|----------|-------------|
| wSegment | Address of the segment to be unlocked |

**Table D.135 Argument of UnlockSegment**

# Sound functions

## CloseSound

This function closes access to the sound device and makes it available for other applications.

```
Declare Sub CloseSound Lib "Sound" ()
```

## CountVoiceNotes

This function returns the number of notes in the nVoice queue.

```
Declare Function CountVoiceNotes Lib "Sound" (ByVal nVoice As Integer) As Integer
```

| Argument | Description |
|----------|-------------|
| nVoice | The voice queue to be counted (first voice is one) |

**Table D.136 Argument of CountVoiceNotes**

## GetThresholdEvent

This function obtains a flag that identifies a threshold event.

```
Declare Function GetThresholdEvent Lib "Sound" () As Integer
```

## GetThresholdStatus

This function obtains the status of the threshold event for each voice.

```
Declare Function GetThresholdStatus Lib "Sound" () As Integer
```

## OpenSound

This function opens the sound device and prevents any other applications from utilizing it.

```
Declare Function OpenSound Lib "Sound" () As Integer
```

## SetSoundNoise

This function determines the source (nSource) and duration of the noise hardware of the sound device.

```
Declare Function SetSoundNoise Lib "Sound" (ByVal nSource As Integer, ByVal nDuration As Integer) As
Integer
```

| Argument | Description |
|----------|-------------|
| nSource | Noise source can be any of the values in Table D.138 |
| nDuration | Duration of the noise |

**Table D.137 Arguments of SetSoundNoise**

| Value | Description |
|-------|-------------|
| S_PERIOD512 | Frequency N/512 |
| S_PERIOD1024 | Frequency N/1024 |
| S_PERIOD2048 | Frequency N/2048 |
| S_PERIODVOICE | Frequency from voice channel |
| S_WHITE512 | Frequency N/512 |
| S_WHITE1024 | Frequency N/1024 |
| S_WHITE2048 | Frequency N/2048 |
| S_WHITEVOICE | Frequency from voice channel |

**Table D.138 Values of SetSoundNoise**

## SetVoiceAccent

This function puts an accent in the voice queue. An accent consists of a combination of tempo (nTempo), volume (nVolume), mode (nMode), and pitch (nPitch).

```
Declare Function SetVoiceAccent Lib "Sound" (ByVal nVoice As Integer, ByVal nTempo As Integer, ByVal
nVolume As Integer, ByVal nMode As Integer, ByVal nPitch As Integer) As Integer
```

| Argument | Description |
|----------|-------------|
| nVoice | Voice queue (first voice queue is one) |
| nTempo | Number of quarter notes played per minute (32-255, Default 120) |
| nVolume | Volume level (0 low to 255 high) |
| nMode | One of the values in Table D.140 |
| nPitch | Pitch of the notes played (0 to 83) |

**Table D.139 Arguments of SetVoiceAccent**

| nMod Values | Description |
|-------------|-------------|
| S_LEGATO | Note is of full duration and blends with next note |
| S_NORMAL | Note is of full duration and stops before next note |
| S_STACCATO | Note is only partially held creating a stop between it and the next note |

**Table D.140 Description of nMode Values**

| Returned Values | Description |
|-----------------|-------------|
| S_SERDMD | Invalid mode |
| S_SERDTP | Invalid tempo |
| S_SERDVL | Invalid volume |
| S_SERQFUL | Queue full |

**Table D.141 Description of returned values**

## SetVoiceEnvelope

This function puts the Voice envelope (wave shape and repeat counts) in the voice queue.

```
Declare Function SetVoiceEnvelope Lib "Sound" (ByVal nVoice As Integer, ByVal nShape As Integer,
ByVal nRepeat As Integer) As Integer
```

| Argument | Description |
|----------|-------------|
| nVoice | Voice queue |
| nShape | Index to OEM wave-shape table |
| nRepeat | Number of times to repeat the wave shape during one note |

Table D.142 Arguments of SetVoiceEnvelope

## SetVoiceNote

This function places a note in the voice queue with the qualities indicated in the nValue, nLength, and nCdots arguments.

```
Declare Function SetVoiceNote Lib "Sound" (ByVal nVoice As Integer, ByVal nValue As Integer, ByVal
nLength As Integer, ByVal nCdots As Integer) As Integer
```

| Argument | Description |
|----------|-------------|
| nVoice | Voice queue |
| nValue | Contains a value between 1 and 84 representing the seven octaves |
| nLength | Reciprocal of the duration of the note. 1 is whole note, 2 is half note, and 4 is quarter note |
| nCdots | Duration of note in dots |

Table D.143 Arguments of SetVoiceNote

| Returned Value | Description |
|----------------|-------------|
| S_SERDCC | Dot count incorrect |
| S_SERDLN | Note length incorrect |
| S_SERDNT | Note incorrect |
| S_SERQFUL | Full queue |

Table D.144 Description of returned values

## SetVoiceQueueSize

This function sets up a queue named nVoice in the size indicated by the nBytes argument. The default value is 192 bytes.

```
Declare Function SetVoiceQueueSize Lib "Sound" (ByVal nVoice As Integer, ByVal nBytes As Integer) As
Integer
```

| Argument | Description |
|----------|-------------|
| nVoice | Voice queue |
| nBytes | Number of bytes in the queue |

Table D.145 Arguments of SetVoiceQueueSize

| Returned Values | Description |
|-----------------|-------------|
| S_SERMACT | Active music |
| S_SEROFM | Not enough memory |

Table D.146 Description of returned values

## SetVoiceSound

This function stores the sound frequency and duration in the voice queue named by the nVoice argument.

```
Declare Function SetVoiceSound Lib "Sound" (ByVal nVoice As Integer, ByVal lFrequency As Long, ByVal nDuration As Integer) As Integer
```

| Argument | Description |
|----------|-------------|
| nVoice | Voice queue |
| lFrequency | Frequency of the sound |
| nDuration | Duration of the sound (measured in clock ticks) |

**Table D.147 Arguments of SetVoiceSound**

## SetVoiceThreshold

This function determines the voice threshold of a voice queue named in the nVoice argument. When the number of notes in the queue falls below the number in the nNotes argument, the threshold flag is set.

```
Declare Function SetVoiceThreshold Lib "Sound" (ByVal nVoice As Integer, ByVal nNotes As Integer) As Integer
```

| Argument | Description |
|----------|-------------|
| nVoice | Voice queue |
| nNotes | Threshold level in number of notes |

**Table D.148 Arguments of SetVoiceThreshold**

## StartSound

This function starts to play each voice queue. The contents of the voice queues are not erased by this function and can be played any number of times.

```
Declare Function StartSound Lib "Sound" () As Integer
```

## StopSound

This function stops the playing of the voice queues. The contents of each voice queue are flushed and the sound driver is turned off.

```
Declare Function StopSound Lib "Sound" () As Integer
```

## SyncAllVoices

This function places a sync mark in each queue. The sync mark has the effect of turning off the voice until sync marks are found in all of the other queues.

```
Declare Function SyncAllVoices Lib "Sound" () As Integer
```

## WaitSoundState

This function pauses until the sound driver enters the state indicated in the nState argument.

```
Declare Function WaitSoundState Lib "Sound" (ByVal nState As Integer) As Integer
```

| Value | Description |
|-------|-------------|
| S_ALLTHRESHOLD | Each voice queue is at threshold |
| S_QUEUEEMPTY | Each voice queue is empty and its sound drivers are off |
| S_THRESHOLD | Voice queue reaches threshold and restores voice |

**Table D.149 Values for WaitSoundState**

**Sound Declarations in CONSTANT.TXT**

```
Global Const S_QUEUEEMPTY = 0
Global Const S_THRESHOLD = 1
Global Const S_ALLTHRESHOLD = 2
Global Const S_NORMAL = 0
Global Const S_LEGATO = 1
Global Const S_STACCATO = 2
Global Const S_PERIOD512 = 0
Global Const S_PERIOD1024 = 1
Global Const S_PERIOD2048 = 2
Global Const S_PERIODVOICE = 3
Global Const S_WHITE512 = 4
Global Const S_WHITE1024 = 5
Global Const S_WHITE2048 = 6
Global Const S_WHITEVOICE = 7
Global Const S_SERDVNA = (-1)
Global Const S_SEROFM = (-2)
Global Const S_SERMACT = (-3)
Global Const S_SERQFUL = (-4)
Global Const S_SERBDNT = (-5)
Global Const S_SERDLN = (-6)
Global Const S_SERDCC = (-7)
Global Const S_SERDTP = (-8)
Global Const S_SERDVL = (-9)
Global Const S_SERDMD = (-10)
Global Const S_SERDSH = (-11)
Global Const S_SERDPT = (-12)
Global Const S_SERDFQ = (-13)
Global Const S_SERDDR = (-14)
Global Const S_SERDSR = (-15)
Global Const S_SERDST = (-16)
```

# String-manuipulation functions

### AnsiLower

This function converts the character string named in the lpString argument into lowercase.

```
Declare Function AnsiLower Lib "User" (ByVal lpString As String) As Long
```

| Argument | Description |
|----------|-------------|
| lpString | Character string to convert |

**Table D.150 Argument of AnsiLower**

### AnsiLowerBuff

This function converts a character string in a buffer named in the lpString to lowercase.

```
Declare Function AnsiLowerBuff Lib "User" (ByVal lpString As String, ByVal aWORD As Integer) As Integer
```

| Argument | Description |
|----------|-------------|
| lpString | Buffer containing the character string |
| nLength | Number of characters in the buffer (0 represents 64K) |

**Table D.151 Arguments of AnsiLowerBuff**

### AnsiNext

This function changes the pointer in a character string to the next character.

```
Declare Function AnsiNext Lib "User" (ByVal lpString As String) As Long
```

| Argument | Description |
| --- | --- |
| lpCurrentChar | Indicates a character in a string |

**Table D.152 Argument of AnsiNext**

## AnsiPrev

This function changes the pointer in a character string to the previous character.

```
Declare Function AnsiPrev Lib "User" (ByVal lpString As String, ByVal lpString As String) As Long
```

| Argument | Description |
| --- | --- |
| lpStart | Points to the start of the string |
| lpCurrentChar | Indicates a character in a string |

**Table D.153 Arguments of AnsiPrev**

## AnsiToOem

This function changes the string named in the lpAnsiStr argument from the ANSI character set to an OEM-defined character set.

```
Declare Function AnsiToOem Lib "Keyboard" (ByVal lpAnsiStr As String, ByVal lpOemStr As String) As Integer
```

| Argument | Description |
| --- | --- |
| lpAnsiStr | String to convert |
| lpOemStr | Indicates the place to put the newly converted string |

**Table D.154 Arguments of AnsiToOem**

## AnsiToOemBuff

This function converts the string in the buffer named in the lpAnsiStr argument from the ANSI character set to an OEM-defined character set.

```
Declare Sub AnsiToOemBuff Lib "Keyboard" (ByVal lpAnsiStr As String, ByVal lpOemStr As String, ByVal nLength As Integer)
```

| Argument | Description |
| --- | --- |
| lpAnsiStr | Buffer that holds the character string to convert |
| lpOemStr | Buffer to put the converted character string into |
| nLength | Number of characters in the buffer that holds the string to convert |

**Table D.155 Arguments of AnsiToOemBuff**

## AnsiUpper

This function changes the character string in the lpString argument to uppercase.

```
Declare Function AnsiUpper Lib "User" (ByVal lpString As String) As String
```

| Argument | Description |
| --- | --- |
| lpString | Character string to be converted |

**Table D.156 Argument of AnsiUpper**

## AnsiUpperBuff

This function converts a character string in a buffer named in the lpString to uppercase.

```
Declare Function AnsiUpperBuff Lib "User" (ByVal lpString As String, ByVal aWORD As Integer) As Integer
```

| Argument | Description |
| --- | --- |
| lpString | Buffer holding the character string to convert |
| nLength | Number of characters in the buffer (0 means 64K) |

**Table D.157 Arguments of AnsiUpperBuff**

## IsCharAlpha

This function indicates whether the character in the cChar argument is an alphabetical character.

```
Declare Function IsCharAlpha Lib "User" (ByVal cChar As Integer) As Integer
```

| Argument | Description |
| --- | --- |
| cChar | Character to be checked |

**Table D.158 Argument of IsCharAlpha**

## IsCharAlphaNumeric

This function indicates whether a character is alphabetical or numerical. If the return value is TRUE, then the character is alphanumeric.

```
Declare Function IsCharAlphaNumeric Lib "User" (ByVal cChar As Integer) As Integer
```

| Argument | Description |
| --- | --- |
| cChar | Character to be tested |

**Table D.159 Argument of IsCharAlphaNumeric**

## IsCharLower

This function indicates if a character is lowercase. If the return value is TRUE, then the character is lowercase.

```
Declare Function IsCharLower Lib "User" (ByVal cChar As Integer) As Integer
```

| Argument | Description |
| --- | --- |
| cChar | Character to be tested |

**Table D.160 Argument of IsCharLower**

## IsCharUpper

This function indicates if a character is uppercase. If the return value is TRUE, then the character is uppercase.

```
Declare Function IsCharUpper Lib "User" (ByVal cChar As Integer) As Integer
```

| Argument | Description |
| --- | --- |
| cChar | Character to be tested |

**Table D.161 Argument of IsCharUpper**

## OemToAnsi

This function converts the string in the lpOemStr argument from the OEM-defined character set to the ANSI character set.

```
Declare Function OemToAnsi Lib "Keyboard" (ByVal lpOemStr As String, ByVal lpAnsiStr As String) As
Integer
```

| Argument | Description |
| --- | --- |
| lpOemStr | Character string to convert |
| lpAnsiStr | Indicates where to place the newly converted string |

**Table D.162 Arguments of OemToAnsi**

## OemToAnsiBuff

This function converts the string in the buffer named in the lpOemStr from the OEM-defined character set to the ANSI character set.

```
Declare Sub OemToAnsiBuff Lib "Keyboard" (ByVal lpOemStr As String, ByVal lpAnsiStr As String, ByVal nLength as Integer)
```

| Argument | Description |
|---|---|
| lpOemStr | Buffer which contains the string to convert |
| lpAnsiStr | Location to place the newly converted string |
| nLength | Number of characters in the lpOemStr buffer |

**Table D.163 Arguments of OemToAnsiBuff**

## ToAscii

This function converts the virtual-key code in the wVirtKey argument and the keyboard state set in the lpKeyState argument to ANSI character or characters.

```
Declare Function ToAscii Lib "Keyboard" (ByVal wVirtKey As Integer, ByVal wScanCode As Integer, lpKeyState As Any, lpChar As Any, Byval wFlags As Integer) As Integer
```

| Argument | Description |
|---|---|
| wVirtKey | Virtual-key code to be translated |
| wScanCode | Raw scan code of the key to be converted |
| lpKeyState | Indicates an array of 256 bytes that identifies the state of the keys on the keyboard |
| lpChar | Buffer that will receive the ANSI characters |
| wFlags | Bit 0 flag's menu display |

**Table D.164 Arguments of ToAscii**

# Task functions

## Catch

This function makes a copy of the current execution environment and places it in a buffer.

```
Declare Function Catch Lib "Kernel" (lpCatchBuf As Any) As Integer
```

| Argument | Description |
|---|---|
| lpCatchBuf | Indicates the CATCHBUF structure that will accept the execution environment |

**Table D.165 Argument of Catch**

## ExitWindows

This function generates a normal Windows shutdown.

```
Declare Function ExitWindows Lib "User" (ByVal dwReserved As Long, wReturnCode) As Integer
```

| Argument | Description |
|---|---|
| dwReserved | Reserved (should be 0) |
| wReturnCode | Return value to pass to DOS |

**Table D.166 Arguments of ExitWindows**

### GetCurrentPDB

This function provides the current DOS Program Data Base (PDB)

```
Declare Function GetCurrentPDB Lib "Kernel" () As Integer
```

### GetCurrentTask

This function provides the task handle of the present task.

```
Declare Function GetCurrentTask Lib "Kernel" () As Integer
```

### GetDOSEnvironment

This function returns the environment string of the present task.

```
Declare Function GetDOSEnvironment Lib "Kernel" () As Long
```

### GetNumTasks

This function provides the number of tasks presently running.

```
Declare Function GetNumTasks Lib "Kernel" () As Integer
```

### SetErrorMode

This function determines if Windows controls DOS Function 24H errors or permits the application to control them.

```
Declare Function SetErrorMode Lib "Kernel" (ByVal wMode As Integer) As Integer
```

| Argument | Description |
| --- | --- |
| wMode | Error mode flag |

**Table D.167 Argument of SetErrorMode**

### Throw

This function returns the execution environment to the indicated values.

```
Declare Sub Throw Lib "Kernel" (lpCatchBuf As Any, ByVal nThrowBack As Integer)
```

| Argument | Description |
| --- | --- |
| lpCatchBuf | Indicates an array that contains the execution environment |
| nThrowBack | Indicates the value to be given to the Catch function |

**Table D.168 Arguments of Throw**

### Yield

This function stops the present task and begins a waiting task.

```
Declare Sub Yield Lib "Kernel" ()
```

# The Sound Project

## Project Overview

The Sound project demonstrates how to incorporate Windows API calls into a Visual Basic application. By examining the code for this project, you will learn how to use API calls in Visual Basic applications.

The explaination of this project begins with the assembly of the controls and subroutines of the Sound form. Table D.169 lists the different elements of the form's controls along with a picture of how the form looks with these controls. Next, there is a list of the code subroutines to enter for this form. Please read this information carefully and use the pictures of the form as guides in putting this project together.

## Assembling the Project

1. Make a new form (the Reference form) with the objects and properties in Table D.169.

| Object | Property | Setting |
|---|---|---|
| Form | FormName | Sound |
|  | BorderStyle | 1 - Fixed Single |
|  | Caption | Sound |
|  | ControlBox' | False |
|  | MaxButton | False |
|  | MinButton | False |
| ScrollBar | CtlName | Octave |
|  | Maximum | 84 |
|  | Minimum | 1 |
|  | Value | 1 |
| ScrollBar | CtlName | Length |
|  | Maximum | 32 |
|  | Minimum | 1 |
|  | Value | 32 |
| ScrollBar | CtlName | Duration |
|  | Maximum | 32767 |
|  | Minimum | 1 |
|  | Value | 32767 |
| TextBox | CtlName | Octave_Display |
|  | Text | 1 |
| TextBox | CtlName | Length_Display |
|  | Text | 32 |
| TextBox | CtlName | Duration_Display |
|  | Text | 3767 |
| Label | Caption | nValue |
|  | CtlName | Octave_Label |
| Label | Caption | nLength |
|  | CtlName | Length_Label |
| Label | Caption | nCdots |
|  | CtlName | Duration_Label |
| CommandButton | Caption | Play Stored Sounds |
|  | CtlName | Play |
| CommandButton | Caption | Play Scales |
|  | CtlName | Play_Scales |
| CommandButton | Caption | Exit |
|  | CtlName | Exit_Program |

**Table D.169 Settings for the Reference form in the Reference project**

2. Size the objects on the screen as shown in Figure D.1 below.

3. Enter the following code in the General Declarations section. This code defines the API functions to be used in the Sound project.

```
Declare Sub CloseSound Lib "Sound" ()
Declare Function OpenSound Lib "Sound" () As Integer
Declare Function SetVoiceNote Lib "Sound" (ByVal nVoice As Integer, ByVal nValue As Integer,
ByVal nLength As Integer, ByVal nCdots As Integer) As Integer
Declare Function SetVoiceQueueSize Lib "Sound" (ByVal nVoice As Integer, ByVal nBytes As
Integer) As Integer
Declare Function StartSound Lib "Sound" () As Integer
```

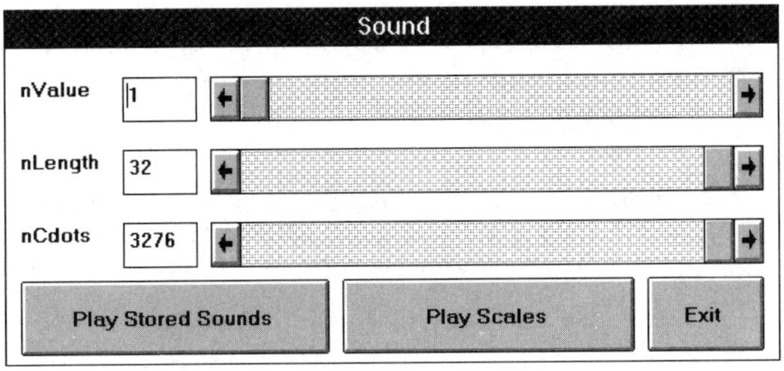

| | Sound | |
|---|---|---|
| nValue | 1 | |
| nLength | 32 | |
| nCdots | 3276 | |

| Play Stored Sounds | Play Scales | Exit |

**Figure D.1 How the Reference form should look**

4. Enter the following code in the General Declarations section to create the new function Store_Sound. This code stores the sound represented by the settings of the scroll bar.

```
Sub Store_Sound ()
    Status% = SetVoiceNote(1, Octave.Value, Length.Value, Duration.Value)
End Sub
```

5. Enter the following code in the Duration_Change event subroutine. This code triggers when the user changes the position of the scroll box on the Duration scroll bar. The text property displays the new value represented on the scroll bar. This code also stores the new sound represented by this scroll bar and the two other scroll bars to the buffer.

```
Sub Duration_Change ()
    Duration_Display.Text = Str$(Duration.Value)
    Store_Sound
End Sub
```

6. Enter the following code in the Exit_Program event subroutine. This code closes the Sound project.

```
Sub Exit_Program_Click ()
    End
End Sub
```

7. Enter the following code in the Form_Load event subroutine. This code triggers at program startup. This code opens the sound device of the current computer to input from the Sound project and prevents access from all other applications.

```
Sub Form_Load ()
    Status% = OpenSound()
    Status% = SetVoiceQueueSize(1, 5376)
End Sub
```

8. Enter the following code in the Form_Unload event subroutine. This code triggers when the form is unloaded from memory and restores other applications' access to the sound device.

```
Sub Form_Unload (Cancel As Integer)
    CloseSound
End Sub
```

9. Enter the following code in the Length_Change event subroutine. This code triggers when the user changes the position of the scroll box on the Length scroll bar. The text property displays the new value represented on the scroll bar. This code also stores the new sound represented by this scroll bar and the two other scroll bars to the buffer.

```
Sub Length_Change ()
    Length_Display.Text = Str$(Length.Value)
    Store_Sound
End Sub
```

10. Enter the following code in the Octave_Change event subroutine. This code triggers when the user changes the position of the scroll box on the Octave scroll bar. The text property

displays the new value represented on the scroll bar. This code also stores the new sound represented by this scroll bar and the two other scroll bars to the buffer.

```
Sub Octave_Change ()
  Octave_Display.Text = Str$(Octave.Value)
  Store_Sound
End Sub
```

11. Enter the following code in the Play_Click event subroutine. This code triggers when the user clicks the command button labeled Play Stored Sounds. This causes the sound device to play the sounds stored by manipulating the scroll bar controls.

```
Sub Play_Click ()
  Status% = StartSound()
End Sub
```

12. Enter the following code in the Play_Scales_Click event subroutine. This code triggers when the user presses the command button labeled Play Scales. This code plays a series of notes on the sound device.

```
Sub Play_Scales_Click ()
  Status% = SetVoiceQueueSize(1, 5376)
  For Note = 1 To 84
      Status% = SetVoiceNote(1, Note, 32, 32767)
  Next Note
  While Note > 1
      Status% = SetVoiceNote(1, Note, 32, 32767)
      Note = Note - 1
  Loop
  Status% = StartSound()
End Sub
```

## How It Works

The Sound project demonstrates the use of Windows API function calls within a Visual Basic application. Each of the scroll bars on the Sound form represents a variable that determines the kind of sound produced. The top scroll bar controls the octave in which the scale will be played, the middle scroll bar sets the length of the sound, and the bottom scroll bar determines the duration. Each time the user changes one of these settings, the sound is stored in a buffer. These sounds will only play when the user presses the command button labeled Play Stored Sounds. To get the program to play the scales, the user presses the command button labeled Play Scales. Pressing the comand button labeled Exit ends the program.

The Sound project uses the sound API functions to produce sounds on the computer's speaker. In order to make these functions accessible to the Sound project, the declaration statements listed for each API must appear in the General Declarations area of the Sound form. This makes these functions accessible to the Sound project.

The process of producing sounds is simple. The OpenSound function allows sounds to be played on the computer's speaker. Each change made to the settings of the scroll bar control triggers the Store_Sound function that uses the new settings to store a sound. The Store_Sound function uses the SetVoiceNote API function to store this sound. To play these sounds, the user simply presses the command button labeled Play Stored Sounds. The StartSound API function produces the sounds on the computer speaker.

# Appendix E
# Further Reading

If you want to learn more about Visual Basic and explore advanced programming techniques, there are three kinds of books you should consider. First, of course, are books written specifically about Visual Basic, such as the one you are reading now and our companion volume, *The Waite Group's Visual Basic How-To*. Besides books, you might want to check out the MSBASIC forum on CompuServe (*go msbasic* at the prompt). There you will find hundreds of Visual Basic applications written by your fellow programmers.

Second, since Visual Basic is intimately involved with the Windows environment, you may want to learn more about the general concepts of Windows programming. While our Visual Basic books show you all you *really* need to know about Windows to write a Visual Basic application, you may want to explore such matters as the Windows Application Program Interface (API), the creation of dynamic link libraries (DLLs), and Dynamic Data Exchange (DDE) in more detail.

Finally, since Visual Basic incorporates a version of the BASIC language, you will find that many books on BASIC have useful routines that can be adapted to Visual Basic. In general, routines that deal with calculation, string formatting, data file management, sorting, and other hardware-independent matters will easily translate into Visual Basic, particularly if they are written in QuickBASIC or QBasic. Routines dealing with the screen and graphics, the printer, the speaker, the serial port, and other devices probably won't be as useful. This is because Visual Basic and the Windows environment handle devices differently than conventional DOS programs do. The best way to extend Visual Basic in these areas is through the use of the API, as shown in Appendix D, *Using the Windows API*.

The brief reading list that follows cannot attempt to be complete, since numerous new titles appear each month. Nevertheless, the titles we describe have proven reliable and useful to us in writing this book and in our other work with Visual Basic and with Windows.

*Master C++.* Rex Woollard, Robert Lafore, Harry Henderson (Waite Group Press, 1992). This is a package consisting of an interactive disk-based tutor and a reference book. Instant and precise feedback on your answers to each question enables you to proceed without confusion. Unlike a book, the software can make sure you've mastered each concept before introducing the next one. If Visual Basic has whetted your appetite for Windows programming, the popular C++ language is probably your best next step. Once you've mastered C++, you can move into the mainstream of Windows programming with the other Windows titles below.

*Programming Windows.* Charles Petzold (Microsoft Press, 1990, second edition). This is Microsoft's "official" guide to Windows programming. It is a thorough exploration of Windows features with numerous short, easy to understand examples. The programs are in C, and reflect the older style of Windows programming with the Microsoft SDK, but they can easily be transferred to the friendlier Turbo C++ and QuickC for Windows environments. This would be a good book to use in tandem with the *Windows Programming Primer Plus* below.

*The Waite Group's Microsoft QuickBASIC Bible.* Mitchell Waite, Robert Arnson, Christy Gemmell, Harry Henderson (Microsoft Press, 1990). This book is structured much like the *Visual Basic SuperBible*, but it deals with Microsoft's popular QuickBASIC, Visual Basic's immediate ancestor. Since Visual Basic shares so many statements and functions with QuickBASIC, the reference entries in the *QuickBASIC Bible* can supplement those in Appendix B of the *Visual Basic SuperBible*. The tutorials that introduce each chapter can also provide useful programming techniques.

*The Waite Group's Microsoft QuickBASIC Primer Plus.* Stephen Prata with Harry Henderson (Microsoft Press, 1990). This book is the primer companion to the *Microsoft QuickBASIC Bible.* The chapters in the first three parts, dealing with the structure, data types, flow control, and file management of QuickBASIC, are fully applicable to Visual Basic. We especially recommend this book if you come to Visual Basic without any prior experience with the BASIC language.

*The Waite Group's Visual Basic How-To.* Robert Arnson, Daniel Rosen, Mitchell Waite, Jonathan Zuck (Waite Group Press, 1992). As you know, Visual Basic makes many programming tasks much easier than ever before. But Visual Basic's wealth of features sometimes makes it hard to know just where to begin. This book presents hundreds of programming problems and situations with complete steps for solving them in Visual Basic. With this book in hand you can quickly implement the standard features used by nearly every program, and move on to the touches that will make your application unique.

*The Waite Group's Windows API Bible.* James L. Conger (Waite Group Press, 1992). As you know, Appendix C of the *Visual Basic SuperBible* introduces the Windows API and briefly summarizes the many API functions. The *Windows API Bible* goes far beyond that in providing a complete reference for the programmer who needs to use many of the more than 600 API calls available. The API functions are grouped into logical categories, each of which is introduced by a tutorial. The reference entry for each function fully describes the syntax and gives usage and program examples. All of the Windows messages are also explained in context, and the new features of Windows 3.1 are included.

*Windows Programming Primer Plus.* James L. Conger (Waite Group Press, 1992). This book is a very accessible way to learn more about the fundamental structure and concepts of Windows "from the ground up." It follows in the tradition of other Waite Group primers such as *C Primer Plus,* and features a step by step, always friendly approach. The book broadens your programming horizons by showing you how to program Windows in C or C++ using the new easy to use Turbo C++ for Windows and Quick C for Windows environments, which are much like Visual Basic in their integrated, graphical approach to programming. C and C++ can give you a more direct access to the Windows environment than is usually possible in Visual Basic. The new features of Windows 3.1 are included. (This book is compatible with C++ but does not discuss features specific to C++. A beginning knowledge of C is recommended, but the author is careful to explain the more advanced C programming techniques.)

# Appendix F
# How to Use the Program Disk

## What's on the Program Disk

Starting with Chapter 4, *Setting Up Forms*, each chapter of the *Visual Basic SuperBible* concludes with a project that illustrates the Visual Basic features covered in the chapter. The Program Disk contains a subdirectory for each chapter that includes everything you need to run the project, including the .MAK file, form (.FRM) files, and Basic code (.BAS) files. Table F.1 lists all of the files on the Program Disk.

| Chapter | Make File | Form Files | Code Files |
|---|---|---|---|
| 4 | SETUP.MAK | DISPLAY.FRM | |
| | SETUP.FRM | | |
| 5 | APPEAR.MAK | APPEAR.FRM | |
| | WARNING.FRM | | |
| 6 | REFERENC.MAK | REFERENC.FRM | REFERENC.BAS |
| | DATAENTR.FRM | | REFER.BAS |
| | LETTER.FRM | | |
| 7 | CHANGE.MAK | CHANGE.FRM | |
| 8 | GRAPHICS.MAK | GRAPHICS.FRM | GRAPHICS.BAS |
| | SCREEN_B.FRM | | |
| 9 | COORDIN.MAK | COORDIN.FRM | |
| 10 | SHAPE.MAK | SHAPE.FRM | |
| 11 | TEXT.MAK | TEXT.FRM | |
| 12 | FONT.MAK | FONT.FRM | |
| | FONTLIST.FRM | | |
| 13 | TEXTBOX.MAK | TEXTBOX.FRM | |
| 14 | MOUSE.MAK | MOUSE.FRM | |
| 15 | DRAG.MAK | DRAG.FRM | |
| 16 | KEYS.MAK | KEYS.FRM | |
| 17 | DIALOG.MAK | | DIALOG1.BAS |
| | | | DIALOG2.BAS |
| 18 | LISTBOX.MAK | LISTBOX.FRM | |
| 19 | DRIVE.MAK | DRIVE.FRM | |
| 20 | SCROLL.MAK | SCROLL.FRM | |

Table F.1 (continued)

| Chapter | Make File | Form Files | Code Files |
|---------|-----------|------------|------------|
| 21 | FOCUS.MAK | FOCUS.FRM | FOCUS.BAS |
| | | ENVELOPE.FRM | |
| | TIME.MAK | TIME.FRM | |
| 23 | CLIP.MAK | CLIP.FRM | CLIP.BAS |
| 24 | PRINTER.MAK | PRINTER.FRM | |
| 25 | DDE.MAK | DDE.FRM | DDELINK.BAS |
| | | SALES_DI.FRM | |
| APPX C | SOUND.MAK | SOUND.FRM | SOUND.BAS |
| APPXD | DEBUG.MAK | DEBUG.FRM | DEBUG.TXT (data file) |

**Table F.1  Files on the Program Disk**

The discussion of the project in each chapter also includes complete specifications for all forms and listings of all code needed to build the project. You can, therefore, either create the project yourself by following the directions, or simply run the project using the files provided on the Program Disk. Since the programs are provided for you on the disk, why would you want to type in everything yourself? Well, if you have not had much experience with Visual Basic, setting up the forms and other objects for a project yourself will help you get used to Visual Basic's program design features. At any rate even if you run programs using the disk files, you should read the chapter project discussions carefully so you can see how the parts of the program fit together and better understand what happens when you run the program. Your understanding of the structure of these programs will allow you to modify them and use them in your applications.

### Installing the Program Disk

You do not need to install the projects to run them. All will run directly from the floppy diskette. However, there are three projects which rely on Visual Basic's CONSTANT.TXT file to operate as described. For this reason we suggest that you install the program disk to the same hard disk that holds your Visual Basic subdirectory. (Or you may modify the projects as described in the appropriate chapters of this book.) Please see the README.TXT file on the floppy disk for complete details and last minute notes.

Installing the Program Disk is very simple. The first thing you should do is to make a copy of the Program Disk and use the copy for installing the programs. This will protect you against possible mishaps. The easiest way to copy the Program Disk is to use the DOS DISKCOPY command. Assuming you have put the Program Disk in drive B:, you can use the following command to copy the disk:

```
DISKCOPY B: B: <Enter>
```

(The <Enter> means to press the <Enter> key as you normally do after any DOS command.) DOS will prompt you periodically to insert your blank disk and swap it for the Program Disk. Of course if you are using a different drive use that drive's letter instead.

Now that you've copied the Program Disk, put away the original and insert the copy in your floppy drive. Change to your Visual Basic directory on drive C:

```
C:\>cd \vb <Enter>
```

Here we assume that you installed Visual Basic in the default VB directory on drive C:. If your Visual Basic directory is different, change to that directory instead.

Next, make a subdirectory called VBSB in your VB directory:

```
C:\VB>md vbsb <Enter>
```

Now change to your VBSB subdirectory:

```
C:\VB>cd vbsb <Enter>
```

Make sure there's at least 500K of space left on your hard disk. (You can use the DOS CHKDSK command to find out how much space is available.) You're now ready to copy the files from the Program Disk to your VBSB directory:

```
C:\VB\VBSB>xcopy b: /s <Enter>
```

This command tells the DOS XCOPY utility to copy all the files on drive B: to the VBSB subdirectory. The /s switch tells DOS to include all the subdirectories. If your Program Disk is in a drive other than B:, use that drive letter instead.

## How to Run the Programs

To run a program, choose Open from Visual Basic's File menu. You will see the Open Project dialog box. In this dialog box, click on the VBSB subdirectory in the directory list on the right side of the window. This list will change to show the subdirectories of the VBSB directory. Click on the chapter or appendix whose project you want to run. The name of the project's .MAK file will appear in the file window on the left side of the dialog box. Click on this file name to load the project.

Once you have loaded a project you can use the Project Window to examine forms or to view code. When you are ready to run the project, simply choose Start from the Run menu, or press <F5>.

We encourage you to experiment by making changes to the forms and code of each project. We suggest however that you make a separate directory for program testing (called perhaps TEST). Before changing a project, copy it to your Test directory. You can do this by clicking on the name of the .MAK file in the Project Window and using the Save Project As... option on the File menu to save the .MAK file with a pathname starting with \VB\TEST. You can then click in turn on each of the other files in the project window and use the Save File As... option on the File menu to save the files to the \VB\TEST path. Finally, reload the project from the TEST directory, responding Yes to the dialog box that asks you whether to save the changes to the project. You can now safely make changes to the project without affecting the original files.

We hope you enjoy exploring the projects on the Program Disk!

# INDEX

# ABOUT THE AUTHORS

Taylor Maxwell works in a consulting firm which specializes in Windows and Visual Basic programming solutions. He began his programming career in 1985 and works extensively in the xBase and Basic languages. He is a graduate of Alma College in Alma, Michigan. He is a member of the Association of Shareware Professionals (ASP).

Bryon Scott graduated from Coleman College, a computer trade school, in September of 1986. Since then he has worked for a group of ceramic tile distributors developing in-house inventory control/order processing software. He is currently modifying this software for distribution in the retail market. Bryon uses QuickBASIC, Visual Basic, Microsoft Assembler, and a smattering of C in his programming efforts.

# COLOPHON

Production for this book was done using desktop publishing techniques and every phase of the book involved the use of computer technology. Never did production use traditional typesetting, stats, or photos, and virtually everything for this book, from the illustrations to the formatted text, was saved on disk.

While this book was written on IBM-PC compatible computers, Apple Macintosh computers were used for desktop publishing. The following method was used to go between machines: A design template for the book was created in Aldus PageMaker for the Macintosh. This template was saved as a Microsoft Word document and then translated into Word for Windows version 1.1. The authors wrote into the WinWord files, which used style sheets to apply formatting. The finished documents were transferred directly to a Macintosh on 3.5-inch diskettes, using Insignia's Access PC. These text files were then opened in Microsoft Word for the Macintosh, which interpreted the RTF formatting.

All book design and page formatting was done in Aldus PageMaker 4.01 on the Macintosh, using the imported Microsoft Word files. Adobe Postscript fonts were used. Line art work was created in Aldus FreeHand.

PC screen dumps were captured as .PCX files and .BMP files and translated to TIFF files. To create the chapter opener pages, the cover photo was photographed in black and white, scanned in grey scale, and saved as a TIFF file. This file was imported into PageMaker.

Final page files were sent on Syquest data cartridges to Courier Printing, where they were directly imposed on film. Plates were then made from the film.

AS A PUBLISHER AND WRITER WITH OVER 360,000 BOOKS SOLD EACH YEAR, IT CAME AS A GREAT SHOCK TO DISCOVER THAT OUR RAIN FORESTS, HOME FOR HALF OF ALL LIVING THINGS ON EARTH, ARE BEING DESTROYED AT THE RATE OF 50 ACRES PER MINUTE  AT THIS RATE THE RAIN FORESTS WILL COMPLETELY DISAPPEAR IN JUST 50 YEARS  BOOKS HAVE A LARGE INFLUENCE ON THIS RAMPANT DESTRUCTION  FOR EXAMPLE, SINCE IT TAKES 17 TREES TO PRODUCE ONE TON OF PAPER, A FIRST PRINTING OF 30,000 COPIES OF A TYPICAL 480 PAGE BOOK CONSUMES 108,000 POUNDS OF PAPER WHICH WILL REQUIRE 918 TREES  TO HELP OFFSET THIS LOSS, WAITE GROUP PRESS WILL PLANT TWO TREES FOR EVERY TREE FELLED FOR PRODUCTION OF THIS BOOK  THE DONATION WILL BE MADE TO RAINFOREST ACTION NETWORK (THE BASIC FOUNDATION, P.O. BOX 47012, ST. PETERSBURG, FL 33743), WHICH CAN PLANT 1,000 TREES FOR $250.

# NO ONE CAN DO A BETTER JOB RAVING ABOUT OUR BASIC BOOKS THAN OUR READERS.

## Here are just a few of the hundreds of comments we have received:

# Windows API Bible

by James L. Conger

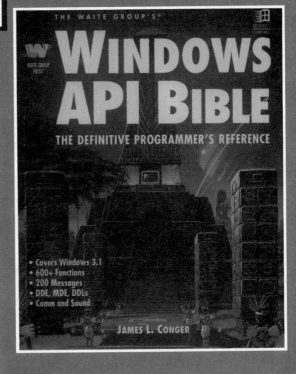

With over 800 functions and messages to learn, Windows presents programmers with a steep and complex learning curve. Windows API Bible cuts through this complexity by breaking the Windows Application Programming Interface (API) into manageable pieces. Chapters are arranged by usage category, beginning with an overview of key concepts, followed by detailed descriptions of every function and message. And:

- More than 350 source code examples demonstrate each function in context, including related messages, support functions, and variable declarations

- Inside cover jump tables and a handy pocket reference card make finding and understanding each API function a snap

Beginners and experienced C and C++ programmers will find invaluable detailed coverage of menus, scroll bars, dialog boxes, graphics, text output, bitmaps, icons, file input and output, character conversions, metafiles, messages, resources, memory management, and clipboard.

You'll also find subjects typically not covered in other Windows books including:

- Color palette control for Super VGA and IBM 8514 systems

- Sound support showing how Windows applications can make music using the PC speaker or add-in sound boards like the Sound Blaster

- Execution profiling and debugging functions for "tuning applications"

With the Waite Group's Windows API Bible by your side you'll never again say "I don't do Windows!"

**Windows API Bible**
by James L. Conger
1992 * 1,040 pages * ISBN: 1-878739-15-8
$39.95 * companion disk available
For IBM PC and compatibles

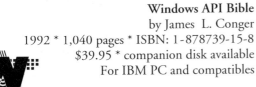

**1** **The definitive guide to Windows Application Programming Interface (API) functions presented in Microsoft's own Windows Software Development Kit**

**2** **Addresses the needs of the working programmer as a complete reference to the complexities of Windows programming, rather than an incomplete tutorial**

**3** **Organized for both quick reference and in-depth analysis**

**4** **Supports the new Windows version 3.1 functions**

# BREAK into Windows Programming

Subscribe to **Windows Tech Journal**,
the new magazine of tools and techniques for
Windows programmers.

(see other side for more information)

## Plan for a programming breakthrough.

To get your free issue and start your no-risk subscription, simply fill out this form and
send it to **Windows Tech Journal**, PO Box 70087, Eugene OR 97401-0143 or
you can FAX it to 503-746-0071.

You'll get a full year—12 issues in all—of Windows tools and techniques for only **$29.95.**
If you're not completely satisfied write "no thanks" on the subscription bill.
The free issue is yours to keep and you owe nothing.

**Windows Tech** JOURNAL

NAME

COMPANY

ADDRESS

CITY                    STATE        ZIP

PHONE

For fastest service call **800-234-0386** or FAX this card to **503-746-007**

491

## Solving Visual Basic Problems Is Simply Knowing How To

**1** Learn to use Window's powerful APIs, create your own ribbon buttons, access the Sound Blaster DLL

**2** Determine system resources, available memory, keyboard types, perform serial I/O

**3** Also includes thousands of bytes worth of custom controls, VBX files, even a custom fractal DLL written in C++ on the companion disk

# Visual Basic How-To

## The Definitive Visual Basic Problem Solver

### by Robert Arnson, Daniel Rosen, Mitchell Waite, Jonathan Zuck

Visual Basic (VB)—long sought after as the "dream" programming language and environment—is here, and The Waite Group has the perfect book. With Visual Basic, Microsoft has created a simple, elegant, and powerful object-oriented language that lets you create full-blown Windows 3 programs! And you don't need a Ph.D. to use Visual Basic: it is built on the immensely popular BASIC programming language known by millions of students.

With Visual Basic How-To you won't have to re-invent the wheel every time you confront a common challenge; just turn here for the solutions you seek—along with expert techniques, custom controls, dynamic link libraries, and more.

Questions and answers are arranged by category for easy reference. Each How-To contains a program solution with complete construction details. And all the code, bitmaps, fonts, icons, forms, and DLLs are included on the bundled disk.

*"This book goes considerably beyond refer-ence without catering to the lowest common denominator of typical tutorials. Think of it as a guide to enjoyable learning ..."*
— Alan Cooper
Director, Applications Software
Coactive Computing Corp.
(Alan Cooper is considered the father of Visual Basic.)

**Visual Basic How-To**
by Robert Arnson, Daniel Rosen, Mitchell Waite,
Jonathan Zuck
1992 * 560 pages * 1 Disk
ISBN: 1-878739-09-3
$34.95
For IBM PC and compatibles
Requires Windows 3

WAITE GROUP
PRESS™

# SoundBytes

## Sound Blaster® MIDI, Synthesizer, and Digitized Voice Controls from Waite Group Software

**G**ive your Visual Basic application exciting sound effects, MIDI music, and digitized speech with Waite Group Software SoundBytes—a set of custom controls for manipulating the famous Sound Blaster audio board. Three controls allow you to play MIDI music in the background while your application is running, control up to eleven channels of the Sound Blaster FM Synthesizer, and give your applications full voice narration. Design-time only samples of the controls are provided in the disk supplied with this book and their operation is detailed in Chapter 8. If you like them, you can purchase the run-time version for only $39.95 plus postage. See ordering details on the next page.

**Music Player**—Play beautiful Midi music while your Visual Basic applications are running or waiting for user interaction with this powerful music player control. Plays standard .MID type midi files as found on CompuServe and allows you to set the filename, start and stop the music, set the tempo, transpose the notes, pause the music, and control how the music fades in and out. 22 different properties may be set with this control from Visual Basic. All music plays in the background and will not interfere with the processing of your running application.

**FM Synthesizer**—Add special sounds effects and musical notes to your VB application by controlling every detail of up to eleven Sound Blaster FM channels. Download custom instrument sounds from CompuServe so you can switch between a piano, a guitar, or an alien ship blasting off. Over 40 different properties may be set with this control. Each channel allows complete control over the carrier and modulator waveforms, so you can set the note, octave, attack, decay, sustain, and release properties as well as vibrato, tremolo, and level. Control such subtle effects as making the volume rise as the frequency goes up. The carrier waveform can be set from a sine to a rectified sine and the feedback between the carrier and the sine can be altered.

**Voice Player**—Give your applications full voice narration or record and play back any sound with this digitized recorder and player control. Voice player allows setting any of 16 properties, including the filename for the recording, pause, play, record, and more. A PlayEnd event notifies you when the recording is completed.

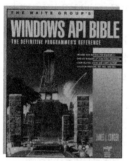
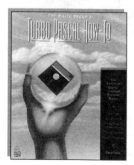

# SOFTWARE LICENSE AGREEMENT

This is a legal agreement between you, the enduser and purchaser, and The Waite Group, Inc. By opening the sealed disk package, you are agreeing to be bound by the terms of this Agreement. If you do not agree with the terms of this Agreement, promptly return the unopened disk package and the accompanying items (including the related book and other written material) to the place you obtained them for a refund.

## SOFTWARE LICENSE

1. The Waite Group, Inc. grants you the right to use one copy of the enclosed software program (the program) on a single computer system (whether a single CPU, part of a licensed network, or a terminal connected to a single CPU). Each concurrent user of the program must have exclusive use of the related Waite Group, Inc. written materials.

2. The program, including the copyright in the program, is owned by The Waite Group, Inc. and is therefore protected under the copyright laws of the United States and other nations, under international treaties. You may make only one copy of the program exclusively for backup or archival purposes, or you may transfer the program to one hard disk drive, using the original for backup or archival purposes. You may make no other copies of the program, and you may make no copies of all or any part of the related Waite Group, Inc. written materials.

3. You may not rent or lease the program, but you may transfer ownership of the program and related written materials (including any and all updates and earlier versions) if you keep no copies of either, and if you make sure the transferee agrees to the terms of this license.

4. You may not decompile, reverse engineer, disassemble, copy, create a derivative work, or otherwise use the program except as stated in this Agreement.

## GOVERNING LAW

This Agreement is governed by the laws of the State of California.

## LIMITED WARRANTY

The following warranties shall be effective for 90 days from the date of purchase: (i) The Waite Group, Inc. warrants the enclosed disks to be free of defects in materials and workmanship under normal use; and (ii) The Waite Group, Inc. warrants that the program, unless modified by the purchaser, will substantially perform the functions described in the documentation provided by The Waite Group, Inc. when operated on the designated hardware and operating system. The Waite Group, Inc. does not warrant that the program will meet client's requirements or that operation of the program will be uninterrupted or error-free. The program warranty does not cover any program that has been altered or changed in any way by anyone other than The Waite Group, Inc. The Waite Group, Inc. is not responsible for problems caused by changes in the operating characteristics of computer hardware or computer operating systems that are made after the release of the program, nor for problems in the interaction of the program with other software.

THESE WARRANTIES ARE EXCLUSIVE AND IN LIEU OF ALL OTHER WARRANTIES OF MERCHANTABILITY OR FITNESS FOR A PARTICULAR PURPOSE OR OF ANY OTHER WARRANTY, WHETHER EXPRESSED OR IMPLIED.

## EXCLUSIVE REMEDY

The Waite Group, Inc. will replace any defective disk without charge if the defective disk is returned to The Waite Group, Inc. within 90 days from the date of purchase.

This is the Purchaser's sole and exclusive remedy for any breach of warranty or claim for contract, tort or damages.

## LIMITATION OF LIABILITY

THE WAITE GROUP, INC. SHALL NOT IN ANY CASE BE LIABLE FOR SPECIAL, INCIDENTAL, CONSEQUENTIAL, INDIRECT, OR OTHER SIMILAR DAMAGES ARISING FROM ANY BREACH OF THESE WARRANTIES EVEN IF THE WAITE GROUP, INC. OR ITS AGENT HAS BEEN ADVISED OF THE POSSIBILITY OF SUCH DAMAGES.

THE WAITE GROUP, INC.'S LIABILITY FOR DAMAGES HEREUNDER SHALL IN NO EVENT EXCEED THE PURCHASE PRICE PAID.

## COMPLETE AGREEMENT

This Agreement constitutes the complete agreement between The Waite Group, Inc. and you, the purchaser.

Some states do not allow the exclusion or limitation of implied warranties or liability for incidental or consequential damages, so the above exclusions or limitations may not apply to you. This limited warranty gives you specific legal rights; you may have others, which vary from state to state.

# Visual Basic Task Jump Table

## Clipboard

Transfer text or graphics data between windows or applications: **Clipboard** (object), 43

Find out whether the clipboard has graphics or text: **GetFormat**, 593

Get graphics from the clipboard: **GetData**, 591

Get text from the clipboard: **GetText**, 594

Send graphics to the clipboard: **SetData**, 595

Send text to the clipboard: **SetText**, 596

Clear the contents of the clipboard: **Clear**, 591

## Controls (General)

Examine attributes of active control: **ActiveControl**, 167

Respond to user change in contents: **Change**, 197

Manipulate controls in a control array: **Index**, 176

Identify a particular control: **Tag**, 181

Find form that contains the control: **Parent**, 178

Label a control on a form: **Label**, 64

## Debugging

Halt program execution: **Stop**, 809

Output program values for debugging: **Debug** (object), 806

Execute a Visual Basic statement immediately: **Immediate Window**, 806

Set and clear breakpoints: **Toggle Breakpoint, Clear All Breakpoints**, 805, 810

Step through code including procedures: **Single Step**, 809

Step through code without showing procedures: **Procedure Step**, 807

Set or show next statement to be executed: **Set Next Statement, Show Next Statement**, 807, 808

## Dialog Boxes (and related controls)

Display a message in a box with standard icons: **MsgBox** (function and statement), 440

Get text from a user by displaying a box: **InputBox$**, 439

Specify choices that can be on or off: **Check box** (control), 41

Define a group of choices of which only one can be selected: **Option button** (control), 71

Create a group of related controls: **Frame** (control), 62

Label part of a dialog box: **Label**, 64

Display a button that executes a specified action: **Command button** (control), 48

## Drive, Directory, and File List Boxes

Set up boxes for working with the disk: **Drive list box, Directory list box, File list box** (objects), 51

Set or read the current drive in a Drive list box: **Drive**, 476

Set or read the name of the currently selected file: **FileName**, 477

Set or read the search path for a Directory or File list box: **Path**, 488

Specify what happens when the search path is changed: **PathChange**, 490

Set or read the file search pattern for a File list box: **Pattern**, 491

Specify what happens when file search pattern is changed: **PatternChange**, 492

Specify DOS attributes of files to be displayed in list: **Archive, Hidden, ReadOnly, System**, 473, 479, 494, 497

Obtain items in a Drive, Dir, or File box's list: **List, ListCount, ListIndex**, 483, 485

## Dynamic Data Exchange (DDE)

Specify type of link (hot/cold and server status): **LinkMode**, 651

Specify actions to take when a link is opened: **LinkOpen**, 654

Get information from a linked application: **LinkRequest**, 658

Specify item and topic to be used in a link: **LinkItem, LinkTopic**, 647, 664

Send contents of a picture box to a linked application: **LinkSend**, 660

Send a command to a linked application: **LinkExecute**, 644

Send information from a client to a server: **LinkPoke**, 656

Deal with errors or timeouts during link: **LinkError, LinkTimeout**, 640, 662

Specify what happens when a link is closed: **LinkClose**, 638

## Focus

Specify which application gets the focus: **AppActivate**, 522

Specify which form or control gets the focus: **SetFocus**, 532

Specify what happens when a form or control gets the focus: **GotFocus**, 528

Specify what happens when a form or control loses the focus: **LostFocus**, 530

Specify whether a control can respond to user input: **Enabled**, 524

Control use of Tab key to move between controls: **TabIndex, TabStop**, 534, 536

## Fonts

Set or get name of current font: **FontName**, 339

Find out what fonts are available: **FontCount, Fonts**, 335, 34

Set point size of font: **FontSize**, 343

Set typestyle: **FontBold, FontItalic, FontStrikethru, FontTransparent, FontUnderline**, 332, 336, 345, 347, 349

## Forms (General)

Position form on screen: **Left, Top**, 142, 149

Set dimensions of form on screen: **Height, Width**, 136, 154

Display form title: **Caption**, 130

Set up menu for a form: **Menu** (control), 69

Set up button to perform a specified action: **Command button** (control), 48

Set color and style: **BackColor, BorderStyle, ForeColor**, 123, 125, 133

Allow resizing of form: **ControlBox, MaxButton, MinButton**, 91, 100, 102

Respond to user actions: **Icon, MousePointer, Resize, WindowState**, 139, 104, 110, 144

Show or hide form: **Hide, Show, Visible**, 93, 106, 151

Load form without showing: **Load** (statement), 97

Refer to forms in code: **FormName**, 175

Activate a particular form or control at run time: **Screen** (object), 78

Examine attributes of active form: **ActiveForm**, 170

Specify actions to take place when form is loaded: **Load** (event), 95

Remove form: **Unload**, 109

# Sound Bytes Order Form

Okay, I have tried the Waite Group Software SoundByte sample controls provided with this book and I am fully addicted. I want my applications to talk to my users and to lull them into a sense of security and contentment. I understand that these three controls work under Windows 3.0 and come with a complete manual that explains the details of using them, how the waveforms work, etc. I also understand that the MIDI player works with standard MIDI files and the FM Synthesizer will work with standard SBI instrument files. I'm raring to go so rush my order now.

## To order by phone, call 800-368-9369 or 415-924-2576 (FAX)

Name

Company

Address
Street Address Only, No P.O. Box

City          State          ZIP          —

Daytime Phone

## Quantity and Type

*SoundBytes VB Controls*     WGS-1     Quantity ☐     x $39.95 =

Sales Tax—California addresses add 7.25% sales tax.

Shipping—Add $5 USA, $10 Canada, or $30 Foreign for shipping and handling. Standard shipping is UPS Ground. Allow 3 to 4 weeks. Prices subject to change. Purchase orders subject to credit approval, and verbal purchase orders will not be accepted.

Sales Tax

Shipping

Total Due

Disk Type: ☐ 5.25-inch   ☐ 3.5-inch

## Method of Payment

Checks or money orders, payable to The Waite Group. To pay by credit card, complete the following:

☐ Visa   ☐ MasterCard     Card Number

Cardholder's Name _____     Exp. Date

Cardholder's Signature _____

## BUSINESS REPLY MAIL

FIRST CLASS MAIL    PERMIT NO. 9    CORTE MADERA, CA

POSTAGE WILL BE PAID BY ADDRESSEE

**Waite Group Press, Inc.**

**Attention: SOUNDBYTES DISK**

**200 Tamal Plaza**

**Corte Madera, CA 94925**

FOLD HERE

# Waite Group Satisfaction Report Card

## Please fill out this card if you wish to know of future updates to
*The Waite Group's Visual Basic SuperBible,* or to receive our catalog.

Company Name: _____

Division: _____  Mail Stop: _____

Last Name: _____  First Name: _____  Middle Initial: _____

Street Address: _____

City: _____  State: _____  Zip: _____

Daytime telephone:  (_____)  _____

Date product was acquired:  Month _____  Day _____  Year _____  Your Occupation: _____

---

**Overall, how would you rate *The Waite Group's Visual Basic SuperBible?***

| | Excellent     | | Very Good       | | Good
| | Fair          | | Below Average   | | Poor

**What did you like MOST about this product?** _____
_____
_____

**What did you like LEAST about this product?** _____
_____
_____

**How do you use this book (tutorial, reference, problem-solver...)?**
_____
_____

**What types of BASIC are you familiar with?** _____
_____

**What is your level of Visual Basic expertise?**
☐ New user     ☐ Dabbler      ☐ Hacker
☐ Power user   ☐ Programmer   ☐ Experienced professional

**Please describe your computer hardware:**

Computer _____  Hard disk _____
5.25" disk drives _____  3.5" disk drives _____
Video card _____  Monitor _____
Printer _____  Peripherals _____
Sound board _____  CD ROM _____

**What other computer languages are you familiar with?** _____
_____

**Where did you buy this book?**

| | Bookstore (name: _____ )
| | Discount store (name: _____ )
| | Computer store (name: _____ )
| | Catalog (name: _____ )
| | Direct from WGP          | | Other _____

**What price did you pay for this book?** _____

**What influenced your purchase of this book?**
☐ Recommendation              ☐ Advertisement
☐ Magazine review             ☐ Store display
☐ Mailing                     ☐ Book's format
☐ Reputation of The Waite Group  ☐ Other _____

**How many computer books do you buy each year?** _____

**How many other Waite Group books do you own?** _____

**What is your favorite Waite Group book?** _____

_____

**Is there any program or subject you would like to see The Waite Group cover in a similar approach?** _____

_____

**Additional comments?** _____

_____
_____

☐ **Check here for a free Waite Group catalog**

---

## BUSINESS REPLY MAIL

FIRST CLASS MAIL     PERMIT NO. 9     CORTE MADERA, CA

POSTAGE WILL BE PAID BY ADDRESSEE

**Waite Group Press, Inc.**
**Attention:** *Visual Basic SuperBible*
**200 Tamal Plaza**
**Corte Madera, CA 94925**

FOLD HERE